SOLDIERS DIED IN THE GREAT WAR 1914-19.

Part 11.

The Royal Warwickshire Regiment.

J. B. HAYWARD & SON
POLSTEAD · SUFFOLK
1989

PREFACE.

These rolls have been compiled from information furnished to Officers-in-Charge of Records through the Official Casualty Lists.

They are published to enable information, which has from time to time been circulated during the war, to be available in volume form.

Attention is invited to the explanations of abbreviations which are printed at the commencement of each part.

Nothing whatever contained in these rolls is to be quoted or made use of in any representation which it may be desired to make on the subject of rank, decoration, nature or date of casualty, or anything consequent upon any casualty

The War Office,
August, 1921.

ISBN 1 871505 11 9

Published by J. B. Hayward & Son
in association with
The Imperial War Museum
Department of Printed Books

CONTENTS

Printed in Great Britain by
Antony Rowe Ltd, Chippenham, Wiltshire

The Royal Warwickshire Regiment.

EXPLANATION OF ABBREVIATIONS.

"b."	"born."	"d. of w." ...	"died of wounds."
"e."	"enlisted."	"k. in a." ...	"killed in action."
"d."	"died."	"F. & F." ...	"France & Flanders" (including Italy).

N.B.—When the place of enlistment is followed by the name of another place in brackets, the latter represents the deceased soldier's place of residence.

1st Battalion.

Accleton, William Charles, b. Luddesdown, Kent, e. Gravesend, Kent (Luddesdown), 648, Pte., k. in a., F. & F., 12/10/16.
Adams, Charles Henry, b. Birmingham, e. Birmingham, 7050, Pte., k. in a., F. & F., 25/4/15.
Adams, Harry, b. All Saints, Evesham, Worcs, e. Worcester (Evesham), 2537, Pte., d. of w., F. & F., 14/10/16, formerly 9997, Oxford & Bucks L.I.
Adamson, Albert, e. Nottingham, 27293, Pte., k. in a., F. & F., 3/5/17, formerly 4774, Notts & Derby Regt.
Adcock, William, b. Birmingham, e. Birmingham, 9402, Pte., k. in a., F. & F., 25/4/15.
Adkins, Albert Charles, b. Knowle, Warwicks, e. Stratford-on-Avon, Warwicks (Henley-in-Arden, Warwicks), 21459, Pte., d. of w., F. & F., 13/5/17.
Ainscough, William Frederick, b. Liverpool, e. Liverpool, 20561, Pte., k. in a, F. & F., 15/4/18, formerly 10120, A. Cyclist Corps.
Ainsworth, George, b. Rishton, Lancs, e. Rochdale, Lancs, 33013, Pte., k. in a., F. & F., 10/7/18, formerly GS/25503, D.G.
Albrighton, Thomas Charles, b. Baddesley, Warwicks, e. Atherstone, Warwicks (Baddesley), 24136, Pte., d. of w., F. & F., 3/9/18.
Alcock, Frank, b. Warwick, e. Warwick, 30428, Pte., k. in a., F. & F., 3/5/18.
Allder, Leonard, b. Sparkbrook, Birmingham, e. Birmingham, 2365, L/Cpl., k. in a., F. & F., 11/4/17.
Allen, Albert, b. Vauxhall, Birmingham, e. Stoneleigh, Warwicks (Vauxhall, Birmingham), 138, Pte., k. in a., F. & F., 24/5/15.
Allen, Arthur, b. Birmingham, e. Birmingham, 11186, Pte., d. of w., F. & F., 20/6/16.
Allen, John Thomas, b. Tremington, Norfolk, e. Norwich (Eye Green, Peterborough), 27602, Pte., k. in a., F. & F., 12/10/16, formerly 5526, S. Staffs Regt.
Allen, Walter James, b. Smethwick, Staffs, e. Birmingham (Smethwick), 12278, Pte., k. in a., F. & F., 25/6/16, formerly 53145, R.G.A.
Allen, Walter Rowland, b. Coventry, e. Coventry (Ryton-on-Dunsmore, Coventry), 23951, Pte., k. in a., F. & F., 5/7/17.
Allton, William, b. Bedworth, Warwicks, e. Nuneaton, Warwicks (Bedworth), 15280, Pte., k. in a., F. & F., 21/6/16.
Amey, William, b. Grafton-under-Wood, Kettering, Northants, e. Coventry (Kettering), 438, Pte., k. in a., F. & F., 25/4/15.
Amos, Fred, b. Martin, Kent, e. Dover (Martin), 27607, Pte., k. in a., F. & F., 10/12/16, formerly 5595, S. Staffs Regt.
Amy, Gordon Samuel, b. St. Teath, Cornwall, e. Truro, Cornwall (St. Teath), 36210, Pte., d., F. & F., 15/9/18.
Anderson, William, b. St. Leonard's, Edinburgh, e. Edinburgh, 34182, Pte., k. in a., F. & F., 30/8/18, formerly 8199, Dragoons.
Andrews, Edward, e. Dublin, 33185, Pte., d. of w., F. & F., 20/11/17, formerly 23647, Lancers.
Andrews, George, b. Washwood Heath, Warwicks, e. Coventry, 9810, L/Cpl., k. in a., F. & F., 12/10/16.
Andrews, Thomas William, b. St. Paul's, Warwick, e. Warwick, 1101, Pte., k. in a., F. & F., 13/10/14.
Andrews, Walter, b. Birmingham, e. Birmingham, 14291, Pte., d. of w., F. & F., 26/6/16.
Angus, David, b. London, e. Birmingham (London), 9384, Pte., k. in a., F. & F., 25/4/15.
Antley, John, b. Birmingham, e. Worthing (Birmingham), 9183, C.S.M., k. in a., F. & F., 23/10/16.
Arculus, Alfred, e. Birmingham, 267481, Pte., k. in a., F. & F., 14/4/17.
Armfield, John, b. Birmingham, e. Birmingham, 9071, Pte., k. in a., F. & F., 25/4/15.
Armstrong, Willie, b. Heptonstall, Yorks, e. Heywood, Lancs (Hopwood, Heywood), 33014, Pte., k. in a., F. & F., 22/4/18, formerly GS/21097, Dragoon Gds.
Arthurs, Walter, b. St. Paul's, Birmingham, e. Warwick (Birmingham), 2386, Pte., k. in a., F. & F., 26/8/14.
Ash, Arthur Douglas, b. Gt. Barr, Staffs, e. Birmingham, 16124, Pte., k. in a., F. & F., 11/4/17.
Ashford Arthur Henry, b. Birmingham, e. Birmingham, 8132, Pte., k. in a., F. & F., 1/12/14.
Astell, Bertie Thomas, b. All Saints, Leamington, Warwicks, e. Leamington, 9887, Pte., k. in a., F. & F., 25/4/15.
Astill, Albert, b. Wolvey, Warwicks, e. Nuneaton, Warwicks, 9509, A/Sgt., k. in a., F. & F., 3/5/17.
Atherton, John William, b. Adlington, Lancs, e. Horwich, Lancs (Adlington), 33012, Pte., d. of w., F. & F., 16/4/18, formerly GS/21488, Dragoon Gds.
Atkins, Albert, b. St. Mark's, Coventry, e. Coventry, 2334, Pte., k. in a., F. & F., 25/4/15.
Atkins, Walter, b. All Saints, Coventry, e. Coventry, 2258, Pte., k. in a., F. & F., 23/10/16.
Austin, Cecil, b. Stratton, Northampton, e. Rugby, 34801, Pte., k. in a., F. & F., 30/8/18.
Austin, Frederick James, e. Ilminster, Som., 25409, Pte., k. in a., F. & F., 12/10/17.
Austin, Joseph, b. Harborne, Birmingham, e. Birmingham, 4025, Pte., k. in a., F. & F., 9/5/15.
Austin, William Henry, b. Rochester, Staffs, e. Warwick (Hadley, Ombersley, Worcs), 10190, L/Cpl., d. of w., F. & F., 11/4/17.
Ayres, William, b. Fleet, Hants, e. Alton, Hants, 40145, Pte., k. in a., F. & F., 11/6/18.
Bacon, James, b. Stockingford, Nuneaton, Warwicks, e. Nuneaton, 1840, Pte., k. in a., F. & F., 25/4/15.
Bailey, George, b. Anstey, Warwicks, e. Nuneaton, Warwicks (Anstey), 4508, Cpl., k. in a., F. & F., 5/4/16.
Baines, Arthur Wilfred, b. Ladywood, Birmingham, e. Warwick (Ladywood, Birmingham), 2427, Pte., k. in a., F. & F., 19/9/14.
Baker, Alfred, b. Lozells, Birmingham, e. Birmingham, 765, Pte., k. in a., F. & F., 30/8/18.
Baker, Colin Langsford, b. Birmingham, e. Birmingham, 9768, Pte., k. in a., F. & F., 19/10/15.
Baker, James, b. St Thomas, Birmingham, e. Manchester, 1830, L/Cpl., k. in a., F. & F., 8/7/15.
Baker, John Albert, b. Birmingham, e. Birmingham, 7511, Pte., k. in a., F. & F., 20/10/14.
Baker, Sidney, b. Kilburn, Middx., e. London, 20602, Pte., k. in a., F. & F., 12/10/16. formerly 11247, Army Cyc. Corps.
Baker, Walter, b. Birmingham, e. Birmingham, 6314, Pte., k. in a., F. & F., 25/4/15.
Baker, William Alfred, b. Dudley, Worcs, e. Dudley, 34803, Pte., d. of w., F. & F., 25/8/18.
Baldwin, Fred, b. Lewisham, London, e. Lewisham (Catford), 34804, Pte., k. in a., F. & F., 20/7/18.
Ball, Arthur, e. Birmingham, 21049, Pte., d. of w., F. & F., 18/10/18.
Ball, George Thomas Henry, b. Belgrave, Leicester, e. Nuneaton, Warwicks, 2387, Pte., k. in a., F. & F., 29/4/15.
Ball, John James, b. All Saints, Birmingham, e. Birmingham, 3849, Pte., k in a., F & F., 10/5/15.
Ballard, Ernest, b. Harborne, Birmingham, e. Hereford (Birmingham), 4114, Pte., k. in a, F. & F., 25/4/15.
Barclay, Alexander, b. Teddington, Middx., e. London (Teddington, Middx.), 1485, Pte., k. in a., F. & F., 25/4/15.
Barefoot, Charles Henry, b. Smethwick. Staffs, e. Birmingham (Smethwick), 2572, Pte., k. in a., F. & F., 19/6/15.
Barley, Frank, b. Ladywood, Birmingham, e. Birmingham, 2288. Pte., k. in a., F. & F., 26/4/15.
Barnbrook, Reuben, e. Warwick (Barford, nr. Warwick), 15976, Pte., k. in a., F. & F., 12/10/16, formerly R.F.A.
Barnes, George Ernest, b. Windsor, Bucks, e. Warwick (Tamworth, Warwicks), 7273, Pte., k. in a., F. & F., 13/10/14.
Barnett, George, b. Broadway, Worcs, e. Stratford-on-Avon, Warwicks (Broadway, Worcs), 9562, Pte., k. in a., F. & F., 9/7/15.
Barnett, Henry, b. Coventry, e. Coventry, 9614, Pte., k. in a., F. & F., 18/12/14.
Barnickle, Harry, b. Birmingham, e. Birmingham, 276, Pte., k. in a., F. & F., 3/1/15.
Barrett, Charles, b. Weston-on-Avon, Stratford-on-Avon, Warwicks, e. Warwick (Shripston-on-Stour, Worcs), 9167, A/Sgt., k. in a., F. & F., 25/4/15.
Barrett, William Alfred, b. Wheatley, Oxon, e. Oxford (Wheatley), 18516, Pte., k. in a., F. & F., 30/8/18, formerly 25301, Som. L.I.
Barrow, Reginald Harold, b. Woolwich, Kent, e. Woolwich, Kent, 33186, L/Cpl., k. in a., F. & F., 30/8/18, formerly 7056, Lancers.
Basnett, Thomas, b. Birmingham, e. Birmingham, 3424, Pte., k. in a., F. & F., 7/11/15
Batchelor, Charles, b. Rochford, Essex, e. Rugby, Warwicks, 21511, Pte., k. in a., F. & F., 11/4/17.

(28808—50) Wt. 0983—4774/707 500 9/21 H. St. G. 2

Batchelor, Fred, b. Ettington, Stratford-on-Avon, Warwicks, e. Alcester, Warwicks (Ettington), 626, Pte., k. in a., F. & F., 18/10/14.

Batchelor, John, b. St. Mary's, Nuneaton, Warwicks, e. Nuneaton, Warwicks, 2362, Pte., k. in a., F. & F., 29/4/15.

Batchelor, Richard, b. Elmanton, Stratford-on-Avon, Warwicks, e. Oakfield, Rugby (Stratford-on-Avon), 761, Pte., d. of w., F. & F., 6/6/15.

Batchelor, Sydney, b. Bretford, Warwicks, e. Rugby, Warwicks (Church Lawford, Rugby, Warwicks), 10559, A/Sgt., d. of w., F. & F., 1/12/17.

Bate, Frank Clifford, b. Moseley, Warwicks, e. Birmingham, 20856, Pte., d. of w., F. & F., 28/10/18.

Bates, Arthur, b. St. Peter's, Coventry, e. Warwick (Coventry), 412, L/Cpl., k. in a., F. & F., 13/10/14.

Bates, Herbert, b. Holy Trinity, Coventry, e. Warwick (Coventry), 2433, Pte., k. in a., F. & F., 29/10/14.

Bates, Thomas Healey, e. Coventry (Ryton-on-Dunsmore, nr. Coventry), 9074, Cpl., k. in a., F. & F., 31/3/18.

Batho, Richard Thomas, b. Whitmore, Staffs, e. Nuneaton, Warwicks, 24525, L/Cpl., k. in a., F. & F., 12/10/17.

Battin, Charles, b. Worcester, e. Birmingham, 3027, Pte., k. in a., F. & F., 19/6/15.

Battin, Henry Archibald, b. Nechells, Birmingham, e. Birmingham (Nechells, Birmingam), 11067, Pte., d. of w., F. & F., 28/4/16.

Baugh, John, b. Aston, Birmingham, e. Warwick (Birmingham), 528, Pte., k. in a., F. & F., 26/4/15.

Baughan, Henry, b. Berkswell, nr. Coventry, e. Coventry (Berkswell, nr. Coventry), 23124, Pte., k. in a., F. & F., 30/8/18.

Baxter, Willie, b. Heckmondwike, Yorks, e. Newcastle-on-Tyne (Doncaster, Lincs), 1982, L/Cpl., d. of w., F. & F., 16/4/18, formerly 140411, Gnr., R.F.A.

Bayliss, Ernest Frederick, b. Moseley, Birmingham, e. Warwick (Birmingham), 9991, Pte., k. in a., F. & F., 13/10/14.

Bayliss, Fred, b. Kenilworth, Warwicks, e. Warwick (Kenilworth), 1682, Pte., k. in a., F. & F., 19/6/15.

Bayliss, Harry, b. Sparkbrook, Birmingham, e. Birmingham, 3578, Pte., k. in a., F. & F., 11/5/15.

Beach, Charles Thomas, b. Birmingham, e. Warwick (Birmingham), 9458, Pte., k. in a., F. & F., 25/4/15.

Beacham, Charles James, b. Bournbrook, Birmingham, e. Warwick (Bournbrook), 1723, Pte., d. of w., F. & F., 6/8/15.

Beacher, Louis George Barton, b. St. Gregory, Canterbury, e. Shorncliffe, Kent (Cheriton, Kent), 2276, L/Cpl., d. of w., F. & F., 14/10/14.

Beale, George John, b. Birmingham, e. Birmingham, 9939, Pte., d. of w., F. & F., 30/1/15.

Beale, James Arthur, b. Birmingham, e. Birmingham, 8966, Pte., k. in a., F. & F., 25/4/15.

Beales, William, b. Coventry, e. Coventry, 16391, Pte., k. in a., F. & F., 17/4/17.

Beasley, Alfred, b. Birmingham, e. Birmingham (Dennington, near Rotherham), 41119, Pte., k. in a., F. & F., 18/7/18.

Beck, Frank, b. All Saints, Coventry, e. Warwick (Coventry), 1964, L/Cpl., k. in a., F. & F., 2/7/16.

Beddington, William Henry, b. All Saints, Leamington, Warwicks, e. Warwick (Leamington), 581, Sgt., k. in a., F. & F., 26/8/14.

Beecham, Paola Reginald George, b. Clerkenwell, London, e. Holloway, London (Canonbury, London), 34809, Pte., d. of w., F. & F., 16/4/18.

Beesley, John Edward, b. Birmingham, e. Birmingham, 9240, Pte., k. in a., F. & F., 26/4/15.

Beeson, Reginald, b. Erdington Birmingham, e. Birmingham, 1285, Pte., k. in a., F. & F., 8/6/15.

Beezley, William, b. Langley, Stratford-on-Avon, e. Warwick (Langley, Stratford-on-Avon), 9051, Pte., k. in a., F. & F., 31/8/18.

Bembridge, Henry, b. Bordesley, Birmingham, e. Birmingham, 3342, Pte., k. in a., F. & F., 25/4/15.

Bench, Charles William, b. Warwick, e. Warwick, 6266, Sgt., k. in a., F. & F., 23/7/17.

Bench, Joseph, b. St. Mary's, Warwick, e. Warwick, 1558, Sgt., k. in a, F. & F., 11/4/17.

Bennett, Henry, b. Leyland, Lancs, e. Leyland, Lancs (Farington, nr. Preston), 33093, L/Cpl., d. of w., F. & F., 27/4/18, formerly 19140, Dragoons.

Bennett, William, b. St. Saviour's, Birmingham, e. Birmingham, 4304, Pte., k. in a., F. & F., 25/5/15.

Benson, William Eli, b. Coventry, e. Coventry, 9482, L/Cpl., k. in a., F. & F., 25/4/15.

Bentley, Walter Thomas, b. Battersea, Surrey, e. Guildford, Surrey (Battersea), 931, L/Cpl., k. in a., F. & F., 9/12/14.

Berry, Arthur, b. Coventry, e. Warwick (Coventry), 16579, Pte., k. in a., F. & F., 4/10/17.

Berry, William Henry, b. Old Church, Warrington, Lancs, e. Lancaster (Stalybridge, Lancs), 6501, Pte., k. in a., F. & F., 13/10/14.

Betteridge, Harold Walter Christopher, b. Bassett, Hants, e. Southampton (Bassett), 36221, Pte., k. in a., F. & F., 13/8/18.

Betts, Francis Gordon, b. Birmingham, e. Birmingham, 9473, Sgt., d. of w., F. & F., 25/11/16.

Bickley, Arthur, b. Birmingham, e. Birmingham, 1922, L/Sgt., k. in a., F. & F., 25/4/15.

Biddle, Arthur Edward, b. Foxley, Warwicks, e. Warwick, 1018, Dmr., k. in a., F. & F., 26/8/14.

Bidwell, Charles, b. Holloway, London, e. London, 12272, Pte., d. of w., F. & F., 23/10/16, formerly 53927, R.G.A.

Biffin, Albert Samuel, b. Atherstone, Warwicks, e. Nuneaton, Warwicks (Atherstone), 2782, Pte., k. in a., F. & F., 25/4/15.

Billett, Lewin James, b. Kington St. Michael, Wilts, e. Chippenham, Wilts (Kington St. Michael), 306675, Pte., d. of w., F. & F., 26/4/18.

Billingham, Albert, b. Birmingham, e. Birmingham, 1388, Pte., k. in a., F. & F., 11/4/17.

Billington, Sidney, b. St. Luke's, Birmingham, e. Birmingham, 2035, Pte., k. in a., F. & F., 13/10/14.

Bilke, Bert, b. St. Mary's, Weymouth, Dorset, e. Nuneaton, Warwicks (Birmingham), 9610, Pte., k. in a., F. & F., 9/7/15.

Bird, Harold, b. Birmingham, e. Birmingham, 1786, Pte., k. in a., F. & F., 3/5/17.

Bird, Harry, b. Darlaston, Staffs, e. Warwick (Darlaston), 971, Pte., k. in a., F. & F., 12/4/18.

Bird, Harry, b. Birmingham, e. Birmingham, 36222, Pte., k. in a., F. & F., 30/8/18.

Bird, Samuel, b. Wednesbury, Staffs, e. Birmingham (West Bromwich, Staffs), 2245, L/Sgt., k. in a., F. & F., 27/4/18.

Birtley, Augustus, b. Dudley, Worcs, e. Birmingham (Bromsgrove, Worcs), 787, Pte., k. in a., F. & F., 11/10/16.

Bishop, Charles Edward, b. Swansea, e. Birmingham (Smethwick, Birmingham), 1898, Pte., d. of w., F. & F., 14/10/14.

Bishop, Henry Victor, b. Lewisham, London, e. Birmingham, 17881, Pte., k. in a., F. & F., 15/4/18.

Bishop, Leonard, b. Brmingham, e. Birmingham, 2172, Pte., k. in a., F. & F., 5/11/14.

Bishop, Oliver Clarence Shenstone, b. Birmingham, e. Birmingham, 38819, Pte., k. in a., F. & F., 30/8/18.

Bishop, Thomas, b. Birmingham, e. Birmingham, 2005, L/Cpl., d. of w., F. & F., 15/4/18.

Blackmoor, Joseph, b. Blakenhall, Walsall, Staffs, e. Nuneaton, Warwicks, 2356, Pte., k. in a., F. & F., 13/10/14.

Blake, Thomas Henry Arthur, b. Kensington, London, e. Newbury (Lambourne, Berks), 32445, Pte., k. in a., F. & F., 30/8/18, formerly R/4/111060, R.A.S.C.

Blakemore, Martin, b. Walsall, Staffs, e. Nuneaton, Warwicks (Arley, Warwicks), 1608, Pte., k. in a., F. & F., 12/10/16.

Blamire, Reginald, b. Hampton-in-Arden, Warwicks, e. Coventry (Hampton-in-Arden), 42502, Pte., d., F. & F., 9/11/18.

Blewitt, John, b. Birmingham, e. Warwick (Birmingham), 7211, C.Q.M.S., d. of w., F. & F., 5/5/18.

Blick, William John, b. Birmingham, e. Birmingham, 7020, Pte., k. in a., F. & F., 25/4/15.

Bloomer, George, b. Yardley, Warwicks, e. Warwick (Yardley), 1502, Pte., d. of w., F. & F., 11/7/15.

Bloxham, George, b. Foleshill, Coventry, e. Coventry, 15022, Pte., d. of w., F. & F., 19/4/18.

Blundell, Albert Harvey, b. Warley, Worcs, e. Birmingham (Warley, Langley), 12746, Pte., k. in a., F. & F., 12/10/16.

Boase, Frank Thorpe, b. Scilly, Cornwall, e. Penzance, Cornwall (Scilly), 25441, Pte., k. in a., F. & F., 30/8/18.

Bocock, George Francis, b. Birmingham, e. Birmingham, 19491, Cpl., k. in a., F. & F., 15/4/18.

Boden, Frederick, b. Hatton, Runcorn, Ches., e. Warrington, Lancs, 4590, Pte., k. in a. F. & F., 10/12/16.

Bodfish, Howard, b. St. Paul's, Birmingham, e. Birmingham, 4974, Pte., d. of w., F. & F., 24/7/15.

Bodman, William, b. St. Mary's, Warwick, e. Birmingham, 16885, Pte., k. in a., F. & F., 12/10/16.

Bolton, Wilfred James, b. Small Heath, Birmingham, e. Birmingham (Wolverhampton), 7364, Pte., k. in a., F. & F., 17/1/15.

Boneham, Herbert, b. Birmingham, e. Birmingham (Folkestone), 1450, Pte., k. in a., F. & F., 29/10/14.

Booth, Charles, b. Sparkbrook, Birmingham, e. Birmingham, 9288, Pte., k. in a., F. & F., 1/7/16.

Boswell, George, b. Harborne, Birmingham, e. Wedgnock Park, Warwick (Harborne), 431, Pte., k. in a., F. & F., 27/4/18.

Bosworth, Walter, b. Attleborough, Nuneaton, Warwicks, e. Coventry (Nuneaton), 1365, Pte., k. in a., F. & F., 19/6/15.

Botterill, Jeremiah, b. All Saints, Birmingham, e. Birmingham, 1373, Pte., d. of w., F. & F., 22/6/16.

Boucher, Albert Henry, b. Gloucester, e. Warwick (Birmingham), 8609, A/Cpl., k. in a., F. & F., 1/7/16.

Boulter, Richard Henry, b. Islington, Middx., e. Birmingham, 11362, Pte., k. in a., F. & F., 30/9/15.

Bousfield, Sidney Robert, b. Coventry, e. Warwick (Nuneaton, Warwicks), 2446, Pte., k. in a., F. & F., 26/4/15.

Bovey, Arthur Albert, b. Eaton, Bucks, e. London (Barking, Essex), 20601, Pte., k. in a., F. & F., 23/7/17, formerly 11239, A. Cyclist Corps.

Bowden, Patrick, b. Dublin, e. Birmingham (Dublin), 803, Pte., d. of w., F. & F., 26/11/15.

Bowen, Percy James, e. Birmingham, 267565, Pte., d., F. & F., 9/1/18

Bowers, Charles, b. Lakenheath, Suffolk, e. Ludlow, Salop (Hungerford, Berks), 27849, Pte., d. of w., F. & F., 2/5/18, formerly 24671, Shrops L.I.

Bradburn, Richard, b. Whitbourne, Worcs, e. Solihull, Warwicks (Birmingham), 21705, Pte., k. in a., F. & F., 15/4/18, formerly 29925, Glos. Regt.

Bradbury, Ernest, b. Aston, Birmingham, e. Birmingham, 2562, Pte., k. in a., F. & F., 16/6/15.

Bradley, Albert, b. London, e. Warwick (Smethwick, Staffs), 14840, Pte., d., F. & F., 25/10/16.

Bradley, Charles William, b. Birmingham, e. Birmingham, 207316, Pte., k. in a., F. & F., 15/4/18.

Bradley, Edward, b. St. Andrew's, Birmingham, e. Birmingham, 4570, Pte., d. of w., F. & F., 27/7/17.

Bradley, George, b. Birmingham, e. Birmingham, 7935, Pte., k. in a., F. & F., 23/11/14.

Bradley, George, b. Walsall, Staffs, e. Coventry, 10971, Pte., k. in a., F. & F., 2/11/15.

Bradshaw, Lewis, b. Harborough Magna, Rugby, Warwicks, e. Coventry, 1858, Pte., k. in a., F. & F., 25/4/15.

Brain, Oliver John, b. Glascote, Warwicks, e. Lichfield, Staffs (Glascote Heath, Tamworth, Warwicks), 25339, Pte., d. of w., F. & F., 15/4/18.

Branford, Frederick, e. Birmingham, 21324, Pte., k. in a., F. & F., 18/4/17, formerly 26764, R. Berks Regt.

Brassington, Harry, b. St. Michael's, Coventry, e. Coventry, 2118, Pte., k. in a., F. & F., 13/10/14.

Britton, Cedric Hartley, b. Welshpool, Mont., e. Birmingham (Smethwick, Staffs), 1117, Pte., k. in a., F. & F., 12/10/16.

Bray, Frederick John, b. Bournville, Birmingham, e. Warwick (Birmingham), 16684, Pte., k. in a., F. & F., 11/10/16.

Brice, Henry, b. Birmingham, e. Warwick (Birmingham), 9007, Pte., k. in a., F. & F., 3/11/14.

Bridgwood, Harold, b. Wednesbury, Staffs, e. Walsall, Staffs (Wednesbury), 41045, Pte., d. of w., F. & F., 26/10/18.

Bright, Edward, b. Mile End, London, e. Birmingham, 16193, Pte., d. of w., F. & F., 28/8/16.

Brimble, Robert, b. Saltley, Birmingham, e. Birmingham, 4807, Pte., k. in a., F. & F., 25/4/15.

Brimble, Walter, b. Nieve, Wilts, e. Devizes, Wilts (Mere, Wilts), 36226, Pte., k. in a., F. & F., 30/8/18.

Brinkworth, Frank George, b. Birmingham, e. Birmingham, 28245, Pte., k. in a., F. & F., 3/5/17, formerly 27264, Hussars.

Broadfield, George, b. St. James, Birmingham, e. Birmingham, 9073, Sgt., k. in a., F. & F., 12/10/17.

Broadfield, Oliver, b. St. Bartholomew's, Birmingham, e. Warwick (Birmingham), 2358, Pte., k. in a., F. & F., 26/5/15.

Brookes, George, b. Birmingham, e. Warwick (Leamington, Warwicks), 9666, L/Cpl., k. in a., F. & F., 26/8/14.

Brookes, John James, b. New Bilton, Rugby, Warwicks, e. Rugby, Warwicks, 28542, Pte., k. in a., F. & F., 30/8/18.

Brooks, Charles, b. Stoke Newington, London, e. New Cross, London (Stoke Newington, London), 815, Cpl., k. in a., F. & F., 13/10/14.

Brown, Alexander Bishop, b. Glasgow, e. Birmingham (Birmingham), 7206, Pte., k. in a., F. & F., 3/5/17.

Brown, Arthur, b. Little Thorpe, Narborough, Leics, e. Coventry (Little Thorpe), 9955, k. in a., F. & F., 13/10/14.

Brown, Ernest, b. Fulham, London, e. London (Kensington, London), 28319, Pte., d. of w., F. & F., 12/4/17, formerly 27322, Hrs.

Brown, George Alfred, b. Hinksey, Oxford, e. Oxford, 306608, Pte., k. in a., F. & F., 15/4/18.

Brown, Henry, b. Herdry, Scotland, e. Warwick, 1616, Pte., k. in a., F. & F., 25/4/15.

Brownlow, Alfred, b. Peterborough, Northants, e. Birmingham, 4792, Pte., k. in a., F. & F., 30/8/18.

Brueton, Theophilus, b. Birmingham, e. Birmingham, 4000, Pte., k. in a., F. & F., 12/10/16.

Bryan, Edmund Frederick, b. Reading, Berks, e. Birmingham, 16/1385, Cpl., d. of w., F. & F., 12/6/18.

Bryan, William, b. Hockley, Birmingham, e. Birmingham, 3923, Sgt., k. in a., F. & F., 12/10/17.

Buckley, John Underwood, b. Coalville, Leicester, e. Atherstone, Warwicks, 10183, Pte., k. in a., F. & F., 6/7/15.

Buckley, Thomas, b. Aston, Birmingham, e. Birmingham, 2043, A/Sgt., k. in a., F. & F., 26/4/15.

Bullock, John, b. St. Dennis, Cornwall, e. Bodmin, Cornwall (St. Austell, Cornwall), 27954, Pte., d., F. & F., 25/2/17.

Bullock, William Thomas, b. West Bromwich, Staffs, e. Birmingham (Sheffield), 1651, L/Cpl., k. in a., F. & F., 25/4/15.

Bunn, James Francis, b. St. John's, Leamington, e. Warwick (Leamington, Warwicks), 777, A/Cpl., k. in a., F. & F., 23/3/15.

Burden, Owen, b. Birmingham, e. Birmingham, 3992, Pte., k. in a., F. & F., 19/6/15.

Burford, Alfred, b. Birmingham, e. Birmingham, 201964, Pte., k. in a., F. & F., 18/7/18.

Burnett, David, b. Glasgow, e. Warwick (Glasgow), 402, Pte., k. in a., F. & F., 3/5/17.

Burnett, Samuel, b. St. Michael's, Coventry, e. Coventry, 10637, Pte., k. in a., F. & F., 3/5/17.

Burrows, Alfred, b. Coventry, e. Coventry, 9762, Pte., k. in a., F. & F., 13/10/14.

Burton, Alfred Ernest, b. Snitterfield, near Warwick, e. Stratford-on-Avon, Warwicks, 10516, Pte., k. in a., F. & F., 13/10/16.

Busson, William, b. Newbold-on-Avon, Rugby, Warwicks, e. Warwick (Newbold-on-Avon), 609, Pte., k. in a., F. & F., 26/8/14.

Butler, Harry, b. Bedworth, Warwicks, e. Nuneaton, Warwicks (Bedworth), 13071, Pte., k. in a., F. & F., 11/4/17.

Butler, Mitham, b. Coleshill, Warwicks, e. Warwick (Birmingham), 1683, Pte., k. in a., F. & F., 26/4/15.

Butler, William Edward, b. Birmingham, e. Birmingham, 1028, L/Cpl., k. in a., F. & F., 19/6/15.

Butt, Thomas, b. St. Mary's, Warwick, e. Birmingham, 9800, Pte., k. in a., F. & F., 11/4/17.

Buxey, Jesse Antony, b. Newbury, Berks, e. Newbury, Berks, 50823, Pte., k. in a., F. & F., 30/8/18.

Byron, John, b. Edgbaston, Birmingham, e. Birmingham, 2418, Pte., k. in a., F. & F., 19/6/15.

Caines, Ernest Benjamin, b. Aston, Birmingham, e. Birmingham, 2345, Pte., k. in a., F. & F., 8/9/14.

Cairns, Walter, b. Balsall Heath, Birmingham, e. Birmingham, 2148, Pte., k. in a., F. & F., 13/10/14.

Calderbank, Joseph, b. St. Paul's, Manchester, e. Manchester, 804, Pte., k. in a., F. & F., 13/10/14.

Callant, Alfred, b. Aston, Birmingham, e. Birmingham, 2460, L/Cpl., d. of w., F. & F., 25/1/15.

Cann, Herbert, b. St. Thomas, Exeter, Devon, e. Exeter, 50822, Pte., k. in a., F. & F., 30/8/18.

Canning, William John, b. St. Michael's, Coventry, e. Warwick (Coventry), 1277, Pte., k. in a., F. & F., 5/4/16.

Carey, George, b. Devonport, e. Warwick (Birmingham), 6803, L/Sgt., k. in a., F. & F., 23/10/16.

Carlow, Harry, b. St. Martin's, Birmingham, e. Birmingham, 2040, Pte., k. in a., F. & F., 3/5/17.

Carr, Frederick Walter, b. Coventry, e. Coventry, 16451, Pte., k. in a., F. & F., 25/6/16.

Carter, Bert, b. Coventry, e. Coventry, 27952, A/Cpl., d. of w., F. & F., 3/5/17.

Carter, Ernest John, b. Reading, Berks, e. Woolwich, Kent (Chelsea, London), 33060, Pte., k. in a., F. & F., 15/4/18, formerly 5535, Dragoons.

Carter, George Alfred, b. Brighton, Sussex, e. Stratford-on-Avon, Warwicks (Brighton), 11353, Pte., k. in a., F. & F., 6/8/15.

Carter, George Henry, b. Cheltenham, Glos., e. Warwick (Cheltenham), 927, Pte., d. of w., F. & F., 21/12/14, formerly 10116, Worcs Regt.

Carter, George Henry, b. St. Peter's, Wolverhampton, Staffs, e. Birmingham, 1535, Pte., k. in a., F. & F., 25/4/15.

Carter, Harold, b. Long Itchington, Leamington, Warwicks, e. Warwick (Leamington), 1701, Pte., k. in a., F. & F., 1/7/16.

Carter, Harvey Bertram, b. Childs Wickham, Broadway, Worcs, e. Warwick (Broadway), 9759, Pte., d. of w., F. & F., 9/7/15.

Carter, Percy, b. Long Itchington, Warwicks, e. Rugby, Warwicks (Stockton, Rugby), 9991, Pte., k. in a., F. & F., 12/10/17.

Carter, William Edward, b. Willesden, Middx., e. Mill Hill London (Willesden), 34132, Pte., d. of w., F. & F., 21/11/17, formerly 8522, Lancers.

Carter, William John, b. St. Anne's, Gloucester, e. Birmingham, 2047, Pte., d. of w., F. & F., 2/4/16.

Carvell, Edmund Harry, b. St. Michael's, Coventry, e. Warwick (Leamington, Warwicks), 10442, Pte., d. of w., F. & F., 30/4/18.

Carver, Bernard, b. Bradford, Yorks, e. Birmingham, 1575, Pte., d. of w., F. & F., 7/10/17.

Casey, Albert Edward, b. Ladywood, Birmingham, e. Birmingham, 2379, L/Cpl., k. in a., F. & F., 29/10/14.

Cashmore, Joseph, b. Holy Trinity, Coventry, e. Coventry, 66, Pte., d. of w., F. & F., 29/4/15.

Cassell, John, b. Hinckley, Leics, e. Nuneaton, Warwicks (Bedworth, Warwicks), 4260, Pte., k. in a., F. & F., 25/4/15.

Casterton, Algernon Alfred, b. Biggleswade, Bedford, e. Leicester (Melton Mowbray, Leics), 30102, Pte., k. in a., F. & F., 30/11/17, formerly 9019, Leics Regt.

Cattermole, Horace, e. Birmingham, 307820, Pte., k. in a., F. & F., 26/7/17.

Cavit, Sydney Norton, e. Birmingham, 267663, Pte., k. in a., F. & F., 4/10/17.

Chamberlain, Samuel, b. Birmingham, e. Birmingham, 11372, L/Cpl., k. in a., F. & F., 11/4/17.

Chance, Thomas, e. Birmingham, 267672, Pte., k. in a., F. & F., 3/5/17.

Chandler, Albert Winslow, b. St. Mary's, Norwich, e. Colchester, Essex (Norwich), 6822, Sgt., k. in a., F. & F., 29/10/14.

Chandler, Wilfred, b. Birmingham, e. Birmingham, 36231, Pte., d. of w., F. & F., 26/10/18.

Chapman, John, b. Leamington, Warwicks, e. Nuneaton, Warwicks (Leamington), 164, L/Cpl., d. of w., F. & F., 4/5/15.

Chappell, Stanley, e. Huddersfield, Yorks, 27317, Pte., k. in a., F. & F., 15/4/18, formerly 3888, W. Riding Regt.

Chapple, Walter Ernest, b. Birmingham, e. Birmingham, 16/1454, Pte., k. in a., F. & F., 9/5/17.

Charles, Albert Edward, b. St. Andrew's, Worcester, e. Birmingham (Worcester), 1239, Sgt., k. in a., F. & F., 8/7/15.

Charles, Leonard, b. Aston, Birmingham, e. Aston, Birmingham, 330863, Pte., k. in a., F. & F., 26/7/17.

Charlwood, John, b. St. Michael's, Coventry, e. Warwick (Coventry), 2352, Pte., k. in a., F. & F., 25/4/15.

Charnell, Walter John, b. Atherstone, Warwicks, e. Atherstone, Warwicks, 20716, Pte., k. in a., F. & F., 1/4/18.

Chatland, William George, b. Coventry, e. Coventry, 229, Pte., d. of w., F. & F., 25/4/15.

Checkley, John, b. Stockton, Warwick, e. Warwick (Southam, Warwicks), 9671, Pte., k. in a., F. & F., 27/10/14.

Cherry, Arthur, b. Enfield, Middx., e. Ponders End, London (Enfield), 3072, Pte., k. in a., F. & F., 25/4/15.

Childs, George Henry, b. Birmingham, e. Birmingham, 9689, Pte., k. in a., F. & F., 9/12/14.

Chinn, James William, e. Warwick (Birmingham), 27870, Pte., d. of w., F. & F., 3/5/17.

Chivers, Fred, b. Forest of Dean, Glos., e. Stratford-on-Avon, Warwicks, 203817, L/Cpl., k. in a., F. & F., 19/9/18, M.M.

Church, Sydney Charles, b. Warrington, Bucks, e. Bletchley, Bucks (Olney, Bucks), 18469, Pte., k. in a., F. & F., 29/3/18, formerly 24310, Som. L.I.

Clark, Percival James, b. Chelsea, London, e. Whitehall, London (Islington, London), 25712, Pte., d. of w., F. & F., 14/5/18, formerly 019212, A.O.C.

Clarke, Alfred, b. Birmingham, e. Birmingham, 1247, Pte., k. in a., F. & F., 29/10/14.

Clarke, Alfred, b. Warwick, e. Tamworth (Warwick), 1029, L/Cpl., d. of w., F. & F., 18/9/14.

Clarke, Frank, b Birmingham, e. Birmingham, 42383, Pte., d. of w., F. & F., 25/10/18.

Clarke, George Henry, b. Hinckley, Leics, e. Birmingham, 4351, Pte., k. in a., F. & F., 15/4/18.

Clarke, John William, b. Alford, Lincs, e. Warwick (Coventry), 7536, Pte., k. in a., F. & F., 25/4/15.

Clarke, Oliver James, b. Willenhall, Coventry, e. Warwick (Kenilworth, Warwicks), 1943, L/Cpl., k. in a., F. & F., 15/7/16.

Clarke, Samuel Francis, b. Leyton, Essex, e. East Ham, London, 34823, Pte., k. in a., F. & F., 15/4/18.

Cleal, Ernest Charles, b. Chedington, Dorset, e. Dorcheser (Chedington), 27961, Pte., d., F. & F., 8/2/17.

Cleaver, Arthur Henry, b. Braunston, Daventry, Northants, e Rugby, Warwicks, 9222, L/Cpl., k. in a., F. & F., 25/4/15.

Cleaver, John, b. Aston, Birmingham, e. Warwick (Birmingham), 225, Pte., k. in a., F. & F., 13/10/14.

Cleaver, Joseph Vincent, b. Oxford, e. Rugby, Warwicks, 17860, Pte., k. in a., F. & F., 11/4/17.

Cleaver, William Edward, b. Cubbington, Leamington, Warwicks, e. Leamington, 9477, Pte., d. of w., F. & F., 17/1/16.

Clemens, John, b. Birmingham, e. Birmingham, 7557, Pte., k. in a., F. & F., 25/4/15.

Clements, Samuel Snape, b. Birmingham, e. Warwick (Birmingham), 1125, L/Sgt., k. in a., F. & F., 16/2/17.

Clements, Thomas, b. Walworth, Surrey, e. Woolwich, Kent (Walworth), 694, Pte., k. in a., F. & F., 25/4/15.

Cleton, Joseph, b. Dudley Port, Staffs, e. Warwick (Birmingham), 6324, Pte., k. in a., F. & F., 25/4/15.

Clews, Colin, b. Tamworth, Warwicks, e. Warwick (Tamworth), 5661, Pte., k. in a., F. & F., 11/4/17.

Clifford, Frederick, b. Springhill, Birmingham, e. Birmingham, 11669, Pte., d. of w., F. & F., 14/10/16.

Clifford, Noel, b. Belgrave, Leicester, e. Leicester, 1420, L/Cpl., k. in a., F. & F., 26/4/15.

Clover, Bernard, b. Sheffield, e. Birmingham (Sheffield), 378, Pte., k. in a., F. & F., 7/7/15.

Coates, Benjamin, b. Birmingham, e. Colchester, Essex (Birmingham), 7242, Pte., k. in a., F. & F., 25/4/15.

Coates, Frederick, b. St. Pauls, Leamington, Warwicks, e. Warwick (Leamington), 306, Pte., k. in a., F. & F., 25/4/15.

Coates, John, b. Polesworth, Warwicks, e. Nuneaton, Warwicks (Atherstone, Warwicks), 9641, Pte., k. in a., F. & F., 11/5/15.

Cockerell, Henry Richard, b. Long Itchington, Warwicks, e. Warwick (Long Itchington), 34825, Pte., k. in a., F. & F., 1/9/18.

Cockerell, Henry, b. Small Heath, Birmingham, e. Birmingham, 2424, Pte., k. in a., F. & F., 25/5/15.

Cockerill, George, e. Coventry (Loughborough, Leic), 4581, Pte., k. in a., F. & F., 7/7/15.

Coldicott, Thomas, b. Aldershot, Hants, e. Warwick (Hampton-in-Arden, Warwicks), 2119, Pte., k. in a., F. & F., 13/10/14.

Cole, Daniel, b. Liverpool, e. Birmingham, 7535, Pte., k. in a., F. & F., 12/11/14.

Cole, Richard, b. Dudley, Worcs, e. Birmingham (Tooting London), 8925, Pte., k. in a., F. & F., 25/4/15.

Collett, Alfred Heber, b. Aston, Birmingham, e. Birmingham, 23199, L/Cpl., d. of w., F. & F., 16/9/18.

Collett, Thomas, b. Smethwick, Staffs, e. Warwick (Smethwick, Staffs), 9821, Pte., d. of w., F. & F., 3/7/17.

Collier, Ernest John, b. Sidmouth, Devon, e. Axminster, Devon (Sidmouth), 36234, Pte., d. of w., F. & F., 24/10/18.

Collier, Frederick Henry Douglas, b. Erdington, Birmingham, e. Birmingham, 23959, Pte., k. in a., F. & F., 11/4/17.

Collins, Cecil, b. Stratford-on-Avon, Warwicks, e. Warwick (Stratford-on-Avon), 2789, Pte., k. in a., F. & F., 26/4/15.

Collins, Charles Henry, b. Aston, Birmingham, e. Warwick (Small Heath, Birmingham), 8328, Pte., d. of w., F. & F., 6/6/15.

Collins, Cuthbert, b. Ford, Devonport, e. Plymouth, Devon, 36235, Pte., k. in a., F. & F., 5/8/18.

Collins, George, b. St. Stephens, Worcester, e. Worcester 28381, Pte., k. in a., F. & F., 30/8/18.

Collins, John, b. Saltley, Birmingham, e. Birmingham, 1144, L/Cpl., k. in a., F. & F., 26/4/15.

Collins, William, b. Wootton Wawen, Birmingham, e. Warwick (Wootton Wawen), 462, Cpl., k. in a., F. & F., 12/10/16.

Compton, William, b. St. John's, Leamington, Warwicks, e. Leamington, Warwicks, 10421, Pte., d. of w., F. & F., 20/10/16.

Conboy, Daniel, b. Birmingham, e. Birmingham, 7487, Pte., d. of w., F. & F., 3/5/15.

Congrave, James, b. Dordon, Warwick, e. Atherstone, Warwicks (Wilnecote, nr. Tamworth, Warwicks), 26246, Pte., k. in a., F. & F., 24/10/18.

Connor, James, b. Birmingham, e. Birmingham, 9695, Pte., k in a., F. & F., 25/4/15.

Cook, Alexander, b. St. George's, Birmingham, e. Birmingham (Walsall, Staffs), 2242, Pte., k. in a., F. & F., 25/4/15.

Cook, Charles Edward, b. Ross, Hereford, e. Ross, Hereford, 27851, Pte., k. in a., F. & F., 2/9/18, formerly 24792, Shrops L.I.

Cook, Frederick, b. Billingford, Norfolk, e. Aldershot, Hants, 18738, Pte, d., F. & F., 15/10/16, formerly 24050, Som.L.I.

Cook, William Albert, b. Hartley Wintney, Hants, e. Winchester, Hants (Winchfield), 34828, Pte., k. in a., F. & F. 15/4/18.

Cook, William Wallace, b. Birmingham, e. Birmingham, 9223, Pte., k. in a., F. & F., 16/6/15.

Coombes, Arthur, b. Shipston-under-Wytchwood, Oxon, e. Rugby, Warwicks (New Bilton, Rugby), 1788, Pte., d. of w., F. & F., 30/6/15.

Cooper, Ernest, b. Ratcliff Caby, Bosworth, Leicester, e. Nuneaton, Warwicks (Ratcliff Caby, Bosworth), 1601, Sgt., d. of w., F. & F., 24/6/15.

Cooper, George, b. Birmingham, e. Birmingham, 8131, Pte., k. in a., F. & F., 27/4/18.

Cooper, John William, b. Newbold, Rugby, Warwicks, e. Rugby Warwicks, 9806, k. in a., F. & F., 26/6/16.

Cooper, Thomas, b. All Saints, Manchester, e. Stalybridge Lancs, k. in a., F. & F., 13/10/14.

Cope, Thomas, b. Aston, Birmingham, e. Worcester (Birmingham), 6838, Pte., d. of w., F. & F., 22/12/14.

Cornell, Arthur, b. Mickleton, Glos., e. Rugby, Warwicks (Mickleton, Campden, Glos.), 18127, Pte., k. in a., F. & F., 12/10/17.

Cornish, Sidney Frank, b. Bradford, Yorks, e. Leyton, Essex (Woolpit, Suffolk), 28984, Pte., d. of w., F. & F., 26/4/18.

Cort, Albert, b. Doncaster, Yorks, e Birmingham, 1072, Pte., k. in a., F. & F., 25/4/15.

Cosford, George, b. Birmingham, e. Warwick (Birmingham), 419, A/Cpl., k. in a., F. & F., 26/4/15.

Cotton, Fred Charles, b. St. Pancras, Middx., e. London, 28322 Pte., k. in a., F. & F., 10/5/18, formerly 27354, Hrs.

Cotton, Frederick, b. St. Paul's, Walsall, Staffs, e. Warwick (Coventry), 2350, Pte., d. of w., F. & F., 2/7/15.

Cox, Frederick John, b. Cowley, St. John's, Oxford, e. Reading (Oxford), 9410, L/Cpl., d. of w., F. & F., 13/10/16.

Cox, George, b. Birmingham, e. Ross (Birmingham), 6886, Sgt., k. in a., F. & F., 11/4/17.

Cox, George Burford, b. Birmingham, e. Birmingham, 30234, Pte., k. in a., F. & F., 8/8/18.

Cox, George William, b. Birmingham, e. Birmingham, 97-- Pte., d. of w., F. & F., 14/11/14.

Cox, John, b. St. James, Birmingham, e. Birmingham, 2120, A/Sgt., d. of w., F. & F., 6/8/18.

Cox, William, b. Ashted, Birmingham, e. Birmingham, 4826, L/Cpl., k. in a., F. & F., 22/6/15.

Coxhill, Herbert, b. Preston Bissett, Bucks, e. Bletchley, Bucks (Preston Bissett), 27872, Pte., k. in a., F. & F., 11/4/17.

Coyne, Peter, b. Highgate, Birmingham, e. Birmingham, 1940, Pte., k. in a., F. & F., 25/4/15.

Cracknell, James, b. Birmingham, e. Coventry, 4080, Pte., k. in a., F. & F., 26/4/15.

Craddock, Robert, b. Edgbaston, Birmingham, e. Birmingham, 1614, Pte., k. in a., F. & F., 25/4/15.

Cramp, William, b. Foleshill, Warwicks, e. Warwick (Foleshill), 157, Pte., k. in a., F. & F., 13/10/14.

Cranbrook, William, b. Waltham Green, Middx., e. London (Fulham, London), 6340, A/Sgt., k. in a., F. & F., 25/4/15, formerly 5289, W. Riding Regt.

Crane, Horace Edward, b. St. Martin's, Bucks, e. Oxford (Bletchley, Bucks), 50807, A/C.Q.M.S., k. in a., F. & F., 30/8/18, formerly 13387, Oxford & Bucks L.I.

Crane, John Joseph, b. Birkenhead, Ches., e. Birkenhead, 408, L/Cpl., d. of w., F. & F., 2/11/14.

Creeper, Frederick William Charles, b. Fleet, Hants, e. Hartley Wintney, Hants (Fleet), 34831, Pte., k. in a., F. & F., 15/4/18.

Cross, Basil Richard, b. Claydon, Bucks, e. Aldershot, Hants (Harrow), 15973, Pte., k. in a., F. & F., 23/10/16.

Cross, George William, b. Sutton Coldfield, Warwicks, e. Birmingham, 21345, Pte., d. of w., F. & F., 11/4/17, formerly 27090, R. Berks Regt.

Crowe, William, b. Smethwick, Birmingham, e. Birmingham (Smethwick, Birmingham), 4081, Pte., k. in a., F. & F., 19/6/15.

Crump, Tom, b. Birmingham, e. Birmingham, 9381, Pte., d. of w., F. & F., 20/10/14.

Crumpton, Charles, b. Birmingham, e. Birmingham, 8958, Pte., k. in a., F. & F., 25/4/15.

Crumpton, William, b. Aston, Birmingham, e. Birmingham, 2397, Pte., k. in a., F. & F., 20/12/14.

Curtis, Henry, b. Birmingham, e. Birmingham, 9577, Pte., d. of w., F. & F., 13/10/16.

Cusack, Edward, b. Warwick, e. Warwick, 4438, Cpl., k. in a., F. & F., 31/1/16.

Daft, Herbert, b. Walsall, Staffs, e. Birmingham (Walsall), 717, Pte., k. in a., F. & F., 13/10/14.

Dale, James Austin, b. London, Middx., e. Birmingham, 7687, Pte., k. in a., F. & F., 19/6/15.

Darby, William Henry, b. Birmingham, e. Birmingham (Smethwick, Birmingham), 1271, Pte., k. in a., F. & F., 3/5/17.

Darby, William Thomas, b. All Saints, Birmingham, e. Warwick (Handsworth, Birmingham), 2097, Pte., d. of w., F. & F., 19/5/15.

Daubrey, Reuben, b. Lincoln, e. Portsmouth, Hants, 21116, Pte., k. in a., F. & F., 11/4/17, formerly 146058, R.A.S.C.

Davidson, James, b Old Machar, Aberdeen, e. Aberdeen, 33065, Cpl., d. of w., F. & F., 1/4/18, formerly 9792, Dragoons.

Davies, Francis, b. St. George's, Birmingham, e. Birmingham, 6273, L/Cpl., k. in a., F. & F., 10/5/18.

Davis, Cecil, b Bishops Waltham, Hants, e. Aldershot, Hants (Swanmore, Hants), 43365, Pte., k. in a., F. & F., 30/8/18, formerly P/681, M.M.P.

Davis, George, b. St. James, Bristol, e. Bristol (Durdham Down, Bristol), 28704, Pte., d. of w., F. & F., 2/5/18.

Davis, Henry, b. Birmingham, e. Birmingham (Aston, Birmingham), 6126, Pte., k. in a., F. & F., 9/12/14.

Davis, John Albert, b. St. George's, Birmingham, e. Birmingham, 4793, Sgt., k. in a., F. & F., 11/10/16.

Davis, Reginald Walter, b. Burton, Bradstock, Dorset, e Dorchester, 27754, Pte., d. of w., F. & F., 19/4/18, formerly 5313, Glos Regt.

Davis, Walter, b. Birmingham, e. Birmingham, 707, A/Sgt., d. of w., F. & F., 24/10/15.

Davis, William, e. Birmingham (Lozells, Birmingham), 4087, Pte., k. in a., F. & F., 19/6/15.

Daw, Joseph Leonard, b. Birmingham, e. Birmingham, 831, Pte., k. in a., F. & F., 25/4/15.

Dawson, William, b. Erdington, Birmingham, e. Birmingham (Nechells, Birmingham), 7613, Pte., k. in a., F. & F., 25/4/15.

Day, Albert Joseph, e. Birmingham, 25446, Pte., k. in a., F. & F., 15/4/18.

Day, Alfred John, b. Birmingham, e. Warwick, 9876, Pte., k. in a., F. & F., 21/5/15.

Deeley, Alfred, b. Birmingham, e. Birmingham, 9843, Pte., d of w., F. & F., 1/4/15.

Deeley, David Norman, b. Douglas, I. of M., e. Birmingham, 9597, Pte., d. of w., F. & F., 13/4/17.

Delve, James, b. Barnstaple, Devon, e. Barnstaple, Devon, 35978, Pte., k. in a., F. & F., 9/8/18.

De Meza, George, b. St. John's, Nuneaton, Warwicks, e. Nuneaton, Warwicks, 23988, Pte., k. in a., F. & F., 24/12/17.
Dennis, Harry, b. Birmingham, e. Birmingham, 9779, L/Cpl., k. in a., F. & F., 25/4/15.
Denny, Alfred, b. Smethwick, Birmingham, e. Warwick (Handsworth, Staffs), 7361, Sgt., k. in a., F. & F., 25/6/16.
Denny, Joseph, b. St. Michael's, Coventry, e. Coventry, 9510, Pte., k. in a., F. & F., 12/10/16.
De Ville, Sydney, b. Rollestone, Burton-on-Trent, Staffs, e Burton-on-Trent, Staffs, 33023, L/Cpl., d., F. & F., 27/6/18, formerly GS/13059, Dragoon Gds.
Dewis, John Henry, b. Coventry, e. Coventry, 16842, Sgt., k. in a., F. & F., 15/4/18.
Dignan, John, b. Co. Mayo, e. Nuneaton, Warwicks (Hawkesford, Co. Mayo), 11966, Pte., k. in a., F. & F., 12/10/16.
Dix, Herbert, b. Birmingham, e. Birmingham, 9837, Pte., d. of w., F. & F., 20/5/15.
Dixon, Sidney Freer, b. Durham, e. Newcastle-on-Tyne (Durham), 20604, Pte., k. in a., F. & F., 23/10/16, formerly 11352, A. Cyclist Corps.
Dixon, Wilfred, b. Swindon, Wilts, e. Atherstone, Warwick (New Swindon, Wilts), 9418, Pte., k. in a., F. & F., 26/5/15
Dobinson, William, b. Battersea, Surrey, e. London, 511, Pte., k. in a., F. & F., 25/4/15.
Dobbs, George Norman, b. Croydon, Surrey, e. Stratford-on Avon, Warwicks, 16093, L/Cpl., k. in a., F. & F., 12/10/16.
Dodd, Arthur James, b. Rugby, Warwicks, e. Warwick (Rugby), 9393, C.S.M., k. in a., F. & F., 1/2/15.
Dodd, Harry, b. St. Gregory's, Kent, e. Shorncliffe, Kent (East Haddon, Northants), 28323, Pte., d. of w., F. & F., 18/2/17, formerly 23803, Hussars.
Dodd, W., b. Castleford, Yorks, e. Castleford, 16/2000, Cpl., k. in a., F. & F., 15/4/18, formerly 140414, R.F.A.
Dolan, John, b. Ashted, Birmingham, e. Birmingham, 1609, Pte., k. in a., F. & F., 9/5/15.
Doughty, John Henry, b. Birmingham, e. Warwick (Falkirk, Scotland), 6790, Pte., k. in a., F. & F., 25/4/15.
Downing, John Harold, b. Birmingham, e. Birmingham, 27940, Pte., d. of w., F. & F., 3/5/18.
Draper, Alfred, b. Aston, Birmingham, e. Birmingham, 9767, Pte., k. in a., F. & F., 11/10/16.
Draper, George, b. Kentish Town, Middx., e. London (Hampstead), 28255, Pte., k. in a., F. & F., 11/4/17, formerly 27459, Hussars.
Driver, Harry, b. Birdlip, Glos., e. Bristol, Glos. (Birdlip), 29866, Pte., d. of w., F. & F., 12/10/17.
Duckerin, Frederick William, b. Aston, Birmingham, e. Birmingham, 2413, Pte., k. in a., F. & F., 25/4/15.
Duddy, Timothy, b. Birmingham, e. Birmingham, 1912, Pte., d. of w., F. & F., 10/8/18.
Dunkley, Leonard, e. Birmingham, 305871, Pte., k. in a., F & F., 9/8/17.
Dunn, Harold Leslie, b. Saltley, Birmingham, e. Birmingham, 9200, Pte., k. in a., F. & F., 1/7/16.
Dunn, Joseph, b. Newcastle-on-Tyne, e. Birmingham, 8996, Pte., k. in a., F. & F., 13/10/14.
Dunne, John, b. Monasteravan, Co. Kildare, e. Naas, Co. Kildare (Birmingham), 8851, Pte., k. in a., F. & F., 25/12/15.
Dutton, Percy, b. All Saints, Leamington, e. Leamington, 10077, Sgt., k. in a., F. & F., 15/4/18.
Dyde, John, b. Chipping Campden, Glos., e. Warwick (Chipping Campden), 9668, Pte., k. in a., F. & F., 4/10/17.
Dyke, Othello, b. Stratford-on-Avon, Warwicks, e. Darlaston, Staffs, 7701, A/Cpl., k. in a., F. & F., 12/10/16.
Eadon, George Edmund, b. Napton, Warwicks, e. Warwicks (Napton), 13066, Pte., k. in a., F. & F., 1/7/16.
Eadon, Henry, b. Napton, Warwick, e. Coventry, Napton, 2393, Pte., k. in a., F. & F., 25/4/15.
Eames, Mark, b. Stogumber, Somerset, e. Taunton, Somerset (Stogumber), 36245, Pte., k. in a., F. & F., 29/8/18.
Easey, Harry Charles, b. Trimulgerry, Secunderabad, India, e. Belgaum, India, 9361, A/Sgt., k. in a., F. & F., 13/10/14.
Eaton, Joseph Charles, b. Peartree, Derby, e. Birkenhead, Ches., 3560, A/Sgt., d. of w., F. & F., 22/7/16.
Eden, John Albert, b. All Saints, Warwick, e. Warwick, 2463, Pte., k. in a., F. & F., 4/2/15.
Edge, John William Mallabone, b. Coton, Warwicks, e. Nuneaton, Warwicks, 10682, L/Cpl., k. in a., F. & F., 12/10/17.
Edmonds, Harry, b Olveston, Thornbury, Glos., e. Nuneaton, Warwicks (Measham, Leics), 1890, Sgt., k. in a., F. & F., 12/10/16.
Edmunds, William, b. Smethwick, Staffs, e. Birmingham, 1244, Sgt., d. of w., F. & F., 12/4/17.
Edwards, Edward, b. Small Heath, Birmingham, e. Warwick (Birmingham), 506, Pte., k. in a., F. & F., 21/4/17.
Edwards, James, b. Bradford, Yorks, e. Bradford, 3108, Pte., k. in a., F. & F., 19/6/15.
Edwards, James Henry, b. Hoxton, London, e. Coventry, 4122, Pte., k. in a., F. & F., 23/10/16.
Edwards, James Henry, b. Birmingham, e. Birmingham, 7672, Sgt., k. in a., F. & F., 3/5/17.
Edwards, Patrick, b. St. Martin's, Birmingham, e. Birmingham, 2246, Pte., d. of w., F. & F., 19/9/14.
Edwards, Thomas, b. Birmingham, e. Birmingham, 9726, Pte., k. in a., F. & F., 20/9/14.
Elliott, Frank Edward, b. Trowbridge, Wilts, e. Trowbridge, Wilts, 18735, Pte., k. in a., F. & F., 12/10/16, formerly 23088, Som. L.I.
Elliott, James Oliver, b. St. Paul's, Birmingham, e. Birmingham, 1262, Pte., k. in a., F. & F., 7/11/15.
Elliott, Percy William, b. Ombersladc, Warwicks, e. Nuneaton, Warwicks (Ansley, Atherstone, Warwicks), 16090, Pte., k. in a., F. & F., 16/2/17.
Elwell, Arthur, b. Duddleston, Birmingham, e. Birmingham, 4836, Pte., k. in a., F. & F., 12/10/16.
Elyard, Richard James, e. Leamington (Radford Semele, Leamington), 19966, L/Cpl., k. in a., F. & F., 15/4/18.
England, Charles Edward, b. Ratley, Warwicks, e. Stratford-on-Avon, Warwicks (Banbury, Oxon), 9782, Pte., k. in a., F. & F., 12/12/15.
Ensor, Sidney, b. Birmingham, e. Birmingham, 9707, Pte., d. of w., F. & F., 14/4/17.
Evans, Charles William, b. Hockley, Birmingham, e. Birmingham, 2255, Pte., k. in a., F. & F., 23/10/16.
Evans, Fred, b. Birmingham, Warwicks, e. Birmingham, 26187, Pte., k. in a., F. & F., 25/7/18.
Evans, John, b. St. George's, Wolverhampton, Staffs, e. Nuneaton, Warwicks (Binley, Coventry), 2183, Pte., k. in a., F. & F., 12/10/16.
Evans, Richard John, b. Birmingham, e. Birmingham, 20989, Pte., d. of w., F. & F., 19/4/17.
Evans, Thomas, b. Baddesley Ensor, Atherstone, Warwicks, e. Nuneaton, Warwicks (Atherstone), 2546, L/Cpl., k. in a., F. & F., 12/10/16.
Evetts, Roland Albert, b. Long Itchington, Rugby, Warwicks, e. Warwick (Long Itchington), 16012, Pte., k. in a., F. & F., 26/6/16.
Fairbrother, John William, b. Stockingford, Warwicks, e. Coventry (Nuneaton), 10510, Pte., k. in a., F. & F., 1/7/15.
Fall, William George, b. St. Bartholomew's, Birmingham, e. Birmingham, 2448, Pte., k. in a., F. & F., 3/5/17.
Fallon, Herbert, b. Rochdale, Lancs, e. Rochdale, Lancs, 33025, Pte., k. in a., F. & F., 30/8/18, formerly G.S./21992, D.G.
Fane, Edwin John, b. High Wycombe, Bucks, e. Tamworth, Warwicks, 9617, Pte., k. in a., F. & F., 25/4/15.
Farmer, Albert, b. Erdington, Warwicks, e. Birmingham (Southam, Rugby, Warwicks), 9969, Pte., k. in a., F. & F., 12/10/16.
Faulkner, Charles Henry, b. Cairo, Egypt, e. Birmingham, 3685, Pte., k. in a., F. & F., 3/6/15.
Faulkner, George Frederick, b. Cardiff, Glam., e. Birmingham, 3390, Pte., k. in a., F. & F., 5/6/15.
Faulkner, James, b. Walsall, Staffs, e. Nuneaton, Warwicks, 2786, Pte., k. in a., F. & F., 9/9/15.
Fawson, Herbert Alfred, b. Birmingham, e. Birmingham, 459, Pte., k. in a., F. & F., 30/4/16.
Fellows, Frank Hubert, b. Wolverhampton, Staffs, e. Birmingham, 39918, Pte., d. of w., F. & F., 30/12/18.
Feltham, William Ernest, b. Balsall, Heath, Birmingham, e. Warwick (Birmingham), 2298, L/Cpl., k. in a., F. & F., 25/1/16.
Fereday, Joseph Allen, b. Pensnett, Worcs, e. Birmingham (Pensnett), 19551, Pte., d. of w., F. & F., 18/4/17.
Fevers, William, b. Grandborough, Rugby, Warwicks, e. Rugby, 8377, Pte., k. in a., F. & F., 11/4/17.
Field, Alonzo Leonard, b. Manchester, e. Nuneaton, Warwicks (Marston), 2423, Pte., k. in a., F. & F., 2/10/15.
Field, Alfred, b. Birmingham, e. Birmingham, 12797, L/Cpl., k. in a., F. & F., 9/10/17.
Finch, Arthur Cecil, b. Staines, Middx., e. London (West Ealing), 28260, Pte., k. in a., F. & F., 23/7/17, formerly 27451, 9th Res. Cav. Regt.
Finch, William, b. Bromsgrove, Worcs, e. Warwick (Bromsgrove), 366, Pte., k. in a., F. & F., 25/4/15.
Fincham, Albert Thomas, b. Birmingham, e. Birmingham, 16922, Pte., k. in a., F. & F., 3/5/17.
Fish, Henry, b. Arnold, Notts, e. Arnold, Notts, 27538, Pte., k. in a., F. & F., 30/8/18, formerly Notts & Derby Regt.
Fiske, Herbert, b. Small Burgh, Norwich, e. Coventry, 14320, L/Cpl., k. in a., F. & F., 12/10/16.
Fitzer, Albert, b. Birmingham, e. Ross, Herefordshire (Birmingham), 6878, Pte., d. of w., F. & F., 19/6/15.
Fitzgerald, Joseph, b. Birmingham, e. Birmingham, 9259, Pte., k. in a., F. & F., 8/2/15.
Fitzgerald, Robert, b. St. Annes, Belfast, e. Hereford (Coventry), 11325, Pte., k. in a., F. & F., 10/10/15.
Fletcher, Alfred Charles, b. Nottingham, e. Coventry, 19348, Pte., k. in a., F. & F., 11/4/17.
Fletcher, Isaac, b. Collycroft, nr. Nuneaton, e. Nuneaton, Warwicks (Collycroft), 4477, L/Cpl., d. of w., F. & F., 31/10/17.
Fletcher, William, b. Ash Green, Exhall, Coventry, e. Nuneaton, Warwicks (Ash Green, Exhall), 4528, Pte., k. in a., F. & F., 24/5/15.
Foden, Henry, b. Nechells Birmingham, e. Birmingham, 1227, Pte., k. in a., F. & F., 19/6/15.
Ford, Leonard, b. Birmingham, e. Coventry (Birmingham), 146, L/Cpl., k. in a., F. & F., 23/7/15.
Forrest, Matthew, b. Coughton, Alcester, Warwicks, e. Warwick (Leek Wootton, Warwick), 4481, A/Cpl., k. in a., F. & F., 12/10/16.
Forrest, Richard, b. St. Wilfrid's, Preston, Lancs, e. Preston, 11470, Pte., k. in a., F. & F., 12/10/16.
Fortey, Bert, b. Atherstone, Warwicks, e. Atherstone (Much Marcle, Glos), 10969, Pte., k. in a., F. & F., 16/2/17.
Foster, Frederick Charles, e. Birmingham (Aston, Birmingham), 267682, Pte., k. in a., F. & F., 3/5/17.
Foster, William, b. Birmingham, e. Birmingham (Foleshill, Coventry), 9359, Pte., d. of w., F. & F., 18/9/14.
Fox, Alfred Ernest, b. Birmingham, e. Birmingham (Camp Hill, Birmingham), 5219, Pte., k. in a., F. & F., 1/4/18.
Fox, Thomas, b. Saltley, Birmingham, e. Tamworth, Warwicks (Birmingham), 9546, Pte., k in a., F. & F., 8/7/15.
Fox, Norman Harry, b. Oxford, e. Rugby, Warwicks, 2123, Pte., k. in a., F. & F., 21/3/15.
Foy, John, b. Deritend, Birmingham, e. Birmingham, 3368, Pte., k. in a., F. & F., 11/10/16.
France, Albert, b. Oldham, Lancs, e. Oldham, 33082, Pte., k. in a., F. & F., 15/4/18, formerly 21551, Dragoons.

France, William Henry, b. Birmingham, e. Birmingham, 9169, Pte., d., F. & F., 5/3/15.

Francis, Frederick Charles, b. West Pennard, Som., e. Bristol (Easton, Bristol), 266894, Pte., k. in a., F. & F., 30/8/18.

Francis, Henry, b. Pirton, Worcester, e. Birmingham (Wadborough, Worcester), 4979, Pte., k. in a., F. & F., 3/5/17.

Francis, James, b. Byfleet, Surrey, e. Guildford, Surrey (Byfleet), 33010, A/Cpl., d. of w., F. & F., 20/11/17, formerly No. G.S./5414, 6th D.G.

Franklin, Alexander, b. Chipping Norton, Oxon, e. Chipping Norton (Shipton-under-Wychwood, Oxon), 18380, Pte., d., F. & F., 7/5/17, formerly 23357, Som. L.I.

Fraser, Hugh, b. Kilmarrock, Beauley, Inverness, e. Marylebone, London, 3719, Pte., k. in a., F. & F., 19/6/15.

Freeman, Joseph, b. Birmingham, e. Birmingham, 9325, Pte., k. in a., F. & F., 19/6/15.

French, Walter Constant, b. St Thomas, Birmingham, e. Birmingham, 10660, Pte., k. in a., F. & F., 12/10/17.

Fry, Edmund, b. Saltley, Birmingham, e. Birmingham, 4296, Pte., k. in a., F. & F., 10/10/16.

Fuller, John, b. Saltley, Birmingham, e. Warwick, 9634, Pte., k. in a., F. & F., 21/3/16.

Fynn, George, b. Shipley, Yorks, e. Rochdale, Lancs, 20630, Pte., k. in a., F. & F., 23/10/16, formerly 11115, Army Cycl. Corps.

Gadsby, John, b. Tamworth, Warwicks, e. Sutton Coldfield, Warwicks, 23279, Pte., d. of w., F. & F., 11/4/17.

Gahan, Lawrence, b. Birmingham, e. Birmingham, 7519, Pte., k. in a., F. & F., 26/4/15.

Gains, Stanley, b. Southampton, Hants, e. Southampton, 27955, Pte., k. in a., F. & F., 12/10/17, formerly 2145, Hants Regt.

Galloway, James, b. Horne, Horley, e. Guildford, Surrey (Horley), 932, Pte., k. in a., F. & F., 19/7/15.

Ganley, Thomas, b. Coventry, e. Warwick (Coventry), 9721, A/C.S.M., d. of w., F. & F., 23/12/17.

Gardener, Harry, b. Harbury, Leamington, Warwick, e. Warwick (Harbury), 2137, Pte., d. of w., F. & F., 16/11/14.

Gardner, Charles, b. St. Mary's, Warwick, e. Birmingham, 11163, L/Cpl., d. of w., F. & F., 21/4/17.

Gardner, George, b. Leamington, Warwick, e. Birmingham, 9453, Pte., d. of w., F. & F., 6/6/15.

Gardner, George Harry, b. Whilton, Northants, e. Nuneaton, Warwicks, 28836, Pte., d. of w., F. & F., 24/10/18, formerly S/2016961, R.A.S.C.

Gardner, William, b. Bishops Itchington, Warwick, e. Warwick (Fenny Compton, Leamington), 10169, Pte., k. in a., F. & F., 8/6/15.

Garland, Walter, b. Nuneaton, e. Nuneaton, Warwicks, 1951, Pte., k. in a., F. & F., 8/7/15.

Garland, William Edward, b. St. Martin's, Birmingham, e. Birmingham, 11680, Pte., k. in a., F. & F., 8/8/16.

Garratt, John, b. Nuneaton, Warwicks, e. Nuneaton, 11912, Pte., k. in a., F. & F., 14/4/18.

Garrison, Bert Richard, b. Warwick, e. Warwick, 14780, Pte., k. in a., F. & F., 11/4/17.

Gartenfield, Charles Reginald, b. Long Itchington, Warwicks, e. Rugby, Warwicks, 3274, Pte., d. of w., F. & F., 25/4/15.

Garvey, William Hugh, b. Edgbaston, Birmingham, e. Ross, Herefordshire (Birmingham), 6861, Pte., k. in a., F. & F., 25/4/15.

Gathercole, Charles Benjamin, b. Oakmere, Ches., e. Northwich, Ches., 29499, Pte., k. in a., F. & F., 30/8/18, formerly 61988, Ches. Regt.

Gear, Charles John, b. Worcester, e. Warwick (Birmingham), 6921, Pte., k. in a., F. & F., 25/4/15.

Gibson, Robert, b. Old Brompton, Chatham, Kent, e. Maidstone, Kent (Chatham), 503, C.S.M., k. in a., F. & F., 11/5/18, M.M.

Gifford, William Henry, b. St. Michael's, Coventry, e. Coventry, 2157, Pte., k. in a., F. & F., 25/4/15.

Gilbert, George, b. Birmingham, e. Warwick (Birmingham), 6748, Pte., d. of w., F. & F., 11/2/15.

Gilderson, William Charles, b. London, Middx., e. Birmingham, 1872, Pte., k. in a., F. & F., 18/6/15.

Gilderthorpe, Harry, b. Birmingham, e. Warwick (Birmingham), 9771, L/Cpl., k. in a., F. & F., 2/5/15.

Giles, Henry, b. Abingdon, Berks, e. Abingdon, 33158, Pte., d. of w., F. & F., 30/8/18, formerly 27416, Hussars.

Gilks, William George, b. Birmingham, e. Birmingham, 384, A/Sgt., k. in a., F. & F., 6/1/16.

Gill, Edwin, b. Birmingham, e. Birmingham, 22907, Pte., k. in a., F. & F., 24/10/18.

Gill, Joshua Thomas, b. St. George's, Birmingham, e. Birmingham, 1422, Cpl., k. in a., F. & F., 3/5/17.

Gillard, Frederick George, b. Mountain Ash, South Wales, e. Frome, Som. (Chewton Mendip, Bath, Som.), 36382, Pte., k. in a., F. & F., 30/8/18.

Gilliver, Herbert Harold, b. Lichfield, Staffs, e. Birmingham, 11880, Pte., d. of w., F. & F., 28/4/18.

Golding, Frederick Herbert, b. Derby, e. Aylesbury, Bucks (Marlow), 36260, Pte., d. of w., F. & F., 30/8/18.

Goode, William Edward, b. Beckbury, Salop, e. Coleshill, Warwicks (Maxstoke, Warwicks), 17027, Pte., k. in a., F. & F., 25/4/18.

Goodhead, James, b. Aston, Birmingham, e. Birmingham (Aston, Birmingham), 2371, Pte., k. in a., F. & F., 20/12/14.

Goodley, George Mathew, b. Peterborough, Northants, e. Peterborough, Northants, 23566, Pte., k. in a., F. & F., 12/10/17, formerly 174190, R.E.

Goodman, Walter George, b. Hillmorton, Rugby, Warwicks, e. Warwick (Hillmorton), 228, Pte., k. in a., F. & F., 27/8/14.

Goodyear, Joseph, b. Birmingham, e. Birmingham, 7739, Pte., k. in a., F. & F., 26/4/15.

Gopsill, Alfred, b. Sheldon, Warwick, e. Warwick (Minworth, Warwicks), 27881, Pte., k. in a., F. & F., 23/6/17.

Gordon, Edward Laing, b. Burslem, Staffs, e. Stoke-on-Trent, 2574, Pte., d. of w., F. & F., 11/12/16.

Gordon, William Plant, b. Burslem, Staffs, e. Stoke-on-Trent (Burslem), 2575, Pte., k. in a., F. & F., 25/4/15.

Gorton, James, b. Birmingham, e. Worthing, Sussex (Birmingham), 273, Pte., k. in a., F. & F., 11/4/17.

Gough, Benjamin George, b. Birmingham, e. Birmingham, 9935, Pte., k. in a., F. & F., 25/4/15.

Gough, Walter, b. St. George's, Birmingham, e. Birmingham, 2871, Pte., k. in a., F. & F., 27/12/15.

Gould, George, b. Birmingham, e. Warwick (Birmingham), 6835, Pte., k. in a., F. & F., 17/1/15.

Govett, Alfred Benjamin, e. Camberwell, London (Peckham, London), 10410, Pte., k. in a., F. & F., 25/4/15.

Graves, Arthur, b. South Muskham, Newark-on-Trent, e. Coventry, 4325, Pte., d. of w., F. & F., 17/10/16.

Gray, Walter Charles Henry Ekin, b. Birmingham, e. Birmingham, 1204, Pte., k. in a., F. & F., 25/4/15.

Greatrix, Harry, b. Birmingham, e. Birmingham, 1468, Pte., k. in a., F. & F., 14/3/15.

Greatrix, William, b. Birmingham, e. Birmingham, 171, Pte., k. in a., F. & F., 26/4/15.

Gregory, Ronald Christopher, b. Bagshot, Surrey, e. Wokingham, Surrey (Brackwell, Berks), 35286, Pte., d. of w., F. & F., 8/9/18.

Green, Alfred Edwin, b. Highgate, Birmingham, e. Birmingham, 2133, A/Cpl., k. in a., F. & F., 13/10/14.

Green, Ernest Thomas, b. St. Martin's, Birmingham, e. Birmingham, 13251, Pte., d. of w., F. & F., 16/7/16.

Green, Percy, b. Downend, Bristol, e. Bristol (Downend), 268875, Pte., d. of w., F. & F., 18/12/17

Greening, Arthur, b. Birmingham, e. Birmingham, 9283, Pte., k. in a., F. & F., 20/4/15.

Greenslade, Reginald, b. Cullompton, Devon, e. Tiverton, Devon (Cullompton), 34849, Pte., d., F. & F., 2/4/18.

Greenway, Ernest John, b. Saltley, Birmingham, e. Birmingham, 2139, Pte., d. of w., F. & F., 19/7/15.

Greenway, Walter, b. Radway, Staffs, e. Birmingham, 11668, L/Cpl., k. in a., F. & F., 12/10/17.

Grice, Harry, b. Birmingham, e. Lichfield, Staffs (Birmingham), 1876, L/Cpl., k. in a., F. & F., 25/4/15.

Griffin, Elijah, b. Coventry, e. Birmingham, 4235, Pte., k. in a., F. & F., 18/11/15.

Griffiths, Albert, b. Birmingham, e. Warwick (Birmingham), 9197, Pte., k. in a., F. & F., 19/6/15.

Griffiths, Harry, b Harborne, Birmingham, e. Birmingham, 1000, Pte., d. of w., F. & F., 5/4/18.

Grimes, Ronald, b. St. John's, Newfoundland, e. Warwick (St. John's, Newfoundland), 22837, Pte., d., F. & F., 7/5/17.

Gubbings, Samuel, b. Homerton, London, Middx., e. Hounslow, Middx. (Clapton Park, Middx.), 7608, Pte., d. of w., F. & F., 20/6/17.

Guest, Alfred, b. Birmingham, e. Birmingham, 10014, Pte., k. in a., F. & F., 12/10/16.

Gunn, William Henry, b. St. Mary's, Banbury, Oxon, e. Nuneaton, Warwick, 2457, Pte., d. of w., F. & F., 10/4/15.

Gurney, John Thomas, b. Calthorpe, Rugby, Warwicks, e Warwick (Calthorpe), 316, L/Cpl., k. in a., F. & F., 25/4/15.

Guttery, Albert, b. Birmingham, e. Birmingham, 4054, Pte., d. of w., F. & F., 24/8/15.

Gwinnett, Alfred, b. Tamworth, Warwicks, e. Warwick (Knowle, Birmingham), 1049, Pte., k. in a., F. & F., 25/10/14.

Hackett, Ernest Wilfred, b. Aston, Birmingham, e. Birmingham, 2096, Pte., d. of w., F. & F., 4/12/14.

Haddock, John Marshall, b. Walsall, Staffs, e. Walsall, 41358, Pte., d. of w., F. & F., 25/10/18.

Hadley, Alfred, b. Worcester, e. Warwick (Oldbury, Birmingham), 9549, Pte., k. in a., F. & F., 6/9/15.

Hadley, Francis William, b. Birmingham, e. London, 8781, Pte., d. of w., F. & F., 3/5/15.

Hadley, Thomas, b. Birmingham, e. Coventry, 29624, Pte., d. of w., F. & F., 6/10/17.

Hale, Sidney John, b. St. Paul's, Leamington, Warwicks, e. Warwick (Leamington), 940, Pte., d. of w., F. & F., 31/10/14.

Hales, Harry, b. Stockton, Rugby, Warwicks, e. Rugby, Warwicks (New Bilton, Rugby), 2105, Pte., k. in a., F. & F., 13/10/14.

Hall, Albert, b. Hanley, Staffs, e. Hanley, Staffs, 7594, Pte., k. in a., F. & F., 27/10/14.

Hall, Alfred Abel, b. Honiley, Warwicks, e. Warwick (Knowle), 9619, Pte., k. in a., F. & F., 4/10/15.

Hall, Charles, b. Bedworth, Coventry, Warwicks, e. Nottingham (Bedworth), 2393, Pte., k. in a., F. & F., 20/4/15.

Hall, Frederick, b. Birmingham, e. Birmingham 9619, A/Cpl., k. in a., F. & F., 25/4/15.

Hall, Ralph, b. Derby, e. Warwick (Austrey, near Atherstone), 24121, Pte., d. of w., F. & F., 16/4/18.

Hammond, John, b. Tottenham, London, e. Birmingham (Tottenham), 734, Pte., k. in a., F. & F., 25/4/15.

Hancox, Charles John, b. Long Lawford, Rugby, Warwicks, e Rugby, Warwicks (Long Lawford), 1685, Pte., k. in a., F. & F., 26/4/15.

Hand, Walter, b. Colley Weston, Northants, e. Stamford (Colley Weston, Northants), 27038, Pte., k. in a., F. & F., 3/5/17, formerly 3802, 4th Lincs Regt., M.M.

Hands, James, b. Winson Green, Birmingham, e. Warwick (Winson Green, Birmingham), 2067, Pte., d., F. & F., 1/11/18.

Hankinson, Thomas, b. Birmingham, e. Nuneaton (Attleborough, Nuneaton), 11381, Pte., k. in a., F. & F., 11/10/16.

Hanks, Joseph Harold, b. All Saints, Birmingham, e. Birmingham, 646, Pte., d. of w., F. & F., 31/10/18.

Hanson, Christopher, b. Liverpool, e. Douglas, Isle of Man, 1817, Pte., k. in a., F. & F., 7/7/15.

Hardman, Joseph, b. Highgate, Birmingham, e. Warwick (Highgate, Birmingham), 448, Pte., k. in a., F. & F., 17/12/14.
Hardman, William, b. Stratford-on-Avon, Warwicks, e. Nuneaton, Warwicks, 10665, Pte., k. in a., F. & F., 3/5/17.
Harley, Alfred, b. Willoughby, Leicester, e. Nuneaton, Warwicks, 3503, Pte., k. in a., F. & F., 29/3/18.
Harris, Albert Edward, b. Bidford-on-Avon, Warwicks, e. Stratford-on-Avon (Binton, Stratford-on-Avon), 9910, Pte. k. in a., F. & F., 31/7/15.
Harris, Charles Oscar, b. Portsmouth, e. Welshpool (Portsmouth), 675, Pte., k. in a., F. & F., 10/10/15.
Harris, Frank, b. All Saints, Leamington, Warwicks, e. Warwick (Coventry), 9158, Pte., k. in a., F. & F., 13/10/14.
Harris, George Albert, b. Birmingham, e. Birmingham (Nechells, Birmingham), 9052, Pte., k. in a., F. & F., 10/4/15.
Harris, Thomas, b. Chilvers Coton, Nuneaton, Warwicks, e. Nuneaton (Chilvers Coton, Nuneaton), 4432, Pte., d. of w., F. & F., 27/7/15.
Harris, William Charles, b. Birmingham, e. Birmingham (Sparkbrook, Birmingham), 7357, Pte., k. in a., F. & F., 19/6/15.
Harrison, Joseph Andrew, b. St. Mary's, Nottingham, e. Nottingham, 683, L/Cpl., k. in a., F. & F., 5/1/16.
Hart, James Timothy, b. Aston, Birmingham, e. Birmingham, 2486, Pte., k. in a., F. & F., 25/4/15.
Hartshorne, William, b. St. Michael's, Coventry, Warwicks, e. Warwick (Emscote, Warwick), 4715, Pte., d., F. & F., 7/11/15.
Harvey, Joseph, b. Deritend, Birmingham, e. Birmingham (Digbeth, Birmingham), 2295, Pte., d. of w., F. & F., 12/4/17.
Haseldine, Stanley, b. Olney, Bucks. e. Aylesbury (Olney, Bucks), 36305, Pte., d., F. & F., 30/8/18.
Haskey, Samuel, b. Birmingham, e. Birmingham (Small Heath, Birmingham), 8971, Pte., k. in a., F. & F., 13/10/14.
Hastings, Frank, b. Edgbaston, Birmingham, e. Warwick (Edgbaston, Birmingham), 9648, Pte., d. of w., F. & F., 29/10/16.
Hastings, John Charles, b. Birmingham, e. Birmingham (Banbury, Oxon), 9255, Pte., k. in a., F. & F., 19/6/15.
Hatfield, Percy George, e. Birmingham (Greet, Birmingham), 267622, Pte., d., F. & F., 31/5/17.
Havard, George, b. Small Heath, Birmingham, e. Birmingham (Bordesley Green, Birmingham), 4883, Sgt., k. in a., F. & F., 11/4/17.
Hawker, Edwin James, b. Aston, Birmingham, e. Birmingham (Aston), 8715, L/Cpl., k. in a., F. & F., 7/3/15.
Hawkes, Frederick George, b. Worcester, e. Birmingham (Swansea), 6984, Pte., k. in a., F. & F., 25/4/15.
Hawkswood, Albert, b. Highgate, Birmingham, e. Birmingham, 1553, Pte., d. of w., F. & F., 9/6/17.
Hawley, George Alexander, b. St. Mary's, Lanark, Scotland, e. Birmingham (Falkirk, Scotland), 9774, Pte., k. in a., F. & F., 1/5/16.
Haywood, Charles Henry, b. Walsall, Staffs, e. Nuneaton, Warwicks (Oakham, Rutland), 1636, Pte., k. in a., F. & F., 7/11/15.
Haywood, Herbert, b. Coventry, Warwicks, e. Coventry, Warwicks, 62, Pte., k. in a., F. & F., 11/10/16.
Haywood, William, b. Glascote Heath, Tamworth, e. Atherstone (Glascote Heath), 10882, Pte., k. in a., F. & F., 17/11/15.
Hazelton, Arthur Cecil, b. Hilgay Downham, Market, Norfolk, e. Norwich, 33045, Pte., k. in a., F. & F., 25/7/18, formerly 6591, 7th D.G.
Healey, James Thomas, b. Birmingham, e. Birmingham (Saltley, Birmingham), 8995, Pte., k. in a., F. & F., 25/4/15.
Heard, Alfred, b. Birmingham, e. Birmingham (Lozells, Birmingham), 9257, Pte., k. in a., F. & F., 25/4/15.
Heath, William Thomas, b. Birmingham, e. Birmingham, 42331, Pte., d., F. & F., 17/12/15.
Hedges, Robert, b. Birmingham, e. Birmingham (Aston, Birmingham), 7490, Pte., k. in a., F. & F., 17/4/18.
Height, Harry, b. St. John's, Leamington, Warwicks, e. Warwick (Leamington), 244, Dmr., d. of w., F. & F., 29/4/16.
Hemmings, James William, b. Idlicote, Shipston-on-Stour, Warwicks, e. Birmingham (Ettington, Stratford-on-Avon), 7205, L/Cpl., k. in a., F. & F., 1/9/18.
Hewins, John, b. Clifford Chambers, Stratford-on-Avon, e. Warwick (Clifford Chambers), 1648, L/Cpl., d. of w., F. & F., 12/10/16.
Hewitt, George, b. Deritend, Birmingham, e. Birmingham, 1010, Pte., k. in a., F. & F., 26/4/15.
Hibbert, Henry Walter, b. Clewer, Windsor, Berks, e. Windsor, 9085, L/Cpl., k. in a., F. & F., 1/7/16.
Higgerson, Arthur, b. Hampton-in-Arden, Warwicks, e. Warwick (Hampton-in-Arden), 2489, Pte., k. in a., F. & F., 26/4/15.
Higham, Alfred Charles, b. Rugby, Warwicks, e. Warwick (Rugby), 1002, L/Cpl., k. in a., F. & F., 8/7/15.
Highley, Arthur Edward, b. Coleford, Glos., e. Lydney, Glos. (Coleford), 34857, Pte., k. in a., F. & F., 15/4/18.
Hill, Caleb George, b. Hockton, Northants, e. Nuneaton, Warwicks, 2230, A/Cpl., d. of w., F. & F., 28/10/14.
Hill, George Joseph, b. Hockley, Birmingham, e. Birmingham, 1936, Pte., k. in a., F. & F., 19/6/15.
Hill, Harry, b. Birmingham, e. Birmingham, 9752, Pte., k. in a., F. & F., 25/4/15.
Hill, John, b. Studley, Warwicks, e. Stratford-on-Avon, Warwicks (Studley), 38944, Pte., k. in a., F. & F., 8/8/18.
Hill, John, b. Smethwick, Staffs, e. Birmingham (Smethwick), 10015, L/Cpl., k. in a., F. & F., 12/10/17.
Hill, Reginald Bertram, b. Broadway, Worcs, e. Stratford-on-Avon, Warwicks (Broadway), 9574, Pte., k. in a., F. & F., 4/7/15.
Hill, William, b. Gravesend, Kent, e. Tidworth, Wilts (Basingstoke, Hants), 34165, Pte. k. in a., F. & F., 1/4/18, formerly GS/14701, D.G.
Hirons, George, b. Thurlaston, Warwicks, e. Leamington, Warwicks (Thurlaston), 50866, L/Cpl., d. of w., F. & F., 3/9/18.
Hitchman, William, b. Birmingham, e. Birmingham, 796, A/Sgt., k. in a., F. & F., 1/5/17.
Hobbs, George, b. Cardiff, Glam., e. Birmingham, 1924, A/Sgt., k. in a., F. & F., 17/4/16.
Hobson, Herbert, b. All Saints, Birmingham, e. Birmingham, 2162, Pte., k. in a., F. & F., 27/8/14.
Hoden, William Ogden, b. Lutterworth, Leics, e. Rugby, Warwicks (Hugglescote, Leics), 9066, Pte., k. in a., F. & F., 13/10/14.
Hodgkiss, George, b. Wolverhampton, Staffs, e. Birmingham, 7896, L/Cpl., k. in a., F. & F., 11/4/17.
Hogg, John, b. St. Michael's, Coventry, e. Warwick (Coventry), 2194, Pte., k. in a., F. & F., 26/8/14.
Hogg, Victor, b. Attleborough, Nuneaton, Warwicks, e. Nuneaton, 4560, A/Cpl., k. in a., F. & F., 17/4/16.
Holden, Charles, b. West Bromwich, Staffs, e. Birmingham (West Bromwich), 9055, Sgt., k. in a., F. & F., 9/8/18, D.C.M.
Holdom, James, b. Nuneaton, Warwicks, e. Hinckley, Leics (Nuneaton), 941, Sgt., k. in a., F. & F., 12/10/16.
Holland, James, b. Bromley, Kent, e. Reigate, Surrey (Redhill, Surrey), 8620, Pte., k. in a., F. & F., 30/8/18, formerly Hussars.
Holland, Thomas, b. Nantwich, Ches., e. Crewe, Ches., 7823, Pte., k. in a., F. & F., 25/6/16.
Hollingsworth, Harry, b. Wolverhampton, Staffs, e. Wolverhampton, 37583, Pte., d. of w., F. & F., 31/5/18, formerly 236229, R.A.S.C.
Holmes, Bert, b. Leicester, e. Rugby, Warwicks, 1664, L/Cpl., k. in a., F. & F., 20/11/17, D.C.M.
Holmes, Sidney, e. Walsall, 41980, Pte., d., F. & F., 16/9/19.
Holtham, George, b. Moreton Morrell, Warwicks, e. Birmingham (Moreton Morrell), 1454, Sgt., k. in a., F. & F., 20/6/17.
Holtom, Frederick, b. Stratford-on-Avon, Warwicks, e. Warwick (Stratford-on-Avon), 280, A/Sgt., k. in a., F. & F., 9/4/17.
Hone, John, b. Wellesbourne, Stratford-on-Avon, Warwicks, e. Birmingham (Wellesbourne), 721, Pte., k. in a., F. & F., 24/10/18.
Honner, John, b. Richmond, Middx., e. Liverpool (Richmond), 400, L/Cpl., k. in a., F. & F., 25/4/15.
Hoomans, Bernard, b. Birmingham, e. Birmingham, 1046, Pte., k. in a., F. & F., 17/4/16.
Hornsby, Arthur, b. Lincoln, e. Birmingham (Dorchester, Dorset), 7752, Pte., d. of w., F. & F., 16/10/14.
Hornsby, Richard, b. St. Michael's, Coventry, e. Birmingham, 2402, Pte., d. of w., F. & F., 29/10/16.
Horton, Joseph, b. Gayton Lee Wold, Lincs, e. Manchester (Market Rasen), 9687, Pte., d. of w., F. & F., 24/10/14.
Hoskins, Harry, b. Sutton, Epsom, Surrey, e. Warwick (Uppingham, Rutland), 9423, C/Sgt., k. in a., F. & F., 24/5/15.
Howell, William Arthur, b. Battersea, Surrey, e. Battersea, 10905, Pte., d. of w., F. & F., 15/12/15.
Howes, Harry James, b. Preston, Brighton, Sussex, e. Brighton, 1069, Pte., k. in a., F. & F., 8/9/14, formerly 5490, Scots Gds., 747, R. Highr.
Howlett, George, b. All Saints, Birmingham, e. Birmingham, 201390, L/Cpl., k. in a., F. & F., 30/8/18.
Hubball, Albert Radford, b. Birmingham, e. Birmingham, 742, Pte., k. in a., F. & F., 26/4/15.
Hubbard, Joseph, b. Countesthorpe, Leics, e. Leicester (Countesthorpe), 9278, Pte., d. of w., F. & F., 24/9/14.
Hubball, Frank, b. Birmingham, e. Birmingham, 7603, L/Cpl., k. in a., F. & F., 11/4/17.
Hudson, John, b. Grenstead, Colchester, e. Colchester, Essex, 6911, Pte., d. of w., F. & F., 9/7/15.
Hughes, Albert, b. Aston, Birmingham, e. Birmingham (Aston, Birmingham), 835, Pte., k. in a., F. & F., 12/10/16.
Hughes, Samuel Francis, b. St. Paul's, Birmingham, e. Birmingham, 1975, Pte., d. of w., F. & F., 7/3/15.
Hull, George, b. Worcester, e. Coventry, 3066, Sgt., k. in a., F. & F., 12/10/16.
Hurden, Frederick John, b. Martinstown, Dorset, e. Dorchester, Dorset (Monkton, nr. Dorchester), 34855, Pte., k. in a., F. & F., 17/4/18.
Ingram, Frederick, b. Warwick, e. Warwick, 9831, Pte., k. in a., F. & F., 25/4/15.
Ingram, George John, b. Birmingham, e. Birmingham, 9301, Pte., k. in a., F. & F., 19/9/14.
Ingram, William, b. Good Shepherd, West Bromwich, Staffs, e. Birmingham (West Bromwich), 1878, Pte., k. in a., F. & F., 25/4/15.
Inman, Walter Henry, b. Ladywood, Birmingham, e. Birmingham, 2282, Pte., k. in a., F. & F., 11/10/16.
Irons, Sidney, b. Diddington, Hunts, e. Huntingdon (Diddington), 30260, L/Cpl., k. in a., F. & F., 11/4/17, formerly 954, Hunts Cyclist Battn.
Ives, James Frederick, b. Belfast, e. Bletchley, Bucks (Belfast), 50868, Pte., d. of w., F. & F., 30/8/18.
Jackson, Arthur William, b. St. Martin's, Birmingham, e. Birmingham (Redditch, Worcs), 9628, Pte., k. in a., F. & F., 31/3/18.
Jackson, George Roland, b. Rotherhithe, Surrey, e. Woolwich, Kent (Rotherhithe), 898, Pte., k. in a., F. & F., 23/11/14.
Jacques, Amos William, b. Bedworth, Warwicks, e. Leamington, Warwicks (Bedworth), 41769, Pte, k. in a., F. & F., 24/10/18.
James, John Henry, b. St. John's, Birmingham, e. Birmingham (Aston, Birmingham), 17100, Pte., d. of w., F. & F., 12/12/16.
Jauncey, John, b. Hereford, e. Nuneaton, Warwicks, 2033, Pte., k. in a., F. & F., 24/3/16.
Jarratt, Alfred, b. Birmingham, e. Birmingham, 1760, L/Cpl., k. in a., F. & F., 9/5/15.

Jarvis, Albert Ernest, b. St. Margaret's, Leicester, e. Leicester, 8011, L/Sgt., d. of w., F. & F., 20/8/14.

Jasper, Edward George, b. St. Teath, Cornwall, e. Bude, Cornwall (Boscastle, Cornwall), 25529, Pte., k. in a., F. & F., 12/10/17.

Jay, Arthur, b. Nottingham, e. Grimsby (Lincs), 8130, Cpl., k in a., F. & F., 12/10/17.

Jeary, Albert George, b. Clay-on-Sea, Norfolk, e. London (Clay-on-Sea), 20578, Pte., k. in a., F. & F., 12/10/16, formerly 10718, A. Cyclist Corps.

Jeavons, Alfred James, b. Dudley, e. Dudley, Worcs, 24804 Pte., k. in a., F. & F., 30/8/18.

Jeif, John, b. Aston, Birmingham, e. Birmingham (Aston, Birmingham), 8853, Pte., k. in a., F. & F., 26/4/15.

Jennings, Edward, b. Ashted, Birmingham, e. Birmingham, 1758, Pte., d. of w., F. & F., 6/8/16.

Jennings, James, b. St. Mary's, Leamington, Warwicks, e. Warwick (Leamington), 1969, Pte., k. in a., F & F., 4/10/17.

Jennings, Walter, b. Knowle, Warwicks, e. Warwick (Badlesley Clinton, Knowle), 9427, Pte., k. in a., F. & F., 1/7/16.

Jephcott, Oliver, b. Trinity, Coventry, e. Coventry (Trinity, Coventry), 425, Pte., k. in a., F. & F., 13/10/14.

Jeynes, Edwin Thomas, b. Birmingham, e. Birmingham, 9982, Sgt., k. in a., F. & F., 25/4/15.

Johnsey, Albert Edward, b. Chiseldon, Wilts, e. Birmingham (Portsmouth), 9405, Pte., k. in a., F. & F., 20/9/15.

Johnson, Edward Philip, e. Birmingham, 16/1778, Pte., k. in a., F. & F., 1/12/17.

Johnson, William, b. West Bromwich, Staffs, e. Birmingham (Langley, Worcs), 11173, Pte., d. of w., F. & F., 26/6/16.

Jolley, John, b. Birmingham, e. Birmingham, 6976, Pte., d. of w., F. & F., 1/3/18.

Jolliffe, Earl Reginald, b. Wolverhampton, Staffs, e. Newport, Mon. (Rushey Green, Catford, Kent), 33004, Pte., k. in a., F. & F., 15/4/18, formerly 25090, Dragoon Gds.

Jones, Albert, b. Portwood, Stockport, Ches., e. Stockport (Portwood, Stockport), 31, Pte., k. in a., F. & F., 9/5/15.

Jones, Albert Edward, b. Birmingham, e. Birmingham, 6334, Pte., d. of w., F. & F., 29/5/15.

Jones, Albert Victor, b. Gosport, Hants, e. Warwick (Aston, Birmingham), 16574, Pte., k. in a., F. & F., 12/10/16.

Jones, Alfred, b. St. George's, Birmingham, e. Birmingham, 2117, L/Cpl., k. in a., F. & F., 25/4/15.

Jones, Arthur, b. Nechells, Birmingham, e. Birmingham, 609, L/Cpl., d. of w., F. & F., 12/4/17.

Jones, Arthur Thomas, b. Highbury, Middx., e. Harringay, Middx. (Islington, Middx.), 28332, Pte., k. in a, F. & F., 4/10/17, formerly 27404, Hussars.

Jones, Charles Henry, b. Handsworth, Birmingham, e. Birmingham, 27933, Pte., d. of w., F. & F., 1/4/18.

Jones, John, b. Birmingham, e. Worthing, Sussex (Birmingham), 6230, Pte., k. in a., F. & F., 20/6/18.

Jones, Percy, e. Stourbridge, Worcs, 20656, Pte., d. of w., F. & F., 31/10/19.

Jones, Reuben John, b. Small Heath, Birmingham, e. Warwick (Birmingham), 2233, Pte., k. in a., F. & F., 29/10/14.

Jones, Robert, b. St. James', Hereford, e. Birmingham, 2015, Pte., k. in a., F. & F., 25/4/15, formerly 9370, Coldstream Gds.

Jones, William, b. Birmingham, e. Warwick (Birmingham), 323, A/C.Q.M.S., k. in a., F. & F., 25/4/15.

Jones, William Ernest, b. Birmingham, e. Warwick, 23086, Pte., d. of w., F. & F., 3/5/17.

Juggins, William Levi, b. Birmingham, e. Birmingham, 50830, Pte., d. of w., F. & F., 31/8/18.

Keeling, Joseph James, e. Birmingham, 23214, Sgt., d. of w., F. & F., 25/10/18.

Kelly, Alec, b. St. Thomas, Birmingham, e. Birmingham, 3564, Pte., k. in a., F. & F., 9/5/17.

Kelly, Richard, b. Camberwell, Surrey, e. London, 7095, Pte., k. in a., F. & F., 19/6/15.

Kemp, Albert, b. Birmingham, e. Birmingham, 8548, Pte., k. in a., F. & F., 29/10/14.

Kemp, William Alfred, b. Aston, Birmingham, e. Birmingham, 1768, Pte., k. in a., F. & F., 3/6/15.

Kendall, Reginald George, b. Coventry, e. Warwick (Coventry), 16504, Pte., d. of w., F. & F., 14/7/16.

Kennett, Harry Thomas b. Shustoke, Warwick, e. Warwick (Shustoke), 16042, Pte., k. in a., F. & F., 10/10/16.

Kenyon, Henry, b. Ramsbottom, Lancs, e. Ramsbottom, 33029, Pte., k in a., F. & F., 15/4/18, formerly GS/21982, Dragoon Gds.

Kerr, Henry, b. Sharkhill, Belfast, Antrim, e. Belfast, 34192, Pte., d. of w., F. & F., 23/12/17, formerly 4209, Hussars.

Ketteridge, William, b. Coventry, e. Birmingham, 13106, Pte., k. in a., F. & F., 5/10/17.

Key, Albert, b. Leamington, Warwicks, e. Leamington, Warwicks, 13317, Pte., d. of w., F. & F., 4/7/16.

Kiff, James Frederick, b. Birmingham, e. Birmingham, 284, Pte., k. in a., F. & F., 31/3/15.

Kimberley, Thomas, b. Coventry, e. Coventry, 42394, Pte., k. in a., F. & F., 24/10/18.

Kinchin, Henry, b. Birmingham, e. Birmingham, 57, Cpl., k. in a., F. & F., 9/10/16.

King, Thomas, b. Hove, Sussex, e. Hove, 30485, Pte., k. in a., F. & F., 30/8/18, formerly S/4/087052, R.A.S.C.

King, William George, b. Ladywood, Birmingham, e. Birmingham, 2280, Pte., d. of w., F. & F., 17/4/18.

Kirkoff, George, b. Birmingham, e. Birmingham, 7393, Pte., k. in a., F. & F., 25/4/15.

Kitching, William, b. Birmingham e. Birmingham, 9599, Pte., d. of w., F. & F., 21/10/14.

Knight, Albert, b. St. Mary's, Nuneaton, e. Nuneaton, 983, L/Cpl., k. in a., F. & F., 13/10/14.

Knight, Alfred, b. Curdworth, Birmingham, e. Coleshill, Warwicks (Birmingham), 16736, Pte., k. in a, F. & F., 23/10/16.

Knight, Tom, b. Radford, Coventry, e. Coventry, 79, Pte., k. in a., F. & F., 13/10/14.

Knott, John Henry, b. Kidderminster, Worcs., e. Stourbridge, Worcs (Kidderminster), 40539, Pte., k. in a., F. & F., 29/6/18.

Kyte, Frederick Andrew, b. Malabar Coast, e. Wellington, Madras, India, 9405, Sgt., k. in a., F. & F., 27/8/14.

Lacey, Norman, b. High Wycombe, Bucks, e. High Wycombe, Bucks, 36278, Pte., k. in a., F. & F., 31/8/18.

Lakin, Charles Frederick, b. St. Margarets, Leicester, e. Coventry, 1798, Pte., k. in a., F. & F., 20/4/15.

Lamb, Thomas, b. Aston, Birmingham, e. Aston, Birmingham (Vauxhall, Birmingham), 1015, Pte., k. in a., F. & F., 23/10/16.

Lane, Ephraim, b. Coventry, e. Coventry, 8883, Pte., k. in a., F. & F., 19/6/15.

Lane, Frederick Charles, b. Blandford, Dorset, e. Dorchester, 50869, Pte., d., F. & F., 4/12/18.

Lane, William Alfred, b. Birmingham, e. Birmingham, 15520, Pte., k. in a., F. & F., 23/10/16.

Langford, Howard, b. Birmingham, e. Birmingham, 307408, L/Cpl., k. in a., F. & F., 20/5/18.

Lapham, Charles Richard, b. Chantry, Frome, Som., e. Birmingham, 1448, L/Cpl., k. in a., F. & F., 25/4/15.

Latham, George Henry, b. Birmingham, e. Birmingham, 9184, L/Cpl., k. in a., F. & F., 11/11/14.

Law, Captain, b. Halesowen, Worcs, e. Halesowen, 2478, Pte., k. in a., F. & F., 12/10/17.

Lawrence, Frank, b. Worksop, Notts, e. Newark, Notts (Mansfield, Notts), 27506, Pte., k. in a., F. & F., 12/10/17, formerly 3792, Notts & Derby Regt.

Lawrence, Maurice, e. Birmingham, 20480, Pte., d. of w., F. & F., 13/4/17.

Layland, Alfred, b. Birmingham, e. Warwick (Birmingham), 1000, Pte, d. of w., F. & F., 11/6/18.

Lazonby, Albert, b. Stockton-on-Tees, Durham, e. Nuneaton, Warwicks (Stockton-on-Tees), 513, Pte., k. in a., F. & F., 25/4/15.

Lea, Frederick, b. Ladywowod, Birmingham, e. Birmingham (Ladywood Birmingham), 2496, Pte., k. in a., F. & F., 27/8/14.

Leach, Harry, b. Newark, Notts, e. Newark, Notts, 849, L/Cpl., k. in a., F. & F., 8/9/14.

Leaton, Thomas Henry, b. Long Buckby, Northants, e. Coventry (Northampton), 884, Pte., d. of w., F. & F., 15/9/14.

Leech, John Henry, b. Birmingham, e. Birmingham, 7050, Sgt., k. in a., F. & F., 12/10/16.

Lee, Frederick, e. Exeter, Devon, 25424, Pte., k. in a., F. & F., 12/10/17, formerly 3952, A.P.C.

Lee, Thomas, b. Elkington, Northants, e. Rugby, Warwicks, 3277, Pte., k. in a., F. & F., 15/4/18.

Lee, William Thomas, b. Rugby, Warwicks, e. Coventry, Warwicks (Rugby, Warwicks), 2836, Pte., d. of w., F. & F., 5/6/18.

Leedham, Herbert, b. Stockingford, Nuneaton, Warwicks, e. Nuneaton, Warwicks, 397, Sgt., k. in a., F. & F., 25/10/16.

Lees, Henry, b. St. Paul's, Birmingham, e. Birmingham (Small Heath, Birmingham), 3660, Pte., k. in a., F. & F., 30/8/18.

Leonard, William Stanley, b. Fulham, London, e. Bristol, Glos., 28798, Pte., d. of w., F. & F., 15/4/18.

Lettington, Stephen, b. Bromley, Kent, e. Bromley, 33101, Pte., d., F. & F., 18/6/18, formerly 11864, Dragoons.

Lewis, Ernest, b. St. Paul's, Birmingham, e. Warwick (Hockley, Birmingham), 2264, Pte., k. in a., F. & F., 8/7/15.

Lewis, Thomas, b. Chichester, Sussex, e. Birmingham, 3335, Pte., k. in a., F. & F., 19/6/15.

Lilley, William George, b. Birmingham, e. Birmingham, 9620, Pte., k. in a., F. & F., 24/5/15.

Lincoln, Richard Maurice, b. Stoneythorp, Southam, Warwicks, e. Warwick (Great Malvern, Worcs), 1652, Pte., k. in a., F. & F., 3/5/17.

Line, Samuel, b. Whittick, Coalville, Leics, e. Warwick (Coalville), 4850, Pte., k. in a., F. & F., 12/10/16.

Lines, Ernest, b. Braunston, Northants, e. Rugby, Warwicks (Northampton), 1189, Sgt., k. in a., F. & F., 4/10/17.

Ling, Henry, b. Birmingham, e. Birmingham, 2453, Pte., k. in a., F. & F., 8/7/15.

Ling, John Afred, b. Old Ford, Middx., e. London, 28276, Pte., k. in a., F. & F., formerly 27430, Cavalry.

Link, James Edwin, b. Cleobury Mortimer, Salop, e. Birmingham, 10720, Pte., k. in a., F. & F., 11/4/17.

Lionett, Percival Hugh, b. Trimulgherry, Secunderabad, Madras, India, e. Wellington, India (Secunderabad, Madras, India), 868, Pte., k. in a., F. & F., 1/11/17.

Lionett, Stanley Newton, b. Secunderabad, Madras, India, e. Wellington, Madras (Secunderabad, Madras, India), 935, L/Cpl., d. of w., F. & F., 28/4/15.

Liversage, William, b. St. Michaels, Ashton-under-Lyne, e. Manchester (Ashton-under-Lyne), 8155, Pte., k. in a., F. & F., 9/5/15.

Lloyd, Albert Edward, b. Croydon, e. London, 9281, Pte., k. in a., F. & F., 25/4/15.

Lloyd, John Edward, b. St. Peter's, Nottingham, e. Nottingham, 571, Pte., k. in a., F. & F., 25/4/15.

Lockley, Ernest, b. Spring Hill, Birmingham, e. Birmingham, 3100, Pte., k. in a., F. & F., 12/10/16.

Long, Albert, b. St. Martin's, Warwick, e. Birmingham, 10614, Pte., k. in a., F. & F., 15/4/18, M.M.

Long, Frederick Ernest, b. Henley-in-Arden, Warwicks, e. Warwick (Birmingham), 6922, Pte., k. in a., F. & F., 3/12/14

Longdon, William Henry, b. Burntwood, Staffs, e. Hednesford, Staffs (Walsall, Staffs), 27591, Pte., k. in a., F. & F., 15/4/18, formerly 9567, S. Staff. Regt.

Lowndes, Bernard, b. Cheadle, Stafford, e. Hanley, Staffs, 7626, Pte., k. in a., F. & F., 26/4/15.

Loynes, Charles Edward Thomas, b. Birmingham, e. Warwick (Birmingham), 8875, Pte., k. in a., F. & F., 6/5/15.

Lucas, Arthur William, e. Coventry, 241621, Pte., d., F. & F., 1/11/19.

Lucas, Leonard, b. Hillfields, Coventry, e. Coventry, 1603, Pte., d. of w., F. & F., 14/10/16.

Luckett, George Edward, b. Brentford, Middx., e. Coventry, Warwicks (Brentford), 2633, Pte., k. in a., F. & F., 25/4/15.

Ludford, Charles Henry, e. Coventry, Warwicks (Stretton-on-Dunsmore), 21110, Pte., d. of w., F. & F., 6/10/17.

Lyons, Daniel David, b. Lambeth, Surrey, e. Birmingham (Greet, Birmingham), 19002, Pte., d. of w., F. & F., 24/5/17.

Mace, Charles Stansbie, b. All Saints, Birmingham, e. Birmingham (Handsworth, Birmingham), 1457, Pte., k. in a., F. & F., 3/5/17.

Magson, Samuel, b. Earlsdon, Coventry, Warwicks, e. Warwick (Coventry), 2199, Pte., k. in a., F. & F., 13/10/14.

Maidstone, Albert Victor, b. Burriscombe, Glos., e. Birmingham (Winson Green, Birmingham), 17505, Pte., k. in a., F. & F., 15/4/18.

Mainwaring, John, b. Llanwo, Mountain Ash, Glam., e. Newport, Mon., 705, A/Sgt., k. in a., F. & F., 11/10/16.

Maley, Edwin, b. Birmingham, e. Birmingham (Brookfields, Birmingham), 16/1681, Pte., k. in a., F. & F., 4/6/16.

Maley, Martin France, b. Birmingham, e. Birmingham, 11169, Pte., k. in a., F. & F., 15/4/18.

Malin, Frederick, b. Birmingham, e. Worthing (Birmingham), 150, Pte., k. in a., F. & F., 24/5/15.

Malin, Wilfred, b. Wolvey, Warwicks, e. Nuneaton, Warwicks (Wolvey), 18998, Pte., k. in a., F. & F., 30/8/18.

Mallen, Richard John, b. St. George's, Birmingham, e. Birmingham, 2215, Pte., k. in a., F. & F., 12/7/15.

Malley, Frederick, b. St. Chads, Birmingham, e. Birmingham, 3852, Pte., d. of w., F. & F., 16/1/16.

Manchester, Leonard, b. Chelsea, London, e. London (Chelsea), 812, L/Cpl., k. in a., F. & F., 25/4/15.

Manners, Benjamin, b. Birmingham, e. Birmingham, 9356, Pte., k. in a., F. & F., 21/10/14.

Manning, John, b. Birmingham, e. Birmingham, 5145, Pte., k. in a., F. & F., 11/10/16.

Manning, John Charles, b. Birmingham, e. Birmingham (Balsall Heath, Birmingham), 1597, Pte., k. in a., F. & F., 25/4/15, formerly 9822, R.W. Fus.

Manning, Percy, b. Northampton, e. Rugby, Warwicks (Northampton), 19401, Pte., k. in a., F. & F., 12/2/17.

Mansfield, Henry, b. Birmingham, e. Birmingham, 11662, Pte., k. in a., F. & F., 4/11/15.

Marshall, Edward, b. Epwell, Banbury, Oxon, e. Nuneaton, Warwicks, 1054, Sgt., k. in a., F. & F., 12/10/16.

Marshall, John, b. Ettington, Warwicks, e. Warwick (Knowle, Warwicks), 9556, Pte., k. in a., F. & F., 30/4/16.

Marshall, Thomas Herbert, b. Leamington, e. Coventry, Warwicks (Leamington, Warwicks), 42395, Pte., k. in a., F. & F., 24/10/18.

Marshall, William, b. Doldridge, Berks, e. Kineton (Lighthorne, Warwicks), 19604, Pte., k. in a., F. & F., 3/5/17.

Marshall, William Albert, b. Belfast, e. Dover (Portsmouth), 33167, Drummer, d., F. & F., 14/8/19.

Martin, Charles Edward, b. Longsight, Manchester, e. Warwick (Walsall, Staffs), 9499, Pte., k. in a., F. & F., 28/1/15.

Martin, George Samuel, b. Aldridge, Walsall, Staffs, e. Birmingham (Aldridge, Walsall), 1245, A/Cpl., k. in a., F. & F., 5/10/17.

Martin, Walter E., b. Birmingham, e. Birmingham (Smethwick, Birmingham), 17553, Pte., k. in a., F. & F., 18/7/18.

Martin, Walter George, b. Stratford-on-Avon, Warwicks, e. Nuneaton, Warwicks, 11933, Pte., k. in a., F. & F., 12/10/16.

Mason, Charles, b. St. Mary's, Salop, e. Birmingham (Aston, Birmingham), 13181, Pte., d. of w., F. & F., 25/10/18.

Mason, Fred, b. Gunby, Lincs, e. Selby, Lincs (Grantham, Lincs), 33031, Pte., d. of w., F. & F., 12/5/18, formerly GS/13314, D.G.

Masters, Frank, b. Budbrook, Warwick, e. Warwick, 9759, Pte., k. in a., F. & F., 25/4/15.

Matthews, Alfred Edward, b. Chelford, Gloucester, e. Coventry, 19229, Pte., k. in a., F. & F., 18/7/18.

Matthews, Percy William, b. Harborne, Birmingham, e. Warwick (Leamington, Warwicks), 2635, Pte., k. in a., F. & F., 25/4/15.

Matthews, William, b. Birmingham, e. Warwick (Birmingham), 554, Pte., k. in a., F. & F., 25/8/16.

Matthews, William George, b. Hordle, Lymington, Hants, e. Christchurch, Hants (Hordle, Lymington), 604, Pte., k. in a., F. & F., 19/6/15.

Maughan, Alfred, b. Wandsworth, Surrey, e. London, 1957, L/Cpl., k. in a., F. & F., 25/4/15.

Maund, Eugene Henry, b. Chester, e. Warwick, 3590, Pte., k. in a., F. & F., 8/6/15.

Mawson, Matthew William, b. Leadgate, Durham, e. Consett, Durham (Leadgate), 11428, Pte., k. in a., F. & F., 3/5/17.

Mayoll, Frederick, b. Weddington, Warwicks, e. Warwick (Nuneaton, Warwicks), 21967, Pte., k. in a., F. & F., 12/10/17

McCann, Michael, b. Rathangan, Kildare, e. Curragh Camp (Clane, Co. Kildare), 28337, Pte., k. in a., F. & F., 12/10/17, formerly 27374, Hussars.

McCracken, Charles, b. Birmingham, e. Ross, 6864, Pte., k. in a., F. & F., 25/4/15.

McGill, Alexander Fenwick, b. St Giles, Edinburgh, e. Edinburgh, 31170, Pte., k. in a., F. & F., 11/6/18, formerly 8150, Dragoons.

Meaden, Charley, b. Radford, Nottingham e. Coventry, 1708, L/Cpl., d. of w., F. & F., 12/4/17.

Mears, Herbert, b. Birmingham, e. Birmingham, 8720, A/Cpl., d., F. & F., 14/11/15.

Medlam, Frank, b. Birmingham, e. Birmingham, 15, Pte., k. in a., F. & F., 25/4/15.

Meegh, Abraham Edward, b. St. Nicholas, Nuneaton, e. Warwick (Nuneaton, Warwicks), 2349, Pte., d. of w., F. & F., 30/4/15.

Mellor, William, b. St. Philip's, Sheffield, e. Sheffield, 7759, Pte., k. in a., F. & F., 19/6/15.

Melton, Richard, b. Durham, e. Warwick (Coventry), 8940, Pte., d. of w., F. & F., 25/5/15.

Merrick, Robert Francis, b. St. Andrew's, Birmingham, e. Birmingham (Small Heath, Birmingham), 35731, Pte., k. in a., F. & F., 20/7/18, formerly 29327, Worcs Regt.

Merrick, Thomas, b. St. Mary's, Birmingham, e. Birmingham (Saltley, Birmingham), 9522, Pte., k. in a., F & F., 12/10/16.

Merry, James Frederick, b. Leicester, e. Birmingham (Coventry), 6356, Pte., d of w., F. & F., 29/3/16.

Middleton, William, b. Birmingham, e. Birmingham, 8944, Pte., k. in a., F. & F., 25/4/15.

Miles, Frank, b. St. Michael's, Coventry, e. Warwick (Coventry), 205, Pte., k. in a., F. & F., 5/2/15.

Millington, William Edward, b. Wells, Somerset, e. Taunton, Somerset (Wells), 50833, Pte., k. in a., F. & F., 1/9/18.

Mills, James, b. St. Mary's, Birmingham, e. Birmingham, 3226, Pte., k. in a., F. & F., 31/7/15.

Mills, Sidney Ernest, b. Daventry, Northants, e. Nuneaton, Warwicks (Daventry), 1033, Pte., k. in a., F. & F., 2/5/15.

Mills, William Nathaniel, b. Burton-on-Trent, Staffs, e. Warwick (Burton-on-Trent), 485, Pte., k in a., F. & F., 19/6/15.

Millward, Albert, b. Birmingham, e. Birmingham, 38, Pte., k. in a., F. & F., 19/6/15.

Millward, Edwin, b. Hanley, Staffs, e. Stoke-on-Trent, Staffs (Hanley), 2584, Pte., k. in a., F. & F., 26/4/15.

Millward, Henry, b. Birmingham, e. Birmingham, 278, A/Cpl., k. in a., F. & F., 12/10/16.

Milward, Joseph, b. Salford Priors, Worcs, e. Stratford-on-Avon, Warwicks (Salford Priors, Evesham, Worcs), 9534, Pte., k. in a., F. & F., 12/10/16.

Minshull, Charles, e. Birmingham, 267683, Pte., k. in a., F. & F., 13/4/17.

Mitchell, Arthur William, b. Holwell, Dorset, e. Dorchester, Dorset (Sherborne, Dorset), 50872, Pte., k. in a., F. & F., 9/8/18.

Mitchell, Bert, b. St. Nicholas, Warwick, e. Warwick, 378, Pte., k. in a., F. & F., 26/4/15

Mitchell, Percy, b. Rochdale, e. Rochdale, Lancs, 33032, L/Cpl., k. in a., F. & F., 3/1/18, formerly GS/25501, D.G.

Mole, Benjamin, b. Stoneleigh, Coventry, e. Warwick (Coventry), 9773, Cpl., k. in a., F. & F., 10/12/14.

Montgomery, Frank Thomas, b. Leamington, Warwicks, e. Warwick (Leamington), 9945, Sgt., k. in a., F. & F., 26/4/15.

Moody, Harold Reginald, b. St. Luke's, Bedminster, Glos., e. Bristol, Glos., 203914, Pte., k. in a., F. & F., 29/8/18, formerly 3042, S. Mid. R.E.

Moore, Arthur, b. Kettering, Northants, e. Birmingham, 2753, A/Cpl., d., F. & F., 20/7/18.

Moore, Harry, b. London, e. Birmingham (Acocks Green, Birmingham), 451, Pte., k. in a., F. & F., 3/5/17.

Moore, John George, b. Birmingham, e. Warwick (Birmingham), 8724, Pte., k. in a., F. & F., 25/5/15.

Moore, Thomas Henry, b. Ilmington, Warwick, e. Stratford-on-Avon, Warwicks (Birmingham), 9480, Pte., d., F. & F., 27/7/18,

Moores, Frederick (Yeovil, Somerset), 25426, Pte., k. in a., F. & F., 30/8/18.

Moreton, William Harold, b. All Saints, Wolverhampton, e. Warwick (Wolverhampton), 1639, Pte., k. in a., F. & F., 4/10/17.

Morgan, George, b. West Bromwich, Staffs, e. Birmingham (Selly Oak, Birmingham), 7496, Pte., k. in a., F. & F., 12/10/17.

Morgan, Percy Douglas, b. Gloucester, e. Birmingham (Erdington, Birmingham), 21464, Pte., d. of w., F. & F., 12/10/17

Morrell, Harry, b. Canwell, Staffs, e. Birmingham (Sutton Coldfield, Birmingham), 8950, Pte., k. in a., F. & F., 12/10/16.

Morris, Charles, b. St. Michael's, Nuneaton, Warwicks, e. Warwick (Nuneaton, Warwicks), 1969, Pte., d. of w., F. & F., 16/10/14.

Morris, Francis William, b. Plaistow, Middx., e. Warwick (Birmingham), 9363, Pte., k. in a., F. & F., 25/4/15.

Morris, Henry, e. Birmingham, 23286, Pte., k. in a., F. & F., 17/4/17.

Morton, Thomas, b. Birmingham, e. Birmingham, 8145, L/Cpl., k. in a., F. & F., 12/10/16.

Moseley, Charles Francis, b. Birmingham, e. Coventry (Selly Oak, Birmingham), 9300, Pte., k. in a., F. & F., 13/10/14

Moseley, Harry, b. Berkswell, Warwicks, e. Coventry (Tile Hill, Coventry), 16434, L/Cpl., d. of w., F. & F., 16/4/18.

Moss, James, b. Birmingham, e. Birmingham, 716, L/Cpl., k. in a., F. & F., 26/8/14.

Mott, Edward, b. Kensington, Middx., e. Shepherd's Bush (Notting Hill, London), 11251, Pte., k. in a., F. & F., 20/6/17.

Mould, Charles, b. Birmingham, e. Birmingham, 7497, Pte., k. in a., F. & F., 19/6/15.

Mounce, Wallace John, b. Northam, Devon, e. Exeter, Devon (Northam), 50873, Pte., k. in a., F. & F., 30/8/18.

Muggleston, Ernest Stanley, b. Handsworth, Birmingham, e. Birmingham (Handsworth), 1596, Pte., k. in a., F. & F., 3/5/17.

Mulleague, Charles Henry, b. Huddersfield, Yorks, e. Richmond, Yorks (Burnley, Lancs), 8886, Pte., k. in a., F. & F., 19/6/15.

Mullis, Frederick George, b. Winson Green, Birmingham, e. Birmingham (Winson Green, Birmingham), 8999, Sgt., d. of w., F. & F., 14/10/16.
Mulliss, Sidney, b. Harbury, Leamington, Warwicks, e. Warwick (Birmingham), 6227, L/Sgt., k. in a., F. & F., 25/4/15.
Murphy, Sidney James, b. St. Paul's Parish, Leamington, Warwicks, e. Coventry (Leamington), 50, A/Cpl., k. in a., F. & F., 25/4/15.
Murphy, William, b. Nottingham, e. Nottingham, 27384, Pte., k. in a., F. & F., 3/5/17, formerly 4710, Notts & Derby Regt.
Murrell, Samuel David, b. Birmingham, e. Birmingham (Balsall Heath, Birmingham), 1871, A/Sgt., d. of w., F. & F., 2/2/16.
Mushens, William, b. Sunderland, Durham, e. Sunderland (Monkwearmouth, Durham), 20588, Pte., k. in a., F. & F., 23/10/16, formerly 11011, A.C.C.
Myatt, Joseph, b. Hockley, Birmingham, e. Warwick (Birmingham), 68, Pte., d. of w., F. & F., 22/9/14.
Narborough, Edward Henry, b. Birmingham, e. Birmingham, 9196, Pte., k. in a., F. & F., 13/10/14.
Nash, George Henry, b. Small Heath, Birmingham, e. Warwick (Small Heath, Birmingham), 30036, Pte., d. of w., F. & F., 15/4/18.
Nash, Henry, b. Birmingham, e. Birmingham, 23227, Pte., k. in a., F. & F., 3/5/17.
Nash, William, b. Birmingham, e. Birmingham (Walsall, Staffs), d. of w., F. & F., 14/10/14.
Naunton, Ernest William, b. Bethnal Green, Middx., e. Coventry, 16730, Pte., k. in a., F. & F., 12/10/16.
Neal, Robert Darius, b. Birmingham, e. Birmingham, 8923 Pte., d. of w., F. & F., 27/10/14.
Neal, Sydney, b. Aston, Birmingham, e. Birmingham, 2060, Pte., k. in a., F. & F., 19/6/15.
Neale, Walter Henry, b. St. Michael's, Coventry, e. Warwick (Coventry), 3388, Pte., k. in a., F. & F., 31/3/18, formerly 251466, R.E.
Nelson, Ernest, b. Birmingham, e. Birmingham, 21993, Pte., k. in a., F. & F., 30/8/18.
Nelson, Herbert, b. Coventry, e. Coventry, 27914, Pte., d. of w., F. & F., 3/5/17.
Nevett, Ernest, b. Birmingham, e. Birmingham, 9396, Pte., d. of w., F. & F., 20/8/15.
Newey, David Henry, b. Aston, Birmingham, e. Birmingham 9605, Pte., d. of w., F. & F., 5/12/14.
Newey, Thomas, b. Birmingham, e. Birmingham, 7340, Pte. k. in a., F. & F., 19/6/15, formerly 6390, R.W. Fus.
Newman, George Leonard, b. St. Bartholomew's, Birmingham, e. Warwick (Birmingham), 2548, Pte., k. in a., F. & F., 1/7/16.
Newman, Richard Henry, b. Birmingham, e. Birmingham, 7071, Pte., k. in a., F. & F., 19/6/15.
Newman, Thomas Martin, b. Seacombe, Ches., e. Birkenhead, Ches., 29467, Pte., k. in a., F. & F., 15/5/18, formerly 62127, Ches. Regt.
Newth, Lewis, b. Ware, Herts, e. Guildford, Surrey (Chesham, Bucks), 27975, Pte., k. in a., F. & F., 31/3/18, formerly 16867, R. Berks Regt.
Newton, Alfred, b. Birmingham, e. Birmingham, 9573, Pte., k. in a., F. & F., 21/10/14.
Newton, Edgar, b. St. Margaret, Leics, e. Leicester, 8599, Pte., k. in a., F. & F., 2/7/16.
Newton, Walter Isaac, b. Warwick, e. Warwick, 2831, L/Cpl., k. in a., F. & F., 25/4/15.
Nicholl, Alfred John, b. St. Chad's, Smethwick, Staffs, e. Birmingham (Smethwick, Birmingham), 1217, Pte., d. of w., F. & F., 25/5/15.
Nicholls, Ernest Albert, b. Birmingham, e. Birmingham, 7466, Pte., k. in a., F. & F., 19/6/15.
Nichols, Harry William, b. Norwich, e. Coventry, 20552, Pte., k. in a., F. & F., 20/10/16, formerly 10114, A.C.C.
Nicholls, Jonathan, e. Bury, Lancs (Manchester), 22081, Pte., d. of w., F. & F., 6/5/17, formerly Lancs Fus.
Nolan, Benjamin, b. Leamington, Warwicks, e. Birmingham (Leamington), 357, Pte., d., F. & F., 8/3/15.
Noon, William, b. Birmingham, e. Birmingham, 353, Pte., k. in a., F. & F., 26/4/15.
Norbury, Albert, b. St. Peter's, Coventry, e. Nuneaton, 1816, Pte., k. in a., F. & F., 7/7/15.
Norbury, Charles J., b. Coventry, e. Coventry, 17659, Pte., k. in a., F. & F., 11/4/17.
Norman, Albert, b West Bromwich, Staffs, e. Birmingham. (Smethwick, Birmingham), 7862, L/Cpl., k. in a., F. & F., 8/7/15
Norman, Frederick, b. Knowle, Warwicks, e. Warwick (Knowle), 16623, Pte., d. of w., F. & F., 12/6/17.
Nowell, Richard Henry, e. Birmingham (Balsall Heath, Birmingham), 330113, Pte., k. in a., F. & F., 24/10/18.
Nuthall, Herbert, b. Camberwell, Surrey, e. London (Brixton, London), 7498, Pte., k. in a., F. & F., 25/4/15.
O'Brien, Peter, b. Birmingham, e. Birmingham, 870, Pte. k. in a., F. & F., 21/4/17.
O Brien, Thomas, b. St. Thomas's, Birmingham, e. Birmingham (Birmingham), 2235, Pte., d., F. & F., 2/7/15.
O'Callaghan, James Morris, b. Budbrook, Warwick, e. Birmingham, 2312, L/Sgt., k. in a., F. & F., 26/4/15.
O'Dell, F., b. U.S.A., e. Birmingham (U.S.A.), 200, Pte., k. in a., F. & F., 25/4/15.
O'Hern, Richard, b. Richmond, Yorks, e. Richmond, 2018, Pte., k. in a., F. & F., 11/4/17, formerly 140432, R.F.A.
Oates, Alfred, b. Westwoodside, Lincs, e. Epworth, Doncaster, Yorks (Westwoodside, Doncaster, Yorks), 27570, L/Cpl., k. in a., F. & F., 12/10/16, formerly 25007, S. Staff. Regt.
Oldaker, David, b. St. Martin's, Birmingham, e. Reading, Berks (Warwick), 18582, Pte., d. of w., F. & F., 23/10/16, formerly 24921, S.L.I.
Oldham, Samuel, b. St. Mary's, Nottingham, e. Nottingham, 674, Pte., d., F. & F., 10/9/15.
Oliver, Frederick, b. Cottingham, Northants, e. Warwick (Cottingham), 2083, Pte., k. in a., F. & F., 25/4/15.
Oliver, Owen, b. Handsworth, Staffs, e. Warwick (Sutton Cold field, Birmingham), 20306, Pte., d. of w., F. & F., 27/12/16.
Orton, Charles, b. Wilnecote, Warwicks, e. Atherstone, Warwick (Tamworth, Warwicks), 10757, A/Cpl., k. in a., F. & F., 23/10/16.
Osborne, Horace Ludwig, e. Birmingham (Small Heath, Birmingham), 27966, A/Cpl., k. in a., F. & F., 11/4/17.
Osborne, James, b. Deritend, Birmingham, e. Birmingham (Small Heath, Birmingham), 3344, Pte., k. in a., F. & F., 25/4/15.
Osborne, William Matthew, b. St. John's, Leamington, Warwick, e. Warwick (Leamington), 2229, Pte., d. of w., F. & F., 10/11/14.
Overton, Thomas Christopher, b. Birmingham, e. Birmingham, 21520, Pte., d. of w., F. & F., 2/5/17.
Overy, Arthur, b. Small Heath, Birmingham, e. Warwick (Small Heath, Birmingham), 10, Pte., k. in a., F. & F., 16/6/15.
Owen, Arthur Herbert, b. Grendon, Warwicks, e. Atherstone, Warwicks (Atherstone), 10555, A/Cpl., k. in a., F. & F., 23/10/16.
Owen, David, b. Birmingham, e. Warwick (Birmingham), 1355, Cpl., k. in a., F. & F., 13/10/14.
Owen, George Ernest, b. Wolston, Coventry, e. Coventry (Wolston, Coventry), 2824, Pte., k. in a., F. & F., 25/4/15.
Owen, John, b. Admaston, Salop, e. Wolverhampton, Staffs (Cottingham, Northants), 27569, Pte., k. in a., F. & F., 12/10/16, formerly 24799, S. Staffs Regt.
Owen, William, b. Lillington, Leamington Spa, e. Leamington Spa (Whitnash, Leamington Spa), 658, Cpl., k. in a., F. & F., 18/7/18, M.M.
Owen, William Thomas, b. Kidderminster, Worcs, e. Nuneaton, Warwicks, 4574, Pte., k. in a., F. & F., 30/4/16.
Oxspring, Frank, b. Bishop Weymorell, Sunderland, Durham, e. Swansea, 3209, Pte., k. in a., F. & F., 25/6/16.
Packer, Jasper, b. Wroughton, Swindon, Wilts, e. Reading. Berks (Longcott, Farrington, Berks), 3171, Pte., k. in a., F. & F., 25/4/15.
Paddy, Fred, b. Colyton, Devon, e. London (Colyton), 22085, Pte., k. in a., F. & F., 25/7/18, formerly 4108, 3/2nd London Regt.
Padmore, Charles, b. Wolverhampton, Staffs, e. Coventry, Warwicks (Wolverhampton), 26714, Pte., k. in a., F. & F., 29/8/18.
Page, Samuel, b. Birmingham, e. Coventry, Warwicks, 2761, Pte., k. in a., F. & F., 18/2/15.
Page, William Hewitt, b. Sparkbrook, Birmingham, e. Birmingham, 2153, Pte., k. in a., F. & F., 17/4/18.
Palfrey, Alfred Harold William, b. Wellington, e. Aston (Saltley College, Birmingham), 303006, Pte., k. in a., F. & F., 15/4/18.
Palfreyman, Benjamin Edward, b. Atherstone, Warwicks, e. Nuneaton, Warwicks (Atherstone), 7118, L/Cpl., k. in a., F. & F., 13/10/14.
Palfreyman, Bert, b. Atherstone, Warwicks, e. Coventry (Chilvers Coton, near Nuneaton), 9868, Pte., k. in a., F. & F., 13/10/14.
Pallett, Harold Walter, b. Upton, Warwicks, e. Atherstone, Warwicks (Upton), 9589, L/Cpl., k. in a., F. & F., 3/5/17.
Palmer, Arthur Cecil, b. Wednesbury, Staffs, e. Birmingham (Stafford), 985, L/Cpl., k. in a., F. & F., 3/5/17.
Palmer, Frederick, e. Birmingham, 27889, Cpl., d. of w., F. & F., 15/4/18.
Palmer, Frederick Samuel, b. Birmingham, e. Birmingham, 4954, Sgt., k. in a., F. & F., 2/5/15.
Palmer, Henry Thomas, b. Caversham, Berks, e. Caversham, 29963, Pte., k. in a., F. & F., 18/4/18, formerly 20402, Oxford & Bucks L.I.
Palmer, Robert, e. Birmingham, 30687, Pte., k. in a., F. & F., 20/7/18.
Parker, Edward, b. Springhill, Birmingham, e. Birmingham, 3984, Pte., k. in a., F. & F., 16/6/15.
Parker, Frederick, b. Warwick, e. Warwick, 15211, Pte., k. in a., F. & F., 15/4/18.
Parker, Samuel, b. Bedworth, Warwick, e. Warwick (Bedworth), 14841, Pte., k in a., F. & F., 3/5/17.
Parkes, Charles Albert, b. St. Stephen's, Birmingham, e. Birmingham, 8720, Pte., d. of w., F. & F., 5/11/15.
Parkhouse, Frederick Thomas, b. Exeter, Devonshire, e. Exeter, 25460, Pte., d. of w., F. & F., 5/10/17, formerly 1854, A.P.C.
Parnell, James William, b. Withybrook, Coventry, Warwicks, e. Rugby, Warwicks (Withybrook), 4448, Cpl., k. in a., F. & F., 23/7/17.
Parry, Evan Henry, e. Warwick (Birmingham), 16683, Pte., k. in a., F. & F., 3/5/17.
Parsons, Harold Ernest, b. Handsworth, Birmingham, e. Birmingham, 1831, Pte., k. in a., F. & F., 24/5/15.
Parsons, Thomas, b. St. Peter's, Banbury, Oxon, e. Warwick (Stratford-on-Avon, Warwicks), 9159, L/Cpl., k. in a., F. & F., 25/4/15.
Parton, Thomas, b. Barrow, Staffs, e. Himley (Swindon, near Dudley), 27597, Pte., k. in a., F. & F., 23/10/16, formerly 3849, 6th S. Staffs Regt.
Pask, Thomas, b. Kaxby, Lincs, e. Lincoln (Gainsborough), 27574, Pte., k. in a., F. & F., 3/5/17, formerly 25033, 10th S. Staffs Regt.
Patrick, Joseph, b. Ladywood, Birmingham, e. Birmingham, 1048, Pte., d. of w., F. & F., 13/5/15.
Paybody, Harry, b. Nuneaton, Warwicks, e. Nuneaton, 10225, Pte., k. in a., F. & F., 25/4/15.

Paley, Walter, b. Birmingham, e. Birmingham, 16/1951, Pte., d. of w., F. & F., 12/12/16.
Payne, Harry, b. Long Lawford, Rugby, Warwicks, e. Rugby (Long Lawford), 2031, L/Cpl., k. in a., F. & F., 25/4/15.
Payne, Howard, b. Trimingham, Norfolk, e. Norwich (Trimingham), 27603, Pte., k. in a., F. & F., 12/10/16, formerly 5526, 3/6th S. Staffs Regt.
Peach, Herbert Henry, b. Paddington, London, e. London (Kilburn, N.W.), 20629, Pte., k. in a., F. & F., 12/10/16, formerly 10546, A. Cyclist Corps.
Pearce, William John Hore, b. Tipperary, Ireland, e. Birmingham (Edgbaston, Birmingham), 16/1703, Sgt., k. in a., F. & F., 15/4/18.
Pearson, Charles, b. Dudley, Worcs, e. Dudley, 28702, Pte., k. in a., F. & F., 17/4/18.
Pearson, John William, b. St. Paul's, Maidstone, Kent, e. Chatham (St. Paul's, Maidstone), 446, Pte., k. in a., F. & F., 25/4/15.
Peers, John, b. St. Peter's, Coventry, Warwicks, e. Coventry, 1414, Pte., k. in a., F. & F., 12/10/16.
Peet, Charles William, b. Greenfield, Beds, e. Coventry, Warwicks (Luton, Beds), 22170, Pte., k. in a., F. & F., 3/5/17.
Penn, Albert, b. All Saints, Birmingham, e. Warwick (Smethwick, Birmingham), 2369, L/Cpl., d. of w., F. & F., 31/10/16.
Pennington, Charles, b. Exeter, Devon, e. Exeter, 27775, Pte., k. in a., F. & F., 15/4/18, formerly 4922, Worcs Regt.
Percy, George Frederick, b. Eton Wick, Bucks, e. Slough (Newtown, near Windsor), 34891, Pte., k. in a., F. & F., 15/4/18.
Perks, Albert, b. Shirley, Birmingham, e. Birmingham (Shirley, Birmingham), 9607, Pte., k. in a., F. & F., 11/4/17.
Perks, Albert Sydney, b. St. Saviour's, Birmingham, e. Birmingham, 1684, Pte., k. in a., F. & F., 23/10/16.
Perrin, Percy, b. Nettlebed, Henley, Oxon, e. High Wycombe, 754, Pte., k. in a., F. & F., 19/6/15.
Perry, Harold, b. Lower Milton, Worcs, e. Stourport, Worcs, 27764, Pte., k. in a., F. & F., 12/10/17, formerly 4807, Worcs Regt.
Perry, John Thomas, b. Aston, Birmingham, e. Birmingham, 2344, L/Cpl., k. in a., F. & F., 25/4/15.
Pettengill, Frank Curnock, b. Sevenoaks, Kent, e. Grays, Essex, 33132, Pte., d. of w., F. & F., 20/11/17, formerly 14752, Dragoons.
Phillips, Arthur, b. Birmingham, e. Birmingham, 7193, Pte., k. in a., F. & F., 25/4/15.
Phillips, John, b. Edgbaston, Birmingham, e. Birmingham, 3324, Pte., d. of w., F. & F., 3/4/15.
Phillips, William, b. Ousden, Suffolk, e. Newmarket, Cambs, 12431, Cpl., k. in a., F. & F., 9/4/17, formerly 54431, R.G.A.
Phillips, William, b. Leamington, Warwicks, e. Warwick (Leamington), 7, Pte., k. in a., F. & F., 25/4/15.
Phipps, Millson, b. Birchmoor, Warwicks, e. Atherstone, Warwicks (Chapel End, Atherstone), 23984, Pte., k. in a., F. & F., 23/12/17.
Pimm, George, b. Coventry, Warwicks, e. Birmingham, 1858, Pte., k. in a., F. & F., 26/8/14.
Pinner, Samuel, b. St. Martin, Birmingham, e. Birmingham (Winson Green, Birmingham), 11417, Pte., k. in a., F. & F., 23/10/16.
Piper, Edwin Alfred, b. Walsall, Staffs, e. Rugby, Warwicks (Walsall), 1676, Pte., k. in a., F. & F., 25/4/15.
Pitt, Arthur Charles, b. Balsall Heath, Birmingham, e. Birmingham (Balsall Heath, Birmingham), 3266, Pte., k. in a., F. & F., 25/4/15.
Poole, John, b. St. Nicholas, Birmingham, e. Birmingham, 3204, Pte., d. of w., F. & F., 13/5/17.
Poole, Matthias, b. Ladywood, Birmingham, e. Birmingham (Ladywood, Birmingham), 3431, Pte., k. in a., F. & F., 3/6/15.
Poole, Richard William, b. Bristol, Glos., e. Bristol (Clifton, Bristol), 27760, Pte., k. in a., F. & F., 15/4/18, formerly 5166, Worcs Regt.
Popplewell, Albert, b. Aston, Birmingham, e. Warwick (Aston, Birmingham), 240, A/Sgt., k. in a., F. & F., 23/10/16.
Potter, Albert, b. Hill Top, Staffs, e. Nuneaton (Hill Top), 11627, Pte., k. in a., F. & F., 12/10/16.
Potter, Henry, b. St. John's, Wednesbury, Staffs, e. Warwick (Nuneaton, Warwicks), 2422, Pte., k. in a., F. & F., 24/5/15.
Powell, Albert, b. Worcester, e. Wolverton, Bucks (Stoney Stratford, Bucks), 18506, Pte., d. of w., F. & F., 4/10/17, formerly 25284, Som. L.I.
Powell, Alfred Edward, b. Birmingham, e. Birmingham, 14/1322, Pte., k. in a., F. & F., 23/12/17.
Powell, Edwin, b. Small Heath, Birmingham, e. Birmingham, 2291, Pte., k. in a., F. & F., 25/10/14.
Powell, Ernest William, b. Herefordshire, e. Warwick, 16053, Pte., d. of w., F. & F., 17/2/17.
Powell, Lloyd Stanley, b. Paddington, Middx., e. London, 34193, Pte., k. in a., F. & F., 15/4/18, formerly 10761, Hussars.
Powell, Thomas Henry, b. Birmingham, e. Birmingham, 14402, Pte., k. in a., F. & F., 11/5/17.
Preddy, George, b. St. George's, Bristol, e. Warwick (Bristol), 20499, Pte., k. in a., F. & F., 11/10/16.
Price, Albert Edward, b. Bilton, Rugby, Warwicks, e. Rugby (Ashton-under-Lyne, Lancs), 9760, Pte., k. in a., F. & F., 23/10/14.
Price, Arthur William Norman, b. Ceylon, e. Birmingham (Saltley, Birmingham), 2010, Pte., k. in a., F. & F., 13/10/14.
Price, Frederick Richard, b. Urr, Kirkcudbright, e. Birmingham, 41294, Pte., k. in a., F. & F., 6/8/18.
Price, Herbert William, b. Milverton, Warwick, e. Coventry (Milverton), 1240, Pte., k. in a., F. & F., 26/4/15.
Price, John Marsh, e. Hereford (Beguildy, nr. Knighton, Rads), 27816, Pte., k. in a., F. & F., 30/8/18, formerly 2757, Herefordshire Regt.
Priest, James Edward, b. Birmingham, e. Birmingham, 9346, Pte., k. in a., F. & F., 25/4/15.
Priestley, Herbert, b. Bradford, Yorks, e. Bradford, 16/2059, Cpl., k. in a., F. & F., 11/4/17, formerly 140437, R.F.A.
Pritchard, George Henry, b. Harborne, Birmingham, e. Warwick (Wednesbury, Staffs), 2005, Pte., k. in a., F. & F., 27/10/14.
Probert, Albert James, b. Drybrook, Cinderford, Glos., e. Nuneaton, Warwicks (Stockingford, Warwicks), 1743, Pte., k. in a., F. & F., 25/4/15.
Pryce, Dan O'Connell, b. Devizes, Wilts, e. Birmingham, 1677, Pte., k. in a., F. & F., 8/7/15.
Purnell, Frederick James, b. Daventry, Northants, e. Leamington, Warwicks, 20164, Pte., k. in a., F. & F., 11/4/17.
Pursall, William, b. U.S.A., e. Birmingham, 28626, Pte., k. in a., F. & F., 20/10/18.
Quick, Albert, b. Okehampton, Devon, e. Warwick, 25331, Pte., d. of w., F. & F., 9/5/18.
Quinlan, Thomas Leonard Michael, b. Greenwich, London, e. Stratford, London (Manor Park, Essex), 1877, Pte., k. in a., F. & F., 9/4/15.
Quinney, Sidney, b. St. Mark's, Coventry, e. Coventry, 1629, Pte., d. of w., F. & F., 24/4/16.
Rachel, George, b. St. Mark's, Birmingham, e. Birmingham (Smethwick, Staffs), 3255, Pte., k. in a., F. & F., 25/4/15.
Radford, John, b. Balsall Heath, Birmingham, e. Birmingham, 3979, Pte., k. in a., F. & F., 16/12/17, M.M.
Rafferty, Thomas Henry, b. Birmingham, e. Warwick (Birmingham), 7840, L/Cpl., k. in a., F. & F., 25/4/15.
Ragsdale, Mark, b. Bingham, Notts, e. Warwick (Derby), 21237, Cpl., k. in a., F. & F., 12/10/17.
Ralphs, William Henry, b. Ludlow, Salop, e. St. Pancras, Middx., 20546, Pte., k. in a., F. & F., 11/10/16, formerly 8246, Army Cyc. Corps.
Randall, Ernest, b. Birmingham, e. Birmingham, 42488, Pte., d. of w., F. & F., 25/10/18.
Randle, Charles Edward, b. Chipping Norton, Oxon, e. Warwick (Chilvers Coton, Nuneaton, Warwicks), 20201, Pte., d. of w., F. & F., 16/4/18.
Rathbone, Arthur, b. Southam, Warwicks, e. Coventry (Southam), 27991, Pte., k. in a., F. & F., 15/4/18.
Raven, Henry William, b. Long Itchington, Warwicks, e. Warwick (Long Itchington), 2466, Pte., k. in a., F. & F. 26/8/14, formerly 1475, R. Warwicks Regt.
Ravenhill, Percy Augustus, b. Birmingham, e. Birmingham, 344, Pte., k. in a., F. & F., 8/11/14.
Rawlins, Bert, b. All Saints, Coventry, e. Warwick (Coventry), 7262, Pte., k. in a., F. & F., 25/4/15.
Ray, William, b. Birmingham, e. Birmingham, 1888, Pte., k. in a., F. & F., 17/12/14.
Read, Charles Henry, b. Norwich, e. Rugby, Warwicks (Hackney, London), 3882, Pte., k. in a., F. & F., 11/4/17.
Read, George Edward, b. Birmingham, e. Birmingham, 7051, Pte., k. in a., F. & F., 26/4/15.
Reade, Samuel, b. Cannock, Staffs, e. Cannock, 27576, Pte., k. in a., F. & F., 11/10/16, formerly 24619, S. Staffs Regt.
Reader, Thomas, b. Middx., e. Stratford-on-Avon, Warwicks (Tamworth-in-Arden, Birmingham), 9342, Pte., k. in a F. & F., 5/11/14.
Redfern, Joseph William, b. Snarestone, Ashby-de-la-Zouch, Leics, e. Nuneaton, Warwicks (Snarestone), 638, A/Cpl., k. in a., F. & F., 2/5/15.
Reeves, Albert, b. Birmingham, e. Birmingham, 9901, Pte., d. of w., F. & F., 13/7/16.
Reeves, John, b. Coventry, e. Coventry, 17455, Pte., k. in a., F. & F., 29/4/18.
Renowden, Charles Carne, b. Penzance, Cornwall, e. Bodmin, Cornwall (Penzance), 23712, Pte., k. in a., F. & F., 15/4/18, formerly 39523, Devon Regt.
Revill, Harry, b. nr. Nottingham, e. Carlisle, Cumberland (Rotherham, Yorks), 8013, A/Cpl., k. in a., F. & F., 14/1/16.
Reynolds, James, b. Birmingham, e. Birmingham, 9729, Pte., k. in a., F. & F., 11/11/11.
Rhodes, George L., b. Bilston, Staffs, e. Bilston, 27577, Pte., k. in a., F. & F., 23/10/16, formerly 24793, S. Staffs Regt.
Rhodes, Job B., b. Darlaston, Staffs, e. Bilston, Staffs (Wednesbury, Staffs), 27578, Pte., k. in a., F. & F., 23/10/16, formerly 24766, S. Staffs Regt.
Rhodes, Leonard, b. Dudley, Birmingham, e. Warwick (Dudley), 8, Pte., d. of w., F. & F., 30/11/14.
Rhodes, Thomas, b. Bearwood, Birmingham, e. Birmingham (Smethwick, Staffs), 23964, Pte., k. in a., F. & F., 3/5/17.
Richardson, Arthur, b. Sneinton, Nottingham, e. Nottingham (Sneinton), 706, L/Cpl., k. in a., F. & F., 11/10/16.
Ricketts, Arthur Thomas, b. Birmingham, e. Warwick (Birmingham), 1283, L/Cpl., d. of w., F. & F., 25/10/16.
Riddle, James, b. Enfield, Middx., e. London, 64, Pte., d. of w., F. & F., 3/10/17.
Rider, Dixon George, b. Birmingham, e. Stratford-on-Avon, Warwicks (Aston, Birmingham), 16358, Pte., k. in a., F. & F., 3/5/17.
Ridgewell, George, b. West Ham, Essex, e. Stratford, London (West Ham), 34176, Pte., d. of w., F. & F., 26/10/18, formerly 34176, Hussars.
Riley, Charles, b. Binton, Stratford-on-Avon, Warwicks, e. Warwick (Stratford-on-Avon), 264, Pte., k. in a., F. & F., 13/11/14.
Riley, Henry Herbert, b. London, Middx., e. Leamington, Warwicks (Coventry), 16848, Pte., k. in a., F. & F., 11/4/17.
Riman, Hector, e. Wimborne, Dorset (St. Giles, Salisbury), 25431, Pte., d. of w., F. & F., 28/10/18.

Robbins, Thomas, b. Oldbury, Worcs, e. Warwick (Birmingham), 9502, L/Cpl., k. in a., F. & F., 25/4/15.
Roberts, Albert, b. Birmingham, e. Birmingham (Coventry), 9373, Pte., k. in a., F. & F., 27/8/14.
Roberts, George, b. Birmingham, e. Birmingham, 6826, Pte., k. in a., F. & F., 2/7/15.
Roberts, Gerard, b. Nechells, Birmingham, e. Birmingham (Nechells, Birmingham), 2570, Pte., k. in a., F. & F., 18/2/15.
Roberts, Harry, b. Cradley, Worcs, e. Warwick (Birmingham), 9005, Pte., k. in a., F. & F., 4/11/14.
Roberts, William, b. Birmingham, e. Dublin (Birmingham), 8880, Pte., k. in a., F. & F., 25/4/15.
Roberts, William, b. Nottingham, e. Coventry, 8961, Pte., d. of w., F. & F., 19/10/14.
Robinson, George Edward, b. Scartho, Lincs, e. Grimsby, Lincs (Scartho), 27579, Pte., k. in a., F. & F., 23/10/16, formerly 25130, S. Staffs Regt.
Robinson, Herbert, b. Camberwell, London, e. London (Clapham Junction), 20594, Pte., k. in a., F. & F., 12/10/16, formerly 11088, A. Cyc. Corps.
Robinson, Walter, b. Birmingham, e. Birmingham, 6806, Pte., k. in a., F. & F., 19/6/15.
Robinson, William, b. New Jersey, U.S.A., e. Coventry, 16034, Pte., k. in a., F. & F., 3/5/17.
Rodds, Frederick, b. Leicester, e. Birmingham, 9739, Pte., k. in a., F. & F., 25/4/15.
Rodgers, Frederick, b. Birmingham, e. Birmingham, 166, Pte., k. in a., F. & F., 13/10/14.
Rollason, Mark Welch, b. West Bromwich, Staffs, e. Coventry, 11673, Pte., k. in a., F. & F., 23/10/16.
Rollins, Harry, b. Snitterfield, Warwicks, e. Birmingham (Sutton Coldfield, Birmingham), 18001, Pte., k. in a., F. & F., 11/4/17.
Rollins, John James, b. Snitterfield, Warwicks, e. Stratford-on-Avon, Warwicks, 29625, Pte., k. in a., F. & F., 12/10/17.
Rose, Frank, b. Barton-on-the-Heath, Glos., e. Stratford-on-Avon, Warwicks (Shipston-on-Stour, Worcs.), 9479, Pte., d. of w., F. & F., 12/10/16.
Rose, William Alexander, b. Birmingham, e. Worcester (Birmingham), 28742, Pte., k. in a., F. & F., 30/8/18.
Rossindale, Herbert, b. Bradford, Yorks, e. Bradford, 8904, L/Cpl., k. in a., F. & F., 19/6/15.
Rouse, Charles, b. Lewisham, Kent., e. New Cross, London (Lewisham), 445, Pte., k. in a., F. & F., 25/11/14.
Rowe, Ernest, b. Portsmouth, Hants, e. Portsmouth, 18699, Pte., d. of w., F. & F., 25/10/16, formerly 22901, Som. L.I.
Rowland, Eustace, b. Birmingham, e. Birmingham, 1264, Pte., k. in a., F. & F., 11/4/17.
Rowley, James, b. St. Paul's, Birmingham, e. Birmingham, 16594, Pte., k. in a., F. & F., 24/10/16.
Rowley, John Josiah, b. Atherstone, Warwicks, e. Walsall, Staffs, 9463, Pte., k. in a., F. & F., 9/5/15.
Rowley, William, b. Stockingford, Nuneaton, Warwicks, e. Nuneaton, Warwicks (Stockingford), 97, Pte., k. in a., F. & F., 13/10/14.
Rudd, Samuel, b. Smethwick, Staffs, e. Birmingham (Smethwick, Staffs), 1334, L/Cpl., k. in a., F. & F., 12/10/16.
Rulton, Alfred William, b. Castle Hedingham, Halstead, Essex, e. London (Halstead), 818, Sgt., d. of w., F. & F., 6/7/15.
Russell, Frederick, b. Leicester, e. Coventry (Leicester), 9631, Pte., k. in a., F. & F., 25/4/15.
Russell, Frederick George, b. Stratford-on-Avon, Warwicks, e. Stratford-on-Avon, 10082, Pte., k. in a., F. & F., 10/5/17.
Russell, George James, b. St. John's, Leamington, Warwicks, e. Warwick (Leamington), 9925, L/Cpl., k. in a., F. & F., 25/11/14.
Russell, William Thomas, b. Leamington Spa, Warwicks, e. Warwick (Leamington), 181, A/L/Sgt., k. in a., F. & F., 15/3/15.
Rutter, Arthur Edward, b. Newton Heath, Manchester, e. Lancaster (Preston, Lancs), 33134, Pte., k. in a., F. & F., 20/11/17, formerly 25590, Dragoons.
Ryan, John Michael, b Birmingham, e. Birmingham, 9853, Pte., k. in a., F. & F., 25/4/15.
Sabell, Samuel, b. St. Martin's, Warwick, e. Birmingham, 11295, Pte., k. in a., F. & F., 7/7/15.
Sadler, Tom, b. Snitterfield, Warwicks, e. Birmingham (Henley-in-Arden, Warwicks), 12165, Pte., d. of w., F. & F., 4/4/18.
Sammonds, George Henry, b. Abbott's, Bromley, Warwicks, e. Warwick (Atherstone, Warwicks), 20142, Pte., k. in a., F. & F., 11/4/17.
Sanders, Eli, b. Stony Stratford, Bucks., e. Wedgnock, Warwicks (Stony Stratford, Bucks), 132, A/L/Sgt., d. of w., F. & F., 31/10/14.
Sanders, Frederick, b. Edgbaston, Birmingham, e. Birmingham (Balsall Heath, Birmingham), 2099, Pte., d. of w., F. & F., 30/4/15.
Sansome, Douglas, b. Polesworth, Warwicks, e. Atherstone, Warwicks (Polesworth), 20082, Pte., d. of w., F. & F., 8/5/17.
Saunders, Arthur Tom, b. Bedminster, Bristol, e. Bristol (Bedminster), 35431, Pte., k. in a., F. & F., 15/4/18.
Saunders, Edmund, b. Leamington, Warwicks, e. Bedworth, Warwicks, 28714, Pte., k. in a., F. & F., 15/4/18.
Saunders, John, b. Perth, e. Birmingham (Rutherglen, Glasgow), 9193, Pte., d. of w., F. & F., 26/5/15.
Saunders, Thomas Merrett Evans, b London, e. Birmingham (Harborne, Birmingham), 17318, Pte., d. of w., F. & F., 14/7/18.
Saunders, William, e. Birmingham (West Bromwich, Staffs), 10524, Pte., k. in a., F. & F., 12/10/16.
Savage, John Patrick, b. Saltley, Birmingham, e. Birmingham, 2571, Pte., k. in a., F. & F., 19/6/15.
Saward, Cornelius, b. Islington, Middx., e. London (Islington), 243, L/Cpl., k. in a., F. & F., 19/6/15.
Scattergood, Walter Frederick, b. Atherstone, Warwicks, e. Nuneaton, Warwicks (Stockingford, Warwicks), 50809, L/Sgt., k. in a., F. & F., 30/6/18, formerly 21768, O. & B.L.I.
Scott, Joseph, b. Shieldfield, Northumberland, e. Newcastle-on-Tyne, 20641, Pte., k. in a., F. & F., 30/6/18, formerly 11376, A. Cyc. Corps.
Scragg, Allbert, b. E. Cowes, I. of W., e. Birmingham (Blakenall, Wolverhampton, Staffs), 11924, Pte., k. in a., F. & F., 12/10/16.
Searles, Joseph, b. Birmingham, e. Birmingham, 8921, A/Cpl., k. in a., F. & F., 26/4/15.
Sears, Charles, e. Aldershot, 28347, Pte., d. of w., F. & F., 4/5/17, formerly 27377, Hussars.
Selby, William, b. St. Martin's, Birmingham, e. Birmingham, 1784, Pte., k. in a., F. & F., 9/5/15.
Sennett, James Anderson, b. Chatham, Kent, e. Wolverhampton, Staffs (Chatham), 27609, Pte., k. in a., F. & F., 8/9/17, formerly 5654, S. Staffs Regt.
Setchell, William Henry, e. Stratford-on-Avon, Warwicks, 9198, L/Cpl., k. in a., F. & F., 30/5/18.
Seymour, Charles Henry, b. Redditch, Worcs, e. Birmingham, 3967, Pte., d. of w., F. & F., 5/6/15.
Sharkey, Arthur, b. Gortin, Dungannon, Tyrone, e. Belfast, 34177, Pte., k. in a., F. & F., 13/5/18, formerly 1070, Hussars.
Shaw, Arthur Edwin, b. Wolverhampton, Staffs, e. Birmingham, 1396, Pte., k. in a., F. & F., 26/4/15.
Shears, Albert, b. Rugby, Warwicks, e. Rugby, 16713, Pte., d. of w., F. & F., 2/5/17.
Sheffield, Thomas William Henry, b. Nuneaton, Warwicks, e. Nuneaton, Warwicks (Stockingford, Nuneaton), 1719, Pte., k. in a., F. & F., 19/6/15.
Shell, Albert Victor, b. Clerkenwell, Middx., e. Westminster, Middx. (Barnsbury, London), 28168, Pte., k. in a., F. & F., 12/10/17, formerly 18030, Hussars.
Shepherd, Frank, b. Deritend, Birmingham, e. Warwick (Small Heath, Birmingham), 9953, Pte., k. in a., F. & F., 25/4/15.
Shepherd, Sidney Herbert, b Warwick, e. Birmingham, 3479, Pte., d. of w., F. & F., 8/7/15.
Sherbon, Alfred, b. Birmingham, e. Long Compton, Shipston-on-Stour, Warwicks, k. in a., F. & F., 12/8/16.
Shillton, Henry Harry, b. Atherstone, Warwicks, e. Nuneaton, Warwicks (Atherstone), 12807, Pte., d. of w., F. & F., 16/4/18.
Shilton, William Henry, b. Birmingham, e. Coventry, 27896, Pte., k. in a., F. & F., 11/4/17.
Shilton, William John, b. Kingsbury, Warwicks, e. Tamworth, Warwicks (Hurley, Atherstone, Warwicks), 15602, Pte., k. in a., F. & F., 15/5/18.
Shorthouse, William, b. Bilston, Staffs, e. Birmingham, Warwicks (Bilston), 193, Pte., k. in a., F. & F., 27/8/14.
Sidebotham, Henry, b. Birmingham, e. Birmingham (Aston, Birmingham), 23977, Pte., k. in a. F. & F., 11/4/17.
Sidwell, Thomas, b. Chilvers Coton, Nuneaton, Warwicks, e. Nuneaton, 203788, Pte., k. in a., F. & F., 15/4/18.
Silk, Frederick Augustus, b. Liverpool, Lancs, e. Birmingham, 4011, Pte., k. in a., F. & F., 19/6/15.
Simcox, William Edward, b. Birmingham, e. Warwick (Birmingham), 453, Pte., k. in a., F. & F., 24/5/15.
Simmons, Alfred Edward, b. Aston, Birmingham, e. Birmingham, 3656, Pte., k. in a., F. & F., 11/10/16.
Simmons, Henry, b. Berkswell, Coventry, e. Coventry (Mere End, Kenilworth, Warwicks), 9058, Pte., k. in a., F. & F., 13/10/14.
Simmons, Henry, b. Over Whitacre, Warwick, e. Warwick (Coleshill, Warwicks), 17704, Pte., d. of w., F. & F., 6/9/16.
Simons, John, b. Birmingham, e. Birmingham, 1820, Pte., k. in a., F. & F., 3/11/15.
Simpkins, Robert, b. Gravesend, Kent, e. Canterbury, Kent (Ashford, Kent), 33047, Pte., k. in a., F. & F. 20/11/17, formerly 921, Dragoons.
Siviter, George Henry, b. Blackheath, Birmingham, e. Smethwick, Staffs (Blackheath, Birmingham), 7829, L/Cpl., k. in a., F. & F., 13/4/17.
Skidmore, William Henry, b Birmingham, e. Birmingham, 9395, Cpl., k. in a., F. & F., 25/4/15.
Skinner, Albert Sidney, e. Birmingham (Small Heath, Birmingham), 27857, L/Cpl., k. in a., F. & F., 10/12/16.
Skyrme, Hubert James, e. Chard, Wilts (Swindon, Wilts), 25463, Pte., k. in a., F. & F., 6/10/17.
Slack, James, b. Cannock Chase, Staffs, e. Warwick (Nuneaton, Warwicks), 37731, Pte., k. in a., F. & F., 15/4/18.
Slade, Lewis Henry, b. Lea, Malmesbury, Wilts, e. Malmesbury, 30520, Pte., k. in a., F. & F., 15/4/18.
Slatcher, Alfred, b. Long Lawford, Rugby, Warwicks, e Rugby, 16712, Pte., d. of w., F. & F., 15/5/18.
Slater Harold, b. Staningley, Leeds, Yorks, e. Coventry, 3617, L/Sgt., d. of w., F. & F., 26/8/16.
Slaymaker, David, b. Carshalton, Surrey, e. Lambeth, London (Streatham, London), 10420, Pte., k. in a., F. & F., 25/4/15.
Small, Ernest, e. Coventry (Oakengates, Salop), 22730, Pte., k. in a., F. & F., 11/4/17.
Smart, James, b. Birmingham, e. Warwick (Birmingham), 270, Pte., k. in a., F. & F., 13/10/14.
Smith, Alfred, e. Stratford-on-Avon, Warwicks (Alcester, Warwicks), 267394, Pte., k. in a., F. & F., 4/10/17.
Smith, Arthur, b. Bordesley, Birmingham, e. Birmingham, 3264, Pte., k. in a., F. & F., 25/4/15.
Smith, Arthur Clarence, b. Dartford, Kent, e. Woolwich (Dartford), 28229, Pte., d. of w., F. & F., 14/10/17, formerly 27352, Hussars.

Smith, Edward, b. Birmingham, e. Birmingham (Aston, Birmingham), 2722, Pte., k. in a., F. & F., 11/5/17.
Smith, Ernest Franklin, b. Cradley Heath, Staffs, e. Coventry (Cradley Heath), 16491, Pte., d. of w., F. & F., 12/10/16.
Smith, Frank Whaley, b. March, Cambs, e. March, Cambs, 29376, Pte., k. in a., F. & F., 30/8/18, formerly 36393, Suffolk Regt.
Smith, George, b. Stoke, Coventry, e. Coventry, 9505, Pte., k. in a., F. & F., 30/8/18, M.M.
Smith, George Sidney, b. Birmingham, e. Birmingham, 10011, Pte., k. in a., F. & F., 23/10/16.
Smith, Harry, b. Billsden, Leics, e. Nottingham, 1869, Sgt., k. in a., F. & F., 11/5/15.
Smith, Harry, b. Louth, Lincs, e. Lincoln (Carlton Askes, Grantham), 27581, Pte., k. in a., F. & F., 12/10/16, formerly 25010, S. Staffs Regt.
Smith, Harry, b. Eardesland, Hereford, e. Abergavenny (Leominster), 27808, Pte., k. in a., F. & F., 8/8/18, formerly 24609, Shrops L.I.
Smith, Henry, b. Bath, Som., e. Birmingham, 3933, Pte., k. in a., F. & F., 19/6/15.
Smith, Herbert J., b. Hockley, Birmingham, e. Birmingham, 16547, Pte., k. in a., F. & F., 3/5/17.
Smith, Howard, b. Birmingham, e. Birmingham, 14435, Pte., k. in a., F. & F., 5/10/17.
Smith, James, b. Deritend, Birmingham, e. Coventry, 17491, Pte., k. in a., F. & F., 3/5/17.
Smith, John Thomas, b. Birmingham, e. Birmingham, 7189, Cpl., d. of w., F. & F., 30/5/15.
Smith, Joseph William, b. Higham-on-the-Hill, Leics, e Warwick (Nuneaton), 20305, Pte, d., F. & F., 16/3/17.
Smith, Paul, b. Smethwick, Staffs, e. Coventry (Smethwick), 158, Pte., k. in a., F. & F., 26/4/15.
Smith, Percy, b. Aston, Birmingham, e. Warwick, 398, A/Cpl., d. of w., F. & F., 5/2/15.
Smith, Peter, b. Birmingham, e. Birmingham, 9639, Pte, d., F. & F., 12/11/16.
Smith, Richard, b. Gosport, Hants, e. Coventry (Gosport), 985, Pte., d. of w., F. & F., 24/5/15.
Smith, Thomas, b. Manor Magdalene, Colchester, e. Colchester, 6909, Pte., k. in a., F. & F., 26/4/15.
Smith, Thomas, b. Birmingham, e. Birmingham, 42490, Pte., k. in a., F. & F., 24/10/18.
Smith, Walter, b. Bedworth, Warwicks, e. Nuneaton (Coventry), 4480, L/Cpl., k. in a., F. & F., 10/5/17.
Smith, Walter, b. Aston, Birmingham, e. Birmingham, 7270 Pte., k. in a., F. & F., 25/4/15
Smith, Wilfred, b. Hurley, Warwicks, e. Coventry, 42526, Pte d. of w., F. & F., 3/11/18.
Smith, William, b. Winson Green, Birmingham, e. Smethwick, Staffs, 9377, Pte., k. in a., F. & F. 9/7/15.
Smith, William George, b. Birmingham, e. Nuneaton, 203711 Pte, k. in a., F. & F., 14/10/18.
Smith, William Henry, b. Hillmorton, Warwicks, e. Rugby (Hillmorton), 1672, Pte., k. in a., F. & F., 25/4/15.
Smith, William Henry, b. Knowle, Warwicks, e. Warwick (Knowle), 9443, Pte., d. of w., F. & F., 9/5/15.
Snelling, Oliver e. Dorking, Surrey, 33085, Pte, k. in a., F. & F., 30/8/18, formerly 2284, Surrey Yeo.
Snook, Thomas, e. Taunton, Som. (Tiverton), 25432, Pte., k. in a., F. & F., 12/10/17.
Soden, William, b. Warwick, e. Warwick, 10136, Pte., k in a., F. & F., 9/5/15.
Soles, Walter, b. Birmingham, e. Warwick (Birmingham), 9525 Pte., k. in a., F. & F., 25/4/15.
Solomon, William Isaac Thomas, b. Aston, Birmingham, e. Birmingham, 16016, Pte., d., F. & F., 28/3/17.
Soughan, Frank, b. Yarmouth, Norfolk, e. Colchester, Essex, 6841, Cpl., k. in a., F. & F., 29/10/14.
South, Stephen, b. Ladywood, Birmingham, e. Birmingham, 1718, Pte., k. in a., F. & F., 10/10/16.
Southam, Jonathan, b. Stratford-on-Avon, Warwicks, e. Worcester (Redditch), 28690, Pte., k. in a., F. & F., 31/3/18
Southam, William, b. Coventry, Warwicks, e. Coventry, 6734, Pte., k. in a., F. & F., 19/6/15.
Sparkes, Edward, b. Sheffield, e. Coventry, Warwicks, 8987, L/Cpl., d. of w., F. & F., 10/5/15.
Sparrow, Frederick, b. Coton, Warwicks, e. Bedworth, 16190, Pte. k. in a., F. & F., 11/4/17.
Spencer, Albert, b. Willenhall, Staffs, e. Darlaston (Willenhall), 27617, Pte., d. of w., F. & F., 17/10/16, formerly 16763, S. Staffs Regt.
Spencer, Thomas, b. Birmingham, e. Birmingham 136, L/Cpl., d. of w., F. & F., 4/11/14.
Spiers, Charles, b. Leamington, Warwicks, e. Warwick (Leamington), 4115, Cpl., k. in a., F. & F., 3/5/17.
Spry, Peter Charles, b. Luton, Beds, e. Birmingham, 9355, Pte., d., F. & F., 12/11/18.
Squires, Edgar Cumberland, b. Ruddington, Notts, e. Coventry, 9611, Sgt., k. in a., F. & F., 4/10/17.
Stanley, Albert, b. Henley-on-Thames, Oxon, e. Reading (Wokingham), 28297, Pte., k. in a., F. & F., 12/2/17, formerly 27461, Hussars.
Steadman, Charles George, b. Worcester, e. Warwick (Handsworth, Birmingham), 2442, Pte., k. in a., F. & F., 27/10/14.
Steadman, William, b. Ellesmere Port., Ches., e. Warwick (Birmingham), 8804, Pte. k. in a., F. & F., 25/4/15.
Steele, Frederick, e. Stratford-on-Avon, Warwicks (Willington, Shipston-on-Stour), 9211, Pte, k. in a., F. & F., 30/8/18.
Steels, William, b. Fletton, Peterborough, e. Huntingdon (Fletton), 24798, Pte, k. in a., F. & F., 3/7/17, formerly 1669, Hunts Cyc. Battn
Stevens, John Arthur, b. West Bromwich, Staffs, e. Birmingham, 7003, Pte., k. in a., F. & F., 9/4/17.
Stevenson, Harry, b. Foleshill, Coventry, Warwicks, e. Coventry (Foleshill), 1722, Pte., k. in a., F. & F., 5/7/15.
Steventon, Albert, b. Birmingham, e. Birmingham, 9187, Pte., k. in a., F. & F., 25/4/15.
Stirk, Frank, b. Birmingham, e. Birmingham, 2606, Pte., k. in a., F & F., 19/6/15.
St. Ledger, Henry, b. Willenhall, Staffs, e. Birmingham, 8957, Pte., d. of w., F. & F., 26/10/14.
Stocks, George, b. Birmingham, e. Birmingham, 1063, L/Cpl., k. in a., F. & F., 1/7/16.
Stockwell, Percival Edgar, b. Stonehouse, Glos., e. Stroud, 1608, Cpl., k. in a., F. & F., 25/6/16.
Stokes, Trevor, b. Heath Hay, Staffs, e. Nuneaton, Warwicks. 35418, Pte., d. of w., F. & F., 16/4/18.
Stone, Francis Hubert, b. Bromsgrove, Worcs, e. Birmingham. 13711, A/Sgt., d., F. & F., 8/3/19, formerly 8162, Worcs Regt.
Stopps, Harry Ernest, b. Leamington, Warwicks, e. Rugby, 24328, Pte., k. in a., F. & F., 30/8/18.
Storer, Joseph, b. Birmingham, e. Birmingham, 6714, Pte., k. in a., F. & F., 24/5/15.
Stott, Richard Norman, b. West Rainton, Durham, e. Houghton-le-Spring, Durham, 29741, Pte., d. of w., F. & F., 20/7/18, formerly 40200, D.L.I.
Stratford, William, b. Harborough Magna, Warwicks, e. Rugby (Harborough Magna), 1853, Pte., d. of w., F. & F., 29/10/15.
Stretch, Henry, b. Birmingham, e. Birmingham, 9084, Pte, k. in a., F. & F., 27/8/14.
Stride, Harry, b. Birmingham, e. Birmingham, 3270, L/Cpl., k. in a., F. & F., 16/2/17.
Stuart, Alec, b. Alveston, Warwicks, e. Stratford-on-Avon (Alveston), 9293, A/Cpl., k. in a., F. & F., 30/11/17.
Sturt, Norris, b. Islington, Middx., e. Devonport (Folkestone), 9621, Sgt., k. in a., F. & F., 25/4/15.
Stych, Samuel, b. Birmingham, e. Birmingham, 1051, L/Cpl., k. in a., F. & F., 8/1/16.
Such, Harry, b. Birmingham, e. Birmingham, 21864, Pte., k. in a., F. & F., 3/5/17.
Sullivan, John, b. Huntingdon, e. Coventry (Birmingham), 3613, Pte., k. in a., F. & F., 11/5/15.
Summerfield, Albert, b. Hockley, Birmingham, e. Birmingham, 3627, Pte., k. in a., F. & F., 6/7/15.
Sutton, Sydney, b. Frankton, Warwicks, e. Rugby (Frankton), 2455, Pte., d. of w., F. & F., 24/6/16.
Sutton, William, b. Liverpool, e. Southampton (Bootle), 50916, Pte., k. in a., F. & F., 31/8/18, formerly 54451, Ches. Regt.
Swainston, William, Ernest, b. York, e. Coventry, 9486, Pte., k. in a., F. & F., 26/7/15.
Swan, George Henry, b. Birmingham, e. Warwick (Birmingham), 20313, Pte., k. in a., F. & F., 3/5/17.
Sweeney, David William, b. Whitechapel, Middx., e. Woolwich (Whitechapel), 981, Pte., k. in a., F. & F., 29/10/14.
Tapp, William, b. Birmingham, e. Birmingham (Walton-on-Trent, Staffs), 8970, Pte., d. of w., F. & F., 25/4/15.
Target, Frederick, b. Birmingham, e. Birmingham, 2401, Pte., k. in a., F. & F., 8/9/14.
Tarver, William, b. Solihull, Warwicks, e. Warwick (Hockley Heath), 10167, Pte., k. in a., F. & F., 26/7/15.
Tate, Thomas Tempest, b. Kidderminster, Worcs, e. Birmingham (Kidderminster), 35424, Pte., k. in a., F. & F, 15/4/18.
Taylor, Arthur, b. Birmingham, e. Lichfield, Staffs (Birmingham), 670, Pte., k. in a., F. & F., 14/10/14. formerly 7834, Border Regt.
Taylor, Charles, b. Triston, Yorks, e. Birmingham, 2091, Pte., d. of w., F. & F., 28/4/15.
Taylor, Colin Rowland, b. Birmingham, e. Birmingham, 1027, Pte., k. in a., F. & F., 8/8/18.
Taylor, Edward, b. Bethnal Green, London, E., e. Camberwell, 28298, Pte., d. of w., F. & F., 2/5/17, formerly 27433, Hussars.
Taylor, George Edward, b. Knowle, Warwicks, e. Birmingham, 11418, Pte., k. in a., F. & F., 3/7/17.
Taylor, Henry, b. Bristol, e. Birmingham, 7951, L/Cpl., k. in a., F. & F., 3/5/17.
Taylor, James, b. Wolverhampton, Staffs, e. Birmingham, 9951, Pte., k. in a., F. & F., 13/10/14.
Taylor, John Ross, b. Brendon, Warwicks, e. Warwick (Atherstone), 16681, Pte., k. in a., F. & F., 12/8/16.
Taylor, Joseph, b. Birmingham, e. Warwick (Birmingham), 75113, Pte., k. in a., F. & F., 25/4/15.
Taylor, Robert, b. Birmingham, e. Ross (Birmingham), 6794, Pte., k. in a., F. & F., 10/12/14.
Tayton, John Henry, e. Coventry, 267116, Sgt., d. of w., F. & F., 29/3/18.
Teager, William, b. Bridgnorth, Salop, e. Birmingham (Glasgow), 6711, L/Cpl., d. of w., F. & F., 23/10/16.
Tedd, James, b. Coventry, e. Coventry, 42233, Pte., k. in a., F. & F., 18/10/18.
Templeton, Robert, e. Salisbury, 268558, Pte., k. in a., F. & F., 12/10/17.
Tennant, John, b. Walsall, Staffs, e. Clu Hill, Staffs, 27776, Pte., d. of w., F. & F., 11/1/17, formerly 24133, Shropshire L.I.
Tetsall, Harry, b. Birmingham, e. Birmingham (Smethwick), 970, L/Cpl., k. in a., F. & F., 11/4/17.
Thomas, John, b. Birmingham, e. Birmingham, 2064, Pte., k. in a., F. & F., 25/6/16.
Thomas, Thomas, b. Foxall, Burton-on-Trent, Staffs, e. Warwick (Birmingham), 4573, L/Cpl., d., F. & F., 9/2/15.
Thomas, William, b. Llanhilleth, Cramlin, Mon., e. Merthyr, 1806, Pte., k. in a., F. & F., 26/4/15.
Thompson, Walter b. Bistthorpe, Norfolk, e. Norwich, 27610, Pte., k. in a., F. & F., 11/4/17, formerly 5525, S. Staffs Regt.
Thompson, William, b. Witherly, Leicester, e. Atherstone (Witherly), 9786, Pte., k. in a., F. & F., 23/10/16.

Thorne, Thomas Henry, b. Aston Clinton, Bucks, e. Aylesbury (Aston Clinton), 35419, Pte., k. in a., F. & F., 15/4/18.
Thornhill, George, b. Birmingham, e. Birmingham, 6607, Pte., k. in a., F. & F., 26/4/15.
Thornton, Ernest, b. Birmingham, e. Birmingham, 6443, Pte., k. in a., F. & F., 25/6/16.
Thornton, Philip, b. Holy Trinity, London, e. Birmingham (Sparkhill, Birmingham), 9484, C/Sgt., k. in a., F. & F., 13/10/14.
Thorneycroft, George Thomas, b. Napton, Southam, Warwicks, e. Warwick (Hillmorton, Rugby), 6648, Pte., k. in a., F. & F., 23/10/14.
Timmins, Ernest, b. Oldbury, Worcs, e. Oldbury (Langley, Oldbury), 28371, Pte., k. in a., F. & F., 3/5/17, formerly 29909, Hussars.
Timmins, Wallace Joseph Henry, b. St. George's, Birmingham, e. Birmingham, 3750, L/Cpl., k. in a., F. & F., 12/10/16.
Timms, William George, b. Warwick, e. Warwick, 21405, Pte., d. of w., F. & F., 3/5/17.
Todd, Ernest, b. Birmingham, e. Birmingham, 9148, A/Sgt., k. in a., F. & F., 2/5/15.
Tolley, William, b. Birmingham, e. Birmingham, 13270, Pte., k. in a., F. & F., 12/10/16.
Tomlinson, Horace, b. Birmingham, e. Birmingham, 763, Pte., k. in a., F. & F., 25/4/15.
Toon, William, b. Birmingham, e. Birmingham, 9252, Pte., k. in a., F. & F., 25/4/15.
Tooth, Benjamin, b. Aston, Birmingham, e. Birmingham, 3938, Pte., k. in a., F. & F., 19/6/15.
Topping, George, b. St. Catherine's, Northampton, e. Birmingham, 3226, Pte., k. in a., F. & F., 25/4/15.
Tovey, Samuel, b. Leamington, Warwicks, e. Birmingham, 9602, L/Cpl., d. of w., F. & F., 1/1/15.
Tranter, Harry, e. Birmingham, 9760, Pte., k. in a., F. & F., 4/6/15.
Tranchard, Hugh, b. Winchester, Hants, e. Winchester, 839, Pte., k. in a., F. & F., 11/5/15.
Trentham, Thomas Henry, b. Halford, Shipston-on-Stour, Warwicks, e. Birmingham (Aston, Birmingham), 2915, L/Cpl., k. in a., F. & F., 12/10/16.
Trentham, George Thomas, b. Halford, Shipston-on-Stour, e. Birmingham, 3486, Pte., d. of w., F. & F., 8/6/15.
Truby, Alfred William, b. Brookfield, Birmingham, e. Birmingham (King's Norton, Birmingham), 19169, Pte., k. in a., F. & F., 23/10/16.
Trumpess, Albert, b. Colchester, Essex, e. Colchester, 12463, Pte., d. of w., F. & F., 12/10/16, formerly 54551, R.G.A.
Tuckey, Charles Ernest, b. Princethorpe, Warwicks, E. Rugby (Princethorpe), 242325, Pte., k. in a., F. & F., 4/10/17.
Tunstall, William, b. St. Martin's, Birmingham, e. Birmingham, 4565, L/Cpl., d. of w. F. & F., 27/7/17.
Turner, Aubrey Fred Llewellyn, b. Birmingham, e. Birmingham, 9064, Pte., k. in a., F. & F., 26/8/14.
Turner, George Frederick, b. Fiskerwick, Elford, Staffs, e. Nuneaton, Warwicks (Polesworth, Tamworth, Warwicks), 13782, Pte., k. in a., F. & F., 23/10/16.
Turvey, Harry, b. Hockley, Birmingham, e. Birmingham, 2322, Cpl., k. in a., F. & F., 12/10/16.
Twigger, Amos, b. Stockingford, Nuneaton, Warwicks, e. Nuneaton, 4423, Pte., k. in a., F. & F., 17/4/17.
Twocock, Edward, b. Deptford, Kent, e. Woolwich, Kent (Deptford), 34178, Pte., d. of w., F. & F., 24/12/17, formerly 14474, Hussars.
Twynham, Herbert Richard, b. King's Sutton, Banbury, Oxon, e. Nuneaton, Warwicks (King's Sutton), 2007, Pte., k. in a., F. & F., 19/6/15.
Tyler, Frederick, b. Liverpool, e. Birmingham (Sparkbrook, Birmingham), 9740, Pte., k. in a., F. & F., 3/5/17.
Underhill, Frank, b. Hillfields, Coventry, e. Coventry, 3517, Pte., k. in a., F. & F., 1/7/16.
Underwood, Cyrus, b. Bilton, Rugby, Warwicks, e. Rugby (Bilton), 9535, Pte., k. in a., F. & F., 9/7/15.
Underwood, Samuel Joseph, b. St. Michaels, Birmingham, e. Lichfield, Staffs (Aston, Birmingham), 7408, Cpl., k. in a., F. & F., 11/4/17.
Underwood, William, b. Long Lawford, Rugby, Warwicks, e. Rugby (Long Lawford, Rugby), 9880, Pte., k. in a., F. & F., 18/3/15.
Urquhart, Colin, b. Small Heath, Birmingham, e. London (Birmingham), 1180, L/Cpl., d. of w., F. & F., 26/4/15.
Urry, William Spanner, b. Birmingham, e. Warwick (Aston, Birmingham), 18355, Pte., d. of w., F. & F., 4/10/17, formerly 23133, Som. L.I.
Usher, Thomas Morris, b. Walsall, Staffs, e. Birmingham, 1998, Pte., k. in a., F. & F., 31/3/18.
Vallance, Richard, b. Leamington Spa, e. Coventry (Leamington Spa), 1785, Pte., k. in a., F. & F., 25/4/15.
Varley, Thomas, b. Birmingham, e. Birmingham, 9851, Pte., k. in a., F. & F., 25/4/15.
Varney, James, b. Coventry, e. Coventry, 203698, Pte., k. in a., F. & F., 17/10/18.
Vaughan, Edward Charles, b. Lambeth, Surrey, e. London (West Norwood, Surrey), 2039, Pte., k. in a., F. & F., 25/6/16.
Vickery, Richard John, b. Camberwell, London, e. London (Walworth), 20584, Pte., k. in a., F. & F., 12/10/16, formerly 10831, A. Cyclist Corps.
Vidion, Charles, b. Molash, Kent, e. Canterbury, Kent (Molash), 33183, Pte., k. in a., F. & F., 23/12/17, formerly 23028, Lancers.
Vincent, William, b. Birmingham, e. Birmingham (Walsall, Staffs), 9994, Pte., d. of w., F. & F., 16/5/15.
Wade, William Henry, b. St. Steven's, Birmingham, e. Birmingham (Aston, Birmingham), 18458, Pte., d. of w., F. & F., 3/5/17, formerly 24218, Som. L.I.
Wakelin, Charles, b. New Bilton, Rugby, Warwicks, e. Rugby (New Bilton), 3290, L/Cpl., k. in a., F. & F., 26/7/17.
Wakeman, Frederick, b. Aston, Birmingham, e. Birmingham, 6458, Pte., d. of w., F. & F., 2/4/16.
Waldron, Frederick, b. Birmingham, e. Birmingham, 9530, Pte., k. in a., F. & F., 25/4/15.
Walker, Bertram, b. Birmingham, e. Birmingham (Balsall Heath, Birmingham), 9251, Pte., k. in a., F. & F., 19/6/15.
Walker, Charles George, e. Birmingham, 27901, Pte., d. of w., F. & F., 11/4/17.
Walker, Harry Walter, b. Balsall Heath, Birmingham, e. Warwick (Harborne, Birmingham), 2352, Pte., k. in a., F. & F., 7/4/15.
Walker, Thomas, b. Sutton Cheney, Market Bosworth, Leicester, e. Nuneaton, Warwicks, 4498, Pte., k. in a., F. & F., 3/6/15.
Walker, William, b. Birmingham, e. Stoneleigh, Warwicks (Birmingham), 118, Pte., d. of w., F. & F., 28/8/14.
Wall, Christopher, b. Birmingham, e. Birmingham, 9439, Pte., k. in a., F. & F., 13/10/14.
Wall, Herbert John, b. Birmingham, e. Birmingham, 9296, Pte., k. in a., F. & F., 13/10/14.
Wall, Jesse Hubert, b. Birmingham, e. Birmingham (Handsworth, Birmingham), 18393, A/Cpl., d. of w., F. & F., 12/10/17, formerly 23472, S.L.I.
Wall, John Henry, b. Ribbsford, Worcs, e. Birmingham, 21080, Pte., k. in a., F. & F., 15/4/18.
Wallace, Francis Albert, b. Birmingham, e. Birmingham, 1880, Pte., d. of w., F. & F., 18/10/16.
Wallace, James, b. Islington, Middx., e. London (Holloway), 28354, Pte., k. in a., F. & F., 11/4/17, formerly 27223, Hussars.
Wallen, Alfred, b. Coventry, e. Coventry, 9701, Pte., d. of w., F. & F., 24/11/14.
Walmsley, James Irving, e. Liverpool (Chipping, Lancs), 22042, Pte., k. in a., F. & F., 12/10/17, formerly 3118, Liverpool Regt.
Ward, Arthur, b. Hanley, Staffs, e. Warwick (West Bromwich, Staffs), 24079, Pte., k. in a., F. & F., 15/4/18.
Ward, Charles, b. Coventry, Warwicks, e. Coventry, 148, Pte., k. in a., F. & F., 25/4/15.
Ward, David, b. Foleshill, Coventry, e. Coventry, 9757, Pte., k. in a., F. & F., 27/10/14.
Ward, Samuel, b. Smethwick, Staffs, e. Birmingham, 1455, Pte., k. in a., F. & F., 25/4/15, formerly 8726, Leics Regt.
Waring, John, b. Exhall, Warwicks, e. Warwick (Kenilworth), 9456, Pte., k. in a., F. & F., 27/7/16.
Waring, William, b. Longford, Coventry, Warwicks, e. Coventry, 2204, Pte., k. in a., F. & F., 26/8/14.
Warr, James, b. London, e. London, 25708, Pte., k. in a., F. & F., 29/7/18, formerly 029030, R.A.O.C.
Warren, Victor Harold, b. Tipton, Staffs, e. Birmingham, 28719, Pte., d. of w., F. & F., 18/5/18.
Warwick, George Frederick, b. Westminster, London, e. Lambeth (Brixton), 30468, Cpl., k. in a., F. & F., 5/10/17, formerly 77895, R.E.
Washbourne, Eric, b. Coleshill, Warwicks, e. Nuneaton, 10408, Pte., d. of w., F. & F., 13/10/16.
Watkins, James, b. Brinklow, Rugby, Warwicks, e. Coventry (Brinklow), 458, Pte., k. in a., F. & F., 8/7/15.
Watkins, William, b. St. Matthews, Walsall, Staffs, e. Warwick (Walsall), 8665, L/Cpl., d. of w., F. & F., 2/10/17.
Watson, Alban Thomas, b. St. Paul's, Middlesbrough, Yorks, e. Middlesbrough, 4594, Cpl., k. in a., F. & F., 3/5/17.
Watson, William Henry, b. Kenilworth, Warwicks, e. Leamington (Coventry), 16122, Pte., k. in a., F. & F., 23/10/16, formerly 1871, R.A.S.C.
Watts, Albert, b. St. Michaels, Coventry, e. Coventry, 2210, Pte., k. in a., F. & F., 27/10/14.
Watts, Edward, b. Stogumber, Som., e. Newbury, Berks, 18650, Pte., k. in a., F. & F., 3/5/17, formerly 24524, Som. L.I.
Watts, William, b. Long Compton, Warwick, e. Warwick (Long Compton), 9507, Pte., k. in a., F. & F., 9/5/15.
Watts, William, b. Great Bourton, Oxon, e. Coventry, 15048, Pte., k. in a., F. & F., 11/4/17.
Weale, Charles, b. Birmingham, e. Brighton, 11664, L/Cpl., k. in a. F. & F., 12/10/16.
Weaver, Richard, b. Hyson Green, Nottingham, e. Nuneaton (Hinckley, Leics), 1861, Pte., k. in a., F. & F., 19/6/15.
Webb, Ernest, b. All Saints, Coventry, e. Coventry, 3681, Pte., d., F. & F., 9/11/15.
Webb, George, e. Market Rasen, Lincs, 27019, Pte., d., F. & F., 21/3/18, formerly 5401, Linc. Regt.
Webb, Robert, b. Warwick, e. Warwick, 9666, Pte., k. in a., F. & F., 12/10/16.
Webb, Robert, b. Willington, Beds, e. Mill Hill (Bedford), 27601, Pte., k. in a., F. & F., 23/10/16, formerly 5546, S. Staffs Regt.
Webb, William, b. Nottingam, e. Ely (Warwick), 6473, Sgt., k. in a., 11/1/15, formerly 5147, Suffolk Regt.
Wedge, Edward, b. Deritend, Birmingham, e. Warwick (Birmingham), 130, Sgt., k. in a., F. & F., 31/3/18.
Weeks, Frederick Edwin, b. Ruscombe, Reading, Berks, e. Reading (Rugby, Warwicks), 9367, Pte., k. in a., F. & F., 25/1/15.
Weeks, Percy George, e. Birmingham (Handsworth, Birmingham), 305351, Sgt., k. in a., F. & F., 30/8/18.
Welch, Arthur, b. Coventry, e. Coventry, 17028, Pte., k. in a., F. & F., 31/8/18.
Welch, Charles, b. Wednesbury, Staffs, e. Birmingham, 10839, Pte., k. in a., F. & F., 3/5/17.
Welch, James, b. Bordesley, Birmingham, e. Birmingham (Small Heath, Birmingham), 1798, Pte., k. in a., F. & F., 18/12/14.

Welch, William Alfred, b. Cookshill, Warwicks, e. Redditch, Worcs (Studley, Warwicks), 19602, Pte., k. in a., F. & F., 3/5/17.
Wells, F. W., b. Birmingham, e. Warwick (Birmingham), 22382, Pte., d. of w., F. & F., 22/4/18.
Wells, Walter, b. Marton, Rugby, Warwicks, e. Warwick (Chapel-en-le-Frith, Derby), 9962, Pte., d. of w., F. & F., 20/12/14.
Westall, Sidney George, b. St. Saviour's, Birmingham, e. Warwick (Birmingham), 456, Pte., k. in a., F. & F., 25/4/15.
Weston, William Henry, b. Tividale, Oldbury, Staffs, e. Birmingham (Smethwick, Staffs), 9798, Pte., k. in a., F. & F., 26/8/14.
Wharton, Frederick, b. Birmingham, e. Birmingham (Small Heath, Birmingham), 9785, Pte., k. in a., F. & F., 26/4/15.
Wheatley, Charles Henry, b. Coates, Cambs, e. Coventry, 24125, Pte., d. of w., F. & F., 5/9/18.
Wheeler, Edward, b. St. Nicholl's, Birmingham, e. Birmingham, 2241, Pte., k. in a., F. & F., 22/3/15.
Wheeler, Edwin George, b. Birmingham, e. Birmingham, 3390, Pte., k. in a., F. & F., 19/6/15.
Wheeler, Ernest, b. Tenbury Wells, Worcs, e. London (Wantage, Berks), 28305, Pte., k. in a., F. & F., 3/5/17, formerly 27466, Hussars.
Whelan, Thomas, b. Chiswick, Middx., e. London (Chiswick, Middx.), 7476, Sgt., d. of w., F. & F., 1/7/16.
White, Charles, b. Willowby, Warwicks, e. Worcester (Sedgberrow, Evesham, Worcs), 30390, Pte., k. in a., F. & F., 20/7/18, formerly 19754, Worcs Regt.
White, Albert Stanley, b. Yeovil, Som., e. Taunton (Yeovil), 41286, Pte., d. of w., F. & F., 5/8/18.
Whitehouse, Alfred, b. Birmingham, e. Birmingham, 7623, L/Cpl., k. in a., F. & F., 3/11/14.
Whitehouse, John Thomas, b. West Bromwich, Staffs, e. Birmingham (West Bromwich), 9604, Pte., d. of w., F. & F., 11/7/15.
Whiting, Richard, b. Birmingham, e. Ross (Birmingham), 6901, L/Sgt., k. in a., F. & F., 23/10/16.
Whiting, William Henry, b. Derby, e. Birmingham, 22183, Pte., k. in a., F. & F., 12/5/17.
Whitlock, William, b. Ladywood, Birmingham, e. Birmingham (Ladywood), 20626, Pte., k. in a., F. & F., 3/5/17, formerly 8147, A Cyclist Corps.
Widdows, William, b. All Saints, Birmingham, e. Birmingham (Handsworth, Staffs), 1952, Pte., d., F. & F., 3/1/16.
Wild, George, b. Birmingham, e. Birmingham, 9298, Sgt., k. in a., F. & F., 10/9/14.
Wilde, John, b. Marylebone, Middx., e. Rugby, Warwicks, 20976, Pte., k. in a., F. & F., 15/4/18.
Wilde, James William, b. Roseville, Dudley, Staffs, e. Birmingham (Dudley), 1215, Pte., k. in a., F. & F., 26/4/15.
Wiles, Bertie, b. St. Nicholas, Nuneaton, Warwicks, e. Nuneaton (Chilvers Coton, Nuneaton), 2445, Pte., k. in a., F. & F., 11/10/16.
Wilkins, Herbert, b. St. Mark's, Coventry, e. Warwick, 16531, Pte., k. in a., F. & F., 12/10/16.
Wilkins, Reginald Gerald, b. Rugby, Warwicks, e. Rugby, Warwicks (St. Albans, Herts), 16008, Pte., k. in a., F. & F., 12/10/16.
Wilkins, William, b. Foleshill, Coventry, e. Coventry, 3515, Pte., d. of w., F. & F., 4/5/15.
Wilkinson, Frederick, b. Nechells, Birmingham, e. Warwick (Nechells, Birmingham), 429, Pte., k. in a., F. & F., 25/4/15.
Wikinson, Levi, b. Stoke-on-Trent, e. Longton, Staffs, 9830, Pte., k. in a., F. & F., 19/6/15.
Wilkshire, William, b. Upton-on-Severn, Worcs., e. Warwick (Upton-on-Severn), 498, Pte., k. in a., F. & F., 25/4/15.
Williams, Alfred Edward, b. Newcastle-under-Lyne, Staffs, e. Coventry (Newcastle-under-Lyne), 3, Pte., k. in a., F. & F., 13/10/14.
Williams, Bertrand John, b. Birmingham, e. Birmingham (Smethwick), 10721, Pte., k. in a., F. & F., 25/4/16.
Williams, Edward Stanley, b. Birkenhead, Cheshire, e. Liverpool (Birkenhead), 29336, Pte., k. in a., F. & F., 31/8/18, formerly 61987, Cheshire Regt.
Williams, Edward, b. St. Matthews, Birmingham, e. Birmingham (Perry Barr), 3717, Pte., k. in a., F. & F., 26/7/15.
Williams, Ernest Arnold, b. Birmingham, e. Birmingham, 1406, Pte., d. of w., F. & F., 26/4/15.
Williams, Frederick, b. Wombourne, Staffs, e. Sedgeley, Dudley (Wombourne), 27583, Pte., k. in a., F. & F., 16/2/17, formerly 24644, S. Staff Res
Williams, Harry, b. Merthyr, Glam., e. Cardiff (Aberfan, Merthyr), 2428, Sgt., k. in a., F. & F., 21/6/17, D.C.M., M.M.
Williams, James, b. St. Mary's, Wolverhampton, Staffs, e. Warwick (Wolverhampton), 2223, Pte., d. of w., F. & F., 14/10/14.
Willis, Charles Henry, b. St. Stephen's, Birmingham, e. Birmingham (Aston, Birmingham), 4456, Pte., d. of w., F. & F., 14/10/16.
Willis, Thomas, b. Putney, Surrey, e. London, 20556, Pte., k. in a., F. & F., 12/10/16, formerly 9877, A Cyclist Corps.
Willsdon, John, b. Clerkenwell, Middx., e. London, 28306, Pte., k. in a., F. & F., 11/4/17, formerly 27358, Hussars.
Wilson, Alfred, b. Nuneaton, Warwicks, e. Nuneaton, 10823, Pte., k. in a., F. & F., 24/8/16.
Wilson, Roland, b. Bulkington, Bedworth, Warwicks, e. Bedworth, 17967, Pte., k. in a., F. & F., 12/10/16.
Wilson, Ernest, b. Balcombe, Brighton, Sussex, e. Nuneaton, Warwicks (Balcombe), 1731, Pte., k. in a., F. & F., 19/6/15.
Winkley, Howard, b. Birmingham, e. Birmingham (Handsworth, Staffs), 9910, Pte., k. in a., F. & F., 26/8/14.
Winter, Thomas Ernest, b. Ely, Glam., e. Cardiff (Ely), 34201, Pte., k. in a., F. & F., 17/4/18, formerly 1369, Welsh Horse.
Withers, George Frederick, b. St. John's, Coventry, e. Warwick (Coventry), 2198, Pte., d., F. & F., 13/10/18.
Withey, William, b. Hallow, Worcs, e. Birmingham (Small Heath, Birmingham), 10437, Pte., k. in a., F. & F., 8/7/15.
Wood, John, b. Tranent, Haddington, e. Edinburgh, 33117, Pte., d., F. & F., 10/7/18, formerly 7887, Dragoons.
Woodham, Frederick James e. Bristol (Badminton, Glos.), 38098, Cpl., k. in a., F. & F., 10/7/18, formerly S/24018, Glos. Regt.
Woodhurst, Frederick, b. Tottenham, Middx., e. Warwick (Tottenham, Middx.), 925, Pte., d. of w., F. & F., 1/7/15.
Woodward, William Henry, b. Coventry, e. Coventry, 16911, Pte., d. of w., F. & F., 29/11/15.
Woolfson, Sydney, b. St Andrews, Newcastle-on-Tyne, Northumberland, e. Newcastle-on-Tyne, 24700, Pte., d. of w., F. & F., 1/11/18.
Wooliscroft, William Henry, b Birmingham, e. Birmingham (Small Heath, Birmingham), 17765, Pte., k. in a., F. & F., 11/4/17.
Wootton, Christie, b. Bloxwich, Staffs, e. Birmingham (Bloxwich), 1026, Pte., k. in a., F. & F., 15/4/18.
Wootton, George Lewis, b. Birmingham, e. Birmingham, 39246, Pte., k. in a., F. & F., 11/5/18.
Worroll, George, b. Ladywood, Birmingham, e. Birmingham, 2260, Pte., k. in a., F. & F., 25/4/15.
Wragg, Arthur, b. Birmingham, e. Birmingham, 1237, Pte., k. in a., F. & F., 25/4/15.
Wright, Thomas Truelove, b. Monks Kirby, Rugby, Warwicks, e. Rugby (Monks Kirby), 4500, Pte., k. in a., F. & F., 2/8/15.
Wyatt, William Hedley, b. Christchurch, Manchester, e. Manchester, 307263, Pte., k. in a., F. & F., 4/10/17, formerly 2058, Manchester Regt.
Yapp, Allen, b. Dudley, Worcs, e. Coventry, 3035, Pte., d., F. & F., 8/2/15.
Yates, Frederick, b. St. George's, Birmingham, e. Warwick (Birmingham). 607, Pte., k. in a., F. & F., 10/12/14.
Yates, Thomas, b. Birmingham, e. Birmingham, 9747, A/Cpl., k. in a., F. & F., 25/4/15.
Yeatman, Edward, b. Buckby Meadows, Berks, e. Cardiff (Bristol), 268883, Pte., k in a., F. & F., 12/10/17.
Yeomans, Joseph Oliver, b. Smethwick, Staffs, e. Nuneaton, Warwicks, 11343, Pte., k. in a., F. & F., 23/10/16.
Young, Lewis James, b. Marton, Warwicks, e. Marton, 17408, Pte., d. of w., F. & F., 3/7/17.

2nd Battalion.

Abbott, Harry, b. Highgate, Birmingham, e. Birmingham, 9294, Pte., k. in a., F. & F., 25/9/15.
Adams, Ernest George, b. Edmonton, Middx., e. Birmingham (Walthamstow, Essex), 1951, Pte., d, of w., F. & F., 25/10/14.
Adams, Joseph George, b. Killarney, Co. Kerry, e. Warwick (Coleshill, Birmingham), 17097, Pte., k. in a., F. & F., 3/9/16.
Adams, William Henry, b. Dunchurch, Rugby, Warwicks., e. Rugby, 1288, L/Cpl., k. in a., F. & F., 20/10/14.
Adcock, Edmund, b. Atherstone, Warwicks., e. Warwick (Atherstone), 16522, Pte., d. of w., F. & F., 7/10/17.
Addison, Herbert, b. Cathorpe, Leicestershire, e. Rugby (Leicester), 1686, Pte., k. in a., F. & F., 13/5/17.
Aldred, Alfred, b. Bootle, Lancs, e. Birmingham, 11282, Pte., k. in a., F. & F., 4/5/17.
Aldridge, Richard Thomas, b. Sunderland, Durham, e. High Wycombe, Bucks (Wycombe Marsh), 29961, Pte., d. of w., F. & F., 3/9/16, formerly 22618, O. & B.L.I.
Alford, Harry, b. Stoke, Coventry, e. Coventry, 1962, Pte., k. in a., F. & F., 19/12/14.
Allen, Alfred William, b. Wheatley, Oxford, e. Warwick (Harbury, Warwicks), 9441, Pte., k. in a., F. & F., 23/8/15.
Allen, Harry, e. Lincoln (Bourne, Lincoln), 26982, Pte., d. of w., F. & F., 10/10/16, formerly 5573, Lincs Regt.
Allington, Arthur, b. St. George's, Birmingham, e. Birmingham, 3261, Pte., d. of w., F. & F., 14/3/15.
Allsopp, John William, b. Tibshelf, Derbys, e. Mansfield, Notts (Newtown, Derbys), 54201, Pte., k. in a., F. & F., 23/10/18, formerly 117138, Notts & Derby Regt.
Allwood, Walter, b. St. Paul's, Leamington, Warwicks, e. Warwick (Leamington), 4288, Pte., k. in a., F. & F., 25/9/15.
Anderson, David McGibbon, b. Alyth, Perthshire, e. Blair gowrie, 1749, Pte., d. of w., F. & F., 11/11/14.
Anderson, Robert John, b. Small Heath, Birmingham, e. Small Heath, Birmingham, 2458, Pte., d. of w., F. & F., 17/2/15.
Andrews, Albert, b. Bristol, Glos., e. London (Totterdown, Bristol), 9581, Pte., k. in a., F. & F., 24/10/14.
Andrews, Charles, b. Birmingham, e. Birmingham (Smethwick, Staffs), 6849, Pte., k. in a., F. & F., 13/3/15.
Andrews, George, b. Birmingham, e. Warwick (Birmingham), 1531, Pte., k. in a., F. & F., 26/10/14.
Andrews, Henry, b. Aston, Birmingham, e. Birmingham, 3730, Pte., k. in a., F. & F., 19/12/14.
Andrews, Richard, b. Knowle, Warwicks, e. Warwick (Knowle), 19074, L/Cpl., k. in a., F. & F., 9/10/17.
Andrews, Thomas John, b. Eastleigh, Hants, e. Portsmouth, Hants (Eastleigh), 23631, Pte., k. in a., F. & F., 4/5/17, formerly 1463, R.E.
Andrews, William, b. Birmingham, e. Worthing, Sussex (King's Heath, Birmingham), 8930, L/Cpl., k. in a., F. & F., 25/9/15.
Andrews, William George, e. Falmouth, Cornwall (Liskeard), 23687, Pte., k. in a., F. & F., 4/5/17, formerly 1003, R.E.

Anscombe, Frederick Charles, b. Cuckfield, Haywards Heath, Sussex, e. Haywards Heath (Cuckfield), 241769, Pte., k. in a., F. & F., 1/10/17, formerly 1385, R. Sussex Regt.

Arkley, Alfred, b. Edgbaston, Birmingham, e. Birmingham, 6211, Cpl., k. in a., F. & F., 3/9/16.

Arnold, Alfred Henry, b. Aston, Birmingham, e. Birmingham (Aston), 11123, Pte., k. in a., F. & F., 28/5/16.

Arthur, Edward, b. Ilmington, Warwicks, e. Stratford-on-Avon, Warwicks (Stratford-on-Avon), 12194, Pte., k. in a., F. & F., 9/10/17.

Arthurs, Henry John, b. Forest Hill, Kent, e. New Cross (London), 595, Pte., d. of w., F. & F., 27/9/15.

Ash, William George, b. Oxford, e. Oxford, 29968, L/Cpl., d. of w., F. & F., 11/5/17, formerly 22707, Oxf. & Bucks L.I.

Ashby, Wallace, b. Rudpage, Bucks, e. High Wycombe (West Wycombe), 29932, Pte., k. in a., F. & F., 9/10/17, formerly 23926, Oxf. & Bucks L.I.

Ashford, George Henry, b. Birmingham, e. Birmingham, 22456, Pte., d., F. & F., 12/8/17.

Ashwell, Thomas William, b. Birmingham, e. Warwick (Birmingham), 1224, Pte., d. of w., F. & F., 6/11/14.

Assinder, Charles William, b. Chadwick End, Knowle, Warwicks, e. Warwick (Knowle), 1126, Pte., k. in a., F. & F., 31/10/14.

Attenbarrow, Ernest, b. Nottingham, e. Birmingham, 3384, Pte., k. in a., F. & F., 25/9/15.

Attenborough, Arthur, b. Nuneaton, Warwicks, e. Coventry (Hinckley, Leics), 9719, Pte., k. in a., F. & F., 3/9/16.

Atkin, Willows, b. Grimsby, Lincs, e. Birmingham (Grimsby), 424, Pte., k. in a., F. & F., 18/5/15.

Atkins, Alfred, b. Hughendon, Bucks, e. High Wycombe, 24228, Pte., k. in a., F. & F., 9/10/17.

Atkins, Ernest, b. Aston, Birmingham, e. Birmingham (Aston), 609, Pte., k. in a., F. & F., 4/5/17.

Atkins, Harold Samuel, b. Kidderminster, Worcs, e. Kidderminster, 34642, L/Cpl., k. in a., F. & F., 27/10/17, formerly 4599, Worcs Regt.

Atkins, James, b. Glatton, Peterborough, Northants, e. Nuneaton, Warwicks (Stilton, Peterborough), 3078, Pte., k. in a., F. & F., 16/5/15.

Audley, Arthur, b. All Saints, Birmingham, e. Birmingham (Hockley, Birmingham), 3343, Pte., k. in a., F. & F., 6/5/16.

Ayres, Edward, b. Hunningham Hill, Warwick, e. Southam, Warwicks (Long Itchington, Rugby), 20519, Pte., k. in a., F. & F., 9/10/17.

Baber, Albert William Alfred, b. Eastville, Bristol, e. Bristol, 235092, Pte., k. in a., F. & F., 8/10/17, formerly 204206, Worcs Regt.

Babington, William, b. Small Heath, Birmingham, e. Birmingham, 10612, Pte., k. in a., F. & F., 31/8/16.

Bacon, Henry, b. West Bromwich, Staffs, e. Birmingham, 3391, Pte., k. in a., F. & F., 2/9/16.

Baglin, George, b. Coventry, e. Coventry, 3516, L/Cpl., d. of w., F. & F., 21/3/17.

Bagshaw, Walter, b. Matlock, Derbyshire, e. Derby (Birmingham), 6444, Pte., k. in a., F. & F., 19/12/14.

Bagshaw, William, b. St. George's, Birmingham, e. Neath, Glam. (Birmingham), 1875, Pte., k. in a., F. & F., 23/9/15.

Bailey, Charles, b. Battersea, Surrey, e. London (Battersea), 627, Pte., k. in a., F. & F., 25/9/15.

Bailey, Charles William, b. Birmingham, e. Birmingham, 1350, Pte., k. in a., F. & F., 19/10/14.

Bailey, John, b. Longford, Warwickshire, e. Nuneaton, Warwickshire (Bedworth), 12139, Pte., k. in a., F. & F., 25/3/16.

Baker, Charles William, b. Ladywood, Birmingham, e. Birmingham, 6235, Pte., k. in a., F. & F., 16/5/15.

Baker, James William, b. Langley, Worcs, e. Birmingham (Langley), 885, Pte., k. in a., F. & F., 25/9/15.

Baker, Thomas Edwin, b. Birmingham, e. Birmingham, 1337, L/Cpl., k. in a., F. & F., 29/10/14.

Bakewell, Albert E., b. Birmingham, e. Birmingham, 16687, Pte., k. in a., F. & F., 4/5/17.

Balcombe, Richard Colman, b. Kennishead, Renfrew, e. Glasgow (Pollokshaws, Glasgow), 23556, Pte., k. in a., F. & F., 13/5/17, formerly 174168, R.E.

Baldwin, George Daniel, b. All Saints, Gloucester, e. Birmingham, 2011, Pte., k. in a., F. & F., 31/10/14.

Ball, Algernon John, b. Market Kingsend, Cornwall, e. Plymouth, 23675, Pte., k. in a., F. & F., 1/10/17, formerly 1464, R.E.

Ball, Arthur Bennett, b. Hanley, Staffs, e. Stoke-on-Trent, Staffs, 11529, Pte., k. in a., F. & F., 15/7/16.

Ball, George Henry, b. Evercreach, Som., e. Barry, Cardiff, 10851, L/Cpl., k. in a., F. & F., 18/3/16.

Ball, William, b. Birmingham, e. Birmingham, 6222, Pte., k. in a., F. & F., 7/6/15.

Balls, Samuel, b. Stanway, Essex, e. Colchester, Essex (Stanway Green), 27108, Pte., k. in a., F. & F., 4/5/17, formerly 5256, Lincs Regt.

Bamford, John, b. Saltley, Birmingham, e. Warwick (Saltley, Birmingham), 2068, Pte., k. in a., F. & F., 31/10/14.

Banks, James Ernest, b. Birmingham, e. Witton, Birmingham (Birmingham), 2058, Pte., k. in a., F. & F., 7/6/15.

Barber, George, b. Birmingham, e. Warwick (Birmingham), 1315, Pte., k. in a., F. & F., 14/1/15.

Bareham, William, b. Gorton, Lancaster, e. Warwick (Bromsgrove, Worcs), 14303, Pte., k. in a., F. & F., 20/7/16.

Barker, Richard, e. Grimsby, Lincs, 26983, Pte., k. in a., F. & F., 4/5/17, formerly 5433, Lincs Regt.

Barnes, Albert, b. Hounslow, Middx., e. Shoreham, Kent (Hounslow Heath), 15030, L/Cpl., k. in a., F. & F., 3/9/16.

Barlow, John, b. West Bromwich, Staffs, e. Bedworth, Warwicks, 11987, Pte., k. in a., F. & F., 3/9/16.

Barnes, Bertram, b. Birmingham, e. Birmingham, 13091, Pte., k. in a., F. & F., 25/3/16.

Barnes, Clarence Edward, e. Stapleford, Notts (Beeston, Notts), 27489, Pte., k. in a., F. & F., 9/10/17, formerly 3880, Notts & Derby Regt.

Barnett, Arthur, b. Farnham, Surrey, e. Romsey (Farnham), 25205, Pte., d., F. & F., 5/11/18, formerly R/4/124915, R.A.S.C.

Barratt, Frederick, b. Northampton, e. Birmingham (Northampton), 199, Bdm., k. in a., F. & F., 20/10/14.

Barratt, Harold, b. Wylde Green, Birmingham, e. Birmingham (Erdington), 15/1542, L/Cpl., k. in a., F. & F., 13/3/17.

Barton, Harry, b. Reading, Berks, e. Warwick (Reading), 2662, Pte., d. of w., F. & F. 7/8/16.

Baskott, William, b. Kenilworth, Warwicks, e. Warwick (Leamington), 1538, Pte., d. of w., F. & F., 24/7/16.

Basnett, Ernest, b. Birmingham, e. Birmingham (Hockley), 3810, L/Cpl., k. in a., F. & F., 25/9/15.

Bass, George Kimbell, e. Birmingham, 203535, Pte., k. in a., F. & F., 9/10/17.

Bassett, Raymond, b. Birmingham, e. Worthing, Sussex (Birmingham), 7315, Sgt., k. in a., F. & F., 25/9/15.

Batchelor, Ernest Edward, b. Whitnash, Warwicks, e. Coventry (Leamington), 1301, Pte., k. in a., F. & F., 16/5/15.

Bates, Alfred William, b. Birmingham, e. Birmingham, 3929, Pte., k. in a., F. & F., 25/9/15.

Bates, Charles Ernest, b. Nuneaton, e. Coventry, 306781, Pte., k. in a., F. & F., 9/10/17.

Bates, Ernest Charles, b. Stratford-on-Avon, Warwicks, e. Warwick (Stratford-on-Avon), 3576, Pte., k. in a., F. & F., 25/9/15.

Bates, Frank, b. Foleshill, Coventry, Warwicks, e. Coventry, 265218, Pte., k. in a., F. & F., 12/10/17.

Baverstock, George, e. Southampton, 268824, Pte., k. in a., F. & F., 9/10/17.

Bayliss, Albert, b. Birmingham, e. Nuneaton (Birmingham), 1909, Pte., k. in a., F. & F., 21/10/14.

Beaufoy, Benjamin, b. Coventry, Warwicks, e. Warwick (Coventry), 1122, Pte., k. in a., F. & F., 11/5/15.

Beaver, Robert, b. Kingswood, Bristol, e. Bristol, 235093, Pte., k. in a., F. & F., 8/10/17, formerly 204207, Worcs Regt.

Beck, Arthur, b. Coventry, e. Warwick (Coventry), 1909, Pte., k. in a., F. & F., 25/9/15.

Beddoes, Horace, b. Kidderminster, e. Birmingham (Kidderminster), 884, Pte., k. in a., F. & F., 13/3/15.

Bedford, Harry, b. Highgate, Birmingham, e. Birmingham, 240258, Pte., k. in a., F. & F., 9/10/17.

Bednall, William, b. Coventry, e. Warwick (Coventry), 2554, Pte., k. in a., F. & F., 18/12/14.

Beeston, Harry, b. Warwick, e. Warwick, 2462, Pte., d. of w., F. & F., 27/1/15.

Bell, John, b. Birmingham, e. Birmingham, 1386, Pte., d. of w., F. & F., 17/3/15.

Bell, Joseph, b. Holbeck, Leeds, e. Bradford (Holbeck), 8902, Pte., d. of w., F. & F., 31/10/14.

Bench, Ernest William, b. Warwick, e. Warwick, 950, Pte., k. in a., F. & F., 25/9/15.

Bendall, Arthur Victor, b. Cardiff, e. Cardiff, 23541, Pte., d. of w., F. & F., 21/3/17, formerly 1271, R.E.

Benjamin, William Henry, b. Dunton Bassett, Leics, e. Rugby, Warwicks, 15779, Pte., d. of w., F. & F., 17/7/16.

Bennett, Frank Lewis, b. Birmingham, e. Birmingham, 1535, Pte., k. in a., F. & F., 25/9/15.

Bennett, Percy John, b. Weston, Warwicks.; e. Coventry (Emscote, Warwick), 24055, Pte., k. in a., F. & F., 19/10/17.

Bent, John William, b. Leeds, e. Birmingham, 13344, Pte., k. in a., F. & F., 20/3/16.

Beswick, William, b. Macclesfield, Ches., e. Birmingham, 17344, Pte., k. in a., F. & F., 4/5/17.

Betts, Charles Haddon, b. Hadleigh, Suffolk, e. Bury St. Edmunds (Hadleigh), 27224, Pte., d. of w., F. & F., 21/10/17, formerly 3171, Suffolk Regt.

Bidgood, William Henry, e. Plymouth, 23676, Pte., k. in a., F. & F., 4/5/17, formerly 1987, R.E.

Billing, Percy Arthur, b. Buckingham, e. Birmingham, 9820, Pte., k. in a., F. & F., 12/3/15.

Binnell, Samuel Thomas, b. Birmingham, e. Birmingham, 10435, Pte., k. in a., F. & F., 25/9/15.

Birch, Walter, b. Coventry, e. Coventry, 30032, Pte., k. in a., F. & F., 3/9/16.

Birch, William, b. Birmingham, e. Birmingham, 271, Pte., k. in a., F. & F., 14/7/16.

Bird, George Albert, b. Small Heath, Birmingham, e. Birmingham (Small Heath), 1695, Pte., k. in a., F. & F., 7/11/14.

Bird, John, b. Birmingham, e. Birmingham, 9200, Pte., k. in a., F. & F., 21/10/14.

Bird, Thomas, b. Ashted, Birmingham, e. Birmingham, 3174, Pte., d., F. & F., 12/2/16.

Blackwell, Alfred, b. Birmingham, e. Birmingham, 893, Pte., k. in a., F. & F., 6/5/16.

Blackwell, Frank, b. Chesterfield, Derby, e Bakewell (Stoney Middleton), 12397, L/Cpl., k. in a., F. & F., 9/10/17, formerly 28613, R.G.A.

Blades, Christopher, e. Stamford, 27031, L/Cpl., k. in a., F. & F., 4/5/17, formerly 4777, Lincs Regt.

Blades, William Henry, b. Wellington, Lincs, e. Attercliffe, Sheffield, 10537, Pte., k. in a., F. & F., 25/9/15.

Blick, Alfred, b. Old Swinford, Worcs, e. Warwick (Stourbridge), 9860, Sgt., k. in a., F. & F., 16/5/15.

Bliss, Thomas, b. Birmingham, e. Birmingham, 1763, Pte., k. in a., F. & F., 25/9/15.

Blocksidge, William John, b. Birmingham, e. Tamworth, 1665, Pte., k. in a., F. & F., 25/9/15.

Bloor, Percy, b. Over Whitacre, Warwicks, e. Shustoke (Over Whitacre), 17372, Pte., k. in a., F. & F., 28/6/17.

Bodsworth, John, b. Hockley, Birmingham, e. Warwick (Birmingham), 3317, Pte., k. in a., F. & F., 19/12/14.

Bogue, Frederick, b. Birmingham, e. Smethwick, Staffs, 2449, Pte., d. of w., F. & F., 13/2/15.

Boldy, Thomas, b. Bradford, e. Bradford, 1899, Pte., k. in a., F. & F., 25/11/14.

Bond, Harry, b. Walsall, Staffs, e. Birmingham (Walsall), 764, Pte., k. in a., F. & F., 19/12/14.

Boncham, Frederick, b. Bishops Tachbrook, Warwicks, e. Warwick (Bishops Tachbrook), 15091, Pte., k. in a., F. & F., 11/7/16.

Bonehill, David, b. Birmingham, e. Birmingham, 1340, Pte., k. in a., F. & F., 10/10/14.

Bonner, Bert, b. Hitchin, Herts, e. Halifáx, 7865, Pte., k. in a., F. & F., 7/11/14.

Booth, Robert, b. Birmingham, e. Leicester, 8612, L/Cpl., d. of w., F. & F., 7/11/14.

Booth, William, b. West Retford, Notts, e. Retford, 27477, L/Cpl., k. in a., F. & F., 9/10/17, formerly 4112, Notts & Derby Regt.

Booton, Sydney, b. Polesworth, Warwicks, e. Atherstone (Polesworth), 24404, Pte., k. in a., F. & F., 9/10/17.

Bott, George William, b. Hull, e. Warwick, 15286, Pte., k. in a., F. & F., 4/5/17.

Boucher, Charles John, b. Derby, e. Birmingham, 4021, Pte., k. in a., F. & F., 28/4/16.

Boucher, John William, b. Leamington, Warwicks, e. Leamington, 12722, Pte., k. in a., F. & F., 14/7/16.

Bough, Thomas, b. Yardley, Birmingham, e. Warwick, 9045, Pte., k. in a., F. & F., 19/12/14.

Boulton, John Alfred, b. Ladywood, Birmingham, e. Birmingham (Ladywood), 3221, Pte., k. in a., F. & F., 25/9/15.

Bowen, William Reginald, b. Stourbridge, Worcs, e. Warwick (Alcester), 15580, A/Cpl., k. in a., F. & F., 4/5/17.

Bowstead, Robert Henry, b. Birmingham, e. Birmingham, 894, Pte., k. in a., F. & F., 29/1/15.

Bradford, Ernest Walter, e. Falmouth (Swanage), 23684, Pte., k. in a., F. & F., 13/5/17, formerly 908, R.E.

Bradford, Frank Montague, b. Warwick, e. Warwick, 1315, Pte., k. in a., F. & F., 12/3/15.

Bradley, William Arthur, b. Birmingham, e. Birmingham (West Bromwich), 3971, Pte., k. in a., F. & F., 13/3/15.

Bradshaw, Albert, b. Longton, Staffs, e. Longton (Morley, nr. Leeds), 8163, Pte., k. in a., F. & F., 7/11/14.

Bradshaw, George, e. Liverpool, 268473, Cpl., d. of w., F. & F., 10/10/17, formerly 3689, Liverpool Regt.

Brain, Albert, b. Banbury, Oxon, e. Coventry (Banbury), 1088, Pte., k. in a., F. & F., 21/11/14.

Brereton, Frederick, b. Lydbury North, Salop, e. Ludlow (Lydbury North), 27779, Pte., k. in a., F. & F., 9/10/17, formerly 19757, Shrops L.I.

Bridges, George Henry, b. Stratford-on-Avon, Warwicks, e. Stratford-on-Avon, 21848, Pte., d., F. & F., 27/9/17.

Brind, John, b. Fairford, Glos., e. Coventry, 1533, Pte., d. of w., F. & F., 19/11/14.

Brindley, Thomas, b. Bedworth, Warwicks, e. Nuneaton (Chilvers Coton), 4417, Cpl., k. in a., F. & F., 9/10/17, D.C.M., M.M.

Brittain, Joseph, b. Aston, Birmingham, e. Warwick (Nechells), 798, Cpl., k. in a., F. & F., 14/7/16.

Broadbent, William Frederick, b. Birmingham, e. Birmingham (Ladywood), 10430, Pte., k. in a., F. & F., 3/9/16.

Brooks, George Henry, b. Wolverhampton, e. Birmingham (Wolverhampton), 404, Pte., k. in a., F. & F., 3/9/16.

Brough, Victor Lawrence, b. Kidderminster, e. Birmingham (Kidderminster), 1703, Pte., k. in a., F. & F., 3/9/16.

Brown, Frederick, b. Sutton, Surrey, e. Cardiff, 10852, Pte., d. of w., F. & F., 4/5/17, M.M.

Brown, George, b. Hinckley, Leics, e. Nuneaton (Hinckley), 1002, Pte., k. in a., F. & F., 31/10/14.

Brown, George Frederick, b. Birmingham, e. Birmingham, 7775, Pte., k. in a., F. & F., 11/5/15.

Brown, James, b. Banbury, Oxon, e. Warwick (Banbury), 1720, Pte., k. in a., F. & F., 20/10/14.

Bryan, James, b. Birmingham, e. Birmingham, 7956, Pte., k. in a., F. & F., 16/5/15.

Buckler, Thomas Henry, b. Aston, Birmingham, e. Birmingham, 3938, Pte., k. in a., F. & F., 25/5/15.

Buckmaster, William Charles Henry, b. West Ham, Essex, e. New Cross (West Ham), 765, L/Cpl., k. in a., F. & F., 11/7/16.

Burbridge, Alfred Foster, b. Worcester, e. Birmingham, 1431, Pte., k. in a., F. & F., 15/7/16.

Burden, Richard Thomas, b. Poole, Dorset, e. Coventry, 1641, Pte., k. in a., F. & F., 19/12/14.

Burgess, Charles William, b. Ashton-under-Lyne, Lancs, e. Ashton-under-Lyne, 12356, Pte., k. in a., F. & F., 30/4/16, formerly 55011, R.G.A.

Burnell, William Charles, b. Southam, Warwicks, e. Warwick (Stockton, Rugby), 1884, Pte., k. in a., F. & F., 16/5/16.

Burrow, Tom, b. Atherstone, Warwicks., e. Warwick (Nuneaton), 1946, L/Cpl., k. in a., F. & F., 25/10/14.

Burt, Alfred, e. Bournemouth (Wimborne, Dorset), 18661, Pte., k. in a., F. & F., 9/10/17, formerly 24627, Som. L.I.

Burton, Harold, b. Atherstone, Warwicks, e. Warwick (Atherstone), 1230, Cpl., k. in a., F. & F., 31/10/14.

Busby, Henry Alfred, b. St. Paul's, Balsall Heath, Birmingham, e. Birmingham, 1805, Pte., k. in a., F. & F., 25/9/15.

Busby, Henry Edward, b. Birmingham, e. Birmingham, 3665, Pte., d. of w., F. & F., 16/3/15.

Bush, William Samuel, b. Warwick, e. Warwick, 15955, L/Cpl., k. in a., F. & F., 3/9/16.

Bustin, Walter Henry, b. Northampton, e. Birmingham (Northampton), 7534, Pte., d. of w., F. & F., 15/7/16.

Butcher, William, b. St. George's, Birmingham, e. Birmingham (Hockley. Birmingham), 2857, Pte., k. in a., F. & F., 16/5/15.

Butler, Robert Alexander, b. Millwall, Middx., e. Birmingham, 5190, L/Cpl., k. in a., F. & F., 9/10/17, M.M.

Butwell, Robert, b. West Bromwich, Staffs, e. Birmingham (West Bromwich), 1189, Pte., k. in a., F. & F., 3/3/15.

Bye, John, b. Newmarket, Cambs, e. Bury St. Edmunds, Suffolk (Newmarket), 27268, Pte., k. in a., F. & F., 14/5/17, formerly 2389, Suffolk Regt.

Byford, Walter, b. Clare, Suffolk, e. Clare, 27223, Pte., k. in a., F. & F., 14/1/17, formerly 1328, Suffolk Regt.

Bygraves, Arthur, b. Aynho, Oxon, e. Aynho (Stratford-on-Avon, Warwicks), 1407, Pte., k. in a., F. & F., 23/5/15.

Bythell, Isaiah, b. Small Heath, Birmingham, e. Birmingham (Small Heath, Birmingham), 2278, Pte., d. of w., F. & F., 29/7/16.

Cadmore, John Samuel, b. Birmingham, e. Warwick (Birmingham), 1567, Pte., k. in a., F. & F., 24/10/14.

Cale, Edwin, Albert, b. Birmingham, e. Birmingham, 1067, L/Cpl., k. in a., F. & F., 25/9/15.

Carbutt, Jack, b. St. Martin's, Birmingham, e. Birmingham, 1208, Pte., k. in a., F. & F., 19/12/14.

Carpenter, Frank, b. Birmingham, e. Warwick (Birmingham), 1688, Pte., k. in a., F. & F., 25/9/15.

Carrott, Fred, b. Thorpe Wainfleet, Lincs, e. Spilsby, Lincs (Huttoft, Alford, Lincs), 27084, Pte., k. in a., F. & F., 5/12/16, formerly 5044, Lincs Regt.

Cartwright, Harry, b. St. Paul's, Wolverhampton, Staffs, e. Wolverhampton, 7696, Pte., k. in a., F. & F., 15/1/15.

Cash, Albert, b. Redditch, Worcs, e. Birmingham (Redditch), 11090, Pte., k. in a., F. & F., 4/7/17.

Cash, William James, b. Birmingham, e. Birmingham, 6623, Pte., k. in a., F. & F., 25/9/15.

Chamberlain, John Henry, b. Birmingham, e. Birmingham, 3350, Pte., k. in a., F. & F., 15/7/15.

Chambers, Frank, b. Brinkhill, Alford, Lincs, e. Grimsby, Lincs (Mablethorpe, Lincs), 27102, Pte., k. in a., F. & F., 4/5/17, formerly 4097, Lincs Regt.

Chambers, Thomas Henry, b. St. John's, Stratford-on-Avon, e. Warwick (Stratford-on-Avon), 2343, Pte., k. in a., F. & F., 25/9/15.

Chandler, Ralph, b. Aston, Birmingham, e. Birmingham, 3809, Pte., k. in a., F. & F., 23/4/16.

Chapman, Albert, b. St. Stephen's, Birmingham, e. Warwick (Birmingham), 190, Pte., k. in a., F. & F., 15/7/16.

Charman, Henry John, b. Thornton Heath, Surrey, e. London (Streatham, London), 7964, Pte., k. in a., F. & F., 7/11/14.

Child, George Andrew, b. Portsmouth, Hants, e. Portsmouth, 23632, Pte., k. in a., F. & F., 4/5/17, formerly 1768, R.E.

Child, John, b. Small Heath, Birmingham, e. Warwick (Birmingham), 1623, Pte., k. in a., F. & F., 29/3/15.

Chillington, Charles, b. Winson Green, Birmingham, e. Birmingham, 4745, Pte., k. in a., F. & F., 3/9/16.

Chinery, George, b. Acton, Suffolk, e. Sudbury, Suffolk, 27257, Pte., k. in a., F. & F., 4/5/17, formerly 3074, Suffolk Regt.

Clamp, Albert Edward, b. Birmingham, e. Birmingham, 946, Pte., d. of w., F. & F., 11/4/16.

Clark, Alexander, b. Alyth, Perth, e. Perth (Alyth), 1663, Pte., k. in a., F. & F., 4/7/17.

Clark, Bertie William, b. Langley, Maidstone, Kent, e. Maidstone (Langley), 697, Pte., k. in a., F. & F., 25/9/15.

Clarke, Frederick William, b. Somerstown, London, e. Birmingham, 837, Pte., k. in a., F. & F., 25/9/15.

Clarke, George, b. Hatton, Warwick, e. Warwick (Hatton), 9808, Pte., k. in a., F. & F., 26/10/17.

Clarke, Herbert Mark, b. St. Thomas, Coventry, e. Coventry, 1319, Pte., d. of w., F. & F., 26/12/14

Clarke, Walter John, b. Pepworth, Stratford-on-Avon, e. Warwick (Stratford-on-Avon, Warwicks), 881, Pte., k. in a., F. & F., 31/10/14.

Clay, Ernest Abraham, b. Birmingham, e. Birmingham, 1684, Pte., k. in a., F. & F., 7/11/14.

Clay, Percy, e. Grimsby, Lincs (Gainsborough, Lincs), 27052, Pte., k. in a., F. & F., 4/5/17, formerly 2527, Lincs Regt.

Cleaver, Harry, b. Birmingham, e. Birmingham, 6544, Pte., d. of w., F. & F., 22/12/14.

Cleverley, William Harvey Thomas, b. Coventry, e. Birmingham, 3013, Pte., k. in a., F. & F., 12/3/15.

Cliff, Herbert, b. Leeds, e. Leeds, 5482, Pte., k. in a., F. & F., 19/12/14.

Clinton, John Thomas, b. Claines, Worcs, e. Birmingham (Worcester), 758, Sgt., k. in a., F. & F., 20/10/14.

Clipson, William Ernest, e. Scunthorpe, Lincs, 27081, Pte., d. of w., F. & F., 21/3/17, formerly 2595, Lincs Regt.

Clissett, William Frederick, b. Stoke Prior, Worcs, e. Birmingham, 1061, Pte., k. in a., F. & F., 31/10/14.

Clow, Frederick Levett, b. Gt. Glenham, Suffolk, e. Nuneaton, Warwicks (Gt. Glenham), 18110, L/Cpl., k. in a., F. & F., 9/10/17.

Cobb, George Henry, b. St. Mary's, Leamington, Warwicks, e. Warwick (Leamington), 1611, Pte., k. in a., F. & F., 26/10/14.

Cockerton, William, b. All Saints, Newmarket, Cambs, e. Bury-St.-Edmunds, Suffolk (Newmarket), 27258, Pte., k. in a., F. & F., 29/11/16, formerly 3197, Suffolk Regt.

Codd, Alfred, b. Coleby, Lincs, e. Lincoln, 26992, Pte., k. in a., F. & F., 4/5/17, formerly 5571, Lincs Regt.

Coggins, Charles, b. Warmington, Oxon, e. Coventry, Warwicks (Wyken, Coventry), 265082, Pte., k. in a., F. & F., 26/10/17.

Cole, George Henry, b. Torquay, Devon, e. Wokingham, Berks, 34342, Pte., d., F. & F., 6/11/18, formerly 3574, R. Berks Regt.

Coleman, William Harold, b. Bishops Itchington, Warwicks, e. Stratford-on-Avon, Warwicks, 10515, Pte., k. in a., F. & F., 4/5/17.
Coles, George, b. Kemsing, Kent, e. Tonbridge, Kent, 23698, Pte., k. in a., F. & F., 4/5/17, formerly 173876, R.E.
Coles, Joseph, b. Tysoe, Warwick, e. Warwick (Hatton, Warwick), 9840, Pte., d. of w., F. & F., 2/10/15.
Collins, Frederick, b. Foleshill, Coventry, e. Coventry, 15797, Pte., k. in a., F. & F., 1/10/17.
Collins, Herbert, b. Birmingham, e. Birmingham, 1427, Pte., k. in a., F. & F., 31/8/16.
Collins, Herbert, b. Birmingham, e. Birmingham, 8721, Pte., d. of w., F. & F., 3/11/14.
Collins, Owen, b. Tamworth, Staffs, e. Birmingham (Tamworth), 634, Pte., k. in a., F. & F., 13/3/15.
Connell, Frank William, b. Balsall Heath, Birmingham, e. Birmingham, 4661, Pte., k. in a., F. & F., 4/5/17.
Connell, Thomas Peter, b. St. Alban's, Birmingham, e. Birmingham (Balsall Heath, Birmingham), 2108, Pte., k. in a., F. & F., 7/11/14.
Connery, Charles, b. St. George's, Birmingham, e. Birmingham, 2234, Pte., k. in a., F. & F., 25/9/15.
Connery, William Bernard, b. St. Mary's, Birmingham, e. Birmingham, 8978, Pte., d. of w., F. & F., 18/9/18.
Conroy, Stephen, b. Ladywood, Birmingham, e. Birmingham, 3244, Pte., d. of w., F. & F., 9/9/16.
Cook, Charles Arthur, b. Birmingham, e. Birmingham, 9202, Pte., k. in a., F. & F., 31/10/14.
Cook, James, b. Birmingham, e. Birmingham, 13059, Pte., k. in a., F. & F., 4/7/16.
Cook, John Thomas, b. Lozells, Birmingham, e. Birmingham, 3244, Pte., k. in a., F. & F., 12/3/15.
Cooney, John Bernard, b. Birmingham, e. Birmingham, 956, Pte., k. in a., F. & F., 11/3/15.
Cooper, Alfred, b. Birmingham, e. Birmingham, 1479, Cpl., k. in a., F. & F., 3/9/16.
Cooper, Fred, b. Newport, Salop, e. Birmingham (Lichfield, Staffs), 1252, Pte., k. in a., F. & F., 9/10/17.
Cooper, Harry, b. Bolingbroke, Lincs, e. Lincoln (Spilsby, Lincs), 26993, Pte., k. in a., F. & F., 4/5/17, formerly 4966, Lincs Regt.
Cooper, John Alfred, b. Small Heath, Birmingham, e. Birmingham, 1368, Pte., d. of w., F. & F., 6/10/15.
Cooper, Reginald, b. North Wales, e. Birmingham, 3881, Pte., k. in a., F. & F., 16/5/15.
Cooper, Reginald, b. Bournemouth, Hants, e. Southampton, 18569, L/Cpl., d. of w., F. & F., 9/10/17, formerly 24964, Som. L.I.
Cope, William John, b. St. George's, Birmingham, e. Birmingham, 14327, Pte., k. in a., F. & F., 3/9/16.
Coppage, Edward George, b. Birmingham, e. Birmingham, 1150, Pte., k. in a., F. & F., 25/10/14.
Corbett, Benjamin Thomas, b. St. Martin's, Birmingham, e. Birmingham, 3732, Pte., k. in a., F. & F., 3/7/15.
Corbett, John, b. St. Andrew's, Birmingham, e. Birmingham, 3327, Pte., k. in a., F. & F., 25/9/15.
Costello, Frederick, b. Birmingham, e. Birmingham (Southampton), 7839, Pte., k. in a., F. & F., 19/12/14.
Cotterrell, John Howard, b. Chessett's Wood, Warwicks, e. Knowle, Warwicks (Chessett's Wood), 17400, L/Cpl., k. in a., F. & F., 4/9/16.
Cotton, Joseph, b. Walsall, Staffs, e. Birmingham, 3580, Pte., d. of w., F. & F., 1/4/16.
Cottrell, Henry James, b. Tuffley, Glos., e. Evesham, Worcs (Tuffley), 1605, Pte., k. in a., F. & F., 31/10/14.
Cottrill, Robert William, b. Birmingham, e. Birmingham, 1481, Pte., k. in a., F. & F., 16/4/15.
Cox, Charles Warren, b. Harborne, Birmingham, e. Birmingham (Harborne), 30033, Pte., k. in a., F. & F., 3/9/16.
Cox, George Henry, b. Alcester, Warwicks, e. Warwick (Alcester), 1545, Cpl., k. in a., F. & F., 7/6/15.
Crawford, Arthur, b. Framlingham, Suffolk, e. Bury-St.-Edmunds, Suffolk (Framlingham), 27085, Pte., k. in a., F. & F., 4/5/17, formerly 5214, Lincs Regt.
Crawford, Edwin, b. St. George's, Birmingham, e. Birmingham, 2010, Pte., k. in a., F. & F., 25/9/15.
Craythorne, Alfred, b. Birmingham, e. Birmingham, 1105, Pte., d. of w., F. & F., 28/10/14.
Craythorne, Arthur, b. Birmingham, e. Warwick (Birmingham), 12, Pte., k. in a., F. & F., 16/5/15.
Cressall, Frank, b. Birmingham, e. Birmingham, 11275, L/Cpl., d. of w., F. & F., 4/9/16.
Cresswell, Percy, b. Dimmington, Alcester, Warwicks, e. Warwick (Dimmington), 481, L/Cpl., k. in a., F. & F., 25/9/15.
Cresswell, Sydney William, b. Birmingham, e. Warwick (Birmingham), 1852, L/Cpl., k. in a., F. & F., 25/10/14.
Croft, Thomas Joseph, b. Birmingham, e. Birmingham, 828, Pte., k. in a., F. & F., 19/12/14.
Cronan, Thomas, b. Coventry, e. Coventry, 12173, Pte., k. in a., F. & F., 14/7/16.
Crutchlow, Herman, b. Dewsbury, Yorks, e. Nuneaton, Warwicks (Bedworth, Warwicks), 9609, Pte., k. in a., F. & F., 15/7/16.
Cull, Cornelius, b. Birmingham, e. Birmingham, 1499, Pte., d., F. & F., 24/11/18.
Culley, William James, b. Birmingham, e. Birmingham, 10533, Pte., k. in a., F. & F., 25/9/15.
Cummings, James Walter, b. Aston, Birmingham, e. Birmingham, 4023, Pte., k. in a., F. & F., 25/9/15.
Cunnane, Bernard, b. Erdington, Birmingham, e. Birmingham, 1343, Pte., k. in a., F. & F., 19/12/14.
Cunnington, David John, b. Birmingham, e. Birmingham, 10689, Pte., k. in a., F. & F., 25/9/15.
Cunnington, Mark, b. Birmingham, e. Birmingham, 15394, Pte., k in a., F. & F., 14/7/16.
Currell, John, b. Princes Risborough, Bucks, e. Aylesbury, Bucks (Princes Risborough), 29999, Pte., d. of w., F. & F., 30/7/17, formerly 22943, Oxf. & Bucks L.I.
Curry, Joseph Henry, b. Aston, Birmingham, e. Birmingham (Nechells, Birmingham), 2716, Pte., d. of w., F. & F., 24/7/16.
Curry, Thomas Henry, b. Birmingham, e. Birmingham, 331, Pte., k. in a., F. & F., 19/12/14.
Curtis, James, b. Staplehurst, Kent, e. Maidstone, Kent, 542, Pte., k. in a., F. & F., 18/12/14.
Curtis, Richard Henry, b. Sparkbrook, Birmingham, e. Newport, Mon. (Birmingham), 3017, Pte., k. in a., F. & F., 3/9/16.
Cusick, James, b. Christchurch, Stalybridge, Ches., e. Stalybridge, 8003, Pte., d., F. & F., 31/10/14.
Daly, Daniel, b. Bishop Ryder's, Birmingham, e. Birmingham, 3924, Pte., k. in a., F. & F., 14/7/16.
Daniels, Albert, b. Bucknell, Stoke-on-Trent, e. Longton, Staffs (Stoke-on-Trent), 8058, Pte., k. in a., F. & F., 7/11/14.
Daniels, Arthur, b. St. Martin's, Birmingham, e. Birmingham, 2526, Pte., k. in a., F. & F., 3/9/16.
Danks, William Henry, b. St. Luke's, Birmingham, e. Birmingham, 2498, Pte., k. in a., F. & F., 20/2/15.
Darby, John Frederick, b. Birmingham, e. Warwick (Birmingham), 41, Pte., d., F. & F., 20/12/15.
Davenport, Benjamin, b. Ladywood, Birmingham, e. Warwick (Nuneaton, Warwicks), 3167, Pte., d., F. & F., 3/1/15.
Davidson, William, b. Shandon, Edinburgh, e. Edinburgh, 23622, Pte., k. in a., F. & F., 4/5/17, formerly 1305, R.E.
Davies, Edwin, b. Rotherhithe, Kent, e. Aldershot, Hants (London), 23710, Pte., d. of w., F. & F., 4/6/17, formerly 174284, R.E
Davies, Harry, b. Dudley, Worcs, e. Warwick (Dudley), 1609, L/Cpl., k. in a., F. & F., 1/5/18.
Davis, Charles, b. Westwinch, Norfolk, e. Leamington, Warwicks, 21913, Pte., k. in a., F. & F., 31/3/17
Davis, James, b. St. Martin's, Birmingham, e. Birmingham, 14274, L/Cpl., k. in a., F. & F., 3/9/16.
Davis, James, b. Highgate, Birmingham, e. Warwick (Highgate, Birmingham), 211, Pte., k. in a., F. & F., 19/12/14.
Davis, John, b. Ladywood, Birmingham, e. Warwick (Birmingham), 1341, Pte., d. of w., F. & F., 21/12/14.
Davis, John Francis, b. St. John's, Worcester, e. Birmingham (Watford, Herts), 9979, Pte., k. in a., F. & F., 11/7/16.
Davis, Robert, b. Ashley, Worcs, e. Birmingham (Kidderminster), 1360, Pte., d., Malta, 26/8/14.
Davis, William John, b. Birmingham, e. Birmingham, 10235, Pte., k. in a., F. & F., 16/5/15.
Davis, William Frederick John, b. Birmingham, e. Birmingham, 4134, Pte., k. in a., F. & F., 4/5/17.
Davy, Roland Peter, b. Draycott, Staffs, e. Nuneaton, Warwicks (Stafford), 979, L/Cpl., k. in a., F. & F., 22/3/15.
Dawes, George James, b. Slaughan, Crawley, Sussex, e. Birmingham (Horsham, Sussex), 1676, L/Cpl., d. of w., F. & F., 3/11/14.
Dawson, John Austin, b. Aberystwyth, e. Birmingham, 3064, Pte., k. in a., F. & F., 25/9/15.
Day, Bert, b. Birmingham, e. Birmingham, 1104, Pte., k. in a., F. & F., 19/12/15.
Deakin, Duncan, b. Barrow-in-Furness, e. Portsmouth (Barrow-in-Furness), 368, Dmr., d., F. & F., 9/5/15.
Deakin, Harold, b. Birmingham, e. Birmingham, 18903, Pte., k. in a., F. & F., 13/5/17.
Deane, Frank, b. Hambledon, Bucks, e. Aylesbury (Medmenham, Bucks), 30006, Pte., d. of w., F. & F., 30/12/18, formerly 21049, Oxf. & Bucks L.I.
Deeley, John, b. Birmingham, e. Birmingham, 9042, Pte., k. in a., F. & F., 24/10/14.
Denby, William, e. London, 339, L/Cpl., k. in a., F. & F., 20/10/14.
Dennis, Charles Frederick, b. Birmingham, e. Birmingham, 1132, Pte., k. in a., F. & F., 25/9/15.
Dennis, Walter, b. Birmingham, e. Birmingham, 8452, Pte., k. in a., F. & F., 19/10/14.
Dent, Bertram, b. Birmingham, e. Birmingham, 6276, Pte., k. in a., F. & F., 3/9/16.
Denton, Frederick George, b. Windsor, e. Nuneaton (Windsor), 997, Pte., d. of w., F. & F., 1/12/14.
Derrick, William, b. Bristol, e. Bristol, 1889, L/Cpl., k. in a., F. & F., 25/9/15.
Dilworth, Thomas William, b. Kenilworth, Warwicks, e. Warwick (Kenilworth), 1319, Pte., d. of w., F. & F., 20/6/15.
Dixon, Alfred, b. Birmingham, e. Birmingham, 13110, Pte., k. in a., F. & F., 14/7/16.
Dixon, John Thomas, b. Birmingham, e. Warwick (Birmingham), 9231, Sgt., k. in a., F. & F., 19/12/14.
Dobbs, Robert, b. Tunstall, Staffs, e. Hanley, Staffs (Tunstall), 7868. Pte., k. in a., F. & F., 25/10/14.
Docker, Henry, b. Aston, Birmingham, e. Warwick (Birmingham), 587, Sgt., k. in a., F. & F., 25/9/15.
Dodd, Edwin William, b. Faringdon, Berks, e. Paddington, Middx., 23601, Cpl., k. in a., F. & F., 9/10/17, formerly 176244, R.E.
Dolden, Leonard Charles, b. Poplar, Middx., e. Woolwich (Poplar), 844, L/Cpl., d. of w., F. & F., 29/10/14.
Doughton, Leonard, b. Riddings, Derbys, e. Mansfield (E. Kirkby), 54264, Pte., k. in a., F. & F., 24/10/18, formerly 116100, Notts & Derby Regt.
Doughty, James, e. Smethwick, Birmingham (West Bromwich), 14279, Pte., d. of w., F. & F., 15/10/17.
Doughty, John, b. Ropsley, Lincs, e. Grantham, Lincs, 27089, Pte., d. of w., F. & F., 31/5/17, formerly 5069, Lincs Regt.
Dovey, Albert William, b. Lincoln, e. Lincoln, 27035, L/Cpl., k. in a., F. & F., 28/[illegible]/17, formerly 1964, Lincs Regt.

Downes, Frank Edward, b. Birmingham, e. Birmingham, 19364, Pte., k. in a., F. & F., 4/5/17.
Downes, George Walter, b. Birmingham, e. Birmingham, 4911, L/Cpl., k. in a., F. & F., 7/11/14.
Downey, James, b. Birmingham, e. Birmingham, 1613, Pte., d. of w., F. & F., 8/6/15.
Downs, Arthur Henry, b. Stockingford, Warwicks, e. Nuneaton (Stockingford), 1544, Pte., k. in a., F. & F., 3/9/16.
Drake, Walter, e. Lincoln, 26994, Pte., k. in a., F. & F., 13/5/17, formerly 5504, Lincs Regt.
Drennon, Robert, b. Budbrooke, Warwicks, e. Birmingham, 1817, Pte., k. in a., F. & F., 20/10/14.
Dunster, William, b. Beckley, Sussex, e. Ashford, Kent (Pluckley), 27066, Pte., d., F. & F., 17/1/17, formerly 5282, Lincs Regt.
Dye, Charles, b. Spitalfields, Middx., e. Poplar (Bethnal Green), 3192, Pte., d. of w., F. & F., 3/1/15.
Dyer, Ernest Thomas, b. Birmingham, e. Birmingham, 861, Pte., d. of w., F. & F., 26/9/15.
Dyer, Joseph Harold, b. Stretton-on-Fosse, Warwicks, e. Evesham, Worcs (Stretton-on-Fosse), 16368, Pte., k. in a., F. & F., 14/7/16.
Dyer, William John Smith, b. Birmingham, e. Birmingham, 8939, Pte., d. of w., F. & F., 20/7/15.
Earl, Thomas Richard, b. Broughton, Northants, e. Moulton (Broughton), 23641, Pte., k. in a., F. & F., 4/5/17, formerly 184017, R.E.
Easton, Neil McLeod, b. Glasgow, e. Warwick, 8062, Pte., k. in a., F. & F., 21/11/14.
Eaton, William Henry, b. Birmingham, e. Warwick (Birmingham), 1564, Pte., k. in a., F. & F., 18/5/15.
Eccles, Harry, b. Bishop Ryders, Warwicks, e. Birmingham, 2055, Pte., k. in a., F. & F., 3/9/16.
Eden, Arthur, b. Warwicks, e. Birmingham (Castle Bromwich), 10457, Pte., k. in a., F. & F., 26/5/16.
Edinburgh, Alfred, b. Adelaide, Australia, e. Birmingham, 6283, A/Cpl., k. in a., F. & F., 3/9/16.
Edmunds, Clement, b. Birmingham, e. Birmingham, 6278, Pte., k. in a., F. & F., 18/12/14.
Edwards, James, b. Birmingham, e. Coventry (Birmingham), 1096, Pte., k. in a., F. & F., 23/1/15.
Ecles, John Lawrence, b. Birmingham, e. Warwick, 8723, Pte., k. in a., F. & F., 6/10/17.
Elcock, Frank, b. Birmingham, e. Warwick (Birmingham), 8929, Pte., k. in a., F. & F., 15/12/14.
Elder, Arthur John, b. Birmingham, e. Birmingham, 6299, Pte., k. in a., F. & F., 19/12/14.
Ellis, Arthur Harold, b. Newark, Notts, e. Newark, 1096, Pte., k. in a., F. & F., 25/10/14.
Ellis, Charles, b. Hastings, Sussex, e. Birmingham, 2978, Pte., k. in a., F. & F., 25/9/15.
Ellis, Clifford, b. Mistley, Essex, e. Ipswich, 23643, Pte., k. in a., F. & F., 4/5/17, formerly 180371, R.E.
Ellis, George Herbert, b. New Bilton, Warwicks, e. Warwick (Nuneaton), 6917, Pte., k. in a., F. & F., 7/11/14.
Ellis, John Edward, b. Consett, Durham, e. Consett, 9312, Sgt., d. of w., F. & F., 29/1/17.
Ellis, William Alfred, b. Plymouth, e. Plymouth, 23624, Pte., k. in a., F. & F., 4/5/17.
Elms, Herbert Reginald, b. Ashford, Kent, e. Hull, 1815, Pte., k. in a., F. & F., 19/10/14, formerly 9600, E. Yorks Regt.
Emmett, Robert, b. Haseley, Warwicks, e. Warwick (Attleborough, Warwicks), 3050, Pte., k. in a., F. & F., 19/12/14.
Emms, William Thomas, b. Birmingham, e. Birmingham, 8759, Pte., k. in a., F. & F., 24/10/14.
Ephgrave, John William, b. St. Albans, Herts, e. Birmingham (St. Albans), 1892, Pte., k. in a., F. & F., 18/12/14.
Evans, Alfred, b. Waddesdon, Bucks, e. Aylesbury (Waddesdon), 29929, Pte., d. of w., F. & F., 3/9/16, formerly 22942, Oxf. & Bucks L.I.
Evans, Alfred Henry, b. Stepney, Middx., e. Stratford (Stepney), 10941, Pte., k. in a., F. & F., 9/10/17.
Evans, Edgar, b. Birmingham, e. Birmingham, 1382, Pte., d., F. & F., 26/12/18.
Evans, George, b. St. Gile's, London, e. London (Clay Cross, Chesterfield), 8018, Pte., d. of w., F. & F., 15/11/14.
Evans, George Henry, b. Birmingham, e. Birmingham, 1001, Pte., k. in a., F. & F., 19/12/14.
Evans, Harry, b. Birmingham, e. Birmingham, 7569, Pte., k. in a., F. & F., 25/9/15.
Evans, James, b. Birmingham, e. Birmingham, 1154, Pte., k. in a., F. & F., 18/12/14.
Everill, Herbert, b. Birmingham, e. Birmingham, 6280, L/Cpl., d. of w., F. & F., 9/10/17.
Everill, Joseph Walter, b. Birmingham, e. Birmingham, 201956, L/Cpl., k. in a., F. & F., 9/10/17.
Everton, Thomas William, b. Birmingham, e. Birmingham, 1716, L/Cpl., k. in a., F. & F., 25/9/15.
Evrall, William Arthur, b. Birmingham, e. Birmingham, 1119, Pte., d. of w., F. & F., 29/9/15.
Ewins, John, b. Birmingham, e. Birmingham, 2350, Pte., k. in a., F. & F., 19/12/14.
Excell, Albert, b. Banning, Kent, e. Chatham (Maidstone), 555, Pte., k. in a., F. & F., 25/7/15.
Eyers, George Henry, b. Birmingham, e. Birmingham, 3948, Pte., k. in a., F. & F., 25/9/15.
Fancote, Albert, b. Smethwick, Staffs, e. Birmingham (Smethwick), 3866, Pte., k. in a., F. & F., 25/9/15.
Farmer, Harold Ernest, b. Inkborough, Worcs, e. Birmingham (Redditch), 2472, Pte., k. in a., F. & F., 25/9/15.
Farndon, Herbert, b. Little Beaton, Warwicks, e. Nuneaton, 4275, Pte., k. in a., F. & F., 20/3/16.
Farnsworth, Richard William, b. Birmingham, e. Birmingham, 482, Pte., k. in a., F. & F., 25/9/15.
Farnsworth, William, e. Nottingham, 27338, Pte., k. in a., F. & F., 9/10/17, formerly 2960, Notts & Derby Regt.
Farrant, Stanley, b. Haverhill, Suffolk, e. Haverhill, 27227, Pte., k. in a., F. & F., 9/10/17, formerly 1655, Suffolk Regt.
Farrell, Henry, b. Birmingham, e. Birmingham, 9952, Pte., k. in a., F. & F., 13/2/15.
Fathers, Isaac, b. Summertown, Oxford, e. Oxford, 29953, Pte., d. of w., F. & F., 2/11/16, formerly 22420, Oxford & Bucks L.I.
Faulkner, John, b. Yardley, Birmingham, e. Birmingham, 2004, Pte., d. of w., F. & F., 30/10/14.
Fearn, Wilfred Austin, b. Aston, Birmingham, e. Birmingham, 16573, L/Cpl., d. of w., F. & F., 24/10/16.
Feasey, Joseph Edward, b. Birmingham, e. Birmingham, 1507, L/Cpl., k. in a., F. & F., 31/10/14.
Feist, Jesse, b. Hoo, Strood, Kent, e. Chatham (Hoo), 828, Pte., k. in a., F. & F., 31/10/14.
Fell, Reuben, b. Trinity, Coventry, e. Coventry, 2841, Pte., k. in a., F. & F., 3/9/16.
Felton, Edmund, b. Aston, Birmingham, e. Birmingham (Aston), 2969, Pte., k. in a., F. & F., 4/5/17.
Fereday, Sidney Charles, b. Birmingham, e. Nuneaton, Warwicks (Atherstone, Warwicks), 12126, Pte., k. in a., F. & F., 3/9/16.
Fiddes, Alexander Thomas, b. Edmonton, Middx., e. Chelsea, 23700, Pte., k. in a., F. & F., 4/5/17, formerly 173792, R.E.
Fielding, Howard Arthur, b. Birmingham, e. Birmingham, 11847, Pte., k. in a., F. & F., 1/4/17.
Fielding, Robert, b. Braunston, Rugby, e. Nuneaton, Warwicks (Rugby, Warwicks), 1363, Pte., d., F. & F., 20/5/16.
Figgitt, Wilfred Charles, b. Broadway, Worcs, e. Stratford-on-Avon, Warwicks (Broadway), 10503, Pte., k. in a., F. & F., 25/9/15.
Finch, Charles, b. Birmingham, e. Birmingham, 3837, Pte., k. in a., F. & F., 25/9/15.
Fincher, Frank Walter, b. Aldershot, Hants, e. Stratford-on-Avon, Warwicks (Shottery, Stratford-on-Avon), 203600, L/Cpl., k. in a., F. & F., 10/10/17.
Fisher, Richard William, b. Birmingham, e. Birmingham (Handsworth, Staffs), 7899, Pte., k. in a., F. & F., 18/12/14.
Fisher, William Edward, b. Birmingham, e. Birmingham, 1837, Pte., k. in a., F. & F., 21/10/14.
Fitzgerald, Michael, b. Yardley, Birmingham, e. Birmingham, 3448, Pte., k. in a., F. & F., 19/12/14.
Flanagan, Frederick, b. Leigh, Lancs, e. Leigh, 15605, Pte., k. in a., F. & F., 31/8/16.
Flanagan, Ernest James, b. St. Miichael's, Coventry, e. Warwick (Coventry), 3326, Pte., d. of w., F. & F., 14/9/17.
Flemming, John, b. Birmingham, e. Glasgow (Birmingham), 3707, Pte., k. in a., F. & F., 25/9/15.
Fletcher, Albert, b. Yardley, Birmingham, e. Birmingham, 1498, Pte., k. in a., F. & F., 9/10/17.
Fletcher, Ernest, b. Nuneaton, Warwicks, e. Nuneaton, 1550, Pte., k. in a., F. & F., 11/5/15.
Fletcher, James, b. Kenilworth, Warwicks, e. Birmingham, 4031, Pte., k. in a., F. & F., 13/3/15.
Flintham, Walter, b. Hednesford, Staffs, e. Birmingham, 6297, Pte., k. in a., F. & F., 1/7/16.
Flowers, Henry, b. Nuneaton, Warwicks, e. Nuneaton (Atherstone, Warwicks), 1795, Pte., k. in a., F. & F., 20/10/14.
Foley, Timothy, b. St. Botolph's, Colchester, Essex, e. Colchester, 532, Cpl., k. in a., F. & F., 7/11/14.
Follows, Christopher, b. Wolverhampton, Staffs, e. Coventry, 16382, Pte., d. of w., F. & F., 3/9/16.
Foreshaw, Oliver Robert, b. Hockley Heath, Birmingham, e. Warwick (Birmingham), 10168, Pte., k. in a., F. & F., 3/9/16.
Forshaw, Thomas, b. Birkenhead, Ches., e. Wallasey (Egremont, Ches.), 9814, Pte., k. in a., F. & F., 17/5/15.
Foster, Arthur Joseph, b. Warwick, e. Birmingham, 4030, Pte., k. in a., F. & F., 25/9/15.
Foster, Ernest Thomas, b. Ilmington, Shipston-on-Stour, Warwicks, e. Birmingham (Shipston-on-Stour), 2133, L/Sgt., k. in a., F. & F., 9/10/17.
Francis, Thomas Emanuel, b. St. James, Poole, Dorset, e. Poole, 6455, Pte., d. of w., F. & F., 14/2/15, formerly 5791, Dorset Regt.
Franklin, Albert Williams, b. Overthorpe, Northants, e. Banbury, Oxon (Culworth, Banbury), 30008, Pte., k. in a., F. & F., 3/9/16, formerly 21321, Oxford & Bucks L.I.
Franks, Charles, b. St. Martin's, Birmingham, e. Birmingham, 3798, Pte., k. in a., F. & F., 7/1/15.
Freeman, Charles Edward, b. Handsworth, Staffs, e. Birmingham (Handsworth), 1118, Pte., k. in a., F. & F., 25/12/14.
Frost, Harry, b. Banbury, Oxon, e. Birmingham, 1941, Pte., k. in a., F. & F., 18/12/14.
Fulleylove, Arthur Herbert, b. Higham-on-the-Hill, Nuneaton, Warwicks, e. Coventry (Higham-on-the-Hill), 10526, L/Cpl., k. in a., F. & F., 25/9/15.
Fullylove, Walter, b. Chapel End, Warwicks, e. Coventry (Caldecote, Warwicks), 10527, Pte., k. in a., F. & F., 25/9/15.
Furborough, Thomas, e. Coventry (Ryton, Bulkington, Warwicks), 307757, Pte., k. in a., F. & F., 9/10/17.
Gallagher, Albert Joseph, b. Middlesbrough, Yorks, e. Warwick (Middlesbrough), 414, Dmr., d. of w., F. & F., 31/10/14.
Garbett, George, b. Birmingham, e. Ross (Birmingham), 6902, Pte., k. in a., F. & F., 31/7/15.
Gardiner, Albert, b. Stapleton, Bristol, e. Bristol, 18739, Pte., d., F. & F., 29/10/18, formerly 24122, Som. L.I.
Gardiner, Samuel Jacob, b. Birmingham, e. Birmingham, 465, Pte., k. in a., F. & F., 18/12/14.
Gardner, Arthur James, b. Welford, Campden, Glos., e. Stratford-on-Avon, Warwicks (Welford), 1177, Pte., k. in a., F. & F., 30/10/14.

Gardner, Bertram John, e. Salisbury, 306657, Pte., k. in a., F. & F., 9/10/17.
Gardner, Charles Henry, b. Welford-on-Avon, Warwicks, e. Birmingham (Dorsington, Warwicks), 5337, Pte., d. of w., F. & F., 3/9/16.
Garrington, George, b. St. Martin's, Birmingham, e. Birmingham, 2987, Pte., d. of w., F. & F., 13/9/16.
Garvey, John, b. Handsworth, Staffs, e. Birmingham (Tamworth, Staffs), 7454, Sgt., k. in a., F. & F., 7/11/14.
Gasson, John, b. St. Clement's, Hastings, Sussex, e. Birmingham, 1846, Pte., k. in a., F. & F., 10/1/15.
Gateley, Joseph, b. Budbrooke, Warwick, e. Warwick, 1343, Sgt., k. in a., F. & R., 7/11/14.
Gee, Alfred James, b. Birmingham, e. Birmingham, 9841, Pte., k. in a., F. & F.. 6/1/17.
German, Ernest Joseph, b. Maxstoke, Warwicks, e. Plymouth, 23652, Pte., k. in a., F. & F., 4/5/17, formerly 170487, R.E.
Gibbons, John, b. Guildford, Surrey, e. Birmingham (Harlesden, Middx.), 3177, Pte., k. in a., F. & F., 19/12/14.
Gibbs, Edwin Grosvenor, b. Nuneaton, Warwicks, e. Bolton, Lancs (Larkhall, Lanark), 14252, L/Cpl., k. in a., F. & F., 14/7/16, formerly 1881, A.P.C.
Gibbs, Frederick, b. Birmingham, e. Birmingham, 490, Pte., k. in a., F. & F., 25/9/15.
Gibbs, Herbert, b. Aldeby, Norfolk, e. Beccles, Suffolk, 27259, Pte., k. in a., F. & F., 9/10/17, formerly 3202, Suffolk Regt.
Gibbs, William Edward, b. Birmingham, e. Birmingham, 955, Pte., k. in a., F. & F., 19/12/14.
Gibson, Arthur, b. Birmingham, e. Birmingham, 1405, Pte., k. in a., F. & F., 7/11/14.
Gilbert, John, b. Birkenhead, Ches., e. Birmingham (Liverpool), 1353, Pte., k. in a., F. & F., 31/3/15.
Gilbert, Oscar James, b. U.S.A., e. Warwick (Smethwick, Staffs), 1646, Pte., k. in a., F. & F., 7/11/14.
Gill, Harold, b. Hepworth, Yorks, e. Aldershot, Hants (Cumberworth, Yorks), 23565, Pte., k. in a., F. & F., 2/4/17, formerly 173767, R.E.
Gillman, Walter Harry, b. Islington, Middx., e. Poplar, London, 12552, Pte., k. in a., F. & F., 3/9/16, formerly 56100, R.G.A.
Gittings, Charles Henry, b. Vauxhall, Birmingham, e. Birmingham (Gloucester), 2550, Pte., d. of w., F. & F., 26/9/15.
Glover, Alfred, b. St. Peter's, Birmingham, e. Birmingham, 3860, Pte., d. of w., F. & F., 10/10/17.
Goddard, Henry Percy, b. Warwick, e. Birmingham (Warwick), 768, Pte., d. of w., F. & F., 15/1/15.
Godridge, John, b. Ladywood, Birmingham, e. Birmingham, 2075, Pte., k. in a., F. & F., 25/10/14.
Golder, William, b. Stoke Lynn, Oxon, e. Oxford (Bicester, Oxon), 24231, Pte., d. of w., F. & F., 20/10/17.
Goldman, Abe, b. Birmingham, e. Warwick (Birmingham), 1211, Cpl., k. in a., F. & F., 25/9/15.
Goodchild, John Albert, b. Birmingham, e. Birmingham, 1165, Pte., k. in a., F. & F., 24/10/14.
Goode, Joseph, b. Ladywood, Birmingham, e. Birmingham, 1583, Pte., k. in a., F. & F., 6/6/15.
Goodhall, William James, b. Brookfields, Birmingham, e. Birmingham, 2134, Pte., k. in a., F. & F., 21/2/15.
Goodliff, John Bavin, b. Bardrey, Lincs, e. Louth, Lincs, 27127, Pte., d., F. & F., 14/10/18, formerly 5457, Linc Regt.
Goodsell, Edward, b. St. Leonards, Hythe, Kent, e. Shorncliffe, Kent (Hythe), 533, Pte., d. of w., F. & F., 29/11/14.
Goodwin, Albert, b. Stratford-on-Avon, Warwicks, e. Rugby, Warwicks (Stratford-on-Avon), 1660, Pte., k. in a., F. & F., 1/1/15.
Goodwin, Thomas Arthur, b. Thelsford, Warwicks, e. Coventry (Thelsford), 14, Pte., k. in a., F. & F., 3/9/16.
Gotts, Charles, b. Castessy, Norfolk, e. Nuneaton, Warwicks (Stockingford, Warwicks), 3198, L/Cpl., k. in a., F. & F., 12/3/15.
Gough, Albert Henry, b. Gt. Yew, Oxon, e. Banbury, Oxon (Gt. Yew), 29928, Pte., k. in a., F. & F., 4/5/17, formerly 23042, Oxf. & Bucks L.I.
Gould, Thomas James, b. Birmingham, e. Birmingham, 1895, Pte., d. of w., F. & F., 29/10/14.
Goulden, Herbert George, b. Shrewsbury, Salop., e. Birmingham, 1782, Pte., k. in a., F. & F., 19/12/14.
Govan, Ernest, b. Birmingham, e. Birmingham, 202649, Pte., k. in a., F. & F., 1/10/17.
Govett, William, b. Forest Hill, Kent, e. London, 7960, Sgt., d. of w., F. & F., 1/11/14.
Grace, George, b. Beechwood, Oxon, e. Caversham, Berks (Henley-on-Thames), 24240, Pte., d. of w., F. & F., 5/11/17.
Grant, George Spence, b. Edinburgh, e. Edinburgh, 23621, Pte., k. in a., F. & F., 5/8/17, formerly 2270, R.E.
Gray, William John, b. Hackney, London, e. Stratford, London (Homerton, London), 10535, Pte., k. in a., F. & F., 30/9/15.
Greaves, Cecil George, b. Birmingham, e. Birmingham, 8821, Pte., d. of w., F. & F., 5/10/15.
Greaves, James Robert, b. Birmingham, e. Birmingham, 16/1772, Pte., k. in a., F. & F., 4/5/17.
Green, Arthur Francis, b. Birmingham, e. Birmingham, 16/1765, L/Cpl., k. in a., F. & F., 4/5/17.
Green, Thomas, b. Birmingham, e. Birmingham, 6973, Pte., k. in a., F. & F., 14/7/16.
Green, William, b. Birmingham, e. Birmingham, 1856, Sgt., k. in a., F. & F., 3/9/16.
Greenway, Ernest William, b. Milverton, Warwicks, e. Warwick (Milverton), 1786, Pte., k. in a., F. & F., 30/10/14.
Greenway, Vincent Sidney, b. Tysoe, Warwicks, e. Nuneaton, Warwicks (Tysoe), 4397, Pte., k. in a., F. & F., 4/5/17.
Gretton, Clifford James, b. Birmingham, e. Birmingham, 1191, Pte., k. in a., F. & F., 25/9/15.
Grey, James, b. St. John's, Carlisle, Cumberland, e. Carlisle, 6846, Pte., k. in a., F. & F., 19/12/14.
Griffin, Arthur, b. Plumstead, Kent, e. Birmingham, 1865, Pte., k. in a., F. & F., 7/11/14.
Griffin, Herbert Henry, b. Coventry, e. Coventry, 17953, Pte., d., F. & F., 21/10/18.
Griffiths, Albert Victor, b. Birmingham, e. Birmingham, 11587, Pte., k. in a., F. & F., 19/6/15.
Griffiths, Henry, b. Birmingham, e. Birmingham, 7571, Pte., k. in a., F. & F., 21/10/14.
Griffiths, Samuel, b. Winson Green, Birmingham, e. Birmingham, 3848, Pte., k. in a., F. & F., 25/9/15.
Griffiths, William Henry, b. St. Michael's, Coventry, e. Coventry, 2336, Pte., d. of w., F. & F., 19/12/14.
Grimes, Stanley Edwin, b. Reading, Berks, e. Oxford (Reading), 18476, Pte., k. in a., F. & F., 12/8/17, formerly 24558, Som. L.I.
Grundy, George William, b. Ladywood, Birmingham, e. Birmingham, 1355, Pte., k. in a., F. & F., 18/12/14.
Guest, Harry, b. Aston, Birmingham, e. Birmingham, 3320, Pte., k. in a., F. & F., 4/5/17.
Guest, Thomas, b. Dudley, Worcs, e. Nuneaton, Warwicks (Stockingford, Nuneaton), 11191, Pte., k. in a., F. & F., 3/9/16.
Haas, William, b. Rawal Pindi, India, e. Nuneaton, Warwicks (Stockingford, Nuneaton), 2432, Pte., k. in a., F. & F., 20/1/15.
Hackett, Harold, b. Birmingham, e. Birmingham, 1435, Pte., d. of w., F. & F., 1/6/16.
Hackleton, Harry, b. Gaydon, Warwicks, e. Warwick (Gaydon), 1635, Pte., d., F. & F., 18/11/14.
Hackleton, Thomas, b. North End, Banbury, Oxon, e. Warwick (Banbury), 1143, Pte., d., F. & F., 30/9/17.
Haddon, William Robert, b. Lozells, Birmingham, e. Birmingham (Smethwick), 3045, Cpl., k. in a., F. & F., 28/10/17.
Haden, Richard, b. Birmingham, e. Birmingham, 7163, Pte., k. in a., F. & F., 21/3/17.
Hadley, Frederick, b. Smethwick, Staffs, e. Birmingham (Smethwick), 6818, Pte., d. of w., F. & F., 5/5/15.
Hagram, Charlie Tom, b. Brackley, Northants, e. Leamington, Warwicks, 10419, Pte., k. in a., F. & F., 3/9/16.
Hall, Arthur, b. Birmingham, e. Birmingham, 11663, Pte., d. of w., F. & F., 4/6/16.
Hall, Harry, b. Birmingham, e. Birmingham, 9626, Pte., k. in a., F. & F., 16/5/15.
Hall, Henry, b. Stratford-on-Avon, Warwicks, e. Birmingham (Stratford-on-Avon), 1590, Pte., k. in a., F. & F., 31/10/14.
Hall, James Henry, b. Birmingham, e. Birmingham, 10463, Pte., k. in a., F. & F., 3/9/16.
Halsey, Arthur, b. Birmingham, e. Birmingham, 21835, Pte., d. of w., F. & F., 13/5/17.
Hammond, Arthur Henry, b. Preston Capes, Northants, e. Rugby, Warwicks (Long Lawford, Rugby), 9943, Pte., k. in a., F. & F., 1/7/16.
Hammond, George Frederick, b. St. George's, Bloomsbury, London, e. Ilford, Essex, 20669, Pte., k. in a., F. & F., 4/5/17, formerly 12154, Army Cycl. Corps.
Hammond, J., b. Woolwich, Kent, e. Canterbury, Kent (Woolwich), 716, Pte., k. in a., F. & F., 25/9/15.
Hancox, Ernest, b. Cubbington, Warwicks, e. Warwick (Cubbington), 1573, Pte., d. of w., F. & F., 29/1/15.
Hands, Thomas, b. Birmingham, e. Warwick (Birmingham), 6209, Pte., d., F. & F., 14/3/15.
Hankerson, John, b. St. Nicholas, Coventry, e. Warwick (Coventry), 3038, Pte., k. in a., F. & F., 19/12/14.
Hannibal, Frederick Walter, b. Birmingham, e. Birmingham, 1145, Pte., k. in a., F. & F., 4/5/17.
Hardiker, Joseph, b. Birmingham, e. Birmingham (Handsworth, Staffs), 202137, Pte., k. in a., F. & F., 3/8/18.
Harding, Herbert Henry, b. Polesworth, Warwicks, e. Atherstone, Warwicks, 4170, Pte., d. of w., F. & F., 6/10/15.
Harding, James Henry, b. St. George's, Kidderminster, Worcs, e. West Bromwich, Staffs, 7196, Pte., k. in a., F. & F., 4/10/17.
Harding, Richard, b. Market Drayton, Shropshire, e. Stafford (Stone, Staffs), 16/2030, L/Cpl., k. in a., F. & F., 9/10/17, formerly 140419, R.F.A.
Hargreaves, Frederick, b. St. Michael's, Coventry, e. Warwick (Coventry), 1016, Pte., k. in a., F. & F., 19/12/14.
Hargraves, Richard Woffendon, b. Aston, Birmingham, e. Warwick (Aston), 1333, Pte., k. in a., F. & F., 3/9/16.
Harnden, Henry Albert, b. Ashford, Kent, e. Birmingham (Ashford), 3745, Pte., k. in a., F. & F., 19/12/14.
Harper, Frank Arnold, b. Birmingham, e. Birmingham, 15618, Pte., k. in a., F. & F., 14/7/16.
Harper, Frederick, b. Birmingham, e. Birmingham, 720, Pte., k. in a., F. & F., 19/12/14.
Harper, William, b. Dublin, e. Warwick (Dupear, Sheffield), 9617, Pte., k. in a., F. & F., 3/9/16.
Harris, Arthur William, b. Aston, Birmingham, e. Birmingham, d., F. & F., 3/5/16.
Harris, Fred, b. Aston-le-Walls, Northants, e. Banbury, Oxon (Banbury), 29987, Pte., d. of w., F. & F., 4/5/17, formerly 22940, Oxford & Bucks L.I.
Harris, Frederick Thomas, b. Coventry, e. Coventry, 30052, Pte., k. in a., F. & F., 3/9/16.
Harris, Harry, b. Dunsden, Oxford, e. Caversham, Berks (Thatcham, Berks), 29975, L/Cpl., k. in a., F. & F., 9/10/17, formerly 22714, Oxford & Bucks L.I.
Harris, William, b. Birmingham, e. Birmingham, 381, Sgt., k. in a., F. & F., 13/2/16.
Harrison, Edward Charles, b. St. Paul's, Warwick, e. Warwick, 9745, Pte., k. in a., F. & F., 3/9/16.
Harrison, Thomas, b. Rotherham, Yorks, e. Longton, Staffs (Rotherham), 8056, Pte., k. in a., F. & F., 19/12/14.
Hartle, Bertram, b. Quinton, Birmingham, e. Birmingham, 4328, Pte., k. in a., F. & F., 21/3/17.
Hartley, William, b. Birmingham, e. Birmingham, 7104, Pte., k. in a., F. & F., 19/12/14.

Hartopp George Joseph, b. Redditch, Worcs, e. Coventry (Redditch), 1285, Pte., d. of w., F. & F., 15/1/15.
Hartwell, William Harold, b. Honeybourne, Glos., e. Warwick (Stratford-on-Avon, Warwicks), 10546, Pte., k. in a., F. & F., 25/9/15.
Harvey, Walter, b. St. Michael's, Coventry, e. Coventry, 587, Pte., k. in a., F. & F., 18/12/14.
Harwood, Charles, b. Leamington, e. Warwick (Leamington), 1199, L/Cpl., k. in a., F. & F., 29/4/16.
Harwood, George Daniel, b. Leamington, Warwicks, e. Warwick (Leamington), 9848, Pte., d. of w., F. & F., 10/6/15.
Hassam, William, b. Birmingham, e. Birmingham, 934, Pte., d. of w., F. & F., 15/10/17.
Hateley, Samuel, b. Ashted, Birmingham, e. Warwick (Ashted), 956, Pte., k. in a., F. & F., 7/11/14.
Haughton, Joseph, b. St. Michael's, Coventry, e. Coventry, 7118, Pte., k. in a., F. & F., 29/7/16.
Hawes, Harry Henry, b. Rochester, Kent, e. Chatham, Kent (Rochester), 368, Pte., k. in a., F. & F., 25/9/15.
Hawkes, Henry, b. St. Stephen's, Birmingham, e. Birmingham, 2021, Pte., k. in a., F. & F., 25/9/15.
Hawkins, George, e. Birmingham, 10250, Pte., d. of w, F. & F., 22/3/17.
Hawkins, William Thomas, b. East Tesley, Newbury, Berks, e. Reading (Wantage), 3152, Pte., k. in a., F. & F., 13/3/15.
Hawley, Thomas, b. Birmingham, e. Birmingham 2048, Pte k. in a., F. & F., 12/3/15.
Hawtin, Edward, b. St. Luke's, Leamington, e. Warwick (Leamington), 1218, C.Q.M.S., d. of w., F. & F., 31/7/17.
Hawtin, Stephen, b. Tysoe, Kineton, Warwicks, e. Warwick (Harbury, Warwicks), 6380, Pte., k. in a., F. & F., 29/5/15.
Haynes, William Thomas, b. Smethwick, Staffs, e. Birmingham (Smethwick), 935, Pte., d. of w., F. & F., 4/10/15.
Haywood, Jesse, b. Bedworth, Warwicks, e. Nuneaton (Bedworth), 4415, Pte., k. in a., F. & F., 25/9/15.
Haywood, William, b. Coventry, e. Coventry, 8906, Pte., k. in a., F. & F., 24/10/14.
Head, Arthur Walter, b. Eltham, Woolwich, Kent, e. New Cross, London (Brixton), 725, Pte., k. in a., F. & F., 10/5/15.
Healey, John, b. Stockingford, Warwicks, e. Nuneaton (Stockingford), 1324, Pte., k. in a., F. & F., 3/9/16.
Heath, Charles, b. Marylebone, Middx., e. London (Marylebone), 9973, Cpl., k. in a., F. & F., 13/5/17.
Heath, Charles Frederick, b. St. John, Kidderminster, Worcs, e. Catterick, Yorks (Birmingham), 60177, Pte., d., F. & F., 5/8/19.
Heaton, Arthur, b. Birmingham, e. Birmingham, 15590, Cpl., k. in a., F. & F., 9/10/17.
Heaton, Francis Christopher, b. Barracks, Lichfield, Staffs, e. Birmingham, 3805, Pte., k. in a., F. & F., 3/9/16.
Hemming, Albert William, b. Aston Manor, Birmingham, e. Warwick (Aston Manor), 1689, Pte., d. of w., F. & F., 15/3/15.
Hemmings, Joseph, b. Saltley, Birmingham, e. Birmingham (Sparkbrook), 6321, L/Cpl., k. in a., F. & F., 3/9/16.
Hemmings, William George, b. Wigginton, York, e. Banbury, Oxon, 29988, Pte., d. of w., F. & F., 3/9/16, formerly 22944, Oxford & Bucks L.L.
Henderson, William Ford, b. Birmingham, e. Birmingham, 3962, Pte., k. in a., F. & F., 25/9/15.
Herring, Edgar George, b. Birmingham, e. Birmingham, 16459, Pte., k. in a., F. & F., 9/10/17.
Heson, Alfred Henry, b. Birmingham, e. Warwick (Birmingham), 1182, Pte., d. of w., F. & F., 10/11/14.
Hewitt, William Charles, b. Stoneleigh, Warwicks, e. Warwick (Coventry), 3013, Pte., k. in a., F. & F., 18/12/14.
Heywood, Samuel John, b. Oakford, Devon, e. Exeter (Oakford), 21754, L/Cpl., k. in a., F. & F., 4/5/17, formerly 27597, Glos. Regt.
Hiam, Charles, b. Sutton, Cambs, e. Birmingham, 7849, Pte., k. in a., F. & F., 4/5/17.
Hickling, Samuel, b. Ladywood, Birmingham, e. Birmingham, 3661, Pte., k. in a., F. & F., 25/9/15.
Hickman, Frederick Royston, b. Bilston, Staffs, e. Birmingham, 4866, L/Cpl., k. in a., F. & F., 4/5/17.
Hicks, Owen John, b. Ford, Devonport, e. Devonport (Ford), 173, Sgt., k. in a., F. & F., 21/10/14.
Higman, Charles Edward, b. St. Austell, Cornwall, e. St. Austell, 29201, Pte., k. in a., F. & F., 27/8/17, formerly 24780, D.C.L.I.
Hiley, William, b. Birmingham, e. Birmingham, 14297, L/Cpl., d. of w., F. & F., 4/9/16.
Hill, Alfred, b. Coventry, e. Coventry, 30035, Pte., k. in a., F. & F., 3/9/16.
Hill, Frank, b. Birmingham, e. Birmingham, 6287, Pte., d. of w., F. & F., 19/6/15.
Hill, Frederick, b. Aston, Birmingham, e. Birmingham (Aston), 1554, Pte., k. in a., F. & F., 15/7/16.
Hill, Harry, b. Birmingham, e. Aston, Birmingham, 21613, Pte., k. in a., F. & F., 9/10/17.
Hill, John Thomas, b. Bedworth, Warwicks, e. Nuneaton, Warwicks (Nuneaton), 16356, Pte., k. in a., F. & F., 15/7/16.
Hillman, Albert, b. Ladywood, Birmingham, e. Birmingham, 2980, Pte., k. in a., F. & F., 13/5/17.
Hillson, William Mark, b. Orton, Waterville, Hunts, e. Peterborough, Northants, 30177, Pte., k. in a., F. & F., 9/10/17, formerly 975, Hunts Cyc. Battn.
Hinde, Walter, b. Haggerston, Middx., e. Dalston, London (Clapton Park), 8108, Pte., k. in a., F. & F., 19/12/14.
Hindson, Frank, b. Middx., e. London, 29949, L/Cpl., d. of w., F. & F., 8/9/16, formerly 6796, Oxf. & Bucks L.I.
Hinks, Reuben, b. Small Heath, Birmingham, e. Birmingham, 2468, Pte., k. in a., F. & F., 9/10/17.
Hinton, Reginald, b. Stoke-by-Nayland, Suffolk, e. Haverhill, Suffolk (Halstead, Essex), 27263, Pte., d. of w., F. & F., 22/3/17, formerly 2913, Suffolk Regt.
Hirst, Edward George, b. Holloway, Middx., e. Stratford, London (Ilford, Essex), 7979, Pte., k. in a., F. & F., 24/10/14.
Hitchman, George Thomas, b. Stratford-on-Avon, Warwicks, e. Birmingham, 8144, k. in a., F. & F., 16/5/15.
Hobbs, Frank Alfred, b. Nottingham, e. Coventry (Bulkington, Warwicks), 2580, Pte., k. in a., F. & F., 25/9/15.
Hobday, Harry, b. Walton, Stratford-on-Avon, Warwicks, e. Warwick (Walton), 1970, Pte., k. in a., F. & F., 21/11/14.
Hodgetts, Joseph, b. Aston, Birmingham, e. Birmingham (Aston), 9520, Pte., k. in a., F. & F., 25/9/15.
Hodrien, William, b. Aston, Birmingham, e. Birmingham, 3303, Pte., k. in a., F. & F., 19/12/14.
Holdaway, Arthur Edmund, b. Small Heath, Birmingham, e. Birmingham, 3354, Pte., k. in a., F. & F., 19/12/14.
Holden, Philip Ernest, b. Margate, Kent, e. Havre, France (Paris), 12563, Pte., k. in a., F. & F., 3/9/16, formerly 12870, R.G.A.
Holland, Frank, b. Birmingham, e. Birmingham (Handsworth, Staffs), 17576, Pte., k. in a., F. & F., 1/10/17.
Holt, Albert, b. Birmingham, e. Warwick (Birmingham), 9861, Pte., k. in a., F. & F., 16/5/15.
Holton, Henry, b. Hampton Lucy, Warwicks, e. Birmingham (Coleshill, Warwicks), 2003, Pte., d., F. & F., 8/11/18.
Holton, Thomas Arthur, b. St. John's, Leamington, Warwicks, e. Warwick (Leamington), 2182, L/Cpl., k. in a., F. & F., 25/9/15.
Horner, Joseph William, b. Tipton, Staffs, e. Birmingham (Tipton), 9303, Pte., k. in a., F. & F., 14/7/16.
Hooker, Harry, b. St. Albans, Middx., e. Leicester (London), 287, Pte., k. in a., F. & F., 24/10/14.
Hookvale, Edgar, b. Leek Wootton, Warwicks, e. Warwick (Leek Wootton), 4485, Pte., k. in a., F & F., 25/9/15.
Hooper, Allenby Victor, b. Evenlode, Glos., e. Warwick (Evenlode), 10506, Pte., k. in a., F. & F., 25/9/15.
Hope, George, b. North London, e. Birmingham, 1871. Pte., k. in a., F. & F., 19/12/14.
Hopkins, George, b. King's Norton, Birmingham, e. Birmingham (Smethwick, Staffs), 1512, Pte., k. in a., F. & F., 25/9/15.
Hopkins, Sidney, b. Birmingham, e. Birmingham, 4002, Pte., d. of w., F. & F., 13/3/15.
Hopwood, Peter, b. Ashted, Birmingham, e. Birmingham, 1480, Pte., k. in a., F. & F., 25/9/15.
Horan, George Patrick, b. Armagh, e. London, 23616, Pte., d., F. & F., 12/5/17, formerly 203797, R.E
Horden, Richard, b. Holy Trinity, Coventry, e. Coventry, 1310, Pte., k. in a., F. & F., 26/1/15.
Horne, Fred, b. Offchurch, Warwicks, e. Nuneaton, Warwicks (Exhall, Coventry, Warwicks), 12137, Pte., d. of w., F. & F., 15/4/16.
Horsburgh, Henry, b. St. Mary's, Gateshead, Durham, e. Gateshead, 1883, Pte., k. in a., F. & F., 19/12/14, formerly 4397, R.A.M.C.
Horsley, Albert Thomas, b. Bearley, Warwicks, e. Warwick (Stratford-on-Avon, Warwicks), 10539, Pte., k. in a., F. & F., 25/9/15.
Horton, Albert, b. Birmingham, e. Birmingham, 1767, Pte., k. in a., F. & F., 1/12/14.
Horton, Frederick, b. Hereford, e. Birmingham (Sutton Coldfield, Warwicks), 9808, Pte., k. in a., F. & F., 4/5/17.
Horton, George Frederick, b. Birmingham, e. Birmingham, 7515, Pte., k. in a., F. & F., 17/5/15.
Horton, John, b. Birmingham, e. Birmingham, 20726, Pte., k. in a., F. & F., 9/10/17.
Howes, Fred, b. Coventry, e. Coventry, 242918, Pte., k. in a., F. & F., 11/10/17.
Hughes, Albert Edward, b. Birmingham, e. Birmingham, 9233, Cpl., k. in a., F. & F., 19/12/14.
Hughes, Richard Henry, b. Birmingham, e. Birmingham, 480, A/C.S.M., d. of w., F. & F., 10/9/16.
Hughes, Samuel, b. Aston, Birmingham, e. Birmingham, 5044, Pte., k. in a., F. & F., 3/9/16.
Humphreys, Harry, e. Birmingham, 30059, Pte., k. in a., F. & F., 3/9/16.
Humphreys, John Henry, b Birmingham, e. Birmingham, 9398, L/Cpl., k. in a., F. & F., 8/3/15.
Hunt, Ebenezer, b. Birmingham, e. Birmingham, 769, Pte., d. of w., F. & F., 12/4/15.
Hunt, George, b. Birmingham, e. Birmingham, 3412, Pte., d. of w., F. & F., 4/9/16.
Hunt, Stanley Albert, b. Reading, Berks, e. Warwick (Leamington, Warwicks), 2305, L/Cpl., k. in a., F. & F., 25/9/15.
Hunt, Walter, b. Evesham, Worcs, e. West Bromwich, Staffs, 7238, Pte., d. of w., F. & F., 16/10/15.
Hunt, William, b. Bolton, Lancs, e. Farnworth, Lancs (Little Hulton, Lancs), 12467, Pte., k. in a., F. & F, 14/7/16, formerly 53742, R.G.A.
Ingram, Percy Walter Frederick, b. Withybrook, Coventry, e. Rugby, Warwicks (Withybrook), 4449, Pte., k. in a., F. & F., 21/3/16.
Ingram, Thomas, b. Aston, Birmingham, e. Birmingham, 3117, Pte., k. in a., F. & F., 25/9/15.
Insley, Albert, b. Aston, Birmingham, e. Birmingham, 1400, Pte., k. in a., F. & F., 18/12/14.
Ison, Ernest, b. Nuneaton, Warwicks, e. Warwick (Nuneaton), 9961, Pte., k. in a., F. & F., 25/9/15.
Izzard, Clifford, b. Monks Kirby, Lutterworth, Leics, e. Rugby, Warwicks (Monks Kirby), 4450, Pte., k. in a., F. & F., 8/6/16.
Jackson, Albert, b. Minster, Beverley, Yorks, e. Hull, 1737, Cpl., k. in a., F. & F., 4/5/17, formerly 2302, Hussars.

Jackson, Harry, b. St. Martin's, Birmingham, e. Birmingham, 12952, Pte., k. in a., F. & F., 3/9/16.
Jackson, Joseph, b. Walsall, Staffs, e. Birmingham (Walsall), 9807, Pte., k. in a., F. & F., 25/9/15.
Jackson, Leonard, e. Louth, Lincs, 27047, Pte., k. in a., F. & F., 4/5/17, formerly 5421, Lincs Regt.
Jacobs, David, b. Birmingham, e. Liverpool (Birmingham), 11457, Pte., k. in a., F. & F., 28/2/17.
Jacobs, Jesse, e. Coventry, 9612, Pte., k. in a., F. & F., 4/5/17.
Jacobs, William Charles, b. Hackney, London, e. Stratford, London, 10961, Pte., k. in a., F. & F., 3/9/16
Jakeman, Jesse Phillip, b. St. Nicholas, Warwick, e. Warwick, 1818, Cpl., k. in a., F. & F., 17/6/15.
James, Frank, b. Wilnecote, Warwicks, e. Atherstone (Wilnecote), 16191, Pte., k. in a., F. & F., 3/9/16.
James, George Alexander, b. Kilburn, London, e. Marylebone (Paddington), 11528, L/Sgt., k. in a., F. & F., 4/5/17.
James, Harry Thomas, b. Birmingham, e. Stoke-on-Trent, Staffs (Birmingham), 1731, Cpl., k. in a., F. & F., 4/5/17.
James, John Richard, b. Hockley, Birmingham, e. Warwick (Hockley), 1647, Pte., k. in a., F. & F., 25/9/15.
Janes, Charles, b. Soulbury, Bucks, e. Aylesbury (Hollingdon, Beds), 24224, Pte., k. in a., F. & F., 9/10/17.
Jayes, Philip, b. Winson Green, Birmingham, e. Birmingham, 3845, Pte., k. in a., F. & F., 3/9/16.
Jenkins, Thomas, b. Birmingham, e. Birmingham, 1579, Pte., d. of w., F. & F., 30/1/15.
Jennings, John William, b. Birmingham, e. Birmingham, 3829, Pte., d., F. & F., 9/2/15.
Jephcote, Frank, b. Stockingford, Warwicks, e. Nuneaton, 1979, Pte., k. in a., F. & F., 19/10/14.
Joesbury, William, b. Birmingham, e. Birmingham, 3694, Pte., k. in a., F. & F., 30/12/14.
Johns, Edward, b. Stonehouse, Devon, e. Plymouth, 23626 Pte., k. in a., F. & F., 28/10/14.
Johnson, Charles, b. Exhall, nr. Coventry, Warwicks, e. Coventry (Exhall), 10514, L/Cpl., k. in a., F. & F., 29/5/15.
Johnson, Reginald George, b. St. Pancras, Middx., e. Birmingham (Finsbury Park, London, N.), 1846, Pte., k. in a., F. & F., 18/6/15.
Johnson, Walter, b. Haywood, Lancs, e. Gainsborough, 27054, Pte., k. in a., F. & F., 4/5/17, formerly 1012, Lincs Regt.
Johnson, William, b. St. Martin's, Norwich, e. Birmingham, 2376, Pte., k. in a., F. & F., 9/10/17.
Johnson, William Thomas, b. Bedworth, Warwicks, e. Nuneaton (Bedworth), 15355, Pte., k. in a., F. & F., 4/5/17.
Jones, Charles, b. Lapworth, Warwicks, e. Warwick (Hockley Heath), 10236, L/Cpl., d. of w., F. & F., 25/9/15.
Jones, Daniel, b. Birmingham, e. Birmingham, 1618, Pte., k. in a., F. & F., 19/12/14.
Jones, Ernest, b. Aston, Birmingham, e. Birmingham, 4064, Pte., d. of w., F. & F., 30/9/15.
Jones, Ernest, b. Great Malvern, Worcs, e. Warwick (Birmingham), 9013, Pte., k. in a., F. & F., 2/4/17.
Jones, Frederick, b. Birmingham, e. Birmingham, 2435, Pte., k. in a., F. & F., 19/12/14.
Jones, George Frederick, b. Hereford, e. Birmingham, 1843, C.S.M., k. in a., F. & F., 25/9/15.
Jones, Gilbert Edward, b. Paddington, Middx., e. Willesden (Kensal Rise, N.W.), 1666, Cpl., d. of w., F. & F., 6/11/14.
Jones, Harry William, b. Worcester, e. Coventry (Worcester), 17675, Pte., d. of w., F. & F., 16/9/16.
Jones, James Benjamin, b. Ladywood, Birmingham, e. Birmingham, 11940, Pte., k. in a., F. & F., 14/7/16.
Jones, Osmond, b. Smethwick, Staffs, e. Birmingham (Smethwick), 2883, Pte., k. in a., F. & F., 6/3/15.
Jones, Robert, b. Birmingham, e. Birmingham, 8476, Pte., k. in a., F. & F., 7/11/14.
Jones, Samuel, b. St. Matthew's, Stockport, Ches., e. Manchester (Stockport), 1925, Sgt., k. in a., F. & F., 3/9/16.
Jones, Samuel, b. Walsall, Staffs, e. Birmingham (Walsall), 9727, Pte., k. in a., F. & F., 25/10/14.
Jones, William, b. Smethwick, Staffs, e. Birmingham (Smethwick), 11589, Pte., k. in a., F. & F., 25/9/15.
Jones, William James, b. Ladywood, Birmingham, e. Birmingham, 11124, Pte., d., F. & F., 30/10/18.
Joyce, Jack, b. Birmingham, e. Birmingham, 400, Pte., d. of w., F. & F., 23/8/15.
Jupp, William, b. Brighton, Sussex, e. London (Redhill), 1220, Sgt., d. of w., F. & F., 25/9/15.
Jury, Edward Thomas, b. Peckham, Surrey, e. New Cross, London, S.E. (Peckham), 811, Pte., k. in a., F. & F., 25/9/15.
Kavanagh, James, b. Balsall Heath, Birmingham, e. Birmingham, 1454, Pte., k. in a., F. & F., 19/12/14.
Kelly, John, b. Birmingham, e. Birmingham, 10750, Pte., k. in a., F. & F., 3/9/16.
Kenny, Francis, b. Horn Dean, Hants, e. Warwick (Atherstone), 203040, Pte., k. in a., F. & F., 9/10/17, formerly 3502, Warwicks Yeo.
Kerr, Thomas, b. Birmingham, e. Birmingham, 4015, Pte., k. in a., F. & F., 14/7/16.
Ketch, Robert, b. St. Mary's, Aston Brook, Birmingham, e. Birmingham, 1908, Pte., k. in a., F. & F., 19/12/14.
Kilkenny, James, b. Birmingham, e. Warwick, 9459, Pte., k. in a., F. & F., 24/8/15.
Killion, John, b. St. Thomas, Birmingham, e. Birmingham, 2617, Pte., k. in a., F. & F., 3/9/16.
Kind, Charles Henry, b. Birmingham, e. Birmingham, 519, Pte., d., F. & F., 21/5/15.
King, George Henry, b. Birmingham, e. Birmingham, 1588, L/Cpl., d. of w., F. & F., 7/11/14.
Kingston, George, b. Birmingham, e. Birmingham, 2736, Pte., k. in a., F. & F., 1/3/17.
Kirby, Edwin, b. Birmingham, e. Birmingham, 6406, Pte., k. in a., F. & F., 25/9/15.
Kirk, Harold, b. Kentish Town, Middx., e. Oxford (Kentish Town), 30017, Pte., k. in a., F. & F., 3/9/16, formerly 13505, Oxf. & Bucks L.I.
Kirkham, John, b. Smethwick, Staffs, e. Birmingham (Smethwick), 10519, Pte., k. in a., F. & F., 25/9/15.
Knight, Ernest, b. Nuneaton, Warwicks, e. Nuneaton, 1543, Pte., d. of w., F. & F., 1/11/14.
Knight, Joseph Wilfred, b. Wednesbury, Staffs, e. Birmingham (Wednesbury), 178, Pte., k. in a., F. & F., 4/5/17.
Lacey, Albert, b. Birmingham, e. Birmingham (Bournbrook, Birmingham), 6346, Pte., d. of w., F. & F., 25/9/15.
Lake, George Henry Taylor, b. Tavistock, Devon, e. Tavistock, 43789, Pte., d. of w., F. & F., 4/11/18, formerly 66819, Devon Regt.
Lamboll, Frederick John, b. Haslemere, Surrey, e. Ringwood, Hants, 18702, Pte., k. in a., F. & F., 4/5/17, formerly 24701, Som. L.I.
Lampard, Arthur Charles Stanley, b. Easton, Glos., e. Bristol, 34271, Pte., k. in a., F. & F., 26/10/17.
Lane, Arthur George, b. Hockley, Birmingham, e. Birmingham, 3979, Pte., d., F. & F., 19/9/15.
Lane, Harry, b. Bourne, Lincs, e. Bourne, 27092, Pte., k. in a., F. & F., 4/5/17, formerly 5082, Lincs Regt.
Langley, John Thomas, b. The Redings, Derbys., e. Birmingham, 3738, Pte., k. in a., F. & F., 2/1/15.
Lawrence, John, b. Aston, Birmingham, e. Warwick (Aston), 1295, Pte., k. in a., F. & F., 25/10/14.
Lawson, Bertie, b. Hornley, Norfolk, e. Warwick, 4620, Pte., k. in a., F. & F., 14/7/16.
Lay, Edward, b. Willenhall, Staffs, e. Birmingham, 1811, Pte., k. in a., F. & F., 19/12/14.
Leadbetter, Albert Sydney, b. Saltley, Birmingham, e. Warwick (Saltley), 13, Pte., k. in a., F. & F., 3/9/16.
Lear, Henry David, b. St. Pancras, Middx., e. Holborn (King's Cross), 30011, L/Cpl., k. in a., F. & F., 3/9/16, formerly 2764, Oxford & Bucks L.I.
Lee, George Alfred, b. Hull, e. Chatham (Hull), 23615, Pte., k. in a., F. & F., 4/5/17, formerly 203786, R.E.
Lee, Herbert, b. St. Mary's, Stockport, Ches., e. Nuneaton (Stockport), 1949, Pte., k. in a., F. & F., 25/9/15.
Lee, Herbert, b. St. Peter's, Rugby, Warwicks, e. Rugby, 1095, Pte., k. in a., F. & F., 3/9/16.
Lee, Joseph, b. Preston, Lancs, e. Birmingham, 1738, L/Cpl., d. of w., F. & F., 24/10/14.
Lee, John, b. Birmingham, e. Birmingham (Greet), 4103, Pte., d. of w., F. & F., 13/9/16.
Leigh, Frederick, b. Boddington, Northants, e. Warwick (Boddington), 1397, Pte., k. in a., F. & F., 7/11/14.
Leigh, George, b. Pinkhull, Stoke, Staffs, e. Newcastle (Stoke-on-Trent), 8113, Pte., k. in a., F. & F., 25/9/15.
Lethbridge, Arthur James, b. St. John's, Leamington, Warwicks, e. Liverpool (Garston, Lancs), 3771, Pte., k. in a., F. & F., 13/3/15.
Levine, Barnett, b. London, e. Birmingham (London), 746, Pte., k. in a., F. & F., 19/12/14.
Linder, Edward, b. Rushhall, Norfolk, e. Coventry, 10752, Pte., k. in a., F. & F., 23/4/16.
Lines, John, b. Birmingham, e. Coventry, 9886, Pte., k. in a., F. & F., 25/9/15.
Linforth, John, b. Birmingham, e. Birmingham, 3532, Pte., k. in a., F. & F., 19/12/14.
Linnett, Frederick, b. Stretton, Warwicks, e. Coventry (Stretton-on-Dunsmore), 1155, Pte., k. in a., F. & F., 3/9/16.
Little, Alfred, b. Birmingham, e. Birmingham, 14523, Pte., k. in a., F. & F., 28/8/16.
Llewellyn, Charles, b. Birmingham, e. Oxford (Birmingham), 7005, Pte., k. in a., F. & F., 7/11/14.
Lloyd, Frederick Charles, b. Llandewe, Radnor, e. Stratford-on-Avon, 4065, A/Sgt., k. in a., F. & F., 25/9/15.
Longden, Harry, b. Birmingham, e. Coventry (Birmingham), 1434, Pte., k. in a., F. & F., 25/9/15.
Lowe, Arthur, b. Bradmore, Staffs, e. Wolverhampton (Birmingham), 7697, Pte., d., F. & F., 12/4/15.
Lucas, William Henry, b. Aston Abbott, Bucks, e. Warwick (Buckingham), 2499, Pte., k. in a., F. & F., 19/12/14.
Luckman, William, b. Birmingham, e. Birmingham (Colchester), 6560, Sgt., k. in a., F. & F., 6/11/14.
Lyons, William, b. Birmingham, e. Birmingham, 3908, Pte., k. in a., F. & F., 12/3/15.
Maddocks, Sydney Thomas, b. Dogpool, Birmingham, e. Birmingham, 2019, Pte., k. in a., F. & F., 11/5/15.
Maguire, William, b. St. George's, Birmingham, e. Birmingham, 1291, Pte., d. of w, F. & F., 17/5/15.
Mander, Thomas, b. Birmingham, e. Brentford, Middx. (Braunston, Rugby, Warwicks), 10170, Pte., d. of w., F. & F., 4/9/16.
Mann, Charles, b. Harbury, Leamington, Warwicks, e. Warwick (Rugby), 1978, Pte., d. of w., F. & F., 24/5/16.
Mann, Robert, b. Birmingham, e. Warwick (Birmingham), 1849, L/Cpl., k. in a., F. & F., 25/9/15.
Manton, Albert, b. Stechford, Warwicks, e. Birmingham, 1703, Pte., k. in a., F. & F., 19/10/14.
Marshall, Thomas Valentine, e. Reading, 2525, Pte., k. in a., F. & F., 28/10/17, formerly 2525, Berks Yeo.
Martin, Arthur James, b. Shotley, Suffolk, e. Ipswich, 6450, Pte., k. in a., F. & F., 29/4/15, formerly 5188, Suffolk Regt.
Martin, Alfred, b. Bedworth, Warwicks, e. Bedworth, 16379, Pte., k. in a., F. & F., 3/9/16.
Martin, Christopher, b. Edgbaston, Birmingham, e. Birmingham, 58, Pte., k. in a., F. & F., 9/10/17.
Martin, John Henry Herbert, b. Birmingham, e. Warwick (Birmingham), 21098, Pte., d. of w., F. & F., 9/10/17.
Martin, John Henry, b. Ancaster, Lincs, e. Ancaster, 27134, Pte., d., F. & F., 11/12/16, formerly 5095, Lincs Regt

Mason, James, b. Birmingham, e. Birmingham, 8713, Pte., k. in a., F. & F., 31/10/14.
Mason, James Edward, b. Wigston Magna, Leicester, e. Birmingham (Wigston Magna), 3315, Pte., k. in a., F. & F., 19/12/14.
Mason, Louis, b. West Derby, Liverpool, e. Manchester (Sheffield), 6065, Sgt., k. in a., F. & F., 4/5/17, M.M.
Mason, Sidney, b. Aston, Birmingham, e. Birmingham (Aston), 722, L/Cpl., k. in a., F. & F., 9/10/17.
Matthews, Albert, b. Leamington, Warwicks, e. Coventry, 19356, L/Cpl., k. in a., F. & F., 9/10/17.
Matthews, William Alfred, b. Birmingham, e. Birmingham, 1235, Pte., d. of w., F. & F., 26/10/14.
Maycock, John, b. Emscote, Warwick, e. Warwick (Leamington), 2326, Pte., k. in a., F. & F., 19/12/14.
Mayer, Alfred, b. St. Nicholas, Nuneaton, Warwicks, e Nuneaton, 1089, Pte., k. in a., F. & F., 16/8/15.
Maynard, William, b. Friern Barnet, Middx., e. Mill Hill (London), 27142, Pte., k. in a., F. & F., 9/10/17, formerly 52833, Linc Regt.
McGill, Henry William, b. St. Mathews, Southampton, Hants, e. Dorchester (Branksome, Dorset), 2302, Cpl., k. in a., F. & F., 3/9/16.
McHeron, John, b. Whitehaven, Cumberland, e. Barrow-in-Furness, Lancs, 6548, Pte., k. in a., F. & F., 19/12/14.
McIntosh, James Gordon, b. Scunthorpe, Lincs, e. Frodingham, Lincs (Scunthorpe), 27118, L/Cpl., d. of w., F. & F., 6/12/16, formerly 1405, Lincs Regt.
McKay, Frederick William, b. Small Heath, Birmingham, e. Birmingham (Bournbrook, nr. Birmingham), 7236, Pte., k. in a., F. & F., 16/5/15.
McLathlan, Robert, b. Oban, Argylls, e. Warwick (Coventry), 203553, Pte., d., F. & F., 3/3/18.
McLuckie, James, b. Dessingtown, Glasgow, e. Birmingham, 3104, Pte., d., F. & F., 20/2/15.
McNally, Harry Amos, b. Eastleigh, Hants, e. Eastleigh, 23639, Pte., k. in a., F. & F., 9/10/17, formerly 1125, R.E.
Mead, John William, b. Long Marston, Stratford-on-Avon, Warwicks, e. Birmingham, 6119, Pte., d., F. & F., 15/12/18.
Medley, John William, b. Osgorby, Lincs, e. Lincoln (Eagle, Lincs), 27032, L/Cpl., k. in a., F. & F., 4/5/17 formerly 3243 Lincs Regt.
Meek, Frederick James, b. Birmingham, e. Birmingham, 7233, Pte., k. in a., F. & F., 19/12/14.
Meech, Reginald William, b. Paignton, Devon, e. Birmingham (Paignton), 15/1352, Pte., k. in a., F. & F., 4/5/17.
Melling, William, b. Birmingham, e. Birmingham, 6550, Pte., d. of w., F. & F., 16/12/14.
Meredith, William Reginald, b. Sparkbrook, Birmingham, e. Birmingham, 6779, Pte., k. in a., F. & F., 28/2/17.
Merewether, William, b. London, e. Birmingham, 15958, Pte., k. in a., F. & F., 3/9/16.
Merricks, Alfred, b. St. George's, Birmingham, e. Birmingham, 19134, Pte., k. in a., F. & F., 9/10/17.
Merritt, Sidney Arthur, b. Harlesden, Middx., e. London (Harlesden), 902, Pte., k. in a., F. & F., 25/9/15.
Middleton, Thomas Cecil Herbert, b. Middle Tysoe, Warwicks, e. Warwick (Middle Tysoe), 9757, Pte., d. of w., F. & F., 19/7/16.
Mills, George, b. Birmingham, e. Birmingham (Newbold-on-Avon, Warwicks), 6940, Pte., k. in a., F. & F., 1/1/15.
Mills, James Henry, b. St. Peter's, Rochester, Kent, e. Chatham, Kent (Rochester), 820, Pte., k. in a., F. & F., 19/12/14.
Millward, Titus, b. Winson Green, Birmingham, e. Birmingham, 1593, Pte., k. in a., F. & F., 13/3/15.
Minchin, George, b. Birmingham, e. Birmingham, 3357, Pte., k. in a., F. & F., 3/9/16.
Minchin, Richard Edward, b. Stow-on-the-Wold, Glos., e. Rugby, Warwicks (Rugby), 15866, Pte., k. in a., F. & F., 7/9/16.
Montgomery, Charles Paul, b. Coventry, e. Doncaster, Yorks (Coventry), 9396, Pte., k. in a., F. & F., 24/10/16.
Moreton, George Alfred, b. Birmingham, e. Warwick (Birmingham), 1232, Pte., k. in a., F. & F., 7/11/14.
Moon, Frederick Charles, b. Delhi, India, e. Warwick, 1441, Sgt., k. in a., F. & F., 9/10/17, M.M.
Moore, Frank, b. Moreton Morrell, Warwicks, e. Warwick (Moreton Morrell), 1445, Pte., k. in a., F. & F., 25/9/15.
Moore, Harry, b. Barwell, Leics, e. Warwick (Barwell), 1401, A/Cpl., k. in a., F. & F., 25/9/15.
Moore, Thomas, b. Chapel End, Warwicks, e. Nuneaton, Warwicks, 10965, Pte., k. in a., F. & F., 26/5/16.
Moore, William Thomas, b. Smethwick, Staffs, e. Birmingham (Smethwick, Staffs), 11701, Pte., k. in a., F. & F., 3/9/16.
Morley, David, b. Stakerhill, Burton-on-Trent, e. Lichfield, Staffs (Burton-on-Trent), 1691, Pte., k. in a., F. & F., 29/10/14.
Morris, Charles, b. St. Phillips, Birmingham, e. Birmingham, 2415, Pte., k. in a., F. & F., 25/9/15.
Morris, Frederick Henry, b. St. Michael's, Coventry, e Coventry, 2842, L/Cpl., d., F. & F., 20/2/15.
Morris, William, b. Birmingham, e. Birmingham (Glasgow), 8445, Pte., k. in a., F. & F., 6/11/14.
Motteram, Thomas, b. St. Matthews, Birmingham, e. Birmingham, 10687, Pte., d. of w., F. & F., 4/6/17.
Mountford, James, b. Stafford, e. Birmingham, 3912, Pte., k. in a., F. & F., 13/3/15.
Mowe, George Henry, b. Aston, Birmingham, e. Birmingham, 1474, Pte., k. in a., F. & F., 19/12/14.
Munday, George, b. High Wycombe, Bucks, e. High Wycombe, 30009, Pte., k. in a., F. & F., 3/9/16, formerly 22828, Oxf. & Bucks L.I
Munro, David, b. Middlesbrough, Yorks, e. Warwick (Birmingham), 9104, Pte., k. in a., F. & F., 25/9/15.
Mullis, Frank, b. Birmingham, e. Birmingham, 14312, Pte., k. in a., F. & F., 14/7/16.
Murden, Robert Edward Henry, b. Brinklow, Warwicks, e. Rugby (Brinklow), 1546, Pte., k. in a., F. & F., 3/9/16, M.M.
Mustoe, Frederick, b. Huntley, Glos., e. Stroud, Glos. (Sandhurst, Glos.), 21771, Pte., k. in a., F. & F., 9/10/17, formerly 28299, Glos. Regt.
Myatt, Thomas, b. Willenhall, Staffs, e. Nuneaton, Warwicks (Stockingford, Nuneaton), 2500, Pte., k. in a., F. & F., 19/12/14.
Neale, Harold Edward, b. Edgbaston, Birmingham, e. Birmingham (Edgbaston), 1524, Pte., k. in a., F. & F., 25/9/15.
Near, Harry, b. Grimsby, Lincs, e. Grimsby, 27058, L/Cpl., k. in a., F. & F., 9/10/17, formerly 3848, Lincs Regt.
Needham, Fred, b. Grimsby, Lincs, e. Grimsby, 27057, Pte., k. in a., F. & F., 4/5/17, formerly 4112, Lincs Regt.
Newman, James Herbert, b. Dunedin, Otago, New Zealand, e. Warwick, 4556, C.S.M., k. in a., F. & F., 13/2/16.
Newman, Samuel, b. Aston, Birmingham, e. Birmingham (Aston), 1613, Pte., k. in a., F. & F., 4/2/15.
Newman, Victor Reuben, b. Swindon, Wilts, e. Devizes, Wilts (Wootton Bassett, Wilts), 12577, Pte., k. in a., F. & F., 3/9/16, formerly 56092, R.G.A.
Newnham, William, b. Danehill, Sussex, e. Grimsby (Cuckfield, Sussex), 27146, Pte., k. in a., F. & F., 4/5/17, formerly 5267, Lincs Regt.
Niblett, Sidney, b. Dordon, Warwicks, e. Nuneaton, Warwicks (Bedworth), 21679, Pte., d. of w., F. & F., 9/10/17.
Nicholson, George Charles, b. Grimsby, Lincs, e. Grimsby (Somersby, Lincs), 27147, Cpl., k. in a., F. & F., 4/5/17, formerly 4044, Lincs Regt.
Nicholas, Thomas James, b. Cardiff, Glam., e. Cardiff, 23552, L/Cpl., k. in a., F. & F., 21/3/17, formerly 1409, R.E.
Nicholls, Albert, b. Birmingham, e. Birmingham, 1714, Pte., k. in a., F. & F., 31/10/14.
Nicholls, Frederick, b. Bournbrook, Birmingham, e. Birmingham (Bournbrook), 2565, Pte., k. in a., F. & F., 19/12/14.
Nicholls, Joseph, b. Birmingham, e. Warwick (Birmingham), 1243, Pte., d., F. & F., 5/10/14.
Noble, John William, b. Leeds, e. Leeds, 268254, Pte., k. in a., F. & F., 9/10/17, formerly 714, R.E.
Norman, Albert, b. Ombersley, Worcs, e. Warwick (Birmingham), 23217, Pte., d. of w., F. & F., 9/10/17.
Norman, Joseph, b. West Bromwich, Staffs, e. Birmingham (Smethwick, Staffs), 11427, Pte., d. of w., F. & F., 27/9/15.
Norman, Roland, b. Dunchurch, Warwicks, e. Warwick (Coventry), 6402, Pte., k. in a., F. & F., 19/12/14.
Norman, William John Patrick, b. Kamptee, India, e. Lichfield, Staffs, 1509, Cpl., k. in a., F. & F., 25/10/14.
Northeast, Albert, b. Adderbury, Wilts, e. London (Islington), 22080, Pte., k. in a., F. & F., 3/8/18, formerly 6561, London Regt.
Norton, Edward, b. Smethwick, Staffs, e. Birmingham, 524, Pte., d. of w., F. & F., 26/9/15.
Nunn, Hugh, b. Lye Green, Bucks, e. Aylesbury, Bucks (Lye Green), 24266, Pte., k. in a., F. & F., 9/10/17.
Nutt, George Edward, b. Bordesley, Birmingham, e. Birmingham, 4790, Pte., k. in a., F. & F., 4/5/17.
O'Brien, Michael Bernard, b. Camden St., Birmingham, e. Birmingham, 3697, Pte., k. in a., F. & F., 25/9/15.
O'Dowd, Michael, b. St. Joseph's, Liverpool, e. Newcastle-on-Tyne (Liverpool), 773, Pte., k. in a., F. & F., 24/10/14.
O'Hare, Patrick, b. Ballyconree, Clifton, Galway, e. Nuneaton, Warwicks (Clifton), 1591, Pte., k. in a., F. & F., 19/12/14.
Organ, Thomas Charles, b. Cheltenham, Glos., e. Warwick (Birmingham), 8604, Pte., d. of w., F. & F., 7/11/14.
Orme, Robert, b. Birmingham, e. Birmingham, 6845, Pte., k. in a., F. & F., 18/12/14.
Osborne, Arthur James, b. Vauxhall, Birmingham, e. Birmingham, 1870, Pte., d. of w., F. & F., 1/1/15.
Ostler, Arthur, b. Skirbeck, Lincoln, e. Boston, Lincs (London), 23575, Pte., k. in a., F. & F., 13/5/17, formerly 173749, R.E.
Over, Charles, b. Brinklow, Warwicks, e. Coventry, 1368, Pte., d. of w., F. & F., 20/10/14.
Overs, Alfred, b. Harbury, Warwicks, e. Warwick (Leamington, Warwicks), 1765, Pte., k. in a., F. & F., 19/12/14.
Overton, Albert Ernest, b. Coventry, e. Birmingham (Coventry), 1193, Sgt., k. in a., F. & F., 25/9/15.
Owen, Alfred, b. Ladywood, Birmingham, e. Birmingham, 3983, Pte., k. in a., F. & F., 3/9/16.
Owens, William Ramsey, b. Seago, Armagh, e. Belfast (Aldershot), 2464, Sgt. Drummer, d. of w., F. & F., 27/12/14, formerly 8017, R. Irish Fus.
Ozierbrook, John Henry, b. Atherstone, Warwicks, e. Nuneaton, Warwicks (Atherstone), 831, L/Cpl., k. in a., F. & F., 25/9/15.
Packwood, Thomas, b. Coventry, e. Coventry, 9030, Pte., d. of w., F. & F., 20/11/14.
Padbury, Samuel, b. Kineton, Warwicks, e. Rugby, Warwicks (Kineton), 21915, Pte., d., F. & F., 4/5/17.
Page, Harry, b. Gedney, Lincs, e. Portland (Wisbech, Cambs), 27153, Pte., k. in a., F. & F., 23/9/16, formerly 5192, Lincs Regt.
Palfreyman, Jess, b. Normanton, Derby, e. Nottingham (Normanton), 675, L/Cpl., k. in a., F. & F., 25/9/15.
Pallett, John James, b. Aspull, Wigan, Lancs, e. Leigh, Lancs, 10411, Pte., d. of w., F. & F., 29/9/15.
Palmer, John Wallace, b. Alvechurch, Worcs, e. Birmingham (Coleshill, Warwicks), 3982, Pte., k. in a., F. & F., 19/12/14.
Papworth, Charles, b. Grays, Essex, e. Warley, Essex (London) 9514, Pte., k. in a., F. & F., 31/10/14.
Pare, Albert Ernest, b. St. Mary's, Warwick, e. Warwick, 2012, Pte., d. of w., F. & F., 31/1/15.
Parker, George, b. Bordesley, Birmingham, e. Birmingham 3833, Pte., k. in a., F. & F., 14/7/16.

Parker, Ernest George, b. Balsall Heath, Birmingham, e. Birmingham, 5077, Pte., k. in a., F. & F., 18/5/15.
Parker, Howard, b. Tipton, Staffs, e. Dudley, Worcs (Tipton), 1366, Pte., k. in a., F. & F., 22/10/14.
Parker, Raymond George, b. Stratford-on-Avon, Warwicks, e. Warwick (Stratford-on-Avon), 800, L/Cpl., k. in a., F. & F., 25/9/15.
Parkes, Charles, b. Mancetter, Warwicks, e. Nuneaton, Warwicks (Atherstone), 2431, Pte., d. of w., F. & F., 23/12/14.
Parkes, Charles Leonard, b. Aston, Birmingham, e. Warwick (Birmingham), 9746, Pte., k. in a., F. & F., 19/12/14.
Parkes, Charles Sydney, b. Boultham, Lincs, e. Luton, Beds (Lincoln), 27033, Pte., k. in a., F. & F., 4/5/17, formerly 2649, Lincs Regt.
Parkes, Herbert Arthur, b. Ansley, Warwicks, e. Warwick (Arley, Warwicks), 9972, Pte., k. in a., F. & F., 25/9/15.
Parkes, Sidney Frank, b. Aston, Birmingham, e. Birmingham, 3681, Pte., d., F. & F., 18/8/17.
Parnham, William, e. Birmingham (Smethwick, Staffs), 200723, Pte., k. in a., F. & F., 10/10/17.
Parrish, John Edwin, b. Whittlesea, Cambs, e. Northampton (Newborough, Northants), 27155, Pte., d., F. & F., 4/11/16, formerly 5321, Lincs Regt.
Parry, Alfred, b. Birmingham, e. Warwick (Birmingham), 1301, Pte., d. of w., F. & F., 22/10/14.
Parsons, Henry, b. Loxley, Warwicks, e. Warwick (Kineton), 9949, Pte., d of w., F & F., 1/10/15.
Parsons, Joseph, b. Birmingham, e. Coventry (Birmingham), 387, Sgt., d. of w., F. & F., 7/7/17.
Parsons, Thomas, b. Small Heath, Birmingham, e. Birmingham, 3064, Pte., k. in a., F. & F., 25/9/15.
Parton, Stephen Thomas, b. Hanley, Staffs, e. Hanley, 8673, Pte., k. in a., F. & F., 25/9/15.
Partridge, Bert, b. Aston, Birmingham, e. Birmingham, 3899, Pte., k. in a., F. & F., 30/8/15.
Pascoe, Sampson Thomas, e. Falmouth, Cornwall, 23689, Pte., k. in a., F. & F., 9/10/17, formerly 1013, R.E.
Patrick, James, b. St. Andrews, Birmingham, e. Birmingham, 1781, Pte., k. in a., F. & F., 16/5/15.
Payne, William, b. Ashted, Birmingham, e. Birmingham, 4017, Pte., k. in a., F. & F., 25/9/15.
Payne, William John Henry, b. Wick, Worcs, e. Rugby, Warwicks (Lilbourne, Warwicks), 19336, Pte., k. in a., F. & F., 4/5/17.
Paynter, William, b. Birmingham, e. Birmingham, 549, Pte., k. in a., F. & F., 18/12/14.
Peacock, Harry, b. Nuneaton, Warwicks, e. Coventry (Nuneaton), 978, Pte., k. in a., F. & F., 25/9/15.
Pearl, Charles Joseph, b. Bow, Middx., e. Birmingham, 10714, Pte., k. in a., F. & F., 25/9/15.
Pearsall, Samuel, b. St. Martin's, Birmingham, e. Birmingham, 1294, L/Cpl., k. in a., F. & F., 17/5/15.
Pease, Montague, b. Warwick, e. Warwick, 267984, Pte., k. in a., F. & F., 9/10/17.
Pemberton, John, b. Birmingham, e. Birmingham, 600, Pte., k. in a., F. & F., 19/12/14.
Perkins, George Thomas, b. Weston-sub-Edge, Glos., e. Birmingham (Broadway, Worcs), 14453, Pte., k. in a., F. & F., 4/5/17.
Perkins, Harry, b. Birmingham, e. Birmingham, 16/1641, Pte., k. in a., F. & F., 9/10/17.
Perks, James Frederick, b. Birmingham, e. Birmingham, 1682, Pte., k. in a., F. & F., 7/11/14.
Perrin, George, b. Birmingham, e. Aston, Birmingham, 28613, Pte., d. of w., F. & F., 9/10/17.
Perry, John, b. Birmingham, e. Birmingham, 9574, Pte., k. in a., F. & F., 25/9/15.
Perry, Joseph, b. Balsall Heath, Birmingham, e. Birmingham, 2250, Pte., k. in a., F. & F., 25/9/15.
Perry, William John, b. Wrington, Somerset, e. Bristol, Glos. (Wrington), 23664, Pte., k. in a., F. & F., 1/10/17, formerly 179510, R.E.
Phelan, Frank Daniel, b. St. John's, Birmingham, e. Birmingham, 1328, Pte., k. in a., F. & F., 25/9/15.
Phelps, Edward, b. Foleshill, Coventry, e. Coventry (Foleshill), 206356, Pte., k. in a., F. & F., 9/10/17.
Phillips, Alfred, b. Leamington, Warwicks, e. Birmingham, 3425, Sgt., d. of w., F. & F., 7/11/15.
Phillips, Charles Edgar, b. Cheltenham, Glos., e. Warwick (Birmingham), 23073, Pte, k. in a., F. & F., 9/10/17.
Phillips, Henry James, b. St. Martin's, Birmingham, e. Warwick (Birmingham), 18981, Pte., d. of w., F. & F., 7/10/17.
Phillips, James Thomas, b. Birmingham, e. Birmingham, 9935, Pte., k. in a., F. & F., 25/9/15.
Phillips, Reuben, b. Hampton, Middx., e. Hounslow, Middx. (Hampton), 27151, Pte., d. of w., F. & F., 21/3/17, formerly 5305, Lincs Regt.
Phillips, Thomas Patrick, b. Birmingham, e. Birmingham, 4223, Pte., k. in a., F. & F., 25/9/15.
Phillipson, Frederick Kennington, b. Grimsby, Lincs, e. Grimsby, 7922, Pte., k. in a., F. & F., 31/10/14.
Philpott, Harold, e. Coventry, 24590, Pte., k. in a., F. & F., 9/10/17.
Phipps, Harold Thomas, b. Birmingham, e. Birmingham, 15611, Pte., k. in a., Italy, 26/10/18.
Pickard, Thmas, b. Coventry, e. Coventry, 9134, Pte., k. in a., F. & F., 31/10/14.
Picken, Harry, b. Sparkbrook, Birmingham, e. Birmingham, 2909, Pte., d. of w., F. & F., 18/6/15.
Pickering, John, b. Aston, Birmingham, e. Birmingham (Aston), 1601, Pte., k. in a., F. & F., 3/9/16.
Piper, Frederick, b. Small Heath, Birmingham, e. Warwick (Birmingham), 1996, Pte., k. in a., F. & F., 25/9/15.
Pittaway, Henry Percy, b. Dodwell, Worcs, e. Birmingham, 2879, Pte., d. of w., F. & F., 11/4/15.
Pittaway, Frederick Howlett, b. Kenilworth, Warwicks, e. Kenilworth, 30001, Pte., k. in a., F. & F., 3/9/16.
Plumridge, Frederick, b. Hyde, Bucks, e. High Wycombe, Bucks (Henley-on-Thames), 29986, Pte., k. in a., F. & F., 4/10/17, formerly 22938, Oxf. & Bucks L.I.
Pocklington, Arthur, b. Shadwell, Middx., e. Islington, Middx., 1873, Pte., d. of w., F. & F., 29/9/15.
Podmore, Francis George, b. Wilnecote, Warwicks, e. Nuneaton, Warwicks (Stockingford), 10749, Pte., k. in a., F. & F., 14/7/16.
Pooley, Bert, b. Worlington, Suffolk, e. Mildenhall, Suffolk (Worlington), 27242, Pte., k. in a., F. & F., 4/5/17, formerly 1785, Suffolk Regt.
Pooley, Bertie, b. Chatling, Kent, e. Shorncliffe, Kent (Chatling), 493, Pte., k. in a., F. & F., 19/12/14.
Portlock, Alfred, b. Birmingham, e. Birmingham, 6517, Pte., k. in a., F. & F., 6/12/14.
Potter, John Thomas, b. Nechells, Birmingham, e. Birmingham, 1980, L/Cpl., k. in a., F. & F., 25/9/15.
Potts, James Bowman, b. St. George's, Birmingham, e. Birmingham, 30054, Pte., k. in a., F. & F., 3/9/16.
Powers, Albert Edward, b. Bordesley, Birmingham, e. Birmingham, 3748, Pte., k. in a., F. & F., 17/6/15.
Powis, Charles Joseph, b. Birmingham, e. London (Birmingham), 3327, Pte., k. in a., F. & F., 13/5/17.
Preece, Cyril, b. Lee, London, e. Blackheath (Lee), 22123, Pte., d. of w., F. & F., 24/7/17, formerly 2090, London Regt.
Preedy, John Thomas, b. Curdworth, Birmingham, e. Birmingham (Neithrop, Banbury, Oxon), 1361, Pte., k. in a., F. & F., 6/11/14.
Prescott, Albert, b. Upton, Worcs, e. Coventry, 10518, Pte., k. in a., F. & F., 4/5/17.
Preston, Albert, b. Bale, Norfolk, e. Nottingham (Fakenham, Norfolk), 748, Pte., k. in a., F. & F., 7/11/14.
Preston, Arthur, b. Birmingham, e. Birmingham, 1072, Pte., k. in a., F. & F., 16/5/15.
Preston, Richard, b. Birmingham, e. Birmingham, 9598, Pte., k. in a., F. & F., 17/6/15.
Price, Frederick, b. Stourbridge, Staffs, e. Birmingham (Stourbridge), 597, Pte., k. in a., F. & F., 25/9/15.
Price, George Enos, b. Huddersfield, e. Coventry, 9900, Pte., k. in a., F. & F., 25/9/15.
Price, Richard, b. St. Phillip's, Bristol, e. Bristol, 721, L/Cpl., d. of w., F. & F., 24/8/15.
Price, Thomas, b. Hockley, Birmingham, e. Birmingham, 3746, Pte., d. of w., F. & F., 26/9/15.
Pridmore, Harold, e. Bourne, Lincs, 27005, L/Cpl., k. in a., F. & F., 9/10/17, formerly 5577, Linc. Regt.
Prin, William, b. Tottenham, Middx., e. Birmingham (London), 1965, Pte., k. in a., F. & F., 23/4/16.
Print, Harry Stanley, b. St. John's, Buckingham, e. Rugby, Warwicks, 1715, Pte., k. in a., F. & F., 8/6/15.
Pritchard, Alfred, b. Wolverhampton, Staffs, e. Birmingham, 4891, Pte., k. in a., F. & F., 3/9/16.
Pugh, Thomas Alfred, b. Ashted, Birmingham, e. Birmingham (Ashted), 1258, Pte., k. in a., F. & F., 25/9/15.
Quinney, William George, b. All Saints, Birmingham, e. Birmingham, 2710, Pte., k. in a., F. & F., 3/9/16.
Rachel, Arthur, b. Hockley, Birmingham, e. Birmingham, 3839, Pte., k in a., F. & F., 19/12/14.
Rachel, John Stephen, b. Ladywood, Birmingham, e. Birmingham, 3980, Pte., k. in a., F. & F., 19/12/14.
Rachell, William Henry, b. Birmingham, e. Birmingham, 8073, Pte., k. in a., F. & F., 19/12/14.
Radford, Arthur, b. Spondon, Derby, e. Birmingham, 6535, Pte., k. in a., F. & F., 25/9/15.
Radford, Harold, b. Exeter, Devon, e. Warwick, 10090, Pte., d. of w., F. & F., 3/9/16.
Randall, Arthur Ernest, b. Birmingham, e. Warwick (Birmingham), 6225, Sgt., k. in a., F. & F., 25/9/15.
Randall, Charles, b. Willesden, Middx., e. Harrow, Middx., 23005, Pte., k. in a., F. & F., 4/5/17, formerly 182094, R.E.
Randall, Walter George, b. Snodland, Kent, e. Maidstone (Snodland), 27100, Pte., k. in a., F. & F., 4/5/17, formerly 5347, Linc. Regt.
Ralley, Abram, b. Bedworth, Warwicks, e. Nuneaton, Warwicks (Bedworth), 1980, Pte., k. in a., F. & F., 11/6/15.
Rann, Louis Frederick, b. Birmingham, e. Birmingham, 35, Pte., k. in a., F. & F., 17/5/15.
Rawlings, Bernard Thomas James, b. Birmingham, e. Birmingham, 19483, Pte., k. in a., F. & F., 4/5/17.
Raybould, Arthur, b. Birmingham, e. Birmingham, 770, L/Cpl., k. in a., F. & F., 9/10/17.
Rayson, Herbert, b. Birmingham, e. Birmingham, 1788, Pte, k. in a., F. & F., 25/10/14.
Read, Alfred John, b. Quainton, Bucks, e. Aylesbury, Bucks (Quainton), 29930, Pte., d. of w., F. & F., 3/9/16, formerly 23040, Oxf. & Bucks L.I.
Reid, Michael, b. Atherstone, Warwicks, e. Nuneaton, Warwicks (Atherstone), 11500, Pte., d. of w., F. & F., 28/9/15.
Redgrave, Frederick, b. Birmingham, e. Coventry (Birmingham), 116, L/Cpl., d. of w., F. & F., 24/5/16.
Reeves, Samuel Albert, b. Brookfields, Birmingham, e. Warwick (Birmingham), 7196, Sgt., k. in a., F. & F., 7/11/14.
Richards, Albert, b. Admington, Glos., e. Birmingham (Welford-on-Avon, Warwicks), 5123, Pte., d. of w., F. & F., 17/7/16.
Richards, Albert Edward, b. Bideford, Devon, e. Barnstaple, Devon, 12269, Sgt., k. in a., F. & F., 3/9/16, formerly 7878, Devon Regt., and 31539, R.G.A.
Richards, Arthur, b. South Shields, Durham, e. Rugby, 3291, Cpl., k. in a., F. & F., 14/7/16.
Richards, Frederick William, b. Birmingham, e. Birmingham, 203196, Pte., k. in a., F. & F., 9/10/17.
Richardson, Charles, b. Pelsall, Staffs, e. Nuneaton (Pelsall), 4509, Pte., k. in a., F. & F., 9/10/17.

Richardson, Charles John, b. Bermondsey, Middx., e. Leicester, 8797, Pte., k. in a., F. & F., 21/10/14.
Ridgway, Herbert James, b. Akeley, Bucks, e. Buckingham (Akeley), 928, C.S.M., d. of w., F. & F., 19/6/15, formerly 5431, Oxf. & Bucks L.I.
Rigbey, Gerard, b. Selly Oak, Warwicks, e. Warwick (Birmingham), 1641, L/Cpl., d. of w., F. & F., 5/11/14.
Riley, Joseph, b. St. Michael's, Coventry, e. Coventry, 1293, Pte., d., Malta, 19/8/14.
Robbins, Frederick, b. Stretton-on-Dunsmore, Warwicks, e. Coventry (Stretton-on-Dunsmore), 2833, L/Cpl., k. in a., F. & F., 30/4/16.
Robbins, Raymond Thomas, b. Moor, Worcs, e. Warwick (Moor), 1283, Pte., k. in a., F. & F., 17/5/15.
Roberts, Charles Henry, b. Addlestone, Surrey, e. Guildford (Addlestone), 29942, Pte., d. of w., F. & F., 3/9/16, formerly 19735, Oxf. & Bucks L.I.
Roberts, Frederick, b. St. Michael's, Coventry, e. Coventry, 983, Pte., k. in a., F. & F., 25/9/15.
Roberts, George William, b. Putney, Surrey, e. Kingston-on-Thames (Putney), 571, Pte., k. in a., F. & F., 19/12/14.
Roberts, Harry, b. Wolverhampton, e. Birmingham, 1704, Pte., k. in a., F. & F., 19/12/14.
Roberts, Henry Charles, b. Abingdon, Northants, e. Northampton (Kingsthorpe, Northants), 23707, Pte., k. in a., F. & F., 4/5/17, formerly 174080, R.E.
Robinson, Arthur Robert, b. Aston, Birmingham, e. Warwick (Bordesley Green, Birmingham), 2438, Pte., k. in a., F. F., 19/12/14.
Robinson, Isaac, b. St. Mary's, Derby, e. Birmingham, 1961, Pte., k. in a., F. & F., 25/9/15.
Rochester, Clifford, b. Handsworth, Staffs, e. Birmingham, 1958, Pte., k. in a., F. & F., 31/10/14.
Rockell, Joseph, b. High Wycombe, Bucks, e. High Wycombe, 30018, L/Cpl., k. in a., F. & F., 3/9/16, formerly 18055, Oxf. & Bucks L.I.
Rodwell, Frederick George, b. Upper Winchendon, Bucks, e. Oxford (Upper Winchendon), 29939, L/Cpl., d. of w., F. & F., 4/5/17, formerly 18323, Oxf. & Bucks L.I.
Rogers, Edward, b. Birmingham, e. Birmingham, 760, Pte., k. in a., F. & F., 18/12/14.
Rogers, Edward, b. Birmingham, e. Birmingham, 202270, Pte., k. in a., F. & F., 8/10/17.
Rogers, Michael, b. Birmingham, e. Birmingham, 11471, Pte., d. of w., F. & F., 20/7/15.
Rooke, Harry, b. St. John's, Warwick, e. Nuneaton, 1979, Pte., k. in a., F. & F., 16/5/15.
Rooney, William, b. Birmingham, e. Warwick (Birmingham), 1142, Pte., k. in a., F. & F., 31/10/14.
Rose, Arthur, b. Balsall Heath, Warwicks, e. Birmingham, 3708, Pte., k. in a., F. & F., 25/9/15.
Rose, Frank Benjamin, b. Vauxhall, Birmingham, e. Birmingham, 15861, Pte., k. in a., F. & F., 9/10/17.
Rose, John, b. St. Michael's, Coventry, e. Coventry (Foleshill, Warwicks), 3087, Pte., k. in a., F. & F., 13/3/15.
Rossiter, John William, b. St. Mark's, Coventry, e. Coventry, 530, Pte., k. in a., F. & F., 21/11/14.
Rosten, Benjamin, b. Small Heath, Birmingham, e. Warwick (Small Heath), 1037, Pte., d., F. & F., 25/12/16.
Rowe, William, b. London, e. Birmingham (Whitechapel, Middx.), 4023, Pte., k. in a., F. & F., 19/12/14.
Rowland, Albert, b. Nuneaton, Warwicks, e. Coventry (Nuneaton), 10509, L/Cpl., k. in a., F. & F., 25/9/15.
Rowley, Arthur Ernest, b. Nuneaton, Warwicks, e. Nuneaton, 18032, Pte., k. in a., F. & F., 4/5/17.
Rudder, Henry Thomas, b. Birmingham, e. Birmingham, 8641, Pte., k. in a., F. & F., 3/9/16.
Rudland, Walter, b. Bath, e. Birmingham, 3470, Pte., k. in a., F. & F., 13/3/15.
Rushton, George William, b. Polesworth, Warwicks, e. Warwick (Nuneaton), 2421, A/Cpl., k. in a., F. & F., 28/6/17.
Rushton, John Howard, b. Tipton, Staffs, e. Birmingham (Great Bridge, Staffs), 10456, Pte., k. in a., F. & F., 4/5/17.
Russ, Percy, b. Hanley, Staffs, e. Birmingham, 3326, L/Cpl., d. of w., F. & F., 27/9/15.
Russell, John, b. Small Heath, Birmingham, e. Birmingham (Small Heath), 1222, Pte., k. in a., F. & F., 13/3/15.
Ryan, Albert, b. Birmingham, e. Warwick (Birmingham), 9297, Pte., k. in a., F. & F., 25/9/15.
Sabin, Frank, b. St. John's, Leamington, Warwicks, e. Warwick (Leamington), 3688, Pte., k. in a., F. & F., 25/9/15.
Sabin, William Henry, b. Oldbury, Staffs, e. Birmingham (Oldbury), 5174, L/Cpl., k. in a., F. & F., 10/10/17.
Sadler, Benjamin, b. Halesowen, Worcs, e. Birmingham (Halesowen), 9965, Pte., k. in a., F. & F., 25/9/15.
Sadler, Benjamin Charles, b. Birmingham, e. Warwick (Birmingham), 1158, Pte., k. in a., F. & F., 17/1/15.
Sandall, Harry, e. Spalding, Lincs (Stansfield Bourne, Lincs), 27173, Pte., k. in a., F. & F., 4/5/17, formerly 5057, Lincs Regt.
Sanders, Edward, b. Northampton, e. Birmingham (Northampton), 820, L/Cpl., k. in a., F. & F., 5/4/15.
Sanders, John, b. St. George's, Birmingham, e. Birmingham, 2463, Pte., k. in a., F. & F., 19/12/14.
Sargent, William, b. Gainsborough, Lincs, e. Grimsby (Gainsborough), 27170, Pte., k. in a., F. & F., 21/3/17, formerly 2564, Lincs Regt.
Satterthwaite, Albert Henry, b. Aston, Birmingham, e. Birmingham (Aston), 8630, L/Cpl., d. of w., F. & F., 3/9/16.
Saunders, Edgar, b. Tackley, Oxford, e. Warwick (Tackley), 4084, Pte., k. in a., F. & F., 3/9/16.
Saunders, George, b. Dover, Kent, e. Deal (Dover), 562, Pte., k. in a., F. & F., 19/12/14.
Savage, Henry, b. Derby, e. Birmingham, 1122, Pte., d. of w., F. & F., 26/12/14.
Savage, William, b. Bentham, Lancaster, e. Lancaster (Bentham), 8898, Pte., k. in a., F. & F., 9/11/17.
Savigar, Walter, b. Birmingham, e. Birmingham, 1044, Pte., k. in a., F. & F., 19/12/14.
Sawyer, Arthur, b. Kenilworth, Warwicks, e. Warwick (Kenilworth), 1137, Pte., k. in a., F. & F., 7/11/14.
Scotney, Fred, e. Lincoln (Bourne, Lincs), 26971, Pte., d., F. & F., 20/12/16, formerly 4857, Lincs Regt.
Scrivens, Arthur, b. Birmingham, e. Birmingham, 7944, Pte., k. in a., F. & F., 4/5/17.
Seccull, Joseph Henry, b. Aynho, Oxon, e. Warwick (Ashow, Warwicks), 2516, Pte., k. in a., F. & F., 25/9/15.
Seeley, John, b. All Saints, Warwick, e. Warwick, 1727, Pte., k. in a., F. & F., 2/1/15.
Senior, William August Montague, b. Poplar, Middx., e. London, 10775, Pte., k. in a., F. & F., 4/5/17.
Shakespeare, Arthur, e. Birmingham, 242929, Pte., k. in a., F. & F., 1/10/17.
Sharpe, John, e. Lincoln (Middle Rasen, Lincs), 26980, Pte., k. in a., F. & F., 4/5/17, formerly 3938, Lincs Regt.
Sharpe, Joseph, b. Hinckley, Leics, e. Nuneaton, Warwicks (Hinckley), 1267, Pte., k. in a., F. & F., 25/9/15.
Sharpe, William, b. Hinckley, Leics, e. Nuneaton, Warwicks (Hinckley), 1266, Pte., k. in a., F. & F., 19/12/14.
Sharratt, Joseph, b. St. Michael's, Coventry, e. Coventry, 1716, L/Cpl., k. in a., F. & F., 4/5/17.
Sheldrake, William Herbert, b. Speen, Berks, e. Maidenhead (Remenham, Berks), 23704, Pte., d. of w., F. & F., 5/5/17, formerly 173848, R.E.
Shelly, John Thomas, b. Stafford, e. Birmingham, 8773, C.S.M., k. in a., F. & F., 25/9/15.
Shepherd, Arthur, b. Coningsley, Lincs, e. New Leake, Lincs (Stickford, Lincs), 27179, Pte., k. in a., F. & F., 13/5/17, formerly 4949, Lincs Regt.
Sheppard, Edward, b. Birmingham, e. Birmingham, 6612, Cpl., k. in a., F. & F., 14/7/16.
Sherwin, George, b. Aston, Birmingham, e. Birmingham (Aston), 1244, Pte., k. in a., F. & F., 26/1/15.
Sherwood, William John, b. Chetwynd, Salop, e. Birmingham (Chetwynd), 1005, Pte., k. in a., F. & F., 9/10/17.
Shipway, Herbert Rossel, b. Stonehouse, Glos., e. Leamington, Warwicks, 19529, Pte., k. in a., F. & F., 11/10/17.
Shufflebotham, Edward, b. St. John's, Coventry, e. Coventry, 1645, L/Cpl., k. in a., F. & F., 4/5/17.
Shutt, John, b. St. Cuthbert, Birmingham, e. Birmingham, 1970, Pte., k. in a., F. & F., 25/9/15.
Sidwell, Howard, b. Birmingham, e. Nottingham (Bromsgrove, Worcs), 3211, Pte., k. in a., F. & F., 25/9/15.
Simcox, Henry, b. St. Andrew's, Birmingham, e. Birmingham, 4197, Cpl., k. in a., F. & F., 25/9/15.
Simpson, John, b. St. Mary's, Birmingham, e. Birmingham, 1387, Pte., k. in a., F. & F., 25/9/15.
Simpson, Samuel, b. Leasingham, Lincs, e. Sleaford, Lincs, 27096, Pte., k. in a., F. & F., 13/5/17, formerly 5097, Lincs Regt.
Sirey, Thomas, b. Carlisle, e. Carlisle, 19787, Pte., k. in a., F. & F., 15/7/16.
Sitch, Albert Edward, b. Aston, Birmingham, e. Birmingham (Aston), 1420, L/Cpl., k. in a., F. & F., 4/5/17.
Skinner, Jack, e. Birmingham, 201624, L/Cpl., d., F. & F., 25/6/18.
Slade, Frank, b. St. Peter's, Worcester, e. Worcester, 1579, Pte., k. in a., F. & F., 20/10/14.
Smant, Alfred Edward, b. Langley, Worcester, e. Birmingham (Langley), 30045, Pte., k. in a., F. & F., 3/9/16.
Smart, Frank, b. Birmingham, e. Warwick (Birmingham), 1302, Cpl., d. of w., F. & F., 3/11/14.
Smart, Henry, b. South Kilworth, Leics, e. London (Lichfield), 7653, A/Sgt., k. in a., F. & F., 3/9/16.
Smith, Alfred, b. Birmingham, e. Birmingham (Handsworth, Birmingham), 30055, Pte., k. in a., F. & F., 3/9/16.
Smith, Alfred James, b. Worcester, e. Birmingham, 8907, Pte., d. of w., F. & F., 9/11/14.
Smith, Arthur Thomas, b. Cuxwold, Lincs, e. Louth, Lincs (Holton-le-Clay, Lincs), 27168, Pte., d. of w., F. & F., 17/5/17, formerly 4946, Lincs Regt.
Smith, Arthur Francis, b. Studley, Warwicks, e. Stratford-on-Avon, Warwicks (Studley), 16366, Pte., k. in a., F. & F., 3/9/16.
Smith, Edgar, b. Birmingham, e. Birmingham, 6282, Pte., k. in a., F. & F., 19/12/14.
Smith, Edward John, b. Minworth, Birmingham, e. Warwick (Minworth, nr. Birmingham), 1612, Pte., k. in a., F. & F., 20/10/14
Smith, Edward, b. Birmingham, e. Warwick (Birmingham), 9152, Pte., d. of w., F. & F., 27/9/15.
Smith, Eli, b. Walsgrave-on-Sowe, Coventry, e. Coventry (Walsgrave-on-Sowe), 14563, Pte., k. in a., F. & F., 5/11/15.
Smith, George Edward, b. Birmingham, e. Birmingham, 1008, Pte., k. in a., F. & F., 19/12/14.
Smith, Henry, b. Birmingham, e. Warwick (Birmingham), 4385, Sgt., k. in a., F. & F., 25/9/15.
Smith, Horace, b. Hinckley, Leics, b. Nuneaton, Warwicks, 419, Pte., k. in a., F. & F., 19/12/14.
Smith, Isaac Ernest, b. Birmingham, e. Birmingham, 7423, L/Cpl., k. in a., F. & F., 19/12/14.
Smith, James, b. St. John's, Coventry, e. Coventry, 1888, Pte., k. in a., F. & F., 19/12/14.
Smith, John, b. Norwood, Middx., e. Birmingham (Southall, Middx.), 11849, Pte., d., F. & F., 10/12/15.
Smith, John William, b. Stoke Prior, Worcester, e. Birmingham (Stoke Prior), 257, L/Cpl., k. in a., F. & F., 15/7/16.
Smith, Joseph Harry, b. Birmingham, e. Birmingham, 1526, L/Cpl., k. in a., F. & F., 19/12/14.
Smith, Mark, b. Coventry, Warwicks, e. Warwick (Coventry), 6211, Pte., d. of w., F. & F., 16/5/15.

Smith, Sydney Charles, b. Ladywood, Birmingham, e. Warwick (Birmingham), 2088, Pte., k. in a., F. & F., 19/12/14.
Smith, Thomas, b. Birmingham, e. Birmingham (Smethwick, Staffs), 10722, Pte., k. in a., F. & F., 23/4/16.
Smith, William, b. Rumburgh, Suffolk, e. Thetford, Suffolk, 23668, Pte., d., F. & F., 19/2/17, formerly 176464, R.E.
Snooks, Harry, b. Handsworth, Staffs, e. Birmingham (Handsworth), 1102, Pte., k. in a., F. & F., 16/4/15.
Southam, Ernest Edward, b. Alderminster, Warwicks, e. Stratford-on-Avon, Warwicks, 17984, Pte., k. in a., F. & F., 4/5/17.
Southam, William Thomas, b. Haselor, Warwicks, e. Stratford-on-Avon, Warwicks (Haselor), 10909, Pte., k. in a., F. & F., 25/9/15.
Sparks, Ernest, b. Barton-on-Humber, Lincs, e. Barton-on-Humber, 27113, Pte, k. in a., F. & F., 13/5/17, formerly 3226, Lincs Regt.
Speak, Oliver, b. Birmingham, e. Birmingham, 1588, Pte., d. of w., F. & F., 28/10/14.
Spencer, Albert George Haynes, b. Far Cotton, Northants, e. Bletchley, Bucks (Northampton), 29985, Pte., k. in a., F. & F., 3/9/16, formerly 22961, Oxf. & Bucks L.I.
Spencer, Harold, b. St. Mary's, Torquay, Devon, e. Stockton-on-Tees, Durham (Middlesbrough), 1675, Cpl., d., Italy, 8/11/18.
Spencer, Samuel, b. Hangingheaton, Dewsbury, Yorks, e. Nuneaton, Warwicks (Bedworth, Warwicks), 2052, Pte., k. in a., F. & F., 24/10/14.
Spicer, Arthur Henry, b. Kenilworth, Warwicks, e. Kenilworth, 201676, Pte., d., F. & F., 25/5/18.
Spofford, Charles, b. Sheffield, Yorks, e. Birmingham, 11531, Pte., k. in a., F. & F., 4/5/17.
Spotswood, James, b. St. Marks, Barrow, Lancs, e. Barrow, 6549, Pte., k. in a., F. & F., 10/12/14.
Spriggs, Ephraim, b. St. Paul's, Birmingham, e. Birmingham, 3538, Pte., k. in a., F. & F., 25/9/15.
Standley, Christopher, b. Birmingham, e. Birmingham, 7162, Pte., k. in a., F. & F., 21/3/17.
Stanley, James Thomas, b. Cubbington, Leamington, Warwicks, e. Warwick (Leamington), 1618, Pte., d. of w., F. & F., 12/11/14.
Stanton, Frank, b. All Saints, Warwick, e. Aldershot, Hants (Warwick), 8815, Pte., k. in a.. F. & F., 31/10/14.
Starling, George Baron, e. Plymouth, 23605, Pte., k. in a., F. & F., 4/5/17, formerly 2057, R.E.
Steadman, Bertram, b. St. Thomas, Birmingham, e. Birmingham, 3497, Pte., k. in a., F. & F., 4/5/17.
Steadman, Joe, b. Birmingham, e. Birmingham, 1087, Pte., k. in a., F. & F., 25/9/15.
Steele, James Henry, b. Birmingham, e. Birmingham, 1818, Pte., k. in a., F. & F., 7/11/14.
Stephens, George, b. Birmingham, e. Birmingham, 23670, Pte., d. of w., F. & F., 14/10/17, formerly 188821, R.E.
Stevens, Arthur, b. Leicester, e. Stoneleigh, Warwicks (Leicester), 94, Cpl., k. in a., F. & F., 3/9/16.
Stevens, John Alfred, b. Newtown, Leicester, e. Rugby, Warwicks (Bedworth, Warwicks), 7680, Pte., d. of w., F. & F., 6/10/17.
Stevens, Thomas, b. Stoke Bardolph, Nottingham, e. Luton, Beds (Ashby, Lincs), 26968, Pte., k. in a., F. & F., 4/5/17, formerly 2760, Lincs Regt.
Stevens, William David, b. St George's, Reading, e. Reading, 1566, Pte, k. in a., F. & F., 25/9/15.
Stevenson, William, b. Birmingham, e. Birmingham, 23926, Pte., k. in a., F. & F., 1/10/17.
Stiles, William, b. Sherborne, Warwicks, e. Coventry, 1323, C.S.M., d. of w., F. & F., 26/7/17.
Stirks, Alfred Albert, b. Hockley, Birmingham, e. Birmingham (Hockley), 1559, Pte., k. in a., F. & F., 9/10/17.
Stokes, Albert George, b. Ladywood, Birmingham, e. Warwick (Ladywood), 1658, Pte., k. in a., F. & F., 17/6/15.
Stokes, Alfred, b. Shepton Mallett, Som., e. Birmingham, 3051, Pte., d. of w., F. & F., 27/10/17.
Stokes, Allen, b. Silverdale, Staffs, e. Nuneaton, Warwicks (Silverdale), 4515, Pte., k. in a., F. & F., 25/9/15.
Stone, Christopher James, b Norwich, e. Warwick (Norwich), 1758, Pt., k. in a., F. & F., 3/9/16.
Storer, Oliver Charles, b. Polesworth,, Warwicks, e. Atherstone, Warwicks (Polesworth), 17060, Pte., d. of w., F. & F., 23/7/16.
Storer, William, b. St. Phillips, Birmingham, e. Birmingham, 2016, L/Cpl., k. in a., F. & F., 16/5/15.
Strevens, Albert, b. Camberwell, Surrey, e. London, 1461, L/Cpl., k. in a., F. & F., 7/11/14.
Stubbs, William, b. St. Peters, Oldham, Lancs, e. Birmingham (Oldham), 4700, Pte., k. in a., F. & F., 4/5/19.
Such, Joseph, b. Stratford-on-Avon, Warwicks, e. Stratford-on-Avon (Birmingham), 21864, Pte., d., F. & F., 27/9/17.
Sullivan, Thomas Peter, b. Whitechapel, Middx., e. Stratford, London, 2206, Pte., k. in a., F. & F., 3/9/16.
Sumner, Ernest, b. Kineton, Warwicks, e. Rugby, Warwicks (Southam), 10684, Pte., k. in a., F. & F., 3/9/16.
Swain, George, b. Ladywood, Birmingham, e. Warwick (Birmingham)), 1653, Pte., k. in a., F. & F., 31/10/14.
Swain, Sidney Walter, b. Yardley, Birmingham, e. Birmingham, 3942, Pte., k. in a., F. & F., 17/5/15.
Swallow, Albert, b. Ashted, Birmingham, e. Birmingham, 3692. Pte., k. in a., F. & F., 19/12/14.
Swann, Percy Joseph, b. St. Lukes, Birmingham, e. Birmingham, 8652, Pte., d. of w., F. & F., 3/10/17.
Swash, William, e. Birmingham (King's Norton, Nr. Birmingham), 241629, Pte., k. in a., F. & F., 9/10/17.
Swift, John, b. Birmingham, e. Warwick (Birmingham), 1136, Pte., k. in a., F. & F., 10/10/14.
Swingler, Walter Henry, b. Birmingham, e. Birmingham, 774, Sgt., k. in a., F. & F., 25/9/15.
Swinnerton, Samuel John, b. Stoke-on-Trent, Staffs, e. Warwick (Stoke-on-Trent), 4055, Pte., k. in a., F. & F., 25/9/15.
Taberner, George, b. Woodburn Green, High Wycombe, Bucks, e. Warwick (Nuneaton, Warwicks), 1803, Pte., k. in a., F & F., 11/5/15.
Talbot, John, b. Ashted, Birmingham, e. Birmingham (Ashted), 3190, Pte., k. in a., F. & F., 25/9/15.
Taylor, Ellis, b. Birmingham, e. Birmingham, 7977, Pte., d., F. & F., 22/3/15.
Taylor, Francis, b. St. Mary's, Birmingham, e. Birmingham, 1819, Pte., k. in a., F. & F., 19/12/14.
Taylor, Herbert, b. Holy Trinity, Coventry, e. Coventry, 1222, Pte., d., Italy, 8/11/18, M.M.
Taylor, Richard Scott, b. Leicester, e. Birmingham, 1925, Sgt., k. in a., F. & F., 14/7/16.
Taylor, George William, b. Bury, Lancs, e. Bury, 22092, Pte., k. in a., F. & F., 4/5/17, formerly 2053, Lancs Fus.
Teare, James, b. Liverpool, e Birmingham, 30038, Pte., k. in a., F. & F., 13/5/17.
Tees, William, b. Moseley, Birmingham, e. Warwick (Handsworth, Staffs), 2340, Pte., d. of w., F. & F., 20/12/14.
Tew, Edward Whiteman, b. St. Luke's, Leamington, e. Warwick (Leamington), 2346, Pte., k. in a., F. & F., 16/5/15.
Thomas, Lionel Edward, b. Foleshill, Coventry, e. Nuneaton, Warwicks (Foleshill), 1752, Cpl., k. in a., F. & F., 25/9/15.
Thompson, Alfred, b. St. Michael's, Coventry, e. Coventry, 1073, Pte., d. of w., F. & F, 21/11/14.
Thompson, George Alfred, b. Saltley, Birmingham, e. Birmingham, 3689, Pte., k. in a., F. & F., 25/9/15.
Thompson, Harry Walter, b. Selly Oak, Birmingham, e. Birmingham, 1325, Pte., k. in a., F. & F., 13/3/15.
Thornicroft, Albert, b. Manchester, e. Birmingham, 1783, Pte., k. in a., F. & F., 29/8/15.
Thorpe, Bert, b. Boultham, Lincoln, e. Lincoln (Boultham), 26973, Pte., k. in a., F. & F., 11/10/17, formerly 4215, Lincs Regt.
Thorpe, Walter, b. Worcester, e. Coventry, 5080, Pte., d. of w., F. & F., 26/6/15.
Thrupp, Harry, b. Droitwich, Worcs, e. Birmingham, 13341, Pte., d. of w., F. & F.. 4/4/16.
Tillson, Joseph Edwin, b. Atherstone, Warwicks, e. Nuneaton, Warwicks (Atherstone), 1638, Sgt., k. in a., F. & F., 3/9/16, D.C.M.
Tilsley, Albert, b. Ladywood, Birmingham, e. Birmingham, 1513, Pte., k. in a., F. & F., 30/12/14.
Timby, George Frederick, b. Holy Trinity, Gainsborough, Lincs, e. Gainsborough, 27183, Pte., k. in a., F. & F., 6/1/17, formerly 580, Lincs Regt.
Todd, Frederick Charles, b. Clerkenwell, Middx., e. London, 4006, Pte., k. in a., F. & F., 12/3/15.
Tongue, Frank, b. Sandwell, West Bromwich, Staffs, e. West Bromwich, 3421, Pte., k. in a., F. & F., 25/9/15.
Tonkin, James Edwin, b. Bristol, e. Bristol, 16/2068, Pte., k. in a., F. & F., 5/8/18, formerly 148744, R.F.A.
Tordoff, Isaac, b. Hartshill, Staffs, e. Birmingham (Harts Hill), 1728, Pte., k. in a., F. & F., 31/10/14.
Towers, George Henry, b. Dadlington, Leics, e. Nuneaton, Warwicks (Attleborough, Warwicks), 14980, Pte., k. in a., F. & F., 3/9/16.
Townsend, Andrew, b. St. Michael's, Coventry, Warwicks, e. Coventry, 147, Pte., k. in a., F. & F., 19/12/14.
Townsend, Tom, b. Tamworth, Warwicks, e. Nuneaton, Warwicks, 30477, Pte., d. of w., F. & F., 26/11/18.
Townsend, William Arthur, b. Holy Trinity, Coventry, e. Coventry, 926, Pte., k. in a., F. & F., 26/9/15.
Trinder, Walter Victor, b. Sutton Stanton Harcourt, Oxford, e. Birmingham (Sutton Stanton Harcourt), 30056, Pte., k. in a., F. & F., 4/5/17.
Trowell, Alfred Edgar, b. Sittingbourne, Kent, e. Sittingbourne, 23650, Pte., k. in a., F. & F., 9/10/17, formerly 180674, R.E.
Trueman, Zachariah, b. Birmingham, e. Birmingham, 1542, Pte., k. in a., F. & F., 3/11/14.
Tucker, John Wallis, e. Plymouth, Devon (Yealmpton, Devon), 23547, Pte., d. of w., F. & F., 12/3/17, formerly 1981, R.E.
Turbill, Henry, b. Birmingham, e. Warwick (Birmingham), 9876, Pte., k. in a., F. & F., 19/12/14.
Turley, Frank, b. Birmingham, e. Birmingham, 6988, Pte., k. in a., F. & F., 19/12/14.
Turner, Charles, b. Brent Eleigh, Suffolk, e. Lavenham, Suffolk, 27234, Pte., k. in a., F. & F., 28/2/17, formerly 1689, Suffolk Regt.
Turner, Edwin, b. Birmingham, e. Birmingham. 6999, L/Cpl., d. of w., F. & F., 6/12/14.
Turner, James, b. Epwell, Oxon, e. Banbury, Oxon (Hornton, Oxon), 24221, Pte., k. in a., F. & F., 5/10/17.
Turner, Walter Henry, b. Birmingham, e. Birmingham, 10229, L/Cpl., d. of w., F. & F., 26/10/15.
Turner, William Paul, b. Birmingham, e. Warwick (Birmingham), 1694, Cpl., k. in a., F. & F., 31/10/14.
Turnock, William George, b. All Saints', Birmingham, e. Warwick (Smethwick, Staffs), 2505, Pte., k. in a., F. & F., 16/5/15.
Turrell, Frank, b. St. Paul's, Leamington, e. Coventry (Leamington), 1176, Pte., k. in a., F. & F., 23/4/16.
Turvey, Charles, b. Birmingham, e. Birmingham, 1127, Pte., k. in a., F. & F., 31/10/14.
Twamley, Leonard, b. Birmingham, e. Birmingham, 29946, L/Cpl., k. in a., F. & F., 2/4/17, formerly 22339, Oxford & Bucks L.I.
Twort, Thomas Walter, b. St. Andrew's, Croydon, Surrey, e. London (Croydon), 852, Pte., d. of w., F. & F., 14/11/14.
Varney, Thomas, b. London, e. Warwick (Leamington, Warwicks), 1885, Pte., k. in a., F. & F., 7/11/14.

Varney, David Henry, b. Blanor, Mon., e. Warwick, 2528, Pte., d. of w., F. & F., 14/2/15.
Vaughan, Edward George, b. Birmingham, e. Birmingham, 440, Sgt., k. in a., F & F., 14/7/16.
Vaux, Mark, b. Wolverhampton, Staffs, e. Birmingham, 2455, Pte., d., F. & F., 23/12/14
Vear, Henry, b. Spilsby, Lincs, e. Wainfleet, Lincs, 27073, Pte., k. in a., F & F., 4/5/17, formerly 4943, Lincs Regt.
Verner, Dudley, b. Malta, e. Warwick (Chelsea, London), 2126, L/Cpl., k. in a., F. & F., 7/11/14.
Vickers, Thomas, b. Birmingham, e. Birmingham, 1040, Sgt., k. in a., F. & F., 19/10/14.
Vincent, Charles Henry, b. Grantham, Lincs, e. Northampton (Peterborough, Northants), 2406, Pte., d. of w., F. & F., 17/5/15.
Vowles, William Henry, b. Leamington, Warwicks, e. Warwick (Leamington), 1691, Pte., k. in a., F. & F., 16/5/15.
Wakefield, Charles William Pearson, e. Lincoln, 26975, L/Cpl., k. in a., F. & F., 23/10/18, formerly 4625, Lincs Regt.
Walker, Robert, b. Aston, Birmingham, e. Birmingham (Aston), 1582, Pte., k. in a., F. & F., 4/5/17.
Wallace, Henry, b. Scotswood, Northumberland, e. Birmingham (Newcastle-on-Tyne), 1023, Pte., k. in a., F. & F., 13/5/17.
Wallis, Ernest, b. Hackney, Middx., e. Stepney, Middx. (Shadwell), 23694, Pte., k. in a., F. & F., 9/10/17, formerly 177746, R.E.
Walters, Thomas Francis, b. Hockley, Birmingham, e. Birmingham, 1673, Pte., k. in a., F. & F., 7/6/15.
Walton, Thomas, b. Birmingham, e. Warwick (Birmingham), 8757, Pte., k. in a., F. & F., 28/10/14.
Ward, Fred, b. Desborough, Northants, e. Desborough, 27185, Pte., k. in a., F. & F., 28/2/17, formerly 5318, Lincs Regt.
Ward, Frederick, b. Brixworth, Northants, e. Nuneaton, Warwicks, 11687, Pte., d. of w., F. & F., 17/7/16.
Ward, James, e. Long Sutton, Lincoln (Damsmere, Lincs), 27021, Pte., k. in a., F. & F., 4/5/17, formerly 5562, Lincs Regt.
Ward, Samuel Ernest, b. Smethwick, Staffs, e. Birmingham, 23251, Pte., d. of w., F. & F., 8/7/17.
Ward, William, b. Birmingham, e. Birmingham, 9966, Sgt., k. in a., F. & F., 25/9/15.
Warder, William, b. Birmingham, e. Coventry, 10465, Pte., k. in a., F. & F., 25/9/15.
Waring, George Frederick, b. St. Paul's, Birmingham, e. Birmingham, 3639, Pte., k. in a., F. & F., 4/4/16.
Warner, Walter, b. Stockton, Warwicks, e. Coventry (Leamington, Warwicks), 989, Pte., k. in a., F. & F., 18/5/18.
Warren, Albert, b. St. Stephen's, Birmingham, e. Birmingham, 11820, Pte., k. in a., F. & F., 3/9/16.
Warwick, Arthur Percy, b. St. John's, Leamington, Warwicks, e. Warwick (Leamington), 1568, Pte., k. in a., F. & F., 3/9/16.
Waters, George, b. St. Michael's, Birmingham, e. Birmingham, 11623, Drummer, k. in a., F. & F., 4/5/17.
Watkins, James, b. Brinklow, Warwicks, e. Coventry, 1367, Pte., k. in a., F. & F., 25/10/14.
Watts, Basil Edgar Charles, b. Yardley, Birmingham, e. Birmingham, 2534, Pte., k. in a., F. & F., 25/9/15.
Watts, Frank Allan, b. Edinburgh, e. Richmond, Yorks (Brighton, Sussex), 22093, Pte., k. in a., F. & F., 4/5/17, formerly 4992, Durham L.I.
Wearing, Arthur, b. Handsworth, Staffs, e. Birmingham (Smethwick, Staffs), 1423, Pte., k. in a., F. & F., 7/11/14.
Weatherill, David, e. Lincoln (North Hykeham, Lincs), 27015, Pte., k. in a., F. & F., 10/12/16, formerly 5572, Lincs Regt.
Weaver, Frederick, b. Warwick, e. Birmingham, 7024, Cpl., k. in a., F. & F., 3/9/16.
Webb, Arthur, b. Smethwick, Staffs, e. Birmingham (Smethwick), 1255, Pte., k. in a., F. & F., 25/9/15.
Webb, Ernest Thomas, b. Aston, Birmingham, e. Birmingham, 1832, Pte., k. in a., F. & F., 25/9/15.
Webb, John Reginald, b. Polesworth, Warwicks, e. Nuneaton, Warwicks (Polesworth), 2483, A/Cpl., k. in a., F. & F., 16/5/15.
Webb, William, b. Cinderford, Glos., e. Coventry, 18112, Pte., d. of w., F. & F., 4/5/17.
Webster, John, b. Kildare, e. Birmingham, 7936, Pte., k. in a., F. & F., 7/11/14.
Webster, Reginald Ernest, b. Cowley, St. John's, Oxford, e. Oxford, 29984, Pte., d. of w., F. & F., 3/9/16, formerly 22962, Oxford & Bucks L.I.
Weedon, William, b. Stoke Mandeville, Aylesbury, Bucks, e. London (Stoke Mandeville), 755, Pte., d. of w., F. & F., 24/10/14
Weeks, William Arthur, b. Birmingham, e. Birmingham, 1392, L/Cpl., k. in a., F. & F., 29/3/15.
Welbourn, Jacob, b. Spalding, Lincs, e. Luton, Beds (Spalding), 27213, Pte., k. in a., F. & F., 4/5/17, formerly 2615, Lincs Regt.
Wellings, Edwin, b. Astley, Shrewsbury, Salop, e. Warwick (Southam, Warwicks), 1059, Pte., k. in a., F. & F., 19/12/14.
Wells, Sydney, b. Aston, Birmingham, e. Birmingham (Aston), 1939, Pte., d., F. & F., 19/6/15.
West, Thomas, b. Birmingham, e. Birmingham (Portland, Dorset), 9160, Sgt., k. in a., F. & F., 24/10/14.
Weston, Harry, b. Birmingham, e. Birmingham, 1036, Pte., k. in a., F. & F., 7/11/14.
Whillock, David, b. Winson Green, Birmingham, e. Birmingham, 10426, L/Cpl., k. in a., F. & F., 25/9/15.
Whistlecraft, William Arthur, b. Eye, Suffolk, e. Eye, 27236, Pte., k. in a., F. & F., 24/10/16, formerly 1774, Suffolk Regt.
Whitaker, Harold, b. Linton, Derby, e. Nuneaton, Warwicks (Tamworth, Warwicks), 1787, Pte., d., F. & F., 3/11/14.
White, Charles, b. Surbiton, Surrey, e. Chatham, Kent (Surbiton), 5156, Pte., k. in a., F. & F., 19/10/14.
White, Edward, b. St. Bartholomew's, Birmingham, e. Warwick (Birmingham), 443, Pte., d. of w., F. & F., 25/9/15.
White, Ernest Leonard, b. Stoke, Coventry, e. Coventry, 1318, Pte., k. in a., F. & F., 19/12/14.
White, Fred, b. Sutton Coldfield, Warwicks, e. Birmingham (Sutton Coldfield), 16/1782, Pte., k. in a., F. & F., 28/10/17.
White, George, b. St. Georges, Birmingham, e. Birmingham, 1863, Pte., d. of w., F. & F., 21/3/15.
White, George Henry, b. St. Andrews, Birmingham, e. Birmingham, 2237, Pte., k. in a., F. & F., 13/3/15.
White, William Henry, b. St. Michaels, Coventry, e. Coventry, 11357, Pte., d. of w., F. & F., 8/5/16.
Whitehall, James, b. Thornboro', Bucks, e. Clowne, Derbyshire 54467, Pte., k. in a., F. & F., 27/10/18, formerly 117209, Notts and Derby Regt.
Whitehouse, Henry Howard, b. Birmingham, e. Birmingham, 5066, A/Sgt., k. in a., F. & F., 15/4/18.
Whitehouse, Joseph Charles, b. Aston, Birmingham, e. Birmingham, 8449, Cpl., k. in a., F. & F., 8/10/17, M.M.
Whitehouse, Samuel James, b. Birmingham, e. Ross (Wootton Wawen, Warwicks), 6892, Pte., k. in a., F. & F., 19/12/14.
Whitehouse, William Harold, b. Walsall, Staffs, e. Walsall, 15871, L/Cpl., d., F. & F., 15/9/16.
Whittall, James, b. Birmingham, e. Birmingham, 1160, L/Cpl., k. in a., F. & F., 25/9/15.
Whittaker, George, b. Digbeth, Birmingham, e. Birmingham, 3699, Pte., k. in a., F. & F., 25/9/15.
Wicks, Albert, b. Binfield, Berks, e. Reading, Berks (Binfield), 5088, Pte., k. in a., F. & F., 7/5/18.
Wiggs, John Henry, b. Hitchin, Cambs., e. Rugby, Warwicks (Calvert, Bucks), 15909, L/Cpl. d. of w., F. & F., 22/3/17.
Wilcox, Arthur, b. Foleshill, Coventry, e. Coventry (Longford, nr. Coventry), 9913, Pte., k. in a., F. & F., 25/9/15.
Wilcox, George, b. Woolston, Hants, e. Bristol, Glos., 10484, Pte., k. in a., F. & F., 25/9/15.
Wilkins, George Samuel, b. Branston, Stafford, e. Bedworth, Warwicks (Woodville, Derbyshire), 17677, Pte., k. in a., F. & F., 3/9/16.
Willcock, Frederick Rolling, b. Lostmithiel, Cornwall, e. Grimsby, Lincs (Putney, London), 27191, Pte., d., F. & F., 5/1/17, formerly 5352, Lincs Regt.
Willdey, Gilbert Bennett, b. Water Orton, Warwicks, e. Colchester, Essex (Water Orton), 16044, Pte., k. in a., F. & F., 15/7/16.
Willetts, George, b. Winson Green, Birmingham, e. Warwick (Birmingham), 848, Cpl., k. in a., F. & F., 1/11/14.
Willetts, Thomas Henry, b. Birmingham, e. Birmingham, 1389, Pte., k. in a., F. & F., 7/11/14.
Williams, Arthur, b. Great Washbourne, Glos., e. Warwick, 6554, Pte., k. in a., F. & F., 19/12/14.
Williams, Arthur, b. Birmingham, e. Warwick (Birmingham), 8726, A/Sgt., k. in a., F. & F., 3/9/16.
Williams, Charles Thomas, b. St. Andrews, Birmingham, e. Birmingham, 6451, Sgt., k. in a., F. & F., 28/2/17.
Williams, Reginald, b. Bermondsey, Middx, e. Warwick (Stretton-on-Fosse, Glos), 2506, L/Cpl., d. of w., F. & F., 5/10/15.
Williams, Richard Harry, b. Miles Platting, Manchester, e. Warwick (Manchester), 1983, Pte., k. in a., F. & F., 19/12/14.
Williams, Samuel, b. Saltley, Birmingham, e. Birmingham, 4878, Pte., k. in a., F. & F., 3/6/16.
Will, William Henry, b. Coventry, e. Warwick (Coventry), 965, Pte., k. in a., F. & F., 16/11/14.
Wilson, Horace Harold, b. Nottingham, e. Birmingham, 8959, Pte., k. in a., F. & F., 19/10/14.
Wilson, John, b. Birmingham, e. Birmingham (Upper Dargle, Co. Dublin), 6679, Sgt., k. in a., F. & F., 25/8/15.
Wilson, Thomas Enoch, b. Stockton, Melbourne, Victoria, Australia, e. Nuneaton, Warwicks, 1579, Pte., k. in a., F. & F., 18/12/14.
Windridge, George, b. Hipstock, Leics, e. Warwick (Stockingford, Warwicks), 14834, Pte., k. in a., F. & F., 3/9/16.
Windridge, Lawrence, b. Radford, Coventry, e. Coventry, 2805, Pte., k. in a., F. & F., 9/10/17.
Wingfield, Albert, b. Birmingham, e. Birmingham, 709, L/Cpl., k. in a., F. & F., 13/5/17.
Winn, Arthur, b. Grimsby, Lincs, e. Grimsby (Cleethorpes, Lincs), 27195, Pte., k. in a., F. & F., 10/1/17, formerly 5388, Lincs Regt.
Wise, John Henry, b. St. Mary's, Leamington, Warwicks, e. Warwick (Leamington), 2008, Pte., k. in a., F. & F., 20/4/15.
Wood, Cecil Harry, b. Yeovil, Som., e. Rugby, Warwicks (New Bilton, Warwicks), 10466, A/Cpl., k. in a., F. & F., 4/5/17.
Woods, Harry Aveling, e. Lincoln, 27205, Pte., k. in a., F. & F., 28/2/17, formerly 5516, Lincs Regt.
Wood, James, b. St. Michael's, Coventry, e. Coventry, 1672, Pte., k. in a., F. & F., 21/7/15.
Woodcock, Fred, b. Potterhanworth, Lincs, e. Lincoln (Potterhanworth), 27201, Sgt., k. in a., F. & F., 30/3/17, formerly 5104, Lincs Regt.
Woodcock, Walter, b. Peckham, Middx., e. Birmingham, 860, Pte., k. in a., F. & F., 24/10/14.
Woodhead, Thomas, b. St. Michael's, Coventry, e. Warwick, 1619, Pte., k. in a., F. & F., 20/2/15.
Wooding, Frederick Charles, b. Stratford, Essex, e. London, 858, Sgt., k. in a., F. & F., 25/10/14.
Woodley, Percival Charles, b. St. Ebbes, Oxford, e. Oxford (Cassington, Oxon), 29997, L/Cpl., k. in a., F. & F., 9/10/17, formerly 22963, Oxf. & Bucks L.I.
Wall, Alfred, b. Birmingham, e. Birmingham, 1298, C.S.M., k. in a., F. & F., 2/4/16.
Worrall, William Henry, b. St. Michael's Coventry, e. Coventry 2839, Sgt., k. in a., F. & F., 3/9/16.

Worrall, William John, b. Small Heath, Birmingham, e. Birmingham (Shirley, nr. Birmingham), 19490, Pte., k. in a., F. & F., 11/10/17.
Worrall, Owen Arthur, b. Long Itchington, Warwicks, e. Rugby, Warwicks (Long Itchington), 1678, Pte., d., F. & F., 21/7/16.
Wragg, Thomas Arthur, b. Birmingham, e. Ross (Birmingham), 6121, L/Cpl., k. in a., F. & F., 19/12/14.
Wright, Henry James, b. Birmingham, e. Birmingham, 7392, A/Sgt., k. in a., F. & F., 16/5/15.
Wright, Herbert Joseph, b. Newington, Surrey, e. London (Battersea), 8021, Pte., k. in a., F. & F., 15/11/14.
Wright, James Alfred, b. Stratford-on-Avon, Warwicks, e. Stratford-on-Avon, 1935, Pte., d. of w., F. & F., 7/10/15.
Wright, John, b. Ladywood, Birmingham, e. Birmingham (Ladywood, Birmingham), 1560, Pte., k. in a., F. & F., 19/12/14.
Wright, William, b. Winchmore Hill, Bucks, e. High Wycombe, Bucks (Amersham, Bucks), 18521, L/Cpl., d. of w., F. & F., 21/10/17, formerly 25307, Som. L.I.
Yates, John, b. St. George's, Birmingham, e. Birmingham, 3758, Pte., k. in a., F. & F., 19/12/14.
Yates, William, b. Birmingham, e. Birmingham, 8507, Pte., k. in a., F. & F., 25/10/14.
Yeates, William Henry, b. St. Martin's, Birmingham, e. Birmingham, 14388, Pte., k. in a., F. & F., 3/9/16.
Yeomans, Herbert, b. Balsall Heath, Birmingham, e. Birmingham, 1414, Pte., k. in a., F. & F., 12/3/15.
Yorke, Edward Walter, b. Birmingham, e. Birmingham, 8990, C.S.M., d. of w., F. & F., 30/8/15.
Young, Horace, b. All Saints, Birmingham, e. Warwick (Leamington, Warwicks), 1769, Pte., d. of w., F. & F., 8/11/14.
Young, William, b. High Wycombe, Bucks, e. High Wycombe, 29983, Pte., d. of w., F. & F., 9/10/17, formerly 23028 Oxf. & Bucks L.I.

3rd Battalion.

Blake, Walter, b. Alcester, Warwicks, e. Alcester (Moreton-in-Marsh, Glos.), 9978, Pte., d., Home, 1/7/15.
Blount, John, b. Atherstone, Warwicks, e. Warwick (Mansfield, Notts), 10723, Pte., d., Home, 12/10/16.
Bromage, Arthur Edward, b. Coventry, e. Warwick, 58101, Pte., d., Home, 9/8/18.
Burgess, Robert Sidney, b. Birmingham, e. Birmingham, 58309, Pte., d., Home, 29/8/18.
Cartwright, Benjamin, b. Birmingham, e. Birmingham, 2441, Pte., d., Home, 19/11/16.
Cheshire, Thomas Allen, b. Crewe, Ches., e. Birmingham (Crewe), 291, Cpl., d., Home, 16/10/18.
Clarke, James, b. Foleshill, Warwicks, e. Warwick (Exhall, Coventry), 21516, d., Home, 4/2/17.
Colegate, William George, b. London, e. Birmingham, 17444, Pte., d., Home, 28/4/16.
Coleman, John, b. Walsall, Staffs, e. Birmingham, 14575, Pte., d., Home, 15/10/15.
Conibere, Arthur Victor, b. Bedminster, Bristol, e. Bristol (Bedminster), 18755, Pte., d., Home, 5/10/16, formerly 24121, Som. L.I.
Corrigan, William, e. Birmingham, 15584, Pte., d., Home, 20/4/16.
Daffern, William, b. St. Mary's, Nuneaton, Warwicks, e. Nuneaton, 3131, Pte., d., Home, 29/10/15.
Davis, John, b. Old Hill, Dudley, Staffs, e. Nuneaton, Warwicks 3/1957, Pte., d., Home, 11/11/14.
Deeming, Thomas, e. Atherstone, Warwicks, 11507, Pte., d., Home, 15/9/15.
Dundon, William, b. St. Ann's, Cork, e. Cork, 30409, L/Sgt., d., Home, 3/11/18, formerly 4/6253, R. Muns. Fus., M.M.
Edge, John, b. Ashted, Birmingham, e. Birmingham, 3933, Pte., d., Home, 22/6/15.
Foster, James, b. Birmingham, e. Birmingham, 13393, Pte., d., Home, 4/6/16.
Harrell, Frederick, b. Ladywood, Birmingham, e. Birmingham, 1753, Pte., d., Home, 17/1/16.
Hemming, Henry Thomas, b. Chipping Norton, Oxon, e. Stratford-on-Avon, Warwicks, 8960, Pte., d., Home, 15/12/16.
Higgs, Charles, b. Admington, Glos., e. Coventry (Newport, I. of W.), 6367, Pte., d., Home, 9/6/17.
Hoggarth, Robert Henry, b. Barrow, Lancs, e. Barrow, 6622, Pte., d., Home, 7/3/15.
Jayes, Frank, b. Sparkhill, Birmingham, e. Birmingham, 23727, Pte., d., Home, 16/2/17.
Jones, Lewis Harold, b. Stratford-on-Avon, Warwicks, e. Birmingham, 27724, Pte., d., Home, 12/11/18.
Lyner, John Edward, b. Birmingham, e. Coventry (Coleshill, Warwicks), 58121, Pte., d., Home, 1/9/18.
Mallin, Edwin Walter, e. Birmingham (Coleshill, Warwicks), 21968, Pte., d., Home, 21/3/17.
Maskell, Francis, b. Fulham, Middx., e. Hammersmith, Middx. (Shepherd's Bush), 12261, Pte., d., Home, 5/6/15, formerly 49355, R.G.A.
Millard, John Thomas, b. Heath Town, Staffs, e. Birmingham, 30373, Pte., d., Home, 9/2/17, formerly 24289, Som. L.I.
Phillpott, Alfred George, b. Leicester, e. Birmingham (Leicester), 16/1751, A/Sgt.-Instr., d., Home, 10/10/18.
Pontings, Dennis Lawrence, b. Shepherd's Bush, London, e. Birmingham (Sparkbrook, Birmingham), 60227, Pte., k. in a., N. Russia, 1/9/19.
Potkins, Arthur Henry, b. Deptford, Kent, e. London (Islington, Middx.), 8059, Pte., d., Home, 16/10/15.
Pulling, Charles, b. Birmingham, e. Birmingham, 9291, Pte., d., Home, 1/2/17.
Robertson, Willie, b. Birmingham, e. Birmingham, 553, Pte., d., Home, 5/9/14.
Rock, Sydney James, b. Coventry, e. Coventry, 62845, Pte., d., S. Russia, 1/2/20.
Smith, Howard, b. Halesworth, Suffolk, e. Warwick (Saxmundham, Suffolk), 21907, Pte., d., Home, 22/2/17.
Stewart, Samuel, b. Birmingham, e. Birmingham, 8121, Sgt., d., Home, 26/2/16.
Stiddard, William, b. Bristol, Glos., e. Bristol, 23588, Pte., d., Home, 14/4/18, formerly 28642, Devon Regt.
Swan, Frederick, b. Leamington, Warwicks, e. Birmingham, 4101, Pte., d., Home, 28/2/16.
Wale, James, b. Birmingham, e. Birmingham, 7844, Pte., d., Home, 8/5/16.
Whelan, Frank, b. London, e. Birmingham, 18485, Pte., d., Home, 28/4/17, formerly 24575, Som. L.I.
Whitmore, Cyril Herbert, b. Hampstead, London, e. London (Wembley, Middx), 15644, L/Cpl., d., Home, 11/1/17.
Wood, Charles Benjamin, b. Birmingham, e. Birmingham, 13454, Pte., d., Home, 26/12/15.

4th Battalion.

Allen, John Frederick, b. Birmingham, e. Birmingham, 24362, Pte., d., Home, 3/4/17.
Barrows, Harry, b. Birmingham, e. Birmingham, 37608, Pte., d., Home, 1/10/17.
Clarke, Arthur, b. Birmingham, e. Birmingham, 58384, Pte., d., Home, 14/7/18.
Coldicott, Alfred, b. Pershore, Worcs, e. Birmingham (Pershore), 11405, Pte., d., Home, 6/3/15.
Cooney, James, b. Birmingham, e. Birmingham, 22427, Pte., d., Home, 19/11/18.
Earwicker, Albert Victor, e. Gosport, 24936, Pte., d., Home, 13/5/17.
Hayes, William, b. London, e. Coventry (Fulham, London), 57665, Pte., d., Home, 17/7/18.
Hughes, Joseph, b. Dudley, Worcs, e. Birmingham, 8782, Pte., d., Home, 13/5/15.
Jones, William, b. Birmingham, e. Birmingham, 25933, Sgt., d., Home, 7/6/18.
McCarthy, Bartholomew, b. Dowlais, Glam., e. Merthyr, Glam. (Penydarren, Glam.), 3365, Pte., d., Home, 11/4/15.
Mitchell, Samuel, b. Stafford, e. Walsall, Staffs (Stafford), 58067, Pte., d., Home, 13/7/18.
Neale, Ernest James, b. Naptoft, Leics, e. Long Itchington, Warwicks (Leamington, Warwicks), 57881, Pte. d., Home, 11/7/18.
Smith, George Arthur, b. Birmingham, e. Birmingham, 3374, Pte., d., Home, 2/1/16.
Smith, William, b. Holloway, Derby, e. Birmingham, 4546, Pte., d., Home, 15/4/15.
Stanley, Eli, b. Pelsall, Staffs, e. Birmingham (Leamore, Staffs), 1207, Pte., d., Home, 18/5/15.
Taplin, Frederick George, b. Claverdon, Warwicks, e. Warwick (Leamington, Warwicks), 4287, Pte., d., Home, 22/2/15.
Wainwright, William, e. Warwick (Polesworth, Warwicks), 38076, A/Sgt., d., Home, 2/11/18.

1/5th Battalion—Territorial.

Acwin, James, e. Birmingham, 4934, Pte., k. in a., F. & F., 24/8/16.
Adams, George Henry, b. Nuneaton, e. Nuneaton, Warwicks, 16037, Pte., k. in a., F. & F., 15/6/18.
Adderley, Herbert, b. Birmingham, e. Birmingham, 202031, Pte., k. in a., F. & F., 4/10/17.
Ainsworth, William, e. Preston, 202470, Pte., k. in a., F. & F., 6/10/17, formerly 3465, North Lancs Regt.
Aldridge Frank, e. Birmingham, 3570, Pte., k. in a., F. & F., 27/11/16.
Allen, Alfred, b. Ramsey, Hunts, e. Huntingdon (Ramsey), 203388, Pte., k in a., F. & F., 22/8/17, formerly 849, Hunts Cyclist Battn.
Allen, Herbert Pateshall, b. Camberwell, Surrey, e. Hammersmith, London (Peckham), 2080, Pte., k. in a., F. & F., 4/10/17, formerly 79, A. Cyclist Corps.
Arlett, Frederick George, b. Southampton, e. Bexley Heath, Kent (Erith, Kent), 28973, Pte., k. in a., F. & F., 22/8/17.
Arrowsmith, Edward, b. Newport, Salop, e. Birmingham, 2429, Pte., k. in a., F. & F., 9/5/15.
Aston, Frank Horace, e. Birmingham (Dudley, Worcs), 3301, Pte., d. of w., F. & F., 16/10/16.
Attenborough, James, b. St. Paul's, Birmingham, e. Birmingham, 2578, Pte., d. of w., F. & F., 22/8/16.
Baldwin, James, b. Newbold-on-Stour, Warwicks., e. Stratford-on-Avon, Warwicks, 202026, Pte., k. in a., F. & F., 7/4/17.
Ball, Frank, e. Portsmouth (Wickham, Hants), 241930, Pte., k. in a., F. & F., 4/10/17, formerly 2602, Hamps. Regt.
Barnes, William, b. Winson Green, Birmingham, e. Birmingham, 2069, Pte., k in a., F. & F., 24/4/16.
Bartlett, Frank, e. Birmingham, 3378, Pte., k. in a., F. & F., 2/5/15.
Bashford, George William, b. St. George's, Birmingham, e. Birmingham, 200295, Pte., d. of w., F. & F., 4/10/17.
Bateman, John William, b. Warboys, Hunts, e. Warboys, 20711, Pte., k. in a., F. & F., 22/8/16, formerly 190, Hunts Cyclist Battn.
Bates, Charles Henry, b. Alcester, Warwicks, e. Stratford-on-Avon, Warwicks (Alcester), 202020, Pte., k. in a., F. & F., 19/4/17.
Batten, Arthur, b. Boughton Monchelsea, Kent, e. Maidstone, Kent, 33948, Pte., k. in a., F. & F., 5/10/17, formerly 202949, E. Kent Regt.

Baxter, Edward, b. Gillinhall, Yorks, e. Sutton Coldfield, Warwicks (Knox Bilton, Yorks), 203004, Pte., k. in a., F. & F., 22/8/17, formerly 3505, Warwick Yeo.
Bedford, Arthur, b. Ramsey, Hunts, e. Ramsey, 20719, Pte., k. in a., F. & F., 22/8/16, formerly 251, Hunts Cyc. Battn.
Beet, Frederick, e. Birmingham, 3896, Pte., k. in a., F. & F., 18/7/16.
Beesley, George Leonard, b. Nuneaton, Warwicks, e. Nuneaton, 24518, Pte., k. in a., F. & F., 13/8/17.
Bellgrove, Arthur, e. Birmingham, 3091, Pte., k. in a., F. & F., 31/5/15.
Bellingham, Alfred James, b. Wolverhampton, Staffs. e. Birmingham (Sutton Coldfield, Warwicks), 201665, Pte, d. of w., F. & F., 11/8/17.
Bendall, George, b. Birmingham, e. Birmingham, 1720, Pte., d. of w., F. & F., 22/5/16.
Benjamin, Harry William, b. Haggerston, Middx., e. Walthamstow, 29042, Pte., k. in a., F. & F., 15/8/17.
Bennett, Albert Edward, e. Birmingham, 2905, L/Cpl., k. in a., F. & F., 21/7/16.
Bennett, Herbert, e. Birmingham, 200714, Cpl., d. of w., F. & F., 1/9/17.
Berry, Ernest Charles, b. Shottery, Warwicks, e. Stratford-on-Avon, Warwicks (Shottery), 15585, Pte., k. in a., F. & F., 4/10/17.
Bevan, William, b. All Saints, Birmingham, e. Birmingham, 1721, Pte., k. in a., F. & F., 18/7/16.
Bicknell, Archibald, b. S. Stoke, Sussex, e. Horsham, Sussex, 241804, Pte., k. in a., F. & F., 25/8/17, formerly 1425, R. Sussex Regt.
Biggs, Joseph Thomas, b. Stratford, Bucks, e. Birmingham, 203002, Pte., k. in a., F. & F., 17/4/17, formerly 3410, Warwick Yeo.
Bird, Sidney, e. Old Fletton, Northants (Peterborough, Northants), 20747, Pte., k. in a., F. & F., 18/8/16, formerly 820, Hunts Cyc. Battn.
Blake, Joseph Francis, b. Holloway, London, e. London, 29010, Pte., k. in a., F. & F., 2/11/17.
Blewitt, Albert, e. Birmingham, 4232, Pte., k. in a., F. & F., 18/7/16.
Blore, James, e. Warwick (Coventry), 6433, Pte., d. of w., F. & F., 27/11/16.
Bluck, Thomas, e. Birmingham, 200728, Cpl., d. of w., F. & F., 5/10/17.
Bone, Thomas Warren, e Woolwich, Kent (Shieldfield, Northumberland), 34630, Pte., d. of w., F. & F., 11/9/18, formerly 012768, R.A.O.C.
Boneham, Sidney, b. Chesterton, Warwicks, e. Leamington, Warwicks (Chesterton), 242980, Pte., d. of w., F. & F., 10/7/18.
Bonell, Benjamin Harry, b. Stratford-on-Avon, Warwick, e. Birmingham, 2428, Pte., k. in a., F. & F., 9/5/15.
Boulton, Aaron, b. Norton, Stafford, e. Burslem, Staffs (Stoke-on-Trent), 54629, Pte., d., F. & F., 13/10/18, formerly 48624, S. Staffs Regt.
Boulton, Samuel Joseph, b. Edgbaston, Birmingham, e. Birmingham, 200269, Pte, k. in a., F. & F, 10/8/17.
Bovill, Arthur Sydney, e. Birmingham, 3043, Pte., k. in a., F. & F., 21/7/16.
Bowman, Alfred, b. Poplar, London, e. Stratford, London (Walthamstow), 29047, Pte., k. in a., F. & F., 19/8/17.
Bownes, William Arthur, b. Birmingham, e. Birmingham (Handsworth, Staffs), 203469, L/Sgt., k. in a., F. & F., 22/8/17.
Bradfield, Percy Charles, b. Reading, Berks, e. Exeter, Devon (Reading), 202045, L/Cpl., k. in a., F. & F., 5/10/17.
Bradley, John, b. Kingham, Oxford, e. Oxford (Charlbury, Oxon), 18313, L/Cpl, d. of w., F. & F., 25/8/17, formerly 22951, Som. L.I.
Bradley, John Perry, b. Bordesley, Birmingham, e. Birmingham, 200251, Pte., k. in a., F. & F., 4/10/17.
Bradley, William Thomas, e. Birmingham, 201359, Pte., k. in a., F. & F., 4/10/17.
Bradshaw, Robert, b. St. Peter's, Warrington, Lancs, e. Warrington, 203446, Sgt., k. in a., F. & F., 9/9/18, formerly 1543, S. Lancs Regt.
Bramwell, David, b. Small Heath, Birmingham, e. Birmingham, 2540, Pte., k. in a., F. & F., 16/4/15.
Briggs, Arthur, b. Sparkbrook, Birmingham, e. Birmingham, 1671, Pte., k. in a., F. & F., 24/7/16.
Bright, Harry, b. Winwick, Northants, e. Fletton, Northants (Peterborough, Northants), 20702, Pte., k. in a., F. & F., 22/8/16, formerly 60, Hunts Cyclist Battn.
Brookes, George, b. Bartholomew, Birmingham, e. Birmingham, 2376, Pte., k. in a., F. & F., 9/5/15.
Brooks, George, b Lower Tooting, London, e. Birmingham (Lower Tooting), 200281, Pte., k. in a., F. & F., 16/7/16.
Brooks, William, b. St. Thomas, Birmingham, e. Birmingham, 1690, Cpl., k. in a., F & F., 18/7/16.
Broome, Benjamin Warman, e. Birmingham, 3985, Pte., d., F. & F., 2/11/15.
Brown, Cyril Ewart, e. Birmingham (Handsworth, Staffs), 2050, Pte., k. in a., F. & F., 18/7/16.
Brown, Frank Charles, b. Erdington, Birmingham, e. Birmingham, 1653, Pte., k. in a., F. & F., 19/8/16.
Brown, Herbert, b Gunness, Lincs, e. Windsor, Surrey (Gainsborough, Lincs). 28067, Pte., k. in a. F. & F., 15/6/18, formerly 140064, R.A.S.C.
Brown, Harold Ebenezer, b. Warboys, Hunts, e. Huntingdon (Warboys), 203389, Cpl., k. in a., F. & F., 24/8/17, formerly 949, Hunts Cyclist Battn.
Brown, Thomas Charles, b. St. Ives, Hunts, e. Huntingdon (Godmanchester, Hunts), 203377, Pte., k. in a., F. & F, 22/8/17, formerly 467, Hunts Cyclist Battn.
Brown, Victor Mark, b. Groton, Suffolk, e. Bildeston, Suffolk (Hitcham, Suffolk), 32650, Pte., k. in a., F. & F., 4/10/17, formerly 6344 E. Kent Regt.

Browning, Walter Henry, b. Gloucester, e. Gloucester, 268035, Pte., k. in a., F. & F., 22/8/17, formerly 30525, Glos. Regt.
Brunning, George Albert, b. Stonham Aspal, Suffolk, e. Ipswich, Suffolk (Stonham Aspal), 34620, Pte., k. in a., F. & F., 4/8/18
Brush, Arthur, b. Balsall Heath, Birmingham, e. Birmingham, 200350, Cpl., d. of w., F. & F., 10/8/17.
Bryne, William Edward, b. Birmingham, e. Birmingham, 259, C.S.M., k. in a., F. & F., 19/8/16.
Bunney, George Ewart, e. Birmingham (Dudley, Worcs), 3304, Pte., k. in a., F. & F., 2/7/16.
Bunker, Albert, b. Westoning, Bedford, e. London (Paddington, London), 29072, Pte., k. in a., F. & F., 22/8/17.
Burman, Frank Henry, b. Great Yarmouth, Norfolk, e. Torquay, Devon (Paignton, Devon), 202069, Pte,. k. in a., F. & F., 2/3/17.
Burridge, John Richard, b. East Ham, Essex, e. Stratford, London (East Ham), 203340, Pte., k. in a., F. & F., 4/10/17, formerly 10491, Hussars.
Burton, John William, e. Huntingdon (Woodstone, Northants), 203424, Cpl., k. in a., F. & F., 9/8/18, formerly 1639, Hunts Cyclist Battn.
Busby, Arthur, b. Birmingham, e. Birmingham, 4882, L/Cpl. d. of w. F. & F., 20/8/16.
Butler, Charles Richard, b. St. Ives, Hunts, e. St. Ives, 203348, Pte., k. in a, F. & F., 19/8/16, formerly 389, Beds Regt., and 34, Hunts Cyclist Battn.
Butler, Edwin, b. Aston, Birmingham, e. Birmingham, 2522 Pte., d. of w., F. & F., 27/8/16.
Butler, Henry, b. Wisbech, Cambs, e. Huntingdon, 203354, Pte, d., F. & F., 31/5/18, formerly 155, Hunts Cyclist Battn
Butler, Robert Alfred, b. Wishaw, Warwicks, e. Sutton Coldfield, Warwicks (Middleton, Tamworth, Warwicks), 201789, Pte., k. in a., F. & F., 9/9/18.
Cant, Martin Green, e. Birmingham, 201467, Pte., k. in a., F. & F., 4/10/17.
Carr, Patrick, b. Paddington, London, e. Kennington, London (Lambeth), 235246, Pte., k. in a., F. & F., 15/6/18, formerly 3105, 3/5th London Regt, 9/5099, Middx. Regt., G/60792, R. Fus., and 268256, Herts Regt.
Carrington, Harold George, b. Eaton Locon, Beds, e. St. Neots Hunts, 20731, Pte., k. in a., F. & F., 18/8/16, formerly 377, Hunts Cyclists Battn.
Castle, Thomas Alfred, b. Sparkhill, Birmingham, e. Birmingham, 1358, Pte., k. in a., F. & F., 26/7/15.
Chadaway, Edward, b. St. Martin's, Birmingham, e. Birmingham, 200222, Pte., k. in a., F. & F., 9/9/18.
Chance, Limuel, b. Bordesley, Birmingham, e. Birmingham, 1460, Pte., k. in a., F. & F., 18/8/16.
Chandler, James Frederick, b. Cheriton, Kent, e. Sandwich, Kent, 32937, Pte., k. in a., F. & F., 5/10/17, formerly 4658, E. Kent Regt.
Charles, Ernest, b. Warwick, e. Birmingham, 1502, Pte., k. in a., F. & F., 10/11/16.
Charles, Leslie William, b. Bristol, e. Birmingham (Bristol), 367, Pte., d. of w., F. & F., 9/10/17.
Chester, Frederick, b. Warrington, Lancs, e. Warrington, 203455, Pte., k. in a., F. & F., 18/8/16, formerly 4083, S. Lancs Regt.
Child, Lawrence, b. Hockley, Birmingham, e. Birmingham (Smethwick, Staffs), 2526, Cpl., k. in a., F. & F., 19/8/16.
Childerley, Harry, b. Abbotsley, Hunts, e. Huntingdon (St. Neots, Hunts), 20769, Pte., k. in a., F. & F., 18/8/16, formerly 1453, Hunts Cyclist Battn.
Childs, George, b. Hartford, Hunts, e. Huntingdon (Hartford), 203383, Pte., k. in a., F. & F., 25/8/17, formerly 651, Hunts Cyclist Battn.
Clark, George Alfred, e. Huntingdon (Ellington, Hunts), 20758, Pte., k. in a., F. & F., 18/8/16, formerly 1384, Hunts Cyclist Battn.
Clark, William, b. Warboys, Hunts, e. Warboys, 20713, Pte., k. in a., F. & F., 10/11/16, formerly 197, Hunts Cyclist Battn.
Clarke, George, b. Highgate, Birmingham, e. Birmingham, 200450, Pte., k. in a., F. & F., 16/4/16.
Cleaver, James, b. St. James, Birmingham, e. Birmingham, 1389, Pte., k. in a., F. & F., 7/5/15.
Clifford, William, e. Birmingham, 201660, Pte., k. in a., F. & F., 19/8/16.
Colbert, Edgar Joseph, e. Huntingdon, e. Broughton, Hunts, 20745, Pte., k. in a., F. & F., 18/8/16, formerly 768, Hunts, Cyclist Battn.
Colbert, Frederick Stanley, b. Offord Cluny, Hunts, e. Huntingdon, 203392, Pte., k. in a., F. & F., 15/8/17, formerly 1066, Hunts Cyclist Battn.
Coldman, William Henry, b. Rotherhithe, London, e. Camberwell, London (Herne Hill, London), 28900, Pte., k. in a., F. & F., 16/8/17.
Collett, George Edward Archie, e. Huntingdon (Kettering, Northants), 203402, Pte., k. in a., F. & F., 9/8/17, formerly 1425, Hunts Cyclist Battn.
Colloff, Sydney, b. Brookfields, Birmingham, e. Birmingham, 200605, L/Cpl., k. in a., F. & F., 22/8/17.
Conway, John Edwin, b. India, e. Birmingham, 2249, Pte., k. in a., F. & F., 18/7/16.
Cook, Archibald, b. Pluckley, Kent, e. Canterbury, Kent, 235188, Pte., k. in a., F. & F., 4/10/17, formerly 3298, E. Kent. Regt.
Cooke, John Henry, b. Birmingham, e. Birmingham, 5173, Pte., k. in a., F. & F., 18/7/16.
Corbett, Frederick, e. Birmingham (Smethwick, Staffs), 201386, Pte., k. in a., F. & F., 10/8/17.
Cornelius, John, b. Birmingham, e. Birmingham, 1867, Pte., k. in a., F. & F., 2/5/15.
Cosgrove, Alfred Henry, e. Birmingham, 200863, Pte., d. of w., F. & F., 31/3/18.

Cotterill, Albert, e. Leamington, Warwickshire, 19270, Pte., k. in a., F. & F., 22/8/17.
Cottom, Frederick, e. Birmingham, 2870, Pte., k. in a., F. & F., 18/8/16.
Cottrell, Albert, e. Birmingham, 3045, Pte., k. in a., F. & F., 17/4/15.
Coulson, Thomas William, e. Coventry (Littlethorpe, Leicester), 266508, Pte., d. of w., F. & F., 10/9/18.
Couzens, Reginald Harold, b. Dover, Kent, e. Dover, 260286, Pte., k. in a., F. & F., 4/10/17, formerly 2889, E. Kent Regt.
Cox, Charles, b. Birmingham, e. Birmingham, 1534, Sgt., d. of w., F. & F., 6/9/16.
Cox, Frederick Francis, b. Flecknoe, Warwickshire, e. Rugby, Warwickshire (Flecknoe), 202002, Pte., k. in a., F. & F., 15/8/17.
Crow, William Frederick, b. Dunmow, Essex, e. Braintree, Essex (Dunmow), 33252, Pte., k. in a., F. & F., 5/10/17, formerly 4/6193, E. Kent. Regt.
Cunningham, Thomas, b. Whitechapel, London, e. London, 29050, Pte., k. in a., F. & F., 4/10/17.
Curtis, Edwin, b. St. Saviours, Birmingham, e. Birmingham, 200363, Pte., k. in a., F. & F., 9/9/18.
Daniel, Thomas, b. Mobberley, Cheshire, e. Manchester (Mobberley), 29135, Pte., k. in a., F. & F., 4/10/17, formerly 62229, Cheshire Regt.
Daniels, William, b. Aston, Birmingham, e. Birmingham, 2095, Pte., k. in a., F. & F., 19/8/16.
Dash, Albert, b. Exeter, Devon, e. Exeter, 6534, Pte., k. in a., F. & F., 27/11/16.
Davies, Aaron, b. Glanaman, Carmarthen, e. Swansea, Glam (Garnant, Carmarthen), 20812, Pte., k. in a., F. & F., 18/7/16, formerly 3253, Welsh Regt.
Davies, Cyril, b. Handsworth, Staffs, e. Coventry (Handsworth, Staffs), 202140, Pte., k. in a., F. & F., 4/10/17.
Davis, Edward, b. Birmingham, e. Birmingham, 4886, Pte., k. in a., F. & F., 18/7/16.
Day, Charles, b. Southport, Lancs, e. Birmingham, 1826, Cpl., k. in a., F. & F., 1/7/16.
Daykin, James William, b. Ilkeston, Derbyshire, e. Birmingham (Ilkeston), 88, Sgt., k. in a., F. & F., 26/4/16.
Deakin, John, b. St. Marks, Birmingham, e. Birmingham, 1832, Sergt., k. in a., F. & F., 18/7/16.
Dearn, George, e. Birmingham (Smethwick, Staffs), 200864, Pte., k. in a., F. & F., 4/10/17.
Delaney, Edward, b. Birmingham, e. Birmingham (Bournbrook, nr. Birmingham), 201216, L/Cpl., k. in a., F. & F., 28/6/16.
Depper, William Henry, b. Birmingham, e. Birmingham (Rubery, Worcs.), 5617, Pte., k. in a., F. & F., 18/7/16.
Dixon, James, e. Birmingham (West Bromwich, Staffs). 3987, Pte., k. in a., F. & F., 18/8/16.
Dobson, Ernest, b. Sunderland, Durham, e. Doncaster, Yorks (Castle Eden, Durham), 33308, Pte., k. in a., F. & F., 4/8/18, formerly 1900 R.A.S.C.
Drinkwater, Harry, e. Warwick, 6477, Pte., k. in a., F. & F., 17/11/16.
Duce, Harold Stanley, b. Pelsall, Staffs, e. Walsall, Staffs (Pelsall), 202295, Pte., k. in a., F. & F., 17/4/17.
Duffin, Thomas, b. Packwood, Warwickshire, e. Warwick (Bentley Heath, Warwickshire), 201719, Pte., k. in a., F. & F., 24/8/17.
Dyas, Albert Edward, e. Birmingham, 201027, Pte., k. in a., F. & F., 4/10/17.
Earl, Ernest, b. Sparkbrook, Birmingham, e. Birmingham, 2613, Pte., d. of w., F. & F., 14/4/15.
Easton, William Herbert, b. New Clee, Grimsby, e. Grimsby, Lincs, 27103, Pte., k. in a., F. & F., 9/9/18, formerly 4166, Lincs Regt.
Eaton, Thomas, b. Warwick, e. Warwick, 6210, Pte., k. in a., F. & F., 11/11/16.
Easthall, Horace William, b. Crowfield, Suffolk, e. Ipswich, Suffolk (Chatisham, Suffolk), 33253, Pte., k. in a., F. & F., 15/6/18, formerly 6214, E. Kent. Regt.
Elliott, Bertie, b. Birmingham, e. Birmingham, 201293, Pte., k. in a., F. & F., 17/4/17.
Elliott, Herbert, b. Coventry, e. Coventry, 203302, Pte., k. in a., F. & F., 19/8/17.
Ellis, Albert Henry, b. Ladywood, Birmingham, e. Birmingham (200088, Cpl., k. in a., F. & F., 9/9/18.
Elton, Reginald, e. Birmingham, 3039, Pte., k. in a., F. & F., 1/7/16.
Ennis, William Henry, b. Bordesley, Birmingham, e. Birmingham, 2164, Pte., k. in a., F. & F., 18/7/16.
Etheridge, Walter Charles, b. Spernell, Warwickshire, e. Coventry (Fletchamstead, nr. Coventry), 202006, Pte., k. in a., F. & F., 15/6/18.
Evans, Harold Toussaint, b. Sparkbrook, Birmingham, e. Birmingham, 2477, Pte., d. of w., F. & F., 20/8/16.
Everitt, Harry, b. Bedworth, Warwickshire, e. Warwick (Bedworth), 201736, Pte., k. in a., F. & F., 18/8/16.
Fall, George Frederick, b. London, e. Coventry, 202019, Pte., k. in a., F. & F., 15/6/18
Fallon, Joseph, b. Roscommon, Ireland, e. Nuneaton, Warwicks (Arley, Warwicks), 201808, Pte., k. in a., F. & F., 13/8/17.
Fenn, Bertram, b. Dalton, Middx., e. Stratford, Essex (Leyton, Essex), 29027, Pte., k. in a., F. & F., 4/10/17.
Ferguson, Alfred, b. St. Pauls, Birmingham, e. Birmingham. 2544, Pte., k. in a., F. & F., 17/4/15.
Fisher, Edward, b. Birmingham, e. Handsworth, Staffs (Birmingham), 201601, Pte., k. in a., F. & F., 13/7/16.
Fisher, Howard, b. Bromford, Warwicks, e. Birmingham, 201784, Pte., k. in a., F. & F., 6/2/17.
Fletcher, William, b. Attleboro', Norfolk, e. Warwick (Leeds), 5966, Pte., d. of w., F. & F., 27/7/16.
Foxall, Joseph, b. Birmingham, e. Birmingham, 5114, Pte., k. in a., F. & F., 18/7/16.
Freeman, Arthur David, b. Warwick, e. Nuneaton, Warwicks, 201734, Pte., k. in a., F. & F., 13/10/17.
Freeman, George Clifford, e. Birmingham, 240847, Pte., k. in a., F. & F., 15/6/18
French, Oliver, b. Napton, Warwicks, e. Warwick (Rugby, Warwicks), 6075, Pte., d., F. & F., 10/2/17.
Fudge, Henry William Golding, b. Hoxton, Middx., e. Stratford, Essex (Leyton, Essex), 29035, Pte., k. in a., F. & F., 22/8/17.
Fulford, George, b. Birmingham, e. Birmingham, 4787, Pte., k. in a., F. & F., 27/11/16.
Gaffey, Thomas, b. St. Johns, Birmingham, e. Birmingham, 200170, Pte., k. in a., F. & F., 22/8/17.
Gardner, Arthur William, b. Barford St. John, Oxon., e. Banbury, Oxon., 241704, Pte., k. in a., F. & F., 22/8/17.
Gardner, William, b. Ladywood, Birmingham, e. Birmingham, 1747, Cpl., d. of w., F. & F., 22/5/16.
Garratt, Alfred, b. Birmingham, Warwicks, e. Birmingham, 202028, Pte., k. in a., F. & F., 17/4/17.
George, Harry, b. Ladywood, Birmingham, e. Birmingham (Smethwick, Staffs), 2363, Pte., k. in a., F. & F., 17/9/15.
Gibbins, John, b. Aston, Birmingham, e. Warwick (Sutton Coldfield, Warwicks), 201772, Pte., d., F. & F., 20/2/18.
Gilbert, George James, b. Chelsea, e. Chelsea, London (Fulham, London), 33293, Pte., k. in a., F. & F., 4/10/17, formerly 4859, E. Kent Regt.
Gilberthorpe, John, e. Birmingham (Edgbaston, Birmingham), 2931, Pte., d., F. & F., 22/8/15.
Gilks, William Thomas John, b. Marlboro', Wilts, e. Weymouth (Henley-on-Thames), 34628, Pte., k. in a., F. & F., 9/9/18.
Gillbanks, Creamer Frederick, b. Islington, Middx., e. Highbury, Kent (Islington), 29031, Pte., k. in a., F. & F., 4/10/17.
Golby, Cyril, e. Warwick (Ratley, Warwicks), 21178, Pte., k. in a., F. & F., 4/10/17.
Goldingay, Thomas, e. Birmingham (Nechells, Birmingham), 202656, Pte., k. in a., F. & F., 23/8/17.
Goodby, George Adlington, b. Balsall Heath, Birmingham, e. Birmingham (Balsall Heath), 200151, Cpl., d. of w., F. & F., 5/10/17.
Goode, Frederick George, b. St. Paul's, Birmingham, e. Birmingham, 2404, Pte., k. in a., F. & F., 26/5/15.
Gould, Cyril Crawford, e. Birmingham (Camp Hill, Birmingham), 3121, Pte., k. in a., F. & F., 14/4/15.
Grattage, William Ernest, b. Edgbaston, Birmingham, e. Birmingham (Edgbaston), 373, Sgt., k. in a., F. & F., 18/7/16.
Green, James, b. Ladywood, Birmingham, e. Birmingham, 1472, Pte., k. in a., F. & F., 2/5/15.
Green, Harold Leon, b. Guernsey, Channel Isles, e. Lewisham, Middx. (Guernsey), 34526, Pte., k. in a., F. & F., 9/9/18 formerly 6533, London Regt.
Greening, Charles, b. Birmingham, e. Birmingham, 242370, Pte., k. in a., F. & F., 4/10/17.
Greet, Charles, b. Torpoint, Cornwall, e. Birmingham, 201814, Pte., k. in a., F. & F., 25/8/17.
Griffin, Frederick John, b. Birmingham, e. Birmingham, 241271, L/Cpl., k. in a., F. & F., 5/10/17.
Griffiths, Leonard, e. Birmingham (Sparkbrook, Birmingham), 2895, Pte., k. in a., F. & F., 18/7/16.
Grimmett, Thomas, b. Aston, Birmingham, e. Birmingham, 1529, Pte., d. of w., F. & F., 22/6/15.
Grout, Thomas Alfred, b. Bromley, Kent, e. Stratford, Essex, 29061, Pte., k. in a., F. & F., 23/8/17.
Guest, Samuel, b. Aston, Birmingham, e. Birmingham, 2041, Pte., k. in a., F. & F., 18/7/16.
Hall, Albert, e. Birmingham, 200732, Pte., k. in a., F. & F., 22/8/17.
Hall, Arthur Rowland, b. Warwick, e. Warwick, 203029, Pte., k. in a., F. & F., 4/10/17, formerly 3626, Warwick Yeo.
Hammond, James, b. Small Heath, Birmingham, e. Birmingham, 2577, L/Cpl., k. in a., F. & F., 18/7/16.
Hancox, Alfred, b. Poplar, London, e. Stratford, Essex (East Ham, Essex), 28981, Pte., k. in a., F. & F., 25/8/17.
Handy, Percy Gerald, b. Alderminster, Worcs, e. Warwick (Stratford-on-Avon, Warwicks), 201804, Pte., k. in a., F. & F., 25/8/17.
Harborne, Bert Edward, b. Aston, Birmingham, e. Birmingham (Aston), 200518, Sgt., k. in a., F. & F., 17/4/17.
Harris, Arthur, b. Stratford-on-Avon, Warwicks, e. Birmingham, 4768, Pte., k. in a., F. & F., 19/8/16.
Harris, Ernest, b. Asbury, Worcs, e. Birmingham (Halesowen, Worcs), 201214, Pte., d. of w., F. & F., 1/10/17.
Harris, Joseph Edgar, e. Birmingham (Handsworth, Staffs), 4632, L/Cpl., k. in a., F. & F., 18/7/16.
Harrison, Harold, e. Birmingham (Balsall Heath, Birmingham), 200869, Pte., d., F. & F., 13/2/18.
Hart, Oswald, b. Middlesboro', Yorks, e. Camberwell, Middx. (Sydenham, Surrey), 29011, Pte., k. in a., F. & F., 22/3/17.
Harvey, Frank, b. Shipston-on-Stour, Worcs, e. Coventry, 201737, Pte., k. in a., F. & F., 4/10/17.
Harwood, George Thomas, b. Cubbington, Warwicks, e. Rugby, Warwicks (Cubbington), 25100, Pte., k. in a., F. & F., 15/6/18.
Hatch, Reginald John, b. Highnam, Glos., e. Bristol, Glos. (Highnam), 5350, L/Cpl., d. of w., F. & F., 13/10/17.
Hatcher, Frank, b. Old Ford, Middx., e. Stratford, Essex (Bromley-by-Bow, Kent), 34515, Pte., k. in a., F. & F., 9/9/18, formerly 7052, Beds. Regt.
Hayes, Thomas Edwin, b. Nuneaton, Warwicks, e. Warwick, 6355, Pte., k. in a., F. & F., 11/11/16.
Haynes, Charles, b. Elmdon, Warwick, e. Birmingham (Elmdon), 200523, Sgt., k. in a., F. & F., 4/10/17.
Hedges, James Robert, b. Birmingham, e. Warwick (Birmingham), 6367, Pte., k. in a., F. & F., 17/11/16

Higginson, Benjamin H., e. Birmingham (Sparkbrook, Birmingham), 3308, Pte., k. in a., F. & F., 18/7/16.
Hill, Alfred, b. Pailton, Warwicks, e. Monks Kirby, Leics. (Pailton), 24543, Pte., k. in a., F. & F., 4/10/17.
Hitchman, Arthur, b. Aston, Birmingham, e. Birmingham (Aston), 200204, Dmr., k. in a., F. & F., 10/8/17.
Hoare, John, b. St. Catherines, Birmingham, e. Birmingham, 828, Pte., k. in a., F. & F., 19/8/16.
Hockley, John Henry, b. Leek Wootton, Warwicks, e. Warwick (Leek Wootton), 203031, Pte., d. of w., F. & F., 9/2/17, formerly 3621, Warwick Yeo.
Hogan, John, b. St. Martins, Birmingham, 200324, Pte., k. in a., F. & F., 19/8/16.
Holden, Harold, b. Aston, Birmingham, e. Birmingham (Aston), 200146, Sgt., k. in a., F. & F., 10/8/17.
Holloway, Philip Henry Ernest, b. Birmingham, e. Birmingham, 5610, Pte., k. in a., F. & F., 4/7/16.
Homer, Alfred George, b. Aston, Birmingham, e. Birmingham, 992, L/Cpl., k. in a., F. & F., 19/9/15.
Hood, Llewellyn, e. Stenhousemuire, Stirlingshire, 330378, Pte., k. in a., F. & F., 4/10/17.
Hooper, Albert Edward, b. Small Heath, Birmingham, e. Birmingham, 240319, Pte., k. in a., F. & F., 8/8/18.
Hopston, Frederick, e. Birmingham, 200702, Pte., k. in a., F. & F., 10/8/17.
Horne, Samuel, e. Birmingham, 4697, Pte., k. in a., F. & F., 18/7/16.
Horton, Howard Frederick, b. Felixstowe, Suffolk, e. Birmingham (Aston, Birmingham), 33318, Pte., d. of w., F. & F., 11/10/17, formerly 4704, E. Kent Regt.
Hoult, John, b. St. Matthews, Birmingham, e. Birmingham, 1131, Pte., k. in a., F. & F., 2/5/15.
Howell, John Henry, b. Mile End, Middx., e. Shoreditch, London (Bethnal Green, London), 29014, Pte., k. in a., F. & F., 23/8/17.
Howes, Charles, b. Eccleshall, Staffs, e. Stoke-on-Trent, Staffs (Yarnfield, Staffs), 25002, Pte., d. of w., F. & F., 6/9/17, formerly 32017, R. Berks Regt.
Hughes, Thomas Henry, e. Birmingham, 200933, L/Cpl., k. in a., F. & F., 9/9/18.
Hunt, Bertie, e. Birmingham, 200788, Cpl., k. in a., F. & F., 22/8/17.
Hurley, Henry Thomas, b. Ramsgate, Kent, e. Ramsgate, 235112, Sgt., k. in a., F. & F., 4/10/17, formerly 200821, E. Kent Regt.
Irving, Frederick, b. Sheffield, e. Birmingham, 201150, L/Cpl., k. in a., F. & F., 22/8/17.
Jacka, Gordon Joseph, b. Oakley Wood, Warwicks, e. Leamington Spa, Warwicks, 23857, Pte., k. in a., F. & F., 10/8/17.
Jackson, John Henry, b. Ashted, Birmingham, e. Birmingham, 2612, Pte., k. in a., F. & F., 18/7/16.
Jacques, William, b. Shaw, Oldham, Lancs, e. Oldham (Shaw), 202373, Cpl., k. in a., F. & F., 10/8/17, formerly 1843, Manchester Regt.
Jarrett, Frank Herbert, b. Claverdon, Warwicks, e. Stratford-on-Avon, Warwicks (Claverdon), 201729, Pte., k. in a., F. & F., 22/8/17.
Jarvis, Edward, b. Vauxhall, Birmingham, e. Birmingham, 200272, Pte., k. in a., F. & F., 17/4/17.
Johnson, Arthur, b. Sutton Coldfield, Warwicks, e. Birmingham (Sutton Coldfield), 203036, Pte., k. in a., F. & F., 4/10/17, formerly 3434, Warwick Yeo., M.M.
Johnson, George, e. Birmingham, 3646, Pte., d. of w., F. & F., 27/7/16.
Johnson, John, b. Bedworth, Warwicks, e. Coventry (Bedworth), 201959, Pte., k. in a., F. & F., 9/9/18.
Jones, Albert, b. Birmingham, e. Birmingham, 28855, Pte., k. in a., F. & F., 22/8/17.
Jones, Brinley, b. Aberthaw, Glam., e. Cardiff (Barry, Glam.), 33345, Pte., k. in a., F. & F., 15/6/18, formerly 032307, R.A.S.C.
Jones, George Harold, b. Birmingham, e. Birmingham, 2162, Pte., k. in a., F. & F., 24/7/16.
Jordan, Thomas, b. Ireland, e. Birmingham (Warwick), 5780, Pte., k. in a., F. & F., 13/7/16.
Jordan, Walter James, b. Birmingham, e. Birmingham, 242228, Pte., k. in a., F. & F., 10/8/17.
Keiff, Victor Frank, e. Birmingham, 3575, Pte., k. in a., F. & F., 13/5/15.
Kelley, Walter, b. Foleshill, Warwicks, e. Coventry (Foleshill), 24537, Pte., k. in a., F. & F., 22/8/17.
Kelly, Alfred, b. Sparkbrook, Birmingham, e. Birmingham (Sparkbrook), 200082, Pte., d., F. & F., 20/10/18.
Kemp, Charles Joseph, b. Vauxhall, Birmingham, e. Birmingham, 2276, Pte., k. in a., F. & F., 24/7/16.
Kenealy, John, b. Aston, Birmingham, e. Birmingham, 1571, Pte., k. in a., F. & F., 18/7/16.
Kessey, Ronald Frederick, b. Studley, Warwickshire, e. Birmingham (Studley), 201835, Pte., k. in a., F. & F., 4/10/17.
King, Lionel Malcolm, b. London, e. Maidstone, Kent (London), 33944, Pte., k. in a., F. & F., 4/10/17, formerly 6371, E. Kent Regt.
King, William, b. Birmingham, e. Solihull, Warwickshire, 201732, Pte., k. in a., F. & F., 29/3/17.
Landucci, Fred Henry, b. Shrewsbury, e. Birmingham, 5549, L/Cpl., k. in a., F. & F., 18/7/16.
Lapworth, Arthur, b. Coventry, e. Coventry, 24517, Pte., k. in a., F. & F., 4/10/17.
Lee, John, b. Birmingham, e. Birmingham, 201439, L/Cpl., k. in a., F. & F., 22/8/17.
Lee, William Richard, b. West Bromwich, Staffs, e. Birmingham, 2361, L/Cpl., k. in a., F. & F., 9/5/15.
Lenton, John Henry, b. Coventry, e. Coventry (Hawkesbury, nr. Coventry), 24534, Pte., k. in a., F. & F., 13/8/17.
Leonard, Horace, b. Small Heath, Birmingham, e. Birmingham (Small Heath), 200240, Pte., d. of w., F. & F., 21/4/17.
Lewis, James, b. Bethnal Green, Middx., e. Leyton, Essex (Hackney, London), 29060, Pte., k. in a., F. & F., 24/8/17.
Lewis, William Cramp, e. Birmingham (Handsworth, Staffs), 2938, Pte., k. in a., F. & F., 19/8/16.
Lichfield, Percy, e. Birmingham, 3143, Pte., k. in a., F. & F., 18/7/16.
Lloyd, Brinley Isaac, b. St. Gabriel's, Swansea, e. Swansea (Brynmill, Swansea), 203440, L/Cpl., k. in a., F. & F., 22/8/17, formerly 1441, Welsh Regt.
Lowson, George Baxter, b. Tottenham, Middx., e. Tottenham, 27612, L/Cpl., k. in a., F. & F., 22/8/17, formerly 5547, S. Staffs Regt.
Madden, Alfred, b. Allahabad, India, e. Birmingham (Prestatyn, Flint), 203048, L/Cpl., k. in a., F. & F., 4/10/17, formerly 3497, Warwickshire Yeo.
Marshall, Arthur Alfred, b. Leamington, Warwickshire, e. Leamington, 33617, Pte., k. in a., F. & F., 4/10/17, formerly 4831, E. Kent Regt.
May, George Ernest, b. Tarmorton, Glos., e. Birmingham, 241160, Pte., k. in a., F. & F., 22/8/17.
May, John Thomas, b. Shepherds Bush, Middx., e. Birmingham (Wimbledon, Surrey), 202016, Pte., k. in a., F. & F., 27/8/17.
Maycock, John Arthur, e. Rugby, Warwickshire, 19568, L/Cpl., k. in a., F. & F., 9/9/18.
Mayoh, William, b. Bolton, Lancs, e. London (Bolton), 33311, Pte., d., F. & F., 30/1/19, formerly 074310, R.A.S.C.
Meagher, William, e. Birmingham (Sparkhill, Birmingham), 200766, Pte., k. in a., F. & F., 18/8/16.
Mason, Arthur George, b. Birmingham, e. Birmingham, 200628, Cpl., k. in a., F. & F., 18/8/16.
Miles, Reginald, b. Swanley, Kent, e. Woolwich, Kent (Swanley), 29038, Pte., d. of w., F. & F., 23/8/17.
Miles, Richard Henry, b. Worcester, e. Leamington, 203336, Pte., k. in a., F. & F., 6/2/17.
Miller, John, b. Pendleton, Manchester, e. Birmingham (Pendleton), 200438, L/Cpl., k. in a., F. & F., 29/3/17.
Mills, Albert, b. St. Martin's, Birmingham, e. Birmingham, 200173, Pte., k. in a., F. & F., 4/10/17.
Milton, Frederick, b. Chatham, Kent, e. Sittingbourne, Kent (Rochester, Kent), 33843, Pte., d. of w., F. & F., 8/10/17, formerly 5064, E. Kent Regt.
Mitchell, David Henry, e. Birmingham, 3685, Pte., k. in a., F. & F., 18/7/16.
Moore, Edward Henry, b. Keynsham, Som., e. Tiverton, Devon (Hemyock, Devon), 202038, Pte., k. in a., F. & F., 6/10/17.
Moore, John Elvy, b. Greenhithe, Kent, e. Woolwich, Kent (Stone, Kent), 29044, Pte., k. in a., F. & F., 22/8/17.
Moore, John William, b. Stockingford, Warwickshire, e. Nuneaton, Warwickshire (Stockingford), 241717, Pte., k. in a., F. & F., 19/8/17.
Moore, Thomas, e. Bedworth, Warwickshire (Longford, Coventry), 6462, Pte., k. in a., F. & F., 8/12/16.
Moran, Alfred, b. Coventry, e. Coventry, 201809, Pte., k. in a., F. & F., 19/8/16.
Moynagh, Thomas, e. Birmingham, 5893, Pte., d. of w., F. & F., 23/7/16.
Myers, Harry Thomas, b. Rotton Park, Birmingham, e. Birmingham (Rotton Park), 403, Pte., k. in a., F. & F., 5/10/17.
Myring, James, b. St. Andrew's, Birmingham, e. Birmingham, 1666, Pte., k. in a., F. & F., 23/4/15.
Newey, William James, b. Moseley, Birmingham, e. Birmingham (Moseley), 200505, Pte., k. in a., F. & F., 15/6/18.
Nicholls, William, b. Birmingham, e. Birmingham, 2050, Pte., k. in a., F. & F., 9/5/15.
North, Albert, b. St. Thomas, Birmingham, e. Birmingham, 1083, Cpl., d. of w., F. & F., 22/8/16.
Norton, Harry Austin Ricketts, b. Burton-on-Trent, Staffs, e. Birmingham (Lichfield, Staffs), 203050, Pte., d. of w., F. & F., 24/8/17, formerly 3090, Warwickshire Yeo.
Osborn, Bernard John, e. Coventry, 6144, Pte., k. in a., F. & F., 10/11/16.
Osborne, Alfred, b. Hundon, Suffolk, e. Bury St. Edmunds, Suffolk (Hundon), 27265, Pte., d. of w., F. & F., 28/8/17, formerly 2910, Suffolk Regt.
Packer, Thomas James, b. Barford, Warwickshire, e. Birmingham (Aston, Birmingham), 201225, Pte., k. in a., F. & F., 24/8/17.
Padbury, Fred, b. Chesterton, Warwickshire, e. Warwick (Chesterton), 203055, Pte., d. of w., F. & F., 15/8/17, formerly 3445, Warwickshire Yeo.
Padbury, Francis James Edward, b. Kineton, Warwickshire, e. Leamington, Warwickshire, 201976, Pte., k. in a., F. & F., 16/3/17.
Page, Walter, b. Tysoe, Warwickshire, e. Stratford-on-Avon (Tysoe), 25083, Pte., k. in a., F. & F., 9/9/18.
Parker, Arthur William, b. Godmanchester, Hunts, e. Huntingdon (Godmanchester), 235244, Pte., k. in a., F. & F., 15/6/18, formerly 660, Hunt's Cyclists Batt., 43028, Beds. R., and 268173, Herts. R.
Parker, William, e. Birmingham (Smethwick, Birmingham), 200936, Pte., k. in a., F. & F., 10/8/17.
Parkes, Fred, e. Birmingham (Yardley, Birmingham), 202563, Pte., k. in a., F. & F., 13/8/17.
Parsons, Albert George, b. Banbury, Oxon, e. Warwick, 203054, Pte., k. in a., F. & F., 23/8/17 formerly 3515, Warwick Yeo.
Pearce, William, b. Hednesford, Staffs, e. Birmingham (Hednesford), 5397, Pte., d. of w., F. & F., 17/7/16.
Pemberton, Walter, b. St. Lawrences, Birmingham, e. Birmingham, 1599, Pte., k. in a., F. & F. 18/7/16.
Penn, John George, b. Hoxton, Middx., e. Birmingham, 1482, Pte., d. of w., F. & F., 12/5/15.
Perks, Albert Edward, b. Aston, Birmingham, e. Birmingham, 2618, Pte., k. in a., F. & F. 9/5/15.
Perks, William Herbert, b. Coventry, e. Coventry, 201681, Pte., k. in a., F. & F., 13/7/16.

Perry, Arthur, e. Birmingham (Haymills, Birmingham), 5399, Pte., k. in a., F. & F., 8/8/16.
Phillips, Albert Henry, e Birmingham, 268064, Pte., k. in a., F. & F., 4/10/17.
Phillips, John George, b. St. Martins, Birmingham, e. Birmingham, 2503, Cpl., d. of w., F. & F., 5/10/16.
Phillpot, Percy, b. Tysoe, Warwicks, e. Warwick (Kineton, Warwicks), 201952, Pte., k. in a., F. & F., 24/8/17.
Pickering, Edmund, b. St. Andrews, Birmingham, e. Birmingham, 200177, Pte., k. in a., F. & F. 15/6/18.
Pilling, George, b. Rochdale, Lancs, e. Rochdale, 6278, Pte., k. in a., F. & F., 8/8/16, formerly 9813, Lancs. Fus.
Pilling, William Henry, b. Birmingham, e. Birmingham, 203000, A/Cpl., k. in a., F. & F., 9/9/18, formerly 3066, Warwick Yeo.
Pinchin, Albert Edward, b. Brickle Hampton, Worcs., e. Warwick (Eckington, Worcs.), 2807, Cpl., k. in a., F. & F., 4/10/17.
Plester, William Joseph, b. St. Pauls, Walsall, Staffs, e. Birmingham (Walsall), 200592, Sgt., k. in a., F. & F., 15/6/18.
Porter, George, b. Ladywood, Birmingham, e. Birmingham, 852, Pte., k. in a., F. & F., 9/5/15.
Poulter Howard, b. St. Pauls, Birmingham, e. Birmingham, 2719, Pte., k. in a., F. & F., 18/7/16.
Pratt, William Horace, b. Soho, Birmingham, e. Birmingham (Soho, Birmingham), 200490, Pte., d. of w., F. & F., 23/8/17.
Prew, Ernest Claude, b. Birmingham, e. Birmingham, 14/1437, Pte., k. in a., F. & F., 25/8/17.
Price, Marshall Bates, b. Nottingham, e. Deptford, Kent (Greenwich, Kent), 28978, Pte., d. of w., F. & F., 8/10/17.
Pritchard, Gerald Henry, b. Leicester, e. Birmingham, 15/1384, Pte., d. of w., F. & F., 6/10/17.
Pugh, Gordon, e. Birmingham (Small Heath, Birmingham), 242525, Pte., d. of w., F. & F., 13/10/17.
Pugh, Joseph Edward, b. Ladywood, Birmingham, e. Birmingham, 2235, Pte., d. of w., F. & F. 26/8/17.
Pulling, Frederick, e. Birmingham, 201124, Pte., d. of w., F. & F., 7/10/17.
Quarterman, Ernest Richard, b. Aston, Birmingham, e. Birmingham, 71, Sgt., k. in a., F. & F., 19/8/16.
Randell, Samuel, e. Birmingham, 330137, Pte., k. in a., F. & F., 4/10/17.
Rands, Percy, b. St. Marks, Birmingham, e. Birmingham, 200313, Pte., k. in a., F. & F., 14/8/17.
Reeve, Henry George, b. Stoke, Newington, Middx., e. Hackney, London (Stoke, Newington), 28970, Pte., k. in a., F. & F., 22/8/17.
Reeves, William, e. Birmingham, 200740, Pte., d. of w., F. & F., 13/8/17.
Rhodes, John, b. Wolverhampton, Staffs, e. Birmingham, 2609, Pte., k. in a., F. & F., 18/7/16.
Rickerby, William John, b. St. Thomas, Birmingham, e. Birmingham, 2102, A/Cpl., d. of w., F. & F., 21/11/16.
Ridgley, John Henry, b. Birmingham, e. Birmingham, 241625, Pte., k. in a., F. & F., 4/10/17.
Roberts, Arthur, b. Warrington, Lancs, e. Warrington, 203456, L/Sgt., k. in a., F. & F., 4/10/17, formerly 2394, S. Lancs. Regt.
Roberts, Joseph, b. Rowley Regis, Birmingham, e. Birmingham (Blackheath, Birmingham), 241428, Pte., k. in a., F. & F., 9/8/17.
Robins, Edward George, b. Birmingham, e. Birmingham, 200312, Cpl., d. of w., F. & F., 17/4/17.
Robinson, Harry, e. Birmingham, 3592, Pte., k. in a., F. & F., 18/8/16.
Rock, Thomas, b. Southwick, Durham, e. Winchester, Hants (Southampton), 242315, Pte., k. in a., F. & F., 25/8/17, formerly 9730, Hants R.
Roper, Harry, b. Sutton Coldfield, Warwicks, e. Sutton Coldfield, 241586, Pte., k. in a., F. & F., 4/10/17.
Rowe, Arthur Nathaniel, b. Bermondsey, London, e. Rotherhithe, Kent (Bermondsey). 29054, Pte., k. in a., F. & F., 24/8/17.
Rugman, Victor Henry, e. Birmingham (Huntley, Glos.), 201406, Pte., k. in a., F. & F., 28/6/16.
Sadler, Reginald, b. Plymouth, Devon, e. Birmingham (Plymouth), 200125, L/Cpl., k. in a. F. & F., 29/10/17.
Salt, George Henry, e. Birmingham (Edgbaston, Birmingham), 201380, Pte., k. in a., F. & F., 9/9/18.
Scandrett, William, e. Birmingham, 2914, Pte., k. in a., F. & F., 19/8/16.
Seal, Bertie, b. Tamworth, Warwicks, e. Alveston, Warwicks (Tamworth), 201748, A/Sgt., k. in a., F. & F., 9/9/18.
Selves, Walter, b. Staplehurst, Kent, e. Maidstone, Kent (West Farleigh, Kent), 33937, Pte., d. of w., F. & F., 4/10/17, formerly 202755, E. Kent Regt.
Sharp, James Davidson, b. Warwick, e. Birmingham, 1986, Pte., k. in a., F. & F., 18/7/16.
Shepherd, Samuel, b. Birmingham, e. Birmingham, 4952, Pte., d. of w., F. & F., 25/7/16.
Sheppard, Arthur, b. Birmingham, e. Birmingham, 5243, Pte., k. in a., F. & F., 18/7/16.
Sherrington, James, e. Preston, Lancs, 202516, Pte., k. in a., F. & F., 4/10/17, formerly 3049, N. Lancs Regt.
Showell, Alfred John, b. St. Thomas, Birmingham, e. Birmingham, 200051, Sgt., k. in a., F. & F., 23/8/17.
Siddall, William, b. Birmingham, e. Birmingham, 201312, Cpl., k. in a., F. & F., 4/10/17.
Sims, Bernard, b. Birmingham, e. Birmingham, 202012, Pte., k. in a., F. & F., 15/6/18.
Skett, Edwin, e. Birmingham, 200699, L/Cpl., k. in a., F. & F., 4/10/17.
Smith, Albert, b. Birmingham, e. Birmingham, 201257, Pte., k. in a., F. & F., 25/8/17.
Smith, Frederick, b. Aston, Birmingham, e. Birmingham, 200527, L/Cpl., k. in a., F. & F., 4/10/17.
Smith, Richard, e. Birmingham, 3064, Pte., k. in a., F. & F., 5/10/16.
Smith, Sydney, b. Aston, Birmingham, e. Birmingham, 2572, Pte., k. in a., F. & F., 6/5/15.
Smith, Sydney, e. Birmingham, 200729, Pte., k. in a., F. & F., 22/8/17.
Smith, Thomas, b. Rise, Yorks, e. Hull, Yorks (Withernwick, Yorks), 33370, Pte., k. in a., F. & F., 9/9/18, formerly 188406, R.A.S.C.
Solomons, John, b. Stepney, London, e. London (Stepney), 29058, Pte., k. in a., F. & F., 10/8/17.
Spencer, Wallworth, b. Longton, Staffs, e. Longton, 54603, Pte., k. in a., F. & F., 2/11/18, formerly 49619, S. Staffs Regt.
Stanley, Harry, b. Birmingham, e. Birmingham, 202030, Pte., k. in a., F. & F., 22/8/17.
Starling, Ernest John, b. Plymouth, Devon, e. Plymouth, 202035, Pte., k. in a., F. & F., 29/3/17.
Starling, Percy Frederick, b. Ladywood, Birmingham, e. Birmingham, 2245, L/Cpl., k. in a., F. & F., 8/8/16.
Steane, Clarence, b. St. Mary's, Birmingham, e. Birmingham, 1531, Sgt., d. of w., F. & F., 24/8/16.
Stone, Arthur Henry, b. Birmingham, e. Birmingham, 2419, Dmr., k. in a., F. & F., 18/7/16.
Stone, Francis Albert, b. Uffculme, Devon, e. Derby (Chellaston, Derby), 28871, Pte., k. in a., F. & F., 9/8/17, formerly S/290445, R.A.S.C.
Stringer, Alfred James, b. Small Heath, Birmingham, e. Birmingham (Smethwick, Staffs), 14/1535, Pte., k. in a., F. & F., 10/8/17.
Stokes, Robert, b. Kings Norton, Birmingham, e. Birmingham (Kings Norton), 200366, Sgt., k. in a., F. & F., 4/10/17.
Sullivan, Joseph, b. Highgate, Birmingham, e. Birmingham, 2528, Pte., k. in a., F. & F., 27/4/15.
Summers, Albert, b. Ladywood, Birmingham, e. Birmingham, 200457, Sgt., k. in a., F. & F., 4/10/17.
Swindells, Herbert, e. Birmingham (Smethwick, Birmingham), 4260, Pte., k. in a., F. & F., 17/7/16.
Taylor, Harry, b. Cradley Heath, Staffs, e. Birmingham (Old Hill, Birmingham), 5369, Pte., d. of w., F. & F., 4/8/16.
Taylor, John William, e. Nuneaton, Warwicks (Birmingham), 202734, Pte., k. in a., F. & F., 4/10/17.
Taylor, William Charles, b. Redhill, Warwicks, e. Redditch, Worcs. (Grafton, Warwicks), 203337, Pte., k. in a., F. & F., 26/6/18.
Tedd, Herbert, b. Coventry, e. Coventry, 202021, L/Cpl., k. in a., F. & F., 24/8/17.
Templer, John Harry, b. Grays, Essex, e. Grays, 33939, Pte., k. in a., F. & F., 4/10/17, formerly 202789, E. Kent Regt.
Thomas, Arthur, e. Birmingham, 200700, Pte., k. in a., F. & F., 10/8/17.
Thomas, Henry Francis, b. Birmingham, e. Birmingham, 200369, Pte., d. of w., F. & F., 29/1/17.
Tilley, Richard, e. Birmingham, 5695, Pte., k. in a., F. & F., 18/7/16.
Tomlin, William, b. Aston, Birmingham, e. Birmingham, 4641, Pte., d. of w., F. & F., 24/8/17.
Trigg, Walter, e. Holloway, London, 29021, Pte., k. in a., F. & F., 27/8/17.
Trubody, Abraham, e. Bristol, Glos., 206929, Pte., d. of w., F. & F., 20/10/17.
Trueman, William, b. Birmingham, 200287, Pte., k. in a., F. & F., 29/3/17.
Turner, Alfred Henry, b. St. Georges, Birmingham, e. Birmingham, 2436, Cpl., k. in a., F. & F., 26/7/15.
Turner, Arthur, b. Hockley, Birmingham, e. Birmingham (Handsworth, Staffs), 2573, Pte., k. in a., F. & F., 25/4/16.
Turvey, William Arthur, b. Lozells, Birmingham, e. Birmingham, 2505, Pte., d. of w., F. & F., 24/6/15.
Villers, Arthur Edward, b. West Ham, Essex, e. Stratford, Essex (London), 28987, Pte., k. in a., F. & F., 22/8/17.
Wakelin, Francis Ernest, e. Birmingham, 3323, L/Cpl., k. in a., F. & F., 2/7/16.
Walters, John, e. Birmingham, 24111, Pte., k. in a., F. & F., 9/8/17.
Warder, Arthur Charles, b. Yardley, Birmingham, e. Birmingham, 240742, L/Cpl., d. of w., F. & F., 30/10/17.
Warburton, George, b. St. Pauls, Warrington, Lancs, e. Birmingham (Warrington), 2693, Pte., d. of w., F. & F., 26/6/15.
Warner, Robert, e. Birmingham, 4081, Pte., d. of w., F. & F., 18/6/15.
Waters, John Thomas, b. Birmingham, e. Birmingham, 33942, Pte., k. in a., F. & F., 1/11/17, formerly 4787, E. Kent Regt.
Watkins, Edwin John, b. Clydach, Glam., e. Swansea, Glam., 203439, Pte., k. in a., F. & F., 17/4/17, formerly 1304, Welsh Regt.
Watkins, William George, b. Stoke Newington, London, e. London, 29037, Pte., k. in a., F. & F., 25/8/17.
Watts, Rupert William, b. Soho, Birmingham, e. Birmingham, 200509, Pte., d. of w., F. & F., 19/8/17.
Webb, Ernest, b. Long Compton, Warwick, e. Warwick (Stow-on-the-Wold, Glos.), 203011, Pte., d. of w., F. & F., 10/8/17. formerly 3528, Warwick Yeo.
Webber, Charles James Stuart, b. Stratford, Essex, e. Woolwich, Kent (Plaistow, Kent), 33340, Pte., k. in a., F. & F., 9/9/18, formerly 207410, R.A.S.C.
West, William, b. Saltley, Birmingham, e. Birmingham (Saltley, Birmingham), 193, Sgt., k. in a., F. & F., 18/7/16.
Weston, Harry John, b. Birmingham, e. Birmingham, 201996, Pte., k. in a., F. & F., 22/7/17.
Westwood, Thomas Leonard, b. St. Martin's, Birmingham, e. Birmingham, 2309, Pte., k. in a., F. & F., 4/6/15.
Wharton, John, b. Formby, Lancs, e. Kilburn, Middx. (Harrow Weald, Middx.), 34521, Pte., k. in a., F. & F., 9/9/18, formerly 16064, Middx. Regt.

Ward, Herbert, b. Woolwich, Kent, e. Birmingham (Woolwich), 200040, Sgt., k. in a., F. & F., 1/10/17.
Wheeldon, Arthur, e. Birmingham (Aston, Birmingham), 5997, Pte., k. in a., F. & F., 18/8/15.
White, Albert Arthur, e. Birmingham, 3350, Pte., k. in a., F. & F., 18/7/15.
White, Edwin, b. Chertsey, Surrey, e. Holloway, London (Manor Park, London), 28071, Pte., k. in a., F. & F., 25/8/17.
White, Joseph Sims, e. Birmingham, 2959, Pte., k. in a., F. & F., 24/8/15.
White, William Henry, b. Whitnash, Leamington, e. Leamington, Warwicks, 265363, Pte., d. of w., F.& F., 10/9/18.
Whitehead, John William, b. Sparkbrook, Birmingham, e. Birmingham (Sparkbrook), 200460, Pte., k. in a., F. & F., 25/8/17.
Whitehouse, John, b. Birmingham, Warwicks, e. Birmingham, 201,974, Pte., k. in a., F. & F., 17/4/17.
Whittle, Harry Victor, b. Southwark, London, e. Woolwich, London (Camberwell, London), 29051, Pte., k. in a., F. & F., 4/10/17.
Wiles, Albert, b. Everton, Beds, e. Sandy, Beds, 34506, Pte., d., F. & F., 15/10/18, formerly 9272, Beds Regt.
Williams, George Henry, b. Birmingham, e. Birmingham, 443, Sgt., k. in a., F. & F., 18/7/16. M.M.
Williams, Stanley, b. Birmingham, e. Birmingham, 5285, Pte., k. in a., F. & F., 18/7/16.
Willis, Edward Percy, b. Nechells, Birmingham, e. Birmingham, 200631, Pte., k. in a., F. & F., 22/8/17.
Winfield, Harry James, b. Hanley, Staffs, e. Birmingham, 1902, Pte., k. in a., F. & F., 17/11/16.
Witherford, John Arthur, b. Birmingham, e. Birmingham, 33941, Pte., k. in a., F. & F., 4/10/17, formerly 4736, E. Kent Regt.
Wood, Arthur Thomas, e. Birmingham (King's Norton, Birmingham), 201414, Pte., k. in a., F. & F., 6/2/17.
Wood, Frederick Leonard, b. St. Martin's, Birmingham, e. Birmingham, 66, Pte., d., F. & F., 9/2/16.
Woodroffe, Albert Sydney, b. Birmingham, e. Birmingham, 14/1686, Pte., k. in a., F. & F., 4/10/17.
Woodward, John, b. Birmingham, e. Birmingham, 5371, Pte., d. of w., F. & F., 2/11/16.
Woodward, Richard Henry, b. Birmingham, e. Birmingham, 16/1710, Pte., k. in a., F. & F., 4/10/17.
Woolley, Sydney Albert, b. London, e. Birmingham, 202969, Pte., k. in a., F. & F., 10/8/17.
Wordley, James Thomas George, b. Sydenham, Surrey, e. Southend, Kent (Westcliff-on-Sea, Kent), 29057, Pte., k. in a., F. & F., 4/10/17.
Wright, Alfred William, b. Birmingham, e. Birmingham, 5575, Pte., d. of w., F. & F., 13/11/16.
Wright, Harry, e. Birmingham, 201103, Pte., k. in a., F. & F., 10/8/17.
Wyatt, Harold, b. Llenrhos, Llandudno, Carnarvonshire, e. Birmingham (Llenrhos), 200568, Pte., k. in a., F. & F., 28/6/16.
Yorke, Arthur, b. Birmingham, e. Birmingham, 242350, Pte., k. in a., F. & F., 6/10/17.

2/8th Battalion.

Adams, Bernard, b. Walsall, Staffs, e. Wednesbury, Staffs Walsall), 20391, Pte., k. in a., F. & F., 20/12/16.
Allen, Joseph, b. Hyde, Ches, e. Hyde, 29105, Pte, k. in a., F. & F., 6/9/17, formerly 61930, Ches. Regt.
Amos Ernest, b. Coalville, Leics., e. Nuneaton, Warwicks (Nuneaton), 203195, Pte., k. in a., F. & F., 3/12/17.
Ashmore, Richard William, b. Warwick, e. Warwick, 28392, Pte., k. in a., F. & F., 3/9/17.
Aylesbury, Charles James, e. Abergavenny, Mon. (Abertillery, Mon.), 235035, Pte., k in a., F. & F., 6/9/17, formerly 290656, Mon. Regt.
Ayscough, John Walter, b. Derby, e. Birmingham (Handsworth, Staffs), 7970, L/Cpl., k. in a., F. & F., 6/9/17.
Bailey, Frank Mawson, b. Haworth, Yorks, e. Keighley, Yorks (Haworth), 203252, Pte., k. in a., F. & F., 5/10/17, formerly 140410, R.F.A.
Baker, Frederick Albert, b. Seaford, Sussex, e. Newhaven, Sussex (Seaford), 20369, Pte., k. in a., F. & F., 10/12/16, formerly 148563, R.F.A.
Ball, William, b. Redhill, Surrey, e. Leamington, Warwicks 201983, Pte., k. in a., F. & F., 22/4/17.
Barker, Percy Edgar, b. Birmingham, e. Birmingham, 200645, L/Sgt., k. in a., F. & F., 6/9/17.
Barlow, Joseph, b. St. Mary's, Birmingham, e. Birmingham, 1506, Pte., k. in a., F. & F., 12/9/16.
Barlow, William Edward, b. Bolton, Lancs., e. Bolton, 235007, Pte., k. in a., F. & F., 3/12/17, formerly 291194, Mon. Regt
Batty, John Robert, e. Bolton, Lancs, 202479, Pte., k. in a., F. & F., 3/12/17, formerly 4641, N. Lancs Regt.
Beavers, William Victor, b. Jarrow, Durham, e. Sunderland, Durham, 29813, Pte., k in a., F. & F., 1/9/17, formerly 44920, Yorks Regt.
Bennett, George, e. Birmingham, 201531, Pte., k. in a., F. & F., 4/11/17.
Bentley, Wilfrid, b. Chadderton, Lancs, e. Rochdale, Lancs, 235008, Pte., k. in a., F. & F., 3/12/17, formerly 32883, Mon. Regt.
Berrow, James, e. Birmingham, 201530, Pte., k. in a., F. & F., 17/12/16.
Binnes, Joseph, b. Manchester, e. Salford (Cheetham, Manchester), 201930, L/Sgt., k. in a., F. & F., 6/9/17, formerly 2870, Lancs Fus.
Bishop, Ernest, e. Birmingham, 201009, Pte., d. of w., F. & F., 19/8/17.
Bowkett, George, e. Birmingham (Small Heath, Birmingham), 3648, Sgt., k. in a., F. & F., 18/12/15.
Bretherton, Samuel, b. St. Cuthberts, Lytham, Lancs, e. Lytham, 202480, Pte., k. in a., F. & F., 4/10/17, formerly 1027, N. Lancs. Regt.
Brickell, William Alfred, e. Birmingham (Worcester), 3522, L/Cpl., k. in a., F. & F., 8/8/16.
Brien, James, e. Newport (Aberbeeg, Mon.), 235066, Pte., k. in a., F. & F., 3/12/17, formerly 4036, Mon. Regt., 15018, Welsh Regt., and 292280, Mon. Regt.
Broome, Herbert, b. Boness, Linlithgow, e. Boness, 202530, Pte., k. in a., F. & F., 1/9/17, formerly 2123, R. Scots.
Brown, Alfred James, e. Coventry, 24585, Pte., d. of w., F. & F., 6/12/17.
Brown, Ernest, b. Shelley, Huddersfield, Yorks, e. Huddersfield (Thurstonland, Yorks), 30440, Pte., d. of w., F. & F., 20/11/17, formerly 3/31749, N. Staff. Regt.
Brown, Horace Newland, e. Birmingham (Moseley, Birmingham), 3387, Pte., k. in a., F. & F., 19/10/16.
Burke, Michael, b. St. Mary's, Birmingham, e. Birmingham, 1659, L/Cpl., k. in a., F. & F., 8/8/16.
Bush, William, b. Wrington, Somerset, e. Bristol (Bedminster, Bristol), 27941, Pte., k. in a., F. & F., 3/12/17.
Butler, Albert, b. Rhodes, Lancs, e. Middleton, Lancs (Rhodes), 7325, Pte., k. in a., F. & F., 2/7/16, formerly 8993, Lanc. Fus.
Button, William John, b. Tottenham, Middx., e. Norwood, Surrey (Tulse Hill, Surrey), 203105, Pte., d. of w., F. & F., 14/12/17, formerly 11332, A. Cyclist Corps.
Buxton, Joseph, b. St. Bartholomews, Salford, Lancs, e. Salford, 202408, Pte., k. in a., F. & F., 3/12/17, formerly 1821, Lancs Fus.
Cantrell, John Arthur, e. Birmingham (Sparkbrook, Birmingham), 4100, Pte., d. of w., F. & F., 22/8/16.
Carney, Patrick, e. Lower Broughton, Lancs (Farnworth, Lancs), 7323, Pte., k. in a., F. & F., 2/7/16, formerly 3963, Lancs Fus.
Carter, George, e. Birmingham, 5755, L/Cpl., k. in a., F. & F., 2/7/16.
Carter William, b. Birmingham, e. Birmingham, 5447, Pte., k. in a., F. & F., 10/12/16.
Cemm, Howard, b. St. Lukes, Birmingham, e. Coventry, 266864, L/Sgt., d. of w., F. & F., 19/1/18.
Chapman, Harold Thornton, b. Connecticut, U.S.A., e. Manchester (Urmaston, Manchester), 6225, Pte., d. of w., F. & F., 5/8/16, formerly 1633, Manch. Regt.
Chapman, William, b. Birmingham, e. Birmingham, 202218, Pte., k. in a., F. & F., 6/9/17.
Chappelow, John Harold, e. Birmingham (Tamworth, Staffs), 2947, Pte., d. of w., F. & F., 13/1/17.
Chare, Albert, b. Aston, Birmingham, e. Birmingham, 203298, Pte., k. in a., F. & F., 6/9/17.
Charnley, John William, b. Blackburn, Lancs, e. Blackburn, 203216, Pte., k. in a., F. & F., 6/9/17, formerly 11855, A. Cyclist Corps.
Clarke, William, b. London, e. Crewe, Ches., 29116, Pte., k. in a., F. & F., 3/12/17, formerly 62235, Ches. Regt.
Clements, Ernest, e. Birmingham (Saltley, Birmingham), 200947, Cpl., d. of w., F. & F., 7/9/17.
Coley, Walter, b. Birmingham, e. Birmingham, 2217, Pte., d. of w., F. & F., 1/6/16.
Collins, Horace John, e. Birmingham, 2975, Pte., k. in a., F. & F., 26/7/15.
Cook, John, b. Preston, Lancs, e. Fauldhouse, West Lothian (Penwortham, Lancs), 7284, Pte., k. in a., F. & F., 10/12/16, formerly 2228, R. Scots.
Cooper, Albert, b. Hockley Heath, Birmingham, e. Warwick (Shirley, Birmingham), 203185, Pte., k. in a., F. & F., 28/4/17.
Cooper, Stanley George, e. Birmingham, 200720, Sgt., k. in a., F. & F., 3/12/17.
Cornock, Frederick, b. Coleshill, Warwickshire, e. Birmingham (Handsworth, Staffs), 20256, Pte., k. in a., F. & F., 26/2/17.
Cornwall, Albert, b. Great Alne, Warwickshire, e. Stratford-on-Avon, Warwickshire (Great Alne), 203085, Pte., k. in a., F. & F., 3/12/17.
Corvell, William George, b. Coggeshall, Essex, e. Warley, Essex (Coggeshall), 29792, Pte., k. in a., F. & F., 3/12/17, formerly 21125, Essex Regt.
Cox, George, b. Kilmerston, Somerset, e. Gerrard's Cross, Bucks, 235027, Pte., d. of w., F. & F., 7/9/17, formerly 33651, Worcs. Regt.
Cryer, John, b. Littleborough, Lancs, e. Rochdale, Lancs, 6228, Pte., k. in a., F. & F., 3/7/16, formerly 10255, Lancs. Fus.
Daniels, George Albert, b. Coventry, e. Coventry, 16854, Pte., k. in a., F. & F., 3/12/17.
Davis, Claude, b. Birmingham, e. Birmingham, 5694, Pte., d. of w., F. & F., 8/8/16.
Day, William, b. Stow-on-the-Wold, Glos., e. Kenilworth, Warwickshire, 22781, Pte., k. in a., F. & F., 6/9/17.
Dodds, John Robert, b. Newcastle-on-Tyne, e. Whitehall, London (Newcastle-on-Tyne), 203211, Pte., k. in a., F. & F., 28/4/17, formerly 11755, A. Cyclist Corps.
Doig, Harold, e. Salford, Manchester (Old Trafford, Manchester), 7324, Pte., k. in a., F. & F., 10/7/16, formerly 2783, Lancs. Fus.
Donald, Neil, b. Whitburn, Linlithgow, e. Fauldhouse, West Lothian (Whitburn), 7285, Pte., k. in a., F. & F., 7/8/16, formerly 1027, R. Scots.
Dovey, Sydney William, b. Hockley, Birmingham, e. Birmingham (Handsworth, Staffs), 12616, Pte., k. in a., F. & F., 23/3/18.
Downing, Benjamin, b. Manchester, e. Salford, Lancs (Hulme, Manchester), 201935, Pte., k. in a., F. & F., 1/9/17, formerly 2035, Lancs. Fus.

Drew, Charles Alfred, e. Birmingham (King's Heath, Birmingham), 200887, Sgt., d. of w., F. & F., 13/12/17.
Dronsfield, Herbert, b. Oldham, Lancs, e. Oldham, 7136, Pte., k. in a., F. & F., 8/8/16, formerly 1789, Manchester Regt.
Duckworth, Levi, e. Preston, 7226, Pte., k. in a., F. & F., 8/8/16, formerly 3119, N. Lancs. Regt.
Earl, William, b. Salford, Lancs, e. Salford, 6233, Pte., k. in a., F. & F., 22/8/16, formerly 2868, Lancs. Fus.
Earnshaw, Charles Frederick, b. Salford, Lancs, e. Salford, 202412, Pte., d. of w., F. & F., 6/10/17, formerly 2017, Lancs. Fus.
Elliott, Alfred, b. Bakewell, Derby, e. Bakewell, 203228, Pte., d., F. & F., 16/5/17, formerly 42897, R.F.A.
Ellis, John Henry, b. Rochdale, Lancs, e. Rochdale, 6235, L/Cpl., k. in a., F. & F., 8/8/16, formerly 10427, Lancs. Fus.
Embley, William, e. Birmingham, 2794, Pte., k. in a., F. & F., 8/8/16.
Evans, Edward, e. Birmingham, 3877, Pte., d. of w., F. & F., 13/10/16.
Evans, William, e. Birmingham, 201050, Pte., k. in a., F. & F., 26/3/17.
Faulkner, Samuel Turner, b. Royton, Warwicks, e. Coventry, 201682, Pte., d., F. & F., 25/1/17.
Fellows, Samuel, b. Bubbenhall, Warwicks, e. Warwick, 203184, Sgt., k. in a., F. & F., 6/9/17.
Felton, Percy, b. Birmingham, e. Birmingham, 5516, Pte., k. in a., F. & F., 8/8/16.
Finch, Charles Albert, b. Coventry, e. Leamington, Warwicks, 20287, Pte., k. in a., F. & F., 6/9/17.
Fisher, William Sydney, e. Birmingham, 201496, Pte., k. in a., F. & F., 8/8/16.
Fleming, Joseph, e. Middlesbrough, Yorks, 29805, Pte., d. of w., F. & F., 3/9/17, formerly 30871, Yorks Regt.
Fletcher, Thomas, b. Latham, Lancs, e. Ormskirk, Ches. (Latham), 235048, Pte., d., F. & F., 1/11/18, formerly 5073, R. W. Fus., 4803 Mon. Regt.
Forrest, John, b. Rochdale, Lancs, e. Todmorden, Lancs, 7326, Pte., k. in a., F. & F., 2/7/16, formerly 9091, Lancs Fus.
Foster, Charles, e. Birmingham, 201065, Pte., k. in a., F. & F., 6/9/17.
Franklin, Frederick Cecil, b. Birmingham, e. Birmingham, 5730, L/Cpl., k. in a., F. & F., 10/7/16.
French, Samuel, e. Birmingham, 201524, Pte., k. in a., F. & F., 8/8/16.
Furze, Joseph, e. Birmingham, 2778, Pte., k. in a., F. & F., 10/12/16.
Gardner, William Young, b. Bathgate, Midlothian, e. Leamington, Warwicks, 203232, L/Cpl., d. of w., F. & F., 20/9/17 formerly 148555, R.H.A.
Garmston, James, b. Middle, Salop, e. Shrewsbury, 235077, Pte., k. in a., F. & F., 6/9/17, formerly 203593, Shrops. L.I.
Gaunt, Percy William, b. Wrexham, N. Wales, e. Birmingham (Stourport, Worcs), 5523, Pte., k. in a., F. & F., 2/7/16.
Gilbert, Arthur Victor, b. Balsall Heath, Birmingham, e. Birmingham (Balsall Heath), 200375, L/Cpl., k. in a., F. & F., 28/4/17.
Gladman, Thomas Frederick, b. Catsfield, Sussex, e. Hillsea, Sussex (Fletching, Sussex), 203238, Pte., d. of w., F. & F., 7/12/17, formerly 148559, R.F.A.
Gliddon, William George, b. Holsworthy, Devon, e. Okehampton, Devon (Ashwater, Devon), 203239, Pte., k. in a., F. & F., 3/12/17, formerly 130449, R.F.A.
Green, Walter, b. Stockton, Warwicks, e. Rugby, Warwicks (Long Lawford, Warwicks), 203135, Pte., k. in a., F. & F., 25/4/17.
Gregson, Albert, b. Preston, Lancs, e. Preston, 202492, Pte., k. in a., F. & F., 8/8/16, formerly 3402, N. Lancs. Regt.
Griffiths, James Edward, b. St. Georges, Birmingham, e. Birmingham, 200165, Cpl., k. in a., F. & F., 6/9/17.
Grimley, Harry, b. Coventry, 201695, Pte., k. in a., F. & F., 13/7/16.
Gwynne, Harry, e. Birmingham, 2277, Pte., k. in a., F. & F., 8/8/16.
Hall, Herbert, b. Paddock, Yorks, e. Huddersfield, Yorks, 30447, Pte., k. in a., F. & F., 3/12/17, formerly 3/32362, N. Staff. Regt.
Haley, William, b. Coventry, e. Coventry, 203116, Pte., k. in a., F. & F., 1/9/17.
Haley, William Thomas, b. Birmingham, e. Birmingham, 200023, Cpl., k. in a., F. & F., 1/9/17.
Halstead, Arthur, b. Huddersfield, Yorks, e. Huddersfield (Lockwood, Yorks), 30445, Pte., k. in a., F. & F., 6/9/17, formerly 3/32043, N. Staffs. Regt.
Hambling, Harry, e. Birmingham, 3467, Pte., k. in a., F. & F., 8/8/16.
Hanby, Henry, b. Driffield, Yorks, e. Leeds, Yorks, 29777, Pte., d. of w., F. & F., 3/12/17, formerly 34503, W. Yorks Regt.
Hardwick, Ernest William John, e. Birmingham, 4476, L/Cpl., k. in a., F. & F., 10/12/16.
Harley, Arthur, e. Birmingham, 201584, L/Cpl., k. in a., F. & F., 4/11/17.
Harley, Richard, b. Trotshill, Worcs, e. Bridgnorth, Salop, 235078, Pte., k. in a., F. & F., 6/9/17, formerly 6471 Shrops. L.I.
Hartley, John Robert, b. Manchester, e. Salford, Lancs, (Sale, Cheshire), 6246, Pte., k. in a., F. & F., 2/7/16, formerly 2618, Lancs. Fus.
Harwood, Percy, b. Cubbington, Warwicks, e. Leamington, Warwicks (Cubbington), 203096, Pte., k. in a., F. & F., 6/9/17.
Hawkesford, Clarence, e. Birmingham (Smethwick, Staffs), 201572, Cpl., k. in a., F. & F., 6/9/17.
Hawkins, John, b. Aston, Birmingham, e. Birmingham (Aston), 200174, L/Cpl., k. in a., F. & F., 6/9/17.
Haywood, Francis Harry, e. Birmingham, 201497, Pte., k. in a., F. & F., 3/12/17.
Hickman, William Samuel, e. Birmingham, 5763, L/Cpl., k. in a., F. & F., 8/8/16.
Higgs, William, b. Oakley, Bucks, e. Birmingham, 2074, Pte., k. in a., F. & F., 8/8/16.
Hobson, Joseph, b. Manchester, e. Birkenhead (Manchester), 29106, Pte., k. in a., F. & F., 6/9/17, formerly 62268, Cheshire Regt.
Hodgson, George, b. Manchester, e. Wallasey (New Brighton, Ches.), 29101, Pte., k. in a., F. & F., 6/9/17, formerly 61901, Cheshire Regt.
Hollis, Frederick, b. Coventry, e. Warwick (Foleshill, Coventry) 20300, Pte., d., F. & F., 13/2/17.
Hosgood, Henry Leonard, b Birmingham, e. Birmingham (Aston, Birmingham), 202238, Pte., d. of w., F. & F., 4/12/17.
Houghton, James, b. Whitacre, nr. Coleshill, Warwicks., e. Birmingham (Nether Whitacre), 5450, Pte., k. in a., F. & F., 8/8/16.
Howard, John Alfred, e. Birmingham, 4536, Pte., k. in a., F. & F., 3/7/16.
Howarth, Philip Thomas, e. Preston, 202496, Pte., k. in a., F. & F., 17/1/18, formerly 4282, North Lancs. Regt.
Howell, Arthur, b. Tottenham, Middlesex, e. Fulham, Middx., 29784, Pte., k. in a., F. & F., 3/12/17, formerly 41463, Yorks Regt.
Hughes, Harry, b. St. Mary's, Oldham, Lancs, e. Oldham, 202366, Pte., k. in a., F. & F., 6/9/17, formerly 1823, Manchester Regt.
Hull, Frank Sydney, b. Chardstock, Som., e. Axminster, Som. (Chardstock), 203229, Pte., k. in a., F. & F., 25/4/17, formerly 130487, R.F.A.
Hunter, Alfred, e. Preston, 202500, Pte., k. in a., F. & F., 5/12/17, formerly 3772, North Lancs. Regt.
Hunter, Frederick James, b. Coton, Staffs, e. Atherstone, Warwicks (Glascote, nr. Tamworth), 19084, Pte., k. in a., F. & F., 3/12/17.
Hyatt, Henry, b. Greet, Birmingham, e. Birmingham (Sparkhill, Birmingham), 12257, L/Cpl., d. of w., F. & F., 6/9/17.
Jackson, Frederick, b. Manchester, e. Manchester, 235013, Pte., k. in a., F. & F., 1/9/17, formerly 5148, Mon. Regt.
Jackson, Henry, b. Newcastle, Northumberland, e. Newcastle, 30449, Pte., k. in a., F. & F., 6/9/17, formerly 31607, North Staffs. Regt.
Jackson, Herbert Arthur, e. Birmingham (Sutton Coldfield), 200795, Cpl., d. of w., F. & F., 9/12/17.
James, John, e. Coventry, 266468, Sgt., k. in a., F. & F., 3/12/17.
James, William Pearson, e. Manchester (Ardwick, Manchester), 0312, Pte., k. in a., F. & F., 2/7/16, formerly 1978, Manchester Regt.
Jolly, Harry, b. St. Mary's, Oldham, Lancs, e. Oldham, 202374, Pte., k. in a., F. & F., 3/12/17, formerly 1310, Manchester Regt.
Jones, James, b. Oldham, Lancs, e. Oldham, 7094, Pte., k. in a., F. & F., 21/10/16, formerly 1793 Manchester Regt.
Jones, Joseph, b. St. Michael's, Chester, e. Chester, 29089, Pte., k. in a., F. & F., 3/12/17, formerly 62051, Ches. Regt.
Jones, Robert, b. Edgbaston, Birmingham, e. Birmingham (Edgbaston), 200393, Pte., k. in a., F. & F., 24/7/16.
Jones, Sidney Clifford, e. Birmingham, 200941, C.Q.M.S., k. in a., F. & F., 6/9/17.
Jones, Daniel James, b. Treharris, Glam., e. Birmingham, 18836, Pte., k. in a., F. & F., 6/9/17.
Kelly, John, b. Armagh, Co. Ulster, e. West Calder, Scotland (Midlothian, Scotland), 268305, Pte., k. in a., F. & F., 3/12/17, formerly 2259, Royal Scots.
Kenwrick, Eramus, e. Birmingham, 201209, Pte., k. in a., F. & F., 3/12/17.
Lackleson, Albert Chadwick, b. St. Paul's, Bury, e. Bury, Lancs, 202434, L/Cpl., k. in a., F. & F., 1/9/17, formerly 1659, Lancs. Fus.
Lang, James Thomas, e. Stockport, 29113, Pte., k. in a., F. & F., 3/12/17, formerly 61945, Cheshire Regt.
Leverington, William, b. Blackley, Manchester, e. Middleton (Blackley, Manchester), 201895, L/Cpl., k. in a., F. & F., 8/9/17, formerly 9002, Lancs. Fus.
Lidster, William, b. Sheffield, e. Birmingham (Aston, Birmingham), 203315, Pte., k. in a., F. & F., 16/4/17.
Lovett, Horace Frederick, b. Birmingham, e. Birmingham (Winson Green, Birmingham), 2281, Pte., k. in a., F. & F., 8/8/16.
Lowe, William Henry, b. Birmingham, e. Coventry, 24550, Pte., k. in a., F. & F., 6/9/17.
Lunn, William, e. Coventry, 24579, Pte., k. in a., F. & F., 8/11/17.
Maddocks, John, b. Norbury, Ches., e. Whitchurch, Ches., 235082, Pte., k. in a., F. & F., 3/12/17, formerly 203601, Shrops L.I.
Mann, Albert George, b. Moreton Morrell, Warwicks., e. Leamington Spa, Warwicks (Shutford, Oxon), 330771, Pte., k. in a., F. & F., 4/11/17.
Manock, Thomas, b. Middleton Junction, Lancs, e. Middleton, 6263, Pte., k. in a., F. & F., 8/8/16, formerly 9927, Lancs. Fus.
Maslin, Thomas Henry, b. Devizes, e. Devizes, Wilts, 29237, Pte., d. of w., F. & F., 3/12/17, formerly 9029, Wilts Regt.
Matthews, Frank William, b. Fillongley, Warwicks., e. Coventry (Fillongley), 201746, Pte., k. in a., F. & F., 17/4/17.
McAlpine, George, b. Linlithgow, Scotland, e. Linlithgow, 7299, Pte., k. in a., F. & F., 21/10/16, formerly 889, Royal Scots.
Miller, George Donald, e. Birmingham, 200913, Sgt., d. of w., F. & F., 2/9/17.

Minshull, Thomas, b. Wigan, Lancs, e. Atherton, Lancs (Wigan), 202382, Pte., k. in a., F. & F., 10/11/17, formerly 1520, Manchester Regt.
Moore, Walter, b. Bedworth, Warwicks., e. Nuneaton, Warwicks. (Foleshill, Coventry), 203200, Pte., d. of w., F. & F., 6/9/17.
Moreton, Leonard, b. Sparkbrook, Birmingham, e. Birmingham, 1886, Sgt., k. in a., F. & F., 2/7/16.
Morris, George, b. Kensington, London, e. Kensington, 235016, Pte., k. in a., F. & F., 3/12/17, formerly 5422, East Surrey Regt.
Morse, Robert George, e. Danbury, Essex (Stalham, Norfolk), 201433, Pte., k. in a., F. & F., 1/9/17.
Murphy, Thomas, b. St. George's, Birmingham, e. Birmingham, 200351, Pte., k. in a., F. & F., 3/12/17.
Nash, Frank, e. Birmingham (Shirley, Birmingham), 4103, Dmr., d. of w., F. & F., 2/7/16.
Newbury, Albert John, b. Childswickham, Glos., e. Evesham, Worcs. (Childswickham), 28330, Pte., d. of w., F. & F., 5/11/17, formerly 27375, Hussars.
Newton, John, b. Parkfield, Middleton, e. Middleton, Lancs, 202440, Pte., k. in a., F. & F., 8/8/16, formerly 8547, Lancs. Fus.
Ogden, John William, b. Jarrow, Durham, e. Jarrow, 30460, Pte., k. in a., F. & F., 3/12/17, formerly 3/31705, North Staffs. Regt.
Palmer, Harry, e. Birmingham, 200663, Pte., k. in a., F. & F., 1/9/17.
Patrick, Ernest John, b. Aston, Birmingham, e. Birmingham (Aston), 200569, Pte., k. in a., F. & F., 3/12/17.
Patrick, James, b. Foleshill, Coventry, e. Warwick (Longford, Coventry), 203274, Pte., k. in a., F. & F., 3/12/17.
Patten, John Oultram, b. Bebington, Ches., e. Lower Bebington, Ches. (Higher Bebington, Ches.), 29082, Pte., k. in a., F. & F., 6/9/17, formerly 62244, Ches. Regt.
Pawson, Walter, b. New Shildon, Durham, e. Newcastle-on-Tyne (New Shildon), 203277, Pte., k. in a., F. & F., 28/4/17, formerly 11383, Army Cyclist Corps.
Peach, William Henry, e. Birmingham, 3663, L/Cpl., k. in a., F. & F., 2/7/16.
Pearce, George William Henry, b. London, e. Coventry, 24552, Pte., k. in a., F. & F., 6/9/17.
Pearce, John, b. Salford, Lancs, e. Salford, 201905, Pte., k. in a., F. & F., 6/9/17, formerly 2650, Lancs Fus.
Penman, Peter, b. Bathgate, Linlithgow, e. Bathgate, 202545, L/Cpl., k. in a., F. & F., 1/9/17, formerly 882, R. Scots.
Penny, Harry Cadwallader, b. Culmington, Salop, e. Ludlow, Salop (Craven Arms, Salop), 235084, Pte., k. in a., F. & F., 6/9/17, formerly 203675, Shrops. L.I.
Perks, George Henry, b. St. Georges, Birmingham, e. Birmingham, 330649, Pte., k. in a., F. & F., 6/9/17.
Perks, William, b. Birmingham, e. Birmingham, 201045, Pte., k. in a., F. & F., 16/11/17.
Perry, Arthur, e. Birmingham (Harborne, Birmingham), 201153, Pte., k. in a., F. & F., 6/9/17.
Phillips, Sydney, b. Cheetham, Lancs, e. Manchester, 201910, Pte., k. in a., F. & F., 19/11/17, formerly 1728, Manch. Regt.
Pickman, Alfred, e. Birmingham, 3024, Pte., k. in a., F. & F., 21/10/16.
Pinney, Ernest George, b. Hemel Hempstead, e. Aylesbury, Bucks (Chesham, Bucks), 25661, Pte., k. in a., F. & F., 14/4/18.
Pitton, William Richard, b. Southam, Warwicks, e. Birmingham (Yardley Wood, Birmingham), 5500, Pte., k. in a., F. & F., 2/7/16.
Platt, George Charles, e. Birmingham, 4528, Pte., k. in a., F. & F., 2/7/16.
Plumley, Albert, e. Birmingham, 201503, Pte., d., F. & F., 5/7/18.
Postans, Albert, e Birmingham, 2773, Pte., k. in a., F. & F., 2/7/16.
Powell, Frederick Charles, e. Birmingham, 5761, Pte., k. in a., F. & F., 26/2/17.
Powell, Norman, b. Oakworth, Yorks, e. Halifax, Yorks (Oakworth), 29806, Pte., k. in a., F. & F., 5/9/17, formerly 38164, Yorks Regt.
Price, Albert, b. Warwick, e. Warwick, 203258, Pte., k. in a., F. & F., 1/9/17, formerly 130464, R.F.A.
Prince, George, e. Salford (Manchester), 202446, L/Cpl., k. in a., F. & F., 8/11/17, formerly 2589, Lancs Fus.
Prince, John, b. St. Clements, Salford, Lancs, e. Salford (Lower Broughton, Manchester), 6280, Pte., k. in a., F. & F., 25/8/16, formerly 1571, Lancs Fus.
Prior, Robert Edwood Ernest, e. Birmingham (Moseley, Birmingham), 2787, Pte., d. of w., F. & F., 12/8/16.
Quinton, Harry, e. Bury, Lancs, 202447, Pte., k. in a., F. & F., 6/9/17, formerly 2583, Lancs Fus.
Ray, Albert, e. Birmingham, 3404, L/Cpl., d. of w., F. & F., 13/10/16.
Reeves, Ernest John, e. Birmingham, 201483, L/Cpl., k. in a., F. & F., 6/9/17.
Rhodes, Richard, e. Preston, Lancs, 7258, Cpl., k. in a., F. & F., 12/9/16, formerly 4576, N. Lancs Regt.
Richmond, Harry, e. Birmingham, 201589, Pte., d. of w., F. & F., 24/12/17.
Rimmer, Thomas, b. Parbold, Wigan, e. Wigan, Lancs, 202392, Pte., d. of w., F. & F., 3/9/17, formerly 1637, Manchester Regt.
Roberts, Zaccheaus, b. St. Luke's, Barrow-in-Furness, Lancs, e. Salford, Lancs (Manchester), 7327, Pte., k. in a., F. & F., 3/7/16, formerly 1599, Lancs Fus.
Robinson, Ernest, b. Wootton Park, Birmingham, e. Birmingham, 200246, Sgt., d. of w., F. & F., 2/9/17.
Robinson, James, e. Preston, 7260, Pte., k. in a., F. & F., 10/12/16, formerly 4515, N. Lancs Regt.
Rodgers, Thomas, b. Manchester, e. Salford, Lancs (Pendleton, Lancs), 201918, Pte., k. in a., F. & F., 3/12/17, formerly 2543, Lancs Fus.
Roe, Reginald George, b. Birmingham, e. Birmingham (Moseley, Birmingham), 5588, Pte., k. in a., F. & F., 8/8/16.
Rollason, Frank, b. Ladywood, Birmingham, e. Birmingham, 203295, Cpl., k. in a., F. & F., 3/12/17.
Rothblatt, Solomon, b. London, e. Salford, Lancs (Lower Broughton, Lancs), 235023, Pte., k. in a., F. & F., 3/12/17, formerly 32737, Lancs Fus.
Rowan, Ernest Columbus, b. Dublin, e. Kensington, London, 203223, Pte., k. in a., F. & F., 4/10/17, formerly 11963, Army Cyclist Corps.
Rowe, Arthur Leslie, e Birmingham (Small Heath, Birmingham), 3546, Pte., k. in a., F. & F., 26/2/17.
Ruffle, Harry, b. St. Martins, Birmingham, e. Birmingham, 2319, Pte., k. in a., F. & F., 8/8/16.
Russon, Norman Albert, e. Birmingham (Sparkbrook, Birmingham), 4531, L/Cpl., k. in a., F. & F., 2/7/16.
Scott, William, b. St. Georges, Chorley, Lancs, e. Chorley, Lancs, 202518, C.S.M., k. in a., F. & F., 3/12/17, formerly 1162, N. Lancs Regt.
Scotting, Frederick William, b. Bury, Lancs, e. Bury, 201921, Pte., k. in a., F. & F., 28/4/17, formerly 3242, Lancs Fus
Shaw, George Henry, b. St. Michaels, Coventry, e. Coventry, 28584, Pte., k. in a., F. & F., 3/12/17.
Shirley, Jesse, b. Leamington, Warwicks, e. Leamington, 203137, Cpl., k. in a., F. & F., 1/2/18.
Sidebotham, George Edward, e. Birmingham (Small Heath, Birmingham), 200816, C.Q.M.S., k. in a., F. & F., 1/9/17
Smith, Ernest, b. North Biddick, Durham, e. Washington, Durham, 29810, Pte., d. of w., F. & F., 7/9/17, formerly 44963, Yorks Regt.
Smith, Frederick Arthur, e. Birmingham, 200845, Cpl., k. in a., F. & F., 6/9/17.
Spiers, Emanuel, e. Birmingham (Smethwick, Staffs), 4314, Pte., k. in a., F. & F., 8/8/16.
Spratt, William, e. Birmingham (Ladywood, Birmingham), 200695, Pte., k. in a., F. & F., 6/9/17.
Stamps, Frederick, e. Birmingham (Smethwick, Staffs), 200817, Pte., d. of w., F. & F., 7/12/17.
Staple, John, b. Chesham, Bucks, e. Aylesbury, Bucks (Chesham), 235033, L/Cpl., k. in a., F. & F., 6/9/17, formerly 7903, Worcs Regt.
Steadman, William, e. Birmingham (Sparkhill, Birmingham), 201518, Pte., d. of w., F. & F., 6/9/17.
Steanes, Thomas Herbert, e. Birmingham (Aston, Birmingham), 200739, Pte., k. in a., F. & F., 17/8/17.
Steel, Sydney, e. Birmingham, 200831, Sgt., k. in a., F. & F., 31/8/17.
Stevens, Arthur, b. Cropredy, Oxon, e. Banbury, Oxon (Cropredy), 29970, Pte., k. in a., F. & F., 3/12/17, formerly 22590, Oxford & Bucks L.I.
Stevens, Arthur, e. Birmingham, 4638, Pte., k. in a., F. & F., 4/7/16.
Stokes, Charles, e. Salford, Lancs (Manchester), 6318, Pte., k. in a., F. & F., 2/7/16, formerly 2578, Lancs Fus.
Stopps, Arthur, b. Leamington, e. Leamington, Warwickshire, 203132, Pte., k. in a., F. & F., 3/12/17.
Sutton, Charles Henry, e. Birmingham, 201487, Pte., k. in a., F. & F., 4/11/17.
Sutton, Harold Stafford, e. Birmingham (Saltley, Birmingham), 201621, Pte., d. of w., F. & F., 17/10/17.
Taylor, Alan, e. Birmingham, 3595, Pte., k. in a., F. & F., 8/8/16.
Taylor, John, b. Leeds, e. Birkenhead, Ches., 29115, Pte., k. in a., F. & F., 6/9/17, formerly 62132, Ches. Regt.
Thorn, Charles, e. Birmingham, 200709, Sgt., k. in a., F. & F., 6/9/17.
Tierney, Michael, e. Birmingham, 330168, Pte., k. in a., F. & F., 3/12/17.
Turner, Edwin, b. Royton, Lancs, e. Royton, 203218, Pte., k. in a., F. & F., 6/9/17, formerly 11902, A. Cyclist Corps.
Truman, Frederick, e. Birmingham, 5757, Pte., d. of w., F. & F., 13/10/16.
Usher, Harold, e. Birmingham, 200751, Pte., k. in a., F. & F., 1/9/17.
Vickers, Louis, b. Chester, e. Salford, Lancs (Manchester), 7321, Pte., k. in a., F. & F., 2/7/16, formerly 1735, Lancs Fus.
Wagstaffe, Amos, e. Skipton, Yorks (Keighley, Yorks), 29802, Pte., d. of w., F. & F., 3/12/17, formerly 4342, W. Riding Regt.
Waite, Thomas, e. Birmingham (Smethwick, Staffs), 2737, Pte., k. in a., F. & F., 3/8/16.
Walker, Percy Frank, b. Atherstone, Warwickshire, e. Leamington, Warwickshire (Radford Semele, Warwickshire), 201776, Pte., k. in a., F. & F., 17/12/17.
Wassall, Harry, b. Birmingham, e. Birmingham, 1843, Pte., k. in a., F. & F., 2/7/16.
Waterworth, Harry, b. Burnley, Lancs, e. Burnley, 203306, Pte., k. in a., F. & F., 9/9/17, formerly 12041, A. Cyclist Corps.
Watkinson, Frank, e. Birmingham (Ladywood, Birmingham), 2939, Pte., k. in a., F. & F., 2/7/16.
Westwell, William, b. Leigh, Lancs, e. Leigh, 202369, L/Sgt., k. in a., F. & F., 25/3/18, formerly 1755, Manchester Regt.
Westwood, Herbert, e. Birmingham (Smethwick, Staffs), 201550, Cpl., k. in a., F. & F., 30/9/17.
Whitworth, Harold, b. Birmingham, e. Birmingham, 5505, Pte., k. in a., F. & F., 8/8/16.
Wilson, Joseph, b. Gorton, Manchester, e. Middleton, Lancs (Moston, Manchester), 6299, Pte., k. in a., F. & F., 21/10/16, formerly 8727, Lancs Fus.

Windridge, Stanley James, b. Sparkbrook, Birmingham, e. Birmingham (Sparkhill, Birmingham), 2550, Dmr., k. in a., F. & F., 8/8/16.
Woodcock, Thomas Arthur, b. Birmingham, e. Birmingham, 201158, Pte., k. in a., F. & F., 15/8/17.
Woods, George, b. Dalmeny, Linlithgow, e. S. Queen's Ferry (Dalmeny), 202555, Pte., d. of w., F. & F., 6/12/17, formerly 2205, Royal Scots.
Woolley, Frank, e. Birmingham (Sparkbrook, Birmingham), 200919, Pte., d. of w., F. & F., 24/12/17.
Yates, John, e. Birmingham, 2978, Pte., k. in a., F. & F., 17/7/16.

5th (Reserve) Battalion—Territorial.

Andrews, Arthur Edward, b. Cardiff, Glam., e. Bristol, 59805, Pte., d., Home, 28/10/18.
Babb, George Henry, b. Halberton, Devon, e. Exeter, Devon (Halberton), 59836, Pte., d., Home, 8/11/18.
Beavon, George Edward, b. Birmingham, e. Birmingham (Saltley, Birmingham), 202131, Pte., d., Home, 24/8/17.
Bedford, Thomas, e. Birmingham, 3192, Pte., d., Home, 1/12/14.
Beebee, Thomas Frank, b. Ettingshall, Staffs, e. Wolverhampton, Staffs, 41936, Pte., d., Home, 16/10/18.
Beeley, Rupert, b. Manchester, e. Birmingham, 26888, Pte., d., Home, 22/8/18.
Benbow, John, e. Birmingham, 4123, Pte., d., Home, 14/9/15.
Bishop, James, e. Birmingham, 4167, Pte., d., Home, 24/8/15.
Blunn, Jesse, e. Birmingham (Kings Heath, Birmingham), 202685, Pte., d., Home, 24/8/17.
Bosbury, Francis Reginald, b. Peasmore, Berks, e. Reading, Berks (Abingdon, Berks), 59616, Pte., d., Home, 17/10/18.
Bottomley, William Henry, b. Battersea, London, e. Worcester (Severn Stoke, Worcs.), 59314, Pte., d., Home, 19/10/18.
Broad, Charles George, b. Winchester, Hants, e. Southampton (Winchester, Hants), 59456, Pte., d., Home, 14/10/18.
Brotherton, Samuel, e. Birmingham (Handsworth, Staffs), 3189, Pte., d., Home, 28/11/14.
Brown, Frank Herbert, e. Huntingdon (Little Barford, Hants), 203417, Pte., d., Home, 18/6/17, formerly 1544, Hunts. Cyclist Battn.
Capewell, William, e. Birmingham, 3875, Pte., d., Home 23/6/15.
Carlin, Patrick, b. Birmingham, e. Birmingham, 20022, Pte., d., Home, 11/11/15.
Clark, William, b. Chalfont St. Giles, Bucks, e. Aylesbury, Bucks (Chalfont St. Giles), 59455, Pte., d., Home, 9/11/18.
Cook, Thomas, e. Birmingham, 3387, Pte., d., Home, 4/12/14.
Crease, Henry William, b. Bedminster, Bristol, e. Bristol (Bedminster), 59619, Pte., d., Home, 15/10/18.
Dark, Benjamin, b. Birmingham, e. Birmingham, 201317, Pte., d., Home, 24/8/17.
Davis, Henry, e. Birmingham, 20130, Pte., d., Home, 2/2/16.
Dennis, William Charles, e. Birmingham, 3488, Pte., d., Home, 19/10/14.
Dugmore, Harry, e. Birmingham, 20038, Pte., d., Home, 11/11/15.
Fewtrell, Charles Leslie, b. Birmingham, e. Birmingham (Sparkhill, Birmingham), 4867, Pte., d., Home, 31/1/16.
Glancy, James, e. Birmingham, 3417, A/Sgt., d., Home, 16/9/15.
Hallett, Robert Pretoria, b. Charlton Mackrell, Somerset, e. Taunton, Somerset (Charlton Mackrell), 59647, Pte., d., Home, 16/10/18.
Henderson, William Harry, b. Weston-super-Mare, Somerset, e. Weston-super-Mare, 26392, Pte., d., Home, 24/8/17.
Henn, George e. Birmingham (Bordesley Green, Birmingham), 4393, L/Cpl., Home, 26/4/16.
Hickie, Stanley, e. Birmingham (Aston Manor, Birmingham), 3764, Pte., d., Home, 19/3/16.
Hill, Frederick, b. Birmingham, e. Birmingham, 5263, Pte., d., Home, 24/1/16.
Hill, William, b. St. Thomas, Birmingham, e. Birmingham, 1795, Pte., d., Home, 19/9/16.
Holland, Hugh, e. Birmingham, 3700, Pte., d., Home, 31/12/14.
Holmes, Arthur Harold, b. Gt. Brickhill, Bucks, e. Aylesbury, Bucks (Bletchley, Bucks), 59964, Pte., d., Home, 1/11/18.
Honeybourne, William, b. Birmingham, e. Birmingham (Aston, Birmingham), 20001, Pte., d., Home, 14/9/15.
Hopkins, Thomas Redvers, b. Portsmouth, e. Southampton (Fratton, Portsmouth), 59606, Pte., d., Home, 14/10/18.
Ingram, Richard Austin, e. Birmingham, 2878, Pte., d., Home, 14/12/14.
Jones, Cyril Baden, b. Munslow, Salop, e. Worcester (Bewdley, Worcs.), 59646, Pte., d., Home, 15/10/18.
Keevil, Thomas Joseph, b. Crockerton, Wilts, e. Trowbridge, Wilts (Stourton, Wilts), 59394, Pte., d., Home, 22/10/18.
Kerby, Harry Bradford, e. Birmingham (Olton, Warwicks), 4891, Pte., d., Home 29/3/16.
Lawrence, Robert Charles Carnell, b. Torquay, Devon, e. Exeter, Devon (Torquay), 59568, Pte., d., Home, 19/10/18.
Lloyd, Frederick Oliver, e. Birmingham (Edgbaston, Birmingham), 3538, Dmr., d., Home, 5/6/15.
Marshall, William George, b. Whatcote, Warwicks, e. Coventry (Whatcote), 60073, Pte., d., Home, 9/11/18.
McGonnell, Ernest Frank, b. Ventnor, I.O.W., e. Southampton (Ventnor), 59609, Pte., d., Home, 12/10/18.
Milner, Alfred, b. Moseley, Birmingham, e. Birmingham, 1669, Pte., d., Home, 26/3/16.
Moran, Thomas, e. Birmingham (Balsall Heath, Birmingham), 4201, Pte., d., Home, 12/10/15.
Nicholls, Walter, b. Highgate, Birmingham, e. Birmingham, 2181, Pte., d., Home, 28/8/14.
Noy, Edward Gordon, e. Penzance, Cornwall (Gulval, Cornwall), 26317, Pte., d., Home, 24/8/17.
Owen, Joseph Roger, e. Birmingham (Small Heath, Birmingham), 4745, Sgt., d., Home, 22/5/16.
Parsons, Edwin, e. Birmingham (Aston, Birmingham), 3475, Pte., d., Home, 6/8/15.
Paxton, Hugh, b. Wolverhampton, Staffs, e. Birmingham (Smethwick, Staffs), 3957, Pte., d., Home, 14/12/15.
Poolman, Arthur George, b. Aston, Birmingham, e. Birmingham (Wylde Green, Birmingham), 5098, Pte., d., Home, 23/4/16.
Powell, Walter, b. Tewkesbury, Glos., e. Birmingham (Tewkesbury), 1616, Pte., d., Home, 8/12/14.
Richards, Howard Charles, b. Bedminster, Bristol, e. Taunton, Som. (Chard, Som.), 59584, Pte., d., Home, 19/10/18.
Riley, John, b. St. Thomas, Birmingham, e. Birmingham (Ladywood, Birmingham), 202172, L/Sgt., d., Home, 24/8/17.
Sadler, Harry, b. Willersey, Glouc., e. Worcester (Evesham, Worcs.), 59360, Pte., d., Home, 17/10/18.
Saunders, William Edgar, b. Draycote, Som., e. Taunton, Som. (Ilchester, Som.), 59479, Pte., d., Home, 25/10/18.
Scattergood, Charles William, e. Coventry (Leamington, Warwicks.), 60057, Pte., d., Home, 11/11/18.
Shale, Fred, e. Birmingham (Handsworth, Staffs), 202962, Pte., d., Home, 24/8/17.
Southern, Harry Blanchard, b. Birmingham, e. Birmingham (Erdington, Birmingham), 26694, Pte., d., Home, 24/8/17.
Stockwell, Percy Enoch, b. Stroud, Glos., e. Stroud, 26578, Pte., d., Home, 26/6/18.
Stott, Edward Bleakley, b. Brighouse, Yorks, e. Trowbridge, Som. (Devizes, Wilts.), 59519, Pte., d., Home, 12/10/18
Styler, Frank Wilson, b. Feckenham, Worcs, e. Birmingham (Feckenham), 201713, A/Sgt., d., Home, 30/5/17.
Thompson, Lincoln, b. Sparkbrook, Birmingham, e. Birmingham, 5803, A/Cpl., d., Home, 15/11/16.
Thorn, George, b. Woolston, Southampton, e. Southampton (Woolston), 59626, Pte., d., Home, 9/10/18.
Townley, Frederick, b. Cheltenham, Glos., e. Gloucester (Cheltenham), 59560, Pte., d., Home, 17/10/18.
Vowles, William Henry, b. Bedminster, Glos., e. Bristol (Bedminster), 26914, Pte., d., Home, 23/3/18.
Warr, Albert, b. Chard, Som., e. Taunton, Som. (Broadchard, Som), 59545, Pte., d., Home, 17/10/18.
Williams, Samuel, e. Birmingham (Moseley, Birmingham), 3508, Pte., d., Home, 25/8/15.
Winstone, Lawrence Cyril, b. Maidenhead, Berks, e. Reading, Berks (Maidenhead), 59643, Pte., d., Home, 11/10/18.

1/6th Battalion—Territorial.

Abell, Henry, b. Stanbridge, Beds., e. Luton, Beds. (Leighton Buzzard, Beds.), 29186, Pte., k. in a., F. & F., 4/10/17, formerly 32142, Northumberland Regt.
Acock, Albert John, b. Taynton, Oxon, e. Birmingham (Harborne, Birmingham), 23236, Pte., k. in a., F. & F., 18/8/17.
Adams, Frank, b. Northampton, e. Birmingham (Balsall Heath, Birmingham), 4517, Pte., k. in a., F. & F., 24/8/16.
Adams, Frank William, b. St. Georges, Birmingham, e. Birmingham (Handsworth, Staffs), 2697, Pte., d. of w., F. & F., 2/6/15.
Adams, Harry, b. Whitchurch, Bucks., e. Aylesbury, Bucks. (Whitchurch), 242593, Pte., d., F. & F., 6/3/19.
Adams, Richard William, b. Blaby, Derbys., e. Knowle, Birmingham (Spratton, Northants), 5197, Pte., k. in a., F. & F., 2/12/16.
Aldridge, Alfred Henry John, b. Thrupp, Glos., e. Stroud, Glos. (Thrupp), 241688, Pte., k. in a., F. & F., 16/4/17.
Allen, Alfred Ernest, e. Birmingham (Selly Park, Birmingham), 3585, Pte., k. in a., F. & F., 1/7/16.
Allen, Henry, b. St. Thomas, Birmingham, e. Birmingham, 942, Pte., k. in a., F. & F., 21/6/15.
Allington, Albert, b. St. Mary's, Kidderminster, Worcs., e. Kidderminster, 20847, Pte., d. of w., F. & F., 1/10/10, formerly 1387, Worcs. Regt.
Amos, William Thomas, b. Southam, Warwicks, e. Southam, 20900, Pte., k. in a., F. & F., 4/2/17.
Anderson, Charles Henry, b. Luton, Beds., e. Luton, 29229, Pte., k. in a., F. & F., 4/10/17.
Andrews, Albert Edwin, b. Ladywood, Birmingham, e. Birmingham (Ladywood), 240370, Pte., k. in a., F. & F., 8/3/17.
Andrews, Frederick, b. Birmingham, e. Birmingham, 4524, Pte., k. in a., F. & F., 1/7/16.
Ashford, Sidney Herbert, b. Shepherd's Bush, London, e. Birmingham (Nechells, Birmingham), 241546, Pte., d., F. & F., 6/8/17.
Aston, William, b. Chester, e. Tottenham, Middx., 23530, Pte., d. of w., F. & F., 4/10/17, formerly 193553, R. E.
Atkins, Arthur, b. Coventry, e. Coventry, 241633, L/Cpl., k. in a., F. & F. 1/4/17.
Atkins, Frederick, e. Birmingham, 4451, Pte., k. in a., F. & F., 1/7/16.
Atkinson, Henry, b. Bethnal Green, Middx., e. Mill Hill, London (Tottenham, Middx.), 260081, Pte., k. in a., F. & F., 27/8/17, formerly 32698, Suff. R. and 400342, Essex R.
Austin, Charles, e. Oxford (Bicester, Oxon), 241654, Pte., k. in a., F. & F., 27/8/17.
Bagnall, John Joseph, b. Handsworth, Staffs, e. Birmingham (Handsworth, Staffs), 1510, Cpl., k. in a., F. & F., 1/7/16.
Baker, John, e. Birmingham, 242855 L/Cpl., k. in a., F. & F., 9/3/17.
Ball, George, e. Birmingham (Aston, Birmingham), 200684, Pte., k. in a., F. & F., 19/6/17.
Barnes, Walter Edwin, b. Nuneaton, Warwicks, e. Nuneaton, 242536, L/Cpl., k. in a., F. & F., 4/10/17.
Barr, David Wesley, b. Hackney, Middx., e. Birmingham, 2773, Pte., d of w., F. & F., 10/7/16.
Bartlett, Edgar, b. St. Martins, Birmingham, e. Birmingham, 240063, Pte., k. in a., F. & F. 30/4/18.

Bastable, John, e. Sutton Coldfield, 20705, Pte., k. in a., F. & F., 24/8/16.
Bateman, William, b. Aston, Birmingham, e. Birmingham (Small Heath, Birmingham), 1530, Pte., k. in a., F. & F., 28/6/16.
Bates, Charles Samuel, e. Birmingham (Small Heath, Birmingham), 4615, Pte., k. in a., F. & F., 1/7/16.
Bates, Edward, e. Birmingham (Handsworth, Staffs), 21084, L/Cpl., k. in a., F. & F., 4/2/17.
Baugh, Albert Edgar, b. Soho, Birmingham, e. Birmingham, 2781, Pte., k. in a., F. & F., 1/7/16.
Bayliss, Arthur Edward, b. Sparkbrook, Birmingham, e. Birmingham, 240105, Cpl., k. in a., F. & F., 9/3/17.
Begley, Francis Arthur, e. Bletchley, Bucks (Newport Pagnell, Bucks), 4806, Pte., k. in a., F. & F., 17/8/16.
Bell, George, b. Coventry, e. Coventry, 241592, Pte., k. in a., F. & F., 1/4/17.
Bell, Herbert Edward, b. Seagrave, Leics., e. Leicester (Seagrave), 20348, Pte., k. in a., F. & F., 4/2/17, formerly 25629, Leic. R.
Bennett, Alfred, b. Birmingham, e. Birmingham, 4261, Pte., k. in a., F. & F., 1/7/16.
Bennett, George Henry, b. Tickencote, Lincoln, e. Bristol, 260085, Pte., d. of w., F. & F., 21/10/17, formerly 5925, Essex R.
Bermingham, David Francis, b. Birmingham, e. Birmingham (Erdington, Birmingham), 242537, Pte., k. in a., F. & F., 22/2/17.
Berry, Frederick, b. Radford, Warwicks., e. Rugby, Warwicks. (Offchurch, Warwicks.), 20901, Pte., d. of w., F. & F., 10/12/16.
Best, Frederick, b. Aston, Birmingham, e. Birmingham (Aston), 180, C.S.M., k. in a., F. & F., 22/5/15.
Billingsley, George, e. Birmingham, 3190, Pte., k. in a., F. & F., 1/7/16.
Billington, Frank, e. Leicester, 242181, C.S.M., k. in a., F. & F., 27/8/17, formerly 8369, Leic. R., D.C.M.
Billington, Harold, b. St. Thomas, Birmingham, e. Birmingham, 240446, Pte., k. in a., F. & F., 1/7/16.
Binns, William, b. Birmingham, e. Birmingham (Small Heath, Birmingham), 241314, Pte., k. in a., F. & F., 18/8/16.
Bird, William, b. Aston, Birmingham, e. Birmingham, 1555, Pte., d. of w., F. & F., 2/6/15.
Boden, Frederick, e. Birmingham (Ladywood, Birmingham), 2882, Pte., k. in a., F. & F., 1/7/16.
Bodley, Alfred Henry, b. Bedminster, Bristol, e. Bristol (Bedminster), 242619, Pte., k. in a., F. & F. 27/8/17, formerly 199 Cyclist Batt.
Boffin, Henry Richard, e. Warwick (Kineton, Warwicks), 4928, Pte., k. in a., F. & F., 17/8/16.
Bolton, Jack, b. King's Heath, Birmingham, e. Birmingham, 1836, Pte., k. in a., F. & F., 1/7/16.
Bowcott, Harry, b. St. Martins, Birmingham, e. Birmingham, 240336, Pte., k. in a., F. & F., 1/7/16.
Bowne, Harold, b. St. Marks, Birmingham, e. Birmingham, 240210, Pte., k. in a., F. & F., 1/7/16.
Bowring, George, e. Birmingham, 241195, Pte., d., F. & F., 4/6/17.
Bonner, Frederick, b. Leicester, e. Leicester, 242197, Pte., k. in a., F. & F., 4/10/17, formerly 25488, Leic. Regt.
Bradley, Richard, b. Birmingham, e. Birmingham, 241299, Pte., k. in a., F. & F., 1/7/16.
Braithwaite, George Alfred, b. St. Pauls, Birmingham, e. Birmingham, 1949, Pte., k. in a., F. & F., 1/7/16.
Brancy, Arthur John, b. St. Mary's, Birmingham, e. Birmingham, 109, Sgt., d. of w., F. & F., 12/7/16.
Bridges, Arthur, b. Stratford-on-Avon, e. Stratford-on-Avon, Warwicks, 18236, Pte., d. of w., F. & F., 4/10/17.
Brooks, Walter, b. Tipton Staffs, e. Birmingham (Bordesley Green, Birmingham), 240287, Sgt., k. in a., F. & F., 31/3/18.
Brown, Frederick Louis, b. Edgbaston, Birmingham, e. Birmingham (Edgbaston), 240069, Sgt., k. in a., F. & F., 1/7/16, M.M.
Brown, George, e. Warrington, Lancs, 20830, Pte., d. of w., F. & F., 19/8/16, formerly 3897, S. Lancs Regt.
Brown, John, b. Haverfordwest, Pembroke, e. Milford Haven, Pembroke, 34710, Pte., d., F. & F. 20/11/18 formerly 306051, Ches. R.
Burgess, Harry John, b. Audlem, Ches., e. Birmingham (Newport, Salop), 4526, Pte., k. in a., F. & F., 1/7/16.
Burnham, Wallace Alfred, b. St. Martins, Warwick, e. Birmingham, 20237, Pte., d. of w., F. & F., 28/2/17.
Butler, Herbert John, b. Stratford, London, e. Watford, Herts., 260001, Pte., k. in a., F. & F., 27/8/17, formerly 330759, Camb. R.
Cadwallader, Albert, e. Birmingham (Sparkbrook, Birmingham), 3064, Pte., k. in a., F. & F., 1/7/16.
Calloway, Archie, b. Winsford, Somerset, e. Taunton, Somerset (Winsford), 29236, Pte., k. in a., F. & F., 17/8/17, formerly 21726, Som. L.I.
Camp, William, b. Buntingford, Hertford, e. Bedford (Buntingford), 20268, Pte., k. in a., F. & F., 4/2/17, formerly 5360, Notts & Derby Regt.
Cantwell, William Robert, e. Leyton, Essex, 260089, Pte., k. in a., F. & F., 27/8/17, formerly 7/3830, Essex Regt.
Carrington, Thomas, e. Birmingham (Balsall Heath, Birmingham), 241283, Pte., k. in a., F. & F., 1/7/16.
Carter, Edward James, b. Birmingham, e. Birmingham, 241289, Pte., k. in a., F. & F., 20/8/17.
Cartwright, Wilfred, b. Ladywood, Birmingham, e. Birmingham, 2068, Pte., k. in a., F. & F., 1/7/16.
Causier, William, b. Grimley, Worcs., e. Redditch, Worcs. (Studley, Warwickshire), 242684, Pte., d. of w., F. & F., 18/4/17, formerly 19758, Worcs. Regt.
Chamberlain, Ernest, b. Foleshill, Coventry, e. Coleshill, Birmingham, 241575, Pte., k. in a., F. & F., 27/8/17.
Chapman, Harold Arthur, b. Northampton, e. Northampton, 29158, Pte., k. in a., F. & F., 27/8/17, formerly 23906, Northumberland Regt.
Chaston, Sidney Frank, b. London, e. Birmingham (London), 1690, L/Cpl., k. in a., F. & F., 1/7/16.
Chatwin, John Alfred, b. St. Thomas, Birmingham, e. Birmingham, 1574, L/Cpl., k. in a., F. & F., 1/7/16.
Chester, Norman, b. Salford, Lancs, e. Birmingham (Hockley, Birmingham), 240516, L/Cpl., k. in a., F. & F., 1/7/16.
Chittendon, Henry, b. Stepney, Middx., e. Wantage, Berks, 242585, Cpl., k. in a., F. & F., 16/4/17, formerly 5518, R. Berks. Regt.
Christie, James, b. Scone, Perth, e. Perth, 242532, L/Cpl., k. in a., F. & F., 19/6/17, formerly 1224, Highland Cyclist Battn.
Church, William, b. Darsham, Suffolk, e. Lowestoft, Suffolk (Darsham), 260094, Pte., k. in a., F. & F., 27/8/17, formerly 6412, Essex Regt.
Clarke, Frederick Albert, b. Pakefield, Suffolk, e. Lowestoft, Suffolk (Oulton, Suffolk), 29187, Pte., k. in a., F. & F., 28/8/17, formerly 32168, Northumberland Regt.
Clarke, Horace, b. Leicester, e. Sheerness, Kent, 242159, Pte., k. in a., F. & F., 16/4/17, formerly 25206, Leic. Regt.
Clayton, Albert, e. Birmingham (Balsall Heath, Birmingham), 3358, Pte., k. in a., F. & F., 18/8/16.
Clements, Henry John, e. Birmingham, 2804, Pte., k. in a., F. & F., 1/7/16.
Clifton, Harold, b. Shirley, Warwickshire, e. Birmingham (Small Heath, Birmingham), 4197, Pte., k. in a., F. & F., 1/7/16.
Coare, Thomas, b. Sheffield, Yorks, e. Birmingham, 241290, Pte., d. of w., F. & F., 5/10/17.
Cohen, Frank George, b. Lenton, Notts, e. Birmingham, 1787, Sergt., d. of w., F. & F., 3/4/16.
Cole, Alfred, e. Birmingham (Sparkbrook, Birmingham), 3182, Pte., k. in a., F. & F., 1/7/16.
Coling, Christopher, b. Granborough, Warwickshire, e. Warwick (Granborough), 21008, Pte., k. in a., F. & F., 4/2/17.
Comyns, Charles, b. Halifax, Yorks, e. Carshalton, Surrey, 260092, Pte., k. in a., F. & F., 27/8/17, formerly 5/6760, Essex Regt.
Concanen, Charles, b. Aston, Birmingham, e. Birmingham, 1773, Pte., k. in a., F. & F., 26/11/16.
Constable, Edwin, b. Plaistow, Essex, e. Woolwich, Kent (Plaistow), 29197, Pte., k. in a., F. & F., 20/8/17, formerly 23070, D. of Corn. L.I.
Cooper, Fred, b. Tottenham, Middx, e. Birmingham, 2059, Pte., k. in a., F. & F., 21/4/15.
Cooper, James Albert, b. Birmingham, e. Birmingham (Handsworth, Staffs) 242912, Pte., k. in a., F. & F., 16/4/17.
Cooper, John, b. Shrewsbury, Salop, e. Birmingham, 2178, Pte., k. in a., F. & F., 5/5/15.
Cooper, John Henry, b. Birmingham, e. Birmingham (Sparkbrook, Birmingham), 4655, Pte., d. of w., F. & F., 12/6/16.
Coombes, Walter, b. Coombe, Oxon, e. Oxford (Coombe) 5367, Pte., k. in a., F. & F., 10/12/16.
Cooper, Frederick Percy, e. Birmingham (Solihull, Warwickshire), 2940, Pte., k. in a., F. & F., 1/7/16.
Cordian, William Alfred, b. Wigan, Lancs, e. Warwick (Longford, Coventry), 5154, Pte., k. in a., F. & F., 17/8/16.
Cornelius, William, b. St. Thomas, Birmingham, e. Birmingham (Balsall Heath, Birmingham), 240524, Pte., k. in a., F. & F., 1/7/16.
Corney, Fred, b. Marwood, Devon, e. Chichester, Sussex (Bexhill, Sussex), 33950, Pte., k. in a., F. & F., 4/10/17, formerly 203237, E. Kent Regt.
Coupe, George Henry, b. Rochdale, Lancs, e. Warwick (Rochdale), 5152, Pte., d. of w., F. & F., 14/10/16.
Court, Arthur, b. Stratford-on-Avon, Warwicks, e. Coventry (Stratford-on-Avon), 242717, Pte., k. in a., F. & F., 4/10/17.
Coveney, Edward William, b. Camberwell, Surrey, e. Leyton, Essex (Walthamstow, Essex), 260090, Pte., k. in a., F. & F., 27/8/17, formerly 7/1606, Essex Regt.
Coward, William, b. Sleaford, Lincs, e. Warwick (Balsall Heath, Birmingham), 5156, Pte., k. in a., F. & F., 13/10/16.
Cox, Frank, e. Oxford (Hardwick, Oxon), 241662, Pte., d., F. & F., 28/2/17.
Craddock, Albert John, e. Birmingham (Kings Norton, Birmingham), 3100, Pte., k. in a., F. & F., 1/7/16.
Cramp, Edward James, b. Coventry, e. Coventry, 5111, Pte., k. in a., F. & F., 25/8/16.
Creed, John, b. Banbury, Oxon., e. Banbury, 242589, Pte., d. of w., F. & F., 28/2/18.
Cresswell, Arthur, b. Chesterfield, Derby, e. Chesterfield, 242136, Pte., k. in a., F. & F., 11/3/17, formerly 2738, Notts. & Derby Regt.
Crew, George, b. St. James, Bristol, e. Bristol (Coventry), 20804, Pte., d. of w., F. & F., 4/2/17, formerly 247, Cyclist Coy.
Crick, George, b. Croft, Leicester, e. Leicester, 242158, Pte., k. in a., F. & F., 8/3/17, formerly 20584, Leic. Regt.
Crocker, Arthur James, b. Kingsdown, Bristol, e. Bristol, 5412, Pte., k. in a., F. & F., 4/2/17.
Crofts, Edward Harry Bates, b. Handsworth, Birmingham, e. Birmingham, 2768, Pte., k. in a., F. & F., 17/4/15.
Cross, Archie, b. Eccington, Worcs, e. Birmingham, 240064, L/Sgt., k. in a., F. & F., 1/7/16.
Cross, Thomas, b. Broughton, Lincs, e. Warwick (Brigg, Lincs), 5081, Pte., k. in a., F. & F., 18/8/16.
Crow, William, e. Birmingham (Redditch), 240896, Cpl., k. in a., F. & F., 27/8/17.
Cunningham, Arthur Edward, e. Birmingham, 5312, Pte., k. in a., F. & F., 17/8/16.
Curl, Leonard James, b. Berkhampstead, Herts, e. London (Sevenoaks, Kent), 33445, Pte., d., F. & F., 29/10/18, formerly M/19466, R.A.S.C.

Cutler, Harold, b. Small Heath, Birmingham, e. Birmingham, 2790, Pte., k. in a., F. & F., 1/7/16.
Cummins, Horace, e. Southport, Lancs, 208576, Pte., k. in a., F. & F., 27/8/17, formerly 2751, Liverpool Regt.
Darby, Harold Leonard, b. Edgbaston, Birmingham, e. Birmingham, 1373, Sgt., d. of w., F. & F., 6/6/15.
Dart, Frederick George, b. Bedminster, Bristol, e. Bristol, 242805, Pte., d. of w., 9/3/17, F. & F.
Davidson, Albert, b. Holborn, Middx., e. London, 242688, Sgt., d. of w., F. & F., 1/4/17, formerly 9858, Worcs Regt.
Davies, Albert Edward, b. Leominster, Hereford, e. Gloucester, 20983, Pte., k. in a., F. & F., 4/2/17.
Davis, Frank Edwin, b. Handsworth, Birmingham, e. Birmingham, 2736, Pte., d., F. & F., 12/2/17.
Dawes, George Henry, b. Birmingham, e. Birmingham, 1495, C.S.M., k. in a., F. & F., 19/8/16, M.M.
Dawson, Edwin, e. Birmingham, 240740, Sgt., d., F. & F., 5/3/17.
Dawson, Gilbert Francis, b. Wisbech, Cambs, e. Birmingham (Wisbech), 2526, Pte., k. in a., F. & F., 3/5/15.
Day, Francis John, b. Stockingford, Nuneaton, e. Warwick (Stockingford), 5208, Pte., k. in a., F. & F., 18/8/16.
Deahl, Reginald, b. Southampton, e. Southampton, 242409, Pte., k. in a., F. & F., 4/10/17, formerly 24252, Som. L.I.
Deakin, Percy, b. Birmingham, e. Birmingham, 4191, Pte., k. in a., F. & F., 25/8/16.
Deal, George Bertie, b. Bulmer, Essex, e. Holloway (Upper Holloway), 260095, Pte., k. in a., F. & F., 27/8/17, formerly 400267, Essex Regt.
Dellahunt, Leonard, e. Birmingham (Hockley, Birmingham), 4574, Pte., k. in a., F. & F., 18/8/16.
Denton, Arthur, b. Birmingham, e. Birmingham, 22376, Pte., d., F. & F., 8/4/17.
Derbyshire, Frederick, b. Loughton, Essex, e. Walthamstow (Royden, Essex), 29199, Pte., k. in a., F. & F., 27/8/17, formerly 11080, Duke of Cornwall's L.I.
Dishington, Neil, b. St. Mark's, Birmingham, e. Birmingham, 1800, L/Cpl., k. in a., F. & F., 1/7/16.
Dixon, Bertie, b. Walsall, e. Birmingham (Handsworth, Birmingham), 241230, L/Cpl., k. in a., F. & F., 17/8/17.
Dixon, James Archibald, e. Birmingham (Bilston, Staffs), 242867, Pte., k. in a., F. & F., 17/8/17.
Doody, Charles, e. Birmingham, 242670, Pte., k. in a., F. & F., 14/5/17, M.M.
Douglas, George, b. Pendrift, Cumberland, e. Warwick (Walsall, Staffs), 5082, Pte., k. in a., F. & F., 1/7/16.
Downes, George, b. Birmingham, e. Birmingham, 4416, Pte., k. in a., F. & F., 28/7/16.
Dudley, John Edward, b. Aston, Birmingham, e. Birmingham, 4424, Pte., k. in a., F. & F., 1/7/16.
Durden, Albert Edward, e. Birmingham (Camp Hill, Birmingham), 21054, Pte., k. in a., F. & F., 4/2/17.
Durham, Charles Arthur, b. St. George's, Birmingham, e. Birmingham, 390, Pte., k. in a., F. & F., 6/6/16.
Eaton, George, b. Yardley, Worcs, e. Small Heath, Birmingham, 1917, Pte., d. of w., F. & F., 18/7/16.
Ebbs, William, b. St. Thomas, Preston, Lancs, e. Preston, 202491, Pte., k. in a., F. & F., 27/8/17, formerly 1772, N. Lancs Regt.
Eccles, William Christopher, e. Coventry, 28656, Pte., k. in a., F. & F., 4/10/17.
Edkins, Walter James, b. Aston Cantlow, Warwickshire, e. Stratford-on-Avon (Aston Cantlow), 28892, Pte., k. in a., F. & F., 22/8/17.
Edwards, Charles Frederick, b. Clown, Chesterfield, Derby, e. Birmingham (Clown), 2712, Cpl., k. in a., F. & F., 1/7/16.
Edwards, Ernest, b. Chilton, Bucks, e. Aylesbury (Chilton), 241685, Pte., k. in a., F. & F., 27/8/17.
Edwards, Frank Victor, b. Warwick, e. Warwick, 21043, Pte., k. in a., F. & F., 4/2/17.
Edwards, John Thomas, b. Runcorn, Ches., e. Runcorn, 34718, Pte., k. in a., F. & F., 16/6/18, formerly 44378, Ches. Regt.
Egerton, Harold Alfred, b. Hockley, Warwickshire, e. Birmingham (Hockley), 201818, Cpl., k. in a., F. & F., 17/6/18.
England, Frank, b. Walton, Warwickshire, e. Warwick (Walton), 5083, Pte., d. of w., F. & F., 6/7/16.
Ert, Albert, b. Leicester, e. Leicester, 242153, Pte., k. in a., F. & F., 27/8/17, formerly 10441, Leics. Regt
Etheridge, Charles, b. Cleobury, Mortimer, Shrops, e. Worcester (Cradley Heath, Staffs), 20867, L/Sgt., k. in a., F. & F., 4/2/17, formerly 20300, Worcs Regt.
Etheridge, Ernest Albert, e. Gloucester, 20851, L/Sgt., k. in a., F. & F., 10/12/16, formerly 2211, Glos. Regt.
Evans, Arthur Denby, e. Birmingham, 20986, Pte., k. in a., F. & F., 4/2/17.
Evans, Arthur Wynne, b. Northop, Mold, Flint, e. Wellingborough, Northants (Kingsbridge, S. Devon) 29176, Pte., k. in a., F. & F., 4/10/17, formerly 15781, Northants Regt.
Evans, Samuel John Tasker, b. Balsall Heath, Birmingham, e. Birmingham, 2621, Pte., k. in a., F. & F., 1/7/16.
Farmer, Albert, b. St. Mary's, Birmingham, e. Birmingham, 1866, Pte., k. in a., F. & F., 1/7/16.
Farrington, George, e. Birmingham (Sparkhill, Birmingham), 4575, Pte., k. in a., F. & F., 28/6/16.
Farrington, John, b. Aston, Birmingham, e. Birmingham, 1584, Pte., k. in a., F. & F., 6/5/15.
Field, Charles, b. Brighton, e. Brighton, 260103, Cpl., k. in a., F. & F., 30/4/18, formerly 28211 Suffolk Regt.
Fitzgerald, Joseph, b. St. Thomas, Birmingham, e. Birmingham, 242656, Sgt., d. of w., F. & F., 29/8/17.
Ford, Gilbert Trevor, b. Aston, Birmingham, e. Birmingham (Aston, Birmingham), 2731, Pte., k. in a., F. & F., 23/6/15.
Fortey, Thomas, b. Birmingham, e. Birmingham (Saltley, Birmingham), 243009, Pte., d., F. & F., 24/8/17.
Foulkes, William Bamford, e. Birmingham (Lutterworth, Leics.), 2827, Pte., k. in a., F. & F., 20/6/15.
Fountain, Richard, e. Birmingham (Cotteridge, Birmingham), 3101, Pte., d. of w., F. & F., 22/5/16.
Frier, Samuel, b. Manchester, e. Birmingham, 241615, Pte., d., F. & F., 8/6/18.
Galloway, Walter, b. Leeds, e. York (Leeds), 43730, Pte., k. in a., F. & F., 4/10/18, formerly 36825, W. York Regt.
Gamble, Charles, b. Otley, Yorks, e. Birmingham, 4544, Pte., k. in a., F. & F., 1/7/16.
Gamson, Alfred, b. Ladywood, Birmingham, e. Birmingham, 240465, Pte., k. in a., F. & F., 6/2/16.
Garlick, Frederick William, b. Leicester, e. Coventry, 20909, Pte., d. of w., F. & F., 8/2/17.
Gascoigne, Alan, b. Warwick, e. Warwick, 20717, Pte., d. of w., F. & F., 15/10/16.
Gauntlett, Leonard, e. Birmingham (Ladywood, Birmingham), 3720, Pte., k. in a., F. & F., 28/6/16.
Gibbons, James Leslie, b. Small Heath, Birmingham, e. Birmingham, 2762, Pte., k. in a., F. & F., 15/8/15.
Gibbs, Sidney, b. Birmingham, e. Birmingham (Edgbaston, Birmingham), 4715, Pte., k. in a., F. & F., 1/7/16.
Gillim, Samuel John, b. Coker, Somerset, e. Yeovil, Som. (Weymouth, Dorset), 29252, Pte., k. in a., F. & F., 27/8/17, formerly 12803, Dorset Regt.
Glenn, Charles Edward, b. Norton Lindsay, Warwicks, e. Warwick (Norton Lindsay), 5278, Pte., k. in a., F. & F., 18/8/16.
Glover, Henry Francis, e. Birmingham (Hockley, Birmingham), 240794, L/Cpl., k. in a., F. & F., 1/7/16.
Godridge, Thomas, e. Birmingham (Nechells, Birmingham), 3119, Pte, k. in a., F. & F., 1/7/16.
Goodfellow, Thomas Charles, b. Chilmark, Wilts, e. Salisbury, Wilts (Hendon, Wilts), 30505, Pte., k. in a., F. & F., 4/10/17, formerly 31612, Worcs. Regt.
Gough, George, b. Fort George, Bermuda, e. Birmingham, 2182, Pte., k. in a., F. & F., 1/7/16.
Gray, Charles Albert, b. Henley, Oxon, e. Henley-on-Thames, 5434, Cpl., k. in a., F. & F., 4/2/17.
Green, Alfred Edwin, b. Belper, Derby, e. Derby (Belper), 242115, L/Cpl., k. in a., F. & F., 27/8/17, formerly 4486, Notts. & Derby Regt.
Green, Harry Bertram, b. Humberstone, Leics., e. Leicester (Cricklewood, London), 242168, Pte., k. in a., F. & F. 27/8/17, formerly 16875, Leic. Regt.
Green, Leonard Joseph, b. Coleshill, Warwicks., e. Birmingham, 2030, Pte., k. in a., F. & F., 29/5/15.
Green, Robert, b. Birmingham, e. Birmingham, 241599, Pte., k. in a., F. & F., 4/10/17.
Greenland, Thomas Alfred, b. Totterdown, Bristol, e. Bristol (Easton, Bristol), 242077, Pte., k. in a., F. & F., 4/10/17, formerly 5485, R. Berks. Regt.
Gregory, Charles Alfred, b. Ladywood, Birmingham, e. Birmingham, 2314, Pte., k. in a., F. & F., 1/7/16.
Grendon, William John, b. Birmingham, e. Birmingham (Hockley, Birmingham), 21034, Pte., k. in a., F. & F., 17/6/18.
Griffiths, Robert, b Smethwick, Staffs, e. Birmingham (Smethwick), 2408, Pte., k. in a., F. & F., 9/2/16.
Griffiths, Wilfred, b. Ludlow, Salop, e. Birmingham (Handsworth, Staffs), 243130, Pte., k. in a., F. & F., 18/8/16.
Griffiths, William Edwin, b. Ladywood, Birmingham, e. Birmingham (Ladywood), 240082, Sgt., k. in a., F. & F., 27/8/17.
Grigg, George, b. Birmingham, e. Birmingham, 241399, Pte., k. in a., F. & F., 1/7/16.
Grove, Walter John, b. Ladywood, Birmingham, e. Birmingham, 2047, Pte., k. in a., F. & F., 1/7/16.
Grover, Alfred, b. London, e. London (Bethnal Green, Middx.), 33971, Pte., d. of w., F. & F., 4/10/17, formerly 5340, E. Kent Regt.
Haffenden, Richard Stanley, b. Ramsgate, Kent, e. Ramsgate (Margate, Kent), 33972, Pte., d. of w., F. & F., 5/10/17, formerly 4439, E. Kent Regt.
Hall, Albert Iddisleigh, b. St. Martin's, Birmingham, e. Birmingham (Yardley, Birmingham), 240315, Pte., k. in a., F. & F., 4/10/17.
Hall, George William, b. Whittlesea, Cambs, e. Wisbech, Cambs, 29148, Pte., k. in a., F. & F., 18/8/17, formerly 43983, Northumberland Regt.
Hall, Harry, b. Sparkbrook, Birmingham, e. Birmingham (Sparkbrook), 1829, Pte., k. in a., F. & F., 1/7/16.
Hall, Percy Victor, b. Sparkhill, Birmingham, e. Birmingham (Sparkhill), 240211, L/Cpl., k. in a., F. & F., 27/8/17.
Halsey, Fred, b. Woodford Halse, Northants, e. Birmingham, 1832, Pte., k. in a., F. & F., 27/6/16.
Hambridge, George Louis, b. Ladywood, Birmingham, e. Birmingham, 2711, Cpl., k. in a., F. & F., 1/7/16.
Hampton, Arthur, b. Halesowen, Staffs, e. Birmingham, 2666, L/Cpl., d. of w., F. & F., 27/6/15.
Hancox, George Hugh, b. Bewdley, Worcs, e. Rugby, Warwicks (Bewdley), 20721, Pte., d. of w., F. & F., 27/8/16.
Hancox, Harry, b. Coventry, e. Coventry, 5219, Pte., k. in a., F. & F., 18/8/16.
Harding, Charles, b. Birmingham, e. Birmingham, 21105, Dmr., k. in a., F. & F., 4/2/17.
Harper, Norman William, b. Wolverhampton, Staffs, e. Birmingham, 2497, L/Cpl., k. in a., F. & F., 1/7/16.
Harris, Percy, b. St. Mary's, Kington, Hereford, e. Birmingham, 2718, Sgt., d. of w., F. & F., 10/12/16.
Harrison, William Arthur, b. Handsworth, Staffs, e. Birmingham (Handsworth), 241600, Pte., k. in a., F. & F., 8/8/16.
Harvey, Albert Henry, b. Birmingham, e. Birmingham, 1572, Pte., k. in a., F. & F., 16/5/15.
Harwood, Joseph William, b. Birmingham, e. Birmingham, 241216, Pte., k. in a., F. & F., 1/4/17.
Hasler, Arnold Leslie, b. Newport, Mon., e. Birmingham (Balsall Heath, Birmingham), 20720, Pte., k. in a., F. & F., 24/8/16.
Haylor, Thomas, e. Birmingham (Yardley, Birmingham), 4509, Pte., d., F. & F., 2/8/16.

Hawkes, Dennis, b. Chesham, Bucks, e. Chesham, 242857, Pte., d. of w., F. & F., 27/10/18.
Hayward, Frank, b. Birmingham, e. Birmingham (Edgbaston, Birmingham), 241436, Pte., k. in a., F. & F., 19/6/17.
Heath, John Thomas, b. Aston, Birmingham, e. Aston, 242837, Pte., k. in a., F. & F., 4/10/17.
Henchcliffe, John, b. Gravesend, Kent, e. Gravesend, 260106, Pte., k. in a., F. & F., 4/10/17, formerly 6640, Essex Regt.
Henley, Ernest Frederick, b. Birmingham, e. Coventry, 242811, Pte., k. in a., F. & F., 1/4/17.
Hewitt, Frederick, e. Birmingham, 21106, Pte., k. in a., F. & F., 4/2/17.
Hill, Edgar, b. Scarborough, Yorks, e. Coventry, 20911, Pte., k. in a., F. & F., 10/12/16.
Hill, George William, e. Birmingham, 4530, Pte., k. in a., F. & F., 2/12/16.
Hill, William, b. Blackheath, Worcs., e. Old Hill, Staffs. (Halesowen, Worcs.), 242790, Pte., k. in a., F. & F., 27/8/17.
Hipperson, Albine Gordon, b. Parnham Broon, Norfolk, e. Coventry, 20249, Pte., k. in a., F. & F., 4/2/17.
Hoare, Victor, b. Chipping Norton, Oxon, e. Chipping Norton, 241686, Pte., d., F. & F., 12/2/17.
Hodges, William, b. Birmingham, e. Birmingham (Balsall Heath, Birmingham), 241300, Pte., k. in a., F. & F., 16/4/17.
Hodgetts, Percy William, b. Birmingham, e. Birmingham (Sparkbrook, Birmingham), 4227, L/Cpl., k. in a., F. & F., 18/8/16.
Hogg, Thomas Edgar, e. Coventry, 242785, Pte., k. in a., F. & F., 27/8/17.
Holey, Wilfred, b Castleford, Yorks, e. Whitby, Yorks, 242170, Pte., k. in a., F. & F., 4/10/17, formerly 20233, 13th Res. Cav. Regt.
Holland, George, b. Manchester, e. Aston, Birmingham, 2077, Cpl., k. in a., F. & F., 20/8/16,
Hollis, Enoch, b. Birmingham, e. Birmingham, 25168, Pte., k. in a, F. & F., 25/8/16.
Homer, Horace, b. Cradley Heath, Staffs, e. Worcester (Cradley Heath), 48482, Pte., k. in a., F. & F., 25/9/18, formerly 42246, R. Berks Regt.
Homer, Mark Benson, b. Newcastle, Staffs, e. Birmingham, 2657, L/Sgt., k. in a., F. & F., 11/6/16.
Hook, William Douglas, b. Holy Cross, Worcs, e. Pershore, Worcs, 1941, L/Cpl., d. of w., F. & F., 13/2/17.
Houghton, Charles Henry, b. Kings Norton, Birmingham, e. Birmingham (Kings Heath, Birmingham), 2774, Pte., d. of w., F. & F., 16/8/15.
Hoult, George Henry, b. Smethwick, Staffs, e. Birmingham (Smethwick), 1698, Pte., k. in a., F. & F., 9/2/16.
Howard, Charles, b. Small Heath, Birmingham, e. Birmingham (Small Heath), 1756, L/Cpl., d. of w., F. & F., 18/10/16.
Hudson, James Edward, b. Accrington, Lancs, e. Coventry, 242093, Pte., k. in a., F. & F., 27/8/17.
Hughes, Walter, b. Lozells, Birmingham, e. Aston, Birmingham, 242000, Pte., k. in a., F. & F., 16/4/17.
Hughes, Richard, b. Wasperton, Warwicks, e. Warwick (Newton Nethercote, Leic), 5042, Pte., k. in a., F. & F., 17/8/16.
Hunt, Charles Herbert, b. Ladywood, Birmingham, e. Birmingham, 240543, Cpl., k. in a., F. & F., 4/10/17.
Hunt, Geoffrey, e. Birmingham (Yardley Wood, Birmingham), 4602, Pte., k. in a., F. & F., 1/7/16.
Hunt, George Frank, e. Birmingham, 240716, Pte., k. in a., F. & F., 1/7/16.
Hunt, Harry, b. Rotton Park, Birmingham, e. Birmingham, 240126, Sgt., k. in a., F. & F., 19/6/17.
Hunt, Walter Isaac, e. Birmingham (Brierley Hill, Staffs), 4670, Pte., k. in a., F. & F., 18/7/16.
Hunt, James, b. Nechells, Birmingham, e. Birmingham (Hockley, Birmingham), 240165, Sgt., k. in a., F. & F., 4/10/17, M.M. and Bar.
Hunt, Samuel Henry, b. Warwick, e. Birmingham (Smethwick, Staffs), 4532, Pte., k. in a., F. & F., 1/7/16.
Hunt, Thomas, b. St. Thomas, Birmingham, e. Birmingham, 1692, Pte, k. in a., F. & F., 1/7/16.
Hurley, Frank Leonard May, b. Barnes, Surrey, e. Kingston-on-Thames (Barnes), 29873, Pte., k. in a., F. & F., 25/9/18, formerly 10699, E. Kent Regt.
Jackson, Ernest Alfred, b. Coventry, e. Coventry, 241619, Pte., k. in a., F. & F., 27/8/17.
Jackson, John Edwin, b. Sowfields, Lincoln, e. Newark, Notts, 27562, Pte., k. in a., F. & F., 4/10/17 formerly 2878, Notts & Derby Regt.
Jackson, William Henry, b. St. Pancras, London, e. Westminster, London, St. Pancras, 242040, Sgt., k. in a., F. & F., 27/8/17.
James, Albert, e. Birmingham (Claverdon, Warwicks), 4965, Pte., k. in a., F. & F., 1/7/16.
James, Stanley, b. Erdington, Birmingham, e. Birmingham, 2387, Pte., k. in a., F. & F., 16/5/15.
Jefferies, James, b. St. Paul's, Birmingham, e. Birmingham (Brookfields, Birmingham), 240286, Pte., k. in a., F. & F., 19/617.
Johnson, Frederick George, b. Handsworth, Staffs, e. Birmingham (Handsworth)), 2787, Sgt., k. in a., F. & F., 1/7/16.
Johnson, George, e. Warwick Birmingham), 5065, Pte., k. in a., F. & F., 18/8/16.
Jones, Arthur Edwin, b. Romford, Essex, e. Romford, 260114, Cpl., d. of w., F. & F., 29/8/17, formerly 7/5667, Essex Regt.
Jones, Edward Charles, b. St. Martin's, Birmingham, e. Birmingham, 240601, L/Cpl., k. in a., F. & F., 1/7/16.
Jones, Ernest b. West Bromwich, Staffs, e. Birmingham (West Bromwich), 2618, Pte., k. in a., F. & F., 16/5/15.
Jones, Francis, b. Birmingham, e Birmingham, 241564, Pte., k. in a., F. & F., 18/8/16.
Jordan, Ernest Frederick, b. Sparbrook, Birmingham, e. Birmingham, 2636, Pte., k. in a., F. & F., 29/5/15.
Joyner, Harry Ernest, b. St. George's, Birmingham, e. Birmingham (Handsworth, Staffs), 242095, Pte., k. in a., F. & F., 1/4/17.
Jukes, Arthur, b. Coventry, Warwicks, e. Warwick (Coventry), 5089, Pte., k. in a., F. & F., 18/8/16.
Jukes, Raymond George, b. Tipton, Staffs, e. Birmingham (Tipton), 2559, Sgt., k. in a., F. & F., 1/7/16.
Kench, Henry Frederick, b. Birmingham, e. Birmingham (Hockley, Birmingham), 242730, Pte., d., F. & F., 1/4/17.
Kenney, Herbert Harold, b. Alcester, Warwicks, e. Rugby (Wolston, Coventry), 5224, Pte., k. in a., F. & F., 4/2/17.
Kettle, George, b. Stretton, Oakham, Rutland, e. Oakham, 242172, Cpl., k. in a., F. & F., 16/4/17, formerly 12276, Leics. Regt.
Kettle, Herbert, e. Leicester (Thurleston, near Hinckley, Leics.), 20330, Pte., d., F. & F., 3/12/16, formerly 16788, Leics Regt.
Kettle, Jack, b. Aston, Birmingham, e. Birmingham (Sparkhill, Birmingham), 2336, L/Cpl., d. of w., F. & F., 15/3/16.
Kiddle, William Harold, b. Bristol, e. Bristol, 5421, Pte k. in a., F. & F., 18/8/16.
Kilby, James Edward, b. Ladywood, Birmingham, e. Birmingham, 1630, Pte., k. in a., F. & F., 1/7/16.
Kimberley, Frank Horace, b. Aston, Birmingham, e. Birmingham (Ladywood, Birmingham), 2225, Pte., k. in a., F. & F., 1/7/16.
Kimberley Thomas Berthram, b. Marton, Warwicks, e. Rugby, Warwicks (Birdingbury, near Rugby), 6204, L/Cpl., k. in a., F. & F., 4/10/17.
King, Alfred George, b. Saffron Walden, Essex, e. Saffron Walden, 260116, Pte., k. in a., F. & F., 27/8/17, formerly 28380, Suffolk Regt., and 400282, Essex Regt.
Kitson, Benjamin Thomas, b. Wordsley, Staffs, e. Warwick (Bilston, Staffs), 5031, Pte., d. of w., F. & F., 23/8/16.
Knibb, Alfred, b. Earlswood, Warwicks, e. Warwick (Dorridge, Knowle, Warwicks), 5066, Pte., d. of w., F. & F., 20/8/16.
Knight, George Edward, b. Hethersett, Norfolk, e. Bury St. Edmunds, Suffolk (Attleborough, Norfolk), 29149, Pte., k. in a., F. & F., 4/10/17, formerly 45963, Northants Regt.
Knight, Harold Louis, b. Bedminster, Bristol, e. Bristol (Keynsham, near Bristol), 20822, Pte., k. in a., F. & F., 18/8/16, formerly 129, S. Mid. Div. Clylist Battn.
Lamb, Frederick James, e. Birmingham, 3322, Pte., k. in a., F. & F., 1/7/16.
Lamb, Harry, e. Birmingham, 3340, Pte., k. in a., F. & F., 1/7/16.
Lambert, George Edward, b. Thornbury, Glos., e. Bristol (Crossways, nr. Thornbury), 242041, Pte., k. in a., F. & F., 19/8/17, formerly 3746, Glos. Regt.
Lancaster, Leslie, e. Birmingham, 242516, Pte., d., F. & F., 5/10/17.
Lane, Richard Harold, b. Lowton, Leigh, Lancs, e. Blackwell, Derby (Pinxton, Derby), 242148, Sgt., k. in a., F. & F., 27/8/17, formerly 2447, Notts & Derby Regt., M.M.
Langford, Richard, b. St. Stephens, Birmingham, e. Birmingham, 2170, Pte., k. in a., F. & F., 1/7/16.
Langford, Thomas, b. Small Heath, Birmingham, e. Birmingham, 2460, Pte., d., F. & F., 21/10/16.
Lawrence, Alfred William, b. All Saints, Birmingham, e. Birmingham, 2692, Pte., d. of w., F. & F., 25/6/16.
Laurence, Ernest John, b. Chiswick, Middx., e. Kingston-on-Thames (Kew, Middx.), 260119, Pte., k. in a., F. & F., 27/8/17, formerly 400248, Essex Regt
Leach, Walter Joseph, b. Aston, Birmingham, e. Warwick (Aston, Birmingham), 5032, Pte., d. of w., F. & F., 19/8/16.
Lee, Thomas Harry, b. St. George's, Birmingham, e. Birmingham, 1965, L/Cpl., k. in a., F. & F., 1/7/16.
Lefley, George, b. London, e. Birmingham, 4520, Pte., k. in a., F. & F., 16/8/16.
Lewis, Albert Edward, b. Leytonstone, Essex, e. Stratford, Essex (Leytonstone), 29204, Pte., k. in a., F. & F., 27/8/17, formerly 11733, D.C.L.I.
Licence, John, b. St. Stephens, Birmingham, e. Birmingham, 2209, Pte., k. in a., F. & F., 26/6/16.
Lichfield, Walter, b. Birmingham, e. Birmingham, 3176, Pte., k. in a., F. & F., 18/8/16.
Lilley, Arthur, e. Birmingham (Small Heath, Birmingham), 4585, Pte., k. in a., F. & F., 1/7/16.
Lindsey, Bernard, b. Belper, Derby, e. Birmingham (King's Norton, Birmingham), 2823, Pte., k. in a., F. & F., 13/5/15.
Link, Horace Bert, b. Bethersden, Ashford, Kent, e. Tenterden, Kent, 260303, Pte., k. in a., F. & F., 4/10/17, formerly 2733, E. Kent Regt.
Lissetter, Charles, e. Birmingham (Sparkhill, Birmingham), 240890, Pte., k. in a., F. & F., 4/10/17.
Lombard, Ernest, b. Foleshill, Warwicks, e. Coventry (Foleshill), 242732, Pte., k. in a., F. & F., 19/6/17.
Louch, Frank, b Stratford-on-Avon, Warwicks, e. Leamington (Kineton, Warwicks), 5226, Pte., k. in a., F. & F., 18/8/16.
Loveridge, John William, b. Fenny Stratford, Bucks, e. Coventry, Warwicks, 20921, Pte., d. of w., F. & F., 18/2/17.
Loxton, James Henry, b. St. Martin's, Birmingham, e. Birmingham, 2183, Pte., k. in a., F. & F., 28/6/16.
Lowe, Richard Ernest, b. Aston, Birmingham, e. Aston (Hockley, Birmingham), 20779, Pte., d. of w., F. & F., 4/2/17.
Lucas, George, b. Sutton Coldfield, Warwicks, e. Birmingham (Four Oaks, Birmingham), 10523, Pte., k. in a., F. & F., 27/8/17.
Lutwyche, Harry, e. Birmingham, 241010, d. of w., F. & F., 26/8/17.
Lyndon, John Palmer, b. Shirley, Birmingham, e. Birmingham, 240556, Pte., k. in a., F. & F., 1/7/16.

Lyons, William, b. Birmingham, e. Birmingham (Handsworth, Birmingham), 241220, Pte., d. of w., F. & F., 5/9/17.
McDonald, George, b. St. Paul's, Balsall Heath, Birmingham, e. Warwick (Balsall Heath), 241555, Pte., k. in a., F. & F., 1/7/16.
MacKay, Frank, b. Govan, Glasgow, e. Totnes, Devon (Govan), 242657, Sgt., d. of w., F. & F., 22/8/17, formerly 1540, Devon Regt., D.C.M.
McPike, William, e. Birmingham (Handsworth, Birmingham), 241083, Pte., k. in a., F. & F., 16/4/17.
Maidment, Walter Charles, e. Poole, Dorset, 21036, Pte., k. in a., F. & F., 4/2/17.
Mander, Douglas Fred, b. Darlaston, Staffs, e. Birmingham, 4249, Pte., k. in a., F. & F., 1/7/16.
Mander, Frederick, b. Wootton Wawen, Warwicks, e. Knowle, Warwicks, 241770, Pte., d., F. & F., 16/2/17.
Markwell, Herbert Charles, b. Wortwell, Norfolk, e. Harleston, Norfolk (Wortwell), 29166, Pte., k. in a., F. & F., 4/10/17, formerly 46003, Northants Regt.
Marriage, Edward Henry, b. Tottenham, Middx., e. Tottenham, 260121, Pte., k. in a., F. & F., 27/8/17, formerly 400382, Essex Regt.
Marshall, Christopher John, b. Poplar, Middx., e. St. Paul's Churchyard, London (Poplar), 242701, Pte., k. in a., F. & F., 4/2/17, formerly 11527, A. Cyclist Corps.
Marshall, James, e. Birmingham (Curdworth, near Birmingham), 4513, Pte., d. of w., F. & F., 18/7/16.
Marshall, Thomas Ernest, b. Burford, Oxon, e. Birmingham, 241312, Pte., k. in a., F. & F., 1/7/16.
Maslin, Thomas Henry, b. Devizes, Wilts, e. Devizes (Swindon, Wilts), 29237, Pte., k. in a., F. & F., 3/12/17, formerly 9029, Wilts Regt.
Massey, Herbert John, b. Meriden, Warwicks, e. Warwick (Meriden), 5115, Pte., k. in a., F. & F., 18/8/16.
Matthews, Connard James, b. St. Stephen's, Redditch, Worcs, e. Birmingham, 2121, Pte., k. in a., F. & F., 1/7/16.
Mathews, Harry Stanley, b. St. Mary, Dover, Kent, e. Dover, 260321, Pte., k. in a., F. & F., 4/10/17, formerly 2594, E. Kent Regt.
Maxfield, Thomas, b. Hockley, Birmingham, e. Birmingham (Balsall Heath, Birmingham), 4141, Pte., k. in a., F. & F., 1/7/16.
Mears, Alfred, b. Ditchling, Sussex, e. Hastings, Sussex (Ditchling), 29874, Pte., k. in a., F. & F., 4/10/17.
Meek, Frederick Clarence, e. Coventry, 7647, Pte., k. in a., F. & F., 4/2/17.
Meredith, Alfred, b. Birmingham, e. Birmingham (Hockley, Birmingham), 241644, Pte., k. in a., F. & F., 18/8/16.
Merry, Robert, b. Hanley, Staffs, e. Sutton Coldfield, Warwicks, 242331, Pte., k. in a., F. & F., 27/8/17.
Miller, Charles Percy Joseph, b. Minster, Kent, e. Ramsgate, Kent, 260304, Pte., k. in a., F. & F., 4/10/17, formerly 1691, E. Kent Regt.
Millerchip, Edward James, b. Coventry, Warwicks, e. Warwick (Coventry), 5174, Pte., k. in a., F. & F., 18/8/16.
Mills, George, b. Saltley, Birmingham, e. Birmingham (Saltley), 2572, Cpl., k. in a., F. & F., 18/8/16.
Millward, Jabez Henry, b. Sparkbrook, Birmingham, e. Birmingham (Sparkbrook), 240481, Pte., d., F. & F., 29/3/17.
Minaham, Edward, e. Birmingham (Erdington, Birmingham), 2806, Cpl., d. of w., F. & F., 22/9/16.
Mogg, Albert, b. Tamworth, Warwicks, e. Small Heath, Birmingham, 240247, L/Cpl., k. in a., F. & F., 16/4/17.
Moore, Alfred, b. Ladywood, Birmingham, e. Birmingham, 1702, Pte., k. in a., F. & F., 1/7/16.
Moore, Ephraim, e. Birmingham (Aston, Birmingham), 4633, Pte., k. in a., F. & F., 1/7/16.
Moore, Maurice, b. Saham, Norfolk, e. Norwich (Thetford, Norfolk), 260003, Pte., k. in a., F. & F., 27/8/17, formerly 9862, Cambs. Regt.
Moore, Thomas, b. Birmingham, e. Birmingham (Small Heath, Birmingham), 4154, Pte., k. in a., F. & F., 1/7/16.
Morgan, Gilbert Stanley, b. Drybrook, Cinderford, Glos., e. Nuneaton, Warwicks, 242050, Sgt., k. in a., F. & F., 4/10/17.
Morgan, John Arthur, b. Neath, Glam., e. Ynyshir, Glam., 29190, L/Cpl., d. of w., F. & F., 4/10/17, formerly 12676, Devon Regt.
Morgan, William, b. Aston, Birmingham, e. Birmingham, 1981, Pte., k. in a., F. & F., 1/7/16.
Morgan, William Stanley, e. Birmingham, 3573, Cpl., k. in a., F. & F., 6/6/16.
Morris, Garnet, b. Gt. Rissington, Glos., e. Borton-on-Water, Glos. (Gt. Rissington), 242685, L/Cpl., k. in a., F. & F., 16/4/17, formerly 17757 Worcs Regt.
Mould, James, b. Chilmark, Wilts, e. Warminster, Wilts (Tetfout Magna, nr. Salisbury), 20781, Pte., k. in a., F. & F., 4/2/17.
Mowbray, William, e. Birmingham, 4123, Pte., k. in a., F. & F., 4/2/17.
Moxon, Samuel, b. Birmingham, e. Birmingham, 5574, Pte., d. of w., F. & F., 4/2/17.
Munt, Thomas, e. Oxford (Littleworth, Wheatley, Oxon), 5361, Pte., d. of w., F. & F., 23/8/16.
Murphy, William, e. Leamington, Warwicks (Rugby, Warwicks), 18244, Pte., d., F. & F., 25/12/17.
Murray, Richard, b. Birmingham, e. Birmingham (Harborne, Birmingham), 4662, Pte., k. in a., F. & F., 1/7/16.
Nash, Charles Richard, b. Burton-on-Trent, Staffs, e. Birmingham (Saltley, Birmingham), 2505, Pte., d. of w., F. & F., 1/7/16.
Nash, Samuel, b. Birmingham, e. Birmingham, 4442, Pte., k. in a., F. & F., 1/7/16.
Neville, George, e. Birmingham (Castle Bromwich, Birmingham), 242829, Pte., k. in a., F. & F., 27/8/17.
Newbold, William, b. Birmingham, e. Birmingham, 1871, Pte., k. in a., F. & F., 1/7/16.
Newman, Frederick, b. Birmingham, e. Birmingham (Small Heath, Birmingham), 4418, Pte., k. in a., F. & F., 1/7/16.
Newsome, Henry Alfred, b. St. Thomas, Birmingham, e. Birmingham, 2008, Pte., k. in a., F. & F., 1/7/16.
Newton, Arthur, b. Hockley, Birmingham, e. Birmingham (Sparkhill, Birmingham), 1869, Pte., k. in a., F. & F., 6/6/16.
Newton, Arthur John, b. London, e. London (South Hackney, E.9), 33991, Pte., d. of w., F. & F., 4/10/17, formerly 5195, E. Kent Regt.
Nichols, Henry, b. Coventry, Warwicks, e. Coventry, 242557 Pte., k. in a., F. & F., 11/3/17.
Norman, John Henry, b. Warboys, Hunts, e. Warboys (Herringford, near St. Ives, Hunts), 29164, Pte., k. in a., F. & F., 20/8/17, formerly 39968, Northants Regt.
Nott, Percy Douglas, e. Birmingham (Ladywood, Birmingham), 241155, Pte., k. in a., F. & F., 4/10/17.
O'Dowd, Martin, e. Birmingham (Edgbaston, Birmingham), 242558, Pte., k. in a., F. & F., 19/6/17.
Osborne, Herbert Charles, b. Hockesill, Bishop's Stortford, Herts, e. Birmingham (Bishop's Stortford), 240589, Pte., k. in a., F. & F., 1/7/16.
Palmer, Alfred, b. St. Albans, Birmingham, e. Birmingham, 4252, Pte., d. of w., F. & F., 28/6/16.
Palmer, John, b. Birmingham, e. Birmingham, 241378, L/Cpl., k. in a., F. & F., 19/8/17.
Parker, Edward, b Aston, Birmingham, e. Birmingham, 2585, Cpl., k. in a., F. & F., 1/7/16. M.M.
Parker, George, b. Small Heath, Birmingham, e. Birmingham, 2426, L/Cpl., k. in a., F. & F., 1/7/16.
Parkyn, William Jack, b. Kenilworth, Warwicks, e. Kenilworth, 242560, Pte., k. in a., F. & F., 27/8/17.
Parr, Percy, b. Birmingham, e. Birmingham (Balsall Heath, Birmingham), 241224, Pte., d., F. & F., 10/7/16.
Parry, Richard Louis, e. Birmingham (Smethwick, Staffs), 4745, Pte., k. in a., F. & F., 1/7/16.
Parsonage, Alfred Thomas, b. Birmingham, e. Birmingham, 4683, Pte., k. in a., F. & F., 1/7/16.
Parsons, Frank, e. Birmingham (Aberavon, S. Wales), 5012, Pte., d. of w., F. & F., 7/7/16.
Parsons, Harold Leonard, b. Sparkhill, Birmingham, e. Birmingham (Sparkhill), 1607, Pte., k. in a., F. & F., 18/8/16.
Partridge, William Henry, b. Bordesley, Birmingham, e. Birmingham (Bordesley), 240433, Pte., k. in a., F. & F., 1/7/16.
Patrick, Frederick, b. Sparkbrook, Birmingham, e. Birmingham, 1564, Pte., k. in a., F. & F., 1/7/16.
Patrick, Henry William, b. Edgbaston, Birmingham, e. Birmingham (Edgbaston), 1767, Pte., k. in a., F. & F., 1/7/16.
Pavelin, Percy Albert, b. Witham, Essex, e. Barking, Essex, 29191, Sgt., k. in a., F. & F., 16/6/18, formerly 14815, Duke of Cornwall's L.I.
Payne, Francis, b. Smethwick, Birmingham, e. Birmingham, 2173, Pte., k. in a., F. & F., 18/8/16.
Peak, John Alfred, b. St. Peter's, Birmingham, e. Birmingham, 2065, Pte., k. in a., F. & F., 1/7/16.
Pearce, Frederick, b. Aston, Birmingham, e. Birmingham (Aston), 1729, Pte., k. in a., F. & F., 1/7/16.
Pegg, George Henry, b. Shirley, Warwick, e. Warwick (Shirley), 241721, L/Cpl., k. in a., F. & F., 4/10/17.
Pentrell, Harry, b. Coalville, Leics., e. Leicester, 242151, Cpl., d. of w., F. & F., 2/4/17, formerly 23623, Leics. Regt.
Percival, William Ernest, b. Irchester, e. Irchester, Northants, 242103, Pte., d. of w., F. & F., 17/9/17, formerly T/5414, Notts and Derby Regt.
Perkins, John James, b. Birmingham, e. Birmingham (Camp Hill, Birmingham), 4748, Pte., k. in a., F. & F., 1/7/16.
Perkins, William George, e. Birmingham (Edgbaston, Birmingham), 21093, A/Cpl., k. in a., F. & F., 4/2/17.
Perks, Joseph, b. St. Paul's, Birmingham, e. Birmingham, 2296, Pte., d. of w., F. & F., 23/7/16.
Perks, Sidney, b. Birmingham, e. Birmingham, 242925, Dmr., k. in a., F. & F., 17/8/17.
Pettifer, William, b. Birmingham, e. Birmingham, 242692, Pte., k. in a., F. & F., 4/10/17, formerly 22454, Worcs Regt.
Phillips, Eric, b. All Saints, Birmingham, e. Birmingham (Hockley, Birmingham), 240392, Pte., d. of w., F. & F., 4/10/17.
Phillips, Fred, e. Birmingham (Handsworth, Staffs), 3260, Pte., k. in a., F. & F., 6/6/16.
Phillips, Harry Frank, b. Bromsgrove, Worcs, e. Birmingham (Ladywood, Birmingham), 241157, Pte., k. in a., F. & F., 1/7/16.
Pickering, Ernest William, e. Birmingham, 241303, Pte., k. in a., F. & F., 27/8/17.
Pinckston, Frederick, e. Birmingham, 240720, Pte., k. in a., F. & F., 27/8/17.
Pitt, Harry, b. Norwood, London, e. Birmingham (Tyseley, Birmingham), 1881, Pte., k. in a., F. & F., 1/7/16.
Plows, Edwin, b. London, Middx., e. Birmingham, 21059, Pte., k. in a., F. & F., 4/2/17.
Polden, Reginald Francis, b. Steeple Langford, Wilts, e. Salisbury, Wilts (Steeple Langford), 33406, Pte., k. in a., F. & F., 30/4/18, formerly M/301272, R.A.S.C.
Poole, James Nathaniel, b. Smethwick, Staffs, e. Birmingham, 1486, Pte., k. in a., F. & F., 28/6/16.
Poole, Walter James, b. Friargate, Derby, e. Birmingham (Sparkbrook, Birmingham), 1608, Pte., k. in a., F. & F., 1/7/16.
Powers, Frederick, b. Aston, Birmingham, e. Birmingham, 2729, Pte., d. of w., F. & F., 3/6/15.
Preston, William Ernest, b. Birmingham, e. Birmingham (King's Heath, Birmingham), 241401, Pte., k. in a., F. & F., 1/7/16.

Prett, Thomas Jacob, b. Canterbury, Kent, e. Birmingham (Canterbury), 5298, Pte., d. of w., F. & F., 23/8/16.
Prince, Harry Leslie, e. Birmingham (Ladywood, Birmingham), 240682, Pte., k. in a., F. & F., 1/7/16.
Probert, Herbert, e. Coventry, 266626, Pte., k. in a., F. & F., 27/8/17.
Purnell, Eric Keppell, b. Kenilworth, Warwickshire, e. Warwick (Coventry), 241541, Pte., k. in a., F. & F., 1/7/16.
Ramsay, David, b. Broughty Ferry, Dundee, e. Aston, Birmingham (Nechells, Birmingham), 242877, Pte., k. in a., F. & F., 1/4/17.
Rayner, Percy, b. Maldon, Essex, e. Chelmsford, Essex (Maldon), 260129, Pte., k. in a., F. & F., 4/10/17, formerly 3215, Essex Regt.
Read, Herbert Henry, e. Rugby, Warwickshire, 242564, Pte., k. in a., F. & F., 9/3/17.
Reeve, Basil, b. Swanton, Morley, Norfolk, e. Norwich, Norfolk (Swanton), 242139, Pte., k. in a., F. & F., 1/4/17, formerly 5145, Notts. & Derby Regt.
Readshaw, Herbert W., b. Middlesbrough, Yorks, e. Birmingham (Middlesbrough), 240515, L/Sgt., k. in a., F. & F., 1/7/16.
Reeves, Horace Albert, e. Birmingham (Small Heath, Birmingham), 3709, L/Sgt., k. in a., F. & F., 1/7/16.
Reynolds, Arthur, b. St. Martins, Birmingham, e. Birmingham, 1508, Pte., k. in a., F. & F., 17/5/15.
Reynolds, Herbert Thomas, b. Walworth, Surrey, e. Kingston-on-Thames, Surrey (Ham, Surrey), 260132, Pte., k. in a., F. & F., 4/10/17, formerly 400790, Essex Regt.
Riches, Samuel Robert, b. Woolwich, Kent, e. Woolwich, 29055, Pte., d. of w., F. & F., 2/11/17.
Riley, Arthur, b. Coventry, e. Birmingham, 241366, Pte., k. in a., F. & F., 1/4/17.
Rippon, Victor William, b. Peterborough, Northants, e. Peterborough, 29230, Pte., k. in a., F. & F., 4/10/17.
Rivers, William Thomas John, b. Romford, Essex, e. Romford, 260128, Pte., k. in a., F. & F., 19/8/17, formerly 31199, Suffolk Regt. and 400591 Essex Regt.
Roberson, Jesse, b. Thornaby, Yorks, e. Stockton-on-Tees, Durham, 20676, Cpl., k. in a., F. & F., 27/8/17, formerly 12179, A. Cyclist Corps.
Roberts, Arthur, b. Birmingham, e. Warwick (Small Heath, Birmingham), 5182, Pte., k. in a., F. & F., 17/8/16.
Roberts, Victor, b. Erdington, Birmingham, e. Birmingham (Erdington), 2438, L/Cpl., k. in a., F. & F., 1/7/16.
Roe, Charles Frederick, b. Birmingham, e. Birmingham (Aston, Birmingham), 4337, Pte., k. in a., F. & F., 1/7/16.
Rogers, Frank, b. Aston, Birmingham, e. Birmingham, 240334, Pte., k. in a., F. & F., 1/7/16.
Rogers, Herbert, b. Acocks Green, Birmingham, e. Birmingham (Warwick), 201291, Cpl., k. in a., F. & F., 19/6/17.
Rollo, Lewis Charles, b. Lancaster, e. Birmingham, 2551, Pte., d. of w., F. & F., 3/7/16.
Roper, Louis, b. Aston, Birmingham, e. Birmingham, 2685, Pte., k. in a., F. & F., 1/7/16.
Roscoe, George, b. Norwich, e. Birmingham, 240495, Pte., k. in a., F. & F., 1/7/16.
Rosinsky, Soloman, b. St. George's, London, e. Stratford, Essex (Whitechapel, London), 20210, Pte., k. in a., F. & F., 4/2/17, formerly 22702, Oxford & Bucks L.I.
Rowley, William, b. Duddeston, Birmingham, e. Birmingham, 240080, Pte., k. in a., F. & F., 1/7/16.
Russell, Samuel, b. Bromley, Kent, e. Nuneaton, Warwicks, 20739, Pte., k. in a., F. & F., 24/8/16.
Russell, Thomas, b. Aston, Birmingham, e. Birmingham, 240049, Pte., k. in a., F. & F., 27/8/17.
Sale, Harry, b. Derby, e. Birmingham (Aston, Birmingham), 240206, Sgt., k. in a., F. & F., 27/8/17.
Sanders, Stanley, b. Birmingham, e. Warwick (Rotton Park, Birmingham), 21117, Dmr., k. in a., F. & F., 4/2/17.
Sanders, William Thomas, b. Aston, Birmingham, e. Birmingham, 242804, Pte., k. in a., F. & F., 27/8/17.
Sansom, Albert John, b. Small Heath, Birmingham, e. Swindon, Wilts, 306733, Pte., k. in a., F. & F., 18/8/17.
Sargent, Alfred, e. Birmingham (Harborne, Birmingham), 4619, Pte., k. in a., F. & F., 1/7/16.
Savigar, Arthur, b. Ladywood, Birmingham, e. Birmingham, 1762, Pte., k. in a., F. & F., 1/7/16.
Sayers, William, b. Birmingham, e. Birmingham, 4224, Pte., k. in a., F. & F., 11/7/16.
Scarrott, William, b. Birmingham, e. Birmingham (Nechells, Birmingham), 241478, Pte., d., F. & F., 9/9/17.
Scott, William, b. Stapleford, Wilts, e. Warminster, Wilts (Upton Lovel, Wilts), 242832, Pte., d., F. & F., 9/4/17.
Sefton, James, b. Ladywood, Birmingham, e. Birmingham (Ladywood), 2604, Sgt., k. in a., F. & F., 1/7/16.
Selby, Percy Harold, b. Cuckfield, Sussex, e. Haywards Heath, Sussex (Cuckfield), 241868, L/Cpl., k. in a., F. & F., 4/10/17, formerly 2169, R. Sussex Regt.
Sewell, Ernest, e. Birmingham (Smethwick, Staffs), 4774, Pte., k. in a., F. & F., 19/8/16.
Sewell, John, b. St. Asaph's, Birmingham, e. Birmingham, 2370, Pte., k. in a., F. & F., 1/7/16.
Sewell, William, e. Birmingham, 240925, Pte., k. in a., F. & F., 27/8/17.
Sharp, Harry, b. All Saints, Birmingham, e. Birmingham, 1779, Pte., d. of w., F. & F., 30/4/16.
Sharpe, Ernest, b. Twyford, Leics, e. Leicester (Twyford), 20353, Pte., k. in a., F. & F., 4/2/17, formerly 25863, Leics Regt.
Sharratt, Thomas Patrick, b. Tamworth, Staffs, e. Birmingham (Tamworth), 21094, Pte., k. in a., F. & F., 4/2/17.
Shipway, Harry, b. Birmingham, e. Birmingham, 241187, Pte., d. of w., F. & F., 23/2/17.
Shenton, Fred, b. Birmingham, e. Birmingham (Smethwick, Staffs), 202963, Pte., k. in a., F. & F., 19/6/17.
Shock, Charles, b. Walsall, Staffs, e. Birmingham, 240076, Pte., k. in a., F. & F., 19/6/17.
Simmons, Charles Frederick, b. Uckfield, Sussex, e. Uckfield, 260136, Pte., k. in a., F. & F., 4/10/17, formerly 31728, Suffolk Regt., 400300, Essex Regt.
Simpson, Edwin Terry, b. Brookfields, Birmingham, e. Birmingham (Smethwick, Staffs), 5750, Pte., k. in a., F. & F., 4/2/17.
Skinner, Ernest, b. Framfield, Sussex, e. Salisbury, Wilts (Rollestone, Suffolk), 242851, Pte., d. of w., F. & F., 3/4/17.
Slater, Thomas William Wyatt, e. Ilkeston, Derby, 242120, Pte., d. of w., F. & F., 16/10/17, formerly 2877, Notts & Derby Regt.
Slim, Leonard, b. Langley, Worcs, e. Birmingham (Bournbrook, Birmingham), 4811, Pte., k. in a., F. & F., 1/7/16.
Small, William, e. Birmingham, 240806, Pte., k. in a., F. & F., 1/7/16.
Smith, Albert William, b. Oakham, Rutland, e. Warwick (Oakham), 241557, Pte., k. in a., F. & F., 1/7/16.
Smith, Albert Buchan, b. Aston, Birmingham, e. Birmingham, 2556, Pte., k. in a., F. & F., 1/7/16.
Smith, Alfred Frederick, b. All Saints, Birmingham, e. Birmingham (Warley, Birmingham), 240359, Pte., k. in a., F. & F., 16/4/17.
Smith, Alfred Thomas, b. Birmingham, e. Birmingham (Aston, Birmingham), 20978, Pte., k. in a., F. & F., 4/2/17.
Smith, Archie Douglas, e. Birmingham (Handsworth, Staffs), 3252, Cpl., k. in a., F. & F., 1/7/16.
Smith, David, b. Reading, Berks, e. Swindon, Wilts, 242844, Pte., d. of w., F. & F., 18/4/17.
Smith, Dudley James, b. Bristol, e. Cambridge, 29152, Pte., k. in a., F. & F., 18/8/17, formerly 39980, Northn. Regt.
Smith, Edward, e. Birmingham (Brierley Hill, Staffs), 4590, Pte., k. in a., F. & F., 1/7/16.
Smith, Ernest, b. Cannock Chase, Staffs, e. Birmingham (Tipton, Staffs), 4975, Pte., k. in a., F. & F., 1/7/16.
Smith, George Henry, b. Duddleston, Birmingham, e. Birmingham, 330138, Cpl., k. in a., F. & F., 27/8/17.
Smith, Godfrey Eric, b. Canterbury, Kent, e. Birmingham (South Yardley, Birmingham), 19008, Pte., k. in a., F. & F., 18/8/17.
Smith, Harold Ernest, b. Saltley, Birmingham, e. Birmingham (Saltley), 2287, Pte., k. in a., F. & F., 1/7/16.
Smith, Jesse Herbert, b. Luton, Beds, e. Coventry (Foleshill, Coventry), 242821, Pte., k. in a., F. & F., 1/4/17.
Smith, John James, e. Birmingham (Hockley, Birmingham), 4711, Pte., d. of w., F. & F., 29/7/16.
Smith, Reginald Arthur, b. Kidderminster, Worcs, e. Birmingham (Edgbaston, Birmingham), 2436, Pte., d. of w., F. & F., 30/4/16.
Smitten, George Arthur, e. Birmingham (Sparkhill, Birmingham), 4751, Pte., k. in a., F. & F., 1/7/16.
Sorrell, James, b. St. Thomas', Birmingham, e. Birmingham, 1457, Sgt., k. in a., F. & F., 1/7/16.
South, Amos Joseph, e. Coventry, 20742, Pte., d. of w., F. & F., 6/2/17.
Sparrow, Harold, e. Birmingham (Hockley, Birmingham), 4775, Pte., k. in a., F. & F., 1/7/16.
Spencer, Joseph, b. Burton-on-Trent, Staffs, e. Coventry, 266505, Pte., k. in a., F. & F., 19/6/17.
Spurrier, Charles, e Birmingham, 3328, Pte., d. of w., F. & F., 10/7/16.
Starbuck, Albert William, b. Bordesley, Birmingham, e. Birmingham, 2456, Pte., k. in a., F. & F., 1/7/16.
Steadman, Walter George, b. Bloomsbury, Birmingham, e. Birmingham, 2742, Pte., k. in a., F. & F., 1/6/15.
Steele, Stanley, b. Rotton Park, Birmingham, e. Birmingham, 240256, L/Cpl., d. of w., F. & F., 11/5/17.
Stevens, Charles Leonard, e. Manchester (Blackley, Manchester), 37929, Pte., k. in a., F. & F., 4/10/18, formerly PS/9434, R. Fus.
Stirk, Albert, b. St. Saviour's, Birmingham, e. Birmingham, 1524, Pte., d. of w., F. & F., 11/6/16.
Strachan, Alexander R., e. Aberdeen, 21189, Pte., k. in a., F. & F., 4/2/17, formerly 830, R.E.
Sturmey, Walter, b. East Lulworth, Dorset, e. Wareham, Dorset, 21052, Pte., k. in a., F. & F., 4/2/17.
Styles, Harry, b. Selly Oak, Birmingham, e. Birmingham (Stirchley, Birmingham), 242708, Pte., k. in a., F. & F., 27/8/17.
Summerfield, Walter Ernest, b. Clifton-on-Dunsmore, Warwicks, e. Rugby, Warwicks, 268343, Pte., k. in a., F. & F., 20/8/17.
Sutton, Herbert, b. Bombay, India, e. Pembroke (Angle, Pembroke), 22087, Pte., k. in a., F. & F., 16/4/17, formerly 741, Welsh Regt.
Swann, George Henry, b. Witton, Birmingham, e. Birmingham (Witton), 2645, Pte., k. in a., F. & F., 1/7/16.
Tanswell, Ernest, b. Rockbourne, Hants, e. Gillingham, Kent (East Knowle, Wilts), 30509, Pte., d. of w., F. & F., 13/10/17, formerly 31621, Worcs Regt.
Tapley, Malcolm, b. Lower Hardres, Kent, e. Canterbury, Kent (Lower Hardres, Kent), 260331, Pte., k. in a., F. & F., 4/10/17, formerly 4566, E. Kent Regt.
Taylor, Leonard Birkett, b. Handsworth, Staffs, e. Birmingham (Handsworth), 241403, Pte., d., F. & F., 26/4/17.
Terry, George William, b. Todenham, Glos., e. Bristol (Todenham), 5424, Pte., k. in a., F. & F., 18/8/16.
Thirlby, Thomas, e. Birmingham, 3118, Pte., k. in a., F. & F., 1/7/16.
Thorburn, Jack Addison, e. Birmingham, 3064, L/Sgt., k. in a., F. & F., 18/8/16.
Thorley, Joseph Thomas, b. St. George's, Birmingham, e. Birmingham, 1893, Pte., k. in a., F. & F., 1/7/16.
Thorne, Arthur Thomas, b. Warwick, e. Birmingham (Hockley, Birmingham), 240294, Pte., k. in a., F. & F., 1/7/16.

Thorpe, James Edward, b. St. Saviour's, Leicester, e. Leicester, 20341, Pte., d. of w., F. & F., 27/2/17, formerly 21159, Leics Regt.
Ticehurst, Arthur Edward, b. Birmingham, e. Birmingham (Aston, Birmingham), 17351, Pte., d. of w., F. & F., 20/11/17.
Tidmus, Edward, b. Deritend, Birmingham, e. Birmingham, 2719, Pte., k. in a., F. & F., 14/6/15.
Tilley, Lewis, b. Wylde Green, Birmingham, e. Birmingham (Bournville, Birmingham), 241630, Cpl., k. in a., F. & F., 4/10/17, M.M.
Tinnion, William, b. Workington, Cumberland, e. Birmingham (Smethwick, Staffs), 2816, L/Sgt., k. in a., F. & F., 1/7/16.
Tipper, William, b. Hanbury, Staffs, e. Birmingham, 1722, Cpl., d. of w., F. & F., 22/5/16.
Tomlinson, Arthur Sidney, e. Birmingham (Sparkbrook, Birmingham), 4356, Pte., k. in a., F. & F., 27/6/16.
Tomlinson, John, b. Little Weston, Yorks, e. Warwick, 20891, Pte., d. of w., F. & F., 13/10/16.
Toplis, Arthur, b. Matlock, Derby, e. Matlock, 242127, Pte., k. in a., F. & F., 1/4/17, formerly 4456, Notts & Derby Regt.
Toy, Alfred John, b. Four Oaks, Birmingham, e. Warwick (Four Oaks), 5188, Pte., k. in a., F. & F., 18/8/16.
Tribe, Albert, b. King's Heath, Birmingham, e. Birmingham (King's Heath), 1872, Pte., k. in a., F. & F., 1/7/16.
Trinder, Harry, b. St. George's, Birmingham, e. Birmingham (Hockley, Birmingham), 2014, Pte., k. in a., F. & F., 1/7/16.
Trott, Henry Ernest, e. Birmingham (Edgbaston, Birmingham), 240877, Pte., k. in a., F. & F., 1/7/16.
Turner, Charles Henry, b. Smethwick, Staffs, e. Birmingham (Warley, Birmingham), 2517, L/Cpl., k. in a., F. & F., 1/7/16.
Tyler, Cyril, b. Stourport, Worcs, e. Birmingham (Stourport), 199, Sgt., k. in a., F. & F., 4/2/17.
Upton, John, b. St. Martin's, Birmingham, e. Birmingham (Sparkbrook, Birmingham), 242935, Pte., d. of w., F. & F., 7/10/17.
Vallender, Charles, b. Oldbury, Staffs, e. Birmingham (Smethwick, Staffs), 4776, Pte., k. in a., F. & F., 1/7/16.
Vernals, William Albert, b. Selly Oak, Birmingham, e. King's Norton, Birmingham (Bournbrook, Birmingham), 242617, Pte., d., F. & F., 18/4/17, formerly 1559, Worcs Regt.
Vincent, Reginald James, b. Budbrooke, Warwick, e. Birmingham (Budbrooke), 1271, Cpl., k. in a., F. & F., 1/7/16.
Vinsen, Harry, b. Mooltan, India, e. Hull, Yorks (Cambridge), 238026, Cpl., k. in a., F. & F., 9/8/18, formerly T/4/250659, R.A.S.C. and 64718, Ches. Regt.
Wagg, John, b. St. Paul's, Birmingham, e. Birmingham, 243117, L/Cpl., d., F. & F., 10/6/18.
Waldron, Thomas, b. St. Thomas, Birmingham, e. Birmingham, 1732, C.S.M., d. of w., F. & F., 14/10/16.
Walker, Joseph Needham, b. Winster, Derby, e. Winster, 242142, Pte., d. of w., F. & F., 7/4/17, formerly 3262, Notts & Derby Regt.
Walker, Wilfred Reginald, b. Balsall Heath, Birmingham, e. Birmingham, 2507, Pte., k. in a., F. & F., 1/7/16.
Wallwork, John, e. Bolton, Lancs, 307065, Pte., k. in a., F. & F., 4/10/18, formerly 4890, N. Lancs Regt.
Walton, Wilfred, e. Birmingham (Aston, Birmingham), 3636, Pte., k. in a., F. & F., 28/6/16.
Ward, John Henry, b. Winson Green, Birmingham, e. Birmingham (Winson Green), 1955, Pte., k. in a., F. & F., 1/7/16.
Warder, William James, b. Birmingham, e. Birmingham, 1903, Pte., d. of w., F. & F., 10/10/16.
Wardley, Bernard Samuel, b. Bowdon, Ches., e. Birmingham (Crowborough, Kent), 2785, C.S.M., k. in a., F. & F., 14/10/16.
Warwick, William Henry, b. Birmingham, e. Birmingham (Balsall Heath, Birmingham), 4647, Pte., k. in a., F. & F., 1/7/16.
Waters, Leslie, b. Birmingham, e. Warwick (Olton, Warwicks), 5077, Pte., k. in a., F. & F., 1/7/16.
Watkinson, Samuel Stevens, e. Birmingham (Brookfields, Birmingham), 3508, Pte., k. in a., F. & F., 1/7/16.
Watson, Albert, b. St. George's, Birmingham, e. Birmingham, 240272, Pte., k. in a., F. & F., 4/2/17.
Watters, Thomas Henry, b. Tipton, Staffs, e. Birmingham (Tipton), 1295, Pte., k. in a., F. & F., 1/7/16.
Watts, Joseph Thomas, b. Beeston, Notts, e. Coventry, 241608, Pte., k. in a., F. & F., 18/8/16.
Weale, Albert, e. Birmingham, 4594, Pte., k. in a., F. & F., 1/7/16.
Webb, Harry, b. Burton Latimer, Northants, e. Burton Latimer, 33998, Pte., k. in a., F. & F., 4/10/17, formerly 6207, E. Kent Regt.
West, William Aubrey, e. Birmingham, 3117, Pte., k. in a., F. & F., 1/7/16.
Westley, William, b. Derby, e. Warwick (Coventry), 5102, Pte., k. in a., F. & F., 18/8/16.
Whatcott, Harry, b. Evesham, Worcs, e. Birmingham, 1737, Pte., d. of w., F. & F., 15/6/15.
White, Harold William, e. Birmingham (Sparkbrook, Birmingham), 21013, Pte., d. of w., F. & F., 4/2/17.
Whitehouse, Alfred, b. Ladywood, Birmingham, e. Birmingham (Ladywood), 1797, L/Sgt., k. in a., F. & F., 17/8/16.
Whiting, Thomas, b. St. James, Birmingham, e. Birmingham, 2789, Pte., k. in a., F. & F., 1/7/16.
Whittle, Walter Charles, b. Cork, e. Weymouth (Preston, Devon), 21041, Pte., k. in a., F. & F., 4/2/17.
Whyment, William, b. Swinford, Leicester, e. Dalton, 20746, Pte., k. in a., F. & F., 26/8/16.
Wickham, Frank, b. Hougham, Kent, e. Dover, Kent, 200279, Pte., k. in a., F. & F., 13/10/17, formerly 2746, E. Kent Regt.
Wier, Albert, b. St. George's, Birmingham, e. Birmingham, 1682, Cpl., d. of w., F. & F., 14/10/16.
Wilcox, George William, b. St. Mary's, Birmingham, e. Birmingham, 2176, Dmr., k. in a., F. & F., 1/7/16.
Wild, George, b. Hockley, Birmingham, e. Birmingham, 1545, Pte., k. in a., F. & F., 1/7/16.
Wilkes, Percy, b. Aston, Birmingham, e. Birmingham (Aston), 241142, L/Sgt., k. in a., F. & F., 4/10/17.
Willetts, George Harold, b. St. Paul's, Birmingham, e. Birmingham (Winson Green, Birmingham), 1860, Pte., k. in a., F. & F., 25/8/16.
Williams, Bertram Thomas, b. St. Martin's, Birmingham, e. Birmingham, 1227, Sgt., k. in a., F. & F., 1/7/16.
Williams, Charles, b. Birmingham, e. Birmingham (Small Heath, Birmingham), 202641, Dmr., k. in a., F. & F., 25/8/17.
Williams, Walter, b. Bordesley, Birmingham, e. Birmingham, 240325, Pte., k. in a., F. & F., 27/8/17.
Williamson, Stanley, b. Old Buckenham, Norfolk, e. Birmingham (Ward End, Birmingham), 5585, Pte., k. in a., F. & F., 12/11/16.
Wilson, John Arthur Cecil, b. Northampton, e. Lutterworth, Leicester, 242193, Pte., k. in a., F. & F., 19/6/17, formerly 25861, Leicester Regt.
Winnitt, William, b. Harborne, Birmingham, e. Birmingham (Harborne), 3527, Pte., d. of w., F. & F., 12/2/17.
Winstanley, George, b. Pemberton, Lancs, e. Wigan, Lancs (Pemberton), 243008, Pte., d. of w., F. & F., 25/10/17, formerly 27201, Hrs.
Wintle, Ernest, b. East Ham, London, e. Birmingham (East Ham), 240485, Pte., d., F. & F., 13/7/18.
Wood, Ephraim, e. Birmingham (Blackheath, Birmingham), 4620, Pte., k. in a., F. & F., 1/7/16.
Wood, Ernest Edward, e. Birmingham, 2929, Sgt., k. in a., F. & F., 1/7/16.
Wood, William, e. Birmingham (Saltley, Birmingham), 4759, Pte., k. in a., F. & F., 1/7/16.
Woodward, Henry John Edward, e. Birmingham (Moseley, Birmingham), 4438, Pte., k. in a., F. & F., 1/7/16.
Woolley, William, b. Aston, Birmingham, e. Aston (Lozells, Birmingham), 242063, L/Cpl., k. in a., F. & F., 4/10/17.
Worrall, Charles Thomas, b. Coventry, e. Coventry, 20894, Pte., k. in a., F. & F., 29/11/16.
Worton, Albert, b. Harborne, Birmingham, e. Birmingham (Harborne), 2815, Cpl., k. in a., F. & F., 4/2/17.
Wright, Alfred, b. Amersham, Bucks, e. Aylesbury, Bucks (Amersham), 28877, Pte., d. of w., F. & F., 20/8/17.
Wright, Robert, e. Aylesbury, Bucks (High Wycombe, Bucks), 242663, Cpl., k. in a., F. & F., 27/8/17, formerly 2324, Oxford & Bucks L.I.
Wright, Thomas, b. St. Martin's, Birmingham, e. Birmingham, 1619, Cpl., d. of w., F. & F., 20/8/16.
Wright, William Herbert, e. Birmingham (Lutterworth, Leicester), 2826, Pte., k. in a., F. & F., 1/7/16.
Yeomans, George Chapman, b. St. Mary's, Birmingham, e. Wolston, Coventry, 242671, Cpl., k. in a., F. & F., 27/8/17.
Young, Donald Frederick, e. Birmingham, 3042, Cpl., k. in a., F. & F., 28/6/16.

2/6th Battalion.

Abbott, Joseph Wells, b. Britannia, Bacup, Lancs, e. Oldham, Lancs. 235006, Pte., k. in a., F. & F., 1/9/17, formerly 4952, Mon. Regt.
Adam, John, b. Grangemouth, Stirlingshire, e. Grangemouth, 6152, Pte., k. in a., F. & F., 19/7/16, formerly 1762, High. Cyc. Battn.
Adkins, Charles Edwin, e. Nuneaton, Warwicks (Fillongley, Coventry, Warwicks), 267733, Pte., k. in a., F. & F., 27/5/18.
Agambar, John, b. Bethnal Green, London, e. London (Bethnal Green), 28998, Pte., d. of w., F. & F., 25/10/18.
Allan, Andrew, b. Bannockburn, Stirlingshire, e. Bannockburn, 241891, Sgt., k. in a., F. & F., 19/7/16, formerly 1187, High. Cyc. Battn.
Allan, Leonard Walter, e. Horsham, Sussex, 5504, Pte., k. in a., F. & F., 19/7/16, formerly 2838, R. Sussex Regt.
Allen, Ernest, e. Birmingham, 202679, Cpl., d. of w., F. & F., 7/9/17
Allwood, Frank, b. Bristol, Glos., e. Shaftesbury, Dorset (Charing, Kent), 20153, Pte., k. in a., F. & F., 21/3/18.
Amor, Joseph Henry, b. Sivell, Somerset, e. Taunton, Somerset (Sivell), 260235, Pte., k. in a., F. & F., 11/5/18, formerly 301789, S.L.I.
Anderson, George, b. Dunfermline, Fife, e. Kirkcaldy, Fife, 241890, Pte., k. in a., F. & F., 10/9/16, formerly 1855, High. Cyc. Battn.
Anderson, Robert, b. Middleton, Lancs, e. Middleton, 202399, Pte., k. in a., F. & F., 3/4/18, formerly 8795, Lancs Fus.
Andrews, Charles, b. Bournemouth, Hants, e. Bournemouth, 242421, Pte., k in a., F. & F., 2/9/17, formerly 20220 Hants Regt.
Arnold, Ben, b. Birmingham, e. Birmingham (Lozells, Birmingham), 202127, Pte., k. in a., F. & F., 28/4/18.
Ashcroft, Joseph, b. Egremont, Ches., e. Birkenhead, Ches., 260191, Pte., k. in a., F. & F., 24/9/17, formerly 203838, Shrops L.I.
Askew, Oliver, b. Northend, Warwicks, e. Nuneaton, Warwicks (Kineton, Warwicks), 25304, Pte., k. in a., F. & F., 20/3/18.
Asquith, James Thomas, b. Rochdale, Lancs, e. Rochdale, 202400, Pte., k. in a., F. & F., 21/3/18, formerly 9209, Lancs Fus.
Attwood, Cyril, b. Amblecote, Staffs, e. Brierley Hill, Staffs (Amblecote), 202309, Pte., k. in a., F. & F., 3/12/17.
Atwill, Arthur Edward, b. Broadhempston, Devon, e. Newton Abbot, Devon, 50341, Pte., k. in a., F. & F., 8/5/18.

Backshall, Reginald, e. Haywards Heath, Sussex, 5530, Cpl., k. in a., F. & F., 8/7/16, formerly 2947, R. Sussex Regt
Badger, Alfred, b. Ladywood, Birmingham, e. Birmingham, 2177, Pte., k. in a., F. & F., 19/7/16.
Badger, William Arthur, b. Birmingham, e. Birmingham, 200205, Pte., k. in a., F. & F., 21/3/18.
Bakewell, William Thomas, b. Whitick, Leicester, e. Birmingham (Coalville, Leicester), 241459, Pte., k. in a., F. & F., 9/4/17.
Balch, Frederick Charles, b. Kensington, London, e. Kensington, 35075, Pte., d. of w., F. & F., 21/3/18.
Baldwin, Percy Charles, b. Withyham, Tunbridge Wells, Kent, e. Withyham (Blackham, Langton Wells, Kent), 6296, Cpl., k. in a., F. & F., 19/7/16, formerly 1464, R. Sussex Regt.
Bale, William, b. Corfe, Somerset, e. Taunton, Somerset, 260236, Pte., k. in a., F. & F., 4/12/17, formerly 203751, S.L.I.
Ballinger, George, b. Birmingham, e. Birmingham, 4679, L/Cpl., k. in a., F. & F., 8/10/16.
Band, Ernest, b. Alfrick, Worcs, e. Birmingham (Edgbaston, Birmingham), 240808, A/L/Sgt., k. in a., F. & F., 19/7/16.
Barlow, William Charles, b. Tadby, Hants, e. Abingdon, Berks (Brightwalton, Wantage, Berks), 35076, Pte., k. in a., F. & F., 21/3/18.
Barratt, Rupert, b. Princethorpe, Warwicks, e. Rugby, Warwicks (Cawston, nr. Rugby), 35077, Pte., d., F. & F., 12/7/18.
Barton, Henry Edward, b. Hockley, Birmingham, e. Birmingham (Ladywood, Birmingham), 242467, Sgt., k. in a., F. & F., 22/3/18, M.M.
Barton, Percy Leonard, b. Stourbridge, Worcs, e. West Bromwich, Staffs (Winson Green, Birmingham), 242369, Sgt., k. in a., F. & F., 27/9/17, M.M.
Basketts, George, b St. John's, Coventry, Warwicks, e. Coventry, 1712, Pte., k. in a., F. & F., 31/3/18.
Batchelor, George Frederick, b. Honington, Warwicks, e. Bournemouth, Hants, 242423, Pte., k. in a., F. & F., 3/4/18, formerly 26127, Hants Regt.
Beech, Colin, b. Birmingham, e. Birmingham, 241013, Pte., k. in a., F. & F., 21/3/18.
Beales, Francis Frederick, b. Sutton, Norfolk, e. Wroxham, Norfolk (Norwich), 41309, Pte., d. of w., F. & F., 7/7/18, formerly 46432, Yeo. Cyc. Battn.
Beauvoisin, Louis, b. Sheffield, Yorks, e. Birmingham (Erdington, Birmingham), 4858, Pte., d. of w., F. & F., 6/7/16.
Beecham, Joseph, b. Berkswell, Warwicks, e. Solihull, Birmingham, 203246, Pte., k. in a., F. & F., 22/3/18.
Beahan, John Dennis, b. Birley's Hulme, Manchester, Lancs, e. Manchester (Chorlton-on-Medlock, Manchester), 201864 Pte., k. in a., F. & F., 1/9/17, formerly 1872, Manch. Regt.
Bennett, Harry Jubilee, b. Bedminster, Bristol, e. Bristol (Bedminster), 26013, Pte., d. of w., F. & F., 15/4/18.
Bibey, James, b. Trevthin, Pontypool, Mon., e. Pontypool Mon., 260058, Pte., k. in a., F. & F., 6/12/17, formerly 3061, Mon. Regt.
Bignell, William Henry, e. Horsham, Sussex (Bolton, Lancs), 6054, Pte., k. in a., F. & F., 19/7/16, formerly 3059, R. Sussex Regt.
Billers, William, b. Bermondsey, Middx., e. Birmingham 240420, L/Sgt., k. in a., F. & F., 19/7/16.
Bird, Edward Thomas, b. Holy Trinity, Malvern, Worcs, e. Birmingham (Malvern), 200243, Sgt., k. in a., F. & F., 11/4/18, D.C.M.
Birkby, Arthur, b. Leeds, Yorks, e. Wallasey, Ches. (Seacombe, Ches.), 20428, Pte., k. in a., F. & F., 25/8/17, formerly 62044, Ches. Regt.
Birt, Frederick George, b. Portsmouth, Hants, e. Portsmouth, 35084, Pte., k. in a., F. & F., 22/3/18.
Birtles, Horace Levison, b. Frodsham, Ches., e. Chester (Frodsham), 260194, Pte., d., F. & F., 29/3/18, formerly 203872, Shrops L.I.
Blackford, William, e. Stratford-on-Avon, Warwicks, 242759, Pte., k. in a., F. & F., 2/11/17, formerly 35110, R.D.C.
Bliss, Percy, b. Birmingham, e. Birmingham (Aston, Birmingham), 241352, Pte., k in a., F. & F., 19/7/16.
Booton, John Arthur, b. Shenton, Bosworth, Leics, e. Atherstone, Warwicks, 242371, Pte., k. in a., F. & F., 6/9/17.
Borrows, Arthur Edwin, b. Birmingham, e. Birmingham (Aston, Birmingham), 242470, Cpl., k. in a., F. & F., 30/3/17
Boucher, Ernest Christopher, b Leamington, Warwicks, e. Leamington, 202836, Pte., k. in a., F. & F., 26/8/17.
Bowers, Percy, b. Warrington, Lancs, e. Warrington, 260196, Pte, k. in a., F. & F., 3/9/17, formerly 203831, Shrops L.I.
Boynton, John Henry, b. West Hartlepool, Durham, e. Coventry, Warwicks (Warwick), 242272, Pte, k. in a., F. & F., 26/3/18.
Bracey, Samuel George, b. Kingswood, Bristol, e. Bristol, 50350, Pte., d. of w., F. & F., 7/11/18.
Bradley Arthur, b. Bollington, Ches., e. Macclesfield, Ches (Bollington), 260197, Pte., k. in a., F. & F., 1/7/18, formerly 203882, Shrops L.I.
Bradshaw, Ernest George, b Rugby, Warwicks, e. Rugby, 242340, Pte., k. in a., 24/9/17.
Brindley, Colin John Penrice, b. West Bromwich, Staffs, e. Birmingham (Amblecote, Stourbridge, Worcs), 1781, Pte., d. of w., F. & F., 10/4/18.
Brittle, Bertram, e Birmingham, 3872, Pte., k. in a., F. & F., 19/7/16.
Broadhead, Henry Harold, b. Birmingham, e. Birmingham, 243013, Pte., k. in a., F. & F., 6/12/17.
Brooks, Ernest Francis, b. Ashton Gate, Bristol, Glos., e. Bristol, 39967, Pte., d. of w., F. & F., 11/11/18.
Brooks, John William, b. Ellis Town, Leics, e. Birmingham (Hugglescote, Leicester), 4865, Pte., k. in a., F. & F., 19/7/16.
Brooks, Sidney, e. Portsmouth, Hants (Fantley, Hants), 241935, Pte., k. in a., F. & F., 3/4/18, formerly 2431, Hants Regt.
Brown, Ernest, b. Liverpool, Lancs, e. Liverpool, 260143, Pte., k. in a., F. & F., 4/12/17, formerly 55660, Liverpool Regt., and 6050, Shrops L.I.
Brown, Horace Henry, b. Walsgrave, Coventry, Warwicks, e. Coventry (Walsgrave-on-Sowe, Warwicks), 8421, L/Cpl., d. of w., F. & F., 31/3/18.
Browning, William James, b. Winchester, Hants, e. Birmingham (Northampton), 202629, Sgt., k. in a., F. & F., 5/12/17.
Bryan, Richmond Hammond, b. St. Thomas', Dublin, Ireland, e. Crewe, Ches. (Coventry, Warwicks), 242363, C.S.M., k. in a., F. & F., 25/7/18, D.C.M..
Bull, Clifford, Edgar, b. Poole, Dorset, e. Poole, 35094, Pte., k. in a., F. & F., 25/3/18.
Bumstead, Robert, e. Hastings, Sussex, 242006, L/Cpl., d. of w., F. & F., 31/3/18, formerly 2610, R. Sussex Regt.
Burke, John Edward, b. Birmingham, e. Birmingham (Small Heath, Birmingham), 22443, Sgt., k. in a., F. & F., 20/3/18.
Burton, Claude, b.. Birmingham, e. Birmingham (Hockley, Birmingham), 331336, Pte., k. in a., F. & F., 20/3/18.
Burrows, Charles, b. Kidderminster, Worcs, e. Kidderminster, 268893, Pte., k. in a., F & F., 24/10/18.
Busby, Fred, b. Hook Norton, Oxon, e. Eanbury, Oxen (Hook Norton), 24223, L/Cpl., k. in a., F. & F., 31/3/18.
Cain, Stanley, b. Liverpool, Lancs, e. Liverpool, 35706, Pte., k. in a., F. & F., 15/8/18.
Cameron, Alexander Sim, b. Blairgowrie, Perth, e. Blairgowrie, 41323, Pte., d. of w., F. & F., 13/9/18, formerly 152068, Sco. Horse Yeo.
Capper, George, b. Droglesden, Manchester, Lancs, e. Birmingham (West Bromwich, Staffs), 241497, Pte., d. of w., F. & F., 4/11/17.
Cameron, James, b. Falkirk, Stirling, e. Kirkcaldy, Fife (Falkirk), 241893, L/Cpl., k. in a., F. & F., 3/9/17, formerly 1634, High. Cyc. Battn.
Carr, John, b. St. Mary's, Lancaster, e. Lancaster, 306895, Pte., d. of w., F. & F., 26/3/18, formerly 2354, R. Lan. Regt.
Carter, John, e. Rugby, Warwicks (Stockton, Rugby), 9990, Sgt., k. in a., F. & F., 2/11/18.
Cavana, Simon, b. Helensburgh, Dumbarton, e. Dundee, Forfar, 41318, Pte., k. in a., F. & F., 16/9/18, formerly 2506, Sco. Horse Yeo.
Cave, George, b. Wigan, Lancs, e. Birkenhead, Ches., 203173, Pte., d. of w., F. & F., 6/4/18, formerly 3536, Ches. Regt.
Chance, John, e. Birmingham (Balsall Heath, Birmingham), 240903, Cpl., k. in a., F. & F., 19/7/16.
Chapman, Horace, b. Glascote, Warwicks, e. Coventry, Warwicks, 24551, Pte., k. in a., F. & F., 3/12/17.
Chard, Frederick, b. Bradpole, Dorset, e. Weymouth, Dorset, 250223, Pte., k. in a., F. & F., 24/9/17, formerly 203794, Som. L.I.
Charman, Alfred, e. Horsham, Sussex, 6061, Pte., d. of w., F. & F., 21/7/16, formerly 2550, R. Sussex Regt.
Charman, Albert Henry, b. Southampton, Hants, e. Brockenhurst, Hants (Hythe, Kent), 50361, Pte., k. in a., F. & F., 19/4/18.
Chatterley, Walter, b. Aston, Warwicks, e. Redditch, Worcs (Studley, Warwicks), 203513, k. in a., F. & F., 30/10/18.
Clampton, William, b. Chappel, Essex, e. Colchester, Essex (Chappel), 32838, Pte. d. of w., F. & F., 7/5/18, formerly 20194, Hussars.
Clark, Harry James, b. Fareham, Hants, e. Portsmouth, Hants (Fareham), 6206, Pte., k. in a., F. & F., 19/7/16, formerly 1929, Hants Regt.
Classon, Ermot, b. Belfast, Ireland, e. Liverpool, Lancs, 260074, Pte., k. in a., F. & F., 4/9/17, formerly 41432, Liverpool Regt. and 5089, Mon. Regt.
Clayton, David George, b. Redditch, Worcs, e. Birmingham (Studley, Warwicks), 242230, Pte., d. of w., F. & F., 8/9/17.
Cleaver, William Thomas, b. Rugby, Warwicks, e. Rugby, 242260, Pte., d. of w., F. & F., 24/4/17.
Cleeton, Reginald, b. Malvern, Worcs, e. Birmingham (Balsall Heath, Birmingham), 29853, Pte., d. of w., F. & F., 21/3/18, formerly 27585, Worcs Regt.
Clemmet, Joseph, b. Manchester, Lancs, e. Salford, Lancs (Manchester), 201873, Pte., k. in a., F. & F., 12/4/18, formerly 2686, Lancs Fus.
Clifford, Walter Horace, b. St. Anns, Birmingham, e. Birmingham (Saltley, Birmingham), 2219, Pte., k. in a., F. & F., 26/9/16.
Coleman, Jonathan James, b. King's Heath, Birmingham, e. Birmingham (King's Heath), 240413, Pte, k. in a., F. & F., 6/12/17.
Collett, Charles Edgar, b. Cleeve Prior, Worcs, e. Stratford-on-Avon, Warwicks, 203086, Pte., d., F. & F., 16/7/18
Collins, Edwin, b. St. Martin's, Birmingham, e. Birmingham, 1636, Cpl., k. in a., F. & F., 19/7/16.
Collins, William James, b. Patcham, Sussex, e. Worthing, Surrey (Bradswater, Sussex), 6063, Pte., d., F. & F., 27/1/17, formerly 2274, R. Sussex Regt.
Collister, William, e. Newcastle-on-Tyne (Trockley, Northumberland), 29752, Pte., d. of w., F. & F., 8/5/18.
Connor, Thomas, b. Sparkbrook, Birmingham, e. Birmingham (Sparkbrook), 240735, Pte., d. of w., F. & F., 5/9/17.
Cook, Thomas John, b. Padston, Cornwall, e. Bodmin, Cornwall (S. Issey, Cornwall), 26361, Pte., d., F. & F., 5/9/18.
Cooke, Albert Edward, e. Birmingham, 242971, Pte., d. of w., F. & F., 7/9/17.
Cooke, William, e. Birmingham (Sparkbrook, Birmingham). 3037, L/Cpl., d. of w., F. & F., 26/10/16.
Cooper, Edward, b. Huntingdon, e. Coventry, 202195, Cpl., k. in a, F. & F., 18/4/18.

Cooper, Evan, b. Tarporley, Ches., e. Chester (Tarporley), 29432, Pte., d. of w., F. & F., 1/11/18, formerly 62090, Ches. Reg.
Cooper, Victor, b. Wolverhampton, Staffs, e. Wolverhampton, 2349, Pte., k. in a., F. & F., 19/7/16, formerly 2215, S. Staffs Regt.
Copp, Walter William, e. Birmingham, 267374, Pte., d. of w., F. & F., 10/9/17.
Corrall, Joseph Henry, b. Coventry, e. Coventry, 266062, Pte., d. of w., F. & F., 1/4/18.
Cotterill, Ralph Alfred, b. Salford, Lancs, e. Altrincham, Ches. (Sale, Ches.), 29411, Pte., k. in a., F. & F., 5/9/17, formerly 62035, Ches. Regt.
Cottle, Richard George, b. Abertillery, Mon., e. Pontypool, Mon., 260059, Pte., k. in a., F. & F., 24/9/17, formerly 2420, Mon. Regt.
Cowburn, Frank, b. Westhoughton, Lancs, e. Westhoughton, 235040, Pte., k. in a., F. & F., 19/4/18, formerly 291236, Mon. Regt.
Cox, Joseph William, e. Birmingham (Quinton, Birmingham), 242528, Pte., k. in a., F. & F., 23/4/17.
Cribb, John Arthur, b. Camberwell, London, e. Woolwich, Kent (Peckham, Kent), 25766, Cpl., k. in a., F. & F., 3/4/18.
Croft, James, b Helsby, Ches., e. Frodsham, Ches. (Helsby), 260199, Pte., k. in a., F. & F., 7/9/17, formerly 203870, Shrops L.I.
Crook, Frederick, b. Coventry, e. Coventry, 242287, L/Cpl., k in a., F. & F., 6/9/17.
Crump, John William, b. Welshampton, Salop, e. Ellesmere, Salop (Bradenheath, Salop), 260163, Pte., k. in a., F. & F., 24/9/17, formerly 203562, Shrops L.I.
Cunniff, Pat., b. Co. Galway, e. Chester (Boughton, Ches.), 260200, Pte., k. in a., F. & F., 24/9/17, formerly 203830, Shrops L.I.
Cunliffe, Cyril John, b. Edgbaston, Birmingham, e. Birmingham (Handsworth, Staffs), 331191, Pte., d. of w., F. & F., 10/6/18.
Curtis, Cecil Howard, b. Corby, Northants, e. Southampton, Hants, 242429, Pte., k. in a., F. & F., 31/8/17, formerly 28230, Hants Regt.
Dale, Albert, e. Horsham, Sussex, 6066, Pte., k. in a., F. & F., 19/7/16, formerly 3064, R. Sussex Regt.
Dale, Harry, e. Horsham, Sussex (Lower Beeding, Sussex), 6340, Pte., k. in a., F. & F., 2/7/16, formerly 2703, R. Sussex Regt.
Dancer, John Robinson, b. Wednesbury, Staffs, e. Leamington, Warwicks, 242298, Pte., k. in a., F. & F., 6/9/17.
Darney, James Alfred, b. Sunbury, Middx., e. Birmingham, 3222, Pte., k. in a., F. & F., 19/7/16.
Davey, Wilfred Thomas, b. Southall, Middx., e. Stourbridge, Worcs (Dudley, Worcs), 203835, Pte., k. in a., F. & F., 12/4/18.
Davinson, Frank, b. Ladywood, Birmingham, e. Birmingham, 398, C.S.M., k. in a., F. & F., 19/7/16.
Davies, Edward Reginald, e. Leamington Spa, Warwicks, 242396, Pte., k. in a., F. & F., 25/3/18.
Davis, John, e. Birmingham, 3369, Pte., k. in a., F & F., 30/6/16.
Davis, Thomas Frederick, b. Warwick, e. Warwick, 20491, Pte., d. of w., F. & F., 22/12/16.
Dawe, Samuel George, b. Liverpool, e. Liverpool, 35611, Pte., d. of w., F. & F., 6/9/18.
Debar, Harry, b. Birmingham, e. Birmingham, 242376, Pte., d, (P. of W.) disease, F. & F., 7/10/18.
Dennett, William, e. Horsham, Sussex, 6068, Pte., k. in a., F. & F., 19/7/16, formerly 2425, R. Sussex Regt.
Devey, Albert Edward, e. Birmingham, 242770, Pte., k. in a., F. & F., 24/10/18.
Dickens, John Robert, b. Stockport, e. Stockport, 260230, Pte., d. of w., F. & F., 6/12/17, formerly 5248, S. Lancs Regt.
Dickinson, Ernest, b. Stockport, Ches., e. Stockport, 260164, Pte., k. in a., F. & F., 5/12/17, formerly 203819, Shrops L.I.
Dimbleby, Fred, e. Atherstone, Warwicks (Glascote, Warwicks), 20563, Pte., d., F. & F., 26/10/16.
Dodd, Walter Henry, b. Blackford, Somerset, e. Weston-super-Mare, Somerset (Blackford), 260254, Pte., k. in a., F. & F., 21/3/18, formerly 30612, Som. L.I.
Dolphin, Stanley, e. Birmingham (Bromsgrove, Worcs), 201014, Cpl., k. in a., F. & F., 5/9/17.
Donald, Tom, e. Coupar Angus, Perthshire, 6162, Pte., k. in a., F. & F., 19/7/16, formerly 1862, High. Cycl. Battn.
Doubleday, John, e. Salford, Lancs (Seedley, Ches.), 202411, L/Cpl., k. in a., F. & F., 24/10/18, formerly 2715, Lancs Fus., M.M.
Dovey, Charles, b. Birmingham, e. Birmingham, 203307, Pte., k. in a., F. & F., 21/3/18.
Dowell, Montague, b. Leamington, Warwicks, e. Leamington, 242338, Pte., k. in a., F. & F., 3/9/17.
Downing, Frank Sorton, b. Coalbrookdale, Shrops, e. Birmingham (Coalbrookdale), 3548, Pte., d. of w., F. & F., 1/7/16.
Downing, John, e. Birmingham, 3263, Pte., k. in a., F. & F., 19/7/16.
Duncan, Thomas, b. Jamestown, Dumbarton, e. Kirkcaldy, Fife (Kennaway, Fife), 241896, Pte., k. in a., F. & F., 3/3/18, formerly 1298, High. Cycl. Battn.
Dunkerley, William, b. Urmston, Lancs, e. Salford, Lancs, 260010, Pte., k. in a., F. & F., 4/12/17, formerly 31660, Lancs Fus.
Durbin, Frederick George, b. Wells, Som., e. Wells, 260253, Pte., k. in a., F. & F., 9/12/17, formerly 30719, Som. L.I.
Dyer, Samuel, b. St. Stephens, Cornwall, e. St. Austell, Cornwall (St. Stephens), 35115, Pte., k. in a., F. & F., 6/9/18.
East, William George, b. East Dean, Hants, e. Salisbury, Wilts (East Dean), 50371, Pte., k. in a., F. & F., 2/11/18.
Eddell, Arthur Samuel, b. St. Thomas, Exeter, Devon, e. Reading, Berks, 35271, Pte., k. in a., F. & F., 24/10/18.
Edgar, Charles Vurtha, b. Dumfries, e. Birmingham (Dumfries), 171, Sgt., d., F. & F., 12/8/16.
Edwards, Charles, e. Birmingham, 202234, Pte., k. in a., F. & F., 21/3/18.
Edwards, Frederick John, b. Ashow, Warwicks, e. Coventry, 242258, Pte., d., F. & F., 14/4/17.
Edwards, George, b. Wolverhampton, Staffs, e Birmingham, 25646, Pte., k. in a., F. & F., 3/4/18.
Edwards, Joseph William, b. Dudley, Worcs, e. Stourbridge, Worcs (Dudley), 25860, Pte., k. in a., F. & F., 12/4/18.
Edwards, Victor Charles, b. Chichester, Sussex, e. Chichester, 24819, Pte., k. in a., F. & F., 3/12/17, formerly 2777, Sussex Regt.
Ellgood, Harry, e. Birmingham, 201494, L/Cpl., d., F. & F., 5/8/18.
Ellidge, Leonard, b. Middleton, Lancs, e. Middleton, 260060, Pte., k. in a., F. & F., 24/9/17, formerly 9012, Lancs. Fus.
Emerton, William Paul, b. North Crawley, Bucks, e. Bletchley, Bucks (North Crawley), 25623, Pte., k. in a., F. & F., 19/4/18.
Emus, Harold, e. Birmingham, 2918, Pte., k. in a., F. & F., 26/6/16.
Evans, John, b. Birmingham, e. Birmingham (Greet, Birmingham), 2333, Pte., k. in a., F. & F., 19/7/16.
Evans, Leonard William, b. Waddesdon, Bucks, e. Aylesbury, Bucks (Waddesdon), 26248, Pte., k. in a., F. & F., 19/4/18.
Everitt, Arthur Thomas, e. Birmingham, 39471, Pte., d., F. & F., 10/5/19.
Farr, Edward Frederick, b. St. Peters, Hereford, e. Birmingham (Saltley, Birmingham), 242324, Pte., k. in a., F. & F., 9/10/17.
Farr, Harold John, e. Birmingham, 2828, Pte., k. in a., F. & F., 19/7/16.
Faulkner, Zachariah, b. Birmingham, e. Birmingham (Bournbrook, Birmingham), 241411, Sgt., k. in a., F. & F., 3/12/17.
Fareday, Frank John, b. Smethwick, Staffs, e. Birmingham (Smethwick), 241512, Pte., k. in a., F. & F., 21/3/18.
Field, Percy Frederick, e. Hastings, Sussex (St. Leonards, Sussex), 6307, Pte., k. in a., F. & F., 19/7/16, formerly 2785, R. Sussex Regt.
Fielder, Edward Cecil, b. Plaxted, Kent, e. Hastings, Sussex (Bolebrook, Sussex), 242012, L/Cpl., k. in a., F. & F., 19/7/16, formerly 2253, R. Sussex Regt.
Fitzgerald, Gerald William, b. Gosport, Hants, e. Portsmouth (Gosport), 241945, Pte., k. in a., F. & F., 19/7/16, formerly 1873, Hants Regt.
Fleming, John, b. Uphall, Linlithgow, e. Bathgate, Linlithgow (Uphall), 202556, Pte., k. in a., F. & F., 22/3/18, formerly 1025, R. Scots.
Florey, Charles, b. Lechlade, Glos., e. Birmingham (Lechlade), 1165, Pte., k. in a., F. & F., 3/12/17.
Ford, Vivian Heberdon, b. Chichester, Sussex, e. Chichester, 241821, Pte., k. in a., F. & F., 24/10/18, formerly 2769, R. Sussex Regt.
Formaston, Vernon, b. Salford, Lancs, e. Salford, 202416, Pte., k. in a., F. & F., 29/3/18, formerly 2337, Lancs Fus.
Foster, Alfred, b. Coventry, Warwicks, e. Coventry, 203191, Pte., k. in a., F. & F., 21/3/18.
Foster, Reginald Arthur, e. Hastings, Sussex, 242013, Pte., k. in a., F. & F., 6/9/18, formerly 2640, R. Sussex Regt.
Fowler, Alfred, b. Birmingham, e. Birmingham (Selly Oak, Birmingham), 240929, Pte., k. in a., F. & F., 5/12/17.
Fowles, Sydney, b. Runcorn, Ches., e. Runcorn, 260165, Pte., k. in a., F. & F., 6/9/17, formerly 203854, Shrops L.I.
Freeman, Francis Hubert, b. Warwick, e. Warwick (Barford, Warwicks), 242326, Pte., k. in a., F. & F., 26/8/17.
Freeman, George Henry, b. Wallingford, Berks, e. Abingdon, Berks (Wallingford), 26214, Pte., d., F. & F., 27/8/18.
Freeman, John, b. Sparkbrook, Birmingham, e. Birmingham, 242224, Pte., k. in a., F. & F., 21/3/19.
Frederick, George, e. Birmingham, 3074, Pte., k. in a., F. & F., 19/7/16.
Fright, Leonard Arthur Duncan, b. Ramsgate, Kent, e. Worthing, Sussex, 6341, Pte., d. of w., F. & F., 6/7/16, formerly 2353, R. Sussex Regt.
Fuller, Reginald Joseph, b. Manchester, e. Grimsby, Lincs, 19373, Sgt., d. of w., F. & F., 24/4/18.
Gage, George Ernest, b. Manchester, e. Manchester (Blackley, Lancs), 235050, Pte., k. in a., F. & F., 3/12/17, formerly 5042, Mon. Regt.
Gamblin, Ernest, b. Fleeland, Hants, e. Fareham, Hants (Titchfield, Hants), 6226, Pte., k. in a., F. & F., 19/7/16, formerly 1656, Hants Regt.
Ganzbery, Harry, b. Manchester, e. Birmingham (Erdington, Birmingham), 4786, Pte., k. in a., F. & F., 27/7/16.
Garbett, Fred, b. St. Edward's, Birmingham, e. Birmingham (Hockley, Birmingham), 3277, Cpl., k. in a., F. & F., 19/7/16.
Gardiner, Fred, b. Wildboar Clough, Staffs, e. Chester (Macclesfield, Ches.), 29562, Pte., d. of w., F. & F., 1/4/18, formerly 40336, S. Lancs Regt.
Gardner, William, b. Temple Balsall, Warwicks, e. Coventry (Far Cotton, Northants), 5386, Pte., k. in a., F. & F., 21/3/18.
Garratt, David Edward, b. Attleborough, Warwicks, e. Nuneaton, Warwicks (Attleborough), 3303, Pte., k. in a., F. & F., 6/9/17.
Geary, William, b. Southsea, Hants, e. Portsmouth (Portsea, Hants), 241950, L/Sgt., k. in a., F. & F., 4/12/17, formerly 1730, Hants Regt.
Gibbins, George Henry, b. Birmingham, e. Birmingham (Aston, Birmingham), 201812, Pte., k in a., F. & F., 21/3/18.
Gilder, Ernest Alfred, b. Bromsgrove, Worcs, e. Worcester (Bromsgrove), 50448, Pte., k. in a., F. & F., 4/9/18.

Gittins, Charles Anthony, b. Coventry, e. Birmingham (Coventry), 240065, Pte., k. in a., F. & F., 26/8/17.
Glover, Alfred William, e. Birmingham (Hockley, Birmingham), 2825, Pte., d. of w., F. & F., 25/7/16.
Goodall, Frederic George, b. Whitchurch, Hants, e. Winchester, Hants (Itchen, Hants), 26156, Pte., k. in a., F. & F., 20/8/18.
Goodfellow, Henry Thomas, b. Birmingham, e. Birmingham, 50381, Pte., k. in a., F. & F., 28/5/18.
Gorton, William Gilbert, b. Easton, Glos., e. Bristol (Easton), 35129, Pte., d. of w., F. & F., 12/2/18.
Gorse, Harry, b. Sheffield, e. Hanneton (Bournemouth, Hants), 242433, Pte., k. in a., F. & F., 9/4/18, formerly 26210, Hants Regt.
Goulding, Matthew, b. Belfast, Antrim, e. Birmingham, 240901, Sgt., d. of w., F. & F., 9/12/17.
Gray, Robert George Freeman, b. Burnley, Lancs, e. Preston (Preston), Pte., k. in a., F. & F., 8/8/16.
Green, Oliver, b. Ladywood, Birmingham, e. Birmingham, 2200, Pte., k. in a., F. & F., 19/7/16.
Green, Sidney, b. Balsall Heath, Birmingham, e. Birmingham, 242346, L/Cpl., k. in a., F. & F., 21/3/18.
Greenfield, Ernest Alfred, e. Worthing, Dorset (Patching, Dorset), 6079, Pte., k. in a., F. & F., 19/7/16, formerly 2910, R. Sussex Regt.
Grice, Herbert William, b. St. Martin's, Birmingham, 240356, Cpl., d. of w., F. & F., 12/4/17.
Griffiths, Harry, b. Birmingham, e. Birmingham (Winson Green, Birmingham), 4395, Pte., k. in a., F. & F., 19/7/16.
Grigg, Walter William, e. Birmingham (Hockley, Birmingham), 3121, Sgt., k. in a., F. & F., 30/6/16.
Grieves, Austin, b. Birmingham, e. Birmingham (Sparkhill, Birmingham), 4841, Pte., k. in a., F. & F., 19/7/16.
Grindod, Oliver William, b. Birmingham, e. Birmingham, 26730, Pte., d., F. & F., 12/4/18.
Hackett, Edgar Jones, b. Cranley Heath, Staffs, e. Birmingham (Cranley Heath), 4873, Pte., k. in a., F. & F., 5/7/16.
Hadley, Horace Hewin, e. Birmingham (Quinton, Birmingham), 3743, A/L/Sgt., k. in a., F. & F., 19/7/16.
Hadley, Joseph, b. Haley Green, Worcs, e. Worcester (Halesowen, Worcs), 242479, Pte., k. in a., F. & F., 6/12/17.
Hague, Thomas, b. St. George's, Hulme, Lancs, e. Salford, Lancs (Hulme), 202424, Pte., k. in a., F. & F., 12/4/18, formerly 2060, Lancs Fus.
Halford, Thomas Edward, b. Birmingham, e. Birmingham (Ladywood, Birmingham), 241437, L/Cpl., k. in a., F. & F., 3/12/17.
Hall, Sidney George, e. Coventry (Rugby, Warwicks), 266586, L/Cpl., k. in a., F. & F., 11/4/18, M.S.M.
Hamilton, Michael James, b. Liverpool, e. Southampton, 20600, Pte., d., F. & F., 26/1/17, formerly 26147, Hants Regt.
Hancox, Percy, b. Tysoe, Warwicks, e. Warwick (Tysoe), 203545, Pte., k. in a., F. & F., 12/4/18.
Hands, Henry Thomas, b. Birmingham, e. Birmingham (Bordesley Green, Birmingham), 240859, C.Q.M.S., k. in a., F. & F., 2/11/18.
Hanson, Arthur John, b. Birmingham, e. Birmingham (Aston, Birmingham), 240861, Pte., k. in a., F. & F., 22/3/18.
Hanson, John Edward, b. Crewe, e. Crewe, Ches., 29079, Pte., k. in a., F. & F., 31/3/18, formerly 62119, Ches. Regt.
Hardwick, Samuel, b. Tipton, Staffs., e. Chester (Ellesmere Port, Cheshire), 29568, Pte., k. in a., F. & F., 5/9/17, formerly 40337, S. Lancs. Regt.
Harries, Owen, b. Pembroke, South Wales, e. Birmingham (Pembroke), 240791, Sgt., d. of w., F. & F., 17/12/17.
Harris, Albert, b. Fraddon, Cornwall, e. Bodmin, Cornwall (Fraddon), 50389, Pte., k. in a., F. & F., 20/8/18.
Harris, Peter James, b. Everton, Lancs, e. Birmingham (Seedley, Lancs), 2569, Sgt., d. of w., F. & F., 20/7/16.
Harris, Richard Henry, e. Kenilworth, Warwicks, 242775, Pte., k. in a., F. & F., 3/4/18.
Harris, William Alfred, e. London (Plaistow, Essex), 260247, Pte., k. in a., F. & F., 2/9/17, formerly 5236, London Regt.
Harrison, Walter Langley, b. New York, U.S.A., e. Birmingham (Perry Barr, Staffs), 240349, C.S.M., k. in a., F. & F., 30/3/17.
Harvey, Owen, e. Southam, Warwicks (Radford Semele, Warwicks), 24582, Pte., k. in a., F. & F., 1/6/18.
Hayes, Frederick Ernest, b. Torquay, Devon, e. Newton Abbot, Devon (Torquay), 50393, Pte., k. in a., F. & F., 24/10/18.
Hemming, Bernard John, b. Birmingham, e. Birmingham (Edgbaston, Birmingham), 3268, Pte., d. of w., F. & F., 22/7/16.
Hemming, George, b. Worcester, e. Birmingham (Ladywood, Birmingham), 241078, Pte., k. in a., F. & F., 5/11/18.
Hewett, William, b. Crowley, Sussex, e. Horsham, Sussex, 6085, Pte., k. in a., F. & F., 19/7/16, formerly 2382, R. Sussex Regt.
Higgins, George, b. Birmingham, e. Birmingham (Sparkbrook, Birmingham), 4944, Pte., d. of w., F. & F., 7/7/16.
Hill, Ivor, b. Cardiff, e. Cardiff, 260015, Pte., k. in a., F. & F., 4/9/17, formerly 291007, Mon. Regt.
Hill, Leonard Charles, e. Birmingham (Saltley, Birmingham), 4769, Pte., d. of w., F. & F., 6/7/16.
Hillman, George, b. Wolverhampton, Staffs, e. Birmingham (Spring Hill, Birmingham), 2867, Sgt., k. in a., F. & F., 19/7/16.
Hindley, William, b. Reddish, Ches., e. Chester, 29529, Pte., d. of w., F. & F., 25/10/18, formerly 62079, Ches. Regt.
Hirons, Walter, b. Warwick, e. Warwick, 38037, Pte., k. in a., F. & F., 13/4/18.
Hoar, Stephen Charles Alfred William, b. Handsworth, Staffs, e. Birmingham (Handsworth), 37969, Pte., k. in a., F. & F., 5/9/18.
Hodgkiss, Herbert, b. Farnworth, Lancs, e. Farnworth, 260017, Pte., k. in a., F. & F., 31/3/18, formerly 291279, Mon. Regt.
Holden, Harry, b. West Bromwich, Staffs, e. Birmingham (Smethwick, Staffs), 242481, Pte., k. in a., F. & F., 7/9/16.
Hollier, Wallace Austin, b. King's Heath, Birmingham, e. Birmingham (Bourneville, Birmingham), 3355, Cpl., k. in a., F. & F., 19/7/16.
Homer, William, b. Solihull, Warwicks, e. Birmingham (Sparkhill, Birmingham), 1943, Sgt., d. of w., F. & F., 22/4/18.
Hood, Jack, b. Barnton, Ches., e. Northwich, Ches. (Barnton), 35631, Pte., k. in a., F. & F., 4/9/18.
Hopkins, Benjamin, b. Birmingham, e. Birmingham (Tipton, Staffs), 4874, Pte., k. in a., F. & F., 19/7/16.
Horrocks, Joe, b. Quarton, Lancs, e. Bolton, Lancs (Tottington, Lancs), 35632, Pte., d. of w., F. & F., 10/10/18.
Howard, Arthur, b. Frodsham, Ches., e. Chester (Frodsham), 260167, Pte., k. in a., F. & F., 4/12/17, formerly 203858, Shrops L.I.
Howard, Isaiah, b. Middleton, Lancs, e. Middleton (Rhodes, Lancs), 27723, Pte., k. in a., F. & F., 30/3/18, formerly 9038, Lancs Fus.
Howcroft, William, e. Salford, Lancs, 260018, Pte., d. of w., F. & F., 8/9/17, formerly 32852, Lancs Fus.
Howse, James, b. Handsworth, Staffs, e. Birmingham (Handsworth), 240829, R.S.M., k. in a., F. & F., 3/12/17.
Hubbard, George, b. Coventry, Warwicks, e. Coventry, 266018, Pte., k. in a., F. & F., 2/11/18.
Hughes, Frederick, b. Emstrey, Salop, e. Ellesmere Port, Ches. (Shrewsbury, Salop), 29404, Pte., d. of w., F. & F., 6/9/17, formerly 62065, Ches. Regt.
Hughes, William, b. Yardley, Worcs, e. Birmingham (Small Heath, Birmingham), 240322, L/Cpl., k. in a., F. & F., 19/7/16.
Humphreys, Arthur, e. Portsmouth (Havant, Hants), 241963, Sgt., k. in a., F. & F., 12/4/18, formerly 2097, Hants Regt., Croix de Guerre.
Humphreys, Harold, b. Brighton, Sussex, e. Coventry, 22779, Pte., d. of w., F. & F., 22/3/18.
Hyett, Charles Edward, b. St. Martin's, Birmingham, e. Birmingham, 1864, Dmr., k. in a., F. & F., 19/7/16.
Ingram, Edwin, b. Bromsgrove, Worcs, e. Birmingham (Small Heath, Birmingham), 241446, Pte., d. of w., F. & F., 24/11/18.
Ireland, David L., b. Scoonie Leven, Fife, e. Leven, 6170, Pte., k. in a., F. & F., 19/7/16, formerly 1527, High. Cyc. Battn.
Irlam, William, b. Salford, Lancs, e. Salford, 260020, Pte., k. in a., F. & F., 6/9/17, formerly 31667, Lanc. Fus.
Isham, Frank Walter, b. Brackley, Northants, e. Bletchley, Northants, 307763, Pte., k. in a., F. & F., 21/3/18.
Jackson, Frederick, b. Stockport, Ches., e. Stockport, 260168, Pte., k. in a., F. & F., 6/9/17, formely 203812, Shrops, L.I.
Jacobs, Thomas James, b. Andover, Hants, e. Salisbury, Wilts, 50404, Pte., k. in a., F. & F., 24/10/18.
James, Frederick, b. Ruddington, Notts, e. Birmingham (Ruddington), 330227, Pte., d., F. & F., 16/9/18.
James, Joseph Christopher, b. Portsea, Hants, e. Portsea, 6246, L/Cpl., d. of w., F. & F., 26/8/16, formerly 1411, Hants Regt.
James, Thomas, b. Morristown, Glam., e. Blackwood, Glam., 260021, Pte., k. in a., F. & F., 6/12/17, formerly 291415, Mon. Regt.
Jenner, Alfred Ernest, e. Hastings, Sussex (Mark Cross, Kent), 6314, Pte., k. in a., F. & F., 19/7/16, formerly 2987, R. Sussex Regt.
Jobson, John Thomas, b. Shrewsbury, Salop, e. Crewe, Ches. (Winclermere, Salop), 29446, Pte., k. in a., 3/9/17, formerly 62219, Ches. Regt.
Johnson, George, b. Balsall Heath, Birmingham, e. Birmingham (Winson Green, Birmingham), 240454, Pte., d. of w., F. & F., 3/9/17.
Johnson, Henry, b. Witton, Ches., e. Northwich, Ches., 29130, Pte., k. in a., F. & F., 9/4/18, formerly 62252, Ches. Regt.
Jones, Andrew Oliver, b. Chester, e. Wallasey, Ches (Egremont, Ches.), 260169, Pte., k. in a., F. & F., 4/12/17, formerly 203896, Shrops L.I.
Jones, Arthur Percy, b. Merthyr, Glam., e. Merthyr, 260023, Pte., k. in a., F. & F., 3/9/17, formerly 4051, Mon. Regt.
Jones, Bert, b. Birmingham, e. Birmingham, 241016, Pte., k. in a., F. & F., 30/3/18.
Jones, Edward David, b. Bromley-by-Bow, Essex, e. Stratford, Essex (Plaistow, Kent), 41293, Pte., d. of w., F. & F., 4/7/18, formerly 5796, D.L.I.
Jones, Fred Clifford, e. Birmingham (Stirchley, Birmingham), 3536, Pte., k. in a., F. & F., 3/7/16.
Jones, James William, b. Birmingham, e. Birmingham (Smethwick, Staffs), 4825, Pte., k. in a., F. & F., 19/7/16.
Jones, Robert Ellesmere, b. Harborne, Staffs, e. Birmingham (Smethwick, Staffs), 2847, Pte., k. in a., F. & F., 19/7/16.
Joyce, Albert Henry, b. Steyning, Sussex, e. Steyning, 5515, L/Cpl., d. of w., F. & F., 22/7/16, formerly 1629, R. Sussex Regt.
Jukes, Leonard, b. Tipton, Staffs, e. Birmingham (Tipton), 242203, Cpl., d. of w., F. & F., 4/9/17.
Kane, Robert Henry, b. Liverpool, e. Liverpool, 260024, Pte., d of w., F. & F., 1/9/17, formerly 32639, Liverpool Regt., 291917, Mon. Regt.
Kaye, Lister Walter, b. Workington, Cumberland, e. Coventry, 202712, Sgt., k. in a., F. & F., 21/3/18.
Kennedy, Harold William, b. Aston, Birmingham, e. Birmingham (Small Heath, Birmingham), 2338, Sgt., d. of w., F. & F., 8/10/16.
Kenny, George, b. Birmingham, e. Birmingham, 3545, Pte., d. of w., F. & F., 21/7/16.
Kent, William Francis, e. Horsham, Sussex (Arundel, Sussex), 241886, Pte., k. in a., F. & F., 3/9/17, formerly 2871, R. Sussex Regt.

Kerr, James, b. Addiewell, West Calder, Middx., e. West Calder (Addiewell), 202541, Pte., k. in a., F. & F., 12/4/18, formerly 2260, R. Scots.
Keys, William Henry, e. Birmingham (Edgbaston, Birmingham), 242065, Pte., d. of w., F. & F., 13/4/18.
King, Charles, b. St. Christopher's, Birmingham, e. Birmingham, 1660, Pte., d. of w., F. & F., 20/7/16.
King, William John, b. Bedminster, Glos., e. Bristol (Bedminster), 25798, Pte., k. in a., F. & F., 19/8/18.
Kingstone, Ernest, b. All Saint's, Birmingham, e. Birmingham, 240290, Sgt., k. in a., F. & F., 24/9/17.
Kingsley, James, b. St. Paul's, Bristol, e. Bristol, 26903, Pte., k. in a., F. & F., 13/4/18.
Kneale, John Alexander, b. Liverpool, e. Liverpool, 35645, Pte., k. in a., F. & F., 6/9/18.
Knight, Charles Percy, b. Birmingham, e. Birmingham (Harborne, Birmingham), 15/1350, Sgt., k. in a., F. & F., 9/4/18.
Knight, Sydney Malyan, b. Reigate, Surrey, e. Clapham, Middx. (Reigate), 263031, Pte., k. in a., F. & F., 2/11/18, formerly 45697, Surrey Yeo., 52024, R. Irish Rif.
Knowles, Alfred John, b. Barton Hill, Bristol, e. Bristol, 25808, Pte., k. in a., F. & F., 12/4/18.
Lacey, Frederick George, b. Morriott, Som., e. Crewkerne, Som. (Merriott), 260261, L/Cpl., k. in a., F. & F., 6/9/17, formerly 4646, Som. L.I.
Lake, Charles, b. Stewkley, Bucks, e. Aylesbury, Bucks (Wing, Bucks), 203768, Pte., k. in a., F. & F., 24/10/18.
Lamb, William Owen, b. Corwen, North Wales, e. Birmingham (Small Heath, Birmingham), 241019, L/Cpl., k. in a., F. & F., 19/7/16.
Larnach, Primrose Logan, b. Birmingham, e. Birminggham (Sutton Coldfield, Warwicks), 202922, Pte., k. in a., F. & F., 5/12/17.
Law, William John, b. Birmingham, e. Birmingham, 4876, Pte., k. in a., F. & F., 19/7/16.
Lawrence, Lawrence, e. Birmingham (Ladywood, Birmingham), 201608, Cpl., k. in a., F. & F., 7/9/17.
Leckey, Francis John, b. Walsham, Norfolk, e. Nuneaton, Warwicks, 202693, A/Cpl., k. in a., F. & F., 5/9/17.
Leishman, Richard, b. Falkirk, Stirling, e. Falkirk, 6175, Pte., k. in a., F. & F., 19/7/16, formerly 1601, High. Cyc. Battn.
Leonard, Evan John, b. Wootton-under-Edge, Glos., e. Wootton-under-Edge, 203250, Pte., d., F. & F., 16/1/19, formerly 148538, R.F.A.
Lett, Thomas, b. St. Mary's Birmingham, e. Birmingham, 200390, L/Cpl., k. in a., F. & F., 21/3/18.
Lewis, Edward Albert, e. Abergavenny, Mon., 260027, Pte., d. of w., F. & F., 15/12/17, formerly 2747, Mon. Regt.
Lissaman, Edwin, b. Coventry, e. Coventry, 19466, Pte., k. in a., F. & F., 20/8/18.
Lloyd, Alfred, e. Birmingham (Bordesley, Birmingham), 3725, Pte., k. in a., F. & F., 19/7/16.
Lloyd, George Edward, b. Birmingham, e. Birmingham (Selly Oak, Birmingham), 50257, Pte., k. in a., F. & F., 24/10/18.
Lockley, Walter Henry, b. Birmingham, e. Birmingham (Small Heath, Birmingham), 26235, Pte., d. of w., F. & F., 12/4/18.
Longfield, George, b Sittingbourne, Kent, e. Sittingbourne, 260265, Cpl., k. in a., F. & F., 5/10/17, formerly 2912, E. Kent Regt.
Loynds, Edward, b. Stalybridge, Ches., e. Chester (Stalybridge), 29577, Pte., d. of w., F. & F., 24/3/18, formerly 40360, S. Lancs Regt.
Luck, Percy, b. Playden, Sussex, e. Rye, Sussex, 5534, C.Q.M.S., k. in a., F. & F., 5/7/16, formerly 439, R. Sussex Regt.
Lucking, Maxwell, b. Birmingham, e. Birmingham (Moseley, Birmingham), 4935, Pte., k. in a., F. & F., 19/7/16.
Luckman, Charles, b. King's Heath, Birmingham, e. Birmingham (King's Heath), 3354, Cpl., k. in a., F. & F., 19/7/16.
Luxton, Bertram Edward, b. Dratton, Portsmouth, e. Portsmouth, 6251, Pte., k. in a., F. & F., 19/7/16, formerly 2143, Hants Regt.
Lyon, James, b. Southport, Lancs, e. Port Talbot, Mon. (Aberavon, Mon.), 260075, Pte., k. in a., F. & F., 24/9/17, formerly 3809, Mon. Regt.
McMain, Robert, b. Almondbank, Perth, e. Perth (Almondbank), 6182, Pte., k. in a., F. & F., 3/10/16, formerly 1902, High. Cyc. Battn.
McDonald, Charles, b. Birmingham, e. Birmingham (Handsworth, Staffs), 202129, Pte., k. in a., F. & F., 7/12/17.
McGorty, Joseph, b. St. Helens, Lancs, e. St. Helens, 29578, Pte., d. of w., F. & F., 21/11/18, formerly 40516, S. Lancs Regt.
McKie, David, b. Birkdale, Liverpool, e. Liverpool (Sefton Park, Liverpool), 35657, Pte., d. of w., F. & F., 11/11/18.
Mace, John William, e. Birmingham (Chesterfield, Derbys), 202108, Pte., k. in a., F. & F., 6/12/17.*
Mackereth, John, b. Kendal, Westmorland, e. Kendal, 35653, Pte., k. in a., F. & F., 24/10/18.
Maggs, Ernest Frederick, b. St. Philips, Bristol, e. Bristol (Avonmouth, Glos.), 26887, Pte., d., F. & F., 12/4/18.
Major, William Herbert, e. Birmingham (Small Heath, Birmingham), 3615, Pte., k. in a., F. & F., 19/7/16.
Mantle, Philip, b. Grimsby, Lincs, e. Grimsby, 27132, Pte., k. in a., F. & F., 31/3/18, formerly 4999, Lincs Regt.
Mallabone, Joseph, b. Nuneaton, Warwicks, e. Warwick (Nuneaton), 21969, Pte., k. in a., F. & F., 21/3/18.
Mannion, William, b. Birkenhead, Ches., e. Birkenhead, 35654, Pte., k. in a., F. & F., 8/8/18.
Mansbridge, Frank, b. Hurstpierpoint, Sussex, e. Hurstpierpoint, 241846, Pte., d., F. & F., 1/4/18, formerly 1708, R. Sussex Regt.
Marston, Henry, b. Lubenham, Leics, e. Nuneaton, Warwicks (Foleshill,, Coventry, Warwicks), 242469, L/Sgt., k. in a., F. & F., 3/4/18.
Martin, Edward, b. Higham-on-the-Hill, Leics, e. Nuneaton, Warwicks, 268937, Pte., d., F. & F., 5/7/18.
Matthews, Herbert, b. Chillington, Somerset, e. Crewkerne, Somerset (Lower Chillington, Ilminster, Somerset), 260248, Pte., k. in a., F. & F., 6/4/18, formerly 203469, Som. L.I
Matthews, Joseph William, b. Barby, Rugby, Warwicks, e. Coventry, Warwicks (Dunchurch, nr. Rugby), 3609, Cpl., k. in a., F. & F., 12/4/18.
Medlicott, Samuel John, b. Burwater, Shropshire, e. Shrewsbury, Shropshire, 235083, Pte., k. in a., F. & F., 3/12/17, formerly 203605, Shrops L.I.
Mellor, Charles Henry, b. St. Martin's, Birmingham, e. Birmingham (Aston, Birmingham), 242244, Cpl., k. in a., F. & F., 7/9/17.
Meredith, Arthur Philip, b. St. Martin's, Birmingham, e. Birmingham (Balsall Heath, Birmingham), 202168, Pte., k. in a., F. & F., 6/9/17.
Middleton, David, b. Stourport, Worcs, e. Birmingham (Stourport), 241032, Pte., k. in a., F. & F., 6/12/17, M.M.
Millard, Arthur John, b. Pontypridd, S. Wales, e. Widnes, Lancs, 35659, Pte., k. in a., F. & F., 24/10/18.
Miller, William, e. Atherstone, Warwicks (Dordon, Tamworth, Warwicks), 242514, Pte., d. of w., F. & F., 25/8/17.
Millership, William, b. Oldbury, Worcs, e. Slough, Bucks (Burham, Bucks), 50264, Pte., k. in a., F. & F., 24/10/18.
Milnes, Arthur Sandford, b. St. Helens, Lancs, e. St. Helens, 242993, Sgt., d., F. & F., 23/4/18, formerly 7951, R.E.
Minchin, George Victor, b. Birmingham, e. Rugby, Warwicks, 36285, Pte., k. in a., F. & F., 4/9/18.
Minett, George Henry, b. Birmingham, e. Birmingham (Solihull, Birmingham), 2937, Pte., k. in a., F. & F., 19/7/16.
Minstrell, Herbert, b. Coventry, Warwicks, e. Coventry (Hillfields, Coventry), 42135, Pte., k. in a., F. & F., 3/9/18.
Mitchell, Henry Morley, b. Crowan, Cornwall, e. Bodmin Barracks, Cornwall (Camborne, Cornwall), 37981, L/Cpl., k. in a., F. & F., 31/3/18.
Mitchell, Maxwell, b. Muiravonaide, Linlithgow, e. Falkirk, Stirling, 241904, Pte., k. in a., F. & F., 19/7/16, formerly 1656, High. Cyc. Battn.
Moore, James, e. Birmingham (Aston, Birmingham), 240832, Pte., k. in a., F. & F., 26/4/18.
Moore, Walter, b. Foleshill, Coventry, Warwicks, e. Coventry, 37971, Pte., d., F. & F., 15/8/18.
Moorhouse, James Arthur, e. Burnley, Lancs, 260064, Pte., k. in a., F. & F., 6/9/17, formerly 19155, R. Lancs Regt.
Morris, Norman Leslie, b. St. Thomas, Birmingham, e. Birmingham, 2741, Pte., k. in a., F. & F., 19/7/16.
Morris, William Herbert, b. Birmingham, e. Birmingham, 202150, Pte., k. in a., F. & F., 1/11/18.
Moss, William, e. Woodstock, Oxon, 28874, Pte., k. in a., F. & F., 31/3/18.
Moulds, Charles, b. Aldershot, Hants, e. Birmingham, 241377, Pte., k. in a., F. & F., 3/12/17.
Mullard, Arthur, b. Birmingham, e. Birmingham, 50439, Pte., k. in a., F. & F., 24/10/18.
Mulraney, Alexander Stuart, b. Manchester, Lancs, e. Liverpool, Lancs, 35664, Pte., k. in a., F. & F., 8/8/18.
Nash, Albert Henry, b. Birmingham, Warwicks, e. Birmingham, 242365, Pte., k. in a., F. & F., 10/9/17.
Neale, Clifford Ernest, b. Birkenhead, Ches., e. Birkenhead, 29407, Pte., k. in a., F. & F., 6/9/17, formerly 45146, Ches. Regt.
Neale, William George, e. Marlborough, Wilts (Collingbourne Ducis, Wilts), 260066, Pte., k. in a., F. & F., 22/3/18, formerly 24079, Som. L.I.
Nelson, Richard, b. Horwich, Lancs, e. Horwich, 260032, Pte., k. in a., F. & F., 22/3/18, formerly 4697, Mon. Regt.
Newby, William Alfred, e. Birmingham, 3716, Pte., k. in a., F. & F., 19/7/16.
Newcombe, John William, b. Leicester, e. Altrincham, Ches., 260176, Pte., d. of w., F. & F., 10/9/17, formerly 203820, Shrops. L.I.
Newman, Cecil, b. Birmingham, e. Birmingham (Ladywood, Birmingham), 201215, Pte., k. in a., F. & F., 12/4/18.
Newton, John, b. Middleton, Lancs, e. Middleton, 202440, Pte., k. in a., F. & F., 8/8/16, formerly 8547, Lancs Fus.
Niblett, Leonard Charles, b. Evesham, Worcs, e. Birmingham, 241468, Pte., d. of w., F. & F., 28/8/17.
Nicklin, Harold, b. Walsall, Staffs, e. Walsall, 203314, Pte., k. in a., F. & F., 6/9/17.
Noke, William Joseph, b. Birmingham, e. Birmingham (Winson Green, Birmingham), 12945, Cpl., d. of w., F. & F., 27/10/18, M.M.
Norman, Thomas George, b. Shottermill, Haslemere, Surrey, e. Petersfield, Hants (Grayshott, Surrey), 6256, Pte., k. in a., F. & F., 19/7/16, formerly 2043, Hamps Regt.
North, Frank Thomas, b. Portsmouth, Hants, e. Birmingham, 41044, Pte., k. in a., F. & F., 24/10/18.
Norton, Norman, b. Northwich, Ches., e. Northwich, 29565, Pte., k. in a., F. & F., 5/9/17, formerly 40341, S. Lancs Regt.
Oakes, John Alfred, b. St. Michael's, Headingley, Leeds, e. Leeds, Yorks, 235139, Pte., d., F. & F., 15/6/18, formerly 15579, A. Cyclist Corps.
Ogden, Robert, b. Manchester, Lancs, e. Manchester, 201904, Pte., k. in a., F. & F., 3/12/17, formerly 2589, Manchester Regt.
Oliver, Cecil James, b. Kettlebrook, Staffs, e. Tamworth, Staffs (Kettlebrook), 17040, Sgt., k. in a., F. & F., 24/10/18.
Orme, Richard, e. Birmingham (Sparkbrook, Birmingham), 3375, Pte., k. in a., F. & F., 31/7/16.
Orton, Arthur, b. Hinckley, Leics, e. Nuneaton, Warwicks, 203119, Pte., k. in a., F. & F., 1/9/17.
Osborn, Fred, e. Birmingham (Nechells, Birmingham), 242061, Pte., k. in a., F. & F., 6/9/17.
Osborne, Henry Joseph, e. Aston, Birmingham (Hockley, Birmingham), 242764, Pte., k. in a., F. & F., 11/4/18.

Osborne, William, e. Chichester, Sussex, 241852, Pte., d. of w., F. & F., 9/12/17, formerly 2509, R. Sussex Regt.
Owen, Frederick Thomas, b. Higher Broughton, Manchester, e. Salford, Lancs (Higher Broughton), 235004, Pte., k. in a., F. & F., 3/12/17, formerly 29258, Lancs Fus.
Owen, Matthew, b. Nechells, Birmingham, e. Birmingham, 241135, L/Cpl., k. in a., F. & F., 17/4/18.
Oxton, William Robert, b. Little Neston, Ches., e. Birkenhead, Ches. (Little Neston), 29090, Pte., k. in a., F. & F., 24/10/18, formerly 62270, Ches. Regt.
Palfreman, James, b. Warrington, Lancs, e. Warrington, 29582, Pte., k. in a., F. & F., 4/12/17, formerly 40473, S. Lancs Regt.
Palmer, Henry Joseph, b. Bicester, Oxon, e. Leamington Spa, Warwicks (Rugby, Warwicks), 42159, Pte., d. of w., F. & F., 24/10/18.
Parker, Archibald John, e. Midhurst, Sussex, 5547, Pte., d. of w., F. & F., 10/7/16, formerly 2744, R. Sussex Regt.
Parker, John, e. Birmingham (Wilnecote, nr. Tamworth, Staffs), 242526, Pte., d. of w., F. & F., 1/9/17.
Parnell, Loftus Samuel John, b. Harberton, Devon, e. Newton Abbot, Devon (Harberton, nr. Totnes), 50272, Pte., d. of w., F. & F., 18/5/18.
Parslow, Joseph, b Birmingham, e. Birmingham, 241011, Pte., k. in a., F. & F., 3/4/18.
Patrick, John, e. Chichester, Sussex, 241745, Pte., k. in a., F. & F., 5/10/18, formerly 2712, R. Sussex Regt.
Pattenden, Edwin, e. Uckfield, Sussex (Heathfield, Sussex), 242025, Pte., k. in a., F. & F., 21/3/18, formerly 2965, R. Sussex Regt., M.M.
Peart, Thomas Ridley, b. Newborough, Northumberland, e. Hexham, Northumberland (Fourstones, Northumberland), 29801, Pte., k. in a., F. & F., 24/10/18, formerly 27284, Yorks Regt.
Pearson, James Appleton, b. St. John's, Manchester, Lancs, e. Manchester, 201906, L/Cpl., d., F. & F., 31/3/18, formerly 1576, Manchester Regt.
Peat, Arthur Robert, b. Midhurst, Sussex, e. Horsham, Sussex (Midhurst), 5519, Pte., d. of w., F. & F., 22/7/16, formerly 2929, R. Sussex Regt.
Peesley, Edgar, b. Cleveley, Euston, Oxon, e. Oxford (Glympton, nr. Woodstock, Oxon), 50278, Pte., k. in a., F. & F., 24/10/18.
Pegler, Howard Richard, b. Stroud, Glos., e. Stroud, 50280, Pte., d. of w., F. & F., 30/10/18.
Penny, Horace, b. Birmingham, e. Birmingham, 240701, Cpl., k. in a., F. & F., 24/10/18.
Pepper, William, b. Coventry, Warwicks, e. Coventry, 203310, Pte., k. in a., F. & F., 31/3/18.
Perrins, Harold, b. Ladywood, Birmingham, e. Birmingham, 1704, Pte., d. of w., F. & F., 20/7/16.
Peters, James Henry, b St. Asaph, Birmingham, e. Birmingham, 3486, Pte., k. in a., F. & F., 19/7/16.
Phillips, Charles William, b. Ledbury, Herefordshire, e. Worcester (Uphampton, Worcs), 50281, Pte., k. in a., F. & F., 20/4/18.
Phillips, Edmund Llewellyn, b. Pengam, Glam., e. Bargoed, Glam. (Pengam), 30461, Pte., k. in a., F. & F., 3/12/17, formerly 25958, Welsh Regt.
Phillips, Idris, b. Llanrug, Carnarvon, e. Chester, Ches. (Hoole, Chester), 260177, Pte., d. of w., F. & F., 8/9/17, formerly 203803, Shrops L.I.
Pickering, Albert, e. Birmingham (Highgate, Birmingham), 201536, Sgt., k. in a., F. & F., 31/3/18.
Pinfold, John, b. Walsall, Staffs, e. Birmingham, 3123, Pte., d. of w., F. & F., 8/7/16.
Pitman, Edgar Victor, e. Hastings, Sussex (Eastbourne, Sussex), 6324, Pte., k. in a., F. & F., 19/7/16, formerly 3043, R. Sussex Regt.
Pitts, Frederick James, b. Pinhoe, Devon, e. Barnstaple, Devon (Lynton, N. Devon), 26451, Pte., d. of w., F. & F., 31/10/18.
Platford, Robert James, b. Horning, Norfolk, e. Norwich, Norfolk (Horning, Norfolk), 38409, Pte., k. in a., F. & F., 11/10/18, formerly G/11865, R. Sussex Regt.
Playforth, Frederick Asbury, e. Birmingham (Aston, Birmingham), 242496, Pte., k. in a., F. & F., 12/4/18.
Pollard, Arthur, b. Singleton, Sussex, e. Horsham, Sussex (Midhurst, Sussex), 6113, Pte., k. in a., F. & F., 10/7/16, formerly 2981, R. Sussex Regt.
Porter, Ernest James, b. Aldershot, Hants, e. Farnham, Surrey, 25924, Pte., k. in a., F. & F., 3/4/18.
Poulton, John Samuel, e. Birmingham (Smethwick, Staffs), 15206, Sgt., d. of w., F. & F., 25/10/18, M.M.
Powell, William George, b. All Saints, Birmingham, e. Birmingham (Winson Green, Birmingham), 3821, Pte., k. in a., F. & F., 19/7/16.
Plumridge, Robert, b. Bisham, Berks, e. Portsmouth, Hants, 241980, Pte., k. in a., F. & F., 6/12/17, formerly 1949, Hants Regt.
Powell, Maldwyn Emlyn, b. Merthyr Tydvil, Glam., e. Merthyr Tydvil, 260038, Pte., k. in a., F. & F., 19/4/18, formerly 4710, Mon. Regt.
Powley, Alfred George, e. Portsmouth, Hants (Tilchfield Common, Hants), 6266, Pte., k. in a., F. & F., 19/7/16, formerly 2622, Hamps. Regt.
Prescott, Samuel, b. Wigan, Lancs, e. Wigan, 202388, Pte., k. in a., F. & F., 3/12/17, formerly 1723, Manchester Regt.
Price, Ernest, b. Saltley, Birmingham, e. Birmingham (Saltley), 242367, Pte., k. in a., F. & F., 6/9/17.
Price, Herbert William, b. St. Martin's, Birmingham, e. Birmingham (Ladywood, Birmingham), 240356, Cpl., d. of w., F. & F., 12/4/17.
Pukit, William A., b. Liverpool, Lancs, e. Bootle, Lancs 260140, Pte., k. in a., F. & F., 4/12/17, formerly 55840, Liverpool Regt.
Purves, Harry, b. Woolwich, Kent, e. Weston-Super-Mare, Somerset (Bideford, Devon), 260258, Sgt., k. in a., F. & F., 6/9/17, formerly 21485, Som. L.I.
Rae, Charles, b. Kirkcaldy, Fife, e. Kirkcaldy, 242044, Sgt., k. in a., F. & F., 21/3/18, formerly 1852, High. Cyclist Battn., D.C.M.
Rafferty, John, b. Ballinasloe, Ireland, e. St. Helens, Lancs (Balliinasloe), 29584, Pte., d. of w., F. & F., 12/4/18, formerly 40517, S. Lancs. Regt.
Ralph, Arthur James, b. Newhaven, Sussex, e. Horsham, Sussex (Slinfold, nr. Horsham), 5523, Pte., k. in a., F. & F., 19/7/16, formerly 2423, R. Sussex Regt.
Randall, Ernest William, b. Wivelsfield, Sussex, e. Haywards Heath, Sussex (Wivelsfield), 6117, Pte., k. in a., F. & F., 19/7/16, formerly 2948, R. Sussex Regt.
Reading, William, b. Birmingham, e. Birmingham (Rotton Park, Birmingham), 242957, Pte., k. in a., F. & F, 11/4/18.
Redding, Thomas, e. Birmingham, 201516, Pte., d. of w., F. & F., 7/6/17.
Reeves, Albert Edward, b. Birmingham, e. Birmingham, 3558, Pte., d. of w., F. & F., 20/7/16.
Reeves, Edward George, b. St. George's, Edgbaston, Birmingham, 242352, L/Cpl., k. in a., F. & F., 14/8/18.
Rhodes, George, e. Hastings, Sussex (Rye, Sussex), 242032, Pte., d. of w., F. & F., 5/4/18, formerly 2691, R. Sussex Regt.
Richardson, Arthur, b. Birmingham, e. Birmingham (Saltley, Birmingham), 28574, Pte., k. in a., F. & F., 24/10/18.
Ridge, Harry, b Chivnor, Devon, e. Barnstaple, Devon (Wrafton, Devon), 50289, Cpl., d. of w., F. & F., 21/8/18.
Riley, Harry, b. Birmingham, e. Birmingham, 50451, Pte., k. in a., F. & F., 24/10/18.
Roberts, Charles James, b. London, e. Birmingham (Smethwick, Staffs), 4882, Pte., k. in a., F. & F., 3/10/16.
Robinson, William, b. Saltley, Birmingham, e. Birmingham (Small Heath, Birmingham), 240125, Cpl., d., F. & F., 13/6/17.
Rowe, Sidney James, b. Penzance, Cornwall, e. Birkenhead, Ches., 29429, Pte., k. in a., F. & F., 6/12/17, formerly 10968, Ches. Regt.
Rowson, Harry, b. Digbeth, Birmingham, e. Birmingham, 3904, Pte., k. in a., F. & F., 19/7/16.
Ruttens, Edward, e. Horsham, Sussex (Westburton, Sussex), 6123, Pte., k. in a., F. & F., 19/7/16, formerly 2554, R. Sussex Regt.
Robinson, Ernest, e. Midhurst, Sussex (Eastbourne, Sussex), 241864, Pte., k. in a., F. & F., 21/3/18, formerly 2747, R. Sussex Regt.
Robotham, Alfred Arthur, b. King's Norton, Worcester, e. Birmingham (King's Norton), 240759, C.S.M., k. in a., F. & F., 24/10/18.
Roche, John, b. Birmingham, e. Birmingham, 241064, Cpl., k. in a., F. & F., 6/9/17.
Rodgers, Thomas, e. Birmingham (Smethwick, Staffs), 242354, Pte., k. in a., F. & F., 22/3/18.
Rogers, Francis Bernard, b. Upper Mytton, Worcs, e. Taunton, Som. (Ilminster, Som.), 260241, Pte., k. in a., F. & F., 6/12/17, formerly 203627, Som. L.I.
Rogers, Arthur, b. St. Bartholomew's, Birmingham, e. Birmingham, 241087, Cpl., k. in a., F. & F., 3/9/17.
Rogers, George, b. Studham, Beds, e. Winchester, Hants (Southampton), 25034, Pte., k. in a., F. & F., 30/3/18.
Rose, William Edward, b. St. Luke's, Birmingham, e. Birmingham, 200407, C.S.M., k. in a., F. & F., 12/4/18.
Ross, Colin Alex, b. Hitchin, Herts, e. Norwich, Norfolk, 33190, Pte., k. in a., F. & F., 24/10/18, formerly 3327, Lancers.
Ruddle, George, e. Rugby, Warwicks, 242389, Pte., k. in a., F. & F., 3/9/17.
Russell, Albert, b. Birmingham, e. Cardiff (Aberavon, Glam.), 57756, Pte., d., F. & F., 29/12/18.
Sanders, Charles Edward, e. Birmingham (King's Heath, Birmingham), 3783, Pte., k. in a., F. & F., 19/7/16.
Sands, William Thomas, b. Forest Row, Sussex, e. Horsham, Sussex (Forest Row), 241867, Pte., k. in a., F. & F., 31/8/17, formerly 2290, R. Sussex Regt.
Saunders, Walter Joseph, e. Birmingham (Balsall Heath, Birmingham), 2885, Sgt., k. in a., F. & F., 19/7/16.
Savage, Thomas, b. Chadderton, Lancs, e. Oldham, Lancs (West Chadderton), 260041, Pte., k. in a., F. & F., 4/12/17, formerly 5403, Mon. Regt.
Searle, John James, b. Greatham, Sussex, e. Horsham, Sussex (Greatham), 6125, Pte., k. in a., F. & F., 19/7/16, formerly 2531, R. Sussex Regt.
Selby, Alfred, e. Coventry, 242506, Pte., d. of w., F. & F., 9/9/17.
Sergeant, William, e. Horsham, Sussex, 241870, Pte., k. in a., F. & F., 21/3/18, formerly 2285, R. Sussex Regt.
Shannon, Samuel, b. Pumpherston, Midlothian, e. Falkirk (Polmond, Stirling), 241916, Cpl., d. of w., F. & F., 18/12/17, formerly 1661, Highland Cyclist Battn.
Shaw, Fred, b. Birmingham, e. Birmingham (Sparkbrook, Birmingham), 241348, Pte., d. of w., F. & F., 5/9/17.
Shaw, Frank Matthew, b. Urmston, Lancs, e. Manchester (Urmston), 260045, Pte., d. of w., F. & F., 11/12/17, formerly 5433, Mon. Regt.
Shaw, Lawrence, b. Stalybridge, Ches., e. Hyde, Ches. (Stalybridge), 29081, Pte., k. in a., F. & F., 24/10/18, formerly 61882, Ches. Regt.
Sheasby, George, e. Warwick (Fenny Compton, Warwicks), 202101, Pte., k. in a., F. & F., 21/3/18.
Sheasby, Thomas Roland, e. Stratford-on-Avon, Warwicks, 242527, Pte., k. in a., F. & F., 3/9/17.
Shields, Arthur Robert, b. Llandudno, e. Bangor (Llandudno), 35709, Pte., k. in a., F. & F., 20/8/18.
Simkins, Arthur, b. Cherrington, Warwicks, e. Warwick (Cherrington), 242474, Sgt., d. of w., F. & F., 19/7/18.

Simms, Percival Arthur, b. Sparkbrook, Birmingham, e. Birmingham (Sparkbrook), 200261, Pte., k. in a., F. & F., 20/3/18.

Simpkins, Samuel, b. Manchester, e. Manchester (Salford, Manchester), 35776, Pte., k. in a., F. & F., 24/10/18.

Smallwood, Ernest, e. Birmingham (Smethwick, Staffs), 240088, Pte., k. in a., F. & F., 19/7/16.

Smith, Albert, b. Canterbury, e. Canterbury, 241872, Pte., k. in a., F. & F., 12/4/18, formerly 903, Kent Cyclist Battn.

Smith, Bertie, b. Melton Mowbray, Leics, e. Birmingham, 3497, Pte., k. in a., F. & F., 19/7/16.

Smith, George Albert, b. Lymington, Hants, e. Brockenhurst, Hants (Lymington), 242441, Pte., k. in a., F. & F., 1/7/17.

Smith, Michael, b. Hanslope, Bucks, e. Bletchley, Bucks (Hanslope), 26173, Pte., d. of w., F. & F., 4/9/18.

Smith, William Thomas, b. Bedhampton, Hants, e. Havant, Hants (Bedhampton), 241987, C.S.M., k. in a., F. & F., 2/11/18, formerly 898, Hants Regt., M.M.

Snooke, John Thomas, e. Newport, Isle of Wight (Ventnor, Isle of Wight), 242415, Pte., k. in a., F. & F., 27/5/18, formerly 26240, Hamps Regt.

Stainer, Edward George, b. Winterburnstoke, Wilts, e. Salisbury, Wilts, 267760, Pte., k. in a., F. & F., 31/3/18.

Stanton, Frederick William, b. Leamington, Warwicks, e. Leamington, 202834, Pte., d. of w., F. & F., 17/10/17.

Starling, Frederick, b. Birmingham, e. Birmingham, 240909, L/Cpl., k. in a., F. & F., 19/7/16.

Stayte, Albert Victor, b. Charlbury, Oxon, e. Birmingham (Northfield, Birmingham), 37693, Pte., k. in a., F. & F., 12/4/18.

Stephens, George William, b. Fishponds, Bristol, e. Bristol (Fishponds), 36307, Pte., k. in a., F. & F., 24/10/18.

Stephens, Sydney, b. Birmingham, e. Birmingham (Smethwick, Staffs), 2853, Sgt., k. in a., F. & F., 19/7/16.

Stevens, Charles William, b. Northampton, e. Northampton, 27177, Pte., k. in a., F. & F., 21/3/18, formerly 5327, Lincs Regt.

Stevens, Harry, b. Cuckfield, Sussex, e. Worthing, Sussex (Hove, Sussex), 241873, A/Cpl., k. in a., F. & F., 19/7/16, formerly 2091, R. Sussex Regt.

Stevenson, George William, e. Horsham, Sussex (Coleman's Hatch, Sussex), 5546, Pte., k. in a., F. & F., 5/7/16, formerly 2857, Sussex Regt.

Stiff, Charles Samuel, e. Birmingham (Lozells, Birmingham), 240982, Pte., k. in a., F. & F., 17/8/17.

Stockton, Frederick, b. Tarporley, Ches., e. Chester (Hoole, Chester), 260186, Pte., k. in a., F. & F., 3/9/17, formerly 203892, Shrops. L.I.

Stubbs, George, b. Madeley, Staffs, e. Chester (Madeley), 29504, Pte., d. of w., F. & F., 12/4/18, formerly 62233, Ches. Regt.

Sturman, Sidney, e. Coventry (Whitley, Warwicks), 242502, Pte., k. in a., F. & F., 6/9/17.

Summerfield, Louis Henry, b. Birmingham, e. Birmingham (Aston, Birmingham), 241420, Cpl., k. in a., F. & F., 2/9/17.

Surgenor, Leslie, e. Bournemouth (Belfast, Ireland), 6276, Pte., k. in a., F. & F., 19/7/16, formerly 2151, Hants Regt.

Tainty, Leonard, b. Birmingham, e. Birmingham (Sparkbrook, Birmingham), 241502, Pte., k. in a., F. & F., 4/12/17.

Tapp, John, e. Birmingham (Hockley, Birmingham), 243022, Pte., d. of w., F. & F., 6/12/17.

Taplin, James William, b. Stratford-on-Avon, Warwicks, e. Stratford-on-Avon, 242761, Pte., k. in a., F. & F., 1/4/18, formerly 13600, R.D.C.

Taylor, Albert, b. Toddington, Glos., e. Cheltenham, Glos. (Tewkesbury, Glos.), 26580, Pte., k. in a., F. & F., 24/10/18.

Taylor, Alfred Owen, b. Gt. Missenden, Bucks, e. Gt. Missenden, 202749, Pte., d. of w., F. & F., 25/12/17.

Taylor, Edmund, b. Rochdale, Lancs, e. Rochdale, 35683, Pte., k. in a., F. & F., 20/8/18.

Taylor, William Thomas, b. Forest Gate, London, e. Birmingham (Bournbrook, Birmingham), 240740, L/Cpl., k. in a., F. & F., 19/7/16.

Teague, George Edwin, b. Havant, Hants, e. Portsmouth (Northam, Hants), 6277, Pte., k. in a., F. & F., 10/9/16, formerly 2055, Hants Regt.

Teasdale, Bertie Leonard, e. Birmingham (Erdington, Birmingham), 3578, Pte., k. in a., F. & F., 19/7/16.

Tew, William, e. Birmingham (Harborne, Birmingham), 4885, Pte., d. of w., F. & F., 13/9/16.

Thomas, Arthur William, b. Birmingham, e. Birmingham (Ladywood, Birmingham), 240819, Pte., k. in a., F. & F., 4/12/17.

Thomas, Charles, b. Birmingham, e. Handsworth, Staffs (Birmingham), 242307, Pte., k. in a., F. & F., 20/3/18.

Thomas, David Brinley, b. Morriston, Swansea, e. Cardiff (Morriston), 260049, Sgt., k. in a., F. & F., 24/10/18, formerly 4005, Mon Regt.

Thompson, Harold Frederick, b. Ramsgate, Kent, e. Bournemouth, Hants, 6278, Pte., d. of w., F. & F., 19/7/16, formerly 1225, Hants Regt.

Thorne, Charles, e. Birmingham, 242521, Pte., k. in a., F. & F., 6/9/17.

Thorpe, Herbert, b. Stalybridge, Ches., e. Chester (Stalybridge), 29438, Pte., d. of w., F. & F., 4/9/17, formerly 62094, Ches. Regt.

Tilley, Ernest Sidney, b. Worthing, Sussex, e. Chichester, Sussex, 6135, Pte., k. in a., F. & F., 19/7/16, formerly 2677, R. Sussex Regt.

Tipper, William Thomas, b. Eastebourne, Midhurst, e. Midhurst, Sussex (Eastebourne), 6136, Pte., k. in a., F. & F., 19/7/16, formerly 2043, R. Sussex Regt.

Tomkins, Ernest Daniell, b. Brislington, Som., e. Bristol (Brislington), 260250, Pte., k. in a., F. & F., 29/1/18, formerly 203453, S.L.I.

Tonks, William, e. Birmingham (Balsall Heath, Birmingham), 3868, Pte., k. in a., F. & F., 19/7/16.

Tribbeck, Harold, b. Stubbington, Hants, e. Stubbington, 241990, L/Cpl., d., F. & F., 20/10/18, formerly 1270, Hants Regt.

Trim, Arthur William Thomas, b. Horsington, Som., e. Taunton, Som. (Templecombe, Som.), 200243, Pte., k. in a., F. & F., 24/3/18, formerly 202514, S.L.I.

Turley, Sidney, e. Birmingham (Edgbaston, Birmingham), 3919, L/Cpl., d. of w., F. & F., 1/7/16.

Turner, William, b. Worcester, e. Birmingham (Sparkhill, Birmingham), 37695, Pte., k. in a., F. & F., 12/4/18.

Turner, William, e. Birmingham, 201519, Pte., k. in a., F. & F., 15/8/18.

Vanner, Frank Albert Victor, e. Ryde, I. of W., 35435, Pte., k. in a., F. & F., 31/3/18.

Veitch, George, b. Medomsley, Durham, e. Consett, Durham (Leadgate, Durham), 242377, Pte., k. in a., F. & F., 29/3/18.

Voisey, Robert, b. St. Andrews, Taunton, Som., e. Taunton, Som., 260244, Pte., d., F. & F., 23/10/18, formerly 265244, S.L.I.

Walker, George, b. Sheffield, e. Salford, Lancs (Birmingham), 3191, Pte., k. in a., F. & F., 4/2/17.

Walker, William John, b. Wharton, Ches., e. Northwich, Ches. (Winsford, Ches.), 260214, Pte., k. in a., F. & F., 4/9/17, formerly 203840, Shrops L.I.

Walton, Arthur, b. Birmingham, e. Birmingham (Winson Green, Birmingham), 242309, Pte., k. in a., F. & F., 12/4/18.

Ward, Leonard, b. Coventry, e. Coventry, 242493, Cpl., k. in a., F. & F., 8/12/17.

Warden, Edward Alfred, b. Over Whitacre, Warwicks, e. Atherstone, Warwicks, 203712, Pte., k. in a., F. & F., 4/9/18.

Warren, Wilfred, b. Hog Island, Leicester, e. Birmingham (Ladywood, Birmingham), 240252, Pte., k. in a., F. & F., 2/4/17.

Waterman, Clinton Stewart, e. Petersfield, Hants (Horndean, Hants), 6285, Pte., d. of w., F. & F., 19/7/16, formerly 2672, Hants Regt.

Watkins, Frederick, b. Southam, Warwicks, e. Leamington, Warwicks, 20498, Pte., d. of w., F. & F., 24/10/16.

Watkins, Tom, b. St. George's, Birmingham, e. Birmingham, 1997, Dmr., k. in a., F. & F., 19/7/16.

Webb, Francis Henry, b. Bridgewater, Som., e. Bristol, 18708, Pte., k. in a., F. & F., 31/3/18, formerly 23418, S.L.I.

Webb, Frederick Harold, b. Kidmorend, Oxon, e. Stratford-on-Avon, Warwicks, 202702, Pte., k. in a., F. & F., 3/9/17.

Webb, Frederick John, b. Liverpool, Lancs, e. Chester, (Wallasey, Ches.), 29443, Pte., d. of w., F. & F., 9/2/17, formerly 62059, Ches. Regt.

Webb, William, e. Birmingham (Aston, Birmingham), 242524, Pte., k. in a., F. & F., 7/9/17.

Webber, Stuart Godfrey, b. Timberscombe, Som., e. Minehead, Som., 260245, Pte., k. in a., F. & F., 12/4/18, formerly 203741, S.L.I.

Webster, Frederick, b. Edgbaston, Birmingham, e. Birmingham (Selly Oak, Birmingham), 3799, Pte., k. in a., F. & F., 19/7/16.

Wedge, William Henry, b. Bordesley Green, Birmingham, e. Warwick (Birmingham), 202198, Sgt., k. in a., F. & F., 2/11/18.

Wellen, Albert, b. Northchapel, Petworth, Sussex, e. Horsham, Sussex (Petworth), 241763, Pte., k. in a., F. & F., 18/8/16, formerly 1944, R. Sussex Regt.

Wells, Frank, b. Coventry, e. Coventry (Allesley, Coventry), 20413, Pte., d. of w., F. & F., 27/10/16.

Wells, Harold George, e. Hastings, Sussex (Flimwell, Kent), 6339, Pte., k. in a., F. & F., 19/7/16, formerly 3094, R. Sussex Regt.

Weston, Leslie, b. Birmingham, e. Birmingham (Balsall Heath, Birmingham), 240091, Pte., k. in a., F. & F., 19/7/16.

Weston, Herbert Arthur, b. Birmingham, e. Birmingham (King's Heath, Birmingham), 242380, Pte., k. in a., F. & F., 3/9/17.

Wheeler, Ernest, b. Birmingham, e. Birmingham (Aston, Birmingham), 241381, Pte., k. in a., F. & F., 12/4/18.

Whitby, Charles E., b. Liverpool, e. Liverpool, 260051, Pte., k. in a., F. & F., 31/3/18, formerly 3495, Liverpool Regt., 6844, Hereford Regt., and 292186, Mon. Regt.

Whitehead, John George, b. Aston, Birmingham, e. Birmingham (Lozells, Birmingham), 266736, Pte., k. in a., F. & F., 12/4/18.

Whitmore, Henry, e. Petersfield, Hants (Bordon, Hants), 241996, Pte., k. in a., F. & F., 19/7/16, formerly 2248, Hants Regt.

Wilcox, Edward, b. Wordsley, Staffs, e. Birmingham (Wordsley), 242385, Pte., k. in a., F. & F., 20/3/18.

Whyley, John Ernest, b. Sparkbrook, Birmingham, e. Birmingham, 2363, Pte., d. of w., F. & F., 27/6/16.

Wilkins, John, b. St. George's, Birmingham, e. Birmingham (Small Heath, Birmingham), 3961, Pte., k. in a., F. & F., 30/6/16.

Wille, Richard, b. Burgess Hill, Sussex, e. Burgess Hill, 241757, Sgt., k. in a., F. & F., 21/3/18, formerly 2853, Sussex Regt.

Williams, Thomas, b. Bordesley Green, Birmingham, e. Birmingham (Bordesley Green), 200275, Sgt., k. in a., F. & F., 3/4/18.

Williams, William, b. Chester, e. Chester, 29398, Pte., k. in a., F. & F., 24/9/17, formerly 45941, Ches. Regt.

Wilson, James, b. Scarborough, e. Warwick (Blackpool, Lancs), 25784, Pte., k. in a., F. & F., 9/4/18.

Wilson, James Stanley, b. Arlecdon, Cumb., e. Workington, Cumb. (Arlecdon), 35699, Pte., k. in a., F. & F., 24/10/18.

Wilson, William, b. Ashford, Kent, e. Canterbury, Kent (Ashford), 50906, Pte., d., F. & F., 13/9/19.
Wincott, Lorenzo Claude, b. Stockton, Warwicks, e. Rugby, Warwicks (Stockton), 202886, Pte., k. in a., F. & F., 9/4/18.
Winscombe, Arthur, e. Warwick (Coventry), 242771, Pte., k. in a., F. & F., 3/4/18.
Winter, Frank, e. Hastings, Sussex (Jarvis Brook, Sussex), 6336, Pte., d. of w., F. & F., 12/9/16, formerly 2998, R. Sussex Regt.
Witten, Frederick, b. Beeding, Sussex, e. Steyning, Sussex (Upper Beeding), 6151, Pte., k. in a., F. & F., 10/7/16, formerly 3002, R. Sussex Regt.
Witten, Thomas, b. Beeding, Sussex, e. Steyning, Sussex (Upper Beeding), 5528, Pte., k. in a., F. & F., 19/7/16, formerly 3001, R. Sussex Regt.
Wood, Arthur William, b. Birmingham, e. Birmingham, 242202, L/Cpl., k. in a., F. & F, 6/12/17.
Wood, Frank, b. Hailsham, Sussex, e. Hailsham, 242039, Cpl., k. in a., F. & F., 24/10/18, formerly 1394, R. Sussex Regt.
Wood, George Cyril, e. Birmingham (Smethwick, Staffs), 2835, Pte., k. in a., F. & F., 19/7/16.
Wood, Richard, b. West Bromwich, Staffs, e. Coventry, 202347, Pte., k. in a., F. & F., 12/4/18.
Wood, Robert, e. Salford, Lancs, 203012, Cpl., k. in a., F. & F., 4/12/17, formerly 32848, Lancs Fus., and 291174, Mon. Regt.
Woodcock, William, b. St. Paul's, Birmingham, e. Birmingham, 242204, Pte., k. in a., F. & F., 21/3/18.
Woods, Frederick, e. Preston, Lancs, 202526, Pte., k. in a., F. & F., 3/12/17, formerly 2777, N. Lancs Regt.
Woodhatch, William, e. Horsham, Sussex, 241887, Pte., k. in a., F. & F., 19/7/16, formerly 2427, R. Sussex Regt.
Woodward, George William Courtnay, e. Portsmouth (Southsea, Hants), 6288, Pte., k. in a., F. & F., 19/7/16, formerly 2339, Hants Regt.
Woodward, James, b. Barnton, Ches., e. Northwich, Ches. (Barnton), 260215, Pte., k. in a., F. & F., 5/9/17, formerly 203833, Shrops L.I.
Woodward, Thomas, b. St. Paul's, Warwick, e. Warwick, 242257, Sgt., k. in a., F. & F., 20/3/18.
Wright, Albert, b. St. Martin's, Birmingham, e. Birmingham (Hockley, Birmingham), 240906, Pte., k. in a., F. & F., 21/3/18.
Wright, John, e. Birmingham (Aston, Birmingham), 242974, Pte., k. in a., F. & F., 8/12/17.
Yates, John, b. Middleton, Lancs, e. Middleton, 202468, Sgt., k. in a., F. & F., 18/4/18, formerly 8679, Lancs Fus.
Young, Frank, b. Acton, Ches., e. Chester (Broxton, Ches.), 29442, Pte., k. in a., F. & F., 8/8/18, formerly 62056, Ches. Regt.

1/7th Battalion.

Ackford, Thomas, e. Stratford-on-Avon, Warwicks, 3233, Pte., k. in a., F. & F., 14/7/16.
Adams, John, b. Smethwick, Staffs, e. Coventry, 2406, Pte., k. in a., F. & F., 9/5/15.
Allard, James, e. Worcester (Knighton, Warwicks), 267043, Pte., k. in a., F. & F., 22/8/17.
Allibone, Henry James Sidney Green, e. Coventry, 266607, Pte., d., F. & F., 30/10/18.
Anderson, Roland Brookes, e. Coventry, 2998, Pte., k. in a., F. & F., 15/7/16.
Ashford, Samuel George, b. Kenilworth, Warwicks, e. Coventry, 1939, Pte., k. in a., F. & F., 14/7/16.
Ayres, Thomas, e. Coventry, 4599, Pte., k. in a., F. & F., 25/7/16.
Bailey, Frederick George, b. Gt. Wakering, Essex, e. Coventry (Leamington, Warwicks), 265740, Sgt., k. in a., F. & F., 8/10/17.
Bailey, Roland Huntley, e. Birmingham (Edgbaston, Birmingham), 4768, Pte., k. in a., F. & F., 5/8/16.
Baker, George Edwin, e. Birmingham, 4754, Pte., d. of w., F. & F., 25/12/16.
Baker, Samuel, e. Coventry (Derby), 266453, Pte., k. in a., F. & F., 20/4/17.
Ballard, Henry Herbert, b. St. Paul's, Warwick, e. Coventry (Warwick), 265501, Cpl., k. in a., F. & F., 27/8/17.
Bannard, Bertie Charles, b. St. Nicholas, Kenilworth, Warwicks, e. Coventry (Kenilworth), 265657, L/Sgt., k. in a., F. & F., 13/8/17.
Barker, Sydney Allen, b. Ravenham, Norfolk, e. Norwich, Norfolk (Ravenham), 29258, Pte., k. in a., F. & F., 27/8/17, formerly 27326, Norfolk Regt.
Barnes, Herbert John Ellard, e. Leamington, Warwicks, 266703, Pte., k. in a., F. & F., 4/10/17.
Barnett, Ellis William, e. Rugby, Warwicks (Edgehills, Warwicks), 266821, Pte., k. in a., F. & F., 11/8/17.
Barrett, Frederick, b. Old Fletton, Northants, e. Fletton (Woodston, Northants), 203365, Pte., k. in a., F. & F., 17/6/18, formerly 264, Hunts Cyc. Corps.
Bartlett, William, b. St. John's, Coventry, Warwicks, e. Coventry, 265381, Pte., d. of w., F. & F., 12/8/18.
Bastable, William Henry, e. Tewkesbury, Glos. (Sturminster Newton, Dorset), 266964, Pte., k. in a., F. & F., 11/8/17.
Bates, Oliver, b. St. Michael's, Coventry, Warwicks, e. Coventry, 2506, Sgt., d. of w., F. & F., 6/8/16.
Batt, Sidney Alfred, b. Chelsea, London, S.W., e. Wandsworth, S.W., 300007, Pte., k. in a., F. & F., 4/10/17, formerly 13306, E. Surrey Regt.
Beal, Ernest, b. Coalville, Leics, e. Coventry, Warwicks, 2401, Pte., k. in a., F. & F., 23/3/16.
Beard, John Stanley, e. Birmingham (Sparkhill, Birmingham), 266755, Pte., d. of w., F. & F., 5/10/17.
Bearley, George, e. Stratford-on-Avon, Warwicks, 265959, Pte., k. in a., F. & F., 25/7/16.
Beaumont, Ernest Charles, b. Coventry, Warwicks, e. Coventry, 4544, Pte., k. in a., F. & F, 19/7/16.
Beech, William, b. Birmingham, e. Birmingham, 267510, Pte., k. in a., F. & F., 8/10/17.
Bennett, Charlie, e. Bristol, Glos., 5069, Pte., d. of w., F. & F., 23/8/16.
Bennett, Ernest, b. Twyford, Berks, e. Bridport, Dorset, 300020, Pte., k. in a., F. & F., 22/8/17, formerly 4465, E. Surrey Regt.
Benny, Richard, e. Coventry, Warwicks, 266525, Pte., k. in a., F. & F., 4/10/17.
Biggs, George Cecil, b. Chilvers Coton, Nuneaton, Warwicks, e. Nuneaton, 1625, Cpl., k. in a., F. & F., 14/7/16.
Birch, Donald Sydney, e. Coventry (Stratford-on-Avon, Warwicks), 2931, Pte., k. in a., F. & F., 18/2/16.
Bird, Albert, b. St. Martin's, Birmingham, e. Birmingham (South Yardley, Birmingham), 19091, Pte., k. in a., F. & F., 4/10/17.
Bird, Frank, b. Chilvers Coton, Nuneaton, Warwicks, e. Nuneaton (Chilvers Coton), 1944, Pte., k. in a., F. & F., 28/8/16.
Birdsey, Hubert Fred, b. Watford, Herts, e. Coventry, Warwicks (Watford), 2539, L/Cpl., k. in a., F. & F., 14/7/16.
Birtwistle, John Harold, e. Rugby, Warwicks, 3079, Pte., k. in a., F. & F., 8/10/15.
Bishop, Raymond, b. Quinton, Warwicks, e. Birmingham (Wolverhampton, Staffs), 25046, Pte., k. in a., F. & F., 27/8/17.
Bodin, Walter, e. Coventry, Warwicks, 2912, L/Cpl., d. of w., F. & F., 4/9/16.
Boon, John, e. Warwick (Haseley Manor, Warwick), 266880, Pte., d., F. & F., 12/3/17.
Borrill, Fred, e. Grimsby, Lincs (Stickford, nr. Boston, Lincs), 300055, Pte., k. in a., F. & F., 22/8/17, formerly 3364, Lincs Regt.
Bowley, Joseph Samuel, b. Birmingham, e. Birmingham (Ladywood, Birmingham), 309099, Pte., k. in a., F. & F., 8/10/17, formerly 7287, Norfolk Regt.
Boxwell, Arnold Francis, e. Gloucester (Newtown, Sharpness, Glos.), 267024, Pte., k. in a, F. & F., 10/8/17.
Brabben, Fred, e. Loddon, Norfolk (Hardley, Loddon), 300006, Pte., k. in a., F. & F., 28/8/17, formerly 3699, Norfolk Regt.
Bradbury, Tom, b. Bedworth, Warwicks, e. Nuneaton, Warwicks (Bedworth), 265158, Pte., k. in a., F. & F., 12/8/17.
Bradley, William Walter Armstrong, b. Longhope, Glos., e. Gloucester (Longhope), 300100, Pte., d. of w., F. & F., 24/8/17, formerly 203758, Norfolk Regiment.
Bradshaw, John Welch, b. St. John's, Kenilworth, Warwicks, e. Coventry, Warwicks (Kenilworth), 265706, Cpl., k. in a., F. & F., 4/10/17.
Bradshaw, Paul, b. Edgbaston, Birmingham, e. Birmingham (Handsworth, Birmingham), 268604, Pte., d. of w., F. & F., 4/10/17.
Brain, Frederick, b. Hanham, Bristol, Glos., e. Bristol (Hanham), 266903, Pte., k. in a., F. & F., 27/8/17.
Brewer, Albert Edward, e. Coventry, Warwicks, 2877, Cpl., k. in a., F. & F., 25/7/16.
Bridges, Albert, e. Birmingham, 4730, Pte., k. in a., F. & F., 14/7/16.
Briggs, Horace Henry, b. Aldwinckle, Thrapston, Northamptonshire, e. Nuneaton, Warwicks, 1941, L/Cpl., k. in a., F. & F., 26/7/16.
Brislen, John, b. St. John's, Coventry, Warwicks, e. Coventry, 2587, Pte., k. in a., F. & F., 10/5/15.
Bromage, William, b. St. Mary's, Warwick, e. Warwick (New Cubbington, Warwicks), 266522, Cpl., k. in a., F. & F., 25/7/16, formerly 1854, Warwick Yeo.
Bromhead, John, e. Birmingham, 267519, Pte., k. in a., F. & F., 17/10/17.
Brookes, Edward, b. Willenhall, Staffs, e. Coventry, Warwicks, 1168, Sgt., k. in a., F. & F., 11/5/15.
Brooks, Alfred Clarence, e. Birmingham (King's Heath, Birmingham), 4753, Pte., k. in a., F. & F., 14/7/16.
Brown, Bertram, e. Coventry, Warwicks, 266558, Pte., k. in a., F. & F., 11/8/17.
Brown, Ernest, e. Coventry, Warwicks, 265999, Sgt., k. in a., F. & F., 18/4/17.
Brown, Leonard, b. St. Mary's, Bedford, e. Bedford, 29299, Pte., k. in a., F. & F., 4/10/17, formerly 32418, Norfolk Regt.
Brown, William Henry, b. Sileby, Leics, e. Nuneaton, Warwicks, 1621, Pte., d. of w., F. & F., 22/5/16.
Bryant, William John, b. St. Andrew's, Rugby, Warwicks, e. Rugby, 308, C.S.M., k. in a., F. & F., 25/7/16.
Bull, James Albert, b. Hanham, Bristol, Glos., e. Bristol (Hanham), 300101, Pte., k. in a., F. & F., 27/8/17, formerly 7926, Norfolk Regt.
Bunney, Arthur George, e. Leamington Spa, Warwicks (Wolston, Warwicks), 266712, Pte., d. of w., F. & F., 21/4/17.
Butler, Arthur William, b. All Saints, Leamington Spa, Warwicks, e. Leamington Spa, 265323, Pte., k. in a., F. & F., 8/10/17.
Burden, Edward Harley, e. Leamington Spa, Warwicks, 2290, Pte., d. of w., F. & F., 8/11/16.
Burton, John Wathon, b. St. Mark's, Coventry, Warwicks, e. Coventry, 2416, Sgt., k. in a., F. & F., 26/6/16.
Carpenter, Francis William, e. Coventry, Warwicks, 4161, Pte., d. of w., F. & F., 28/6/16.
Carroll, John James, b. Holy Trinity, Coventry, Warwicks, e. Coventry (Foleshill, Coventry), 2039, Cpl., d. of w., F. & F., 11/5/15.

Cartwright, James, b. Smethwick, Staffs, e. Birmingham (Winson Green, Birmingham), 20451, Pte., k. in a., F. & F., 4/2/17, formerly 3432, Warwick Yeo.
Case, Charles Henry James, b. St. Phillips, Bristol, Glos, e. Bristol, 5044, Pte., k. in a., F. & F., 12/11/16.
Chambers, Edward, b. Walton, Bucks, e. Watford, Herts (Radlett, Herts), 29262, Pte., k. in a. F. & F., 27/8/17, formerly 27416, Norfolk Regt.
Chambers, George, b. St. Nicholas, Warwick, e. Coventry (Leamington Spa, Warwicks), 265487, L/Cpl., k. in a., F. & F., 15/5/18.
Chapman, Robert, b. St. Clemens, Aberdeen, e. Coventry, Warwicks (Leamington, Warwicks), 2383, Cpl., d., F. & F., 8/7/16.
Chapman, Richard Charles, b. Birmingham, e. Birmingham, 300102, Pte., k. in a., F. & F., 27/8/17, formerly 7507, Norfolk Regt.
Chattaway, George Henry, b. Bridlington, Yorks, e. Warwick (Coventry, Warwicks), 268224, Pte., k. in a., F. & F., 2/3/17, formerly 3411, Warwick Yeo.
Cleaver, Joseph Turton, e. Coventry, Warwicks, 4302, Pte., k. in a., F. & F., 1/7/16.
Clews, Leonard, b. Coventry, Warwicks, e. Coventry, 265907, Pte., k. in a., F. & F., 11/8/17.
Clowes, Reginald, b. Christ Church, Crewe, Ches., e. Rugby, Warwicks, 1402, L/Cpl., d. of w., F. & F., 2/6/15.
Coleman, Charles, e. Romford, Essex (Corsham, Wilts), 267709, Pte., d., F. & F., 15/2/17.
Collett, Albert Henry, e. Stratford-on-Avon, Warwicks, 265814, Pte., k. in a., F. & F., 15/7/16.
Collumbell, Herbert, b. Birmingham, e. Birmingham, 16/1885, Pte., d. of w., F. & F., 26/11/18.
Colwell, Lewis, e. Bristol, Glos. (Cinderford, Glos.), 5243, Pte., k. in a., F. & F., 28/8/16.
Compton, Daniel, b. St. John's, Leamington Spa, Warwicks, e. Leamington Spa, 1487, Pte., k. in a., F. & F., 14/7/16.
Cook, Ernest Charles, b. Moreton-in-the-Marsh, Glos., e. Coventry, Warwicks, 2847, Pte., k. in a., F. & F., 16/10/15.
Cooke, Irvine, b. Bristol, Glos., e. Newport, Mon. (Bristol), 265430, Sgt., k. in a., F. & F., 4/10/17, formerly 1860, Mon. Regt.
Cooke, William Frederick, b. St. Steven's, Hounslow, Middx., e. Coventry, Warwicks, 2409, Pte., k. in a., F. & F., 17/3/16.
Copson, Jonathan, e. Coventry, Warwicks (Exhall, Coventry), 4242, Pte., d. of w., F. & F., 31/7/16.
Corbett, Ernest, b. Brentwood, Lichfield, Staffs, e. Nuneaton, Warwicks (Attleborough, Nuneaton), 1943, Pte., k. in a., F. & F., 9/5/15.
Core, Cecil John, b. Dulwich, Middx., e. Camberwell, Middx. (Dulwich), 34023, Pte., d. of w., F. & F., 8/10/17, formerly 202196, E. Kent Regt.
Cosford, Alfred, e. Huntingdon (Kettering, Northamptonshire), 20757, Pte., k. in a., F. & F., 21/8/16, formerly 1375, Hunts. Cyclist Battn.
Cox, Lawrence Cecil, e. Coventry, Warwicks, 4515, Pte., k. in a., F. & F., 14/7/16.
Crawley, John Patrick, e. Rotherhithe, London, S.E. (Bermondsey, S.E.16), 300013, Pte., k. in a., F. & F., 28/8/17, formerly 6056, R. Fus.
Crick, Harold Ernest, e. Huntingdon (Kettering, Northamptonshire), 268502, Pte., k. in a., F. & F., 16/6/18, formerly 1503, Hunts Cyclist Battn.
Crutchlow, William Joseph, b. Coventry, Warwicks, e. Coventry, 266116, Pte., k. in a., F. & F., 8/10/17.
Cuff, Charles Leonard, e. Blandford, Dorset, 6568, Pte., d. of w., F. & F., 18/12/16.
Cunnington, William, b. Fletton, Northants, e. Fletton (Old Fletton), 268476, Pte., k. in a., F. & F., 11/8/17, formerly 74, Hunts Cyclist Battn.
Cusling, Charles, b. St. Phillip's, Norwich, e. Norwich, 29302, Pte., k. in a., F. & F., 8/10/17.
Dadge, Albert Oliver, e. Birmingham, 4894, Pte., k. in a., F. & F., 26/7/16.
Darvill, Ernest William, e. Coventry, 4537, Pte., k. in a., F. & F., 27/11/16.
Davies, Charles William, b. Milverton, Warwick, e. Coventry (Nuneaton, Warwicks), 265455, Sgt., k. in a., F. & F., 27/8/17.
Dawson, John, e. Cowie, Stirling (Fallinby, Stirling), 267220, Pte., k. in a., F. & F., 14/8/17, formerly 5603, H. Cyc. Battn.
Deakin, Benjamin, b. Baddesley, Warwicks, e. Nuneaton, Warwicks (Atherstone, Warwicks), 2788, Pte., k. in a., F. & F., 8/10/17.
Denny, Walter, e. Coventry, 4531, Pte., k. in a., F. & F., 14/7/16.
Dever, John, b. Westport, Co. Mayo, e. Coventry, 265465, Pte., k. in a., F. & F., 27/8/17.
Dickenson, Henry, b. Evesham, Worcs, e. Wootton-under-Edge, Worcs (Charfield, Glos.), 267023, Pte., k. in a., F. & F., 8/10/17.
Dockerill, James, b. Warboys, Hunts, e. Warboys, 268478, Pte., k. in a., F. & F., 27/8/17, formerly 191, Hunts Cyc. Battn.
Dowswell, Herbert, e. Coventry, 4504, Pte., k. in a., F. & F., 14/7/16.
Drake, John James, e. Leamington, Warwicks, 4669, Pte., k. in a., F. & F., 14/7/16.
Dransfield, Clifford, b. Lees, Lancs, e. Oldham, Lancs (Lees), 54528, Pte., d., F. & F., 28/1/19, formerly 14381, Manchester Regt.
Duckett, Ernest, e. Birmingham (Ladywood, Birmingham), 4762, Pte., d. of w., F. & F., 12/8/16.
Duckett, Jesse, b. St. Nicholas, Nuneaton, Warwicks, e. Nuneaton, 2275, Pte., k. in a., F. & F., 29/4/15.
Dunn, Thomas William, b. South Shields, Northumberland, e. Coventry, 265603, Pte., d. of w., F. & F., 5/10/17.
Durrant, Sidney, e. Huntingdon (Kettering, Northants), 20758, Pte., k. in a., F. & F., 19/8/16, formerly 1431, Hunts Cyc. Battn.
Eagles, Alfred Samuel, e. Coventry (Birmingham), 4435, Pte., k. in a., F. & F., 14/7/16.
Eardley, John William, b. Coventry, e. Coventry, 266713, Pte., k. in a., F. & F., 14/7/16.
Earl, Joseph, e. Warwick (Small Heath, Birmingham), 20522, Pte., k. in a., F. & F., 8/10/17.
Eaves, Harold, b. Coventry, e. Coventry, 1778, Pte., k. in a., F. & F., 14/7/16.
Edwards, Herbert Alfred, b. Witley, Surrey, e. Godalming, Surrey, 33559, Pte., d., F. & F., 26/12/18, formerly 18923, R.F.C.
Eldridge, Albert, b. Langton, Kent, e. Maidstone, Kent, 300023, Pte., k. in a., F. & F., 4/10/17, formerly 6480, R.W. Kent Regt., and 201739, Norfolk Regt.
Elliman, Percy, b. Stoke, Coventry, e. Coventry, 2532, Pte., k. in a., F. & F., 14/7/16.
Ellis, Bertie, e. Stratford-on-Avon, Warwicks (Tiddington, Warwicks), 265989, Pte., d., F. & F., 5/2/18
Etteridge, Robert William, b. Attleborough, Norfolk, e. Norwich Norfolk (Attleborough), 300025, Pte., k. in a., F. & F., 4/10/17, formerly 2700, Norfolk Regt.
Evans, Harry, b. Birmingham, e. Birmingham (Small Heath, Birmingham), 33541, Pte., k. in a., F. & F., 16/6/18, formerly M/301281, R.A.S.C.
Faragher, John, b. St. John's, I. of M., e. Coventry, 3898, Pte., k. in a., F. & F., 14/7/16.
Fardon, Arthur, b. St. Mark's, Coventry, e. Coventry, 2568, Pte., k. in a., F. & F., 14/7/16.
Faulks, Leonard, e. Coventry, 3261, Pte., k. in a., F. & F., 11/11/16.
Fellows, Thomas, e. Birmingham, 4783, Pte., k. in a., F. & F., 4/8/16.
Feltham, William Henry, b. St. Michael's, Coventry, e. Coventry, 2443, Pte., k. in a., F. & F., 6/9/15.
Fidler, William George, b. Harborough Magna, Warwicks, e. Rugby (Harborough Magna), 1797, Pte., d., F. & F., 7/3/16.
Field, David, b. St. Nicholas, Warwick, e. Warwick, 267126, C.S.M., d., F. & F., 8/8/18.
Field, Harry, e. Birmingham, 266756, Pte., k. in a., F. & F., 22/8/17.
Finch, William Samuel, e. Marazion, Cornwall, e. Long Rock, Cornwall, 6575, Pte., d., F. & F., 3/2/17.
Ford, William, e. Coventry, 4852, Pte., k. in a., F. & F., 25/7/16.
Forder, John Edwin, e. Coventry (Coombe, Warwicks), 4447, Pte., d. of w., F. & F., 31/7/16.
Fothergill, William Alfred, b. Millwall, Middx., e. Rugby, Warwicks (New Bilton, Warwicks), 2020, Pte., k. in a., F. & F., 28/8/16.
Frazer, Ernest, b. Kenilworth, Warwicks, e. Kenilworth, 265270, Pte., k. in a., F. & F., 27/8/17.
Freeman, George Matthew, e. Huntingdon, 268546, Pte., k. in a., F. & F., 22/8/17, formerly 1490, Hunts Cyc. Battn.
Frisby, Edward Hedley, b. Melton Mowbray, Leics, e. Coventry (Radford, Coventry), 4338, Pte., d. of w., F. & F., 1/9/16.
Frost, Sidney Albert, b. St. Pancras, Middx., e. Holborn, Middx., 34026, Pte., k. in a., F. & F., 4/10/17, formerly 202118, E. Kent Regt.
Fuller, Walter George, b. St. Ives, Hunts, e. St. Ives, 268512, Pte., k. in a., F. & F., 27/8/17, formerly 124, Hunts Cyc. Battn.
Gaisford, William, b. Fisherson, Wilts, e. Coventry (Salisbury), 2516, Pte., k. in a., F. & F., 20/8/16.
Gardner, Henry Victor, b. Kenilworth, Warwicks, e. Kenilworth, 2025, Cpl., k. in a., F. & F., 18/8/16.
Gardner, Thomas, b. Grantham, Lincs, e. Coventry, 2510, Pte., d. of w., F. & F., 25/7/16.
Gardner, William, b. All Saints, Leamington, e. Leamington, Warwicks, 265317, Pte., k. in a., F. & F., 25/10/17.
Garner, Arthur Cecil, b. Warwick, e. Aston, Birmingham, 306119, Pte., k. in a., F. & F., 16/8/18, formerly 63646, R.D.C.
Garner, Harold, b. St. Helens, Lancs, e. St. Helens, 268265, Pte., k. in a., F. & F., 21/8/17, formerly 3659, R.E.
Gay, Frank, b. Banbury, Oxon, e. Birmingham, 268599, Pte., k. in a., F. & F., 21/8/17.
Gayton, Frank, b. Stoke, Coventry, e. Coventry, 265499, Pte., k. in a., F. & F., 14/7/16.
Gee, John, b. Washingley, Hunts, e. Fletton, Hunts (Washingley), 268526, L/Cpl., d. of w., F. & F., 4/3/17, formerly 388, Hunts Cyclist Battn.
Gilchrist, George, b. Kilmarnock, Ayrshire, e. Glasgow (Kilmarnock), 268270, Pte., k. in a., F. & F., 4/10/17, formerly 5386, H.L.I.
Gilliver, Ernest, e. Coventry, Warwicks (Nuneaton, Warwicks), 3203, Pte., k. in a., F. & F., 14/7/16.
Gitsom, Frederick Oliver, e. Bristol, 267022, Pte., k. in a., F. & F., 22/8/17.
Glenn, Percy, b. Peterborough, Northants, e. Fletton, Northants (Peterborough), 268520, Pte., k. in a., F. & F., 27/8/17, formerly 382, Hunts Cyclist Battn.
Goakes, Albert, b. Ramsey, Hunts, e. Huntingdon (Newtown, Ramsey), 268533, Pte., d., F. & F., 29/10/18, formerly 908, Hunts Cyclist Battn.
Godfrey, Thomas Joseph, b. St. Paul's, Leamington, Warwicks, e. Leamington 1651, Pte., k. in a. F. & F., 26/7/16.
Gray, Ernest William, e. Huntingdon (Hull), 20821, Pte., k. in a., F. & F., 28/8/16, formerly 1585, Hunts Cyclist Battn.
Green, Frederick Joseph Lee, b. Hapton, Norfolk, e. Norwich, 29314, Sgt., k. in a., F. & F., 28/8/17, formerly 7531, Norfolk Regt.

Green, William Robert, b. Birmingham, e. Birmingham (Ladywood, Birmingham), 266883, Pte., d. of w., F. & F., 16/6/18.
Greengrass, William, e. Coventry, Warwicks, 4525, Pte., k. in a. F. & F., 14/7/16.
Gunn, Henry Edwin, b. Coventry, Warwicks, e. Coventry, 265749, Pte., d. of w., F. & F., 26/6/18.
Hall, Albert, b. Hartford, Hunts, e. Huntingdon (Hartford), 20707, Pte., k. in a., F. & F., 11/11/16, formerly 868, Hunts Cyclist Battn.
Hammond, Ralph Edward, e. Stratford-on-Avon, Warwicks, 3402, Pte., k. in a., F. & F., 14/7/16.
Harber, Wentworth, b. Redditch, Worcs, e. Birmingham (Redditch), 268608, Pte., k. in a., F. & F., 16/6/18.
Harborne, Walter, e. Coventry, Warwicks, 4495, Pte., k. in a., F. & F., 1/7/16.
Harris, Douglas Walter, b. Peckham, Surrey, e. Camberwell, Surrey (Peckham), 34049, Pte., d. of w., F. & F., 8/10/17, formerly 202205, E. Kent Regt.
Harrison, William, b. Solihull, Warwicks, e. Birmingham (Solihull), 2190, Cpl., d. of w., F. & F., 10/6/15.
Hatfield, Harry Walter, b. Marston, St. Lawrence, Oxon, e. King's Lynn, Norfolk (Todmorton, Oxon), 303022, Pte., d., Egypt, 2/6/19, formerly 3176, Q.O. Ox. Hrs.
Hathaway, Albert Frederick, b. St. Paul's, Coventry, Warwicks, e. Coventry, 1937, Pte., k. in a., F. & F., 3/4/16.
Hatton, Alfred, e. Coventry, Warwicks, 4512, Pte., d. of w., F. & F., 3/9/16.
Hawker, Fred, e. Tewkesbury, Glos., 266938, Pte., k. in a., F. & F., 16/8/17.
Hawkes, Walter, b. Birmingham, e. Birmingham (Saltley, Birmingham), 300115, Pte., k. in a., F. & F., 8/10/17, formerly 7721, Norfolk Regt.
Hayes, George Hinde, b. Brinklow, Warwicks, e. Rugby, Warwicks, 265385, C.S.M., d. of w., F. & F., 10/10/17, M.C.
Hebblewhite, Edward, b. Thulby, Lincs, e. Coventry, Warwicks, 1810, Pte., k. in a., F. & F., 14/7/16, M.M.
Henton, Wilfred, b. Mexborough, Yorks, e. Coventry, Warwicks (Longford, Coventry), 266863, Pte., k. in a., F. & F., 3/11/18.
Hewitt, William Henry, b. Coventry, Warwicks, e. Coventry, 2553, Pte., k. in a., F. & F., 25/7/16.
Hextall, Harold Jarvis, b. Nuneaton, Warwicks, e. Nuneaton, 1118, Sgt., d. of w., F. & F., 24/8/16.
Hill, Fred, e. Huntingdon (Brampton, Hunts), 20798, Pte., k. in a., F. & F., 19/8/16, formerly 681, Hunts. Cyclist Batt.
Hill, Lewis Henry, b. Newbold-on-Avon, Warwicks, e. Rugby, Warwicks, 1932, Pte., k. in a., F. & F., 28/5/15.
Hindle, William, e. Chorley, Lancs, 202501, L/Cpl., k. in a., F. & F., 8/10/17, formerly 3656, N. Lanc. Regt.
Hitch, Walter, b. St. John's, Peterborough, Northants, e. Fletton, Northants (Peterborough), 20772, Pte., k. in a., F. & F., 21/8/16, formerly 91, Bedford Regt.
Hobbs, Tom, e. Huntingdon (Ramsay, Hunts), 20802, Pte., k. in a., F. & F., 28/8/16, formerly 946, Hunts Cyclist Battn.
Hobbs, Walter Rueben, b. St. John's, Coventry, Warwicks, e. Coventry, 2632, Pte., d. of w., F. & F. 15/5/15.
Hogan, Thomas, e. Coventry, 4458, Pte., k. in a., F. & F., 26/7/16.
Hollins, Frederick, b. All Saints, Leamington, Warwicks, e. Leamington, 1523, Pte., d. of w., F. & F., 25/6/16.
Hopkins, Harold, e. Coventry, Warwicks (New Bilton, Warwicks), 4345, Pte., k. in a., F. & F., 14/7/16.
Horton, William Henry, b. Holy Trinity, Coventry, Warwicks, e. Coventry, 2309, Pte., k. in a., F. & F., 14/7/16, M.M.
Houghton, William Thomas, b. Rugby, Warwicks, e. Rugby, 202847, Pte., d. of w., F. & F., 4/10/17.
Houghton Victor, e. Coventry, Warwicks, 3075, Pte., k. in a., F. & F., 14/7/16.
Howes, Arthur Roland, b. Moulton, Norfolk, e. Norwich, 29255, Pte., k. in a., F. & F., 8/10/17, formerly 27461, Norfolk Regt.
Hubbard, Herbert, b. Necton, Norfolk, e. Coventry, Warwicks, 2447, Cpl., k. in a., F. & F. 28/6/16.
Huey, William, b. Carncullugh, Dervock, Co. Antrim, e. Belfast (Carncullugh), 33483, Pte., k. in a., F. & F., 3/8/18, formerly M2/224557, R.A.S.C.
Hughes, John William George, b. Kings Newnham, Warwicks, e. Rugby, Warwicks, 2006, L/Cpl., k. in a., F. & F., 18/6/15.
Hughes, Thomas William, e. Coventry, Warwicks (Foleshill, Warwicks), 4244, Pte., d. of w., F. & F., 1/4/16.
Hulett, Percival Charles Eaton, b. Clapham, Surrey, e. Hitchin, Herts, 34032, L/Cpl., k. in a., F. & F., 16/6/18, formerly 202661, E. Kent Regt.
Humpage, Arthur, b. Dudley, Staffs, e. Coventry, Warwicks, 2113, Pte., k. in a., F. & F., 17/2/16.
Hunt, Francis William, e. Coventry, Warwicks, 266873, Pte., k. in a., F. & F., 28/8/17.
Hunt, Philip, b. Pershore, Worcs, e. Pershore, 27767, Pte., d. of w., F. & F., 8/10/17, formerly 4881, Worc. Regt.
Hunt, William George, b. Kettering, Northants, e. Coventry, Warwicks, 1571, Sgt., k. in a., F. & F., 14/7/16.
Hurdley, George Harold, b. Broseley, Salop, e. Coventry, Warwicks, 268853, Pte., k. in a., F. & F., 4/10/17.
Hurt, Alfred Thomas, b. Marylebone, London, e. London (South Hampstead, London), 29312, Pte., k. in a., F. & F., 27/8/17, formerly 2980, A.P. Corps.
Hutchings, Leslie, e. Coventry, Warwicks, 3175, Pte., k. in a., F. & F., 25/6/15.
Iliff, Edward George, b. Dunchurch, Warwicks, e. Rugby, Warwicks (Dunchurch), 927, Cpl., k. in a., F. & F., 26/7/16.
Ireland, Edward, b. Coventry, Warwicks, e. Coventry, 266604, Pte., k. in a., F. & F., 13/8/17.
Jackson, Rex, b. St. Mary's, Warwick, e. Warwick, 242838, Sgt., d., F. & F., 8/8/18.
James, Alfred, b. Woodhouse, Yorks, e. Coventry, Warwicks (Hull), 2329, L/Cpl., d. of w. F. & F., 4/12/15.
Jeanes, George Edward Francis, b. Stoke Line, Oxon, e. Birmingham (Sutton Coldfield, Warwicks), 268201, Pte., k. in a., F. & F., 2/3/17, formerly 3336, Warwicks Yeo.
Jeffs, Albert, b. St. John's, Coventry, Warwicks, e. Coventry, 2626, Pte., k. in a., F. & F., 14/7/16.
Jennings, Walter, e. Coventry, Warwicks, 4522, Pte., k. in a., F. & F., 1/7/16.
Johnson, John Robert, b. St. Mary's, Ramsey, Hunts, e. Huntingdon (Ramsey), 29254, Pte., k. in a., F. & F., 8/10/17.
Johnson, Thomas Frederick, b. Atherstone, Warwicks, e. Rugby, Warwicks, 751, Cpl., k. in a., F. & F., 9/5/15.
Jones, Harold Randall, e. Leamington, Warwicks, 3843, Pte., k. in a., F. & F., 24/6/16.
Jones, Tudor Stanley, e. Bristol (Cheltenham, Glos.), 5115, Pte., k. in a., F. & F., 23/11/16.
Jones, William Henry, e. Coventry, 3068, Pte., k. in a., F. & F., 14/7/16.
Jones, William Henry, e. Coventry, 4367, Pte., k. in a., F. & F., 24/6/16.
Jones, William James, b. Bloxwich, Staffs, e. Nuneaton, Warwicks. (Stockingford, Warwicks), 265311, Pte., k. in a., F. & F., 29/8/17.
Jukes, William, e. Birmingham (Balsall Heath, Birmingham), 4816, Pte., d. of w., F. & F., 31/8/16.
Keefe, Frederick Richard, b. All Saints, Coventry, e. Coventry, 3936, Pte., d. of w., F. & F., 22/8/16.
Kenney, Richard, b. Brinklow, Warwicks, e. Coventry (Brinklow), 2096, Sgt., k. in a., F. & F., 14/7/16.
Kimberley, Reuben, e. Coventry (Bedworth, Warwicks.), 4303, Pte., k. in a., F. & F., 1/7/16.
King, James Herbert, b. Hadley, Suff., e. Hammersmith, London (West Kensington, London), 300116, Pte., k. in a., F. & F., 13/8/17, formerly 4232, East Surrey Regt.
Lapworth, Bernard William, b. St. Mary's, Nuneaton, e. Nuneaton, Warwicks, 1620, Pte., k. in a., F. & F., 30/6/16.
Lapworth, Cecil, b. Chilvers Coton, Warwicks, e. Nuneaton, Warwicks., 849, L/Cpl., d. of w., F. & F., 18/12/15.
Lawrence, Walter, e. Birmingham, 4727, Pte., d. of w., F. & F., 5/8/16.
Lawrence, Walter Joseph, e. Leamington, Warwicks. (Warwick), 2921, Pte, d., F. & F., 5/12/15.
Leake, William James, e. Nuneaton, Warwicks (Castle Bromwich, nr. Birmingham), 266831, Pte., k. in a., F. & F., 24/6/17.
Lee, William, e. Coventry (Stoneleigh, Warwicks.), 266050, Pte., k. in a., F. & F., 27/8/17.
Lee, William, e. Coventry, 4243, Pte., d. of w., F. & F., 29/7/16.
Linforth, John Richard, b. Birmingham, e. Birmingham, 267465, Pte., k. in a., F. & F., 16/6/18.
Lloyd, Harry, e. Coventry, 2965, Pte., k. in a., F. & F., 25/7/16.
Loone, George, e. Birmingham, 266807, Pte., k. in a., F. & F., 16/8/17.
Louvel, Theodore, b. Norwood, Surrey, e. Kingston-on-Thames, Surrey (South Norwood), 29294, Pte., k. in a., F. & F., 21/8/17.
Lowe, Henry Arthur, e. Coventry, 266861, Pte., d. of w., F. & F., 12/8/17.
Lucas, Bertie, b. St. Michael's, Coventry, e. Coventry, 265476, C.S.M., k in a., F. & F., 11/8/17.
Lucas, Frederick, b. St. John's. Coventry, e. Coventry, 2595, L/Cpl., k. in a., F. & F., 14/7/16.
Ludford, Lawrence, b. Greyfriars, Coventry, e. Coventry, 2646, Pte., k. in a., F. & F., 14/7/16.
Lugg, Henry, b. St. Ives, Cornwall, e. Hayle, Cornwall (St. Ives), 300319, Pte., k. in a., F. & F., 29/9/17, formerly 202868, Duke of Cornwall's L.I.
McLean, Thomas Wright, e. Rutherglen, Glasgow (Bridgeton, Glasgow), 268242, Pte., k. in a., F. & F., 22/8/17, formerly 1150, R.E.
McLeod, Charles Frederick, e. Warwick (Leamington, Warwicks.), 4956, Pte., k. in a., F. & F., 18/8/16.
McLuckie, John Robertson, b. Troon, Ayrshire, e. Birmingham (Aston, Birmingham), 241262, Pte., d., F. & F., 27/12/17.
MacNamara, Charles Henry, e. Coventry, 27022, Pte., d. of w., F. & F., 27/8/17.
Manders, Arthur, e. Birmingham, 201057, Pte., k. in a., F. & F., 4/10/17.
Marchant, Henry John, e. Stratford-on-Avon, Warwicks., e. Stratford-on-Avon, 3237, Pte., k. in a., F. & F., 19/6/15.
Marshall, Arthur Sidney, b. Burley, Yorks, e. Coventry, 1634, Pte., d. of w., F. & F., 19/7/16.
Martin, Albert, e. Coventry, 265877, Pte., k. in a, F. & F., 14/7/16.
Matthews, Bertram, e. Birmingham, 5203, Pte., k. in a., F. & F., 21/8/16.
Maynard, Alfred, e. Stratford-on-Avon, Warwicks., 266093, Pte., k. in a., F. & F., 8/10/17.
Mence, Frederick Henry, b. Coventry, e. Coventry, 1802, Pte., k. in a., F. & F., 8/10/15.
Merriman, Frank, b. Rowington, Warwicks., e. Birmingham (Rowington), 25040, Pte., k. in a., F. & F., 14/8/17.
Metcalfe, Harry John, b. St. Peter's, Coventry, e. Coventry, 2543, L/Cpl., k. in a., F. & F., 12/9/15.
Miles, Percy Henry, b. St. Thomas, Coventry, e. Coventry, 265525, Cpl., k. in a., F. & F., 22/8/17.
Miles, Reginald Harry, e. Oxford (Highfield, Oxford), 266890, Pte., k. in a., F. & F., 27/3/17.

Miller, Osborne, e. Atherstone, Warwicks., 266791, Pte., k. in a., F. & F., 2/3/17.
Miller, Vincent, b. Longsight, Manchester, e. Manchester (West Gorton, Manchester), 306949, Pte., k. in a., F. & F., 8/10/17, formerly 2019, Manchester Regt.
Mills, Harry, e. Oldbury, Staffs, 267056, Pte., k. in a., F. & F., 19/6/17.
Morfett, Harry, b. Peckham, London, e. Coventry, 1885, Pte., d. of w., F. & F., 4/6/16.
Morris, Leonard, b. St. Michaels, Coventry, e. Coventry, 1754, L/Cpl., k. in a., F. & F., 14/7/16.
Morris, Thomas, e. Coventry, 266046, Pte., k. in a., F. & F., 27/3/17
Morritt, Richard Francis, b. Liversedge, Yorks, e. Dudley, Worcs., 266912, Pte., k. in a., F. & F., 8/10/17.
Murray, Patrick, b. Motherwell, Lanark, e. Hamilton (Motherwell), 268225, Pte., k. in a., F. & F., 20/4/17, formerly 52646, R.E.
Naseby, Thomas, b. Bow, Middx., e. East Ham, Essex, 34004, Pte., k. in a., F. & F., 8/10/17, formerly 202006, East Kent Regt.
Nash, Harold Whitehouse, b. Aston, Birmingham, e. Coventry (Leamington, Warwicks.), 265710, Pte., k. in a., F. & F., 18/4/17.
Nash, Thomas, e. Stourbridge, Worcs., 266921, Pte., d. of w., F. & F., 7/3/17.
Naylor, Joseph, e. Warwick (Ashbourne, Derby), 5000, Pte., k. in a., F. & F., 25/7/16.
Neale, Arthur, b. Kidderminster, Worcs, e. Worcester (Kidderminster), 266948, Pte., d., F. & F., 21/10/18.
Newcombe, Christopher, b. Foleshill, Coventry, e. Coventry, 2091, Pte., k. in a., F. & F., 14/7/16.
Newman, John Charles, e. Coventry, 265785, Pte., k. in a., F. & F., 27/8/17.
Norris, William Charles, b. Camberwell, London, e. Coventry, 265566, L/Sgt., d. of w., F. & F., 16/6/18, M.M.
North, Harry, b. Wimbdlen, Soms., e. Exeter, Devon (Taunton, Som.), 34675, L/Cpl., d., F. & F., 14/2/19, formerly 35306, R.A.S.C.
Osborne, Harold Colin Jesse, b. Worcester, e. Coventry, 4540, Pte., k. in a., F. & F., 4/6/16.
Page, Cyril Morson, b. Bedworth, Warwicks, e. Nuneaton, Warwicks, 1622, Cpl., k. in a., F. & F., 15/7/16. M.M.
Pagett, Harry, b. St. Peter's, Coventry, e. Coventry, 2529, Pte., k. in a., F. & F., 2/7/16.
Palmer, William, b. St. Philip's, Bristol, e. Coventry, 1862, Pte., d. of w., F. & F., 29/9/16.
Parker, Ernest Arthur Edward, e. Coventry, 266551, Pte., k. in a., F. & F., 27/8/17.
Parker, Harold Thomas, b. Coventry, e. Coventry, 265491, L/Cpl., k. in a., F. & F., 23/9/18.
Parratt, Lewis, b. Farnham, Surrey, e. Rye, Sussex (Mecclesham, Surrey), 44055, Pte., d., F. & F., 13/7/19, formerly 4068, R. Sussex Regt.
Parriss, George Valentine, e. Stratford-on-Avon, Warwicks (Welford-on-Avon, Glos.), 266961, L/Cpl., k. in a., F. & F., 22/8/17.
Parrock, Alfred, e. Worcester (Woolescote, Worcs.), 266947, Pte., k. in a., F. & F., 4/10/17.
Pentecost, Frederick, b. Otham, Kent, e. Maidstone, Kent (Maidstone), 300120, Pte., k. in a., F. & F., 29/9/18, formerly G/11731, R.W. Kent Regt.
Perks, George Henry, e. Bromsgrove, Worcs. (Sidmoor, Worcs.), 266917, Pte., k. in a., F. & F., 27/8/17.
Perry, Albert George, e. Bristol, 267016, Pte., k. in a., F. & F., 27/8/17.
Pettitt, Horace, b. West Dereham, Norfolk, e. Downham Market, Norfolk (Dereham), 33072, Pte., d. of w., F. & F., 10/10/17, formerly 201230, Norfolk Regt.
Phillips, Thomas, b. Birmingham, e. Birmingham (Handsworth, Staffs), 268206, Pte., k. in a., F. & F., 4/10/17, formerly 3504, Warwicks Yeo.
Philpott, Martin, e Coventry, Warwicks (Nuneaton, Warwicks), 265973, Pte., k. in a., F. & F., 3/3/17.
Pickering, Henry, e. Birmingham (Ladywood, Birmingham), 4709, Pte., k. in a., F. & F., 14/7/16.
Piggott, Albert, e. Coventry, Warwicks, 3269, Pte., k. in a., F. & F., 25/6/15.
Postle, Cecil, b. Burlingham, Norfolk, e. Norwich (Newton Flotman, Norfolk), 300074, Pte., k. in a., F. & F., 4/10/17, formerly 6197, Norfolk Regt.
Potter, Alfred Higham, b. Shrewsbury, Salop, e. Leamington, Warwicks (Shrewsbury), 470, Sgt., k. in a., F. & F., 19/7/16.
Preedy, Herbert, b. St. Paul's, Cheltenham, Glos., e. Warwick, 265768, C.Q.M.S., d. of w., F. & F., 21/3/18.
Price, Ernest, e. Coventry, Warwicks, 266540, Pte., k. in a., F. & F., 13/8/17.
Prince, John, b. St. Clement's, Salford, Lancs, e. Salford (Lower Broughton, Lancs), 6280, Pte., k. in a., F. & F., 25/8/16.
Reddington, John, b. Coventry, Warwicks, e. Coventry, 1828, Sgt., d. of w., F. & F., 18/7/16.
Reeve, Thomas Bertie, b. Stediham, Norfolk, e. Wroxham, Norfolk (Kirstead Brooke, Norfolk), 29281, Pte., k. in a., F. & F., 28/8/17, formerly 27355, Norfolk Regt.
Reeves, Alfred, e. Warwick (Kenilworth, Warwicks), 4733, Pte., k. in a., F. & F., 25/7/16.
Revell, Thomas Edgar, b. Herne Bay, Kent, e. Canterbury, Kent (Herne Bay), 300272, Pte., k. in a., F. & F., 4/10/17, formerly 4554, E. Kent Regt.
Robinson, Sidney Herbert, b. St. Mark's, Coventry, Warwicks, e. Coventry, 265613, Pte., d., F. & F., 30/7/18.
Roddy, Harry, b. Coventry, Warwicks, e. Coventry, 3770, Pte., k. in a., F. & F., 14/10/16.
Rolfe, Frederick, b. St. Giles, Reading, Berks, e. Reading, 300057, Pte., k. in a., F. & F., 27/8/17, formerly 2543, R. Berks Regt.
Rollason, William Thomas, e. Coventry, 4908, Pte., k. in a., F. & F., 20/8/16.
Round, Howard, b. Hollyhall, Worcs., e. Coventry, Warwicks, 2404, Pte., k. in a., F. & F., 25/7/16.
Rowe, Bertram Thomas, b. Coventry, Warwicks, e. Coventry, 206599, Pte., k. in a., F. & F., 8/10/17.
Russell, Thomas, b. Edinburgh, e. Edinburgh (Stockbridge, Edinburgh), 268245, Pte., k. in a., F. & F., 28/8/17, formerly 7145, R.E.
Sadler, Robert, b. Hardley, Norfolk, e. Harleston, Norfolk (Alburgh, Norfolk), 300093, Pte., k. in a., F. & F., 27/8/17, formerly 2906, Norfolk Regt.
Sanigar, Frederick Thomas John, e. Bristol, 5062, Pte., k. in a., F. & F., 22/8/18.
Saunders, Arthur Edward, b. Strood, Kent, e. Rochester, Kent (Strood), 300076, Pte., k. in a., F. & F., 27/8/17, formerly 6527, R.W. Kent Regt.
Savage, Alfred Victor, e. Worcester, 267072, Pte., k. in a., F. & F., 27/8/17.
Scott, John, b. Mereworth, Kent, e. Maidstone, Kent, 300039, Pte., k. in a., F. & F., 22/8/17, formerly 12753, R.W. Kent Regt.
Scott, Thomas Henry, b. Stoke Lacey, Hereford, e. Worcester, 268843, Pte., k. in a., F. & F., 8/10/17.
Searle, Ernest Thomas, e. Bristol, 268029, Pte., k. in a., F. & F., 22/8/17, formerly 30481, Glos. Regt.
Shergold, James Ernest, b. Aston, Birmingham, e. Coventry, Warwicks, 203568, Pte., k. in a., F. & F., 4/10/17.
Sheward, William Charles, e. Coventry, Warwicks, 4424, Pte., k. in a., F. & F., 14/10/16.
Shrapnell, Percy, e. Trowbridge, Wilts, 306640, Pte., k. in a., F. & F., 16/6/18.
Sidwell, William Harry, b. St. Paul's, Warwick, e. Warwick, 1343, Pte., k. in a., F & F., 18/5/15.
Simmons, William, b. Coventry, Warwicks, e. Coventry, 2567, Pte., k. in a., F. & F., 23/6/15.
Simpson, Frederick, e. Coventry, Warwicks (Foleshill, Coventry), 266371, Pte., k. in a., F. & F., 8/10/17.
Sims, William, b. Heston, Middx., e. Teddington, Middx. (Hampton, Middx.), 34003, Pte., d. of w., F. & F., 23/9/18, formerly 203275, E. Kent Regt.
Skidmore, Frederick George, e. Coventry, Warwicks (Berkswell, Coventry), 266850, Pte., d. of w., F. & F., 22/8/17.
Skitmore, Walter Charles, b. Little Ettingham, Norfolk, e. Attleborough, Norfolk, 34046, Pte., d., F. & F., 8/3/18, formerly 202667, E. Kent Regt.
Slade, Albert James, e. Rugby, Warwicks (Aylesbury, Bucks), 3067, Pte., k. in a., F. & F., 28/8/16.
Smith, Enoch, e. Birmingham (Marston Green, Warwicks), 4865, Pte., k. in a., F. & F., 25/7/16.
Smith, Percival James, b. Newton Abbot, Som., e. Coventry, Warwicks, 265402, Pte., d., F. & F., 7/3/17.
Smith, Reginald, b. Baxterley, Warwicks, e. Warwick (Mancetter, Warwicks), 34759, Pte., k. in a., F. & F., 16/6/18.
Smith, William, e. Lincoln, 27026, Pte., k. in a., F. & F., 27/8/17, formerly 5594, Lincs Regt.
Smithies, Joshua, b. Withnell, Lancs, e. Chorley, Lancs (Wheelton, Lancs), 268227, Pte., k. in a., F. & F., 20/4/17, formerly 127287, R.E.
Snell, Albert, e. Birmingham (Sparkhill, Birmingham), 266842, Pte., d. of w., F. & F., 30/8/17.
Snow, Charles Richard, e. Coventry, Warwicks, 266577, Pte., d. of w., F. & F., 14/8/17.
South, Frederick Henry, e. Stratford-on-Avon, Warwicks, 206091, Pte., k. in a., F. & F., 4/10/17.
Spencer, James Thomas, b. St. Mark's, Coventry, Warwicks, Coventry, 2610, L/Cpl., k. in a., F. & F., 1/7/16.
Spencer, William Edward, b. Winchester, Hants., e. Coventry, Warwicks, 2191, Pte., k. in a., F. & F., 26/6/16.
Springall, Arthur Charles, b. Halvergate, Norwich, e. Norwich (Halvergate), 300042, Pte., k. in a., F. & F., 27/8/17, formerly 201844, Norfolk Regt.
Stevens, Stephen Ward, b. Burham, Kent, e. Tunbridge Wells, Kent (Pembury, Kent), 300078, Pte., k. in a., F. & F., 22/8/17, formerly 12102, R.W. Kent Regt.
Stock, George, e. Warwick, 1424, Sgt., k. in a., F. & F., 7/5/15.
Stollery, Edgar Musk, b. Stratford-on-Avon, Warwicks, e. Stratford-on-Avon, 18237, Pte., k. in a., F. & F., 27/8/17.
Stone, Cecil Edward, b. Southam, Warwicks, e. Leamington, Warwicks, 265101, Pte., k. in a., F. & F., 5/10/17.
Stone, Herbert Edward, b. Earl Soham, Suffolk, e. Ipswich, Suffolk (Swefling, Suffolk), 29283, Pte., k. in a., F. & F., 8/10/17, formerly 27409, Norfolk Regt.
Swann, Albert Edward, b. Hadstock, Essex, e. Luton, Beds., 34011, Pte., k. in a., F. & F., 4/10/17, formerly 202635, E. Kent Regt
Swingler, Percy, b. Stanton, Northants., e. Coventry, Warwicks, 268854, Pte., k. in a., F. & F., 8/10/17.
Talbot, William Henry, b. St. Pauls, Warwick, e. Warwick, 267106, Sgt., k. in a., F. & F., 27/8/17.
Taylor, Jack, b. Warwick, e. Warwick, 1518, Pte., k. in a., F. & F., 14/7/16.
Taylor, Thomas, b. Trinity, Coventry, e. Coventry, Warwicks, 2598, Cpl., k. in a., F. & F., 14/7/16.
Taylor, William Albert, b. All Saints, Coventry, Warwicks, e. Coventry, 2386, Sgt., k. in a., F. & F., 14/7/16.
Thompson, Edwin, e. Coventry, Warwicks, 265784, Pte., k. in a., F. & F., 6/4/17.
Thompson, Leonard, b. St. Johns, Coventry, Warwicks, e. Coventry, 265511, L/Sgt., k. in a., F. & F., 9/8/18.
Thurston, Albert Arthur, b. Great Ormesby, Norfolk, e. Great Yarmouth, Norfolk (Great Ormesby), 29289, Pte., k. in a., F. & F., 8/10/17, formerly 27304, Norfolk Regt.

Tims, William, b. Foleshill, Warwicks, e. Coventry, Warwicks (Foleshill), 1868, Pte., k. in a., F. & F., 7/6/15.
Tizard, Albert Victor, b. Dorchester, Dorset, e. Dorchester, 307237, Pte., k. in a., F. & F., 16/8/18.
Tod, Alexander, e. Coventry, Warwicks, 265788, Cpl., k. in a., F. & F., 4/10/17.
Tookey, James Pressley, b. Rawtenstall, Lancs, e. Coventry, Warwicks (Kenilworth, Warwicks), 266230, Pte., k. in a., F. & F., 4/10/17.
Toon, Charlie, b. Derby, e. Coventry, Warwicks, 265215, Cpl., k. in a., F. & F., 26/3/17.
Townsend, William, b. Leamington, Warwicks, e. Coventry, Warwicks (Leamington), 2731, Pte., k. in a., F. & F., 9/10/15.
Treadgold, William Henry, b. St. Michaels, Coventry, Warwicks, e. Coventry (Stoke, Coventry), 266273, L/Cpl., k. in a., F. & F., 8/10/17.
Tyler, George William, e. Warwick, 266798, Pte., k. in a., F. & F., 27/8/17.
Underwood, Harry, e. Birmingham (Small Heath, Birmingham), 266809, Pte., k. in a., F. & F., 21/8/17.
Upton, Reginald, b. Deal, Kent, e. Sandwich, Kent (Deal, Kent), 300287, Pte., k. in a., F. & F., 16/5/18, formerly 4310, E. Kent Regt.
Viner, Albert Victor, b. Allesley, Coventry, Warwicks, e. Coventry (Allesley), 2602, Pte., k. in a., F. & F., 23/3/16.
Wagstaff, Thomas Herbert, b. Nuneaton, Warwicks, e. Nuneaton, 265342, Pte., k. in a., F. & F., 11/8/17.
Wagstaff, William, b. Nuneaton, Warwicks, e. Nuneaton, 265374, Sgt., k. in a., F. & F., 4/10/17, D.C.M.
Wall, George Henry, b. St. Thomas, Coventry, e. Coventry, 265568, Sgt., k. in a., F. & F., 18/4/17.
Walton, Joseph John, b. Nuneaton, Warwicks, e. Coventry (Attleborough, Warwicks), 266241, Pte., d. of w., F. & F., 6/4/17.
Warden, Frederick Harold Bert, b. St. Andrews, Rugby, e. Rugby, Warwicks, 265369, L/Cpl., k. in a., F. & F., 27/8/17.
Waring, Ernest Edward, b. St. John's, Coventry, e. Coventry, 1773, Pte., k. in a., F. & F., 14/7/16.
Waring, James John, e. Coventry, 266460, Pte., d. of w., F. & F., 7/3/17.
Watts, Archie William, b. Boxwell, Glos., e. Tetbury, Glos., 266073, Pte., k. in a., F. & F., 28/8/17.
Watts, Walter John, e. Coventry, 266520, Pte., k. in a., F. & F., 13/8/17
Watson, Arthur James, b. Long Lawford, Warwicks, e. Rugby, Warwicks (New Bilton, Warwicks), 2270, Pte., k. in a., F. & F., 2/7/16.
Webley, Ernest Harry, e. Leamington, Warwicks, 266843, Pte., d. of w., F. & F., 17/12/17.
Webster, Robert William, b. St. Georges, London, e. Coventry, 2243, Pte., k. in a., F. & F., 3/4/16.
Wellard, John Caleb, b. Battersea, London, e. Chichester, Sussex (Eastbourne, Sussex), 34000, Pte., d. of w., F. & F., 8/10/17, formerly 203249, E. Kent Regt.
West, Frederick, b. Coventry, e. Coventry, 4663, Pte., k. in a., F. & F., 1/7/16.
Weston, Joseph, e. Worcester (Uphampton, Worcs.), 267077, Pte., d., F. & F., 16/6/17.
Weyman, Charles Frederick, b. St. Pauls, Worcester, e. Warwick, 266627, Pte., d., F. & F., 31/10/17.
Whetstone, Andrew, e. Coventry, 4572, Pte., d. of w., F. & F., 31/7/16.
White, Ernest Arthur Gordon, b. Mandalay, Burmah, e. Birmingham (Mandalay), 1171, Pte., k. in a., F. & F., 11/8/17.
White, Leslie, e. Birmingham, 4719, Pte., d., F. & F., 24/7/16.
White, William Thomas, b. Milverton, Warwick, e. Leamington, Warwicks, 2261, Cpl., k. in a., F. & F., 25/7/16.
Whitehead, Noah, b. Wellington, Salop, e. Birmingham (Aston, Birmingham), 300131, Pte., k. in a., F. & F., 27/8/17, formerly, 7740, Norfolk Regt.
Whittaker, James Thomas, b. Lincoln, e. Coventry, 1785, L/Cpl., d. of w., F. & F., 23/8/16.
Wilcox, James William, b. Trinity, Coventry, e. Coventry, 676, Pte., k. in a., F. & F., 14/7/16.
Wild, Herbert, b. All Saints, Warwick, e. Warwick, 267103, Sgt., k. in a., F. & F., 16/6/18.
Wilde, Robert, e. Birmingham, 5299, Pte., d. of w., F. & F., 28/11/16.
Williams, Albert John, b. St. Johns, Worcester, e. Worcester, 265444, Pte., d., F. & F., 26/10/18, formerly 1753, Worcs. Regt.
Willis, Sydney John, b. Sheffield, Yorks, e. Sheffield, 268279, Pte., k. in a., F. & F., 8/10/17, formerly 3884, R.E.
Wilson, Horace Llewellyn, b. Stoke, Coventry, e. Coventry, 2397, Pte., k. in a., F. & F., 25/7/16.
Wilson, William John, e. Pontypridd, Glam, 267192, Pte., k. in a., F. & F., 26/8/16, formerly 3479, Welsh Regt.
Wing, Walter, b. Princethorpe, Warwicks, e. Coventry, 266583, Pte., k. in a., F. & F., 27/3/17.
Wing, William Francis, e. Coventry, 265828, Pte., k. in a., F. & F., 16/6/18.
Witherford, George Frank Leslie, b. Birmingham, e. Birmingham (Quinton, Birmingham), 267492, Pte., k. in a., F. & F., 16/6/18.
Wit(h)erington, Joseph Charles, b. Battersea, London, e. Battersea, 300053, Pte., d. of w., F. & F., 12/8/17, formerly 201834, Norfolk Regt.
Wood, William Henry Croft, b. St. Giles, Kensington, London, e. Coventry (Kensington), 8, C.S.M., d. of w., F. & F., 24/7/16.
Woodman, William, e. Coventry, 4527, Pte., k. in a., F. & F., 25/7/16.
Woodward, Reginald Joseph, e. Stratford-on-Avon, Warwicks, 265048, Cpl., k. in a., F. & F., 14/7/16.
Worrall, Alfred Thomas, e. Coventry, 4573, Pte., k. in a., F. & F., 14/7/16.
Wright, George Alfred, e. Leamington, Warwicks, 2974, Pte., k. in a., F. & F., 8/10/15.
Wright, George Reginald, e. Abertillery, Mon. (Newbridge, Mon.), 266994, Pte., k. in a., F. & F., 25/8/17.
Wright, Herbert George, e. Coventry, 4481, Pte., d. of w., F. & F., 15/11/16.
Wykes, Frank, b. Cotton, Nuneaton, e. Nuneaton, Warwicks, 1879, Cpl., k. in a., F. & F., 14/7/16.
Wyman, Charles, b. St. Mary, Peterborough, Northants, e. Fletton, Northants (Peterborough), 20841, Pte., k. in a., F. & F., 18/8/16.

2/7th Battalion.

Ackrill, Harold Richard, b. Crowthorne, Berks, e. Wokingham, Berks (Sandhurst, Berks), 40932, Pte., d., F. & F., 9/10/18.
Adcock, Albert Thomas, b. St. Nicholas, Nuneaton, Warwicks, e. Nuneaton, 265361, Pte., k. in a., F. & F., 5/12/17.
Adler, Edward, b. Coventry, e. Coventry, 266855, Pte., k. in a., F. & F., 3/12/17.
Agg, Arthur, b. Childswickham, Worcs, e. Cheltenham, Glos. (Broadway, Worcs.)) 26500, Pte., k. in a., F. & F., 21/8/18.
Aldhouse, Albert, b. Birmingham, e. Birmingham (Aston, Birmingham), 38030, Pte., k. in a., F. & F., 24/10/18.
Allchurch, Harold, b. Stourbridge, Worcs., e. Stourbridge, 40933, Pte., k. in a., F. & F., 14/4/18.
Allen, William Allan, b. Worcester, e. Coventry, Warwicks, 266110, L/Cpl., k. in a., F. & F., 23/3/18, M.M.
Allen, William John, b. Bedworth, Warwicks, e. Coventry, Warwicks. (Bulkington, Warwicks.), 3660, Cpl., d. of w., F. & F., 16/7/16.
Andrews, Reuben, b. Halesowen, Worcs., e. Halesowen, 266924, Pte., k. in a., F. & F., 5/12/17.
Arden, John Ellis, b. Disley, Ches., e. Stockport, Ches. (Disley), 29603, Pte., k. in a., F. & F. 7/8/18, formerly 39367, S. Lancs Regt.
Ashford, Henry Albert, b. Birmingham, e. Birmingham (Handsworth, Staffs), 43413, Pte., k. in a., F. & F., 7/9/18.
Ashton, Colin, b Darwin, Lancs, e. Accrington, Lancs (Barnoldswick, Lancs), 32886, Pte., k. in a., F. & F., 24/3/18, formerly 24779, Hrs.
Ashton, Richard, b. Pilton, Devon, e. Slough, Bucks, 35027, Pte., k. in a., F. & F., 24/3/18, formerly 22924, Ox. & Bucks, L.I.
Athersuch, Walter, b. All Saints, Coventry, Warwicks, e. Coventry, 265352, L/Cpl., k. in a., F. & F., 21/3/18.
Atkins, William Thomas, b. Birmingham, e. Birmingham (Stirchley, Birmingham), 40935, Pte., k. in a., F. & F., 7/8/18.
Austin, Harry, e. Coventry, Warwicks., 266487, Pte., k. in a., F. & F., 19/7/16.
Austin, Syndey Arthur, b. Kettlebrook, Warwicks, e. Tamworth, Warwicks (Kettlebrook), 268339, Pte., k. in a., F. & F., 9/4/17.
Ayres, William Thomas, b. Eynsham, Oxon, e. Oxford (Eynsham), 28920, Pte., k. in a., F. & F., 3/12/17.
Bailey, Christopher, e. Coventry, Warwicks, 3224, Sgt., k. in a., F. & F., 19/7/16.
Bailey, Leonard, b. Aston, Birmingham, e. Aston (Birmingham), 328022, Pte., d., F. & F., 9/9/19.
Bailey, Robert, b. Chalfont St. Giles, Bucks, e. High Wycombe, Bucks (Chalfont St. Giles), 26723, Pte., k. in a., F. & F., 13/4/18.
Bailey, William, b. Sponden, Derby, e. Woolwich, Kent (Sponden), 32510, Pte., k. in a., F. & F., 18/4/18, formerly 4072, Lrs.
Bailey, William, b. Stockingford, Warwicks, e. Nuneaton, Warwicks (Stockingford), 42683, Pte., k. in a., F. & F., 1/11/18.
Balchin, Alfred Horace, b. Leamington, Warwicks, e. Leamington, 266305, Pte., k. in a., F. & F., 5/12/17.
Ball, Samuel, b. Birmingham, e. Birmingham, 24138, Pte., k. in a., F. & F., 25/4/18.
Banks, William, b. Fazeley, Warwicks, e. Tamworth, Warwicks (Fazeley), 42810, Pte., k. in a., F. & F., 1/11/18.
Bann, James, e. Bathgate, Linlithgow (Winchburgh, Linlith), 307294, Pte., d. of w., F. & F., 21/4/18, formerly 2604, R. Scts.
Bannister, Walter, b. Burton on Trent, Staffs, e. Coventry, Warwicks, 3755, Pte., d. of w., F. & F., 20/7/16.
Barber, John, b. Kenilworth, Warwicks, e. Kenilworth, 1980, Pte., k. in a., F. & F., 28/8/16.
Barlow, Ernest, b. Tamworth, Staffs, e. Tamworth, 42674, Pte., k. in a., F. & F., 1/11/18.
Barlow, Henry, b. Alderman's Green, Coventry, e. Coventry (Alderman's Green), 266144, Pte., k. in a., F. & F., 19/7/16.
Barnett, Stephen, e. Coventry, Warwicks, 3367, Pte., k. in a., F. & F., 19/7/16.
Barnett. William Henry, e. Leamington, Warwicks (Warwick), 3654, Pte., k. in a., F. & F., 19/7/16.
Barnfield, Charles Henry, b. Birmingham, e. Birmingham, 268362, Pte., d. of w., F. & F., 9/4/17.
Barnwell, Harry, e. Rugby, Warwicks (Old Bilton, Rugby), 268127, Pte., k. in a., F. & F., 19/11/17.
Barr, Russell, b. Birmingham, e. Birmingham (Nechells, Birmingham), 42646, Pte., k. in a., F. & F., 1/11/18.
Baseley, Arthur, e. Coventry, Warwicks (Keresley Heath, Coventry), 3413, Pte., d. of w., F. & F., 12/1/17.
Bates, Edwin, b. Two Gates, Warwickshire, e. Atherstone, Warwicks (Dosthill, Warwicks), 41883, Pte., k. in a., F. & F., 1/11/18.
Bates, Harold, e. Coventry, Warwicks (Bedworth, Warwicks), 3435, Pte., k. in a., F. & F., 19/7/16.
Baxendale, Thomas, b. All Saints, Southport, Lancs, e. Southport, 268488, L/Cpl., k. in a., F. & F. 28/3/18, formerly 2688, Liverpool Regt.

Bayne, Herriot, e. Ladybank, Fife, 267203, Pte., k. in a., F. & F., 29/4/17, formerly 1185, Highl. Cyclist Battn.

Beale, Arthur, b. Glascote, Warwicks, e. Warwick (Glascote), 43415, Pte., k. in a., F. & F., 7/9/18.

Beardmore, Harold, b. Birmingham, e. Birmingham (Handsworth, Birmingham), 22579, Pte., k. in a., F. & F., 20/8/18.

Beasley, Harry, b. Walsgrave-on-Sowe, Warwicks, e. Coventry, Warwicks, (Walsgrave-on-Sowe), 266139, L/Cpl., k. in a., F. & F., 21/3/18.

Beathe, John, b. Nechells, Birmingham, e. Aston, Birmingham (Nechells), 305274, Cpl., k. in a., F. & F., 22/3/18.

Beckett, Harry, e. Stratford-on-Avon, Warwicks, 3456, Pte., d., F. & F., 19/7/16.

Beesley, Albert, e. Stratford-on-Avon, Warwicks, 266208, Pte., k. in a., F. & F., 19/7/16.

Begley, Samuel, b. Shipston-on-Stour, Worcs, e. Birmingham (Shipston-on-Stour), 7216, Sgt., k. in a., F. & F., 19/8/18.

Bell, Francis John, b. Bootle, Lancs, e. Bootle, 267140, L/Cpl., k. in a., F. & F., 22/3/18 formerly 5334, Liverpool Regt.

Benson, Fergus John, e. Coventry, Warwicks, 3123, Pte., k. in a., F. & F., 27/11/16.

Beresford, William, b. All Souls, Coventry, Warwicks, e. Coventry, 3851, L/Cpl., d. of w., F. & F. 15/2/16.

Berry, Harry, e. Rugby, Warwicks, 4628, L/Cpl., k. in a. F. & F., 19/7/16.

Bessant, Thomas, e. Ashton, Birmingham, 305992, Pte., d. of w., F. & F., 18/4/18.

Best, Edward Robert Charles, b. Sunninghill, Berks, e. Reading, Berks (Sunninghill), 40944, Pte., d. of w., F. & F., 8/11/18.

Bewsher, Tom, e. Ulverston, Lancs, 306955, Pte., k. in a., F. & F., 22/3/18, formerly 2881, R. Lancs. Regt.

Bicknell, Leonard, b. Coventry, Warwicks, e. Coventry (Stoke, Coventry), 19700, Pte., d. of w., F. & F., 2/9/17.

Billington, Albert, b. Nantwich, Ches., e. Crewe, Ches. (Nantwich), 29460, Pte., k. in a., F. & F. 18/4/18, formerly 61936, Ches. Regt.

Binnell, John, b. Stockton, Bridgnorth, Salop, e. Stoney Lane, Birmingham (Small Heath, Birmingham), 306516, Pte., k. in a., F. & F., 14/4/18.

Birchall, John, b. Westhead, Ormskirk, Lancs, e. Ormskirk (Lathom, near Ormskirk), 5488, Pte., k. in a., F. & F., 19/7/16, formerly 2274, Liverpool Regt.

Birchall, Thomas, b. Scarisbrick, Ormskirk, Lancs., e. Liverpool (Ormskirk), 267143, L/Cpl., k. in a., F. & F., 19/7/16, formerly 2291, Liverpool Regt.

Bird, Alfred Abraham, b. Lane End, Bucks, e. High Wycombe, Bucks, 30002, Pte., d. of w., F. & F., 5/5/18, formerly 21043, Oxf. and Bucks L.I.

Bishop, Lancelot, b. Newton-le-Willows, Lancs, e. Warrington, Lancs (Newton-le-Willows), 29616, Pte., k. in a., F. & F., 5/12/17, formerly 40081, S. Lancs Regt.

Blacoe, Herbert, b. Liverpool, Lancs, e. Chester (Birkenhead, Ches.), 29454, Pte., k. in a., F. & F. 3/12/17, formerly 61398, Ches. Regt.

Blake, Leonard, b. Birmingham, e. Birmingham (Nechells, Birmingham), 40948, Pte., k. in a., F. & F., 13/4/18.

Blakemore, Albert James, e. Leamington Spa, Warwicks (Warwick), 2922, Sgt., k. in a., F. & F., 19/7/16.

Blakemore, Charles, b. Warwick, e. Warwick, 268340, Pte., k. in a., F. & F., 1/11/18.

Blatchford, Edward George, b. St. John's, Devonport, Devon, e. Plymouth, 268382, L/Cpl., d. of w., F. & F., 22/11/17, formerly 56862, R.G.A.

Blunt, Sidney John, b. Farcotton, Northampton, e. Nuneaton. Warwicks, 42682, Pte., k. in a., F. & F., 1/11/18.

Bolton, Sidney Thomas, b. Birmingham, Warwicks; e. Birmingham (Ballsall Heath, Birmingham), 203825, L/Cpl., k. in a., F. & F., 12/4/18.

Bond, John Frederick, e. Redditch, Worcs (Studley S.O., Warwicks), 267966, Pte., k. in a., F. & F., 9/4/17.

Boot, Alfred Alexander, e. Birmingham (Handsworth, Birmingham), 266769, Pte., k. in a., F. & F., 9/4/17.

Borthwick, Alfred, b. Kirkcaldy, Fife, e. Kirkcaldy, 267207, Pte., k. in a., F. & F., 13/10/17, formerly 781 Highl. Cyclist Battn.

Bowers, Thomas, b. Haverhill, Suffolk, e. Coventry, Warwicks, 268138, Pte., d., F. & F. 18/11/18.

Bowns, Thomas Henry, e. Coventry, Warwicks (Bedworth, Warwicks), 266446, Pte., d. of w., F. & F., 5/7/17.

Boyles, Frank, b. Banbury, Oxon, e. Banbury, 267728, Pte. k. in a., F. & F., 21/11/17.

Brace, Leslie, b. St. Thomas, Birmingham, e. Birmingham, 201415, Pte., k. in a., F. & F. 16/4/18.

Bradshaw, Joseph Edmund, b. Birmingham, e. Birmingham (Aston, Birmingham), 43416, Pte., k. in a., F. & F., 7/9/18.

Brain, George William, b. Rugby, Warwicks, e. Leamington, Spa, Warwicks (Dunchurch, Warwicks), 43437 Pte., k. in a., F. & F., 1/11/18.

Brazier, Charles, b. Micheldiver, Hants, e. Winchester, Hants (Micheldiver), 28923, Pte., k. in a., F. & F., 12/4/18.

Brett, Sidney Alfred, b. Wandsworth, Surrey, e. Hornchurch, Essex (Upper Tooting, London, S.W.), 37944, Pte., k. in a., F. & F., 24/3/18, formerly 1858, R. Fus.

Britton, Thomas Hughes, b. Plymouth, Devon, e. Bristol, Glos. (Brislington, Bristol), 40954, Pte. k. in a., F. & F., 8/8/18.

Brookes, George, b. Birmingham, e. Birmingham, 307486, Pte., k. in a., F. & F., 10/5/18.

Brown, Frank, e. Coventry, Warwicks, 3285, L/Cpl., d., F. & F., 30/9/16.

Brown, Herbert, b. Coventry, Warwicks, e. Coventry, 266318, Pte., k. in a., F. & F., 14/7/16.

Brunton, Thomas Arthur, e. Coventry, Warwicks, 4434, Pte., k. in a., F. & F., 25/6/16.

Buckingham, Edgar Herbert, b. Coventry, Warwicks, e. Cheltenham, Glos. (Coventry), 37766, Pte., k. in a., F. & F., 14/4/18.

Buckley, Sam, b. Rochdale, Lancs, e. Rochdale, 32697, Pte., k. in a., F. & F., 24/3/18, formerly 21937, Dragoons.

Bunker, Harold, b. Coventry, Warwicks, e. Coventry, 266069, Pte., k. in a., F. & F., 18/4/18.

Burman, Walter Insull, b. Coleshill, Birmingham, e. Birmingham, 523, Pte., k. in a., F. & F., 25/4/18.

Burrows, Ernest John, b. Chapel End, Warwicks, e. Coventry, Warwicks (Walsgrave, Warwicks), 3609, L/Cpl., k. in a., F. & F., 6/6/16.

Butlin, Thomas, b. Minworth, Warwicks, e. Birmingham (Minworth), 208352, Pte., k. in a., F. & F., 22/3/18.

Cadden, Herbert, e. Coventry, Warwicks, 265870, Pte., k. in a., F. & F., 9/4/17.

Calloway, Arthur James, b. Coventry, e. Coventry (Walsgrave-on-Sowe, Warwicks), 3469, Pte., d., F. & F., 21/7/16.

Campbell, Francis, e. Kirkcaldy, Fife, 5591, Pte., d. of w., F. & F., 8/8/16, formerly 2164, Highl. Cyclist Battn.

Camplin, Harry, b. Hoyland, Yorks, e. Barnsley, Yorks (Tankersley, nr. Barnsley), 29753, L/Cpl., d. of w., F. & F., 21/9/18.

Cannon, Walter, b. Hockley, Birmingham, e. Aston, Birmingham, 305273, Pte., k. in a., F. & F., 13/4/18.

Carton, William, b. Pendleton, Lancs, e. Warwick (Minworth, Warwicks), 40963, Pte., k. in a., F. & F., 12/4/18.

Cashmore, George, b. West Bromwich, Staffs, e. Coventry, Warwicks (Foleshill, Warwicks), 266361, A/C.S.M., d. of w., F. & F., 2/4/18, M.M.

Charlwood, James Helme, b. St. Michaels, Coventry, Warwicks, e. Coventry, 265155, Pte., k. in a., F. & F., 15/8/17.

Chatwin, Alfred, b. Trinity, Coventry, Warwicks, e. Coventry, 265148, L/Cpl., k. in a., F. & F., 19/7/16.

Cheney, Albert George, b. Rockhampton, Dorset, e. Dorchester, 28945, Pte., k. in a., F. & F., 24/3/18.

Chester, Francis John, b. Smethwick, Staffs, e. Birmingham Smethwick), 202570, Pte., d. of w., F. & F., 23/8/18.

Christie, Frank, b. Everton, Lancs, e. Liverpool (Everton), 267150, Pte., k. in a., F. & F., 19/7/16, formerly 1831, Liverpool Regt.

Clarke, John Alfred, b. Kenilworth, Warwicks, e. Coventry, Warwicks, 266690, Pte., k. in a., F. & F., 19/7/16.

Clarke, Victor Leslie, b. Radford, Warwicks, e. Coventry, Warwicks, 266061, L/Cpl., d. of w., F. & F., 3/7/18.

Clarke, William, b. Shrewsbury, Shrops, e. Birmingham, 268301, Pte., k. in a., F. & F., 3/12/17.

Clarkson, Edward, b. Sunderland, Durham, e. Kirkliston, West Lothian, N.B. (Dalmeny, Edinburgh), 307375, Pte., k. in a., F. & F., 1/7/18, formerly 967, R. Scots.

Clements, Frederick Charles, b. Roade, Northants, e. Rugby, Warwicks, 307487, Cpl., d., F. & F., 10/1/18.

Clements, Thomas Henry, b. Cliftonvale, Glos., e. Bristol, Glos., 268014, Pte., k. in a., F. & F., 5/12/17, formerly 30472, Glouc. Regt.

Clews, Arthur Ernest, b. Coventry, Warwicks, e. Coventry, 24570, Pte., d. of w., F. & F., 20/5/18.

Clowes, Albert Victor, b. Birmingham, e. Birmingham (Sparkbrook, Birmingham), 306312, L/Cpl., k. in a., F. & F., 24/10/18.

Cole, Edward David, b. Rowley's Green, Coventry, Warwicks, e. Coventry, 265550, Pte., k. in a., F. & F., 5/12/17.

Coley, George, b. Earl's Shilton, Leics., e. Nuneaton, Warwicks, 268332, Pte., k. in a., F. & F., 20/8/18.

Coley, Henry George, b. Birmingham, e. Birmingham (Lozells, Birmingham), 266745, Pte., k. in a., F. & F., 22/3/18.

Colley, Thomas, e. Bolton, Lancs, 307056, Pte., k. in a., F. & F., 18/4/18, formerly 7766, N. Lancs Regt.

Collins, Matthew, b. Tipton, Staffs, e. Birmingham (West Bromwich, Staffs), 41851, Pte., k. in a., F. & F., 24/10/18.

Collins, Mitchell, e. Kirkcaldy, Fife, 267217, Pte., k. in a., F. & F., 19/7/16, formerly 1402, Highl. Cyclist Batn.

Compton, Thomas, b. Oldbury, Worcester, e. Oldbury, 28695, Pte., k. in a., F. & F., 1/11/18.

Constable, Stafford Reginald, b. Knowle, Glos., e. Bristol (Knowle), 28912, L/Cpl., k. in a., F. & F., 5/12/17.

Cook, John, b. Kegworth, Leics., e. Derby (Sutton Bonnington, Leics.), 29696, Pte., k. in a., F. & F., 14/4/18.

Copeland, Samuel Herbert, b. Tamworth, Warwicks, e. Birmingham (Bonehill, Staffs), 300233, Pte., k. in a., F. & F., 28/4/18, formerly 204353, Oxf. and Bucks. L.I.

Cooke, John James, b. Birmingham, e. Birmingham (Sparkhill, Birmingham), 328033, Pte., k. in a., F. & F., 1/11/18.

Cornock, Harold Victor, b. Birmingham, e. Birmingham (Nechells, Birmingham), 39855, Pte., d. of w., F. & F., 25/10/18.

Coughlan, John, b. Pimlico, Dublin, e. Dublin, 32452, Pte., d., F. & F., 7/11/18, formerly 16083, Lancers.

Coull, George, b. Aberchirder, Banff., e. Perth (Aberchirder), 5598, Pte., d., F. & F., 19/7/16, formerly 1701, Highl. Cyclist Battn.

Cowhern, Harold, b. Radcliffe, Lancs, e. Nuneaton, Warwicks, 42087, Pte., k. in a., F. & F., 1/11/18.

Cox, Frederick William, b. Westbury-on-Leven, Glos., e. Cinderford, Glos. (Gloucester), 307449, Pte., k. in a., F. & F., 20/4/18, formerly 26745, R. Berks Regt.

Cox, William James, b. Yarnton, Oxon, e. Oxford (Yarnton), 35024, Pte., k. in a., F. & F., 24/3/18, formerly 29007, Oxf. and Bucks. L.I.

Crane, Harold, b. Bromsgrave, Worcs, e. Birmingham (Spring Hill, Birmingham), 42647, Pte., k. in a., F. & F., 1/11/18.

Critchlow, Richard Harold, b. Birkenhead, Ches., e. Birkenhead, 29475, Pte., k. in a., F. & F., 13/10/17, formerly 62033, Ches. Regt.

Crompton, Harold, e. Ormskirk, Ches., 268583, Pte., k. in a., F. & F., 19/7/16, formerly 2350, Liverpool Regt.

Crump, William James, e. Birmingham (Harborne, Birmingham), 305750, Pte., k. in a., F. & F., 11/5/18.

Cunningham, Robert, e. Leven, Fife, 267218, L/Cpl., k. in a., F. & F., 19/7/16, formerly 2268, Highl. Cyclist Batn.
Daniels, Harold Walker, b. Birmingham, e. Birmingham, 268327, L/Cpl., k. in a., F. & F., 15/5/18.
Dare, Leonard, e. Bargoed, Glam., 5499, Pte. d. of w., F. & F., 8/8/16, formerly 2834, Welsh Regt.
Darrall, Ben, b. Dawley, Salop, e. Wellington, Salop (Horsehay, Salop), 268326, Pte., k. in a., F. & F., 5/12/17.
Davenport, Charles, b. Coventry, e. Coventry, 3858, Pte., k. in a., F. & F., 28/8/16.
Davenport, Henry Charles, b. Stoneleigh, Warwicks, e. Coventry, 3492, L/Cpl., d., F. & F., 19/7/16.
Davidson, Henry Victor, e. Bristol (Bedminster, Glos.), 268000, Pte., k. in a., F. & F., 9/4/17, formerly 30631, Glos. Regt.
Davies, Gilbert, e. Southport, Lancs, 300177, Pte., d. of w., F. & F., 5/11/17, formerly 55681, Liverpool Regt.
Davies, George Edward, b. Shrewsbury, Salop, e. Worcester (Dudley, Worcs), 40973, Pte., k. in a., F. & F., 13/4/18.
Davies, James Ernest, b. Gorseinon, Glam., e. Carmarthen (Penygres, Carnarvon), 5949, Pte., k. in a., F. & F., 19/7/16, formerly 4124, Welsh Regt.
Davies, Robert Clifford, b. Llanelly, Carmarthen, e. Llanelly, 267414, L/Cpl., k. in a., F. & F., 19/7/16, formerly 5338, Welsh Regt.
Davies, Walter, b. Bramley, Yorks, e. Bradford, Yorks (Wibsey, Yorks), 35068, Pte., k. in a., F. & F., 22/3/18, formerly 022171, R.A.O.C.
Davis, Thomas Henry, e. Stratford-on-Avon, Warwicks, 3231, Pte., k. in a., F. & F., 19/7/16.
Daw, Augustus Thomas, b. Birmingham, e. Birmingham (Camp Hill, Birmingham), 306311, Pte., d. of w., F. & F., 1/4/18.
Day, George William, b. Denham, Bucks, e. London (Pinner, Middx.), 28752, Pte., k. in a., F. & F., 22/3/18, formerly S4/125707, R.A.S.C.
Deacon, Richard, e. Nuneaton, Warwicks., 268155, Pte., d., F. & F., 26/6/18.
Dearlove, George William Dix, b. Banbury, Oxon, e. Aston, Birmingham, 306326, Pte., d. of w., F. & F., 25/10/18.
Dennison, Fred, e. Arnold, Notts, 27522, Pte., k. in a., F. & F., 20/8/18, formerly 3838, Notts and Derby Regt.
Desborough, Thomas, b. Birmingham, e. Coventry, Warwicks, 206259, Pte., k. in a., F. & F., 19/7/16.
Dimoned, Albert Edward, b. Clew Magna, Somerset, e. Bristol, Glos. (Clew Magna), 28926, Pte., k. in a., F. & F., 3/12/17.
Dobbins, Jack, e. Coventry, 3000, Pte., k. in a., F. & F., 19/7/16.
Doney, Nathan Hart Coad, b. North Hill, Cornwall, e. Bodmin, Cornwall, 26368, Pte., d. of w., F. & F., 24/10/18.
Dorsett, Leonard, b. Dudley, Worcs., e. Worcester (Dudley), 40976, Pte., k. in a., F. & F., 24/10/18.
Drinkwater, Frederick James, e. Stratford-on-Avon, Warwicks., 265990, Pte., k. in a., F. & F., 19/7/16.
Druce, Raymond Victor, Stokenchurch, Bucks, e. High Wycombe, Bucks (Fingest, Bucks), 40977, Pte., d. of w., F. & F., 2/9/18.
Dryburgh, Alexander, b. Wemyss, Kirkcaldy, e. East Wemyss (Coaltown of Wemyss), 267224, Pte., k. in a., F. & F., 19/7/16, formerly 958, Highland Cyclist Battn.
Duncan, Donald, b. Rescobie, Forfar, e. Forfar, 5609, Pte., d. of w., F. & F., 8/7/16, formerly 645, Highland Cyclist Battn.
Duncan, Edmund, b. Huncott, Leics., e. Leicester (Huncott), 29690, Pte., d. of w., F. & F., 24/3/18, formerly 23791, Leicester Regt.
Duncan, William Hepburn, e. Kirkcaldy, Fife (Dunfermline, Fife), 267228, Pte., k. in a., F. & F., 9/4/17, formerly 1184, Highland Cyclist Battn.
Dyer, Joseph, b. St. Helen's, Lancs, e. Warrington, Lancs (St. Helen's), 29627, Pte., k. in a., F. & F., 3/12/17, formerly 40052, South Lancs Regt.
Eaton, Harry Wilfred, b. Langley, Bucks, e. Slough, Bucks, 28927, Pte., d. of w., F. & F., 6/12/17.
Elkin, John, b. Congleton, Ches., e. Congleton, 300146, Pte., k. in a., F. & F., 3/12/17, formerly 27478, S. Lancs Regt.
Elks, David, b. Pendlebury, Lancs, e. Middlewich, Ches. (Holmes Chapel, Ches.), 29630, Pte., k. in a., F. & F., 1/11/18, formerly 40011, South Lancs Regt.
Ellen, Thomas James Samuel, b. Birmingham, e. Birmingham (Aston, Birmingham), 241490, Pte., k. in a., F. & F., 24/10/18.
Ellis, George, b. Aston, Birmingham, e. Aston, 306299, Pte., k. in a., F. & F., 1/11/18.
Ellison, William, b. Walton, Lancs, e. Bootle, Liverpool (Orrell, Lancs), 300180, Pte., d. of w., F. & F., 6/4/18, formerly 41405, Liverpool Regt.
Elson, Ernest, e. Birmingham (Sparkhill, Birmingham), 266804, Pte., d. of w., F. & F., 9/4/17.
Emms, George, e. Market Harborough, Northants, 32880, Pte., k. in a., F. & F., 24/10/18, formerly R/4/108877, R.A.S.C.
Evans, William James, b. Cheltenham, Glos., e. Cheltenham, 40979, Pte., d. of w., F. & F., 22/6/18.
Ewers, Harold Richmond, b. Burton-on-Trent, Staffs, e. Derby (Southwell, Notts), 29699, Pte., k. in a., F. & F., 24/10/18.
Fagan, Thomas, b. Liverpool, Lancs, e. Liverpool, 267159, Pte., k. in a., F. & F., 13/5/18, formerly 1514, Liverpool Regt.
Farren, Joseph, b. London, e. Coventry, 265409, Pte., k. in a., F. & F., 19/7/16.
Fidoe, Arthur Oliver, b. Leamington, Warwicks., e. Leamington, 266884, Pte., d. of w., F. & F., 4/12/17.
Field, Walter, b. Wick, Bristol, e. Bristol, Glos., 26913, Pte., d. of w., F. & F., 1/11/18.
Fisher, Hubert John, b. Shipton-on-Stour, Worcs., e. Stratford-on-Avon, Warwicks, 268147, Sgt., k. in a., F. & F., 14/4/18.
Fletcher, Charles Norman, e. Lydney, Glos., 40981, Pte., k. in a., F. & F., 1/11/18.
Fletcher, George Edward, b. Napton, Warwicks., e. Rugby, Warwicks. (Napton), 268321, Pte., k. in a., F. & F., 27/8/17.
Foley, William, e. Bootle, Liverpool, 20851, Pte., d., F. & F., 19/7/16, formerly 3277, Liverpool Regt.
Foss, Herbert, e. Brockenhurst, Hants, 268109, Pte., k. in a., F. & F., 6/9/17, formerly 26337, Hampshire Regt.
Fowles, Charles, e. Salford, Lancs, 300182, Pte., k. in a., F. & F., 3/12/17, formerly 2731, Lancs. Fus.
Francis, George, b. St. Helen's, Lancs, e. St. Helen's, 29632, Pte., k. in a., F. & F., 19/11/17, formerly 40256, South Lancs Regt.
Franklin, Arthur Edward, b. Luton, Beds., e. Aston, Birmingham (Saltley, Birmingham), 330831, Pte., k. in a., F. & F., 18/4/18.
Fraser, Donald, b. Inverness, e. Coventry, Warwicks., 23861, Pte., k. in a., F. & F., 20/8/18.
Frear, John William, b. Chapeltown, Yorks, e. Leeds, Yorks, 25228, Pte., d. of w., F. & F., 12/4/18, formerly R/258935, R.A.S.C.
Furnival, Alfred, b. Coventry, Warwicks., e. Coventry (Foleshill, Coventry), 3764, L/Cpl., k. in a., F. & F., 20/9/16.
Galloway, George, b. Wemyss, Fife, e. East Wemyss (Buckhaven, Fife), 267233, Pte., k. in a., F. & F., 19/7/16, formerly 851, Highland Cyclist Battn.
Gardner, Charles Percy, b. Gloucester, e. Coventry, Warwicks., 266881, Pte., k. in a., F. & F., 24/10/18.
Gardner, Percy, b. London, e. New York, U.S.A., 35033, Pte., k. in a., F. & F., 23/8/18, formerly T/331127, R.A.S.C.
Gardner, Thomas Harris, b. Edgehill, Warwicks., e. Warwick (Coventry, Warwicks), 328046, Pte., d. of w., F. & F., 11/6/18.
Garner, John Alec, e. Coventry, Warwicks., 3062, Pte., k. in a., F. & F., 19/3/16.
Garnsey, William John Bonding, b. Milverton, Som., e. Taunton, Som. (Norton-Fitz-Warren, Som.), 28929, Pte., k. in a., F. & F., 22/3/18.
Garrad, Charles Ashton, b. Camberwell, Middx., e. Petersfield, Hants (Liphook, Hants), 300149, Pte., k. in a., F. & F., 5/12/17, formerly 23481, Somerset L.I.
Gibson, James Arthur, e. Atherstone, Warwicks. (Hurley, Warwicks.), 266844, Pte., k. in a., F. & F., 9/4/17.
Gilbert, John Thomas, e. Rugby, Warwicks., 2914, Sgt., d. of w., F. & F., 1/8/16.
Gillett, George, b. Winsford, Ches., e. Northwich, Ches., 29465, Pte., k. in a., F. & F., 5/12/17, formerly 61613, Cheshire Regt.
Gleave, Thomas William, b. Runcorn, Ches., e. Frodsham, Ches. (Runcorn), 29522, Pte., d. of w., F. & F., 31/3/18, formerly 62100, Cheshire Regt.
Glenn, Henry, b. Southam, Warwicks., e. Rugby, Warwicks. (Southam), 202898, Pte., d. of w., F. & F., 28/12/17.
Goble, Cecil Leslie, b. Waterlooville, Hants, e. Horndean, Hants, 268389, Pte., k. in a., F. & F., 22/3/18, formerly 24954, Somerset L.I.
Godsell, Horace, b. Foleshill, Coventry, Warwicks., e. Coventry, 3009, Pte., k. in a., F. & F., 19/7/16.
Godwin, Ernest Thomas, b. Aston, Birmingham, e. Aston, 330870, Pte., k. in a., F. & F., 5/12/17.
Goode, Absolom, b. Blackheath, Birmingham, e. Coventry, Warwicks., 3930, Cpl., k. in a., F. & F., 19/7/16.
Goode, William John, b. Keresley, Coventry, e. Coventry, 266673, Pte., d., F. & F., 5/7/18.
Gordon, David Ogilvie, b. Dundee, e. Perth, 5628, Pte., k. in a., F. & F., 10/7/16, formerly 2018, Highland Cyclist Battn.
Grady, George Andrew, b. Liverpool, e. Liverpool, 267165, Pte., k. in a., F. & F., 19/7/16, formerly 3677, Liverpool Regt.
Grant, Frederick James, b. Dewsbury, Devon, e. Exeter, Devon, 42532, Pte., k. in a., F. & F., 7/9/18, formerly 55654, Devon Regt.
Gray, Alex, b. Glasgow, e. Kirkcaldy, Fife (Cupar, Fife), 267239, Pte., k. in a., F. & F., 10/7/16, formerly 1304, Highland Cyclist Battn.
Green, Bernard Lawdon, b. Leamington, Warwicks., e. Coventry, Warwicks. (Leamington), 42828, Pte., k. in a., F. & F., 24/10/18.
Green, Frank, b. Birmingham, e. Warwick (Birmingham), 242373, Pte., k. in a., F. & F., 13/4/18.
Greenway, Harry, b. Brierley Hill, Staffs, e. Birmingham, 40992, Pte., d., F. & F., 12/3/19.
Grieve, Walter, b. St. Andrews, Kingsbarns, Fife, e. Kirkcaldy, Fife (Windygates, Fife), 267241, L/Cpl., k. in a., F. & F., 8/8/18, formerly 11051, Highland Cyclist Battn.
Griffiths, Ernest George, b. Birmingham, e. Oxford (Birmingham), 24818, Pte., d., F. & F., 25/10/18.
Griffiths, John, e. Cardigan, 5958, Pte., k. in a., F. & F., 19/7/15, formerly 2528, Welsh Regt.
Griffiths, John McPearson, e. Liverpool, 20860, Pte., d., F. & F., 10/7/16.
Griffiths, William Ernest, b. Aston, Birmingham, e. Aston, 306182, Pte., k. in a., F. & F., 3/12/17.
Grimsley, John Edward, b. Harborough Magna, Rugby, e. Rugby, Warwicks, 330743, Pte., k. in a., F. & F., 1/11/18.
Gulliver, Henry, b. Broadwell, Warwicks, e. Leamington Spa, Warwicks (Cubbington, Warwicks), 268317, Pte., k. in a., F. & F., 25/12/17.
Hadley, William James, b. Smethwick, Staffs, e. Birmingham (Winson Green, Birmingham), 29841, Cpl., d. of w., F. & F., 11/11/18, formerly 28651, Oxf. and Bucks L.I.
Hall, John Gardner, b. Glasgow, Lanark, e. Rugby, Warwicks, 268328, Pte., d., F. & F., 6/5/17.

Hamilton, Stanley John, b. Bristol, Glos., e. Bristol, 41000, Pte., k. in a., F. & F., 1/11/18.
Hammersley, Thomas Charles, e. Bedworth, Warwicks, 268167, Cpl., k. in a., F. & F., 27/8/17.
Harris, Daniel, e. Landilo, Carmarthen, 5970, L/Cpl., k. in a., F. & F., 19/7/16, formerly 5411, Welsh Regt.
Harris, David, e. Landilo, Carmarthen, 207427, Sgt., k. in a., F. & F., 22/3/18, formerly 514, Welsh Regt.
Harris, Josiah, e. Llanelly, Carmarthen, 5728, Pte., k. in a., F. & F., 17/7/16, formerly 5385, Welsh Regt.
Harris, Percy, b. Leamington, Warwicks, 41003, Pte., k. in a., F. & F., 14/4/18.
Harrison, Thomas, b. Bedworth, Warwicks, e. Coventry, Warwicks (Bedworth), 266445, L/Cpl., k. in a., F. & F., 30/3/18.
Harte, James, b. Templeby, Co. Sligo, e. Boyle, Co. Roscommon (Templeboy), 35053, Pte., d. of w., F. & F., 31/8/18, formerly 06887, R.A.O.C.
Hartle, Harry, b. Birmingham, e. Aston, Birmingham (Bartley Green, Birmingham), 306342, Pte., k. in a., F. & F., 5/12/17.
Haspey, Arthur, b Oscroft, Ches., e. Chester (Tarvin, Ches.), 29492, Pte., d., F. & F., 16/12/18, formerly 62138, Ches. Regt.
Hastead, Sidney John, b. Great Yarmouth, Norfolk, e. London (Chelsea, London), 34344, Pte., d. of w., F. & F., 8/9/18, formerly 3585, R. Berks Regt.
Hatto, Charles Edward, b. Small Heath, Birmingham, e. Birmingham (Washwood Heath, Birmingham), 22572, Pte., k. in a., F. & F., 24/10/18.
Hawkins, Walter Edward, e. Coventry, Warwicks (Exhall, Coventry), 37725, Pte., k. in a., F. & F., 1/11/18.
Hawtin, George, e. Coventry, Warwicks (Leamington, Warwicks), 268047, Pte., k. in a., F. & F., 9/4/17.
Hayes, Frank Hinde, b. Brinklow, Warwicks, e. Rugby, Warwicks, 2216, Pte., k. in a., F. & F., 19/7/16.
Haynes, William, b. Pontege, Pontypool, Mon., e. Morriston, Glam., 267400, Pte., k. in a., F. & F., 18/4/18, formerly 1447, Welsh Regt.
Hazelwood, James, e. Coventry, Warwicks, 265933, Pte., k. in a., F. & F., 19/7/16.
Hazlewood, Walter George, e. Birmingham, 19451, Pte., k. in a., F. & F., 24/10/18.
Heath, Arthur Alfred, b. Aston, Birmingham, e. Aston, 305602, Pte., k. in a., F. & F., 24/3/18.
Henning, Arthur George, e. Coventry, 266074, L/Cpl., d., F. & F., 9/6/17.
Herd, Alexander, e. Kirkcaldy, Fife, 267243, L/Cpl., k. in a., F. & F., 23/3/18, formerly 2144, Highland Cyclist Battn.
Herringshaw, John, b. Leamington Spa, Warwicks, e. Leamington Spa, 203504, Pte., k. in a., F. & F., 13/4/18.
Hesp, Eric Tom, b. Birmingham, e. Birmingham (Hands worth Staffs), 328011, Pte., k. in a., F. & F., 24/10/18.
Higgs, Augustus Silvester, b. Wells, Som., e. Weston-super Mare, Som. (Wedmore, Som.), 26406, Pte., k. in a., F. & F., 1/11/18.
Harris, Ernest, b. Alcester, Warwicks, e. Stratford-on-Avon, Warwicks, 265880, Pte., k. in a., F. & F., 21/3/18.
Hill, Frank, e. Bristol, 268024, Pte., d., F. & F., 6/2/17, formerly 30470, Glos. Regt.
Hill, Harry Stanley, b. St. Helens, Lancs, e. Warrington, Lancs (St. Helens), 29602, Pte., d. of w., F. & F., 11/12/17 formerly 39413, S. Lancs Regt.
Hillier, Charles George, b. London, e. Bristol (Sandhurst, Glos.), 41006, Pte., k. in a., F. & F., 24/10/18.
Hinton, Gerald Charles, e. Warwick (Broadway, Worcs.), 307582, Pte., k. in a., F. & F., 18/4/18, formerly 3645, Warwicks Yeo.
Hobbs, Frederick Charles, b. Sinbridge, Glos., e. Stroud, Glos (Stonehouse, Glos.), 57806, Pte., d. of w., F. & F., 9/8/18.
Hodge, John Walter, b. Bristol, Glos., e. Bristol, 41009, Pte, k. in a., F. & F., 8/8/18.
Holder, John Robert, b. Gayton, Warwicks, e. Rugby, Warwicks (Light Horne, Warwick), 208160, Pte., k. in a., F. & F., 3/12/17.
Holder, Reginald Charles, b. Rockhampton, Glos., e. Cheltenham, Glos., 41011, Pte., d. of w., F. & F., 18/5/18.
Holland, Joseph, e. Liverpool, 5524, Pte., k. in a., F. & F., 26/6/16, formerly 4927, Liverpool Regt.
Holly, Robert Ballington, e. Liverpool, 5525, Pte., k. in a., F. & F., 19/7/16, formerly 4358, Liverpool Regt.
Holt, Herbert, b. St. John's, Coventry, e. Coventry, 265532, Pte., d. of w., F. & F., 8/12/17. M.M.
Holt, John, b. Barnston, Ches., e. Northwich, Ches. (Barnston), 29463, Pte., d. of w., F. & F., 6/12/17, formerly 61872, Ches. Regt.
Hopkins, George, e. Coventry, 266418, Pte., k. in a., F. & F., 6/9/18.
Hough, Charles, b. Norland, Yorks, e. Halifax, Yorks (Sheffield, Yorks), 29735, Pte., d. of w., F. & F., 13/4/18, formerly 04463, R.A.S.C.
Hough, Stanley, b. Middlewich, Ches., e. Middlewich, 29469, Pte., k. in a., F. & F., 13/10/17, formerly 62298, Ches. Regt.
Hulligan, Michael, e. Liverpool (Bootle, Liverpool), 268591, Pte., k. in a., F. & F., 19/7/16, formerly 2731, Liverpool Regt.
Hunt, Charles Edward, e. Coventry, 268095, Pte., k. in a., F. & F., 24/3/18.
Hutt, Bertie, b. Trinity, Coventry, e. Coventry, Warwicks, 330755, Pte., k. in a., F. & F., 25/12/17.
Irons, William, e. Birmingham (Oldbury, Staffs), 307390, Pte., k. in a., F. & F., 24/3/18.
Isaacs, Thomas, b. Birmingham, e. Birmingham, 17650, Pte., k. in a., F. & F., 14/4/18.
Ison, John William, e. Coventry, Warwicks, 267964, Pte., k. in a., F. & F., 17/4/17.
Jakeman, William Alfred, e. Coventry, Warwicks (Norton Lindsay, Warwicks), 24655, Pte., d. of w., F. & F., 22/11/18.
James, Benjamin, e. Pontypridd, Glam., 267174, Pte., k. in a. F. & F., 19/7/16, formerly 2896, Welsh Regt.
James, William, e. Birmingham, 266781, Pte., d. of w., F. & F., 31/8/17.
Jephcott, John, b. Hillfields, Coventry, Warwicks, e. Coventry, 266263, Pte., k. in a., F. & F., 19/7/16.
Jocelyn, Ernest, b. Kensington, London, e. Coventry, War wicks (London), 266351, L/Sgt., k. in a., F. & F., 19/7/16.
Jocelyn, Herbert Charles, e. Stratford-on-Avon, Warwicks (Stratford-on-Avon), 3649, Sgt., k. in a., F. & F., 25/6/10.
Johnson, Albert, b. Brightwell, Oxon, e. Oxford (Watlington. Oxon), 29994, L/Cpl., d. of w., F. & F., 14/11/18, formerly 22947, Oxf. and Bucks L.I.
Johnson, Albert Joseph, b. St. Leonards, Bridgnorth, Salop, e. Coventry, Warwicks (Bridgnorth), 266341, Sgt., k. in a., F. & F., 17/9/16.
Johnson, Edward, b. Birmingham, e. Birmingham (Small Heath, Birmingham), 268150, Pte., k. in a., F. & F., 30/3/18.
Johnson, George Plant, b. Birmingham, e. Coventry, Warwicks, 66637, Pte., k. in a., F. & F., 5/12/17.
Jones, Daniel, b. Pontypridd, Glam., e. Pontypridd (Mountain Ash, Glam.), 267172, Pte., k. in a., F. & F., 8/8/18, formerly 3424, Welsh Regt.
Jones, David John, e. Carmarthen (Llandibie, Carmarthen), 6673, Pte., k. in a., F. & F., 8/7/16, formerly 565, Welsh Regt.
Jones, George, b. Llanwonno, Glam., e. Mountain Ash, Glam., 5532, Pte., d. of w., F. & F., 5/6/16.
Jones, John Thomas, b. Methyr Tydvil, Glam., e. Merthyr Tydvil, 5983, Pte., k. in a., F. & F., 19/7/16, formerly 1826, Welsh Regt.
Jones, William Henry, b. Liverpool, e. Liverpool, 267175, Pte., d. of w., F. & F., 13/9/17, formerly 2062, K. Liverpool Regt.
Kavanagh, Bryan, e. Bootle, Liverpool (New Bass, Co. Wexford), 267176, Pte., d., F. & F., 17/5/18, formerly 6001, Liverpool Regt.
Kay, William, e. Falkirk, 5641, Pte. d., F. & F., 23/7/16, formerly 1598, Highland Cyclist Battn.
Keatley, John, b. Nether Whitacre, Warwicks., e. Nuneaton, Warwicks. (Griff, Warwicks.), 28498, Pte., k. in a., F. & F., 14/4/18.
Kehoe, Martin, e. Liverpool, 20730, Pte., k. in a., F. & F., 11/1/17, formerly 2717, Liverpool Regt.
Kendall, Arthur, e. Coventry, Warwicks., 4624, Pte., d. of w., F. & F., 20/7/16.
Kendrick, Henry, e. Coventry, Warwicks, 266406, L/Cpl., k. in a., F. & F., 4/10/17.
Kent, George Harold, b. Stapleton, Glos., e. Bristol, 35156, Pte., k. in a., F. & F., 30/3/18.
Kerley, Walter Gordon, b. Newton Valance, Hants, e. Winchester, Hants (Itchen Abbott, Hants), 268391, Pte., k. in a., F. & F., 9/4/17, formerly 24397, Som. L.I.
King, Richard, b. Liverpool, e. Liverpool, 300165, Pte., k. in a., F. & F., 5/12/17, formerly 54499, Liverpool Regt.
Kitchen, Joseph William, b. Kilburn, Middx., e. Oxford (Chadlington, Oxon), 41023, Pte., d. of w., F. & F., 18/4/18.
Kite, Edward Frederick, b. Redfield, Glos., e. Bristol, Glos. (Redfield), 26212, Pte., d. of w., F. & F., 15/4/18.
Knight, Herbert Spencer, b. Birmingham, e. Birmingham (Aston, Birmingham), 24073, Pte., k. in a., F. & F., 14/8/18.
Knight, Joseph, e. Exeter, Devon, 268040, Pte., k. in a., F. & F., 9/4/17, formerly 30146, Glos. Regt.
Knighton, Frederick William, b. Sheffield, Yorks, e. Coventry, Warwicks., 4571, Pte., k. in a., F. & F., 24/3/18.
Lamb, Alfred, e. Coventry, Warwicks, 3206, Pte., k. in a., F. & F., 19/7/16.
Lane, Alfred Richard, e. Birmingham, 268074, Pte., k. in a., F. & F., 14/4/18.
Lapworth, George William, b. Warwick, e. Warwick, 41026, Pte., k. in a., F. & F., 13/4/18.
Lardner, Thomas Richard, b. Buscot, Berks, e. Abingdon, Berks (Farringdon, Berks), 57807, Pte., k. in a., F. & F., 11/11/18.
Larvin, Arthur Thomas, b. Birmingham, e. Birmingham (Winson Green, Birmingham), 239990, Pte., d. of w., F. & F., 22/8/18, formerly 22936, Ox. & Bucks L.I.
Laverty, Robert, e. Liverpool, 267177, Pte., k. in a., F. & F., 6/9/17, formerly 2785, Liverpool Regt.
Leach, William George, b. Littlemoor, Oxon, e. Oxford (Littlemoor), 24919, L/Cpl., k. in a., F. & F., 1/11/18.
Lewis, Frederick, b. Bromsgrove, Worcs., e. Coventry, Warwicks., 15070, Pte., k. in a., F. & F., 24/10/18.
Lewis, Thomas, e. Llandilo, Carmarthen (Manordilo, Carmarthen), 5727, L/Cpl., d. of w., 16/7/16, formerly 5196, Welsh Regt.
Lewis, William John, e. Blackpool, Lancs, 267179, Pte., k. in a., F. & F., 19/7/16, formerly 3440, Liverpool Regt.
Little, William, b. Stockport, Ches., e. Stockport, 29649, Pte., d. of w., F. & F., 2/11/18, formerly 40208, S. Lancs Regt.
Lloyd, Thomas, e. Gloucester, 266944, Pte., d. of w., F. & F., 7/4/17.
Lockyer, Percy, b. Fordingbridge, Hants, e. Fordingbridge (Frogham, Hants), 29828, Pte., d. of w., F. & F., 5/4/18, formerly 29279, Ox. & Bucks L.I.
Long, Alick, b. Nottingham, e. Nottingham, 27378, Pte., k. in a., F. & F., 25/4/18, formerly 33940, Notts & Derby Regt.
Lovell, William, b. Plymouth, Devon, e. Plymouth, 300212, Pte., k. in a., F. & F., 5/12/17, formerly 30231, D. of Corn. L.I.

Lucas, Ernest, e. Coventry, Warwicks, 266383, L/Cpl., k. in a., F. & F., 18/4/18.
Luscombe, Frederick Walter, b. Birmingham, e. Birmingham (Sparkhill, Birmingham), 39843, Pte., k. in a., F. & F., 24/10/18.
McGarry, James, e. Dunfermline, Fife (Cantsdam, Fife), 267265, Pte., k. in a., F. & F., 8/11/17, formerly 1577, Highland Cyclist Battn., M.M.
McGregor, William, e. Kirkcaldy, Fife (Dysart, Fife), 267266, Pte., d. of w., F. & F., 4/12/17, formerly 928, Highland Cyclist Battn.
McNab, William, b. Forfar, e. Forfar, 5664, Pte., k. in a., F. & F., 2/10/16, formerly 822, Highland Cyclist Battn.
McNulty, Andrew, b. Darlaston, Staffs, e. Darlaston, 41842, Pte., d. of w., F. & F., 2/11/18.
Macdonald, Arthur, b. Inverallan, Banff, e. Perth (Bufftown, Banff), 5658, L/Cpl., d., F. & F., 19/7/16, formerly 1235, Highland Cyclist Battn.
Macro, Arthur, e. Norwich, Norfolk (Great Ellingham, Norfolk), 29278, Pte., d., F. & F., 6/6/18, formerly 27350, Norfolk Regt.
Makin, Harry, b. Macclesfield, Ches., e. Macclesfield, 29652, Cpl., d. of w., F. & F., 3/11/18, formerly 40335, S. Lancs Regt.
Malin, William, e. Leamington, Warwicks. (Warwick), 3896, Pte., d. of w., F. & F., 28/7/16.
Mapley, Arthur William, e. Coventry, Warwicks., 4209, Pte., d. of w., F. & F., 21/8/16.
Marchant, Arthur Henry, b. Marlboro', Wilts, e. Marlboro, 306729, L/Cpl., k. in a., F. & F., 5/12/17.
Marsh, Edgar, b. Wareham, Dorset, e. Pontypridd, Glam. (Merthyr Tydvil, Glam.), 5541, Pte., d. of w., F. & F., 6/6/16, formerly 3401, Welsh Regiment.
Marshall, David, b. Scone, Perth, e. Scone, 267261, L/Cpl., k. in a., F. & F., 19/7/16, formerly 664, Highland Cyclist Battn.
Marshall, James Brown, b. Doune-Doune, Perth, e. Icome, Perth (Perth), 5654, L/Cpl., k. in a., F. & F., 2/7/16, formerly 965, Highland Cyclist Battn.
Masters, Herbert, e. Coventry, Warwicks., 268139, Pte., k. in a., F. & F., 21/3/18.
Masters, John Robert, e. Atherstone, Warwicks, 267955, Pte., k. in a., F. & F., 14/4/18.
Maxwell, George, e. Falkirk (Braehead, Falkirk), 5666, Pte., d. of w., F. & F., 25/7/16, formerly 1831, Highland Cyclist Battn.
Maynard, Frank, b. Weston, Oxon, e. Oxford (Swyncombe, Oxon), 28870, Pte., k. in a., F. & F., 14/4/18.
Mead, Fred Henry, b. Old Bradwell, Bucks, e. Wolverton Bucks (Old Bradwell), 29998, Pte., k. in a., F. & F. 7/9/18, formerly 22934, Ox. and Bucks L.I.
Melville, John, e. Perth, 267272, L/Cpl., k. in a., F. & F., 19/7/16, formerly 2020, Highland Cyclist Battn.
Miles, Stanley John, b. Rimpton, Som., e. Frome, Som. (Downhead, Som.), 26668, Pte., k. in a., F. & F., 21/8/18.
Millar, Robert, e. Kirkcaldy, Fife (North Queensferry, Fife), 267270, Pte., k. in a., F. & F., 5/12/17, formerly 1841, Highland Cyclist Battn.
Moore, Harold, b. Stockingford, Warwicks, e. Nuneaton, Warwicks (Stockingford), 2132, Cpl., k. in a., F. & F., 19/7/16.
Moore, Thomas, b. Coventry, Warwicks, e. Coventry, 266167, Pte, k. in a., F. & F., 19/7/16.
Morgan, Richard, e. Treharris, Glam., 5984, Pte., k. in a., F. & F., 19/7/16, formerly 1842, Welsh Regt.
Morris, Charles William, b. Wolverhampton, Staffs, e. Ashton, Birmingham (Witton, Birmingham), 305884, Pte., k. in a., F. & F., 1/11/18.
Morris, William, b. Dunfermline, Fife, e. Kirkcaldy, Fife (Dunfermline), 267277, Pte., k. in a., F. & F., 4/11/17, formerly 1773, Highland Cyclist Battn.
Morton, Matthew, b. Stockingford, Warwicks, e. Nuneaton, Warwicks (Stockingford), 1013, Pte., d. of w., F. & F., 22/4/18.
Mowbray, Charles, e. Rugby, Warwicks, 4785, Pte., d., F. & F., 8/1/17.
Muckalt, James, b. St. John's, Lancaster, e. Lancaster, 306976, Pte., d. of w., F. & F., 12/4/18, formerly 1733, R. Lanc. Regt.
Musson, Alfred Thomas, b. Birmingham, e. Birmingham, 40843, Pte., d. of w., F. & F., 14/4/18.
Nash, Edna Reginald, b. St. George's, Bristol, e. Bristol (Fishponds, Bristol), 37470, Pte.. d. of w., F. & F., 31/8/18.
Nash, William Henry, b. St. Luke's, Birmingham, e. Birmingham, 268372, Cpl., k. in a., F. & F., 14/4/18.
Neale, Alexander Grant, e. Coventry (Bedworth, Warwicks), 266506, Pte., k. in a., F. & F., 19/7/16.
Neil, Frederick George, b. Birkenhead, Ches., e. Birkenhead (Lower Tranmere, Ches.), 29551, Pte., k. in a., F. & F., 5/5/18, formerly 62010, Ches. Regt.
Nelson, Cornelius, b. Liverpool, e. Liverpool, 267185, L/Cpl., k. in a., F. & F., 3/12/17, formerly 3500, Liverpool Regt., M.M.
Ness, Andrew, b. Dysart, Fife, e. Kirkcaldy, Fife (Guardbridge, Fife), 267281, Pte., k. in a., F. & F., 18/8/18, formerly 2285, Highland Cyclist Battn.
Neville, Percy Frank, e. Stratford-on-Avon, Warwicks, e. Stratford-on-Avon, 266133, Pte., k. in a., F. & F., 29/4/17.
Nice, Zachariah Fuller Percy, b. Hayes, Middx., e. Ealing, Middx. (Hayes), 268292, Pte., k. in a., F. & F., 9/4/17, formerly 12191, A. Cyclist Corps.
Nicholl, Duncan, b. Berkswell, Coventry, e. Coventry (Berkswell), 2851, C.Q.M.S., d. of w., F. & F., 16/12/16.
Nicholson, Charles Alister, b. Coventry, Warwicks, e. Coventry, 267371, Pte., k. in a., F. & F., 1/11/18.
Nicol, Robert, e. Birmingham (Moseley, Birmingham), 268169, Sgt., k. in a., F. & F., 7/12/17.
Nixon, Joseph, b. Ryton, Warwicks, e. Nuneaton, Warwicks (Ryton), 268131, Pte., k. in a., F. & F., 1/11/18.
Noakes, Francis, b. Nunney, Som., e. Frome, Som. (Holwell, Som.), 57810, Pte., k. in a., F. & F., 16/9/18.
Noakes, Robert Foster, e. Stratford-on-Avon, Warwicks, 2943, Sgt., k. in a., F. & F., 19/7/16.
Norton, John Frederick, e. Rugby, Warwicks (Shotteswell, Warwicks), 268078, Pte., k. in a., F. & F., 4/10/17.
O'Dell, Ernest William, e. Stratford-on-Avon, Warwicks (Ardens Grafton, Warwicks), 3530, Pte., k. in a., F. & F., 12/12/16.
O'Dell, George Alexander, b. Kasauli, India, e. Dover, Kent, 3445, Cpl., d. of w., F. & F., 1/6/18.
Oldham, Henry John, b. Long Lawford, Warwicks, e. Rugby, Warwicks (Long Lawford), 42268, Pte., k. in a., F. & F., 24/10/18.
Oughton, Ernest Henry, b. Keresley, Coventry, Warwicks, e. Coventry (Brownshill Green, Warwicks), 266298, L/Cpl., k. in a., F. & F., 23/3/18.
Over, Albert Edward, b. St. Michaels, Coventry, e. Coventry, 2827, Pte., d. of w., F. & F., 18/5/18.
Over, Walter, b. Foleshill, Coventry, Warwicks, e. Coventry (Foleshill), 266203, Cpl., k. in a., F. & F., 29/9/17.
Overton, Ernest Henry, b. Coventry, Warwicks, e. Coventry, 265902, Pte., k. in a., F. & F., 3/12/17.
Parish, Herbert, b. Doncaster, Yorks, e. Coventry, Warwicks (Stainforth, Yorks), 24644, Pte., k. in a., F. & F., 14/4/18.
Parry, Herbert, b. Merthyr, Glam., e. Merthyr, 325130, Pte., k. in a., F. & F., 25/4/18, formerly 4964, Mon. Regt.
Passmore, Dennis Edmund, b. Bristol, Glos., e. Bristol, 41050, Pte., d. of w., F. & F., 24/5/18.
Paton, Ernest, b. Forfar, e. Forfar, 5683, Pte., k. in a., F. & F., 19/7/16, formerly 814, Highland Cyclist Battn.
Pattie, Alex., b. Sconull, Leven, Fife, e. Kirkcaldy, Fife (Leven), 267285, Sgt., k. in a., F. & F., 5/12/17, formerly 1109, Highland Cyclist Battn.
Pearce, Alfred, b. Avonmouth, Glos., e. Shirehampton, Glos. (Avonmouth), 32879, Pte., k. in a., F. & F., 23/3/18, formerly 27609, Hrs.
Pearman, Arthur William, e. Rugby, Warwicks, 2991, Pte., d. of w., F. & F., 29/7/16.
Perkins, Arthur, b. Sunninghill, Berks, e. Reading, Berks (Windlesham, Surrey), 41051, L/Cpl., d. of w., F. & F., 29/10/18.
Phillips, Victor, b. Wednesbury, Staffs, e. Warwick, 23855, Pte., d. of w., F. & F., 15/7/18.
Pickerill, Sydney, b. Sutton Coldfield, Warwicks, e. Coventry, 265917, Pte., k. in a., F. & F., 23/3/18.
Pickering, William Harold, b. Buckingham, e. Coventry, Warwicks, 268075, Pte., k. in a., F. & F., 21/3/18.
Pickles, Arthur, b. Newchurch-in-Pendle, Lancs, e. Nelson, Lancs (Newchurch-in-Pendle), 325151, Pte., d. of w., F. & F., 8/4/18, formerly 27649, S. Lan. Regt.
Pinn, Edwin Charles, e. Hounslow, Middx. (New Cross, London, S.E.), 20350, Pte., k. in a., F. & F., 12/1/17, formerly 10855, A. Cyclist Corps.
Pinnegar, Albert, b. Stoney Stanton, Leics., e. Nuneaton, Warwicks (Attleborough, Warwicks), 203814, Pte., k. in a., F. & F., 23/3/18.
Place, William, b. Rawtenstall, Lancs., e. Preston, Lancs. (Cloughfold, Lancs.), 325131, Pte., k. in a., F. & F., 13/5/18, formerly 27620, S. Lan. Regt.
Portman, Albert, e. Coventry, 266488, Pte., k. in a., F. & F., 19/7/16.
Powell, Herbert, b. Totterdown, Glos., e. Bristol (Totterdown), 37444, Pte., d. of w., F. & F., 31/8/18.
Powers, James, b. Shirley, Warwicks, e. Birmingham (Shirley), 26254, Pte., k. in a., F. & F., 24/10/18.
Pratt, Clarence Arthur Meynell, b. Birmingham, e. Birmingham (Ashton, Birmingham)- 16948, Pte., k. in a., F. & F., 14/4/18.
Pratt, George, b. Kettle Hill, King's Kettle, Fife, e. Kirkcaldy, Fife (Methil, Fife), 5687, Pte., k. in a., F. & F., 19/7/16, formerly 1095, Highland Cyclist Battn.
Price, Alonzo, b. Birmingham, e. Warwick (Birmingham), 23237, Pte., k. in a., F. & F., 5/12/17.
Price, Edward John, e. Gloucester (Arlingham, Glos.), 268028, Pte., k. in a., F. & F., 14/4/18, formerly 30491, Gloucester Regt.
Price, Harold Gwillym, e. Merthyr Tydfil, Glam. (Penywern, Dowlais, Glam.), 6000, Pte., d. of w., F. & F., 4/9/16, formerly 2575, Welsh Regt.
Prince, Alfred Percival, b. Ashton, Birmingham, e. Birmingham (Balsall Heath, Birmingham), 26450, Pte., d., F. & F., 15/11/18.
Pringle, William, b. Liverpool, e. Birkenhead, Ches. (Hoylake, Ches.), 29660, Pte., k. in a., F. & F., 14/4/18, formerly 40435, S. Lan. Regt.
Pryde, John, b. Newburn, Largo, Fife, e. Kirkcaldy, Fife (Colinsburgh, Fife), 5688, L/Cpl., d., F. & F., 19/7/16, formerly 1336, Highland Cyclist Battn.
Pullinger, William, b. N. Waltham, Basingstoke, Hants, e. Basingstoke, 306918, Cpl., d. of w., F. & F., 6/4/18, formerly 2065, Hamps Regt.
Pye, George, b. Coltishall, Norfolk, e. Coltishall, 300122, Pte., k. in a., F. & F., 18/8/18, formerly 1480 Norfolk Regt.
Randall, Albert, e. Birmingham, 268616, Pte., k. in a., F. & F., 19/11/17.
Ravenhall, William, b. Birmingham, e. Birmingham (Ashton, Birmingham), 300250, Pte., k. in a., F. & F., 29/9/17, formerly 204381, Ox. and Bucks. L.I.
Rawlinson, Charles, b. Preston, Lancs, e. Preston, 37473, Pte., d. of w., F. & F., 13/4/18, formerly 19611, E. Lan. Regt.
Rayner, Edwin Henry, b. Windsor, Berks, e. Windsor, 7010, Pte., k. in a., F. & F., 4/6/18, M.M.

Raynor, Stephen, b. Longham, Norfolk, e. Chester, 29524, Pte., k. in a., F. & F., 23/3/18, formerly 61949, Ches. Regt.
Read, Edwin, b. Aylesbury, Bucks, e. Rugby, Warwicks, 266155, Pte., k. in a., F. & F., 5/12/17.
Readhead, John, b. Bridlington, Yorks, e. Driffield, Yorks (Bridlington), 35035, Pte., k. in a., F. & F., 24/3/18, formerly 1089, R.A.S.C.
Reading, Archibald George, b. Mile End, Middx., e. East Ham, London, E. (Forest Gate, Essex), 32482, Pte., k. in a., F. & F., 14/4/18, formerly 6487, Lancers.
Reading, George Victor, e. Kineton, Warwicks (Tysoe, Warwicks), 207986, Pte., k. in a., F. & F., 9/4/17.
Rees, William Simon, e. Llandilo, Carmarthen, 5962, Pte., k. in a., F. & F., 19/7/16, formerly 5408, Welsh Regt.
Reynolds, John Henry, b. Rugby, Warwicks, e. Rugby, 268059, Pte., k. in a., F. & F., 8/5/18.
Rice, Leonard, b. Easton, Bristol, Glos., e. Bristol (Easton), 203904, Pte., k. in a., F. & F., 27/4/18, formerly 2596, R.E.
Richards, David, e. Swansea, Glam. (Cwmbwrla, Swansea), 267403, Pte., k. in a., F. & F., 24/10/18, formerly 2490, Welsh Regt.
Richardson, William, b. Perth, e. Scone, Perth (Perth), 267290, L/Cpl., k. in a., F. & F., 19/7/16, formerly 848, Highland Cyclist Battn.
Richardson, William Ernest, b. Bicester, Oxon, e. High Wycombe, Bucks, 26856, Pte., k. in a., F. & F., 24/10/18.
Riches, Albert Edward, b. Camberwell, London, e. Camberwell (Peckham, London, S.E.), 40401, Pte., k. in a., F. & F., 24/10/18.
Riddle, William Randolph, b. Netley, Hants, e. Portsmouth (Netley), 12590, L/Cpl., k. in a., F. & F., 25/4/18, formerly 56099, R.G.A.
Robb, Kinnaird, b. St. Peter's, Dundee, Forfar, e. Dundee, 32720, Cpl., k. in a., F. & F., 14/4/18, formerly 1797, Fife and Forfar Yeo.
Robbins, George, b. Birmingham, Warwicks, e. Birmingham (Sutton Coldfield, Birmingham), 307585, Pte., k. in a., F. & F., 22/3/18, formerly 3415, Warwicks Yeo.
Robertson, William, b. Markinch, Cameron Bridge, Fife, e. Kirkcaldy, Fife (Cameron Bridge), 5693, Cpl., k. in a., F. & F., 20/7/16, formerly 1107, Highland Cyclist Battn.
Robins, George Henry, b. Henley-on-Thames, Oxon, e. Caversham, Oxon (Henley-on-Thames), 37458, Pte., k. in a., F. & F., 14/4/18.
Rollason, Walter James, b. Winson Green, Birmingham, e. Birmingham (Hockley, Birmingham), 23839, Pte., k. in a., F. & F., 28/3/18.
Rowden, Leonard Harold, b. Chesham, Bucks, e. Oxford (Chesham), 29832, Pte., d. of w., F. & F., 11/4/18, formerly 27946, Oxf. and Bucks L.I.
Rowe, Arthur Price, b. Madeley, Wellington, Shrops., e. Birmingham (Balsall Heath, Birmingham), 457, Pte., d., F. & F., 12/3/18.
Rowlands, Arthur Ernest, b. Bridgnorth, Salop, e. Birmingham (Saltley, Birmingham), 26739, Pte., k. in a., F. & F., 16/4/18.
Russ, Sidney Ernest, b. Birmingham, e. Birmingham (Aston, Birmingham), 33652, Pte., d. of w., F. & F., 22/3/18, formerly 155313, R.A.S.C.
Russell, Horace Richard, b. Birmingham, e. Birmingham (Aston, Birmingham), 40855, Pte., k. in a., F. & F., 25/4/18.
Russell, James, e. Kirkcaldy, Fife (Camelon, Falkirk, Stirling), 5695, Pte., k. in a., F. & F., 8/7/16, formerly 1607, Highland Cyclist Battn.
Ryan, Christopher, b. Liverpool, e. Liverpool, 20871, L/Cpl., k. in a., F. & F., 19/7/16, formerly 2034, Liverpool Regt.
Ryman, Frederick, b. Stratford-on-Avon, Warwicks, e. Stratford-on-Avon, 3785, Pte., d., F. & F., 6/2/17.
Sanderson, David, e. Liverpool (Islington, Liverpool), 268586, L/Cpl., k. in a., F. & F., 19/7/16, formerly 3383, Liverpool Regt.
Satchwell, Arthur, b. Alvechurch, Worcester, e. Birmingham (Quinton, Birmingham), 202217, Pte., k. in a., F. & F., 7/9/18.
Saunders, James Charles, b. Birmingham, e. Birmingham, 37789, Pte., k. in a., F. & F., 22/3/18.
Scapleton, Edward Leonard Charles, b. Bristol, Glos., e. Bristol, 40861, Pte., k. in a., F. & F., 13/4/18.
Series, John Robert, b. Stratford, London, e. Winchester, Hants (Hickfield, Hants), 306920, Pte., d. of w., F. & F., 15/4/18, formerly 3173, Hamps. Regt.
Shaffir, Herbert Meredith, b. Coventry, e. Coventry, 266007, Sgt., d. of w., F. & F., 21/3/18.
Sharlott, Thomas Charles, e. Stratford-on-Avon, Warwicks, 266353, Pte., k. in a., F. & F., 19/7/16.
Sharp, Joseph Martin, b. N. Woolwich, London, S.E., e. Winchester, Hants, 306930, L/Cpl., d. of w., F. & F., 29/4/18, formerly 2190, Hamps. Regt.
Shaw, John Henry, b. Birmingham, e. Birmingham, 268366, Pte., d., F. & F., 10/4/17.
Shaw, William, b. Bannockburn, Stirling, e. Bannockburn, 267295, Cpl., k. in a., F. & F., 18/5/18, formerly 2054, Highland Cyclist Battn.
Shaw, William Harry, b. Birmingham, e. Birmingham (Handsworth, Birmingham), 267988, Pte., k. in a., F. & F., 14/4/18.
Sheargold, Sidney George Allen, b. Cheltenham, Glos., e. Warwick (Coventry, Warwicks), 40863, Pte., k. in a., F. & F., 14/4/18.
Sheeley, Frederick George, e. Bristol, Glos., 20202, L/Cpl., k. in a., F. & F., 10/1/17, formerly 30483, Glos. Regt.
Sheffield, Sidney, e. Coventry, Warwicks (Stoke, Coventry), 4618, L/Cpl., d., F. & F., 19/7/16.
Shepherd, Charles, b. Kendal, Westmoreland, e. Crosby, Westmoreland (Bootle, Lancs), 268573, Pte., k. in a., F. & F., 19/7/16, formerly 1987, Liverpool Regt.
Sheppard, Herbert Benjamin, b. Coventry, Warwicks, e. Coventry, 265192, Pte., k. in a., F. & F., 19/7/16.
Shird, George, b. Stockport, Ches., e. Manchester (Stockport), 29484, Pte., k. in a., F. & F., 5/12/17, formerly 61809, Ches. Regt.
Simmons, Frank, e. Wallasey, Ches. (Fishponds, Bristol), 267002, Pte., d., F. & F., 24/12/18.
Simpson, David, b. Pathead, Fife, e. Kirkcaldy, Fife, 267298, Cpl., k. in a., F. & F., 19/7/16, formerly 711, Highland Cyclist Battn.
Skevey, William, e. Salford, Lancs (Liverpool), 300136, Pte., k. in a., F. & F., 29/9/17, formerly 2885, Lancs Fus.
Smith, Alec James Victor, e. Leamington, Warwicks (Warwick), 3859, L/Cpl., k. in a., F. & F., 19/7/16.
Smith, Ernest Richard, b. Reading, Berks, e. Birmingham (Bordesley Green, Birmingham), 300256, Pte., k. in a., F. & F., 18/8/18, formerly 204379, Oxf. and Bucks L.I.
Smith, Frederick James, b. Malta, e. Coventry, Warwicks, 9699, Pte., d. of w., F. & F., 31/12/17.
Smith, John, b. Forfar, e. Forfar, 5704, Pte., d., F. & F., 19/7/16, formerly 830, Highland Cyclist Battn.
Smith, Henry, b. Stratford-on-Avon, Warwicks, e. Stratford-on-Avon, 266253, Pte., k. in a., F. & F., 11/8/18.
Smith, John, e. Birmingham (Hednesford, Staffs), 306315, Pte., d. of w., F. & F., 14/4/18.
Smith, Thomas, e. Coventry, Warwicks (Stoke, Coventry), 265979, Cpl., d. of w., F. & F., 28/10/18. M.M.
Smith, William, b. Southam, Warwicks, e. Rugby, Warwicks (Southam), 37934, L/Cpl., d. of w., F. & F., 19/4/18.
Snead, Charles Edward, b. Birmingham, e. Warwick (Small Heath, Birmingham), 37843, Pte., k. in a., F. & F., 27/10/18.
Southgate, Charles Rowland, b. Norton, Bury St. Edmunds, Suffolk, e. Bury St. Edmunds (Harleston, Norfolk), 32999, Pte., k. in a., F. & F., 23/3/18, formerly 8850, Hussars.
Sparkes, Frederick, b. Thurlaston, Warwicks, e. Rugby, Warwicks (Bilton, Warwicks), 268140, Pte., k. in a., F. & F., 11/8/18.
Stannard, George, b. Earlsfield, Surrey, e. Gosport, Hants (Newtown, Eastleigh, Hants), 29827, Pte., k. in a., F. & F., 3/12/17, formerly 29278, Oxf. and Bucks L.I.
Stanway, Herbert William, b. Aberdeen, e. Coventry, Warwicks, 265295, Cpl., k. in a., F. & F., 19/7/16.
Stevens, George, b. Leamington, Warwicks, e. Slough, Bucks (Burnham, Bucks), 34978, Pte., k. in a., F. & F., 24/10/18, formerly 286472, Oxf. Hussars.
Stevens, William James, b. Newton Abbot, Devon, e. Totnes, Devon, 300208, Pte., k. in a., F. & F., 5/11/17, formerly 202655, Duke of Cornwall's L.I.
Stevenson, Frederick, b. Hockley, Warwicks, e. Birmingham (Springhill, Birmingham), 268370, Pte., k. in a., F. & F., 9/4/17.
Stiles, Harold George, b. Malvern, Worcs., e. Birmingham, 26776, Pte., k. in a., F. & F., 13/4/18.
Stirrup, James Hope, b. Southport, Lancs, e. Seaforth, Lancs (Southport), 300193, Pte., k. in a., F. & F., 5/12/17, formerly 56617, Liverpool Regt.
Stocker, Joseph William, b. St. Ives, Hunts, e. Huntingdon (St. Ives), 30280, Pte., k. in a., F. & F., 31/5/18, formerly 674, Hunts Cyclist Battn.
Stockton, James, b. Shrewsbury, Shrops, e. Oswestry, Shrops (Dudleston Heath, near Oswestry), 208258, Pte, k. in a., F. & F., 9/4/17, formerly 63026, R.E.
Stockwell, Bertram Arthur, b. Reading, Berks, e. Reading, 40870, Pte., k. in a., F. & F., 7/8/18.
Stokes, Horace, b. Haugham, Kent, e. Dover, Kent, 35063, Pte., d. of w., F & F., 17/4/18, formerly 012701, R.A.O.C.
Storrar, David, b. Kirkcaldy, Fife, e. Kirkcaldy (Dysart, Fife), 5711, Pte., k. in a., F. & F., 20/9/16, formerly 704, Highland Cyclist Battn.
Stroud, Charles Henry, b. Gloucester, e. Bristol, Glos. (Gloucester), 40872, Pte., d. of w., F. & F., 19/4/18.
Stuart, Arthur Charles, e. Coventry, Warwicks, 4206, Pte., k. in a., F. & F., 22/8/16.
Stych, Joseph, b. Birmingham, e. Birmingham, 23869, Pte., k. in a., F. & F., 18/4/18.
Styles, William Ewart, b. Tysoe, Warwicks, e. Kineton, Warwicks (Church Tysoe, Warwicks), 203510, Pte., k. in a., F. & F., 21/3/18.
Summers, Frederick, b. Eathorpe, Warwicks, e. Rugby, Warwicks (Clifton, Warwicks), 265906, Pte., k. in a., F. & F., 23/3/18.
Summers, Walter, e. Birmingham (Springhill, Birmingham), 306402, Pte., k. in a., F. & F., 24/3/18.
Sutherland, Thomas, b. Leamington Spa, Warwicks, e. Coventry, Warwicks (Leamington Spa), 267960, Pte., k. in a., F. & F., 14/4/18.
Sweetzer, Ernest Frank, b. Birmingham, e. Birmingham, 25627, Pte., k. in a., F. & F., 24/10/18.
Swift, John Charles, e. Rugby, Warwicks. (Bourne, Lincs), 265915, Pte., k. in a., F. & F., 19/7/16.
Symonds, Frederick Ebenezer, b. Bermuda, British West Indies, e. Portsmouth, Hants, 268043, L/Cpl., k. in a., F. & F., 28/3/18, formerly 29175, Glos. Regt.
Tagg, George Edward, b. Crewe, Ches., e. Crewe, 29595, Pte., k. in a., F. & F., 29/8/17, formerly 40446, S. Lancs Regt.
Tallis, Thomas, e. Coventry, Warwicks. (Bedworth, Warwicks.), 4233, Pte., k. in a., F. & F., 19/7/16.
Tams, Henry Francis, e. Coventry (Foleshill, Coventry, Warwicks.), 3343, Pte., d. of w., F. & F., 20/7/16.
Taylor, George Albert, e. Coventry, Warwicks., 4309, Dmr., k. in a., F. & F., 19/7/16.
Taylor, Ralph Henry, b. Enstone, Oxon., e. Oxford (Charlbury, Oxon.), 35200, Pte., k. in a., F. & F., 8/8/18.
Terry, Frederick, e. Coventry, 265956, Pte., k. in a., F. & F., 29/9/17.

Thom, David Low, b. Forfar, e. Kirkcaldy, Fife (Forfar), 5712, Pte., d., F. & F., 19/7/16, formerly 1135, Highland Cyclist Battn.
Thompson, Edwin, b. Luton, Beds., e. Bedford (Luton), 307504, Pte., d., F. & F., 22/3/18, formerly 3354, R.E.
Thorpe, Dennis, b. Kidlington, Oxon, e. Coventry, Warwicks. (Kidlington), 43621, Pte., d. of w., F. & F., 7/9/18.
Tibbles, George Edward, e. Stratford-on-Avon, Warwicks. (Alcester, Warwicks.), 268077, Pte., k. in a., F. & F., 9/4/17.
Timms, Harold, b. Wootton Wawen, Warwicks., e. Warwick (Tiddington, Warwicks.), 24675, Pte., d. of w., F. & F., 2/5/18.
Timms, William Frank, b. Milton-under-Wychwood, Oxon, e. Bristol, Glos. (Shipton-under-Wychwood, Oxon), 41081, Pte., d. of w., F. & F., 29/10/18.
Tonks, John, b. Birmingham, e. Warwick (Dorridge, Warwicks.), 41082, Pte., k. in a., F. & F., 14/4/18.
Topp, Aubrey, e. Coventry, Warwicks, 4386, Pte., k. in a., F. & F., 19/7/16.
Towey, Patrick, b. Ardcull, Co. Mayo, e. Chester (Ardcull), 29479, Pte., k. in a., F. & F., 3/12/17, formerly 61855, Ches. Regt.
Townley, Frederick, b. Hook Norton, Oxon, e. Coventry, Warwicks (Foleshill, Coventry), 4638, Pte., k. in a., F. & F., 19/7/16.
Townley, William, b. Lancaster, Lancs, e. Liverpool (Aigburth, Liverpool), 325128, Pte., d. of w., F. & F., 2/11/18, formerly 41359, Liverpool Regt.
Townsend, Arthur, b. Tysoe, Warwicks, e. Fenny Compton, Warwicks. (Upper Tysoe), 23152, Pte., d. of w., F. & F., 6/12/17.
Townsend, John, b. West Bromwich, Staffs, e. Birmingham (Small Heath, Birmingham), 20098, Pte., k. in a., F. & F., 6/12/17.
Trinder, Percy, b. South Cerney, Cirencester, Glos., e. Bristol, Glos. (South Cerney), 41084, Pte., d. of w., F. & F., 27/10/18.
Troupe, William, e. Kirkcaldy, Fife (Bannockburn, Stirling), 5715, Pte., d. of w., F. & F., 16/7/16, formerly 2076, Highland Cyclist Battn.
Turnbull, Henry, e. Stenhousemuir, Stirling (Denny, Stirling), 267305, Pte., k. in a., F. & F., 19/7/16, formerly 2081, Highland Cyclist Battn.
Turnbull, James, b. Markinch, Fife, e. E. Wemyss, Fife (Windygates, Fife), 267306, Pte., d. of w., F. & F., 20/3/17, formerly 942, Highland Cyclist Battn.
Twamley, Leonard, b. Coventry, Warwicks, e. Leamington, Warwicks., 266675, Pte., k. in a., F. & F., 19/7/16.
Tyler, William Alfred, b. Harbury, Warwicks., e. Coventry, Warwicks. (Leamington, Warwicks.), 265351, L/Cpl., d. of w., F. & F., 4/10/17.
Unitt, Amos Latham, b. Stratford-on-Avon, e. Stratford-on-Avon, Warwicks., 24305, Pte., k. in a., F. & F., 23/3/18.
Vernon, John, b. Coventry, Warwicks., e. Coventry, 268162, Pte., k. in a., F. & F., 9/4/17.
Vince, Thomas Cyril, b. Breamore, Hants, e. Ringwood, Hants (Breamore), 35212, Pte., k. in a., F. & F., 28/3/18.
Vosper, Albert Thomas, e. Harborne, Birmingham, 26763, Pte., k. in a., F. & F., 24/10/18.
Wale, William, b. Coventry, Warwicks., e. Coventry, 266674, Pte., k. in a., F. & F., 19/7/16.
Walker, Alfred, e. Birmingham (Aston, Birmingham), 267783, Pte., k. in a., F. & F., 29/11/17.
Walker, Arthur, b. Foleshill, Coventry, e. Coventry, Warwicks., 265279, Pte., d., F. & F., 9/3/19.
Walker, Augustus Harry, b. Birmingham, e. Handsworth, Staffs, 36440, Sgt., d. of w., F. & F., 1/12/18, formerly 24343, Ox. & Bucks. L.I.
Walker, Cuthbert, b. Little Bytham, Lincs, e. Coventry, Warwicks, 21204, Pte., k. in a., F. & F., 30/8/17.
Walker, Edward Albert, b. Hotwells, Bristol, Glos., e. Bristol (Hotwells), 28915, Pte., d. of w., F. & F., 6/9/17.
Walker, Joshua, e. Bathgate, Linlithgow (East Benhar, Linlithgow), 307147, Pte., k. in a., F. & F., 30/3/18, formerly 2587, R. Scots.
Walker, Joseph Evan, b. Burton-on-Trent, Staffs, e. Warwick (New Bilton, Rugby, Warwicks.), 23770, Pte., k. in a., F. & F., 30/3/18.
Walker, Thomas William, b. Birmingham, e. Birmingham (Ladywood, Birmingham), 267990, Pte., k. in a., F. & F., 9/4/17.
Walker, Walter, b. Stratford-on-Avon, Warwicks., e. Warwick (Stratford-on-Avon), 22503, Pte., k. in a., F. & F., 3/12/17.
Ward, Herbert, e. Coventry, Warwicks (Whitley, Coventry), 3354, L/Sgt., k. in a., F. & F., 19/7/16.
Ward, Joseph, b. Holy Trinity, Coventry, Warwicks., e. Coventry, 266345, Pte., k. in a., F. & F., 14/7/16.
Warner, George Percy, e. Coventry, Warwicks., 3274, L/Cpl., k. in a., F. & F., 8/10/15.
Watkins, Archie Kenneth, e. Newbury, Berks (Lambourne, Berks), 32046, Pte., k. in a., F. & F., 1/11/18, formerly 27429, Hrs.
Watkins, Henry Percival, b. Haverfordwest, Pembroke, e. Haverfordwest (Milford Haven, Pembroke), 5948, L/Cpl., k. in a., F. & F., 19/7/16, formerly 354, Welsh Regt.
Watkins, William Richard, b. Rhondda, Glam., e. Putne, Glam., 25017, Pte., d. of w., F. & F., 4/4/18, formerly 106629, R.A.S.C.
Watson, Joseph William, e. Tamworth, Warwicks (Glascote, Warwicks), 242402, Pte., k. in a., F. & F., 6/9/18.
Watts, Charles Henry, b. Long Lawford, Warwicks, e. Long Lawford, 266560, Pte., k. in a., F. & F., 5/12/17.
Webb, Alfred Thomas, e. Coventry, Warwicks, 268097, Pte., k. in a., F. & F., 15/11/17.
Webb, Francis Edward, b. Pangbourne, Oxon, e. Coventry, Warwicks (Honington, Shipston-on-Stour, Worcs), 25640, Pte., k. in a., F. & F., 24/10/18.
Webb, James, b. Stratford-on-Avon, Warwicks, e. Coventry, Warwicks, 266321, Sgt., d. of w., F. & F., 22/4/18.
Webster, George Chawner, b. Lancaster, Lancs, e. Lancaster, 306999, L/Cpl., k. in a., F. & F., 23/3/18, formerly 2540, R. Lanc. Regt.
Weeks, Thomas Henry, b. Easton, Bristol, Glos., e. Bristol (Bedminster, Glos.), 35203, Pte., k. in a., F. & F., 22/3/18.
Wells, Sydney Charles, e. Cheltenham, Glos., 307461, Pte., k. in a., F. & F., 24/3/18, formerly 27109, R. Berks Regt.
Welsh, Robert, b. Bortley, Durham, e. Gallamien, Stirling (Cowie, Stirling), 5718, L/Cpl., d., F. & F., 19/7/16, formerly 924, Highland Cyclist Battn.
Wenmouth, William James, b. Crewkerne, Som., e. Crewkerne (Broadshard, Som.), 28942, Pte., k. in a., F. & F., 22/3/18.
West, Frank Mansell, b. Aylesbury, Bucks, e. Oxford (Aylesbury), 29838, Pte., d. of w., F. & F., 5/10/17, formerly 28539, Oxf. and Bucks L.I.
West, George, e. Birmingham, :42989, Pte., d. of w., F. & F., 19/8/18.
West, Ralph Montague, b. Bristol, Glos., e. Bristol, 40878, Pte., d. of w., F. & F., 28/6/18.
Weston, George, b. Liverpool, e. Liverpool, 267196, Pte., k. in a., F. & F., 12/4/18, formerly 4599, Liverpool Regt.
Westwood, Charles Patrick, e. Bristol, Glos., 43651, Pte., k. in a., F. & F., 20/9/18, formerly 35887, Glouc. Regt.
Whatley, Joseph Edward, b. Coventry, Warwicks, e. Coventry, 268082, Pte., k. in a., F. & F., 22/3/18.
Whateley, Joseph Robert, e. Stratford-on-Avon, Warwicks, 2987, L/Sgt., k. in a., F. & F., 19/7/16.
Whatley, Reginald, b. Bletchley, Bucks, e. Bletchley, 26171, Pte., k. in a., F. & F., 19/8/18.
Whitcroft, Tom, e. Coventry, Warwicks (Bedworth, Warwicks), 266485, Pte., k. in a., F. & F. 19/7/16.
White, George Edgar, b. Leicester, e. Rugby, Warwicks, 22140, Pte., k. in a., F. & F. 14/4/18.
White, Reginald, b. Fritwell, Oxon, e. Banbury, Oxon (Fritwell), 29844, Pte., d. of w., F. & F., 22/3/18, formerly 29006, Oxf. and Bucks L.I.
White, William, b. Bristol, Glos., e. Bristol (Kingswood, near Wootton-under-Edge, Glos.), 25801, Pte., d. of w., F. & F., 27/8/18.
White, William Harvey, b. Frankton, Rugby, Warwicks, e. Coventry, Warwicks (Rugby), 2497, Sgt., d., F. & F., 19/7/16.
Whyte, Andrew Thomson, e. Aberdeen, 307509, Pte., k. in a., F. & F., 24/3/18, formerly 843, R.E.
Wiggins, Harold, b. Crewe, Cheshire, e. Crewe, 29598, Pte., k. in a., F. & F., 3/12/17, formerly 40445, S. Lancs. Regt.
Wilkins, George, b. Birmingham, e. Aston, Birmingham, (Aston Manor, Birmingham), 328049, Cpl., k. in a., F. & F., 1/11/18.
Williams, David George, b. Llanelly, Carmarthen, e. Llanelly, 267421, Pte., d., F. & F., 7/6/17, formerly 883, Welsh Regt.
Williams, Edward Ernest, e. Bristol, Glos. (Bedminster, Som.), 203915, Pte., k. in a., F. & F. 14/4/18, formerly 20081, R.E.
Williams, George Edward, b. Finmere, Oxon, e. Bletchley, Bucks (Buckingham), 29834, Pte., k. in a., F. & F., 29/9/17, formerly 28369, Oxf. and Bucks L.I.
Williams, Robert Henry, b. Penzance, Cornwall, e. Truro, Cornwall (Helston, Cornwall), 300211, Pte., d. of w., F. & F., 20/8/18, formerly 202942, D. of Corn. L.I.
Williams, Thomas John, b. Blaenavon, Mon., e. Pontypool, Mon. (Blaenavon), 325155, Sgt., k. in a., F. & F., 24/10/18, formerly 3133, Mon. R.
Willis, Percy, b. Polesworth, Warwicks, e. Atherstone, Warwicks (Polesworth), 41797, Pte., k. in a., F. & F., 24/10/18.
Willits, Thomas Righton, b. Eckington, Worcs e. Stratford-on-Avon, Warwicks, 266366, Pte., k. in a., F. & F., 22/12/17.
Willmott, Harry Ross, b. Winchester, Hants, e. Reading, Berks, 35208, Pte., d. of w., F. & F., 16/4/18.
Wilson, Aubrey, b. Stockingford, Warwicks, e. Nuneaton, Warwicks (Stockingford), 12780, Pte., k. in a., F. & F., 24/10/18.
Wilson, Robert Harold, b. Northampton, e. Bristol (Staplehill, Bristol), 40882, Pte., k. in a., F. & F., 1/11/18.
Wiseman, William, b. Birmingham, Warwicks, e. Birmingham (Handsworth, Birmingham), 43631, Pte., k. in a., F. & F., 1/11/18.
Wood, David Joseph, e. Pontypridd, Glam. (Brecon), 267198, Pte., k. in a., F. & F., 22/3/18, formerly 3261, Welsh Regt.
Woodcock, Walter, b. Birmingham, e. Birmingham (Aston, Birmingham), 43645, Pte., k. in a., F. & F., 7/9/18.
Woodman Percy, b. Warnham, Sussex, e. Winchester, Hants (Horsham, Sussex), 26599, Pte., d. of w., F. & F., 5/9/18.
Woolley, Thomas Edward, b. Birmingham, e. Birmingham (Hockley, Birmingham), 26774, Pte., k. in a., F. & F., 22/3/18.
Woolloff, Horace, e. Birmingham (Rowington, Warwicks), 266730, Pte., d. of w., F. & F., 1/3/17.
Wright, Ernest, e. Tiverton, Devon (Mardon Down, near Wellington, Som.), 267991, Pte., k. in a., F. & F., 29/4/17.
Wright, Frank Edward, e. Birmingham (Polesworth, Warwicks), 268073, Pte., k. in a., F. & F., 1/3/17.
Wright, Herbert Steven, b. Shaftesbury, Dorset, e. Shaftesbury, 35211, Pte., d. of w., F. & F. 13/4/18.
Wright, James, b. Sutton Coldfield, Warwicks, e. Warwick (Wilde Green, Birmingham), 267992, Pte., k. in a., F. & F., 5/4/18.
Wright, Robert, b. Ormskirk, Lancs, e. Ormskirk, 267199, Pte., d., F. & F., 8/1/18, formerly 1997, Liverpool Regt.
Wright, William Henry, b. Birmingham, e. Birmingham (Sparkhill, Birmingham), 266720, Cpl., k. in a., F. & F., 9/4/17.
Yoxall, Robert, e. Redditch, Worcs, 266943, Pte., k. in a., F. & F., 9/4/17.

7th Reserve Battalion.

Adkins, Charles, e. Coventry, 3194, Pte., d., Home, 8/3/16.
Ashton, Wilfred Thomas, b. St. Mary's, Shrewsbury, Salop, e. Birmingham (Shrewsbury), 1641, Pte., d., Home, 28/3/15.
Baker, Albert Edward, e. Huntingdon (Catworth, Hunts.), 203414, Pte., d., Home, 31/3/18, formerly 1531, Hunts. Cyclist Battn.
Beresford, Ernest George, e. Aston, Birmingham (Kinver, Staffs), 4058, Pte., d., Home, 20/11/15.
Branson, Harry, b. Boddington, Northants, e. Warwick (Byfield, Northants), 4633, Pte., d., Home, 3/7/16.
Garrett, Samuel H., e. Coventry, Warwicks, 3065, Pte., d., Home, 15/7/15.
Gilks, William Henry, b. Pillerton, Warwicks, e. Warwick, 4550, Pte., d., Home, 11/4/16.
Hesketh, Harry, e. Birmingham, 2915, Pte., d., Home, 26/1/15.
Hewitt, Walter, e. Leamington, Warwicks, 3589, Pte., d., Home, 13/6/16.
Horsley, Christopher, b. St. Nicholas, Kenilworth, Warwicks, e. Kenilworth, 2142, Pte., d., Home, 21/1/15.
Huby, William Frederick Hacket, b. Derby, e. Coventry, Warwicks (Bretford, Warwicks), 202001, Pte., d., Home, 7/10/18.
Lippitt, Leonard, e. Birmingham (Perry Barr, Birmingham), 3790, Pte., d., Home, 16/11/16.
Loxley, Charles William, e. Stratford-on-Avon, Warwicks (Ardens Grafton, Warwicks), 3531, Pte., d., Home, 31/1/15.
Mountford, John Edward, e. Birmingham (Handsworth, Staffs), 2725, Pte., d., Home, 14/2/15.
O'Connell, James, b. Athy, Co. Kildare, e. Coventry, Warwicks, 3088, Pte., d., Home, 17/4/15.
Reeves, Thomas, e. Birmingham (King's Heath, Birmingham), 267637, Pte., d., Home, 28/3/17.
Satchwell, William Charles, b. Chapelfields, Coventry, Warwicks, e. Coventry, 1473, Pte., d., Home, 7/1/16.
Sturgess, Samuel, e. Dorchester, Dorset (Upper Parkstone, Dorset), 5845, Pte., d., Home, 16/7/16.
Taylor, Arthur, e. Aston, Birmingham (Lozells, Birmingham), 4270, Pte., d., Home, 6/12/15.

1/8th Territorial Battalion.

Ackrill, Sidney, e. Birmingham (Edgbaston, Birmingham), 305096, Pte., k. in a., F. & F., 7/1/16.
Adams, Herbert William, e. Bletchley, Bucks (Wolverton, Bucks), 306555, Pte., k. in a., F. & F., 1/7/16.
Albrow, Herbert, e. Coventry, Warwicks, 307642, Pte., k. in a., F. & F., 27/8/16.
Alcock, Percy, e. Birmingham (Witton, Birmingham), 305639, Pte., k. in a., F. & F., 1/7/16.
Alford, Ernest, e. Birmingham, 307598, Pte., k. in a., F. & F., 3/11/18
Allen, Alfred, b. Birmingham, e. Birmingham (Aston, Birmingham), 306270, Pte., k. in a., F. & F., 1/7/16.
Allen, Percival Arthur, b. Berkhamstead, Herts, e. Slough, Bucks (Uxbridge, Middx.), 306528, Pte., d. of w., F. & F., 10/11/18.
Allport, Ernest John, b. Witton, Birmingham, e. Aston, Birmingham, 4121, Pte., k. in a., F. & F., 1/7/16.
Allsopp, Albert, e Birmingham (Balsall Heath, Birmingham), 2444, Pte., d. of w., F. & F., 5/7/15.
Ambrose, James, b. Lavenham, Suffolk, e. Lavenham, 27217, Cpl., k. in a., F. & F., 6/10/18, formerly 1403, Suffolk Regt.
Amphlett, James Andrew, e. Birmingham, 306472, Pte., k. in a., F. & F., 1/7/16.
Andrews, Ernest Dorton, b Whitechapel, London, E., e. W. London (Upper Clapton, London, N.), 33257, Pte., k. in a., F. & F., 10/8/18, formerly 33820, Hampshire Regt.
Apthorpe, Harold Wakeling, e. Birmingham (Bedford), 3009, Cpl., k. in a., F. & F., 1/7/16.
Archer, Alfred, e. Birmingham (Saltley, Birmingham), 2854, Pte., k. in a., F. & F., 1/7/16.
Aris, Walter Edwin, e. Oxford (Steeple Claydon, Bucks), 306575, Pte., k. in a., F. & F., 27/8/16.
Armitt, John, e. Birmingham, 305229, Pte., k. in a., F. & F., 1/7/16.
Armstrong, Frederick, e. Salisbury, Wilts, 4914, Pte., k. in a., F. & F., 27/8/16.
Arnold, Sidney Graham, e. Birmingham (Balsall Heath, Birmingham), 305435, Pte., k. in a., F. & F., 1/7/16.
Ashley, Philip Joseph, e. Birmingham (Edgbaston, Birmingham), 306451, Pte., d. of w., F. & F., 18/8/17.
Atkinson, Arthur, e. Birmingham (Washwood Heath, Birmingham), 305333, Sgt., k. in a., F. & F., 6/10/18.
Atwood, Frank, e. Chippenham, Wilts, 306674, Pte., k. in a., F. & F., 27/8/16.
Attwood, Henry James, b. Saltley, Birmingham, e. Birmingham (Saltley), 2312, Pte., k. in a., F. & F., 1/7/16.
Austin, Fred, b. Aston Cantlow, Warwicks, e. Aston, Birmingham (Plymouth), 4264, Pte., k. in a., F. & F., 1/7/16.
Austin, George, e. Aston, Birmingham (Witton, Birmingham), 305857, Pte., k. in a., F. & F., 27/8/16.
Ayles, Robert, e. Bournemouth, Hants (Christchurch, Hants), 325159, A/Cpl., k. in a., F. & F., 25/10/17, formerly 717, Hampshire Cyclist Battn.
Bacon, Ernest Jesse, b. Wood Lane, Mortimer, Essex, e. Maldon, Essex, 325004, Pte., k. in a., F. & F., 6/10/18, formerly 28303, Suffolk Regt.
Backwell, Wallace, e. Birmingham, 306779, Pte., k. in a., F. & F., 27/8/16.
Bagg, Ross, b. Aston Manor, Birmingham, e. Aston, Birmingham, 305974, Pte., k. in a., F. & F., 1/7/16.
Bailey, Thomas, e. Birmingham, 2628, Pte., k. in a., F. & F., 1/7/16.
Bailey, Thomas Percival, b. Birmingham, e. Aston, Birmingham (Nechells, Birmingham), 1828, Pte., k. in a., F. & F., 25/7/15.
Baker, Frank, e. Malmesbury, Wilts (Charlton, near Malmesbury), 4916, Pte., d., F. & F., 12/9/16.
Baker, George Frederick, e. Warwick (Handsworth, Birmingham), 5085, Pte., k. in a., F. & F., 27/11/16.
Baker, James Gammery, e. Warwick (Birmingham), 20875, Pte., k. in a., F. & F., 4/2/17.
Barber, Ernest, b. Birmingham, e. Aston, Birmingham (Brookfields, Birmingham), 306323, Pte., k. in a., F. & F., 1/7/16.
Barnes, Norman Stanley, e. Aston, Birmingham (Amblecote, Worcs.), 305858, Pte., k. in a., F. & F., 1/7/16.
Barnsley, John, b. St. Edward's, Birmingham, e. Aston, Birmingham 2178, Pte., d. of w., F. & F., 26/7/16.
Bashford Sidney, e. Aston, Birmingham, 306053, Pte., k. in a., F. & F., 1/7/16.
Batchelor, Frederick James, e. Oxford (Fringford, Bicester, Oxon), 306529, Pte., k. in a., F. & F., 27/8/17.
Bates, William, b. Birmingham, e. Birmingham, 1064, Pte., k. in a., F. & F., 1/7/16.
Beard, Edward, e. Birmingham (Aston, Birmingham), 2435, Pte., k. in a., F. & F., 3/12/15.
Bearley, Horace John, b. Hockley, Birmingham, e. Birmingham, 2382, Pte., k. in a., F. & F., 1/7/16.
Beevor, Harold, b. Haddiscoe, Norfolk, e. Wroxham, Norfolk (Loddon, Norwich), 29321, Pte., k. in a., F. & F., 4/10/17. formerly 45285, Norfolk Regt.
Bell, Joseph, e. Birmingham (Lozells, Birmingham), 305522, Pte., k. in a., F. & F., 1/7/16.
Belson, Ernest Edwin, e. Wallingford, Berks. 4756, Pte., k. in a., F. & F., 1/7/16.
Bembridge, Alfred John, b. Aston, Birmingham, e. Birmingham (Nechells, Birmingham), 2311, Pte., k. in a., F. & F., 7/6/15.
Bennett, Alfred, b. Small Heath, Birmingham, e. Aston, Birmingham (Nechells, Birmingham), 305681, A/L/Sgt., k. in a., F. & F., 13/3/17.
Bennetts, William John, e. Padston, Cornwall, (St. Issey, Cornwall) 267836, Pte., k. in a., F. & F., 10/10/18.
Benton, John, b. St. Stephen's, Birmingham, e. Aston, Birmingham (Nechells, Birmingham), 305769, Pte., k. in a., F. & F., 1/7/16.
Benwell, Harry James, b. Aston, Birmingham, e. Birmingham (Vauxhall, Birmingham), 2355, Cpl., k. in a., F. & F., 1/7/16.
Bevan, Harold Bernard, e. Birmingham (Lozells, Birmingham), 2635, Pte., k. in a. F. & F., 27/7/16.
Billiard, John Thomas, b. Birmingham, e. Aston, Birmingham, 1764, Cpl., k. in a., F. & F., 22/8/15.
Bingham, Joseph William, b. Derby, e. Nuneaton, Warwicks., 20727, Pte., k. in a., F. & F., 27/8/16.
Bird, Henry George, e. Birmingham (S. Lowestoft, Suffolk), 2844, Pte., d., F. & F., 5/5/15.
Bird, Reginald, e. Birmingham, 305100 Pte., k. in a., F. & F., 1/7/16.
Bliss, Arthur James, e. Aston, Birmingham (Wylde Green, nr. Birmingham), 305963, Pte., k. in a., F. & F., 27/8/16.
Bloomer, Albert, e. Aston, Birmingham (Witton, Birmingham), 3305, Pte., k. in a., F. & F., 1/7/16.
Blunn, Frederick Ernest, b. Aston, Birmingham, e. Aston, 305674, Pte., d., F. & F., 1/7/16.
Bolton, Thomas, b. Birmingham, e. Aston, Birmingham, 306188, Pte., k. in a., F. & F., 1/7/16.
Bonnard, Charles, e. Birmingham (Nechells, Birmingham), 3150, Pte., k. in a., F. & F., 30/5/15.
Boraston, Richard James, b. St. George's, Birmingham, e. Birmingham, 200, C.S.M., k. in a., F. & F., 24/12/15.
Bottomley, William James, e. Aston, Birmingham (Stirchley, Birmingham), 3412, A/Sgt., k. in a., F. & F., 9/2/16.
Boulton, Frederick, b. Aston, Birmingham, e. Aston (Witton, Birmingham), 305263, Pte., k. in a., F. & F., 1/7/16.
Bowcott, Donald, b. Lower Mitton, Stourport, Worcs., e. Saltley, Birmingham, 305134, Pte., k. in a., F. & F., 1/7/16.
Bowen, George Montague, e. Birmingham (Handsworth, Birmingham), 2585, L/Cpl., d., F. & F., 16/8/15.
Brackstone, Robert William, e. Poole, Dorset (Upper Parkstone, Dorset), 267838, Pte., k. in a., F. & F., 2/11/18.
Bradley, Charles, b. London, Middx., e. Aston, Birmingham (Ashted, Birmingham), 305399, Pte., k. in a., F. & F., 1/7/16.
Bradley Frank, b. Aston, Birmingham, e. Aston, 1879, Pte., k. in a., F. & F., 10/6/16.
Bradley, George, b. Lincoln, e. Pembrey, Carmarthenshire (Burry Port, Carmarthenshire), 306557, Pte., k. in a., F. & F., 15/6/18.
Bragg, Alfred Joseph John, e. Birmingham (Winson Green, Birmingham), 2863, Pte., d. of w., F. & F., 18/7/16.
Brailey, Henry Charles, e. Aston, Birmingham (King's Heath, Birmingham), 305000, Pte., k. in a., F. & F., 1/7/16.
Breese, Harold, b. Aston, Birmingham, e. Aston, 305808, Cpl., k. in a., F. & F., 16/8/17.
Brewster, George Douglas, e. Birmingham (Witton, Birmingham), 305207, Pte., k. in a., F. & F., 1/7/16.
Brindley, James William, e. Aston, Birmingham (Handsworth, Birmingham), 3932, Pte., k. in a., F. & F., 18/7/16.
Bristow, William James, e. Swindon, Wilts, 4960, Pte., k. in a., F. & F., 2/2/17.
Broadway, George Howard, e. Birmingham (Perry Barr, Birmingham), 305168, Sgt., k. in a., F. & F., 1/7/16.
Brogan, Daniel, b. Ladywood, Birmingham, e. Aston, Birmingham (Nechells, Birmingham), 4195, Pte., k. in a., F. & F., 28/2/16.
Brooks, Thomas John, e. Birmingham, 3152, Pte., k. in a., F. & F., 15/11/16.

Brown, Frederick, e. Birmingham, 305723, Pte., k. in a., F. & F., 1/7/16.

Brown, John, b. Birmingham, Warwicks., e. Aston, Birmingham, 305593, Pte., k. in a., F. & F., 1/7/16.

Brown, William Alfred, b. St. Stephen's, Birmingham, e. Aston, Birmingham, 306248, Pte., k. in a., F. & F., 1/7/16.

Brown, William Charles, e. Huntingdon (Bridlington, Yorks), 20855, Pte., k. in a., F. & F., 12/11/16, formerly 898 Hunts Cyclist Battn.

Browning, Reginald Frederick Leslie, e. Birmingham, 3059, Pte., d. of w., F. & F., 5/7/16.

Brunker, Albert, e. Trowbridge, Wilts, 4970, Pte., k. in a., F. & F., 27/8/16.

Bryant, Joseph, e. Birmingham, 306507, Pte., k. in a., F. & F., 1/7/16.

Buck, Thomas James, e. Birmingham, 4573, Pte., k. in a., F. & F., 1/7/16.

Bull, Frank, e. Birmingham (Walsall, Staffs), 305313, Pte., k. in a., F. & F., 1/7/16.

Bullows, Richard Eric, e. Birmingham (Castle Bromwich, Birmingham), 3009, L/Cpl., k. in a., F. & F., 11/11/16.

Bundy, Cecil Reginald James, e. Salisbury, Wilts (West Cholderton, Wilts), 5257, Pte., d. of w., F. & F., 26/11/16.

Bunegar, Albert Clifford, b. Birmingham, e. Birmingham, 3809, Pte., d., F. & F., 5/3/16.

Burke, James William, e. Birmingham, 305221, Pte., k. in a., F. & F., 1/7/16.

Burke, William Michael, e. Birmingham, 3058, Pte., d., F. & F., 9/7/16.

Burr, Alexander William, b. Aston, Birmingham, e. Birmingham (Aston), 1770, Dmr., k. in a., F. & F., 1/7/16.

Burr, Leonard, b. London, e. Birmingham (Aston, Birmingham), 305359, Sgt., k. in a., F. & F., 1/7/16.

Burrows, Arthur William, b. Chingwell, Essex, e. Epping, Essex (Chingwell), 29325, Pte., d. of w., F. & F., 15/8/17, formerly 45321, Suffolk Regt.

Busby, George Smith, b. Monk's Kirby, Warwicks, e. Coventry, Warwicks. (Brockhurst, Warwicks.), 307750, Cpl., d. of w., F. & F., 24/10/18.

Bushell, James, b. Erdington, Birmingham, e. Birmingham, 306120, Pte., k. in a., F. & F., 1/7/16.

Butler, Frank, e. Birmingham (Erdington, Birmingham), 331034, Pte., k. in a., F. & F., 17/8/17.

Butwright, Stanley, b. Wisbech, Cambs, e. Wisbech, 29326, Pte., k. in a., F & F., 27/8/17, formerly 36370, Suffolk Regt.

Cahill, Edward J., e. Birmingham (Walkerville P.O., Essex Co., Ontario, Canada), 20954, Pte., d. of w., F. & F., 9/12/16.

Caldicott, George, e. Aston, Birmingham, 305965, Sgt., k. in a., F. & F., 1/7/16.

Calloway, Joseph, e. Birmingham (Oldbury, Staffs), 307638, Pte., k. in a., F. & F., 21/4/17.

Cantrell, Frederick George, e. Slough, Bucks (Farnham Royal, Bucks), 4809, Pte., k. in a., F. & F., 20/8/16.

Cashmore, Howard Victor, e. Birmingham (Erdington, Birmingham), 3157, Sgt., k. in a., F. & F., 1/7/16.

Caswell, Joseph, b. Birmingham, e. Aston, Birmingham, 305394, Pte., k. in a., F. & F., 1/7/16.

Chalk, Arthur, b. St. Paul's, Birmingham, e. Aston, Birmingham, 305766, C.S.M., k. in a., F. & F., 27/8/17, M.M.

Chapman, Edgar Leslie, e. Birmingham (Rotton Park, Birmingham), 307634, Pte., k. in a., F. & F., 27/8/16.

Chapman, William Albert, b. Nechells, Birmingham, e. Aston, Birmingham (Saltley, Birmingham), 305006, Sgt., k. in a., F. & F., 27/8/17.

Chatham, Rupert, e. Birmingham (Edgbaston, Birmingham), 305438, Pte., k. in a., F. & F., 1/7/16.

Chesworth, Frederick Charles, b. Coseley, Staffs, e. Wolverhampton, Staffs (Deepfields, Staffs), 57288, Pte., d. of w., F. & F., 6/11/18.

Chetwynd, Thomas, b. Glascote, Warwicks., e. Atherstone, Warwicks. (Glascote), 41887, Pte., k. in a., F. & F., 4/11/18.

Chillingsworth, Ernest George, b. Birmingham, e. Birmingham (Handsworth, Staffs), 307645, Pte., k. in a., F. & F., 27/8/17.

Church, Hugh, e. Bletchley, Bucks (Olney, Bucks), 306561, L/Cpl., k. in a., F. & F., 7/10/17.

Churchill, John, e. Birmingham (Castle Bromwich, Birmingham), 305644, Pte., k. in a., F. & F., 1/7/16.

Clanchy, Bertram, e. Birmingham (Sparkbrook, Birmingham), 2637, Pte., d. of w., F. & F., 13/5/15.

Clark, Albert, b. Godmanchester, Hunts, e. Huntingdon, 203355, Pte., k. in a., F. & F., 10/10/18, formerly 160, Hunts Cyclist Battn.

Clark, Henry, e. Birmingham (Perry Barr, Birmingham), 2728, Sgt., d., F. & F., 5/5/16.

Clarke, Walter James, b. Aberystwyth, Cardiganshire, e. Birmingham (Whitstable, Kent), 305044, Pte., d. of w., F. & F., 5/6/17.

Clements, William George, e. Birmingham (Sparkbrook, Birmingham), 305188, Pte., k. in a., F. & F., 1/7/16.

Cliff, Alfred, e. Birmingham, 306457, Pte., k. in a., F. & F., 1/7/16.

Coleman, Arthur Benjamin, e. Aston, Birmingham (Nechells, Birmingham), 306168, Pte., k. in a., F. & F., 17/7/16.

Coleman, George Joshua, e. Aston, Birmingham, 4611, Pte., k. in a., F. & F., 1/7/16.

Coleman, John William, b. St. Faith's, Lincs., e. Aston, Birmingham (Lincoln), 4098, Pte., k. in a., F. & F., 20/8/16.

Coles, Charles Henry, b. Birmingham, e. Aston, Birmingham, 305773, L/Cpl., d., F. & F., 8/2/17.

Collett, George William, e. Aston, Birmingham (Erdington, Birmingham), 3270, Pte., k. in a., F. & F., 18/7/16.

Colley, John, e. Aston, Birmingham, 3677, Pte., k. in a., F. & F., 1/7/16.

Commander, Bert, e. Birmingham, 2478, Pte., k. in a., F. & F., 1/7/16.

Cook, William John, b. Seend, Wilts, e. Troubridge, Wilts (Seend), 306049, Pte., k. in a., F. & F., 2/11/18.

Cooper, Thomas, b. Knowle, Warwicks., e. Aston, Birmingham (Knowle), 306173, Pte., k. in a., F. & F., 1/7/16.

Corbey, Ernest, b. Coventry, Warwicks., e. Rugby, Warwicks., 307616. Pte., k. in a., F. & F., 27/8/16.

Corns, Benjamin Leonard, b. Duxhill, Salop, e Aston, Birmingham (Hockley, Birmingham), 306187, Pte., k. in a., F. & F., 1/7/16.

Cornwell, Frederick George, b. Buswell Green, Norfolk, e. King's Lynn, Norfolk (Great Dunham, Norfolk), 29333, Pte., k. in a., F. & F., 27/8/17, formerly 45358, Suff. Regt.

Couchman, Arthur Charles, b. Birmingham, e. Birmingham (Aston, Birmingham), 4096, Pte., d. of w., F. & F., 25/7/16.

Cox, Albert Thomas, e. Birmingham (Winson Green, Birmingham). 3281, Pte., k. in a., F. & F., 15/5/15.

Cox, William, b. Birmingham, e. Aston, Birmingham (Nechells, Birmingham), 305252, Pte., k. in a., F. & F., 1/7/16.

Cracknell, Harold, b. Erdington, Birmingham, e. Aston, Birmingham (Erdington), 1797, Pte., k. in a., F. & F., 1/7/16.

Crane, Albert George, b. Woodbridge, Suffolk, e. Woodbridge, 29338, Pte., d., F. & F., 27/7/18, formerly 36498, Suff. Regt.

Cranmer, Thomas, b. Wroxall, Warwickshire, e. Birmingham (Hockley Heath, Birmingham), 23944, L/Cpl., k. in a., F. & F., 5/10/18.

Crook, Robert Alfred, e. Waddesdon, Bucks, 306533, Pte., k. in a., F. & F., 1/7/16.

Crowdy, Thomas David, e. Oxford, 4718, Pte., k. in a., F. & F., 18/7/16.

Crowe, Alan Davy, b. Woodbridge, Suffolk, e. Woodbridge, 29339, Pte., k. in a., F. & F., 27/8/17, formerly 36500, Suff. Regt.

Cureton, James, b. Soho, London, e. Staines, Middx., 305007, Sgt., k. in a., F. & F., 8/10/18.

Curzon, James, e. Birmingham (Hockley, Birmingham), 305460, Pte., k. in a., F. & F., 1/7/16.

Darby, James William, e. Birmingham (Handsworth, Staffs), 2881, Pte., k. in a., F. & F., 1/7/16.

Davies, John, b Nutton, Staffs. e. Aston, Birmingham, 305814, Pte., k. in a., F. & F., 1/7/16.

Davis, Albert George, e. Birmingham (Erdington, Birmingham), 2810, Pte., k. in a., F. & F., 23/6/15.

Davis, Percival Arthur, e. Birmingham (Aston, Birmingham), 2468, Pte., k. in a., F. & F., 1/7/16.

Davis, Robert Percy, e. Birmingham (Sparkbrook, Birmingham), 305434, Pte., k. in a., F. & F., 1/7/16.

Dawes, Sydney, e. Aston, Birmingham (Saltley, Birmingham), 305944, Pte., k. in a., F. & F., 27/8/16.

Dawson, Leonard, e. Coventry, Warwicks. (Foleshill, Coventry), 266818, Pte., k. in a., F. & F., 27/8/17.

Dawson, William Nathaniel, e. Rugby, Warwicks., 307611, Pte., k. in a., F. & F., 27/8/16.

Day, Albert Edwin, e. Warwick (Stratford-on-Avon, Warwicks.), 5147, Pte., d. of w., F. & F., 24/8/16.

Deacon, William Henry, e. Devizes, Wilts. (Southampton, Hants), 4976, Pte., d. of w., F. & F., 25/8/16.

Deakin, John, b. Aston, Birmingham, e. Birmingham, 2331, Pte., d., F. & F., 6/4/15.

Debar, John, e. Birmingham (Warwick), 305528, Pte., k. in a., F & F., 1/7/16.

Dell, John Henry, e. Birmingham (Bearwood, Birmingham), 305855, Pte., k. in a., F. & F., 1/7/16.

Dewsbery, Harold Edwin, b. Bolton, Lancs, e. Aston, Birmingham, 1874, Pte., k. in a., F. & F., 5/5/15.

Dicks, Frederick William, e. Aston, Birmingham (Hockley, Birmingham), 3800, Pte., k. in a., F. & F., 1/7/16.

Dobbins, Walter Frederick, e. Birmingham (Redditch, Worcs.), 2829, Pte., d. of w., F. & F., 2/7/16.

Dodd, Joseph Philip, b. Birmingham, e. Birmingham (Aston, Birmingham), 2327 Pte., k. in a., F. & F., 22/6/15.

Doggett, Charles Kimpton, b. Destwich, Cambs, e. Cambridge (Oakington, Cambs), 29341, Pte., k. in a., F. & F., 4/10/17, formerly 36501, Suffolk Regt.

Dolling, Herbert, b. Coombe Down, Somerset, e. Bristol, Glos. (Thornbury, Glos.), 28894, Pte., k. in a., F. & F., 27/8/17.

Doughty, Harry, e. Birmingham (Hockley, Birmingham), 4635, Pte., k. in a., F. & F., 27/8/16.

Dow, Ernest, b. West Bergholt, Essex, e. Hendon, Middx., 325022, Pte., d., F. & F., 15/8/18, formerly 32450, Suff. Regt.

Downing, Henry James, b. Aston, Birmingham, e. Aston, 305283, Pte., k. in a., F. & F., 27/8/16.

Downsbrough, Smith, b. Halifax, Yorks, e. Halifax (Huddersfield, Yorks), 33664, Pte., d. of w., F. & F, 7/10/18, formerly 22227, R.A.S.C.

Druce, Arthur, b. Penn, Bucks, e. High Wycombe, Bucks (Penn), 20885, Pte., d. of w., F. & F., 29/11/16.

Dugmore, Henry, b. Smethwick, Staffs, e. Coventry, 307851, Pte., k. in a., F. & F., 4/10/17.

Dugmore, Thomas John, e. Birmingham (Brookfields, Birmingham), 2886, Pte., k. in a., F. & F., 23/5/15.

Dunlop, William, e. Trowbridge, Wilts (Bradford-on-Avon, Wilts), 306604, Pte., k. in a., F. & F., 27/8/17.

Durber, Sidney, b. St. James, Birmingham, e. Birmingham, 1565, Pte., k. in a., F. & F., 1/7/16.

Durnford, Eric Charles, e. Aston, Birmingham (Bamford, Derby), 3289, Pte., d. of w., F. & F., 7/6/16.

Durrant, Edward William, b. St. Saviour's, Eastbourne, Sussex, e. Hastings, Sussex (Ipswich, Suffolk), 242010, Pte, k. in a., F. & F., 4/10/17, formerly 2913, R. Sussex Regt.

Eade, Arthur Henry, b. Birmingham, e. Birmingham (Warley, Birmingham), 57290, Pte., k. in a., F. & F., 4/11/18.

Eaves, Thomas, e. Sutton Coldfield, Warwicks (Minworth, Birmingham), 306753, Pte., k. in a., F. & F., 27/8/16.

Edwards, Hedley Charles, b. Small Heath, Birmingham, e. Birmingham (Ashted, Birmingham), 306786, Pte., k. in a., F. & F., 23/10/18.
Edwards, James, b. Mattishall, Norfolk, e. Attleborough, Norfolk (Mattishall), 20343, Pte., k. in a., F. & F., 27/8/17, formerly 45346, Suffolk Regt.
Edwards, Walter, e. Birmingham (Ward End, Birmingham), 307879, Pte., d. of w., F. & F., 3/9/17.
Ellesmere, Arthur John, e. Birmingham (Balsall Heath, Birmingham), 2835, Sgt., k. in a., F. & F., 29/5/15.
Ellis, William Edward, e. Aston, Birmingham, 330829, Pte., k. in a., F. & F., 16/8/17.
Elsmore, Reginald, e. Birmingham (Witton, Birmingham), 2612, L/Cpl., d. of w., F. & F., 25/8/16.
Evans, Ernest, b. Gloucester, e. Bristol (Shirehampton, Bristol), 307855, Pte., k. in a., F. & F., 4/10/17.
Evans, Gurlim Philip, b. Merthyr, Glam., e. Pontypridd, Glam. Maisycoed, Glam.), 267451, Pte., k. in a., F. & F., 4/10/17, formerly 3335, Welsh Regt.
Everitt, Percy, b. Birmingham, e. Aston, Birmingham, 305684, Cpl., k. in a., F. & F., 13/3/17.
Eversden, Charles, b. Little Buckhill, Notts, e. Nuneaton, Warwicks (Coventry, Warwicks), 307756, Pte., k. in a., F. & F., 23/10/18.
Eyles, Frank, e. Birmingham (Erdington, Birmingham), 2654, L/Cpl., d. of w., F. & F., 3/7/16.
Farmer, George Herbert, b. Victoria, Melbourne, Australia, e. Birmingham (Tamworth, Staffs), 306399, Pte., k. in a., F. & F., 1/7/16.
Farrell, John Stewart, b. Old Monkland, Lanark, e. Glasgow (Baillieston, Glasgow), 33653, Pte., k. in a., F. & F., 15/6/18, formerly 190866, R.A.S.C.
Fennell, Edward Arthur, b. Lowestoft, e. Lowestoft, Suffolk, 325024, Pte., k. in a., F. & F., 27/8/17, formerly 6495, Suffolk Regt.
Ferrier, John, b. Glasgow, e. Rutherglen, Lanark, 23339, Pte., k. in a., F. & F., 9/10/18, formerly 7132, R.E.
Findlater, John, e. Birmingham (Saltley, Birmingham), 306447, Pte., k. in a., F. & F., 1/7/16.
Finlayson, Albert, e. Birmingham, 305534, Pte., k. in a., F. & F., 1/7/16.
Fisher, Arthur Edward, b. Birmingham, e. Aston, Birmingham (Nechells, Birmingham), 306118, Pte., k. in a., F. & F., 1/7/16.
Fisher, Benjamin, e. Aston, Birmingham (Witton, Birmingham), 4130, Pte., k. in a., F. & F., 18/7/16.
Fisher, Geoffrey, b. St. George's, Birmingham, e. Aston, Birmingham, 305975, Pte., k. in a., F. & F., 1/7/16.
Fisher, Stanley, b. Birmingham, e. Aston, Birmingham, 1739, Pte., k. in a., F. & F., 27/8/16.
Flear, Thomas Edward, e. Birmingham (Burton-on-Trent, Staffs), 2819, Pte., d. of w., F. & F., 14/10/16.
Flowers, Daniel, b. Birmingham, e. Birmingham (Small Heath, Birmingham), 307796, Pte., k. in a., F. & F., 27/8/17.
Forrest, Bert, b. Camp Hill, Birmingham, e. Aston, Birmingham, 306226, Cpl., k. in a., F. & F., 4/10/17.
Fowkes, Thomas Edwin, b. Birmingham, e. Aston, Birmingham, 3969, Pte., k. in a., F. & F., 1/7/16.
Frain, George, b. St. George's, Birmingham, e. Birmingham (Nechells, Birmingham), 2317, L/Cpl., d. of w., F. & F., 5/7/16.
Frampton, John, b. Birmingham, e. Aston, Birmingham, 2254, Cpl., d., F. & F., 16/6/15.
Franks, George, b. Birmingham, e. Birmingham, 307822, Pte., d., F. & F., 6/7/18.
French, Ernest, b. Oldbury, Staffs, e. Aston, Birmingham, 306215, Pte., k. in a., F. & F., 28/8/17.
Frost, Arthur James, b. Marylebone, Middx., e. Birmingham (Berkhampstead, Herts), 305045, Pte., k. in a., F. & F., 1/7/16.
Fry, Frank Stannard, b. Hampton Wick, Middx., e. Staines, Middx. (Teddington, Middx.), 325028, Pte., d. of w., F. & F., 2/9/17, formerly 31136, Suffolk Regt.
Fuller, George Wesley, b. Uckfield, Sussex, e. Uckfield, 325030, Pte., k. in a., F. & F., 27/8/17, formerly 31294, Suffolk Regt.
Gaffney, Edward, b. Salford, Lancs, e. Aston, Birmingham (Witton, Birmingham), 305011, Cpl., k. in a., F. & F., 27/8/16.
Gage, William Alfred, b. Birmingham, e. Birmingham, 307637, Pte., k. in a., F. & F., 27/8/17.
Gardiner, Harry, b. Wing, Bucks, e. Seaford, Sussex, 325035, Pte., k. in a., F. & F., 4/10/17, formerly 31295, Suffolk Regt.
Garrett, Frank John, b. Harborough, Warwicks, e. Rugby, Warwicks, 268342, Pte., k. in a., F. & F., 23/10/18.
Gibbins, Charles, b. London, e. Birmingham (Bearwood, Staffs), 4339, Pte., k. in a., F. & F., 26/7/16.
Gibbs, Bertie, b. Wandsworth, London, e. Coventry, Warwicks (Rugby, Warwicks), 42579, Pte., d. of w., F. & F., 5/11/18.
Gibson, Thomas Henry, b. Islington, Middx., e. London (Palmer's Green, London), 325031, Pte., k. in a., F. & F., 5/10/18, formerly 32451, Suffolk Regt.
Gleave, James, e. Aston, Birmingham (Warrington, Lancs), 306106, Pte., k. in a., F. & F., 1/7/16.
Goddard, Cecil Henry, b. Framlingham, Suffolk, e. Framlingham, 325032, Pte., d. of w., F. & F., 6/10/18, formerly 1914, Suffolk Regt.
Golding, Robert, e. Malmesbury, Wilts (Brokenborough, Wilts), 4933, Pte., d., F. & F., 31/12/16.
Goodall, Percy Victor, e. High Wycombe, Bucks (Beaconsfield, Bucks), 4721, Pte., k. in a., F. & F., 1/7/16.
Goodey, Peter Joseph, b. Standon, Massey, Herts, e. Epping, Essex (Magdalen, Essex), 29347, Pte., d. of w., F. & F., 27/9/17, formerly 45305, Suffolk Regt.
Goodwin, Sydney Charles, b. Small Heath, Birmingham, e. Birmingham (Edgbaston, Birmingham), 307823, Cpl., d. of w., F. & F., 17/8/17.
Goodwin, Thomas Alfred, b. Longfield, Kent, e. Gravesend, Kent, 325033, Pte., k. in a., F. & F., 27/8/17, formerly 32679, Suffolk Regt.
Gower, William Rowland, b. Wolverhampton, Staffs, e. Wolverhampton, 57272, Pte., k. in a., F. & F., 23/10/18.
Grant, Charles, e. Westbury, Wilts (Chapmanslade, Wilts), 306775, Sgt., k. in a., F. & F., 27/8/17.
Gray, Alfred Walter, e. Birmingham (Perry Barr, Birmingham), 305538, Pte., k. in a., F. & F., 1/7/16.
Green, Arthur, b. Hale, Surrey, e. Grove Park, Surrey (Hale), 33615, Pte., k. in a., F. & F., 4/10/18, formerly DM2/171954, R.A.S.C.
Green, Herbert William, e. Chippenham, Wilts (Calne, Wilts), 306659, Pte., k. in a., F. & F., 27/8/16.
Green, Richard, e. Birmingham, 4606, Pte., k. in a., F. & F., 1/7/16.
Green, William, b. Walsall, Staffs, e. Aston, Birmingham, 305697, Pte., k. in a., F. & F., 1/7/16.
Greening, Frederick, e. Birmingham (Aston, Birmingham), 306462, Pte., k. in a., F. & F., 4/2/17.
Greenway, Arthur William, b. Long Handborough, Oxon, e. Kingston-on-Thames, Surrey (Wimbledon, Surrey), 325034, Pte., k. in a., F. & F., 27/8/17, formerly 6434, Suffolk Regt.
Griffith, Arthur, b. Birmingham, e. Birmingham (Handsworth, Staffs), 203076, Pte., k. in a., F. & F., 4/10/17, formerly 3490, Warwicks Yeo.
Griffiths, Ernest, e. Birmingham (Ward End, Birmingham), 2446, Pte., k. in a., F. & F., 4/7/16.
Griffiths, Noah, b. Christchurch, West Bromwich, Staffs, e. Birmingham (Smethwick, Staffs), 25001, Pte., k. in a., F. & F., 25/8/18.
Griffiths, Walter, b. Kinder, Staffs, e. Aston, Birmingham, 305268, Pte., k. in a., F. & F., 1/7/16.
Guest, George, b. Soho, Birmingham, e. Aston, Birmingham, 305601, Pte., k. in a., F. & F., 1/7/16.
Haddock, William Allan, b. Mitcheldean, Glos., e. Nuneaton, Warwicks (Stockingford, Warwicks), 42709, Pte., k. in a., F. & F., 4/11/18.
Hale, Archibald William, b. Aston, Birmingham, e. Aston (Lozells, Birmingham), 305704, Sgt., k. in a., F. & F., 27/8/17.
Hales, Henry, e. Birmingham (Aston, Birmingham), 2590, Pte., k. in a., F. & F., 1/7/16.
Hancocks, Ernest John, b. Coventry, Warwicks, e. Coventry, (Appleby Magna, Warwicks), 42895, Pte., k. in a., F. & F., 23/10/18.
Handley, Alfred William, b. Northampton, e. Coventry, Warwicks (Leamington Spa, Warwicks), 57322, Pte., d. of w., F. & F., 20/10/18.
Hands, Albert, b. St. Matthews, Birmingham, e. Aston, Birmingham, 1801, Pte., k. in a., F. & F., 1/7/16.
Hands, Thomas Philip, e. Birmingham (Lozells, Birmingham), 305439, Sgt., k. in a., F. & F., 1/7/16.
Harding, Alfred Sidney, e. Gillingham, Kent (Mere, Wilts.), 306722, Pte., k. in a., F. & F., 27/8/17.
Harlond, Hugh, b. Sutton Coldfield, Warwicks, e. Birmingham Sutton Coldfield, 20486, Pte., k. in a., F. & F., 27/8/17.
Harris, George, b. Manchester, e. Aston, Birmingham (Nechells, Birmingham), 4150, Pte., d., F. & F., 31/8/16.
Harrison, William, e. Birmingham (Aston, Birmingham), 305223, Cpl., k. in a., F. & F., 27/8/17.
Hatton, Walter, e. Birmingham (Oldswinford, Worcs.), 305648, Pte., k. in a., F. & F., 1/7/16.
Hatton, William, b. Aston, Birmingham, e. Aston, 305688, Cpl., k. in a., F. & F., 1/7/16.
Hawker, Thomas Henry, e. Birmingham (Lozells, Birmingham), 306480, Pte., k. in a., F. & F., 19/8/17.
Haynes, William Henry, e. Birmingham (Ladywood, Birmingham), 306481, Pte., k. in a., F. & F., 1/7/16.
Hayward, Frederick Charles, b. Leamington, Warwicks, e. Leamington, 267962, Pte., k. in a., F. & F., 6/10/18, formerly 19390, R.A.S.C.
Heading, Gilbert Arthur, e. Birmingham (Handsworth, Staffs), 305101, Pte., k. in a., F. & F., 1/7/16.
Heath, Arthur, b. Aston, Birmingham, e. Aston, 1852, Pte., d. of w., F. & F., 7/7/16.
Heath, Joseph, e. Birmingham, 3905, Pte., k. in a., F. & F., 1/7/16.
Heath, Leonard Beale, b. St. Georges, Worcester, e. Worcester, 2032, Sgt., k. in a., F. & F., 1/7/16, formerly 1772, Worcs. Regt.
Heatley, William, e. Birmingham, 305822, Pte., d. of w., F. & F., 31/10/17.
Hedges, George, b. Duddeston, Birmingham, e. Aston, Birmingham, 305002, Cpl., k. in a., F. & F., 27/8/17.
Hemmell, Percy George, b. Thorpe Hamlet, Norfolk, e. Norwich, Norfolk, 325050, Pte., k. in a., F. & F., 27/8/17, formerly 6226, Suffolk Regt.
Hewson, Arthur, b. Birmingham, e. Coventry, Warwicks (Foleshill, Coventry), 23940, Pte., k. in a., F. & F., 27/8/17.
Hill, Frederick Walter, e. Birmingham, 305824, Pte., k. in a., F. & F., 1/7/16.
Hines, John William, b. Oulton Broad, Suffolk, e. Lowestoft, Suffolk, 29350, Pte., k. in a., F. & F., 15/6/18, formerly 36503, Suffolk Regt.
Hitchman, Basil, e. Birmingham (Soho, Birmingham), 306475, Pte., k. in a., F. & F., 1/7/16.
Hoad, John Ernest, b. Hythe, Kent, e. Canterbury, Kent (Folkestone, Kent), 325039, Pte., k. in a., F. & F., 27/8/17, formerly 6082, Suffolk Regt.
Hobbs, William, b. Birmingham, e. Aston, Birmingham, 305265, Pte., k. in a., F. & F., 1/7/16.

Hobson, Albert, b. Stalybridge, Ches., e. Stalybridge, 29566, Pte., k. in a., F. & F., 4/11/18, formerly 40402, S. Lan. Regt.
Hodgetts, John, e. Halesowen, Worcs, 20993, A/Cpl., k. in a., F. & F., 4/2/17.
Holley, Percy John, e. Huntingdon (Thrapston, Northants.), 307703, Pte., k. in a., F. & F., 27/8/16, formerly 1508, Hunts. Cyclist Battn.
Hollins, Henry, b. St. Edward's, Birmingham, e. Aston, Birmingham, 305783, Cpl., k. in a., F. & F., 13/3/17.
Hollis, Frederick Edwin, b. Knowle, Warwicks, e. Aston, Birmingham (Dorridge, Warwicks), 306171, Pte., k. in a., F. & F., 27/8/16.
Hollyoake, Albert, e. Birmingham (Small Heath, Birmingham), 306755, Pte., k. in a., F. & F., 23/2/17.
Holman, Harold Walker, b. Small Heath, Birmingham, e. Aston, Birmingham (Sparkbrook, Birmingham), 1912, Pte., k. in a., F. & F., 20/4/15.
Holmes, John Herbert Hector, e. Birmingham (Balsall Heath, Birmingham), 2540, L/Cpl., k. in a., F. & F., 25/1/16.
Holt, Ernest, b. Birmingham, e. Birmingham (Hockley, Birmingham), 23920, Pte., k. in a., F. & F., 16/5/17.
Hook, Horace Frederick, b. Eareth, Hunts., e. Huntingdon (Offord d'Arc, Hunts.), 307676, Pte., k. in a., F. & F., 27/8/16, formerly 598, Hunts. Cyclist Battn.
Hook, Sidney Pevensey, e. Devizes, Wilts. (Swindon, Wilts.), 5013, Pte., d. of w., F. & F., 29/12/16.
Hook, Thomas Henry, e. Birmingham (Witton, Birmingham), 2663, Pte., k. in a., F. & F., 21/5/15.
Hooker, Albert Edward, b. Colchester, Essex, e. Portsmouth, Hants., 28406, Pte., k. in a., F. & F., 27/8/17.
Hooper, Frederick William, e. Trowbridge, Wilts. (Southwick, Wilts.), 5297, Pte., d. of w., F. & F., 18/9/16.
Hopley, Percy, b. Eardisley, Hereford, e. Aston, Birmingham (Nechells, Birmingham), 305481, L/Cpl., k. in a., F. & F., 9/2/17.
Horobin, Arthur, b. Nuneaton, Warwicks, e. Coventry, Warwicks (Nuneaton), 18135, Pte., k. in a., F. & F., 4/11/18.
Horrocks, Fred, b. Aston, Birmingham, e. Aston, 305286, Pte., k. in a., F. & F., 1/7/16.
Horton, William, b. Birmingham, e. Aston, Birmingham, 305784, L/Cpl., k. in a., F. & F., 1/7/16.
Hotson, Lionel, e. Huntingdon (West Mersea, Essex), 307710, Pte., k. in a., F. & F., 27/8/16, formerly 1675, Hunts. Cyclist Battn.
Hounsham, Walter George, b. Fletton, Peterborough, Northants., e. Fletton (Old Fletton, nr. Peterborough), 20784, Pte., k. in a., F. & F., 27/8/16, formerly 317 Hunts Cyclist Battn.
Howard, Edward Arthur, b. Aston, Birmingham, e. Aston, 306152, Pte., k. in a., F. & F., 27/8/16.
Howell, Francis, b. Aston, Birmingham, e. Birmingham (Erdington, Birmingham), 305054, Pte., k. in a., F. & F., 1/7/16.
Hudson, Cecil Stanley, e. Warwick (Emscote, Warwick), 5162, Pte., k. in a., F. & F., 21/8/16.
Hudson, William, e. Birmingham (Bordesley Green, Birmingham), 307800, Pte., k. in a., F. & F., 16/6/17.
Hudson, William Mark, e. Birmingham (Harborne, Birmingham), 306502, Pte., k. in a., F. & F., 27/8/16.
Huggins, Charles Robert, b. Great Yarmouth, Norfolk, e. Woodbridge, Suffolk, 20355, Pte., d. of w, F. & F., 4/10/17, formerly 36499, Suffolk Regt.
Hughes, George Thomas, e. Aston, Birmingham (Witton, Birmingham), 305951, Pte., k. in a., F. & F., 1/7/16.
Hulme, Harry Jackson, e. Huntingdon (Tunstall, Staffs), 20820, Pte., k. in a., F. & F., 27/8/16, formerly 1408, Hunts. Cyclist Battn.
Humphrey, Thomas, e. Horsham, Sussex (Tunbridge Wells, Kent), 33438, Pte., k. in a., F. & F., 9/10/18, formerly 202826, E. Kent Regt.
Hurren, Hugh Maurice, b. Yoxford, Suffolk, e. Saltley College, Birmingham (Yoxford), 1664, Sgt., k. in a., F. & F., 1/7/16, M.M.
Hutt, Frederick William, b. Kettering, Northants., e. Aston, Birmingham, 306183, Pte., d. of w., F. & F., 29/7/17.
Hutton, Charles, e. Birmingham (Erdington, Birmingham), 2652, Pte., k. in a., F. & F., 20/4/15.
Inge, Alfred, b. Cannock Chase, Staffs, e. Birmingham (Hammerwich, Staffs), 20725, Pte., k. in a., F. & F., 12/11/16.
Ingles, Richard Ernest, b. Studley, Warwicks, e. Coventry, Warwicks (Studley), 42898, Pte., k. in a., F. & F., 25/10/18.
Inglis, James, e. Aston, Birmingham (Musselburgh, Edinburgh), 2535, Pte., k. in a., F. & F., 1/7/16.
Jackson, Alfred, b. Birmingham, e. Aston, Birmingham (Handsworth, Birmingham), 306243, Pte., k. in a., F. & F., 1/7/16.
Jackson, Ellis, b. Manchester, e. Birmingham (Sparkhill, Birmingham), 242198, L/Cpl., k. in a., F. & F., 4/10/17.
Jackson, George, b. Foleshill, Warwicks, e. Coventry, Warwicks (Longford, Warwicks), 57226, Pte., k. in a., F. & F., 4/11/18.
Jackson, Sidney, e. Birmingham (Erdington, Birmingham), 2482, Pte., k. in a., F. & F., 1/7/16.
Jackson, William, e. Aston, Birmingham, 3924, Pte., k. in a., F. & F., 1/7/16.
Jacques, Frank, e. Huntingdon (St. Neots, Hunts.), 307709, Pte., k. in a., F. & F., 27/8/16, formerly 1658, Hunts. Cyclist Battn.
James, Alfred George, e. Poole, Dorset (Parkstone, Dorset), 267777, Pte., k. in a., F. & F., 17/8/17.
James, Edwin Bowater, e. Birmingham (Smethwick, Staffs), 2474, Pte., k. in a., F. & F., 1/7/16.
Jamieson, John, b. New York, U.S.A., e. Liverpool (Holbeck, Leeds), 33666, Pte., k. in a., F. & F., 9/10/18, formerly 081768, R.A.S.C.
Jarvis, Elijah, e. Aston, Birmingham, 3316, Pte., k. in a., F. & F., 1/7/16.
Jeans, Charley, e. Devizes, Wilts., 4937, Pte., d., F. & F., 30/12/16.
Jennings, Arthur Thomas, e. Birmingham (Selly Oak, Birmingham), 306465, Pte., k. in a., F. & F., 4/2/17.
Jeynes, James Frederick, b. Aston, Birmingham, e. Aston, 1426, Sgt., d. of w., F. & F., 25/8/16.
Jeynes, Thomas George, e. Birmingham (Homerton, London), 305441, Cpl., k. in a., F. & F., 1/7/16.
John, Arthur Morgan, b. Saundersfoot, Pembroke, e. Neath, Glam., 33698, Pte., k. in a., F. & F., 10/10/18, formerly 032611, R.A.S.C.
Johnson, Herbert William, b. Shurning, Oundle, Northants., e. Fletton, Peterborough, Northants. (Stanground, Hunts.), 307660, Pte., k. in a., F. & F., 27/8/16, formerly 310, Hunts. Cyclist Battn.
Johnson, Percival, e. Birmingham (Erdington, Birmingham), 2656, Pte., k. in a., F. & F., 1/7/16.
Johnson, Raymond Gladstone, e. Birmingham (Aston, Birmingham), 306138, Pte., k. in a., F. & F., 1/7/16.
Jones, Albert Oscar, e. Aston, Birmingham, 306185, Pte., k. in a., F. & F., 9/10/18.
Jones, Edwin William, b. Erdington, Birmingham, e. Aston, Birmingham (Erdington), 4257, Pte., d. of w., F. & F., 3/7/16.
Jones, Joseph Thomas, b. Birmingham, e. Birmingham (Handsworth, Birmingham), 307742, L/Cpl., k. in a., F. & F., 23/10/18.
Jones, Leslie Thomas, b. Coventry, Warwicks, e. Warwick (Coventry), 42908, Pte., k. in a., F. & F., 4/11/18.
Jones, Sidney, e. Salisbury, Wilts. (Tidworth, Wilts.), 306644, Pte., k. in a., F. & F., 27/8/17.
Keen, George, b. Naphill, Bucks., e. High Wycombe, Bucks., 306543, Pte., k. in a., F. & F., 4/10/17.
Keen, Harry Gilbert, b. Birmingham, e. Aston, Birmingham (Tyburn, Birmingham), 4116, Pte., d. of w., F. & F., 16/8/16.
Kelsall, Alfred, b. Hanley, Staffs, e. Sheffield, Yorks (Hanley), 307540, Pte., d., F. & F., 5/9/18, formerly 2821, R.E.
Kentish, David George, e. Watford, Bucks (Chalfont St. Peter's, Bucks), 4733, Pte., k. in a., F. & F., 26/7/16.
Kimmence, William, b. Withersfield, Suffolk, e. Haverhill, Suffolk, 325061, Pte., k. in a., F. & F., 27/8/17, formerly 2591, Suffolk Regt.
King, George Edward, e. Salisbury, Wilts (Southampton), 306662, Pte., k. in a., F. & F., 27/8/16.
King, John Frederick, e. Devizes, Wilts, 4939, Pte., k. in a., F. & F., 26/7/16.
Kirby, William, b. Rugby, Warwicks, e. Aston, Birmingham (Witton, Birmingham), 305597, L/Cpl., k. in a., F. & F., 1/7/16.
Kirk, Harry George, b. Smethwick, Staffs, e. Aston, Birmingham (Smethwick), 1442, Pte., k. in a., F. & F., 1/7/16.
Kiteley, George Henry, b. Finchley, Middx., e. Barnet, Middx., 325060, Pte., k. in a., F. & F., 27/8/17, formerly 31512, Suffolk Regt.
Knight, Henry Charles, e. Huntingdon (Wilburton, Cambs), 307696, L/Cpl., k. in a., F. & F., 27/8/16, formerly 1416, Hunts Cyclist Battn.
Knight, John James, e. Birmingham (Sparkhill, Birmingham), 305551, Sgt., k. in a., F. & F., 1/7/16.
Knighton, Arthur William, e. Birmingham, 2664, Pte., k. in a., F. & F., 1/7/16.
Laight, James Henry Sydney, e. Birmingham (Erdington, Birmingham), 307765, Pte., d. of w., F. & F., 22/3/17.
Lampard, James John, e. Salisbury, Wilts (Amesbury, Wilts), 306727, Pte., k. in a., F. & F., 27/8/16.
Lancaster, Edward, b. Studley, Warwicks, e. Leamington, Warwicks (Studley), 42106, Pte., k. in a., F. & F., 23/10/18.
Lancaster, Frank, b. Hounslow, Middx., e. Hounslow, 20575, Pte., d., F. & F., 26/11/17, formerly 10597, A. Cyclist Corps.
Lander, Richard Robert Augustus, b. Birmingham, e. Birmingham (Balsall Heath, Birmingham), 42910, Pte., k. in a., F. & F., 23/10/18.
Langford, Clarence Adrian, b. Sheffield, Yorks, e. Coventry, Warwicks, 42725, Pte., k. in a., F. & F., 4/11/18.
Latimer, Hubert George, b. Smethwich, Staffs, e. Ashton, Birmingham (Smethwick), 1298, Sgt., k. in a., F. & F., 1/7/16.
Lavender, Oliver, b. Brampton, Hunts, e. Huntingdon (Brampton), 307662, Pte., k. in a., F. & F., 27/8/16, formerly 332, Hunts Cyclist Battn.
Lavin, Charles, b. Birmingham, e. Aston, Birmingham (Nechells, Birmingham), 305482, Pte., k. in a., F. & F., 1/7/16.
Leach, George Frederick, e. Birmingham, 201018, Pte., k. in a., F. & F., 27/10/17.
Lee, Albert, e. Birmingham (Bourneville, Birmingham), 305215, Pte., k. in a., F. & F., 1/7/16.
Leggett, Firth, b. March, Cambs, e. Huntingdon (Ramsey, Hunts), 20802, Pte., d. of w., F. & F., 27/8/16, formerly 642, Hunts Cyclist Battn.
Leonard, Howard, b. Aston, Birmingham, e. Aston, 1725, Pte., k. in a., F. & F., 1/7/16.
Lewis, Frank Albert, b. Yarby, Peterborough, Northants, e. Fletton, Northants (Woodstone, Peterborough), 307661, Pte., k. in a., F. & F., 10/8/18, formerly 311, Hunts Cyclist Battn.
Liddington, Octavius Saxby, b. St. Lucia, B.W.I., e. Aston, Birmingham, 306113, Pte., k. in a., F. & F., 1/7/16.
Ling, Herbert, e. Peterborough, Northants, 307680, Pte., k. in a., F. & F., 27/8/16, formerly 780, Hunts Cyclist Battn.
Lister, Harry, b. Walsall, Staffs, e. Saltley, Birmingham, 305160, Pte., k. in a., F. & F., 1/7/16.
Littlehales, Harry Jarrett, b. Penarth, Glam., e. Barry, Glam., 307522, Pte., k. in a., F. & F., 4/10/17, formerly 938, R.E.

Lolley, John, b. Redditch, Worcs., e. Redditch, 307409, Pte., k. in a., F. & F., 12/10/18.
Longland, Charles, e. Huntingdon (Ramsey, Hunts), 20801, Pte., d. of w., F. & F., 11/9/16, formerly 641, Hunts Cyclist Battn.
Love, James, e. Birmingham (Nechells, Birmingham), 305832, Pte., k. in a., F. & F., 1/7/16.
Loveday, Ernest, b. Nechells Birmingham, e. Aston, Birmingham (Nechells), 305939, Pte., k. in a., F. & F., 4/11/18.
Loveridge, Elias, e. Leamington, Warwicks (Warwick), 265806, Pte., k. in a., F. & F., 2/11/18.
Lowe, Charles, b. Hughendon, Bucks, e. High Wycombe, Bucks, 306622, Pte., d., F. & F., 22/10/18.
Lowe, Wilfred, e. Birmingham (Sparkhill, Birmingham), 3209, Pte., d. of w., F. & F., 23/6/15.
Luckett, George Edward, b. Birmingham, e. Birmingham, 23891, Pte., k. in a., F. & F., 4/11/18.
Ludlow, Ernest Frederick, e. Birmingham (West Bromwich, Staffs), 305454, Sgt., k. in a., F. & F., 4/10/17.
Luke, Frederick, e. Birmingham, 305219, Pte., k. in a., F. & F., 1/7/16.
Luker, John, e. Birmingham (Aston, Birmingham), 2629, Cpl., k. in a., F. & F., 1/7/16.
Lunniss, Frank, e. Huntingdon (Great Paxton, Hunts), 20856, Pte., k. in a., F. & F., 27/8/16, formerly 1414, Hunts Cyclist Battn.
Lusker, Sydney James, b. St. John's, Huntingdon, e. Huntingdon, 307669, Pte., k. in a., F. & F., 27/8/16, formerly 444, Hunts Cyclist Battn.
McAdam, Alfred, e. Birmingham, 3063, Cpl., k. in a., F. & F., 1/7/16.
McCormick, Joseph, e. Birmingham, 306503, Pte., d. of w., F. & F., 17/8/17.
McKay, Hugh, e. Birmingham, 306827, Cpl., k. in a., F. & F., 27/8/17, M.M.
McKenzie, Francis Charles, e. Birmingham (Balsall Heath, Birmingham), 2935, Pte., k. in a., F. & F., 18/7/16.
McManus, Albert, b. Aston, Birmingham, e. Aston (Lozells, Birmingham), 305616, Pte., k. in a., F. & F., 27/8/16.
McManus, Charles Henry, b. Aston, Birmingham, e. Aston, 305583, Pte., k. in a., F. & F., 1/7/16.
McManus, Harold, e. Birmingham (Handsworth, Staffs), 2653, Pte., k. in a., F. & F., 10/9/15.
Maile, Harry, b. Brampton, Hunts, e. Huntingdon (Brampton), 307656, Cpl., k. in a., F. & F., 27/8/16, formerly 207, Hunts Cyclist Battn.
Male, Charles, e. Aston, Birmingham, 305928, Sgt., k. in a., F. & F., 4/10/17
Mander, Thomas Archibald, e. Birmingham (Handsworth, Staffs), 307831, Pte., k. in a., F. & F., 25/8/17.
Mann, Arthur Charles, e. Aston, Birmingham (Harborne, Birmingham), 4242, Pte., d. of w., F. & F., 29/11/16.
Mann, Charles, e. Birmingham, 305833, Pte., k. in a., F. & F., 1/7/16.
Mansell, David, e. Birmingham (Greet, Birmingham), 20897, Pte., k. in a., F. & F., 4/12/17.
Marks, Frederick, e. Aston, Birmingham (Vauxhall, Birmingham), 306169, Pte., d. of w., F. & F., 28/8/17.
Marshall, Arthur Sam, b. Birmingham, e. Aston, Birmingham, 306184, Pte., k. in a., F. & F., 27/8/17.
Maskell, Arthur, e. Birmingham (Perry Barr, Birmingham), 305554, Pte., k. in a., F. & F., 1/7/16.
Mason, Charles, e. Barrow-in-Furness, Lancs, 306898, Pte., k. in a., F. & F., 16/8/17, formerly 2205, R. Lancs. Regt.
Mason, Frederick Edmund, e. Birmingham, 305176, Pte., k. in a., F. & F., 1/7/16.
Mason, Joseph, b. Wolverhampton, Staffs, e. Aston, Birmingham, 305401, Pte., k. in a., F. & F., 10/10/18,
Mason, Thomas, e. Huntingdon (St. Ives, Hunts), 307706, Pte., k. in a., F. & F., 27/8/16, formerly 1563, Hunts Cyclist Battn.
Masters, Thomas Stevens, e. Coventry, Warwicks, 306486, Pte., k. in a., F. & F., 1/7/16.
Mavity, Harry, e. Aston, Birmingham, 3382, Pte., k. in a., F. & F., 1/7/16.
May, Stanley Ernest, b. Gt. Yarmouth, Norfolk, e. Saltley, Birmingham, 20116, L/Cpl., k. in a., F. & F., 1/7/16.
Meakin, George, e. Birmingham, 2936, k. in a., F. & F., 1/7/16.
Melvin, John, e. Birmingham, 2937, Pte., k. in a., F. & F., 1/7/16.
Merrick, Sidney George, b. Aston, Birmingham, e. Aston (Bordesley Green, Birmingham), 305020, C.S.M., k. in a., F. & F., 6/10/18, D.C.M.
Merry, Thomas, b. Aston, Birmingham, e. Birmingham (Erdington, Birmingham), 306482, Cpl., k. in a., 4/10/17.
Mickleburgh, Cecil Robert, b. Walthamstow, Essex, e. Walthamstow, 34036, Pte., k. in a., F. & F., 4/11/18, formerly 202034, E. Kent Regt.
Middleton, Arthur, e. Birmingham, 305204, Pte., k. in a., F. & F., 27/8/16.
Middleton, Frank, e. Birmingham, (Lozells, Birmingham), 305112, Pte., k. in a., F. & F., 4/10/17.
Miles, Arthur, e. Devizes, Wilts, 306664, Pte., k. in a., F. & F., 27/8/16.
Miles, Charles, e. Aylesbury, Bucks (Holmer Green, Bucks), 306545, Pte., k. in a., F. & F., 27/7/16.
Milner, Horace, b. Birmingham, e. Aston, Birmingham (Erdington, Birmingham), 2184, Pte., k. in a., F. & F., 18/8/16.
Milsom, Arthur James, e. Devizes, Wilts (Marlborough, Wilts), 5276, Pte., d. of w., F. & F., 29/8/16.
Ming, William, e. Aylesbury, Bucks (Weedon, Bucks), 29980, Pte., k. in a., F. & F., 27/8/17, formerly 23036, Ox. and Bucks L.I.
Moon, Sidney Herbert, e. Birmingham (South Yardley, Birmingham), 2804, Sgt., k. in a., F. & F., 1/7/16.
Morgan, Archibald, b. Gloucester, e. Gloucester, 1843, Pte., k. in a., F. & F., 1/7/16. formerly 1745, Glos. Regt.
Morris, Edwin Christopher, e. Birmingham (Witton, Birmingham), 305553, Pte., k. in a., F. & F., 1/7/16.
Morris, Westley, e. Birmingham (Stirchley, Birmingham), 2509, Pte., k. in a., F. & F., 1/7/16.
Morse, Frederick Charles, e. Swindon, Wilts, 306846, Pte., k. in a., F. & F., 27/8/16.
Mott, William, b. Surbiton, Surrey, e. Birmingham (Witton. Birmingham), 305484, Pte., k. in a., F. & F., 1/7/16.
Moulton, Robert Freeman, b. St. Ives, Hunts, e. St. Ives, 20774, Pte., k. in a., F. & F., 12/11/16, formerly 133, Hunts Cyclist Battn.
Mucklow, William James, b. Birmingham, e. Birmingham. 306278, Cpl., k. in a., F. & F., 27/8/17.
Musselle, George Leonard, b. Nottingham, e. Aston, Birmingham, 1554, L/Sgt., d. of w., F. & F., 19/10/15.
Musson, Ernest, e. Nuneaton, Warwicks (Stockingford, Warwicks), 307648, Pte., k. in a., F. & F., 27/8/16.
Nash, Arthur, b. Birmingham, e. Aston, Birmingham, 1805, Pte., k. in a., F. & F., 1/7/16.
Nash, John Reginald, b. Wilnecote, Warwicks, e. Stratford-on-Avon, Warwicks (Wilnecote), 23936, Pte., k. in a., F. & F., 15/6/18.
Neal, Frank James, b. London, e. St. Neot's, Hunts, 307664, Sgt., k. in a., F. & F., 27/8/16, formerly 354, Hunts Cyclist Battn.
Neale, Arthur, b. Balsall Heath, Birmingham, e. Coventry, Warwicks, 307594, Pte., k. in a., F. & F., 24/10/18.
Nesbit, Henry Robert, b. Newcastle-on-Tyne, Northumberland, e. Coventry, Warwicks (Gateshead-on-Tyne, Durham), 57327, Pte., k. in a., F. & F., 9/10/18.
Newbery, John, b. Birmingham, e. Aston, Birmingham (Handsworth, Staffs), 306282, Pte., k. in a., F. & F., 1/7/16.
Newell, George, b. Northampton, e. Huntingdon (Kettering, Northants), 307701, A/Sgt., k. in a., F. & F., 4/11/18, formerly 1472, Hunts Cyclist Battn.
Newey, George, b. Nechells, Birmingham, e. Aston, Birmingham, 1465, Pte., k. in a., F. & F., 1/7/16.
Newey, George, b. St. Paul's, Birmingham, e. Aston, Birmingham, 2119, Pte., k. in a., F. & F., 1/7/16.
Newman, George Edward, b. Stechford, Birmingham, e. Birmingham (Stechford), 27887, Pte., k. in a., F. & F., 27/8/17.
Newman, Joseph William, b. Birmingham, e. Birmingham (Handsworth, Staffs), 23888, Pte., k. in a., F. & F., 6/8/17.
Newman, Wilfred, e. Huntingdon (Warboys, Hunts), 307679, Pte., k. in a., F. & F., 27/8/16, formerly 693, Hunts Cyclist Battn.
Nicholls, Arthur Frederick, b. Birmingham, e. Aston, Birmingham, 1556, Pte., d. of w., F. & F., 7/7/16.
Nicholson, John, e. Bathgate, Linlithgow, 307112, Pte., k. in a., F. & F., 7/10/17, formerly 2388, R. Scots.
Nickerson, Frank, b. Woodstone, Northants, e. Fletton, Northants (Old Fletton), 307651, Pte., k. in a., F. & F., 6/10/17, formerly 68, Hunts Cyclist Battn.
Norton, Bertram Joseph, b. Wandsworth, Birmingham, e. Saltley, Birmingham, 305163, Pte., k. in a., F. & F., 1/7/16
Nunn, Arthur, b. Wrentham, Suffolk, e. Ipswich, Suffolk (Wrentham), 29365, Pte., k. in a., F. & F., 4/10/17, formerly 26497, Suffolk Regt.
Oates, Frederick Alexander, b. Birmingham, e. Birmingham, 307572, Pte., k. in a., F. & F., 16/8/17.
Oldham, Harry, b. St. Neot's, Hunts, e. St. Neot's, 307667, L/Sgt., k. in a., F. & F., 27/8/17, formerly 370, Hunts Cyclist Battn.
Osborne, Horace, b. Wilbraham, Cambs, e. Bury St. Edmunds, Suffolk (Great Wilbraham), 28366, Pte., d. of w., F. & F., 27/8/17, formerly 36363, Suffolk Regt.
Overton, John Henry, b. Terrington, St. Clement, Norfolk, e. Norwich, Norfolk (Terrington, St. Clement), 29367, Pte., k. in a., F. & F., 7/10/17, formerly 45345, Suffolk Regt.
Overy, Walter, e. Aston, Birmingham (Hockley, Birmingham), 3483, Pte., k. in a., F. & F., 1/7/16.
Owen, Alfred Ernest, e. Birmingham, 305432, Pte., k. in a., F. & F., 23/10/18.
Owen, William Alfred Ernest, e. Birmingham (Moseley, Birmingham), 2679, Pte., k. in a., F. & F., 25/4/15.
Page, Edwin George, b. Fenstanton, Hunts, e. St. Ives, Hunts (Fenstanton), 307653, Cpl., d. of w., F. & F., 5/11/18, formerly 125, Hunts Cyclist Battn.
Page, John James, b. Hemingford Grey, Hunts, e. Huntingdon (Fomersham, Hunts), 307677, L/Cpl., k. in a., F. & F, 27/8/17, formerly 624, Hunts Cyclist Battn.
Pallett, John Charles, e. Birmingham (Handsworth, Staffs), 2691, Pte., d. of w., F. & F., 12/11/15.
Palmer, Arthur Leonard, e. Aston, Birmingham (Sparkhill, Birmingham), 305907, Pte., k. in a., F. & F., 1/7/16.
Palmer, Harry, b. Bedworth, Warwicks, e. Nuneaton, Warwicks (Collycroft, Bedworth), 57199, Pte., k. in a., F. & F., 23/10/18.
Palmer, Reginald Orlando, e. Birmingham (Langley, Birmingham), 2613, Pte., d. of w., F. & F., 4/7/16.
Palmer, Wilfred Harry, b. Wednesbury, Staffs, e. Birmingham (Sparkhill, Birmingham), 305068, Pte., k. in a., F. & F., 1/7/16.
Parker, Alfred, b. Liverpool, Lancs, e. Seaforth, Liverpool, 325150, Pte., k. in a., F. & F., 4/11/18, formerly 43425, Liverpool Regt.
Parker, Joseph, e. Birmingham (Hockley, Birmingham), 305556, Pte., k. in a., F. & F., 27/8/17.

Parkes, Horace, e. Birmingham, 305836, L/Cpl., k. in a., F. & F., 16/8/17.
Parkins, Francis John, b. Ickleford, Herts, e. Hitchin, Herts, 325078, Pte., k. in a., F. & F., 10/10/18, formerly 5984, Suffolk Regt.
Parkinson, Tom, b. Boston, Lincs, e. Stafford, 20370, Pte., k. in a., F. & F., 4/2/17, formerly 2832, R.E.
Parratt, Ernest, e. Henley-on-Thames. Oxon, 4830, Pte., k. in a., F. & F., 25/8/16.
Parrott, Thomas James, e. Huntingdon (Thrapston, Northants), 307685, Pte., k. in a., F. & F., 27/8/16, formerly 965, Hunts Cyclist Battn.
Parsons, James Alfred, b. St. Mary's, Birmingham, e. Aston, Birmingham, 305584, Pte., k. in a., F. & F., 27/8/16.
Paterson, George, b. Hillview, Bannockburn, Stirlingshire, e. Stirling (Bannockburn), 33602, Pte., k. in a., F. & F., 10/10/18, formerly M/2/134559, R.A.S.C.
Payne, Charles Austin, b. St. Margaret's, Oxon, e. Oxford, 307768, Pte., d. of w., F. & F., 20/10/18.
Payne, Granville, b. Heywood, Lancs, e. Bury, Lancs (Heywood), 33681, Pte., k. in a., F. & F., 23/10/18, formerly 075422, R.A.S.C.
Peach, Thomas, e. Aston, Birmingham (Ward End, Birmingham), 2466, Cpl., k. in a., F. & F., 18/7/16.
Pearce, Charles Matthew, e. Slough, Bucks (Wraysbury, Middx.), 306547, Pte., k. in a., F. & F., 1/7/16.
Pearson, Thomas, e. High Wycombe, Bucks, 306571, Pte., k. in a., F. & F., 1/7/16.
Perkins, Ambrose, e. Birmingham, 2550, Pte., d. of w., F. & F., 4/7/16.
Perkins, Herbert Henry, b. Henley-in-Arden, Birmingham, e. Warwick (Handsworth, Birmingham), 305396, L/Sgt., k. in a., F. & F., 1/7/16.
Perry, Thomas, b. Birmingham, e. Aston, Birmingham (Ladywood, Birmingham), 306446, Pte., k. in a., F. & F., 1/7/16.
Pettitt, Cecil George, e. Huntingdon (Ramsay, Hunts), 307716, L/Cpl., k. in a., F. & F., 27/8/17, formerly 960, Hunts Cyclist Battn.
Phelps, Philip, b. Vauxhall, Birmingham, e. Aston, Birmingham (Nechells, Birmingham), 306133, Pte., k. in a., F. & F., 1/7/16.
Phibbs, Harold Edward, e. Birmingham (Sparkbrook, Birmingham), 305737, Pte., k. in a., F. & F., 1/7/16.
Phillimore, Leslie Eneas, e. Bournemouth, Hants (Parkstone, Dorset), 307226, Pte., d. of w., F. & F., 22/3/17.
Phillips, Thomas, e. Birmingham (Nechells, Birmingham), 305169, Sgt., k. in a., F. & F., 13/3/17.
Phillips, Thomas, e. Birmingham (Aston, Birmingham), 306468, Cpl., k. in a., F. & F., 16/8/17.
Pinfield, Alfred, b. Aston, Birmingham, e. Aston, 4120, Pte., d. of w., F. & F., 5/7/16.
Piper, Hubert, e. Birmingham (Wolverhampton, Staffs), 305452, Pte., k. in a., F. & F., 1/7/16.
Pitt, Samuel Thomas, b. Worcester, e. Birmingham, 241423, Pte., k. in a., F. & F., 4/10/17.
Plant, Arthur, e. Birmingham (Kings Heath, Birmingham), 2713, Cpl., k. in a., F. & F., 1/7/16.
Ponting, Frank, e. Swindon, Wilts (Newtonbishopstone, Shrivenham, Berks), 5300, Pte., k. in a., F. & F., 5/10/16.
Poole, John William, e. Devizes, Wilts (Cricklade, Wilts), 4986, Pte., d. of w., F. & F., 16/9/16.
Potter, Alfred, e. Devizes, Wilts (Market Lavington, Wilts), 306847, Pte., d., F. & F., 15/2/17.
Potts, Frederick Arthur, e. Huntingdon (Leeds, Yorks), 307718, Pte., k. in a., F. & F., 4/10/17, formerly 1727, Hunts Cyclist Battn.
Powell, Arthur, e. Aston, Birmingham (Lozells, Birmingham), 3514, L/Cpl., k. in a., F. & F., 1/7/16.
Powell, George, e. Birmingham (Small Heath, Birmingham), 2700, Pte., k. in a., F. & F., 1/7/16.
Powell, James, e. Aston, Birmingham, 4022, Pte., k. in a., F. & F., 1/7/16.
Powell, William, b. Aston, Birmingham, e. Aston, 306149, Pte., k. in a., F. & F., 1/7/16.
Pratley, Hubert, e. Burford, Oxon, 307771, Pte., d. of w., F. & F., 8/7/18.
Pratt, Ernest, e. Southam, Warwicks, 306800, Pte., k. in a., F. & F., 27/8/16.
Preston, Edward, b. Small Heath, Birmingham, e. Aston, Birmingham (Witton, Birmingham), 1885, Pte., k. in a., F. & F., 5/5/15.
Price, George, b. Aston, Birmingham, e. Aston, 1582, Pte., k. in a., F. & F., 1/7/16.
Proctor, Alfred Charles, e. Birmingham, 305446, Pte., k. in a., F. & F., 1/7/16.
Purnell, Frederick Arthur, b. Trowbridge, Wilts, e. Trowbridge, 306709, L/Cpl., k. in a., F. & F., 10/10/18.
Pysden, George Ernest Savin, b. St. John's, Margate, Kent, e. Margate, 33635, Pte., k. in a., F. & F., 24/10/17, formerly MT/182199, R.A.S.C.
Pywell, Charles, e. Huntingdon (Buckden, Hunts), 307733, Pte., k. in a., F. & F., 27/8/17, formerly 1578, Hunts Cyclist Battn.
Rainsford, Wilfred John, b. St. John's Kidderminster, Worcs, e. Saltley, Birmingham (Saltley College), 2021, Pte., k. in a., F. & F., 19/4/15.
Rance, Thomas, b. Wendover, Bucks, e. Aylesbury, Bucks (Tring, Herts), 307772, Pte., k. in a., F. & F., 4/11/18.
Randall, Claude, e. Kenilworth, Warwicks, 306526, Pte., k. in a., F. & F., 1/7/16.
Randle, Albert, b. Attleborough, Warwicks, e. Nuneaton, Warwicks (Attleborough), 241542, Pte., d. of w., F. & F., 31/10/18.
Rands, Herbert, b. St. John's Peterborough, Northants, e. Old Fletton, Peterborough (Peterborough), 307722, A/Sgt., k. in a., F. & F., 4/10/17, formerly No. 1 Hunts Cyclist Battn.
Reading, James, b. Birmingham, e. Aston, Birmingham (Erdington, Birmingham), 305693, Pte., k. in a., F. & F., 1/7/16.
Reed, Jack, b. Newport, Mon., e. Birmingham, 240511, Pte., k. in a., F. & F., 4/10/17.
Redgrave, Alfred Llewellyn, b. Swansea, Glam., e. Huntingdon (Warboys, Hunts), 307724, Pte., k. in a., F. & F., 27/8/16, formerly 557, Hunts Cyclist Battn.
Reece, Herbert, e. Aston, Birmingham, 306003, L/Cpl., k. in a., F. & F., 1/7/16.
Reeve, William George, e. Devizes, Wilts (West Kensington, London), 4987, Pte., k. in a., F. & F., 14/11/16.
Reynolds, Frank, e. Trowbridge, Wilts, 306687, Pte., k. in a., F. & F., 27/8/17.
Reynolds, Joseph Edward, b. Birmingham, e. Birmingham (Saltley, Birmingham), 42937, Pte., d. of w., F. & F., 11/10/18.
Reynolds, Samuel, e. Bedworth, Warwicks, 306801, Pte., k. in a., F. & F., 27/8/17.
Rice, Denis, b. Rackheath, Norfolk, e. Norwich (Pauxworth, nr. Norwich), 29370, Pte., k. in a., F. & F., 27/8/17, formerly 4575, Suffolk Regt.
Richards, Alfred Thomas, b. Edgbaston, Birmingham, e. Aston, Birmingham, 305400, Pte., k. in a., F. & F., 1/7/16.
Richardson, Edwin, b. Aston, Birmingham, e. Aston (Lozells, Birmingham), 2274, Pte., k. in a., F. & F., 1/7/16.
Richardson, George Harry, b. Ramsey, Hunts, e. Ramsey (Warboys, Hunts), 307726, Pte., k. in a., F. & F., 27/8/17, formerly 253 Hunts Cyclist Battn.
Ridding, Arthur, b. Birmingham, e. Aston, Birmingham, 305793, Pte., k. in a., F. & F., 1/7/16.
Ridgway, Fred, e. Aston, Birmingham (Hockley, Birmingham), 4094, Pte., d., F. & F., 17/6/16.
Righton, Walter William, b. Small Heath, Birmingham, e. Shipston-on-Stour, Worcs. (Ilmington, Warwicks.), 242953, Pte., k. in a., F. & F., 4/10/17.
Riley, Stanley, b. Colne, Lancs, e. Bradford, Yorks (Colne), 33673, Pte., d. of w., F. & F., 5/10/18, formerly 162519, R.A.S.C.
Rix, Walter Ernest, e. Huntingdon (Norwich), 307728, L/Cpl., k. in a., F. & F., 27/8/16, formerly 1725, Hunts Cyclist Battn.
Roach, Edward, e. Birmingham, 305622, Pte., k. in a., F. & F., 27/8/17.
Robinson, James Thomas, b. Yalding, Kent, e. Maidstone, Kent (Yalding), 325084, Pte., k. in a., F. & F., 6/10/18, formerly 6375, Suffolk Regt.
Robinson, Simeon, b. Netherton, Worcs., e. Netherton, 28900, Pte., k. in a., F. & F., 27/8/17.
Roden, John, b. Birmingham, e. Coventry, Warwicks., 202806, Pte., k. in a., F. & F., 4/11/18.
Rogers, Charles William, b. Oldbury, Worcs., e. Birmingham (Small Heath, Birmingham), 306124, L/Cpl., k. in a., F. & F., 1/7/16.
Rogers, James, e. Birmingham (Aston, Birmingham), 305843, Pte., k. in a., F. & F., 27/8/17.
Rose, Charles Ernest, e. Birmingham (Erdington, Birmingham), 2526, Pte., k. in a., F. & F., 1/7/16.
Rose, George Henry, e. Birmingham (Handsworth, Birmingham), 305301, L/Cpl., k. in a., F. & F., 1/7/16.
Rousham, Alfred, b. Warwick, e. Aston, Birmingham (Nechells, Birmingham), 306205, Pte., k. in a., F. & F., 1/7/16.
Rudd, Harry, e. Birmingham (Castle Bromwich, Birmingham), 305661, Pte., k. in a., F. & F., 1/7/16.
Ryland, William Henry, b. Aston, Birmingham, e. Birmingham (Aston), 305071, Pte., k. in a., F. & F., 15/6/18.
Sadler, James, e. Birmingham, 27893, Pte., k. in a., F. & F., 27/8/17.
Salisbury, William Henry, e. Marlboro', Wilts, 306671, L/Cpl., k. in a., F. & F., 6/10/18.
Salter, Louis, b. Wolverhampton, Staffs, e. Birmingham (Kinver, Stourbridge, Worcs.), 306254, Cpl., k. in a., F. & F., 27/8/16.
Sanders, Hubert Wedgwick, b. Lichfield, Staffs, e. Saltley College, Birmingham (Walsall, Staffs), 1680, Pte., k. in a., F. & F., 5/5/15.
Sargent, William Edward, b. Edgbaston, Birmingham, e. Birmingham, 2388, Pte., k. in a., F. & F., 1/7/16.
Sartin, Albert Victor, e. Trowbridge, Wilts., 306863, Pte., k. in a., F. & F., 20/4/17.
Satchwell, George Albert Victor, e. Birmingham (Handsworth, Birmingham), 307809, Pte., k. in a., F. & F., 25/3/17.
Saunders, William Harry, b. Studham, Beds., e. Luton, Beds. (Studham), 29372, Pte., k. in a., F. & F., 7/10/17, formerly 45331, Suffolk Regt.
Sayers, William George, e. Birmingham (Aston, Birmingham), 3108, Pte., k. in a., F. & F., 1/7/16.
Scriven, George Arthur, b. Enville, Stourbridge, Worcs., e. Aston, Birmingham (Nechells, Birmingham), 305385, Sgt., k. in a., F. & F., 15/8/17.
Scrivens, William Harold, b. Leicester, e. Birmingham, 14/1560, Pte., k. in a., F. & F., 4/10/17.
Seaton, Percy Alexander, e. Swindon, Wilts., 306849, Pte., k. in a., F. & F., 27/8/16.
Shaw, Archie, e. Coventry, Warwicks. (Stoke, Coventry), 307745, Pte., k. in a., F. & F., 15/6/18.
Shaylor, Frederick Henry, b. St. Andrews, Birmingham, e. Birmingham (Erdington, Birmingham), 8535, Pte., d. of w., F. & F., 4/9/17.
Shearman, Joseph, e. Birmingham (Handsworth, Birmingham), 306830, Pte., k. in a., F. & F., 27/8/16.
Shearman, William Henry, b. Aston, Birmingham, e. Aston, 2152, L/Cpl., k. in a., F. & F., 1/7/16.

Sheil, Bernard Reginald, b. St. John's, Leamington, Warwicks., e. Saltley College, Birmingham, 305148, Sgt., k. in a., F. & F., 1/7/16, D.C.M.
Sheppard, Samuel, b. Sparkbrook, Birmingham, e. Birmingham (Small Heath, Birmingham), 241040, Pte., k. in a., F. & F., 4/10/17.
Sheppard, Alfred, e. Birmingham (King's Heath, Birmingham), 305845, Sgt., k. in a., F. & F., 1/7/16.
Sheppard, Frederick, e. Aston, Birmingham (King's Heath, Birmingham), 305892, Pte., k. in a., F. & F., 1/7/16.
Shock, Harold, e. Birmingham (Aston, Birmingham), 305846, Pte., k. in a., F. & F., 27/8/16.
Simmons, George, b. Manchester, e. Aston, Birmingham, 2076, Pte., k. in a., F. & F., 17/9/15.
Sissen, John, b. Costessey, Norfolk, e. Norwich (Costessey), 29375, Pte., k. in a., F. & F., 27/8/17, formerly 45246, Suffolk Regt.
Small, Samuel, b. Birmingham, e. Aston, Birmingham, 1979, Pte., k. in a., F. & F., 22/6/15.
Smith, Arthur, e. Witton, Birmingham, 305941, Pte., k. in a., F. & F., 1/7/16.
Smith, Charles, b. Talke, Staffs, e. Burslem, Staffs (Talke Pitts, Staffs), 57215, Pte., k. in a., F. & F., 4/11/18.
Smith, Claud Humphrey, b. Islington, London, e. Salisbury, Wilts (Durrington, Salisbury), 306822, Pte., k. in a., F. & F., 27/8/17.
Smith, Edward, e. Birmingham (Aston, Birmingham), 2554, Pte., k. in a., F. & F., 23/11/15.
Smith, Edwin, e. Aston, Birmingham, 305996, Pte., k. in a., F. & F., 1/7/16.
Smith, Frank, e. Coventry, Warwicks., 307778, Pte., k. in a., F. & F., 27/8/17.
Smith, Frank Edmund, e. Oxford (Witney, Oxon), 4871, Pte., k. in a., F. & F., 25/8/16.
Smith, George, e. Birmingham, 305664, Pte., k. in a., F. & F., 1/7/16.
Smith, George, b. Aston, Birmingham, e. Aston, 305384, Pte., k. in a., F. & F., 1/7/16.
Smith, George Henry, b. Birmingham, e. Birmingham (Aston, Birmingham), 306394, Pte., k. in a., F. & F., 27/8/16.
Smith, Harry, b. Sheffield, Yorks, e. Aston, Birmingham, 305383, Pte., k. in a., F. & F., 1/7/16.
Smith, Henry Edward, b. Birmingham, e. Aston, Birmingham, 1105, L/Cpl., k. in a., F. & F., 25/4/15.
Smith, John Edward, b. Birmingham, e. Aston, Birmingham (Ashted, Birmingham), 2044, Pte., k. in a., F. & F., 25/1/16.
Smith, Leonard, e. Aston, Birmingham, 305958, Pte., k. in a., F. & F., 1/7/16.
Smith, Richard James, b. Solihull, Birmingham, e. Aston, Birmingham (Small Heath, Birmingham), 306239, Pte., k. in a., F. & F., 1/7/16.
Smith, Thomas, b. Ross, Herefordshire, e. Warwick (Four Oaks, Birmingham), 5935, Pte., k. in a., F. & F., 27/7/16.
Smith, Thomas, b. Birmingham, e. Birmingham (Handsworth, Birmingham), 20912, Pte., d. of w., F. & F., 7/10/16.
Smith, Walter Thomas, e. Coventry, Warwicks., 306768, Pte., d. of w., F. & F., 1/9/17.
Smith, William, e. Birmingham (Aston, Birmingham), 200872, Pte., k. in a., F. & F., 7/10/17.
Smith, William Albert, e. Birmingham, 305665, Pte., k. in a., F. & F., 1/7/16.
Smith, William Gordon, b. Birmingham, e. Aston, Birmingham, 1599, Pte., k. in a., F. & F., 1/7/16.
Sneath, Arthur, b. Aston, Birmingham, e. Aston, 305592, Cpl., k. in a., F. & F., 4/11/18.
Sneath, Thomas, b. Birmingham, e. Aston, Birmingham, 1529, Sgt., k. in a., F. & F., 1/7/16.
South, Percy, b. Snitterfield, Warwicks, e. Atherstone, Warwicks (Hurley, Warwicks), 42753, Pte., k. in a., F. & F., 4/11/18.
Spencer, William Henry, b. Springhill, Birmingham, e. Birmingham (Springhill), 267902, Sgt., k. in a., F. & F., 15/8/17.
Spicer, John, e. Bath, Som. (Ashley Box, Wilts), 4962, Pte., d., F. & F., 10/9/16.
Spiers, John Alfred, e. Birmingham (King's Heath, Birmingham), 307782, Pte., k. in a., F. & F., 4/10/17.
Spreadbury, Frederick Daniel, e. Pewsey, Wilts (Enford, Wilts), 306735, Pte., k. in a., F. & F., 27/8/16.
Sprules, Francis William, e. Marlborough, Wilts, 306641, Pte., k. in a., F. & F., 22/6/17.
Squires, Stephen Henry, e. Birmingham (Handsworth, Staffs), 305449, Pte., k. in a., F. & F., 1/7/16.
Stanton, Robert Went, e. Birmingham (Evesham, Worcs.), 305437, Pte., k. in a., F. & F., 1/7/16.
Steele, Harry, b. Birmingham, e. Aston, Birmingham, 482, Cpl., d., F. & F., 26/2/16.
Stephenson, William, b. Gold's Hill, Staffs, e. Aston, Birmingham (West Bromwich, Staffs), 1216, C.S.M., k. in a., F. & F., 1/7/16.
Stevens, Henry, b. Wollaston, Worcs., e. Saltley, Birmingham (Stourbridge, Worcs), 1393, L/Cpl., d. of w., F. & F., 24/6/15.
Stew, Thomas, e. Coventry, Warwicks (Foleshill, Coventry), 306495, Pte., k. in a., F. & F., 1/7/16.
Steward, Alfred Joseph, e. Birmingham, 3236, Pte., k. in a., F. & F., 1/7/16.
Stockall, Harry, e. Warwick (Aston, Birmingham), 5118, Pte., d. of w., F. & F., 28/8/16.
Stokes, Alfred, e. Birmingham (Hockley, Birmingham), 305173, Pte., k. in a., F. & F., 1/7/16.
Stook, Albert Edgar, b. South Lambeth, Surrey, e. Coventry, Warwicks, 307646, Pte., k. in a., F. & F., 27/8/17.
Stone, Edward, e. Birmingham (Sparkbrook, Birmingham), 305356, Pte., d., F. & F., 15/10/18.
Stone, Harold, b. Derby, e. Coventry, Warwicks, 42745, Pte., d. of w., F. & F., 13/11/18.
Stoneman, Reginald Harry, e. Birmingham (Gloucester), 307784, Pte., d. of w., F. & F., 4/10/17.
Stowe, William Hayward, e. Ipswich, Suffolk (Needham Market, Suffolk), 325092, Pte., d. of w., F. & F., 15/8/17, formerly 31078, Suffolk Regt.
Street, Edgar, e. Devizes, Wilts (London, N.), 5210, L/Cpl., k. in a., F. & F., 28/8/16.
Sturgess, Herbert Harry, e. Burnham, Som., 307871, Pte., k. in a., F. & F., 27/8/17.
Summers, Oliver, b. Studley, Warwicks, e. Saltley, Birmingham (Studley), 1678, Sgt., k. in a., F. & F., 1/7/16. D.C.M.
Surplice, Harry, b. Aston, Birmingham, e. Birmingham (Nechells, Birmingham), 2362, Pte., k. in a., F. & F., 1/7/16.
Swain, George Alexander, e. Birmingham, 2575, Pte., k. in a., F. & F., 1/7/16.
Swift, Richard Neville, b. Edgbaston, Birmingham, e. Birmingham, 305078, Pte., d. of w., F. & F., 23/10/18. M.M.
Talbott, Walter James, b. Wincanton, Som., e. Aston, Birmingham (Nechells, Birmingham), 306274, Pte., k. in a., F. & F., 1/7/16.
Tayles, Charles Francis, e. Aston, Birmingham (West Smethwick, Staffs), 3409, Pte., k. in a., F. & F., 27/8/16.
Taylor, Arthur, e. Coventry, 267856, Pte., k. in a., F. & F., 27/3/17.
Taylor, Albert Cooper, e. Moseley, Birmingham (Small Heath, Birmingham), 23969, Pte., k. in a., F. & F., 23/10/18.
Taylor, Arthur Frederick, e. Birmingham (Edgbaston Birmingham), 201130, Cpl., d. of w., F. & F., 7/11/18.
Taylor, David, b. Peterhead, Aberdeenshire, e. Aberdeen, 307564, Pte., k. in a., F. & F., 25/3/17, formerly 946, R.E.
Taylor, Edward, e. Birmingham, 5247, Pte., d., F. & F., 10/10/16.
Taylor, Frank, b. Coventry, e. Coventry, 4705, Pte., k. in a., F. & F., 18/7/16.
Taylor, Frederick, e. Birmingham, 306805, Pte., k. in a., F. & F., 27/8/17.
Taylor, George Ernest, b. Small Heath, Birmingham, e. Warwick (Aston, Birmingham), 305612, Pte., k. in a., F. & F., 27/8/16.
Taylor, George Frederick, b. Bratton, Sussex, e. Salisbury, Wilts, 307574, Pte., k. in a., F. & F., 27/8/17, formerly 23400, E. Lancs. Regt.
Taylor, John, b. Birmingham, e. Birmingham, 42919, Pte., d. of w., F. & F., 12/11/18.
Taylor, James Alfred, b. Worcester, e. Birmingham (Balsall Heath, Birmingham), 23897, Pte., k. in a., F. & F., 4/10/17.
Taylor, William, e. Newcastle-on-Tyne, Northumberland. 307550, Pte., k. in a., F. & F., 27/8/17, formerly 3686, R.E.
Theobald, Sidney Victor Hugo, b. Aylesford, Kent, e. Aston, Birmingham, 2096, L/Cpl., k. in a., F. & F., 1/7/16.
Thicke, William Roy, e. Oxford, 306551, Pte., k. in a., F. & F., 27/8/17.
Thompson, Albert, b. Aston, Birmingham, e. Aston (Nechells, Birmingham), 305796, Pte., k. in a., F. & F., 1/7/16.
Thompson, William, e. Birmingham (Whitehaven, Cumberland), 305456, Pte., k. in a., F. & F., 1/7/16.
Thorpe, Robert Arnold, e. Oxford (Middle Clayton, Bucks), 4885, Pte., k. in a., F. & F., 12/11/16.
Thurstans, William Henry, b. St. Thomas, Birmingham, e. Birmingham, 2392, Pte., d. of w., F. & F., 23/4/15.
Tilley, John Edward, b. Aston, Birmingham, e. Birmingham (Handsworth, Staffs), 307609, Pte., k. in a., F. & F., 27/8/16.
Titley, Walter, e. Birmingham (Witton, Birmingham), 2487, Pte., k. in a., F. & F., 29/4/15.
Tomkins, Henry James, b. Edgbaston, Birmingham, e. Birmingham (Edgbaston), 28519, Pte., k. in a., F. & F., 5/10/18.
Tomlinson, Thomas Henry, b. Aston, Birmingham, e. Aston, 305278, Pte., k. in a., F. & F., 1/7/16.
Tonks, Albert, b. Birmingham, e. Birmingham (Handsworth, Staffs), 242962, Pte., d. of w., F. & F., 11/10/18.
Toomer, James, e. Salisbury, Wilts (Durrington, Wilts), 306691, Pte., k. in a., F. & F., 27/8/16.
Troop, Albert Edward, e. Wareham, Dorset (Corfe Castle, Dorset), 307238, Pte., k. in a., F. & F., 18/6/18.
Towner, Frederick Charles, e. Aston, Birmingham, 3938, Pte., k. in a., F. & F., 1/7/16.
Townsend, Charlie, b. Swindon, Wilts, e. Swindon, 306600, Pte., k. in a., F. & F., 15/6/18.
Tranter, Thomas, e. Aston, Birmingham (Nechells, Birmingham), 305998, Pte., k. in a., F. & F., 1/7/16.
Trewern, Richard, b. Sennen, Cornwall, e. St. Just, Cornwall (Tregiffian, Cornwall), 306870, Cpl., k. in a., F. & F., 6/10/18.
Tropman, William Thomas, b. Shirley, Birmingham, e. Birmingham (Shirley), 202200, Pte., k. in a., F. & F., 4/10/17.
Troughton, Percy George, b. Greet, Glos., e. Aston, Birmingham (Bengeworth, Worcs.), 306369, Pte., k. in a., F. & F., 27/8/16.
Tweedy, John Reginald, b. Barnard Castle, Durham, e. Birmingham (Witton, Birmingham), 4260, Pte., k. in a., F. & F., 1/7/16.
Tye, George, b. Aston, Birmingham, e Aston, Birmingham (Nechells, Birmingham), 306216, Pte., k. in a., F. & F., 1/7/16.
Tye, Thomas James, b. Lower Broughton, Lancs, e. Birmingham, 8310, Pte., k. in a., F. & F., 4/11/18.
Tyler, Thomas, e. Birmingham (Aston), 20757, Pte., k. in a., F. & F., 20/8/16.

Underwood, Thomas, e. Birmingham (Nechells, Birmingham), 3596, Pte., k. in a., F. & F., 25/4/15.
Uffindell, Henry Lester, e. Purley, Surrey, 325096, Pte., k. in a., F. & F., 27/8/17, formerly 31580, Suffolk Regt.
Wadams, Gilbert Harry, e. Birmingham (Wolverhampton, Staffs), 305667, Pte., k. in a., F. & F., 1/7/16.
Waddup, Albert, e. Oxford (Bicester, Oxon), 4886, Pte., k. in a., F. & F., 25/8/16.
Wadman, William, e. Birmingham, 306088, L/Cpl., k. in a., F. & F., 3/10/17.
Waghorn, Charles Alfred, b. Allington, Kent, e. Maidstone, Kent, 325101, Sgt., k. in a., F. & F., 5/10/18, formerly 31374, Suffolk Regt.
Waldron, Thomas Henry, e. Birmingham, 3245, Pte., k. in a., F. & F., 1/7/16.
Walker, Alfred Charles, b. Birmingham, e. Birmingham (Sparkbrook, Birmingham), 57267, Pte., d. of w., F. & F., 5/11/18.
Walker, George, b. Birmingham, e. Birmingham (Erdington, Birmingham), 305314, L/Cpl., k. in a., F. & F., 1/7/16.
Walker, Henry, b. Brailes, Warwicks, e. Warwick (Lower Brailes), 28899, Pte., k. in a., F. & F., 16/8/17.
Walker, William, b. Birmingham, e. Aston, Birmingham (Nechells, Birmingham), 2278, L/Cpl., k. in a., F. & F., 30/4/15.
Wallace, John, b. Aberdeen, e. Aberdeen, 307559, Pte., k. in a., F. & F., 6/10/18, formerly 949, R.E.
Wallis, William Henry, e. Birmingham (Hockley, Birmingham), 306521, Pte., k. in a., F. & F., 27/8/16.
Walters, Herbert, e. Birmingham (Wolverhampton, Staffs), 2828, Pte., d. of w., F. & F., 2/5/16.
Ward, Alfred, b. Boston, Lincs, e. Aston, Birmingham (Small Heath, Birmingham), 1915, Pte., k. in a., F. & F., 1/7/16.
Ward, John, b. Horton-on-the-Hill, Warwick, e. Coventry, Warwicks (Dordon, Warwicks), 57354, Pte., k. in a., F. & F., 4/11/18.
Ware, Thomas, b. Torrington, Devon, e. Coventry, Warwicks (Buckfastleigh, Devon), 20984, Pte., d., F. & F., 16/12/16.
Ware, William John, b. Birmingham, e. Birmingham, 23928, Pte., k. in a., F. & F., 4/10/17.
Wassal, Christopher, e. Birmingham (Stourbridge, Worcs), 305669, L/Cpl., k. in a., F. & F., 1/7/16.
Watts, Frank, b. Birmingham, e. Birmingham (Aston, Birmingham), 42046, Pte., k. in a., F. & F., 18/10/18.
Watts, Wallace, e. Banbury, Oxon (Deddington, Oxon), 306574, Pte., k. in a., F. & F., 27/8/17.
Weatherby, David, e. Coventry (Longford, Coventry, Warwicks), 307840, Pte., k. in a., F. & F., 4/10/17.
Webb, Walter, e. Birmingham (Small Heath, Birmingham), 201080, Pte., k. in a., F. & F., 9/10/18.
Webber, Walter, b. Cardiff, Glam., e. Cardiff (Cathays, Cardiff), 307526, Pte., k. in a., F. & F., 26/8/17, formerly 937, R.E.
Weblin, William, e. Aston, Birmingham (Handsworth, Staffs), 305959, Pte., k. in a., F. & F., 1/7/16.
Webster, James, b. Solihull, Birmingham, e. Aston, Birmingham, 305380, Pte., k. in a., F. & F., 1/7/16.
Weetman, Charles Sidney, e. Birmingham, 4570, Pte., k. in a., F. & F., 15/11/16.
Wells, Frank Herbert, b. Hednesford, Staffs, e. Sutton Coldfield, Warwicks (Hednesford), 20723, Pte., k. in a., F. & F., 4/2/17.
West, Cecil Edward, b. West Raynham, Norfolk, e. Norwich, Norfolk (Fakenham, Norfolk), 29384, Pte., k. in a., F. & F., 27/8/17, formerly 45347, Suffolk Regt.
Weston, George Leonard, e. Birmingham, 3079, Pte., k. in a., F. & F., 5/5/15.
Wharton, Robert Charles, b. Ipswich, Suffolk, e. Ipswich, 325103, Pte., k. in a., F. & F., 27/8/17, formerly 219088, R.A.S.C.
Wheeldon, Hubert Horace, b. Dudley, Worcs, e. Birmingham, 305820, Sgt., k. in a., F. & F., 27/8/17, D.C.M., M.M.
Wheller, Leonard, e. Bridport, Dorset (North Chidcock, Dorset), 307240, Pte, k. in a., F. & F., 27/8/17.
White, Ashton Fuller, b. Hampton, Middx., e. London (Hampton), 33694, Cpl., k. in a., F. & F., 18/10/18, formerly 032571, R.A.S.C.
White, John, b. Birmingham, e. Aston, Birmingham, 306167, Pte., k. in a., F. & F., 27/7/16
White, William, e. Westbury, Wilts (Edington, Wilts), 306730, Pte., k. in a., F. & F., 27/8/16.
White, William George, b. Cirencester, Glos., e. Birmingham (Saltley, Birmingham), 307499, Pte., k. in a., F. & F., 16/8/17.
Whitehall, Charles, e. Aston, Birmingham (Witton, Birmingham), 306108, Pte., k. in a., F. & F., 1/7/16.
Whitehead, Arthur, b. Stroud Green, London, e. Brighton, Sussex (Muswell Hill, London), 235158, Pte., k. in a., F. & F., 18/10/18, formerly 18906, Army Cyclist Corps, 311350, Hussars, and 52123, R. Irish Rifles.
Whitehouse, Joseph, e. Birmingham, 2537, Cpl., d., F. & F., 11/9/16.
Whiting, Graham, e. Trowbridge, Wilts, 306642, Pte., k. in a., F. & F., 17/8/17.
Whittel, John Howard, b. Overbury, Worcs, e. Aston, Birmingham (Solihull, Birmingham), 306176, Pte., k. in a., F. & F., 23/10/18.
Wightman, Charles Norman, b. St. Leonard's, Bridgnorth, Salop, e. Saltley, Birmingham, 305149, Pte., k. in a., F. & F., 1/7/16.
Wilcox, Harry, b. Erdington, Birmingham, e. Aston, Birmingham (Erdington), Pte., 306284, d. of w., F. & F., 16/10/17.
Wilkinson, George Bertram, b. Christchurch, West Bromwich, Staffs, e. Birmingham (Harborne, Birmingham), 2322, A/Cpl., k. in a., F. & F., 4/5/15.
Wilkinson, Harry, b. Nechells, Birmingham, e. Birmingham (Nechells), 467, Sgt., k. in a., F. & F., 26/3/16.
Williams, Clive, b. Oldbury, Worcs, e. Tamworth, Warwicks (Wilnecote, Warwicks), 57334, Pte., d. of w., F. & F., 20/11/18.
Williams, Ernest, e. Bodmin, Cornwall (Mere, Cornwall), 5334, Pte., k. in a., F. & F., 14/11/16.
Williams, Frank, b. All Saints, Coventry, e. Coventry, 307883, Pte., d., F. & F., 19/1/18.
Williams, Harry Reginald, e. Aston, Birmingham, 3862, Pte., d. of w., F. & F., 13/4/16.
Williamson, George Edwin, b. Wigston, Leics, e. Aston, Birmingham, 305387, L/Cpl., k. in a., F. & F., 4/2/17.
Willis, Oscar Potter, e. Birmingham (Saltley, Birmingham), 305348, Cpl., k. in a., F. & F., 1/7/16
Willis, Robert, b. Urchfont, Wilts, e. Devizes, Wilts (Urchfont), 306694, Pte., k. in a., F. & F., 4/10/17.
Wilson, Ernest Harold, e. Aston, Birmingham (Lozells, Birmingham), 306164, Pte., k. in a., F & F., 1/7/16.
Wilson, George Alfred, b. Birmingham, e. Birmingham (Small Heath, Birmingham), 42406, Pte., d. of w., F. & F., 8/11/18.
Wilson, John, b. Leyton, Essex, e. London, Middx. (Forest Gate, Essex), 33686, Pte., k in a., F. & F., 15/6/18, formerly 3709, R.A.S.C.
Wilson, Philip, b. Stockingford, Warwicks, e. Atherstone, Warwicks (Nuneaton, Warwicks), 42760, Pte., k. in a., F. & F., 4/11/18.
Winter, Charles Edward, e. Birmingham (Handsworth, Birmingham), 305234, Pte., k. in a., F. & F., 1/7/16.
Withey, Thomas, e. Birmingham (Winson Green, Birmingham), 307841, Pte., d. of w., F. & F., 23/6/17.
Wood, Paul Herbert, e. Birmingham (Winson Green, Birmingham), 4661, Pte., d., F. & F., 22/12/16.
Woodhoods, George, e. Birmingham (Erdington, Birmingham), 306512, Pte., k. in a., F. & F., 1/7/16.
Woodman, Albert Frederick James, b. Swindon, Wilts, e. Devizes, Wilts (Swindon), 4857, Pte., k. in a., F. & F., 1/7/16.
Wootton, James, b. Hanley, Staffs, e. Birmingham, 306771, Pte., d. of w., F. & F., 29/10/18.
Worrall, Henry, b. St. George's, Edgbaston, Birmingham, e. Birmingham, 307876, L/Cpl., d. of w., F. & F., 11/10/17.
Wort, Cecil Jack, e. Salisbury, Wilts, 5288, Pte., k. in a., F. & F., 20/8/16.
Wright, Herbert, b. Chapel End, Warwicks, e. Atherstone, Warwicks (Chapel End), 57286, Pte., d. of w., F. & F., 24/10/18.
Wynn, Robert, e. Aston, Birmingham, 305962, Pte., k. in a., F. & F., 1/7/16.
Yates, Thomas, b. Aston, Birmingham, e. Aston (Lozells, Birmingham), 1876, Pte., k in a., F. & F., 16/5/15.
Yates, William, e. Birmingham, 306810, Pte., k. in a., F. & F., 17/8/17.
Young, Henry, b. Handsworth, Birmingham, e. Aston, Birmingham (Handsworth), 306246, Pte., k. in a., F. & F., 1/7/16.
Young, William, e. Birmingham (Balsall Heath, Birmingham), 305231, Cpl., k. in a., F. & F., 27/8/16.

2/8th Battalion

Adie, Andrew, b. Sunderland, Durham, 29747, Pte., k. in a., F. & F., 5/12/17.
Allen, Frank Louis, e. Birmingham (Winson Green, Birmingham), 305741, Pte., k. in a., F. & F., 5/9/17.
Anderson, James Carlan, e. Bathgate, Linlithgow, 5689, Pte., k. in a., F. & F., 28/9/16, formerly 4325, Royal Scots.
Angell, Frederick Edward George, b. Calne, Wilts, e. Chippenham, Wilts (Calne), 306854, Pte., k. in a., F. & F., 27/8/16.
Bacon, John, e. Devizes, Wilts (Bapton, Wilts), 4999, Pte., k. in a., F. & F., 20/8/16.
Ball, Edward, e. Devizes, Wilts (Whitchurch, Bristol), 5001, Pte., k. in a., F. & F., 4/10/16.
Barton, James Edward, b. Saltley, Birmingham, e. Aston, Birmingham (Nechells, Birmingham), 306388, Pte., k. in a., F. & F., 30/3/17.
Bateman, Cecil Henry, b. Birkenhead, Cheshire, e. Hoylake, Cheshire (Birkdale, Cheshire), 325145, Pte., k. in a., F. & F., 7/9/16, formerly 55682, Liverpool Regt.
Bates, John Thomas, b. Farnworth, Lancs, e. Farnworth, 307158, Cpl., k. in a., F. & F., 6/9/17, formerly 2142, North Lancs Regt.
Beach, Thomas Richard, e. Aston, Birmingham, 3730, Pte., k. in a., F. & F., 26/6/16.
Beesley, William Henry, b. Coventry, Warwicks., e. Coventry, 306782, Pte., k. in a., F. & F., 27/8/16.
Bell, George Henry, b. Northampton, e. Aston, Birmingham (Witton, Birmingham), 305471, Pte., k. in a., F. & F., 1/7/16.
Bennett, Thomas Bracey, e. Aston, Birmingham (Lozells, Birmingham), 3691, Pte., k. in a., F. & F., 18/8/16.
Bermingham, James, b. Bolton, Lancs, e. Bolton, 5461, Pte., d. of w., F. & F., 20/10/16, formerly 1292, N. Lancs Regt.
Berry, Godfrey Charles, e. Southampton, 5524, Pte., d. of w., F. & F., 15/1/17, formerly 2131, Hampshire Regt.
Berry, Harold, e. Aston, Birmingham (Handsworth, Birmingham), 3261, Pte., d. of w., F. & F., 28/10/16.
Birch, Harold, b. Halliwell, Lancs, e. Bolton, Lancs, 307377, Cpl., k. in a., F. & F., 6/12/17, formerly 1448, North Lancs Regt.
Bodger, Roland, b. Saltley, Birmingham, e. Aston, Birmingham, 305276, Pte., k. in a., F. & F., 27/8/16.
Bowers, John William, e. Bury, Lancs (Heywood, Lancs), 5779, Pte., k. in a., F. & F., 25/8/16, formerly 3028, Lancs Fus.

Bradbury, Alfred, b. All Souls, Manchester, e. Manchester, 5742, Pte., k. in a., F. & F., 16/10/16, formerly 2096, Manchester Regt
Bragg, Horace, b. Birmingham, e. Aberbargoed, Cardiff (New Tredegar, Cardiff), 203812, Pte., k. in a., F. & F., 31/3/18.
Brazier, William, e. Aston, Birmingham (Six Ways, Birmingham), 3713, Pte., d., F. & F., 23/10/16.
Bright, James, e. Salisbury, Wilts (Winterbourne, Wilts), 306648, Pte., k. in a., F. & F., 27/8/16.
Brown, Alexander, b. West Calder, Midlothian, e. West Calder, 5731, Pte., d. of w., F. & F., 8/9/16, formerly 2215, Royal Scots.
Brown, Frederick George, b. Wimborne, Dorset, e. Poole, Dorset (Wimborne), 27968, Pte., d. of w., F. & F., 15/4/18.
Brown, Peter, e. Bathgate, Linlithgow, 307141, Pte., d. of w., F. & F., 6/9/17, formerly 2336, Royal Scots.
Butler, Charles, b. Yateley, Hants, e. Winchester, Hants (Yateley), 307201, L/Sgt., k. in a., F. & F., 14/4/18, formerly 3230, Hant Regt.
Calder, James, b. Mid Calne, Midlothian, e. West Calder, Midlothian, 307171, Sgt., k. in a., F. & F., 24/9/17, formerly 2219, R. Scots.
Casey, Arthur Harry Roland, b. Birmingham, e. Aston, Birmingham, 306324, Pte., k. in a., F. & F., 3/9/17.
Chambers, William, e. Aston, Birmingham (Handsworth, Staffs), 306102, Pte., k. in a., F. & F., 7/9/17.
Chatterley, Oscar M., b. Snitterfield, Warwicks, e. Warwick (Leamington, Warwicks), 24054, Pte., k. in a., F. & F., 22/8/17.
College, Archer, b. Brinklow, Warwicks, e. Coventry, Warwicks, 24649, Pte., k. in a., F. & F., 3/9/17.
Collier, Fred, e. Bolton, Lancs, 306965, Pte., d. of w., F. & F., 19/4/17, formerly 3471, N. Lancs Regt.
Collins, Ernest Alfred, e. Pewsey, Wilts (Bottleford, Wilts), 306699, Pte., k. in a., F. & F., 27/8/16.
Cornhill, Herbert Charles, b. Broxburne, Herts, e. Coventry, Warwicks, 267924, Pte., k. in a., F. & F., 22/4/18.
Corless, James, e. Bolton, Lancs, 307254, Sgt., k. in a., F. & F., 4/9/17, formerly 3203, N. Lanc. Regt.
Cotterhill, Howard, b. St. Paul's, Birmingham, e. Aston, Birmingham, 1570, Pte., k. in a., F. & F., 18/7/16.
Crisp, Arthur William, e. Wolverton, Bucks, 4773, Pte., d. of w., F & F., 5/10/16.
Cowie, James Donald, e. Birmingham (Sparkbrook, Birmingham), 3646, Sgt., k. in a., F. & F., 5/9/16.
Crawford, William James, b. Folkestone, Kent, e. Aston, Birmingham (Gravelly Hill, Birmingham), 1815, Pte., d. of w., F. & F., 10/7/16.
Croshaw, Frank Herbert, e. Birmingham (Aston, Birmingham), 3647, Dmr., d. of w., F. & F., 14/10/16.
Dale, Charles Redwood, b. Macclesfield, Ches., e. Macclesfield, 307359, Sgt., k. in a., F. & F., 3/9/17, formerly 1309, Ches. Regt.
Davis, William, b. Birmingham, e. Birmingham, 5010, A/R.S.M,. k. in a., F. & F., 19/4/17.
Downard, Charles Henry, e. Birmingham, 2742, Sgt., d. of w., F. & F., 16/8/16.
Drew, Frederick, e. Winchester, Hants, 5760, Pte., d. of w., F. & F., 20/7/16, formerly 3163, Hants Regt.
Drummond, Peter Frederick, b. Linlithgow, e. Bo'ness, West Lothian, 5704, Pte., d. of w., F. & F., 14/12/16, formerly 2032, R. Scots.
Dyer, Frederick Percy, b. Hound, Hants, e. Southampton (Hound), 307022, Pte., k. in a., F. & F., 3/12/17, formerly 1339, Hants Regt.
Eccott, Alfred, b. Old Basing, Basingstoke, Hants, e. Basingstoke (Mapledurwell, Basingstoke), 5403, L/Sgt., d. of w., F. & F., 12/7/16, formerly 2087, Hants Regt.
Farmer, Arthur, e. Birmingham (Erdington, Birmingham), 4160, Pte., k. in a., F. & F., 18/7/16.
Fisher, Frank Ambrose, b. Winchcombe, Glos., e. Cheltenham, Glos., 307465, Pte., k. in a., E. & F., 27/8/17, formerly 28814, R. Berks Regt.
Flynn, Alfred, b. Nantwich, Ches., e. Crewe, Ches., 29523, Pte., d. of w., F. & F., 10/9/17, formerly 62007 Ches. Regt.
Foster, Harry, e. Aston, Birmingham, 306093, Cpl., k. in a., F. & F., 27/8/16.
French, George, b. Birmingham, e. Aston, Birmingham (Wylde Green, Birmingham), 305711, L/Sgt., k. in a., F. & F., 30/3/17.
Friend, Herbert, b. Aston, Birmingham, e. Aston (Nechells, Birmingham), 305611, Pte., k. in a., F. & F., 26/6/16.
Gaines, George, e. Aldershot, Hants (Farnborough, Hants), 307425, Pte., k. in a., F. & F., 15/12/17
Gardener, William, b. Horten Heath, Hants, e. Newbury, Berks (Brambridge, Eastleigh, Hants), 307437, Sgt., k. in a., F. & F., 6/12/17, formerly 26318, R. Berks Regt.
Gibbard, George, e. Oxford (Banbury, Oxon), 4877, Pte., d. of w., F. & F., 19/7/16.
Gilkes, Reginald William, b. Ratley, Warwicks, e. Banbury, Oxon (Ratley), 328039, Pte., k. in a., F. & F., 5/9/17.
Glaister, James Robert, e. Bolton, Lancs, 328055, Pte., k. in a., F. & F., 27/8/17, formerly 3646, N. Lancs Regt.
Gordon, Robert, b. Birkenhead, Ches., e. Chester (Birkenhead), 29667, Pte., k. in a., F. & F., 24/3/18, formerly 40458, S. Lanc. Regt.
Grant, Arthur, b. Birmingham, e. Birmingham, 306379, Cpl., k. in a., F. & F., 7/9/17.
Grant, Charles Alfred, e. Devizes, Wilts (Yarnbrook, nr. Trowbridge, Wilts), 5010, Pte., d., F. & F., 22/12/16.
Hall, Harry, e. Bletchley, Bucks (Great Horwood, Bucks), 307466, Pte., d. of w., F. & F., 30/4/17, formerly 22660, Oxf. & Bucks L.I.
Hanson, Sydney, e. Birmingham, 4473, Pte., k. in a., F. & F., 7/7/16.
Harris, John Frederick, e. Aston, Birmingham, 306033, L/Sgt., k. in a., F. & F., 3/9/17.
Hartle, Harry, b. Birmingham, e. Aston, Birmingham (Bartley Green, near Birmingham), 306342, Pte., k. in a., F. & F., 5/12/17.
Hawkins, Ernest Edward, b. Birmingham, e. Birmingham, 24299, Pte., k. in a., F. & F., 10/10/17.
Hirons, Alfred Ernest, b. Combroke, Warwicks, e. Leamington, Warwicks (Combroke), 24670, Pte., d. of w., F. & F., 13/4/18.
Hodges, Sydney Philip, e. Swindon, Wilts, 306819, Pte., k. in a., F. & F., 27/8/16.
Hodgson, Sam., e. Bolton, Lancs, 6533, Pte., k. in a., F. & F., 10/7/16, formerly 4004, N. Lancs Regt.
Holden, Ernest Howard, b. Devizes, Wilts, e. Devizes (Seend, Wilts), 306703, Cpl., d. of w., F. & F., 10/10/18.
Hough, Walter, b. Buglawford, Congleton Ches., e. Congleton, 6417, Pte., k. in a., F. & F., 6/9/16, formerly 1231, Ches. Regt.
Houlder, James, e. Bolton, Lancs, 307205, Pte., d., F. & F., 10/3/17, formerly 1598, N. Lancs Regt.
Hunter, John, b. Kirkpatrick, Glasgow, e. Aston, Birmingham, 305600, Pte., k. in a., F. & F., 1/7/16.
Ingram, William, e. Westbury, Wilts (Leigh, Westbury), 306638, Pte., k. in a., F. & F., 27/8/16.
Jones, Albert, e. Birmingham (Balsall Heath, Birmingham), 3200, Pte., k. in a., F. & F., 9/7/16.
Jones, Arnold, e. Aston, Birmingham (Saltley, Birmingham), 305878, Pte., k. in a., F. & F., 1/7/16.
Jones, Harry, e. Preston, Lancs, 307030 Pte., k. in a., F. & F., 30/3/17, formerly 3500, N. Lancs. Regt.
Jones, William, b. Runcorn, Ches., e. Runcorn, 29526, Pte., k. in a., F. & F., 14/4/18, formerly 62143, Ches. Regt.
Kemp, Herbert Ernest, b. Birmingham, e. Birmingham, 306398, Pte., k. in a., F. & F., 30/3/17.
Kendall, Walter Emerson, b. Whitehaven, Cumberland, e. Aston, Birmingham (Witton, Birmingham), 305810, Cpl., k. in a., F. & F., 6/9/17.
Kenny, John, b. Linlithgow, e. Linlithgow, 307156, Pte., d. of w., F. & F., 8/9/17 formerly 2050, R. Scots.
Key, Alfred, b. Kensington, London, e. Kensington, 35390, Pte., d., F. & F., 5/4/18, formerly 5390, Middx. Regt.
Kidner, Walter James, b. Aston, Birmingham, e. Aston, 1788, Pte., k. in a., F. & F., 21/7/16.
Langston, Samuel Elmer, e. Birmingham (Small Heath, Birmingham), 306795, Pte., k. in a., F. & F., 27/8/16.
Lawrence, Percy Hayward, b. Birmingham, e. Aston, Birmingham (Small Heath, Birmingham), 306406, Pte., k. in a., F. & F., 27/8/16.
Leedham, George Edward, e. Aston, Birmingham (Burton-on-Trent, Staffs), 4428, L/Sgt., k. in a., F. & F., 14/8/16.
Lester, Thomas, e. Birmingham (Aston, Birmingham), 306019, Pte., k. in a., F. & F., 1/7/16.
Lewis, Albert Victor, b. Kingston-on-Thames, Surrey, e. Winchester, Hants, 5407, Pte., k. in a., F. & F., 20/7/16, formerly 2179, Hants Regt.
Lightfoot, Ernest, b. Runcorn, Ches., e. Runcorn, 29686, Pte., k. in a., F. & F., 1/11/17, formerly 273555, R.A.S.C.
Lockley, Joseph, b. Chester, e. Chester; 29550, Pte., k. in a., F. & F., 4/9/17, formerly 61947, Ches. Regt.
McKenzie, James, b. Uphall, Linlithgow, e. Uphall, 5671, Pte., d. of w., F. & F., 11/1/17, formerly 2276, R. Scots.
Macauley, Ernest, e. Devizes, Wilts, 4943, Pte., d. of w., F. & F., 4/2/17.
Mallin, Edward Henry, e. Aston, Birmingham (Hockley, Birmingham), 305966, Pte., k. in a., F. & F., 14/4/17.
Mander, William, e. Birmingham (Hockley, Birmingham), 305175, Pte., k. in a., F. & F., 17/8/17.
March, Caleb, b. Evesham, Worcs, e. Pershore, Worcs (Bengeworth, Worcs), 28954, Pte., k. in a., F. & F., 7/9/17, formerly 31162, Worcs Regt.
Meredith Edward, e. Lancaster, Lancs, 306983, L/Cpl., k. in a., F. & F., 5/12/17, formerly 3353, R. Lancs Regt., M.M.
Miles, Archie, Frederick, b. Worthing, Sussex e. Worthing, 29706, Pte., d. of w., F. & F., 17/12/17, formerly 144999, R.A.S.C.
Miller, Christopher Sidney, b. Bilston, Staffs, e. Birmingham (Pattingham, Wolverhampton, Staffs), 306418, Pte., k. in a, F. & F., 7/9/16.
Miller, William John, e. Salisbury, Wilts (Teffont Manor, Salisbury), 306708, Pte., k. in a., F. & F., 27/8/16.
Milward, Ernest, e. Birmingham (Aston, Birmingham), 3040, Pte., d. of w., F. & F., 21/7/16.
Morgan, David William, e. Devizes, Wilts (Nursteed, Devizes), 306685, Pte., k. in a., F. & F., 27/8/16.
Morris, John, e. Aston, Birmingham, 305885, Pte., k. in a., F. & F., 1/7/16.
Moss, Harry, b. Wrinehall, Staffs, e. Crewe, Ches. (Wrinehall), 29654, Pte., k. in a., F. & F., 3/12/17, formerly 40451, S. Lancs Regt.
Nicholls, Esmond Herbert Lawson, e. Aston, Birmingham (Handsworth, Birmingham), 4381, Sgt., k. in a., F. & F., 5/12/16.
Oakes, Arthur Edward, e. Aston, Birmingham (Solihull, Birmingham), 3973, Pte., k. in a., F. & F., 18/12/16.
Owen, John Richard, e. Birmingham (Chin, Salop), 305658, Pte., k. in a., F. & F., 1/7/16.
Oxley, Frederick Stephen, e. Morecambe, Lancs, 307352, Sgt., k. in a., F. & F., 7/9/17, formerly 3273, R. Lancs Regt.
Pain, Aaron, b. Littleport, Cambridge, e. Birmingham (Wellesbourne, Warwick), 307471, Pte., k. in a., F. & F., 4/10/17.
Painter, Joseph, e. Aston, Birmingham, 306040, Pte., k. in a., F. & F., 1/7/16.
Pearce, Harold Leslie, e. Birmingham (Moseley, Birmingham), 306414, Pte., k. in a., F. & F., 21/4/17.

Perks, Joseph, e. Birmingham (Winson Green, Birmingham), 305659, Pte., k. in a., F. & F., 1/7/16.
Portman, Bert, b. Smethwick, Staffs, e. Birmingham (Smethwick), 306364, Cpl., d. of w., F. & F., 1/4/17.
Povey, George Peter, e. Chester (Holt, Wrexham, Denbigh), 307273, Pte., d. of w., F. & F., 4/9/17.
Povey, John, b. Birmingham, e. Birmingham, 306302, Pte., k. in a., F. & F., 6/9/17.
Pratley, Frederick John, b. Witney, Oxon, e. Oxford (Witney), 35182, Pte., k. in a., F. & F., 30/3/18.
Ray, Charles Edward, b. Redditch, Worcs., e. Birmingham (Webb Heath, Redditch), 305024, Cpl., d., F. & F., 29/10/18, M.M.
Reddell, Henry Thomas, e. Aston, Birmingham (Witton, Birmingham), 3341, L/Cpl., d. of w., F. & F., 25/6/16.
Reid, Jeremiah, b. Liverpool, Lancs, e. Liverpool, 325136, Pte., k. in a., F. & F., 28/3/18, formerly 46128, Liverpool Regt.
Reynolds, William Arthur, b. Portswood, Southampton, Hants, e. Southampton, 5413, L/Cpl., d. of w., F. & F., 29/10/16, formerly 1602, Hamps. Regt.
Richardson, Alfred, b. Shirley, Warwicks, e. Aston, Birmingham (Shirley), 306370, Pte., k. in a., F. & F., 4/9/17.
Rigby, James, b. Liverpool, e. Seaforth, Lancs, 325119, Pte., d., F. & F., 5/5/18, formerly 4982, York & Lancs Regt.
Roberts, Clifford, b. Dolgelly, Merioneth, e. Leamington, Warwicks (Warwick), 268942, Pte., d., F. & F., 30/10/18.
Robertson, Alexander Clyne, e. Aberdeen, 307510, Pte., k. in a., F. & F., 30/3/17, formerly 781, R.E.
Robinson, Alexander George, b. Coventry, Warwicks, e. Coventry (Foleshill, Warwicks), 22209, Cpl., d., F. F., 14/1/18.
Robinson, Alexander George, b. Coventry, Warwicks, e. Coventry (Foleshill, Warwicks), 22209, Cpl., d., F. & F., 14/1/18.
Rose, Herbert, e. Aston, Birmingham (Witton, Birmingham), 3752, Pte., k. in a., F. & F., 25/8/16.
Rose, William Arthur, b. Handsworth, Birmingham, e. Aston, Birmingham (Handsworth), 306334, L/Cpl., d. of w., F. & F., 2/4/17.
Rowe, Ernest, b. Birmingham, e. Aston, Birmingham, 1922, Pte., k. in a., F. & F., 1/7/16.
Rudge, Leonard, b. Birmingham, e. Aston, Birmingham, 306407, Cpl., k. in a., F. & F., 30/3/18.
Salmond, Henry, b. Linlithgow, e. Linlithgow, 5684, Pte., k. in a., F. & F., 23/10/16, formerly 2092, R. Scots.
Scrivener, John Henry, e. Birmingham (Sparkhill, Birmingham), 3229, C.S.M., d. of w., F. & F., 19/9/16.
Sears, George, b. Birmingham, e. Birmingham, 305623, Pte., k. in a., F. & F., 1/7/16.
Seeley, Thomas Nelson, b. Handsworth, Staffs, e. Worcester (Halesowen, Worcs.), 35189, Pte., k. in a., F. & F., 22/3/18.
Shakespeare, David Arthur, e. Birmingham (South Yardley, Birmingham), 4321, Pte., d. of w., F. & F., 12/7/16.
Sheppard, Percy John, b. Wroughton, Wilts, e. Grove Park, Middx. (Swindon, Wilts), 29691, Pte., k. in a., F. & F., 28/9/17, formerly 268018, R.A.S.C.
Shiner, Frank Thomas, e. Birmingham (Edgbaston, Birmingham), 4396, Pte., d., F. & F., 12/7/16.
Sillitoe, Thomas, b. Heswall, Ches., e. Birkenhead, Ches. (Heswall), 29525, Pte., k. in a., F. & F., 3/9/17, formerly 62289, Ches. Regt.
Singleton, William, e. Preston, Lancs, 307373, Pte., k. in a., F. & F., 7/1/18, formerly 3543, N. Lancs Regt.
Smith, Fred, b. Cowling, Yorks, e. Halifax, Yorks (Skipton, Yorks), 29718, Pte., d. of w., F. & F., 31/3/18.
Smith, George, b. Addiewell, Edinburgh, e. West Calder, Edinburgh, 5673, Pte., d. of w., F. & F., 25/6/16, formerly 2304, R. Scots.
Smith, Hugh Rice Arthur, b. Bladon, Oxon, e. Birmingham (Balsall Heath, Birmingham), 306371, L/Cpl., k. in a., F. & F., 5/12/17.
Smith, Leonard, b. Birmingham, e. Birmingham (Aston, Birmingham), 306425, Pte., d. of w., F. & F., 2/10/17.
Smith, Percy William, e. Stratford-on-Avon, Warwicks (Studley, Warwicks), 306803, Pte., k. in a., F. & F., 27/8/16.
Stone, Arthur Campbell Brain, e. Bristol, Glos. (Easton, Bristol), 35197, Pte., d. of w., F. & F., 8/10/19.
Stott, William, b St. Paul's, Farnsworth, Lancs, e. Little Hulton, Lancs (Walkden, Lancs), 307374, Pte., k. in a., F. & F., 7/12/17, formerly 1672, N. Lancs Regt.
Strickland, Hugh, e. Lancaster (Kirkby Lonsdale, Westmoreland), 5388, Pte., d. of w., F. & F., 30/7/16, formerly 2323, R. Lancs Regt.
Sutcliffe, Isherwood Edmonds, e. Birmingham (Handsworth, Staffs), 5190, Pte., d. of w., F. & F., 2/9/16.
Tarrant, Sidney Archibald, b. Andover, Hants, e. Shirley, Hants, 306922, Pte., k. in a., F. & F., 16/12/16, formerly 1512, Hants Regt.
Thornton, Bertram Harry, b. Fenny Compton, Warwicks, e. Coventry, Warwicks (Farnborough, Warwicks), 24646, Pte., k. in a., F. & F., 15/11/17.
Tompkins, William, b. Upton-on-Severn, Worcs., e. Worcester (Uckinghall, Glos.), 28938, Pte., k. in a., F. & F., 8/12/17.
Topliss, Arthur, b. Rollaston, Burton-on-Trent, Staffs, e. Saltley, Birmingham (Rollaston), 4434, Cpl., k. in a., F. & F., 5/9/16.
Tory, John Thomas, b. Spalding, Lincs, e. Lincoln (Peterborough, Northants), 29745, Pte., k. in a., F. & F., 24/9/17.
Turner, Edward, e. Aston, Birmingham, 3821, Pte., k. in a., F. & F., 26/6/16.
Turner, James, e. Bolton, Lancs, 5601, Pte., k. in a., F. & F., 12/8/16, formerly 3336, N. Lancs Regt.
Twamley, Joseph, b. Coventry, Warwicks, e. Aston, Birmingham, 779, Pte., d., F. & F., 11/7/16.
Tyler, Peter, e. Coventry, Warwicks (Bedworth, Warwicks), 328043, Pte., k. in a., F. & F., 15/12/17.
Veitch, Ernest, b. Aston, Birmingham, e. Birmingham (Aston), 328034, Pte., k. in a., F. & F., 24/3/18.
Walker, Robert J., e. Lancaster (Halton, Lancs), 306996, L/Cpl., k. in a., F. & F., 30/3/17, formerly 2538, R. Lancs Regt.
Walker, Thomas, b. Whitburn, Linlithgow, e. West Calder, Edinburgh (Fauld House, Linlithgow), 307157, Sgt., k. in a., F. & F., 6/9/17, formerly 5707, R. Scots.
Walsh, John, e. Bolton, Lancs, 5559, Pte., k. in a., F. & F., 26/6/16, formerly 4468, N. Lancs Regt.
Ward, Alexander, e. Bolton, Lancs, 306951, Pte., k. in a., F. & F., 26/6/16, formerly 3432, N. Lancs Regt.
Wasley, Frederick Charley, e. Birmingham (Alum Rock, Birmingham), 305633, Pte., k. in a., F. & F., 1/7/16.
Watson, Frank, b. Linlithgow, e. Bathgate, Linlithgow, 5665, Pte., d. of w., F. & F., 31/7/16, formerly 2771, R. Scots.
Watson, James, e. Lancaster, 5391, L/Cpl., k. in a., F. & F., 9/9/16, formerly 2432, R. Lancs Regt.
Watson, William, b. Birmingham, e. Birmingham, 27904, Pte., k. in a., F. & F., 4/12/17.
Watts, Harry, e. Aston, Birmingham, 306100, Pte., k. in a., F. & F., 2/4/17.
Weavers, George Frederick, e. Southampton, 307009, Pte., k. in a., F. & F., 14/12/17, formerly 2811, Hants Regt.
Weedon, Peter, e. Aylesbury, Bucks (Weston Turville, Bucks), 4750, Pte., d., F. & F., 21/12/16.
Wells, Alfred Steven, e. Southampton, Hants (Romsey, Hants), 5523, Pte., k. in a., F. & F., 19/8/16, formerly 2559, Hants Regt.
West, Herbert, e. Birmingham, 2994, Pte., d. of w., F. & F., 26/6/16.
White, George, b. Bournemouth, Hants, e. Southampton, Hants (Bournemouth), 306923, Pte., k. in a., F. & F., 7/9/16, formerly 1924, Hants Regt.
White, Lawrence, b. 'Boness, Linlithgow, e. 'Boness, 5646, Pte., d. of w., F. & F., 20/12/16, formerly 992, R. Scots.
Wilson, John, b. Mid-Calder, Edinburgh, e. Uphall, West Lothian (Winchburgh, West Lothian), 5657, L/Cpl., k. in a., F. & F., 28/6/16, formerly 644, R. Scots.
Woolagham, b. Cleator Moor, Cumberland, e. Cleator Moor, 29677, Pte., k. in a., F. & F., 5/10/17, formerly 1298, Northumberland Fus.
Yates, Albert b. Chorley, Lancs, e. Chorley, 29543, Pte., k. in a., F. & F., 24/3/18, formerly 44001, Ches. Regt.

9th Battalion.

Adams, William James, b. Liverpool, e. Bristol, 15930, Cpl., d. of w., Gallipoli, 15/11/15.
Adkins, Ernest Gilbert, b. Saltley, Birmingham, e. Birmingham (Saltley), 8979, Pte., k. in a., Gallipoli, 9/8/15.
Ainsworth, Walter, b. Padiham, Lancs, e. Burnley, Lancs 12496, Pte., d., Gallipoli, 25/9/15, formerly 51437, R.G.A.
Allen, John, b. Birkenhead, Cheshire, e. Birmingham (Handsworth, Birmingham), 13386, Pte., k. in a., Mesopotamia, 19/4/16.
Allen, William Francis, b. Birmingham, e. Birmingham (Handsworth, Birmingham), 12047, Pte., k. in a., Mesopotamia, 10/3/17.
Amos, Charles Henry, b. Willinghall, Wolverhampton, Staffs, e. Coventry, Warwicks, 1614, Pte., d., Mesopotamia, 13/7/16.
Angel, Nicholas, b. Huntingdon, e. Leamington, Warwicks. (Brislington, Bristol), 16931, Pte., k. in a., Mesopotamia, 25/1/17.
Ansell, Frederick James, b. Birmingham, e. Birmingham (Small Heath, Birmingham), 13053, Pte., k. in a., Mesopotamia, 25/1/17.
Arnold, Charles, b. Walsall, Staffs, e. Birmingham, 11095, Pte., d. of w., Mesopotamia, 25/10/15.
Arnold, Frederick, b. Winson Green, Birmingham, e. Birmingham, 5371, Pte., d. of w., Gallipoli, 10/8/15.
Arnold, Sidney, b. Bedworth, Warwicks., e. Nuneaton, Warwicks. (Bedworth), 14337, Pte., k. in a., Mesopotamia, 11/2/17.
Ash, Walter, b. St. Thomas's, Birmingham, e. Birmingham 2959, Pte., k. in a., Mesopotamia, 10/8/15.
Ashford, Albert, b. St. Mary's, Birmingham, e. Birmingham (Winson Green, Birmingham), 3000, Cpl., d., Gallipoli, 17/12/15.
Ashley, John Henry, b. Sutton, Birmingham, e. Birmingham, 2184, Pte., d., Mesopotamia, 19/6/16.
Astle, Arthur, b. St. Paul's, Birmingham, e. Birmingham 4741, Pte., d. of w., Mesopotamia, 26/8/16.
Atkins, David, b. Hartshill, Warwicks, e. Warwick (Hartshill), 12813, Pte., k. in a., Mesopotamia, 5/4/16.
Atkins, John Thomas G., b. Nuneaton, Warwick, e. Nuneaton (Astley, Nuneaton), 4507, Cpl., k. in a., Mesopotamia, 12/1/17.
Austin, Lawrence, b. Bedworth, Warwicks., e. Nuneaton, Warwicks. (Bedworth), 9537, Cpl., d., Mesopotamia, 12/7/16.
Ayres, George William, b., Holme, Huntingdon, e. Bedworth, Warwicks., 22345, L/Cpl., d., Mesopotamia, 23/6/17.
Bacon, William Thomas, b. Birmingham, e. Birmingham (Small Heath, Birmingham), 22851, Pte., d., Mesopotamia, 23/6/17.
Baker, Edwin, b. Tamworth, Warwicks, e. Atherstone, Warwicks. (Tamworth), 10755, Pte., k. in a., Gallipoli, 20/8/15.
Ball, Jonah, b. Wombridge, Wellington, Salop, e. Coventry, Warwicks. (Wellington), 8566, Cpl., k. in a., Mesopotamia, 25/6/16.
Bampton, Leonard, b. Birmingham, e. Birmingham (Winson Green, Birmingham), 15676, Cpl., d., Mesopotamia, 18/10/17.
Banks, Francis Hubert, b. Sparkbrook, Birmingham, e. Birmingham, 4137, Cpl., d. of w., Mesopotamia, 10/4/16.

Barlow, Albert William, b. Leamington, Warwicks., e. Leamington, 15571, Pte., d., Mesopotamia, 24/9/16.
Barratt, John, b. Bulkington, Warwicks., e. Nuneaton, Warwicks. (Bulkington), 15017, Pte., d. of w., Mesopotamia, 29/3/17.
Bartlett, James Thomas, b. Birmingham, e. Birmingham (Aston, Birmingham), 3488, Pte., k. in a., Gallipoli, 10/8/15.
Barton, Jesse, b. Langley Green, Oldbury, Worcs, e. Birmingham (Aston, Birmingham), 8028, Pte., k. in a., Gallipoli, 5/1/16.
Bate, William Henry, b. Cheltenham, Glos., e. Birmingham (Wylde Green, Birmingham), 10817, Pte., d., Gallipoli, 30/9/15.
Bates, Alfred, b. Digbeth, Birmingham, e. Birmingham, 5301, Pte., d., Mesopotamia, 1/7/16.
Bates, Frederick George, b. Saltley, Birmingham, e. Consett, Co. Durham (Castle Side, Co. Durham), 12215, Cpl., d., Mesopotamia, 1/9/18.
Batty, Henry, b. Balsall Heath, Birmingham, e. Birmingham, 4/2071, Pte., k. in a., Mesopotamia, 10/8/15.
Beach, Frederick Leonard, b. Birmingham, e. Birmingham (Erdington, Birmingham), 16024, Pte., d. of w., Mesopotamia, 8/1/17.
Bean, Claude Hollis, b. Bristol, Glos., e. Cardiff, 10846, Pte., k. in a., Gallipoli, 10/8/15.
Beardmore, Albert, b. Birmingham, e. Birmingham, 5459, Pte., k. in a., Gallipoli, 10/8/15.
Beardsmore, George, b. Bentley, Willenhall, Staffs, e. Nuneaton, Warwicks. (Stockingford, Warwicks.), 3523, Pte., d., Mesopotamia, 24/11/18.
Beasley, Albert, b. Birmingham, e. Birmingham, 22546, Pte., d., Mesopotamia, 1/9/18.
Beaton, Frank, e. Portsmouth (Havant, Hants), 241932, Pte., d., Mesopotamia, 30/10/18, formerly 2123, Hamps. Regt.
Beck, Joseph Arthur, b. Trinity, Coventry, Warwicks., e. Coventry, 2764, Pte., d., Mesopotamia, 1/9/18.
Beddow, John Phil, b. Aston, Birmingham, e. Birmingham (Aston), 11041, Pte., k. in a., Mesopotamia, 5/4/16.
Beddow, Thomas, b. Smethwick, Staffs, e. Smethwick, 12747, Pte., k. in a., Gallipoli, 16/12/15.
Behagg, Arthur, b. Warboys, Huntingdon, e. Ramsey, Huntingdon (Wister Fen, Huntingdon), 203359, Pte., d., Mesopotamia, 1/10/18, formerly 213, Hunts Cyclist Battn.
Belfield, Ralph, b. Leeds, Yorks, e. Bradford, Yorks (Shelf, Halifax, Yorks), 4/2042, Pte., k. in a., Gallipoli, 10/8/15.
Bennett, Joseph, b. Liverpool, e. Liverpool, 12352, Pte., k. in a., Mesopotamia, 25/1/17, formerly 53070, R.G.A.
Bent, Arthur, b. Westcoates, Leics, e. Leicester (Byfield, Northants), 8826, Pte., k. in a., Mesopotamia, 19/4/16.
Benting, George Evans, b. Church Stretton, Salop, e. Warwick (Welshpool, Salop), 16653, Pte., k. in a., Mesopotamia, 29/3/17.
Biggs, John, b. Nechells, Birmingham, e. Birmingham (Smethwick, Staffs), 11995, Pte., d. of w., Mesopotamia, 18/4/16.
Biller, Edward John, b. St. John's, Royston, Hereford, e. Jarrow, Durham, 3162, Cpl., k. in a., Mesopotamia, 25/1/17.
Bilney, Walter, b. Brandeston, Framlingham, Suffolk, e. Ipswich, Suffolk (Framlingham), 12532, Pte., d. of w., Gallipoli, 13/10/15, formerly 54559, R.G.A.
Bilston, John, b. Birmingham, e. Birmingham (Nechells, Birmingham), 3359, Pte., k. in a., Gallipoli, 10/8/15.
Birch, Albert James, b. Ettington, Stratford-on-Avon, Warwicks., e. Stratford-on-Avon (Ettington), 11451, Pte., d., Gallipoli, 27/11/15.
Bishop, Alfred Thomas, b. Birmingham, e. Birmingham (Ladywood, Birmingham), 16512, Pte., k. in a., Mesopotamia, 25/1/17.
Bladon, Raymond, b. Witton, Birmingham, e. Birmingham (Small Heath, Birmingham), 16/532, Sgt., d. of w., Mesopotamia, 3/3/17.
Blake, James Vincent, b. Edgbaston, Birmingham, e. Birmingham, 2849, Pte., k. in a., Gallipoli, 9/8/15.
Bloomer, John Wood, b. Perry Bank, Staffs, e. Birmingham (Perry Bank), 6192, Pte., d., Mesopotamia, 26/9/18.
Bodilly, Frank, b. New York, U.S.A., e. Worcester (Crumhampton, Worcs), 15454, Pte., d., Mesopotamia, 2/7/16.
Boobyer, Francis Edward, b. Helen Broadwich, Devon, e. Portsmouth (Cosham, Hants), 12530, L/Sgt., d., Mesopotamia, 26/1/17, formerly 6877, R.G.A.
Bourne, Augustus, b. Leicester, e. Coventry, Warwicks (Hawkesbury, Warwicks), 30050, Pte., d. of w., Mesopotamia, 1/9/18.
Boyne, William, b. Birmingham, e. Birmingham (Ashted, Birmingham), 3398, Pte., k. in a., Gallipoli, 10/8/15.
Brackstone, Herbert Cherrett, b. Kinson, Dorset, e. Poole, Dorset (Upper Parkstone, Dorset), 12274, Pte., d., Gallipoli, 16/11/15, formerly 53479, R.G.A.
Bradbury, Thomas William, b. Birmingham, e. Birmingham (Deritend, Birmingham), 3216, L/Cpl., k. in a., Gallipoli, 10/8/15.
Bramley, James Daniel, e. Preston, Lancs, 202474, Pte., d. of w., Mesopotamia, 4/10/18, formerly 3358, N. Lancs Regt.
Branford, Oliver, b. Wolverhampton, Staffs, e. Birmingham, 10378, Pte., d., Gallipoli, 12/9/15.
Bridges, Fred, b. Stratford-on Avon, Warwicks, e. Stratford-on-Avon (Shottery, Warwicks), 9634, Pte., d., Mesopotamia, 12/5/16.
Briggs, Bernard, b. Birmingham, e. Birmingham (Soho, Birmingham), 15357, Pte., k. in a., F. & F., 25/1/17.
Broadhurst, George, b. Dordon, Warwicks, e. Nuneaton, Warwicks (Dordon), 11980, Pte., k. in a., Mesopotamia, 5/4/16.
Broadmore, George Howard, b. Winson Green, Birmingham, e. Birmingham, 3943, Sgt., k. in a., Mesopotamia, 25/1/17.
Brookes, John Taylor, b. Rochdale, Lancs, e. Bacup, Lancs (Rochdale), 9952, Pte., d. of w., Mesopotamia, 27/4/16.
Brookes, Archie Percival, b. Lugwardine, Hereford, e. Rugby, Warwicks (Lugwardine), 3077, Pte., k. in a., Gallipoli, 9/8/15.
Brooks, Tom, b. Chesterfield, Derby, e. Birmingham, 3190, L/Cpl., k. in a., Gallipoli, 8/8/15.
Brookes, William, b. Alvecote, Warwicks, e. Atherstone, Warwicks (Tamworth, Warwicks), 10741, Pte., k. in a., Mesopotamia, 19/4/16.
Brooks, Henry James, b. Powick, Worcs, e. Pontefract, Yorks (Worcester), 11691, Pte., k. in a., Mesopotamia, 9/4/16.
Brown, Arthur, b. Atherstone, Warwicks, e. Nuneaton, Warwicks (Atherstone), 13221, Pte., k. in a., Mesopotamia, 29/3/17.
Brown, Albert William, b. Gloucester, e. Birmingham (Aston, Birmingham), 18159, Pte., k. in a., Mesopotamia, 11/4/17.
Brown, Lionel, b. Buxton, Derby, e. Banbury, Oxon (St. Alban's, Herts), 18407, Pte., d., Mesopotamia, 11/11/18, formerly 23629, Som. L.I.
Bruen, Frank, b. Newcastle-under-Lyne, Staffs, e. Nuneaton, Warwicks (Newcastle-under-Lyne), 1510, L/Sgt., k. in a., Mesopotamia, 1/9/18.
Buckler, Harry, b. Birmingham, e. Birmingham, 3559, Pte., k. in a., Gallipoli, 5/1/16.
Buhler, Frederick, b. Battersea, London, e. Canning Town, London (Plaistow, Kent), 11116, Pte., k. in a., Mesopotamia, 5/4/16.
Bunce, Harry, b. Yardley Wood, Birmingham, e. Birmingham (King's Heath, Birmingham), 8848, Pte., d., Mesopotamia, 28/6/16.
Bunce, Albert Percival, b. Hursley, Hants, e. Winchester, Hants (Hursley), 4767, Pte., d of w., Gallipoli, 16/8/15.
Bunker, Frederick Alfred, b. Luton, Beds, e. Coventry, Warwicks, 16769, Pte., k. in a., Mesopotamia, 25/1/17.
Burnett, Eli, b. Stogumber, Som., e. Taunton, Som. (Bagborough, Som.), 12275, Pte., k. in a., Mesopotamia, 25/1/17, formerly 53327, R.G.A.
Burrows, Arthur, b. Birmingham, e. Birmingham (Aston, Birmingham), 8577, Sgt., k. in a., Mesopotamia, 9/4/16.
Butler, Alfred William, b. Welland, Worcs, e. Warwick (Upper Welland, Worcs.), 16654, Pte., d., Mesopotamia, 20/10/16.
Caffrey, Walter, b. Tottenham, Middx., e. Holborn, Middx. (London), 11356, Pte., d. of w., Gallipoli, 17/12/15.
Caldwell, Charles, b. Galashiels, Selkirk, e. Shorncliffe, Kent (Edinburgh), 2504, Sgt., d. of w., Mesopotamia, 4/2/17.
Capewell, David, b. St. Wolfstans, Birmingham, e. Birmingham (Bournbrook, Birmingham), 8977, Pte., d. of w., Gallipoli, 10/8/15.
Capewell, Frederick Joseph, b. Birmingham, e. Birmingham, 11805, L/Cpl., d., Mesopotamia, 13/10/18.
Carey, Albert, b. Sutton-under-Brailes, Oxon, e. Warwick (Sutton-under-Brailes), 12897, L/Cpl., k. in a., Mesopotamia, 5/4/16.
Carter, Walter Harry, b. Bedworth, Warwicks, e. Nuneaton, Warwicks (Bedworth), 12830, Pte., k. in a., Mesopotamia, 25/1/17.
Cartwright, John, b. Birmingham, e. Birmingham, 1075, Pte., d., Mesopotamia, 5/7/16.
Carver, William Robert, b. St. Thomas, Birmingham, e. Birmingham, 6260, Pte., d. of w., Gallipoli, 22/7/15.
Cashmore, John, b. Shustoke, Warwicks, e. Warwick (Sutton Coldfield, Warwicks), 4766, Pte., k. in a., Gallipoli, 10/8/15.
Caswell, Wilfred, b. St. Nicholls, Gloucester, e. Coventry, Warwicks, 12628, Pte., d., Mesopotamia, 1/7/17.
Catch, Albert, b. Birmingham, e. Birmingham, 6262, Pte., k. in a., Gallipoli, 9/8/15.
Chamberlain, Charles Henry, b. Temple, Balsall Heath, Warwicks, e. Coventry, Warwicks (Burton Green, Warwicks), 3312, Pte., k. in a., Mesopotamia, 29/3/17.
Chapman, Alfred, b. Hanwell, Middx., e. Carmarthen (Cardiff, Glam.), 10853, Pte., d. of w., Gallipoli, 30/8/15.
Chater, William Thomas, b. Rugby, Warwicks, e. Warwick (Rugby), 14788, Pte., d. of w., Mesopotamia, 23/1/17.
Chatterton, George William, b. Birmingham, e. Birmingham, 4554, Pte., d. of w., Mesopotamia, 16/4/17.
Chittem, William, b. Coventry, Warwicks, e. Coventry, 19760, Pte., d., Mesopotamia, 21/9/18.
Clark, Joseph, b. St. Matthew's, Birmingham, e. Birmingham (Smethwick, Staffs), 2917, Pte., k. in a., Mesopotamia, 10/8/15.
Clark, Reginald, b. Cardiff, Glam., e. Cardiff, 10858, Pte., k. in a., Mesopotamia, 25/1/17, formerly 13729, Welsh Regt.
Clark, William, b. Milton, Hants, e. Christchurch, Hants (Old Milton), 12533, Pte., k. in a., Mesopotamia, 5/4/16, formerly 53778, R.G.A.
Clarke, George, e. Mansfield, Notts (Mansfield Woodhouse, Notts), 27505, Pte., d., Mesopotamia, 29/9/18, formerly 34950, Notts & Derby Regt.
Clarke, William Henry, b. St. Stephen's, Birmingham, e. Birmingham, 7992, Pte., k. in a., Mesopotamia, 29/3/17.
Clayton, William, b. Small Heath, Birmingham, e. Birmingham, 1586, Pte., k. in a., Mesopotamia, 9/4/16.
Cleaver, James, b. Corston, Warwicks, e. Warwick (Nuneaton, Warwicks), 3947, Pte., k. in a., Gallipoli, 10/8/15.
Cleaver, Walter, b. Small Heath, Birmingham, e. Birmingham, 6264, Pte., k. in a., Gallipoli, 10/8/15.
Clements, Robert William, b. Tunbridge Wells, Kent, e. Woolwich, Kent (Tunbridge Wells), 12414, Pte., d. of w., Mesopotamia, 9/4/16, formerly 40013, R.G.A.
Climpson, Frederick, b. Loudwater, Bucks, e. High Wycombe, Bucks (Loudwater), 12290, Pte., d., Mesopotamia, 7/7/16, formerly 53870, R.G.A.
Cogger, William Allen, b. Portsmouth, Hants, e. Portsmouth, 12489, Pte., k. in a., Gallipoli, 5/10/15, formerly 56866, R.G.A.

Colclough, William, b. Stockport, Lancs, e. Nuneaton, Warwicks (Atherstone, Warwicks), 15576, Pte., d., Mesopotamia, 4/7/16.
Coldicott, John, b. Hockley, Birmingham, e. Birmingham (Hockley), 5468, Pte., k. in a., Gallipoli, 18/7/15.
Coles, James, b. Blana, Mon., e. Nuneaton, Warwicks (Exhall, Warwicks), 11653, Pte., d., Mesopotamia, 23/5/15.
Collett, Christopher, b. Diss, Norfolk, e. Coventry, Warwicks (Diss), 9673, Pte., d., Mesopotamia, 15/5/18.
Collett, Oliver, b. All Saints, Birmingham, e. Birmingham, 2179, Pte., d., Mesopotamia, 4/10/18.
Collett, Percy, e. Birmingham (Edgbaston, Birmingham), 202612, Sgt., k. in a., Mesopotamia, 1/9/18.
Collins, George, b. Leamington, Warwicks, e. London (Leamington), 13245, Pte., d., Mesopotamia, 24/8/16.
Colledge, William, b. Nuneaton, Warwicks, e. Nuneaton (Chilvers Coton, Nuneaton), 12152, Pte., d., Mesopotamia, 29/4/16.
Connelly, James, b. Birmingham, e. Birmingham (Aston, Birmingham), 5253, Pte., d. of w., Mesopotamia, 3/9/15.
Conway, John Henry, b. Stratford-on-Avon, Warwicks, e. Stratford-on-Avon, 4069, Pte., k. in a., Gallipoli, 10/8/15.
Cooke, Percy John, b. Astwood Bank, Worcs, e. Redditch, Worcs, 15342, Pte., d., Mesopotamia, 7/7/16.
Cooke, Stanley Waterton, b. Meriden, Warwicks, e. Coventry, Warwicks (Meriden), 9674, L/Cpl., d., Mesopotamia, 28/11/15.
Cooper, Henry, b. Chelsea, London, e. London (Walworth, London), 12717, Pte., k. in a., Mesopotamia, 5/4/16.
Cooper, Harry Harold, b. Studley, Warwicks, e. Redditch, Worcs (Studley), 16987, Pte., k. in a., Mesopotamia, 25/1/17.
Cooper, Thomas, b. Nuneaton, Warwicks, e. Nuneaton, 12657, Pte., d. of w., Mesopotamia, 30/3/17.
Cooper, William, b. Birmingham, e. Birmingham, 812, Pte., k. in a., Mesopotamia, 19/4/16.
Cope, George, b. Warton, Warwicks, e. Nuneaton, Warwicks (Hinckley, Leics), 12665, Pte, d., Mesopotamia, 30/6/16.
Corbett, George, b. Birmingham, e. Warwick (Smethwick, Staffs), 21406, Pte., d., Mesopotamia, 23/6/17.
Cowley, William, b. West Bromwich, Staffs, e. Birmingham (West Bromwich), 2953, Pte., k. in a., Mesopotamia, 10/8/15.
Craggs, John, b. St. Andrews, Newcastle-on-Tyne, Northumberland, e. Newcastle-on-Tyne, 749, Pte., k. in a., Mesopotamia, 9/4/16.
Crane, James, b. Warwick, e. Warwick (Milverton, Leamington, Warwicks), 15356, Pte., d., Mesopotamia, 26/6/16.
Crawshaw, Samuel George, b. Ashted, Birmingham, e. Birmingham (Small Heath, Birmingham), 8717, Pte., d., Mesopotamia, 12/5/16.
Cresser, George Roland, b. St. Georges, Bristol, Glos., e. Birmingham, 3546, Pte., d., Mesopotamia, 28/8/16.
Crimming, John, b. Roath, Cardiff, Glam., e. Cardiff, 10855, L/Cpl., k. in a., Gallipoli, 10/8/15, formerly 11800, Welsh Regt.
Crisp, Clarence, b. Molding, Essex, e. Nuneaton, Warwicks (Foleshill, Warwicks), 12728, Pte., d. of w., Gallipoli, 14/4/16.
Croft, Arthur Benjamin, b. Stone, Staffs, e. Birmingham (Stone), 12103, Cpl., k. in a., Mesopotamia, 25/1/17.
Crofts, Charles Harry, b. Burton-on-Trent, Staffs, e. Coventry, Warwicks (Nuneaton, Warwicks), 13176, Pte., k. in a., Mesopotamia, 5/4/16.
Cross, Robert William, b. Nechells, Birmingham, e. Birmingham, 2684, L/Cpl., k. in a., Gallipoli, 23/7/15.
Crowder, Alfred, b. St. Georges, Birmingham, e. Birmingham, 3135, Pte., d., Mesopotamia, 15/6/15.
Crowe, Edward, b. Stratford-on-Avon, Warwicks, e. Stratford-on-Avon, 13398, A/Sgt., k. in a., Mesopotamia, 19/4/16.
Crutchlow, Arthur, b. Batley, Yorks, e. Bedworth, Warwicks (Nuneaton, Warwicks), 15415, Pte., k. in a., Mesopotamia, 16/1/17.
Daley, John, b. Birmingham, e. Birmingham, 12198, Pte., k. in a., Mesopotamia, 19/4/16.
Davenport, Frank, b. Pailton, Rugby, Warwicks, e. Coventry, Warwicks (Pailton), 2055, L/Cpl., k. in a., Mesopotamia, 25/1/17.
Davenport, Samuel, b. Collycroft, Warwicks, e. Nuneaton, Warwicks, 4257, Pte., d. of w., Mesopotamia, 4/2/17.
Davis, Percy, b. Coventry, Warwicks, e. Nuneaton, Warwicks (Attleborough, Warwicks), 16733, Pte., k. in a., Mesopotamia, 25/1/17.
Davies, Samuel, b. Smallwood, Ches., e. Crewe, Ches. (Smallwood), 13241, Pte., k. in a., Mesopotamia, 29/3/17.
Dawn, Albert, b. Beeston, Notts, e. Coventry, Warwicks (Beeston), 22887, Pte., d., Mesopotamia, 24/7/17.
Dawson, Philip, b. Aston, Birmingham, e. Birmingham (Winson Green, Birmingham), 12719, Pte., k. in a., Mesopotamia, 25/1/17.
Day, Alfred Ernest, b. Balsall Heath, Warwicks, e. Birmingham (Springhill, Birmingham), 5892, Pte., k. in a., Gallipoli, 10/8/15.
Day, Charles, b. Knowle, Warwicks, e. Leamington, Warwicks (Cubbington, Leamington), 12702, Pte., d. of w., Gallipoli, 9/1/16.
Day, George, b. Birmingham, e. Birmingham, 11863, Pte., d. of w., Gallipoli, 7/12/17.
Deacon, Percival John, b. Worcester, e. Birmingham (Coventry, Warwicks), 16791, Pte., k. in a., Mesopotamia, 25/1/17.
Dean, Albert Reuben, b. St. George's, Birmingham, e. Warwick, 1828, A/C.S.M., k. in a., Mesopotamia, 19/4/16.
Derrington, Charles Edwin, b. Handsworth, Birmingham, e. Birmingham (Stirchley, Birmingham), 13102, Pte., d. Gallipoli, 8/12/15.
Dewis, Jabez, b. Chapel End, Warwicks, e. Nuneaton, Warwicks (Stockingford, Warwicks), 3309, Pte., d., Mesopotamia, 25/9/18.
Dickenson, Horace, b. Balsall Heath, Birmingham, e. Birmingham (Kings Heath, Birmingham), 1521, Pte., k. in a., Mesopotamia, 19/4/16.
Dickinson, John, b. Gateshead, Durham, e. Sunderland, Durham, 12484, Pte., k. in a., Mesopotamia, 29/3/17, formerly 45593, R.G.A.
Digman, Joseph, b. Birmingham, e. Warwick (Kidderminster, Worcs), 9585, Pte., d. of w., Mesopotamia, 27/1/17.
Dixon, Robert William, b. Consett, Durham, e. Newcastle-on-Tyne, Northumberland (Consett), 11636, Pte., k. in a., Mesopotamia, 25/1/17.
Dobson, Vincent, b. Burnley, Lancs, e. Birmingham (Erdington, Birmingham), 15406, Pte., d., Mesopotamia, 24/9/18.
Docker, Albert, b. Smethwick, Staffs, e. Smethwick, 5279, Pte., d. of w., Mesopotamia, 10/8/15.
Downey, Joseph, b. Birmingham, e. Poplar, London (Birmingham), 12123, Pte., k. in a., Mesopotamia, 19/4/16.
Duffin, Albert, b. Redditch, Worcs, e. Worcester (Headless Cross, Redditch), 13244, Pte., d. of w., Mesopotamia, 27/4/17.
Dukes, Ernest Edward, b. Bordesley Green, Birmingham, e. Birmingham, 2930, Pte., d. of w., Mesopotamia, 19/8/15.
Dunn, James, b. St. Chad's, Birmingham, e. Birmingham (Handsworth, Birmingham), 11870, Pte., d. of w., Gallipoli, 5/11/15.
Dyer, Albert, b. Lostwithiel, Cornwall, e. London, Middx., 12213, Pte., d. of w., Mesopotamia, 14/4/16.
Eaglesfield, George Dennis, b. Birmingham, e. Birmingham, 11227, Pte., d. of w., Gallipoli, 22/7/15.
Eaves, Ernest, b. Coventry, Warwicks, e. Warwick (Coventry), 16502, Pte., d., Mesopotamia, 14/11/16.
Edgar, Thomas William, b. Foxteth, Lancs, e. Warwick (Liverpool), 9656, Pte., k. in a., Mesopotamia, 19/4/16.
Edge, Joseph, b. Crewe, Ches., e. Birmingham, 11823, Pte., k. in a., Mesopotamia, 25/1/17.
Edkins, Frank, b. Birmingham, e. Warwick (Birmingham), 1617, Pte., d. of w., Mesopotamia, 25/1/17.
Edwards, Arthur William, b. Birmingham, e. Birmingham (Hockley, Birmingham), 8968, Pte., k. in a., Mesopotamia, 9/4/16.
Edwards, George, e. Basingstoke, Hants (Aston, Birmingham), 5006, Cpl., k. in a., Mesopotamia, 19/4/16.
Edwards, Herbert Henry, b. Hartlebury, Worcs, e. Stratford-on-Avon, Warwicks (Alcester, Warwicks), 13004, Pte., d., Mosopotamia, 13/7/16.
Edwards, Jesse, b. Fenny Compton, Warwicks, e. Coventry, Warwicks, 16828, Pte., d. of w., Mesopotamia, 15/9/18.
Edwards, John, b. St. Stephens, Birmingham, e. Birmingham, 3406, Pte., k. in a., Gallipoli, 9/8/15.
Edwards, Richard, b. St. Julien's, Shrewsbury, Shrops, e. Birmingham, 6288, Pte., d. of w., Mesopotamia, 10/8/15.
Elliott, Francis John, b. Bubbenhall, Warwicks, e. Coventry, Warwicks (Wolston, Warwicks), 3300, Pte., k. in a., Gallipoli, 10/8/15.
Ellis, Henry Reuben, b. Ringmer, Sussex, e. Brighton, Sussex (Ringmer), 12546, Pte., d., Mesopotamia, 2/8/17, formerly 56556, R.G.A.
Embrey, Arthur, b. Lozells, Birmingham, e. Birmingham, 3570, L/Cpl., d. of w., Gallipoli, 8/8/15.
Evans, Henry, b. St. Peter's, Carmarthen, e. Carmarthen, 10863, Pte., d. of w., Gallipoli, 20/7/15, formerly 11674, Welsh Regt.
Evans, Samuel, b. Middlesbrough, Yorks, e. Rugby, Warwicks (Middlesbrough), 2802, Cpl., d. of w., Gallipoli, 21/8/15.
Everett, Albert, b. Maldon, Essex, e. Coventry, Warwicks, 16431, Pte., d., Mesopotamia, 4/7/16.
Everall, George Henry, b. Hinckley, Leics, e. Nuneaton, Warwicks, 11874, Pte., k. in a., Mesopotamia, 25/1/17.
Evetts, Albert Thomas, b. Bascote, Warwicks, e. Warwick (Long Itchington, Warwicks), 11790, L/Cpl., k. in a., Mesopotamia, 5/4/16.
Farley, Frederick James, b Walton, Warwicks, e. Warwick (Walford-on-Avon, Warwicks), 2822, L/Cpl., d. of w., Gallipoli, 17/8/15.
Faulkner, Walter Frederick, b. Stratford-on-Avon, Warwicks, e. Warwick (Stratford-on-Avon), 2701, Pte., k. in a., Gallipoli, 10/8/15.
Feeney, Patrick, b. Birmingham, e. Birmingham, 7934, L/Cpl., d., Mesopotamia, 12/11/16.
Fenn, Edwin, b. Birmingham, e. Handsworth, Staffs (Birmingham), 202106, Pte., d., British East Africa, 31/5/17.
Field, Charles, b. Birmingham, e. Birmingham, 16992, Pte., k. in a., Mesopotamia, 25/1/17.
Fielder, Bertram Edwin, b Hammersmith, London, e. Hammersmith, 12283, Pte., k. in a., Mesopotamia, 9/4/16, formerly 53971, R.G.A.
Fildes, Albert Edward, b. St. George's, Worcester, e. Birmingham (Sparkbrook, Birmingham), 4813, Pte., k. in a., Gallipoli, 10/8/15.
Flanagan, Frank, b. St. Peter's, Coventry, e. Coventry, Warwicks, 9680, Pte., k. in a., Gallipoli, 22/7/15.
Fleetwood, William Henry, b. Redditch, Worcs, e. Birmingham (Redditch), 12271, Pte., d. of w., 12/11/15, formerly 51225, R.G.A.
Fleming, George Leslie, e. Warwick (Small Heath, Birmingham), 16690, Pte., d. of w., Mesopotamia, 28/1/17.
Florence, Thomas, b. Wythall, Warwicks, e. Birmingham (King's Heath, Birmingham), 22187, Pte., d., Mesopotamia, 3/8/18.

Ford, Edward, b. Bedworth, Warwicks, e. Nuneaton, Warwicks (Bedworth), 11497, Pte., k. in a., Mesopotamia, 25/1/17.

Ford, John, b. St. George's Birmingham, e. Birmingham (Witton, Birmingham), 6298, Pte., d. of w., Mesopotamia, 27/8/15.

Foster, John, b. St. Martin's, Birmingham, e. Birmingham (Aston, Birmingham), 10013, Pte., k. in a., Gallipoli, 8/8/15.

Fox, Alfred George, b. Atherstone, Warwicks, e. Nuneaton, Warwicks (Atherstone), 3318, Pte., k. in a., Gallipoli, 10/8/15.

Freeman, Harvey, b. Weethly, Warwicks, e. Stratford-on-Avon, Warwicks (Weethly), 17983, Pte., k. in a., Mesopotamia, 25/1/17.

French, Arthur James, b. Bishops Itchington, Warwicks, e. Coventry, Warwicks (Lillington, Warwicks), 8573, L/Cpl., k. in a., Mesopotamia, 5/4/16.

Freshwater, George, b. St. Mary's, St. Neot's, Hunts, e. Birmingham (St. Neot's), 2846, Pte., d., Mesopotamia, 20/7/16.

Fuller, Victor, b. Ware, Herts, e. Hounslow, Middx. (Bedfont, Middx.), 20586, Pte., k. in a., Mesopotamia, 14/9/18, formerly 10881, A.C.C.

Gamble, George, b. Nuneaton. Warwicks, e. Nuneaton, 16175, Pte., d. of w., Mesopotamia, 18/2/17.

Gardner, Frederick Thomas, b. Crewkerne, Som., e. Birmingham, 11667, Pte., d. of w., Gallipoli, 1/10/15.

Gaskell, Albert, b. St. Mary's, Wigan, Lancs, e. Wigan, 202363, Pte., d., Mesopotamia, 21/5/18, formerly 1322, Manch. Regt.

Gaston, Albert Harold, b. Cliffe, Lewes, Sussex, e. Lewes (Cliffe), 242015, Pte., k. in a., Mesopotamia, 1/9/18, formerly 1788, R. Sussex Regt.

Gee, Sidney George, b. Atherstone, Warwicks, e. Atherstone, 16312, Pte., k. in a., Mesopotamia, 25/1/17.

Gibbard, George, b. Chalfont, St. Giles, Bucks, e. Aylesbury, Bucks (Chalfont St. Giles), 18470, Pte., k. in a., Mesopotamia, 25/1/17, formerly 24309, S.L.I.

Gibbard, Harry, b. Towcester, Northants, e. Birmingham (Adstone, Northants), 11921, Pte., d. of w., Mesopotamia, 1/2/17.

Gilbert, George Arthur, b. Atherstone, Warwick, e. Atherstone (Warwick), 16363, Pte., d., Mesopotamia, 6/4/17.

Giles, Arthur, b. Edgbaston, Birmingham, e. Warwick (Birmingham), 12737, Pte., d. of w., Mesopotamia, 1/5/16.

Giles, Henry Horace, b. Wilnecote, Warwicks, e. Leamington, Warwicks (Wilnecote), 16298, Pte., d. of w., Mesopotamia, 1/4/17.

Gittens, Chas. William, b. Birmingham, e. Birmingham (Winson Green, Birmingham), 12037, Pte., k. in a., Mesopotamia, 9/4/16.

Glazebrook, George, b. Aston Manor, Birmingham, e. Birmingham, 2960, Pte., k. in a., Mesopotamia, 10/8/15.

Gleaves, John, b. Liverpool, e. Liverpool (Bootle, Liverpool), 12354, Pte., k. in a., Mesopotamia, 9/4/16, formerly 53062, R.G.A.

Godwin, George, b. Plaistow, Essex, e. Canning Town, London (Plaistow), 9501, Pte., d., Mesopotamia, 3/7/16.

Goulden, Frederick, b. Rubery, Worcs., e. Birmingham (Hockley, Birmingham), 8967, Pte., d. of w., Gallipoli, 28/11/15.

Goulding, William Henry, b. Deritend, Birmingham, e. Birmingham, 2605, Pte., k. in a., Gallipoli, 8/8/15.

Gower, Thomas Henry, b. Tring, Hertford, e. Birmingham (Lozells, Birmingham), 13238, Pte., k. in a., Mesopotamia, 9/4/16.

Graver, Ernest, b. Wendling, Norfolk, e. Norwich, 12553, Pte., k. in a., Mesopotamia, 14/4/17, formerly 54557, R.G.A.

Green, Frederick Thomas, e. Birmingham (Ladywood, Birmingham), 25594, Pte., d., Mesopotamia, 25/5/18.

Green, George Oliver Gilbert, b. Northampton, e. Birmingham (Sutton Coldfield, Warwicks), 15258, Pte., k. in a., Mesopotamia, 25/1/17.

Green, Leonard, b. Kenilworth, Warwicks, e. Warwick (Kenilworth), 16644, Pte., k. in a., Mesopotamia, 18/1/17.

Greenway, Alfred, b. Tysoe, Warwicks, e. Warwick (Tysoe), 3/4649, Pte., d. of w., Gallipoli, 13/8/15.

Greenway, James Victor, b. Warwick, e. Warwick (Coventry), 14786, Pte., k. in a., Mesopotamia, 25/1/17.

Gregory, Frank, b. Sandridge, Wilts, e. Southwark, London, 10970, Pte., k. in a., Gallipoli, 18/11/15.

Gregory, Harry, b. Southampton, e. Newton Abbot, Devon (Southsea, Hants), 12445, Pte., d., Mesopotamia, 14/6/16, formerly 5636, R.G.A.

Griffin, John, b. Hampton Lucy, Warwicks, e. Coventry, Warwicks (Stratford-on-Avon, Warwicks), 12758, Sgt., d., Mesopotamia, 16/6/16.

Griffin, Walter, b. Bedworth, Warwicks, e. Ilkeston, Derby, 12804, Pte., d. of w., Mesopotamia, 9/5/16.

Griffiths, Charles Henry, e. Birmingham, 22913, Pte., d., Mesopotamia, 3/9/17.

Griffiths, John Zephaniah, b. Birmingham, e. Birmingham (Ladywood, Birmingham), 21403, Pte., d., Mesopotamia, 24/2/17.

Grimsdell, John George, b. Ashley Green, Bucks, e. Aylesbury, Bucks (Chesham, Bucks), 18528, Pte., d., Mesopotamia, 21/10/18, formerly 25376, S.L.I.

Grinham, Arthur, b. Birmingham, e. Birmingham, 22914, Pte., d., Mesopotamia, 30/9/18.

Gummol, Edwin, b. Smethwick, Staffs, e. Birmingham (Stirchley, Birmingham), 5851, Pte., k. in a., Gallipoli, 10/8/15.

Gwilliam, Arthur, b. Hockley, Birmingham, e. Warwick (Birmingham), 2080, L/Cpl., d. of w., Mesopotamia, 15/2/17.

Hackett, Charles Arthur, b. Nuneaton, Warwicks, e. Nuneaton, 16297, Pte., d., Mesopotamia, 16/7/16.

Hadley, Charles, b. Aston, Birmingham, e. Birmingham, 5342, Pte., k. in a., Gallipoli, 13/11/15.

Hadley, Ernest Leonard, b. Liverpool, e. Birmingham (Bearwood, Birmingham), 16/1689, Pte., k. in a., Mesopotamia, 29/3/17.

Hadley, Jeremiah, b. Hill Top, Staffs, e. Birmingham (Hill Top), 11091, Pte., k. in a., Mesopotamia, 10/8/15.

Hall, David, b. Nuneaton, Warwicks, e. Warwick (Nuneaton), 2021, Pte., d., Mesopotamia, 18/8/16.

Hall, Frank William Thomas, b. St. John's, Bedminster, Glos., e. Bristol (Bedminster), 5319, Pte., d. of w., Gallipoli, 8/8/15.

Hall, George, b. Nechells, Birmingham, e. Birmingham (Nechells), 1565, Pte., k. in a., Mesopotamia, 10/4/16.

Hall, Sidney Walter Robert, b. Ilmington, Worcs, e. Birmingham (Ilmington), 5114, Pte., d., Mesopotamia, 7/7/16.

Hancocks, James, b. Offenham, Worcs, e. Birmingham, 3405, Pte., d., Gallipoli, 15/8/15.

Hancocks, Jesse, b. Southam, Warwicks, e. Long Itchington, Warwicks, 16704, Pte., d. of w., Mesopotamia, 3/2/17.

Hancox, John Edwin, b. Tysoe, Warwicks, e. Kineton, Warwicks (Lower Tysoe, 19446, Pte., d., Mesopotamia, 24/5/17.

Hancox, Thomas, b. Longford, Warwicks, e. Coventry, Warwicks (Bishopston, Warwicks), 9684, Pte., k. in a., Mesopotamia, 10/8/15.

Handy, John, b. Ardens Grafton, Warwicks, e. Stratford-on-Avon, Warwicks (Ardens Grafton), 16248, Pte., d. of w., Mesopotamia, 13/4/17.

Harbage, George, e. Kineton, Warwicks (Chacombe, Oxon), 17964, Pte., d., Mesopotamia, 8/11/17.

Harding, William Ernest, b. Weston-Super-Mare, Som., e. Birmingham, 16919, Pte., d. of w., Mesopotamia, 25/1/17.

Harries, William Meurig, b. Llanrhian, Pembroke, e. Haverfordwest, Pembroke (Llanrhian), 10872, Pte., k. in a., Gallipoli, 10/8/15, formerly 13746, Welsh Regt.

Harrington, John Denis, b. Kidderminster, Worcs, e. Coventry, Warwicks, 5423, Pte., k. in a., Gallipoli, 10/8/15.

Harris, Henry, b. Bordesley, Birmingham, e. Birmingham, 5323, Pte., k. in a., Mesopotamia, 25/1/17.

Harris, L. Arthur, b. Speenham Lane, Newbury, Berks, e. Warwick (Newbury), 2700, Pte., d. of w., Gallipoli, 14/8/15.

Harrison, Arthur, b. All Saints, Warwick, e. Warwick (Emscote, Warwick), 1570, L/Cpl., k. in a., Mesopotamia, 1/9/18.

Harrison, George, b. St. George's, Birmingham, e. Birmingham, 3346, Pte., k. in a., Gallipoli, 10/8/15.

Harrison, Wilfred John Henry, b. Braunston, Northants, e. Rugby, Warwicks (Braunston), 16011, Pte., k. in a., Mesopotamia, 25/1/17.

Harrison, William, b. St. Helens, Lancs, e. Atherstone, Warwicks, 4454, Pte., k. in a., Mesopotamia, 14/9/18.

Hart, Albert, b. Blackhill, Durham, e. Consett, Durham, 11494, Pte. k. in a., Mesopotamia, 19/4/16.

Hart, Richard Edward, b. Birmingham, e. Birmingham (Sparkhill, Birmingham), 14651, Pte., d., Mesopotamia, 21/7/17.

Haslam, John Walter William, b. Ladywood, Birmingham, e. Birmingham (Ladywood), 8576, Pte., d., Mesopotamia, 11/12/15.

Hatton, William Bernard, b. St. Mary's, Stafford, e. Lichfield, Staffs (Stafford), 7421, Pte., k. in a., Gallipoli, 5/4/16.

Hawkins, Reuben William, b. Aston, Birmingham, e. Birmingham (Handsworth, Birmingham), 16950, Pte., d., Mesopotamia, 11/7/17.

Hayden, Albert Walter, b. Hartshill, Warwicks, e. Nuneaton, Warwicks (Hartshill), 11645, Pte., d., Mesopotamia, 29/6/16.

Haynes, Edward Theodore, b. Priors Hardwick, Warwicks, e. Rugby, Warwicks (Priors Hardwick), 10193, Pte., d., Mesopotamia, 15/12/15.

Heap, George, b. Saltley, Birmingham, e. Birmingham, 3027, Pte., k. in a., Gallipoli, 10/8/15.

Heinrick, Joseph, b. St. Paul's, Birmingham, e. Birmingham (Hockley, Birmingham), 3116, Pte., k. in a., Gallipoli, 10/8/15.

Hemming, Alexander, b. Wilnecote, Warwicks, e. Atherstone, Warwicks (Wilnecote), 16407, Pte., d., Mesopotamia, 31/5/17.

Hemmings, Percy John, b. Long Compton, Warwicks, e. Stratford-on-Avon, Warwicks (Long Compton), 16047, Pte., d. of w., Mesopotamia, 28/12/16.

Hemming, George, b. Alcester, Warwicks, e. Warwick (Alcester), 9948, C.S.M., k. in a., Mesopotamia, 14/4/17.

Hemmingway, John, b. Slay Cross, Derby, e. Manchester, 12389, Pte., d., Mesopotamia, 2/12/15, formerly 51331, R.G.A.

Hewitt, Samuel, b. Caverswall, Staffs, e. Longton, Staffs, 8112, Pte., d. of w., Gallipoli, 4/12/15.

Higgs, William, b. St. Peter's, Walsall, Staffs, e. Birmingham (Walsall), 1588, Pte., k. in a., Mesopotamia, 17/12/16.

Hill, William, b. West Bromwich, Staffs, e. Bilston, Staffs, 14306, Pte., d., Mesopotamia, 8/11/18.

Hillman, Frederick William, b. Frome, Som., e. Warwick (Frome), 16626, Pte., k. in a., Mesopotamia, 25/1/17.

Hillston, John James, b. Burton-on-Trent, Staffs, e. Birmingham (Burton-on-Trent), 12295, Pte., d., Mesopotamia, 10/12/15, formerly 53914, R.G.A.

Hirons, William, b. Thurlaston, Warwicks, e. Rugby, Warwicks (Thurlaston), 8947, Pte., k. in a., Gallipoli, 10/8/15.

Hodges, William Ernest, b. Saltley, Birmingham, e. Birmingham, 10391, Pte., k. in a., Gallipoli, 10/8/15.

Hodgetts, William, b. Birmingham, e. Birmingham (Winson Green, Birmingham), 6715, Pte., k. in a., Gallipoli, 4/10/15.

Hodgkins, Frederick William, b. Stratford-on-Avon, Warwicks, e. Stratford-on-Avon, 15640, Pte., d., Mesopotamia, 29/6/16.

Holden, Frederick, b. Birmingham, e. Darlaston, Staffs (Small Heath, Birmingham), 13489, Pte., k. in a., Mesopotamia, 17/4/16.

Holden, Walter, e. Blackburn, Lancs, 12936, Pte., d. of w., Gallipoli, 4/11/15, formerly 55812, R.G.A.

Holdsworth, John Thomas, b. Barnwood, Glos., e. Merthyr Tydfil, Glam. (Gloucester), 12558, Pte., d. of w., Mesopotamia, 26/1/17, formerly 54552, R.G.A.
Hollis, Edward William, e. Basingstoke, Hants (Frankton, Warwicks), 10120, Pte., k. in a., Mesopotamia, 10/8/15.
Holmes, William Ewart, b. Nuneaton, Warwicks, e. Atherstone, Warwicks, 16290, L/Cpl., k. in a., Mesopotamia, 3/2/17.
Hooker, Frank Samuel, b. Daventry, Northants, e. Rugby, Warwicks, 12791, Pte., k. in a., Mesopotamia, 9/4/16.
Hopkins, Edward, b. Henley-in-Arden, Warwicks, e. Stratford-on-Avon, Warwick (Henley-in-Arden), 11466, Pte., d. of w., Gallipoli, 8/10/15.
Hopkins, John, b. Earl Shilton, Leics, e. Nuneaton, Warwicks, 2647, Pte., k. in a., Gallipoli, 10/8/15.
Hopkins, John Henry, b. St. Mary's, Birmingham, e. Birmingham, 3397, Sgt., d. of w., Gallipoli, 15/8/15.
Horner, Peter, b. Manchester, Lancs, e. Manchester, 12309, Pte., k. in a., Mesopotamia, 30/10/15, formerly 53096, R.G.A.
Horton, Arthur, b. West Bromwich, Staffs, e. Birmingham (West Bromwich), 2113, Pte., k. in a., Mesopotamia, 13/2/17.
Horton, Robert, b. Aston, Birmingham, e. Birmingham (Hay Mills, Birmingham), 13476, Pte., k. in a., Mesopotamia, 9/4/16.
Horton, William Benjamin, b. Atherstone, Warwicks, e. Nuneaton, Warwicks (Atherstone), 15601, Pte., d., Mesopotamia, 30/6/16.
Hubball, James, b. Birmingham, e. Birmingham, 1867, Cpl., k. in a., Mesopotamia, 21/4/16.
Hubbard, Robert, b. Bethnal Green, London, e. Finsbury Barracks, London (Homerton, London, N.E.), 3123, C.Q.M.S., k. in a., Mesopotamia, 1/9/18.
Hughes, George, b. St. Martin's, Birmingham, e. Birmingham, 5264, Pte., d. of w., Gallipoli, 10/8/15.
Humpherson, Joseph, b. Willenhall, Staffs, e. Birmingham, 3464, Pte., d. of w., Gallipoli, 10/8/15.
Hutchins, Frederick Thomas, e. Birmingham (Stirchley, Birmingham), 22933, Pte., d., Mesopotamia, 17/7/17.
Hutchinson, James Jackson, b. Helsington, Westmoreland, e. Kendal, Westmoreland (Crosthwaite, Kendal), 12297, L/Sgt., k. in a., Mesopotamia, 25/1/17, formerly 53019, R.G.A.
Hyde, Edward, b. Bulwell, Notts, e. Coventry, Warwicks (Daybrook, Notts), 11619, Pte., k. in a., Mesopotamia, 5/4/16.
Iles, Horace John, e. Warwick (Birmingham), 14887, Pte., d. of w., Mesopotamia, 3/4/17.
Irons, Edward Arthur, b. Castle Bromwich, Warwicks, e. Birmingham (Castle Bromwich), 22937, Pte., d., Mesopotamia, 6/6/19.
Isley, John Rowland, b. Didlington, Brandon, Norfolk, e. Hull, Yorks, 12564, Pte., k. in a., Mesopotamia, 25/1/17. formerly 56726, R.G.A.
Jacques, Thomas, b. Collycroft, Warwicks, e. Warwick (Bedworth, Warwicks), 9309, Pte., d. of w., Gallipoli, 22/10/15.
James, Harry Archibald Hawkins, b. Leytonstone, Essex, e. Birmingham (Middx.), 1585, Pte., d. of w., Mesopotamia, 13/4/16.
James, Edward, b. St. Martin's, Birmingham, e. Birmingham (Small Heath, Birmingham), 14355, Pte., d., Mesopotamia, 21/8/18.
James, John, b. Exeter, e. Ferndale, Glam. (Pontygwaith, Glam.), 12421, Pte., k. in a., Gallipoli, 27/9/15, formerly 44171, R.G.A.
Jeffries, John, b. Stafford, e. Birmingham, 5974, Pte., d. of w., Gallipoli, 13/8/15.
Jenkins, Frank Henry, b. Ashley, Bristol, Glos., e. Birmingham (Bristol), 5975, Pte., k. in a., Mesopotamia, 5/4/16.
Jenson, William Walter, b. Coventry, Warwicks e. Coventry, 16030, Pte., d., Mesopotamia, 22/9/18.
Jiggle, Edgar, b. St. Andrew's, Rugby, Warwicks, e. Rugby, 2806, Pte., k. in a., Gallipoli, 10/8/15.
Jinks, Arthur, b. St. Bartholomews, Birmingham, e. Coalville, Leics. (Birmingham), 200406, Sgt., d., Mesopotamia, 11/10/18, formerly 1723, Leics. Regt.
Johnson, Albert, b. Birmingham, e. Birmingham, 9965, Pte., k. in a., Mesopotamia, 9/4/16.
Johnston, Andrew, b. Houghton-le-Spring, Durham, e. Houghton-le-Spring, 12565, Pte., d., Mesopotamia, 29/6/17, formerly 16703, R.G.A., M.M.
Johnson, Alfred, b. Aberdeen, e. Shepherd's Bush, London, 12567, Cpl., k. in a., Mesopotamia, 9/4/16, formerly 54550, R.G.A.
Johnson, Albert William, b. Willesden, London, e. Rugby, Warwicks, 3382, Pte., k. in a., Gallipoli, 5/1/16.
Johnson, Charles James, b. Alcester, Warwicks, e. Warwick (Alcester), 2634, L/Cpl., d., Mesopotamia, 12/6/16.
Johnson, John, b. St. Michael's, Coventry, Warwicks, e. Birmingham, 3156, Pte., d., Mesopotamia, 31/5/16.
Johnson, Samuel, b. Smethwick, Staffs, e. Birmingham (Smethwick), 3797, Pte., d., Gallipoli, 20/10/15.
Johnson, William, b. St. Bartholomew, Birmingham, e. Birmingham (Small Heath, Birmingham), 5460, Pte., k. in a., Mesopotamia, 9/4/16.
Johnson, William, b. St. Martin's, Birmingham, e. Birmingham, 12089, Pte., k. in a., Mesopotamia, 9/4/16
Jones, Arthur, b. Studley, Warwicks, e. Stratford-on-Avon, Warwicks (Studley), 15439, Pte., d., Mesopotamia, 1/7/16.
Jones, Charles, b. Birmingham, e. Birmingham, 12226, Pte., k. in a., Mesopotamia, 19/4/16.
Jones, Frederick, b. Castlethorpe, Bucks, e. Rugby, Warwicks, 203596, Pte., d., Mesopotamia, 28/9/18.
Jones, John, b. Birmingham e. Birmingham (Shirley, Warwicks), 13111, Pte., k. in a., Mesopotamia, 25/1/17.
Jordan, Albert Edward, b. Small Heath, Birmingham, e. Warwick (Nechells, Birmingham), 3/3117, Sgt., k. in a., Gallipoli, 10/8/15.
Joseph, Charles, b. All Saints, Stourbridge, Worcs, e. Birmingham, 4865, Pte., k. in a., Mesopotamia, 9/4/16.
Joyce, Patrick Joseph, b. St. Mary's, Rugby, Warwicks, e. Rugby, 3386, L/Cpl., k. in a., Gallipoli, 10/8/15.
Judge, Ronald Melville, b. Ardley, Bicester, Oxon, e. Winchester, Hants (Bicester), 4682, Pte., k. in a., Mesopotamia, 5/4/16.
Juggins, Harry, b. Grendon, Warwicks, e. Nuneaton, Warwicks (Grendon), 11981, Pte., k. in a., Mesopotamia, 5/4/16.
Juxon, William Horace, b. Sutton Coldfield, Warwicks, e. Warwick (Sutton Coldfield), 21983, Pte., d., Mesopotamia, 23/7/17.
Kean, Frank, b. Greet, Worcs, e. Warwick (Greet), 890, Pte., d. of w., Mesopotamia, 19/4/16.
Keightley, Tom, b. Accrington, Lancs, e. Haslingden, Lancs, 12310, Pte., d. of w., Mesopotamia, 27/11/15, formerly 53863, R.G.A.
Kelly, Edward Arthur, b. Foleshill, Warwicks, e. Coventry, Warwicks, 16449, Pte., d. of w., Mesopotamia, 16/3/17.
Kemp, Albert, b. St. Asaphs, Birmingham, e. Birmingham, 3399, L/Cpl., d. of w., Gallipoli, 30/8/15.
Kenning, George, b. Birmingham, e. Birmingham, 17044, Pte., k. in a., Mesopotamia, 25/1/17.
Kenny, Francis, b. Aston, Birmingham, e. Birmingham, 8956, Pte., k. in a., Gallipoli, 10/8/15.
Kenny, John, b. St. Thomas, Birmingham, e. Birmingham, 3201, Pte., d., Mesopotamia, 13/7/16.
Kenney, Noel Algar, b. Sparkhill, Birmingham, e. Birmingham, 8954, Pte., d. of w., Mesopotamia, 20/12/16.
Kent, Charles Ernest, b. Sutton Coldfield, Warwicks, e. Sutton Coldfield, 15568, Pte., d., Mesopotamia, 30/6/16.
Kent, Francis Joseph Henry Hinks, b. Handsworth Birmingham, e. Sutton Coldfield, Warwicks, 16786, Pte., k. in a., Mesopotamia, 25/1/17.
Kent, Louis Victor, b. Brodwell, Wolverton, Bucks, e. Warwick (Brodwell), 7526, Cpl., k. in a., Mesopotamia, 5/4/16.
Kippen, George William, b. St. Mark's, Birmingham, e. Birmingham, 3578, Pte., k. in a., Mesopotamia, 5/4/16.
Knight, Edmund, b. Berkswell, Warwicks, e. Rugby, Warwicks (New Bilton, Warwicks), 25267, Pte., d., Mesopotamia, 9/10/18.
Knight, George, b. Stratford-on-Avon, Warwicks, e. Stratford-on-Avon, 15641, Pte., d., Mesopotamia, 17/10/16.
Knight, Thomas, b. Dewsbury, Yorks, e. Birmingham (Dewsbury), 11281, Pte., k. in a., Mesopotamia, 12/2/17.
Labrum, John James, b. Attleborough, Warwicks, e. Nuneaton, Warwicks, 11639, L/Cpl., k. in a., Mesopotamia, 19/4/16.
Lander, Arthur, b. Aston, Birmingham, e. Birmingham (Aston), 3129, Pte., k. in a., Gallipoli, 10/8/15.
Lander, Albert William, b. Nottingham, e. Nottingham, 14359, Pte., d., Mesopotamia, 14/7/17.
Landers, William, b. St. Lawrence, Birmingham, e. Birmingham, 2848, Pte., k. in a., Mesopotamia, 31/8/15.
Langford, Thomas, b. Birmingham, e. Leamington, Warwicks (Birmingham), 17002, Pte., d., 17/7/17.
Lapworth, Sidney Ernest, b. Aston, Birmingham, e. Birmingham, 1896, Pte., k. in a., Mesopotamia, 25/1/17.
Latham, Robert, b. West Derby, Liverpool, e. Bolton, Lancs, 12346, Pte., d., Mesopotamia, 5/11/15, formerly 49393, R.G.A.
Lavin, John, b. Nechells, Birmingham, e. Birmingham, 4077, L/Cpl., k. in a., Gallipoli, 10/8/15.
Lawrence, John, b. Birmingham, e. Birmingham, 2604, Pte., k. in a., Gallipoli, 10/8/15.
Laycock, Arthur William, b. Scarborough, Yorks, e. Coventry, Warwicks, 3083, Pte., k. in a., Gallipoli, 31/12/15.
Leather, William, b. Coventry, Warwicks, e. Coventry, 9580, Pte., k. in a., Gallipoli, 10/8/15.
Leather, William, b. Radford, Coventry, e. Coventry, Warwicks (Radford), 10468, Cpl., d. of w., Mesopotamia, 29/4/16.
Lees, Walter, b. Norton Juxta, Warwicks, e. Nuneaton, Warwicks (Norton Juxta), 12653, Pte., k. in a., Mesopotamia, 25/1/17.
Liddamore, George, b. Bury St. Edmunds, Suffolk, e. Coventry, Warwicks (Berkswell, Warwicks), 3088, Pte., k. in a., Mesopotamia, 21/4/16.
Lilley, Arthur, b. Birmingham, e. Birmingham, 241301, Pte., d., Mesopotamia, 24/7/18.
Linskey, Thomas, b. St. Michael's, Birmingham, e. Birmingham, 3258, Cpl., Home, 25/12/14.
Litchfield, Frank, b. Birmingham, e. Birmingham, 11242, Pte., d., Mesopotamia, 29/9/18.
Litchfield, Harold, b. Blackley, Lancs, e. Warwick (Leigh, Lancs), 12676, Pte., d., Mesopotamia, 1/10/18.
Lockley, Harry, e. Birmingham, 10729, Pte., d., Mesopotamia, 29/6/18.
Long, Joseph, b. Bilston, Staffs, e. Nuneaton, Warwicks (Bedworth, Warwicks), 10992, Pte., k. in a., Mesopotamia, 10/8/15.
Lord, Fred, b. Rochdale, Lancs, e. Manchester (Rochdale), 15619, Pte., d., Mesopotamia, 25/7/16.
Mansell, William Henry, b. St. George's, Birmingham, e. Birmingham (Aston, Birmingham), 5182, L/Cpl., k. in a., Mesopotamia, 19/4/16.
Mapp, Frederick, b. Arley Kings, Worcs, e. Coventry, Warwicks, 16752, Pte., d., Mesopotamia, 26/10/17.
Marsh, Thomas, b. Ashted, Birmingham, e. Birmingham, 10107, Pte., Mesopotamia, k. in a., 9/4/16.
Marsh, Bertram Thomas, b. Dudley, Worcs, e. Coventry, Warwicks (Dudley), 16256, Pte., d., Mesopotamia, 26/9/18.
Marles, Frank Edward, b. Granton, Warwicks, e Nuneaton, Warwicks, 16766, Pte., k. in a., Mesopotamia, 25/1/17.
Marshall, Kenneth, b. Walsall, Staffs, e. Birmingham (Walsall), 13237, Pte., k. in a., Gallipoli, 2/1/16.
Martin, John William, b. Consett, Durham, e. Consett, 9435, Pte., d. of w., Mesopotamia, 20/9/18.

Mason, Frederick Thomas, b. Skethrury, South Wales, e. Coventry, Warwicks (Broad Marston, Warwicks), 16261, Pte., k. in a., Mesopotamia, 7/1/17.
Mason, Percy, b. Bourton, Warwicks, e. Warwick, 16778, Pte., k. in a., Mesopotamia, 29/3/17.
Maull, James Henry, b. Stratford-on-Avon, Warwicks, e. Birmingham (Aston, Birmingham), 3058, Pte., d., Mesopotamia, 5/7/16.
Maycock, William Edward, b. Yardley Fields, Banbury, Oxon, e. Nuneaton, Warwicks (Stockingford, Warwicks), 8625, Sgt., d., Mesopotamia, 27/7/16, formerly 3774, Cavalry.
Maynard, Harold, b. Coventry, Warwicks, e. Warwick (Coventry), 16602, Pte., k. in a., Mesopotamia, 25/1/17.
McCann, Christopher, b. Aston, Birmingham, e. Birmingham, 3573, Pte., k. in a., Gallipoli, 10/8/15.
McGee, Reginald Harry, b. Portsmouth, Hants, e. Portsmouth, 12469, Pte., k. in a., Gallipoli, 1/10/15, formerly 40400, R.G.A.
McKnight, George, b. St. Mary's, Bristol, e. Birmingham (Liverpool), 2034, Pte., d., Gallipoli, 22/12/15.
McKnight, Leonard, b. Hillfields, Coventry, Warwicks, e. Coventry, 9689, Pte., k. in a., Mesopotamia, 5/4/16.
Meaney, Michael, b. Bally Bricken, Waterford, e. Waterford, 12504, Pte., k. in a., Gallipoli, 5/1/16, formerly 46108, R.G.A.
Meredith, William Robert, b. Birmingham, e. Birmingham (Warley, Birmingham), 4648, Pte., k. in a., Gallipoli, 10/8/15.
Metcalfe, Edward, b. Dunsdale, Yorks, e. Nuneaton, Warwicks (Guisborough, Yorks), 11973, Pte., k. in a., Mesopotamia, 29/11/15.
Middleton, Richard Benjamin, b. Stockingford, Warwicks, e. Nuneaton, Warwicks (Stockingford), 11612, Pte., d., Mesopotamia, 13/7/16.
Miller, John, b. Chatteris, Cambs, e. Atherstone, Warwicks (Chatteris), 203572, Pte., d., Mesopotamia, 4/10/18.
Miller, Percy Arnold, b. Birmingham, e. Birmingham (Smethwick, Staffs), 24107, Pte., d. of w., Mesopotamia, 16/10/18.
Millerchip, Joseph, b. Foleshill, Warwicks, e. Nuneaton, Warwicks (Stockingford, Warwicks), 10424, Pte., k. in a., Gallipoli, 10/8/15.
Mills, Benjamin, b. Alcester, Warwicks, e. Birmingham (Alcester), 7468, Pte., d. of w., Gallipoli, 14/11/15.
Mills, James, e. Birmingham (Aston, Birmingham), 16/1773, Pte., k. in a., Mesopotamia, 31/8/18.
Milnthorpe, Herbert, b. Plumstead, Kent, e. Stratford, London (Leytonstone, London), 12574, Pte., k. in a., Mesopotamia, 25/1/17, formerly 56566, R.G.A.
Moore, Richard Cecil, b. Northampton, e. Oxford (Chipping Norton, Oxon), 22967, Pte., k. in a., Mesopotamia, 14/9/18.
Morgan, Harry, b. Birmingham, e. Birmingham (Spring Hill, Birmingham), 12081, Pte., k. in a., Mesopotamia, 27/9/15.
Morrell, William, b. All Saints, Birmingham, e. Birmingham (Handsworth, Birmingham), 3913, Pte., d., Home, 9/1/15.
Morris, Samuel James, b. Leicester, e. Birmingham (Barwell, Leics), 4916, Pte., d. of w., Gallipoli, 9/8/15.
Moseley, Thomas, b. Handsworth, Birmingham, e. Warwick (Brookfields, Birmingham), 3/1825, A/Sgt., k. in a., Mesopotamia, 9/4/16.
Moult, Leonard, b. Nottingham, e. Birmingham, 3333, Sgt., k. in a., Mesopotamia, 19/4/16.
Mountford, Frank, b. Stoke-on-Trent, Staffs, e. Warwick (Hartshill, Stoke-on-Trent), 16587, Pte., k. in a., Mesopotamia, 25/1/17.
Moxey, Ernest Lancelot Lionel, b. St. Peter's, Cheltenham, Glos., e. Cheltenham, 12619, Pte., d. of w., Mesopotamia, 19/4/16.
Mitchell, Albert Bertie, e. Parkhurst, I. of W. (Sparkbrook, Birmingham), 15058, Pte., k. in a., Mesopotamia, 9/4/16.
Mullis, Herbert George, b. Kineton, Warwicks, e. Stratford-on-Avon, Warwicks, 13381, Pte., d. of w., Mesopotamia, 18/4/16.
Murphy, John, b. Digbeth, Birmingham, e. Birmingham, 2687, Pte., d. of w., Gallipoli, 18/8/15.
Musson, George, b. Burbage, Hinckley, Leics., e. Nuneaton, Warwicks (Stockingford, Nuneaton), 2048, Sgt., d., Mesopotamia, 19/12/16.
Musto, Frank, b. Oxford, e. Warwick, 11532, A/Sgt., d. of w., Mesopotamia, 15/2/17.
Nash, Walter, b. Warley, Birmingham, e. Birmingham (Bournbrook, Birmingham), 5850, Pte., d. of w., Gallipoli, 14/8/15.
Neale, William, b. St. Martin's, Birmingham, e. Birmingham, 2691, Pte., d. of w., Gallipoli, 11/8/15.
Neighbour, Charles Herbert, b. High Wycombe, Bucks, e. High Wycombe, 18446, Pte., k. in a., Mesopotamia, 25/1/17, formerly 24032, Som. L.I.
Nestling, Wilfred Ronald, b. Kilburn, London, e. Loughton, Essex, 12384, Pte., d., Mesopotamia, 3/1/16, formerly 26759, R.G.A.
Niblett, Frank, b. Hockley, Birmingham, e. Birmingham (Winson Green, Birmingham), 3678, Pte., k. in a., Gallipoli, 8/8/15.
Nightingale, Harry, b. Birmingham, e. Birmingham, 10103, Pte., d. of w., Mesopotamia, 2/9/18.
Nixon, Alfred, b. Chilvers Coton, Nuneaton, Warwicks, e. Nuneaton, 1887, Pte., k. in a., Mesopotamia, 29/3/17.
Noon, Harry, b. Tamworth-in-Arden, Warwicks, e. Rugby, 21881, Pte., d., Mesopotamia, 4/2/18.
Norris, Frederick, b. St. Luke's, Shoreditch, Middx., e. Nuneaton (Stockingford, Nuneaton), 11125, Pte., k. in a., Gallipoli, 10/8/15.
Oakes, William, b. Small Heath, Birmingham, e. Birmingham, 8052, Sgt., d., Mesopotamia, 4/9/17.
Oram, Frank, b. Tinhead, Wilts, e. Nuneaton, Warwicks, 12080, Pte., k. in a., Mesopotamia, 19/4/16.
Osborne, Frederick Arthur, b. Netherfield, Notts, e. Birmingham (Netherfield), 6378, Pte., k. in a., Gallipoli, 10/8/15.
Osborn, Harold, b. Stowe, Northants, e. Nuneaton, Warwicks (Fenny Drayton, Nuneaton), 13217, Pte., k. in a., Mesopotamia, 9/4/16.
Overton, Ernest Alexander, b. Nuneaton, Warwicks, e. Nuneaton (Coton, Nuneaton), 11604, Pte., k. in a., Mesopotamia, 25/1/17.
Owen, John, b. Holyhead, Anglesey, e. Nuneaton, Warwicks, 13076, Pte., k. in a., Mesopotamia, 5/4/16.
Owen, William Alfred, b. Holy Trinity, Coventry, Warwicks, e. Coventry, 2490, Pte., k. in a., Mesopotamia, 25/1/17.
Palmer, Frank, b. Birmingham, e. Birmingham (Aston, Birmingham), 9964, Cpl., k. in a., Mesopotamia, 25/1/17.
Palmer, Frederick George, b. Highgate, Birmingham, e. Birmingham, 6395, Pte., d., Mesopotamia, 11/5/16.
Pane, Alfred Harold, b. St. Martin's, Birmingham, e. Birmingham (Edgbaston, Birmingham), 8932, Pte., d., Mesopotamia, 1/9/18.
Parker, John, b. Studley, Warwicks, e. Stratford-on-Avon, Warwicks (Coughton, Warwicks), 19601, Pte., d., Mesopotamia, 10/7/17.
Paul, Thomas Jones, b. Attleborough, Warwicks, e. Nuneaton, Warwicks (Attleborough), 10979, Pte., d., Mesopotamia, 3/7/16.
Payne, Alfred George, b. Stratford-on-Avon, Warwicks, e. Warwick (Stratford-on-Avon), 2651, Pte., d. of w., Mesopotamia, 6/4/16.
Pearson, Henry James, b. Aston, Birmingham, e. Birmingham (Aston), 11656, Pte., d. of w., Mesopotamia, 19/4/16.
Pegler, George, b. Smethwick, Staffs, e. Birmingham (Smethwick), 11206, L/Cpl., k. in a., Mesopotamia, 5/4/16.
Pendergast, Joseph, b. St. Martin's, Birmingham, e. Birmingham, 3173, Pte., k. in a., Gallipoli, 10/8/15.
Penticost, Herbert George, b. Kingston Deverill, Warminster, Wilts, e. Bristol (Clifton, Bristol), 5359, Pte., k. in a., Mesopotamia, 18/12/16.
Percox, Victor Arthur John, b. Tatchbrook, Warwicks, e. Leamington, Warwicks (Tatchbrook), 21437, Pte., d. of w., Mesopotamia, 31/8/18.
Perrott, Alfred James, b. Erdington, Warwicks, e. Parkhurst, I. of W. (Erdington), 14718, Pte., d., Mesopotamia, 26/7/16.
Perry, William Henry, b. Harbourne, Staffs, e. Birmingham (Erdington, Birmingham), 16727, Pte., k. in a., Mesopotamia, 25/1/17.
Philbin, Michael, b. Clifford Wetherby, Yorks, e. Keighley, Yorks 21821, A/Sgt., d., Mesopotamia, 3/7/18.
Philpotts, George, b. Hoxton, London, e. Birmingham (Primrose Hill, London), 8617, L/Cpl., d. of w., Mesopotamia, 7/4/16.
Pickering, Arthur, b. Winson Green, Birmingham, e. Birmingham (Winson Green), 3012, Pte., k. in a., Gallipoli, 10/8/15.
Pickford, Frederick, b. St. Mark's, Birmingham, e. Birmingham (Saltley, Birmingham), 6048, Pte., k. in a., Gallipoli, 29/11/15.
Pitman, Frank Henry, b. Eastleigh, Hants, e. Southampton (Bishopstoke, Hants), 12370, Pte., d. of w., Mesopotamia, 19/4/16, formerly 53489, R.G.A.
Pollard, George William James, b. Hackney, London, e. Birmingham (Sparkbrook, Birmingham), 8285, Sgt., d. of w., Mesopotamia, 9/4/16.
Pope, Stanford, b. Balsall Heath, Birmingham, e. Birmingham (Sparkbrook, Birmingham), 2737, Pte., k. in a., Gallipoli, 16/7/15.
Porter, Ernest, b. St. Michael's, Coventry, Warwicks, e. Coventry (Little Heath, Coventry), 12889, Pte., k. in a., Mesopotamia, 5/4/16.
Potts, John Charles Stanley, b. Southam, Warwicks, e. Coventry, Warwicks (Small Heath, Birmingham), 2814, Pte., d. of w., Gallipoli, 12/8/15.
Powell, Sydney Percy, b. St. George's, Birmingham, e. Birmingham, 8962, Pte., k. in a., Gallipoli, 10/8/15.
Powers, George Frederick, b. Allesley, Warwicks, e. Warwick (Allesley), 16652, Pte., k. in a., Mesopotamia, 25/1/17.
Price, George, b. Aston, Birmingham, e. Warwick (Aston), 1226, Sgt., k. in a., Mesopotamia, 9/4/16.
Price, John Aubrey, b. Ludlow, Hereford, e. Birmingham (Small Heath, Birmingham), 6388, Pte., d. of w., Gallipoli, 7/8/15.
Prince, Charles Frederick, b. Atherstone, Warwicks, e. Atherstone, 16299, Pte., d., Mesopotamia, 9/9/16.
Prince, David John, b. Ladywood, Birmingham, e. Birmingham (Ladywood), 3032, Pte., d. of w., Gallipoli, 10/8/15.
Prince, Thomas Daniel, b. Tipton, Dudley, Staffs, e. Birmingham, 3643, Cpl., d., Mesopotamia, 9/6/16.
Pulford, Frank, b. Ellesmere Port, Ches., e. Gosport, Hants (Ellesmere Port), 12342, L/Cpl., d., Mesopotamia, 8/8/16, formerly 51407, R.G.A.
Quinn, Charles, b. Glasgow, e. Birmingham (Paisley, Renfrewshire), 3103, Pte., k. in a., Gallipoli, 10/8/15.
Quinsey, Richard, b. St. Bartholomew's, Birmingham, e. Birmingham, 3673, Pte., k. in a., Gallipoli, 7/8/15.
Raby, William Ernest, b. St. John's, Coventry, Warwicks, e. Coventry, 3314, Pte., k. in a., Gallipoli, 10/8/15.
Rachel, William, b. Hockley, Birmingham, e. Birmingham, 3815, L/Cpl., k. in a., Gallipoli, 10/8/15.
Ratcliffe, William, b. Leigh, Lancs, e. Atherton, Lancs (Lowton, Lancs), 12438, Pte., d., Mesopotamia, 10/9/18, formerly 49243, R.G.A.
Ravenhall, William Sidney, b. Birmingham, e. Coventry, Warwicks (Birmingham), 1819, Pte., d., Mesopotamia, 2/7/16.
Rayner, Alfred, b Wandsworth, Surrey, e. London (Blenheim, Ontaria, Canada), 21822, L/Cpl., d.. Mesopotamia, 18/2/18, formerly 8944, W. Riding Regt.

Rayson, James Albert, b. Nuneaton, Warwicks, e. Warwick (Nuneaton), 4/2090, Pte., k. in a., Mesopotamia, 10/8/15.
Reader, Percy Hutchinson, b. St Paul's, Warwick, e. Warwick (Birmingham), 4688, Pte., k. in a., Gallipoli, 10/8/15.
Redgrave, Herbert, b. Coventry, Warwicks, e. Coventry, 15374, Pte., k. in a., Mesopotamia, 25/1/17.
Reid, Walter James, b. St. Thomas, Coventry, Warwicks, e. Coventry, 3302, Sgt., k. in a., Gallipoli, 10/8/15.
Reynolds, Arthur Thomas, b. Vauxhall, Birmingham, e. Birmingham (Ashted, Birmingham), 4032, Cpl., k. in a., Gallipoli,, 22/7/15.
Reynolds, James, b. Ryton, Warwicks, e Bedworth, Warwicks, 22091, Pte., d., Mesopotamia, 11/11/18.
Rhodes, George William, b. Birmingham, e. Birmingham (Selly Oak, Birmingham), 13479, Pte., d. of w., Mesopotamia, 27/1/17.
Richards, Percy, b. Sidbury, Devon, e Exeter, Devon (Sidbury), 12317, d., Mesopotamia, 23/6/16, formerly 53895, R.G.A.
Rickards, George, b. Birmingham, e. Birmingham, 3495, Pte., k. in a., Gallipoli, 10/8/15.
Robbins, Frederick George, b. Hindley, Lancs, e. Leigh, Lancs, 12320, Pte., d. of w., Mesopotamia, 6/4/16, formerly 53798, R.G.A.
Roberts, Edward William, b. Coventry, Warwicks, e. Warwick (Coventry), 10895, Pte., k. in a., Gallipoli, 7/8/15.
Roberts, Edward Harry, b. Nechells, Birmingham, e. Birmingham (Nechells), 4107, Pte., k. in a., Gallipoli, 10/8/15.
Roberts, Sidney Herbert Harold, b. Holy Trinity, Coventry, Warwicks, e. Coventry, 9605, Pte., d., Mesopotamia, 22/8/15.
Roberts, Thomas, b. Welshpool, Mont., e. Warwick, 13061, Pte., d. of w., Mesopotamia, 6/4/16.
Robins, William, b. Walworth, Surrey, e. Southwark, Surrey (Walworth), 12592, Pte., d. of w., Mesopotamia, 16/4/16, formerly 56860, R.G.A.
Robinson, Ernest Edward, b. Burton-on-Trent, Staffs, e. Coventry, Warwicks (Burton-on-Trent), 3873, Pte., k. in a., Gallipoli, 10/8/15.
Robinson, James, b. Deritend, Birmingham, e. Birmingham, 10403, Pte., k. in a., Gallipoli, 10/8/15.
Robinson, John, b. Perry Barr, Staffs, e. Birmingham (Winson Green, Birmingham), 3251, Pte., d. of w., Gallipoli, 13/8/15.
Robson, Thomas, b. Annfield Plain, Durham, e. Newcastle-on-Tyne (Consett, Durham), 11556, Pte., d., Mesopotamia, 14/6/16.
Roderick, Alfred, b. Balsall Heath, Birmingham, e. Birmingham, 3347, Pte., k. in a., Gallipoli, 10/8/15.
Rogers, Albert, b. Small Heath, Birmingham, e. Birmingham, 3896, Pte., k. in a., Gallipoli, 10/8/15.
Rogers, Alfred Edward, e. Birmingham (Sparkbrook, Birmingham), 9252, Pte., k. in a., Gallipoli, 11/11/15.
Rogers, Harold, b. Birmingham, e. Warwick (Erdington, Birmingham), 15880, Pte., k. in a., Mesopotamia, 25/1/17.
Rogers, James, b. St. Thomas, Birmingham, e. Birmingham, 3262, Pte., d. of w., Gallipoli, 24/12/15.
Rogers, Richard, b. St. Phillip's, Bristol, Glos., e. Bristol, 5425, Pte., d., Gallipoli, 19/9/15.
Rollason, William, b. Birmingham, e. Birmingham, 12005, Pte., k. in a., Mesopotamia, 9/4/16.
Rollins, Joseph William, b. Brisnell Fields, Worcs, e. Birmingham, 3047, Pte., k. in a., Gallipoli, 10/8/15.
Rolls, Alfred, b. Moordown, Hants, e. Bournemouth, Hants (Winton, Hants), 12455, Pte., d., Mesopotamia, 16/6/16, formerly 5626, R.G.A.
Roper, William, b. Wolverhampton, Staffs, e. Coventry, Warwicks, 2504, Pte., k. in a., Gallipoli, 10/8/15.
Ross, John, b. Birmingham, e. Birmingham, 1076, L/Cpl., d., Mesopotamia, 27/9/18.
Rottenbury, Henry John, b. Parracombe, Devon, e. Coventry, Warwicks (Parracombe), 5004, L/Cpl., d., Gallipoli, 26/7/15.
Roughton, Albert, b. St. Andrew's, Birmingham, e. Birmingham, 2325, Pte., k. in a., Gallipoli, 5/1/16.
Rowlands, William, b. Birmingham, e. Birmingham, 13367, Pte., k. in a., Mesopotamia, 25/1/17.
Ruane, Justin Joseph, b. Carnarvon, e. Birmingham (Erdington, Birmingham), 9694, Pte., k. in a., Mesopotamia, 10/8/15.
Rushton, Arthur, b. Hoar Cross, Burton-on-Trent, Staffs, e. Birmingham, 3826, Pte., k. in a., Gallipoli, 10/8/15.
Russell, George Walter, b. Bulkington, Warwicks, e. Nuneaton, Warwicks (Bulkington), 3513, Pte., d., Mesopotamia, 9/3/18.
Russell, Joe Edgar, b. Broadway, Worcs, e. Stratford-on-Avon, Warwicks (Broadway), 9570, Pte., k. in a., Mesopotamia, 19/4/16.
Rye, Walter Harold, b. Hoo, Kent, e. Coventry, Warwicks, 16748, Pte., k. in a., Mesopotamia, 25/1/17.
Ryman, Leonard James, b. Holy Trinity, Oxford, e. Oxford, 11120, Pte., k. in a., Gallipoli, 10/8/15.
Salt, Edward, b. Wolverhampton, Staffs, e. Warwick (Foleshill, Coventry), 241543, Pte., d., Mesopotamia, 6/10/18.
Salt, George, b. Armitage, Staffs, e. Stafford (Blithbury, Staffs), 12214, Pte., k. in a., Mesopotamia, 9/4/16.
Salt, William, b. Handsacre, Staffs, e. Nuneaton, Warwicks (Handsacre), 11037, Pte., d., Mesopotamia, 16/7/16.
Sandbrook, Alfred Samuel, b. All Saints, Birmingham, e. Birmingham, 4053, Pte., k. in a., Gallipoli, 10/8/15.
Sandford, Thomas, b. Stratford-on-Avon, Warwicks, e. Warwick (Stratford-on-Avon), 3072, Pte., d., Mesopotamia, 2/8/16.
Savvin, James, b. Liverpool, e. Liverpool, 12611, Pte., k. in a., Mesopotamia, 5/4/16.
Scarlett, Walter, b. Hillmorton, Rugby, Warwicks, e. Rugby, 1685, Pte., k. in a., Mesopotamia, 29/3/17.
Seagar, Harry, e. Consett, Durham, 11305, Pte., d., Mesopotamia, 9/4/18.
Sergeant, Thomas Henry, b. Liverpool, e. Liverpool, 12315, Pte., k. in a., Mesopotamia, 5/4/16, formerly 53563, R.G.A.
Shale, William John, b. All Saints, Birmingham, e. Birmingham, 6410, Pte., k. in a., Gallipoli, 8/8/15.
Sharrott, Edward Michael, b. Baddesley Ensor, Warwicks, e. Atherstone, Warwicks, 3/4639, A/Sgt., k. in a., Mesopotamia, 19/4/16.
Sheen, John, b. Birmingham, e. Birmingham, 520, Pte., k. in a., Mesopotamia, 9/4/16.
Shilton, Arthur, b. Hurley, Warwicks, e. Atherstone, Warwicks (Hurley), 10742, Pte., d., Mesopotamia, 29/5/16.
Shield, Walton, b. Murton, Durham, e. Sunderland, Durham (Murton), 13097, Pte., k. in a., Mesopotamia, 19/4/16.
Shipway, Charles James, b. London, e. Winchester, Hants (London), 4683, Pte., k. in a., Gallipoli, 20/7/15.
Shorten, Frank Clinton, b. Salford, Lancs, e. Manchester (Salford), 12313, Pte., k. in a., Mesopotamia, 15/11/15, formerly 53831, R.G.A.
Simmonds, Thomas, b. Holy Trinity, Coventry, Warwicks, e. Coventry, 3324, Pte., d. of w., Gallipoli, 21/8/15.
Simmons, Alfred Edward, b. Aston, Birmingham, e. Aston (Birmingham), 3656, Pte., k. in a., Gallipoli, 11/10/16.
Simpson, Sidney, b. Stratford-on-Avon, Warwicks, e. Stratford-on-Avon, 11855, Pte., d., Mesopotamia, 17/7/17.
Slim, Samuel, b. Birmingham, e. Birmingham, 12171, Pte., k. in a., Mesopotamia, 9/4/16.
Smart, Albert, b. Nechells, Birmingham, e. Birmingham, 6434, Pte., d. of w., Gallipoli, 10/8/15.
Smith, Arthur, b. St. Michael's, Coventry, e. Coventry, 15692, Pte., d., Mesopotamia, 4/7/16.
Smith, Frank Leonard, b. Hanbury, Worcs, e. Coventry, Warwicks, 18246, Pte., k. in a., Mesopotamia, 25/1/17.
Smith, George, b. St. Davids, Birmingham, e. Birmingham, 3900, Pte., k. in a., Gallipoli, 7/8/15.
Smith, George Edward, b. Birmingham, e. Birmingham (Winson Green, Birmingham), 11139, Pte., d., Mesopotamia, 26/8/16.
Smith, Joseph, b. Bordesley, Birmingham, e. Birmingham (Bordesley), 10432, Pte., k. in a., Mesopotamia, 16/2/16.
Smith, Percy Francis, b. Coventry, Warwicks, e. Coventry, 16323, Cpl., k. in a., Mesopotamia, 29/3/17.
Smith, Reginald, b. Stafford, e. Stafford, 9637, Pte., d., Gallipoli, 24/10/15.
Smith, Samuel Thomas Kimberley, b. Aston, Birmingham, e. Birmingham, 3847, Pte., d., Home, 20/12/14.
Smith, Sidney, b. Birmingham, e. Birmingham, 17883, L/Cpl., d., Mesopotamia, 30/9/18.
Sparkes, Ernest Harry, b. Atherstone, Warwicks, e. Nuneaton, Warwicks (Atherstone), 2774, Pte., d., Gallipoli, 12/11/15.
Speak, Percy, b. Madeley, Salop, e. Birmingham (Iron Bridge, Salop), 4036, Cpl., k. in a., Mesopotamia, 19/4/16.
Spratt, Sidney, b. Ladywood, Birmingham, e. Birmingham (Ladywood), 4777, Pte., k. in a., Mesopotamia, 9/4/16.
Stagg, William, b. Coventry, Warwicks, e. Coventry, 8936, Pte., k. in a., Gallipoli, 8/8/15.
Stallard, George William, b. Portsmouth, Hants, e. Portsmouth, 12594, Pte., d. of w., Mesopotamia, 23/4/16, formerly 10844, Worcs Regt.
Stanley, Freeman, b. Sheffield, Yorks, e. Halifax, Yorks (King's Lynn, Norfolk), 21826, Pte., k. in a., Mesopotamia, 25/1/17, formerly 7183, W. Riding Regt.
Stanton, Walter, b. Leamington, Warwicks, e. Manchester (Leamington), 3874, Pte., d., Gallipoli, 23/8/15.
Steenton, Charles, b. St. Mary's, Worcester, e. Birmingham, 21431, Pte., d., Mesopotamia, 28/6/17.
Stevens, William Thomas, b. Chetwood, Bucks, e. Oxford (Bicester, Oxon), 18372, Pte., d., Mesopotamia, 20/3/17, formerly 23305, Som. L.I.
Stone, Albert George, b. Ilminster, Somerset, e. Birmingham (Smethwick, Staffs), 11826, Pte., k. in a., Mesopotamia, 29/3/17.
Summerfield, Edwin, b. Rotton Park, Birmingham, e. Birmingham, 4660, Pte., d., Mesopotamia, 21/4/16.
Summers, James, e. Hackney Baths, London (Dalston, N.E.), 20697, Pte., k. in a., Mesopotamia, 1/9/18, formerly 12213, Army Cycl. Corps.
Summers, Joseph Henry, b. Handsworth, Birmingham, e. Birmingham (Winson Green, Birmingham), 5408, Pte., d. of w., Gallipoli, 13/8/15.
Sutton, Ernest, b. Darlaston, Birmingham, e. Birmingham (Perry Barr, Birmingham), 6417, Pte., k. in a., Gallipoli, 27/9/15.
Tacy, William, b. St. Andrew's, Birmingham, e. Birmingham, 16548, Pte., k. in a., Mesopotamia, 3/2/17.
Tandy, Wilfred, b. Broadway, Worcs, e. Warwick (Broadway), 10754, Pte., k. in a., Gallipoli, 7/8/15.
Tate, Robert Smith, b. Birmingham, e. London, Middx. (Sunderland, Durham), 12236, Pte., d. of w., Mesopotamia, 13/4/17.
Taylor, Charles, b. St. David's, Birmingham, e. Birmingham (Camp Hill, Birmingham), 10505, Pte., d. of w., Gallipoli, 9/8/15.
Taylor, Clarence Charles, b. St. Martin's, Birmingham, e. Birmingham, 12922, Pte., d., Mesopotamia, 1/7/16.
Taylor, Frederick, b. Ibstock, Leics, e. Coventry, Warwicks (Longford, Coventry), 203507, Pte., k. in a., F. & F., 31/8/18.
Taylor, Frederick Oscar, e. Birmingham (Walsall, Staffs), 16/1610, Cpl., k. in a., Mesopotamia, 1/9/18.
Taylor, Joseph William, b. Birmingham, e. Birmingham, 10494, Pte., d. of w., Gallipoli, 13/8/15.
Taylor, William, b. Coventry, Warwicks, e. Warwick (Coventry), 16665, Pte., d., Mesopotamia, 9/5/17.
Terry, Ambrose Joseph, b. Weldon, Northants, e. Warwick (Crick, Rugby, Warwicks), 16529, Pte., d. of w., Mesopotamia, 7/6/17.

Thacker, Thomas Richard, b. Bishops Itchington, Warwicks, e. Warwick (Bishops Itchington), 2645, Dmr., d., Mesopotamia, 16/3/18.
Thatcher, Stanley Alfred, b. Kerby Moorside, Yorks, e. Birmingham (Acocks Green, Birmingham), 6444, Pte., k. in a., Gallipoli, 10/8/15.
Thomas, Arthur, b. Birmingham, e. Birmingham (Stirchley, Birmingham), 23019, Pte., d., Mesopotamia, 7/11/17.
Thompson, Herbert Charles, b. South Hackney, London, e. Stratford, London, E. (Hackney), 10634, L/Cpl., d. Gallipoli, 29/12/15.
Thompson, William George, b. Coventry, Warwicks, e. Warwick (Coventry), 16641, Pte., k. in a., Mesopotamia, 25/1/17.
Thorley, Samuel Ernest, b. Nuneaton, Warwicks, e. Coventry, Warwicks (Nuneaton), 3593, L/Cpl., d. of w., Gallipoli, 25/8/15.
Thornley, William, b. Little Hulton, Bolton, Lancs, e. Bolton (Little Hulton), 12332, Pte., d. of w., Mesopotamia, 13/4/16, formerly 51313, R.G.A.
Thursfield, Thomas, b. St. Martin's, Birmingham, e. Birmingham (Small Heath, Birmingham), 13405, Pte., d., Mesopotamia, 23/5/16.
Thurston, William, b. Birmingham, e. Birmingham (Hockley, Birmingham), 3389, Pte., k. in a., Gallipoli, 27/7/15.
Tidman, Walter, b. Shilton, Warwicks, e. Coventry, Warwicks (Walsgrave-on-Sowe, Coventry), 12785, Pte., d., Mesopotamia, 26/9/18.
Tilston, Leonard, b. Milford, Stafford, e. Coventry, Warwicks (Milford), 1326, Pte., d., Mesopotamia, 20/7/16.
Tims, Frederick, b. Leamington Spa, Warwicks, e. Warwick (Leamington), 16552, Pte., d. of w., Mesopotamia, 1/4/17.
Townley, William, b. Manchester, e. Birmingham, 11753, Pte., d. of w., Mesopotamia, 20/4/16.
Townsend, Ernest, b. St. George's, Birmingham, e. Birmingham, 3037, Pte., k. in a., Mesopotamia, 14/9/18.
Townsend, Percival Stanley, b. Manor Park, Essex, e. East Ham, London (Manor Park), 12601, Pte., d. of w., Mesopotamia, 12/4/16, formerly 54544, R.G.A.
Truby, John, b. St. Martin's, Birmingham, e. Birmingham (Smethwick, Staffs), 11583, Pte., k. in a., Mesopotamia, 5/4/16.
Turley, Harold, b. Wolverhampton, Staffs, e. Birmingham (Wolverhampton), 7919, Cpl., d. of w., Mesopotamia, 12/4/17.
Turner, Archibald Francis, b. West Bromwich, Birmingham, e. Warwick (West Bromwich), 428, C.S.M., k. in a., Gallipoli, 10/8/15.
Turner, James, b. Stoke Newington, London, e. Holloway, London (Stoke Newington), 11539, Pte., d., Mesopotamia, 28/9/18.
Turner, Tom, b. Solihull, Warwicks, e. Birmingham, 7070, Pte., k. in a., Gallipoli, 10/8/15.
Tustin, James Henry, b. Neithrop, Banbury, Oxon, e. Rugby, 11686, Pte., d. of w., Gallipoli, 11/4/16.
Twigger, Ernest, b. Bedworth, Warwicks, e. Nuneaton, Warwicks (Bedworth), 10988, Pte., d. of w., Gallipoli, 5/8/15.
Varney, George, b. Napton, Warwicks, e. Warwick (Southam, Warwicks), 1455, Pte., d. of w., Mesopotamia, 8/4/16.
Vaughan, Harry, b. Birmingham, e. Birmingham, 8909, Pte., d., Gallipoli, 6/10/15.
Wagstaff, Alfred, b. Handsworth, Birmingham, e. Birmingham (Handsworth), 2893, C.S.M., k. in a., Mesopotamia, 25/1/17.
Wainman, Charles Frederick, b. Birmingham, e. Birmingham (Sparkbrook, Birmingham), 23033, Pte., d., Mesopotamia, 23/7/17.
Wall, George Thomas, b. Bordesley, Birmingham, e. Birmingham (Bordesley), 5442, Pte., k. in a., Mesopotamia, 19/4/16.
Walmsley, Harry, b. St. Stephen's, Birmingham, e. Birmingham, 11949, L/Cpl., d., Mesopotamia, 27/7/16.
Ward, Alfred James, b. Stratford-on-Avon, Warwicks, e. Warwick (Stratford-on-Avon), 13119, Pte., d. of w., Mesopotamia, 10/4/16.
Ward, Harry, b. Banbury, Oxon, e. Plymouth, Devon (Redditch, Worcs), 15333, Pte., d., Mesopotamia, 10/3/17.
Ward, Louis Richard, e. Birmingham (Saltley, Birmingham), 240683, Pte., d., Mesopotamia, 30/9/18.
Ward, Walter, b. Rugeley, Staffs, e. Birmingham (Nechell's Green, Birmingham), 7305, Pte., d., Mesopotamia, 9/4/16.
Ward, William, b. Hockley, Birmingham, e. Birmingham, 1330, Pte., d. of w., Mesopotamia, 4/9/16.
Wardle, Brown, b. Cockfield, Durham, e. Spennymoor, Durham, 12713, Pte., k. in a., Mesopotamia, 17/9/15, formerly 51003, R.G.A.
Warner, Henry, b. St. Paul's, Birmingham, e. Birmingham, 3094, Pte., k. in a., Gallipoli, 10/8/15.
Warren, John, b. Stoke Golding, Leics, e. Nuneaton, Warwicks, 10623, Pte., d. of w., Mesopotamia, 22/5/16.
Watkins, James, b. Birmingham, e. Birmingham, 2825, Pte., k. in a., Gallipoli, 10/8/15.
Watton, Arthur, b. Ashwood Bank, Worcs, e. Stratford-on-Avon, Warwicks (Earlswood, Birmingham), 11481, Pte., d. of w., Gallipoli, 5/4/16.
Watts, Harold Percy, b. Rugby, Warwicks, e. Rugby (New Bilton, Warwicks), 12212, Pte., k. in a., Mesopotamia, 5/4/16.
Webster, James Gordon, b. Erdington, Birmingham, e. Birmingham (Wylde Green, Birmingham), 4092, Pte., k. in a., Mesopotamia, 19/4/16.
Webster, William, b. Burbage, Leics, e. Nuneaton, Warwicks (Barwell, Leics), 10681, Pte., d. of w., Gallipoli, 10/4/16.
West, George Henry, b. Pudsey, Yorks, e. Warwick (Atherstone, Warwicks), 13146, Pte., d. of w., Gallipoli, 7/12/15.
West, Jabez, b. Vauxhall, Birmingham, e. Birmingham (Winson Green, Birmingham), 5414, Pte., k. in a., Gallipoli, 10/8/15.
Weston, Bowden Harry, b. Eddisbury, Ches., e. Birmingham (Kensall, Ches.), 8916, Pte., k. in a., Gallipoli, 10/8/15.
Weychan, Charles, b. St. Thomas, Stourbridge, Worcs, e. Birmingham, 9889, A/C.Q.M.S., k. in a., Mesopotamia, 19/4/16.
Wheeler, William, b. Stratford-on-Avon, Warwicks, e. Coventry, Warwicks (Birmingham), 9743, L/Cpl., d. of w., Mesopotamia, 6/4/16.
White, Christopher, b. Consett, Durham, e. Consett, 11472, Pte., d., Mesopotamia, 26/5/16.
White, James, b. Hulme, Lancs, e. Birmingham (Camp Hill, Birmingham), 14331, Pte., d. of w., Mesopotamia, 11/4/17.
Whittaker, Benjamin, b. Birmingham, e. Birmingham, 13272, Pte., d., Mesopotamia, 27/6/16.
Wilkes, Charles, b. Bloomsbury, Birmingham, e. Birmingham, 11716, Sgt., k. in a., N. Russia, 1/9/19.
Wilkes, Thomas, b. Birmingham, e. Birmingham, 12181, Pte., k. in a., Mesopotamia, 5/4/16.
Wilkins, John James, b. Birmingham, e. Birmingham, 21649, Pte., d., Mesopotamia, 29/9/18
Williams, Edward, b. Swansea, Glam., e. Neath, Glam., 12372, Pte., d. of w., Mesopotamia, 3/2/17, formerly 4736, R.G.A.
Williams, Ernest John, b. Leamington, Warwicks, e. Leamington, 16740, Pte., k. in a., Mesopotamia, 25/1/17.
Williams, Harry, b. Birmingham, e. Birmingham (Deritend, Birmingham), 5109, Pte., d. of w., Gallipoli, 10/1/16.
Williams, Herbert Marklew, b. Ladywood, Birmingham, e Birmingham, 4879, Pte., k. in a., Gallipoli 10/8/15.
Williams, John, b. All Saint's, Southport, Lancs, e. Warwick (Southport), 2661, Pte., k. in a., Gallipoli, 10/8/15.
Williams, Joseph, b. Barston, Warwicks, e. Warwick (Knowle, Warwicks), 9555, Pte., d. of w., Gallipoli, 13/8/15.
Willits, Frederick, b. Birmingham, e. Birmingham (Winson Green, Birmingham), 11744, Pte., d., Mesopotamia, 28/11/15.
Willson, Arthur, b. Hackney, Middx., e. Coventry, Warwicks (Stoneleigh, Warwicks), 3606, Pte., k. in a., Gallipoli, 10/8/15.
Wilshire, John Henry, b. Fieldharrin, Wilts, e. Pewsey, Wilts (Fiddliton, Wilts), 306740, Pte., d., Mesopotamia, 8/10/18.
Wiltshire, Richard, Henry, b. Saltley, Birmingham, e. Birmingham (Saltley), 5308, Pte., k. in a., Mesopotamia, 29/3/17.
Winkley, Howard, b. Small Heath, Birmingham, e. Birmingham (Small Heath), 488, Pte., k. in a., Mesopotamia, 29/3/17.
Winstanley, Harry Ashford, b. Liverpool, e. Liverpool, 12328, Pte., d., Mesopotamia, 29/6/16, formerly 53803, R.G.A.
Witcomb, Harold, e. Birmingham, 3832, Cpl., d., Mesopotamia, 19/3/17.
Wood, Charles, b. Mitcham, Surrey, e. Birmingham, 3223, Pte., d., Mesopotamia, 14/1/17.
Wood, Frank, b. Womborne, Staffs, e. Birmingham (Polesworth, Warwicks), 3983, Pte., k. in a., Gallipoli, 10/8/15.
Woods, Francis John, b. Marsh Gibbon, Bucks, e. Birmingham (Hay Mills, Birmingham), 3700, Sgt., k. in a., Gallipoli, 10/8/15.
Woodward, Warren Thomas, b. Edgbaston, Birmingham, e. Birmingham (Bridgwater, Som.), 12189, Pte., k. in a., Mesopotamia, 5/4/16.
Wookey, George, b. Bristol, Glos., e. Birmingham (Bordesley, Birmingham), 13019, Pte., k. in a., Mesopotamia, 29/3/17.
Woolford, Wilfred Reginald, b. Reading, Berks, e. Birmingham (Bromsgrove, Worcs), 6455, L/Cpl., k. in a., Gallipoli, 10/8/15.
Woolley, John Samuel, b. Birmingham, e. Birmingham, 10263, Pte., d., Mesopotamia, 2/10/18.
Woolley, Robert, b. Pluckley, Kent, e. Chatham, Kent (Ashford, Kent), 12428, Pte., d., Gallipoli, 29/11/15, formerly 56434, R.G.A.
Worthington, Arthur, b. St. John's, Birmingham, e. Birmingham (Acock's Green, Birmingham), 8984, L/Cpl., d., Mesopotamia, 11/7/16.
Wrench, James Stephen, b. St. Paul's, Leamington, Warwicks, e. Warwick (Solihull, Warwicks), 12650, Pte., d., Mesopotamia, 6/7/16.
Wright, Arthur Egbert, b. New Evington, Leic., e. Birmingham (Erdington, Birmingham), 18296, Pte., d. of w., Mesopotamia, 28/1/17.
Wright, John, b Bromsgrove, Worcs, e. Birmingham, 1383, Sgt., d. of w., Mesopotamia, 26/1/17.
Yeandle, Robert, b. Williton, Som., e. Taunton, Som. (Williton), 12325, Pte, d. of w., Mesopotamia, 24/2/17, formerly 53804, R.G.A.
Yorke, Wilfred, b. Ansley Village, Warwicks, e. Swanage, Dorset (Ansley Village), 4523, Pte., d. of w., Mesopotamia, 12/4/16.

10th Battalion.

Adams, Eric Thomas, e. Witton, Birmingham (Harborne, Birmingham), 28673, Pte., d. of w., F. & F., 21/10/18, formerly 777, R.A.S.C.
Adams, George Howard, b. Radway, Warwicks, e. Kineton, Warwicks, 20240, Pte., k. in a., F. & F., 21/9/17.
Addison, Ralph, b. Seacombe, Ches., e. Birkenhead, Ches (Egremont, Ches.), 25771, Pte., d. of w., F. & F., 26/10/18, formerly 024648, R.A.O.C.
Ainger, Joseph, b. Arnold, Notts, e. Arnold, 27473, Pte., d of w., F. & F., 8/5/17, formerly 34108, Notts & Derby Regt.
Akerman, Rupert, b. Leamington, Warwicks, e. Leamington, 20953, Pte., d. of w., F. & F., 21/9/17.
Albrighton, John, b. Baddesley Ensor, Atherstone, Warwicks, e. Atherstone, 4655, Pte., k. in a., F. & F., 23/7/16.
Alder, Samuel, b. Gloucester, e. Gloucester, 35559, L/Cpl., k. in a., F. & F., 25/9/18, formerly 26782, Glos. Regt.

Allamby, James Edward, b. Leeds, Yorks, e Leeds, 12740, Pte., k. in a., F. & F., 3/7/16.
Allan, Thomas, b. Kilkerra, Co. Tyrone, e. Paisley, Lanarks, 30403, Pte., k. in a., F. & F., 18/11/16, formerly 8/25737, R. Innis. Fus.
Allbrighton, Henry, b. Dordon, Warwicks, e. Atherstone, Warwicks (Dordon), 42799, Pte., k. in a., F. & F., 25/9/18.
Allen, Archibald, b. St. Gabriel's, Bristol, e. Bristol, 5439, Pte., k. in a., F. & F., 3/7/16.
Allen, Ernest John, b. Reading, Berks, e. Reading, 18756, Pte., d. of w., F. & F., 11/5/18, formerly 24527, Som. L.I.
Allen, Thomas, b. Birmingham, e. Northampton (Warwick), 10587, Pte., k. in a., F. & F., 18/11/16.
Allen, Thomas Henry, b. Lambeth, London, e. London (Lambeth), 43271, Pte., d. of w., F. & F., 27/3/18.
Allsop, George Arthur, b. Balsall Heath, Birmingham, e. Birmingham, 4567, Pte., k. in a., F. & F., 7/11/18.
Allsopp, Ernest, b Stafford, e. Birmingham, 2649, Pte., d., F. & F., 4/3/16.
Allsopp, William George, e. Nottingham, 27206, Pte., k. in a., F. & F., 18/11/16, formerly 3683, Notts & Derby Regt.
Allwood, George, b. St. Paul's, Leamington, Warwicks, e. Warwick (Leamington), 4286, Pte., k. in a., F. & F., 16/12/15.
Antill, Sibery, b. Sutton-in-Ashfield, Notts, e. Sutton-in-Ashfield, 27499, Pte., k. in a., F. & F., 18/11/16, formerly 34749, Notts & Derby Regt.
Arkley, Alfred, b. Edgbaston, Birmingham, e. Birmingham, 2159, Pte., d. of w., F. & F., 3/4/18.
Armstrong, Tom, b. Elswick, Newcastle-on-Tyne, e. Coventry, Warwicks, 5801, Sgt., k. in a., F. & F., 16/12/15.
Arnold, Richard Charles, b. Oxton-on-the-Hill, Warwicks, e. Warwick (Anstey, Warwicks), 23155, Pte., d. of w., F. & F., 28/7/17.
Ashton, Harold Victor, b. Birmingham, e. Warwick (Wingate, Leeds), 12739, Cpl., k. in a., F. & F., 19/4/18.
Askin, Archie, b. Sheffield, Yorks, e. Ripley, Derby, 27285, Pte., d. of w., F. & F., 22/11/16, formerly 5593, Notts & Derby Regt.
Aston, Henry Amos, e. Coventry, Warwicks (Warwick), 266556, Pte., k. in a., F. & F., 22/3/18.
Aston, Thomas Henry, b. Colway, Glos., e. Bristol, Glos. (Coleford, Glos.), 34799, Pte., d., F. & F., 11/4/18.
Atkins, Arthur, b. Nottingham, e. Nottingham, 27292, Pte., k. in a., F. & F., 18/11/16, formerly 5590, Notts & Derby Regt.
Atkins, Arthur Thomas, b. Birmingham, e. Birmingham (Aston, Birmingham), 8871, Cpl., k. in a., F. & F., 25/3/18.
Atkins, Wilfred, b. Kidderminster, Worcs, e. Coventry, Warwicks, 16857, Pte., d. of w., F. & F., 28/9/17.
Attewell, Henry, b. Letcombe Regis, Berks, e. Wantage, Berks, 16/1979, Pte., d. of w., F. & F., 19/11/16, formerly 150145, R.F.A.
Attle, Harry Walter, b. Ipswich, Suffolk, e. Colchester, Essex, 27300, Pte., k. in a., F. & F., 18/11/16, formerly 5815, Notts & Derby Regt.
Austin, Albert, b. Woodstock, Oxon, e. Coventry, Warwicks (Steeple Aston, Oxon), 9986, Pte., k. in a., F. & F., 28/4/16.
Axford, Arthur, b. Boddington, Glos., e. Birmingham, 7968, Cpl., k. in a., F. & F., 19/4/18.
Ayres, Thomas Henry, b. Royston, Herts, e. Marylebone, London, 28825, Pte., k. in a., F. & F., 23/3/18, formerly S/4/143711, R.A.S.C.
Baker, Ernest George, b. Mollington, Oxon, e. Leamington, Warwicks (Wormleighton, Warwicks), 28007, Pte., d. of w., F. & F., 8/5/17.
Baker, James William, b. Amblecote, Worcs, e. Birmingham (Handsworth, Staffs), 202148, Pte., k. in a., F. & F., 22/3/18.
Ball, Edwin Joshua, b. Wolverhampton, Staffs, e. Birmingham (Barnbrook, Birmingham), 20470, Pte., k. in a., F. & F., 23/3/18.
Ball, Frederick Hewitt, b. Battersea, London, e. Battersea, 50490, Pte., k. in a., F. & F., 8/11/18, formerly 324794, London Regt.
Baller, Thomas Henry, b. Birmingham, e. Warwick (King's Norton, Birmingham), 16662, Pte., k. in a., F. & F., 3/7/16.
Bannerman, Wallace, b. St. Mark's, Dublin, e. Birmingham (Dublin), 3935, Pte., k. in a., F. & F., 26/10/16.
Bannister, Albert, e. Nottingham, 27312, Pte., k. in a., F. & F., 18/11/16, formerly 4727, Notts & Derby Regt.
Barker, Albert Edward, b. Portsmouth, e. Portsmouth, 43313, Pte., k. in a., F. & F., 2598, Hants Yeo.
Barker, Alfred, b. Broughton, Hunts, e. Huntingdon (Broughton), 203386, Pte., k. in a., F. & F., 19/4/18, formerly 764, Hunts Cyc. Battn.
Barker, Edward Vernon, b. Barston, Warwicks, e. Coventry, Warwicks (Kenilworth, Warwicks), 27998, Pte., k. in a., F. & F., 22/3/18.
Barker, William, b. Wollaston, Warwicks, e. Coventry, Warwicks (Wollaston), 30065, Pte., d. of w., F. & F., 15/12/17.
Barlow, Reuben, b. Clapham, London, e. Birmingham (London), 8501, Pte., k. in a., F. & F., 14/10/15.
Bartlett, Alex, b. Cirencester, Glos., e. Cirencester, 35477, Pte., k. in a., F. & F., 13/5/18.
Bartlett, John, b. Hillfields, Coventry, e. Coventry, 266302, Pte., d. of w., F. & F., 8/11/18.
Bassett, Charles, b. St. Martin's, Tipton, Staffs, e. West Bromwich, Staffs (Tipton), 7193, Pte., k. in a., F. & F., 18/11/16.
Bates, James, b. Woodsetton, Dudley, Staffs, e. Dudley, Staffs (West Tipton, Staffs), 8739, Sgt., d. of w., F. & F., 24/3/18.
Bateson, Charles, b. Dunkeswick, Yorks, e. Warwick (Dunkeswick), 1829, Sgt., k. in a., F. & F., 10/4/18.
Battell, Henry, b. Langley, Bucks, e. Portsmouth (Southsea, Hants), 59210, Pte., k. in a., F. & F., 20/10/18, formerly 15041, Hants Regt.
Baxter, Frederick, b. Rugby, Warwicks, e. Coventry, Warwicks, 5487, Pte., d. of w., F. & F., 5/2/16.
Beagley, Frank, b. Newton Valance, Hants, e. Alton, Hants (Newton Valance), 43338, Pte., d. of w., F. & F., 18/6/18, formerly 2631, Hants Yeo.
Beale, Leonard, b. West Bromwich, Staffs, e. Birmingham, 5586, Sgt., k. in a., F. & F., 10/4/18.
Belson, Arthur, b. Chippenham, Bucks, e. Cowley Barracks, Oxford (Chippenham), 35478, Pte., k. in a., F. & F., 19/4/18.
Bench, Joseph, b. Rugby, Warwicks, e. Rugby, 16211, Pte., d., F. & F., 5/3/17.
Bennett, George Thomas, b. Derby, e. Sutton Coldfield, Warwicks, 22477, Pte., d., F. & F., 25/2/17.
Bennett, Joseph, b. St. George's, Birmingham, e. Birmingham, 4667, Pte., k. in a., F. & F., 1/11/16.
Bennett, Leonard Ernest, b. Kinver, Staffs, e. Stourbridge, Worcs (Kidderminster, Worcs), 35436, Pte., d., F. & F., 23/10/18.
Bennett, Victor, b. Birmingham, e. Birmingham (Edgbaston, Birmingham), 15109, Cpl., k. in a., F. & F., 3/7/16.
Bennett, William Henry, b. Birmingham, e. Birmingham (Selly Oak, Birmingham), 36203, Pte., d. of w., F. & F., 8/11/18.
Benson, Thomas Joseph, b. Birmingham, e. Birmingham (Erdington, Birmingham), 5152, Pte., d., F. & F., 7/12/15.
Beresford, George William, b. Eckington, Derbyshire, e. Newark, Notts (Mansfield Woodhouse, Notts), 27493, Pte., k. in a., F. & F., 6/1/17, formerly 3662, Notts & Derby Regt.
Bestley, Archie Harold, b. Cuddeston, Oxon, e. Oxford (Chislehampton, nr. Oxford), 36180, L/Cpl., d. of w., F. & F., 1/12/18, formerly 30758, Hussars.
Bevington, Ernest, b. Hanley, Staffs, e. Stoke-on-Trent, Staffs (Hanley), 15714, Pte., d. of w., F. & F., 4/8/16.
Bicknell, Albert, b. Rugby, Warwicks, e. Birmingham (Saltley, Birmingham), 8031, L/Cpl., k. in a., F. & F., 21/3/18.
Bicknell, Harry, b. Southam, Warwicks, e. Rugby, Warwicks, 28034, Pte., d., F. & F., 16/6/18.
Billingham, Clarence, b. Adstone, Towcester, Northants, e. Coventry, Warwicks (Adstone), 9029, L/Cpl., d. of w., F. & F., 14/6/17.
Billingham, Oscar, b. Ladywood, Birmingham, e. Birmingham (Ladywood), 3122, Pte., d., F. & F., 18/5/18.
Bint, Frank, b. Birmingham, e. Birmingham (Witton, Birmingham), 306497, Pte., d. of w., F. & F., 21/10/18.
Birch, William, b. Nottingham, e. Nottingham (Old Basford, Nottingham), 27310, Pte., k. in a., F. & F., 21/9/17, formerly 5543, Notts & Derby Regt.
Bird, Gordon Herbert, b. Birmingham, e. Birmingham (Small Heath, Birmingham), 36162, Pte., d. of w., F. & F., 22/9/18.
Blackburn, James, e. Lincoln, 26977, Pte., d. of w., F. & F., 4/4/18, formerly 4708, Lincs Regt.
Blake, Albert John, b. Birmingham, e. Warwick, 14848, Pte., k. in a., F. & F., 18/11/16.
Blakeman, Hubert, b. Wellington, Shrops, e. Birmingham (Snow Beach, Salop), 7978, Sgt., k. in a., F. & F., 30/12/17.
Blenkinsop, Gordon Lionel, b. Norton, Yorks, e. Newark, Notts (Dinnington, Yorks), 27463, L/Sgt., k. in a., F. & F., 18/11/16, formerly 3656, Notts & Derby Regt.
Bligh, Edmond, b. St. George's, Birmingham, e. Birmingham, 5685, Sgt., d. of w., F. & F., 4/6/18.
Bloxham, Percy George Bird, b. Birmingham, e. Biimingham, 39115, Pte., k. in a., F. & F., 23/10/18.
Bodfish, Ernest, b. Birmingham, e. Birmingham 11331, Pte., k. in a., F. & F., 20/9/17.
Bodfish, Joseph, b. Birmingham, e. Birmingham (Ladywood, Birmingham), 5316, Pte., k. in a., F. & F., 3/7/16.
Bohan, Charles, b. Port Glasgow, Lanarks, e. Boyle, Co. Roscommon (Ballymote, Co. Sligo), 30396, Sgt., k. in a., F. & F., 26/4/18, formerly 6/1863, Con. Rangers.
Boswell, Thomas James, b. Wootton Wawen, Warwicks, e. Birmingham (Deritend, Birmingham), 23871, Pte., k. in a., F. & F., 22/3/18.
Bott, William Henry, e. Warwick (Coventry, Warwicks), 20520, Pte., d. of w., F. & F., 13/4/18.
Bourne, Benjamin Thomas, b. Sparkbrook, Birmingham, e. Birmingham, 1906, Pte., k. in a., F. & F., 23/7/16.
Bowden, Joseph Henry, b. Torquay, Devon, e. Newton Abbot, Devon (Torquay), 50585, Pte., k. in a., F. & F., 20/9/18.
Bower, Matthew James, b. Birmingham, e. Warwick (Birmingham), 14850, Pte., k. in a., F. & F., 18/11/16.
Bowers, George, b. Denby Main, Yorks, e. Nuneaton, Warwicks (Bedworth, Warwicks), 14400, Pte., k. in a., F. & F., 30/7/16.
Box, Frank, b. Stratford-on-Avon, Warwicks, e. Stratford-on-Avon, 20166, Pte., k. in a., F. & F., 26/10/17.
Boyce, Walter Thomas, b. Temple Grafton, Warwicks, e. Stratford-on-Avon, Warwicks, 28559, Pte., k. in a., F. & F., 23/9/17.
Boyer, Thomas William, b. Peterborough, Northants, e. Rugby, Warwicks, 16083, Cpl., k. in a., F. & F., 10/5/17.
Boyles, Joseph, b. Falkirk, Stirling, e. Birmingham (Aston, Birmingham), 7976, Pte., d. of w., F. & F., 9/2/17.
Bracey, Fred, e. Birmingham (Edgbaston, Birmingham), 1173, Pte., k. in a., F. & F., 7/6/17.
Bracken, Hugh Alexander, b. Ballinashaw, Co. Galway, e. Birmingham (Galway), 521, Cpl., k. in a., F. & F., 22/3/18.
Bradbury, Arthur Ernest, b. Willenhall, Warwicks, e. Coventry, Warwicks, 266630, Pte., d. of w., F. & F., 30/5/18.
Bradbury, John William, b. Birmingham, e. Birmingham, 26181, Pte., d. of w., F. & F., 9/11/18.

Braddock, William Edward Richard, b. St. Mary's, Birmingham, e. Birmingham, 4744, Cpl., k. in a., F. & F., 15/10/16.
Bradshaw, John Henry, b. Leamington, Warwicks e. Birmingham, 14612, Pte., k. in a., F. & F., 3/7/16.
Bradshaw, Thomas Henry, b. Ipsley, Worcs, e. Birmingham (Redditch, Worcs), 9174, L/Cpl., d. of w., F. & F., 10/6/17.
Brandon, William James, b. Oxhey, Herts, e. Watford, Herts (Oxhey), 25879, Pte., d. of w., F. & F., 23/3/18, formerly 25879, R.A.S.C.
Bratt, James, b. Coton, Nuneaton, e. Nuneaton, Warwicks (Attleborough, Nuneaton), 14316, Pte., k. in a., F. & F., 30/7/16.
Breeze, Arthur, b. Warrington, Lancs, e. Warrington, 22057, Pte., k. in a., F. & F., 28/7/17, formerly 1430, S. Lancs Regt.
Breeze, Guy Porter, b. Alcester, Warwicks, e. Birmingham (Alcester), 8409, Sgt., d. of w., F. & F., 20/9/17.
Brenton, Arthur James, b. Enniscanen, Cornwall, e. St. Austell, Cornwall (Enniscanen), 35483, Pte., k. in a., F. & F., 10/4/18, formerly 202777, D.C.L.I.
Brett, Leslie James, b. Birmingham, e. Birmingham (Selly Park, Birmingham), 10946, Cpl., k. in a., F. & F., 30/7/16.
Brickell, Victor Robert, e. Shaftesbury, Dorset (Butts Knapp, Dorset), 28387, Pte., d., F. & F., 27/3/17.
Bright, Leonard, b. Bilston, Staffs, e. Wolverhampton, Staffs (Bilston), 57485, Pte., d. of w., F. & F., 21/11/18.
Bristoll, James, b. Birmingham, e. Birmingham (Aston, Birmingham), 16351, Pte., k. in a., F. & F., 25/7/17.
Bristow, Frederick John, b. Calstone, Wilts, e. Chippenham, Wilts (Calne, Wilts), 43350, Pte., k. in a., F. & F., 4/9/18, formerly 2681, Hants Regt.
Brogden, John, b. Stockingford, Warwicks, e. Nuneaton, Warwicks, 17913, Cpl., d. of w., F. & F., 26/6/18.
Bromwich, Benjamin, e. Birmingham (Hockley, Birmingham), 28647, Pte., k. in a., F. & F., 18/10/18.
Brooks, Clifford, b. Halifax, Yorks, e. Birmingham, 9998, Pte., k. in a., F. & F., 18/11/16.
Brough, Bernard Harry Fairfax, b. Sparkbrook, Birmingham, e. Birmingham (Sparkbrook), 12974, Pte., k. in a., F. & F., 3/7/16.
Brown, Henry Robert, b. Bermondsey, Surrey, e. East Ham, Essex, 32585, Pte., d., F. & F., 27/9/18, formerly AS/15262, R.A.S.C.
Brown, John William, b. Priors Marston, Warwicks, e. Rugby, Warwicks (Old Bilton, Rugby), 18075, Pte., d., F. & F., 13/7/18.
Bryant, William, b. Birmingham, e. Warwick (Birmingham), 18013, Pte., k. in a., F. & F., 20/10/18.
Buckingham, Albert Edward, b. Hampstead, London, e. Coventry, Warwicks (Kenilworth, Warwicks), 42677, Pte., k. in a., F. & F., 25/9/18.
Buckler, Frederick Hubbard, b. Nuneaton, Warwicks, e. Nuneaton, 10662, Pte., d. of w., F. & F., 8/8/16.
Bullivant, Christopher, b. Birmingham, e. Birmingham (Greet, Birmingham), 5235, Pte., k. in a., F. & F., 6/11/15.
Burden, Jonah, b. Pokesdown, Hants, e. Bournemouth, Hants (Pokesdown), 28764, Pte., k. in a., F. & F., 8/11/18, formerly S/4/094538, R.A.S.C.
Burgess, Charles Henry, b. Liverpool, e. Birmingham (Ladywood, Birmingham), 8450, Pte., d. of w., F. & F., 22/3/16.
Burrell, Albert Edward, b. Thaxted, Essex, e. Greensted Hall, Essex (Ongar, Essex), 32889, Pte., k. in a., F. & F., 20/9/18, formerly 5362, Hussars.
Bursnall, Frederick William, b. Birmingham, e. Birmingham (Small Heath, Birmingham), 58580, Pte., k. in a., F. & F., 7/11/18.
Burton, Charles Silvester, b. Minworth, Warwicks, e. Warwick (Coventry, Warwicks), 28657, Pte., k. in a., F. & F., 23/3/18.
Burton, John, b. Hayden, Cambs, e. Melbourne, Cambs. 28706, Pte., d., F. & F., 23/10/16, formerly S/4/158768, R.A.S.C.
Burton, Sidney Walter, b. Birmingham, e. Warwick (Small Heath, Birmingham), 37822, Pte., k. in a., F & F., 30/5/18.
Burton, Walter, b. Aldridge, Staffs, e. Birmingham (Saltley, Birmingham), 8422, Pte., k. in a., F. & F., 30/7/16.
Burton, William, b. Arnold, Notts, e. Arnold, 27488, Pte., k. in a., F. & F., 15/6/17, formerly 34974, Notts & Derby Regt.
Butler, Arthur Richard Charles, b. Poplar, London, e. Rotherhithe, Kent (London), 34817, Pte., d. of w., F. & F., 8/11/18.
Butler, Charles William, b. Aston, Birmingham, e. Birmingham, 7260, Pte., k. in a., F. & F., 18/11/16.
Butler, Frederick, b. Birmingham, e. Birmingham, 17746, Pte., d., F. & F., 21/11/18.
Butler, Frederick Henry, b. St. Thomas, Birmingham, e. Birmingham, 4161, Pte., k. in a., F. & F., 3/7/16.
Butler, Harold, b. Edgbaston, Birmingham, e. Moseley, Birmingham (Balsall Heath, Birmingham), 1206, Cpl., k. in a., F. & F., 21/10/18.
Butler, Harold George, b. Aston Manor, Birmingham, e. Birmingham, 9172, Sgt., k. in a., F. & F., 18/11/16
Butt, William John, b. Walsall, Staffs, e. Birmingham, 4704, Pte., k. in a., F. & F., 3/7/16.
Buttress, Henry Albert William, b. Portsmouth, Hants, e. Portsmouth, 43316, Pte., k. in a., F. & F., 16/4/18, formerly 2594, Hants Regt.
Buxton, John, b. Belper, Derby, e. Coventry, Warwicks, 17773, Pte., k. in a., F. & F., 10/4/18.
Carter, Arthur, b. Sutton Coldfield, Warwicks, e. Sutton Coldfield, 21024, Pte., k. in a., F. & F., 20/9/17.
Casey, Tom, b. St. Ann's, Cork, e. Cork, 30410, L/Cpl., k. in a., F. & F., 18/11/16, formerly 4/7598, R.M. Fus.
Cashmore, Arthur, b. Budbrooke, Warwick, e. Rugby, Warwicks, 9844, Pte., d. of w., F. & F., 3/7/16.
Caswell, Jack Reading, b. St. Peter's Wolverhampton, Staffs, e. Birmingham (Wolverhampton), 55, Cpl., d. of w., F. & F., 15/5/18.
Caudle, Frank, b. Worksop, Notts, e. Worksop, 27513, Pte., d. of w., F. & F., 5/11/16, formerly 3817, Notts & Derby Regt.
Chambers, Herbert Victor, b. Preston Baggott, Warwicks, e. Warwick (Hall Green, Birmingham), 4751, Pte., d. of w., F. & F., 4/9/18.
Chambers, Percy Arthur, e. Nottingham, 27321, Pte., k. in a., F. & F., 18/11/16, formerly 3645, Notts & Derby Regt.
Chapman, Edward, b. Leamington, Warwicks, e. Warwick, 9950, Pte., k. in a., F. & F., 30/7/16.
Chapman, Joseph, b. Bolehall, Warwicks, e. Tamworth, Warwicks (Bolehall), 9432, Pte., d. of w., F. & F., 7/11/18.
Chapman, Thomas Henry, b. Leamington, Warwicks, e. Birmingham, 4587, Sgt., k. in a., F. & F., 21/5/17.
Chappell, Harry, b. Hucknall, Notts, e. Hucknall (Radford, Notts), 27501, Pte., d., F. & F., 29/10/16, formerly 4107, Notts & Derby Regt.
Chatman, Frank Henry, b. Birmingham, e. Birmingham, 22407, Pte., k. in a., F. & F., 8/6/17.
Cheshire, John, e. Kimberley, Notts (Bulwell, Notts), 27516, Pte., k. in a., F. & F., 16/4/18, formerly 3869, Notts & Derby Regt.
Child, Hubert Charles, b. Andover, Hants, e. Tidworth, Hants (Andover), 25725, Pte., k. in a., F. & F., 23/3/18, formerly 7643, R.A.O.C.
Childs, John, b. New Radford, Notts, e. Nottingham, 27315, Drummer, k. in a., F. & F., 19/4/18, formerly 3040, Notts & Derby Regt.
Childs, William, b. Eynesbury, St. Neots, Hunts, e. St. Neots, 203370, Pte., k. in a., F. & F., 5/3/18, formerly 342, Hunts Cyclist Battn.
Clapp, James, b. Nuneaton, Warwicks, e. Nuneaton (Coventry, Warwicks), 4443, Pte., k. in a., F. & F., 26/9/18.
Clark, Francis Gollar, b. Stepney, London, e. Portsmouth, 18686, Pte., d. of w., F. & F., 19/4/18, formerly 24587, Som. L.I.
Clark, Frederick, b. Burmington, Shipston-on-Stour, Worcs, e. Birmingham (Burmington), 7219, L/Cpl., k. in a., F. & F., 3/7/16.
Clarke, Charles, b. Norton, Worcs, e. Birmingham (Blackheath, Birmingham), 9970, Pte., k. in a., F. & F., 6/9/16.
Clarkson, Harry, b. Leamington, Warwicks, e. Leamington, 18994, L/Cpl., k. in a., F. & F., 7/11/18.
Clayton, Joseph, b. Huddersfield, Yorks, e. Liverpool (Liscard, Ches.), 32665, Pte., k. in a., F. & F., 19/4/18, formerly 5247, Dragoon Gds.
Cleaver, Henry Francis, b. Barston, Warwicks, e. Warwick (Knowle, Warwicks), 10447, Pte., d. of w., F. & F., 17/6/18.
Cleverley, Frank, b. St. Michaels, Coventry, Warwicks, e. Coventry, 186, Pte., k. in a., F. & F., 23/8/18, M.M.
Clifford, Edward Samuel, b. Birmingham, e. Warwick (Birmingham), 9933, Pte., k. in a., F. & F., 6/9/18.
Clifford, George, b. St. Mark's, Coventry, Warwicks, e. Warwick (Coventry), 4714, Pte., k. in a., F. & F., 27/2/16.
Clifford, Walter John, b. Islington, London, e. Holloway, London (Islington), 40296, Pte., k. in a., F. & F., 17/8/18.
Cockbill, Harry, b. St. Ebbes, Oxford, e. Oxford, 4476, C.Q.M.S., k. in a., F. & F., 10/4/18.
Cockbill, Samuel, b. Aston, Birmingham, e. Birmingham, 10487, Pte., k. in a. F. & F., 30/7/16.
Cocks, Leonard Henry, b. Battersea, London, e. Battersea, 50513, Pte., d. of w., F. & F., 6/6/18, formerly 536625, London Regt.
Coldicott, Fred, b. Ettington, Stratford-on-Avon, Warwicks, e. Birmingham (Ettington), 7204, Pte., k. in a., F. & F., 18/11/16.
Cole, Alfred Joseph, b. Chilvers Coton, Nuneaton, Warwicks, e. Birmingham (Handsworth, Birmingham), 8006, Pte., k. in a., F. & F., 30/7/16, M.M.
Collett, Walter Victor, b. Blackwell, Worcs, e. Stratford-on-Avon, Warwicks (Blackwell), 15221, Pte., k. in a., F. & F., 23/7/16.
Comer, Stanley John, b. St. Werburgh's, Bristol, e. Bristol (St. Werburgh's), 34827, Pte., k. in a., F. & F., 5/4/18.
Compton, Richard, b. Hoxton, London, e. Kingston-on-Thames, Middx. (Eastbourne, Sussex), 48262, Pte., d. of w., F. & F., 12/10/18, formerly 32040, R.A.S.C.
Congrave, John James Patrick, e. Atherstone, Warwicks (Tamworth, Warwicks), 16380, Pte., k. in a., F. & F., 23/3/18.
Cook, Alexander George, b. Pimlico, London, e. Piccadilly, London (Pimlico), 40298, Pte., d. of w., F. & F., 8/5/18.
Cook, George Henderson, b. Edinburgh, Midlothian, e. Worcester (Gt. Witley, Worcs), 28717, Pte., k. in a., F. & F., 19/4/18, M.M.
Cook, George Watson, b. Tottenham, Middx., e. Tottenham (Lower Edmonton, Middx.), 41325, Pte., k. in a., F. & F., 6/6/18, formerly 46468, Yeo. Cyclist Regt.
Cooley, Frederick, b. St. Nicholas, Birmingham, e. Birmingham (Aston, Birmingham), 7998, Pte., k. in a., F. & F., 23/11/15.
Cooper, Albert Victor, b. Hockley, Birmingham, e. Birmingham (Small Heath, Birmingham), 2138, Pte., d., F. & F., 28/7/18.
Cooper, Edward, b. St. Martin's, Birmingham, e. Birmingham, 7246, Pte., d. of w., F. & F., 3/11/16.
Cooper, Ernest Arthur, b. Yardley, Warwicks, e. Birmingham (Hay Mills, Birmingham), 1389, A/Cpl., k. in a., F. & F., 6/6/18.
Cooper, William, b. West Bromwich, Staffs, e. Tipton, Staffs (Horsley Heath, Tipton), 11449, Pte., k. in a., F. & F., 23/3/18.
Cooper, William Ernest, b. Strentham, Surrey, e. Fulham, Surrey, 23535, Pte., d. of w., F. & F., 31/5/18, formerly 188002, R.E.
Copeland, John Robert, e. Nottingham (New Lenton, Nottingham), 27322, Pte., k. in a., F. & F., 18/11/16, formerly 4760, Notts & Derby Regt.

Cornthwaite, George Henry, b. Lancaster, e. Garstang, Lancs (Lancaster), 28071, Pte., d., F. & F., 22/1/17, formerly 29640, Hrs.
Cotterill, Samuel, b. Balsall Heath, Birmingham, e. Birmingham (Small Heath, Birmingham), 17544, Pte., k. in a., F. & F., 17/6/18.
Court, Ernest James, b. Wick, St. Lawrence, Som., e. Weston-Super-Mare, Som. (Wick, St. Lawrence), 35461, Pte., k. in a., F. & F., 19/4/18, formerly 36061, Hrs.
Cowley, Henry, b. Rugby, Warwicks, e. Rugby, 307605, Pte., k. in a., F. & F., 19/10/17.
Cox, Ernest, b. Hempstead, Essex, e. Saffron Walden, Essex (Littlebury, Essex), 39800, Cpl., k. in a., F. & F., 1/6/18, formerly G/4655, R. Fus.
Cox, Thomas, b. Balsall Heath, Birmingham, e. Birmingham (Bordesley Green, Birmingham), 240213, Pte., k. in a., F. & F., 27/3/18.
Craig, William, b. Dufftown, Banffshire, e. Hawick, Roxburghshire (Dufftown), 34830, Pte., d. of w., F. & F., 25/3/18.
Crampton, Albert, b. Sutton-in-Ashfield, Notts, e. Sutton-in-Ashfield, 27514, Pte., d. of w., F. & F., 5/12/16, formerly 1927, Notts & Derby Regt.
Crew, Alfred Henry, b. Great Barr, Birmingham, e. Birmingham (Great Barr), 5482, Pte., k. in a., F. & F., 10/1/16.
Crew, Frederick, b. Netherton, Worcs, e. Dudley, Worcs (Netherton), 266914, Pte., k. in a., F. & F., 22/3/18.
Cribbin, Daniel Joseph, b. Birmingham, e. Birmingham (Erdington, Birmingham), 20990, Pte., k. in a., F. & F., 11/1/17.
Crooks, George, e. Nottingham, 27316, Pte., d. of w., F. & F., 8/6/17, formerly 2905, Notts & Derby Regt.
Curry, Walter Bertram, b. Birmingham, e. Birmingham (Sparkbrook, Birmingham), 4990, Pte., k. in a., F. & F., 3/7/16.
Daffern, Arthur, b. St. Mary's, Nuneaton, Warwicks, e. Nuneaton, Warwicks (Attleborough, Warwicks), 14897, Pte., k. in a., F. & F., 3/7/16.
Daniells, Reginald, b. Newport Pagnell, Bucks, e. Newport Pagnell, 26724, Pte., d. of w., F. & F., 26/4/18.
Danks, Eric, b. Studley, Warwicks, e. Redditch, Worcs (Studley), 22204, Pte, d. of w., F. & F., 8/5/18.
Davies, Henry William, b. Sparkbrook, Birmingham, e. Birmingham (Sparkbrook, Birmingham), 4971, Pte., k. in a., F. & F., 3/9/16.
Davies, Thomas Cecil, b. Yardley, Birmingham, e. Birmingham (Hockley Heath, Birmingham), 7207, Pte., k. in a., F. & F., 29/8/15.
Davies, William Frederick, b. St. Mary, Birmingham, e. Birmingham, 5986, L/Cpl., d. of w., F. & F., 5/7/16.
Davis, Alfred Charles, b. St. Phillip's, Birmingham, e. Birmingham (Ladywood, Birmingham), 2396, Pte., k. in a., F. & F., 3/7/16.
Davis, Frederick Stephen, b. Bristol, Glos., e. Bristol, 27774, Pte., d. of w., F. & F., 7/6/18, formerly 5176, Worcs Regt
Davis, William, b. St. Paul's, Birmingham, e. Birmingham, 7966, Pte., d. of w., F. & F., 24/7/16.
Dawes, George Arthur, b. Small Heath, Birmingham, e. Birmingham, 1927, Sgt., k. in a., F. & F., 3/7/16.
Dawson, Ephraim, b. Birmingham, e. Birmingham (Aston, Birmingham), 20992, Pte., k. in a., F. & F., 23/9/17.
Day, John Herbert Taylor, b. Fulham, London, e. Fulham, 34833, Pte., d., F. & F., 8/7/18.
Dean, David, b. St. Bartholomew's, Salford, Lancs, e. Salford (Pendleton, Lancs), 201874, Dmr., k. in a., F. & F., 20/9/17, formerly 1908, Lancs Fus.
Dewis, Sidney, b. Nuneaton, Warwicks, e. Nuneaton, 16346, Pte., d. of w., F. & F., 1/9/16.
Dimbleby, William, b. Tamworth, Warwicks, e. Tamworth (Glascote, Warwicks), 16215, Pte., d. of w., F. & F., 30/7/16.
Dixey, Joseph Edward, b. Bampton, Oxon, e. Exeter (Budleigh, Devon), 35464, Pte., k. in a., F. & F., 18/4/18, formerly 5293, Devon Regt.
Dixon, Frederick James, b. Plymouth, Devon, e. Plymouth, 34836, Pte., k. in a., F. & F., 23/3/18.
Dodson, John William, b. Ashby, Lincs, e. Gainsborough, Lincs (Retford, Notts), 27519, Pte., k. in a., F. & F., 18/11/16, formerly 4105, Notts & Derby Regt.
Donnelly, Thomas, b. St. George's, Birmingham, e. Birmingham, 8008, Pte., d. of w., F. & F., 7/8/15.
Dooley, Charles Henry, b. Nottingham, e. Nottingham, 27326, Pte., k. in a., F. & F., 18/11/16, formerly 6076, Notts & Derby Regt.
Dorrell, John, b. St. Paul's, Worcester, e. Birmingham (Hay Mills, Birmingham), 19170, Pte., k. in a., F. & F., 18/11/16.
Dowell, Sidney William, b. Bubbenhall, Warwicks, e. Coventry, Warwicks, 19233, Pte., k. in a., F. & F., 18/11/16.
Downton, Frederick Alfred, b. Winton, Hants, e. Bournemouth, Hants, 43321, Pte., k. in a., F. & F., 20/9/18, formerly 2672, Hants Yeo. (Cyc.).
Doyle, William Henry, e. Nottingham, 27332, Pte., d. of w., F. & F., 2/11/16, formerly 2431, Notts & Derby Regt.
Drew, James, b. Solihull, Warwicks, e. Coventry, Warwicks (Kenilworth, Warwicks), 16230, Pte., k. in a., F. & F., 25/3/18.
Druce, Harry Lionel, e. Oxford, 29981, Pte., k. in a., F. & F., 6/6/18, formerly 22933, Oxf. & Bucks L.I.
Dunn, Oliver, b. Coventry, Warwicks, e. Coventry, 23862, Pte., d. of w., F. & F., 16/8/18.
Durber, Thomas Richard, b. Aston, Birmingham, e. Birmingham, 42775, Pte., k. in a., F. & F., 23/10/18.
Dutton, Arthur, b. Salford Priors, Warwicks, e. Stratford-on-Avon, Warwicks (Salford Priors), 28886, Pte., d. of w., F. & F., 16/11/18.
Dyer, Harry Emanuel, b. Sevenhampton, Wilts, e. Rugby, Warwicks (Sevenhampton), 9042, Pte., d. of w., F. & F., 16/9/15.
Dykes, Albert, b. Hanley, Staffs, e. Nuneaton, Warwicks (Stockingford, Warwicks), 15063, Dmr., k. in a., F. & F., 23/3/18.
Earle, Edward Stephen, b. Stroud, Glos., e. Stroud, 268036, Pte., k. in a., F. & F., 7/6/18, formerly 30402, Glos. Regt.
Eaton, Harold, b. Birmingham, e. Birmingham, 241551, Pte., d. of w., F. & F., 14/5/18.
Eden, Herbert, b. Chesterton, Warwicks, e. Coventry, Warwicks (Chesterton), 21901, Pte., k. in a., F. & F., 10/4/18.
Edgecombe, Edwin, b. Himbleton, Worcs, e. Birmingham (Droitwich, Worcs), 4915, Sgt., d. of w., F. & F., 23/11/16.
Edgeworth, Wilfred Henry, b. Birmingham, e. Birmingham (Sparkhill, Birmingham), 15389, Pte., k. in a., F. & F., 18/11/16.
Edwards, Henry Humpherson, b. Birmingham, e. Birmingham (Acocks Green, Birmingham), 36204, Pte., d. of w., F. & F., 25/10/18.
Edwards, William Arthur, b. Bethnal Green, Middx., e. Bethnal Green, 50495, Pte., d. of w., F. & F., 1/6/18, formerly 324776, London Regt.
Elden, Percy James, b. Broome, Norfolk, e. Coventry, Warwicks, 19613, Pte., k. in a., F. & F., 20/9/18.
Elliott, Frederick William Edward, b. South Petherton, Som., e. Taunton, Som. (South Petherton), 50625, Pte., k. in a., 4/9/18.
Elliott, Harry, b. Walsall, Staffs, e. Walsall, 12071, Pte., d., F. & F., 9/11/18.
Ellis, Benjamin John, e. Bristol, Glos., 29855, Pte., k. in a., F. & F., 10/4/18, formerly 36657, Worcs Regt.
Ellis, Jeoffrey Philip, b. Mile End, Middx., e. Tottenham, London (Lower Edmonton, London), 38260, Pte., d. of w., F. & F., 31/5/18.
Ellis, Herbert, e. Bradford, Yorks, 27532, Pte., k. in a., F. & F., 18/11/16, formerly 5119, W. Yorks Regt.
Ellis, William Daniel, b. Nuneaton, Warwicks, e. Nuneaton, 16091, Pte., d. of w., F. & F., 14/5/18.
Ells, Byron Benjamin, b. Margate, Kent, e. Canterbury, Kent (Margate), 38673, Pte., k. in a., F. & F., 20/9/18.
Elphick, Leslie Strudwick, b. Forest Gate, Essex, e. Stratford, London, E. (Forest Gate), 50539, Pte., d. of w., F. & F., 8/5/18.
Embleton, Arthur Charles, b. Harrow, Middx., e. West London (North Kensington, London, W.), 50478, Pte., d. of w., F. & F., 24/10/18.
Ensor, Harold, b. Birmingham, e. Birmingham (Aston, Birmingham), 8461, Sgt., k. in a., F. & F., 3/9/16.
Esam, George, e. Newark, Notts, 27530, Pte., k. in a., F. & F., 8/5/18, formerly 3255, Notts & Derby Regt.
Evans, Albert, b. Great Barr, Staffs, e. In the Field (Birmingham), 3529, Pte., k. in a., F. & F., 30/7/16.
Evans, Albert Edward, b. Birmingham, e. Birmingham, 10588, Pte., k. in a., F. & F., 22/11/15.
Evans, Alfred Joseph, b Shoreditch, London, e. Newbury, Berks, 18783, Pte., k. in a., F. & F., 19/4/18, formerly 24242, Som. L.I.
Evans, George, b. Aston, Birmingham, e. Birmingham, 5726, Pte., d of w., F. & F., 1/3/16.
Eversden, William, b. Little Brittle, Bucks, e. Nuneaton, Warwicks (Coventry, Warwicks), 17458, Pte., d. of w., F. & F., 12/11/17.
Evison, Jim, b. Norton Woodsets, Derby, e. Newark, Notts (Tuxford, Newark), 27529, Pte., d., F. & F., 7/10/18, formerly 4035, Notts & Derby Regt.
Farmer, Albert Edward, b. Leamington Spa, Warwicks, e. Coventry, Warwicks, 16881, Pte., k. in a., F. & F., 25/6/17.
Fearn, Frank, b. Ashbourne, Derby, e. Ashton-under-Lyne, Lancs (Mossley, Lancs), 235062, Pte., k. in a., F. & F., 16/4/15, formerly 5014, Mon. Regt.
Fearn, William, e. Nottingham, 27342, Pte., k. in a., F. & F., 20/9/17, formerly 3652, Notts & Derby Regt.
Feetham, Joseph, b. Sheffield, Yorks, e. Birmingham, 14/1372, Pte., k. in a., F. & F., 6/6/18.
Felton, John Howard, b. Sutton Coldfield, Warwicks, e. Sutton Coldfield, 35505, Pte., k. in a., F. & F., 10/4/18.
Fentem, Joseph, b. Derby, e. Nuneaton, Warwicks (Hartshill, Warwicks), 10072, Pte., k. in a., F. & F., 25/3/16.
Ferguson, William, b. Newington, Edingburgh, e. Coventry, Warwicks (Longford, Warwicks), 202139, Pte., k. in a., F. & F., 19/4/18.
Fisher, William, e. Blackpool, Lancs, 268461, Pte., k. in a., F. & F., 20/9/17, formerly 3531, Liverpool Regt.
Fisher, William Robert, b. Birmingham, e. Birmingham, 241241, Pte., k. in a., F. & F., 23/3/18.
Flitton, George William, b. Flamstead, Herts, e. Bedford (Kensworth, Beds), 36172, Pte., k. in a., F. & F., 18/9/18, formerly 57251, Hussars.
Flood, Joseph, b. Nuneaton, Warwicks, e. Nuneaton (Stockingford, Warwicks), 15653, Pte., k. in a., F. & F., 18/11/16.
Ford, Charles, b. Birmingham, e. Birmingham, 22364, Pte., k in a., F. & F., 27/9/18.
Ford, Edward, b. Atherstone, Warwicks, e. Nuneaton, Warwicks (Atherstone), 15524, Pte., k. in a., F. & F., 23/7/16.
Forrest, William, b. Arnold, Notts, e. Nottingham (Arnold), 27341, Pte., k. in a., F. & F., 26/10/16, formerly 4791, Notts & Derby Regt.
Forsythe, Joseph, b. Ballycastle, Co. Antrim, e. Ballycastle, 30401, Pte., k. in a., F. & F., 18/11/16, formerly 8/24309, R. Innis. Fus.
Foster, Alfred Ralph, b. Birmingham, e. Birmingham, 14494, Pte., k. in a., F. & F., 30/7/16.
Foxall, James Ernest, b. Hanley, Staffs, e. Birmingham (Cradley Heath, Staffs), 7096, Pte., k. in a., F. & F., 3/7/16.

Francis, George, b. Ladywood, Birmingham, e. Birmingham (Ladywood), 5180, L/Cpl., k. in a., F. & F., 18/11/16.
Franklin, James, b. Meriden, Warwicks, e. Coventry, Warwicks (Meriden), 28567, Pte., k. in a., F. & F., 20/4/18.
Freeman, Ernest Robert, b. Ladywood, Birmingham, e. Birmingham (Winson Green, Birmingham), 8657, C.S.M., k. in a., F. & F., 23/10/18.
Freeman, Francis, b. Mancetter, Warwicks, e. Nuneaton, Warwicks, 15784, Pte., d. of w., F. & F., 26/10/16.
Fretter, Charles James, b. Rugby, Warwicks, e. Rugby, 18034, Pte., k. in a., F. & F., 22/3/18.
Fuguel, Walter, b. York, e. Newark, Notts (Retford, Notts), 27536, Pte., k. in a., F. & F., 20/9/17, formerly 3400, Notts & Derby Regt.
Fulcher, Thomas Henry, b. Worcester, e. Worcester, 50633, Pte., d. of w., F. & F., 3/10/18.
Gadd, George Henry, b. West Norwood, Surrey, e. Lewisham, London (Sydenham, London), 34845, Pte., k. in a., F. & F., 20/10/18.
Gardner, George, b. Shipston-on-Stour, Worcs, e. Birmingham (Shipston-on-Stour), 7300, Pte., k. in a., F. & F., 28/2/16.
Gardner, Harry, b. Banbury, Oxon., e. Coventry, Warwicks (Banbury), 17787, Pte., k. in a., F. & F., 31/5/18.
Garfield, Harold, b. Langwith, Derby, e. Mansfield, Notts (Langwith), 27543, Pte., k. in a., F. & F., 19/4/18, formerly 4057, Notts & Derby Regt.
Garraway, Frank, b. St. James, Westminster, London, e. London (West Ealing, London), 28263, L/Cpl., k. in a., F. & F., 25/9/18, formerly 27398, Hussars.
Gibbons, Francis William, b. Portsmouth, Hants, e. Portsmouth, 43287, Pte., d., F. & F., 11/10/18, formerly 18474, Hants Regt.
Gibbs, Albert Henry, b. Duddeston, Warwicks, e. Birmingham, 12014, Pte., k. in a., F. & F., 23/7/16.
Gibson, Edwin, b. Saltley, Birmingham, e. Birmingham (Saltley, Birmingham), 1998, Pte., k. in a., F. & F., 3/7/16.
Gilbert, William, e. Sutton Coldfield, Warwicks (Four Oaks, Sutton Coldfield), 28009, Pte., d. of w., F. & F., 28/3/18.
Giles, Ernest Edward, b. Bromsgrove, Worcs, e. Birmingham (Bromsgrove), 17901, Pte., k. in a., F. & F., 19/9/18.
Gilmore, Thomas, b., Birmingham, e. Birmingham (Digbeth, Birmingham), 57845, Pte., d. of w., F. & F., 9/11/18.
Glenn, John, b. Rugby, Warwicks, e. Rugby, 20054, Pte., d., F. & F., 8/12/16.
Glover, Thomas Howard, b. Knowle, Warwicks, e. Knowle, 19835, Pte., k. in a., F. & F., 18/11/16.
Goddard, Victor, b. Quinton, Stratford-on-Avon, Warwicks, e. Warwick (Dunnington, Warwicks), 7264, Pte., k. in a., F. & F., 30/7/16.
Godwin, Percival, b. Rubery Hill, Worcs, e. Birmingham (Winson Green, Birmingham), 20388, Pte., d., F. & F., 28/10/18.
Golder, Herbert, b. Wednesbury, Staffs, e. Birmingham (Wednesbury), 8466, A/C.S.M., k. in a., F. & F., 4/5/18.
Golding, Hubert James, e. Coventry, Warwicks, 19375, Pte., d. of w., F. & F., 28/7/17.
Goldstraw, Edwin Walter, b. Erdington, Birmingham, e. Birmingham (Erdington), 234, Pte., d. of w., F. & F., 21/9/17
Goodier, George James, e. Birmingham (Small Heath, Birmingham), 57818, Pte., k. in a., F. & F., 4/9/18.
Goodman, George, b. Milverton, Warwicks, e. Warwick (Leamington, Warwicks), 20516, Pte., k. in a., F. & F., 23/3/18.
Gould, Gerald, b. Bidford-on-Avon, Warwicks, e. Warwick (Bidford-on-Avon), 36145, Pte., k. in a., F. & F., 8/11/18, formerly H/57222, Queen's Own Oxford Hussars.
Gray, Sydney, b. All Saints, Birmingham, e. Birmingham (Hockley, Birmingham), 6303, Pte., k. in a., F. & F., 23/10/18.
Green, Arthur Edward, b. Kenilworth, Warwicks, e. Coventry, Warwicks (Kenilworth), 50766, Pte., k. in a., F. & F., 21/10/18.
Green, Albert Leonard, e. Birmingham (Brookfields, Birmingham), 19668, Pte., k. in a., F. & F., 25/7/17.
Green, Idris, b. Llyn Pier, Glam., e. Worksop, Notts, 27539, Pte., k. in a., F. & F., 18/11/16, formerly 2836, Notts & Derby Regt.
Green, Robert Walter, b. Balsall Heath, Birmingham, e. Birmingham, 5779, Pte., k. in a., F. & F., 23/7/16.
Green, William Jonathan, b. Handsworth, Staffs, e. Birmingham (Handsworth), 7851, Pte., k. in a., F. & F., 5/7/16.
Greenfield, James Edward, b. Netherton, Staffs, e. Nuneaton, Warwicks (Stockingford, Warwicks), 15671, Pte., k. in a., F. & F., 3/7/16.
Greenland, Wilfred Robert, b. Keynsham, Bristol, e. Bristol (Bedminster Down, Bristol), 50767, Pte., d. of w., F. & F., 5/6/18.
Gregory, Frank, b. Fishponds, Bristol, e. Bristol (Staple Hill, Bristol), 242631, Pte., d. of w., F. & F., 20/9/17, formerly 2375, Glos. Regt.
Gregson, Robert, b. Blackbburn, Lancs, e. Burnley, Lancs (Padiham, Lancs), 35527, Pte., k. in a., F. & F., 10/4/18, formerly 37252, E. Lancs. Regt.
Grew, Joseph, b. Birmingham, e. Birmingham (Bordesley, Birmingham), 36176, Pte., d. of w., F. & F., 3/9/18, formerly 57352, Hussars.
Grigg, Alfred, b. Aston, Birmingham, e. Birmingham (Hockley, Birmingham), 10624, Pte., d. of w., F. & F., 13/1/17.
Grisedale, Thomas Watson, b. Durham, e. Birmingham, 16618, Pte., k. in a., F. & F., 18/11/16.
Gubbins, George Henry, b. Wroxall, Warwicks, e. Warwick (Haseley Knob, Warwicks), 20051, Pte., d. of w., F. & F., 21/5/17.
Gulliver, Albert, b. Cubbington, Warwicks, e. Stratford-on-Avon, Warwicks (Shottery, Stratford-on-Avon), 9916, Pte., d. of w., F. & F., 25/11/16.
Gurney, George Henry, b. Wolston, Warwicks, e. Rugby, Warwicks (Church Lawford, Rugby), 9846, Pte., k. in a., F. & F., 30/7/16.
Guy, William John, b. Ilminster, Som., e. Birmingham (Ilminster), 9824, Pte., k. in a., F. & F., 6/11/15.
Haddon, William, b. Coventry, Warwicks, e. Coventry, 15027, Pte., k. in a., F. & F., 19/4/18.
Hadley, Alfred, b. Blackheath, Birmingham, e. Old Hill, Staffs (Blackheath), 2026, Pte., k. in a., F. & F., 20/9/17, formerly 148827, R.F.A.
Hall, George, b. Reading, Berks, e. Reading, 35397, Pte., k. in a., F. & F., 23/3/18, formerly 329912, Camb. Regt.
Hall, William, b. Alvecote, Warwicks, e. Nuneaton, Warwicks, 14902, Pte., d. of w., F. & F., 30/7/16.
Hall, William Ewart, b. Harborough Magna, Warwicks, e. Birmingham (Stourbridge, Worcs), 15011, Pte., k. in a., F. & F., 26/3/18.
Halley, Edward, b. St. Martin's, Birmingham, e. Birmingham, 3823, L/Cpl., k. in a., F. & F., 18/11/16.
Hamblin, Cecil William, b. Kettering, Northants, e. Nuneaton, Warwicks, 4268, Pte., d. of w., F. & F., 29/8/16.
Hancock, Claude Thomas, b. St. Columb, Cornwall, e. Bodmin, Cornwall (St. Columb Major), 35486, Pte., k. in a., F. & F., 19/4/18.
Hancox, Frank Louis, e. Southam, Warwicks (Rugby, Warwicks), 19338, Pte., d. of w., F. & F., 5/6/18.
Handley, Edward, b. Dudley, Worcs, e. Birmingham (Handsworth, Birmingham), 27984, Pte., k. in a., F. & F., 22/3/18.
Hannaford, William Henry, b. Rattery, Devon, e. Plymouth (Laira, Devon), 260365, Sgt., k. in a., F. & F., 19/4/18, formerly 1965, Devon Regt.
Hanson, Christopher, b. Aston, Birmingham, e. Birmingham, 8123, Pte., k. in a., F. & F., 23/3/18.
Hanson, Frederick, e. Birmingham (Balsall Heath, Birmingham), 23918, Pte., k. in a., F. & F., 9/6/18
Harborne, Herbert John, b. Stratford-on-Avon, Warwicks, e. Stratford-on-Avon, 19988, Pte., k. in a., F. & F., 20/9/17.
Hardings, William Frederick, b. Bermondsey, Surrey, e. London (Bermondsey), 28200, Pte., k. in a., F. & F., 26/2/17, formerly 27333, Hussars.
Hardy, John Henry, b. Sutton-in-Ashfield, Notts, e. Mansfield, Notts (Sutton-in-Ashfield), 27546, Pte. d. of w., F. & F., 1/2/17, formerly 3771, Notts and Derby Regt.
Harper, Charles Edward, e. Manchester, Lancs, 20822, Pte., k. in a., F. & F., 9/5/17, formerly 12021, A. Cycl. Corps.
Harrington, William, b. Stourbridge, Staffs, e. Birmingham (Kidderminster, Worcs), 8381, Pte., k. in a., F. & F., 1/11/16.
Harris, Edwin, b. Shrewsbury, Salop, e. Birmingham, 7212, Pte., k. in a., F. & F., 30/7/16.
Harris, George Arthur, b. Daventry, Northants, e. Warwick (Hatton, Warwick), 28029, Pte., d. of w., F. & F., 5/7/17.
Harris, Hubert Archibald, b. Sparkbrook, Birmingham, e. Birmingham (King's Norton, Worcs), 5475, Sgt., d., F. & F., 13/1/19.
Harrison, Alfred, b. Birmingham, e. Birmingham (Nechells, Birmingham), 5218, Cpl., d. of w., F. & F., 4/8/16.
Harrison, George Robson, b. Sheraton, Durham, e. West Hartlepool, Durham (Southampton, Hants), 25892, Pte., d. of w., F. & F., 14/8/18, formerly R/4/069103, R.A.S.C.
Hart, Maurice, b. Midleton, Cork, e. Cardiff, Glam., 30106, Pte., k. in a., F. & F., 26/7/17, formerly 7989, R. Munster Fus.
Harvey, Arthur, b. Shipston-on-Stour, Worcs, e. Birmingham (Shipston-on-Stour), 7221, Pte., k. in a., F. & F., 20/1/16.
Hasler, Horace, b. Birmingham, e. Birmingham (Edgbaston, Birmingham), 16135, Pte., d. of w., F. & F., 23/7/16.
Haskey, William Alfred, b. Fazeley, Staffs, e. Birmingham, 8048, Pte., d. of w., F. & F., 22/1/16.
Hawker, Leonard, e. Birmingham (Hockley, Birmingham), 201089, Pte., k. in a., F. & F., 10/4/18.
Hawkesford, Clarence Henry, b. Hartshill, Warwicks, e. Birmingham, 6320, Pte., k. in a., F. & F., 12/10/15.
Hawkins, Thomas, b. Birmingham, e. Birmingham (Smethwick, Staffs), 15365, Pte., d. of w., F. & F., 7/7/16.
Haworth, Dennis, b. Burnley, Lancs, e. Burnley, 35532, Pte., k. in a., F. & F., 10/4/18, formerly 37242, East Lancs Regt.
Hayes, Daniel, b. Birmingham, e. Birmingham, 8804, Pte., k. in a., F. & F., 18/10/18.
Haynes, George Herbert, b. Priors Hardwick, Warwicks, e. Southam, Warwicks (Priors Hardwick), 17857, Pte., k. in a., F. & F., 30/5/18.
Hazlewood, Harry, b. Herne Hill, Kent, e. Canterbury, Kent (Faversham, Kent), 35496, Pte., k. in a., F. & F., 19/4/18, formerly 13667, Dragoons.
Hazelwood, John Frederick, b. Tottenham, Middx., e. Tottenham, 50497, Pte., k. in a., F. & F., 31/5/18.
Heard, Albert Ernest, b. Exeter, Devon, e. Southampton, Hants (Exeter), 43332, L/Cpl., k. in a., F. & F., 20/9/18, formerly 2494, Hamps. Yeo. Cycl.
Heath, John, b. All Saints', Leamington, Warwicks, e. Warwick (Leamington), 4679, Sgt., k. in a., F. & F., 2/7/16.
Heffer, Stanley George, b. Waltham Cross, Herts, e. Cheshunt, Herts (Waltham Cross), 41326, Pte., d. of w., F. & F., 2/6/18, formerly 46469, Surrey Yeo.
Henderson, John James, b. Woolstone, Hants, e. Portsmouth, Hants, 43359, Pte., d. of w., F. & F., 8/6/18, formerly Hampshire Yeo. Cyc.
Hendy, Joseph Sydney, b. Cury, Cornwall, e. Helston, Cornwall (Cury), 28082, Pte., d., F. & F., 26/3/17, formerly 27512, Hussars.

Henstridge, Frederick, b. Shanklin, Isle of Wight, e. Southampton, Hants (Shanklin), 35880, Pte., d. of w., F. & F., 22/9/18, formerly 43428, Hampshire Regt.

Heron, Thomas James, b. Poplar, London, e. Poplar, 34941, Pte., d. of w., F. & F., 5/6/18.

Hewitt, Ernest John, e. Warwick, 235269, Pte., k. in a., F. & F., 6/9/18, formerly 310658, Warwick Yeo.

Hickin, Edwin, b. Gloucester, e. Birmingham, 2310, Pte., k. in a., F. & F., 29/8/15.

Higgins, Frank William, b. Aston, Birmingham, e. Birmingham (Moseley, Birmingham), 8383, Pte., k. in a., F. & F., 30/7/16.

Higgins, Thomas Frederick, b. Aston, Birmingham, e. Birmingham, 5281, Sgt., d. of w., F. & F., 18/11/16.

Higgs, Charles Arthur, b. Sutton Coldfield, Warwicks, e. Sutton Coldfield, 17050, Pte., k. in a., F. & F., 10/4/18.

Higham, Peter, b. Sunderland, Durham, e. Consett, Durham, 11906, Cpl., k. in a., F. & F., 10/4/18.

Highton, Percy, b. St. Mark's, Dukinfield, Lancs, e. Ashton-under-Lyne, Lancs (Dukinfield), 22101, Pte., k. in a., F. & F., 20/9/17, formerly 1724, Manchester Regt.

Hiley, Joseph, b. Yardley, Birmingham, e. Birmingham (Yardley), 9183, Pte., d. of w., F. & F., 31/7/16.

Hill, Alfred James, e. Birmingham (Small Heath, Birmingham), 7065, Pte., k. in a., F. & F., 30/8/15.

Hill, Arthur James, e. Birmingham, 24796, Pte., k. in a., F. & F., 7/8/17, formerly 15550, R. Berkshire Regt.

Hill, Edward, e. Huddersfield, Yorks, 27358, Pte., d. of w., F. & F., 20/11/16, formerly 6235, W.R. Regt.

Hill, Rowland William, b. Yardley, Birmingham, e. Nuneaton, Warwicks (Bedworth, Warwicks), 8693, Pte., k. in a., F. & F., 18/11/16, formerly 21355, Hussars.

Hinchcliffe, Thomas William, b. Burton-on-Trent, Staffs, e. Coventry, Warwicks, 19238, Pte., d. of w., F. & F., 1/11/16.

Hines, Thomas, b. Canning Town, Essex, e. Woolwich, Kent, 34608, Pte., k. in a., F. & F., 8/9/18, formerly 6735 Dragoons.

Hinson, Thomas George, b. St. Thomas, Birmingham, e. Birmingham, 8473, L/Cpl., k. in a., F. & F., 30/7/16.

Hinton, Alfred, b. Long Ashton, Wilts, e. Bristol, Glos., 5346, Pte., d. of w., F. & F., 23/7/16.

Hite, Albert Charles, b. Birmingham, e. Birmingham (Camp Hill, Birmingham), 6320, Cpl., k. in a., F. & F., 23/3/18.

Hocking, Joseph, b. Shipley, Notts, e. Mansfield, Notts (Newark, Notts), 27551, Pte., k. in a., F. & F., 17/4/18, formerly 4128, Notts & Derby Regt.

Hodge, Herbert, b. Rhayader, Radnor, e. Birmingham (Leighton Buzard, Beds), 6325, Pte., k. in a., F. & F., 29/8/15.

Hodgetts, Benjamin, b. Northfield, Birmingham, e. Birmingham (Selly Oak, Birmingham), 5095, L/Cpl., k. in a., F. & F., 25/3/16.

Hodgkinson, Albert, b. Old Basford, Notts, e. Nottingham (Old Basford), 27349, Pte., k. in a., F. & F., 7/8/17, formerly 3211, Notts & Derby Regt.

Hoe, Arthur, b. Madras, India, e. Birmingham (Clapton, London, N.E.), 155, L/Cpl., k. in a., F. & F., 10/6/17.

Hollamby, Frank, b. Tunbridge Wells, Kent, e. Maidstone, Kent (Tunbridge Wells), 38296, Pte., k. in a., F. & F., 10/4/18.

Hollyhead, George, b. Pedbury, Staffs, e. Birmingham, 13018, Pte., k. in a., F. & F., 21/5/17, M.M.

Holmes, John, b. Sutton-in-Ashfield, Notts, e. Sutton-in-Ashfield, 27557, Pte., d., F. & F., 25/10/18, formerly 4885, Notts & Derby Regt.

Homer, George, b. St. George's, Birmingham, e. Birmingham, 10171, Pte., d. of w., F. & F., 27/12/16.

Hood, Charles, b. London, e. Birmingham (Sparkhill, Birmingham), 15101, Pte., k. in a., F. & F., 30/7/16.

Hooper, Charles Henry, b. Birmingham, e. Birmingham (Nechells, Birmingham), 15693, L/Cpl., k. in a., F. & F., 3/7/16.

Hopcroft, Ben, e. Birmingham (Hockley, Birmingham), 260723, Pte., k. in a., F. & F., 19/1/18.

Hopper, George William, e. Whitby, Yorks (Loftus, Yorks), 27351, Pte., d. of w., F. & F., 20/9/17, formerly 3759, Yorks Regt.

Horton, Colin Charles, b. Sparkbrook, Birmingham, e. Birmingham (Sparkbrook), 5064, Pte., d. of w., F. & F., 20/9/17.

Horton, Frederick, b. Smethwick, Staffs, e. Smethwick, 5793, Sgt., k. in a., F. & F., 3/7/16.

Horton, William John, b. Birmingham, e. Coventry, Warwicks, 58250, Pte., d. of w., F. & F., 8/11/18.

Howell, Joseph Edwin, b. Sparkbrook, Birmingham, e. Birmingham (Sparkbrook), 267334, Pte., d. of w., F. & F., 11/5/18.

Howkins, Charles, b. Stretton, Warwicks, e. Coventry, Warwicks (Wolston, Warwicks), 16900, Pte., k. in a., F. & F., 18/11/16.

Hoyles, Percy, b. Pinchbeck, Lincs, e. Spalding, Lincs, 16/2032, Pte., d. of w., F. & F., 8/6/17, formerly 140642, R.F.A.

Hudson, Henry, b. Trinity, Birmingham, e. Birmingham, 7194, Pte., k. in a., F. & F., 30/7/16.

Hughes, Edward Philip, b. Redditch, Worcs, e. Birmingham (Small Heath, Birmingham), 16/905, Pte., k. in a., F. & F., 10/4/18.

Hughes, Harry, b. Wolverhampton, Staffs, e. Warwick (Nuneaton, Warwicks), 20174, Pte., k. in a., F. & F., 23/3/18.

Hughes, John, b. Birmingham, e. Birmingham, 7210, Pte., d., F. & F., 6/11/18.

Hughes, William, e. Birmingham, 202602 Pte., k. in a., F. & F., 20/9/17.

Hunt, Ernest, b. Aston Manor, Birmingham, e. Birmingham, 9186, Pte., k. in a., F. & F., 7/8/17.

Hunt, Robert Stanley, b. Collingham, Notts, e. Newark, Notts (North Collingham), 27555, Pte., k. in a., F. & F., 25/10/16, formerly 4663, Notts & Derby Regt.

Husselbee, William, b. Penkridge, Staffs, e. Atherstone, Warwick (Baddesley Ensor, Warwicks), 28033, Pte., d. of w., F. & F., 24/10/17.

Huyton, Roland Frederick, b. Leeds, Yorks, e. Nottingham, 27353, L/Cpl., d. of w., F. & F., 25/5/17, formerly 35262, Notts & Derby Regt.

Ingamells, Reuben, b. Amber Hill, Lincs, e. Goldthorpe, Lincs, 25898, Pte., k. in a., F. & F., 26/3/18, formerly R/4/068493, R.A.S.C.

Ingram, Ernest, b. Fillongley, Warwicks, e. Seaham Harbour, Durham, 15086, Pte., d. of w., F. & F., 10/7/16.

Ingram, Herbert, b. St. Mary's, Oxford, e. Birmingham (Yardley, Birmingham), 16720, Pte., k. in a., F. & F., 23/7/16.

Ingram, William, b. Walsall, Staffs, e. Birmingham, 12012, Pte., k. in a., F. & F., 19/4/18.

Ingram, William Henry, b. Saltley, Birmingham, e. Birmingham (Balsall Heath, Birmingham), 20973, Pte., k. in a., F. & F., 6/9/18.

Innes, James Stanley, b. St. Simon's, Bristol, e. Bristol, 260395, Dmr., k. in a., F. & F., 19/4/18, formerly 2158, Glos. Regt.

Isham, Henry, b. Edgcote, Oxon, e. Leamington, Warwicks (Warwick), 19987, Pte., k. in a., F. & F., 19/4/18.

Jackson, John William, b. Harrogate, Yorks, e. Bradford, Yorks, 28735, Pte., k. in a., F. & F., 16/4/18, formerly 04145, R.A.S.C.

Jackson, William, b. Coventry, Warwicks, e. Coventry, 24270, Pte., k. in a., F. & F., 19/4/18.

James, Willie, b. Norton, Herts, e. Bedford (Baldock, Herts) 38172, Pte., k. in a., F. & F., 20/9/18.

Jameson, John, e. Leeds, Yorks, 27564, Pte., k. in a., F. & F. 18/11/16, formerly 2635, W. Yorks Regt.

Jarvis, Joseph, b. Birmingham, e. Birmingham (Aston, Birmingham), 9835, Pte., d. of w., F. & F., 20/11/16.

Jenkins, Leonard, b. Coventry, Warwicks, e. Coventry, 16863, Pte., d. of w., F. & F., 6/7/16.

Jennings, Edward, b. Hetherton, Staffs, e. Nuneaton, Warwicks (Stockingford, Warwicks), 34865, Pte., k. in a., F. & F., 23/3/18.

Jeyes, Joseph, b. Saltley, Birmingham, e. Birmingham (Saltley, Birmingham), 8429, Pte., d. of w., F. & F., 3/9/16.

Johnson, Arthur Edward, b. St. Mary's, Birmingham, e. Birmingham, 10471, L/Cpl., d. of w., F. & F., 3/7/16.

Johnson, Frank, b. Birmingham, e. Birmingham (Hockley, Birmingham), 36132, Pte., k. in a., F. & F., 20/9/18.

Johnson, George Alfred, b. Smethwick, Staffs, e. Birmingham (Smethwick), 10005, Pte., k. in a., F. & F., 25/3/16.

Johnson, Robert, e. Nottingham, 27287, Sgt., d. of w., F. & F., 23/3/18, formerly 2859, Notts & Derby Regt.

Johnson, William Alfred, b. Ulverston, Lancs, e. Coventry, Warwicks, 26218, Pte., k. in a., F. & F., 18/10/18.

Johnston, Walter, b. Belfast, e. Belfast, 23345, Pte., d. of w., F. & F., 23/3/18, formerly 12939, R. Irish Rif.

Jones, Arthur Douglas, b. Haselor, Warwicks, e. Warwick (Haselor), 9770, Sgt., k. in a., F. & F., 2/11/16.

Jones, Edward, b. Haselor, Warwicks, e. Warwick (Haselor), 9771, L/Cpl., k. in a., F. & F., 3/7/16.

Jones, Ernest Henry, b. Birmingham, e. Birmingham, 8019, Cpl., k. in a., F. & F., 3/7/16

Jones, George, b. Bromford, Hereford, e. Stourbridge, Worcs (Wolverley, Worcs), 16/2033, Pte., k. in a., F. & F., 18/11/16, formerly 148829, R.F.A.

Jones, George, b. Liverpool, e. Liverpool, 12608, Pte., k. in a., F. & F., 23/7/16.

Jones, George William, b. Islington, Middx., e. Canning Town, London, 6124, Pte., k. in a., F. & F., 22/3/16.

Jones, Horace, b. Birmingham, e. Birmingham (Sutton Coldfield, Warwicks), 241452, L/Cpl., k. in a., F. & F., 26/10/17.

Jordan, William George, b. Ladywood, Birmingham, e. Birmingham (Ladywood), 10490, Pte., k. in a., F. & F., 25/3/16.

Judd, Alfred John, b. Mile End, London, e. Stepney, London Mile End), 34866, Pte., k. in a., F. & F., 23/3/18.

Keal, Frederick John, b. Buckrill, Lincs, e. Lincoln (Bourne, Lincs), 27001, Pte., k. in a., F. & F., 25/3/18, formerly 5059, Lincs Regt.

Kemp, James Everett, b. Hellingham, Norfolk, e. Bury St. Edmund's, Suffolk (Oulton Broad, Norfolk), 50499, Pte., d. of w., F. & F., 5/9/18.

Kennell, William Samuel, b. Easenhall, Warwicks, e. Coventry, Warwicks, 42516, Pte., k. in a., F. & F., 8/11/18.

Kenning, John William, b. Coventry, Warwicks, e. Warwick (Coventry), 16542, Pte., k. in a., F. & F., 1/11/16.

Kidby, George, b. Caversham, Oxon, e. Reading, Berks, 21280, Pte., d., F. & F., 31/1/18, formerly 26487, R. Berks Regt.

King, William Stephen, b. Wootton Wawen, Warwicks, e. Birmingham (Gt. Alne, Warwicks), 8656, Pte., d. of w., F. & F., 30/5/18.

Kirkbright, John, b. Smethwick, Staffs, e. Coventry, Warwicks, 11327, Pte., d. of w., F. & F., 4/8/16.

Kite, Albert James, b. Woolwich, Kent, e. Stratford, Essex (East Ham, Essex), 38688, A/Sgt., d. of w., F. & F., 31/5/18, formerly 17574, Oxf. & Bucks L.I.

Knibb, Joseph Harold, b. St. Mary's, Leamington Spa, Warwicks, e. Moseley, Birmingham (Leamington Spa), 16/1130, Pte., d. of w., F. & F., 17/12/16.

Knott, Arthur Edward, e. Leamington Spa, Warwicks, 267907, Pte., d. of w., F. & F., 9/9/17, formerly 13573, R.D.C.

Knott, George Albert, b. Dudley, Worcs, e. Dudley, 28749 Pte., k. in a., F. & F., 23/3/18.

Lacey, George John, b. Pittsburgh, U.S.A., e. Bristol (Warmley, Bristol), 24840, Pte., k. in a., F. & F., 23/3/18.

Lake, Arthur, b. Kenilworth, Warwicks, e. Warwick (Kenilworth), 888, Sgt., d. of w., F. & F., 21/10/18.

Lancaster, Joseph, b. Higher Hints, Lancs, e. Atherstone, Warwicks (Ratcliffe Culey, Warwicks), 9878, L/Cpl., k. in a., F. & F., 18/11/16.

Lailey, Frederick St. Quinton Victor, b. Barkham, Berks, e. Wokingham, Berks (Barkham), 34867, Pte., d. of w., F. & F., 6/6/18.
Lang, Thomas, b. Bury, Lancs, e. Blackburn, Lancs, 35538, Pte., k. in a., F. & F., 19/4/18, formerly 37292, E. Lancs Regt.
Lapworth, Thomas, b. St. Stephen's, Birmingham, e. Birmingham (Winson Green, Birmingham), 5376, Sgt., k. in a., F. & F., 23/3/18.
Law, Harry, b. Birmingham, e. Birmingham (Winson Green, Birmingham), 8483, Pte., d. of w., F. & F., 30/7/16.
Lawley, Benjamin, b. Rugby, Warwicks, e. Warwick (New Bilton, Rugby), 18116, Pte., k. in a., F. & F., 23/3/18.
Lawley, William John, b. Balsall Heath, Birmingham, e. Birmingham, 10491, Pte., k. in a., F. & F., 30/7/16.
Lawrence, James Thomas, e. Birmingham (Gravelly Hill, Birmingham), 20997, Pte., k. in a., F. & F., 11/1/17.
Lawrence, Thomas, b. Shepton Beauchamp, Som., e. Taunton, Som. (Shepton, Beauchamp), 27743, Pte., d. of w., F. & F., 1/6/18, formerly 5934, Glos. Regt.
Lee, Harold, b. Leamington, Warwicks, e. Rugby, Warwicks (New Cubbington, Warwicks), 9945, L/Sgt., d. of w., F. & F., 6/8/16.
Lees, James Edward, b. Shirley, Warwicks, e. Shirley, 28020, Pte., d., F. & F., 13/5/17.
Legh, Gerald, b. St. Austell, Cornwall, e. Birmingham (St. Austell), 64, Pte., k. in a., F. & F., 23/5/17.
Leigh, John, b. Strood, Kent, e. Rochester, Kent (Strood), 27372, Pte., k. in a., F. & F., 18/11/16, formerly 5962, Notts & Derby Regt.
Letting, George William, b. Harlington, Beds, e. Nottingham (Beeston, Notts), 27373, Pte., k. in a., F. & F., 18/11/16, formerly 34679, Notts & Derby Regt.
Lines, Henry, b. Napton, Warwicks, e. Rugby, Warwicks (Napton), 9938, Pte., k. in a., F. & F., 30/7/16.
Llewellyn, Frederick, b. Birmingham, e. Birmingham (Small Heath, Birmingham), 28005, Pte., k. in a., F. & F., 20/9/17.
Lloyd, Harry, b. St. Martin's, Birmingham, e. Birmingham, 267354, L/Cpl., k. in a., F. & F., 22/3/18.
Lomas, John Thomas, b. Burntwood, Staffs, e. Lichfield, Staffs (Chasetown, Staffs), 15014, L/Cpl., k. in a., F. & F., 23/7/16.
Long, Ernest Harold, b. Berkswell, Warwicks, e. Northampton (Coventry, Warwicks), 4765, A/Sgt., k. in a., F. & F., 31/5/18, formerly 13994, Northumberland Regt., D.C.M., M.M.
Lord, Thomas Arthur, b. Barwell, Leics, e. Birmingham (Barwell), 6344, Pte., d., Home, 21/1/15.
Love, Stanley Ernest, b. North Waltham, Hants, e. Bristol (North Waltham), 24838, Pte., d., F. & F., 10/4/18.
Lovegrove, William, b. Solihull, Birmingham, e. Birmingham (Solihull), 6952, Pte. d., F. & F., 25/1/16.
Lowe, William, b. St. George's, Birmingham, e. Birmingham (Ladywood, Birmingham), 5250, Pte., k. in a., F. & F., 30/7/16.
Lowndes, George, e. Newark, Notts (Worksop, Notts), 27469, L/Cpl., k. in a., F. & F., 18/11/16, formerly 3509, Notts & Derby Regt.
Luckett, Albert Edward, b. Chesterfield, Derby, e. Birmingham (Small Heath, Birmingham), 8142, Sgt., k. in a., F. & F., 25/9/18.
Luckman, Daniel George, b. Small Heath, Birmingham, e. Birmingham, 3413, Pte.. k. in a., F. & F., 23/3/18.
Lysons, William, b. Madeley, Salop, e. Birmingham (Madeley) 25455, Pte., d. of w., F. & F., 21/9/18.
Maiden, Bertram, b. Leiester, e. Birmingham (King's Heath, Birmingham), 39764, L/Cpl., d., F. & F., 5/11/18.
Makepeace, Ernest, b. Kirby, Warwicks, e. Rugby, Warwicks, 4749, L/Cpl, d., F. & F., 4/5/16.
Malaney, John, e. Ashton-under-Lyne, Lancs, 22104, Pte., d. of w., F. & F., 7/6/17, formerly 2825, Manchester Regt.
Mallett, Clement, b. Halvergate, Norfolk, e. Norwich (Halvergate), 29362, Pte., d. of w., F. & F., 26/9/18, formerly 45165, Suffolk Regt.
Mann, Henry John, b. Birmingham, e. Birmingham (Handsworth, Staffs), 9963, Sgt., d. of w., F. & F., 18/11/16.
Mann, William John, b. Bascote, Warwicks, e. Leamington, Warwicks (Lillington, Warwicks), 19984, Pte., d. of w., F. & F., 25/4/18.
Manttan, Charles James, b. Warwick, e. Warwick, 16738, Pte., k. in a., F. & F., 18/11/16.
Marlow, William Thomas, b. Wootton, Northants, e Northampton (Wootton), 27141, Pte., d., F. & F., 31/10/18, formerly 5328, Lincs Regt.
Marriott, Bertram James, e. Rugby, Warwicks (Byfield, Northants), 10601, Pte., k. in a., F. & F., 23/3/18.
Marriott, Joseph, b. Foleshill, Warwicks, e. Coventry, Warwicks (Foleshill), 16218, Pte., k. in a., F. & F., 30/7/16.
Marshall, Charles Cynric, b. Birmingham, e. Birmingham (Small Heath, Birmingham), 202946, Pte., k. in a., F. & F., 1/10/17.
Marshall, Samuel, b. Hinckley, Leics, e. Hinckley, 19163, Pte., k. in a., F. & F., 18/11/16.
Marshall, Thomas, b. Aston, Birmingham, e. Aston, 306103, Pte., k. in a., F. & F., 19/4/18.
Marston, Thomas, b. Bedworth, Warwicks, e. Nuneaton, Warwicks (Bedworth), 14336, L/Cpl., k. in a., F. & F., 1/9/16.
Martin, Thomas, b. Bedworth, Warwicks, e. Bedworth, 19254, Pte., k. in a., F. & F., 7/8/17.
Mason, Norman, b. Birmingham, e. Birmingham (King's Heath, Birmingham), 14935, Pte., k. in a., F. & F., 21/3/18.
Masters, William Albert, b. Birmingham, e. Smethwick, Staffs (Winson Green, Birmingham), 10718, Pte., k. in a., F. & F., 11/5/18.
Matthews, Jesse, b. Hadlow, Kent, e. Tonbridge, Kent (Hadlow), 27390, Pte., k. in a., F. & F., 18/11/16, formerly 5980, Notts & Derby Regt.
Mathews, John, e. Birmingham, 20999, Pte., d., F. & F., 22/1/17
Matthews, William Thomas, b. Portsmouth, Hants, e. Portsmouth, 43333, Pte., k. in a., F. & F., 30/5/18, formerly 2815, Hants Yeo. Cyc. Battn.
Maull, Tom, b. Wellesbourne, Warwicks, e. Stratford-on-Avon, Warwicks (Wellesbourne), 19392, Pte., k. in a., F. & F., 8/5/18.
Mayer, William Henry, b. Hanley, Staffs, e. Mexborough, Yorks (Swinton, Yorks), 2316, Pte., k. in a., F. & F., 3/7/16.
Maynard, Thomas Alfred, b. St. Thomas, Coventry, Warwicks, e. Coventry, 5800, Pte., k. in a., F. & F., 21/10/18.
Mayo, Frank, b. Nottingham, e. Nottingham, 27386, Pte., k. in a., F. & F., 18/11/16, formerly 34620, Notts & Derby Regt.
McCullum, Edwin Ted, b. Clifton, Bristol, e. Bristol, 5356, L/Cpl., k. in a., F. & F., 21/3/18.
McDonagh, William Hannaford, b. Nuneaton, Warwicks, e. Nuneaton, 22540, Pte., d. of w., F. & F., 9/6/18.
McDonnell, Thomas Vincent, e. Coventry, Warwicks, 19824, Pte., k. in a., F. & F., 19/4/18.
McLaughlin, John Patrick, b. Glasgow, Lanarks, e. Hilsea, Hants (Glasgow), 10/2038, Pte., d., F. & F., 24/2/17, formerly 135665, R.F.A.
McMahon, Alfred Eric, e. Liverpool (Bootle, Lancs), 22037, Pte., k. in a., 20/9/17, formerly 5445, Liverpool Regt.
Mead, Harry, b. Bristol, Glos., e. Port Talbot, Glam. (Bristol), 22077, Pte., k. in a., F. & F., 8/7/17, formerly 34906, R. Welsh Fus.
Mellor, Tom, b. Ilkeston, Derbyshire, e. Ilkeston, 27385, Pte., k. in a., F & F., 21/6/17, formerly, 34227, Notts & Derby Regt.
Mew, Edwin Herbert, b. Brixton, London, e. Lambeth, London (Kennington, London, S.E.), 50533, Pte., k. in a., F. & F., 30/5/18, formerly 536646, London Regt.
Meyrick, James Ivor, b. Foleshill, Warwicks, e. Coventry, Warwicks (Bedworth, Warwicks), 57351, Pte., d. of w., F. & F., 8/11/18.
Mills, Cecil Owen, b. Birmingham, e. Liverpool (Egremont, Ches.), 14/1736, Cpl., k. in a., F. & F., 28/2/17.
Mills, George Maxwell, b. Bromsgrove, Worcs, e. Birmingham (Halesowen, Worcs), 5390, Pte., d. of w., F. & F., 23/7/16.
Mills, Walter, b. St. Thomas, Birmingham, e. Birmingham, 6041, L/Cpl., d. of w., F. & F., 5/7/16.
Missenden, George, b. Newton, Longville, Bucks, e. Bletchley, Bucks, 35576, Pte., k. in a., F. & F., 19/4/18.
Mitchell, Arthur, b. Burnley, Lancs, e. Burnley, 35541, Pte., k. in a., F. & F., 10/4/18, formerly 37294, E. Lanc. Regt.
Mitchell, William Henry Robert, b. Redditch, Worcs, e. Redditch (Studley, Warwicks), 25161, L/Cpl., k. in a., F. & F., 20/9/18.
Molloy, Thomas William, b. Coventry, Warwicks, e. Coventry, 20902, Pte., k. in a., F. & F., 24/7/17.
Monaghan, John, b. Workington, Cumberland, e. Middlesbrough, Yorks, 4493, Pte., d. of w., F. & F., 17/4/18.
Monahan, Patrick, b. Manor Hamilton, Leitrim, Ireland, e. Paisley, Scotland, 30109, Pte., d. of w., F. & F., 11/1/17, formerly 7907, R. Muns. Fus.
Moore, Arthur, b. Benthall, Shropshire, e. Birmingham (Kidderminster, Worcs), 5300, Cpl., k. in a., F. & F., 8/6/17.
Moore, Charles Frederick, b. Dunsford, Exeter, Devon, e. Exeter (Dunsford), 35454, Pte., k. in a., F. & F., 10/4/18, formerly 21850, Devon Regt.
Moore, Herbert John, b. Ladywood, Birmingham, e. Birmingham, 8433, Pte., d. of w., F. & F., 9/2/17.
Morgan, John Albert, b. Bishop's Itchington, Warwicks, e. Warwick, 6567, Sgt., k. in a., F. & F., 30/7/16.
Morgan, John Charles, b. Coventry, Warwicks, e. Coventry (Kenilworth, Warwicks), 22464, Pte., d. of w., F. & F., 10/6/17.
Moring, Frederick, b. Kingswood, Oxon, e. Oxford (Kingswood Common, Oxon), 34777, Pte., d. of w., F. & F., 6/6/18, formerly 204451, Oxf. & Bucks L.I.
Morris, Frederick Charles, b. Birmingham, e. Birmingham (Aston, Birmingham), 14/1666, Pte., k. in a., F. & F., 7/11/18.
Morris, William, b. Isycoed, Denbigh, e. Southam, Warwicks, 20058, Pte., k. in a., F. & F., 23/3/18.
Morton, Arthur, b. Small Heath, Birmingham, e. Smethwick, Staffs (Handsworth, Birmingham), 5243, Sgt., k. in a., F. & F., 7/6/17.
Morton, Arthur, b. Iver, Middx., e. Slough, Bucks (Iver), 41676, Pte., k. in a., F. & F., 19/10/17.
Moss, William, John, b. Whichford, Warwicks, e. Stratford-on-Avon, Warwicks (Shipston-on-Stour, Worcs), 16678, Pte., k. in a., F. & F., 23/7/16.
Mulligan, William Moses, b. Birmingham, e. Birmingham, 39034, Pte., d of w., F. & F., 4/9/18.
Mumford, William, e. Birmingham (West Bromwich, Staffs), 24782, Pte., k. in a., F. & F., 23/3/18.
Murden, Lewis Arthur, b. New Basford, Notts, e. Nottingham (New Basford), 27387, Pte., k. in a., F. & F., 31/10/16, formerly 33455, Notts & Derby Regt.
Myers, William, b. Birmingham, e. Warwick (King's Heath, Birmingham), 20972, Pte., k. in a., F. & F., 22/3/18.
Myring, Albert Edward Victor, b. Bordesley, Birmingham, e. Birmingham, 5470, L/Cpl., k. in a., F. & F., 18/11/16.
Naylor, Thomas, b. Methley, Leeds, e. Leeds, 30437, Pte., d. of w., F. & F., 21/5/17, formerly 6881, Hussars.
Neale, Ernest William, b. Copt Heath, Nnowle, Warwicks, e. Warwick (Copt Heath), 202887, Pte., k. in a., F. & F., 23/3/18.
Neale, Thomas, b. Gosport, Hants, e. Birmingham, 3918, C.S.M., k. in a., F. & F., 3/7/16.

Newborn, David Victor, e. Grays, Essex (S. Ockendon, Essex), 33885, Pte., k. in a., F. & F., 4/9/18, formerly 6379, E. Kent Regt.
Nicholls, Raymond William, b. Studley, Warwicks, e. Birmingham (Studley), 8547, L/Sgt., k. in a., F. & F., 12/11/16.
Nichols, Robert, e. Birmingham, 17008, L/Sgt., k. in a., F. & F., 23/10/18.
Norris, Edward Thomas, b. Fulham, London, e. White City, London (Fulham), 50504, Pte., k. in a., F. & F., 20/9/18, formerly 494286, London Regt.
Northcott, Reginald John, b. Teignmouth, Devon, e. Bodmin, Cornwall, 35497, Pte., k. in a., F. & F., 26/4/18, formerly 34959, Res. Cav. Regt.
Novis, Frederick Davis, b. Eastbourne, Sussex, e. Chichester, Sussex (Eastbourne), 38254, Pte., d. of w., F. & F., 14/6/19.
Olver, Leslie, e. Nottingham, 27275, Cpl., d., F. & F., 14/1/17, formerly 2506, Notts & Derby Regt.
O'Neary, Francis Joseph, b. Sutton Coldfield, Warwicks, e. Birmingham, 12066, Pte., k. in a., F. & F., 3/7/16.
Osborne, Frank George, b. Farringdon, Berks, e. Winchester, Hants (Petersfield, Hants), 244187, Pte., k. in a., F. & F., 6/6/18, formerly 1633, Hants Carabiniers.
Overend, William, b. Warrington, Lancs, e. Birmingham (Nechells, Birmingham), 202944, Pte., k. in a., F. & F., 23/3/18.
Page, Harold, b. Aston-on-Trent, Derbyshire, e. Long Eaton, Derby, 27400, Pte., k. in a., F. & F., 18/11/16, formerly 34889, Notts & Derby Regt.
Paget, Arthur, b. Roxhall, Warwicks, e. Knowle, Warwicks (Hockley Heath, Birmingham), 18204, Pte., k. in a., F. & F., 21/9/17.
Palmer, Edgar James, b. Balsall Heath, Birmingham, e. Birmingham (Cape Hill, Staffs), 6394, Pte., k. in a., F. & F., 3/7/16.
Palmer, Harry, b. Birmingham, e. Birmingham (Stechley, Birmingham), 16228, Pte., k. in a., F. & F., 20/9/17.
Papworth, Frank Henry, b. Hartford, Hunts, e. Huntingdon, 307671, Pte., d. of w., F. & F., 29/10/18, formerly 459, Hunts Cyc. Battn., M.M.
Parish, William, b. Bordesley, Birmingham, e. Birmingham (Small Heath, Birmingham), 5265, Pte., k. in a., F. & F., 30/7/16.
Parker, Ambrose, b. St. Jude's, Bristol, e. Bristol, 18721, Cpl., k. in a., F. & F., 23/3/18, formerly 23420, Som. L.I.
Parker, Frederick, b. Birmingham, e. Birmingham, 16925, Pte., k. in a., F. & F., 19/6/17.
Parry, Frederick David, b. King's Norton, Birmingham, e. Birmingham (King's Norton), 666, A/Cpl., k. in a., F. & F., 31/5/18.
Partridge, Thomas, e. Birmingham, 9168, Pte., k. in a., F. & F., 30/7/16.
Pawley, Horace, b. Nottingham, e. Nottingham, 27403, Pte., k. in a., F. & F., 26/4/18, formerly 34163, Notts & Derby Regt.
Paxford, Thomas Frank, b. Whimpston, Warwicks, e. Stratford-on-Avon, Warwicks (Armscote, Warwicks), 14947, Pte d. of w., F. & F., 25/8/16.
Peacock, Fred, b. Ruddington, Notts, e. West Bridgford, Notts (Ruddington), 27401, Pte., d., F. & F., 6/2/17, formerly 34901, Notts & Derby Regt.
Pearce, Alfred, b. Nyke, Dorset, e. Dorchester, 16/2056, Pte., k. in a., F. & F., 10/11/16.
Pearce, George Henry, b. Stroud, Glos., e. Birmingham (Winson Green, Birmingham), 14378, Pte., d. of w., F. & F., 13/4/16.
Pearce, Harry Herbert, b. Poole, Dorset, e. Poole, 34889, Pte., k. in a., F. & F., 23/3/18.
Pegg, Henry, b. Nuneaton, Warwicks (Ryton-on-Dunsmore, Warwicks), 10078, Pte., d. of w., F. & F., 9/4/18.
Penn, Joseph Henry, b. Birmingham, e. Birmingham (Spring Hill, Birmingham), 37712, Pte., k. in a., F. & F., 20/10/18.
Perkins, Harry, b. Edgbaston, Birmingham, e. Birmingham (Edgbaston), 962, Pte., k. in a., F. & F., 9/7/17.
Phelps, Charles, b. Aston, Birmingham, e. Birmingham, 5774, Cpl., d. of w., F. & F., 28/7/17.
Phelps, William Arthur, b. Camberwell, London, e. Camberwell, 40399, Pte., k. in a., F. & F., 17/4/18.
Phillips, George Noel, b. Stockingford, Warwicks, e. Coventry, Warwicks (Bedworth, Warwicks), 12986, Pte., d. of w., F. & F., 24/3/18, formerly 3520, Life Gds.
Phillips, John, b. St. Nicholas, Warwick, e. Warwick, 4653, L/Sgt., d. of w., F. & F., 11/3/19, M.M.
Phillips, Sydney, b. Barnet, Harpenden, Herts, e. London (Harpenden), 20686, Pte., d. of w., F. & F., 23/5/17, formerly 12107, A. Cyc. Corps.
Philpott, Horace Leonard, b. Camberwell, Surrey, e. Camberwell (Peckham, S.E.), 40397, Pte., k. in a., F. & F., 30/5/18.
Pickering, Andrew, b. Hartshill, Warwicks, e. Nuneaton, Warwicks, 11854, L/Cpl., k. in a., F. & F., 3/7/16.
Pike, Ernest Campbell, e. London, 33897, L/Cpl., d. of w., F. & F., 8/11/18, formerly 075316, R.A.S.C.
Pinson, George Edward, b. Bloxwich, Staffs, e. Sutton Coldfield, Warwicks, 15702, Pte., k. in a., F. & F., 23/7/16.
Piper, Frank, b. Stourbridge, Worcs, e. Coventry, 268807, Pte., k. in a., F. & F., 22/9/17.
Poole, Rowland Howard, b. Birmingham, e. Birmingham (Hall Green, Birmingham), 36123, Pte., d. of w., F. & F., 17/8/18.
Porter, Albert Stanley, b. Upton Park, Essex, e. London (Upton Park), 32602, Pte., d. of w., F. & F., 27/4/18, formerly 2250, Dns.
Potter, William Henry, b. Bideford, Devon, e. Barnstaple, Devon (Bideford), 260362, Sgt., k. in a., F. & F., 20/9/18, formerly 2128, Devon Regt.
Powers, John Thomas, b. Small Heath, Birmingham, e. Birmingham, 5407, Pte., k. in a., F. & F., 7/8/17.
Pratt, Edward Joseph, b. Westwood Heath, Warwicks, e. Warwick (Foleshill, Warwicks), 2469, R.S.M., d. of w., F. & F., 20/9/17.
Pratt, George Rupert, b. Aston, Birmingham, e. Birmingham, 8778, Pte., d., F. & F., 15/7/18.
Price, Henry John, b. Southwark, Surrey, e. London, 28096, Pte., d. of w., F. & F., 8/10/17, formerly 27596, Hussars.
Price, Thomas Henry, b. Hockley, Birmingham, e. Birmingham (Greet, Birmingham), 7936, Pte., k. in a., F. & F., 3/7/16.
Price, William Thomas, b. Balsall, Warwicks, e. Nuneaton, Warwicks (Coleshill, Warwicks), 28004, Pte., k. in a., F. & F., 12/1/17.
Priest, Joseph, b. Oldbury, Worcs, e. Smethwick, Staffs (Oldbury), 7900, Pte., d. of w., F. & F., 24/3/18, M.M.
Pritchard, Alfred, b. Brierley Hill, Staffs, e. Birmingham (Ladywood, Birmingham), 2389, L/Cpl., k. in a., F. & F., 3/7/16.
Prosser, William Frank, b. Ladywood, Birmingham, e. Birmingham (Ladywood), 8390, Pte., k. in a., F. & F., 30/7/16.
Pugh, William, b. Birmingham, e. Birmingham (Hockley, Birmingham), 17885, L/Cpl., k. in a., F. & F., 5/7/17.
Purvey, George Edwin, b. Bordesley, Birmingham, e. Birmingham (Small Heath, Birmingham), 8391, Pte., k. in a., F. & F., 1/1/18.
Quill, Michael, b. Langhill, Limerick, e. Limerick (Langhill), 30117, Pte., k. in a., F. & F., 25/7/17, formerly 3001, R. Munster Fus.
Rachael, Ernest Edward, b. Icombe, Glos., e. Birmingham (Ladywood, Birmingham), 14441, L/Cpl., d. of w., F. & F., 3/7/16.
Radnor, Thomas Harold, b. Dudley, Worcs, e. Birmingham (Moseley, Birmingham), 37838, Pte., k. in a., F. & F., 30/5/18.
Randall, Charles, b. Coventry, Warwicks, e. Coventry, 16333, Pte., d. of w., F. & F., 6/4/18.
Randle, George, b. Nuneaton, Warwicks, e. Warwick (Nuneaton), 16582, Pte., d. of w., F. & F., 27/2/17.
Randle, Oliver, b. Shipston-on-Stour, Worcs, e. Coventry, Warwicks (Coleshill, Warwicks), 16635, L/Cpl., k. in a., F. & F., 18/11/14.
Rea, William, b. Bromsgrove, Worcs, e. Birmingham (Hockley, Birmingham), 15139, Pte., k. in a., F. & F., 3/7/16.
Read, Joseph, e. Wigan, Lancs, 28345, Pte., k. in a., F. & F., 23/3/18, formerly 27203, Res. Cav. Regt.
Reason, Charles Joseph, b. Tysoe, Warwicks, e. Coventry, Warwicks, 5451, L/Cpl., d. of w., F. & F., 30/7/16.
Reed, John Leslie Burnett, b. Pill, Bristol, Glos., e. Bristol (Pill), 5353, Pte., k. in a., F. & F., 18/11/16.
Redding, Thomas, b. Birmingham, e. Birmingham, 201516, Pte., d. of w., F. & F., 7/6/17.
Reeves, John, b. St. Luke, Cannock, Staffs, e. Birmingham (Saltley, Birmingham), 4999, Pte., k. in a., F & F., 22/9/17.
Rew, Thomas, b. Cardiff, Glam., e. Winchester, Hants (Upper Bonchurch, I. of W.), 43335, Pte., k. in a., F. & F., 31/5/18, formerly 2710, Hants Yeo. Cyc.
Richmond, Fred, b. Blackburn, Lancs, e. Blackburn, 35549, Pte., k. in a., F. & F., 19/4/18, formerly 37200, E. Lancs Regt.
Ricketts, William Hampton, b. Birmingham, e. Warwick (Birmingham), 10670, Pte., k. in a., F. & F., 23/7/16.
Ridlinton, Lawrence Percy, e. Birmingham (Coventry, Warwicks), 202857, Pte., k. in a., F. & F., 10/6/17
Riley, Frank, b. Burnley, Lancs, e. Burnley, 35552, Pte., d. of w., F. & F., 14/6/18, formerly 37227, E. Lancs Regt.
Riley, James, b. Birmingham, e. Birmingham, 8906, Pte., k. in a., F. & F., 10/5/17.
Roach, William, b. Deptford, Kent, e. Deptford (New Cross, London, S.E.), 40400, Pte., k. in a., F. & F., 1/6/18.
Roberts, Herbert, b. Coventry, Warwicks, e. Coventry, 14619, Pte., k. in a., F. & F., 20/9/17.
Roberts, Harold Martin, b. Semley, Wilts, e. Fulham, London, 40405, Pte., k. in a., F. & F., 25/9/18.
Robins, Edgar Ernest, b. Pilton, Devonshire, e. Birmingham, 19770, Pte., d. of w., F. & F., 11/5/18.
Robinson, George, b. Radford, Notts, e. Nottingham (Radford), 27406, Pte., k. in a., F. & F., 23/3/18, formerly 1837, Notts & Derby Regt.
Robinson, Thomas George, b. Knowle, Warwicks, e. Birmingham (Knowle), 6958, L/Cpl., d. of w., F. & F., 9/2/18.
Roden, Ernest Clement, b. Nuneaton, Warwicks, e. Nuneaton, 17434, A/Cpl., k. in a., F. & F., 7/11/18.
Rooker, Albert, b. Birmingham, e. Birmingham, 27990, Pte., k. in a., F. & F., 18/4/18.
Rose, George Charles, e. Aston, Birmingham, 306198, Pte., k. in a., F. & F., 12/4/18.
Rose, James, b. Leith, Edinburgh, e. Edinburgh (Leith), 32596, L/Cpl., k. in a., F. & F., 20/9/18, formerly 5025, Scot. Horse.
Rose, Sidney Arnold, b. Atherstone, Warwicks, e. Atherstone, 16362, L/Cpl., k. in a., F. & F., 27/2/17.
Rose, William John Henry, b. Maidenhead, Berks, e. Reading, Berks (Maidenhead), 35488, Pte., d., F. & F., 13/11/18.
Round, Jacob, b. Netherton, Staffs, e. Birmingham (Dudley, Worcs), 9989, Pte., d. of w., F. & F., 20/4/18.
Rouse, Frederick, b. Newbold-on-Stour, Warwicks, e. Warwicks (Stratford-on-Avon, Warwicks), 2641, Pte., d. of w., F. & F., 24/10/15.
Rouse, Norman Edward, e. Stratford-on-Avon, Warwicks (Great Wolford, Warwicks), 9246, Pte., d. of w., F. & F., 26/9/18.
Rowberry, William, b. Stone, Kidderminster, Worcs, e. Birmingham (Kidderminster), 7906, A/L/Sgt., k. in a., F. & F., 18/11/16, M.M.
Rowels, John, b. Burford, Oxon, e. Devizes, Wilts (Burford), 28611, Pte., d., F. & F., 19/4/18.

Rowland, Sydney Leslie, b. Cwmbran, Mon., e. Newport, Mon. (Cwmbran), 39769, Pte., k. in a., F. & F., 19/4/18, formerly S.4/157479, R.A.S.C.
Rowley, Harry, b. Copston Magna, Warwicks, e. Nuneaton, Warwicks, 17120, Pte., d. of w., F. & F., 1/8/16.
Rumsey, Leonard, b. West Ham, London, e. Stratford, London (Leytonstone, London, E.), 40403, Pte., k. in a., F. & F., 25/9/18.
Russell, Alfred Charles, b. Wednesbury, Staffs, e. Coventry, Warwicks, 16337, Pte., k. in a., F. & F., 3/7/16.
Russell, Charles, b. Ogley Hay, Brownhills, Staffs, e. Birmingham (Brownhills), 5240, A/Sgt., k. in a., F. & F., 30/5/18.
Rutherford, Harry, e. Birmingham, 240760, Pte., k. in a., F. & F., 10/6/17.
Sabin, Edward Herbert, b. Long Itchington, Warwicks, e. Rugby, Warwicks (Long Itchington), 34900, Pte., k. in a., F. & F., 19/10/18.
Sadler, Thomas, e. Stratford-on-Avon, Warwicks (Willersley, near Broadway, Worcs), 10042, Pte., k. in a., F. & F., 30/7/16.
Sanders, George, b. St. Thomas, Birmingham, e. Birmingham, 8494, Pte., d. of w., F. & F., 4/7/16.
Sanford, George, b. Birmingham, e. Birmingham, 8537, Pte., k. in a., F. & F., 23/10/15.
Sargeant, Tom, b. Lapley, Staffs, e. West Bromwich, Staffs (Tipton, Staffs), 7312, Sgt., k. in a., F. & F., 30/7/16.
Saunders, George Henry, b. Grusline, Carnarvon, e. Warwick (Grusline), 1456, Pte., k. in a., F. & F., 20/9/17.
Savage, Frederick, b. Bulwell, Notts, e. Newark, Notts (Mansfield-Woodhouse, Notts), 27468, L/Cpl., d. of w., F. & F., 20/11/16, formerly 3727, Notts & Derby Regt.
Savage, William, b. Birmingham, e. Aston, Birmingham, 306241, Pte., d. of w., F. & F., 24/10/18.
Sawers, George, b. Edinburgh, e. Bristol, Glos., 22454, Pte., k. in a., F. & F., 21/5/17, formerly 29259, Gloucester Regt.
Scandrett, George, e. Stratford-on-Avon, Warwicks (Moreton Morrell, Warwicks), 9955, Dmr., d. of w., F. & F., 20/5/18.
Scantlebury, Alfred, b. Clerkenwell, London, e. Stratford, London, E. (Walthamstow, London, E.), 40424, Pte., k. in a., F. & F., 30/5/18.
Scott, Harry Walter, b. Birmingham, e. Birmingham, 202651, Pte., d. of w., F. & F., 6/4/18.
Scott, Joseph William, e. Exeter, Devon, 27894, Pte., d., F. & F., 8/7/18.
Scott, Samuel, b. Aston, Birmingham, e. Birmingham (Aston), 8042, Pte., k. in a., F. & F., 18/11/16.
Scull, John, b. St. George's, Bristol, e. Bristol (Hanham, Bristol), 28104, L/Cpl., k. in a., F. & F., 24/7/17, formerly 27747, Res. Cavalry Regt.
Searle, John Stanley, b. Wellington, Som., e. Bristol (Cotham, Bristol), 39775, Pte., k. in a., F. & F., 19/4/18.
Sears, Ernest, b. West Wycombe, Bucks, e. Oxford (West Wycombe), 241668, Pte., k. in a., F. & F., 23/3/18, M.M.
Seeney, William George, b. Thurlaston, Warwicks, e. Rugby, Warwicks (Bourton, Warwicks), 8399, Pte., k. in a., F. & F., 3/7/16.
Sharman, Edward John, b. Kenilworth, Warwicks, e. Leamington, Warwicks, 266184, Pte., k. in a., F. & F., 20/9/17.
Sharman, Thomas Henry, b. Old Humberstone, Leics, e. Coventry, Warwicks (Old Humberstone), 21673, Pte., k. in a., F. & F., 5/4/18.
Shaw, James, b. Rochdale, Lancs, e. Rochdale, 28419, Pte., k. in a., F. & F., 23/9/18, formerly 8650, Lancs Fus.
Sheasby, John, b. Harbury, Warwicks, e. Rugby, Warwicks (Bishops Itchington, Warwicks), 7725, Pte., k. in a., F. & F., 18/11/16.
Shelley, George, b. Oxford, e. Birmingham (Witton, Birmingham), 27093, Pte., d. of w., F. & F., 19/4/18.
Sheppard, Frederick, b. Enford, Wilts, e. Newbury, Berks (Enford), 7095, Pte., k. in a., F. & F., 22/3/18.
Shilvock, Rowland, b. Leamington, Warwicks, e. Leamington, 16056, Pte., k. in a., F. & F., 30/5/18, M.M.
Shirley, Percy John, b. Meriden, Warwicks, e. Coventry, Warwicks (Stonebridge, Warwicks), 10481, Cpl., k. in a., F. & F., 20/9/17.
Shuker, Herbert, b. Birmingham, e. Birmingham (Balsall Heath, Birmingham), 240840, Pte., d. of w., F. & F., 13/6/17.
Simkins, William, b. St. Stephen's, Birmingham, e. Aston, Birmingham (Saltley, Birmingham), 4701, L/Cpl., k. in a., F. & F., 30/7/16.
Simmonds, Aubrey Henry, b. Exhall, Coventry, Warwicks, e. Leamington, Warwicks (Exhall), 39403, Pte., k. in a., F. & F., 22/10/18.
Simmons, Albert Edward, b. Clerkenwell, London, e. London (Holloway, London), 22490, Pte., d. of w., F. & F., 31/3/18, formerly 9965, A. Cyclist Corps.
Simpson, James, b. Aston-on-Trent, Derby, e. Atherstone (Aston-on-Trent), 4756, L/Cpl., k. in a., F. & F., 6/8/17.
Slaughter, Robert George, b. Englefield Green, Egham, Surrey, e. Windsor, Berks, 7050, Pte., k. in a., F. & F., 3/7/16.
Smallwood, John, b. St. George's, Birmingham, e. Birmingham, 8041, Pte., k. in a., F. & F., 20/9/18.
Smith, Albert, b. Coventry, Warwicks, e. Coventry, 22516, Pte., k. in a., F. & F., 26/4/18.
Smith, Ernest Alfred, b. Leigh Sinton, Worcs, e. Worcester (Malvern, Worcs), 26901, Pte., k. in a., F. & F., 21/9/18.
Smith, Frank, b. Birmingham, e. Birmingham (Ladywood, Birmingham), 18460, Pte., d. of w., F. & F., 11/6/18, formerly 24222, Som. L.I.
Smith, Fred, b. Old Sawley, Derby, e. Long Eaton, Derby (Sawley), 27416, Pte., k. in a., F. & F., 31/10/16, formerly 34904, Notts & Derby Regt.
Smith, George, e. Bristol, Glos., 7063, Pte., d. of w., F. & F., 12/11/15
Smith, George Henry, e. Birmingham (Eggington, Staffs), 6775, L/Cpl., k. in a., F. & F., 25/12/15.
Smith, Henry, b. Hackney, Middx., e. Hackney (Homerton, N.E.), 25900, Pte., d. of w., F. & F., 31/3/18.
Smith, Jabez, b. Bilston, Staffs, e. Birmingham, 14917, Pte., k. in a., F. & F., 21/10/16.
Smith, John, b. Sneinton, Notts, e. Nottingham, 27423, Pte. k. in a., F. & F., 19/6/17, formerly 3148, Notts & Derby Regt.
Smith, John Corbett, b. Bidford-on-Avon, Warwicks, e. Stratford-on-Avon, Warwicks (Bidford-on-Avon), 10098, Pte., d. of w., F. & F., 10/10/15.
Smith, Joseph Edward, b. Higham-on-the-Hill, Leics, e. Nuneaton, Warwicks, 7701, Cpl., k. in a., F. & F., 8/11/18.
Smith, Joseph Percy, b. Halesowen, Worcs, e. Birmingham (Halesowen), 15303, Pte., k. in a., F. & F., 23/3/18.
Smith, James Thomas, b. Coventry, Warwicks, e. Coventry, 58432, Pte., k. in a., F. & F., 7/11/18.
Smith, Percy Arthur, b. Hillfields, Coventry, e. Coventry, 4060, Pte., d. of w., F. & F., 26/2/16.
Smith, Roland, b. Saltley, Birmingham, e. Birmingham, 11299, Pte., k. in a., F. & F., 3/7/16.
Smith, William, b. Meriden, Warwicks, e. Coleshill, Warwicks (Meriden), 15432, Pte., k. in a., F. & F., 3/7/16.
Smith, William, b. St. Columbus, Leeds, Yorks, e. Leeds, 27415, Pte., k. in a., F. & F., 18/11/16, formerly 1951, W. Yorks Regt.
Smith, William Alfred, e. Birmingham (Ladywood, Birmingham), 14/1622, L/Cpl., d. of w., F. & F., 24/3/18.
Smith, William Enos, b. Solihull, Warwicks, e. Birmingham (Solihull), 7242, Cpl., k. in a., F. & F., 1/9/15.
Smith, William George, b. Colchester, Essex, e. Colchester, 235032, Pte., d. of w., F. & F., 18/4/18, formerly 10344, Hants Regt.
Solan, Michael, b. Keltymigh, Co. Mayo, e. Warwick (Co. Mayo), 2302, Pte., k. in a., F. & F., 23/3/18.
Soper, Edward William, b. Loddeswell, Devon, e. Bristol, Glos. (Newton Abbot, Devon), 28108, Pte., k. in a., F. & F., 20/10/18, formerly 27427, Res. Cav. Regt.
Sowden, Ernest Albert, b. Thelbridge, Devon, e. Tiverton, Devon (Mill Barton, Devon), 35441, Pte., k. in a., F. & F., 19/4/18, formerly 20964, Devon Regt.
Sparks, George Henry, b. Birmingham, e. Birmingham, 15218, Pte., k. in a., F. & F., 23/7/16.
Sparkes, William Henry, b. Sheffield, Yorks, e. Coventry, Warwicks, 24280, Cpl, k. in a., F. & F., 23/3/18.
Sparrow, Arthur, e. Birmingham, 200761, Pte., d. of w., F. & F., 9/5/18.
Spencer, Reginald George Percy, b. Wilnecote, Warwicks, e. Atherstone, Warwicks (Wilnecote), 19339, Cpl., k. in a., F. & F., 20/9/18.
Spiers, Thomas John, b. Dudley, Worcs, e. Stratford-on-Avon, Warwicks (Evesham, Worcs), 23991, Pte, k. in a., F. & F., 26/8/17.
Stafford, Alfred Joseph, b. Whitley, Warwicks, e. Coventry, Warwicks, 9843, Pte, k. in a., F. & F., 30/7/16.
Stanley, Frederick, e. Dudley, Worcs, 57816, Pte., k. in a., F. & F., 19/10/18.
Stanley, Harry, b. Anstey, Warwicks, e. Coventry, Warwicks, 1702, Pte., k. in a., F. & F., 23/3/18.
Stanley, Richard, b. Henley-on-Thames, Oxon, e. Faversham, Kent (Boughton, Kent), 22471, Pte., k. in a., F. & F., 27/2/17.
Stapley, Henry, b. Crewe, Ches., e. Birmingham (Crewe), 5000, Pte., k. in a., F. & F., 3/7/16.
Steele, Albert, b. Alcester, Warwicks, e. Stratford-on-Avon, Warwicks (Alcester), 20855, A/Cpl., k. in a., F. & F., 7/11/18.
Stenson, William, b. Peterborough, Northants, e. Peterborough, 268810, Pte., k. in a., F. & F., 25/3/18.
Stevenson, John, b. Beeston, Notts, e. Nottingham (Beeston), 27424, Pte., k. in a., F. & F., 31/10/16, formerly 3143, Notts & Derby Regt.
Stone, James, b. Islington, Middx., e. Whitehall, London, 40420, Pte., k. in a., F. & F., 1/6/18.
Stonehouse Thomas, b. Polesworth, Warwicks, e. Atherstone, Warwicks (Dordon, Warwicks), 20875, Pte., k. in a., F. & F., 20/9/17.
Stringer, Leonard Frank, b. Hillfields, Coventry, e. Coventry, Warwicks, 307496, L/Cpl., k. in a., F. & F., 21/3/18.
Sturch, Edward, b. Shipston-on-Stour, Worcs, e. Birmingham (Shipston-on-Stour), 7299, Pte., d. of w., F. & F., 26/3/16.
Sturge, Edwin, b. Bethnal Green, London, e. Stratford, Essex (Bethnal Green), 40413, Pte., d. of w., F. & F., 7/5/18.
Styler, Charles, b. Redditch, Worcs, e. Redditch, 15348, Pte., k. in a., F. & F., 26/10/16.
Surch, Thomas, b. Chipping Norton, Oxon, e. Birmingham, 21048, Pte., k. in a., F. & F., 7/6/17.
Surman, Ernest Albert, b. Alvechurch, Worcs, e. Nuneaton, Warwicks (Stockingford, Warwicks), 2408, Cpl., d., F. & F., 21/7/16.
Summersby, Albert John, b. Rotherhithe, Kent, e. Camberwell, London, 40416, Pte., k. in a., F. & F., 16/4/18.
Swann, William Joseph Richard, b. Birmingham, e. Warwick (Birmingham), 1313, A/C.S.M., d. of w., F. & F., 14/6/17.
Swift, Isaac, b. St. Mark's, Birmingham, e. Birmingham (Ladywood, Birmingham), 6409, L/Cpl., k. in a., F. & F., 23/7/16.
Tabberner, Sidney Victor, b. Birmingham, e. Birmingham (Camp Hill, Birmingham), 21321, Pte., d., F. & F., 27/11/18, formerly 26759, R. Berks Regt.
Tandy, William, b. St. Paul's, Warwick, e. Warwick, 4089, L/Sgt., k. in a., F. & F., 23/7/16.
Tansley, Alfred James Richard, b. Camberwell, Surrey, e. Lambeth, London (Camberwell), 40420, Pte., k. in a., F. & F., 5/6/18.

Tarbet, John George, b. Sunderland, Durham, e. Rugby, Warwicks) (Wallsend, Northumberland), 20383, Pte., k. in a., F. & F., 1/6/18.
Taylor, Benjamin, e. Birmingham, 202663, Pte., k. in a., F. & F., 31/7/17.
Taylor, Frank Albert Victor, b. Birmingham, e. Birmingham (Erdington, Birmingham), 19541, Pte., k. in a., F. & F., 27/2/17.
Taylor, Harry, b. Kingswood, Birmingham, e. Birmingham (Hockley Heath, Birmingham), 7792, Sgt., k. in a., F. & F., 20/9/17, M.M.
Taylor, Hollis, b. Hinchley Heath, Warwicks, e. Atherstone, Warwicks (Birchley Heath), 10655, Pte., k. in a., F. & F., 30/7/16.
Taylor, Henry Joseph, b. Digbeth, Birmingham, e. Attercliffe, Yorks (Sheffield, Yorks), 10536, Pte., d., F. & F., 5/11/18.
Taylor, John, b. St. John's, Birmingham, e. Birmingham (Ladywood, Birmingham), 2337, Pte., k. in a., F. & F., 2/7/16.
Taylor, Joseph, b. Dudley, Worcs, e. Smethwick, Staffs, 7837, Pte., k. in a., F. & F., 30/7/16.
Taylor, Thomas, b. Peckham, London, e. Camberwell, London (Peckham), 40427, Pte., d. of w., F. & F., 8/5/18.
Taylor, Thomas Edwin, b. Brailsford, Derby, e. Birmingham (Ettington, Warwicks), 7293, Pte., d., F. & F., 12/11/18.
Terry, Benjamin, b. Aston, Birmingham, e. Birmingham, 5447, Pte., k. in a., F. & F., 23/7/16.
Thewlis, Clarence, b. St. Patrick's, Leeds, Yorks, e. Leeds, 27431, Pte., k. in a., F. & F., 19/6/17, formerly 1772, W. Yorks Regt.
Thomas, Charles Edwin, b. Wendron, Cornwall, e. Bodmin, Cornwall (Redruth, Cornwall), 35492, Pte, k. in a., F. & F., 1/6/18, formerly 202798, D.C.L.I.
Thomas, David James, b. Talgareg, Carm., e. Worcester (Tibberton, Worcs), 29865, Pte., d. of w., F. & F., 15/4/18, formerly 36168, Worcs Regt.
Thompson, Arthur James, b. Derby, e. Birmingham, 14/1621, Pte., k. in a., F. & F., 18/11/16.
Thompson, Thomas, b. Coventry, Warwicks, e. Leamington, Warwicks (Coventry), 50738, Pte., k. in a., F. & F., 3/6/18.
Thompson, William Henry, b. St. John's, Leamington, Warwicks, e. Warwick (Leamington), 2103, L/Cpl., k. in a., F. & F., 7/9/17.
Thornborough, James Sylvester, b. Mosley Hill, Ches., e. Leamington, Warwicks, 202832, Pte., d. of w., F. & F., 23/10/17.
Thornett, Albert, b. Llandwrog, Carnarvonshire, e. Birmingham (Coventry, Warwicks), 16581, Pte., k. in a., F. & F., 10/4/18.
Thornhill, Charles Henry, b. Maryvale, Warwicks, e. Warwick (Erdington, Birmingham), 17749, Pte., k. in a., F. & F., 18/11/16.
Thorning, William Henry, b. St. Andrew's, Plymouth, Devon, e. Plymouth, 25435, Pte., d. of w., F. & F., 8/11/18, formerly 011476, R.A.O.C.
Thornton, Fred, b. Pailton, Warwicks, e. Coventry, Warwicks, 28006, Pte., d. of w., F. & F., 30/10/18.
Thornton, Sydney Herbert, b. Sutton Coldfield, Warwicks, e. Sutton Coldfield, 202201, Pte., d. of w., F. & F., 9/6/17.
Timms, Albert, b. Hockley, Birmingham, e. Birmingham, 7862, Pte., k. in a., F. & F., 26/4/18.
Tippin, George, b. Highfields, Sheffield, Yorks, e. Warwick (Hockley, Birmingham), 11798, Pte., k. in a., F. & F., 4/9/16.
Tippin, William, b. Bloxwich, Staffs, e. Warwick (Sheffield, Yorks), 14709, Pte., k. in a., F. & F., 23/3/18.
Tonks, Walter, b. Atherstone, Warwicks, e. Atherstone, 4324, Pte., k. in a., F. & F., 23/7/16.
Tovey, Charles, b. Kidderminster, Worcs, e. Kidderminster, 28730, Pte., k. in a., F. & F., 23/3/18.
Townsend, Abraham, b. Birmingham, e. Birmingham (King's Norton, Birmingham), 5467, Pte., d. of w., F. & F., 31/7/16.
Train, Edward, b. Burton Hastings, Warwicks, e. Nuneaton, Warwicks, 12834, Pte., d. of w., F. & F., 25/3/18.
Trickett, Alfred, b. Birmingham, e. Birmingham (Handsworth, Staffs), 1130, Pte., d. of w., F. & F., 2/6/18.
Tuckett, Arthur Leonard, e. Wickford, Essex, 35519, Pte., k. in a., F. & F., 19/4/18, formerly 3564, Devon Regt.
Tulk, Arthur James, b. Birmingham, e. Birmingham (Small Heath, Birmingham), 15157, Pte., k. in a., F. & F., 9/11/16.
Turner, Edwin Samuel, b. St. Lawrence, Birmingham, e. Birmingham (Saltley, Birmingham), 5299, A/Cpl., k. in a., F. & F., 30/7/16.
Twiss, John Henry, b. Birmingham, e. Birmingham (Aston Manor, Birmingham), 50739, Pte., k. in a., F. & F., 23/10/18.
Tyler, Albert, b. Barking, Essex, e. Stratford, Essex (Barking), 40445, Pte., k. in a., F. & F., 4/9/18.
Underhill, Frank Arthur, b. Thornbury, Glos., e. Bristol, Glos. (Thornbury), 35558, Pte., k. in a., F. & F., 19/4/18, formerly 35827, Glos.
Vanderwolf, William, b. Lantrydoch, Cornwall, e. Bodmin, Cornwall (Lantrydoch), 35498, Pte., d. of w., F. & F., 15/4/18.
Varnum, Charles Hedmond, b. Clifton, Bristol, e. Bristol (Bedminster, Glos.), 50742, Pte., d. of w., F. & F., 15/6/18.
Vatcher, Onesimus, e. Brockenhurst, Hants (Christchurch, Hants), 35425, Pte., k. in a., F. & F., 19/4/18.
Vaughan, Arthur, b. St. Martin's, Birmingham, e. Birmingham, 8071, Pte., d. of w., F. & F., 24/3/18.
Vinall, Henry Edward, b. Birmingham, e. Aston, Birmingham (Hockley, Birmingham), 19305, Pte., k. in a., F. & F., 18/11/16.
Vinnicombe, Hubert, b. Otterton, Devon, e. Exeter, Devon (Exmouth, Devon), 16/2073, Pte., k. in a., F. & F., 19/6/17, formerly 135663, R.F.A.
Wadey, Walter, b. Sutton Coldfield, Warwicks, e. Birmingham (Erdington, Birmingham), 19280, Pte., k. in a., F. & F., 6/6/18.
Wain, George, b. Wootton Wawen, Warwicks, e. Stratford-on-Avon, Warwicks (Wootton Wawen), 16250, Pte., d., F. & F., 17/8/18.
Wakeford, George Edward, b. Petersfield, Hants, e. Petersfield (Hawkley, Hants), 241993, Pte., d., F. & F. 3/11/18, formerly 101, Hampshire Regt.
Walker, James Alfred, b. Rochdale, Lancs, e. Bury, Lancs, 32773, Pte., d. of w., F. & F., 1/9/18, formerly 21787, Dragoon Gds.
Walker, William Harold, b. Birmingham, e. Birmingham (Holloway Head, Birmingham), 35474, Pte., k. in a., F. & F., 10/4/18, formerly 30139, Devon Regt.
Waller, Sydney Frank, b. Cambridge, e. Bury St. Edmunds, Suffolk (Cambridge), 38242, Pte., d. of w., F. & F., 4/6/18.
Walters, Frederick, b. Walsall, Staffs, e. Birmingham, 9196, Pte., d. of w., F. & F., 29/7/16.
Walton, Albert Archie, b. Ashted, Birmingham, e. Birmingham, 5273, Pte., k. in a., F. & F., 17/10/15.
Ward, Alfred, b. Bordesley, Birmingham, e. Birmingham (Hockley, Birmingham), 4815, Pte., k. in a., F. & F., 30/7/16.
Ward, Amos, b. Radford, Warwicks, e. Coventry, Warwicks (Radford), 8363, Pte., d. of w., F. & F., 31/8/15.
Ward, Albert Edward, b. Birmingham, e. Birmingham (Aston, Birmingham), 23219, A/Cpl., d. of w., F. & F., 5/9/18.
Ward, George, b. Coventry, Warwicks, e. Coventry, 42875, Pte., k. in a., F. & F., 21/10/18.
Ward, George, b. Leamington, Warwicks, e. Newport, Mon., 14985, Pte., d. of w., F. & F., 15/9/16.
Ward, James Arthur, b. St. Martin's, Birmingham, e. Birmingham, 7883, Pte., d. of w., F. & F., 7/6/17.
Ward, John Henry, b. Birmingham, e. Birmingham, 14458, Pte., k. in a., F. & F., 3/7/16.
Ward, Reginald, b. Leamington, Warwicks, e. Leamington, 20852, Pte., k. in a., F. & F., 7/8/17.
Wareing, Stanley Wilfred, b. Northampton, e. Rugby, Warwicks, 12624, Pte., k. in a., F. & F., 23/7/16.
Warren, John, b. Kidderminster, Worcs, e. Birmingham (Kidderminster), 12000, Pte., k. in a., F. & F., 25/10/16.
Watkins, George Henry, b. Flecknoe, Warwicks, e. Warwick (Long Lawford, Warwicks), 23121, Pte., k. in a., F. & F., 25/9/18.
Watson, Edgar Eustace, b. Bow, London, e. Salisbury, Wilts (Zeals, Wilts), 17671, Pte., k. in a., F. & F., 21/3/18, formerly 24728, Som. L.I.
Watts, John Sidney, b. Rugby, Warwicks, e. Rugby, 28015, Pte., d. of w., F. & F., 30/7/17.
Webb, John Thomas, e. Coventry, Warwicks, 267332, Pte., d., F. & F., 16/10/18.
Wesselhoeft, Frederick Grange, e. Nottingham, 27272, Sgt., k. in a., F. & F., 20/9/17, formerly 2544, Notts & Derby Regt.
Wheal, Alfred James, b. Waterhales, Navestock, Essex, e. Ilford, Essex (Romford, Essex), 50487, Pte., k. in a., F. & F., 8/5/18, formerly 30645, Oxf. & Bucks L.I.
Whillock, Samuel, b. St. Thomas, Birmingham, e. Birmingham, 4535, Pte., k. in a., F. & F., 19/4/18.
White, Albert, b. Lapworth Brook, Warwicks, e. Birmingham (Lapworth Brook), 34025, Pte., k. in a., F. & F., 23/3/18.
White, Arthur Charles Ferrebe, b. Ashley, Bristol, e. Bristol (Kingsdown, Bristol), 35518, Pte., k. in a., F. & F., 19/4/18.
White, Sidney, b. Harden, Staffs, e. Birmingham (Rugby, Warwicks), 16/1899, Pte., k. in a., F. & F., 23/3/18.
White, Samuel, b. Rugby, Warwicks, e. Rugby, 10053, L/Cpl, k. in a., F. & F., 3/7/16.
Whitesman, Nathan, b. Whitechapel, Middx., e. London, 20655, Pte., d. of w., F. & F., 9/6/17, formerly 11551, A. Cyc. Corps.
Whitehouse, William, b. Aston, Birmingham, e. Birmingham, 5118, L/Sgt., k. in a., F. & F., 3/7/16.
Whittingham, Ernest Alfred, b. St. Alban's, Birmingham, e. Birmingham, 6466, Pte., k. in a., F. & F., 3/7/16.
Whittle, Sidney James, b. Wareham, Dorset, e. Winchester, Hants (Wareham), 244176, Cpl., k. in a., F. & F., 26/4/18, formerly 100497, Hants Yeo. Cyc.
Widekind, Carl Rudulph, b. Aston, Birmingham, e. Birmingham (Erdington, Birmingham), 2536, Pte., k. in a., F. & F., 19/10/17.
Wilkes, Alfred James, b. Spring Hill, Birmingham, e. Warwick (Spring Hill), 14884, Pte., k. in a., F. & F., 30/7/16.
Wilkes, Samuel Alfred, b. Birmingham, e. Birmingham (Balsall Heath, Birmingham), 201215, Pte., k. in a., F. & F., 20/9/18.
Wilkins, Sidney, b. Foleshill, Warwicks, e. Coventry, Warwicks, 7270, Pte., k. in a., F. & F., 30/7/16.
Williams, Albert, b. Birmingham, e. Birmingham, 20099, Pte., k. in a., F. & F., 21/3/18.
Williams, George, b. Newent, Glos., e. Birmingham, 16905, Pte., k. in a., F. & F., 1/11/16.
Williams, John, b. Balsall Heath, Birmingham, e. Birmingham (Balsall Heath), 19590, Pte., k. in a., F. & F., 30/5/18.
Williams, Orlando, b. St. Stephen's, Cornwall, e. Birmingham (Sparkbrook, Birmingham), 26910, Pte., k. in a., F. & F., 31/5/18.
Willmott, Edward Henry, b. St. George's, Birmingham, e. Birmingham (Notting Hill Gate, London, W.), 8313, Pte., d. of w., F. & F., 27/3/18.

Wills, Almon John, b. Chepstow, Glos., e. Warwick (Shirley, Warwicks), 22495, Pte., k. in a., F. & F., 7/6/17.
Wilson, David, b. Kettlebrook, Warwicks, e. Dosthill, Warwicks, 16232, Pte., k. in a., F. & F., 3/7/16.
Wilson, Harry James, e. Birmingham, 12932, Pte., d. of w., F. & F., 26/3/18.
Winston, George, b. West Bromwich, Staffs, e. Birmingham (West Bromwich), 5379, Cpl., d. of w., F. & F., 16/8/16.
Winwood, George, e. Birmingham (Witton, Birmingham), 267342, Pte., k. in a., F. & F., 27/9/17.
Wisedale, John, b. St. George's, Birmingham, e. Birmingham, 4738, Pte., k. in a., F. & F., 9/1/16.
Withers, Thomas Percy, b. Wednesbury, Staffs, e. Birmingham (Aston, Birmingham), 5973, L/Cpl., k. in a., F. & F., 5/11/15.
Wood, Edward, e. Nottingham (Old Basford, Notts), 27443, Pte., k. in a., F. & F., 18/11/16, formerly 4958, Notts & Derby Regt.
Wood, Frederick Marshall, b. Birmingham, e. Birmingham (Greet, Birmingham), 50756, Pte., k. in a., F. & F., 30/5/18.
Wood, Joseph, b. Amington, Warwicks, e. Atherstone, Warwicks (Tamworth, Warwicks), 4734, Pte., k. in a., F. & F., 3/7/16.
Woodford, Percy Henry, b. Budbrooke, Warwicks, e. Coventry, Warwicks (Wolverton, Warwicks), 26256, Pte., d. of w., F. & F., 23/10/18.
Woodley, Albert Edward, b. Fulham, London, e. Fulham, 40438, Pte., k. in a., F. & F., 17/4/18.
Woodward, Francis Harry, b. Henley-in-Arden, Warwicks, e. Stratford-on-Avon, Warwicks (Henley-in-Arden), 21199, Pte., k. in a., F. & F., 11/1/17.
Woodward, Thomas, b. Birmingham, e. Warwick (Birmingham), 38943, Pte., k. in a., F. & F., 8/9/18.
Woollaston, William Richard, b. Birmingham, e. Birmingham (Ladywood, Birmingham), 14491, Pte., k. in a., F. & F., 18/11/16.
Wootton, Sidney William, b. Bournemouth, Hants, e. Winchester, Hants, 4684, Pte., d. of w., F. & F., 30/8/15.
Workman, Joseph Richard, b. St. James, Aston, Birmingham, e. Birmingham, 4908, Pte., d. of w., F. & F., 7/2/17.
Wormleighton, Alfred, b. Higham-on-the-Hill, Warwicks, e. Nuneaton, Warwicks, 7702, Pte., k. in a., F. & F., 18/11/16.
Worwood, Bertram, b. Exhall, Warwicks, e. Coventry, Warwicks, 50758, Pte., d. of w., F. & F., 6/6/18.
Wright, Ernest, b. Nuneaton, Warwicks, e. Nuneaton (Stockingford, Warwicks), 15042, Pte., k. in a., F. & F., 8/11/16.
Wright, Frederick, b. Bingham, Notts, e. Newark, Notts (Barnstone, Notts), 27435, Pte., k. in a., F. & F., 18/11/16, formerly T/35272, Notts & Derby Regt.
Wright, George, b. Willey, Leics, e. Rugby, Warwicks (Willey), 4521, Pte., d. of w., F. & F., 9/8/16.
Yapp, Joseph Charles, b. Herefordshire, e. Harborne, Birmingham, 22496, Pte., k. in a., F. & F., 19/4/18.
Yates, Arthur, b. Birmingham, e. Birmingham, 14439, Pte., d. of w., F. & F., 4/7/16.
Yates, Charles Alfred, b. St. George's, Birmingham, e. Birmingham, 6513, Pte., d. of w., F. & F., 6/7/16.
Yates, William, b. Birmingham, e. Birmingham (Aston, Birmingham), 12010, Pte., k. in a., F. & F., 23/7/16.
Yeomans, Ernest George, b. Warwick, e. Warwick, 17578, Pte., k. in a., F. & F., 10/11/16.
Yeomans, Frederick, b. Dunton Frean, Kent, e. Sevenoaks, Kent (Otford, Kent), 27458, Pte., k. in a., F. & F., 9/11/16, formerly 5983, Notts & Derby Regt.
Young, Albert Edward, b. Salisbury, Wilts, e. Salisbury, 50762, Pte., k. in a., F. & F., 31/5/18.
Young, Frederick Arthur, b. Mortlake, Surrey, e. Richmond, Surrey (Mortlake), 27457, Pte., k. in a., F. & F., 18/11/16, formerly 5995, Notts & Derby Regt.

11th Battalion.

Adams, Ernest, b. Spring Hill, Birmingham, e. Birmingham (Nechells, Birmingham), 8097, Sgt., k. in a., F. & F., 24/4/17.
Adshead, Charles Herbert, b. Birmingham, e. Birmingham (Sparkbrook, Birmingham), 17687, Pte., k. in a., F. & F., 11/10/16.
Agg, John Henry, b. Birmingham, e. Birmingham (Nechells, Birmingham), 10275, Pte., d. of w., F. & F., 10/7/16.
Aldridge, Jesse, b. St. Mary's, Reading, Berks, e. Reading, 10051, Pte., k. in a., F. & F., 11/7/16.
Allbright, Herbert, b. Gosta Green, Birmingham, e. Birmingham (Digbeth, Birmingham), 8820, L/Cpl., k. in a., F. & F., 15/7/16.
Allcock, Arthur, b. Rubery, Worcs, e. Bromsgrove, Worcs, 27762, Pte., k. in a., F. & F., 10/4/17, formerly 4680, Worcs Regt.
Allcott, James, b. Birmingham, e. Birmingham, 11297, Pte., k. in a., F. & F., 29/4/17.
Allen, Frederick, b. Chipping Norton, Oxon, e. Warwick (Chipping Norton), 1466, Sgt., k. in a., F. & F., 16/7/16.
Allison, Frederick Charles, b. Aston, Birmingham, e. Birmingham (Aston), 17345, Pte., k. in a., F. & F., 13/8/16.
Allman, Albert John, b. Clifford Chambers, Warwicks, e. Birmingham (Clifford Chambers), 8237, Pte., k. in a., F. & F., 11/8/16.
Allsop, William Henry, b. St. Edward's, Birmingham, e. Birmingham, 6213, L/Cpl., d. of w., F. & F., 25/10/17.
Andrews, Charles William, b. Reading, Berks, e. Reading, 27770, Pte., k. in a., F. & F., 16/11/16, formerly 5219, Worcs Regt.
Andrews, George William, b. Henley-in-Arden, Warwicks, e. Stratford-on-Avon, Warwicks (Henley-in-Arden), 22523, Pte., k. in a., F. & F., 28/4/17.
Andrews, Joseph George Patrick, b. Kingstown, Dublin, e. Birmingham, 16/1582, Pte., k. in a., F. & F., 27/4/17.
Arnold, Edward, e. York (Norwich), 2488, Sgt., d. of w., F. & F., 17/11/16, formerly 4857, Lancers.
Ashmore, Thomas, b. Birmingham, e. Birmingham, 15400, Pte., k. in a., F. & F., 13/2/17.
Bacon, William Stevnitt, e. Nottingham, 27309, Pte., k. in a., F. & F., 9/12/17, formerly 4705, Notts & Derby Regt.
Badger, William Edgar, b. Billesley, Warwicks, e. Stratford-on-Avon, Warwicks (Snitterfield, Warwicks), 10650, Sgt., k. in a., F. & F., 11/4/17.
Bagnall, Thomas Israel, b. Walsall, Staffs, e. Birmingham (Small Heath, Birmingham), 10311, Pte., k. in a., F. & F., 11/18/16.
Baker, Edgar, b. Bexhill, Sussex, e. Hastings, Sussex (Wadhurst, Sussex), 28737, Pte., k. in a., F. & F., 8/10/17, formerly S4/144931, R.A.S.C.
Baker, John Henry, b. Tinstall, Worcs, e. Leamington, Warwicks, 19438, Pte., k. in a., F. & F., 9/4/17.
Baker, Thomas, b. Birmingham, e. Birmingham, 21191, Pte., k. in a., F. & F., 12/8/17.
Balding, James, b. Sutton Coldfield, Warwicks, e. Nuneaton, Warwicks, 4277, Pte., k. in a., F. & F., 11/8/16.
Ball, George, b. Nechells, Birmingham, e. Birmingham (Nechells), 9072, Pte., k. in a., F. & F.,, 16/7/16.
Bannister, James Hartley, b. Burnley, Lancs, e. Nelson, Lancs, 28744, Pte., k. in a., F. & F., 10/10/17, formerly S4/144121, R.A.S.C.
Barber, Charles Walter, b. Chilvers Coton, Warwicks, e. Warwick (Nuneaton, Warwicks), 3235, Sgt., k. in a., F. & F., 16/7/16.
Barker, George, b. Bordesley, Birmingham, e. Birminggham (Balsall Heath, Birmingham), 8889, Pte., k. in a., F. & F., 25/4/17.
Barlow, Henry, b. Tamworth, Warwicks, e. Coventry, Warwicks, 14894, Pte., k. in a., F. & F., 11/8/16.
Barnett, Reginald, b. Ashton-under-Hill, Glos., e. Evesham, Worcs (Ashton-under-Hill), 12364, L/Cpl., d. of w., F. & F., 29/4/17, formerly 53889, R.G.A.
Barrett, Sydney, b. Honiton, Som., e. Weston-super-Mare (Tarnock, Som.), 27752, Pte., d. of w., F. & F., 19/11/16, formerly 5809, Glos. Regt.
Bartlett, Harold, b. Stratford-on-Avon, Warwicks, e. Birmingham (Stratford-on-Avon), 10947, Pte., k. in a., F. & F., 15/7/16.
Barwick, Edward Sidney, b. Wiveliscombe, Som., e. Coventry, Warwicks, 20206, Pte., d. of w., F. & F., 14/4/17.
Bastable, Leonard, b. Halesowen, Birmingham, e. Birmingham (Halesowen), 8870, Pte., k. in a., F. & F., 16/7/16.
Batchelor, George Walter Raymond, b. Broadway, Worcs, e. Stratford-on-Avon, Warwicks (Ardens Grafton, Warwicks), 19269, Pte., k. in a., F. & F., 22/3/18.
Batsford, William, b. Knowle, Warwicks, e. Birmingham (Northfield, Birmingham), 24162, Pte., k. in a., F. & F., 12/8/17.
Battams, Frank Harry, b. Neasdon, Middx., e. Bletchley, Bucks (Verne Junction, Bucks), 28775, Pte., d. of w., F. & F., 23/9/17.
Bayliss, Arnold Thomas, b. Leamington, Warwicks, e. Birmingham, 763, L/Cpl., d. of w., F. & F., 29/4/17.
Bayley, Leslie Morris, b. Birmingham, e. Moseley, Birmingham (King's Heath, Birmingham), 1225, L/Cpl., k. in a., F. & F., 23/5/17.
Beddoes, Charles Joseph, b. Toxteth, Lancs, e. Birmingham (Liverpool), 778, L/Cpl., k. in a., F. & F., 14/11/16.
Bellamy, Horace, b. Aston, Birmingham, e. Aston, 28547, Pte., d. of w., F. & F., 10/8/17.
Benjamin, Herbert Leslie, b. Welton, Northants, e. Rugby, Warwicks (Welton), 13458, Pte., k. in a., F. & F., 11/7/16.
Bennett, Frederick Henry, b. Birmingham, e. Birmingham (Lozells, Birmingham, 17785, Pte., k. in a., F. & F., 13/8/16.
Bentley, Harry, b. London, e. Birmingham (Hay Mills, Birmingham), 24188, Pte., d. of w., F. & F., 29/9/17.
Berrill, John, b. Clifton, Bucks, e. Bletchley, Bucks (Olney, Bucks), 18311, Pte., d. of w., F. & F., 11/8/16, formerly 22949, Som. L.I.
Betts, George, b. Aston, Birmingham, e. Warwick (Birmingham), 2203, Pte., k. in a., F. & F., 7/11/15.
Bickley, William Richard, b. Westminster, Middx., e. Maidstone, Kent, 20351, L/Cpl., k. in a., F. & F., 13/8/16, formerly T/4/039970, R.A.S.C.
Biddle, Charles Ernest, b. Warwick, e. Warwick, 10137, Cpl., d. of w., F. & F., 28/9/17.
Biddle, John Evelyn, b. Aston, Birmingham, e. Birmingham (Olton, Warwicks), 781, Pte., k. in a., F. & F., 29/4/17.
Billington, Archibald, b. Nantwich, Ches., e. Birmingham (Worcester), 4952, Pte., d. of w., F. & F., 26/4/17.
Bishop, Charles, b. Honington, Shrops., e. Knowle, Warwicks (Dorridge, Warwicks), 19594, Pte., d. of w., F. & F., 22/5/17.
Bishop, Frederick John, b. Hastings, Sussex, e. Coventry, Warwicks, 15318, Pte., k. in a., F. & F., 9/8/16.
Bittle, Bernard, b. Plumstead, Kent, e. Woolwich, London (Plumstead), 330453, Pte., k. in a., F. & F., 24/11/17.
Blewer, John James, b. Birmingham, e. Birmingham, 9404, Pte., d. of w., F. & F., 7/12/15.
Bolton, Robert, b. Sunbury-on-Thames, Middx., e. Coventry, Warwicks, 9084, Pte., k. in a., F. & F., 13/8/16.
Booth, George, b. Gateshead, Durham, e. Gateshead, 28770, Pte., k. in a., F. & F., 22/7/17, formerly DM/2/171069, R.A.S.C.
Booton, Charles Edwin, b. Kidderminster, Worcs, e. Birmingham (Moseley, Birmingham), 2243, Pte., d. of w., F. & F., 11/7/16.

Bowley, Edward, b. West Bromwich, Staffs, e. Birmingham (Aston, Birmingham), 9131, Sgt., d. of w., F. & F., 20/7/16.
Bowstead, Sidney, b. Birmingham, e. Birmingahm, 8860, Pte., k. in a., F. & F., 16/7/16.
Brain, James, b. Bedminster, Glos., e. Bristol, Glos., 27750, Pte., d. of w., F. & F., 15/8/17, formerly 5719 Glos. Regt.
Bramley, Thomas, b. Jekinston, Derbyshire, e. Nuneaton, Warwarks (Bedworth, Warwicks). 12637, Cpl., k. in a., F. & F., 10/4/17.
Branch, Francis, b. Clapton, London, e. Warwick (Hoddesdon, Herts), 14843, Pte., k. in a., F. & F., 15/7/16.
Brandish, Fred, b Tysoe, Warwicks, e. Birmingham (Ettington, Warwicks), 8243, Pte., k. in a., F. & F., 11/8/16.
Brandon, Albert Henry, b. Chesham, Bucks, e. Aylesbury, Bucks (Chesham), 18504, Pte., k. in a., F. & F., 11/8/16, formerly 25281, Som. L.I.
Brandrick, Cecil Arthur, b. Bicester, Oxon., e. Oxford (Walton-on-Thames, Surrey), 18495, Pte., d. of w., F. & F., 28/8/16, formerly 25265, Som. L.I.
Brannon, Albert William, b. St. Thomas, Birmingham, e. Birmingham (Balsall Heath, Birmingham), 1226, Pte., k. in a., F. & F., 1/8/16.
Brinsley, George, b. Stockport, Ches., e. Stockport, 27786, Pte., d. of w., F. & F., 29/4/17, formerly 22332, Shrops L.I.
Bromwich, Harry, b. King's Norton, Birmingham, e. Birmingham, 21085, Pte., d. of w., F. & F., 29/4/17.
Brookes, Frederick George, b. Binton, Warwicks, e. Birmingham (Binton), 7987, Cpl., k. in a., F. & F., 29/4/17.
Brooks, William Frederick, b. Flecknoe, Warwicks, e. Rugby, Warwicks (Flecknoe), 22658, Pte., d. of w., F. & F., 3/3/17.
Brown, Frank, b. Erdington, Birmingham, e. Birmingham (Erdington), 20991, Pte., k. in a., F. & F., 29/4/17.
Brown, Frederick Charles, b. Birmingham, e. Birmingham (Hockley, Birmingham), 20376, Pte., k. in a., F. & F., 12/8/17.
Brown, Jack, e. Warwick (Ettington, Warwicks), 267626, Pte., k. in a., F. & F., 25/4/17.
Browne, John Edward, b. Ladywood, Birmingham, e. Birmingham (Ladywood), 8690, Pte., k. in a., F. & F., 13/7/16.
Brownhill, Frederick, b. Birmingham, e. Birmingham (Aston, Birmingham), 3626, Pte., k. in a., F. & F., 13/8/16.
Bryan, Albert Ernest, b. Bridgnorth, Salop, e. Bridgnorth, 27787, Pte., k. in a., F. & F., 14/11/16, formerly 18611, Shrops L.I.
Burgess, William Charles, b. Gorton, Manchester, Lancs, e. Warwick, 28830, Pte., k. in a., F. & F., 9/10/17 formerly 7333, A.P.C.
Burns, William, b. Saltley, Birmingham, e. Birmingham, 10658, L/Cpl., k. in a., F. & F., 16/7/16.
Burrows, David, b. Stratford-on-Avon, Warwicks, e. Birmingham (Stratford-on-Avon), 8838, Pte., k. in a., F. & F., 15/7/16.
Burton, Horace Victor, b. Birmingham, e. Birmingham, 17543, Pte., k. in a., F. & F., 16/11/16.
Burton, William Edward, b. Crewe, Ches., e. Birmingham (Smethwick, Staffs), 11015, L/Cpl., k. in a., F. & F., 13/8/16.
Busswell, Francis, b. Saltisford, Warwick, e. Warwick, 15/1575, Pte., k. in a., F. & F., 25/4/17.
Buttfield, Albert James, e. Birmingham (New Oscott, Birmingham), 22133, Pte., k. in a., F. & F., 11/4/17.
Byles, Arthur Walter, b. Lighthorne, Warwicks, e. Leamington, Warwicks (Heathcote Hill, Warwicks), 17386, Pte., k. in a., F. & F., 16/11/16.
Byrd, Samuel, b. Wallasey, Ches., e. Stratford-on-Avon, Warwicks (Broadway, Worcs), 10044, Pte., d. of w., F. & F., 7/3/17.
Caddick, Frederick, b. Birmingham, e. Birmingham, 17072, Pte., k. in a., F. & F., 24/5/17.
Cain, John, b. St. George's, Birmingham, e. Birmingham, 9091, Pte., d. of w., F. & F., 23/10/16.
Canton, Lewis, b. St. Adaens, Liverpool, e. Pembroke Dock, 11825, C.S.M., k. in a., F. & F., 10/7/16.
Carpenter, Albert Henry, b. Foleshill, Coventry, Warwicks, e. Warwick, 16666, Pte., k. in a., F. & F., 8/10/17.
Carter, Edgar, b. Wolvey, Warwicks, e. Nuneaton, Warwicks (Wolvey), 17459, L/Cpl., k. in a., F. & F., 21/11/16.
Carter, Lionel Ernest, b. St. George's, Kidderminster, Worcs, e. Worcester (Kidderminster), 9341, Pte., k. in a., F. & F., 1/8/16, formerly 18608, Worcs Regt.
Caste, William, b. Minworth, Warwicks, e. Birmingham (Minworth), 18033, Pte., k. in a., F. & F., 13/8/16.
Cauldwell, Henry, e. Birmingham (Aston, Birmingham), 17035, Pte., k. in a., F. & F., 11/8/16.
Cawley, William, b. Hornton, Oxon, e. Banbury, Oxon (Hornton), 18421, Pte., d. of w., F. & F., 13/8/16, formerly 23812, Som. L.I.
Chapple, Alfred James, b. Torquay, Devon, e. Birmingham (Sparkhill, Birmingham), 8793, Pte., k. in a., F. & F., 7/11/15.
Charnell, Joseph, b. Atherstone, Warwicks, e. Atherstone, 10187, L/Cpl., k. in a., F. & F., 14/11/16.
Chatten, Thomas, b. Birmingham, e. Birmingham, 9128, Pte., k. in a., F. & F., 21/11/16.
Chatterton, Albert Edward, b. Wolverhampton, Staffs, e. Birmingham (Dudley, Worcs), 9088, Pte., k. in a., F. & F., 15/7/16.
Checkley, Arthur, b. Foleshill, Warwicks, e. Coventry, Warwicks, 266693, Pte., k. in a., F. & F., 23/4/17.
Chew, Albert Henry, b. St. George's, Birmingham, e. Birmingham (Hockley, Birmingham), 14328, Pte., d. ot w., F. & F., 21/11/16.
Childs, William Joseph, e. Birmingham (Aston, Birmingham), 28375, Pte., k. in a., F. & F., 8/10/17.
Chilton, John Henry, b. Cannock, Staffs, e. Stourbridge, Worcs, 25053, Pte., k. in a., F. & F., 11/10/17.
Chilton, Samuel George, b. Penn, Bucks, e. High Wycombe, Bucks (Beaconsfield, Bucks), 18520, Pte., k. in a., F. & F., 10/8/16, formerly 25306, Som. L.I.
Chipman, Walter, b. Birmingham, e. Birmingham, 22762, Pte., d. of w., F. & F., 29/4/17.
Clark, Edward, b. Binton, Warwicks, e. Birmingham (Stratford-on-Avon, Warwicks), 8105, Pte., d., Home, 29/5/15.
Clark, Charles Thomas, b. Long Compton, Warwicks, e. Birmingham (Long Compton), 8590, Pte., d. of w., F. & F., 15/7/16.
Claydon, Jonathan Whing, b. Brailes, Warwicks, e. Stratford-on-Avon, Warwicks (Upper Brailes), 24306, Pte., k. in a., F. & F., 10/8/17.
Clements, Thomas George Henry, b. Halesowen, Worcs, e. Birmingham (Rubery, Birmingham), 10230, Pte., k. in a., F. & F., 13/8/16.
Clissold, Henry Stephen, b. Stroud, Glos., e. Birmingham (Ladywood, Birmingham), 8786, Pte., d. of w., F. & F., 15/7/16.
Clowes, Harry, e. Birmingham (Sparkbrook, Birmingham), 9210, Pte., k. in a., F. & F., 10/7/16.
Cole, Albert Edward, b. Westminster, Middx., e. London (South Lambeth, London), 8541, L/Cpl., k. in a., F. & F., 16/7/16.
Coleman, Ernest Edwin, b. Birmingham, e. Birmingham, 629, L/Cpl., k. in a., F. & F., 27/4/17.
Coleman, George Bertram, b. Priors Hardwick, Warwicks, e. Coventry, Warwicks (Binley, Warwicks), 11059, L/Cpl., k. in a., F. & F., 10/4/17.
Coleman, James, b. Longton, Staffs, e. Coventry, Warwicks, 3808, Pte., d., F. & F., 9/4/16.
Collins, Harry Ernest, b. Stratford-on-Avon, Warwicks, e. Stratford-on-Avon, 10083, Pte., k. in a., F. & F., 21/11/16.
Cooke, Arthur Thomas, b. Birmingham, e. Birmingham, 10058, L/Cpl., k. in a., F & F., 14/11/16, M.M.
Cooper, Harry Ashley, b. Bedworth, Warwicks, e. Warwick (Bedworth), 9797, Pte., k. in a., F. & F., 24/9/17.
Cooper, Herbert William, b. Rushall, Staffs, e. Walsall, Staffs, 11267, Pte., d. of w., F. & F., 20/10/15.
Cope, John Thomas, b. Hartshill, Warwicks, e. Warwick (Hinckley, Leics), 29852, Pte., d. of w., F & F., 12/8/17, formerly 35955, Worcs Regt.
Cornish, Edward Henry Louis, b. Forest Gate, London, e. Rugby, Warwicks (Priors Marston, Warwicks), 7909, Pte., k. in a., F. & F., 23/4/17.
Coton, William John, b. Erdington, Birmingham, e. Warwick (Bordesley, Birmingham), 2541, L/Cpl., d. of w., F. & F., 25/4/17.
Cox, Arthur, b. Aston, Birmingham, e. Smethwick, Staffs (Birmingham), 4958, Pte., k. in a., F. & F., 16/7/16.
Cox, Charles Joseph, b. Emscote, Warwicks, e. Warwick, 10549, Pte., d. of w., F. & F., 16/7/16.
Cox, John, b. St. Martin's, Birmingham, e. Birmingham (Edgbaston, Birmingham), 17714, Pte., k. in a., F. & F., 11/4/17.
Cozens, Alfred Henry, b. Norwich, Norfolk, e. Coventry, Warwicks, 15250, Pte., k. in a., F. & F., 15/7/16.
Craddock, Alfred Thomas, b. Fromeshill, Herefordshire, e. Rugby, Warwicks (Stoneleigh, Warwicks), 10298, Pte., k. in a., F. & F., 2/6/16.
Crewe, Sidney Hubert, b. St. Michael's, Salop, e. Whitchurch, Salop, 27780, Pte., d. of w., F. & F., 7/12/16, formerly 24734, Shrops L.I.
Croker, Reginald Clifford, b. Eastville, Glos., e. Bristol, Glos., 10140, Pte., d. of w., F. & F., 7/11/15.
Crossby, Charles Bertie, b. Birgstock, Northants, e. Rugby, Warwicks, 17864, Pte., d. of w., F. & F., 16/11/16.
Cuckow, George, b. Ladywood, Birmingham, e. Birmingham, 4231, Pte., k. in a., F. & F., 7/11/15.
Curran, William, b. Stanton Lacey, Salop, e. Ludlow, Salop (Stanton Lacey), 27777, Pte., k. in a., F. & F., 16/11/16, formerly 19595, Shrops L.I.
Curry, John Emerson, e. Coventry (Foleshill, Coventry, Warwicks), 9163, Pte., k. in a., F. & F., 9/7/16.
Curtis, John, b. Aston, Birmingham, e. Birmingham (Aston), 9518, Pte., k. in a., F. & F., 29/4/17.
Cutler, John Thomas, b. Dudley, Worcs, e. Worcester (Dudley), 28774, Pte., k. in a., F. & F., 25/7/17.
Dabbs, Thomas James, b. Coleshill, Birmingham, e. Nuneaton, Warwicks (Stockingford, Warwicks), 12639, Pte., k. in a., F. & F., 16/7/16.
Dadd, Albert, b. London, e. Birmingham (London), 9135, Pte., d. of w., F. & F., 9/10/17.
Dale, Harley, b. Dunstew, Oxon, e. Rugby, Warwicks (Long Lawford, Warwicks), 22633, Pte., k. in a., F. & F., 10/4/17.
Darwood, W. Richard, b. Ladywood, Birmingham, e. Birmingham, 8215, Pte., k. in a., F. & F., 12/7/16.
Davis, Edward, b. Aston, Birmingham, e. Birmingham (Sutton Coldfield, Warwicks), 8219, Pte., d. of w., F. & F., 9/10/17.
Davis, James, b. Wellington, Som., e. Taunton, Som., 16/1996, Pte., k. in a., F. & F., 10/4/17, formerly 148548, R.F.A.
Davies, Charles Bertram Hine, b. Leamington, Warwicks, e. Leamington, 17839, Pte., k. in a., F. & F., 13/8/16.
Davies, William, b. Bloomsbury, Birmingham, e. Birmingham, 2884, Pte., k. in a., F. & F., 16/7/16.
Davies, William, b. Bordesley, Birmingham, e. Birmingham, 4385, L/Cpl., k. in a., F. & F., 28/4/17.
Davies, William, b. Birmingham, e. Birmingham, 8249, Pte., k. in a., F. & F., 2/3/17.
Dawes, Sidney Frank, b. Slough, Bucks e. Slough (Harlington, Middx.), 18322, Pte., d., F. & F., 8/11/16, formerly 22962, Som. L.I.
Dawes, Sidney William, e. Aston, Birmingham (Dorridge, Warwick), 306237, Pte., d. of w., F. & F., 30/4/17.
Day, Thomas, b. Birmingham, e. Birmingham (Deritend, Bir mingham), 15126, Pte., k. in a., F. & F., 16/7/16.

Dayus, James Sidney, b. All Saints, Worcester, e. Worcester, 8736, Pte., k. in a, F. & F., 1/8/16.
Dealey, Lewis James Bartholomew, b. Smethwick, Birmingham, e. Birmingham (Smethwick), 361, Pte., d. of w., F. & F., 29/4/17.
Derrington, William Henry, b. Birmingham, e. Birmingham, 10066, Pte., d., Home, 8/3/15.
Diffley, Thomas, b. St. Martin's, Birmingham, e. Birmingham, (Bordesley Green, Birmingham), 10061, Pte., k. in a., F. & F., 11/8/16.
Dillon, Robert, b. Birmingham, e. Birmingham, 10736, Pte., d. of w., F. & F., 19/7/17.
Dingley, Albert Bert, b. St. Michael's, Coventry, Warwicks, e. Coventry, 12802, Pte., k. in a., F. & F., 13/8/16.
Dixon, William, b. Birmingham, e. Warwick (Birmingham), 8625, Pte., k. in a., F. & F., 15/7/16.
Down, Frank, e. Romsey, Hants (West Wellon, Romsey), 27753, Pte., d. of w., F. & F., 10/4/17, formerly 5425, Glos Regt.
Draper, George, b. Saltley, Birmingham, e. Birmingham (Small Heath, Birmingham), 8598, Pte., k. in a., F. & F., 16/7/16.
Drinkwater, Walter, b. St. Paul's, Birmingham, e. Birmingham (Sparkbrook, Birmingham), 8695, Pte., k. in a., F. & F., 28/4/17.
Driver, Percy James, b. Tachbrook, Warwicks, e. Coventry, Warwicks, 14968, Pte., k. in a., F. & F., 29/4/17.
Duckett, Arthur John, b. Southam, Warwicks, e. Leamington, Warwicks (Witnash, Leamington), 28809, Pte., d. of w., F. & F., 9/10/17.
Duggins, Francis William, b. Cubbington, Warwicks, e. Leamington, Warwicks, 16977, Pte., k. in a., F. & F., 13/8/16.
Dunn, William Henry, b. Sparkbrook, Birmingham, e. Birmingham (Small Heath, Birmingham), 9337, Pte., k. in a., F. & F., 29/12/15.
Eagle, George Frederick, b. Little Paxton, Hunts, e. Huntingdon (Godmanchester, Hunts), 268491, Pte., k. in a., F. & F., 6/9/17, formerly 652, Hunts Cyc. Battn.
Eaton, John, b. Myddle, Salop, e. Warwick (Myddle), 14842, Pte., k. in a., F. & F., 9/7/16.
Eden, William Herbert, b. Lighthorne, Warwicks, e. Leamington, Warwicks (Lighthorne), 20404, Pte., k. in a., F. & F., 26/2/17.
Edge, Alfred, b. Glasgow, e. Birmingham (Erdington, Birmingham), 202230, Pte., k. in a., F. & F., 11/4/17.
Edgington, James, b. Leamington, Warwicks, e. Leicester (Whitnash, Leamington), 16946, L/Cpl., k. in a., F. & F., 1/10/16.
Egerton, William, b. Bicester, Oxon, e. Oxford (Bicester), 28677, Pte., k. in a., F. & F., 23/5/17.
Eley, Albert John, b. St. Giles, Oxford, e. Birmingham (Greet, Birmingham), 9122, Pte., k. in a., F. & F., 22/3/18.
Elley, Albert Thomas, b. Battersea, London, e. London (Croydon, Surrey), 2081, Pte., k. in a., F. & F., 22/7/17, formerly 10236, D.C.L.I. and 1177, Army Cyc. Corps.
Evans, Alfred, b. Aston, Birmingham, e. Birmingham, 4099, Pte., k. in a., F. & F., 1/8/16.
Evans, Charles Robert, b. Winchcombe, Glos., e. Nuneaton, Warwicks, 15319, Pte., k. in a., F. & F., 8/10/17.
Evans, Frederick William, b. Tenbury, Worcs, e. Coventry, Warwicks, 15859, L/Cpl., k. in a., F. & F., 13/8/16.
Eykelbosch, Jack, b. Coventry, Warwicks, e. Coventry, 16405, Pte., d. of w., F. & F., 20/7/16.
Fairbrother, Alfred George, b. Aston, Birmingham, e. Birmingham (Bordesley Green, Birmingham), 8556, Pte., k. in a., F. & F., 10/4/17.
Farmer, Alfred, b. Whitefield, Lancs, e. Nuneaton, Warwicks, 16361, Pte., k. in a., F. & F., 25/7/17.
Farquhar, John, b. Calcutta, India, e. Birmingham (Redditch, Worcs), 1894, Pte., k. in a., F. & F., 9/10/17.
Farrington, Daniel, b. Bloomsbury, Birmingham, e. Birmingham, 8108, C.S.M., k. in a., F. & F., 23/4/17, M.C.
Faulkner, William, b. Hinckley, Leics, e. Nuneaton, Warwicks (Hinckley), 11430, L/Cpl., d. of w., F. & F., 21/11/16.
Featherstone, William, b. Aston, Birmingham, e. Birmingham (Aston), 7958, Pte., k. in a., F. & F., 29/4/17.
Finch, Henry Charles, b. Baughton, Worcs, e. Birmingham (King's Heath, Birmingham), 15806, Pte., k. in a., F. & F., 29/8/16.
Finch, William Henry, b. Birmingham, e. Warwick (King's Heath, Birmingham), 14794, Pte., k. in a., F. & F., 16/7/16.
Fisher, Harry, b. Upper Bentley, Worcs, e. Redditch, Worcs (Burrow Hill, Redditch), 28792, Pte., k. in a., F. & F., 22/3/18.
Fisher, James, b. Codicott, Herts, e. Leamington, Warwicks, 19439, Pte., k. in a., F. & F., 29/4/17.
Fisher, Thomas Enoch, b. Erdington, Birmingham, e. Birmingham (Erdington), 8782, L/Sgt., d. of w., F. & F., 9/8/17.
Fletcher, Arthur Thomas, b. Birmingham, e. Birmingham (Brookfield, Birmingham), 18299, Pte., k. in a., F. & F., 1/8/16.
Flowers, William Henry, b. Foleshill, Coventry, Warwicks, e. Coventry (Foleshill), 17323, Pte., k. in a., F. & F., 28/9/16.
Floyd, Thomas Albert, b. Birmingham, e. Birmingham (Ladywood, Birmingham), 18058, Pte., k. in a., F. & F., 3/9/16.
Ford, John, b. Henstride, Somerset, e. Milborne Port, Somerset (Sherborne, Dorset), 27744, Pte., k. in a., F. & F., 23/4/17, formerly 5846, Glos. Regt.
Ford, Leonard, b. Nuneaton, Warwicks, e. Nuneaton, 12143, Pte., k. in a., F. & F., 11/8/16.
Ford, Sydney, b. Long Compton, Worcs, e. Stratford-on-Avon, Warwicks (Long Compton), 16048, Pte., k. in a., F. & F., 12/9/16.
Fossett, John, b. Preston, Lancs, e. Bristol (Selly Oak, Birmingham), 21710, Pte., k. in a., F. & F., 10/10/17, formerly 29258, Glos. Regt.
Foster, Lewis, b. Bolton, Lancs, e. St. Helens, Lancs (Bolton), 23307, Pte., k. in a., F. & F., 12/8/17, formerly 8048, R.E.
Fowler, Henry George, b. Birmingham, e. Birmingham, (Bournbrook, Birmingham), 14653, Pte., k. in a., F. & F., 13/8/16.
Frampton, Frederick, b. Birmingham, e. Birmingham, 5232, Pte., d., F. & F., 26/3/16.
Francis, Harry, b. Groombridge, Kent, e. Caversham, Kent, 18500, Pte., d. of w., F. & F., 13/8/16, formerly 25274, Som. L.I.
Franklin, James, b. Charlgrove, Oxon, e. Oxford (Charlgrove), 18439, Pte., d. of w., F. & F., 5/12/16, formerly 24023, Som. L.I.
Freeman, Charles, b. King's Norton, Birmingham, e Birmingham, 7956, Pte., k. in a., F. & F., 11/8/16.
Freeman, Charles Bertie, b. St. Thomas, Birmingham, e. Birmingham, 11397, Pte., k. in a, F. & F., 9/7/16, formerly 13942, D.C.L.I.
French, Thomas, b. Llanwrst, Denbighshire, e. Wolverhampton, Staffs (Walsall, Staffs), 11045, Pte., k. in a., F. & F., 7/11/15.
Frost, Charles, b. Bordesley, Birmingham, e. Birmingham (Small Heath, Birmingham), 8257, Pte., k. in a., F. & F., 11/7/16.
Frost, Frank William, b. Gosport, Hants, e. Portsmouth, Hants, 28766, Pte., k. in a., F. & F., 22/7/17, formerly 18745, Hants Regt.
Fuller, Thomas, b. Dublin, e. Birmingham, 8724, Pte., k. in a., F. & F., 29/4/17.
Gabbitas, Charles Edwin, b. Newark, Notts, e. Blandford, Dorset (Newark), 15937, L/Cpl., d. of w., F. & F., 26/8/16.
Gadsby, Benjamin Alfred, b. Nuneaton, Warwicks, e. Nuneaton, 15210, Pte., k. in a., F. & F., 22/3/18.
Gameson, William Henry, b. Lozells, Birmingham, e. Birmingham, 20377, Pte., d. of w., F. & F., 18/7/17.
Gammage, Albert Arthur, b. Abbington, Northants, e. Nuneaton, Warwicks (Rugby, Warwicks), 17916, L/Cpl., k. in a., F. & F., 13/8/16.
Gardner, John Edward, b. Birmingham, e. Coventry, Warwicks, 16867, Pte., k. in a., F. & F., 14/7/16.
Garner, Alfred, b. Letton Green, Norfolk, e. Ledbury, Hereford, 27807, Pte., d. of w., F. & F., 9/10/17, formerly 24631, Shrops L.I.
George, Sydney Henry, b. Reading, Berks, e. Reading (Woodley, Reading), 28566, Pte., k. in a., F. & F., 24/9/17, formerly 31370, R. Berks Regt.
Gibbs, Alfred James, b. Saltley, Birmingham, e. Birmingham, 5440, Pte., k. in a., F. & F., 16/7/16.
Gibbs, Thomas, b. Lichfield, Staffs, e. Atherstone, Warwicks (Lichfield), 16074, A/Sgt., d. of w., F. & F., 16/2/17.
Gilbert, Joseph Gatcliff, b. Bedworth, Warwicks, e. Coventry, Warwicks (Bedworth), 20369, Pte., d. of w., F. & F., 12/5/17.
Gilks, Albert, b. Kineton, Warwicks, e. Coventry, Warwicks (Kenilworth, Warwicks), 37907, Pte., d., F. & F., 27/1/18.
Glithero, Edwin, b. Birmingham, e. Birmingham, 11869, Pte., k. in a., F. & F., 28/4/17.
Goddard, John, b. Birmingham, e. Birmingham, 8259, Pte., k. in a., F. & F., 13/8/16.
Goddard, William, b. Birmingham, e. Birmingham (Harborne, Birmingham), 17446, Pte., k. in a., F. & F., 22/11/16.
Godson, Albert, b. Cherrington, Warwicks, e. Stratford-on-Avon, Warwicks (Cherrington), 10026, Pte., k. in a., F. & F., 9/10/17.
Godson, Joseph, b. Snowshill, Glos., e. Stratford-on-Avon, Warwicks (Cherrington, Warwicks), 10025, Pte., k. in a., F. & F., 9/10/17.
Goodall, Herbert, b. Ladywood, Birmingham, e. Birmingham, 240552, Pte., k. in a., F. & F., 29/4/17.
Goodey, Harry, b. Langley, Bucks, e. Slough, Bucks, 18366, Pte., k. in a., F. & F., 13/8/16, formerly 23226, Som. L.I.
Goodfield, Cornelius, b. Wick, Glos., e. Bristol, Glos. (Fish-Ponds, Glos.), 21711, Pte., d. of w., F. & F., 26/7/17, formerly 29667, Glos. Regt.
Goodyear, Victor John, b. Birmingham, e. Birmingham (Handsworth, Staffs), 17783, Pte., d. of w., F. & F., 28/4/17.
Gosling, Eli, b. Offwell, Devon, e. Bristol, Glos. (Totterdown, Glos.), 21712, Pte., k. in a., F. & F., 16/11/17, formerly 29660, Glos. Regt.
Gosling, Frank, b. Nottingham, e. Nuneaton, Warwicks (Nottingham), 11708, L/Cpl., d., F. & F., 27/12/16.
Gough, James, b. All Stretton, Salop, e. Rugby, Warwicks (All Stretton), 10240, Pte., k. in a., F. & F., 2/6/16.
Gowers, Henry George, b. Enfield, Middx., e. Cheshunt, Herts, 20745, Pte., d. of w., F. & F., 14/4/17, formerly 11457, Army Cycl. Corps.
Grainger, James, b. Cardiff, Glam., e. Cardiff (Abertrednor, Glam.), 9267, L/Cpl., k. in a., F. & F., 11/4/17.
Gray, Harry, b. Homerton, London, e. Stratford, Essex (Homerton), 10680, Pte., k. in a., F. & F., 12/6/16.
Green, Kelynge, b. Kineton, Warwicks, e. Stratford-on-Avon, Warwicks (Kineton), 17862, L/Cpl., k. in a., F. & F., 31/5/18.
Green, William Henry, b. Ashted, Birmingham, e. Birmingham (Saltley, Birmingham), 8659, L/Cpl., k. in a., F. & F., 15/7/16.
Greenman, Herbert Charles, b. Leamington, Warwicks, e. Warwick (Leamington), 9616, L/Cpl., k. in a., F. & F., 29/5/16.
Greenwood, Willie, b. Salford, Lancs, e. Manchester (Heaton Park, Manchester), 23309, Pte., d. of w., F. & F., 29/4/17, formerly 127014, R.E.
Gregory, Harold, b. Cheltenham, Glos., e. Cheltenham, 20661, L/Cpl., k. in a., F. & F., 24/4/17, formerly 12138, Army Cyc. Corps.
Greville, Albert Edward, b. Cheltenham, Glos., e. Birmingham (Nechells, Birmingham), 8684, Sgt., d. of w., F. & F., 12/4/17.

Griffin, L., b. Birmingham, e. Birmingham (Small Heath, Birmingham), 241444, Pte., k. in a., F. & F., 29/4/17.
Griffin, William, e. Leamington, Warwicks, 267904, Pte., k. in a., F. & F., 25/4/17.
Griffiths, John Henry, b. Birmingham, e. Birmingham (Hockley, Birmingham), 17715, Pte., k. in a., F. & F., 15/11/16.
Grimley, Sidney, b. Coventry, Warwicks, e. Warwick (Coventry), 202193, Pte., d. of w., F. & F., 23/4/17.
Grimmett, George, b. Birmingham, e. Worcester (Handsworth, Staffs), 28716, Pte., k. in a., F. & F., 24/9/17.
Grosvenor, Edward, e. Birmingham (West Bromwich, Staffs), 10207, Pte., d., Home, 20/10/15.
Gunby, Ernest William, b. Leicester, e. Nuneaton, Warwicks (Leicester), 11484, Pte., k. in a., F. & F., 14/2/17.
Gurton, Marcus Ward, b. Atherstone, Warwicks, e. Warwick (Atherstone), 17595, Pte., k. in a., F. & F., 13/8/16.
Hackett, Arthur, e. Birmingham (Small Heath, Birmingham), 267335, Pte., d. of w., F. & F., 30/10/17.
Hackett, Joseph, e. Birmingham (Dudley, Worcs), 9374, Pte., k. in a., F. & F., 11/8/16.
Haines, Job, b. Quarry Bank, Stourbridge, Worcs, e. Birmingham (Stourbridge), 401, Sgt., k. in a., F. & F., 21/11/16.
Hammond, William Henry, b. St. Martin's, Birmingham, e. Birmingham, 8129, Pte., k. in a., F. & F., 10/7/16.
Hampton, Frederick Edward, b. Ladywood, Birmingham, e. Birmingham (Ladywood), 8767, A/Cpl., d. of w., F. & F., 1/12/16.
Hancox, Edward, b. Birmingham, e. Kineton, Warwicks (Lower Tysoe, Warwicks), 18896, Pte., d. of w., F. & F., 9/5/17.
Harding, Levi, b. Birmingham, e. Birmingham (Winson Green, Birmingham), 10123, Pte., d. of w., F. & F., 15/7/16, formerly 38065, R.A.M.C.
Harris, Arthur Joseph, b. Henley, Oxon, e. Caversham, Oxon (Reading, Berks), 18501, Pte., d. of w., F. & F., 28/4/17, formerly 25276, Som. L.I.
Harris, Frank Martin, b. Potter's Bar, Middx., e. Rugby, Warwicks, 10239, L/Cpl., k. in a., F. & F., 21/11/16.
Harris, Harry, b. Warwick, e. Warwick, 17583, Pte., d. of w., F. & F., 14/11/16.
Harris, Thomas Charles, b. Birmingham, e. Birmingham (Balsall Heath, Birmingham), 11360, Pte., d., F. & F., 9/6/16.
Harrison, Benjamin, b. St. Martin's, Birmingham, e. Warwick (Birmingham), 17549, Pte., k. in a., F. & F., 1/10/16.
Harrison, William, b. Bedworth, Warwicks, e. Warwick (Bedworth), 14833, Pte., k. in a., F. & F., 16/7/16.
Hartley, George, b. Nechells, Birmingham, e. Birmingham (Nechells, Birmingham), 8128, Pte., k. in a., F. & F., 24/9/17.
Hartup, Harry, b. Newport Pagnell, Bucks, e. Bletchley, Bucks (Newport Pagnell), 18382, Pte., k. in a., F. & F., 13/8/16, formerly 23359, Som. L.I.
Harvey, Arthur Cecil, b. Swadlincote, Derby, e. Burton-on-Trent, Staffs (Swadlincote), 28753, Pte., d. of w., F. & F., 28/8/17, formerly D.M.2/231625, R.A.S.C.
Harwood, Albert, b. Whichford, Warwicks, e. Stratford-on-Avon, Warwicks (Whichford), 16249, Pte., d. of w., F. & F., 17/7/16.
Hastings, William, b. Coleshill, Warwicks, e. Coventry, Warwicks (Bedworth, Warwicks), 10087, Pte., d. of w., F. & F., 22/11/16.
Hatton, Albert, b. Fazeley, Staffs, e. Birmingham (Fazeley), 8654, Pte., d. of w., F. & F., 11/7/16.
Hatton, William, b. Birmingham, e. Birmingham, 22820, Pte., k. in a., F. & F., 27/4/17.
Havard, Frederick William, b. Birmingham, e. Birmingham (Bournville, Birmingham), 17692, Pte., k. in a., F. & F., 10/10/17.
Hawling, Clement Aubrey, b. Brierley Hill, Staffs, e. Warwick (Small Heath, Birmingham), 17077, Pte., k. in a., F. & F., 13/8/16.
Haynes, Arthur Thomas, b. Ashton, Bristol, e. Bristol, Glos. (Totterdown, Bristol), 28832, Pte., k. in a., F. & F., 24/9/17.
Haynes, Arthur Trevor, e. Birmingham (Sparkhill, Birmingham), 267598, Pte., d., F. & F., 29/4/17.
Hayton, Percy Daniel Gilling, b. Hereford, e. Hereford, 27835, Pte., d. of w., F. & F., 23/7/17, formerly 24591, Shrops L.I.
Haywood, George Alfred, b. Birmingham, e. Birmingham, 15169, Pte., k. in a., F. & F., 11/8/16.
Hearne, Frederick, b. North Curry, Som., e. Taunton, Som., 27755, Pte., k. in a., F. & F., 24/4/17, formerly 5939, Glos. Regt.
Hearne, John, b. Leicester, e. Northampton, 24315, Pte., d. of w., F. & F., 11/12/17.
Hedges, Zachariah, b. New Invention, Staffs, e. Nuneaton, Warwicks (Polesworth, Warwicks), 11914, Pte., k. in a., F. & F., 24/9/15.
Height, Herbert, b. Leamington Spa, Warwicks, e. Leamington Spa, 20197, Pte., k. in a., F. & F., 11/4/17.
Hemmings, James, b. Wroxton, Banbury, Oxon, e. Birmingham, 17896, Pte., k. in a., F. & F., 15/11/16.
Hemmings, Leonard John, b. Newbold-on-Stour, Glos, e. Stratford-on-Avon, Warwicks (Shipston-on-Stour, Worcs), 16422, Pte., k. in a., F. & F., 24/9/17.
Henshall, Albert, b. Whitchurch, Salop, e. Whitchurch, 27784, Pte., d. of w., F. & F., 14/11/16, formerly 19562, Shrops L.I.
Herrick, Frederick, b. Birmingham, e. Birmingham (Bordesley, Birmingham), 202326, Pte., k. in a., F. & F., 11/4/17.
Hewitt, James, b. Leeds, Yorks, e. Birmingham (Nechells, Birmingham), 17739, Pte., k. in a., F. & F., 25/4/17.
Hewitt, John Douglas, b. Wolverhampton, Staffs, e. Birmingham (Erdington, Birmingham), 8563, Pte., d. of w., F. & F., 20/11/16.
Higginson, James, b. Bentley, Warwicks, e. Atherstone, Warwicks, 11055, Pte., d. of w., F. & F., 19/7/16.
Hill, Frederick, b. Menheniot, Cornwall, e. Coventry, Warwicks (Menheniot), 16438, Cpl., k. in a., F. & F., 28/4/17.
Hillier, John, b. Birmingham, e. Birmingham, 28751, Pte., d. of w., F. & F., 25/7/17, formerly S/4/144977, R.A.S.C.
Hirons, George Albert, b. Heathcote, Warwicks, e. Warwick, 20198, Pte., d. of w., F. & F., 25/9/17.
Hirons, Joseph Henry, b. Warwick, e. Rugby, Warwicks, 22640, Pte., k. in a., F. & F., 10/4/17.
Hiskins, Charlie, b. Chelsea, London, e. Abingdon, Berks, (Steventon, Berks), 28698, Pte., k. in a., F. & F. 26/9/17.
Hitchman, Sydney Charles, b. Leamington Spa, Warwicks, e. Tunstall, Staffs (Longport, Staffs), 8727, A/Cpl., k. in a., F. & F., 16/7/16.
Hobbs, John Allen, b. Nottingham, e. Nuneaton, Warwicks, 4629, L/Cpl., k. in a., F. & F., 9/7/16.
Hobday, George, b. Ryton-on-Dunsmore, Warwicks, e. Coventry, Warwicks (Marton, Warwicks), 9076, Pte., k. in a., F. & F., 16/7/16.
Hodson, Thomas, b. St. Martin's, Birmingham, e. Warwick (Aston, Birmingham), 12177, Pte., d. of w., F. & F., 11/7/16.
Holland, Joseph, b. St. Mary's, Birmingham, e. Birmingham, 8803, Pte., d., F. & F., 11/1/17.
Holloway, William, b. Saltley, Birmingham, e. Birmingham (Saltley), 8119, L/Cpl., k. in a., F. & F., 2/3/17.
Holmes, George, b. Aston Manor, Birmingham, e. Birmingham, 305370, Cpl., k. in a., F. & F., 18/10/17.
Holt, Walter James, b. Mancetter, Warwicks, e. Atherstone, Warwicks (Mancetter), 10291, Pte., k. in a., F. & F., 11/8/16.
Holtom, Edward, b. Combroke, Warwicks, e. Coventry, Warwicks, 19719, Pte., k. in a., F. & F., 22/7/17.
Hooper, John Henry, b. Northfield, Worcs, e. Birmingham (Selly Oak, Birmingham), 16799, Cpl., k. in a., F. & F., 29/4/17.
Hopkins, Arthur, b. Willersey, Worcs, e. Warwick (Barford, Warwicks), 20152, Pte., d., F. & F., 20/1/17.
Hopkins, Harold Charles, b. Redditch, Worcs, e. Warwick (Studley, Warwicks), 28724, Pte., k. in a., F. & F., 9/10/17.
Hopkins, Richard, b. Milton-under-Wychwood, Oxon, e. Oxford (Milton-under-Wychford), 18436, Pte., k. in a., F. & F., 11/10/16, formerly 24035, Som. L.I.
Hornby, Herbert, b. Welford-on-Avon, Glos., e. Birmingham (Welford-on-Avon), 8060, Pte., k. in a., F. & F., 20/5/17.
Hornsey, Sidney, b. Alderminster, Worcs, e. Warwick (Alderminster), 2783, L/Cpl., k. in a., F. & F., 23/4/17.
Horrocks, William, e. Birmingham, 9226, Pte., k. in a., F. & F., 10/4/17.
Horsley, Levi, b. Warwick, e. Warwick (Erdington, Birmingham), 17750, Pte., k. in a., F. & F., 11/8/16.
Hoult, Percy, b. Sparkbrook, Birmingham, e. Sutton Coldfield, Warwicks (Sparkhill, Birmingham), 1162, Pte., d. of w., F. & F., 24/4/17.
Hounsell, Henry Frank, e. Chard, Som., 27756, Pte., k. in a., F. & F., 8/10/17, formerly 5035, Glos. Regt.
Howard, Stephen, b. Dunchurch, Warwicks, e. Rugby, Warwicks (Long Lawford, Warwicks), 17855, Pte., d. of w., F. & F., 1/8/16.
Howkins, W. H., b. Loxley, Warwicks, e. Stratford-on-Avon, Warwicks, 12733, Pte., k. in a., F. & F., 15/7/16.
Huggins, Arthur Percival, b. Birmingham, e. Birmingham (Olton, Warwicks), 17308, Pte., k. in a., F. & F., 13/8/16.
Hughes, Edward, e. Coventry, Warwicks, 15656, Pte., k. in a., F. & F., 16/7/16.
Hughes, Francis Charles, b. Upton-on-Severn, Worcs, e. Droitwich, Worcs, 28733, Pte., k. in a., F. & F., 12/8/17.
Hughes, Henry, b. Birmingham, e. Birmingham (Spring Hill, Birmingham), 22580, Pte., k. in a., F. & F., 28/4/17.
Humpage, Benjamin, b. Nechells, Birmingham, e. Birmingham (Nechells), 8120, Pte., d. of w., F. & F., 28/4/17.
Humphries, Percy, b. Long Lawford, Warwicks, e. Rugby, Warwicks (Long Lawford), 14608, Pte., k. in a., F. & F., 9/4/17.
Hunt, Albert Edward, b. Aston, Birmingham, e. Birmingham, 8349, Pte., d. of w., F. & F., 9/7/16.
Hunt, William George, b. Sparkbrook, Birmingham, e. Birmingham, 24189, Pte., k. in a., F. & F., 26/9/17.
Hyde, Charles Herbert, b. Tewkesbury, Glos., e. Birmingham (Tredington, nr. Tewkesbury), 20349, Pte., k. in a., F. & F., 6/9/17.
Insell, William Henry, b. Stratford-on-Avon, Warwicks, e. Warwick (Alveston, Warwicks), 5651, Pte., k. in a., F. & F., 16/11/16.
Ison, Henry, b. Chapel End, Warwicks, e. Nuneaton, Warwicks, 10071, Pte., k. in a., F. & F., 15/11/16.
Ivatts, Edwin Harold, b. Ladywood, Birmingham, e. Birmingham (Ladywood), 368, L/Cpl., k. in a., F. & F., 1/8/16.
Jacobs, Ralph Ernest, b. Marlow, Bucks, e. Oxford (Marlow), 18350, Pte., d. of w., F. & F., 16/11/16, formerly 23074, Som. L.I.
James, Christopher, b. St. Leonards, Herts, e. Warwick (Solihull, Warwicks), 10616, Pte., k. in a., F. & F., 3/5/16.
Jeffries, Thomas Charles, b. Winchcombe, Glos., e. Cheltenham, Glos. (Winchcombe), 585, L/Cpl., k. in a., F. & F., 1/10/16.
Jeffrey, William, b. Hardwicke, Lancs, e. Warwicks (Tachbrook, Warwicks), 10444, Pte., k. in a., F. & F., 15/7/16.
Jelfs, George Wilfred, b. Willersey, Worcs, e. Stratford-on-Avon, Warwicks (Willersey), 10046, Pte., k. in a., F. & F., 23/4/17.

Jennings, Albert Victor, b. Warwick, e. Stratford-on-Avon, Warwicks (Moreton Morrell, Warwicks), 19207, Pte., k. in a., F. & F., 15/11/16.
Johnson, George, b. Marton, Warwicks, e. Warwick (Shirley, Warwicks), 20188, L/Cpl., d. of w., F. & F., 4/1/18.
Johnson, George William, b. St. Luke's, Kettering, Northants, e. Birmingham (Bromsgrove, Worcs), 8269, Pte., k. in a., F. & F., 24/4/17.
Johnson, James, b. St. Bartholomew, Birmingham, e. Birmingham (Saltley, Birmingham), 8805, Pte., k. in a., F. & F., 29/4/17.
Johnson, James, b. Vange, Essex, e. Reading, Berks (Vange), 28756, Pte., k. in a., F. & F., 26/9/17.
Johnson, Oscar, b. Birmingham, e. Birmingham (Hurley, Warwicks), 16073, Cpl., k. in a., F. & F., 24/4/17.
Jones, Alfred, e. Birmingham, 9233, Pte., k. in a., F. & F., 15/7/16.
Jones, Archibald Edwin, b. Warwick, e. Coventry, Warwicks 16410, Pte., k. in a., F. & F., 11/11/17.
Jones, Ernest, b. Birmingham, e. Birmingham, 11707, Pte., d., F. & F., 14/12/15.
Jones, Ernest Albert Emanuel, b. Birmingham, e. Birmingham (Aston, Birmingham), 22760, Pte., d. of w., F. & F., 25/4/17.
Jones, George Herbert, b. Tamworth, Staffs, e. Atherstone, Warwicks (Tamworth), 10745, Pte., k. in a., F. & F., 13/8/16.
Jones, Ishmael, b. Bilston, Staffs, e. Nuneaton, Warwicks (Stockingford, Warwicks), 9510, L/Cpl., k. in a., F. & F., 10/8/16.
Jones, John Edward, b. Birmingham, e. Birmingham, 17693, Pte., k. in a., F. & F., 25/4/17.
Jones, Sidney Frederick, b. Smethwick, Staffs, e. Birmingham (Ladywood, Birmingham), 23082, Pte., d. of w., F. & F., 29/4/17.
Jordan, John Ernest, b. Knighton, Radnor, e. Knighton, 27796, Pte., k. in a., F. & F., 21/11/16, formerly 24573, Shrops L.I.
Keaveney, Thomas, b. Birmingham, e. Birmingham (Ladywood, Birmingham), 16994, Pte., d. of w., F. & F., 13/8/16.
Keeling, Charles Craddock, b. Hall End, Tamworth, Warwicks, e. Warwick (Dordon, Warwicks), 17596, Pte., k. in a., F. & F., 1/8/16.
Kelly, Thomas, b. Birmingham, e. London (Birmingham), 28223, Pte., d., F. & F., 10/8/17, formerly 14783, Hussars.
Kemp, Charles, b. Stratford-on-Avon, Warwicks, e. Stratford-on-Avon (Shottery, Warwicks), 16710, Pte., d. of w., F. & F., 25/9/17.
Kench, Albert Edward, b. Birmingham, e. Birmingham (Smethwick, Staffs), 20150, Pte., k. in a., F. & F., 24/9/17.
Kennings, Thomas, b. West Bromwich, Staffs, e. Birmingham (Smethwick, Staffs), 8980, Pte., k. in a., F. & F., 15/7/16.
Kirby, John, b. Aston, Birmingham, e. Birmingham (Aston), 11416, Pte., d. of w., F. & F., 9/3/17.
Kirkland, John William, b. Ashbourne, Derby, e. Birmingham (Ashbourne), 10285, L/Cpl., d. of w., F. & F., 18/7/16.
Knaggs, William Edward, b. Sunderland, Durham, e. Consett, Durham (Sunderland), 11907, Sgt., k. in a., F. & F., 11/4/17.
Knight, George Henry, b. Meriden, Warwicks, e. Coventry, Warwicks (Claybrook, Leics), 10563, Pte., k. in a., F. & F., 11/4/17.
Knight, Harry Henry, b. Birmingham, e. Birmingham, 10610, Pte., k. in a., F. & F., 13/8/16.
Knight, John James, b. Small Heath, Birmingham, e. Birmingham (Small Heath), 10256, Cpl., d. of w., F. & F., 23/8/16.
Lackey, Percival, b. St. Bartholomew, Birmingham, e. Birmingham, 2458, Pte., k. in a., F. & F., 7/11/15.
Lamb, William Thomas, b. Walsall, Staffs, e. Coventry, Warwicks, 3295, L/Cpl., k. in a., F. & F., 1/8/16.
Lambert, William Charles David, b. Birmingham, e. Warwick (Aston, Birmingham), 8563, Pte., k. in a., F. & F., 15/7/16.
Lambeth, Arthur, b. Aston, Birmingham, e. Aston, 305702, Pte., k. in a., F. & F., 27/4/17.
Latham, Alfred, b. Aston, Birmingham, e. Birmingham, 8273, Pte., k. in a., F. & F., 16/7/16.
Laugher, Frank, b. Bromsgrove, Worcs, e. Bromsgrove, 267054, Pte., d., F. & F., 17/9/17.
Lawrence, Ernest, b. Bocking, Essex, e. Coventry, Warwicks (Bocking), 19406, Pte., d. of w., F. & F., 4/5/17.
Lawrence, Ralph Frederick, b. Birmingham, e. Warwick (Handsworth, Birmingham), 17627, Pte., d. of w., F. & F., 27/8/16.
Lax, Gilbert, b. Stockton, Durham, e. Consett, Durham (Stockton), 11073, L/Cpl., k. in a., F. & F., 10/10/17.
Layton, James, b. Coddington, Hereford, e. Hereford (Weston Biggard, Hereford), 27800, Pte., d. of w., F. & F., 29/11/16, formerly 24630, Shrops L.I.
Lee, John Gilbert, b. Sheffield, Yorks, e. Birmingham (Aston, Birmingham), 13029, L/Cpl., k. in a., F. & F., 15/7/16.
Liddington, Wallace, b. Rugby, Warwicks, e. Rugby, 21021, Pte., d. of w., F. & F., 25/4/17.
Loakes, George, b. Blackburn, Lancs, e. Coventry, Warwicks, 265845, Pte., k. in a., F. & F., 23/4/17.
Lockyer, Frederick, b. Bordesley, Birmingham, e. Birmingham (Philadelphia, U.S.A.), 8271, Pte., k. in a., F. & F., 27/4/17.
Long, Percy, b. Brailes, Staffs, e. Birmingham (Oldbury, Worcs), 15273, Pte., k. in a., F. & F., 16/7/16.
Lott, Albert Leonard, b. Church Stretton, Salop, e. Church Stretton, 27802, Pte., k. in a., F. & F., 25/11/16, formerly 24709, Shrops L.I.
Lovell, William Henry, b. Leamington, Warwicks, e. Leamington, 17391, L/Cpl., d. of w., F. & F., 15/8/16.
Loveridge, Ernest, b. Birmingham, e. Birmingham, 11026, L/Cpl., k. in a., F. & F., 10/7/16.
Lynes, Thomas, b. Coventry, Warwicks, e. Coventry, 9590, Pte., d. of w., F. & F., 19/7/16.
Mabberley, William, b. Cheltenham, Glos., e. Gloucester (Cirencester, Glos.), 27699, Pte., k. in a., F. & F., 14/11/16, formerly 5728, Glos. Regt.
McCarthy, Alfred Charles, b. Holborn, Middx., e. London (King's Cross, London), 20597, Pte., k. in a., F. & F., 27/4/17, formerly 11108, A.C.C.
McClure, Samuel, b. Radford, Nottingham, e. Birmingham, 4860, Pte., d. of w., F. & F., 20/7/16.
Mallabone, Thomas, b. Chilvers Coton, Warwicks, e. Coventry, Warwicks (Collycroft, Warwicks), 12694, L/Cpl., k. in a., F. & F., 12/3/16.
Mann, William, b. Birmingham, e. Birmingham (Sparkbrook, Birmingham), 8143, L/Sgt., k. in a., F. & F., 24/4/17.
Mansell, Thomas, b. Birmingham, e. Birmingham (Small Heath, Birmingham), 9260, Pte., d. of w., F. & F., 10/7/16.
Markham, Thomas, b. Upton, Warwicks, e. Southam, Warwicks (Bascote Heath, Warwicks), 17859, Pte., d., F. & F., 5/6/18.
Martin, Frank Louis, e. West Bromwich, Staffs, 19666, Pte., k. in a., F. & F., 12/8/17.
Martin, John Thomas, b. Husbands Bosworth, Leics, e. Coventry, Warwicks (Husbands Bosworth), 24287, Pte., k. in a., F. & F., 9/10/17.
Martin, William Joseph Charles, e. Bristol, Glos., 267000, Pte., k. in a., F. & F., 25/7/17.
Mason, Frederick, b. Ferndale, Glam., e. Ferndale (Pembroke Dock, Glam.), 27782, Pte., d. of w., F. & F., 21/11/16, formerly 15237, Shrops L.I.
Mason, Frederick Henry, b. Coughton, Warwicks, e. Worcester (Coughton), 9212, L/Cpl., d. of w., F. & F., 9/8/17.
Matthews, Albert George, b. Walton, Bucks, e. Aylesbury, Bucks, 18428, Pte., k. in a., F. & F., 13/8/16, formerly 23820, Som. L.I.
Maycock, Robert Henry, b. Ryton-on-Dunsmore, Warwicks, e. Coventry, Warwicks (Ryton-on-Dunsmore), 17374, Pte., k. in a., F. & F., 13/8/16.
Maynard, William, b. Stratford-on-Avon, Warwicks, e. Stratford-on-Avon, 11421, Pte., k. in a., F. & F., 16/11/16.
Melton, John James, b. Swaffham, Norfolk, e. Worcester (Clifton-on-Teme, Worcs), 21719, Pte., k. in a., F. & F., 29/4/17, formerly R7/8266, Glos. Regt.
Merchant, Edward Massey, b. Nottingham, e. Nottingham, 27388, Pte., d., F. & F., 18/4/18, formerly 35036, Notts & Derby Regt.
Merchant, Henry, b. West Bromwich, Staffs, e. Birmingham (Smethwick, Staffs), 14524, Pte., k. in a., F. & F., 16/7/16.
Merrell, Albert, b. Bromsgrove, Worcs, e. Birmingham (King's Norton, Birmingham), 17542, Pte., k. in a., F. & F., 21/11/16.
Miles, James, b. Temple Balsall, Warwicks, e. Knowle, Warwicks, 18043, Pte., k. in a., F. & F., 23/4/17.
Miller, Alfred Fred William, b. S. Prested, Sussex, e. Coventry, Warwicks, 24154, Pte., k. in a., F. & F., 9/10/17.
Mitchell, Benjamin Henry, b. Aston Manor, Birmingham, e. Birmingham, 1828, Pte., k. in a., F. & F., 13/8/16.
Mitchell, Ernest, b. St. Pancras, London, e. St. Pancras (Kentish Town, London, N.W.), 9112, Sgt., k. in a., F. & F., 9/7/16.
Mitchell, Percy Charles, b. Portsmouth, Hants, e. Reading, Berks (Maidenhead, Berks), 28846, Pte., k. in a., F. & F., 6/9/17, formerly S4/145130, R.A.S.C.
Montague, Sydney, b. London, e. Ramsgate, Kent, 28772, Pte., k. in a., F. & F., 22/7/17, formerly S4/122492, R.A.S.C.
Moore, George Thomas, b. Bristol, Glos., e. Birmingham (Rickmansworth, Herts), 9521, Pte., d. of w., F. & F., 13/7/16.
Moore, Herbert, b. Atherstone, Warwicks, e. Nuneaton, Warwicks (Ansley Common, Warwicks), 14341, Pte., d. of w., F. & F., 30/7/16.
Moore, John, b. St. John's, Birmingham, e. Parkhurst, I. of W. (Birmingham), 12869, Pte., k. in a., F. & F., 15/7/16.
Mouzer, Albert John, b. Norton Lindsay, Warwicks, e. Warwick (Lower Norton, Warwicks), 19435, Pte., k. in a., F. & F., 29/4/17.
Muddiman, George Henry Wickers, b. Cobham, Kent, e. Birmingham (Small Heath, Birmingham), 20471, Pte., k. in a., F. & F., 7/10/17.
Mullaley, Thomas, b. Birmingham, e. Birmingham, 11756, Pte., k. in a., F. & F., 29/4/17.
Nash, Stanley George, b. Chesham, Bucks, e. Aylesbury, Bucks (Chesham), 18529, Pte., d. of w., F. & F., 16/11/16, formerly 25377, Som. L.I.
Neal, David, b. Banbury, Oxon, e. Coventry, Warwicks (Longford, Warwicks), 16843, Pte., d. of w., F. & F., 19/7/16.
Neal, Walter Ernest, b. Fillongley, Warwicks, e. Coventry, Warwicks (Allesley, Warwicks), 17456, Pte., k. in a., F. & F., 26/11/16.
Neary, Charles, b. Vauxhall, Birmingham, e. Birmingham (Small Heath, Birmingham), 8216, Pte., k. in a., F. & F., 11/8/16.
New, Percy Samuel, b. Basingstoke, Hants, e. Fordingbridge, Wilts (Breamore, Wilts), 241971, Pte., k. in a., F. & F., 24/4/17, formerly 2010, Hampshire Regt.
Nixon, Thomas Parker, b. Nuneaton, Warwicks, e. Nuneaton (Leicester), 17920, L/Cpl., k. in a., F. & F., 13/8/16.
Oldrey, George, b. Birmingham, e. Birmingham (Small Heath, Birmingham), 8149, Pte., k. in a., F. & F., 13/8/16.
O'Neil, Albert, b. Coventry, Warwicks, e. Coventry, 17674, Pte., k. in a., F. & F., 13/8/16.
Osborne, Francis Edward, b. St. Mary's, Wolverhampton, Staffs, e. Birmingham, 8694, Pte., k. in a., F. & F., 15/7/16.

Overs, William John Drane, b. Kenilworth, Warwicks, e. Warwick (Kenilworth), 9594, L/Sgt., d. of w., F. & F., 19/8/16.

Page, Victor Scott, b. Claybrook, Leics, e. Rugby, Warwicks (Walton-on-Thames, Surrey), 9265, L/Sgt., k. in a., F. & F., 16/7/16.

Parker, Frank, b. Ladywood, Birmingham, e. Birmingham (Harborne, Birmingham), 17763, Pte., k. in a., F. & F., 14/11/16.

Parker, Frederick, b. Stapenhill, Derby, e. Nuneaton, Warwicks (Stockingford, Warwicks), 12460, Pte., k. in a., F. & F., 13/8/16, formerly 53760, R.G.A.

Parratt, Samuel William, b. Bradford, Yorks, e. Coventry, Warwicks, 15038, L/Cpl., k. in a., F. & F.., 10/4/17.

Parsons, Albert Joseph, b. St. Martin's, Birmingham, e. Birmingham (Sparkbrook, Birmingham), 17764, Pte., k. in a., F. & F., 13/8/16.

Partridge, Alfred, b. Great Bridge, Staffs, e. Birmingham (Tipton, Staffs), 11424, Pte., d. of w., F. & F., 25/6/16.

Paston, Charles, e. Nuneaton, Warwicks (Attleborough, Warwicks), 10528, Pte., k. in a., F. & F., 9/8/17.

Patrick, Felix, b. Ipswich, Suffolk, e. Nuneaton, Warwicks (Leigh-on-Sea, Essex), 12244, Sgt., d. of w., F. & F., 12/4/17.

Paul, William, b. Coventry, Warwicks, e. Ross, Herts (Winson Green, Birmingham), 6865, Pte., k. in a., F. & F., 10/4/17.

Payne, Charles, b. Vauxhall, Birmingham, e. Birmingham (Vauxhall), 10254, Pte., k. in a., F. & F., 12/7/16.

Payne, Ernest, b. Pailton, Warwicks, e. Rugby, Warwicks 10122, L/Cpl., k. in a., F. & F., 15/7/16.

Pemberton, George Reece, b. Birmingham, e. Birmingham (Aston, Birmingham), 28794, Pte., k. in a., F. & F., 9/10/17.

Peplow, John, b. Bromsgrove, Worcs, e. Stratford-on-Avon, Warwicks, 19218, Pte., d., F. & F., 17/2/17.

Pepper, James Frederick, b. Birmingham, e. Birmingham (Aston, Birmingham), 202892, Pte., k. in a., F. & F., 9/10/17.

Perry, Joseph, b. Birmingham, e. Birmingham, 14505, Pte., k. in a., F. & F., 23/7/16.

Perkins, Horace Thomas, b. Olney, Bucks, e. Bletchley, Bucks (Olney), 18448, Pte., k. in a., F. & F., 10/4/17, formerly 24031, Som. L.I.

Pettipher, George, b. Warwick, e. Warwick, 18263, Pte., d. of w., F. & F., 12/4/17.

Phelps, Harry, b. Duddeston, Birmingham, e. Birmingham (Saltley, Birmingham), 8155, Pte., d. of w., F. & F., 12/4/17.

Phipps, Henry Albert, b. Aston, Warwicks, e. Birmingham (Lozells, Birmingham), 17630, Pte., k. in a., F. & F., 13/8/16.

Phipps, James Richard, b. West Dean, Glos., e. Bristol, Glos. (Coleford, Glos.), 21722, L/Cpl., d. of w., F. & F., 3/12/16, formerly 29260, Glos. Regt.

Pickard, James, b. Coventry, Warwicks, e. Coventry, 15252, Pte., k. in a., F. & F., 9/10/17.

Pickering, John Wiiliam, b. Swannington, Leics, e. Warwick (Nuneaton, Warwicks), 14837, Pte., k. in a., F. & F., 9/7/16.

Pitcher, Bernard Harold, e. Stratford-on-Avon, Warwicks (Bidford-on-Avon, Warwicks), 9249, L/Cpl., k. in a., F. & F., 10/4/17.

Player, Wilfred James, e. Worcester, 266975, Pte., d. of w., F. & F,. 24/4/17.

Plowman, Ernest, b. Haddon, Hunts, e. Huntingdon (Peterborough, Northants), 30225, Pte., k. in a., F. & F., 23/4/17, formerly 1254, Hunts Cyc. Battn.

Pointon, Thomas, e. Nuneaton, Warwicks (Little Packington, Warwicks), 267740, Pte., k. in a., F. & F., 23/5/17.

Pope, William Tom, b. Upton-on-Severn, Worcs, e. Worcester (Upton-on-Severn), 30066, Pte., d. of w., F. & F., 7/6/17, formerly 27889, Worcs Regt.

Postins, Sidney Colin, b. Titchfield, Hants, e. Birmingham (Stourbridge, Worcs), 18375, Pte., k. in a., F. & F., 13/8/16, formerly 23288, Som. L.I.

Potter, Arnold Anderton, b. Ladywood, Birmingham, e. Birmingham, 8794, L/Sgt., k. in a., F. & F., 23/4/17.

Povey, Frank, b. Manchester, e. Manchester, 23314, Pte., d. of w., F. & F., 29/4/17, formerly 3460, R.E.

Power, Ernest Reginald, b. Saltley, Birmingham, e. Birmingham, 24178, Pte., k. in a., F. & F., 9/10/17.

Preece, Arthur Henry, b. Birmingham, e. Birmingham (Ladywood, Birmingham), 16940, Pte., d. of w., F. & F., 9/10/17.

Preen, Richard, b. Small Heath, Birmingham, e. Birmingham, 8841, Pte., k. in a., F. & F., 8/10/17.

Price, Irvine, b. Birmingham, e. Birmingham (Aston, Birmingham), 330528, Pte., k. in a., F. & F., 7/10/17.

Price, Oscar Leonard, b. Aston, Birmingham, e. Birmingham, 8883, L/Cpl., k. in a., F. & F., 11/4/17.

Priest, William Joseph, b. Bedworth, Warwicks, e. Hucknall, Notts, 11038, L/Cpl., d., F. & F., 29/1/17.

Probets, Walter, b. Brill, Bucks, e. Birmingham (Brill), 14864, Pte., k. in a., F. & F., 16/7/16.

Puffer, Harry Henry, b. Birmingham, e. Birmingham, 8879, Pte., k. in a., F. & F., 15/7/16.

Quelch, Alfred Thomas, b. Pentless, Hants, e. Newbury, Berks (Midgham, Berks), 34805, Pte., k. in a., F. & F., 3/1/18.

Radburn, Joseph, b. Holy Trinity, Coventry, Warwicks, e. Coventry, 28544, Pte., k. in a., F. & F., 29/4/17.

Ralph, Richard, b. Redditch, Worcs, e. Redditch, 28827, Pte., k. in a., F. & F., 25/7/17.

Ransom, James Edward, b. Birmingham, e. Birmingham, 8613, A/Sgt., k. in a., F. & F., 18/11/16.

Raybould, Albert Alfred, b. Coventry, Warwicks, e. Coventry, 16849, Pte., k. in a., F. & F., 8/7/16.

Reeves, Alfred Thomas, b. Reading, Berks, e. Caversham, Berks, 307773, Pte., k. in a., F. & F., 24/9/17.

Rennie, William, b. Glasgow, e. Glasgow, 18103, Sgt., k. in a., F. & F., 23/4/17, formerly 12344, Dragoons.

Reynolds, James, b. Kinton, Staffs, e. Coventry, Warwicks (Kenilworth, Warwicks), 22782, Pte., k. in a., F. & F., 28/4/17.

Reynolds, James Henry, b. Birmingham, e. Birmingham, 11715, Pte., d. of w., F. & F., 13/8/17.

Richards, Clay, e. Nuneaton, Warwicks (Bedworth, Warwicks), 9880, Cpl., d. of w., F. & F., 26/7/17.

Richards, John, b. St. Georges, Birmingham, e. Birmingham (Balsall Heath, Birmingham), 8164, C.S.M., k. in a., F. & F., 22/5/17.

Richardson, Ernest Charles, b. Tringford, Oxon, e. Oxford (Tringford), 18398, Pte., k. in a., F. & F., 13/8/16, formerly 23459, Som. L.I.

Ricarby, Henry, b. Deptford, Kent, e. Warwick (Leamington, Warwicks), 1734, Pte., k. in a., F. & F., 10/5/16.

Riddle, William, b. St. Phillips', Bristol, e. Bristol, 21724, Pte., k. in a., F. & .,F 23/5/17, formerly 20663, Glos. Regt.

Rider, Joseph, b. Coventry, Warwicks, e. Warwick (Bedworth, Warwicks), 28555, Pte., k. in a., F. & F., 10/4/17.

Robbins, George William, b. Wookey, Som., e. Birmingham (Aston, Birmingham), 876, L/Cpl., k. in a., F. & F., 1/8/16.

Roberts, Ben, b. Liverpool, Lancs, e. Oldham, Lancs, 12307, Pte., d. of w., F. & F., 8/8/16, formerly 53386, R.G.A.

Roberts, George Harold, b. Nottingham, e. Coventry, Warwicks, 17421, Pte., d. of w., F. & F., 12/8/17.

Robertson, Henry Thomas, b. Cardiff, Glam., e. Birmingham (Edgbaston, Birmingham), 17810, Pte., k. in a., F. & F., 29/4/17.

Robinson, Alfred, b. Oxford, e. Oxford (New Headington, Oxon), 18509, Pte., d. of w., F. & F., 23/4/17, formerly 25201, Som. L.I.

Robotham, Arthur, b. Walsall, Staffs, e. Smethwick, Staffs (Walsall), 15778, Pte., k. in a., F. & F., 23/4/17.

Ross, Alexander, e. Warwick (Troon, Ayrshire), 20966, Pte., d. of w., F. & F., 29/4/17.

Rowland, William John, b. Eton, Bucks, e. Oxford (Streatham, London), 18403, Cpl., k. in a., F. & F., 25/4/17, formerly 23465, Som. L.I.

Rowland, Samuel, b. Nuneaton, Warwicks, e. Nuneaton, 11266, Pte., d. of w., F. & F., 14/2/16.

Rowley, Richard Francis, b. Wolvey, Warwicks, e. Birmingham (Northfield, Birmingham), 9869, Sgt., d. of w., F. & F., 27/10/15.

Ruffles, George Henry, b. Plumbtree, Notts, e. Birmingham (Mapperley Plains, Notts), 12099, C.S.M., k. in a., F. & F., 16/7/16.

Russell, Edgar, b. St. Lukes, Derby, e. Birmingham, 9100, Pte., k. in a., F. & F., 15/7/16.

Russell, Thomas, b. Aston, Birmingham, e. Birmingham (Small Heath, Birmingham), 9016, Pte., k. in a., F. & F., 24/6/16.

Russell, William, b. Bordesley, Birmingham, e. Birmingham (Sparkbrook, Birmingham), 8161, Pte., k. in a., F. & F., 15/7/16.

Sanders, Henry, b. Derby, e Birmingham (Amey, Detroit, U.S.A.), Pte., k. in a., F. & F., 15/7/16.

Sanders, Henry Charles, b. Birmingham, e. Manchester, 14931, Pte., k. in a., F. & F., 13/8/16, formerly 14594, S. Lancs Regt.

Saunders, Ernest Alfred, b. Bardon, Leics, e. Birmingham (Bromsgrove, Worcs), 28784, Pte., d. of w., F. & F., 10/12/17.

Saunders, Frank, b. Feckenham, Worcs, e. Redditch, Worcs, 28833, Pte., k. in a., F. & F., 8/10/17.

Saunders, Frank William, b. Aston, Birmingham, e. Birmingham (Saltley, Birmingham), 8168, Pte., d. of w., F. & F., 7/7/16.

Saunders, Godfrey William, b. Birmingham, e. Birmingham, 9021, Pte., k. in a., F. & F., 29/4/17.

Saunders, William, b. Ladywood, Birmingham, e. Birmingham, 8302, Pte., k. in a., F. & F., 12/7/16.

Scandrett, William, b. Warwick, e. Warwick, 2280, Pte., k. in a., F. & F., 15/7/16.

Scrivens, William, b. Aston, Birmingham, e. Birmingham (Selly Oak, Birmingham), 8298, Pte., k. in a., F. & F., 11/7/16.

Seaton, Hugh Victor Alexander, b. Aston, Birmingham, e. Birmingham, 240621, Pte., k. in a., F. & F., 28/5/17.

Shale, Edward, e. Birmingham (Erdington, Birmingham), 267652, Pte., k. in a., F. & F., 8/9/17.

Sharpe, Francis Phillip, b. Nuneaton, Warwicks, e. Nuneaton, 9907, Pte., k. in a., F. & F., 15/7/16.

Shaw, James, e. Nottingham, 27413, L/Cpl., k. in a., F. & F., 23/4/17, formerly 3350, Notts & Derby Regt.

Shaw, John, b. St. Michael's, Coventry, Warwicks, e. Coventry, 1751, L/Cpl., k. in a., F. & F., 15/11/16.

Shaw, John Charles, b. Dunchurch, Warwicks, e. Rugby, Warwicks (Dunchurch), 18100, Pte., k. in a., F. & F., 1/8/16.

Shear, Arthur, b. Birmingham, e. Coventry, Warwicks (Warwick), 3562, R.S.M., k. in a., F. & F., 14/11/16.

Sheldon, William, b. Tewkesbury, Glos., e. Birmingham (Ladywood, Birmingham), 14516, Pte., k. in a., F. & F., 11/8/16.

Sheridan, Leslie, b. Saffron Walden, Essex, e. Stratford-on-Avon, Warwicks, 10628, Pte., k. in a., F. & F., 16/7/16.

Silvester, Frank, b. Coombe Farm, Stratford-on-Avon, e. Stratford-on-Avon, Warwicks (Coombe Farm), 28734, Pte., k. in a., F. & F., 9/10/17.

Simkins, Richard, b. Aston, Birmingham, e. Birmingham, 8783, Pte., k. in a., F. & F., 27/5/17.

Simmonds, John, b. Birmingham, e. Birmingham (Balsall Heath, Birmingham), 8836, Pte., d. of w., F. & F., 4/6/16.

Simms, Thomas Frederick, b. Birmingham, e. Birmingham (Witton, Birmingham), 16/1739, Pte., k. in a., F. & F., 29/4/17.

Simpson, Hubert, e. Birmingham (Marston Green, Warwicks), 20841, Pte., k. in a., F. & F., 10/8/17.

Siviter, Samuel, b. Blackheath, Staffs, e. Birmingham (Blackheath), 8846, Pte., k. in a., F. & F., 13/8/16.

Skelton, Charles Frederick, b. Stone, Staffs, e. Warwick (Burton-on-Trent, Staffs), 16539, Pte., d. of w., F. & F., 22/7/17.

Skidmore, Arthur, b. Aston, Birmingham, e. Birmingham, 21087, Pte., k. in a., F. & F., 24/9/17.

Smith, Alfred, b. Lapworth, Warwicks, e. Stratford-on-Avon, Warwicks (Hockley Heath, Warwicks), 21726, Pte., k. in a., F. & F., 28/4/17, formerly 29413, Gloucester Regt.

Smith, Alfred Ernest, b. Wolstanton, Stoke-on-Trent, e. Stoke-on-Trent, Staffs (Wolstanton), 9144, Pte., d. of w., F. & F., 16/7/16.

Smith, Alfred William, b. Nechells, Birmingham, e. Birmingham (Aston, Birmingham), 11370, Pte., k. in a., F. & F., 15/7/16.

Smith, Harold Herbert, b. Coventry, Warwicks, e. Coventry (Foleshill, Coventry), 28685, Pte., k. in a., F. & F., 17/7/17.

Smith, John Henry, b. Highgate, Birmingham, e. Birmingham, 8863, Pte., d. of w., F. & F., 24/5/17.

Smith, John Henry, b. Langley, Warwicks, e. Warwick (Langley), 9053, L/Cpl., k. in a., F. & F., 10/4/17.

Smith, John Joseph, b. Wallasey, Ches., e. Birkenhead, Ches. (Wallasey), 28678, Pte., k. in a., F. & F., 19/8/17, formerly 2118, R.A.S.C.

Smith, Joseph, b. St. George's, Birmingham, e. Birmingham (Hockley, Birmingham), 8166, Pte., k. in a., F. & F., 15/7/16.

Smith, Leonard Clifford, b. St. Mary's, Warwick, e. Warwick, 430, Sgt., k. in a., F. & F., 11/7/16.

Smith, Oliver Thomas, b. Bulkington, Warwicks, e. Bedworth, Warwicks (Bulkington), 16441, Pte., d., F. & F., 14/4/18.

Smith, William, b. Bedworth, Warwicks, e. Nuneaton, Warwicks (Collycroft, Bedworth), 12661, Pte., k. in a., F. & F., 13/8/16.

Smith, Ernest, b. Birmingham, e. Birmingham (Hockley, Birmingham), 10127, Pte., d. of w., F. & F., 15/7/16.

Smith, William Henry, b. Coventry, Warwicks, e. Coventry, 10115, L/Sgt., k. in a., F. & F., 24/9/17.

Smithson, George, b. Stoke, Coventry, e. Coventry, Warwicks, 10088, Pte., k. in a., F. & F., 15/7/16.

Sorrell, William, b. Harrington, Worcs, e. Birmingham, 4823, Pte., k. in a., F. & F., 16/7/16.

Southam, Francis James, b. Grendon, Warwicks, e. Atherstone, Warwicks (Stoke-on-Tern, Salop), 16216, Pte., k. in a., F. & F., 23/9/17.

Southorn, William Charles, b. Tipton, Staffs, e. Birmingham (Tipton), 10270, A/Cpl., k. in a., F. & F., 23/4/17.

Spears, Alfred John, b. Birmingham, e. Birmingham, 10261, Pte., d. of w., F. & F., 15/7/16.

Spencer, Elliott, b. Upton-on-Severn, Worcs, e. Warwick (Olton, Warwicks), 20228, Pte., k. in a., F. & F., 29/4/17.

Spencer, James Bartlett, e. Rugby, Warwicks, 267322, Pte., k. in a., F. & F., 22/7/17.

Spink, Harry, b. Leeds, Yorks, e. Bradford, Yorks (Holbeck, Leeds), 8900, Pte., k. in a., F. & F., 13/8/16.

Stapleford, William Henry, b. Buxton, Derbyshire, e. Birmingham (Buxton), 14697, Pte., k. in a., F. & F., 15/7/16.

Stanley, John, b. St. Nicholas, Coventry, Warwicks, e. Warwick (Coventry), 2321, Sgt., k. in a., F. & F., 1/10/16.

Stevens, Albert, b. Birmingham, e. Birmingham, 391, Cpl., d. of w., F. & F., 10/8/17.

Stevens, William, b. Sutton Coldfield, Warwicks, e. Birmingham, 9014, Pte., k. in a., F. & F., 15/7/16.

Stock, Clarence, b. St. Paul's, Leamington, Warwicks, e. Leamington, 266174, Pte., k. in a., F. & F., 23/4/17.

Stoddard, Walter, b. Ladywood, Birmingham, e. Birmingham (Ladywood), 5168, Pte., k. in a., F. & F., 16/2/16.

Stokes, George, b. Ladywood, Birmingham, e. Birmingham, 1590, Pte., k. in a., F. & F., 13/8/16.

Stonehouse, Walter, b. Polesworth, Warwicks, e. Birmingham (Polesworth), 9155, Pte., d. of w., F. & F., 10/7/16.

Storry, Albert, b. New Wortley, Yorks, e. Birmingham (Small Heath, Birmingham), 17685, Pte., k. in a., F. & F., 24/4/17.

Street, Frank, b. Birmingham, e. Birmingham (Saltley, Birmingham), 17633, Pte., k. in a., F. & F., 16/11/16.

Sumner, William, b. Milverton, Warwicks, e. Warwick (Leamington, Warwicks), 9939, L/Cpl., k. in a., F. & F., 11/8/17.

Swift, Charles Edward, b. Caversham, Oxon, e. Caversham, 18442, Pte., d. of w., F. & F., 13/8/16, formerly 24025, Som. L.I.

Tacey, Ernest, b. Shepshead, Leics, e. Nuneaton, Warwicks (Shepshead), 11513, Cpl., d. of w., F. & F., 18/11/16.

Tandy, Jack, b. Knowle, Warwicks, e. Knowle, 17974, Pte., k. in a., F. & F., 16/11/16.

Tansley, Percy William, b. Coventry, Warwicks, e. Coventry, 16758, Pte., k. in a., F. & F., 15/7/16.

Tatton, Horace William, b. Small Heath, Birmingham, e. Birmingham (Balsall Heath, Birmingham), 22561, Pte., k. in a., F. & F., 23/5/17.

Taylor, Daniel, b. Coventry, Warwicks, e. Coventry, 18808, Pte., k. in a., F. & F., 29/4/17.

Taylor, George, b. Crabb's Cross, Redditch, Worcs, e. Redditch (Crabb's Cross), 9316, C.Q.M.S., k. in a., F. & F., 22/7/17.

Taylor, Harry, b. Darlington, Durham, e. Darlington, 28710, Pte., k. in a., F. & F., 10/10/17, formerly S/4/145342, R.A.S.C.

Taylor, John Edmund, b. Stockingford, Warwicks, e. Warwick (Nuneaton, Warwicks), 16560, Pte., k. in a., F. & F., 12/8/16.

Thomas, Alfred, b. Wolverhampton, Staffs, e. Birmingham (Balsall Heath, Birmingham), 240402, L/Cpl., k. in a., F. & F., 7/10/17.

Thomas, Henry, b. Wroxeter, Salop, e. Shrewsbury, Salop (Wroxeter), 27790, Pte., k. in a., F. & F., 21/11/16, formerly 24539, Shrops L.I.

Thompson, James, b. Bell Green, Coventry, Warwicks, e. Coventry (Bell Green), 10047, Pte., d. of w., F. & F., 5/7/17.

Thompson, Wallace, e. Birmingham (Perry Barr, Birmingham), 267472, Pte., k. in a., F. & F., 9/10/17.

Thornley, Francis Edward, b. Birmingham, e. Birmingham (Yardley, Birmingham), 15406, Pte., k. in a., F. & F., 29/4/17.

Thorpe, Richard, b. Bedworth, Warwicks, e. Nuneaton, Warwicks (Bedworth), 17378, Pte., k. in a., F. & F., 13/8/16.

Tiff, George Edgar, b. Stockton, Warwicks, e. Warwick (Stockton), 20910, L/Cpl., k. in a., F. & F., 28/5/17.

Timerick, Norbert, b. Coventry, Warwicks, e. Coventry, 16780, Pte., k. in a., F. & F., 9/7/16.

Timmins, A., e. Birmingham (Vauxhall, Birmingham), 9309, L/Cpl., k. in a., F. & F., 14/7/16, M.M.

Tompkins, Edward, b. St. Thomas, Stourbridge, Worcs, e. Worcester (Stourbridge), 8734, Pte., k. in a., F. & F., 12/7/16.

Townsend, Frederick, b. Bampton, Oxon, e. Oxford (Bampton), 18423, Pte., k. in a., F. & F., 12/8/16, formerly 23814, Som. L.I.

Townsend, Frederick Bert, b. Birmingham, e. Warwick (Kings Norton, Birmingham), 17551, Pte., d. of w., F. & F., 1/10/16.

Trudgett, George, b. Westbourne, Sussex, e. Gosport, Hants (Westbourne), 28736, Pte., k. in a., F. & F., 12/8/17, formerly S/4/143751, R.A.S.C.

Truelove, Victor James, b. Billinghurst, Sussex, e. Horsham, Sussex (Billinghurst), 28728, L/Cpl., k. in a., F. & F., 9/10/17, formerly S/4/145548, R.A.S.C.

Tunnicliffe, Ernest, b. Coventry, Warwicks, e. Coventry, 19610, Pte., k. in a., F. & F., 7/10/17.

Turley, Ralph, b. Viney Hill, Glos., e. Bristol (Oldcroft, Glos.), 21729, Pte., k. in a., F. & F., 11/4/17, formerly 29261, Glos. Regt.

Tustin, Levi, b. Elmbridge, Worcs, e. Birmingham (Rotton Park, Birmingham), 17350, Pte., d. of w., F. & F., 29/8/16.

Underhill, Henry, b. Aston, Birmingham, e. Birmingham (Sparkbrook, Birmingham), 6764, Pte., d. of w., F. & F., 21/8/16.

Vickers, Richard, e. Birmingham (Small Heath, Birmingham), 21703, Pte., k. in a., F. & F., 10/4/17.

Vickery, Frederick Richard, b. Lower Froyle, Hants, e. Winchester, Hants (Lower Froyle), 28815, Pte., k. in a., F. & F., 9/10/17.

Vigurs, Charles Alfred, b. Birmingham, e. Birmingham (Yardley, Birmingham), 11187, Pte., k. in a., F. & F., 22/2/17.

Village, Thomas Herbert, b. Sparkbrook, Birmingham, e. Birmingham (Sparkbrook), 8612, Cpl., k. in a., F. & F., 20/5/16.

Villiers, William, b. All Saints, Coventry, Warwicks, e. Coventry, 12627, Pte., k. in a., F. & F., 16/7/16.

Vines, William, b. St. George's, Bristol, e. Bristol (Eastville, Bristol), 21730, Pte., k. in a., F. & F., 10/4/17, formerly 29348, Glos. Regt.

Wainwright, John, b. Alveley, Salop, e. Ludlow, Salop, 27825, Pte., k. in a., F. & F., 9/10/17, formerly 23792, Shrops L.I.

Wainwright, Richard, b. Leicester, e. Nuneaton, Warwicks (Bagworth, Leics), 10222, Pte., k. in a., F. & F., 15/7/16.

Waldron, Robert William, b. Sutton Coldfield, Warwicks, e. Sutton Coldfield (Four Oaks, Sutton Coldfield), 10314, Pte., d. of w., F. & F., 22/3/18.

Walker, Harry, b. Coventry, Warwicks, e. Coventry, 15480, Pte., d. of w., F. & F., 18/7/16.

Wallin, James, b. Birmingham, e. Birmingham, 9124, Pte., k. in a., F. & F., 15/7/16.

Ward, Albert Edward, b. Woolwich, Kent, e. Coventry, 17758, Pte., k. in a., F. & F., 13/8/16.

Ward, Benjamin George, b. Aston, Birmingham, e. Birmingham, 8311, Pte., k. in a., F. & F., 11/8/16, D.C.M.

Ward, William Ernest, b. Cubbington, Warwicks, e. Warwick (Leamington, Warwicks), 17584, Pte., d. of w., F. & F., 29/4/17.

Wardle, Joseph Walter, b. Rusholme, Manchester, e. Portslade, Sussex (Brighton, Sussex), 9469, Sgt., d., F. & F., 17/2/18.

Warmington, George Henry, b. West Bromwich, Staffs, e. Coventry, Warwicks, 10188, Pte., d. of w., F. & F., 15/7/16.

Waters, Charles, b. Wilnecote, Warwicks, e. Warwick (Hatton, Warwicks), 267952, Pte., k. in a., F. & F., 29/4/17, formerly 2464, Warwicks Yeo.

Watson, George, b. Hartshill, Warwicks, e. Nuneaton, Warwicks (Hartshill), 12647, Pte., k. in a., F. & F., 23/9/17.

Waters, Edward, b. Warwick, e. Warwick, 10138, Pte., k. in a., F. & F., 16/11/16.

Watson, Harry, b. Hartshill, Warwicks, e. Nuneaton, Warwicks (Hartshill), 15363, Pte., k. in a., F. & F., 15/7/16.

Watson, Walter, b. Atherstone, Warwicks, e. Atherstone (Hartshill, Warwicks), 16313, Pte., k. in a., F. & F., 9/10/17.

Watts, James, b. Moseley, Birmingham, e. Knowle, Warwicks (Shirley, Birmingham), 19073, Pte., k. in a., F. & F., 11/8/17.

Watts, Thomas, b. Deritend, Birmingham, e. Birmingham (Sparkbrook, Birmingham), 8186, L/Cpl., k. in a., F. & F., 12/8/16.

Weaver, Alfred John, b. St. Luke's, Gloucester, e. Birmingham (Stourport, Worcs), 7890, Cpl., k. in a., F. & F., 11/4/17.

Webb, Charles, e. Birmingham (Hockley, Birmingham), 27905, Pte., k. in a., F. & F., 24/11/17.

Webb, Frank, b. Berkswell, Warwicks, e. Coventry, Warwicks, 12757, Sgt., k. in a., F. & F., 26/4/17.

Webb, John David, e. Birmingham, 9203, Pte., k. in a., F. & F., 15/7/16.

Webb, Thomas, b. Ashted, Birmingham, e. Birmingham (Edgbaston, Birmingham), 4564, Pte., k. in a., F. & F., 7/11/15.
Westerman, Albert, b. Ecclesfield, Yorks, e. Birmingham (Chapeltown, Yorks), 17504, Pte., k. in a., F. & F., 13/8/16.
Westley, Frederick William, b. Warwick, e. Coventry, Warwicks, 28629, Pte., k. in a., F. & F., 10/8/17.
Weston, Arthur Clement, b. Birmingham, e. Birmingham (Bordesley Green, Birmingham), 18305, Pte., k. in a., F. & F., 11/8/16, formerly 22930, Som. L.I.
Westwood, Howard, b. Woolescote, Worcs, e. Stourbridge, Worcs (Lye, Worcs), 27765, Pte., d. of w., F. & F., 15/11/16, formerly 4597, Worcs Regt.
Whitbread, Frederick Henry, e. Bletchley, Bucks (Hanslope, Bucks), 18369, Pte., d., F. & F., 14/4/17, formerly 23300, Som. L.I.
White, James, b. Hawkchurch, Devon, e. High Wycombe, Bucks, 18367, Pte., d. of w., F. & F., 28/4/17, formerly 23224, Som. L.I.
Whitehouse, Albert Victor, e. Birmingham (Smethwick, Staffs), 12357, Pte., k. in a., F. & F., 27/4/17, formerly 55785, R.G.A.
Wickers, Arthur James, b. Coventry, Warwicks, e. Coventry, 17383, Pte., k. in a., F. & F., 10/4/17.
Wilcox, Albert, b. St. Mark's, Coventry, Warwicks, e. Coventry, 9276, L/Cpl., k. in a., F. & F., 16/7/16.
Wildblood, William Samuel, b. Shrewsbury, Salop, e. Shrewsbury, 27846, Pte., k. in a., F. & F., 25/4/17, formerly 24669, Shrops L.I.
Wilkes, Archie James, b. Edgbaston, Birmingham, e. Warwick (Radford, Leamington, Warwicks), 22565, Pte., k. in a., F. & F., 11/4/17.
Wilkes, Arthur Richard, b. Hockley, Birmingham, e. Birmingham (Sparkbrook, Birmingham), 8721, Pte., k. in a., F. & F., 8/7/16.
Wilkins, Joseph, b. Rugby, Warwicks, e. Warwick (Rugby), 17598, Pte., k. in a., F. & F., 29/4/17.
Wilkinson, George, b. Stockingford, Warwicks, e. Coventry, Warwicks, 16420, Pte., d. of w., F. & F., 15/7/16.
Willets, William, b. Old Hill, Staffs, e. Birmingham (Dudley, Worcs), 8686, Pte., k. in a., F. & F., 10/7/16.
Williams, Arthur Joseph, e. Hereford (Bartestree, Hereford), 27820, Pte., d. of w., F. & F., 29/4/17, formerly 2845, Hereford Regt.
Williams, Ernest, b. Bromsgrove, Worcs, e. Birmingham (Shepley, Worcs), 10202, Pte., k. in a., F. & F., 16/7/16.
Williams, Frank, b. Dudley, Worcs, e. Worcester (Dudley), 8735, Sgt., k. in a., F. & F., 11/4/17.
Williams, George, b. Kerry, Montgomery, e. Ludlow, Salop (Church Stretton, Salop), 27844, Pte., k. in a., F. & F., 25/7/17, formerly 24707, Shrops L.I.
Williams, Thomas Henry, b. Hereford, e. Hereford, 27845, Pte., d. of w., F. & F., 16/11/16, formerly 24717, Shrops L.I.
Williams, William, b. Worcester, e. Hereford, 27843, Pte., d. of w., F. & F., 29/4/17, formerly 24714, Shrops L.I.
Williams, William Alfred, b. New Oscott, Birmingham, e. Birmingham (Wylde Green, Birmingham), 17814, Pte., k. in a., F. & F., 13/8/16.
Williamson, William, b. West Bromwich, Staffs, e. West Bromwich (Oldbury, Staffs), 7863, Pte., k. in a., F. & F., 25/4/17.
Wills, Herbert, b. Atherstone, Warwicks, e. Atherstone, 10584, Pte., d. of w., F. & F., 22/7/16.
Wilmott, Frank Ernest, b. Lozells, Birmingham, e. Birmingham, 6627, Pte., k. in a., F. & F., 22/7/17
Wilson, Albert Alfred, b. Smethwick, Staffs, e. Birmingham (Erdington, Birmingham), 15068, Pte., k. in a., F. & F., 29/4/17.
Wilson, George Harold, e. Birmingham (Lozells, Birmingham), 18335, Pte., d. of w., F. & F., 13/8/16, formerly 22075, Som. L.I.
Wilson, Harry, b. St. Thomas', Coventry, Warwicks, e. Warwick (Coventry), 8871, Pte., k. in a., F. & F., 1/7/16.
Winslow, Shirley Cuthbert, e. Wells, Som. (Ramsgate, Kent), 27747, Pte., k. in a., F. & F., 16/11/16, formerly 5806, Glos. Regt.
Winspear, Victor, b. Bordesley, Birmingham, e. Manchester (Salford, Manchester), 2013, Pte., k. in a., F. & F., 15/7/16.
Wood, David, b. St. Paul's, Birmingham, e. Birmingham, 8054, Pte., k. in a., F. & F., 10/4/17.
Wood, William Frederick, e. Hereford, 27810, L/Cpl., k. in a., F. & F., 27/9/17, formerly 2842, Hereford Regt.
Woodbridge, William, b. Birmingham, e. Birmingham (Hay Mills, Birmingham), 11016, Pte., k. in a., F. & F., 14/3/16.
Woodward, Richard, b. Horninton, Staffs, e. Coventry, Warwicks, 1715, Pte., d., F. & F., 16/9/15.
Woodward, Walter Edward, b. Knowle, Warwicks, e. Hampton-in-Arden, Warwicks, 19802, Pte., k. in a., F. & F., 22/2/17.
Woolley, John Henry, b. Castle Bromwich, Birmingham, e. Birmingham (Water Orton, Birmingham), 5026, Pte., k. in a., F. & F., 7/11/15.
Worrall, Thomas East, b. Grandborough, Warwicks, e. Rugby, Warwicks (Grandborough), 9266, Pte., d., Home, 9/1/15.
Worviell, Alfred Thomas, b. Dunstew, Oxon, e. Stratford-on-Avon, Warwicks (Newbold-on-Avon, Warwicks), 14948, Pte., k. in a., F. & F., 16/7/16.
Wright, Bertie, b. Foleshill, Coventry, e. Coventry, Warwicks, 2631, Pte., d. of w., F. & F., 2/8/16.
Wright, Samuel Thomas, b. Dudley, Worcs, e. Birmingham, 8884, Pte., k. in a., F. & F., 16/7/16.
Wyatt, Arthur C., b. Westbury-on-Severn, Glos., e. Bristol (Rodley, Glos.), 21734, Pte., k. in a., F. & F., 10/4/17, formerly 20552, Glos. Regt.
Wylie, Matthew, e. Glasgow, 23342, Pte., k. in a., F. & F., 9/10/17, formerly 2853, H.L.I.
Yardley, Joseph Harry, b. Stourbridge, Worcs, e. Birmingham (Sparkbrook, Birmingham), 8857, Pte., k. in a., F. & F., 24/9/17.
Yates, Thomas, b. Birmingham, e. Birmingham (Bournville, Birmingham), 1188, Cpl., k. in a., F. & F., 7/10/17.
Yates, Thomas, b. Holborn, Middx., e. Warley, Middx., 4876, Sgt., k. in a., F. & F., 9/7/16, M.M.
Yeomans, James, b. Silverdale, Staffs, e. Nuneaton, Warwicks (Stockingford, Warwicks), 11741, Cpl., k. in a., F. & F., 1/1/17.

12th Battalion.

Davies, William Harold Pryce, b. London, e. Warwick, 16400, Pte., d., Home, 6/3/16.
Jones, Arthur, b. St. Mark's, Birmingham, e. Birmingham, 3254, L/Cpl., d., Home, 1/7/15.
Lester, William, b. Aston, Birmingham, e. Birmingham (King's Heath, Birmingham), 11659, Pte., d., Home, 5/9/17.
Stanley, George Harold, b. Birmingham, e. Birmingham (Saltley, Birmingham), 16137, Pte., d., Home, 26/2/16.
Wilson, William James, b. Northampton, e. Bristol, Glos. (Staple Hill, Bristol), 5351, Pte., d., Home, 18/9/15.

13th Battalion.

Aldous, Albert Guthrie, b. Hampstead, London, e. Kilburn, London (Hampstead, London), 3316, Sgt., d., Home, 7/10/15.
Brailee, John Edward, b. Worcester, e. Birmingham (Broadheath, Worcs), 14704, Pte., d., Home, 3/2/16.
Butler, John, b. Sunderland, Durham, e. Birmingham (Aston, Birmingham), TR/8/1840, Pte., d., Home, 19/4/17.
Goodyear, Fred, b. Basing, Hants, e. Basingstoke, Hants (Kempshott, Hants), TR/8/1800, Pte., d., Home, 26/3/17.
Griffin, Sidney, b. Shirley, Hants, e. Southampton, Hants (Shirley), TR/8/1369, Pte., d., Home, 25/3/17.
Horsnett, Maurice Edward, b. Warwick, e. Stratford-on-Avon, Warwicks (Henley-in-Arden, Warwicks), TR/8/1449, Pte., d., Home, 8/4/17.
Humphries, Bert William, b. St. Mary's, Wolverhampton, Staffs, e. Warwick (Stoke, Coventry, Warwicks), 4559, Pte., d., Home, 13/8/15.
Jarvis, William, b. Marlborough, Devon, e. Newton Abbot, Devon (Batsom, Devon), TR/8/1081, Pte., d., Home, 6/2/17.
Newey, Frederick Hirons, b. Witton, Birmingham, e. Birmingham (Aston, Birmingham),) TR/8/1697, Pte., d., Home, 29/3/17.
Newman, William John, b. Axford, Wilts, e. Marlborough, Wilts (Axford), TR/8/823, Pte., d., Home, 8/2/17.
Palmer, Howard Alfred, e. Birmingham (Erdington, Birmingham), TR/8/1511, Pte., d., Home, 31/3/17.
Pearce, Thomas Leonard, b. Hayling Island, Hants, e. Portsmouth, Hants (S. Hayling Island), TR/8/2092, Pte., d., Home, 11/3/17.
Shelton, James Frederick, b. Charlbury, Bucks, e. Slough, Bucks (Langley, Bucks), TR/8/1245, Pte., d., Home, 8/4/17.
Stiff, William Henry, b. Birmingham, e. Birmingham (Small Heath, Birmingham), TR/8/1736, Pte., d., Home, 21/3/17.
Trussler, Albert James, b. Mills, Som., e. Stroud, Glos., TR/8/1541, Pte., d., Home, 10/4/17.
West, Alfred, b. Herriard, Hants, e. Basingstoke, Hants (Herriard), TR/8/1488, Pte., d., Home, 6/4/17.
Wilson, Ewart Leslie, b. Topsham, Devon, e. Exeter, Devon (Topsham), TR/8/1273, Pte., d., Home, 5/4/17.
Winter, John Charles, b. Wellington, Som. (Hillcommon Oake, Som.), TR/8/937, Pte., d., Home, 4/2/17.

14th Battalion.

Abbott, Frederick Charles, b. Barnstaple, Devon, e. Birmingham (Barnstaple), 28388, L/Cpl., k. in a., F. & F., 13/4/18.
Abbott, Percy Zechariah, b. Ipswich, Suffolk, e. Ipswich, 25406, Pte., d. of w., F. & F., 15/9/18, formerly S/19243, R.A.S.C.
Ackland, George Henry, b. Newdigate, Surrey, e. Chichester, Sussex (Newdigate), 32610, Pte., d., F. & F., 8/2/19, formerly 2016, R. Sussex Regt.
Adams, Alfred, b. St. Andrews, Northampton, e. Northampton, 32509, Pte., k. in a., F. & F., 26/10/17, formerly 5793, Lancers.
Adams, Albert George, b. Bordesley, Birmingham, e. Birmingham, 843, Sgt., k. in a., F. & F., 23/7/16.
Adams, Edwin John, b. Towcester, Northants, e. Solihull, Warwicks (Catherine-de-Barnes, Warwicks), 19146, L/Cpl., k. in a., F. & F., 4/10/17, formerly 78692, R.G.A.
Adams, Henry Stanley, b. Hanmer, Flint, e. Hanmer (Whitchurch, Salop), 29888, Pte., k. in a., F. & F., 13/4/18, formerly 694, Welsh Horse.
Adams, James Boyce, b. St. Mary's, Lichfield, Staffs, e. Sutton Coldfield, Warwicks (Lichfield), 1206, Pte., k. in a., F. & F., 23/7/16.
Aldred, Frank Watson, b. Leigh, Lancs, e. Atherton, Lancs (Leigh), 28389, Pte., k. in a., F. & F., 23/5/18, formerly 2822, Manchester Regt.
Aldridge, William George, b. Bishops Cleeve, Glos., e. Cheltenham, Glos. (Bishops Cleeve), 28041, Pte., k. in a., F. & F., 27/9/18.
Alexander, Frederick Herbert, b. Guildford, Surrey, e. Sutton Coldfield, Warwicks (South Yardley, Birmingham), 1133, Pte., k. in a., F. & F., 23/7/16.

Allcock, Lancelot, b. Annesley Woodhouse, Notts, e. Newark, Notts (Annesley Woodhouse), 27474, Pte., k. in a., F. & F., 7/5/17, formerly 3201, Notts & Derby Regt.
Allen, Arthur William, b. Wherwell, Hants, e. Sutton Coldfield, Warwicks, 1168, Pte., k. in a., F. & F., 23/7/16.
Allen, Claude Benjamin, b Moseley, Birmingham, e. Birmingham (Moseley), 30, Pte, k. in a., F. & F., 23/7/16.
Allen, Richard, b. Coventry, Warwicks, e. Coventry (Stoke, Warwicks), 16633, Pte.. d. of w., F. & F., 15/6/17.
Allen, Thomas Alfred, b. Farnworth, Lancs, e. Manchester (Pendlebury, Lancs), 36516, Pte., k. in a., F. & F., 27/9/16, formerly 46479, S. Lancs Regt.
Allen, William, e. Nuneaton, Warwicks (Stockingford, Warwicks), 11075, Pte., k. in a., F. & F., 4/10/17.
Allum, Wilfred, b. Woodston, Hunts, e. Huntingdon (Woodston), 30201, Pte., k. in a., F. & F., 3/9/16, formerly 1316, Hunts Cyc. Battn.
Anderton, Sydney, b. Edgbaston, Birmingham, e. Birmingham (Moseley, Birmingham), 565, Pte., k. in a., F. & F., 23/7/16.
Andrew, George Hubert, b. Sheffield, Yorks, e. Sheffield, 25234, Pte., k. in a., F. & F., 14/4/18, formerly Rx/4/263656, R.A.S.C.
Andrews, Jacob, b. Calne, Wilts, e. Devizes, Wilts (Calne), 34503, Pte., k. in a., F. & F., 29/5/18.
Anstey, John Darrall, b. Erdington, Birmingham, e. Birmingham (Erdington), 28, Pte., k. in a., F. & F., 23/7/16.
Anthony, Arthur John, b. Hampstead, London, N.W., e. Whitehall, London (St. Pancras, London), 35217, Pte., k. in a., F. & F., 19/9/18.
Appleton, William Thomas, b. Leyton, London, e. Walthamstow, London, E., 35815, Pte., k. in a., F. & F., 8/7/18.
Asbury, Ernest, b. Birmingham, e. Birmingham, 19771, Pte., k. in a., F. & F., 14/4/18.
Asbury, William John, b. Birmingham, e. Birmingham, 503, Pte., k. in a., F. & F., 23/7/16.
Ashford, Alfred George, e. Huntingdon (St. Neots, Hunts), 28391, Pte., k. in a., F. & F., 23/3/17, formerly 1742, Hunts Cyc. Battn.
Ashmead, Thomas Francis, b. Birmingham, e. Birmingham (Aston, Birmingham), 14/1253, Pte., k. in a., F. & F., 30/7/16.
Ashton, Joseph Edward, b Birmingham, e. Birmingham, 19139, Pte., k. in a., F. & F., 4/10/17.
Ashwell, William James, b. St. Neots, Hunts, e. Hunts (St. Neots), 30219, Pte., k. in a., F. & F., 26/10/17, formerly 1694, Hunts Cyc. Battn.
Askew, Wilfred, b. Harrold, Beds, e. Kettering, Northants, 32435, Pte., d. of w., F. & F., 2/5/18, formerly R/4/125027, R.A.S.C.
Aspey, Albert, b. Bradford, Yorks, e. Bradford (Sturry, Canterbury, Kent), 34195, Pte., k. in a., F. & F., 14/4/18, formerly 989 Lancers.
Badham, William Henry, b. Birmingham, e. Birmingham (Harborne, Birmingham), 14/1455, Pte., k. in a., F. & F., 23/7/16.
Bailey, Benjamin Thomas, b. Lugwardine, Hereford (Lugwardine), 48205, Pte., k. in a., F. & F., 27/9/18, formerly 217649, R.A.S.C.
Bailey, Herbert William, b. Oakham, Rutland, e. Coventry, Warwicks (Northampton), 16915, Pte., k. in a., F. & F., 3/9/16.
Baker, Richard, b. Birminghm, e. Birmingham, 9326, Pte., d., F. & F., 29/3/18, formerly 17445, Worcs. Regt.
Baker, Walter, b. Croydon, Surrey, e. Birmingham, 558, L/Cpl., k. in a., F. & F., 4/10/17.
Ballard, George, e. Moseley, Birmingham (Pershore, Worcs), 1071, Pte., k. in a., F. & F., 5/10/17.
Barker, James, b. Coventry, Warwicks, e .Coventry, 16833, Pte., k. in a., F. & F., 12/9/16.
Barker, William, b. Liverpool, e. Birmingham, 17753, Pte., k. in a., F. & F., 8/7/17.
Barlow, Benjamin Bertram, b. Rawal Pindi, India, e. Birmingham (Washwood Heath, Birmingham), 854, Sgt., d. of w., F. & F., 23/12/15.
Barlow, Matthew Richard, b. Shirley, Warwicks, e. Birmingham (Solihull, Birmingham), 14/1382, Pte., k. in a., F. & F., 4/6/16.
Barlow, Percy Charles, b. Somersham, Hunts, e. Huntingdon (Somersham), 30217, Pte., k. in a., F. & F., 3/9/16, formerly 1083, Hunts Cyc. Battn.
Barnacle, Charles William, b. Birmingham, e. Birmingham (Balsall Heath, Birmingham), 14/1701, Pte., k. in a., F. & F., 23/7/16.
Barrett, Arthur, b. Lichfield, Staffs, e. Birmingham (Lichfield), 358, Pte., k. in a., F. & F., 23/7/16.
Barrett, Joseph Frederick, b. Tipton, Staffs, e. Birmingham (Tipton), 855, Pte., k. in a., F. & F., 23/7/16.
Barrett, Walter James, b. Birmingham, e. Birmingham (Vauxhall, Birmingham), 14/1421, Pte., k. in a., F. & F., 23/5/16.
Barrow, Charles Henry Brindley, b. Edgbaston, Birmingham, e. Sutton Coldfield, Warwicks (Edgbaston), 1149, Pte., k. in a., F. & F., 3/9/16.
Bartholomew, William Christopher, b. Leamington, Warwicks, e. Leamington, 38895, Pte., k. in a., F. & F., 8/7/18.
Bast, Ernest Arthur, b. Bournemouth, Hants, e. Bournemouth, 50576, Pte., k. in a., F. & F., 27/8/18.
Bates, Thomas Herbert, b. Coventry, Warwicks, e. Leamington, Warwicks, 15813, Pte., k. in a., F. & F., 3/9/16.
Bates, Walter, b. Chilvers Coton, Warwicks, e. Nuneaton, Warwicks, 17376, Pte., k. in a., F. & F., 30/7/16.
Baxter, Albert Ernest, b. Birmingham, e. Birmingham (Hockley, Birmingham), 36100, Pte., k. in a., F. & F., 26/8/18.
Bayliss, William Henry, b. Mickleton, Glos., e. Leamington, Warwicks, 17837, Pte., k. in a., F. & F., 3/9/16.
Beale, John Henry, b. Aston, Birmingham, e. Birmingham (Aston), 22354, Pte., k. in a., F. & F., 26/10/17.
Beasley, Clement Ful, b. Napton, Warwicks, e. Southam, Warwicks (Napton), 23762, Pte., k. in a., F. & F., 26/10/17.
Beddard, Arthur James, b. Nottingham, e. Birmingham (Nottingham), 104, Pte., d. of w., F. & F., 13/4/18.
Beddoes, Charles Edward, b. Birmingham, e. Birmingham, 50453, L/Cpl., d. of w., F. & F., 17/10/18.
Bedford, Charles Ernest, b. Leicester, e. Coventry, Warwicks, 16822, Pte., k. in a., F. & F., 30/7/16.
Beer, Fred, b. Birmingham, e. Birmingham, 1306, Pte., k. in a., F. & F., 4/10/17.
Belcher, James, b. Ratby, Leics, e. Leamington, Warwicks (Nuneaton, Warwicks), 43425, Pte., k. in a., F. & F., 7/9/18.
Bellamy, Frederick William, b. Birmingham, e. Birmingham (Winson Green, Birmingham), 14/1646, Pte., k. in a., F. & F., 23/7/16.
Bellamy, William Miles Coverdale, b. Birmingham, e. Birmingham (Sparkbrook, Birmingham), 1003, Pte., k. in a., F. & F., 23/7/16.
Bench, Frederick George, b. Leamington, Warwicks, e. Leamington, 22675, Pte., k. in a., F. & F., 10/3/17.
Benfield, Brian William, b. Chipping Barnet, Herts, e. Birmingham (High Barnet, Herts), 510, Pte., k. in a., F. & F., 23/7/16.
Bennett, Harold, b. Birmingham, e. Birmingham (Nechells, Birmingham), 16/1691, Pte., d. of w., F. & F., 2/8/16.
Bennett, Henry James, b. Bristol, Som., e. Chatham, Kent, 48310, Pte., k. in a., F. & F., 23/8/18, formerly R/355168, R.A.S.C.
Bennett, Job Haddon, b. Newton Regis, Warwicks, e. Atherstone, Warwicks (Newton Regis), 17829, Pte., k. in a., F. & F., 3/9/16.
Bennett, John William, b. Kidderminster, Worcs, e. Birmingham (Kidderminster), 14/1334, Pte., k. in a. F. & F., 30/7/16.
Bennett, Percy, b. Hockley, Birmingham, e. Birmingham (Aston, Birmingham), 18076, Pte., d. of w., F. & F., 7/9/16.
Benson, William, b. Maryport, Cumberland, e. Birmingham, 859, Pte., k. in a., F. & F., 23/7/16.
Benwell, Wilfred Frank, b. Bexhill, Sussex, e. Birmingham (Gravelly Hill, Birmingham), 14/1649, Pte., d. of w., F. & F., 23/7/16.
Berry, Frank Leslie, b. Christchurch, Burton-on-Trent, Staffs, e. Sutton Coldfield, Warwicks (Burton-on-Trent), 1127, L/Cpl., d. of w., F. & F., 11/9/16.
Bertin, Benjamin John, b. Birmingham, e. Piccadilly, London, 32521, Pte., d. of w., F. & F., 26/12/17, formerly 17144, Lancers.
Best, William, b. Belbroughton, Worcs, e. Birmingham (Bearwood, Birmingham), 14/1647, Pte., d. of w., F. & F., 20/8/16.
Billett, John Henry, b. Carshalton, Surrey, e. London (Carshalton), 29893, Pte., d. of w., F. & F., 31/10/17, formerly 5548, Lancers.
Billingley, Charles Henry, b. Wordsley, Worcs, e. Birmingham (Handsworth, Staffs), 14/1684, Pte., k. in a., F. & F., 23/7/16.
Birch, Henry, b. Curdworth, Warwicks, e. Coleshill, Warwicks, 17021, Pte., d. of w., F. & F., 15/9/16.
Birch, John Clements, b. St. Paul's, Birmingham, e. Birmingham, 14/513, Pte., d. of w., F. & F., 31/7/16.
Bird, Alexander, b. Birmingham, e. Birmingham, 14/1584, Pte., k. in a., F. & F., 3/9/16.
Bishop, Sydney Stewart, e. Chelsea, London (Herne Hill, London), 32514, Pte., k. in a., F. & F., 3/10/17, formerly 4448, London Yeo.
Blanch, James, b. Evesham, Worcs, e. Birmingham (Ladywood, Birmingham), 16/1447, Pte., k. in a., F. & F., 22/7/16.
Blight, Clarence, b. Shebbear, Devon, e. Exeter, Devon (Buckland, Filleigh, Devon), 35830, Pte., k.in a., F. & F., 28/9/18.
Bliss, Frank Humphreys, b. Banbury, Oxon, e. Birmingham (Banbury), 156, Pte., k. in a., F. & F., 23/7/16
Blood, Joseph Vallance, b. Normanton, Derby, e. Warwick (Tamworth, Warwicks), 20510, Pte., k. in a., F. & F., 26/10/17.
Blower, John, e. Birmingham (Ladywood, Birmingham), 28525, Pte., d. of w., F. & F., 20/10/17.
Bolton, Ralph James, b. Warrington, Lancs, e. Rugby, Warwicks, 25269, Pte., k. in a., F. & F., 14/4/18.
Bott, Sydney George, b. Sheffield, Yorks, e. Birmingham (Great Barr, Birmingham), 14/1516, Sgt., d. of w., F. & F., 18/5/17.
Bough, William, b. Birmingham, e. Birmingham, 21096, Pte., k. in a., F. & F., 14/4/18
Bowen, Arthur Samuel, b. Coventry, Warwicks, e. Coventry, 50587, Pte., d. of w., F. & F., 29/5/18.
Bowmer, Joseph, b. West Hartlepool, Durham, e. Birmingham (Aston, Birmingham), 14/1505, Pte., k. in a., F. & F., 23/7/16.
Boyd, Charles Frederick, b. Rolleston, Staffs, e. Birmingham, 863, Pte., k. in a., F. & F., 23/7/16.
Boyd, William, b. Glasgow, e. Glasgow (Motherwell, Lanark), 34089, Pte., d., F. & F., 5/6/18, formerly 8374, Dragoons.
Brace, Albert Sydney, b. Redcliffe, Bristol, e Bristol (Bedminster, Bristol), 43058, Pte., k. in a., F. & F., 27/9/18, formerly 29396, Glos. Regt.
Brain, Herbert James, b. Snitterfield, Warwicks, e. Birmingham (Locksley, Warwicks), 9257, Sgt., d. of w., F. & F., 8/10/18.
Brain, Joseph Charles, b. St. Martin's, Birmingham, e. Birmingham, 7971, Cpl., k. in a., F. & F., 13/4/18.

Branch, William, b. Birmingham, e. Birmingham, 28518, Pte., k. in a., F. & F., 24/6/17.
Brandham, George, b. Old Fletton, Northants, e. Old Fletton, 30171, Pte., k. in a., F. & F., 4/10/17, formerly 823, Hunts Cyclist Battn.
Brettell, Frank Bernard, b. Handsworth, Staffs, e. Birmingham (Handsworth), 362, L/Cpl., d., F. & F., 16/4/16.
Bridge, Valentine, b. Stanwick, Northants, e. Peterborough, Northants, 30221, Pte., k. in a., F. & F., 3/9/16, formerly 1701, Hunts Cyclist Battn.
Bridgwater, Frederick Horace, b. Blackheath, Worcs, e. Birmingham (Blackheath), 16/1938, Pte., k. in a., F. & F., 23/7/16.
Britt, Edward George, b. Hastings, Sussex, e. Sutton Coldfield, Warwicks (Halesowen, Worcs), 14/1434, Pte., k. in a., F. & F., 11/6/16.
Brittain, Harry Amos, e. Coventry, Warwicks, 16760, Pte., k. in a., F. & F., 3/6/17.
Brodie, Arthur, b. Birmingham, e. Birmingham (Handsworth, Staffs), 16181, L/Cpl., d. of w., F. & F., 30/7/16.
Bromley, Harry, e. Salford, Manchester (Weaste, Manchester), 202405, Pte., k. in a., F. & F., 8/7/18, formerly 2029, Lan. Fus.
Bromley, Wilfred, b. Hinckley, Leics, e. Nuneaton, Warwicks (Hinckley), 10914, Pte., d. of w., F. & F., 23/10/17.
Brooks, Percival John, b. Mitcheldean, Glos., e. Gloucester (Mitcheldean), 36354, Pte., k. in a., F. & F., 27/9/18.
Broughton, Ernest William, b. Banbury, Oxon, e. Birmingham (Banbury), 871, Pte., k. in a., F. & F., 23/7/16.
Broughton, Herbert, b. Warboys, Hunts, e. Huntingdon (Warboys), 30208, Pte., k. in a., F. & F., 24/4/17, formerly 1463, Hunts Cyclist Battn.
Brown, Albert, b. Sledfield, Bristol, Glos., e. Bristol (Barton Hill, Bristol), 21261, Pte., d., F. & F., 27/2/17, formerly 23345, R. Berks Regt.
Brown, Ebenezer, b. Queensland, Australia, e. Birmingham (Aston, Birmingham), 15/1325, Pte., k. in a., F. & F., 23/7/16.
Brown, Edward, b. Sutton Coldfield, Warwicks, e. Sutton Coldfield, 1093, L/Cpl., k. in a., F. & F., 23/7/16.
Brown, Frederick, b. Portsmouth, Hants, e. Portsmouth, 50591, Pte., k. in a., F. & F., 29/6/18.
Brown, Frederick Herbert, b. Stechford, Birmingham, e. Birmingham, 579, Sgt., k. in a., F. & F., 30/7/16.
Brown, George Holland, e. Birmingham (Small Heath, Birmingham), 28448, Pte., k. in a., F. & F., 9/3/17.
Brown, Robert, b. Rutherglen, Lanark, e. Grove Park, London (Rutherglen), 33723, Pte., d. of w., F. & F., 5/5/18, formerly 176868, R.A.S.C.
Bruce, Herbert, b. Cubbington, Warwicks, e. Warwick (Cubbington), 17745, Pte., k. in a., F. & F., 3/9/16.
Bruce, Thomas Harold, b. Long Malford, Suffolk, e. Croydon, Surrey (Lavenham, Suffolk), 29884, Pte., d. of w., F. & F., 26/10/17, formerly 4257, Lancers.
Buckle, Charles Leonard, b. Wandsworth, London, e. Wandsworth (Earlsfield, London), 38600, Pte., k. in a., F. & F., 20/10/18.
Buckley, Clifford, b. Rugeley, Staffs, e. Birmingham (Edgbaston, Birmingham), 14/1399, Pte., k. in a., F. & F., 23/7/16.
Bugby, William John, b. Birmingham, e. Birmingham (Stirchley, Birmingham), 28458, Pte., k. in a., F. & F., 7/5/17.
Bullivant, Frederick Ralph, b. York, e. York, 32592, Pte., k. in a., F. & F., 10/5/18, formerly 15454, Dragoons.
Burgess, Frederick, e. Warminster, Wilts, 28046, Pte., k. in a., F. & F., 26/10/17.
Burnell, Axel Walter Alexander, b. St. Warburgh's, Bristol, Glos., e. Bristol, 35838, Pte., k. in a., F. & F., 30/8/18.
Burness, William Henry, b. King's Heath, Birmingham, e. Birmingham (Bordesley, Birmingham), 22194, Pte., k. in a., F. & F., 26/10/17.
Burnside, John Barr, b. Ladywood, Birmingham, e. Birmingham (Ladywood), 356, L/Cpl., k. in a., F. & F., 30/12/15.
Burnside, William Dickson, b. All Saints, Birmingham, e. Birmingham, 361, L/Cpl., k. in a., F. & F., 23/7/16.
Burrows, Alfred Richard, b. Gloucester, e. Lydney, Glos. (Parkend, Gloucester), 50443, Pte., k. in a., F. & F., 27/9/18.
Burrows, Joseph, b. Hanley, Staffs, e. Nuneaton, Warwicks (Atherstone, Warwicks), 1930, Pte., d. of w., F. & F., 20/5/18.
Burt, Charles, b. St. Jude's, Bristol, Glos., e. Birmingham (Balsall Heath, Birmingham), 15/1409, Pte., k. in a., F. & F., 23/7/16.
Burton, John, e. Birmingham (Nechells, Birmingham), 330602, Pte., k. in a., F. & F., 15/9/18.
Burton, Joseph, b. Aston, Birmingham, e. Birmingham (Aston), 17101, Pte., k. in a., F. & F., 30/7/16.
Busby, William John, b. Curbridge Downs, Oxon, e. Oxford (Holwell, Burford, Oxon), 34969, Pte., k. in a., F. & F., 26/10/17, formerly 286430, Q.O. Oxf. Hussars.
Butcher, Ernest Leonard, b. Epsom, Surrey, e. Winchester, Hants (Micheldever, Hants), 32518, Pte., k. in a., F. & F., 5/10/17, formerly 17145, Lancers.
Butler, Alfred Charles, b. Birmingham, e. Birmingham (Aston, Birmingham), 21166, Pte., d. of w., F. & F., 26/10/17.
Butler, Francis Walter, e. Gloucester (Cheltenham, Glos.), 27657, Pte., k. in a., F. & F., 27/9/18, formerly 2474, Glos. Yeo.
Butler, Leigh Stanley Latham, b. Handsworth, Birmingham, e. Birmingham, 592, Pte., k. in a., F. & F., 21/7/16.
Butler, Robert William, b. St. Andrew's, Plymouth, Devon, e. Plymouth, 35839, Pte., k. in a., F. & F., 20/9/18.
Byrd, Frank, b. Barcheston, Worcs, e. Stratford-on-Avon, Warwicks, 17416, Pte., k. in a., F. & F., 30/7/16.
Callis, John, b. Acton, London, e. London (Acton), 32525, Pte., k. in a., F. & F., 4/10/17, formerly 23030, Lancers.
Candler, Francis John, b. Bampton, Devon, e. Exeter, Devon (Bampton), 50595, L/Cpl., k. in a., F. & F., 27/9/18.

Carr, Richard Gardener, b. Darlaston, Staffs, e. Warwick (Harborne, Birmingham), 38775, Pte., k. in a., F. & F., 28/8/18.
Carter, Edwin, b. Walsall, Staffs, e. Birmingham (Walsall), 14/1303, Pte., k. in a., F. & F., 21/7/16.
Cartwright, Harry, b. Northampton, e. Bedford (Northampton), 23429, Pte., d. of w., F. & F., 5/10/17, formerly 3121, R.E.
Castle, Reginald Lancelot, b. Derby, e. Birmingham (Derby), 14/59, Pte., d. of w., F. & F., 21/7/16.
Chalcroft, Walter, b. Epsom, Surrey, e. Hounslow, London (Epsom), 32615, Pte., k. in a., F. & F., 4/10/17, formerly 6461, Dragoons.
Challis, George, b. Portsmouth, Hants, e. Southampton (East Ham, London), 18599, Pte., k. in a., F. & F., 8/7/18, formerly 24766, Som. L.I.
Chamberlain, John Pearton, b. Walsall, Staffs, e. Sutton Coldfield, Warwicks (Erdington, Birmingham), 1187, Pte., k. in a., F. & F., 23/7/16.
Chandler, Edward Ray, b. Newton Heath, Lancs, e. Birmingham (Manchester), 585, Pte., k. in a., F. & F., 23/7/16.
Chaney, Wilfred George, b. Lenham, Kent, e. Maidstone, Kent (Farleigh, Kent), 33880, L/Cpl., k. in a., F. & F., 8/7/18, formerly 120579, R.A.S.C.
Charter, Sydney, b. Colne, Hunts, e. Huntingdon (Colne), 30194, Pte., k. in a., F. & F., 27/12/16, formerly 1223, Hunts Cyc. Battn.
Chatwin, George Frederick, b. Smethwick, Staffs, e. Birmingham (Smethwick), 678, Pte., k. in a., F. & F., 26/10/17.
Checketts, Henry Wilfred, b. Birmingham, e. Birmingham (Balsall Heath, Birmingham), 873, Cpl., k. in a., F. & F., 3/9/16.
Cherry, William, b. Birmingham, e. Birmingham, 14/1403, Pte., k. in a., F. & F., 23/7/16.
Cherry, William Henry, b. Oxford, e. Aylesbury, Bucks (Ickford, Oxon), 34957, Pte., k. in a., F. & F., 26/10/17, formerly 286431, Queen's Own Oxford Hussars.
Child, William Henry, b. Moseley, Birmingham, e. Birmingham (Moseley), 601, L/Cpl., k. in a., F. & F., 23/7/16.
Chonlarton, John, b. Manchester, Lancs, e. Manchester, 16771, Pte., k. in a., F. & F., 3/9/16.
Christie, Robert Locke, b. Bordesley, Birmingham, e. Birmingham, 604, L/Cpl., k. in a., F. & F., 30/7/16.
Churchill, Albert Ernest, b. Blackheath, Worcs, e. Birmingham (Blackheath), 14/1336, Pte., k. in a., F. & F., 23/7/16.
Clapham, Frederick Thomas, b. Stockton-on-Tees, Durham, e. Stockton-on-Tees (Thornaby-on-Tees, Yorks), 20691, Pte., d. of w., F. & F., 22/9/18, formerly 12207, A. Cyc. Corps.
Clare, Francis Cyril, b. Staveley, Derby, e. Birmingham (Edgbaston, Birmingham), 868, Pte., k. in a., F. & F., 30/7/16.
Clarke, Alfred, b. West Smethwick, Staffs, e. Birmingham (West Smethwick), 1432, Pte., d., F. & F., 1/8/16.
Clarke, Henry, b. Coventry, Warwicks, e. Coventry, 16829, Pte., k. in a., F. & F., 3/9/16.
Clarke, Percy, b. Coventry, Warwicks, e. Coventry, 17907, Pte., k. in a., F. & F., 10/6/17.
Clarkson, Francis Richard, b. Kensington, London, e. Fulhom, London, 34470, Pte., k. in a., F. & F., 29/6/18, formerly 43117, R.A.S.C.
Cleaver, Thomas, b. Stockton, Warwicks, e. Warwick (Stockton), 945, C.S.M., d. of w., F. & F., 9/5/17.
Clements, Charles, b. Ladywood, Birmingham, e. Birmingham (Ladywood), 102, Sgt., k. in a., F. & F., 23/7/16.
Clements, George, b. Coventry, Warwicks, e. Coventry, 22421, Pte., k. in a., F. & F., 27/6/17.
Climer, Heber, b. Wellesbourne, Warwicks, e. Stratford-on-Avon, Warwicks, 16989, Pte., k. in a., F. & F., 27/6/17.
Clow, Bert Turner, b. Exning, Suffolk, e. Atherstone, Warwicks, 17816, Pte., k. in a., F. & F., 30/7/16.
Clow, Frank, b. Sandy, Beds, e. Sandy, 32523, Pte., k. in a., F. & F., 26/10/17, formerly 2488, Bedford Yeo.
Cockerill, Herbert, b. Birmingham, e. Birmingham (Nechells, Birmingham), 15/1582, Pte., k. in a., F. & F., 23/7/16.
Codling, Reginald, b. Manchester, e. Salford, Manchester (Moss Side, Manchester), 27706, Pte., k. in a., F. & F., 14/4/18, formerly 2057, Lancs Fus.
Coffen, Newton Reginald, b. Arreton, I. of W., e. Winchester (Walton, London), 50603, Pte., d. of w., F. & F., 5/10/18.
Cogbill, Edwin, b. Birmingham, e. Birmingham (Cotteridge, Birmingham), 16/1679, Pte., k. in a., F. & F., 23/7/16.
Cole, Henry Stanley, b. St. George's, Birmingham, e. Birmingham (Hockley, Birmingham), 14/1300, Pte., k. in a., F. & F., 30/7/16.
Coleman, Frederick George, b. Birmingham, e. Birmingham, 15/1619, Pte., k. in a., F. & F., 25/12/16.
Coley, William, b. Birmingham, e. Birmingham (Hockley, Birmingham), 1150, Pte., k. in a., F. & F., 14/4/18.
Collett, Albert, b. Bidford-on-Avon, Warwicks, e. Stratford-on-Avon, Warwicks (Bidford-on-Avon), 16326, Pte., d. of w., F. & F., 5/9/16.
Collins, Francis Bertram, b. Kidderminster, Worcs, e. Kidderminster, 22001, Pte., k. in a., F. & F., 26/10/17.
Collins, Joseph, b. Birmingham, e. Birmingham (Small Heath, Birmingham), 14/1265, Pte., k. in a., F. & F., 4/6/16.
Connolly, John Newman, b. Ladywood, Birmingham, e. Birmingham (Harborne, Birmingham), 16/1852, Pte., k. in a., F. & F., 7/5/17.
Constable, George Frederick, b. Brixton, Surrey, e. York (Forest Gate, London), 32601, Pte., k. in a., F. & F., 27/10/17, formerly 15328, Dragoons.
Cook, Ernest, b. Leighton Bromswold, Hunts, e. Huntingdon (Leighton Bromswold), 30245, Pte., k. in a., F. & F., 26/10/17, formerly 1145, Hunts Cyc. Battn.
Cooke, Francis Charles, b. Birmingham, e. Birmingham (Small Heath, Birmingham), 28530, Pte., k. in a., F. & F., 23/8/18.

Cooper, Alfred Samuel, b. Kidderminster, Worcs, e. Birmingham (Kidderminster), 16/1647, L/Cpl., k. in a., F. & F. 23/7/16.
Cooper, John Henry, b. Ibstock, Leics, e. Nuneaton, Warwicks, 12140, Cpl., k. in a., F. & F., 13/4/18.
Cooper, John William, b. Hartford, Hunts, e. Huntingdon (Warboys, Hunts), 30302, Pte., d. of w., F. & F., 9/10/17, formerly 1253, Hunts Cyc. Battn.
Cooper, James William, b. Banbury, Oxon, e. Oxford (Banbury), 35846, Pte., k. in a., F. & F., 23/8/18.
Cooper, Leonard Simion, b. Redditch, Worcs, e. Warwick (Redditch), 1241, L/Cpl., k. in a., F. & F., 7/5/17.
Cope, Ernest Arthur George, b. Camden, London, e. Huntingdon (Hardwick, Hunts), 30246, Pte., k. in ac., F. & F., 8/5/17, formerly 1286, Hunts Cyc. Battn.
Coslett, Thomas Charles, b. Northfield, Birmingham, e. Birmingham, 50, Pte., k. in a., F. & F., 23/7/16.
Couch, Harold Jerome, b. Aston, Birmingham, e. Birmingham (Aston), 599, Sgt., k. in a., F. & F., 30/7/16.
Couldwell, Harold, b. Sheffield, Yorks, e. Sheffield, 33771, Pte., k. in a., F. & F., 27/9/18, formerly 081038, R.A.S.C.
Couling, Frederick James, b. Great Malvern, Worcs, e. Birmingham (Great Malvern), 543, Sgt., k. in a., F. & F., 7/5/17.
Coulthard, Harold Douglas, b. Handsworth, Birmingham, e. Birmingham, 870, A/Sgt., k. in a., F. & F., 3/9/16.
Cox, Albert Joseph, b. Camp Hill, Birmingham, e. Sutton Coldfield, Warwicks (Small Heath, Birmingham), 14/1268, Pte., k. in a., F. & F., 30/7/16.
Cox, Bertie, e. Birmingham (Blackheath, Birmingham), 28374, Cpl., k. in a., F. & F., 27/10/17.
Cox, Francis Albert, b. Winterbourne, Glos., e. Bristol (Hambrook, Glos.), 50411, Pte., k. in a., F. & F., 8/7/18.
Cox, Frederick William, b. Nechells, Birmingham, e. Birmingham, 58, L/Sgt., k. in a., F. & F., 30/7/16.
Crake, Frederick William, b. Hebburn, Durham, e. Woolwich, Kent (Hebburn), 32449, Pte., d. of w., F. & F., 3/10/17, formerly 4888, Lancers.
Crane, George, b. Gainsborough, Lincs, e. Birmingham (Saltley, Birmingham), 15/1457, Pte., d. of w., F. & F., 28/7/16.
Crates, Henry, b. Birmingham, e. Birmingham, 16/1509, Pte., k. in a., F. & F., 21/7/16.
Crisp, Charles Henry, b. St. Cuthbert's, Birmingham, e. Birmingham (Winson Green, Birmingham), 8508, Pte., k. in a., F. & F., 3/9/16.
Cross, Frank William, b. Weston-super-Mare, Som., e. Weston-super-Mare, 50613, Pte., k. in a., F. & F., 26/6/18.
Cross, Harold Clement, b. Balsall Heath, Birmingham, e. Sutton Coldfield, Warwicks (Moseley, Birmingham), 1220, Pte., k. in a., F. & F., 21/7/16.
Cross, Kenneth Leslie, b. Weddington, Warwicks, e. Nuneaton, Warwicks (Weddington), 23128, Pte., d. of w., F. & F., 4/10/17.
Crowe, Justin James, b. Liverpool, Lancs, e. Ormskirk, Ches. (Warrington, Lancs), 34433, Pte., k. in a., F. & F., 14/4/18, formerly 43001, R.A.S.C.
Curtis, William Guy, b. Clapham, Middx., e. Birmingham (London), 64, Pte., k. in a., F. & F., 23/7/16.
Cutler, Samuel, b. Birmingham, e. Birmingham, 37878, Pte., k. in a., F. & F., 27/9/18.
Dain, John Leslie, b. Bridgnorth, Salop, e. Birmingham, 882, Pte., d. of w., F. & F., 4/7/16.
Dale, Albert Edward, b. Crowland, Northants, e. Huntingdon (Crowland), 30174, Pte., k. in a., F. & F., 3/9/16, formerly 872, Hunts Cyclist Battn.
Daniels, Walter Ernest, b. Chelsea, London, e. Huntingdon (Great Gransden, Hunts), 30248, L/Cpl., d. of w., F. & F., 21/10/18, formerly 798, Hunts Cyclist Battn.
Datson, Charles, e. Rugby, Warwicks (Peterborough, Northants), 21310, Pte., d. of w., F. & F., 9/2/17, formerly 26728, R. Berks Regt.
Davey, Robert, b. Ebsone Hill, Som., e. Taunton, Som. (Littleton, Som.), 36104, Pte., k. in a. F. & F., 8/7/18.
Davies, John William, b. Ironbridge, Salop, e. Warwick, 17520, Pte., k. in a., F. & F., 30/7/16.
Davies, William, b. Bridgnorth, Salop, e. Bridgnorth (Glazeley, Salop), 27821, Pte., k. in a., F. & F., 27/9/18, formerly 24082, Shrops L.I.
Davies, William Henry, b. Birmingham, e. Birmingham (Saltley, Birmingham), 8769, Cpl., k. in a., F. & F., 14/4/18.
Davis, Arthur Thomas, b. Birmingham, e. Birmingham (Aston, Birmingham), 14/1599, Pte., k. in a., F. & F., 18/3/16.
Daw, Ernest William, b. Small Heath, Birmingham, e. Birmingham, (Acock's Green, Birmingham), 24348, Pte., k. in a., F. & F., 26/10/17.
Day, Thomas, b. All Saints, Warwick, e. Birmingham (Small Heath, Birmingham), 17442, Pte., k. in a., F. & F., 26/10/17.
Dean, William James, b. Birmingham, e. Birmingham (Sparkhill, Birmingham), 16/1705, Pte., k. in a., F. & F., 3/9/16.
Delamy, Thomas, b. Derby, e. Birmingham, 15/1670, Pte., k. in a., F. & F., 12/6/16.
Dent, Wilfred Henry, b. Birmingham, e. Birmingham, 14/1251, Pte., k. in a., F. & F., 27/9/18.
Devereux, George Albert Francis, b. Birmingham, e. Birmingham, 17960, Pte., k. in a., F. & F., 3/9/16.
Devey, Thomas George, b. Alcester, Warwicks, e. Sutton Coldfield, Warwicks (Alcester), 14/1277, Pte., k. in a., F. & F., 23/7/16.
Dewbury, John Percy, b. Small Heath, Birmingham, e. Birmingham, 331, L/Cpl., k. in a., F. & F., 21/7/16.
Deykin, Cecil John, b. Penkridge, Staffs, e. Birmingham, 328, Pte., k. in a., F. & F., 23/7/16.
Dingley, Percy Groves, b. Edgbaston, Birmingham, e. Birmingham (Edgbaston), 1037, Pte., k. in a., F. & F., 23/7/16.
Dipper, William Ambrose, b. Headington, Oxon, e. Oxford (Headington), 34971, Pte., k. in a., F. & F., 26/10/17, formerly 3455, Queens Own Oxford Hussars.
Dobson, William, b. Manchester, e. Manchester (Acock's Green, Birmingham), 14/1256, Pte., k. in a., F. & F., 30/7/16.
Docker, William Ernest, b. Nechells, Birmingham, e. Birmingham (Nechells), 14/1639, Pte., k. in a., F. & F., 23/7/16.
Dockerill, John, b. Warboys, Hunts, e. Huntingdon (Warboys), 30250, A/Cpl., k. in a., F. & F., 12/9/16, formerly 587, Hunts Cyclist Battn.
Dodd, Alfred Henry, e. Birmingham (Hockley, Birmingham), 27721, Pte., k. in a., F. & F., 1/12/16.
Dolman, Percy Archibald, b. Devizes, Wilts, e. Chippenham, Wilts (Calne, Wilts), 50623, Pte., k. in a., F. & F., 23/8/18.
Dowler, Arthur Reginald, b. Handsworth, Birmingham, e. Birmingham (Handsworth), 876, L/Cpl., k. in a., F. & F., 23/7/16.
Dowler, Frank, b. Moss Side, Manchester, e. Birmingham (Moss Side), 613, Cpl., k. in a., F. & F., 3/9/16.
Dowling, George Albert, e. East Ham, Essex (Canning Town, Essex), 34115, Pte., d. of w., F. & F., 31/10/17, formerly 19598, Dragoons.
Dowling, Robert, b. Harpenden, Herts, e. Birmingham (Moseley, Birmingham), 875, Pte., k. in a., F. & F., 30/7/16.
Drake, Robert John, b. Marylebone, London, e. Huntingdon (St. Neots, Hunts), 30307, L/Cpl., k. in a., F. & F., 26/10/17, formerly 1283, Hunts Cyclist Battn.
Drake, Walter, b. Middlesbrough, Yorks, e. Middlesbrough, 30415, Pte., k. in a., F. & F., 14/4/18, formerly 12951, Hussars.
Dreyheller, Wilfred Elwin, b. Sparkhill, Birmingham, e. Birmingham, 551, Pte., k. in a., F. & F., 14/4/18.
Drinkwater, Willie, b. Wootton, Oxon, e. Birmingham (Cape Hill, Birmingham), 14/1468, Pte., k. in a., F. & F., 23/7/16.
Druce, Harold, b. Garsington, Oxon., e. Oxford (Garsington, Oxon.), 18478, Pte., k. in a., F. & F., 4/10/17, formerly 24556, Som. L.I.
Duffill, Francis Harry, b. Bromsgrove, Worcs, e. Birmingham (Sparkbrook, Birmingham), 14/1568, Pte., k. in a., F. & F., 23/7/16.
Dumbell, Walter, b. Penketh, Lancs, e. Widnes, Lancs, 36522, Pte., d. of w., F. & F., 28/9/18, formerly 46470, S. Lancs Regt.
Dunkley, Harry, b. Newbold, Warwicks, e. Rugby, Warwicks, 16711, Pte., k. in a., F. & F., 30/7/16.
Dwane, John William, b. Birmingham, e. Birmingham (Edgbaston, Birmingham), 14/1575, Pte., k. in a., F. & F., 23/7/16.
Eacott, Henry William Thomas, b. St. Clement's, Oxford, e. Oxford (Headington Hill, Oxon.), 34958, Pte., k. in a., F. & F., 26/10/17, formerly 286126, Queens Own Oxford Hussars.
Ebourne, Leonard Ernest, b. Edgbaston, Birmingham, e. Birmingham, 552, Pte., k. in a., F. & F., 23/7/16.
Eden, George, b. Chipping Norton, Oxon., e. Stow-on-the-Wold, Glos. (Little Compton), 17802, Pte., k. in a., F. & F., 30/7/16.
Edmonds, Joseph Henry, b. Birmingham, e. Birmingham, 15151, Pte., d. of w., F. & F., 8/1/18, M.M.
Edwards, Herbert Lionel, e. Birmingham (Launceston, Cornwall), 17694, Pte., k. in a., F. & F., 3/9/16.
Eldridge, Charles, b. Avening, Glos., e. Stroud, Glos. (Avening), 35859, Pte., d. of w., F. & F., 31/8/18.
Elliott, Harry, b. Long Parish, Winchester, Hants, e. Birmingham (Long Parish), 223, Cpl., k. in a., F. & F., 15/6/16.
Elmer, Thomas, b. Peterborough, Northants, e. Huntingdon (Peterborough), 30309, L/Cpl., d. of w., F. & F., 17/10/16, formerly 1264, Hunts Cyclist Battn.
Elsey, Charles, b. Gosberton, Lincs, e. Manchester (Hulme, Manchester), 36544, Pte., d., F. & F., 17/9/18, formerly 46453, S. Lan. Regt.
Emery, William Francis, b. Malmesbury, Wilts, e. Chippenham, Wilts, 50626, Pte., k. in a., F. & F., 27/9/18.
England, Albert Henry, b. Merthyr Tydvil, Glam., e. Birmingham (Sparkhill, Birmingham), 28514, Pte., k. in a., F. & F., 7/5/17.
England, Reginald Frank, b. Bideford, Devon, e. Exeter, Devon (Barnstaple, Devon), 35860, Pte., d. of w., F. & F., 27/8/18.
Evans, George Henry, b. Birmingham, e. Birmingham (Sparkhill, Birmingham), 14/1532, Pte., k. in a., F. & F., 30/7/16.
Evans, Philip Marsh, b. Wylde Green, Birmingham, e. Birmingham (Wylde Green), 14/222, Pte., d., F. & F., 25/11/16.
Evans, William, b. Walsall, Staffs, e. Windsor, Berks (Thurlaston, Warwicks), 16082, Pte., k. in a., F. & F., 10/6/17.
Everill, James, e. Birmingham, 28478, Pte., d. of w., F. & F., 8/11/17.
Eyre, Harry Percival, b. Bagilt, Flint, e. Birmingham (Gravelly Hill, Birmingham), 1157, L/Cpl., k. in a., F. & F., 30/7/16.
Fair, Robert, b. Talybont, Brecon, e. Holyhead, Anglesey (Rhosneiger, Anglesey), 32532, Pte., k. in a., F. & F., 26/10/17, formerly 1102, Welsh Cavalry Regt.
Fairbairn, John, e. Dunbar, Haddington (Belhaven, Dunbar), 34119, Pte., k. in a., F. & F., 13/4/18, formerly 22093, Dragoons.
Fairclough, William, b. St. Clement's, Rochdale, Lancs, e. Manchester (Rochdale), 46, Cpl., k. in a., F. & F., 3/9/16.
Farnell, Arthur Benjamin, b. Aston, Birmingham, e. Birmingham (Aston), 149, Pte., k. in a., F. & F., 23/7/16.
Farnell, Alfred Charles, b. Aston, Birmingham, e. Birmingham (Aston), 150, L/Cpl., k. in a., F. & F., 23/7/16.
Farr, Frances Harry, b. Huntingdon, e. Huntingdon, 30253, L/Sgt., d. of w., F. & F., 11/9/16, formerly 708, Hunts Cyclist Battn.

Faulks, James George, b. Warwick, e. Leamington, Warwicks (Warwick), 15/1416, Pte., k. in a., F. & F., 23/7/16.
Fellows, Harold John, b. Darlaston, Staffs, e. Sutton Coldfield, Warwicks, 1117, Pte., k. in a., F. & F., 22/7/16.
Felton, Joseph Henry, b. Smethwick, Staffs, e. Birmingham (Smethwick), 14/1430, Pte., d. of w., F. & F., 26/5/16.
Fennell, John Lissamer, b. Attleborough, Warwicks, e. Nuneaton, Warwicks, 16347, Pte., k. in a., F. & F., 13/4/18.
Fermor, Charles, b. Withyam, Sussex, e. Warwick (Exeter, Devon), 22387, Pte., k. in a., F. & F., 4/10/17.
Field, Alan, b. Harborne, Warwicks, e. Birmingham (Harborne), 147, Pte., k. in a., F. & F., 23/7/16.
Field, John, b. West Bromwich, Staffs, e. Birmingham (West Bromwich), 231, Pte., k. in a., F. & F., 23/7/16.
Finch, Walter, b. Birmingham, e. Birmingham (Smethwick, Staffs), 14/1546, Pte., k. in a., F. & F., 23/7/16.
Findon, Richard, b. Hereford, e. Birmingham (Hereford), 233, Sgt., k. in a., F. & F., 23/7/16.
Fletcher, John William, b. Ripley, Derby, e. Coventry, Warwicks (Ripley), 16301, Pte., k. in a., F. & F., 24/10/17.
Fletcher, Reginald Vickers, b. Small Heath, Birmingham, e. Birmingham (Yardley, Birmingham), 646, Pte., k. in a., F. & F., 11/6/16.
Flynn, Harold, b. Birmingham, e. Birmingham, 15/1439, Pte., d. of w., F. & F., 5/8/16.
Ford, Albert James, b. Bristol, Glos., e. Bristol, 21336, Pte., k. in a., F. & F., 26/10/17, formerly 26800, R. Berks Regt.
Ford, Ernest, b. Gt. Gransden, Hunts, e. Huntingdon (Gt. Gransden), 30166, Pte., k. in a., F. & F., 3/9/16, formerly 795, Hunts Cyclist Battn.
Fox, Arthur Alfred, b. Weston, Warwicks, e. Warwick (Cawston, Warwicks), 17614, L/Cpl., k. in a., F. & F., 27/9/18.
Franklin, Harold Edwin, b. Chesham, Bucks, e. Aylesbury, Bucks (Chesham), 43277, Pte., k. in a., F. & F., 26/10/17, formerly 3694, Queen's Own Oxford Hussars.
Froggatt, George Elias, b. Warwick, e. Birmingham (Small Heath, Birmingham), 1441, Pte., k. in a., F. & F., 23/7/16.
Frost, James, b. Daventry, Northants, e. Warwick (Bell Green, Warwicks), 18052, Pte., d. of w., F. & F., 9/5/17.
Fulford, Frederick Henry, b. Kenilworth, Warwicks, e. Leamington, Warwicks, 14/1602, Pte., d. of w., F. & F., 24/7/16.
Fuller, Thomas George, b. Birmingham, e. Birmingham (Small Heath, Birmingham), 43669, Pte., k. in a., F. & F., 17/9/18.
Gabriel, Henry Michael, b. Liverpool, Lancs, e. Sutton Coldfield, Warwick (Birmingham), 1155, Pte., k. in a., F. & F., 30/7/16.
Gale, Victor, b. Astwood Bank, Worcs, e. Redditch, Worcs (Astwood Bank), 28471, Pte., k. in a., F. & F., 8/5/17.
Gamble, Lawrence Ernest, b. Retford, Notts, e. Hyde, Ches. (Neasden, Middx.), 34106, Pte., k. in a., F. & F., 26/10/17, formerly 4876, Dragoons.
Gardner, John, e. Coventry, Warwicks (Fen End, Warwicks), 27691, Pte., k. in a., F. & F., 21/5/17.
Gardner, William, b. Smethwick, Staffs, e. Birmingham (Smethwick), 9656, Pte., k. in a., F. & F., 11/9/16.
Garner, Edward, b. Liverpool, e. Birmingham (Saltley, Birmingham), 16/1496, Pte., k. in a., F. & F., 30/7/16.
Garner, George, b. Southam, Warwicks, e. Stockton, Warwicks, 17393, Pte., k. in a., F. & F., 2/10/17.
Garner, Percy Albert, b. St. Saviours, Walthamstow, Essex, e. Birmingham (Walthamstow), 7, Pte., d. of w., F. & F., 23/7/16.
Garratt, Harold Wheale, b. West Bromwich, Staffs, e. Birmingham (West Bromwich), 896, Pte., k. in a., F. & F., 23/7/16.
George, James Joseph, b. Nuneaton, Warwicks, e. Warwick (Coventry, Warwicks), 18049, Pte., k. in a., F. & F., 11/11/17.
George, John William, b. Crowland, Lincs, e. Huntingdon (Crowland), 30311, Pte., k. in a., F. & F., 3/9/16, formerly 1707, Hunts Cyclist Battn.
Gilkes, Frank, b. Stoke Newington, London, e. Stratford-on-Avon, Warwicks (Salford Priors, Warwicks), 21922, Pte., k. in a., F. & F., 13/4/18.
Gilroy, William Wilson, b. Edgbaston, Birmingham, e. Birmingham (Nechells, Birmingham), 28441, Pte., k. in a., F. & F., 26/8/18.
Given, Sydney James, b. West Bromwich, Staffs, e. Birmingham, 14/906, A/Sgt., k. in a., F. & F., 11/9/16.
Glover, Leslie Frank, b. Small Heath, Birmingham, e. Birmingham (Small Heath, Birmingham), 615, Pte., d. of w., F. & F., 1/8/16.
Glydon, Rupert, b. Handsworth, Birmingham, e. Sutton Coldfield, Warwicks (Handsworth), 1191, Pte., k. in a., F. & F., 23/7/16.
Goldsmith, Frank Thomas, b. Wadhurst, Sussex, e. Wadhurst, 28400, Pte., k. in a., F. & F., 27/6/17, formerly 1630, R. Sussex Regt.
Goodchild, William, b. Brookfields, Birmingham, e. Birmingham (Brookfields), 402, Sgt., k. in a., F. & F., 6/5/17.
Goswell, Thomas, b. Bangor-on-Dee, Denbigh, e. Overton, Flint (Bangor-on-Dee), 32538, Pte., k. in a., F. & F., 26/10/17, formerly 710, Welsh Cavalry.
Grainger, William Henry, b. Kenilworth, Warwicks, e. Kenilworth, 18045, Pte., k. in a., F. & F., 13/4/18.
Graley, John, b. Walsall, Staffs, e. Birmingham (Lozells, Birmingham), 18172, Pte., k. in a., F. & F., 3/9/16.
Gray, Albert Percival, b. Gillingham, Dorset, e. Salisbury, Wilts (Patchway, Bristol), 36421, Pte., k. in a., F. & F., 27/9/18, formerly 208888, R. Bucks Hussars.
Greaves, Ernest John, b. Birmingham, e. Birmingham (Hockley, Warwicks), 28473, Pte., k. in a., F. & F., 26/10/17.
Green, Abraham Philip, b. Bordesley, Birmingham, e. Birmingham (Bordesley), 205, Pte., k. in a., F. & F., 23/7/16.
Green, Charles Walter, b. Waldon, Essex, e. Cambridge, 34571, Pte., d. of w., F. & F., 30/4/18.
Green, James, b. Quarry Bank, Staffs, e. Birmingham (Netherton, Worcs), 1165, Pte., k. in a., F. & F., 22/7/16.
Green, Joseph, b. Coventry, Warwicks, e. Coventry, 27983, Pte., k. in a., F. & F., 4/10/17.
Green, Norman Frederick, b. Mosely, Birmingham, e. Birmingham (Moseley), 606, Pte., k. in a., F. & F, 23/7/16.
Green, Robert Charles, b. Greenhithe, Kent, e. Wantage, Berks (Greenhithe), 32456, Pte., k. in a., F. & F., 26/10/17, formerly 16484, R.A.S.C.
Greenhouse, Joseph, e. Birmingham (Small Heath, Birmingham), 28062, Pte., k. in a., F. & F., 8/5/17.
Greenwood, Frank, b. Ramsey, Hunts, e. Huntingdon (Ramsey), 30312, Pte., d. of w., F. & F., 20/5/18, formerly 959, Hunts Cyclist Battn.
Griffiths, Thomas, b. Wrexham, Denbigh, e. Ashton-in-Makerfield, Lancs, 36543, Pte., d., F. & F., 27/9/18, formerly 46467, S. Lan. Regt.
Grimes, Leonard Cecil, b. Moseley, Birmingham, e. Birmingham (Moseley), 609, Pte., k. in a., F. & F., 30/7/16.
Gunter, William Edward James, b. Birmingham, e. Birmingham (Aston, Birmingham), 18298, Pte., k. in a., F. & F., 4/10/17, formerly 22931, Som. L.I.
Habgood, George, b. Gibraltar, e. Dublin, Ireland, 32429, Sgt., k. in a., F. & F., 23/8/18, formerly 5/6644, Lancers.
Hackett, Arthur, b. Moseley, Birmingham, e. Sutton Coldfield, Warwicks (King's Heath, Birmingham), 1202, Pte., k. in a., F. & F., 8/12/15.
Haden, William, b. Birmingham, e. Birmingham (Gosta Green, Birmingham), 14/1541, Pte., k. in a., F. & F., 13/5/16.
Haigh, Henry, b. Leicester, e. Birmingham (Erdington, Birmingham), 656, Pte., k. in a., F. & F., 8/5/17.
Halford, Sidney Arthur, b. Wyken, Warwicks, e. Coventry, Warwicks (Binley, Warwicks), 16433, Pte., d. of w., F. & F., 3/9/16.
Hall, Ernest, b. Wirksworth, Derby, e. Coventry, Warwicks, 17023, Pte., k. in a., F. & F., 8/5/17.
Hall, Frederick Harold, b. St. Barnabas, Birmingham, e. Birmingham, 907, L/Cpl., k. in a., F. & F., 23/7/16.
Hall, John, b. Lower Boddington, Warwicks, e. Leamington, Warwicks (Warmington, Warwicks), 16978, Pte., d., F. & F., 5/9/16.
Hall, James Walton, b. Twyford, Bucks, e. Oxford (Twyford), 43278, Pte., d. of w., F. & F., 25/5/18, formerly 3846, Queen's Own Oxford Hussars.
Hall, Thomas, b. Sutton Coldfield, Warwicks, e. Sutton Coldfield, 1169, Pte., k. in a., F. & F., 31/12/15.
Hamlet, John Dudley, e. Aylesbury, Bucks (High Wycombe, Bucks), 260357, Pte., k. in a., F. & F., 26/10/17, formerly 2680, Oxf. & Bucks L.I.
Hammond, Arthur Dudley, b. Aldershot, Hants, e. Portsmouth, Hants (Southsea, Hants), 18776, Pte., k. in a., F. & F., 13/4/18, formerly 24476, Som. L.I.
Hammond, Arthur Henry, b. Holy Trinity, Malvern, Worcs, e. Worcester (Malvern), 238051, Pte., k. in a., F. & F., 27/9/18, formerly 4305, Worcs Regt.
Hammond, Basil, b. Friskney, Lincs, e. Huntingdon (Wrangle, Lincs), 30313, Pte., k. in a., F. & F., 25/12/16, formerly 1686, Hunts Cyclist Battn.
Hancox, John Frederick, b. Stretton-on-Dunsmore, Warwicks, e. Coventry, Warwicks (Stretton-on-Dunsmore), 25543, Pte., k. in a., F. & F., 14/4/18.
Hand, Henry, b. Coseley, Staffs, e. Birmingham (Coseley), 16/1928, Pte., k. in a., F. & F., 30/8/16.
Handley, James, b. Bradford, Yorks, e. Birmingham (Bloxwich, Staffs), 14/1279, Pte., d. of w., F. & F., 26/7/16.
Hannigan, Thomas, b. Liverpool, Lancs, e. Liverpool, 34094, Pte., d. of w., F. & F., 28/10/17, formerly 7586, Dragoons.
Hanson, Thomas Reginald, b. Birmingham, e. Birmingham, 380, L/Cpl., k. in a., F. & F., 23/7/16, M.M.
Hardiman, John Bertram, b. Moreton-in-the-Marsh, Glos., e. Cheltenham, Glos. (Moreton-in-the-Marsh), 50652, Pte., k. in a., F. & F., 8/7/18.
Harker, Frank, e. Skelton, Yorks (North Skelton), 27360, Pte., k. in a., F. & F., 27/9/18, formerly 2612, Yorks Regt.
Harland, Albert Edward, b. Scarborough, Yorks, e. Birmingham (Scarborough), 6, Pte., d. of w., F. & F., 23/7/16.
Harris, Frederick, b. Northampton, e. Northampton, 32460, Sgt., k. in a., F. & F., 15/9/18, formerly 42023, Lancers.
Harris, Thomas Harvey, b. Birmingham, e. Birmingham (Hall Green, Birmingham), 14/1631, Pte., k. in a., F. & F., 23/7/16.
Harrison, Walter Edward, b. Bordesley, Birmingham, e. Birmingham (Ashted, Birmingham), 15/1637, Pte., k. in a., F. & F., 4/2/17.
Hartland, Frederick Harold, b. Birmingham, e. Coventry, Warwicks, 37435, Pte., k. in a., F. & F., 8/7/18.
Hartley, Ralph, b. Manchester, Lancs, e. Stratford-on-Avon, Warwicks (Weston-Super-Mare, Som.), 11585, Pte., k. in a., F. & F., 25/10/17.
Hartwell, William, b. Walsall, Staffs, e. Birmingham (Walsall), 14/1650, Pte., k. in a., F. & F., 23/7/16.
Harvey, William James, b. Gloucester, e. Gloucester, 50655, Pte., k. in a., F. & F., 27/8/18.
Harwood, William, b. Great Bridge, Staffs, e. Birmingham, 14/1630, Pte., k. in a., F. & F., 23/7/16.
Hastings, Cyril John, b. Moseley, Birmingham, e. Birmingham (Small Heath, Birmingham), 917, L/Cpl., k. in a., F. & F., 30/7/16.
Hawcroft, George, b. Swinton, Yorks, e. Mexborough, Yorks (Swinton), 29907, Pte., d. of w., F. & F., 26/10/17, formerly 4902, Lancers.
Hawker, Percival Clarence, b. Tewkesbury, Glos., e. Birmingham (Saltley, Birmingham), 15/1636, Pte., k. in a., F. & F., 23/7/16.

Haynes, Charles, b. Aston, Birmingham, e. Birmingham (Aston), 408, L/Cpl., d. of w., F. & F., 8/10/16.
Haynes, Ernest James, b. Paris, e. Birmingham (Sparkbrook, Birmingham), 14/1651, Pte., k. in a., F. & F., 23/7/16.
Haynes, John William, b. Eaton Locon, Hunts, e. Huntingdon (Wyboston, Hunts), 30209, Pte., k. in a., F. & F., 14/4/18, formerly 1651, Hunts Cyclist Battn., M.M.
Heafield, Henry Clarence, b. Birmingham, e. Birmingham (Handsworth, Staffs), 15/1597, Pte., k. in a., F. & F., 23/7/16.
Hearn, Harry, b. Godmanchester, Hunts, e. Huntingdon, 30175, Pte., k. in a., F. & F., 7/5/17, formerly 910, Hunts Cyclist Battn.
Heath, Alfred Harold, b. Burslem, Staffs, e. Birmingham (Burslem), 409, Cpl., k. in a., F. & F., 23/7/16.
Heath, Abraham Richard, b. Birmingham, e. Birmingham (Aston, Birmingham), 0843, Sgt., k. in a., F. & F., 4/10/17.
Heath, John, b. Birmingham, e. Birmingham (Winson Green, Birmingham), 15/1594, Pte., d. of w., F. & F., 29/8/16.
Heathcote, Herbert Harold, b. Brampton, Hunts, e. Huntingdon (Brampton), 30258, Pte., k. in a., F. & F., 24/9/16, formerly 1269, Hunts Cyclist Battn.
Heathfield, William, b. Lambeth, London, e. Marylebone, London, 13406, Pte., k. in a., F. & F., 30/7/16.
Hebbert, Joseph William, b. Christchurch, Stafford, e. Birmingham (Christchurch, Stafford), 112, Cpl., d. of w., F. & F., 20/7/16
Herbert, Richard Thomas, b. Lozells, Birmingham, e. Birmingham (Small Heath, Birmingham), 8013, Pte., k. in a., F. & F., 5/10/17.
Herrick, Henry Douglas, b. Saltley, Birmingham, e. Birmingham (Saltley), 635, Sgt., k. in a., F. & F., 23/7/16.
Herriman, George, b. Moreton Saye, Market Drayton, Salop, e. Sutton Coldfield, Warwicks (Market Drayton), 1130, L/Cpl., k. in a., F. & F., 30/7/16.
Herring, John Ivor, b. Atherstone, Warwicks, e. Birmingham (Ladywood, Birmingham), 18073, Pte., k. in a., F. & F., 3/9/16.
Hewitt, Ellis John, b. New Bilton, Warwicks, e. Rugby, Warwicks, 2772, Pte., k. in a. F. & F., 27/2/17.
Hewitt, William Henry, b. Birmingham, e. Birmingham, 413, Cpl., k. in a., F. & F., 30/7/16.
Hewson, Ernest Singleton, b. Leeds, Yorks, e. Huntingdon, 30344, Pte., k. in a., F. & F., 3/9/16, formerly 1045, Hunts Cyc. Battn.
Hibell, Alfred Rupert, b. Bromsgrove, Worcs, e. Birmingham (Aston, Birmingham), 16/1445, Pte., d. of w., F. & F., 6/8/16.
Hill, Ernest Clifford, b. Small Heath, Birmingham, e. Birmingham (Small Heath), 371, Cpl., k. in a., F. & F., 23/7/16.
Hill, Frederick Elthorne, b. Devonport, Devon, e. Plymouth, Devon (Stoke, Devonport), 35296, Pte., k. in a., F. & F., 27/9/18.
Hill, George, b. Birmingham, e Birmingham, 19175, Pte., k. in a., F. & F., 4/10/17
Hilton David Thomas, b. Birmingham, e. Birmingham, 9857, Dmr., k. in a., F. & F., 3/9/16.
Hirons, William Thomas, b. Banbury, Oxon, e. Coventry, Warwicks, 16763, Pte., k. in a., F. & F., 14/4/18.
Holden, Sidney Naldrett, b. Navan, Neath, e. Birmingham (Sparkhill, Birmingham), 693, Pte., k. in a., F. & F., 31/8/16.
Holmes, John Frederick William, b. St. Marks, Bath, Som., e. Birmingham (Sparkhill, Birmingham), 641, Pte., d. of w., F. & F., 31/8/16.
Homer, Bernard Harold, b. Edgbaston, Birmingham, e. Birmingham (Edgbaston), 417, Pte., k. in a., F. & F., 23/7/16.
Hopkin, Fred Head, b. Leicester, e. Leicester, 30316, Pte., d. of w., F. & F., 13/4/18, formerly 1538, Hunts. Cyc. Battn.
Hopkins, Basil Piermont, b. Edgbaston, Birmingham, e. Birmingham, 672, A/L/Sgt., d. of w., F. & F., 11/9/16.
Hopkins, John Stanley, b. Birmingham, e. Birmingham (Sparkhill, Birmingham), 14/1570, Sgt., k. in a., F. & F., 26/10/17.
Houghton, Peter, b. Blackbrook, Lancs, e. St. Helen's, Lancs, 36536, Pte., k. in a. F. & F. 17/9/18, formerly 46498, S. Lancs. Regt.
Hoult, Douglas George, b. Penarth, Glam., e. Grove Park, London (Penarth), 33704, Pte., k. in a., F. & F., 14/4/18, formerly 181357, R.A.S.C.
Howe, Joseph, b. Coventry, Warwicks, e. Warwick (Coventry), 16003, Sgt., k. in a., F. & F., 29/6/18, M.M.
Howell, Daniel, b. Carmarthen, e. Birmingham (Carmarthen), 113, Pte., k. in a., F. & F., 25/3/16.
Howells, Henry Harcourt, b. Rhymney, Mon., e. Cardiff (Rhymney), 32543, Pte., k. in a., F. & F., 5/10/17, formerly 642, Welsh Horse.
Hucker, William Thomas, b. Aveton Gifford, Devon, e. Uckfield, Sussex (Abbey Wood, London), 33703, Pte., k. in a., F. & F., 13/4/18, formerly 105651, R.A.S.C.
Hudson, Leonard Charles, b. Balsall Heath, Birmingham, e. Birmingham (Balsall Heath), 912, Pte., k. in a., F. & F., 4/6/16.
Hudson, Walter, b. Nuneaton, Warwicks, e. Warwick (Nuneaton), 17729, Pte., k. in a., F. & F., 26/10/17.
Hughes, William, b. Ashstead, Surrey, e. New Cross, London (Southfields, London), 32546, Pte., k. in a., F. & F., 5/10/17, formerly 3008, Lancers.
Hulbert, Henry Horace Stanley, b. Handsworth, Staffs, e. Sutton Coldfield, Warwicks (Handsworth), 14/1292, Pte., d. of w., F. & F., 13/1/17.
Humber, William Thomas, b. Birmingham, e. Birmingham (Hockley, Birmingham), 16159, Pte., d. of w., F. & F., 30/7/16.
Hunter, Joseph Finlayson, b. Glasgow, e. Glasgow (Berwick-on-Tweed), 29911, Pte., d. of w., F. & F., 6/7/18, formerly 9783, K.O.S.B.
Huntley, Arthur William Ernest, e. Birmingham (King's Heath, Birmingham), 330222, Pte., d. of w., F. & F., 3/5/18.
Hurley, Victor Hubert, b. Dublin, e. Birmingham (Small Heath, Birmingham), 15/1609, Pte., d., F. & F. 23/7/16.
Hurrell, Steward, b. Birmingham, e. Birmingham (Selly Park, Birmingham), 14/1350, Pte., k. in a., F. & F., 23/7/16.
Hutchinson, Howard John, b. St. Mark's, Birmingham, e. Birmingham (Hall Green, Birmingham), 682, Pte., k. in a., F. & F., 30/7/16.
Ingle, David, b. Upwood, Hunts, e. Huntingdon (Upwood), 30199, Pte., k. in a., F. & F., 25/6/17, formerly 1298, Hunts. Cyc. Battn.
Izard, Frank Thomas, b. Aston, Birmingham, e. Birmingham (Aston), 925, Pte., k. in a., F. & F., 4/10/17.
Jackman, George, b. Coventry, Warwicks, e. Coventry, 17815, L/Cpl.., k. in a., F. & F. 13/4/18.
Jackson, Albert Ernest, b. Coventry, Warwicks, e. Coventry, 17668, Pte., k. in a., F. & F., 11/11/17.
Jackson, Arnold Ernest, b. Manchester, e. Sutton Coldfield, Warwicks (Sparkbrook, Birmingham), 14/1487, A/Sgt., k. in a., F. & F., 27/9/18.
Jackson, Clifford York, b. Moseley, Birmingham, e. Birmingham (Moseley), 1034, L/Cpl., k. in a., F. & F., 23/7/16.
Jackson, Percy Thomas, b. Northampton, e. Northampton, 168, Pte., k. in a., F. & F., 22/7/16.
James, Joseph, b. Marsh Green, Lancs, e. Parkhurst, I. of W. (Grodrergraig, Glam.), 17116, Cpl., k. in a., F. & F., 7/5/17.
James, Thomas, b. Bearley, Warwicks, e. Stratford-on-Avon, Warwicks (Birmingham), 16251, Pte., k. in a., F. & F., 3/6/17.
Jarratt, Cecil Ambrose, b. Walsall Staffs, e. Birmingham (Kings Norton, Birmingham), 15/1347, Pte., k. in a., F. & F., 10/6/17.
Jarrett, Thomas, b. Cherrington, Warwicks, e. Stratford-on-Avon, Warwicks (Shipston-on-Stour, Warwicks), 10018, Pte., d. of w., F. & F., 3/9/16.
Jarvis, Herbert John, b. Stokenham, Devon e. Newton Abbott, Devon (Torcross, Devon), 50463, Pte., k. in a., F. & F., 28/8/18.
Jarvis, John Thomas, b. West Bromwich, Staffs, e. Birmingham (West Bromwich), 16/1688, A/Sgt., k. in a., F. & F., 3/9/16.
Jeffery, Frank, b. Bugbrooke, Northants, e. Coventry, Warwicks (Weedon, Northants), 9956, Pte., k. in a., F. & F., 30/7/16.
Jeffs, George Oliver, b. Oadby, Leics, e. Nuneaton Warwicks (Bulkington, Warwicks), 17095, Pte., k. in a., F. & F., 30/7/16.
Jenkins, John Richard, b. Dudley, Staffs, e. Birmingham, 14/631, Pte,, d. of w., F. & F., 24/1/16.
Jinks, Joseph, b. Birmingham, e. Birmingham (Deritend, Birmingham), 16722, Pte., k. in a., F. & F., 13/4/18.
Jinks, William Mace, b. Peterborough, Northants, e. Peterborough, 30178, Pte., k. in a., F. & F., 7/5/17, formerly 994, Hunts. Cyc. Battn.
Johnson, Arthur Edgar, b. Birmingham, e. Birmingham (Wylde Green, Birmingham), 827, Pte., k. in a., F. & F., 30/7/16.
Johnson, Ernest Emil Victor, b. London, e. Birmingham (Ladywood, Birmingham), 9137, Pte., k. in a., F. & F., 3/9/16.
Jolliffe, Leslie Donald, b. Moseley, Birmingham, e. Birmingham (Moseley), 176, Pte., d. of w., F. & F. 24/7/16.
Jones, Alfred, b. Ladywood, Birmingham, e. Birmingham (Ladywood), 174, L/Cpl., k. in a., F. & F., 23/7/16.
Jones, Collins Jeffreys, b. Churchill, Kidderminster, Worcs., e. Sutton Coldfield, Warwicks (Hampton-in-Arden, Warwicks), 1134, L/Cpl., k. in a., F. & F., 22/7/16.
Jones, Charles Victor, b. Churchill, Kidderminster, Worcs, e. Sutton Coldfield, Warwicks (Hampton-in-Arden, Warwicks), 1135, L/Cpl., k. in a., F. & F., 23/7/16.
Jones, Frederick, b. Birmingham, e. Birmingham, 1572, Pte., k. in a., F. & F., 23/7/16.
Jones Frederick George, b. King's Norton, Birmingham, e Birmingham (King's Norton), 169, Pte., k. in a., F. & F., 23/7/16, M.M.
Jones, George Frederick, b. Great Malvern, Worcs, e. Birmingham (Malvern), 14/1397, Pte., d. of w., F. & F., 26/4/16.
Jones, George Henry, e. Birmingham (Smethwick, Staffs), 27714, Pte., d. of w., F. & F., 7/10/17.
Jones, Hubert William, b. Hockley, Birmingham, e. Birmingham (Handsworth, Birmingham), 342, Sgt., k. in a., F. & F., 3/9/16.
Jones, Leslie William, b. Birmingham, e. Birmingham (Handsworth, Birmingham), 14/1254, Pte., k. in a., F. & F., 23/7/16.
Jones, Noel Edward, b. Handsworth, Birmingham, e. Birmingham (Handsworth), 831, L/Cpl., k. in a., F. & F., 22/7/16.
Jones, Richard, b. Small Heath, Birmingham, e. Birmingham (Small Heath), 2281, Pte., k. in a., F. & F., 14/4/18.
Jones, Thomas James, b. Birmingham, e. Birmingham (Hockley, Birmingham), 22805, Pte., k. in a., F. & F., 9/10/17.
Jones, William, b St. Helens, Lancs, e. Birmingham, 14/1379, Pte., k. in a., F. & F., 23/7/16.
Jones, William Richard, b. Cannock, Staffs, e. Birmingham (Cannock), 109, L/Cpl., k. in a., F. & F., 23/7/16.
Jordon, Lawrence, b. St. Catherine, Dublin, Ireland. e. Dublin, 16/2084, Pte., k. in a., F. & F., 23/7/16, formerly 8560, R. Dublin Fus.
Joseph, Evelyn, b. Pretoria, South Africa, e. Birmingham (Edgbaston, Birmingham), 336, Sgt., k. in a., F. & F., 23/7/16.

Kay, Alfred Styles, b. Birmingham, e. Birmingham (Saltley, Birmingham), 428, Pte., k. in a., F. & F., 23/7/16.
Kefford, Leonard, b. Moulton, Northants, e. Aldershot, Hants, 25399, Pte., d., F. & F., 23/4/18, formerly S/4/218736, R.A.S.C.
Kemp, George, b. Bedworth, Warwicks, e. Nuneaton, Warwicks (Bedworth), 15281, Pte., k. in a., F. & F., 3/9/16.
Kenyon, Arthur Austin, b. St. Lukes, Birmingham, e. Birmingham (Bournbrook, Birmingham), 17905, Pte., k. in a., F. & F., 30/7/16.
Kightley, Sidney Frank, b. Coventry, Warwicks, e. Coventry, 17427, Pte., k. in a., F. & F., 30/7/16.
Killick, William, b. Poplar, London, e. London (Rotherhithe, London, S.E.), 32549, Pte., k. in a., F. & F., 29/4/18, formerly 7540, Lancers.
Kimsey, Walter, e. Hertford (St. Albans, Herts), 34114, Pte., k. in a., F. & F., 24/10/17, formerly 3434, Dragoons.
King, Frederick, e. Birmingham (Winson Green, Birmingham), 21154, Pte., k. in a., F. & F., 27/9/18.
Kingwell, William, b. London, e. Birmingham (Moseley, Birmingham), 931, Sgt., k. in a., F. & F., 23/3/16.
Kirby, George Felix, b. Swindon, Wilts, e. Birmingham (West Bromwich, Staffs), 14/1263, Pte., k. in a., F. & F., 23/7/16.
Kirby, Joseph Sidney Walter, b. Birmingham, e. Birmingham (Aston, Birmingham), 24293, Pte., k. in a., F. & F., 27/9/18.
Kirby, Robert Harold Edward, b. Brookfields, Birmingham, e. Sutton Coldfield, Warwicks (Handsworth, Birmingham), 1111, Pte., k. in a., F. & F., 23/7/16.
Kisby, Cyril, b. Kexby, Lincs, e. Huntingdon (Horncastle, Lincs), 30215, Pte., k. in a., F. & F., 24/10/17, formerly 1659, Hunts Cyc. Battn.
Kitchen, James Mole, b. St. Philip's, Birmingham, e. Sutton Coldfield, Warwicks (Birmingham), 1088, C.S.M., d. of w., F. & F., 16/12/15.
Knight, William George, b. Morice Town, Devonport, e. Plymouth, Devon, 36107, Pte., k. in a., F. & F., 8/7/18.
Knowles, William Edwin, b. Cradley, Worcs, e. Stourbridge, Worcs (Cradley), 35307, Pte., k. in a., F. & F., 29/5/18.
Lake, Harry Charles, b. Birmingham, e. Birmingham (Small Heath, Birmingham), 1219, Pte., k. in a., F. & F., 23/7/16.
Lalby, George, b. Dublin, Ireland, e. Dublin, 32500, L/Cpl., k. in a., F. & F., 26/8/18, formerly 16265, Lancers.
Langford, Alfred, b. Finstock, Oxon, e. Oxford (Finstock), 18426, Pte., d. of w., F. & F., 30/7/16, formerly 23818, Som. L.I.
Law, Arthur, b. Birmingham, e. Birmingham (Northfield, Birmingham), 15/1378, Pte., k. in a., F. & F., 23/7/16.
Lawson, George, b. Barony, Glasgow, e. Waterford, Ireland (Glasgow), 32551, Pte., k. in a., F. & F., 26/10/17, formerly 24123, Lancers.
Lawson, George William, b. Birmingham, e. Coventry, Warwicks, 25136, Pte., k. in a., F. & F., 23/8/18.
Lediard, George Henry, b. St. Thomas', Birmingham, e. Birmingham, 1754, Pte., k. in a., F. & F., 3/9/16.
Lee, Harold, b. Erdington, Birmingham, e. Birmingham (Erdington), 804, Sgt., k. in a., F. & F., 30/4/18, M.S.M.
Leeding, Tom, b. Wormwood Scrubbs, Middx., e. London (Cheam, Surrey), 33762, Pte., d. of w., F. & F., 5/5/18, formerly 021112, R.A.S.C.
Leeson, Ernest Reuben, b. Selly Park, Worcs, e. Moseley, Birmingham (Aston, Birmingham), 1109, Pte., k. in a., F. & F., 23/7/16.
Lewis, Albert Edward, b. Kenilworth, Warwicks, e. Birmingham (Kenilworth), 634, Pte., k. in a., F. & F., 26/10/17.
Lewis, Ernest, b. St. Mary's, Birmingham, e. Birmingham, 186, Pte., k. in a., F. & F., 23/7/16.
Lilley, Frederick, b. St. Albans, Herts, e. Huntingdon (St. Ives, Hunts), 30319, Pte., d. of w., F. & F., 24/9/16, formerly 809, Hunts Cyc. Battn.
Lilley, Leonard, b. St. Mary's, Huntingdon, e. Huntingdon (Ramsey Heights, Hunts), 30206, L/Cpl., d. of w., F. & F., 25/6/17, formerly 1608, Hunts Cyc. Battn.
Liminton, Walter Ernest, b. Horfield, Bristol, Glos., e. Bristol, 22171, Pte., k. in a., F. & F., 8/5/17, formerly 26309, R. Berks Regt.
Limmage, George, b. Glatton, Hunts, e. Huntingdon (Leighton, Hunts), 30320, Pte., k. in a., F. & F., 14/4/18, formerly 1146, Hunts Cyc. Battn.
Lincoln, William, b. St. Ives, Hunts, e. Huntingdon, 30218, Pte., k. in a., F. & F., 3/9/16, formerly 1687, Hunts Cyc. Battn.
Lines, William, b. Aston, Birmingham, e. Birmingham (Aston), 1289, Pte., d. of w., F. & F., 5/5/17.
Lister, Edward, b. Wakefield, Yorks, e. Birmingham (Small Heath, Birmingham), 437, Pte., k. in a., F. & F., 23/7/16.
Lloyd, John, b. Neen Sollars, Shrops, e. Worcester (Neen Sollars), 30381, Pte., k. in a., F. & F., 20/4/18, formerly 22537, Worcs Regt.
Lock, Sydney Victor, b. Windsor, Bucks, e. Oxford (Henley-on-Thames, Oxon), 260358, Pte., k. in a., F. & F., 26/10/17, formerly 2592, Queen's Own Oxf. Hussars.
Lockwood, Sydney, b. London, e. Birmingham (Manor Park, London, E.), 16/1408, Pte., k. in a., F. & F., 23/7/16.
Longmore, Cyril Raymond, b. Birmingham, e. Birmingham (Edgbaston, Birmingham), 14/1223, Pte., k. in a., F. & F., 30/7/16.
Lord, Frederick William, b. Aston, Birmingham, e. Sutton Coldfield, Warwicks (Handsworth, Staffs), 1192, Pte., k. in a., F. & F., 30/7/16.
Lord, Harold Crane, b. Nuneaton, Warwicks, e. Warwick (Nuneaton), 16562, Pte., k. in a., F. & F., 3/9/16.
Lucas, Alfred, b. Aston, Birmingham, e. Birmingham (Handsworth, Staffs), 16/1413, Pte., k. in a., F. & F., 27/3/16.
Lucas, Charles John, b. Bridport, Dorset, e. Dorchester (Yetminster, Dorset), 35892, Pte., d. of w., F. & F., 27/8/18.
Mahady, Frederick, b. Leeds, Yorks, e. Birmingham, 14/1461, Pte., k. in a., F. & F., 30/7/16.
Malin, John, b. Ladywood, Birmingham, e. Warwick (Ladywood), 18019, Pte., k. in a., F. & F., 11/9/16.
Malin, Robert, b. Hampton-in-Arden, Warwicks, e. Birmingham (Sparkhill, Birmingham), 1030, C.S.M., k. in a., F. & F., 23/7/16.
Manning, John, b. London, e. Birmingham (Solihull, Warwicks), 16481, L/Cpl., d. of w., F. & F., 30/7/16.
Mansfield, Harold, b. Queensborough, Leics, e. Leamington, Warwicks (Queensborough), 16500, L/Cpl., k. in a., F. & F., 3/9/16.
Marks, Frances Alfred, b. Wantage, Berks, e. Birmingham (Erdington, Birmingham), 34409, Pte., k. in a., F. & F., 26/10/17, formerly 4016, Worcs Yeo.
Marlow, Arthur Edward, b. Birmingham, e. Birmingham (Rednall, Birmingham), 15/1371, Pte., k. in a., F. & F., 23/7/16.
Marlow, Harold, b. Kettering, Northants, e. Kettering, 34471, Pte., d. of w., F. & F., 16/4/18, formerly R/4/125022, R.A.S.C.
Marsh, George William, b. Rugby, Warwicks, e. Rugby, 17293, Pte., k. in a., F. & F., 26/10/17.
Marshall, John Henry, b Birmingham, e. Warwick (Ladywood, Birmingham), 17740, Pte., k. in a., F. & F., 7/5/17.
Marshall, William Peter, b. Brinsted, Hants, e. Alton, Hants (Hartley Mandritt, Hants), 35311, Pte., k. in a., F. & F., 14/4/18.
Martin, Arthur James Samuel, b. Plymouth, Devon, e. Plymouth, 50261, Pte., k. in a., F. & F., 27/9/18.
Martin, James Arthur, e. Birmingham (Saltley, Birmingham), 28408, Pte., k. in a., F. & F., 18/5/17.
Martin, William Charlton, b. Birmingham, e. Birmingham (Acock's Green, Birmingham), 14/1720, Pte., k. in a., F. & F., 23/7/16.
May, Walter Francis, b. Sparkhill, Birmingham, e. Warwick (Hall Green, Birmingham), 16630, Sgt., d. of w., F. & F., 24/5/18.
Maycock, Walter James, b. Warwick, e. Nuneaton, Warwicks (Stockingford, Warwicks), 23905, Pte., d. of w., F. & F., 5/3/19.
Mayrick, Thomas, b. Bidford-on-Avon, Warwicks, e. Stratford-on-Avon, Warwicks (Bidford-on-Avon), 17806, Pte., d. of w., F. & F., 28/9/16.
McGown, Henry, b. Glasgow, e. Glasgow, 34121, Pte., k. in a., F. & F., 11/11/17, formerly 8702, Dragoons.
McKey, Matthew Charles, b. Small Heath, Birmingham, e. Birmingham (South Yardley, Birmingham), 948, Cpl., d. of w., F. & F., 11/10/17.
McQuay, Fred, b. Redditch, Worcs, e. Birmingham (Redditch), 215, Pte., k. in a., F. & F., 30/7/16.
Medlock, Ernest, b. Stanground, Hunts, e. Old Fletton, Northants (Stanground), 30170, Cpl., d. of w., F. & F., 12/9/16, formerly 822, Hunts Cyc. Battn.
Meese, William Henry, b. Dudley, Worcs, e. Stourbridge, Worcs (Dudley, Worcs), 50467, Pte., k. in a., F. & F., 10/5/18.
Mendham, Percy Wilfred, b. Old Fletton, Northants, e. Old Fletton, 30172, Pte., k. in a., F. & F., 3/9/16, formerly 834, Hunts Cyc. Battn.
Mercer, Howard Norman, b. Willenhall, Staffs, e. Birmingham (Handsworth, Staffs), 14/1491, Cpl., k. in a., F. & F., 23/7/16.
Merrick, Alfred Sidney, b. Madley, Herefordshire, e. Birmingham (Small Heath, Birmingham), 949, Pte., k. in a., F. & F., 23/7/16.
Merrick, Thomas, e. Birmingham, 9238, Pte., d. of w., F. & F., 28/8/16.
Millar, David, b. Small Heath, Birmingham, e. Birmingham (Handsworth, Staffs), 16/948, Pte., k. in a., F. & F., 26/8/18.
Mills, Harry, b. Birmingham, e. Birmingham (Small Heath, Birmingham), 16/1946, Pte., k. in a., F. & F., 30/8/16.
Mills, Harold Frederick, b. Perry Barr, Birmingham, e. Sutton Coldfield, Warwicks (Edgbaston, Birmingham), 14/1147, Pte., k. in a., F. & F., 23/7/16.
Millward, James Howard, b. St. George's, Edgbaston, Birmingham, e. Birmingham (Edgbaston), 1075, Pte., k. in a., F. & F., 30/7/16.
Milton, Charlie, b. Gt. Grandson, Hunts, e. Huntingdon (Gt. Grandson), 30165, Pte., k. in a., F. & F., 7/5/17, formerly 792, Hunts Cyc. Battn.
Mitchell, Arthur, b. Halifax, Yorks, e. Halifax, 16/2042, L/Cpl., d. of w., F. & F., 28/8/18, farmerly 140540, R.F.A.
Momber, Harry, b. Bristol, Glos., e. Birmingham, 16/1500, Cpl., k. in a., F. & F., 30/7/16.
Montgomery, Albert, b. Ashby St. Ledgers, Northants, e. Coventry, Warwicks, 21139, Pte., d. of w., F. & F., 26/10/17.
Moon, Alfred, b. Chilvers Coton, Warwicks, e. Nuneaton, Warwicks, 17033, Pte., k. in a., F. & F., 3/9/16.
Mooney, Nicholas, b. St.Andrew's, Dublin, e. Dublin (Kingstown, Dublin), 32474, Pte., k. in a., F. & F., 2/5/18, formerly 1386, Lancers.
Morgan, William, b. Smethwick, Staffs, e. Birmingham (Erdington, Birmingham), 17517, Pte., k. in a., F. & F., 13/4/18.
Morley, Ernald Walter, b. Etwall, Derby, e. Birmingham (Etwall), 40, L/Cpl., k. in a., F. & F., 23/7/16.
Morris, John, b. Vauxhall, Birmingham, e. Sutton Coldfield, Warwicks (Acock's Green, Birmingham), 14/1248, Pte., d. of w., F. & F., 3/8/16.
Morris, Sydney, b. Wolverton, Bucks, e. Bletchley, Bucks, 34951, Pte., k. in a., F. & F., 27/9/18, formerly 286469, Q.O. Oxf. Hussars.
Moulding, Albert, b. Ladywood, Birmingham, e. Birmingham (Ladywood), 14/1474, Pte., k. in a., F. & F., 30/7/16.

Moulton, Edward Joseph, b. London, e. London, 34110, Pte., k. in a., F. & F., 11/11/17, formerly 9168, Dragoons.
Mountney, James, b. Bilton, Leics, e. Birmingham, 14/1307, Pte., k. in a., F. & F., 23/7/16.
Mousley, Henry George, b. St. George's, Birmingham, e. Birmingham, 166941, Pte., k. in a., F. & F., 3/9/16.
Mucklow, Charles William, b. Bishopston, Warwicks, e. Stratford-on-Avon, Warwicks, 17942, Pte., k. in a., F. & F., 30/7/16.
Mullis, Harold, b. Birmingham, e. Birmingham (Small Heath, Birmingham), 7923, A/Cpl., k. in a., F. & F., 3/9/16.
Murphy, Albert Dennis, b. Erdington, Birmingham, e. Birmingham, 14/1638, Pte., k. in a., F. & F., 23/7/16.
Murrell, Percival Christopher, b. West Ham, Middx., e. Whitehall, Middx. (East Ham, Essex), 32471, Pte., k. in a., F. & F., 4/10/17, formerly 24116, Lancers.
Neale, Dick, b. Claverdon, Warwicks, e. Birmingham (Sparkbrook, Birmingham), 14/1318, Pte., d. of w., F. & F., 22/7/16.
Negus, Percy Archibald, b. Chatteris, Cambs, e. Huntingdon (Chatteris), 30209, Pte., k. in a., F. & F., 26/10/17, formerly 961, Hunts Cyc. Battn.
Nelson, Alfred, b. Birmingham, e. Birmingham, 14/1623, Pte., k. in a., F. & F., 30/7/16.
Newberry, Frederick Walter, b. Saltley, Birmingham, e. Birmingham (Saltley), 192, Pte., k. in a., F. & F., 14/4/18.
Newey, Henry, e. Aston, Birmingham (Sparkbrook, Birmingham), 305886, A/Sgt., k. in a., F. & F., 18/8/18, D.C.M.
Newman, Alfred, b. Coventry, Warwicks, e. Coventry, 42137, Pte., k. in a., F. & F., 27/9/18.
Newman, James Albert, b. Pimlico, London, e. Stratford-on-Avon, Warwicks, 24638, Pte., k. in a., F. & F., 27/9/18.
Newton, Conrad, b. Preston, Lancs, e. Preston, 34097, Pte., d., F. & F., 27/1/18, formerly 7816, Dragoons.
Newton, George, b. Wollescote, Worcs, e. Worcester (Wollescote), 8748, Pte., k. in a., F. & F., 26/10/17.
Niblett, Alfred Thomas, b. Brighton, Sussex, e. Brighton, 235170, Pte., k. in a., F. & F., 27/9/18, formerly 18852, A. Cyc. Corps.
Nickless, William John, b. Sparkbrook, Birmingham, e. Birmingham (Sparkbrook), 953, Cpl., k. in a., F. & F., 23/7/16.
Nickson, Stuart, b. Acock's Green, Birmingham, e. Birmingham (Acock's Green), 44, Pte., k. in a., F. & F., 23/7/16.
Nix, John, b. Knowle, Warwicks, e. Birmingham (Knowle), 14/1330, Pte., k. in a., F. & F., 23/7/16.
Noak, Alfred, b. Birmingham, e. Birmingham (Clayton, Manchester), 17530, Pte., k. in a., F. & F., 27/9/16.
Noden, Frederick William, b. Aston, Birmingham, e. Birmingham (Erdington, Birmingham), 456, L/Cpl., k. in a., F. & F., 23/7/16.
North, George Henry, b. Hallavington, Hants, e. Bristol, Glos. (Tetbury, Glos.), 25367, Pte., k. in a., F. & F., 13/4/18, formerly S4/056357, R.A.S.C.
North, William James, b. Aston, Birmingham, e. Birmingham (Aston), 45, Pte., k. in a., F. & F., 23/7/16.
Northfield, Charles, b. Stepney, Middx., e. Poplar, Middx. (Bow, London), 35171, Pte., k. in a., F. & F., 30/8/18.
Norton, Horace John, b. Edgbaston, Birmingham, e. Birmingham (Handsworth, Staffs), 1070, Pte., k. in a., F. & F., 18/5/16.
Nurse, John James, b. Birmingham, e. Birmingham, 16/1736, Pte., k. in a., F. & F., 3/9/16.
O'Dowd, Bernard, b. Bolton, Lancs, e. Birmingham (King's Heath, Birmingham), 21141, Pte., k. in a., F. & F., 18/5/17.
Ogburn, Henry, b. Cannock, Staffs, e. Rugby, Warwicks, 14967, Pte., k. in a., F. & F., 30/7/16.
Oldham, Herbert Hadland, b. Combrook, Warwicks, e. Gloucester (Rudcombe, Glos.), 35904, Pte., d. of w., F. & F., 28/9/17.
Oliver, George, b. Hillmorton, Warwicks, e. Birmingham (Small Heath, Birmingham), 14/1665, Pte., k. in a., F. & F., 28/8/18.
Oliver, Harold Thomas, b. Forest Gate, Essex, e. Birmingham (London), 792, Pte., k. in a., F. & F., 3/9/16.
Olley, William Benjamin, b. Gt. Yarmouth, e. Gt. Yarmouth, 35797, Pte., k. in a., F. & F., 17/9/18, formerly 3011, Yeo. Cyclist.
Onions, William Leslie, b. Aston, Birmingham, e. Birmingham (Four Oaks, Birmingham), 816, Pte., k. in a., F. & F., 23/7/16.
Orme, John, b. Tamworth, Warwicks, e. Tamworth (Glascote, Warwicks), 20731, Pte., k. in a., F. & F., 4/6/17.
Owen, William, e. Birmingham (Lozells, Birmingham), 28412, Pte., k. in a., F. & F., 20/5/17.
Oxford, Arthur, b. Bentley, Warwicks, e. Nuneaton, Warwicks (Bentley), 16045, Cpl., k. in a., F. & F., 23/8/18.
Oxton, Sydney, b. Birkenhead, Ches., e. Birmingham (Birkenhead), 33706, Pte., k. in a., F. & F., 13/4/18, formerly 152, R.A.S.C.
Packer, Edward George, b. Swindon, Wilts, e. Swindon, 35323, L/Cpl., k. in a., F. & F., 26/9/18.
Palmer, Arthur, b. Hackney, London, e. Stratford, Essex (Athboy, Meath, Ireland), 32562, Pte., k. in a., F. & F., 26/10/17, formerly 7761, Dragoons.
Parker, Charles William, b. Ramsey, Hunts, e. Huntingdon (Ramsey), 30224, Pte., k. in a., F. & F., 3/9/16, formerly 1003, Hunts Cyc. Battn.
Parker, Ernest Harold, b. Brettle Lane, Staffs, e. Birmingham (Handsworth, Birmingham), 17070, Pte., k. in a., F. & F., 28/7/16.
Parkes, Henry Thomas, b. Birmingham, e. Birmingham (Small Heath, Birmingham), 16/1592, Pte., k. in a., F. & F., 13/4/18.
Parsons, Charles William, b. Hereford, e. Birmingham (Selly Park, Birmingham), 22497, Pte., d., F. & F., 9/2/17.
Payne, William, b. Birmingham, e. Birmingham, 3985, Pte., k. in a., F. & F., 3/9/16.
Peach, Henry, b. Hockley, Birmingham, e. Birmingham (Hockley), 470, Pte., k. in a., F. & F., 23/7/16.
Pearce, George, b. Peckham, Surrey, e. Battersea, London, S.W., 330529, Pte., d. of w., F. & F., 24/5/18.
Pearce, Harry William, b. Birmingham, e. Birmingham (Saltley, Birmingham), 15/1487, Pte., d. of w., F. & F., 21/7/16.
Pearson, Alfred William, b. St. Thomas, Birmingham, e. Birmingham (Hockley, Birmingham), 904, Pte., k. in a, F. & F., 3/9/16.
Pegg, Thomas, b. Bedworth, Warwicks, e. Nuneaton, Warwicks, 17497, Pte., k. in a., F. & F., 3/9/16.
Pilling, William Arthur, e. Stratford-on-Avon, Warwicks, 28463, Pte., d. of w., F. & F., 10/11/17.
Penn, William James, b. Northampton, e. La Havre, France (Newcastle-on-Tyne), 34276, Pte., k. in a., F. & F., 27/8/18, formerly 367458, R.A.S.C.
Perkes, Reginald, b. Stone, Staffs, e. Sutton Coldfield, Warwicks, 16785, Pte., k. in a., F. & F., 7/7/17.
Perkins, Charles Leonard, b. Birmingham, e. Birmingham (Aston, Birmingham), 1420, Pte., d. of w., F. & F., 11/9/10.
Perry, Percy Henry, b. Small Heath, Birmingham, e. Birmingham (Wylde Green, Warwicks), 15/1401, L/Sgt., k. in a., F. & F., 23/7/16.
Phelps, Alfred Charles, b. Box, Wilts, e. Chippenham, Wilts (Box), 40700, Pte., d. of w., F. & F., 24/8/18.
Phelps, William Henry, b. Vauxhall, Birmingham, e. Birmingham (Aston, Birmingham), 17550, Pte., k. in a., F. & F., 30/7/16.
Phillips, Albert Henry, b. St. Martin's, Birmingham, e. Birmingham (Balsall Heath, Birmingham), 14/1628, Sgt., k. in a., F. & F., 3/9/16, formerly 87468, R.F.A.
Pilgrim, Arthur Charles, b. Linslade, Bucks, e. Aylesbury, Bucks (Leighton Buzzard, Beds.), 18314, Pte., d. of w., F. & F., 4/10/18, formerly 22952, Som. L.I., M.M.
Pinchin, William Heath, b. Handsworth, Birmingham, e. Birmingham (Handsworth), 125, Pte., k. in a., F. & F., 23/7/16.
Pitts, Albert, b. Honeybourne, Worcs, e. Birmingham (Ashted, Birmingham), 3689, Pte., d. of w., F. & F., 16/1/19.
Platt, Samuel Woodgate, b. Wetherley, Yorks, e. Birmingham (Wetherley), 14/126, Pte., k. in a., F. & F., 23/7/16.
Poole, Frank, b. Rugby, Warwicks, e. Rugby, 20895, Pte., k. in a., F. & F., 24/4/17.
Poole, Frank George, e. Nottingham, 27398, Pte., k. in a., F. & F., 27/9/18, formerly 33279, Notts & Derby Regt.
Poole, Leonard Arthur, b. Huntley, Glos., e. Dorchester, Dorset (Bearminster, Dorset), 35910, Pte., k. in a., F. & F., 27/9/18.
Pope, Herbert, b. Ely, Cambs, e. Huntingdon (St. Ives, Hunts), 30270, Pte., k. in a., F. & F., 3/9/16, formerly 1567, Hunts Cyc. Battn.
Portch, Richard Daniel, b. Kensington, London, e. Hammersmith, London, W. (West Kensington), 32555, Pte., d. of w., F. & F., 13/10/17, formerly 6454, Lancers.
Powell, James, b. Manchester, Lancs, e. Manchester, 36528, Pte., k. in a., F. & F., 27/9/18, formerly 40448, S. Lancs Regt.
Powell, John, e. Nottingham, 27290, Cpl., k. in a., F. & F., 26/10/17, formerly 3489, Notts & Derby Regt.
Powell, William, b. West Bromwich, Staffs, e. Birmingham (West Bromwich), 16/1398, Pte., k. in a., F. & F., 23/7/16.
Powell, William Arthur, b. Wylde Green, Birmingham, e. Birmingham (King's Heath, Birmingham), 1001, Pte., k. in a., F. & F., 23/7/16.
Power, Brian Christopher, b. Coleshill, Birmingham, e. Birmingham, 296, L/Cpl., k. in a, F. & F., 23/7/16.
Prescott, Thomas Peter, b. Prescot, Lancs, e. Birmingham (Prescot), 119, Pte., k. in a., F. & F., 23/7/16.
Preston, William Albert, b. Coventry, Warwicks, e. Birmingham (Coventry), 131, L/Cpl., k. in a., F. & F., 23/7/16.
Pretty, William Henry, b. Coventry, Warwicks, e. Coventry, 35329, Pte., d. of w., F. & F., 14/4/18.
Price, John Edward Chilton, b. Edgbaston, Birmingham, e. Birmingham, 295, Pte., k. in a., F. & F., 23/7/16.
Price, Joseph, b. Walsall, Staffs, e. Birmingham (Coventry, Warwicks), 962, A/Sgt., d. of w., F. & F., 1/9/16.
Price, John William, b. St. Thomas-in-Moor, Birmingham, e. Birmingham, 967, Pte., k. in a., F. & F., 3/9/16.
Pridmore, Henry Alfred, b. Desborough, Northants, e. Coventry Warwicks, 22532, Pte., k. in a., F. & F., 27/9/18.
Pritchard, Frank, b. Warwick, e. Warwick (Coventry, Warwicks), 21959, L/Cpl., k. in a., F. F., 18/5/17.
Proud, Albert Ernest, b. Aston, Birmingham, e. Sutton Coldfield, Warwicks (Aston), 1201, Pte., k. in a., F. & F., 30/7/16.
Pryer, Aubrey Oliver, b. Luton, Beds, e. Bedford (Luton), 23418, Pte., d. of w., F. & F., 6/5/17, formerly 1606, R.E.
Quarton, Philip Bryan Davis, b. Birmingham, e. Sutton Coldfield, Warwicks (Rhyl, Flint), 16819, Pte., k. in a., F. & F., 3/9/16.
Quinn, William Edward, b. Liverpool, e. Widnes, Lancs, 25390, Pte., k. in a., F. & F., 28/8/18, formerly S4/217635, R.A.S.C.
Rafferty, Edwin Patrick, b. Hornsey, Middx., e. Mill Hill, London (Bowes Park, London), 38252, Pte., k. in a., F. & F., 27/9/18.
Ranford, William Henry, b. Birmingham, e. Birmingham, 43687, Pte., k. in a., F. & F., 27/9/18.
Rann, Leslie Claud, b. Newport, I. of W., e. Newport, 35331, Pte., k. in a., F. & F., 13/4/18.
Ravenscroft, John Samuel, b. Pendleton, Lancs, e. Salford, Lancs (Pendleton), 36527, Pte., k. in a., F. & F., 27/9/18, formerly 46459, S. Lancs Regt.

Raymond, Arthur, b. Peterborough, Northants, e. Huntingdon (Stanground, Northants), 30226, Pte., k. in a., F. & F., 3/9/16, formerly 1612, Hunts Cyc. Battn.
Reader, Charles Edward, b. Newton Castleacre, Norfolk, e. King's Lynn, Norfolk (Great Massingham, Norfolk), 32481, L/Cpl., k. in a., F. & F., 27/9/18, formerly 32400, Lancers.
Reed, Frank Arthur, b. Yelling, Hunts, e. Huntingdon (Offord D'Arcy, Hunts), 30227, Pte., k. in a., F. & F., 24/4/17, formerly 1225, Hunts Cyc. Battn.
Reid, James, e. Birmingham (Sutton Coldfield, Warwicks), 15/1511, L/Cpl., d. of w., F. & F., 11/5/17.
Reid, James, b. Aberdeen, e. Aberdeen, 34435, Pte., d. of w., F. & F., 1/6/18, formerly 43013, R.A.S.C.
Rhodes, James Peter, b. Birmingham, e. Birmingham, 39085, Pte., k. in a., F. & F., 8/7/18.
Richards, David, b. West Bromwich, Staffs, e. Birmingham (West Bromwich), 1218, Pte., k. in a., F. & F., 3/9/16.
Richards, Thomas Henry, b. St. Cuthbert's, Birmingham, e. Birmingham, 972, Pte., k. in a., F. & F., 20/9/18.
Richardson, Wilson Thomas, b. Alcester, Warwicks, e. Stratford-on-Avon, Warwicks (Alcester), 20854, Pte., k. in a., F. & F., 7/5/17.
Ricketts, Walter, b. Birmingham, e. Birmingham, 14/1405, Pte., k. in a., F. & F., 23/7/16.
Rider, Frank, b. Gloucester, e. Birmingham (Small Heath, Birmingham), 833, A/Cpl., k. in a., F. & F., 3/9/16.
Ridgway, Alfred, e. Market Harborough, Leics (Atherstone, Warwicks), 34098, Pte., d. of w., F. & F., 27/10/17, formerly 108717, R.A.S.C.
Ridley, Reginald George, b. Worcester, e. Stourbridge, Worcs (Old Swinford, Worcs), 35332, Pte., k. in a., F. & F., 13/4/18.
Rigg, Leonard, b. Rochdale, Lancs, e. Blackburn, Lancs, 48298, Cpl., k. in a., F. & F., 27/9/18, formerly 011901, R.A.O.C.
Riley, Thomas, b. St. Thomas, Lancaster, e. Birmingham (Lancaster), 976, Pte., k. in a., F. & F., 23/7/16.
Robbins, Thomas Henry, e. Aston, Birmingham (Adminton, Worcs), 28477, Pte., k. in a., F. & F., 27/2/18.
Robert, Charles Thomas, b. St. Helier's, Jersey, e. Fort Regent, Jersey (St. Helier's), 50423, Cpl., d. of w., F. & F., 8/7/18.
Roberts, George Arthur, b. Handsworth, Staffs, e. Birmingham, 14/1501, Pte., k. in a., F. & F., 23/7/16.
Robertson, James, b. Dundee, Forfar, e. Cowdenbeath, Fife (Kelty, Fife), 34124, Pte., d. of w., F. & F., 26/10/17, formerly 8325, Dragoons.
Robinson, Arthur James, b. Sparkbrook, Birmingham, e. Warwick (Sparkbrook), 17537, Pte., k. in a., F. & F., 30/7/16.
Robinson, James, b. Sutton Coldfield, Warwicks, e. Sutton Coldfield, 1173, L/Cpl., d. of w., F. & F., 27/9/16.
Robinson, Victor Arthur, b. Bethnal Green, London, e. London (Clapton, E.), 34962, Pte., k. in a., F. & F., 26/10/17, formerly 5401, R.W. Kent Regt.
Roe, Frederick Hubert, b. Sparkhill, Birmingham, e. Birmingham (Sparkhill), 9, Pte., k in a., F. & F., 30/7/16.
Rogers, Frank Roster, b. Streatham, London, e. Sutton Coldfield, Warwicks (London), 1203, L/Cpl., k. in a., F. & F., 23/7/16.
Rose, James William, b. Ladywood, Birmingham, e. Birmingham (Ladywood), 483, A/Sgt., k. in a., F. & F., 3/9/16.
Rosenthall, Louis Montague, b. Glasgow, Renfrewshire, e. Birmingham (Glasgow), 484, Pte., k. in a., F. & F., 23/7/16.
Rowan, Walter John, b. Birmingham, e. Birmingham, 14/1414, Pte., k. in a., F. & F., 23/7/16.
Rowcroft, George Arthur, b. Hunslet, Yorks, e. Birmingham (Hunslet), 33, Sgt., k. in a., F. & F., 23/7/16.
Rowlands, Thomas Samuel, b. Kingswinford, Worcs, e. Birmingham (Erdington, Birmingham), 16/1944, Pte., k. in a., F. & F., 23/7/16.
Rudd, Oliver, b. Northfield, Birmingham, e. Birmingham (Northfield), 486, L/Cpl., k. in a., F. & F., 23/7/16.
Rushton, Thomas, b. Liverpool, Lancs, e. Liverpool, 34109, Pte., k. in a., F. & F., 11/11/17, formerly 3036, Dragoons.
Russell, Leonard, b. Meriden, Warwicks, e. Coventry, Warwicks (Meriden), 9114, Pte., k. in a., F. & F., 13/4/18.
Russell, William George, b. Chippenham, Wilts, e. Birmingham (Chippenham), 993, Sgt., k. in a., F. & F., 26/10/17.
Sabin, Harold, b. Aston, Birmingham, e. Birmingham (Sparkbrook, Birmingham), 703, Pte., d. of w., F. & F., 4/8/16.
Sabin, Thomas Edward, b. Gloucester, e. Smethwick, Staffs (Oldbury, Worcs), 36113, Pte., k. in a., F. & F., 27/9/18.
Sackett, Frederick Henry, b. Brighton, Sussex, e. Sutton Coldfield, Warwicks, 14/1416, Pte., d. of w., F. & F., 20/9/16.
Salt, George Goodwin, b. Moseley, Birmingham, e. Sutton Coldfield, Warwicks, 14/1271, L/Cpl., k. in a., F. & F., 3/9/16.
Sanders, Frederick, b. St. George's, Birmingham, e. Birmingham (Sparkhill, Birmingham), 20094, Pte., k. in a., F. & F., 26/10/17.
Sanders, Thomas Frederick Procter, b. Ladywood, Birmingham, e. Birmingham, 272, Pte., d. of w., F. & F., 20/4/16.
Saunders, John Ernest Albert, b. Brill, Bucks, e. Coventry, Warwicks, 1446, Pte., k. in a., F. & F., 29/5/18, M.M.
Saunter, Harry Charles, b. Folkestone, Kent, e. Birmingham, 21149, Pte., k. in a., F. & F., 27/9/18.
Scarborough, Raymond Joseph, b. Wisbech, Cambs, e. Birmingham, 714, Pte., k. in a., F. & F., 24/9/16.
Scarff, Albert Edward, b. Ipswich, Suffolk, e. Ipswich, 33708, Pte., k. in a., F. & F., 14/4/18, formerly 081517, R.A.S.C.
Scott, Reginald Walker, b. Aston, Birmingham, e. Birmingham, 274, Pte., k. in a., F. & F., 3/9/16.
Seabrook, Frederick George, e. London (New Cross, London, S.E.), 32490, Pte., k. in a., F. & F., 23/5/18, formerly 5582, Hussars.
Sellars, Francis, b. Spalding, Lincs, e. Huntingdon (Billingborough, Lincs), 30228, L/Cpl., k. in a., F. & F., 11/9/16, formerly 955, Hunts Cyc. Battn.
Severn, Ernest Cyril, b. Birmingham, e. Birmingham, 14/1613, Pte., k. in a., F. & F., 3/9/16.
Seymour, Sidney Herbert, b. Wargrave, Berks, e. Maidenhead, Berks, 35340, Pte., k. in a., F. & F., 14/4/18.
Sharples, William Arnold, b. Bury, Lancs, e. Coventry, Warwicks, 18155, Pte., k. in a., F. & F., 3/9/16.
Sharps, Edward William Squires, b. South Marston, Wilts, e. Swindon, Wilts (South Marston), 35342, Pte., k. in a., F. & F., 14/4/18.
Shattock, George Henry, b. St. Phillip's, Bristol, Glos., e. Bristol, 27356, Pte., k. in a., F. & F., 8/5/17, formerly 27254, R. Berks Regt.
Sheldon, George William Augustus, b. Birmingham, e. Birmingham, 14/1255, Pte., k. in a., F. & F., 23/7/16.
Shenton, Horace Edgar, b. Hints, Tamworth, Staffs, e. Birmingham (Sutton Coldfield, Warwicks), 709, L/Sgt., d. of w., F. & F., 27/8/17.
Shinton, George Henry, b. Kidderminster, Worcs, e. Kidderminster, 34964, Cpl., k. in a., F. & F., 23/8/18, formerly 5353, R.W. Surrey Regt.
Shore, James Harold, b. London, Middx., e. Coventry, Warwicks, 35343, Pte., k. in a., F. & F., 14/4/18.
Shutt, Harry, b. Chesterton, Staffs, e. Birmingham (Handsworth, Birmingham), 203792, Pte., k. in a., F. & F., 14/4/18, Bronze Medal for Military Valour, Italy.
Sice, William Charles, b. Birmingham, e. Birmingham, 14/1338, Pte., k. in a., F. & F., 3/9/16.
Silk, Bernard Ward, b. Redditch, Worcs, e. Birmingham (Redditch), 15/1415, Pte., k. in a., F. & F., 23/7/16.
Silk, Edwin Guy, b. Solihull Warwicks, e. Birmingham, 80, Pte., k. in a., F. & F., 20/9/18.
Simmons, Edward, b. Birmingham, e. Birmingham, 14/1527, Pte., k. in a., F. & F., 23/7/16.
Simmons, John Albert, b. Aston, Birmingham, e. Birmingham (Aston), 214, Sgt., k. in a., F. & F., 23/7/16.
Simpson, Walter, b. Eastria, Cambs, e. Huntingdon (Old Fletton, Northants), 30229, Pte., k. in a., F. & F., 3/9/16, formerly 1571, Hunts Cyc. Battn.
Sinclair, William, b. Ramsey Heights, Hunts, e. Huntingdon (Ramsey Heights), 30331, Pte., k. in a., F. & F., 3/9/16, formerly 1614, Hunts Cyc. Battn.
Skelsey, Frederick, b Cubbington, Warwicks, e. Warwick, 289, A/Sgt., k. in a., F. & F., 3/9/16.
Skidmore, Frederick Arthur, b. Birmingham, e. Birmingham (Balsall Heath, Birmingham), 15/1459, L/Cpl., k. in a., F. & F., 3/9/16.
Slough, Philip Cecil, b. Christchurch, Birmingham, e. Birmingham, 14/789, Sgt., k. in a., F. & F., 23/7/16.
Smallwood, John William, b. Redditch, Worcs, e. Birmingham (Redditch), 712, Pte., k. in a., F. & F., 21/7/16.
Smith, Alfred, b. Princethorpe, Warwicks, e. Coventry, Warwicks (Princethorpe), 371, Pte., k. in a., F. & F., 9/5/17.
Smith, Alfred, b. Eccleshall, Yorks, e. Manchester (Salford, Lancs), 32568, Pte., k. in a., F. & F., 14/4/18, formerly 6980, Lancers.
Smith, Austen Benedict, b. Princethorpe, Warwicks, e. Birmingham (Harborne, Birmingham), 17637, Pte., k. in a., F. & F., 3/9/16.
Smith, Albert Owen, b. Deritend, Birmingham, e. Birmingham (Deritend), 254, Pte., k. in a., F. & F., 23/7/16.
Smith, Albert William, b. Birmingham, e. Birmingham (Small Heath, Birmingham), 14/1444, Pte., k. in a., F. & F., 23/7/16.
Smith, Charles Ernest, b. Bangalore, India, e. Birmingham (Sparkbrook, Birmingham), 708, Pte., k. in a., F. & F., 23/7/16.
Smith, David, b. Halesowen, Worcs, e. Birmingham (Blackheath, Birmingham), 14/1387, Pte., k. in a., F. & F., 28/7/16.
Smith, George, b. Atherstone, Warwicks, e. Atherstone, 18068, Pte., k. in a., F. & F., 3/9/16.
Smith, James Albert, b. Birmingham, e. Birmingham (Soho, Birmingham), 17071, Pte., k. in a., F. & F., 8/5/17.
Smith, Joseph Banks, b. Bewdley, Worcs, e. Kidderminster, Worcs (Bewdley), 1764, Pte., k. in a., F. & F., 3/9/16.
Smith, Joseph Bertram, b. Balsall Heath, Birmingham, e. Birmingham (Balsall Heath), 21, Pte., k. in a., F. & F., 23/7/16.
Smith, Joseph Henry, b. Peterborough, Northants, e. Old Fletton, Northants (New Fletton), 30236, Pte., k. in a., F. & F., 3/9/16, formerly 810, Hunts Cyc. Battn.
Smith, John William, b. Hammerton, Hunts, e. Huntingdon (Upton, Hunts), 30288, Pte., k. in a., F. & F., 3/9/16, formerly 1203, Hunts Cyc. Battn.
Smith, Sidney, b. Kings Norton, Worcs, e. Birmingham (Kings Norton), 144, Pte., k. in a., F. & F., 17/3/16.
Smith, Stanley Frederick, b. Ross, Hereford, e. Bridgend, Glam., 235227, Pte., k. in a., F. & F., 27/9/18, formerly 2333, Welsh Regt.
Smith, William, b. Linslade, Bucks, e. Aylesbury, Bucks (Linslade), 35351, Pte., k. in a., F. & F., 13/4/18.
Smith, William Gregory, b. Winson Green, Birmingham, e. Birmingham (Handsworth, Staffs), 987, Pte., k. in a., F. & F., 23/7/16.
Smith, William Harry, b. Studley, Warwicks, e. Redditch, Worcs (Middletown, Studley), 17415, Pte., k. in a., F. & F., 30/7/16.
Smith, Walter Henry, b. Kenilworth, Warwicks, e. Bedworth, Warwicks, 42742, Pte., d., F. & F., 29/10/18.
Smith, William John, b. Birmingham, e. Coventry, Warwicks, 28048, Sgt., k. in a., F. & F., 7/5/17.
Sowerby, Wilfred, b. Barnsley, Yorks, e. Barnsley, 25721, Pte., k. in a., F. & F., 5/7/18, formerly 29068, R.A.O.C

Spall, Henry, e. Aston, Birmingham, 331344, Pte., d. of w., F. & F., 17/9/18.
Stanley, Charles, b. Stratford-on-Avon, Warwicks, e. Stratford-on-Avon, 17985, Pte., d. of w., F. & F., 28/8/16.
Stanley, John, b. Hatton, Warwicks, e. Leamington, Warwicks (Warwick), 11677, Pte., k. in a., F. & F., 23/8/18.
Stanworth, George, b. St. Helens, Lancs, e. St. Helens, 36018, Pte., k. in a., F. & F., 27/9/18.
Stawford, Alfred, b. Birmingham, e. Birmingham (Kings Norton, Worcs), 16/1864, Pte., k. in a., F. & F., 23/7/16.
Stevenson, Charles, b. Birmingham, e. Birmingham (Perry Barr, Birmingham), 34411, Pte., d. of w., F. & F., 27/8/18, formerly 4046, Worcs Regt.
Stevenson, Thomas Edward, b. Fletton, Northants, e. Huntingdon (Old Fletton), 30289, Pte., k. in a., F. & F., 26/10/17, formerly 1631, Hunts Cyc. Battn.
Stockton, Richard Henry, b. Birmingham, e. Warwick (Stoke, Coventry, Warwicks), 14818, L/Cpl., k. in a., F. & F., 22/6/17.
Stokes, Albert,, e. Birmingham, 14471, Pte., k. in a., F. & F., 4/10/17.
Stokes, Alfred William, b. Claverley, Salop, e. Birmingham (Handsworth, Staffs), 14/1689, Pte., k. in a., F. & F., 3/9/16.
Stokes, James, b. Birmingham, e. Birmingham, 15006, Pte., k. in a., F. & F., 3/9/16.
Stokes, William David, b. Oldbury, Staffs, e. Birmingham (Ladywood, Birmingham), 16/1407, Pte., k. in a., F. & F., 23/7/16.
Stone, John, b. Leighton Buzzard, Beds, e. Coventry, Warwicks, 17700, Pte., k. in a., F. & F., 3/9/16.
Storer, Ernest, b. Erdington, Birmingham, e. Sutton Coldfield, Warwicks (Erdington), 28438, Pte., k. in a., F. & F., 7/5/17.
Storey, William Ernest, b. Pentney, Norfolk, e. St. Neot's, Hunts, 30279, Pte., k. in a., F. & F., 8/5/17, formerly 1671, Hunts Cyc. Battn.
Stratford, William Edward, b. Bourton-on-the-Water, Glos., e. Birmingham (Bourton-on-the-Water), 16999, Pte., k. in a., F. & F., 13/9/16.
Stretton, Cecil Harry, b. Lilford, Northants, e. Huntingdon (Lilford), 30335, Pte., d. of w., F. & F., 9/11/17, formerly 1106, Hunts Cyc. Battn.
Stubbs, William Ernest, b. Edgbaston, Birmingham, e. Birmingham (Edgbaston), 996, Pte., k. in a., F. & F., 23/7/16.
Styles, Arthur Edward, b. Coventry, Warwicks, e. Birmingham, 10155, Pte., k. in a., F. & F., 30/7/16.
Styles, Ernest Lazenby, b. Bloxwich, Staffs, e. Birmingham (Bloxwich), 463, Pte., k. in a., F. & F., 27/7/16.
Styles, Frederick, b. Kidderminster, Worcs, e. Birmingham (Trimpley, Worcs), 14/1756, Pte., d. of w., F. & F., 28/7/16.
Suart, Robert, b. Stockport, Ches., e. Stockport (Edgeley, Stockport), 29593, Pte., k. in a., F. & F., 27/9/18, formerly 40332, S. Lancs Regt.
Summers William Frederick b. Moseley Birmingham e. Birmingham (Moseley), 19, Pte., k. in a., F. & F., 23/7/16.
Suter, Frank William, b. Attleborough, Warwicks, e. Nuneaton, Warwicks, 10030, L/Cpl., k. in a., F. & F., 26/10/17.
Sutton, Alfred Leonard, b. Fenny Drayton, Warwicks, e. Nuneaton, Warwicks, 27697, Pte., k. in a., F. & F., 13/10/16.
Sutton, Arthur Moswood, b. Hunmanly, York, e. York (New Earswick, York), 32486, Pte., k. in a., F. & F., 26/10/17, formerly 4411, Lancers.
Sweeney, Thomas, e. Liverpool, 30476, Pte., k. in a., F. & F., 1/11/17, formerly 130387, R.A.S.C.
Tasker, Ernest, b. Birmingham, e. Birmingham (Harborne, Birmingham), 16/1405, Pte., k. in a., F. & F., 23/7/16.
Taunton, Robert, b. Moseley, Birmingham, e. Birmingham (Handsworth, Staffs), 14/1351, Pte., k. in a., F. & F., 23/7/16.
Taylor, Richard Alfred, b. Worcester, e. Sutton Coldfield, Warwicks (West Bromwich, Staffs), 14/1247, Pte., d., F. & F., 24/7/16.
Taylor, Sidney Arthur, b. Aston, Birmingham, e. Basingstoke, Hants (Saltley, Birmingham), 10395, L/Cpl., k. in a., F. & F., 27/9/18.
Taylor, Thomas Henry, b. Stratford-on-Avon, Warwicks, e. Birmingham (Warwick), 6317, R.S.M., d. of w., F. & F., 1/5/18.
Taylor, Wallace, b. Birmingham, e. Birmingham (Handsworth, Staffs), 15/1291, Pte., k. in a., F. & F., 13/4/18.
Taylor, William, b. Stourton, Worcs, e. Birmingham, 14/1606, Pte., k. in a., F. & F., 23/8/18.
Taylor, William Arthur, b. St. Nicholas, Coventry, Warwicks, e. Coventry, 27698, L/Cpl., k. in a., F. & F., 31/3/17.
Taylor, William Henry, b. Birmingham, e. Birmingham, 16/1962, Pte., k. in a., F. & F., 30/7/16.
Tedman, Walter, b. Grays, Essex, e. Gravesend, Kent (Grays), 32502, Cpl., d. of w., F. & F., 10/11/17, formerly 3627, Lancers.
Tedstone, Reginald Richard, b. Ladywood, Birmingham, e. Birmingham (Edgbaston, Birmingham), 746, L/Cpl., k. in a., F. & F., 23/7/16.
Tennant, Herbert, b. Alethorpe, Norfolk, e. Middleton Cheney, Oxon (Thenford, Oxon), 32491, Pte., k. in a., F. & F., 26/10/17, formerly 24175, Lancers.
Terry, Henry Arthur, b. St. Michael's, Coventry, e. Coventry, Warwicks, 28459, Pte., k. in a., F. & F., 7/5/17.
Thackwell, Frank, b. Oxhill, Warwicks, e. Stratford-on-Avon, Warwicks (Oxhill), 21020, Pte., d. of w., F. & F., 26/10/17.
Thompson, Albert Edwin, b. Edgbaston, Birmingham, e. Birmingham, 76, Pte., k. in a., F. & F., 23/7/16.
Thompson, Henry, b. St. Paul's, Birmingham, e. Birmingham (Handsworth, Staffs), 797, Pte., k. in a., F. & F., 23/7/16.
Thompson, Victor Herbert, b. Malvern, Worcs, e. Birmingham (Malvern), 311, Pte., k. in a., F. & F., 23/7/16.
Thompson, Walter, b. Holy Trinity, Coventry, Warwicks, e. Coventry, 28446, Pte., d. of w., F. & F., 7/5/17.
Thomson, Colin Moffat, b. Edinburgh, e. Edinburgh, 34113, Pte., d. of w., F. & F., 20/10/17, formerly 7975, Dragoons.
Thorn, Frank Edwin, b. St. Martin's, Birmingham, e. Birmingham (Handsworth, Staffs), 14/1443, Pte., k. in a., F. & F., 26/10/17.
Thurston, Arthur, b. Birmingham, e. Birmingham (Ashted, Birmingham), 17522, Pte., k. in a., F. & F., 30/7/16.
Tierney, John Terence Freer, b. Moseley, Birmingham, e. Birmingham, 82, Pte., k. in a., F. & F., 23/7/16.
Tilbury, William George, b. Portsmouth, Hants, e Huntingdon (Kettering, Northants), 30336, Cpl., k. in a., F. & F., 26/10/17, formerly 1380, Hunts Cyc. Battn.
Tinknell, Frederick Charles, b. Devonport, e. Plymouth, Devon, 35358, Pte., k. in a., F. & F., 14/4/18.
Toney, Jack Samuel, b. Birmingham, e. Birmingham (Nechells, Birmingham), 15/1544, Pte., k. in a., F. & F., 23/7/16.
Tonge, John Thomas, b. Astley, Lancs, e. Atherton, Lancs (Astley), 36524, Pte., d. of w., F. & F., 28/9/18, formerly 46449, S. Lancs Regt.
Tongue, Frank, b. Birmingham, e. Birmingham (Greet, Birmingham), 14/1551, Pte., k. in a., F. & F., 23/7/16.
Tonks, William Henry, b. St. Mary's Atherstone, Warwicks, e. Atherstone, 4072, L/Cpl., d. of w., F. & F., 20/5/17.
Tovey, Percy, b. Aston, Birmingham, e. Birmingham, 28422 Pte., k. in a., F. & F., 27/9/18.
Toye, Leslie, e. Birmingham (Camp Hill, Birmingham), 267989, Pte., k. in a., F. & F., 1/9/18.
Tranter, Alfred, b. Coleshill, Warwicks, e. Birmingham (Coleshill), 312, Sgt., d. of w., F. & F., 21/7/16.
Tranter, Arnold Samuel, b. Aston, Birmingham, e Birmingham (Aston), 22215, Pte., k. in a., F. & F., 6/5/17.
Treble, William Henry, b. Birmingham, e. Birmingham (Aston, Birmingham), 27734, Pte., k. in a., F. & F., 3/12/16.
Treglown, Robert Cecil, b. Handsworth, Staffs, e. Birmingham (Handsworth), 1000, Pte., k. in a., F. & F., 23/7/16.
Trickett, Arthur, b. Coventry, Warwicks, e. Coventry, 26204, Pte., k. in a., F. & F., 28/8/18.
Trickett, Charles, b. Birmingham, e. Birmingham (Edgbaston, Birmingham), 17534, Pte., k. in a., F. & F., 8/5/17.
Troman, Charles Gordon, b. Solihull, Warwicks, e. Birmingham, 83, Pte., k. in a., F. & F., 23/7/16.
Trowman, Alfred, b. Ladywood, Birmingham, e. Birmingham (Edgbaston, Birmingham), 14/999, Pte., d. of w., F. & F., 4/8/16.
Trueman, William, b. Birmingham, e. Birmingham, 28450, Pte., k. in a., F. & F., 26/10/17.
Turley, David Edward, b. Smethwick, Staffs, e. Birmingham (Smethwick), 14/1459, Pte., d. of w., F. & F., 31/7/16.
Turner, Alfred, b. Coventry, Warwicks, e. Coventry, 203718, Pte., k. in a., F. & F., 14/4/18.
Turner, Arthur Leslie Hinkley, b. Great Barr, Staffs, e. Birmingham (Great Barr), 16/1557, Pte., d. of w., F. & F., 28/11/16.
Tustin, Jack, b. Broadway, Worcs, e. Worcester (Broadway), 36116, L/Cpl., d. of w., F. & F., 13/9/18.
Tustin, Sidney Arthur, b. Ladywood, Birmingham, e. Birmingham (Acock's Green, Birmingham), 14/313, Pte., d. of w., F. & F., 6/8/16.
Twittey, George, b. Birmingham, e. Birmingham, 14716, Pte., k. in a., F. & F., 24/1/17.
Tyler, Edward, b. Putney, London, e. Fulham, London (Putney), 32492, Pte., k. in a., F. & F., 4/10/17, formerly 6576, Lancers.
Vallis, Noel Arthur John, b. Birmingham, e. Birmingham (Handsworth, Staffs), 28439, Pte., d. of w., F. & F., 28/10/17.
Verney, Tom, b. St. George's, Bristol, e. Bristol, 21277, Pte., k. in a., F. & F., 26/10/17, formerly 26317, R. Berks Regt.
Vint, Stanley Arthur, b. Holy Trinity, Aldershot, Hants, e. Birmingham (Aldershot), 94, Pte., k. in a., F. & F., 23/7/16.
Virr, Samuel, b. Smethwick, Staffs, e. Sutton Coldfield, Warwicks (West Smethwick), 1144, Sgt., k. in a., F. & F., 8/5/17.
Waddup, William, b. Bucknell, Oxon, e. Oxford (Fritwall, Oxon), 18467, Pte., k. in a., F. & F., 30/7/16, formerly 24312, Som. L.I.
Wakelin, Herbert Samuel, b. Handsworth, Staffs, e. Birmingham (Olton, Warwicks), 719, Pte., d., Home, 19/5/15.
Wales, Bertram William, b. York, e. Birmingham (York), 1025, L/Cpl., k. in a., F. & F., 23/7/16.
Walker, Ernest Albert, b. Birmingham, e. Birmingham, 14/1862, L/Cpl., k. in a., F. & F., 23/7/16.
Walker, Ernest Sydney, b. Coventry, Warwicks, e. Coventry, 9507, Pte., k. in a., F. & F., 8/11/17.
Walker, Oliver John, b. Hemsworth, Yorks, e. Coventry, Warwicks, 25120, Pte., k. in a., F. & F., 14/4/18.
Walker, Thomas, b. Melrose, Roxburgh, e. Melrose, 32586, Pte., k. in a., F. & F., 26/10/17, formerly 3321, Dragoons.
Walkley, Victor Norman, b. Handsworth, Birmingham, e. Sutton Coldfield, Warwicks (Birmingham), 14/1509, Pte., k. in a., F. & F., 23/7/16.
Wallis, Hubert John, b. Bexhill, Sussex, e. Piccadily, London (Hindley, Lancs), 32569, Pte., k. in a., F. & F., 26/10/17, formerly Rx/4/126593, R.A.S.C.
Wallis, Thomas, b. Birmingham, e. Birmingham, 34415, Pte., d., F. & F., 26/10/17, formerly 3957, Worcs Regt.
Walters, William, b. Kidderminster, Worcs, e. Birmingham (Smethwick, Staffs), 14/1540, Sgt., k. in a., F. & F., 3/9/16.
Waltho, Alfred, b. Birmingham, e. Warwick (Greet, Birmingham), 22161, Pte., k. in a., F. & F., 7/5/17.

Ward, William Arthur, e. Smethwick, Staffs (Winson Green, Birmingham), 23495, Pte., k. in a., F. & F., 14/4/18, formerly 2661, R.E.
Warren-Boulton, Reginald Palmer, b. Edgbaston, Birmingham, e. Birmingham (Edgbaston), 14/496, Pte., k. in a., F. & F., 23/7/16.
Warwood, Frank Joseph, b. King's Norton, Birmingham, e. Birmingham (Northfield, Birmingham), 727, Pte., k. in a., F. & F., 30/7/16.
Watkins, Edward William, b. London, e. Warwick (Nechells, Birmingham), 17741, Pte., k. in a., F. & F., 30/7/16.
Watson, George, b. Westminster, London, e. Slough, Bucks, 28931, Cpl., k. in a., F. & F., 8/7/18, formerly 27484, Glos. Regt.
Watson, John Stanley, b. Langley, Birmingham, e. Birmingham (Langley), 259, L/Cpl., k. in a., F. & F., 23/7/16.
Watson, Walter, b. Stirchley, Birmingham, e. Birmingham (Stirchley), 21055, Pte., k. in a., F. & F., 8/5/17.
Watts, George Robinson Ernest, b. Hartford, Hunts, e. Huntingdon (Hartford), 30233, A/Cpl., k. in a., F. & F., 3/9/16, formerly 590, Hunts Cyc. Battn.
Watts, Maurice Henry, b. Chalton, Beds, e. Bedford (Chalton), 32548, Pte., k. in a., F. & F., 26/10/17, formerly 2108, Beds Yeo.
Weatherhead, James, b. Hanley, Staffs, e. Birmingham, 1086, Sgt., k. in a., F. & F., 23/7/16.
Webb, George Albert, b. Sevenhampton, Glos., e. Birmingham (Harborne, Birmingham), 17683, Pte., k. in a., F. & F., 30/7/16.
Webb, John, b. Sutton Coldfield, Warwicks, e. Sutton Coldfield, 20734, Pte., k. in a., F. & F., 4/6/17.
Webb, Samuel Ignatius, b. Ashted, Birmingham, e. Birmingham (Aston, Birmingham), 15449, A/Cpl., k in a., F. & F., 3/9/16.
Webber, Garfield Leonard, e. Pontypridd, Glam., 260446, Pte., k. in a., F. & F., 17/9/18, formerly 5220, Welch Regt.
Wells, John Thomas, b. Kempston, Beds, e. London (Bedford), 33746, L/Cpl., k. in a., F. & F., 17/9/18, formerly 050476, R.A.S.C.
Westwood, William Amos, e. Dudley, Worcs, 30087, Pte., k. in a., F. & F., 27/9/18, formerly 27863, Worcs Regt.
Whatley, Walter, b. Stow-on-the-Wold, Glos., e. London (Charlton Kings, Glos.), 33720, Pte., k. in a., F. & F., 27/2/18, formerly 019421, R.A.S.C.
Wheeler, Edwin, b. Birmingham, e. Birmingham, 7839, Sgt., d. of w., F. & F., 28/9/18.
Whiley, William, b. Birmingham, e. Birmingham (Hockley, Birmingham), 14/1462, Pte., k. in a., F. & F., 30/7/16.
Whitbrook, Edwin James, b. Birmingham, e. Birmingham (Smethwick, Staffs), 14/1635, Pte., k. in a., F. & F., 23/7/16.
Whitcombe, Beresford, b. All Saints, Birmingham, e. Birmingham, 785, L/Cpl., k. in a., F. & F., 3/9/16.
White, Fred, b. Dowsdale, Lincs, e. Lincoln (Dowsdale), 27194, Pte., k. in a., F. & F., 23/5/18, formerly 5086, Lincs Regt.
White, John Robert, b. Upton, Hunts, e. Huntingdon (Upton), 30349, Pte., k. in a., F. & F., 1/10/17, formerly 1748, Hunts Cyc. Battn.
White, Richard Thomas, b. Wiggington, Oxon, e. Banbury, Oxon (Wiggington), 34965, Pte., k. in a., F. & F., 26/10/17, formerly 286052, Queen's Own Oxf. Hussars.
Whitehouse, Wilfred Tyrone, b. Sparkhill, Birmingham, e. Birmingham (Sparkhill), 665, Pte., d. of w., F. & F., 22/7/16.
Whittaker, Nathaniel Edward, b. Stakenbridge, Worcs, e. Birmingham (Edgbaston, Birmingham), 14/1426, Pte., d. of w., F. & F., 26/7/16.
Whittet, Frank, b. Brampton, Hunts, e. Huntingdon, 30337, Pte., k. in a., F. & F., 3/9/16, formerly 1756, Hunts Cyc. Battn.
Wickens, Arthur Edward, b. Mortimer, Berks, e. Newbury, Berks (Mortimer), 50409, Pte., k. in a., F. & F., 27/9/18.
Wicks, Henry John, b. Chippenham, Wilts, e. Warwick (Chippenham), 16604, Pte., d. of w., F. & F., 30/7/16.
Wilcox, Leslie Claude, b. Birmingham, e. Birmingham (Sparkbrook, Birmingham), 15/1367, Pte., k. in a., F. & F., 23/7/16.
Willcock, Robert Cecil, b. St. Mark's, Wolverhampton, Staffs, e. Birmingham (Wolverhampton), 285, Cpl., k. in a., F. & F., 23/7/16.
Willetts, George, b. Colleygate, Worcs, e. Stourbridge, Worcs (Cradley Heath, Staffs), 24787, Pte., k. in a., F. & F., 29/9/18.
Willetts, George John, b. Birmingham, e. Birmingham (Handsworth, Birmingham), 43703, Pte., k. in a., F. & F., 27/9/18.
Williams, Arthur Harry, b. Court House Green, Coventry, e. Coventry, Warwicks, 17730, Pte., k. in a., F. & F., 30/7/16.
Williams, Alfred James, b. Portsmouth, Hants, e. Birmingham (Edgbaston, Birmingham), 1328, Pte., k. in a., F. & F., 23/7/16.
Williams, Clement, e. Bristol, Glos., 21264, Pte., k. in a., F. & F., 7/11/17, formerly 23340, R. Berks Regt.
Williams, Edward, b. St. Paul's, Birmingham, e. Birmingham (Nechells, Birmingham), 9219, L/Cpl., k. in a., F. & F., 26/10/17.
Williams, Edward Wallace, b. Handsworth, Birmingham, e. Birmingham, 281, Sgt., k. in a., F. & F., 23/7/16, M.M.
Williams, George William, b. Mansell Lacey, Hereford, e. Cardiff, Glam. (Barry, Glam.), 43714, Pte., k. in a., F. & F., 27/9/18, formerly 5732, Mon. Regt.
Williams, Harry Cyril, b. Smethwick, Staffs, e. Birmingham (Ladywood, Birmingham), 14/1240, Pte., d., F & F., 20/1/18.
Williams, Jack, b. Wargrave, Berks, e. Reading, Berks (Wargrave), 36117, Pte., k. in a., F. & F., 27/9/18.
Williams, John Arthur, b. Tipton, Staffs, e. Dudley, Worcs, 19238, Pte., k. in a., F. & F., 22/10/17, formerly 21933, Glos. Regt.
Williams, Thomas, b. Henley, Ches., e. Birmingham (Harborne, Birmingham), 14/1402, Pte., k. in a., F. & F., 23/7/16.
Willis, Percy Ward, b. Birmingham, e. Birmingham, 16/1474, Pte., k. in a., F. & F., 29/5/18.
Wilsdon, Frederick George, b. Barston, Warwicks, e. Knowle, Warwicks (Barston), 17395, Pte., d. of w., F. & F., 3/9/16.
Winbury, Arthur Charles, b. Kidderminster, Worcs, e. Stourbridge, Worcs (Kidderminster), 15/1662, Pte., k. in a., F. & F., 13/4/18.
Wincup, John, b. Birmingham, e. Birmingham (Aston, Birmingham), 15956, Pte., k. in a., F. & F., 26/10/17.
Windres, William, b. Birmingham, e. Birmingham, 17638, Pte., k. in a., F. & F., 13/4/18.
Windridge, Harry, b. Ward End, Birmingham, e. Birmingham, 288, Pte., k. in a., F. & F., 23/7/16.
Witcombe, Robert Arthur, b. Sparkbrook, Birmingham, 1020, Pte., k. in a., F. & F., 23/7/16.
Wood, Albert Victor, b. Bromsgrove, Worcs, e. Birmingham (Bromsgrove), 14/1305, Pte., k. in a., F. & F., 23/7/16.
Wood, George, b. Kettering, Northants, e. Rugby, Warwicks (Coventry, Warwicks), 16755, Pte., k. in a., F. & F., 8/5/17.
Wood, John Charles, b. New Ferry, Ches., e. Birkenhead, Ches. (New Ferry), 36023, Pte., d. of w., F. & F., 8/7/18.
Wood, Samuel, b. Holly Hall, Worcs, e. Worcester (Dudley, Worcs), 30378, Pte., k. in a., F. & F., 3/9/16, formerly 29806, Worcs Regt.
Woodstock, Frederick Arthur, b. Sheffield, Yorks, e. Birmingham (Sheffield), 286, Pte., d., F. & F., 3/2/18.
Woodward, Harry, b. Sutton Coldfield, Warwicks, e. Birmingham (Erdington, Birmingham), 723, L/Cpl., d., F. & F., 6/6/17.
Wookey Edwin, b. Bristol, Glos., e. Birmingham, 14/1502, Pte., k. in a., F. & F., 23/7/16.
Worth, Charlie, e. Worcester (Tattenhall, Ches.), 28040, Pte., k. in a., F. & F., 26/10/17.
Wright, Albert, b. Ladywood, Birmingham, e. Birmingham, 288, Pte., k. in a., F. & F., 23/7/16
Wright, Alfred, b. St. Peter, Birkenhead, Ches., e. Birkenhead (Liverpool), 32582, Cpl., k. in a., F. & F., 4/10/17, formerly 4643, Dragoons.
Wright, Ernest, b. Cheadle, Staffs, e. Coventry, Warwicks, 17489, Pte., k. in a., F. & F., 3/9/16.
Wright, Robert Alban, b. Bedford, e. Birmingham (Shirley, Warwicks), 662, Sgt., k. in a., F. & F., 13/4/18.
Wyatt, Frederick John, b. Charlton, Northants, e. Birmingham (Castle Bromwich, Birmingham), 14/1693, Pte., k. in a., F. & F., 23/7/16.
Wyness, James Thomas Watt, b. Shrewsbury, Salop, e. Birmingham (Small Heath, Birmingham), 23238, Pte., k. in a., F. & F., 24/10/17.
Yates, Percy William, b. Laverstock, Wilts, e. Salisbury, Wilts (Tilshead S.O., Wilts), 28052, L/Cpl., k. in a., F. & F., 24/5/18.
Yeandle, Henry William, b. Edgbaston, Birmingham, e. Birmingham (Acocks Green, Birmingham), 664, Cpl., k. in a., F. & F., 20/5/17.
Young, Henry Alfred, b. Guernsey, Channel Islands, e. Northwich, Ches. (Hartford, Ches.), 34416, Pte., d., F. & F., 26/10/17, formerly 4428, Worcs Regt.
Young, Herbert Lionel, b. Holloway, London, e. London (High Barnet, London, N.), 34203, Pte., k. in a., F. & F., 26/10/17, formerly 5090, Lancers.

15th Battalion.

Abbott, Alfred, b. Kidlington, Oxon, e. Coleshill, Warwicks (Minworth, Birmingham), 15621, Cpl., d. of w., F. & F., 23/12/16.
Abkin, Thomas William, b. Glasgow, e. Birmingham (Northfield, Birmingham), 38354, Pte., k. in a., F. & F., 25/7/18.
Adam, Robert, b. Littleton, Wilts, e. Windsor, Berks (Datchet, Bucks), 30128, Pte., k. in a., F. & F., 3/9/16, formerly 22167, Oxf. & Bucks L.I.
Adams, William Ernest, b. Hampstead, London, e. Ilford, Essex (Seven Kings, Essex), 20567, Pte., d. of w., F. & F., 3/7/17, formerly 10360, A. Cyc. Corps.
Airey, Albert, e. Howick, Lancs (Haigh, Lancs), 32689, Pte., k. in a., F. & F., 14/4/18, formerly GS/21524, D. Gds.
Alexander, Henry James, b. Islington, Middx., e. Stratford, Essex (Darlinghurst, Sydney, Australia), 32659, Pte., k. in a., F. & F., 8/10/17, formerly 7497, Dragoons.
Alexander, James Philip, b. Urquhart, Moray, e. Grove Park, London (Lossiemouth, Moray), 33788, Pte., d. of w., F. & F., 29/6/18, formerly 206041, R.A.S.C.
Allen, George Frederick, b. Birmingham, e. Birmingham, 18340, Pte., d. of w., F. & F., 19/1/19, formerly 22999, Som. L.I.
Allen, Herbert Henry, b. Small Heath, Birmingham, e. Birmingham (Balsall Heath, Birmingham), 1002, Pte., k. in a., F. & F., 30/4/16.
Allen, Thomas, b. Beaconsfield, Bucks, e. High Wycombe, Bucks, 30129, Pte., k. in a., F. & F., 24/9/16, formerly 18508, Oxf. & Bucks L.I.
Allen, Thomas Edward, b. Birmingham, e. Birmingham, 15/1482, Pte., k. in a., F. & F., 23/7/16.
Allison, John Maskil, b. Doncaster, Yorks, e. Birmingham (Aston, Birmingham), 1161, Sgt., k. in a., F. & F., 27/9/18.
Allton, Joseph, b. Bedworth, Warwicks, e. Warwick (Bedworth), 22397, Pte., k. in a., F. & F., 8/5/17.
Andrews, George Phoenix, b. Bradford, Yorks, e. Bradford (Lidget Green, Bradford), 32742, Pte., k. in a., F. & F., 4/10/17, formerly 6241, Dragoons.

Andrews, Walter Henry, b. Leeds, Yorks, e. Birmingham (Hockley, Birmingham), 22651, Pte., d. of w., F. & F., 28/7/17.
Anstey, Thomas Reginald, b. West Bromwich, Staffs, e. Birmingham (West Bromwich), 317, Pte., k. in a., F. & F., 3/9/16.
Anthony, Frederick Arthur, e. Huntingdon (Old Fletton, Northants), 203415, Pte., k. in a., F. & F., 26/10/17, formerly 1539, Hunts Cyc. Battn.
Antrobus, Alfred Percy, b. Allesley, Warwicks, e. Birmingham (Maxstoke, Warwicks), 15/1643, Pte., k. in a., F. & F., 4/6/16.
Appleton, Arthur, b. Manchester, e. Warrington, Lancs, 22047, Pte., k. in a., F. & F., 26/10/17, formerly 3112, S. Lancs Regt.
Ashby, James Edman, e. Atherstone, Warwicks (Dordon, Warwicks), 11882, Pte., d. of w., F. & F., 18/2/17.
Astell, George Hawtin, b. Claydon, Oxon, e. Brackley, Northants (Leamington, Warwicks), 203710, Pte., k. in a., F. & F., 26/8/18.
Aston, Percy, b. Wednesbury, Staffs, e. Birmingham (Wednesbury), 1260, A/C.S.M., k. in a., F. & F., 29/8/16.
Atkins, Percy Frederick, b. Handsworth, Birmingham, e. Birmingham, 279, Pte., k. in a., F. & F., 4/6/16.
Attwood, Frederick Charles, b. Birmingham, e. Birmingham (Aston, Birmingham), 16/1785, Pte., k. in a., F. & F., 5/6/16.
Audley, William, b. Walsall, Staffs, e. Birmingham, 7232, Cpl., k. in a., F. & F., 28/6/18.
Austen, Frederick, b. Smarden, Kent, e. Sevenoaks, Kent, 27299, Pte., k. in a., F. & F., 27/9/18, formerly 5974, Notts & Derby Regt.
Baddeley, Frank, b. Tunstall, Staffs, e. Burslem, Staffs, 23555, Pte., d. of w., F. & F., 10/5/17, formerly 173764, R.E.
Bagshaw, Charles, b. Rugby, Warwicks, e. Stratford-on-Avon, Warwicks, 26348, Pte., d. of w., F. & F., 16/9/18.
Bailey, Harry, b. Brockmoor, Staffs, e. Birmingham (West Bromwich, Staffs), 16/1959, Pte., k. in a., F. & F., 23/7/16.
Baker, Alfred James, b. Royston, Herts, e. Birmingham (Aston, Birmingham), 15/1342, Pte., k. in a., F. & F., 3/9/16.
Baker, Oswald Ernest, b. Redditch, Worcs, e. Birmingham (Kings Heath, Birmingham) 15/1584, Pte., k. in a., F. & F., 4/6/16.
Baldwin, William, b. Atherstone, Warwicks, e. Nuneaton, Warwicks (Atherstone), 9426, Pte., k. in a., F. & F., 28/7/16.
Ballard, Thomas John, b. Coventry, Warwicks, e. Coventry, 241729, Pte., d. of w., F. & F., 28/5/18.
Balleny, George Wilfred, b. Erdington, Birmingham, e. Birmingham (Handsworth, Staffs), 334, Pte., k. in a., F. & F., 23/7/16.
Barnett, Leonard Powell, b. Handsworth, Staffs, e. Birmingham (Handsworth), 324, L/Cpl., k. in a., F. & F., 3/9/16.
Barrett, Ernest, b. Small Heath, Birmingham, e. Birmingham (Saltley, Birmingham), 30125, Cpl., k. in a., F. & F., 26/9/16, formerly 10837, Oxf. & Bucks L.I.
Barrett, Frederick, b. Birmingham, e. Birmingham (Handsworth, Staffs), 333, Sgt., k. in a., F. & F., 3/9/16.
Bartlett, Henry, b. Birmingham, e. West Hartlepool, Durham (Saltley, Birmingham), 16/1968, Pte., d. of w., F. & F., 6/10/16.
Bassett, William, b. Birmingham, e. Birmingham, 14/1581, Pte., k. in a., F. & F., 4/6/16.
Bate, William Thomas, b. Peterhead, Aberdeen, e. Birmingham (Peterhead), 1006, Cpl., d. of w., F. & F., 20/5/17.
Bates, George, b. Saltley, Birmingham, e. Birmingham (Saltley, Birmingham), 332, Pte., k. in a., F. & F., 4/6/16.
Bates, Samuel Harold, b. Edgbaston, Birmingham, e. Birmingham (Edgbaston), 617, Sgt., k. in a., F. & F., 28/8/16.
Baugust, Ronald Henry, b. Hilderstone, Staffs, e. Birmingham (Harborne, Birmingham), 1389, Pte., k. in a., F. & F., 3/9/16.
Baxter, Charles, e. Forfar (Dundee, Forfar), 235117, Pte., k. in a., F. & F., 26/10/17, formerly 5117, Scottish Horse.
Baxter, Ernest Harold, e. Huntingdon (Brampton, Hunts), 203393, Pte., k. in a., F. & F., 26/10/17, formerly 1308, Hunts Cyc. Battn.
Beach, George Bloxam Bury, e. Bailleul, France (Whitehall, Bristol), 34290, Pte., k. in a., F. & F., 27/7/18, formerly 362967, R.A.S.C.
Beal, William Ernest, b. Birmingham, e. Birmingham, 22704, Pte., k. in a., F. & F., 5/10/17.
Beale, Albert, b. Wellingborough, Northants, e. Birmingham, 1199, Pte., d. of w., F. & F., 9/7/18.
Beames, Charles Thomas, b. Birmingham, e. Birmingham (Nechells, Birmingham), 15/1644, Pte., k. in a., F. & F., 12/6/16.
Beardmore, John Henry, b. Stafford, e. Stafford, 34127, Pte., d. of w., F. & F., 29/10/17, formerly 19283, Hussars.
Bearman, Robert, b. Sevenoaks, Kent, e. Warwick (Leamington Spa, Warwicks), 32798, Cpl., k. in a., F. & F., 27/5/18, formerly 15824, Hussars.
Beaumont, Charles Eugene, b. Willesden, London, e. Birmingham (Willesden), 988, Pte., k. in a., F. & F., 9/5/17.
Bednall, Benjamin Charles, b. Birmingham, e. Birmingham (Rotton Park, Birmingham), 1254, Pte., k. in a., F. & F., 30/8/16.
Bell, Robert, b. St. Stephen's, Newcastle-on-Tyne, e. Gateshead, Durham (Elswick, Newcastle-on-Tyne), 32692, Pte., k. in a., F. & F., 4/10/17, formerly 5591, Dragoons.
Bennett, John, b. Erdington, Birmingham, e. Birmingham (Sparkhill, Birmingham), 325, L/Cpl., k. in a., F. & F., 4/6/16.
Bennitt, Ernest Gordon, b. Harborne, Birmingham, e. Birmingham (Harborne), 326, L/Cpl., k. in a., F. & F., 4/6/16.
Berry, Edward Bayes, b. Stratford-on-Avon, Warwicks, e. Birmingham (Stratford-on-Avon), 2030, L/Sgt., k. in a., F. & F., 3/9/16.
Berry, George Edward, b. Quedgeley, Glos., e. Birmingham (Erdington, Birmingham), 1229, Pte., k. in a., F. & F., 23/7/16.
Betty, William George, b. Moorfields, Bristol, e. Bristol (Moorfields), 35975, Pte., k. in a., F. & F., 30/8/18.
Bevan, Henry Joseph, b. Birmingham, e. Birmingham (Aston, Birmingham), 16/1551, Pte., k. in a., F. & F., 28/8/16.
Beynon, Thomas Hughes, b. Llangendeirne, Carm., e. Carmarthen, 32748, Pte., k. in a., F. & F., 4/10/17, formerly 25566, Dragoons.
Bird, John Alfred, b. Aston, Birmingham, e. Birmingham (Aston), 8244, Pte., k. in a., F. & F., 26/10/17.
Bird, George, b. Balsall Heath, Birmingham, e. Birmingham, 3570, L/Cpl., k. in a., F. & F., 2/7/17.
Birch, Harry Richard Adolphus, b. Yardley, Birmingham, e. Birmingham (Yardley), 97, Cpl., d. of w., F. & F., 29/8/16.
Blake, Leonard, b. Birmingham, e. Birmingham, 16/1633, Pte., d. of w., F. & F., 2/7/17.
Blakeman, William, b. All Saints, Northampton, e. Bedford (Northampton), 34225, A/Cpl., k. in a., F. & F., 12/4/18, formerly 5255, Dragoons.
Blakemore, Reginald Milnes, b. Knowle, Warwicks, e. Birmingham (Sparkbrook, Birmingham), 342, Pte., d. of w., F. & F., 1/8/16.
Blick, Richard Albert, b. Birmingham, e. Aston, Birmingham (Nechells, Birmingham), 330860, Pte., k. in a., F. & F., 26/10/17.
Blundell, Alfred Sidney, b. Aylestone, Leics, e. Leicester (Aylestone), 1824, Sgt., k. in a., F. & F., 3/9/16.
Boland, Sydney, b. Birmingham, e. Birmingham (Sparkbrook, Birmingham), 1123, Pte., k. in a., F. & F., 23/7/16.
Bolton, Allen, b. St. Michael's, Coventry, Warwicks, e. Warwick (Leamington, Warwicks), 3/2954, Cpl., k. in a., F. & F., 24/9/16.
Bond, Charles, b. Birmingham, e. Birmingham (Aston, Birmingham), 24858, Pte., k. in a., F. & F., 26/10/17.
Boss, Noah, b. Birmingham, e. Birmingham (Saltley, Birmingham), 14/1752, Pte., d. of w., F. & F., 22/9/16.
Bowen, Richard Biggs, b. Birmingham, e. Birmingham, 330024, Pte., k. in a., F. & F., 13/4/18.
Box, Frederick Archibald, b. Birmingham, e. Birmingham (Stirchley, Birmingham), 28660, Pte., k. in a., F. & F., 15/7/17.
Boyes, Ernest Charles, b. Colbury, Hants, e. Winchester, Hants (Hounsdown, nr. Southampton), 18757, Pte., k. in a., F. & F., 27/10/17, formerly 23846, Som. L.I.
Bradbury, William, b. Balsall Heath, Birmingham, e. Birmingham (Balsall Heath), 849, Pte., d., F. & F., 26/4/17.
Bradley, Clarence Austin, b. Birmingham, e. Birmingham (Kings Norton, Birmingham), 1164, Pte., k. in a., F. & F., 4/6/16.
Brain, Clifford, b. Kingswood, Bristol, e. Bristol (Kingswood), 18749, Pte., d. of w., F. & F., 27/12/16, formerly 24508, Som. L.I.
Brassington, Arthur, b. Betley, Staffs, e. Crewe, Ches., 29613, Pte., k. in a., F. & F., 27/8/18, formerly 40452, S. Lancs Regt.
Brassington, Henry Wilfrid, b. Aston, Birmingham, e. Birmingham (Aston), 255, Pte., k. in a., F. & F., 3/9/16.
Brember, Andrew, e. Aldershot, Hants (Burntisland, Fife), 32663, Pte., k. in a., F. & F., 4/10/17, formerly 19046, Dragoon Gds.
Bridge, Joseph Reginald, b. St. Helens, Lancs, e. Birmingham (Selly Oak, Birmingham), 15/1374, Cpl., k. in a., F. & F., 9/5/17.
Bridger, Alex William John, b. Folkestone, Kent, e. Folkestone, 33210, Pte., d. of w., F. & F., 26/10/17, formerly 23880, Lancers.
Brierly, Charles William, b. Rochdale, Lancs, e. Rochdale, 32747, Pte., k. in a., F. & F., 26/10/17, formerly 21933, Dragoons.
Bristow, Charles Henry, b. St. Faiths, Lincoln, e. Birmingham (Lincoln), 579, Pte., k. in a., F. & F., 7/5/16.
Brittain, George, b. Meriden, Warwicks, e. Coventry, Warwicks, 16731, Pte., k. in a., F. & F., 3/9/16.
Britton, Albert Sherwood, b Birmingham, e. Birmingham (Pontyrhyl, Glam.), 15/1568, Pte., k. in a., F. & F., 23/7/16.
Bromwich, Edgar John, b. Sutton Coldfield, Warwicks, e. Birmingham (Sutton Coldfield), 312, Pte., k. in a., F. & F., 4/6/16.
Bromwich, Frederick, b. Rugby, Warwicks, e. Rugby (Long Lawford, Warwicks), 22391, Pte., k. in a., F. & F., 8/5/17.
Bromwich, Leslie Francis, b. Sutton Coldfield, Warwicks, e. Birmingham (Sutton Coldfield), 308, L/Cpl., k. in a., F. & F., 4/6/16.
Brookes, Vernon John, b. Smethwick, Staffs, e. Birmingham (Cheltenham, Glos.), 349, L/Cpl., k. in a., F. & F., 2/6/16.
Brookfield, Percy William, b. Walsall, Staffs, e. Birmingham (Walsall), 585, Pte., k. in a., F. & F., 31/7/16.
Broomfield, Percy Taylor, b. Ditton, Maidstone, Kent, e. Birmingham (Marston Green, Warwicks), 831, Cpl., k. in a., F. & F., 15/12/15.
Brown, Archibald Henry, b. S. Croydon, Surrey, e. Solihull, Warwicks (Hampton-in-Arden, Warwicks), 17721, Pte., k. in a., F. & F., 3/9/16.
Brown, Ernest, b. Conisborough, Yorks, e. Sheffield, Yorks (Conisborough), 12492, Pte., d. of w., F. & F., 29/6/18, formerly 56625, R.G.A.

Brown, Frank, b. Rochdale, Lancs, e. Manchester (Broughton, Manchester), 20612, Pte., d., F. & F., 17/10/18, formerly 11442, Army Cyc. Corps.

Brown, Herbert Avery, b. Franche, Kidderminster, Worcs, e. Birmingham (Harborne, Birmingham), 939, Pte., k. in a., F. & F., 23/5/16.

Brown, Henry Samuel, b. London, e. London, 33211, Pte., k. in a., F. & F., 26/10/17, formerly 23209, Lancers.

Bryant, Christopher George, b. Small Heath, Birmingham, e. Birmingham (Small Heath), 351, Pte., k. in a., F. & F., 23/7/16.

Bryers, William, b. Rainford, Lancs, e. Rainford, 34495, Pte., d. of w., F. & F., 15/4/18, formerly 204220, S. Lancs Regt.

Buckland, Thomas Henry, b. West Hartlepool, Yorks, e. Birmingham (Ladywood, Birmingham), 14/1323, Pte., k. in a., F. & F., 30/7/16.

Buckley, William Francis, b. Birmingham, e. Birmingham, 1066, L/Sgt., k. in a., F. & F., 4/6/16.

Buffey, Frederick William, b. Westmeon, Hants, e. Portsmouth, Hants (Westmeon), 18767, L/Cpl., d. of w., F. & F., 24/4/17, formerly 23626, Som. L.I.

Bulley, Alfred James, b. St. Luke's, Bristol, e. Bristol (Barton Hill, Bristol), 18707, Pte., k. in a., F. & F., 2/7/17, formerly 24512, Som. L.I.

Burgess, Rowland Hill, b. Stockport, Ches., e. Birmingham (Stockport), 185, Pte., k. in a., F. & F., 3/9/16.

Burn, James Ernest, b. Aston, Birmingham, e. Birmingham, 261, Pte., k. in a., F. & F., 9/5/17.

Burnett, Alfred, b. Vauxhall, Birmingham, e. Birmingham (Sparkbrook, Birmingham), 11411, Pte., k. in a., F. & F., 27/9/18.

Burnett, William Charles, b. All Saints, Birmingham, e. Birmingham (Aston, Birmingham), 16/1818, Pte., k. in a., F. & F., 10/10/17.

Burns, John, b. Barony, Lanark, e. London (Glasgow), 33703, Pte., k. in a., F. & F., 14/4/18, formerly 040146, R.A.S.C.

Burton, Charles Lamley, b. Nottingham, e. Coleshill, Warwicks (Water Orton, Warwicks), 203845, Pte., d., F. & F., 13/10/18.

Butcher, Harold, b. Trowbridge, Wilts, e. Trowbridge, 18595, Pte., d. of w., F. & F., 4/6/17, formerly 24716, Som. L.I.

Capers, Clarence Charles Arthur Albert Edward, b. Warwick, e. Warwick, 202344, Pte., k. in a., F. & F., 26/10/17.

Carpenter, Wilfred John, b. Chipping Norton, Oxon, e. Stoney Lane, Birmingham, 16/1759, Pte., d. of w., F. & F., 16/9/16.

Carter, Frank, b. Birmingham, e. Birmingham (Spring Hill, Birmingham), 16/1619, Pte., d. of w., F. & F., 28/8/16.

Cattle, Fred, b. Parkstone, Dorset, e. Poole, Dorset, 38718, Pte., k. in a., F. & F., 28/6/18.

Challen, Reginald Frederick, e. Horsham, Sussex (Billingshurst, Sussex), 33213, Pte., d. of w., F. & F., 15/4/18, formerly 16036, Lancers.

Chantler, Robert, b. Acton, London, e. Southampton, Hants (Acton Green, London), 32732, Pte., k. in a., F. & F., 4/10/17, formerly 6374, Dragoons.

Chapman, Arthur, b. Polesworth, Warwicks, e. Nuneaton, Warwicks (Freasley, Warwicks), 14896, Cpl., k. in a., F. & F., 9/5/17.

Chasey, Henry, b. Redcliffe, Bristol, e. Bristol (Bedminster, Glos.), 18748, Pte., k. in a., F. & F., 9/5/17, formerly 24513, Som. L.I.

Chattock, Claude Arthur, b. Hampstead, London, e. Birmingham (Edgbaston, Birmingham), 15/704, Pte., k. in a., F. & F., 4/6/16.

Cheetham, Ferdinand, b. Birmingham, e. Birmingham (Lozells, Birmingham), 16/1709, Pte., d. of w., F. & F., 21/4/17.

Chirgwin, John Charles, b. Penzance, Cornwall, e. Rugby, Warwicks, 17031, Cpl., d. of w., F. & F., 15/7/17.

Chopping, Reginald Bertram Clive, b. Grassingdale, Lancs, e. Birmingham (Grassingdale), 163, Pte., k. in a., F. & F., 28/8/16.

Church, Arthur Percival, b. Ashford, Kent, e. Newport, I. of W., 18567, Pte., k. in a., F. & F., 22/12/16, formerly 24957, Som. L.I.

Clackett, Albert, b. Birmingham, e. Birmingham, 14/1610, Pte., k. in a., F. & F., 4/6/16.

Clare, Samuel, b. Birkenhead, Ches., e. Birkenhead, 29532, Pte., k. in a., F. & F., 27/9/18, formerly 62239, Ches. Regt.

Clark, Charles Phillip, b. Erdington, Warwicks, e. Birmingham (Erdington), 164, Pte., k. in a., F. & F., 3/9/16.

Clarke, Frederick William, b. Haverhill, Suffolk, e. Haverhill, 27228, Pte., k. in a., F. & F., 13/4/18, formerly 1337, Suffolk Regt.

Clarke, William Henry, b. Dudley, Worcs, e. Birmingham (Dudley), 168, Cpl., k. in a., F. & F., 3/7/17.

Clarke, William John, b. Birmingham, e. Birmingham (Handsworth, Birmingham), 28662, Pte., k. in a., F. & F., 26/10/17.

Cleaver, Albert Ernest, b. Coventry, Warwicks, e. Coventry, 18877, Pte., k. in a., F. & F., 26/10/17.

Clements, Harold, b. Birmingham, e. Birmingham, 16/1831, Pte., d. of w., F. & F., 30/7/16.

Clews, Joseph Henry Sharrard, b. Aston, Birmingham, e. Birmingham (Aston), 170, L/Cpl., k. in a., F. & F., 4/6/16.

Clifford, John Robert, b. Beeston, Notts, e. Coventry, Warwicks, 28601, Pte., k. in a., F. & F., 26/8/18.

Cole, Alfred James, b. Flixton, Ches, e. Birmingham (Hockley, Birmingham), 8976, Pte., k. in a., F. & F., 28/7/16.

Cole, Percy Baden, b. Prittlewell, Essex, e. Southend, Essex (London), 35966, Pte., d. of w., F. & F., 11/8/18.

Coley, Harry, b. Birmingham, e. Birmingham (Quinton, Birmingham), 16/1734, Pte., k. in a., F. & F., 5/10/17.

Collins, Arthur, b. Willey, Warwicks, e. Rugby, Warwicks (New Bilton, Warwicks), 17406, Pte., k. in a., F. & F., 26/10/17.

Collins, Arthur, b. Sutton Coldfield, Warwicks, e. Sutton Coldfield (Balsall Heath, Birmingham), 16200, Pte., d. of w. F. & F., 9/5/17.

Collins, Joseph Henry, b. Aston, Birmingham, e. Birmingham, 1562, Pte., k. in a., F. & F., 30/8/16.

Connell, Frederick, b. Isleworth, Middx., e. Aldershot, Hants, 18765, Pte., k. in a., F. & F., 9/5/17, formerly 24239, Som. L.I.

Cook, William Henry, e. Birmingham, 19206, Pte., k. in a., F. & F., 4/10/17.

Cooling, Alfred Tom, b. North Barrow, Som., e. Castle Cary, Som. (N. Barrow), 34946, Pte., k. in a., F. & F., 28/6/18, formerly 55501, Devon Regt.

Cooney, Joseph, b. Manchester, e. Birmingham (King's Norton, Birmingham), 35967, Pte., d., F. & F., 27/6/18.

Cooper, David Petty, b. London, e. Birmingham (London), 15/194, Pte., k. in a., F. & F., 4/6/16.

Cooper, Frank William, b. Aldeburgh-on-Sea, Suffolk, e. Ipswich, Suffolk (Aldeburgh), 34133, Pte., k. in a., F. & F., 26/10/17, formerly GS/23507, Lancers.

Cooper, Hubert Arthur, b. Rotten Park, Birmingham, e. Birmingham (Rotten Park), 31, Pte., k. in a., F. & F., 3/9/16.

Cooper, Joseph, b. Sutton Coldfield, Warwicks, e. Birmingham (Erdington, Birmingham), 1163, Pte., d. of w., F. & F., 24/7/16.

Cooper, Thomas, b. Burroughs Grove, Bucks, e. Marlow, Bucks (Burroughs Grove), 29830, Pte., k. in a., F. & F., 24/8/18, formerly 28598, Oxf. & Bucks L.I.

Cooper, Thomas, b. Islington, Middx., e. Newport, Mon. (Brighton, Sussex), 32728, Pte., k. in a., F. & F., 25/10/17, formerly 25589, Dragoons.

Corless, Hall Laing, b. Newton-le-Willows, Lancs, e. Warrington, Lancs (St. Helens, Lancs), 36073, Pte., k. in a., F. & F., 24/8/18.

Corns, Isaac, b. St. Mary's, Birmingham, e. Birmingham (Gosta Green, Birmingham), 330207, Pte., k. in a., F. & F., 27/9/18.

Cottrell, Charles, b. Edgbaston, Birmingham, e. Birmingham, 933, Sgt., k. in a., F. & F., 23/5/16.

Cotterill, George Thomas, b. Willenhall, Staffs, e. Shotton, Ches. (Queen's Ferry, Chester), 36075, Pte., k. in a., F. & F., 27/9/18, formerly 4/21619, Ches. Regt.

Cowles, Francis James, b. Smethwick, Staffs, e. Birmingham (Smethwick), 15/848, L/Cpl., d., F. & F., 12/6/17.

Cox, Clifford, b. Hurst Hill, Bilston, Staffs, e. Birmingham (Hurst Hill), 16/1846, Pte., k. in a., F. & F., 23/7/16.

Cox, Cecil Herbert, b. Salisbury, Wilts, e. Birmingham (Salisbury), 370, Pte., d. of w., F. & F., 27/10/17.

Cox, Fritz James, b. Kidderminster, Worcs, e. Birmingham (Kidderminster), 15/1661, Pte., k. in a., F. & F., 23/7/16.

Cox, Herbert, b. King's Norton, Birmingham, e. Birmingham (Handsworth, Birmingham), [illegible]69, Sgt., k. in a., F. & F., 3/9/16.

Crabb, John, b. Brentwood, Essex, e. Leamington, Warwicks, 11889, Pte., d. of w., F. & F., 24/5/17.

Craddock, William Henry, b. Stratford-on-Avon, Warwicks, e. Birmingham (Nechells, Birmingham), 15/1318, Pte., k. in a., F. & F., 3/9/16.

Craven, James Alexander, b. Streetly, Birmingham, e. Birmingham (Streetly), 16/1657, Cpl., k. in a., F. & F., 29/5/18.

Crennell, George, b. Balsall Heath, Warwicks, e. Birmingham (Balsall Heath), 196, Pte., k. in a., F. & F., 3/9/16.

Cresswell, Ernest, b. St. Martin's, Birmingham, e. Birmingham (Small Heath, Birmingham), 24075, Pte., k. in a., F. & F., 28/6/18.

Crome, John Leslie, b. Small Heath, Birmingham, e. Birmingham (Worcester), 645, L/Cpl., k. in a., F. & F., 4/6/16.

Cross, James, b. Salford, Lancs, e. Birmingham (Salford), 9731, Pte., k. in a., F. & F., 30/8/16.

Cross, Valentine, b. St. Thomas, Birmingham, e. Birmingham, 431, Pte., k. in a., F. & F., 27/8/16.

Crossley, Thomas Horler, b. Frome, Somerset, e. Leamington, Warwicks, 17398, Pte., k. in a., F. & F., 29/8/16.

Cubbison, William James, b. Liverpool, Lancs, e. Liverpool, 36074, Pte., k. in a., F. & F., 28/6/18.

Curtis, Charles Edward, b. Derby, e. Caversham, Oxon (Reading, Berks), 34592, Sgt., k. in a., F. & F., 27/9/18, formerly 832, R.A.V.C.

Dance, Lionel Bert, b. Gloucester, e. Birmingham (Vauxhall, Birmingham), 16/1780, L/Cpl., k. in a., F. & F., 3/9/16.

Dangerfield, James Henry, b. Marlborough, Wilts, e. Bristol, Glos. (Wootton Bassett, Wilts), 32848, Pte., k. in a., F. & F., 10/10/17, formerly 32836, Hussars.

Darlington, William, b. Liverpool, Lancs, e. Liverpool, 36081, Pte., k. in a., F. & F., 28/6/18, formerly 4/22698, Ches. Regt.

Davies, Hugh Richard, b. Nottingham, e. Birmingham (Nottingham), 15/1069, Pte., d., F. & F., 18/9/16, M.M.

Davies, James, b. Salford, Lancs, e. Salford (Manchester), 27909, Pte., d. of w., F. & F., 15/4/18, formerly 1861, Lancs Fus.

Davies, James, b. Kingsbury, Salop, e. Aldershot, Hants (Worcester), 23561, Pte., d. of w., F. & F., 9/5/17, formerly 163152, R.E.

Davies, Norman Hayden, b. Liverpool, Lancs, e. Old Haymarket, Liverpool (Southport, Lancs), 32752, Pte., k. in a., F. & F., 4/10/17, formerly 37177, Dragoon Gds.

Davis, Alfred Edward, b. Birmingham, e. Birmingham, 15/1445, Pte., k. in a., F. & F., 12/4/18.

Davis, James Thomas, b. Saltley, Birmingham, e. Birmingham, 3647, Pte., k. in a., F. & F., 9/5/17.

Dawkins, Thomas, b. Birmingham, e. Birmingham, 378, Pte., k. in a., F. & F., 1/6/16.

Dawson, Robert, b Birmingham, e. Birmingham (Erdington, Birmingham), 14/1471, Pte., k. in a., F. & F., 3/9/16.
Deacon, Frederick, b. Aston, Birmingham, e. Birmingham (Aston), 968, L/Cpl., k. in a., F. & F., 9/5/17.
Dean, William, b. Coldstream, Dumfries, e. Edinburgh (Fauldhouse, West Lothian), 34597, Pte., k. in a., F. & F., 28/6/18, formerly 6179, R.A.V.C.
Dear, Charles James, e. Pewsey, Wilts, 26937, Pte., k. in a., F. & F., 5/5/17.
Deeley, Albert James, b. Birmingham, e. Birmingham (Bournbrook, Birmingham), 1237, Pte., k. in a., F. & F., 9/5/17.
Denchfield, Harry James, b. St. Peter's, Cheltenham, Glcs., e. Birmingham (Small Heath, Birmingham), 911, Pte., k. in a., F. & F., 23/5/16.
Dewar, Neil Somerville, b. St. Cuthbert's, Edinburgh, e. In the Field (Edinburgh), 34649, Cpl., k. in a., F. & F., 12/4/18, formerly 1608, Lothian & Border Horse.
Dicks, Benjamin Thomas, e. Birmingham (Aston, Birmingham), 28658, Pte., k. in a., F. & F., 26/10/17.
Dingley, John, b. Coventry, Warwicks, e. Coventry, 16855, Pte., d. of w., F. & F., 3/9/16.
Doble, Henry Wood, b. Johannesburg, South Africa, e. Birmingham (Solihull, Birmingham), 14/1747, L/Cpl., k. in a., F. & F., 3/9/16.
Dodgson, Thomas Culshaw, b. Pilling, Lancs, e. Fleetwood, Lancs (Poulton-le-Fylde, Lancs), 12286, Pte., k. in a., F. & F., 3/9/16, formerly 53783, R.G.A.
Dowler, Arthur Gordon, e. Moseley, Birmingham, e. Birmingham, 376, Pte., k. in a., F. & F., 4/6/16.
Downing, Ernest, b. Birmingham, e. Birmingham (Sutton Coldfield, Birmingham), 1267, Pte., d. of w., F. & F., 1/8/16.
Doyle, Frederick Clarence, b. Sparkbrook, Birmingham, e. Birmingham, 539, L/Cpl., k. in a., F. & F., 25/7/16.
Driscoll, Harold Cornelius, b. St. Catherine, Birmingham, e. Birmingham, 240470, Pte., d. of w., F. & F., 9/10/17.
Drury, Frederick George, b. Pucklechurch, Glos., e. Bristol (Pucklechurch), 18754, Pte., k. in a., F. & F., 24/9/16, formerly 24129, Som. L.I.
Duckett, Edward Charles Albert Victor, b. Stratford-on-Avon, Warwicks, e. Warwick, 19076, Pte., d. of w., F. & F., 9/10/17.
Duckett, Thomas French, b. Napton, Warwicks, e. Warwick (Napton), 18101, Pte., k. in a., F. & F., 26/10/17.
Duncan, Charles, b. Sunderland, Durham, e. Sunderland, 12393, Pte., k. in a., F. & F., 3/9/16, formerly 52401, R.G.A.
Durnall, John Owen, b. West Bromwich, Staffs, e. Birmingham (West Bromwich), 16/1580, Pte., d. of w., F. & F., 4/9/16.
Dury, Sidney, b. St. Margaret's, Birmingham, e. Birmingham, 483, L/Cpl., k. in a., F. & F., 22/9/16.
Dutton, Frederick, b. Birmingham, e. Birmingham (Winson Green, Birmingham), 17654, Pte., k. in a., F. & F., 9/5/17.
Dyson, William, b. Birmingham, e. Birmingham, 15/1314, Pte., k. in a., F. & F., 28/6/18.
Eden-Hurlstone, Ernest John, b. Perry Barr, Staffs, e. Birmingham (Gravelly Hill, Birmingham), 14/1742, Pte., k. in a., F. & F., 3/9/16.
Edge, Philip Reginald Freegarde, b. Erdington, Birmingham, e. Birmingham (Erdington), 189, L/Sgt., k. in a., F. & F., 22/12/16.
Edson, Alfred Sear, b. Coventry, Warwicks, e. Birmingham (Coventry), 382, Pte., k. in a., F. & F., 3/9/16.
Edwards, Frederick James, b. Great Alne, Warwicks, e. Stratford-on-Avon, Warwicks (Alcester, Warwicks), 19393, L/Cpl., d. of w., F. & F., 9/5/17.
Edwards, Alfred, b. Coventry, Warwicks, e. Coventry, 19060, Pte., d. of w., F. & F., 2/7/17.
Elcock, Edward, b. Kidderminster, Worcs, e. Birmingham (Sparkbrook, Birmingham), 203732, Pte., k. in a., F. & F., 13/4/18.
Ellis, Edgar William, b. Tipton, Staffs, e. Birmingham, 203696, Pte., k. in a., F. & F., 21/4/18.
Elmore, John Harold, b. Walsall, Staffs, e. Birmingham (Walsall), 16/1945, Pte., k. in a., F. & F., 9/5/17.
Emptage, Charles Edwin, b. Broadstairs, Kent, e. Broadstairs, 33192, Pte., d. of w., F. & F., 26/10/17, formerly 10329, Lancers.
England, Fred, b. Pontefract, Yorks, e. Pontefract, 34128, Pte., d. of w., F. & F., 29/6/18, formerly 28839, Hussars.
Essex, Harry, b. Banbury, Oxon, e. Birmingham (Banbury), 14/1587, Pte., d. of w., F. & F., 19/4/16.
Essex, Thomas, b. St. Mary's, Warwick, e. Coventry, Warwicks, 28615, Pte., k. in a., F. & F., 24/8/18.
Eustace, Henry, b. High Wycombe, Bucks, e. Warwick (Erdington, Birmingham), 17751, Pte., k. in a., F. & F., 26/10/17.
Evans, Horace John, b. Guildford, Surrey, e. Rugby, Warwicks, 201774, Pte., k. in a., F. & F., 9/5/17.
Evans, James Havard, b. Edgbaston, Birmingham, e. Birmingham, 503, Pte., d. of w., F. & F., 11/9/16.
Evans, Walter, b. St. Matthew's, Sheffield, Yorks, e. Birmingham (Yardley, Birmingham), 649, Pte., k. in a., F. & F., 8/5/17.
Farmer, William Joseph, b. Aston, Birmingham, e. Birmingham (Aston), 20848, Pte., d. of w., F. & F., 29/8/18.
Faulkner, William John Henry, b. Birmingham, e. Birmingham (Small Heath, Birmingham), 26017, Pte., k. in a., F. & F., 28/6/18.
Fencott, Roland, b. Bristol, Glos., e. Worcester (Hanley Castle, Worcs), 16/1400, Pte., k. in a., F. & F., 4/6/16.
Fielding, William Ewart, b. Hulme, Manchester, e. Redditch, Worcs (Studley, Warwicks), 19316, Pte., k. in a., F. & F., 26/10/17.
Fisher, George Edward, b. Tooting, Middx., e. Birmingham Tooting), 154, Pte., d. of w., F. & F., 4/9/16.
Fisher, Harry Bernard, b. Belper, Derby, e. Birmingham (Derby), 393, L/Cpl., d. of w., F. & F., 10/5/16.
Fitcherd, Harry, b. Dudley Rd., Birmingham, e. Birmingham, 16/1599, Pte., k. in a., F. & F., 23/7/16.
Fitzpatrick, Thomas, b. Dublin, e. Dublin, 32803, Pte., k. in a., F. & F., 25/10/17, formerly 13631, Hussars.
Flannigan, Francis, b. Falkirk, Stirling, e. Edinburgh, 33218, Pte., k. in a., F. & F., 26/10/17, formerly 4989, Lancers.
Flavell, David Charles, b. Coventry, Warwicks, e. Coventry (Bell Green, Coventry), 242262, Pte., k. in a., F. & F., 26/10/17.
Flavell, Herbert Spencer, b. Birmingham, e. Birmingham (Small Heath, Birmingham), 1186, Pte., k. in a., F. & F., 23/7/16.
Fletcher, John, b. Sparkhill, Birmingham, e. Birmingham (Sparkhill), 478, L/Cpl., k. in a., F. & F., 4/6/16.
Ford, John Frederick, b. Aston, Birmingham, e. Birmingham, 1064, Pte., d. of w., F. & F., 29/5/16.
Foster, Alexander, b. Crieff, Perthshire, e. Perth (Crieff), 32843, Pte., k. in a., F. & F., 13/4/18, formerly 331384, Yorks Hussars.
Foster, Frederick, b. Redditch, Worcs, e. Birmingham (Moseley Birmingham), 966, Pte., k. in a., F. & F., 23/8/16.
Foster, Harry, b. Pokesdown, Hants, e. Bournemouth, Hants, 16/2005, Pte., k. in a., F. & F., 5/5/17, formerly 141511, R.F.A.
Foulks, Arthur, b. Guisboro', Yorks, e. Birmingham (Ladywood, Birmingham), 37848, Pte., k. in a., F. & F., 27/9/18.
Foy, Richard, b. Curragh, Co. Kildare, e. Naas, Co. Kildare, 32607, Cpl., k. in a., F. & F., 3/10/17, formerly 4609, Dragoons.
France, Herbert George, b. Wellington, Madras, India, e. Birmingham (Edgbaston, Birmingham), 921, Pte., d. of w., F. & F., 24/5/16.
Franklin, Arthur, b. Hillfields, Coventry, e. Coventry, Warwicks, 8548, L/Cpl., k. in a., F. & F., 28/8/16.
Franklin, Arthur William, b. Inverness, e. Birmingham (Sparkhill, Birmingham), 15/1497, Pte., k. in a., F. & F., 4/6/16.
Freeman, George, b. Birmingham, e. Birmingham (Ladywood, Birmingham), 1247, Pte., k. in a., F. & F., 3/9/16.
Freeman, Sidney, b. Wroxton, Oxon, e. Coventry, Warwicks, 19581, Pte., k. in a., F. & F., 9/5/17.
Freeth, Ernest, b. Birmingham, e. Aston, Birmingham, 28594, Pte., k. in a., F. & F., 21/4/17.
French, John, e. Parkhurst, I. of W. (Long Itchington, Warwicks), 15057, Pte., k. in a., F. & F., 26/10/17, M.M.
French, William Arthur, b. Boxford, Berks, e. Reading, Berks (Haydon Wick, Wilts), 40651, Pte., k. in a., F. & F., 28/6/18.
Friend, Thomas Francis, b. Leamington, Warwicks, e. Leamington, 18270, Pte., d. of w., F. & F., 25/5/17.
Fuidge, James Courtenay, b. Addlestone, Surrey, e. Guildford, Surrey (Addlestone), 30135, Pte., k. in a., F. & F., 24/9/16, formerly 19701, Oxf. & Bucks L.I.
Galtress, George, b. Stantonbury, Bucks, e. Bletchley, Bucks (Stantonbury), 32756, Pte., k. in a., F. & F., 25/10/17, formerly 7218, Dragoons.
Gandy, Jack, e. Altrincham, Ches., 325163, Pte., k. in a., F. & F., 24/8/18, formerly 2574, Ches. Regt.
Ghent, John Edgar, b. Polesworth, Warwicks, e. Birmingham (Handsworth, Staffs), 20478, Pte., k. in a., F. & F., 28/6/18.
Gibbon, Charles, b. Birmingham, e. Birmingham (Small Heath, Birmingham), 15/1336, Pte., k. in a., F. & F., 4/6/16.
Gibbons, Harry, b. Aston, Birmingham, e. Birmingham (Camp Hill, Birmingham), 705, Pte., k. in a., F. & F., 30/8/16.
Gibson, Arthur, b. St. Thomas, Birmingham, e. Birmingham, 990, Pte., k. in a., F. & F., 29/8/16.
Gilbert, George, b. Bodmin, Cornwall, e. Birmingham (Truro, Cornwall), 389, Pte., k. in a., F. & F., 4/6/16.
Gilks, Albert, b. Ladbrook, Warwicks, e. Warwick, 17611, Cpl., d., F. & F., 7/3/17.
Gill, Frederick William, b. Coventry, Warwicks, e. Coventry, 330744, Pte., k. in a., F. & F., 10/10/17.
Gittins, Charles Rowland, b. St. Thomas, Stourbridge, Worcs, e. Birmingham (Stourbridge), 536, Pte., k. in a., F. & F., 4/6/16.
Godfrey, Harry, b. Aston, Birmingham, e. Birmingham (Saltley, Birmingham), 16/1673, Pte., k. in a., F. & F., 9/5/17.
Godfrey, Robert Charles, b. St. Ebb's, Oxford, e. Oxford, 18401, Pte., d., F. & F., 9/9/16, formerly 23463, Som. L.I.
Godwin, Alexander John, b. Birmingham, e. Birmingham (Erdington, Birmingham), 21350, Pte., k. in a., F. & F., 28/7/17, formerly 27098, R. Berks Regt.
Goodall, Harry, b. Ladywood, Birmingham, e. Birmingham (Ladywood), 246, L/Cpl., k. in a., F. & F., 3/9/16.
Gossage, Thomas, e. Leamington, Warwicks, 242395, Pte., k. in a., F. & F., 26/10/17.
Gossage, Walter William, b. Birmingham, e. Birmingham (Ladywood, Birmingham), 15/1200, Pte., k. in a., F. &. F., 4/6/16.
Gough, Frederick, b. Edgbaston, Birmingham, e. Birmingham (Moseley, Birmingham), 15/1583, Pte., k. in a., F. & F., 3/9/16.
Granger, Victor, b. York, e. Dublin (Derby), 33159, Pte., k. in a., F. & F,. 27/9/18, formerly 13273, Hussars.
Gratton, Wilfrid Lawson, b. Tideswell, Derby, e. Birmingham (Redditch, Worcs), 1420, Pte., d. of w., F. & F., 23/7/16.
Gray, Victor Lionel James, b. Birmingham, e. Birmingham (Hall Green, Birmingham), 241787, Pte., k. in a., F. & F., 9/5/17.
Grazier, Frederick Charles, b. Bromsgrove, Worcs, e. Birmingham (Bromsgrove), 1136, Pte., k. in a., F. & F., 9/5/15.
Greasley, Daniel Joseph, b. Birmingham, e. Birmingham, 870, Cpl., k. in a., F. & F., 15/12/15.
Greaves, Richard John, b. Birmingham, e. Birmingham, 14/1683, Sgt., k. in a., F. & F., 23/7/16.

Greaves, Willoughby Frank George, b. Birmingham, e. Birmingham (Aston, Birmingham), 14/1252, Pte., k. in a., F. & F., 4/6/16.
Green, Albert, b. West Bromwich, Staffs, e. Wednesbury, Staffs (West Bromwich), 16/1552, L/Cpl., k. in a., F. & F., 3/7/17.
Green, Albert, b. Badley, Northants, e. Coventry, Warwicks (Lilburn, Warwicks), 16883, Pte., k. in a., F. & F., 3/9/16.
Green, Albert John, b. Sutton, Warwicks, e. Birmingham (Erdington, Birmingham), 16/1667, L/Cpl., k. in a., F. & F., 26/10/17.
Green, Peter Thomas, b. Breedon, Worcs, e. Birmingham, 203707, Pte., k. in a., F. & F., 12/4/18.
Greenlees, Howard, b. West Hartlepool, Durham, e. Birmingham, 1085, Pte., k. in a., F. & F., 4/6/16.
Griffin, John William, b. Hammersmith, London, e. Marylebone, London (Hammersmith), 34190, Pte., k. in a., F. & F., 26/10/17, formerly 6818, Lancers.
Griffiths, George, b. Birmingham, e. Birmingham (Edgbaston, Birmingham), 15/1528, Pte., k. in a., F. & F., 23/7/16.
Groom, Ernest, b. Leamington, Warwicks, e. Leamington, 17930, L/Cpl., d. of w., F. & F., 29/7/17.
Grosvenor, Christopher, b. Deritend, Birmingham, e. Birmingham (Saltley, Birmingham), 16797, Pte., d. of w., F. & F., 18/4/17.
Grimsell, Gordon, b. Lymington, Hants, e. Birmingham (Lymington), 396, Cpl., k. in a., F. & F., 13/6/16.
Gurney, Gordon Thomas, b. Worcester, e. Birmingham, 4/1617, L/Cpl., k. in a., F. & F., 27/9/18.
Haines, Arthur Charles, b. Brighton, Sussex, e. Brighton, 32991, Pte., k. in a., F. & F., 26/10/17, formerly 4997, Lancers.
Hall, Thomas, b. Birmingham, e. Birmingham, 1172, Pte., k. in a., F. & F., 3/9/16.
Hall, William George, b. Birmingham, e. Birmingham (Stechford, Birmingham), 28633, Pte., k. in a., F. & F., 26/10/17.
Hambidge, Edward, b. Birmingham, e. Birmingham (Bearwood, Birmingham), 14/1558, Pte., d. of w., F. & F., 8/9/16.
Hancock, Frederick Sydney, b. Old Milverton, Warwicks, e. Coventry, Warwicks, 17055, Pte., k. in a., F. & F., 3/9/16.
Hancox, John Tate, b. Lincoln, e. Lincoln, 35968, Pte., k. in a., F. & F., 24/8/18.
Hanks, George Henry, b. All Saints, Birmingham, e. Birmingham, 85, L/Cpl., k. in a., F. & F., 5/10/17.
Hardman, Frederick Harcourt, b. Northwood, Middx., e. Slough, Bucks (Piccadilly, London), 18312, Pte., k. in a., F. & F., 3/9/16, formerly 22050, Som. L.I.
Hardman, William John, e. Rugby, Warwicks, 242403, Pte., k. in a., F. & F., 27/10/17.
Harling, Cecil, b. Wasperton, Warwicks, e. Leamington, Warwicks (Coventry, Warwicks), 16762, Pte., k. in a., F. & F., 24/4/17.
Harnett, John Henry, b. Camberwell, London, e. London (Maida Vale, London), 32540, Pte., d. of w., F. & F., 16/10/18, formerly 11416, Lancers.
Harnett, Wilfred Sidney, b. Teffent, Wilts, e. Bournemouth, Hants, 18729, Pte., k. in a., F. & F., 24/9/16, formerly 24055, Som. L.I.
Harper, John, b. Glass, Aberdeen, e. Huntly, Aberdeen, 23568, Pte., d. of w., F. & F., 9/5/17, formerly 173667, R.E.
Harper, Herbert William, b. Coventry, Warwicks, e. Coventry, 17912, L/Sgt., k. in a., F. & F., 21/4/17.
Harris, Albert George, b. Coventry, Warwicks, e. Coventry, 37824, Pte., k. in a., F. & F., 13/4/18.
Harris, Frederick William, b. Leamington, Warwicks, e. Leamington, 17397, Pte., k. in a., F. & F., 23/7/16.
Harris, William George, b. Birmingham, e. Birmingham (Small Heath, Birmingham), 16/1884, L/Cpl., d. of w., F. & F., 28/10/17.
Harrison, William, b. Droitwich, Worcs, e. Worcester (Droitwich), 35984, Pte., d. of w., F. & F., 15/9/18.
Harrop, Arthur Rex, b. Nechells, Birmingham, e. Sutton Coldfield, Warwicks (Wylde Green, Birmingham), 22636, Pte., k. in a., F. & F., 27/9/18.
Hart, Harold Edward, b. Reading, Berks, e. Reading, 35983, Pte., k. in a., F. & F., 30/8/18.
Hart, Thomas, b. Birmingham, e. Birmingham (Hall Green, Birmingham), 203701, Pte., k. in a., F. & F., 14/4/18.
Hartland, William, b. Birmingham, e. Birmingham (Small Heath, Birmingham), 1191, Cpl., k. in a., F. & F., 31/10/17.
Hartland, William Henry, b. Birmingham, e. Birmingham, 1109, Dmr., k. in a., F. & F., 7/11/17.
Hawkes, Alfred Victor, b. Birmingham, e. Birmingham (Saltley, Birmingham), 22438, Pte., k. in a., F. & F., 27/9/18.
Hawkes, Ernest William, b. Aston, Birmingham, e. Birmingham, 400, Pte., k. in a., F. & F., 4/6/16.
Hawkins, George, b. Birmingham, e. Birmingham (Smethwick, staffs), 15/1464, Pte., k. in a., F. & F., 3/9/16.
Hawkins, Thomas, b. Birmingham, e. Birmingham (King's Heath, Birmingham), 14/1620, Pte., k. in a., F. & F., 3/9/16.
Hawthorne, Herbert William, b. Coventry, Warwicks, e. Warwick (Stoke, Coventry), 235259, Cpl., d. of w., F. & F., 4/7/18, formerly H/310505, Warwicks Yeo.
Hayes, John Reginald, b. Chippenham, Wilts, e. Chippenham, 26642, Pte., k. in a., F. & F., 24/8/18.
Haynes, Albert, b. Leamington, Warwicks, e. Leamington (Cubbington, Warwicks), 17294, Pte., d. of w., F. & F., 27/8/16.
Haywood, Stanley James, b. Canterbury, Kent, e. Birmingham (Canterbury), 309, Pte., k. in a., F. & F., 4/6/16.
Heath, William Reginald, b. Aston, Birmingham, e. Birmingham (Aston), 242, Pte., k. in a., F. & F., 3/9/16.
Hedges, Herbert Arthur, b. Bury St. Edmunds, Suffolk, e. Leamington, Warwicks, 18995, Pte., k. in a., F. & F., 12/4/18.
Hedley, William, b. Seaton Sluice, Northumberland, e. Newcastle, Northumberland (Seaton Sluice), 32796, Cpl., d. of w., F. & F., 28/10/17, formerly 25026, Hussars.
Hemming, John, b. Birmingham, e. Birmingham, 22776, Pte., d. of w., F. & F., 9/5/17.
Hendra, Patrick, b. Stirling, e. Warwick (Stirling), 1766, Pte., k. in a., F. & F., 9/5/17.
Henning, William, b. Portsmouth, Hants, e. Portsmouth, 18656 Pte., d. of w., F. & F., 9/5/17, formerly 24591, Som. L.I.
Henton, Cecil, b. Ashby-de-la-Zouch, Leics, e. Southam, Warwicks (Rugby, Warwicks), 16787, Pte., d. of w., F. & F., 9/9/16.
Hession, Charles William, b. Saltley, Birmingham, e. Birmingham (Saltley), 4475, Pte., k. in a., F. & F., 14/4/18.
Hewitt, Archibald, b. Walsall, Staffs, e. Stoney Lane, Birmingham (Walsall), 15/1613, Pte., k. in a., F. & F., 4/6/16.
Hewitt, George, b. Abbeydale, Sheffield, Yorks, e. Birmingham (Harborne, Birmingham), 977, Pte., k. in a., F. & F., 23/5/16.
Hiatt, John Corbett, b. Uppenwell, Glos, e. Nuneaton, Warwicks (Fillongley, Warwicks), 16331, Pte., d. of w., F. & F., 14/9/16.
Hickman, Isaac, e. Birmingham (Handsworth, Birmingham), 28569, Pte., k. in a., F. & F., 5/10/17.
Hill, Alfred, b. Digbeth, Birmingham, e. Birmingham, 2746, Pte., k. in a., F. & F., 9/5/17.
Hills, Robert Fish, b. Cunhill-on-Tweed, Northumberland, e. Birmingham (Spittal, Berwick-on-Tweed), 1096, Pte., k. in a, F. & F., 9/3/16.
Hirons, John Henry, b. Rugby, Warwicks, e. Rugby (New Bilton, Warwicks), 9056, Pte., d. of w., F. & F., 13/9/16.
Hitchings, Albert Charles, b. Amblecote, Worcs, e. Birmingham (Wollaston, Stourbridge, Worcs), 913, L/Cpl., k. in a., F. & F., 23/7/16.
Hitchman, Francis Percival, b. Stratford-on-Avon, Warwicks, e. Stratford-on-Avon, 16/1812, L/Cpl., d. of w., F. & F., 6/10/17.
Hobbs, George James, b. Balsall Heath, Birmingham, e. Birmingham, 554, Pte., k. in a., F, & F., 30/8/16.
Hobbs, William Henry Bagley, b. Birmingham, e. Warwick (Stirchley, Birmingham), 28570, Pte., k. in a., F. & F., 9/5/17.
Hodgetts, Frank Horace, b. Sparkbrook, Birmingham, e. Birmingham (King's Heath, Birmingham), 903, Sgt., k. in a., F. & F., 27/9/18.
Holbrook, Frederick Thomas, b. Birmingham, e. Birmingham, 15/1312, Pte., k. in a., F. & F., 18/4/16.
Holdstock, William, b. Hathfield, Kent, e. Ashford (Norwich), 32451, Sgt., d. of w., F. & F., 26/10/17, formerly 32451, Lancers.
Hollick, Edgar, b. Pershore, Worcs, e. Worcester (Evesham, Worcs), 35982, Pte., k. in a., F. & F., 28/6/18.
Hollier, Thomas, b. St. Phillips, Birmingham e. Birmingham, 1912, Pte., k. in a., F. & F., 28/5/17.
Hollis, Christopher Alex, b. Birmingham, e. Birmingham (Blackpool, Lancs), 920, Sgt., k. in a., F. & F., 28/6/18.
Holt, Ernest, b. St. Mary's, Birmingham, e. Birmingham, 506, Pte., k. in a., F. & F., 3/9/16.
Holt, Norman, b. Coventry, Warwicks, e. Coventry, 16397, Pte., d. of w., F. & F., 8/9/16.
Holt, Stanley, b. Birmingham, e. Birmingham (Edgbaston, Birmingham), 1187, Pte., k. in a., F. & F., 4/6/16.
Holtom, Joseph Henry, b. Birmingham, e. Birmingham (Bournville, Birmingham), 1189, Pte., d. of w., F. & F., 30/8/16.
Homer, Chester Joseph, b. Handsworth, Birmingham, e. Birmingham (Handsworth), 15/87, Cpl., k. in a., F. & F., 15/6/16.
Honeywill, Walter Reginald, b. Ipplepen, Devon, e. Exeter, Devon (Newton Abbott), 12373, Cpl., d. of w., F. & F., 3/11/17, formerly 43167, R.G.A.
Hooper, Albert, b. Liversidge, Yorks, e. Wakefield, Yorks (Dewsbury), 34140, Pte., k. in a., F. & F., 26/10/17, formerly 9521, Hussars.
Hooper, James, b. Battersea, London, e. London (Battersea), 32687, L/Cpl., k. in a., F. & F., 26/10/17, formerly 5991, Dragoon Guards.
Hooper, Norris, b. Worcester, e. Worcester, 33798, Pte., k. in a., F. & F., 28/6/18 formerly 032688, R.A.S.C.
Hopkins, Harry Gordon, b. Harborne, Birmingham, e. Birmingham (Harbone), 204, Pte., k. in a., F. & F., 15/6/16.
Hopkins, John Walter, b. Birmingham, e. Birmingham (Sparkhill, Birmingham), 14/1658, Pte., k. in a., F. & F., 23/7/16.
Hopkins, William, b. Warwick, e. Coventry, Warwicks (Warwick), 16087, Pte., d. of w., F. & F., 7/9/16.
Horton, Albert, b. St. Alban's, Birmingham, e. Birmingham (St. Alban's), 225, Sgt., k. in a. F. & F., 21/12/15.
Horton, Frank Horatio, b. St. Mark's, Lincoln, e. Lincoln, 34186, Pte., d. of w., F. & F., 30/6/18, formerly 4093, Lancers.
Horton, Harold Frederick, b. Sparkbrook, Birmingham, e. Birmingham, 79, Cpl., k. in a., F. & F., 3/9/16.
Hough, John, b. Birmingham e. Birmingham, 28378, Pte., k. in a., F. & F., 9/5/17.
Howard George, b. Birmingham, e. Birmingham (Sparkbrook, Birmingham), 330589, L/Cpl., k. in a., F. & F., 26/10/17.
Howard, Harry Lee, b. Rugby, Warwicks, e. Rugby, 32857, Pte., k. in a., F. & F., 26/10/17, formerly 29965, Hussars.
Howell, Alfred, b. Birmingham, e. Birmingham, 15/1635, Pte., k in a., F. & F., 9/5/17.
Howes Horace Ernest, b. Southtown, Great Yarmouth, Norfolk, e. Birmingham (Balsall Heath, Birmingham), 897, Pte., k. in a., F. & F., 26/9/16.
Hudson, Conor George, e. Birmingham (Sparkbrook, Birmingham), 203491, Pte., k. in a., F. & F., 26/1/18.

Hughes, Charles Henry, b. Edgbaston, Birmingham, e. Birmingham (Edgbaston), 414, L/Cpl., k. in a., F. & F., 4/6/16.
Hughes, Harry, b. Birmingham, e. Birmingham, 16350, Pte., d. of w., F. & F., 29/6/18.
Hughes, William, b. Kettering, Northants, e. Kettering, 38424, Pte., k. in a., F. & F., 28/6/18.
Hundy, William James, b. All Saints, Birmingham, e. Birmingham, 1, L/Cpl., k. in a., F. & F., 21/5/16.
Hutchence, Fred, b. Cyprus, Essex e. Hull, Yorks, 12562, Pte., k. in a., F. & F., 9/5/17, formerly 56725, R.G.A.
Hutton, William, b. Lynn, Mass., U.S.A., e. Rugby, Warwicks (Coventry, Warwicks), 34156, Sgt., k. in a., F. & F., 27/9/18, formerly 16023, Lancers.
Iggulden, Walter, b. Erdington, Birmingham, e. Warwick (Erdington), 952, L/Cpl., k. in a., F. & F., 24/9/16.
Illingworth, Charles Chester, b. Headingly, Yorks, e. Birmingham (Leeds, Yorks), 74, L/Cpl., k. in a., F. & F., 3/9/16.
Ingram, Leonard, b. Rugby, Warwicks, e. Coventry, Warwicks (New Bilton, Warwicks), 260513, Pte., d. of w., F. & F., 29/5/18.
Izzard, Robert Earl, b. Peckham, London, e. Camberwell, London (Blackheath), London), 34031, Pte., k. in a., F. & F., 30/8/18, formerly 202197, E. Kent Regt.
Jackson, Archibald George, b. Aston, Birmingham, e. Birmingham, 505, Pte., k. in a., F. & F., 3/9/16.
Jackson, Herbert, b. Erdington, Birmingham, e. Birmingham (Erdington), 1120, L/Cpl., d. of w., F. & F., 30/7/16.
Jacobs, Isaac Elias, b. Birmingham, e. Birmingham, 16/1508, Pte., k. in a., F. & F., 23/7/16.
James, Albert, b. Woollaston, Northants, e. Coventry, Warwicks, 201738, Pte., k. in a., F. & F., 26/10/17.
James, William, b. Crumlin, Mon., e. Newport, Mon. (Crumlin), 34147, Pte., k. in a., F. & F., 26/10/17, formerly 24064, Hussars.
Jarvis, Ewart White, b. Aston, Birmingham, e. Birmingham, 523, Sgt., k. in a., F. & F., 9/5/17.
Jeeves, Percy, b. Dewsbury, Yorks, e. Birmingham (Dewsbury), 611, Pte., k. in a., F. & F., 22/7/16.
Jeffrey, John Walter, b. Kettering, Northants, e. Warwick (Small Heath, Birmingham), 22763, Pte., d. of w., F. & F., 26/10/17.
Jelfs, George Watkin, b. Birmingham, e. Birmingham (Bromsgrove, Worcs), 1313, L/Cpl., k. in a., F. & F., 4/6/16.
Jennings, Fred, b. Warrington Lancs, e. Warwick (Warrington), 22515, Pte., k. in a., F. & F., 28/6/18.
Jervis, Joseph Stephen, b. Duddeston, Birmingham, e. Birmingham (Sparkbrook, Birmingham), 823, Cpl., k. in a., F. & F., 25/7/16.
Jinks, Phillip Gordon, b. Birmingham, e. Birmingham (Harbourne, Birmingham), 15/1369, Pte., k. in a., F. & F., 14/6/16.
Johnson, Cyril Harry, b. Bures, Suffolk, e. Birmingham (Bures), 222, Sgt., k. in a., F. & F., 5/10/17.
Johnson, Frederick, e. Birmingham (Bordesley Green, Birmingham), 26955, Pte., k. in a., F. & F., 12/4/18.
Johnson, Frank Cecil, b. Oxford, e. Birmingham (Moseley, Birmingham), 1041, Sgt., k. in a., F. & F., 1/7/17.
Jolly, Frederick William, b. Norwich Norfolk e. Sutton Coldfield, Birmingham (Neatishead, Norfolk), 15/1492, Pte., d. of w., F. & F., 11/8/16.
Jones, Austin Edward Clule, b. King's Norton, Birmingham, e. Birmingham, 987, Pte., k. in a., F. & F., 3/9/16.
Jones, Albert Victor, b. Birmingham, e. Birmingham (Nechells Birmingham), 16/1450, Pte., d. of w., F. & F., 24/9/16.
Jones, Harry Francis, b. Birmingham, e. Birmingham (Vauxhall, Birmingham), 28649, Pte., k. in a., F. & F., 26/10/17.
Jones, James Henry, b. Oldbury, Staffs, e. Birmingham (Saltley, Birmingham), 15/1577, Pte., k. in a., F. & F., 22/5/16.
Jordan, Arthur Leonard, b. Birmingham, e. Stoney Lane, Birmingham (Small Heath, Birmingham), 15/1612, Pte., k. in a., F. & F., 20/5/16.
Joyce, Walter, b. Gravesend, Kent, e. Woolwich, Kent (Eltham, Kent), 34476, Pte., k. in a., F. & F., 27/8/18, formerly 257882, R.A.S.C..
Jump, Gilbert George, b. Salford, Lancs, e. Sale, Ches. (Middleton Junction, Lancs), 32703, Pte., d. of w., F. & F., 23/5/18, formerly 25510, Dragoons.
Kemp, Ernest Richard, b. Deptford, Kent, e. Woolwich, Kent (Deptford), 48369, Pte., k. in a., F. & F., 29/9/18, formerly 023917, R.A.O.C.
Kent, Stedman Francis, b. Handsworth, Birmingham, e. Birmingham, 71, Pte., d., F. & F., 30/8/16.
Kentell, Ivor Frederick, b. Bournemouth, Hants, e. Bournemouth, 18735, Pte., d. of w., F. & F., 26/9/16, formerly 24378, Som. L.I.
King, Albert Sidney, b. Birmingham, e. Birmingham (Balsall Heath, Birmingham), 14/1739, Pte., k. in a., F. & F., 4/6/16.
King, Edgar, b. Upper Priory, Birmingham, e. Birmingham, 3902, Pte., k. in a., F. & F., 30/8/16.
King Roy, b. Bangalore India, e. Marylebone, London (Woking, Surrey), 32825, Pte., k. in a., F. & F., 26/10/17, formerly 28641, Hussars.
Kings, Edward Clement, b. Yardley, Birmingham, e. Birmingham (Yardley), 806, Pte., k. in a., F. & F., 23/7/16.
Kiteley, William Bernard, b. Sauldem, Oxon., e. Warwick (Gt. Borten, Oxon.), 16889, Pte., k. in a., F. & F., 3/9/16.
Knaggs, George, e. Bridlington, Yorks, 32837, Pte., k. in a., F. & F., 26/10/17, formerly 064097, R.A.S.C.
Knight, Arthur, b. Ladywood, Birmingham, e. Birmingham (Ladywood), 782, Sgt., k. in a., F. & F., 23/7/16.
Kyte, Herbert, b. Tilshead, Wilts, e. Devizes, Wilts (Tilshead), 306744, Pte., k. in a., F. & F., 24/8/18.
Lambert, Walter William, b. Chesham, Bucks, e. Chesham, 30147, Pte., d. of w., F. & F., 14/5/17, formerly 22331, Oxf. & Bucks L.I.
Lamble, Robert Reginald, b. Moseley, Birmingham, e. Birmingham (Moseley), 943, Pte., d. of w., F. & F., 21/12/16.
Lancaster, George, b. Birmingham, e. Birmingham (King's Heath, Birmingham), 28640, Pte., k. in a., F. & F., 9/5/17.
Lawrence, William, b. Edgbaston, Birmingham, e. Birmingham, 6350, Pte., k. in a., F. & F., 28/8/16.
Lawton, Harry, b. St. Mary's, Chesterfield, Derby, e. Chesterfield, 34187, Pte., k. in a., F. & F., 24/8/18, formerly 963, Lancers.
Lea, John, b. Tamworth, Staffs, e. Birmingham, 15679, Pte., d. of w., F. & F., 25/10/18.
Leafe, George Edward, b. Suttonbridge, Leics, e. Warwick (Wilnecote, Warwicks), 20511, Pte., k. in a., F. & F., 9/5/17.
Leake, Albert Ernest, b. Birmingham, e. Birmingham (Balsall Heath, Birmingham), 15/1630, Pte., d. of w., F. & F., 26/7/16.
Lebourne, Henry, b. Hedge End, Hants, e. Southampton, Hants (Woolston, Hants), 18768, Pte., k. in a., F. & F., 24/9/16, formerly 24383, Som. L.I.
Leigh, Austin Geoffrey, b. Hampton-in-Arden, Warwicks, e. Birmingham (Hampton-in-Arden), 420, L/Cpl., k. in a., F. & F., 4/6/16.
Lennane, Frank, b. Clare, Ireland, e. Aldershot, Hants (Dublin), 32733, Pte., k. in a., F. & F., 4/10/17, formerly 6271, Dragoons.
Lerrigo, William George, b. Sparkbrook, Birmingham, e. Birmingham, 63, Cpl., k. in a., F. & F., 3/9/16.
Lester, Ernest Samuel, b. Southampton, Hants, e. Totton, Hants, 18715, Pte., d. of w., F. & F. 9/4/17, formerly 23258, Som. L.I.
Lewis, Bernard Robert, b. Sparkbrook, Birmingham, e. Birmingham (Sparkbrook), 421, L/Cpl., k. in a., F. & F., 23/7/16.
Leyland, Thomas, b. Liverpool, Lancs, e. Liverpool, 34487, Pte., k. in a., F. & F., 27/9/18, formerly 204113, S. Lan. Regt.
Lindley, Joseph, e. Rugby, Warwicks, 20368, Pte., d. of w., F. & F., 5/10/17.
Lloyd, Walter George, b. Lozells, Birmingham, e. Birmingham (Lozells), 898, Pte., k. in a., F. & F., 7/3/16.
Loam, Gilbert Henry, b. Reading, Berks, e. Birmingham (Selly Oak, Birmingham), 929, Pte., k. in a., F. & F., 30/8/16.
Lord, Alfred Walter, b. Birmingham, e. Birmingham (Small Heath, Birmingham), 28635, Pte., d. of w., F. & F., 10/4/17.
Lord, Frederick, b. St. Matthew's, Birmingham, e. Birmingham (Walsall, Staffs), 15/1607, Pte., k. in a., F. & F., 3/9/16.
Lowe, Samuel, b. Nottingham, e. Nottingham (East Kirkby, Notts), 33850, Pte., d., F. & F., 9/10/17, formerly 106221, R.A.S.C.
Ludlow, John Edwin, b. Langley, Worcs, e. Birmingham, 902, Pte., k. in a., F. & F., 4/6/16.
Lunnon, Dennis, b. High Wycombe, Bucks, e. High Wycombe, 18507, Pte., d. of w., F. & F., 11/9/16, formerly 25287, Som. L.I.
Lyon, Ernest, b. Birmingham, e. Birmingham, 18302, Pte., k. in a., F. & F., 3/9/16, formerly 22936, Som. L.I.
Macaulay, Angus, b. St. Mary's, Birmingham, e. Birmingham (High Barnet, Herts), 906, Pte., k. in a., F. & F., 23/7/16.
Machin, Edwin, e. Stoke-on-Trent, Staffs (Longport, Staffs), 9243, C.S.M., k. in a., F. & F., 26/10/17, M.M.
Macklin, Frederick George, b. Small Heath, Birmingham, e. Birmingham, 10957, L/Cpl., k. in a., F. & F., 28/8/16.
Mansbridge, Alfred Ernest, b. Birmingham, e. Birmingham (Camp Hill, Birmingham), 1563, Pte., k. in a., F. & F., 27/9/18.
Marley, William, b. Bishop Auckland, Durham, e. Bishop Auckland, 48322, Pte., k. in a., F. & F., 28/8/18, formerly 5636, R.A.S.C.
Marshall, Thomas, b. Eccles, Lancs, e. Patricroft, Lancs (Eccles), 201899, L/Cpl., k. in a., F. & F., 28/6/18, formerly 2564, Manchester Regt.
Mason, Benjamin, b. Birmingham, e. Aston, Birmingham, 20420, Pte., k. in a., F. & F., 2/7/17.
Maspers, Albert Francis, b. Leatherhead, Surrey, e. Birmingham (Leatherhead), 836, L/Sgt., k. in a., F. & F., 23/5/16.
Masters, Herbert Edward, b. Portsmouth, Hants, e. Portsmouth, 18714, Pte., k. in a., F. & F., 24/4/17, formerly 22905, Som. L.I.
Maylott, Arthur, b. Ladywood, Birmingham, e. Birmingham (Bournebrook, Birmingham), 922, Pte., k. in a., F. & F., 26/10/17.
McCrum, James Alexander Cameron, b. Limavady, Co. Londonderry, e. Birmingham (Stourbridge, Worcs), 15/1370, Pte., d. of w., F. & F., 23/7/16.
McDermid, John, b. Govan, Lanark, e. Glasgow, 48336, Pte., k. in a., F. & F., 27/9/18, formerly R/4/089442, R.A.S.C.
McDonald, Donald, b. Barony, Lanark, e. Glasgow, 32673, Pte., d. of w., F. & F., 8/10/17, formerly 6457, Dragoon Gds.
McFarland, Edward James, b. All Saints, Antrim, e. Belfast, 32820, Pte., k. in a., F. & F., 19/10/18, formerly 24560, Hussars, M.M.
McGrath, James Nugent, b. Lasswade, Edinburgh, e. Edinburgh (Cowdenbeath, Fife), 34153, Pte., d., F. & F., 14/12/17, formerly 6375, Lancers.
McGrevy, James, b. Newcastle-on-Tyne, e. Scarborough, Yorks (Shieldfield, Northumberland), 32845, Pte., k. in a., F. & F., 26/10/17, formerly 28988, Hussars.
McMillan, William, b. Edgbaston, Birmingham, e. Birmingham, 88, Sgt., k. in a., F. & F., 9/5/17.
McRill, George, b. Sholing, Hants, e. Southampton, Hants (Sholing), 26437, Pte., k. in a., F. & F., 27/9/18.

Meadows, William Henry, b. Birmingham, e. Birmingham (Handsworth, Staffs), 15/1349, Pte., d. of w., F. & F., 11/9/16.
Meredith, James, b. All Saints, Birmingham, e. Birmingham, 253, Cpl., k in a., F. & F., 3/9/16.
Meyler, Llewellyn John, b. Huddersfield, Yorks, e. Aylesbury, Bucks (Southport, Lancs), 59191, Pte., k. in a., F. & F., 27/9/18.
Middleton, James, b. Smethwick, Staffs, e. Birmingham, 89, Pte., k. in a., F. & F., 4/6/16.
Middleton, Walter, b. Birmingham, e. Birmingham, 703, Pte., k. in a., F. & F., 25/7/16.
Miller, Arthur, b. Ashted, Birmingham, e. Birmingham (Ashted), 258, Pte., d. of w., F. & F., 15/5/16.
Miller, Emanuel, b. Aldgate, London, e. London (Bethnal Green, London), 30149, Pte., k in a., F. & F., 5/10/17, formerly 22231, Oxf. & Bucks L.I.
Mills, Wilfred Hiram, e. Hartley Winchfield, Hants (Aldershot, Hants), 22735, Pte., k. in a., F. & F., 26/10/17.
Mitchard, Ernest Victor, b. Aston, Birmingham, e. Birmingham (Saltley, Birmingham), 28572, Pte., k. in a., F. & F., 3/7/17.
Milton, John, b. Landport, Hants, e. Taunton, Som. (Yeovil, Som.), 32764, Pte., k. in a., F. & F., 26/10/17 formerly 4346, Dragoons.
Mitchell, Percy James, e. Bath, Som. (Oakhill, Bath), 238033, Pte., k. in a., F. & F., 12/4/18, formerly 897, Som. Yeo.
Mockford, John, b. Southwark, London, e. Dalston, London (St. Pancras, London), 30124, L/Cpl., k. in a., F. & F., 24/9/16, formerly 6684, Oxf. & Bucks L.I.
Molesworth, Ernest, b. Coventry, Warwicks, e. Coventry, 19486, Pte., k. in a., F. & F., 24/4/17.
Moon, Frederick Oscar Warburton, b. Glenelg, South Australia, e. Wolverhampton, Staffs (Benoni, South Africa), 34129, Pte., d. of w., F. & F., 26/10/17, formerly 12182, Hussars.
Morgan, William, b. Cardiff, Glam., e. London (Cardiff), 32822, Pte., k. in a., F. & F., 26/10/17, formerly 24350, Hussars.
Morley, Alfred, b. Lambeth, Surrey, e. Camberwell, Surrey (Vauxhall, London), 34477, Pte., k. in a., F. & F., 27/9/18, formerly 43153, R.A.S.C
Morris, Arthur, b Birmingham, e. Birmingham, 16/1591, Pte., k. in a., F. & F., 22/3/16.
Morris, Ernest, b. Islington, London, e. Stratford, London (Islington), 34148, Pte., k. in a., F. & F., 26/10/17, formerly 5432, Hussars.
Morris, Percy John, b. Aston, Birmingham, e. Birmingham, (Aston), 256, L/Cpl., k. in a., F. & F., 4/6/16.
Mould, Clarence, b. St. Mark's, Birmingham, e. Birmingham, 533, Pte., d. of w., F. & F., 4/9/16.
Mulroy, John Henry, b. Aston, Birmingham, e. Birmingham, 15/1361, Pte., k. in a., F. & F., 4/6/16.
Musselwhite, Sidney James, e. Salisbury, Wilts (Bishopstone, Salisbury), 28603, Pte., k. in a., F. & F., 9/5/17.
Mutlow, Percy Arnold, b. Ledbury, Herefordshire, e. Birmingham (Ladywood, Birmingham), 15/1433, Pte., k. in a., F. & F., 9/5/17.
Napper, Reginald Harold, b. Henlade, Som., e. Yeovil, Som. (Quickleas, Som.), 48351, Pte., k. in a., F. & F., 26/8/18, formerly R/278218, R.A.S.C.
Neighbour, Henry Alford, b. Plumstead, Kent, e. Warwick (Plumstead), 330524, Pte., k. in a., F. & F., 26/10/17.
Newbury, Guy, b. Handsworth, Birmingham, e. Birmingham, 52, L/Cpl., d. of w., F. & F., 27/1/17.
Nicholls, Reginald Alexander, b. Gt. Bridge, West Bromwich, Staffs, e. Birmingham (West Bromwich), 73, Pte., d. of w., F. & F., 14/5/17.
Noakes, Edward Charles, b. Newbury, Berks, e. Aldershot, Hants, 18613, Pte., k. in a., F. & F., 9/10/17, formerly 24065, S.L.I.
Nokes, George, b. Bromsgrove, Worcs, e. Birmingham (Selly Park, Birmingham), 16800, Pte., k. in a., F. & F., 27/9/18.
Noon, William, b. Kennington, London, e. Camberwell, London (Peckham, London), 21691, Pte., k. in a., F. & F., 4/10/17, formerly 13009, R. Berks Regt.
North, Charles William, b. Coventry, Warwicks, e. Coventry, 15430, Pte., k. in a., F. & F., 3/9/16.
Ogden, Albert, e. Halifax, Yorks (Luddenden, Yorks), 32776, Pte., k. in a., F. & F., 26/10/17, formerly 6288, Scot. Horse.
Oldbury, Edgar Joseph, b. Aston, Birmingham, e. Birmingham, 46, Pte., k. in a., F. & F., 4/6/16.
Olds, George Frederick, b. Kineton, Warwicks, e. Warwick (Kineton), 1133, Pte., k. in a., F. & F., 30/8/16.
Ollier, Ernest, b. Wharton, Ches., e. Winsford, Ches. (Winsford), 42082, Pte., k. in a., F. & F., 27/9/18, formerly 2254 Ches. Yeo.
Orange, Cecil, b. Leamington, Warwicks, e. Coventry, Warwicks (Leamington), 18276, Pte., k. in a., F. & F., 9/4/17.
Osborne, Thomas Joseph, b. Oldbury, Worcs, e. Warwick (Oldbury), 203051, Pte., d. of w.. F. & F., 25/4/18, formerly 3510, Warwick Yeo.
Osbourn, Charles Edward, b. Porchfield, I. of W., e. Winchester, Hants (Carisbrooke, I. of W.), 50682, Pte., k. in a., F. & F., 26/8/18.
Overton, John Stanley, b. Birmingham, e. Birmingham (Balsall Heath, Birmingham), 14/1741, Pte., d. of w., F. & F., 16/7/17.
Paddy, George Frederick, b. Aston, Birmingham, e. Birmingham, 28368, Pte., k. in a., F. & F., 9/5/17, formerly 29779, Hussars.
Page, Albert Arthur, b. Camberwell, Surrey, e. Southwark, London (Kensington, London), 50695, Pte., d. of w., F. & F., 30/6/18, formerly G/44500, R. Fus.
Page, Albert Edward, b. Abbotsley, Hunts, e. Huntingdon (Abbotsley), 30223, Pte., k. in a., F. & F., 27/9/18, formerly 1160, Hunts Cyc. Battn.
Page, Sidney, b. Balsall Heath, Birmingham, e. Birmingham (Balsall Heath), 176, Cpl., k. in a., F. & F., 3/9/16.
Palmer, Herbert John, b. St. Matthew's, Birmingham, e. Birmingham, 692, Cpl., k. in a., F. & F., 3/9/16.
Parish, Charles Ernest, b. Oldbury, Worcs, e. Birmingham (Halesowen, Birmingham), 830, Pte., k. in a., F. & F., 23/7/16.
Parker, Frederick William, b. Smethwick, Staffs, e. Birmingham, 557, Cpl., k. in a., F. & F., 30/8/16.
Parker, William, b. Sparkbrook, Birmingham, e. Birmingham, 1008, L/Cpl., k. in a., F. & F., 4/6/16.
Parkes, Frederick Liddell, b. St. Stephen's Birmingham, e. Birmingham, 914, L/Cpl., k. in a., F. & F., 23/7/16.
Parkinson, Norman, b. Liverpool, Lancs, e. Liverpool, 34494, Pte., k. in a., F. & F., 27/9/18, formerly 204212, S. Lancs Regt.
Parry, William Richard, b. Birmingham, e. Birmingham (Hockley Heath, Birmingham), 18145, Pte., k. in a., F. & F., 26/10/17.
Parsons, Herbert, e. Taunton, Som. (Rowbarton, Som.), 23434, L/Cpl., k. in a., F. & F., 13/4/18, formerly 4581, R.E.
Parsons, Stephen, b. Winchester, Hants, e. Basingstoke, Hants, 32767, Pte., k. in a., F. & F., 26/10/17, formerly 1848, Dragoons.
Paskin, George Edward, b. St. Martin's, Birmingham, e. Birmingham, 441, Pte., k. in a., F. & F., 9/1/16.
Patch, Frederick Robert, b. Lewisham, Kent, e. Birmingham (Lewisham), 150, L/Cpl., k. in a., F. & F., 4/6/16.
Pay, Roland, b. Ringwood, Hants, e. London (Ringwood), 33783, Pte., d., F. & F., 14/4/18, formerly 115881, R.A.S.C.
Payne, Moses, b. East End, Hants, e. Lymington, Hants (East End), 18621, Pte., d. of w., F. & F., 3/5/17, formerly 24489, Som. L.I.
Payton, Frank Edwin, b. Lichfield, Staffs, e. Birmingham (Lichfield), 433, Pte., d. of w., F. & F., 10/6/16.
Peakman, Harold Ethelbert, b. Birmingham, e. Birmingham (Moseley, Warwicks), 1118, L/Cpl., k. in a., F. & F., 4/6/16.
Pearson, Richard, b. Birmingham, e. Birmingham, 201203, Pte., d. of w., F. & F., 16/4/18.
Pearson, Sidney, b. Edgbaston, Birmingham, e. Birmingham (Ladywood, Birmingham), 882, Pte., k. in a., F. & F., 24/9/16.
Peel, Edwin, b. Farnley, Yorks, e. Coventry, Warwicks, 19255, Pte., k. in a., F. & F., 5/10/17.
Penn, Ernest, b. Birmingham, e. Coventry, Warwicks, 16221, Pte., d., F. & F., 26/6/17.
Penn, Fred, b. Birmingham, e. Birmingham (Sparkhill, Birmingham), 15/1624, Pte., k. in a., F. & F., 14/4/18.
Penny, Herbert, b. Wilton, Wilts, e. Salisbury, Wilts (Wilton), 18725, Pte., k. in a., F. & F., 9/5/17, formerly 23278, Som. L.I.
Percival, Philip Job, b. Stockingford, Warwicks, e. Warwick (Nuneaton, Warwicks), 22787, Pte., d. of w., F. & F., 9/5/17.
Perks, Alfred, b. Dudley, Worcs, e. Warwick (Dudley), 28631, Pte., k. in a., F. & F., 6/10/17.
Perks, Fred, b. Shirley, Warwicks, e. Warwick (Shirley), 17581, Pte., d. of w., F. & F., 25/4/17.
Perrow, William, b. Cross Keys, Newport, Mon., e. Aberdare, Glam. (Aberavon, Glam.), 32734, Pte., d. of w., F. & F., 28/10/17, formerly 9617, Dragoons.
Perry, Cecil, b. Birmingham, e. Birmingham (Harborne, Birmingham), 1259, Pte., d. of w., F. & F., 7/9/16.
Perry, George, b. Ladywood, Birmingham, e. Birmingham, 961, Pte., k. in a., F. & F., 6/1/16.
Peters, Frank Terrial, b. Bath, Som., e. Barnstaple, Devon (Weston, Bath), 50680, Pte., k. in a., F. & F., 27/9/18.
Phillips, Thomas Henry, b. Penn, Wolverhampton, Staffs, e. Birmingham (Penn), 38, A/C.S.M., k. in a., F. & F., 23/7/16.
Pilch, William Fuller, b. Sheringham, Norfolk, e. Birmingham, 814, Sgt., k. in a., F. & F., 3/9/16.
Pilley, Thomas Edward, e. Birmingham (Balsall Heath, Birmingham), 26950, Pte., k. in a., F. & F., 14/4/18.
Pitt, William, b. Oldswinford, Worcs, e. Birmingham (Oldswinford), 8286, Pte., k. in a., F. & F., 26/10/17.
Pittman, Sydney, b. Chickerell, Weymouth, Dorset, e. Crewkerne, Som. (Rollaston Camp, Wilts), 18690, Pte., k. in a., F. & F., 9/5/17, formerly 24612, Som. L.I
Plant, Charles, b. Edgbaston, Birmingham, e. Birmingham, 3361, Pte., k. in a., F. & F., 26/10/17.
Plowman, Leonard David, b. Bournemouth, Hants, e. Bournemouth, 18688, Pte., k. in a., F. & F., 12/4/18, formerly 24373, Som. L.I.
Pollard, William Frederick, b. Cirencester, Glos., e. Cirencester, 50690, Pte., k. in a., F. & F., 28/6/18.
Poole, Alexander, b. Gravelly Hill, Birmingham, e. Birmingham, 17742, Pte., k. in a., F. & F., 30/8/16.
Poplett, William Henry, e. Kingston-on-Thames, Surrey (Epsom, Surrey), 30152, Pte., k. in a., F. & F., 30/8/18, formerly 18373, R. Fus.
Porter, James, b. Foleshill, Warwicks, e. Coventry, Warwicks, 19115, Pte., k. in a., F. & F., 24/4/17.
Poulton, George, b. Banbury, Oxon, e. Wolverhampton, Staffs (Chaomoc, nr. Banbury), 33845, Pte., k. in a., F. & F., 14/4/18, formerly 078042, R.A.S.C.
Powell, Christopher William, e. Cardiff, Glam. (Elliotstown, Glam.), 23433, Pte., d. of w., F. & F., 15/4/18, formerly 697, R.E.
Powell, Ernest, b. Winson Green, Birmingham, e. Birmingham (Hockley, Birmingham), 22718, Pte., k. in a., F. & F., 8/5/17.

Pratt, Samuel, b. Bedworth, Warwicks, e. Nuneaton, Warwicks (Bedworth), 12036, Pte., k. in a., F. & F., 9/5/17.
Preece, Arthur, b. Pear Tree, Derby, e. Birmingham (Bosbury, Herefordshire), 17748, Pte., d. of w., F. & F., 7/9/16.
Priest, Hubert, b. Edgbaston, Birmingham, e. Birmingham, 1048, Pte., k. in a., F. & F., 4/6/16.
Pugh, Henry Richard, b. Hughoftka, Russia, e. Birmingham (Dawley, Salop), 700, Pte., d. of w., F. & F., 19/4/18.
Purdew, Henry John William, b. Southampton, Hants, e. Petersfield, Hants (West Meon, Petersfield), 18658, Pte., d. of w., F. & F., 12/5/17, formerly 24469, Som. L.I.
Purnell, William John, b. Henbury, Glos., e. Bristol, Glos. (Horfield, Glos.), 50692, Pte., d. of w., F. & F., 26/8/18.
Raby, Sydney Herbert, b. Aston, Birmingham, e. Birmingham, 140, L/Cpl., k. in a., F. & F., 27/9/18.
Radburn, Bertram, b. Warwick, e. Warwick, 16550, Pte., k. in a., F. & F., 9/5/17.
Randall, Walter, b. Stourton, Warwicks, e. Stratford-on-Avon, Warwicks (Shipston-on-Stour, Worcs), 33181, Pte., k. in a., F. & F., 20/10/18.
Randle, John, b. Stratford-on-Avon, Warwicks, e. Birmingham (Stratford-on-Avon), 992, Pte., d. of w., F. & F., 16/10/18.
Raper, Claud William, b. Clapton, London, e. Birmingham (Clapton), 141, Pte., k. in a., F. & F., 4/6/10.
Rayner, Charles Edwin, b. Felixstowe, Suffolk, e. Colchester, Essex (Halstead, Essex), 32812, Pte., k. in a., F. & F., 25/10/17, formerly 6377, Hussars.
Reardon, William, b. Portland, Dorset, e. Dublin, Ireland, 34154, L/Cpl., k. in a., F. & F., 27/9/18, formerly 2594, Lancers.
Redhead, Frank, b. Cleckheaton, Yorks, e. Dewsbury, Yorks, 19498, Dmr., k. in a., F. & F., 4/3/17.
Rees, Timothy, b. Tondu, Glam., e. Birmingham, 28630, Pte., k. in a., F. & F., 9/5/17.
Reeve, Lewis Frederick, b. Brookfields, Birmingham, e. Birmingham, 973, Sgt., k. in a., F. & F., 14/4/18.
Reeve, Vincent Charles, b. St. Stephen's, Birmingham, e. Birmingham, 173, Pte., k. in a., F. & F., 15/6/16.
Reeves, Alfred George, b. Newchurch, I. of W., e. Newport, I. of W. (Sandown, I. of W.), 18625, Pte., d. of w., F. & F., 6/2/18, formerly 24491, Som. L.I.
Reid, Alexander, e. Dunkeld, Perth (Clanemore, Perth), 235131, Pte., k. in a., F. & F., 13/4/18, formerly 5230, Scot. Horse.
Rhodes, Cecil, b. Bampton, Oxon, e. Gloucester, 50701, Pte., k. in a., F. & F., 28/6/18.
Richardson, Reece Edward, b. Ladywood, Birmingham, e. Birmingham (Ladywood), 143, Pte., d., F. & F., 3/7/18.
Rideout, Harry Spicer, b. Bedchester, Dorset, e. Bournemouth, Hants, 18623, Pte., d. of w., F. & F., 11/4/17, formerly 23389, Som. L.I.
Ring, Patrick, b. Macroon, Cork, e. Birmingham, 202724, Pte., k. in a., F. & F., 9/5/17.
Risley, Sidney Albert, b. Stratford, London, E., e. Birmingham (Edgbaston, Birmingham), 14/1626, Pte., k. in a., F. & F., 25/10/17.
Roberts, Edward, b. Kenley, Salop, e. Shrewsbury, Salop (Kenley), 30526, L/Cpl., k. in a., F. & F., 27/9/18, formerly 3111, Shrops Yeo.
Roberts, Seth Hixon, b. Tottenham, London, e. Birmingham, 458, Pte., k. in a., F. & F., 22/9/16.
Roberts, William Lawton, b. Ruabon, Denbighshire, e. Birmingham (Ruabon), 172, Pte., d. of w., F. & F., 30/7/16.
Robinson, Harry George, b. Islington, London, e. London, 35013, Pte., d. of w., F. & F., 28/9/18, formerly M/2/074289, R.A.S.C.
Robinson, James Richard, b. Drakes Cross, Redditch, Worcs, e. Birmingham (King's Heath, Birmingham), 16/894, Pte., k. in a., F. & F., 23/7/16.
Robotham, William Henry, b. Birmingham, e. Birmingham (Ladywood, Birmingham), 14/1449, Pte., d. of w., F. & F., 28/8/18.
Rockingham, Thomas, b. Olton, Middx., e. Southam, Warwicks, 28588, Pte., k. in a., F. & F., 30/6/18.
Roper, Alfred Marshall, b. Newent, Glos., e. Birmingham (Newent), 146, Cpl., k. in a., F. & F., 30/7/16.
Rouse, Reginald, b. Malvern, Worcs, e. Handsworth, Birmingham (Hockley, Birmingham), 17046, Pte., k. in a., F. & F., 7/5/18.
Row, Charles Edward, b. Braunton, Devon, e. Barnstaple, Devon (Torrington, Devon), 202044, Pte., k. in a., F. & F., 5/5/17.
Rowbury, Bertram Harry, b. Todenham, Glos., e. Birmingham (Aston, Birmingham), 26571, Pte., k. in a., F. & F., 30/8/18.
Russell, Joseph, b. Oldbury, Worcs, e. Birmingham (Smethwick, Staffs), 14/1659, Pte., d. of w., F. & F., 12/5/16.
Rycroft, Leslie Clare, b. St. Paul's, Warwick, e. Birmingham (Sparkhill, Birmingham), 14/1714, Pte., k. in a., F. & F., 9/5/17.
Ryley, James, b. Small Heath, Birmingham, e. Birmingham (Small Heath), 817, Sgt., d. of w., F. & F., 30/6/18.
Rymer, Harry, b. Camberwell, London, e. Camberwell (Forest Hill, London), 32684, Cpl., k. in a., F. & F., 4/10/17, formerly 10457, Dragoons.
Sadler, Frederic John, b. Saltley, Birmingham, e. Birmingham (Handsworth, Birmingham), 785, L/Cpl., k. in a., F. & F., 3/9/16.
Sadler, John Jordan, b. Oldbury, Birmingham, e. Birmingham (Oldbury), 982, Pte., k. in a., F. & F., 23/5/16.
Sainsbury, William James, e. Swindon, Wilts (Purton, Swindon), 26939, Pte., k. in a., F. & F., 14/4/18.
Sale, Henry Richard, b. Blockley, Worcs, e. Birmingham, 14/1702, Pte., k. in a., F. & F., 4/6/16.
Salt, Edward, b. Sutton Coldfield, Warwicks, e. Warwick (Sutton Coldfield), 16680, Pte., k. in a., F. & F., 3/9/16.
Sanders, James McMillan, b. Arley, Kidderminster, Worcs, e. Birmingham (Arley), 133, Pte., k. in a., F. & F., 3/9/16.
Sanders, James William, b. Birmingham, e. Birmingham (Small Heath, Birmingham), 1147, Cpl., k. in a., F. & F., 24/4/17.
Saunders, John, b. Ashted, Birmingham, e. Birmingham, 17735, Pte., k. in a., F. & F., 29/8/16.
Savage, John, b. Durham, e. Wakefield, Yorks (Ryhill, nr. Wakefield), 203242, Pte., k. in a., F. & F., 27/9/18, formerly 140585, R.F.A.
Scott, Charles Robert, b. Kennington, London, e. Battersea, London, 50416, Pte., k. in a., F. & F , 30/8/18.
Scrivens, George Ernest, b. Birmingham, e. Birmingham, 1446, Sgt., d. of w., F. & F., 11/6/16.
Sharlott, Hubert William, b. Stratford-on-Avon, Warwicks, e. Stratford-on-Avon (Shipston-on-Stour, Worcs), 16986, Pte., d. of w., F. & F., 2/10/18.
Sharpe, Frederick, b. Sheffield, Yorks, e. York (Grimsby, Lincs), 32768, Pte., k. in a., F. & F., 4/10/17, formerly 11126, Dragoons.
Sharrocks, William Arthur, b. Nordon, Lancs, e. Nordon, 32709, Pte., k. in a., F. & F., 4/10/17, formerly 21748, Dragoon Gds.
Shaw, Ernest Charles, b. Bethnal Green, Middx., e. London (Bethnal Green), 43222, Pte., k. in a., F. & F., 27/9/18, formerly 6002, W. Kent Regt.
Shaw, Herbert, e. Bolton, Lancs (Haulgh, Bolton), 26929, Pte., k. in a., F. & F., 26/10/17, formerly 3281, N. Lancs Regt.
Sheppard, Ernest Frederick, b. Bristol, Glos., e. Bristol (Clifton, Bristol), 34812, Pte., k. in a., F. & F., 27/9/18.
Shergold, Charles, b. Birmingham, e. Birmingham (Aston, Birmingham), 1258, Pte., d of w., F. & F., 25/5/16.
Shergold, Charles James, b. Chalford, Glos., e. Stroud, Glos. (Chalford), 50710, Pte., d. of w., F. & F., 17/6/18, formerly G/44509, R. Fus.
Sherwood, John Martin, b. Edgbaston, Birmingham, e. Birmingham (Edgbaston), 841, L/Cpl., k. in a., F. & F., 6/2/17.
Shingleton, James, b. Glasgow, e. Birmingham (Smethwick, Staffs), 1220, Pte., k. in a., F. & F., 4/6/16.
Short, Edward, e. Birmingham (Small Heath, Birmingham), 330147, Pte., k. in a., F. & F., 7/11/17.
Simkins, Alfred, b. St. Paul's, Warwick, e. Birmingham (Aston, Birmingham), 1194, Pte., d. of w., F. & F., 4/2/17.
Simmons, Frank, e. Horwich, Lancs, 32710, Pte., k. in a., F. & F., 26/10/17, formerly 21688, Dragoons.
Simmons, William James Henry, b. Falmouth, Cornwall, e. Plymouth, Devon (Devonport), 50712, Pte., k. in a., F. & F., 27/9/18.
Simpson, John Charles, b. High Leigh, Ches, e. Altrincham, Ches. (Bollington, Ches.), 48330, Pte., k. in a., F. & F., 27/9/18, formerly R.X./4/235093, R.A.S.C.
Skinner, Harry, b. Birmingham, e. Warwick (Small Heath, Birmingham), 37817, Pte., k. in a., F. & F., 28/6/18.
Skinner, William, b. Stockton Heath, Ches., e. Birmingham, (Newton, Denver, Colorado, U.S.A.), 14/1711, Pte., k. in a., F. & F., 3/9/16.
Sloper, Ernest, b. Milton Hill, Berks, e. Winchester, Hants (Alresford, Hants), 32850, Pte., k. in a., F. & F., 25/10/17, formerly 18534, Hussars.
Smith, Arthur, b. Witherley, Leics, e. Nuneaton, Warwicks (Bedworth, Warwicks), 17832, Pte., k. in a., F. & F., 29/8/16.
Smith, Albert Edward, b. Stourbridge, Worcs, e. Coventry, Warwicks (Foleshill, Coventry), 12763, Sgt., k. in a., F. & F., 26/10/17.
Smith, Benjamin, b. Erdington, Birmingham, e. Birmingham (Smethwick, Staffs), 460, Pte., k. in a., F. & F., 4/6/16.
Smith, Cecil, b. St. Chad's, Stafford, e. Birmingham (Stafford), 598, Pte., k. in a., F. & F., 31/7/16.
Smith, Eli, b. Portsmouth, Hants, e. Portsmouth (Gosport, Hants), 18635, Pte., k. in a., F. & F., 23/11/16, formerly 24764, Som. L.I.
Smith, Ernest Rowland, e. Coventry, Warwicks, 26947, Pte., k. in a., F. & F., 22/10/16.
Smith, Frederick, b. Alcester, Warwicks, e. Redditch, Worcs (Studley, Warwicks), 21119, Pte., d. of w., F. & F., 26/10/17.
Smith, Garnet, b. Grantham, Lincs, e. Birmingham (Olton, Warwicks), 891, Pte., k. in a., F. & F., 3/9/16.
Smith, George Aaron, b. Kingswood, Glos, e. Bristol, 18679, L/Cpl., k. in a., F. & F., 26/10/17, formerly 24504, Som. L.I.
Smith, George Edward, b. Coventry, Warwicks, e. Coventry, 17368, Pte., k. in a., F. & F., 30/7/16.
Smith, Peter Stephen, b. Fyfield, Essex, e. Epping, Essex (Fyfield), 34553, Pte., k. in a., F. & F., 29/9/18, formerly 271554, Herts Regt.
Smith, Robert Henry, b. Solihull, Warwicks, e. Leamington, Warwicks (Solihull), 50717, Pte., k. in a., F. & F., 28/6/18.
Smith, Stewart, b. Manchester, e. Birmingham (Erdington, Birmingham), 1103, Pte., k. in a., F. & F., 4/6/16.
Smith, Thomas Harold, b. Birmingham, e. Birmingham (Bournville, Birmingham), 201199, Pte., k. in a., F. & F., 4/10/17.
Smith, Victor Silverthorne, e. London (Tottenham, London), 235132, L/Cpl., k. in a., F. & F., 26/10/17, formerly 206380, R. Bucks Hussars.
Smith, Walter, b. Collycroft, Warwicks, e. Nuneaton, Warwicks (Collycroft), 24120, Pte., k. in a., F. & F., 27/9/18.
Snell, Edwin Charles, e. Wimborne, Dorset, 26933, Pte., k. in a., F. & F., 26/10/17.
Snewing, Arthur Elkington, b. Rugby, Warwicks, e. Birmingham, (Handsworth, Staffs), 908, Pte., k. in a., F. & F., 18/4/16.
Sommers, John Percival, b. Lichfield, Staffs, e. Lichfield, 16462, Pte., d. of w., F. & F., 26/2/17.
Southam, George Henry, b. Birmingham, e. Birmingham (Erdington, Birmingham), 50729, Pte., d. of w., F. & F., 13/10/18.
Southgate, Percy Thomas, b. Bury St. Edmunds, Suffolk, e. St. Omer, France (Brentwood, Essex), 34297, Pte., d. of w., F. & F., 29/6/18, formerly 199927, E.F. Canteens.

Spare, Frank Victor, b. Birmingham, e. Birmingham, 6435, Pte., k. in a., F. & F., 30/6/17.
Sparrow, Alfred William, e. London (Walthamstow, London), 20572, Pte., k. in a., F. & F., 9/5/17, formerly 10562, A. Cyc. Corps.
Spencer, Charles Arthur, b. Birmingham, e. Birmingham, 28618, Pte., k. in a., F. & F., 22/4/17.
Spencer, Samuel Horace, b. Sutton-in-Ashfield, Notts, e. Sutton-in-Ashfield, 32821, Pte., k. in a., F. & F., 4/10/17, formerly 25017, Hussars.
Spraggitt, George, e. Coventry, Warwicks (Keresley, Warwicks), 330794, Pte., k. in a., F. & F., 7/10/17.
Spring, Albert Henry, b. Birmingham, e. Manchester (Salford, Lancs), 12341, Pte., k. in a., F. & F., 21/10/16, formerly 49369, R.G.A.
Stacey, Harry, b. Leicester, e. Birmingham, 16/1788, Pte., k. in a., F. & F., 14/3/17.
Stainton, Harold, b. Birmingham, e. Birmingham (Tyseley, Birmingham), 16/1693, Pte., k. in a., F. & F., 4/6/16.
Stait, Horace Edward, b. Aston, Birmingham, e. Birmingham (Handsworth, Staffs), 890, Pte., k. in a., F. & F., 26/9/16.
Stallard, Harry, b. Mullingar, Co. Meath, e. Birmingham (Ladywood, Birmingham), 18376, Pte., d. of w., F. & F., 27/10/17, formerly 23291, Som. L.I.
Standing, Samuel Pope, b. Birmingham, e. Birmingham, 15/1307, Pte., k. in a., F. & F., 29/8/16.
Stanford, John Henry, b. Edgbaston, Birmingham, e. Birmingham (Edgbaston), 132, Pte., k. in a., F. & F., 28/8/16.
Stanley, William Bernard, b. Birmingham, e. Birmingham (Selly Park, Birmingham), 23305, Pte., d. of w., F. & F., 12/10/17, formerly 32521, R. Berks Regt.
Statham, Ernest, b. Aston, Birmingham, e. Birmingham (Aston), 482, Pte., k. in a., F. & F., 3/9/16.
Statham, James, b. Wilnecote, Warwicks, e. Atherstone, Warwicks (Wilnecote), 10699, Pte., k. in a., F. & F., 28/6/18.
Steer, Harry William, b. Woking, Surrey, e. Brighton, Sussex (Datchet, Bucks), 32744, L/Cpl., d. of w., F. & F., 6/10/17, formerly 3430, Dragoons.
Stephens, Francis William, b. St. Saviour's, Bath, Somerset, e. Birmingham (Stirchley, Birmingham), 240050, Pte., k. in a., F. & F., 9/5/17.
Stephens, Leonard Reginald, b. Cofton, Devon, e. Newton Abbot, Devon (Starcross, Devon), 202040, Pte., k. in a., F. & F., 26/10/17.
Stringer, William, b. Birmingham, e. Birmingham (Hockley, Birmingham), 21352, Pte., k. in a., F. & F., 14/4/18, formerly 27104, R. Berks Regt.
Strong, George Henry, b. Carhampton, Somerset, e. Minehead, Somerset (Carhampton), 267080, Pte., k. in a., F. & F., 2/2/18.
Suffolk, Thomas, b. Nuneaton, Warwicks, e. Nuneaton, 23097, Pte., k. in a., F. & F., 26/10/17.
Sutton, Alfred, b. Ladywood, Birmingham, e. Birmingham (Winson Green, Birmingham), 50726, Pte., k. in a., F. & F., 28/6/18
Sutton, John Lawrence, b. London, e. Birmingham (Small Heath, Birmingham), 28646, Pte., k. in a., F. & F., 5/10/17.
Swadling, Edward, b. Hurst, Berks, e. Camberley, Berks (Wokingham, Berks), 30155, Pte., k. in a., F. & F., 3/9/16, formerly 20731, Oxf. & Bucks L.I.
Swadling, Robert, e. Coventry, Warwicks (Bampton, Oxon), 16452, Pte., d. of w., F. & F., 8/10/17.
Taylor, Arthur Victor, b. Nechells, Birmingham, e. Birmingham (Nechells), 21992, Pte., k. in a., F & F., 5/10/17.
Taylor, Edward, b. Moseley, Birmingham, e. Birmingham, 531, Pte., k. in a., F. & F., 3/9/16.
Taylor, Frank, b. Harpurhey, Lancs, e. Birmingham (Manchester), 869, Cpl., k. in a., F. & F., 28/6/18.
Taylor, Jack, b. Little Sutton, Ches., e. Chester, 32772, Pte., k. in a., F. & F., 6/10/17, formerly 25570, Dragoon Gds.
Taylor, Percy William, b. Tate, Glos., e. Bristol (Kingswood, Bristol), 18639, Pte., d. of w., F. & F., 12/4/17, formerly 24006, Som. L.I.
Taylor, William Thomas, b. Coventry, Warwicks, e. Coventry, 43328, Pte., d. of w., F. & F., 31/10/18, formerly 357282, Hampshire Regt.
Thacker, Percy Harold, b. Wolverhampton, Staffs, e. Sutton Coldfield, Warwicks, 16/1498, Pte., k. in a., F. & F., 3/9/16.
Thexton, John, b. Kendal, Westmoreland, e. Manchester (Kendal), 22089, Pte., k. in a., F. & F., 8/5/17, formerly 2845, Manchester Regt.
Thickett, Leonard, b. Walsall, Staffs, e. Birmingham (Washwood Heath, Birmingham), 16/1684, Pte., k. in a., F. & F., 9/5/17.
Thomas, Daniel Edgar, b. Swansea, Glam., e. Cardiff, Glam. (West Cross Gower, Glam.), 48332, Pte., d. of w., F. & F., 29/9/18, formerly RX/4/235994, R.A.S.C.
Thomas, Frederick Victor, b. Handsworth, Staffs, e. Birmingham (Handsworth), 915, Pte., k. in a., F. & F., 23/7/16.
Thomas, James, b. Duddeston, Birmingham, e. Birmingham, 298, Pte., k. in a., F. & F., 28/7/16.
Thomas, Percy George, b. Iron Acton, Glos., e. Bristol (Iron Acton), 23578, Pte., k. in a., F. & F., 9/5/17, formerly 174176, R.E.
Thompson, Arthur, b. Gravelly Hill, Birmingham, e. Birmingham, 997, Sgt., k. in a., F. & F., 30/8/18.
Thompson, Albert Charles, b. Meriden, Warwicks, e. Coventry, Warwicks, 28586, Pte., d., F. & F., 26/10/17.
Thompson, Leslie Hubert, b. Birmingham, e. Birmingham (King's Heath, Birmingham), 1243, Pte., d. of w., F. & F., 7/6/16.
Thomson, Wallace Robert, b. Birmingham, e. Birmingham (Harborne, Birmingham), 1181, L/Cpl., k. in a., F. & F., 4/6/16.
Timmins, Horace, b. Handsworth, Staffs, e. Birmingham, 851, Cpl., k. in a., F. & F., 29/8/16.
Timmins, Harry Charles, b. St. Luke's, Birmingham, e. Birmingham, 7281, Pte., k. in a., F. & F., 28/8/16.
Tipping, Roland Walter, b. Kineton, Warwicks, e. Stratford-on-Avon, Warwicks (Kineton), 242900, Pte., d. of w., F. & F., 24/8/18.
Tomkins, Frank, b. St. Mark's, Wolverhampton, Staffs, e. Birmingham (Wolverhampton), 461, Sgt., d. of w., F. & F., 8/8/16.
Toney, Charles William, b. Warwick, e. Warwick, 24823, Pte., k. in a., F. & F., 28/6/18.
Tongue, Charles Edward, b. Hockley, Birmingham, e. Birmingham, 15/299, Pte., k. in a., F. & F., 4/6/16.
Tonks, Albert, b. Yardley, Birmingham, e. Warwick (Stechford, Birmingham), 22775, Pte., k. in a., F. & F., 8/5/17.
Tonks, Edward Carrick, b. Small Heath, Birmingham, e. Birmingham (Small Heath), 462, Pte., k. in a., F. & F., 4/6/16.
Tonks, Lionel Anthony Stanley, b. Birmingham, e. Birmingham (Edgbaston, Birmingham), 35930, Pte., k. in a., F. & F., 17/9/18.
Toon, Albert George, b. Birmingham, e. Birmingham, 16/1470, Pte., k. in a., F. & F., 21/4/18.
Towell, Arthur C., e. Birmingham (Ladywood, Birmingham), 241067, Pte., k. in a., F. & F., 25/6/17.
Tremethick, Arthur Clarence, b. Paul, Cornwall, e. Truro, Cornwall (Penzance, Cornwall), 35932, Pte., k. in a., F. & F., 17/9/18, formerly 38160, D.C.L.I.
Trenouth, John Henry, b. North Tamerton, Devon, e. Bude, Cornwall (South Poole, Devon), 33776, Pte., k. in a., F. & F., 28/6/18, formerly 222234, R.A.S.C.
Trinder, Albert Charles, b. Abingdon, Berks, e. Abingdon, 18644, Pte., k. in a., F. & F., 12/4/18, formerly 23426, Som. L.I.
Troman, Henry, b. Solihull, Warwicks, e. Solihull, 17307, Pte., k. in a., F. & F., 3/9/16.
Truscott, Percy Ivor, b. Birmingham, e. Birmingham (Edgbaston, Birmingham), 16/1655, Pte., d. of w., F. & F., 5/6/16.
Tunaley, Edgar Harold, b. St. Paul's, Derby, e. Birmingham (Cotteridge, Birmingham), 738, L/Sgt., k. in a., F. & F., 31/7/16.
Turner, Walter Oliver, b. Dartford, Kent, e. Canning Town, London (Dartford), 32725, Pte., k. in a., F. & F., 5/10/17, formerly 10285, Dragoons.
Turvey, Horace, b. Maney, Sutton Coldfield, Warwicks, e. Birmingham (Sutton Coldfield), 1674, Pte., k. in a., F. & F., 28/8/16.
Tyrer, Eric Walter, b. Newhampton, Staffs, e. Birmingham (Colwyn Bay, Denbigh), 1126, Pte., k. in a., F. & F., 29/8/16.
Vaughan, Leonard, b. St. Martin's, Birmingham, e. Birmingham, 205, Pte., k. in a., F. & F., 4/6/16.
Vickerstaff, Eric Lonsdale, b. Balsall Heath, Birmingham, e. Birmingham (Balsall Heath), 129, Pte., k. in a., F. & F., 28/7/16.
Vince, Horace Leonard, b. Campbelltown, Argyle, e. Gosport, Hants, 32719, Pte., k. in a., F. & F., 4/10/17, formerly 5621, Dragoons.
Viveash, Ernest Arnold, b. Awebridge, Hants, e. Southampton, Hants (Awebridge), 35937, Pte., k. in a., F. & F., 27/9/18, formerly 45459, Hants Regt.
Voyce, Walter Charles, b. Birmingham, e. Birmingham (Handsworth, Birmingham), 1170, Pte., k. in a., F. & F., 4/6/16.
Waldron, Edward James, b. Birmingham, e. Birmingham, 28621, Pte., d. of w., F. & F., 26/10/17.
Walker, Horace John, b. Handsworth, Birmingham, e. Birmingham (Handsworth), 179, Pte., d. of w., F. & F., 4/9/16.
Walker, Harold Wilson, b. London, e. Birmingham (London), 1086, Pte., d. of w., F. & F., 23/7/16.
Walker, William Stanley, b. Sparkhill, Birmingham, e. Birmingham, 281, L/Cpl., k. in a., F. & F., 4/6/16.
Ward, Charles Alfred, b. Rugby, Warwicks, e. Rugby, 41088, Pte., k. in a., F. & F., 27/9/18.
Warnell, William Thomas, e. London (Walthamstow, London. N.), 32652, Pte., k. in a., F. & F., 26/10/17, formerly 21711, Dragoon Gds.
Waterhouse, Frank, b. Langley, Worcs, e. Birmingham (Langley), 16/1906, Pte., k. in a., F. & F., 26/10/17.
Weatherall, Percy, e. Nottingham (Swinton, Notts), 27446, Pte., k. in a., F. & F., 22/7/18, formerly 4779, Notts & Derby Regt.
Webster, William Henry, b. Fakenham, Norfolk, e. Birmingham (Saltley, Birmingham), 657, L/Cpl., k. in a., F. & F., 30/8/16.
Weeks, Harry George, b. Wickham, Hants, e. Winchester, Hants (Shedfield, Hants), 18744, Pte., k. in a., F. & F., 24/9/16, formerly 22911, Som. L.I.
Welch, Arthur, b. Mansfield, Notts, e. Rugby, Warwicks (Mansfield), 9752, Pte., k. in a., F. & F., 21/4/17.
Welch, Victor Charles Henry, b. Petersfield, Hants, e. Winchester, Hants (Petersfield), 18742, Pte., k. in a., F. & F., 24/9/16, formerly 23265, Som. L.I.
Wells, Charles James, b. Portsmouth, Hants, e. Weymouth, Dorset, 33206, Pte., d. of w., F. & F., 26/10/17, formerly 24265, Lancers.
Weston, Alfred Henry, e. London (Uxbridge, Middx.), 34288, L/Cpl., k. in a., F. & F., 28/8/18.
Whiston, Alan Whittall, b. Handsworth, Birmingham, e. Birmingham (Handsworth), 601, Pte., k. in a., F. & F., 2/9/16.
White, Charles Ronald, b. St. Paul's, Walsall, Staffs, e. Birmingham (Walsall), 935, Sgt., k. in a., F. & F., 23/7/16.

White, Frank, b. Bampton, Oxon., e. Oxford (Bampton), 30158, Pte., k. in a., F. & F., 3/9/16, formerly 20886, Oxf. & Bucks L.I.
White, Harold, b. Battersea, London, e. Battersea, 32716, Pte., k. in a., F. & F., 5/10/17, formerly 9639, Dragoons.
White, Jesse William, b. Balsall Heath, Birmingham, e. Birmingham (Bournville, Birmingham), 967, L/Cpl., k. in a., F. & F., 4/6/16.
Whitehead, David, b. Liverpool, Lancs, e. Liverpool, 32649, Pte., k. in a., F. & F., 26/10/17, formerly 63, Dragoons.
Whitehouse, Ernest, b. Moseley, Birmingham, e. Birmingham, 15/989, Pte., k. in a., F. & F., 23/7/16.
Whitehouse, William Edward, b. Tipton, Staffs, e. Birmingham, 241723, Pte., k. in a., F. & F., 13/4/18.
Whiteman, Thomas, b. Bracknell, Berks, e. Rugby, Warwicks, 15720, L/Cpl., k. in a., F. & F., 3/9/16.
Whittle, John, b. Aston, Birmingham, e. Birmingham, 581, Pte., k. in a., F. & F., 9/9/16.
Wilcox, Charles Otto, b. Birmingham, e. Birmingham (Harborne, Birmingham), 16/1614, Pte., d. of w., F. & F., 26/10/16.
Wilcox, David, b. Coventry, Warwicks, e. Coventry, 17370, Pte., k. in a., F. & F., 9/5/17.
Wileman, Evan, b. Mersham, Leics, e. Coventry, Warwicks, 16845, Pte., k. in a., F. & F., 9/5/17.
Wilkes, Christopher, b. Aston, Birmingham, e. Birmingham (Saltley, Birmingham), 11791, Cpl., d. of w., F. & F., 2/10/18.
Wilkins, William Ferdinand, b. Smethwick, Staffs, e. Birmingham, 16/1579, Pte., k. in a., F. & F., 4/6/16.
Wilkinson, Fred, e. Barrow-in-Furness, Lancs, 32717, Pte., k. in a., F. & F., 4/10/17, formerly 21496, Dragoons.
Willday, Cyril Thomas, b. Aston, Birmingham, e. Birmingham (Stechford, Birmingham), 1124, Pte., d. of w., F. & F., 21/7/16.
Williams, Ivor Brierley, b. St. Mary's, Swansea, Glam., e. Birmingham (Swansea), 470, Pte., k. in a., F. & F., 23/7/16.
Williams, Jack, b. Birmingham, e. Small Heath, Birmingham, 28379, Pte., k. in a., F. & F., 9/5/17.
Williams, Lawson, b. Malvern, Worcs, e. Birmingham (Malvern), 469, Pte., k. in a., F. & F., 4/6/16.
Williams, William, b. Lambeth, London, e. London, 34131, Pte., k. in a., F. & F., 26/10/17, formerly 6858, Dragoon Gds.
Williams, William Isaac, e. Bristol, Glos. (Westbury, Bristol), 35949, Pte., k. in a., F. & F., 29/8/18.
Wilson, Edward, b. Mountrath, Queen's Co. Ireland, e. Aldershot, Hants (Bishopston, Bristol), 32831, Pte., d. of w., F. & F., 28/10/17, formerly 32980, Hussars.
Wilson, Timothy, b. Hinckley, Leics, e. Nuneaton, Warwicks (Hinckley), 12095, Pte., d. of w., F. & F., 5/5/17.
Wimbush, Sydney Ernest, b. Marton, Warwicks, e. Stratford-on-Avon, Warwicks 10651, L/Cpl., k. in a., F. & F., 30/8/16.
Wiseman, Joseph Edward, b. Birmingham, e. Birmingham (Handsworth, Birmingham), 28581, Pte., k. in a., F. & F., 27/9/18.
Wood, Albert, b. Rugeley, Staffs, e. Birmingham (Saltley, Birmingham), 16918, Pte., k in a., F. & F., 29/8/16.
Wood, George, b. Dordon, Warwicks, e. Warwick (Dordon), 17594, L/Cpl., k. in a., F. & F., 30/6/17.
Wood, George Edmund, e. Birmingham (King's Heath, Birmingham), 15/1524, Pte., k. in a., F. & F., 20/5/16.
Wood, Henry, b. Birmingham, e. Birmingham, 16/1783, Pte., k. in a., F. & F., 9/5/17.
Wood, Harold Freeman, b. Birmingham, e. Birmingham (Balsall Heath, Birmingham), 16/1690, Pte., d. of w., F. & F., 29/9/18.
Wood, Thomas Edward, b. Knottingley, Yorks, e. Birmingham (Knottingley), 751, Sgt., k. in a., F. & F., 23/7/16.
Wood, Thomas Lionel, b. Erdington, Birmingham, e. Birmingham, 15/292, Sgt., d. of w., F. & F., 8/7/16.
Woodall, William Bernard, b. Stourbridge, Worcs, e. Stourbridge, 35760, Pte., k. in a., F. & F., 27/9/18, formerly 313935, Warwick Yeo.
Woodcock, Andrew, b. Witney, Oxon., e. Cowley, Oxon. (Witney), 32979, Pte., k. in a., F. & F., 26/10/17, formerly GS/24128, Lancers.
Woodings, Edward, e. Birmingham (Sutton Coldfield, Warwicks), 23288, Pte., k. in a., F. & F., 4/10/17.
Woods, Robert, b. Tamworth, Warwicks, e. Warwick (Hockley Heath, Warwicks), 16904, Pte., k. in a., F. & F., 30/8/18.
Woods, William, b. Feltham, Middx., e. Hounslow, Middx., 28357, Pte., d. of w., F. & F., 26/10/17, formerly 27301, Hussars.
Wooliscroft, Walter, b. Macclesfield, Ches., e. Macclesfield (Higher Broughton, Manchester), 33205, Pte., k. in a., F. & F., 27/9/18, formerly 5000, Lancers.
Woollaston, Neville, b. Shirley, Warwicks, e. Moseley Barracks, Birmingham (Shirley), 16/1171, Pte., k. in a., F. & F., 7/11/17.
Worrall, Frank, b. Coventry, Warwicks, e. Coventry, 28583, Pte., d. of w., F. & F., 10/4/17.
Worsfield, Alfred William, b. Gosport, Hants, e. Portsmouth, Hants, 35952, Pte., d. of w., F. & F., 29/6/18.
Wright, Harold, b. King's Heath, Birmingham, e. Birmingham, 592, Pte., d. of w., F. & F., 23/4/17.
Wright, Robert, b. Sprowston, Norwich, e. Birmingham (Sprowston), 188, Pte., k. in a., F. & F., 3/9/16.
Wyatt, Edmund Leonard, b. Birmingham, e. Birmingham (Edgbaston, Birmingham), 1696, Pte., k. in a., F. & F., 3/9/16.
Yard, Walter, b. Glascote, Warwicks, e. Birmingham (Walsall, Staffs), 15/1562, Pte., d. of w., F. & F., 6/6/16.
Yardley, William Edgar, b. St. Thomas, Coventry, Warwicks, e. Coventry, 28595, Pte., k. in a., F. & F., 4/10/17.
Yates, Arthur Bennion, b. Walsall, Staffs, e. Birmingham (Walsall), 117, Pte., k. in a., F. & F., 9/5/17.
Yates, Francis Herbert, b. Great Barr, Walsall, Staffs, e. Birmingham (Great Barr), 116, Cpl., k. in a., F. & F., 3/9/16.
Young, George Jacob, b. Limehouse, Middx., e. East Ham, London (Dover, Kent), 32741, Pte., k. in a., F. & F., 4/10/17, formerly 10017, Dragoons.
Young, Harry James, b. Small Heath, Birmingham, e. Birmingham 6473, Pte., k. in a., F. & F., 26/10/17.
Young, Sidney, b. Skipton, Yorks, e. Birmingham (Skipton), 114, L/Cpl., k. in a., F. & F., 30/6/17.

16th Battalion.

Ackrill, Albert James, b. Birmingham, e. Birmingham (Ladywood, Birmingham), 16/1366, Pte., k. in a., F. & F., 24/7/16.
Adcock, Donald, b. Thurlaston, Leics, e. Leicester, 52202, Pte., k. in a., F. & F., 27/9/18, formerly 3148, S. Notts Hussars.
Adderley, William Edward, e. Birmingham, 24895, Pte., d. of w., F. & F., 10/10/18.
Alcock, Arthur Sidney, b. Balsall Heath, Birmingham, e. Birmingham (Sparkbrook, Birmingham), 754, L/Cpl., k. in a., F. & F., 6/10/17.
Aldgate, Wilfred, b. Holy Trinity, Derby, e. Bakewell, Derbyshire (Ashford, Derbyshire), 242145, Pte., k. in a., F. & F., 30/5/18, formerly 2263, Notts & Derby Regt.
Aldridge, Alfred John, b. Newbury, Berks, e. Birmingham (Newbury), 497, Pte., k. in a., F. & F., 27/7/16.
Allen, Alfred, b. Birmingham, e. Birmingham (Edgbaston, Birmingham), 847, Pte., k. in a., F. & F., 3/9/16.
Allen, Isaiah Humphries, b. Lower Heyford, Northants, e. Northampton, 32885, Pte., k. in a., F. & F., 9/10/17, formerly 5375, Hussars.
Allen, Thomas Arthur, b. Birmingham, e. Birmingham (Nechells, Birmingham), 40928, Pte., k. in a., F. & F., 23/8/18.
Allen, Thomas George, b. Birmingham, e. Birmingham (Ladywood, Birmingham), 36556, Pte., k. in a., F. & F., 30/9/18.
Allso, Percival Allen, b. Stratford, Essex, e. Birmingham (Stratford), 252, L/Cpl., k. in a., F. & F., 27/7/16.
Ansell, Frank Benson, b. Middlesborough, Yorks, e. Birmingham (Middlesborough), 251, L/Cpl., k. in a., F. & F., 27/7/16.
Archer, John Arthur Randall, b. Lambley, Notts, e. Lambley, 245162, Pte., d., F. & F., 11/11/18, formerly 305303, Notts & Derby Regt.
Arculus, Herbert, b. Acock's Green, Birmingham, e. Birmingham (Acock's Green), 1056, L/Cpl., k. in a., F. & F., 26/9/16.
Arkell, Henry Serle, b. Aston, Birmingham, e. Birmingham (Moseley, Birmingham), 759, L/Cpl., d. of w., F. & F., 6/10/17.
Ashmall, Alfred Josiah, b. Coventry, Warwicks, e. Coventry, 38350, Pte., k. in a., F. & F., 21/8/18.
Aspery, William Thomas, e. Birmingham, 27929, Pte., k. in a., F. & F., 23/8/18.
Astley, Samuel Loach, b. Birmingham, e. Birmingham (Aston, Birmingham), 21592, Pte., k. in a., F. & F., 5/11/17.
Atkins, William, b. Scotton, Norfolk, e. Norwich (Scotton), 300061, Pte., k. in a., F. & F., 20/6/18, formerly 201846, Norfolk Regt.
Attwood, Lawson, b. Cradley, Staffs, e. Stourbridge, Worcs (Netherend, Staffs), 34697, Pte., k. in a., F. & F., 11/11/17, formerly 204568, Oxf. & Bucks L.I.
Ayres, John, b. Worthorpe, Northants, e. Melton Mowbray, Leics, 32868, Pte., k. in a., F. & F., 23/8/18, formerly 22509, Hussars.
Ayto, John William, b. Beeston, Notts, e. Grantham, Lincs (Hough-on-the-Hill, Lincs), 52239, Pte., k. in a., F. & F., 1/9/18, formerly 106692, Notts & Derby Regt.
Bacon, John, b. Birmingham, e. Birmingham (Rotton Park, Birmingham), 14/1732, Pte., d. of w., F. & F., 26/6/18.
Baggott, George James, b. Dudley, Worcs, e. Birmingham (Dudley), 118, Cpl., k. in a., F. & F., 26/9/16.
Baggott, Joseph, b. Stechford, Birmingham, e. Birmingham, 16/1300, Pte., k. in a., F. & F., 3/9/16.
Bagley, Matthew, b. Halesowen, Worcs, e. Oldbury, Staffs (Blackheath, Birmingham), 50241, Pte., k. in a., F. & F., 24/8/18.
Bagnall, John, b. Birmingham, e. Birmingham (Hay Mills, Birmingham), 200836, Pte., k. in a., F. & F., 28/10/17.
Bailey, John George, b. Birmingham, e. Birmingham (Nechells, Birmingham), 43447, Pte., k. in a., F. & F., 2/9/18.
Bailey, Selwyn, b. Willenhall, Staffs, e. Birmingham (Willenhall), 772, Pte., d. of w., F. & F., 4/9/16.
Baker, Edward Harold, b. Leamington, Warwicks, e. Coventry, Warwicks, 35223, Pte., k. in a., F. & F., 27/9/18.
Baker, Frederick James, e. Oxford (Cowley, Oxford), 235140, Sgt., k. in a., F. & F., 23/8/18, formerly 201692, Oxf. & Bucks L.I.
Baker, Herbert George, b. Clerkenwell, Middx., e. London (Baldwin, Manitoba, Canada), 43237, Pte., d. of w., F. & F., 22/8/18, formerly 35495, R.E.
Baker, Joseph Shirley, b. Acock's Green, Birmingham, e. Birmingham, 522, Pte., k. in a., F. & F., 27/7/16.
Baker, Walter Wallace, b. Birmingham, e. Birmingham 785, L/Cpl., k. in a., F. & F., 3/9/16.
Bakewell, Alfred, b. Birmingham, e. Birmingham (Selly Park, Birmingham), 16/1650, Pte., k. in a., F. & F., 27/7/16.
Bakewell, Walter, b. Dudley, Worcs, e. Dudley, 244153, Pte., k. in a., F. & F., 23/8/18, formerly 3644, Worcs Regt.
Barker, Alfred, b. Birmingham, e. Birmingham, 3854, Sgt., k. in a., F. & F., 9/8/17.

Barker, William, b. Birmingham, e. Birmingham, 17604, L/Cpl., k. in a., F. & F., 9/10/17.
Barnfield, Herbert, b. Edgbaston, Birmingham, e. Birmingham, 505, Pte., k. in a., F. & F., 1/2/16.
Barnsley, William, e. Worcester (Brierley Hill, Staffs), 50219, Pte., d., F. & F., 2/11/18, formerly 22924, Worcs Regt.
Barrett, Paul John, b. Islington, Middx., e. Birmingham, 22505, L/Cpl., k. in a., F. & F., 28/10/17.
Barrett, William Thomas, b. Smethwick, Staffs, e. Birmingham (West Bromwich, Staffs), 16/1708, Pte., k. in a., F. & F., 30/5/18.
Bartlett, Frederick, b. Stratford-on-Avon, Warwicks, e. Stratford-on-Avon, 16/1813, Pte., k. in a., F. & F., 27/7/16.
Barwell, Wilfred, b. Leighton, Hunts, e. Huntingdon (Leighton), 30208, L/Cpl., k. in a., F. & F., 1/9/18, formerly 1627, Hunts Cyc. Battn., M.M. .
Bassnett, Charles Hayward, b. Handsworth, Staffs, e. Birmingham (Handsworth), 494, Pte., k. in a., F. & F., 27/7/16.
Bastable, Harry James, b. Smethwick, Staffs, e. Birmingham (Smethwick), 1201, Pte., k. in a., F. & F., 1/1/17.
Baugh, Charles, b. Winson Green, Birmingham, e. Birmingham, 511, L/Cpl., k. in a., F. & F., 27/7/16.
Bayliss, Thomas, b. West Bromwich, Staffs, e. Birmingham (West Bromwich), 16/1387, Pte., k. in a., F. & F., 14/5/17.
Bedford, George, b. London, e. Southampton, 18720, Pte., k. in a., F. & F., 19/9/16, formerly 24065, Som. L.I.
Belcher, Ernest John Reginald, b. St. Paul's, Leamington, e. Leamington, Warwicks (Milverton, Leamington), 28549, L/Cpl., k. in a., F. & F., 18/4/18.
Bell, Charles Francis, b. Redcliffe, Gloster, e. Birmingham (Bristol), 527, Cpl., d., F. & F., 17/10/16.
Benbow, George Edward, b. Cound, Salop, e. Woolwich, Kent (Cound), 48427, Pte., k. in a., F. & F., 23/8/18, formerly O/22952, R.A.O.C.
Bennett, Charles Henry, b. Stanbridge, Worcs, e. Birmingham (Stanbridge), 274, Cpl., k. in a., F. & F., 7/10/17.
Bennett, George Clarence, b. Handsworth, Birmingham, e. Birmingham (Handsworth), 260, Pte., k. in a., F. & F., 27/9/16.
Bennett, Gilbert Edward, b. Kidderminster, Worcs, e. Birmingham (Kidderminster), 124, Pte., k. in a., F. & F., 27/7/16.
Bennett, Stephen Ernest, b. Gaton, Staffs, e. Stratford-on-Avon, Warwicks, 35232, Pte., k. in a., F. & F., 20/4/18.
Bennion, Percy, b. Stafford, e. Birmingham (Blackheath, Birmingham), 14638, Pte., k. in a., F. & F., 9/10/17.
Benson, Alfred, b. Coventry, Warwicks, e. Birmingham (Bordesley Green, Birmingham), 16/1438, L/Cpl., k. in a., F. & F., 16/4/17.
Benton, William Edwin, b. Cannock, Staffs, e. Birmingham (Cannock), 783, Pte., k. in a., F. & F., 2/9/16.
Berry, John, b. Ashton-in-Makerfield, Lancs, e. Newton-le-Willows, Lancs (Ashton-in-Makerfield), 260428, Pte., k. in a., F. & F., 13/10/18, formerly 3046, S. Lancs Regt.
Bethell, Douglas, b. Stourbridge, Worcs, e. Birmingham (Woolaston, Worcs), 1210, Pte., k. in a., F. & F., 3/9/16.
Bibb, Albert, b. Birmingham, e. Birmingham, 1052, Pte., k. in a., F. & F., 10/5/17.
Bick, Leonard Long, e. Gloucester (Staverton, Glos.), 27653, Pte., k. in a., F. & F., 13/3/17, formerly 2457, Glos. Yeo.
Biddle, Frank, b. Birmingham, e. Warwick (Bedworth, Warwicks), 18122, Pte., k. in a., F. & F., 3/9/16.
Bigden, Albert George Mapp, b. Ascot, Berks, e. Portsmouth, Hants, 33000, Pte., k. in a., F. & F., 6/10/17, formerly 5574, Hussars.
Billson, Cyril Frank, b. Plumstead, Middx., e. Warwick (Hythe, Kent), 7756, Sgt., k. in a., F. & F., 3/9/16.
Birch, Charles Percival, b. Birmingham, e. Birmingham (Bloomsbury, Birmingham), 788, L/Cpl., k. in a., F. & F., 24/7/16.
Blackham, Cyril, b. All Saints, Leamington, Warwicks, e. Leamington, 513, Pte., k. in a., F. & F., 26/7/16.
Blore, Bernard, e. Nottingham (Radford, Nottingham), 245163, Pte., d. of w., F. & F., 4/9/18, formerly 6055, Sherwood Foresters.
Boden, Thomas George, b. Ludlow, Salop, e. Birmingham (Shrewsbury, Salop), 531, Sgt., k. in a., F. & F., 9/10/17.
Bodman, Ambrose, b. Oldland, Glos., e. Bristol, Glos. (Bitton, Bristol), 23258, Pte., d. of w., F. & F., 27/5/17, formerly 30337, Glos. Regt.
Bond, Herbert, b. Bridgwater, Som., e. Pontypridd, Glam. (Bridgwater), 32876, Pte., k. in a., F. & F., 9/10/17, formerly 5284, Hussars.
Boot, John Henry, b. Aston, Birmingham, e. Birmingham (Aston), 201728, Pte., k. in a., F. & F., 23/8/18.
Bosley, Arthur, b. Sparkbrook, Birmingham, e. Birmingham, 528, Pte., k. in a., F. & F., 24/8/18.
Boswell Alfred, b. Worcester, e. Evesham, Worcs (Gt. Hampton, Worcs), 50209, Pte., k. in a., F. & F., 21/8/18, formerly 242577, Worcs Regt.
Bott, Thomas William, b. Birmingham, e. Birmingham (Leamington Spa, Warwicks), 15/1395, Pte., k. in a., F. & F., 9/10/17.
Bourne, Albert, b. St. John's, Birmingham, e. Birmingham, 2135, Pte., d. of w., F. & F., 9/10/17.
Bowen, Albert, b. Stanton Lacey, Salop, e. Wem, Salop (Belan, Salop), 27789, Pte., k. in a., F. & F., 9/10/17, formerly 24189, Shrops L.I.
Bradfield, Maurice Daniel, b. Leighton Buzzard, Beds, e. Warrington, Lancs, 36461, Pte., d. of w., F. & F., 4/9/18, formerly 4216, S. Lancs Regt.
Bradford, Benjamin Arthur, b. Gainsborough, Lincs, e. Gainsborough, 52253, Pte., k. in a., F. & F., 2/9/18, formerly 51836, Notts & Derby Regt
Bradley, Harold, b. Alvechurch, Worcs, e. Birmingham (Alvechurch), 22769, Pte., d. of w., F. & F., 9/10/17.
Brampton, Charles Clifford, b. Sutton Coldfield, Warwicks, e. Birmingham (Sutton Coldfield), 123, Pte., k. in a., F. & F., 26/9/16.
Briggs, Tom, b. Blackburn, Lancs, e. Blackburn, 52252, Pte., k. in a., F. & F., 1/9/18, formerly 16/39179, Liverpool Regt.
Bromwich, John George, b. New Bilton, Warwicks, e. Rugby, Warwicks, 14531, Pte., d. of w., F. & F., 29/7/16.
Brookes, Arnold David, b. Lye, Worcs, e. Birmingham (Lye), 120, Pte., k. in a., F. & F., 15/1/16.
Brookes, Charles, e. Stratford-on-Avon, Warwicks (Loxley, Warwicks), 13474, Pte., k. in a., F. & F., 10/5/17.
Brown, Charles Edward, b. Hanworth, London, e. Hammersmith, London (Fulham, London), 48277, Pte., k. in a., F. & F., 23/8/18, formerly 024893, R.A.O.C.
Brown, Harry William, b. Salwarpe, Worcs, e. Worcester (Clains, Worcs), 50223, Pte., k. in a., F. & F., 23/8/18, formerly 31277, Worcs Regt.
Brown, John, b. Woodcote. Oxon, e. Caversham, Oxon (Woodcote), 34740, Pte., k. in a., F. & F., 28/10/17.
Brown, William Tipton, b. Tetbury, Glos., e. Stroud, Glos. (Tetbury), 35835, Pte., k. in a., F. & F., 20/10/18.
Brown, John Henry, b. Stockingford, Warwicks, e. Warwick (Nuneaton, Warwicks), 22206, Pte., k. in a., F. & F., 14/5/17.
Buckley, Hugo, b. Bentley Heath, Birmingham, e. Birmingham (Hockley Heath, Birmingham), 8240, L/Cpl., k. in a., F. & F., 3/9/16.
Budden, Fred, b. Hay, Brecon, e. Bridlington, Yorks, 245167, Pte., k. in a., F. & F., 2/9/18, formerly 1450, E. Yorks Regt.
Bugg, George, b. Offord, Suffolk, e. Mill Hill, London (Enfield Middx.), 36451, Pte., d. of w., F. & F., 3/9/18, formerly G/22555, Middx. Regt.
Burlison, Robert Roy, b. Edinburgh, e. Birmingham (Edinburgh), 16/518, Pte., k. in a., F. & F., 25/12/15.
Burt, Donald, b. Wardour, Wilts, e. Salisbury, Wilts (Wardour), 35248, Pte., k. in a., F. & F., 23/8/18.
Burt, Henry Thomas, b. Hornsey, Middx., e. London (Walthamstow, Essex), 235150, L/Sgt., k. in a., F. & F., 23/8/18, formerly 202998, Oxf. & Bucks L.I.
Burton, Edwin, b. Birmingham, e. Birmingham (Sparkhill, Birmingham), 16/1660, Pte., k. in a., F. & F., 6/10/17.
Burton, Eric Crossland, e. Moseley, Birmingham (Balsall Heath, Birmingham), 1079, Pte., k. in a., F. & F., 27/7/16.
Burton, Frederick, b. Birmingham, e. Birmingham (Lozells, Birmingham), 27678, Pte., d. of w., F. & F., 21/9/16.
Burton, George Henry, b. Knowle, Warwicks, e. Warwick (Knowle), 18203, Pte., k. in a., F. & F., 10/10/17.
Burton, William, b. Landom, Salop, e. Derby (Much Wenlock, Salop), 32973, Pte., k. in a., F. & F., 9/10/17, formerly 17481, Hussars.
Butcher, Albert William, b. Bray, Berks, e. Maidenhead, Berks (White Waltham, Berks), 32887, Pte., k. in a., F. & F., 9/10/17, formerly 29969, Hussars.
Butler, Thomas Arthur, b. St. Nicholas, Warwick, e. Leamington, Warwicks (Warwick), 512, Pte., k. in a., F. & F., 30/7/16.
Bywater, Arthur Harold, b. Stroud, Glos., e. Birmingham (Aston, Birmingham), 16/1575, Pte., k. in a., F. & F., 16/6/16.
Bywater, Leonard Albert, b. Stroud, Glos., e. Birmingham (Aston, Birmingham), 16/1590, Pte., k. in a., F. & F., 3/4/16.
Cann, Edward Henry, b. Bloomsbury, London, e. London, 32526, Pte., d. of w., F. & F., 9/10/17, formerly 2854, Lancers.
Capon, Alfred Ernest, b. Mile End, London, e. East Ham, London (Forest Gate, London), 35250, Pte., k. in a., F. & F., 27/9/18.
Carless, Arthur, b. St. Thomas, Birmingham, e. Birmingham, 550, Pte., k. in a., F. & F., 27/7/16.
Carr, Harry, b. Nantwich, Ches., e. Birmingham (Witton, Birmingham), 15/1379, Pte., k. in a., F. & F., 3/9/16.
Carr, Harry, b. Carlisle, Cumberlnad, e. York (Harrogate, Yorks), 34068, Pte., k. in a., F. & F., 31/5/18, formerly 11589, Hussars.
Carter, John, b. St. James, Birmingham, e. Birmingham, 1263, Pte., k. in a., F. & F., 2/9/18.
Carter, Walter, b. Birmingham, e. Birmingham (Selly Oak, Birmingham), 14/1695, Pte., d. of w., F. & F., 1/8/16.
Caseley, James Douglas, b. Stratford-on-Avon, Warwicks, e. Birmingham (Acock's Green, Birmingham), 16/1465, Pte., k. in a., F. & F., 27/7/16.
Castle, William Edward, b. Birmingham, e. Birmingham, 1169, Pte., k. in a., F. & F., 25/12/15.
Chable, Rene, b. Lewisham, London, e. Paris, France (Maison Lafitte, Seine et Oise, France), 32604, Pte., k. in a., F. & F., 9/10/17, formerly 15271, Dragoons.
Chance, Albert Stanley, b. Stourbridge, Worcs, e. Stourbridge, 28952, Pte., d. of w., F. & F., 29/9/18, formerly 31115, Worcs Regt.
Chance, Frederick Ernest, b. Birmingham, e. Birmingham (Gravelly Hill, Birmingham), 267315, Pte., k. in a, F. & F., 27/9/18.
Chance, Wilfred George, b. Stamber Mill, Stourbridge, Worcs, e. Stourbridge, 35252, Pte., k. in a., F. & F., 20/10/18.
Chapman, John, b. St. Mary's, Lancaster, e. Lancaster, 32881, L/Cpl., k. in a., F. & F., 9/10/17, formerly 6519, Hussars.
Chatwin, Arthur Josiah, b. Smethwick, Staffs, e. Birmingham (Smethwick), 946, Pte., k. in a., F. & F., 31/8/16.
Clague, William Edward, b. Newport Pagnell, Bucks, e. Birmingham (Newport Pagnell), 291, Pte., k. in a., F. & F 27/7/16.

Clancy, Frank, e. Doncaster, Yorks, 23558, Pte., k. in a., F. & F., 27/10/17, formerly 173677, R.E.

Claridge, William, b. Louth, Lincs, e. Mexborough, Lincs, 48261, Pte., d., F. & F., 20/10/18, formerly 016902, R.A.S.C.

Clark, Stanley, Henry, b. Devonport, e. Plymouth, Devon (Devonport), 35254, Pte., d. of w., F. & F., 27/8/18.

Clarke, George Harold Bayldon, b. Lelas, Yorks, e. Bradford, Yorks, 48282, Pte., k. in a., F. & F., 23/8/18, formerly 017655, R.A.O.C.

Clarke, Herbert Rollason, b. Birmingham, e. Moseley, Birmingham (Bearwood, Birmingham), 1333, Pte., d. of w., F. & F., 3/8/16.

Clarkson, Charles, b. Redditch, Worcs, e. Birmingham (Redditch), 292, Cpl., d. of w., F. & F., 24/8/18.

Cleaver, Albert, b. Bretforton, Worcs, e. Worcester (Bretforton), 35255, Pte., k. in a., F. & F., 29/6/18.

Clement, Harold George, b. St. Paul's, Warwick, e. Leamington, Warwicks (Warwick), 548, Cpl., k. in a., F. & F., 9/10/17.

Coggane, Maurice, b. Bradford, Yorks, e. York (Harrogate, Yorks), 33908, L/Cpl., k. in a., F. & F., 27/9/18, formerly 2414, R.A.S.C.

Cogram, Samuel, b. Peckham, London, e. Camberwell, London (Peckham), 52262, Pte., k. in a., F. & F., 1/9/18, formerly 7013, Notts & Derby Regt.

Coldrick, Herbert, b. Bewdley, Worcs, e. Birmingham (Bewdley), 15/1600, Pte., k. in a., F. & F., 6/10/17.

Cole, Frederick William, b. Sutton Coldfield, Warwicks, e. Birmingham (Sutton Coldfield), 43452, Pte., k. in a., F. & F., 14/10/18.

Coleing, George, b. Aston, Birmingham, e. Birmingham, 540, Pte., d. of w., F. & F., 27/9/16.

Coley, Harold Bert, b. Dudley, Worcs, e. Birmingham (Dudley), 296, Pte., k. in a., F. & F., 25/12/15.

Collett, Sidney b. Coventry, Warwicks, e. Warwick (Coventry), 18137, Pte., d., F. & F., 28/1/17.

Collier, William Charles, b. Newbold-on-Avon, Warwicks, e. Rugby, Warwicks (Southam, Warwicks), 202908. Pte., k. in a., F. & F., 9/10/17.

Conyers, Joseph, b. Hunslet, Leeds, e. Birmingham (Hunslet), 129, Pte., k. in a., F. & F., 2/7/17.

Cook, Oliver, b. Kettlebrook, Warwicks, e. Tamworth, Warwicks (Kettlebrook), 202995, Pte., k. in a., F. & F., 27/10/17, formerly 18109, N. Staffs Regt.

Cook, William James, b. St. John's, Harborne, Birmingham, e. Birmingham (Harborne), 6, L/Cpl., k. in a., F. & F., 6/10/17.

Cooke, Harold William, b. Studley, Warwicks, e. Birmingham (Studley), 131, Pte., d., F. & F., 24/6/16.

Cooper, Frederick Augustus, b. Moor Common, Marlow, Bucks, e. High Wycombe, Bucks (Uxbridge, Middx.), 43206, Pte., d. of w., F. & F., 4/9/18, formerly 7498, R. Berks Regt.

Cooper, Hubert, b. Moseley, Birmingham, e. Birmingham, (Moseley), 136, Pte., k. in a., F. & F., 31/8/16

Cope, Thomas, b. Sparkbrook, Birmingham, e. Birmingham (Sparkbrook), 267595, Pte., d., F. & F., 27/6/18.

Cornish, John Adams, b. Callington, Cornwall e. Birmingham (Callington), 542, Sgt., k. in a., F. & F., 27/7/16.

Cox, Aubrey Samuel, b. Lichfield, Staffs, e. Taunton, Som. (Tiverton, Devon), 36471, Pte., d. of w., F. & F., 9/11/18, formerly 8/27784, Hants Regt.

Coxall, Percy, b. Stanish, Wigan, Lancs, e. Blackpool, Lancs, 245156, Pte., k. in a., F. & F., 2/9/18, formerly 3795, King's Liverpool Regt.

Craner, George Frederick, b. St. Mary's, Studley, Warwicks, e. Birmingham (Studley), 294, Pte., d. of w., F. & F., 3/10/16.

Creasey, Walter, b. Market Rasen, Lincs, e. Birmingham, 807, C.S.M., k. in a., F. & F., 14/4/17.

Crees, Fred, b. West Bromwich, Staffs, e. Oldbury, Worcs, 30070, Pte., k. in a., F. & F., 11/5/17, formerly 27886, Worc. Regt.

Cresswell, Ernest Frank, b. Birmingham, e. Birmingham, 35260, Pte., k. in a., F. & F., 27/9/18.

Cross, Harry, b. St. George's, Birmingham, e. Birmingham (Hockley, Birmingham), 795, Pte., k. in a., F. & F., 16/5/16.

Crosswell, John Tracey, e. Warwick (Emscote, Warwick), 242390, Pte., k. in a., F. & F., 2/10/18.

Crump, Thomas, b. Stourbridge, Worcs, e. Stourbridge, 27771, Pte., k. in a., F. & F., 21/8/18, formerly 5079, Worc. Regt.

Culley, Arthur, b. Calne, Wilts, e. Chippenham, Wilts (Calne), 35262, Pte., k. in a., F. & F., 23/8/18.

Curtis, Charles William, b. Stockton, Warwicks, e. Rugby, Warwicks (Bilton, Warwicks), 21120, Pte., d. of w., F. & F., 8/10/17.

Daft, Bert, e. Birmingham (Stirchley, Birmingham), 50208, Pte., k. in a., F. & F., 20/4/18, formerly 326201, Worc. Regt.

Dance, Lawrence Wilfred, b. Birchfield, Birmingham, e. Birmingham (Birchfield), 18, Pte., d. of w., F. & F., 3/9/16.

Darby, Dennis Bennett, b. Blackheath, Staffs, e. Birmingham (Blackheath), 16/1940, Pte., k. in a., F. & F., 27/10/17.

Dark, Eric, b. Grangetown, Yorks e. Stockton-on-Tees, Durham (Grangetown), 48400, Pte., k. in a., F. & F., 21/8/18, formerly R/258047, R.A.S.C.

Darlow, John Charles, b. Bubbenhall, Warwicks, e. Warwick (Bubbenhall), 18129, Pte., k. in a., F. & F., 3/9/16.

Davies, Alfred James, b. Birmingham, e. Birmingham (Erdington, Birmingham), 24863, Pte., k. in a., F. & F., 27/9/18.

Davies, Frederick John, b. Bideford, Devon, e. Barnstaple, Devon (Bideford), 35264, Pte., k. in a., F. & F., 27/9/18.

Davies, William Edward, b. Wolverhampton, Staffs, e. Birmingham (Wolverhampton), 309, Cpl., k. in a., F. & F., 26/9/16.

Davis, Albert, b. Nechells, Birmingham, e. Birmingham, 27082, Pte., d. of w., F. & F., 12/5/17.

Davis, Archibald Thomas, b. St. Paul's, Worcester, e. Worcester, 30069, Pte., k. in a., F. & F., 26/9/16, formerly 27927, Worcs. Regt.

Daws, Charles, b. Birmingham, e. Birmingham, 13466, Pte., k. in a., F. & F., 6/10/17.

Deacon, William, b. Nuneaton, Warwicks, e. Nuneaton, 35265, Pte., d., F. & F. 8/10/18.

Dean, Charles Conrad, b. Brierley Hill, Staffs, e. Birmingham (Amblecote, Worcs), 16/1769, Pte., d. of w., F. & F., 15/9/16.

Dean, Robert Warren, b. Wollaston, Stourbridge, Worcs, e. Birmingham (Amblecote, Worcs), 313, Sgt., k. in a., F. & F., 2/9/16.

Deeming, Joseph, b. Atherstone, Warwicks, e. Atherstone, 268338, Pte., k. in a., F. & F., 29/9/18.

Dent, Herbert, b. Watermillock, Cumberland e. Penrith, Cumberland, 36082, Pte., k. in a., F. & F., 20/10/18, formerly 4/22780, Ches. Regt.

Denton Arthur, b. Birmingham, e. Birmingham, 22376, Pte., d., F. & F., 8/4/17.

Denton, Frederick, b. Drayton Field, Oxford, e. Evesham, Worcs (Shipston-on-Stour, Worcs), 263010, Pte., k. in a., F. & F., 27/5/18, formerly 203719 Worc. Regt.

Derrick, Albert, b. Lower Weston, Bath, Som., e. Bath (Lower Weston), 35266, Pte., k. in a., F. & F., 27/9/18.

Derry, John Jordan, b. Hednesford, Staffs, e. Coventry, Warwicks (Brinklow, Warwicks), 20465, Pte., k. in a., F. & F., 15/5/18.

Derry, William Percival, b. Olton, Leominster, Herefordshire, e. Birmingham (Leominster), 552, Pte., d. of w., F. & F., 25/6/18.

Dexter, Charles, b. Atherstone, Warwicks, e. Nuneaton, Warwicks, 1629, Pte., k. in a., F. & F., 26/9/16.

Dickinson, Charlie, b. Salford, Lancs, e. Nuneaton, Warwicks, 13410, Pte., d. of w., F. & F., 19/11/17.

Disney, Harry, b. Carlton, Notts, e. Derby, 52214, Pte., d. of w., F. & F., 22/9/18, formerly 95425, Notts & Derby Regt.

Dixon, Jesse, b. Aston, Birmingham, e. Birmingham, 555, L/Cpl., k. in a., F. & F., 9/10/17.

Doggett, Thomas Herbert, b. Grafton, Wilts, e. Devizes, Wilts Stanton St. Bernard, Pewsey, Wilts), 35267, Pte., d. of w., F. & F., 24/8/18.

Dolphin, David, b. Inkberrow, Worcs, e. Warwick (Southhampton, Hants), 21242, A/C.S.M., d. of w., F. & F., 19/5/17.

Doughty, John, b. Birmingham, e. Birmingham (Hockley, Birmingham), 16/1600, Pte., k. in a., F. & F., 27/7/16.

Dowler, Albert, b. Birmingham, e. Birmingham 16/1771, Pte., k. in a., F. & F., 3/9/16

Downey, Andrew Thomas, b. Edgbaston, Birmingham, e. Birmingham, 808, Pte., k. in a., F. & F., 3/9/16.

Doyle Wilfred Joseph, b. Frankton, Warwicks, e. Warwicks (Frankton), 260281, Pte., k. in a., F. & F., 11/11/17, formerly 35567, Oxf. & Bucks L.I.

Draycott, Frederick Ernest, b. Windsor, Berks, e. Windsor, 50232, Pte., d. of w., F. & F., 27/5/18 formerly 39807, Worcs. Regt.

Duce, William, b. Wolverhampton, Staffs, e. Newbury, Berks (Limerick, Ireland), 28076, Pte., d. of w., F. & F., 30/9/18, formerly 27468, Hussars.

Dunbar, John Thomas, b. Hastings, Sussex, e. Hastings 17719, L/Sgt., d., F. & F., 26/11/16.

Dunning, Leonard David, b. Willesden, Middx., e. Aylesbury, Bucks (Chesham, Bucks), 35856, Pte., k. in a., F. & F., 23/8/18.

Eastman, Alfred, b. Pontypool, Mon., e. Worcester (Dudley, Worcs), 50242, Pte., d. of w., F. & F., 26/5/18, formerly 48260, Worcs. Regt.

Edwards, Albert John, b. Harborne, Birmingham, e. Birmingham (Harborne), 20, Pte., k. in a., F. & F., 9/10/17.

Edwards, George, b. Leek Wootton, Warwicks, e. Warwick (Leek Wootton), 21987, Pte., d. of w., F. & F., 11/10/17.

Edwards, Horace Maunder, b. Cheltenham, Glos., e. Birmingham (Cheltenham), 565, A/C.S.M., k. in a., F. & F., 20/4/17.

Elliott, Arthur Leslie, b. Smethwick, Staffs, e. Birmingham (Smethwick), 21, Pte., k. in a., F. & F., 10/5/17.

Elstub, John Edward, b. Castleford, Yorks, e. Pontefract, Yorks (Castleford), 52271, Pte., d. of w., F. & F., 2/9/18, formerly 106754, Notts & Derby Regt.

Emanuel, George, b. St. Lucia, West Indies, e. London (Bridlington, Yorks), 32835, Pte., d. of w., F. & F., 2/8/18, formerly 72188, R.A.S.C.

Ensor, Albert, b. Birmingham, e. Birmingham (Aston, Birmingham), 26223, Pte., k. in a., F. & F., 23/8/18.

Ettle, William, b. Bristol, Glos., e. Bristol, 23261, Pte., k. in a., F. & F., 30/6/17, formerly 29673, Glos. Regt.

Evans, Clifford, b. St. Saviour's, Birmingham, e. Birmingham (Handsworth, Birmingham), 200531, L/Cpl., k. in a., F. & F., 27/9/18.

Evenden, Walter, b. Maidstone, Kent, e. Maidstone, 29900, Pte., k. in a., F. & F., 11/11/17, formerly 5054, Lancers.

Everson, Sidney Walter, b. Plumstead, London, e. London (Brixton, London), 48424, Cpl., d. of w., F. & F., 22/8/18, formerly 012044, R.A.O.C.

Ewings, Walter, b. Stirchley, Birmingham, e. Moseley Barracks, Birmingham (King's Heath, Birmingham), 1285, Pte., k. in a., F. & F., 10/5/17.

Facer, Arthur, b. Moseley, Birmingham, e. Birmingham, 826, Pte., k. in a., F. & F., 21/12/15.

Farndon, Allen Joseph, b. Castle Donnington, Yorks, e. Birmingham (Castle Donnington), 145, Pte., d. of w., F. & F., 28/7/16.

Farrar, Lewis, b. E. Dulwich, Surrey, e. London (East Grinstead, Sussex), 33927, Pte., d. of w., F. & F., 7/2/18, formerly 103754, R.A.S.C.

Fawke, John Edwin, b. Kidderminster, Worcs, e. Birmingham, 14/1730, Pte., k. in a., F. & F., 16/4/17.

Fear, Arthur Cecil, b. St. John's, Weston-super-Mare, Som., e. Weston-super-Mare (Shrewsbury, Salop), 34221, Cpl., k. in a., F. & F., 1/9/18, formerly 926, Dragoon Gds.

Fenney, Joseph, b. St. Helen's, Lancs, e. St. Helen's, 29609, Pte., d. of w., F. & F., 27/9/18, formerly 40197, S. Lancs Regt.

Finch , Henry Charles, b. Halstead, Essex, e. Deptford, Kent (Walthamstow, Essex), 32932, Pte., k. in a., F. & F., 9/10/17, formerly 21054, Hussars.

Findon, Frank Leonard, b. Handsworth, Staffs, e. Birmingham, 68, Pte., k. in a., F. & F., 26/9/16.

Fisher, Joseph, e. Birmingham, 201337, Pte., k. in a., F. & F., 26/5/18.

Fitter, Richard, b. St. Martin's, Birmingham, e. Birmingham (Bournemouth, Hants), 16/1596, Pte., d. of w., F. & F., 22/9/16.

Fletcher, George William, b. Worksop, Notts, e.Worksop, 52215, Pte., k. in a., F. & F., 1/9/18, formerly 95060, Notts & Derby Regt.

Floyd, Arthur Henry, b. Birmingham, e. Birmingham, 16/1644, Pte., k. in a., F. & F., 26/4/18.

Ford, Henry, b. Bootle, Liverpool, e. Morecambe, Lancs (Liverpool), 4617, Cpl., k. in a., F. & F., 27/9/18.

Fortin, Eric Owen, b. Sawston, Cambridge, e. Birmingham (Cambridge), 571, Pte., d. of w., F. & F., 25/5/16.

Foster, Arnold, b. Otley, Yorks, e. Birmingham (Otley), 27679, Pte., d. of w., F. & F., 23/10/18.

Francis, Alfred, b. Clown, Derby, e. Mansfield, Notts, 238048, Pte., k. in a., F. & F., 23/8/18, formerly 305771, Notts & Derby Regt.

French, Albert William, b. London, e. Manchester (Blackpool, Lancs), 23458, Pte., k. in a., F. & F., 14/5/17, formerly 444483, R.E.

Fry, Frederick Charles, b. West Chinnock, Som., e. Crewkerne, Som. (Middle Chinnock), 260238, Pte., k. in a., F. & F., 27/9/18, formerly 30797, Som. L.I.

Fry, Henry, b. Cardiff, Glam., e. Cardiff, 36038, Pte., k. in a., F. & F., 23/8/18, formerly 41443, Ches. Regt.

Gardner, Albert John, b. Handswworth, Staffs, e. Birmingham (Edgbaston, Birmingham), 15/1593, Pte., k. in a., F. & F., 20/4/17.

Garrett, David, b. Banbury, Oxon, e. Warwick (Longford, Coventry, Warwicks), 22414, Pte., d. of w., F. & F., 23/12/17.

Gasser, Frederick John, e. Gloucester (Sharpness, Glos.), 27611, L/Cpl., k. in a., F. & F., 29/9/18, formerly 2363, Glos. Hussars.

Genders, Tom Atherstone, b. Birmingham, e. Birmingham, 28537, Pte., d. of w., F. & F., 30/4/17.

Georgeson, George Frederick, b. Burscough, Lancs, e. Ormskirk, Lancs (Burscough), 36041, Pte., k. in a., F. & F., 1/9/18, formerly 3/3077, Ches. Regt.

German, William Lewis, b. St. Peter's, Wolverhampton, Staffs, e. Birmingham (Wolverhampton), 329, Pte., k. in a., F. & F., 9/10/17.

Gibbon, Edward, b. West Hartlepool, Durham, e. North Shields, Durham (West Hartlepool), 21134, Pte., k. in a., F. & F., 3/9/16, formerly 1407, Durham L.I.

Gibbs, Edward Lewis, b. Birmingham, e. Birmingham (Saltley, Birmingham), 34768, L/Cpl., d. of w., F. & F., 5/5/18, formerly 204358, Oxf. & Bucks L.I.

Gibbs, Hedley, b. Brockley, Glos., e. Moseley, Birmingham (Sparkhill, Birmingham), 1231, Pte., k. in a., F. & F., 27/7/16.

Gibbs, William, b. Birmingham, e. Birmingham (Perry Barr, Staffs), 16/1359, Pte., k. in a., F. & F., 23/1/16.

Gilmore, David Henry, b. Southam, Warwicks, e. Southam, 18893, L/Cpl., d. of w., F. & F., 12/5/17.

Glover, Walter, b. Birmingham, e. Birmingham (Small Heath, Birmingham), 22433, Pte., d. of w., F. & F., 17/10/17.

Glynn, Thomas Nicholas, b. Ashted, Warwicks, e. Birmingham (Saltley, Birmingham), 22749, Pte., k. in a., F. & F., 9/10/17.

Godderidge, John William, b. Nuneaton, Warwicks, e. Nuneaton, 23716, Pte., k. in a., F. & F., 9/10/17.

Golding, Thomas, b. Birmingham, e. Birmingham, 12009, Pte., k. in a., F. & F., 9/10/17.

Goodby, Herbert, b. Aston, Birmingham, e. Birmingham, 578, Sgt., k. in a., F. & F., 16/4/17.

Graham, Thomas, b. Lamplugh, Cumberland, e. Frizington, Cumberland (Lamplugh), 48270, Pte., k. in a., F. & F., 23/8/18, formerly T3/022631, R.A.S.C.

Grant, John William, b. Stoke Canon, Devon, e. Newton Abbot, Devon (Broadhempstone, Devon), 35284, Pte., k. in a., F. & F., 23/8/18.

Green Albert Howard, e. Birmingham (Aston, Birmingham), 28531, Pte., k. in a., F. & F., 9/10/17.

Green, Harold, b. Edgbaston, Birmingham, e. Moseley, Birmingham (Balsall Heath, Birmingham), 1205, Pte., k. in a., F. & F., 24/7/16.

Greenfield, Charles Richard, b. Heckmondwike, Yorks, e. Wakefield, Yorks (Pontefract, Yorks), 23654, Pte., k. in a., F. & F., 21/8/18, formerly 170357, R.E.

Greenhalgh, Harry, b. Bolton, Lancs, e. Birmingham (Dudley, Worcs), 14/1663, Pte., k. in a., F. & F., 3/9/16.

Greenwood, John Ledville, b. Hertford, e. Gloucester (Newham, Glos.), 27663, Pte., k. in a., F. & F., 10/5/17, formerly 3482, Glos. Hussars.

Griffin, Thomas Edward, b. Coventry, Warwicks, e. Coventry, 22678, Pte., d. of w., F. & F., 14/3/17.

Griffin, William Gilbert, b. King's Heath, Birmingham, e. Birmingham (Cotteridge, Birmingham), 16/1572, L/Cpl., d. of w., F. & F., 18/10/17.

Griffiths, William Andrew, b. Swansea, Glam., e. Cardiff, Glam., 48264, Pte., d. of w., F. & F., 8/10/18, formerly 028169, R.A.S.C.

Grimes, Albert Spencer, b. All Saints, Birmingham, e. Birmingham (Erdington, Birmingham), 834, L/Cpl., k. in a., F. & F., 3/9/16.

Gripton, Thomas Leslie, b. Kidderminster, Worcs, e. Birmingham (Kidderminster), 15/1614, Pte., k. in a., F. & F., 10/10/17.

Grove, Frank William, b. Wilnecote, Warwicks, e. Birmingham (Shustoke, Warwicks), 331, Sgt., k. in a., F. & F., 1/1/16.

Groves, Albert Edward, b. Newcastle-under-Lyme, Staffs, e. Birmingham (Balsall Heath, Birmingham), 22562, Pte., k. in a., F. & F., 14/5/17.

Groves, John Wilfred, b. Rotton Park, Birmingham, e. Birmingham (Rotton Park), 200491, L/Cpl., d. of w., F. & F., 6/9/18.

Guest, William, b West Bromwich, Staffs, e. Oldbury, Staffs, 30086, L/Sgt., d., F. & F., 26/8/17, formerly 27862, Worcs Regt.

Gulliver, Arthur, b. Broadwell, Warwicks, e. Southam, Warwicks (Broadwell), 21122, Pte., k. in a., F. & F., 6/10/17.

Gurden, Ernest, b. Harbury, Warwicks, e. Southam, Warwicks (Harbury), 20308, Pte., d. of w., F. & F., 13/5/17.

Haggett, Tom Wellington, b. Newport, Mon., e. Gloucester (Newport), 27666, Pte., k. in a., F. & F., 16/4/17, formerly 3356, R. Glos. Hussars.

Hale, Charles, b. St. Pancras, London, e. Birmingham (London), 586, L/Cpl., k. in a., F. & F., 25/7/16.

Halford, Bert, b. St. Paul's, Leamington, Warwicks, e. Leamington, 882, Pte., k. in a., F. & F., 3/9/16.

Hall, Walter, b. Sheffield, Yorks, e. Sheffield, 48428, Pte., k. in a., F. & F., 14/10/18, formerly 043920, R.A.O.C.

Hallgarth, Albert, b. Birmingham, e. Birmingham (Aston, Birmingham), 15/1590, Pte., k. in a., F. & F., 3/9/16.

Hamilton, Douglas, b. Edinburgh, e. Edinburgh, 35714, Pte., k. in a., F. & F., 15/6/18, formerly 3889, Fife & Forfar Yeo.

Hammett, Robert Henry, b. Monmouth, e. Birmingham (Newport, Mon.), 1833, Pte., d. of w., F. & F., 25/9/16.

Hands, George Edward Joseph, b. Birmingham, e. Birmingham, 22375, Pte., k. in a., F. & F., 30/6/17.

Hands, Reginald, b. Stratford-on-Avon, Warwicks, e. Birmingham (Stratford-on-Avon), 41, Pte., k. in a., F. & F., 27/4/16.

Harper, Frank, e. Birmingham (Aston, Birmingham), 15081, Pte., k. in a., F. & F., 1/9/18.

Harris, George, b. St. Stephen's, Birmingham, e. Birmingham (Handsworth, Staffs), 341, L/Cpl., k. in a., F. & F., 16/4/17.

Harris, Joseph, b. Shipston-on-Stour, Warwicks, e. Worcester (Evesham, Worcs), 30098, Pte., k. in a., F. & F., 3/9/16, formerly 30418, Worcs Regt.

Harris, Sidney, b. Illsgan, Cornwall, e. Nuneaton, Warwicks, 267938, Pte., k. in a., F. & F., 26/10/18.

Hart, Archibald, b. Barony, Lanark, e. London (Bridge-of-Weir, Renfrew), 33860, Pte., d. of w., F. & F., 27/1/19, formerly 073061, R.A.S.C.

Hartwell, Herbert, b. Maunton Beauchamp, Worcs, e. Worcester (Churchill, Worcs), 244152, Pte., k. in a., F. & F., 25/4/18, formerly 4193, Worcs Regt.

Harvey, Frank, b. Birmingham, e. Birmingham, 17450, Pte., d. of w., F. & F., 2/9/16.

Harvey, Frederick William, b. Nuneaton, Warwicks, e. Nuneaton, 17110, Pte., k. in a., F. & F., 13/10/18.

Hastings, Ernest Harry, b. Birmingham, e. Birmingham (Sparkbrook, Birmingham), 16/1711, Pte., k. in a., F. & F., 24/7/16.

Hawley, George, e. Nottingham, 245150, Pte., k. in a., F. & F., 2/9/18, formerly 5150, Notts & Derby Regt.

Hayes, Leonard, b. Birmingham, e. Birmingham (King's Heath, Birmingham), 22381, Pte., k. in a., F. & F., 9/10/17.

Haynes, John Henry, b. Wellesbourne, Warwicks, e. Warwick (Stratford-on-Avon, Warwicks), 18208, Pte., k. in a., F. & F., 2/7/17.

Hayward, Frederick, b. Boughton-Monchelsea, Kent, e. Canterbury (East Farleigh, Kent), 32936, Pte., k. in a., F. & F., 9/10/17, formerly 2570, Hussars.

Hazlewood, Joseph William, b. St. Mary's, Stafford, e. Birmingham (Stafford), 169, Pte., k. in a., F. & F., 9/10/17.

Heafield, John Edward, b. Birmingham, e. Birmingham (Handsworth, Staffs), 15/1598, Pte., k. in a., F. & F., 23/8/18.

Hemming, George Henry, b. Birmingham, e. Birmingham (Edgbaston, Birmingham), 15/1595, Pte., k. in a., F. & F., 14/5/17.

Herbert, Leslie Stafford, b. Barnwood, Glos., e. Gloucester (Hugglecote, Glos.), 27668, Pte., d., F. & F., 14/5/17, formerly 2252, R. Glos. Yeo.

Heywood, William, b. Warrington, Lancs, e. Warrington, 36459, Cpl., k. in a., F. & F., 2/9/18, formerly 28784, South Lancs Regt.

Hicklin, Leonard, b. Ocker Hill, Staffs, e. Hartford, Ches. (Ocker Hill), 36399, L/Cpl., k. in a., F. & F., 24/8/18, formerly 11063, Ches. Regt.

Hicks, Leonard, b. Ladywood, Birmingham, e. Birmingham (Harborne, Birmingham), 893, Pte., k. in a., F. & F., 10/4/16.

Higgins, Alfred Charles, e. Gloucester (Hatfield, Glos.), 27669, Pte., k. in a., F. & F., 9/11/16, formerly 2781, R. Glos. Yeo.

Hildage, Philip, e. Altrincham, Ches., 260421, Pte., k. in a., F. & F., 27/9/18, formerly 240735, Ches Regt.

Hill, Gordon, b. Sunderland, Durham, e. Birkenhead, Ches. (Lower Tranmere, Ches.), 36472, Pte., k. in a., F. & F., 1/9/18.
Hill, John Henry, b. St. Martin's, Birmingham, e. Birmingham (Saltley, Birmingham), 16/1712, Pte., k. in a., F. & F., 27/7/16.
Hodgers, Percy William, b. St. Mary's, Chester, e. Hereford, 32865, Pte., k. in a., F. & F., 9/10/17, formerly H/4987, Hussars.
Hodgkins, Harry, b. Nechells, Birmingham, e. Birmingham (Handsworth, Staffs), 16/1636, Pte., d. of w., F. & F., 4/10/16.
Hodkinson, Henry, b. St. Helens, Lancs, e. Warrington, Lancs (St. Helens), 36404, Pte., k. in a., F. & F., 23/8/18, formerly 62679, Manchester Regt.
Hodson, Percival Clifford, b. Cheltenham, Glos., e. Willesden, London, 29908, Pte., k. in a., F. & F., 8/10/17, formerly 8523, Lancers.
Holland, Arthur, b. Stockport, Ches., e. Stockport, 36411, Pte., k. in a., F. & F., 1/9/18, formerly 245017, R.F.A.
Hollins, Harold, b. Manchester, e. Manchester (Hulme, Manchester), 20633, Pte., k. in a., F. & F., 9/10/17, formerly 61621, R.A.M.C.
Holt, Frank Lacey, b. Small Heath, Birmingham, e. Birmingham (Small Heath), 884, Cpl., k. in a., F. & F., 26/9/16.
Hooper, Harry Edward, b. Newtown, Montgomery, e. Welshpool, Montgomery (Kerry, Montgomery), 36042, Pte., k. in a., F. & F., 27/9/18, formerly 21913, Ches. Regt.
Hope, Robert William, b. Lanercost, Carlisle, e. Birmingham (Lanercost), 1844, L/Cpl., k. in a., F. & F., 27/9/18.
Hopkins, Alfred James, b. Ladywood, Birmingham, e. Birmingham (Small Heath, Birmingham), 3241, L/Cpl., k. in a., F. & F., 16/4/17.
Horne, Robert, b. Nottingham, e. Nottingham (Radford, Nottingham), 27361, Pte., k. in a., F. & F., 2/9/18, formerly 34830, Notts & Derby Regt.
Howe, Charles Frederick, b. Plymouth, Devon, e. Birmingham (Plymouth), 599, Pte., k. in a., F. & F., 3/9/16.
Howlett, William Rathbone, b. Chapel End, Warwicks, e. Nuneaton, Warwicks, 28524, Pte., k. in a., F. & F., 28/6/17.
Hughes, Albert, b. Swansea, Glam., e. Moseley, Birmingham (Ladywood, Birmingham), 1156, Sgt., k. in a., F. & F., 6/10/17.
Hughes, Frederick John, b. Renbury, Ches., e. Birmingham (Newport, Salop), 15/1434, Pte., k. in a., F. & F., 9/11/16.
Hughes, William, b. Colwyn Bay, Denbigh, e. Wrexham, Denbigh (Colwyn Bay), 36044, Pte., k. in a., F. & F., 23/8/18, formerly 4/23417, Ches. Regt.
Humphries, John, b. Aston, Birmingham, e. Birmingham (Aston), 364, Pte., d. of w., F. & F., 21/9/16.
Huntley, Samuel, b. Birmingham, e. Birmingham, 16/1672, Pte., k. in a., F. & F., 27/7/16.
Hyett, Arthur, b. Moreton Hampstead, Devon, e. Exeter, Devon (Moreton Hampstead), 33163, Pte., k. in a., F. & F., 23/8/18 formerly 13769, Hussars.
Iddon, Robert, b. Preston, Lancs, e. Morecambe, Lancs (Lancaster), 48434, Pte., d. of w., F. & F., 20/10/18, formerly 04348, R.A.O.C.
Ince, Albert, b. Cripplegate, London, e. Croydon, Surrey (Thornton Heath, Surrey), 325054, Pte., k. in a., F. & F., 20/7/18, formerly 6155, Suffolk Regt.
Ireland, George, b. Toddington, Glos., e. Birmingham (Toddington), 369, Pte., d. of w., F. & F., 29/6/17.
Ireland, William Sinclair, b. Dundee, Forfarshire, e. London (Dundee), 43236, Pte., d., F. & F., 10/2/18, formerly 137031, R.E.
Ivens, Martin Edward, b. St. Mary's, Warwick, e. Leamington, Warwicks (Warwick), 007, A/C.S.M., k. in a., F. & F., 3/9/16.
Jackson, Thomas Percy, b. Coventry, Warwicks, e. Coventry, 24869, Pte., d. of w., F. & F., 8/9/18.
Jacob, Robert Goldie, b. Gillingham, Kent, e. Roberts Heights, Transvaal (Shepherd's Bush, London), 33242, L/Cpl., k. in a., F. & F., 24/8/18, formerly 6569, Hussars.
James, Charles Henry, b. Pimlico, Middx., e. Fulham, London, 48288, L/Cpl., k. in a., F. & F., 23/8/18, formerly 011189, R.A.O.C.
James, Harry, b. St. Stephen's, Birmingham, e. Birmingham, 200442, Pte., k. in a., F. & F., 9/10/17.
James, John Milton, b. Hailes, Cheltenham, Glos., e. Birmingham (Hailes), 171, Pte., k. in a., F. & F., 23/1/16.
James, Sidney William, b. Parkstone, Dorset, e. Poole, Dorset (Parkstone), 35151, Pte., k. in a., F. & F., 2/9/18.
James, William Hubert, b. St. Issells, Pembroke, e. Haverfordwest, Pembroke, 36053, Pte., k. in a., F. & F., 21/8/18, formerly 4/9038, Ches. Regt.
Jarrett, Frank, b. Horstead, Sussex, e. Bristol, Glos., 48418, Pte., k. in a., F. & F., 23/8/18, formerly T/30751, R.A.S.C.
Jarvis, William Edward, b. Thanington, Canterbury, Kent, e. Birmingham (Canterbury), 51, Cpl., d., F. & F., 16/9/18, M.M.
Jeffs, William Evelyn Cecil, b. St. Mary's, Birmingham, e. Birmingham (Yardley, Birmingham), 7273, Pte., k. in a., F. & F., 23/8/18.
Jenkinson, Alfred Arnold, b. Handsworth, Birmingham, e. Birmingham (Handsworth), 372, Pte., k. in a., F. & F., 27/7/16.
Jenkinson, Thomas, b. St. Michael's, Coventry, Warwicks, e. Coventry, 2795, Cpl., k. in a., F. & F., 9/10/17.
Jenks William Ivor Jeffries, b. Birmingham, e. Birmingham (Bournville, Birmingham), 16/1626, Pte., d. of w., F. & F., 14/5/18.
Jennings, George Henry, b. Builth, Breconshire, e. Birmingham (Aston, Birmingham), 39766, L/Sgt., k. in a., F. & F., 27/9/18, formerly 29150, Glos. Regt.
Jennings, Percy Douglas, b. Hereford, e. Birmingham (Hereford), 375, Pte., k. in a., F. & F., 27/7/16.
Johnson, Frederick, b. Daventry, Northants, e. Atherstone, Warwicks (Kettering, Northants), 22693, Pte., k. in a., F. & F., 9/10/17.
Johnson, Montague, b. Coventry, Warwicks, e. Birmingham (Coventry), 15/1576, Pte., k. in a., F. & F., 3/9/16.
Johnson, Sidney, b. Birmingham, e. Moseley Barracks, Birmingham (Sparkhill, Birmingham), 1176, Pte., k. in a., F. & F., 25/12/15.
Jolly, John, b. Aston, Birmingham, e. Birmingham, 28497, Sgt., k. in a., F. & F., 23/8/18.
Jones, Albert, b. Birmingham, e. Birmingham (Edgbaston, Birmingham), 16/1646, Pte., k. in a., F. & F., 26/9/16.
Jones, Elwy, b. Moseley, Birmingham, e. Birmingham (Moseley), 174, L/Cpl., k. in a., F. & F., 3/9/16.
Jones, Ernest Frederick, b. St. Martin's, Birmingham, e. Birmingham (Selly Oak, Birmingham), 16/1757, Pte., k. in a., F. & F., 27/7/16.
Jones, Frederick, b. Aston, Birmingham, e. Birmingham (Aston), 910, Pte., k. in a., F. & F., 27/7/16.
Jones, Frederick William, b. Birmingham, e. Birmingham (Aston, Birmingham), 1616, Pte., d. of w., F. & F., 3/2/18.
Jones, George Arthur, b. Weston, Yorks, e. Leamington, Warwicks (Weston), 615, A/Cpl., k. in a., F. & F., 26/9/16.
Jones John Bamforth, b. Apperley Bridge, Yorks, e. Wigan, Lancs (Ellesmere Port, Ches.), 18117, L/Cpl., d. of w., F. & F., 26/9/16.
Jones, James Sydney, b. Cradley Heath, Staffs, e. Birmingham (Cradley Heath), 177, Sgt., k. in a., F. & F., 10/5/17.
Jones, Jeremiah, b. Cardiff, Glam., e. Pontypool, Mon. (Ammanford, Carmarthen), 50256, Pte., d. of w., F. & F., 24/8/18, formerly 57225, Worcs Regt.
Jones, John Samuel, b. Dudley, Worcs, e. Dudley, 30075, Pte., k. in a., F. & F., 1/1/17, formerly 27605, Worcs Regt.
Jones, Richard, b. Birmingham, e. Birmingham, 16/1627, Pte., k. in a., F. & F., 25/7/16.
Jones, Thomas Edward, b. Birmingham, e. Birmingham (Ladywood, Birmingham), 22703, Pte., k. in a., F. & F., 9/10/17.
Jones, Sydney, b. Handsworth, Birmingham, e. Birmingham, 917, L/Cpl., d. of w., F. & F., 30/11/16.
Jordon, Joseph George, b. Wing, Bucks, e. Aylesbury, Bucks (Leighton Buzzard, Beds), 32938, Pte., k. in a., F. & F., 9/10/17, formerly 29748, Hussars.
Jordan, James Victor Theodore, b. Keswick, Cumberland, e. Birmingham (Erdington, Birmingham), 22558, Pte., k. in a., F. & F., 9/10/17.
Keighley, Joseph, b. Chapeltown, Leeds, e. Birmingham (Chapeltown), 621, Pte., k. in a., F. & F., 27/7/16.
Kelly, Frank, b. St. John's, Stourbridge, Worcs, e. Birmingham (Stourbridge), 383, Pte., k. in a., F. & F., 6/4/17.
Kelly, Richard Frederick, b. Ballybraik, Co. Dublin, e. Coventry, Warwicks (Allesley, Warwicks), 20324, Pte., d. of w., F. & F., 11/5/17.
King, Frank, b. Henham, Essex, e. Birmingham (Erdington, Birmingham), 1321, Pte., d. of w., F. & F., 24/12/15.
King, Horace, b. Brill, Bucks, e. Willesden, London, N.W. (Harlesden, London, N.W.), 260273, Pte., k. in a., F. & F., 11/11/17, formerly 2832, Oxf. Yeo.
Kirkham, John, b. Manchester, Lancs, e. Manchester, 36491, Pte., k. in a., F. & F., 28/9/18, formerly 6137, Ches. Regt.
Kneale, Fernie, b. Dudley, Worcs, e. Dudley, 30076, Pte., k. in a., F. & F., 3/9/16, formerly 27568, Worcs Regt.
Knight, Alfred James Leonard, b. Duddeston, Birmingham, e. Birmingham (Smethwick, Staffs), 919, L/Cpl., k. in a., F. & F., 27/2/17.
Knight, Ralph, b. St. Andrew's, Walsall, Staffs, e. Walsall, 48405, Pte., k. in a., F. & F., 23/8/18, formerly 11490, R.A.S.C.
Knowles, Frederick, b. Quarry Bank, Worcs, e. Birmingham (Stourport, Worcs), 16/1392, L/Cpl., k. in a., F. & F., 3/9/16.
Lafford, Frederick Charles, b. Ross, Hereford, e. Ross, 27801, Pte., d. of w., F. & F., 10/4/17, formerly 24767, Shrops L.I.
Lamb, Andrew Francis, e. Stratford-on-Avon, Warwicks (Studley, Warwicks), 22743, Pte., d. of w., F. & F., 19/9/18.
Lambert, Benjamin Arthur, b. Stepney, London, e. Birmingham (London), 57, Cpl., k. in a., F. & F., 3/9/16.
Lambert, George William Henry Frederick, b. Nutfield, Surrey, e. Acton, London (Queen's Park, London, N.W.), 33871, Pte., k. in a., F. & F., 29/6/18, formerly M2/134235, R.A.S.C.
Lander, George, b. Norton Caves, Staffs, e. Birmingham (Smethwick, Staffs), 16/1539, Pte., k. in a., F. & F., 23/1/16.
Lane, Frederick John James, b. Birmingham, e. Birmingham, 18186, Pte., d. of w., F. & F., 27/9/18.
Langstone, Albert Henry, b. Worcester, e. Birmingham (Worcester), 16/1741, Pte., k. in a., F. & F., 3/9/16.
Langwell, Walter William, b. Attercliffe, Sheffield, Yorks, e. Birmingham (Attercliffe), 631, Sgt., d. of w., F. & F., 28/7/16.
Lawley, John William, b. Ellastone, Staffs, e. Lichfield, Staffs (Doveridge, Derby), 34227, L/Sgt., k. in a., F. & F., 24/5/18, formerly SE/4412, R.A.V.C.
Lay, Arthur Thomas, b. Bordesley, Birmingham, e. Birmingham, 4201, Pte., k. in a., F. & F., 3/9/16.
Layton, Arthur, e. Chester (Warrington, Lancs), 260417, Pte., k. in a., F. & F., 29/9/18, formerly 1774, Ches. Yeo.

Lea, Crofts Edward, b. Harborough Magna, Warwicks, e. Rugby, Warwicks (Monks Kirby, Warwicks), 21121, Pte., k. in a., F. & F., 30/7/17.
Lee, John, b. Small Heath, Birmingham, e. Birmingham, 387, Pte., k. in a., F. & F., 26/9/16.
Lee, John, b. All Saints, King's Lynn, Norfolk, e. Leamington, Warwicks, 753, Pte., k. in a., F. & F., 3/9/16.
Leonard Michael, b. Glasgow, Lanark, e. Edinburgh, 48419, Pte., d., F. & F., 23/8/18, formerly 2/1972, R.A.S.C.
Lewis, Ivo Frank, b. Birmingham, e. Birmingham (Handsworth, Birmingham), 16/1791, Pte., k. in a., F. & F., 9/10/17.
Lewis, John Grenville, b. Radnor, e. Birmingham, 23295, Pte., k. in a., F. & F., 5/10/17.
Liddiard, Basil, b. Bordesley, Birmingham, e. Birmingham (Small Heath, Birmingham), 931, L/Sgt., k. in a., F. & F., 3/9/16.
Livesey, Reginald Whitaker, b. Dukinfield, Ches., e. Ashton-under-Lyne, Lancs, 48301, Pte., d. of w., F. & F., 3/10/18, formerly 4/214886, R.A.S.C.
Lockington, Arthur James Ralph, b. Greenwich, Kent, e. London (Liverpool), 32861, Pte., d. of w., F. & F., 6/10/18, formerly 133891, R.E.
Lockyer, Alfred Thomas Herbert, e. Birmingham, 43218, L/Cpl., k. in a., F. & F., 23/8/18, formerly 3874, Queen's Own Oxf. Hussars.
Lovell, Frederick Howard Bertram, b. Birmingham, e. Birmingham, 15/1573, Pte., k. in a., F. & F., 27/7/16.
Lovering, George Samuel, b. Torrington, Devon, e. Oxford (Bristol, Glos.), 235177, Pte., d. of w., F. & F., 17/11/17, formerly 204502, Oxf. & Bucks L.I.
Lowe, Cyril Ernest, b. King's Heath, Birmingham, e. Birmingham, 937, L/Cpl., k. in a., F. & F., 9/10/17.
Lowe, John, b. Barrow-in-Furness, Lancs, e. Birmingham, 260297, Pte., k. in a., F. & F., 15/11/17, formerly 35582, Oxf. & Bucks L.I.
Lucas, Harry Edward, b. St. George's, Bristol, Glos., e. Bristol, 48431, Pte., k. in a., F. & F., 27/9/18, formerly 018349, R.A.O.C.
Lunn, Walter, b. Birmingham, e. Birmingham (Saltley, Birmingham), 32942, Pte., k. in a., F. & G., 9/10/17, formerly 29877, Hussars.
Lunn, Walter, b. Rotherhithe, Kent, e. Rotherhithe, 37894, Pte., k. in a., F. & F., 23/8/18, formerly 14325, E. Surrey Regt.
McGuire, Patrick, b. Burnley, e. Burnley, Lancs, 330991, Pte., k. in a., F. & F., 11/5/18, formerly 5156, E. Lancs Regt.
McKay, David, e. Stirling (Gargumock, Stirling), 35765, Pte., k. in a., F. & F., 27/9/18, formerly 150951, Scot. Horse.
McLean, William, b. Paisley, Renfrew, e. Glasgow, Lanark (Paisley), 33883, Pte., d. of w., F. & F., 29/6/18, formerly M/2/133096, R.A.S.C.
McLoughlin, Frederick, b. Dover, Kent, e. Canterbury, Kent (Dover), 38273, Pte., d. of w., F. & F., 23/8/18.
McReynolds, Thomas Anderson, b. Govan, Lanark, e. Glasgow, Lanark (Kings Mills, Co. Tyrone), 32788, Pte., k. in a., F. & F., 9/10/17, formerly GS/3369, Dragoons.
Madge, Walter, e. Launceston, Cornwall (Exeter, Devon), 23462, Pte., d., F. & F., 20/3/17, formerly 4605, R.E.
Malin, Frederick George, b. Stretton, Staffs, e. Birmingham (Moseley, Birmingham), 654, L/Sgt., k. in a., F. & F., 26/9/16.
Manning, Harold Frank Victor, b. Hunstanton, Norfolk, e. Birmingham (Coventry, Warwicks), 16/654, Pte., d., Home, 21/11/15.
Manning, Percy Herbert, b. Great Bentley, Essex, e. Colchester, Essex (Great Bentley), 27613, Pte., k. in a., F. & F., 27/9/18, formerly 5542, S. Staffs Regt.
Mansell, William James, b. London, e. Aylesbury, Bucks (Brill, Bucks), 50207, Pte., d. of w., F. & F., 23/8/18, formerly 203214, Worcs Regt., M.M.
Manton, Arthur James, b. Eastney, Portsmouth, e. Guildford, Surrey (Farncombe, Surrey), 32904, Pte., k. in a., F. & F., 4/10/17, formerly 1745, Hussars.
Margetts, Albert Victor Thomas, b. Cheltenham, Glos., e. Cheltenham, 50213, Cpl., k. in a., F. & F., 23/8/18, formerly 11882, Worcs Regt.
Marshall, Phillip, b. Coleshill, Warwicks, e. Birmingham (Coleshill), 638, Sgt., k. in a., F. & F., 28/10/17.
Marshall, William Thomas, b. Birmingham, e. Birmingham, 18018, Pte., d. of w., F. & F., 9/10/17.
Martin, Edward, b. Bow, Middx., e. Poplar, Middx. (Bow), 34874, Pte., k. in a., F. & F., 27/9/18.
Martin, Frederick, e. St. Peter's, Birkenhead, Ches., 32962, Pte., k. in a., F. & F., 27/10/17.
Massey, Alfred, b. Watton, Liverpool, e. Stafford (Wolverhampton, Staffs), 245148, Sgt., k. in a., F. & F., 2/9/18, formerly 3232, Staffs Yeo.
Matthews, Frederick William, e. Stratford-on-Avon, Warwicks, 300117, Pte., k. in a., F. & F., 21/8/18, formerly 7769, Norfolk Regt.
Matthews, Walter, b. Birmingham, e. Birmingham (Sparkbrook), 48379, Pte., k. in a., F. & F., 23/8/18, formerly 025612, R.A.O.C.
Matthias, Alfred, b. Wallacetown, Ayrshire, e. Ayr, 32633, Pte., k. in a., F. & F., 23/8/18, formerly 2570, Ayrshire Yeo.
Maycock, Arthur Edwin Richard, b. Fenny Compton, Warwicks, e. Fenny Compton, 22748, Pte., k. in a., F. & F., 22/4/17.
Maycock, George Trevor, b. Peshawar, India, e. Warwick, 16/1371, Sgt., k. in a., F. & F., 26/9/16.
Mayes, George Ernest, b. St. Barnabas, Birmingham, e. Birmingham, 951, Pte., d. of w., F. & F., 1/8/16.
Mayhew, Francis Henry, b. Littlemore, Oxon, e. Oxford (Littlemore), 50237, Pte., k. in a., F. & F., 27/9/18, formerly 46358, Worcs Regt.
Meacham, Alfred Ernest, b. Balsall Heath, Birmingham, e. Birmingham (Moseley, Birmingham), 644, Cpl., k. in a., F. & F., 9/10/17.
Medcalf, John James, b. Birmingham, e. Birmingham (Hockley, Birmingham), 1170, Pte., k. in a., F. & F., 27/7/16.
Meggs, George, b. Birmingham, e. Birmingham (Walsall, Staffs), 15/1666, Pte., k. in a., F. & F., 27/7/16.
Mellor, Charles William, b. St. John's, Worcester, e. Birmingham (Worcester), 69, Pte., k. in a., F. & F., 16/4/17.
Menzies, Ernest Reginald, b. Newcastle-on-Tyne, e. Birmingham (Winson Green, Birmingham), 14639, Pte., d. of w., F. & F., 5/9/18.
Millhouse, Theodore, b. St. Peter's, Bolton, Lancs, e. Bolton, 36496, Pte., d. of w., F. & F., 27/9/18, formerly 238015, N. Lancs Regt.
Mills, James Denley, b. London, e. Christchurch, Hants, 32631, Pte., k. in a., F. & F., 9/10/17, formerly 33148, Dragoons.
Millward, Walter Frederick, b. Ashted, Birmingham, e. Birmingham (Ashted), 189, Pte., k. in a., F. & F., 3/9/16.
Minahan, Harold Charles, b. Birmingham, e. Birmingham (Aston, Birmingham), 16/1651, Pte., k. in a., F. & F., 27/7/16.
Minchella, Michael, b. Croydon, Surrey, e. Aldershot, Hants (Reading, Berks), 34209, L/Cpl., k. in a., F. & F., 26/4/18, formerly 7850, Hussars.
Minton, Charles, b. St. George's, Kidderminster, Worcs, e. Birmingham (Kidderminster), 66, L/Cpl., d. of w., F. & F., 3/9/16.
Moorcroft, Harold, e. Lathorn Park, Lancs (Ormskirk, Lancs), 32472, Pte., k. in a., F. & F., 9/10/17, formerly 064273, R.A.S.C.
Moore, John, b. Shankhill, Co. Antrim, e. Belfast, 48247, Pte., d., F. & F., 23/8/18, formerly S/4/127965, R.A.S.C.
Moore, William Alfred, b. Bedworth, Warwicks, e. Bedworth, 17915, Pte., d. of w., F. & F., 26/9/16.
Moreton, Benjamin, b. Madeley, Salop, e. Birmingham (Aston, Birmingham), 17713, Pte., d. of w., F. & F., 29/6/18.
Morgan, Peter Swain, b. Kidderminster, Worcs, e. Moseley, Birmingham (Kidderminster), 856, R.S.M., d. of w., F. & F., 31/12/15.
Morgan, Vincent Harold, b. Stonehouse, Glos., e. Birmingham (Stonehouse), 408, Pte., k. in a., F. & F., 3/9/16.
Morton, William, b. Burbage, Derby, e. Buxton, Derby (Stalybridge, Ches.), 30432, Pte., k. in a., F. & F., 5/10/17, formerly 58952, R.E.
Morris, Arthur, b. Tipton, Staffs, e. Birmingham (Tipton), 650, Pte., d. of w., F. & F., 12/9/16.
Moston, Edward, b. Knutsford, Ches., e. London (Knutsford), 33896, Pte., k. in a., F. & F., 29/6/18, formerly M/2/018473, R.A.S.C.
Moy, Thomas William, b. Shoreditch, London, e. Islington, London (Upper Holloway, London), 32905, Pte., d. of w., F. & F., 9/10/17, formerly 11982, Hussars.
Muir, Leonard Ridley, b. Petsmoor, Yorks, e. Sheffield, Yorks, 48378, Pte., k. in a., F. & F., 3/9/18, formerly 28162, R.A.O.C.
Mulloy, Harry, b. Wolverhampton, Staffs, e. Wolverhampton, 57277, Pte., d. of w., F. & F., 4/11/18.
Nall, Thomas, b. Derby, e. Birmingham (Derby), 17999, Pte., k. in a., F. & F., 3/9/16.
Neate, Robert, b. St. Martin's, Birmingham, e. Birmingham (Washwood Heath, Birmingham), 22220, Pte., k. in a., F. & F., 28/6/17.
Newport, Charles William, b. St. Clement's, Oxford, e. Oxford, 34781, L/Cpl., k. in a., F. & F., 23/8/18, formerly 204373, Oxf. & Bucks L.I.
Newsham, Robert, b. Barrow-in-Furness, Lancs, e. Manchester, 32909, Pte., d. of w., F. & F., 11/10/17, formerly 25072, Hussars.
Nicholls, Harold, b. Ravenstone, Bucks, e. Bletchley, Bucks (Ravenstone), 260290, Pte., k. in a., F. & F., 11/11/17, formerly 35584, Oxf. & Bucks L.I.
Nicholls, William Charles, b. St. Mary's, Kidderminster, Worcs, e. Birmingham (Kidderminster), 193, Pte., k. in a., F. & F., 3/9/16.
Nicholson, Charles Herbert, b. Hull, Yorks, e. Hull, 48426, Pte., d. of w., F. & F., 24/9/18, formerly 025748, R.A.O.C.
Nokes, Benjamin, b. Birmingham, e. Birmingham, 34073, Pte., d., F. & F., 14/2/19, formerly 6571, Lancers.
Norton, Thomas, b. Birmingham, e. Birmingham, 932, Pte., k. in a., F. & F., 23/8/18.
Nurden, Alfred, b. St. Martin's, Birmingham, e. Birmingham, 70, Pte., k. in a., F. & F., 27/7/16.
Offord, Walter Charles, b. Acton, Suffolk, e. Bury St. Edmunds, Suffolk (Sudbury, Suffolk), 27241, Pte., k. in a., F. & F., 9/10/17, formerly 2802, Suffolk Regt.
O'Kane, John, e. Ayr, 32634, Pte., d. of w., F. & F., 19/10/17, formerly 2887, Ayr Yeo.
Orford, Robert John, b. Sparkhill, Birmingham, e. Birmingham (Handsworth, Birmingham), 959, Pte., d. of w., F. & F., 27/7/16.
Orme, Henry, b. Birmingham, e. Birmingham, 16/1912, Pte., k. in a., F. & F., 3/9/16.
Paddock, Richard Harold, b. Woodside, Dudley, Worcs, e. Birmingham (Dudley), 419, L/Cpl., k. in a., F. & F., 27/7/16.
Palmer, Thomas Henry, b. Colley Gate, Cradley Heath, Staffs, e. Birmingham (Cradley Heath), 435, Pte., k. in a., F. & F., 26/9/16.
Parfitt, Maurice, b. Pensnett, Staffs, e. Birmingham (Pensnett), 201, L/Cpl., d. of w., F. & F., 21/4/17.
Parkin, Harold, b. Barnsley, Yorks, e. Birmingham (Barnsley), 1327, Pte., k. in a., F. & F., 3/9/16.
Partridge, Harry, b. Birmingham, e. Birmingham (Small Heath, Birmingham), 14/1503, Pte., d. of w., F. & F., 1/7/17.

Patterson, Reginald Harry, b. Birmingham, e. Birmingham (Balsall Heath, Birmingham), 1166, Pte., k. in a., F. & F., 10/4/16.

Payne, John, b. Southport, Lancs, e. Birmingham (Southport), 417, Pte., k. in a., F. & F., 27/7/16.

Payne, Percy Owen, b. Alvaston, Derby, e. Bulford, Wilts (South Gosforth, Northumberland), 33913, L/Cpl., k. in a., F. & F., 28/5/18, formerly M2/054477, R.A.S.C.

Pearse, Harry, b. Edgbaston, Birmingham, e. Birmingham, 434, Pte., k. in a., F. & F., 26/9/16.

Peevor, Howard Edward, b. Cardiff, Glam, e. Birmingham (Small Heath, Birmingham), 668, Pte., k. in a., F. & F., 27/7/16.

Pegrum, Frederick William, b. Leyton, London, e. Leamington, Warwicks (Leyton), 16/961, Pte., k. in a., F. & F., 15/3/16.

Perkins, Howard, b. Blurton, Staffs, e. Birmingham (Blurton) 418, Pte., d. of w., F. & F., 27/7/16.

Perring, George Charles, b. St. Mary's, Torquay, Devon, e. Torquay, 48210, A/Sgt., k. in a., F. & F., 8/7/18, formerly S/34130, R.A.S.C.

Phillips, James John, b. Aberdaron, Carnarvon, e. Birmingham (Bilston, Staffs), 16/679, Sgt., d., Home, 14/11/15.

Philp, Philip, b. Stoke, Climsland, Cornwall, e. Bodmin, Cornwall (Stoke Climsland), 34782, Pte. k. in a., F. & F., 5/11/17, formerly 4985, D.C.L.I.

Pickersgill, Sidney, b. Edinburgh, e. Birmingham (Handsworth, Birmingham), 48285, Pte., k. in a., F. & F., 13/10/18, formerly 012138, R.A.O.C.

Piggott, Percy, b. Maes-y-cwmmer, Glam., e. Grove Park (Caerphilly, Glam.), 33022, Pte., d. of w., F. & F., 28/5/18, formerly M2/178490, R.A.S.C.

Pillinger, Fred, b. St. Bartholomew, Birmingham, e. Birmingham (Small Heath, Birmingham), 28682, Pte., k. in a., F. & F., 24/8/18.

Pink, Charles William, b. Rugeley, Staffs, e. Birmingham (Rugeley), 424, Cpl., k. in a., F. & F., 27/7/16.

Pink, Sidney Percy, b. Fareham, Hants, e. Portsmouth, Hants (Portsea, Hants), 35993, Pte., k. in a., F. & F., 18/10/18.

Pollard, Frederick John, b. Bow, London, e. London (West Ham, London), 32912, Pte., k. in a., F. & F., 13/4/18, formerly 4475, Hussars

Poole, Harry, b. Nuneaton, Warwicks, e. Nuneaton, 10132, L/Cpl., d., F. & F., 14/5/17.

Poole, Samuel, b. Coventry, Warwicks, e. Coventry, 18862, Pte., k. in a., F. & F., 9/10/17.

Porter, Alfred William, b. Gt. Somerford, Wilts, e. Malmesbury, Wilts (Startley, Wilts), 242636, Pte., d. of w., F. & F., 4/7/18.

Posnette, Harold Latimer, b. King's Norton, Birmingham, e. Birmingham (King's Norton), 431, Pte., d. of w., F. & F., 1/8/16.

Potter, Charles William, b. St. Steven's, Birmingham, e. Birmingham (Handsworth, Birmingham), 969, Pte., d. of w., F. & F., 27/7/16.

Potter, Frank, b. Birmingham, e. Birmingham, 16/1643, Pte., k. in a., F. & F., 16/4/17.

Potts, Thomas, b. Kidderminster, Worcs, e. Stourbridge, Worcs (Birmingham), 35994, Pte., k. in a., F. & F., 23/8/18.

Poulton, Ernest Edward, b. St. Mary's, Southampton, Hants, e. Southampton, 32913, Pte., k. in a., F. & F., 9/10/17, formerly 5817, Hussars.

Powell, Charles, b. Dudley, Worcs, e. Birmingham, 3630, Pte., k. in a., F. & F., 3/9/16.

Powell, Egbert, b. Leek, Staffs, e. Warwick (Coventry, Warwicks), 8930, Pte., k. in a., F. & F., 3/9/16.

Poynter, William Frank, b. Ashford, Kent, e. Stratford, London (West Ham, London), 36502, Pte., d. of w., F. & F., 27/9/18, formerly 506367, London Regt.

Price, Frank Leonard, b. Holy Trinity, Smethwick, Staffs, e. Birmingham (Smethwick), 979, L/Cpl., k. in a., F. & F., 3/9/16.

Probert, Harold Edwin, b. Birmingham, e. Birmingham (Handsworth, Birmingham), 17015, Pte., k. in a., F. & F., 27/5/17.

Puddick, William Frederick, b. Birmingham, e. Birmingham (Lozells, Birmingham), 20725, Pte., k. in a., F. & F., 1/9/18.

Rainbow, Frank Grosvenor, b. St. Paul's, Leamington Spa, Warwicks, e. Leamington Spa, 692, Pte., k. in a., F. & F., 27/10/17.

Ramsbottom, George Arthur, b. St. Barnaby, Norwich, e. Norwich, Norfolk, 35788, Pte., k. in a., F. & F., 27/9/18, formerly 2970, Norfolk Regt.

Randle, Alexander, b. Tipton, Staffs, e. Tipton, 52217, Pte., k. in a., F. & F., 1/9/18, formerly 98249, Notts & Derby Regt.

Randle, George, b. Nuneaton, Warwicks, e. Warwick (Boscombe, Hants), 18136, Pte., d. of w., F. & F., 31/8/16.

Randall, James Edward, b. Bradley, Wolverhampton, Staffs, e. Birmingham (Wolverhampton), 991, Pte., k. in a., F. & F., 27/7/16.

Ray, William Frederick, b. Stourbridge, Worcs, e. Birmingham (Edgbaston, Birmingham), 16/1394, Pte., d. of w., F. & F., 29/9/18.

Read, William, e. Horsham, Sussex, 241862, Pte., k. in a., F. & F., 23/8/18, formerly 2440, R. Sussex Regt.

Reed, Harry Geoffrey, b. Bath, Som., e. Christchurch, Hants (Bath), 23463, Pte., d. of w., F. & F., 22/4/17, formerly 4693, R.E.

Reeve, William Henry, b. Barrow-on-Soar, Leics, e. Birmingham, 24882, Pte., d. of w., F. & F., 22/4/18.

Reeves, Henry Arthur, b. Wednesbury, Staffs, e. Birmingham (Wednesbury), 1159, L/Cpl., k. in a., F. & F., 27/7/16.

Regester, Edgar, b. Islington, Middx., e. London (Upper Holloway, London, N.), 43219, Pte., d. of w., F. & F., 30/9/18, formerly 5690, W. Kent Regt.

Reynolds, Ernest Reginald, b. Aston, Birmingham, e. Birmingham, 22695, Pte., k. in a., F. & F., 9/10/17.

Rickards, Reuben, b. Pontypridd, Glam., e. Woolwich, Kent (Lewisham, London, S.E.), 29919, Pte., k. in a., F. & F., 7/10/17, formerly 8594, Lancers.

Richardson, George, e. Liverpool, Lancs (Bootle, Liverpool), 263019, Pte., k. in a., F. & F., 20/10/18, formerly 13792, Army Cyc. Corps.

Riddell, Harry, b. Birmingham, e. Birmingham (Small Heath, Birmingham), 682, Cpl., k. in a., F. & F., 5/10/17.

Righton, Haydn Gordon, b. Ecclesall, Sheffield, Yorks, e. Sheffield, 48245, A/Sgt., k. in a., F. & F., 21/8/18, formerly S/31483, R.A.S.C.

Robbie, David, b. Paisley, Renfrew, e. Paisley, 32589, Pte., d. of w., F. & F., 11/10/17, formerly GS/22224, Dragoons.

Robins, Benjamin Thomas, b. Birmingham, e. Birmingham (Aston, Birmingham), 28595, Pte., k. in a., F. & F., 5/10/17.

Robinson, Albert Edward, b. Nechells, Birmingham, e. Birmingham (Erdington, Birmingham), 989, L/Cpl., k. in a., F. & F., 26/9/16.

Robinson, George Thomas, b. Birmingham, e. Birmingham (Aston, Birmingham), 35995, Pte., k. in a., F. & F., 27/9/18.

Roffey, William, b. Croydon, London, e. London (West Croydon), 34211, Pte., d. of w., F. & F., 24/8/18, formerly 5558, Lancers.

Rogers, Charles Arthur, b. Bishop's Itchington, Warwicks, e. Warwick, 17301, Pte., d. of w., F. & F., 3/9/16.

Rolinson, John, b. Netherton, Worcs, e. Birmingham (Netherton), 30067, Pte., k. in a., F. & F., 26/9/16, formerly 27648, Worcs Regt.

Rose, Frank, e. Devizes, Wilts (Salisbury, Wilts), 28051, Pte., k. in a., F. & F., 2/9/18.

Rose, Nathaniel, b. Gloucester, e. Gloucester, 30092, Pte., k. in a., F. & F., 3/9/16, formerly 24460, Som. L.I.

Rosenbaum, Samuel, b. Edgbaston, Birmingham, e. Birmingham (Edgbaston), 444, Pte., k. in a., F. & F., 3/9/16.

Routledge, Edgar William, e. Morris Town, Devon, 1270, Pte., k. in a., F. & F., 25/1/16.

Ruane, Michael, b. Glencullen, Co. Mayo, Ireland, e. Wallsend, Northumberland, 48407, Pte., d. of w., F. & F., 27/8/18, formerly 5379, Northumberland Fus.

Rudhall, Norman, b. St. George's, Birmingham, e. Birmingham, 1350, Pte., d. of w., F. & F., 28/7/16.

Russell, Reginald, b. Bidford-on-Avon, Warwicks, e. Warwick (Bidford-on-Avon), 23133, Pte., k. in a., F. & F., 21/8/18.

Saddler, William, b. Elswick, Newcastle-on-Tyne, e. Birmingham (Small Heath, Birmingham), 715, Pte., k. in a., F. & F., 26/9/16.

Salmond, Raymond George, b. Stratford-on-Avon, Warwicks, e. Birmingham (Stratford-on-Avon), 1011, Pte., k. in a., F. & F., 10/4/16.

Sanders, Walter Rupert, b. Aston, Birmingham, e. Birmingham (Handsworth, Staffs), 456, Pte., d. of w., F. & F., 31/7/16.

Saunders, Frank, b. Aston, Birmingham, e. Sutton Coldfield, Warwicks (Birmingham), 16/1493, Pte., d. of w., F. & F., 11/10/17.

Scott, Albert Frederick, b. Waterbury, Connecticut, U.S.A., e. Birmingham (King's Norton, Birmingham), 704, Pte., d. of w., F. & F., 6/8/16.

Scott, James Alexander, b. Darlington, Durham, e. Halifax, Yorks (Hebden Bridge, Yorks), 29719, Pte., d., F. & F., 10/8/18.

Scott, Walter, b. Sutton Coldfield, Warwicks, e. Birmingham (Wylde Green, Birmingham), 448, Pte., k. in a., F. & F., 27/7/16.

Searston, Thomas Henry, b. Nottingham, e. Nottingham (Radford, Notts), 52238, Pte., d. of w., F. & F., 19/9/18, formerly 99929, Notts & Derby Regt.

Sensicall, William, b. Leverton, Lincs, e. Gainsborough, Lincs, 52233, Pte., k. in a., F. & F., 27/9/18, formerly 51665, Notts & Derby Regt.

Sephton, Robert, b. St. Helen's, Lancs, e. St. Helen's, 36500, Pte., k. in a., F. & F., 3/9/18, formerly 443, S. Lancs Regt.

Sewall, John King, b. Lambeth, Surrey, e. London (Dudley, Worcs), 32643, Pte., k. in a., F. & F., 9/10/17, formerly 5780, Dragoons.

Sewell, Edward Harry, b. Birmingham, e. Birmingham (Camp Hill, Birmingham), 16/1595, Pte., d. of w., F. & F., 24/8/18.

Shakespeare, William, b. Birmingham, e. Birmingham (Nechells, Birmingham), 202561, Pte., d. of w., F. & F., 6/11/17.

Sharratt, Albert Edward, b. Birmingham, e. Birmingham Brookfields, Birmingham), 16/1501, Pte., d. of w., F. & F., 31/3/16.

Sharratt, Richard, b. West Bromwich, Staffs, e. Birmingham (West Bromwich), 15238, Pte., k. in a., F. & F., 27/7/16.

Shaw, Arnold, b. Long Eaton, Derby, e. Coventry, Warwicks, 26715, Pte., k. in a., F. & F., 15/3/18.

Shilton, George James Joseph, b. Birmingham, e. Coventry, Warwicks (Foleshill, Coventry), 17955, Pte., k. in a., F. & F., 7/10/17.

Short, William, b. St. Andrew's, Newcastle-on-Tyne, e. Newcastle-on-Tyne, 48268, Pte., k. in a., F. & F., 23/8/18, formerly T/23783, R.A.S.C.

Shorter, Sydney Frank, b. St. Luke's, Dudley, Worcs, e. Birmingham (Dudley), 209, Pte., d. of w., F. & F., 1/8/16.

Shrimpton, Herbert Edward, b. Redditch, Worcs, e. Birmingham (Bournville, Birmingham), 24879, Pte., k. in a., F. & F., 9/10/17.

Simms, Horace, e. Eastbourne, Sussex, 32640, Pte., k. in a., F. & F., 8/10/17, formerly 20354, Dragoons.

Simpson, John, b. Malton, Yorks, e. York (Malton), 32985, Pte., k. in a., F. & F., 9/10/17, formerly M/32105, R.A.S.C. (M.T.).

Skillern, William, b. Redmarley, Glos., e. Upton-on-Severn, Glos. (Redmarley), 30078, Pte., k. in a., F. & F., 3/9/16, formerly 27398, Worcs. Regt.
Skinner, Harry Nicol, b. St. Stephen's, Bristol, e. Bristol (Totterdown, Bristol), 27635, Pte., k. in a., F. & F., 3/6/18, formerly 3390, R. Glos. Hussars.
Skinner, Joseph, e. Stourbridge, Worcs, 33009, Pte., d. of w., F. & F., 7/10/17, formerly 27385, Hussars.
Skipton, William, e. Birmingham (Blackheath, Birmingham), 9225, Pte., k. in a., F. & F., 1/9/16.
Slater, William Edward, b. Riddings, Derby, e. Derby (Riddings), 52219, Pte., k. in a., F. & F., 1/9/18, formerly 98402, Notts & Derby Regt.
Smith, Albert William James, b. Innellen, Argyll, e. London (Innellen), 48271, A/Cpl., k. in a., F. & F., 3/9/18, formerly SE/2789, R.A.V.C.
Smith, Clarence Alfred Sinclair, b. Knowle, Warwicks, e. Birmingham (Small Heath, Birmingham), 16/1555, Pte., k. in a., F. & F., 27/7/16.
Smith, George, e. Gateshead, Durham (Wreckerton, Durham), 21136, Pte., d. of w., F. & F., 13/10/17, formerly 25393, Durham L.I.
Smith, Henry, b. Birmingham, e. Birmingham, 22759, Pte., d. of w., F. & F., 14/10/17.
Smith, Herbert, b. Birmingham, e. Birmingham (Aston, Birmingham), 19741, A/Cpl., k. in a., F. & F., 23/8/18.
Smith, Horace R., b. Stoke Newington, Middx., e. Reading, Berks (Stoke Newington), 21686, Pte., k. in a., F. & F., 6/10/17, formerly 10086, R. Berks Regt.
Smith, Robert, b. Manchester, e. Aldershot, Hants (Catford, London), 32503, Cpl., k. in a., F. & F., 9/10/17, formerly 688, Lancers.
Smout, Albert Henry, b. All Saints, Birmingham (Edgbaston, Birmingham), 16/1278, L/Cpl., k. in a., F. & F., 10/5/17.
Snape, George, e. Moseley, Birmingham (Witton, Birmingham), 1096, Pte., k. in a., F. & F., 27/7/16.
Sneddon, Thomas, b. New Monkland, Lanark, e. Dunfermline, Fife (Lamphinians, Fife), 33855, L/Cpl., k. in a., F. & F., 27/9/18, formerly 099057, R.A.S.C.
Solomon, William John Clement, b. Handsworth, Staffs, e. Birmingham (Sparkhill, Birmingham), 1341, Pte., d. of w., F. & F., 11/10/17, M.S.M.
Souls, Francis Ernest Edward, e. Gloucester (Stonehouse, Glos.), 27636, L/Cpl., k. in a., F. & F., 24/4/18, formerly 2604, R. Glos. Yeo.
Spurr, Hedley, b. Lincoln, e. Birmingham (Lincoln), 22766, Pte., k. in a., F. & F., 10/5/17.
Stanley, James, b. Birmingham, e. Birmingham (King's Heath, Birmingham), 17897, Pte., d., F. & F., 6/3/17.
Stanton, Frank, b. Tamworth, Warwicks, e. Moseley, Birmingham (King's Heath, Birmingham), 1186, Pte., k. in a., F. & F., 27/7/16.
Stanton, Thomas, b. Runcorn, Ches., e. Birmingham (Lichfield, Staffs), 752, Pte., k. in a., F. & F., 27/7/16.
Starkey, Eric Humphrey, b. Kimberley, S. Africa, e. Birmingham (Kingstone, Hereford), 447, Pte., k. in a., F. & F., 27/9/18.
Starmer, William Wesley John, e. Kettering, Northants, 32875, Pte., k. in a., F. & F., 9/10/17, formerly R/4/089048, R.A.S.C.
Steadman, Alfred James, b. Kidderminster, Worcs, e. Birmingham (Acock's Green, Birmingham), 705, Pte., k. in a., F. & F., 9/10/17.
Steel, Clifford, b. Plumstead, Kent, e. Moseley, Birmingham, 16/1057, Pte., k. in a., F. & F., 27/7/16.
Steele, Horace, b. All Saints, Birmingham, e. Birmingham, 210, Pte., k. in a., F. & F., 2/9/16.
Stephens, Alfred, b. Knighton, Hereford, e. Atherstone, Warwicks (Arnington, Warwicks), 18132, Pte., d. of w., F. & F., 10/9/16.
Stevenson, Arthur, b. Sunderland, Durham, e. Leamington, Warwicks (Sunderland), 1007, L/Cpl., d. of w., F. & F., 3/8/16.
Stimpson, Alfred John, b. Boughton, Norfolk, e. Norwich (Down ham Market, Norfolk), 32918, Pte., k. in a., F. & F., 9/10/17, formerly 29226, Hussars.
Stone, George, b. Bath, Som., e. Bath, 33230, Pte., k. in a., F. & F., 20/10/18, formerly GS/17142, Lancers.
Stych, Frank John, b. Birmingham, e. Birmingham (Moseley, Birmingham), 446, Pte., d. of w., F. & F., 10/10/16.
Styles, George Reginald, b. Peterborough, Northants, e. Birmingham (Aston, Birmingham), 450, L/Cpl., k. in a., F. & F., 3/9/16.
Swann, Leslie William, b. Langley Mill, Notts, e. Birmingham (Edgbaston, Birmingham), 701, Cpl., k. in a., F. & F., 9/10/17.
Swann, Sydney, b. Wolverhampton, Staffs, e. Leicester, 16/1548, Pte., k. in a., F. & F., 27/7/16.
Swarsbrick, Douglas Holt, b. Earlstown, Lancs, e. Birmingham (Warrington, Lancs), 1002, L/Cpl., k. in a., F. & F., 27/7/16.
Swede, John Asher, b. London, e. Liverpool, 48423, Pte., d. of w., F. & F., 25/8/18.
Swift, William, b. Stalybridge, Ches., e. Hyde, Ches. (Stalybridge), 36401, Pte., k. in a., F. & F., 27/9/18, formerly 315911, Ches. Regt.
Sylvester, Samuel, b. St. Mary, Exeter, Devon, e. Exeter, 35971, Pte., k. in a., F. & F., 18/10/18.
Symonds, Frederick George, b. Worcester, e. Warwick (Marston Green, Birmingham), 18200, Pte., d. of w., F. & F., 19/9/16.
Talbot, Harry, b. King's Heath, Birmingham, e. Birmingham (King's Heath), 7306, Pte., k. in a., F. & F., 9/10/17.
Tams, Thomas, b. Chebsey, Staffs, e. Birmingham (Stechford, Birmingham), 16/1793, Pte., k. in a., F. & F., 3/9/16.
Taylor, Frederick C., b. Stratford-on-Avon, Warwicks, e. Leamington, Warwicks (New Cubbington, Warwicks), 17946, Pte., k. in a., F. & F., 7/10/17.
Taylor, Harold, b. Manchester, e. Manchester (Miles Platting, Manchester), 35777, Pte., k. in a., F. & F., 20/10/18, formerly 29743, Manch. Regt.
Taylor, Harold Edmund, b. Shepherd's Bush, London, e. Birmingham (Shepherd's Bush), 470, Pte., k. in a., F. & F., 25/12/15.
Taylor, Joseph, b. Birmingham, e. Birmingham, 34401, Pte., k. in a., F. & F., 2/9/18, formerly 34612, Worcs Regt.
Taylor, William, b. Heath, Derby, e. Derby (Chesterfield, Derby), 16/2069, Pte., d. of w., F. & F., 16/4/17, formerly 140549, R.F.A.
Teasdale, Edward George, e. Rugby, Warwicks (Upton, Oxon), 201805, Pte., k. in a., F. & F., 17/3/18.
Tepper, William Henry, b. Chichester, Hants, e. Portsmouth, Hants, 36564, L/Cpl., d. of w., F. & F., 30/9/18.
Tetley, Harold, b. Small Heath, Birmingham, e. Birmingham (Small Heath, Birmingham), 468, Pte., k. in a., F. & F., 30/6/17.
Testall, Charles, e. Warwick (Wolverhampton), 18126, Pte., k. in a., F. & F., 3/9/16.
Thayre, Arthur Henry, b. Hulme, Manchester, e. London (Gorton, Manchester), 33874, L/Cpl., k. in a., F. & F., 27/9/18, formerly M2/020549, R.A.S.C.
Thompson, Richard Kenneth, b. Birmingham, e. Birmingham, 263022, Pte., k. in a., F. & F., 14/10/18, formerly 3244, Warwicks Yeo.
Thorne, William, b. Aston, Birmingham, e. Birmingham (Aston), 96, Pte., k. in a., F. & F., 25/9/16.
Thornton, George Henry, b. South Littleton, Worcs, e. Worcester (South Littleton), 50249, Pte., k. in a., F. & F., 27/4/18, formerly 51340, Worcs Regt.
Todd, John, b. Haverholme, Priory, Lincs, e. Lincoln (Ewerby, Lincs), 238011, Pte., k. in a., F. & F., 7/10/17, formerly 2355, Lincs Yeo.
Todd, William, b. Hull, Yorks, e. Birmingham (Sparkhill, Birmingham), 1354, Pte., k. in a., F. & F., 27/7/16.
Tonkins, Ernest, b. Bristol, G'os., e. Bristol, 23266, Pte., k. in a., F. & F., 23/8/18, formerly 30372, Glos. Regt.
Trevis, Arthur, b. Old Hill, Staffs, e. Nuneaton, Warwicks, 35771, Pte., k. in a., F. & F., 27/9/18, formerly 313808, Warwicks Yeo.
Trill, George Ernest, b. Chislehurst, Kent, e. Colchester, Essex (Chislehurst), 35809, Pte., k. in a., F. & F., 20/10/18, formerly R/35094, K.R.R.
Tudor, Arthur, b. Saltley, Birmingham, e. Birmingham (Saltley, Birmingham), 466, Pte., k. in a., F. & F., 25/12/15.
Tulley, William Thomas, b. Brighton, Sussex, e. Brighton, 260380, Pte., k. in a., F. & F., 27/9/18, formerly 52104, R. Irish Rif.
Tuppen, Thomas, b. St. John's, Brighton, Sussex, e. Brighton, 32921, Pte., k. in a., F. & F., 9/10/17, formerly 5996, Hussars.
Tutty, Frank, e. York (Fishergate, York), 235153, Pte., k. in a., F. & F., 20/10/18, formerly 3087, Yorks Hussars.
Twissell, Albert, b. Berkswell, Warwicks, e. Coventry, Warwicks (Kenilworth, Warwicks), 16/2067, Pte., k. in a., F. & F., 14/5/17.
Tye, Reginald Steven, e. Bromley, Kent (Chislehurst, Kent), 245149, Pte., k. in a., F. & F., 2/9/18, formerly 2352, R.W. Kent Regt.
Tye, Seymour Clinton, b. Handsworth, Staffs, e. Moseley, Birmingham (Hall Green, Birmingham), 1160, Pte., k. in a., F. & F., 3/9/16.
Tyson, Henry John, b. Hoxton, Middx., e. London (Haggerston, Middx.), 48388, Pte., d. of w., F. & F., 24/9/18, formerly R/4072986, R.A.S.C.
Upton, William Thomas, b. Birmingham, e. Birmingham (Vauxhall, Birmingham), 15/1621, Pte., k. in a., F. & F., 9/10/17.
Urpeth, William, b. Kirkee, India, e. Woolwich, Kent, 32591, L/Cpl., k. in a., F. & F., 23/8/18, formerly 5560, Dragoons.
Vincent, Edgar Arthur, b. Kenilworth, Warwicks, e. Kenilworth, 23724, Pte., d. of w., F. & F., 10/5/17.
Vincent, Lewis, e. Devizes, Wilts (Salisbury, Wilts), 28602, Pte., d. of w., F. & F., 14/11/18.
Vise, George Henry, b. Summerfield, Birmingham, e. Birmingham (Ladywood, Birmingham), 723, Pte., k. in a., F. & F., 6/10/17.
Wakefield, Oliver Thomas, b. Aston, Birmingham, e. Birmingham (S. Yardley, Birmingham), 1024, L/Cpl., k. in a., F. & F., 27/7/16.
Wakeling, Major, b. Winson Green, Birmingham, e. Birmingham (Brookfields, Birmingham), 748, L/Sgt., k. in a., F. & F., 23/8/18.
Walby, William, b. Ashington, Northumberland, e. Ashington, 48375, Pte., k. in a., F. & F., 27/9/18, formerly 012758, R.A.O.C.
Walker, Albert, b. St. Martin's, Birmingham, e. Birmingham, 1113, Pte., k. in a., F. & F., 27/7/16.
Walker, John, b. Stapleford, Ches., e. Chester (Tarporley, Ches.), 36419, Pte., d. of w., F. & F., 24/8/18, formerly 65029, Ches. Regt.
Walker, William, b. Stockport, Ches., e. Stockport, 36408, Pte., k. in a., F. & F., 1/9/18, formerly 64902, Ches. Regt.
Wall, Stanley, b. Pontypridd, Glam., e. Pontypool, Glam. (Wainfelin, Glam), 33235, Pte., k. in a., F. & F., 27/9/18, formerly 4996, Lancers.
Walsh, Herbert Frederick, b. Birmingham, e. Moseley, Birmingham, 1263, Pte., k. in a., F. & F., 31/1/16.
Walters, George Ernest, b. Smethwick, Birmingham, e. Birmingham (Smethwick), 727, Pte., k. in a., F. & F., 3/9/16.
Ward, Henry, b. Birmingham, e. Birmingham (Erdington, Birmingham), 16/1733, Pte., k. in a., F. & F., 6/10/17.
Ward, John Percy Grant, b. Fonedon, Northants, e. Birmingham (Kettering, Northants), 16/1925, Pte., k. in a., F. & F., 26/9/16.

Wark, Hector, b. Coylton, Ayrshire, e. London (Coylton), 33882, Pte., d. of w., F. & F., 12/11/17, formerly M2/049792, R.A.S.C.
Warner, William Reginald, b King's Heath, Birmingham, e. Birmingham (Handsworth, Staffs), 749, L/Cpl., k. in a., F. & F., 27/7/16.
Waters, James William, b. Lowestoft, Suffolk, e. Lowestoft, 38291, Pte., d. of w., F. & F., 5/9/18.
Watkin, William Bateman, b. Leamington, Warwicks, e. Warwick (Cubbington, Warwicks), 21918, Pte., k. in a., F. & F., 9/10/17.
Watts, Thomas George, b. Walsall, Staffs, e. Warwick (Birmingham), 20964, A/Sgt., k. in a., F. & F., 30/7/17.
Webb, Albert, b. Abingdon, Berks, e. Abingdon, 32965, Pte., k. in a., F. & F., 8/10/17, formerly 19046, Hussars.
West, Israel, b. Tadley, Hants, e. Basingstoke, Hants (Tadley), 36557, Pte., k. in a., F. & F., 27/9/18, formerly 30787, Hampshire Regt.
Wheeler, Frank Harold, b. Birmingham, e. Moseley, Birmingham, 1197, Pte., k. in a., F. & F., 27/7/16.
Wheeler, Harry, b. Crabb's Cross, Warwicks, e. Redditch, Warwicks (Crabb's Cross), 22202, Pte., k. in a., F. & F., 10/5/17.
White, Cornelius Samuel, b. Charmouth, Dorset, e. Birmingham (Ystradgynlais, Brecon), 16/1801, Pte., k. in a., F. & F., 9/10/17.
White, Henry Joseph, b. Bristol, Glos., e. Bristol, 21340, Pte., k. in a., F. & F., 16/4/17, formerly 26807, R. Berks Regt.
White, Thomas Charles, b. Birmingham, e. Birmingham (Northfield, Birmingham), 1261, P.e., k. in a., F. & F., 27/7/16.
Whitehouse, Joseph, b. Stourport, Worcs, e. Birmingham (West Bromwich, Staffs), 1035, Pte., k. in a., F. & F., 27/7/16.
Whittingham, Albert Edward, b. All Saints, Birmingham, e. Birmingham (All Saints), 243, Pte., k. in a., F. & F., 26/9/16.
Wilcox, Albert, b. Small Heath, Birmingham, e. Birmingham, 28509, Pte., d. of w., F. & F., 8/8/17.
Wilford, George Thomas, b. Northampton, e. Northampton, 33943, Pte., k. in a., F. & F., 1/9/18, formerly 202684, E. Kent Regt.
Wilkes, Charles Henry, b. Dudley, Worcs, e. Dudley, 30089, Pte., k. in a., F. & F., 3/9/16, formerly 27842, Worcs Regt.
Wilkins, Alfred, b. St. Augustine, Birmingham, e. Birmingham, 3046, Pte., k. in a., F. & F., 11/5/17.
Wilkins, Bert, b. Birmingham, e. Birmingham, 34790, Pte., k. in a., F. & F., 11/11/17, formerly 204578, Oxf. & Bucks L.I.
Wilkinson, William Edwin, b. Dudley, Worcs, e. Birmingham (Dudley), 232, Pte., k. in a., F. & F., 10/5/17.
Williams, Frederick, b. Leamington, Warwicks, e. Warwick (Small Heath, Birmingham), 238012, Pte., k. in a., F. & F., 23/8/18, formerly 311282, Warwicks Yeo.
Williamson, David, b. Lochgelly, Fife, e. Dunfermline, Fife, 33856, L/Cpl., k. in a., F. & F., 27/9/18, formerly M/2/099075, R.A.S.C.
Wills, George, b. St. Matthew's, Smethwick, Staffs, e. Birmingham (Smethwick), 1034, Cpl., k. in a., F. & F., 27/7/16.
Wimbush, Ambrose, b. Small Heath, Birmingham, e. Birmingham (Small Heath), 16/481, L/Sgt., k. in a., F. & F., 3/9/16.
Windridge, Alfred, b. Birmingham, e. Birmingham (Bournbrook, Birmingham), 36554, Pte., k. in a., F. & F., 27/9/18.
Wines, John Edwin, b. Runcorn, Ches., e. Cardiff, Glam. (Maesteg, Glam.), 28369, Pte., k. in a., F. & F., 29/6/18, formerly 19176, Hussars.
Wint, John William, b. Pleasley Hill, Derby, e. Mansfield, Notts, 52234, Pte., k. in a., F. & F., 3/9/18, formerly 86519, Notts & Derby Regt.
Wood, Richard Albert, b. Birmingham, e. Birmingham (Winson Green, Birmingham), 16/1533, Pte., d. of w., F. & F., 3/8/17.
Woolley, Frederick William, b. Aston, Birmingham, e. Birmingham (Aston), 240, Sgt., d. of w., F. & F., 27/5/18.
Worley, Joseph, e. High Wycombe, Bucks, 34932, Pte., d., F. & F., 9/8/18.
Wray, Edgar, b. St. Paul's, Birmingham, e. Birmingham (Sparkbrook, Birmingham), 487, L/Cpl., k. in a., F. & F., 3/9/16.
Wright, Ernest John, b. Rotton Park, Birmingham, e. Birmingham (Rotton Park), 231, Pte., d., Home, 26/11/18.
Wright, Sidney, e. Atherstone, Warwicks (Old Kettlebrook, Warwicks), 24455, Pte., k. in a., F. & F., 24/8/18.
Wright, Thomas Hulme, b. Stockport, Ches., e. Stockport, 35786, Pte., k. in a., F. & F., 27/9/18, formerly 2226, Ches. Yeo.
Wright, Walter Henry Percival, b. Leicester, e. Birmingham (Shirley, Birmingham), 724, Pte., d. of w., F. & F., 27/7/16.
Wykes, Albert, b. Coventry, Warwicks, e. Coventry, 17908, Pte., k. in a., F. & F., 23/4/17.
Yardley, Enoch George, b. Birmingham, e. Birmingham, 9623, L/Cpl., k. in a., F. & F., 25/8/17.
Young, Robert, b. Egham, Surrey, e. Guildford, Surrey (Virginia Water, Surrey), 32988, Pte., d. of w., F. & F., 24/6/18, formerly 31002, Hussars.

17th Battalion.

Beechener, Charles Edwin, b. Lincoln, e. Birmingham (Soho, Birmingham), 1717, Pte., d., Home, 16/3/16
Cornaby, Alfred, b. St. Thomas, Birmingham, e. Birmingham (Edgbaston, Birmingham), 15/699, Pte., d., Home, 30/8/15.
Foyle, William, b. Wharton-on-Thames, Middx., e. Birmingham, TR/7/1345, Pte., d., Home, 26/6/17.
Franklin, John, b. Olton, Warwicks, e. Warwick (Olton), 20187, Pte., d., Home, 2/7/16.
Haberfield, Nicholas John, b. Temple, Glos., e. Bristol, TR/7/4835, Pte., d., Home, 1/3/17.
Hasler, Charles George, b. Basingstoke, Hants, e. Basingstoke, TR/7/2110, Pte., d., Home, 30/6/17.
Maybury, George Henry, e. Birmingham (Winson Green, Birmingham), 330234, Pte., d., Home, 1/6/17.
Paine, Cecil John, b. Sherborne Dorset, e. Sherborne, TR/7/2460, Pte., d., Home, 6/6/17.
Parsons, Victor Reginald, b. Leamington, Warwicks, e. Coventry, Warwicks, TR/7/1085, Pte., d., Home, 30/5/17.
Pepper, Herbert Sydney, b. Birmingham, e. Birmingham, TR/7/693, Pte., d., Home, 13/1/17.
Roberts, Joe, b. Coates, Glos., e. Birmingham (Saltley, Birmingham), 16/1514, Pte., d., Home, 4/4/16.
Stevens, Albert, b. Ellesborough, Bucks, e. Aylesbury, Bucks (Princes Risborough, Bucks), TR/7/3704, Pte., d., Home, 29/8/17.
Stubbs, Francis George, b. Upton St. Leonard's, Glos., e. Gloucester (Huntley, Glos.), TR/7/3551, Pte., d., Home, 23/8/17.
Watts, William, b. Coventry, Warwicks, e. Coventry, 17298, Pte., d., Home, 26/3/16.
Willis, George Frederick, b. Birmingham, e. Birmingham, TR/7/3279, Pte., d., Home, 16/7/17.

18th Battalion.

Ball, Ernest, b. Coventry, Warwicks, e. Coventry (Hillfields, Coventry), 331274, Pte., d., Home, 2/7/17.
Edwards, Henry, b. Lydiard, Somerset, e. Taunton, Somerset (Elworthy, Somerset), 24626, Pte., d., Home, 24/7/17, formerly 21097, Som. L.I.
Exon, William James, e. Birmingham (Harborne, Birmingham), 330213, L/Cpl., d., Home, 27/9/17.
Langston, Samuel Ernest, b. St. Barnabas, Birmingham, e. Birmingham, 330099, Cpl., k. in a., F. & F., 4/2/17.
Peyton, Reginald Augustus, b. Birmingham, e. Birmingham (Saltley, Birmingham), 330236, Pte., d., Home, 28/9/17.
Probert, Frederick William, e. Birmingham (Sparkbrook, Birmingham), 330653, Pte., d., Home, 12/3/17.
Reece, Squire, b. Guide Bridge, Lancs, e. Hyde, Ches., 330977, Pte., d., Home, 14/3/17, formerly 18403, Devon Regt.

81st Provisional Battalion.

Beaizley, Owen, e. Birmingham (Bournbrook, Birmingham), 3156, Pte., d., Home, 4/12/15.
Hayfield, Harry, b. Lozells, Birmingham, e. Birmingham, 1896, Pte., d., Home, 28/9/15.
Lawley, Reginald Arthur, e. Birmingham (Edgbaston, Birmingham), 2770, Pte., d., Home, 20/6/16.
Smith, Thomas Charles, b. Ladywood, Birmingham, e. Birmingham (Ladywood), 178, Pte., d., Home, 2/7/16.

Depot.

Baker, James, b. Birmingham, e. Birmingham, 3441, Pte., d., Home, 18/12/18.
Bignall, John, b. Radford., Notts, e. Nottingham, 27304, Pte., d., Home, 15/3/18, formerly 5425, Notts & Derby Regt.
Broadway, A., e. Coventry, Warwicks (Bedford), 14205, Pte., d., Home, 9/11/18, formerly 15321, R. Berks Regt.
Clarke, Joseph, b. Hartshill, Warwicks, e. Nuneaton, Warwicks (Stockingford, Warwicks), 9857, Pte., d., Home, 26/2/15.
Conway, George, b. Leicester, e. Nuneaton, Warwicks (Bedworth, Warwicks), 13080, Pte., d., Home, 14/7/15.
Copley, Joseph, b. Birmingham, e. Birmingham, 2236, Pte., d., Home, 10/6/17.
Crow, William, b. St. Paul's, Birmingham, e. Birmingham (Smethwick, Staffs), 3439, Pte., d., Home, 30/7/18.
Farmer, Thomas, b. Pusey, Wilts, e. Newbury, Berks (Bristol, Glos.), 14235, Pte., d., Home, 18/8/15.
Gateley, John, b. Roscommon, Ireland, e. Birmingham (Hockley, Birmingham), 13005, A/L/Sgt., d., Home, 14/10/15.
Gibbons, Charles, b. Ledbury, Herefordshire, e. Warwick (Nechells, Birmingham), 9036, A/Cpl., d., Home, 19/7/16.
Gibbs, Bert, b. Harbury, Warwicks, e. Warwick (Stockton, Warwicks), 17121, Pte., d., Home, 15/3/16.
Gopsill, Barry Graham, b. Harborne, Birmingham, e. Birmingham (Harborne), 15/11, Pte., d., Home, 16/12/16.
Hall, Frank, b. Birmingham, e. Birmingham (Handsworth, Staffs), 9391, Pte., d., Home, 27/2/15.
Hardaker, William Henry, b. Rugby, Warwicks, e. Ilkeston, Derbyshire, 11021, Pte., d., Home, 2/11/18.
Harris, Charles, b. Oxford, e. Warwick (Leamington, Warwicks), 8209, Pte., d., Home, 14/1/16.
Hewitt, George, b. Gibraltar, e. London (Wood Green, London), 3764, Sgt., d., Home, 11/10/17.
Holt, John, b. St. Martin's, Birmingham, e. Birmingham, 3653, Pte., d., Home, 25/10/18.
Homer, William Henry, b. Tipton, Staffs, e. West Bromwich, Staffs (Tipton), 7454, Pte., d., Home, 7/10/14.
Jones, William, b. Dudley, Worcs, e. Nuneaton, Warwicks (Stockingford, Warwicks), 11076, Pte., d., Home, 2/9/18.
Lory, Victor Alfred Manley, b. Holyhead, Anglesey, e. Warwick (Moseley, Birmingham), 21418, Pte., d., Home, 23/5/17.
Norton, Sidney Albert, b. Gt. Witley, Worcs, e. Birmingham, 41649, Pte., d., Home, 10/7/18.
Parkes, William Henry, b. Aston, Birmingham, e. Warwick, 3254, Q.M.S., d., Home, 2/4/16.

Perkins, Frederick, b. Selly Oak, Birmingham, e. Sutton Coldfield, Warwicks (Edgbaston, Birmingham), 14/1150, Pte., d., Home, 8/10/16.
Phillips, Henry, b. Morton Worrell, Oxon, e. Warwick (Hill Wootton, Warwicks), 60197, Pte., k. in a., N. Russia, 1/9/19.
Shenstone, Amos, b. Coventry, Warwicks, e. Coventry, 18020, Pte., d., Home, 10/4/16.
Shepherd, Frederick John Francis, b. Pillerton, Warwicks, e. Wolston, Warwicks, 21433, Pte., d., Home, 17/1/17.
Smith, George, b. Birmingham, e. Warwick (Selly Park, Birmingham), 11027, Pte., d., Home, 30/10/17.
Turner, Ernest Ephraim, b. Claines, Worcs, e. Birmingham (Worcester), 13495, Pte., d., Home, 10/8/15.
Turner, Henry William, b. Birmingham, e. Birmingham (Aston, Birmingham), 7354, Pte., d., Home, 9/10/14.
Ward, Richard, b. Birmingham, e. Birmingham, 1212, Pte., d., Home, 20/2/16.
Westwood, Herbert, e. Birmingham (Blackheath, Birmingham), 241049, A/L/Cpl., d., Home, 4/11/18.

158 (T.F.) Depot.

Smith, Robert Frederick, e. Birmingham (Ladywood, Birmingham), 200860, Pte., d., Home, 8/11/18.
Tucker, Edwin, b. St. Jude's, Birmingham, e. Birmingham (St. Jude's), 201183, Sgt., d., Home, 17/4/18.

51st Battalion.

Scott, Ernest, e. East Ham, London, 38712, Sgt., k. in a., F. & F., 16/6/18.

1st Garrison Battalion.

Andrews, Arthur George, b. Salford Priors, Warwicks, e. Worcester (Evesham, Worcs), 13872, Pte., d., Egypt, 5/9/15, formerly 21341, Worcs Regt.
Ashton, William, b. Birmingham, e. Birmingham (Small Heath, Birmingham), 14102, Pte., d., Egypt, 17/12/15, formerly 19232, Oxf. & Bucks L.I.
Brown, Arthur, b. Fishponds, Bristol, Glos., e. Bristol (Fishponds), 17135, Pte., d., Egypt, 5/1/17, formerly 10698, Glos. Regt.
Burton Francis Henry, b. Kintbury, Berks, e. Newbury, Berks (Kintbury), 14202, Pte., d., Egypt, 16/6/16, formerly 16552, R. Berks Regt.
Chapman, William, b. St. Phillip's, Gloucester, e. Bristol, Glos., 13501, Sgt., d., Egypt, 19/3/16, formerly 23648, Glos. Regt.
Collett, Joseph George, b. St. Spa, Gloucester, e. Oxford (Gloucester), 13538, Pte., d., Egypt, 10/7/16, formerly 23647, Glos. Regt.
Compton, Frederick, b. Tetbury, Glos., e. Aberdare, Glam. (Tetbury), 14231, Pte., d., Egypt, 4/10/16, formerly 10374, R. Berks Regt.
Gillett, William Francis, b. Moreton-in-the-Marsh, Glos., e. Swindon, Wilts, 17156, Pte., d., Egypt, 5/7/16, formerly 28520, Worcs Regt.
Goring, Alfred, b. Worth, Crawley, Sussex, e. East Grinstead, Sussex (Crawley), 203963, Pte., d., Egypt, 7/6/18, formerly 122, R. Sussex Regt.
Gregory, Arthur, b. Holloway, Middx., e. Whitehall, London (Islington, London), 269350, Pte., d., Egypt, 2/12/17, formerly 203318, Rifle Bde.
Hounslow, William, b. Hardwick, Oxon, e. Oxford (Hincksey, Oxon), 14217, Pte., d., Egypt, 8/9/15, formerly 10504, R. Berks Regt.
Hull, Charles, b. East Hampstead, Berks, e. Manchester, Lancs (Salford, Lancs), 14286, Sgt., d., Egypt, 24/5/16, formerly 10227, R. Berks Regt.
Lewis, William Henry, b. Wordsley, Worcs, e. Worcester (Pershore, Worcs), 17161, A/C.S.M., d., Egypt, 19/6/17, formerly 6456, Worcs Regt.
Lyburn, Edward, b. Kingstown, Dublin, e. West London (Paddington, London, W.), 38979, Pte., d., Egypt, 10/3/18, formerly G/28567, R. Fus.
McGregor, John, b. Wesham, Lanark, e. Cinderford, Glos., 13576, Pte., d., Egypt, 7/6/16, formerly 3269, Glos. Regt.
Munn, William George, b. Dover, Kent, e. Holborn, London (King's Cross, London, N.W.), 13618, Pte., d., Egypt, 24/10/15, formerly 85770, R.F.A.
Murray, William, b. Birmingham, e. Birmingham, 13861, Pte., d., Egypt, 14/11/16, formerly 23518, Worcs Regt.
Nash, George, b. Braywick, Windsor, Berks, e. Reading, Berks (Alloa, Clackmannan), 14125, Sgt., d., Egypt, 23/1/16, formerly 10379, R. Berks Regt.
Neill, Archibald, b. Newington, Edinburgh, e. Worcester (Small Heath, Birmingham), 13507, Cpl., d., Egypt, 29/12/15, formerly 23293, Glos. Regt.
Pearce, William George, b. Clapham, London, e. Camberwell, London, 13524, Pte., d., Egypt, 27/7/16, formerly 40894, R.F.A.
Ratcliffe, Sydney, b. Rodmarton, Glos., e. Cirencester, Glos., 13585, Pte., d., Egypt, 4/6/16, formerly 3187, Glos. Regt.
Rodman, Frederick, b. Berkeley, Glos., e. Wootton-under-Edge, Glos., 13608, Dmr., d., Egypt, 26/12/16, formerly 23343, Glos. Regt.
Smith, John, e. Oxford (Berrick Wallingford, Berks), 14043, Pte., d., Egypt, 3/12/15, formerly 9870, Oxf. & Bucks L.I.
Tilbury, James, b. High Wycombe, Bucks, e. Oxford (High Wycombe), 14089, Pte., d., Egypt, 4/6/17, formerly 19061, Oxf. & Bucks L.I.
Townsend, Walter, b. Stanley Lake, Oxford, e. Wallingford, Berks, 14079, A/Sgt., d., Egypt, 29/10/18, formerly 17903, Oxf. & Bucks L.I.
Weaver, George, b. Dumbleton, Worcs, e. Worcester (Evesham, Worcs), 14736, Pte., d., Egypt, 7/9/15, formerly 23898, Worcs Regt.